SOCIAL THOUGHT

SOCIAL THOUGHT

FROM THE ENLIGHTENMENT
TO THE PRESENT

edited and
with introductions by

ALAN SICA
Pennsylvania State University

PEARSON

Boston   New York   San Francisco
Mexico City   Montreal   Toronto   London   Madrid   Munich   Paris
Hong Kong   Singapore   Tokyo   Cape Town   Sydney

Senior Editor: Jeff Lasser
Series Editorial Assistant: Sara Owen
Senior Marketing Manager: Krista Groshong
Composition and Prepress Buyer: Linda Cox
Manufacturing Manager: JoAnne Sweeney
Cover Coordinator: Kristina Mose-Libon
Production Editor: Won Jang
Electronic Composition: Omegatype Typography

Library of Congress Cataloging-in-Publication Data

Social thought : from the Enlightenment to the present / edited and with introductions by
    Alan Sica.
        p.   cm.
    Includes bibliographical references and index.
    ISBN 0-205-39437-X (paper)
    1. Social sciences—Philosophy.   I. Sica, Alan.

H61.S7753   2004
300'.1—dc22

                                                                        2004044766

Printed in the United States of America

10 9 8 7 6 5 4 3 2 1   09 08 07 06 05 04

To
MAH-LEE KANADAE WOCKADOOWALLI KANAY
and her sponsor in our region,
ANNE LOWELL RYLAND SICA

CONTENTS

Preface   xxi
Acknowledgments   xxii
Credits   xxiii
Refashioning the Social Thought Canon   1

part I | ORIGINS OF THE MODERN WORLDVIEW

JOHN LOCKE, *1632–1704*   10
    Essay Concerning Human Understanding, 1690: "On Hermeneutics"
    "Education as Training for Virtue"

MARY ASTELL, *1668–1731*   14
    Reflections upon Marriage, 1700/06

GIAMBATTISTA VICO, *1668–1744*   18
    The New Science: "Concerning the Course [of Human Things] Taken by the Nations,"
        1725

VOLTAIRE, *1694–1778*   23
    Philosophical Letters, 1733–34: "Of Persons of Rank Who Cultivate Learning"
    Philosophical Dictionary, 1764: "Ancients and Moderns" | "Equality" | "Essay on
        the Manners and Spirit of Nations"

MONTESQUIEU, *1689–1755*   27
    The Spirit of the Laws, 1748: "Of Laws in Relation to the Nature of a Despotic
        Government" | "In What Manner the Laws of Civil Slavery Relate to the
        Nature of the Climate" | "Of Laws in Relation to the Principles Which Form the
        General Spirit, the Morals, and Customs of a Nation"

DENIS DIDEROT, *1713–1784*   33
    Encyclopedié, 1751: "Intolerance" | "Character" | "Negroes"

JEAN-JACQUES ROUSSEAU, *1712–1778*   39
    Discourse on the Origin of Inequality, 1755

ADAM SMITH, *1723–1790*   45
    The Theory of Moral Sentiments, 1759: "Of Sympathy" | "Of Justice and
        Beneficence"

ADAM FERGUSON, *1723–1816*   50
    An Essay on the History of Civil Society, 1767: "Of Moral Sentiment" | "Of
        Happiness" | "Of Luxury"

JOHN MILLAR, *1735–1801*   54
    The Origin of the Distinction of Ranks, 1771/79: "Of the Rank and Condition of
        Women in Different Ages" | "The Usual Effects of Opulence and Civilized
        Manners"
    "Social Consequences of the Division of Labour"

IMMANUEL KANT, *1724–1804*   59
    Lectures on Ethics, 1775–80: "Suicide" | "Duties Towards the Body in Respect of
        Sexual Impulse" | "Wealth"

ETIENNE DE CONDILLAC, *1715–1780*   66
    Commerce and Government Considered in their Mutual Relationship, 1776: "Of the
        Employment of Men in a Society which has Simple Tastes" | "Of Luxury"

DAVID HUME, *1711–1776*   70
    An Enquiry Concerning the Principles of Morals, 1751: "Concerning Moral
        Sentiment" | "Of National Characters"

THOMAS JEFFERSON, *1743–1826*   75
    Notes on the State of Virginia, 1782: "The Particular Manners and Customs that May
        Happen to be Received in that State?"
    Indian Addresses: "Letter for Brother John Baptist de Coigne," 1781 | "To the
        Brothers of the Choctaw Nation," 1803

JOHANN G. HERDER, *1744–1803*   79
    Ideas for a Philosophy of the History of Man, 1784–91: "National Genius and the
        Environment" | "Humanity the End of Human Nature"

JEREMY BENTHAM, *1748–1832*   85
    An Introduction to the Principles of Morals and Legislation, 1789: "On the Principle of
        Utility" | "Of the Four Sanctions or Sources of Pain and Pleasure" | "Value of
        a Lot of Pleasure or Pain, How to be Measured"

part II | REVOLUTION AND ROMANTICISM

EDMUND BURKE, *1729–1797*   90
    Reflections on the Revolution in France, 1790
    A Vindication of Natural Society, 1756: "Discontents in the Kingdom"

MARY WOLLSTONECRAFT, *1759–1797*   95
    A Vindication of the Rights of Men, 1790
    A Vindication of the Rights of Woman, 1792

THOMAS PAINE, *1737–1809*   100
    Rights of Man, 1791/92: "Conclusion"

FRIEDRICH SCHILLER, *1759–1805*   103
    Letters on the Aesthetic Education of Man, 1794–95

MARQUIS DE CONDORCET, *1743–1794*   106
    Sketch for a Historical Picture of the Progress of the Human Mind, 1795:
        Introduction | "The Tenth Stage: The Future Progress of the Human Mind"

GEORG WILHELM FRIEDRICH HEGEL, *1770–1831*   110
    Phenomenology of Spirit, 1807: "Master and Servant"

THOMAS ROBERT MALTHUS, *1766–1834*   115
    An Essay on the Principle of Population, 1798

FRIEDRICH SCHLEIERMACHER, *1768–1834*   119
    On Religion: Speeches to Its Cultured Despisers, 1799: "Religion and Reason" |
        "Sociality and Religion"

JEAN-CHARLES-LEONARD SIMONDE DE DISMONDI, *1773–1842*   123
    New Principles of Political Economy, 1819: "Of Slave Cultivation"

JOHANN GOTTLIEB FICHTE, *1762–1814*   127
    The Vocation of Man, 1800: "Faith"
    Characteristics of the Present Age, 1804: "The Idea of Universal History"

JOSEPH DE MAISTRE, *1753–1821*   131
    On God and Society, 1808–09
    Study on Sovereignty: "The Weakness of Human Power" | "The Best Species
        of Government" | "On the Nature of Sovereignty"

HENRI COMTE DE SAINT-SIMON, *1760–1825*   135
   "Essay on the Science of Man," 1813
   "On Social Organization," 1825

THOMAS CARLYLE, *1795–1881*   139
   "Signs of the Times," 1829

FRANÇOIS-MARIE-CHARLES FOURIER, *1772–1837*   143
   "Social Evolution," 1829
   "On the Rôle of the Passions," 1830
   "The Condition of Women," 1808

part III | THE INVENTION OF MODERN SOCIAL THEORY

AUGUSTE COMTE, *1798–1857*   152
   "Plan of the Scientific Operations Necessary for Reorganizing Society," 1822
   "Conclusion: The Religion of Humanity," 1854

JOHN STUART MILL, *1806–1873*   159
   "The Spirit of the Age," 1831
   "The Subjection of Women," 1869

ADOLPHE QUETELET, *1796–1874*   164
   Research on the Propensity for Crime at Different Ages, 1833

ALEXIS TOCQUEVILLE, *1805–1859*   169
   Democracy in America, 1835–40: "How Equality Suggests to the Americans the Idea of
      the Indefinite Perfectability of Man" | "Unlimited Power of the Majority in the
      United States and Its Consequences" | "The Three Races in the United States"
   The Old Regime and the Revolution, 1856: "Why Feudalism Had Come to be More
      Detested in France than in Any Other Country"

FREDERICK DOUGLASS, *1817–1895*   179
   "The Church and Prejudice," 1841
   "My Slave Experience in Maryland," 1845

KARL MARX, *1818–1883*   184
   "Contribution to the Critique of Political Economy," 1859
   German Ideology, 1845–46
   Contribution to the Critique of Hegel's *Philosophy of Right*, 1843
   Economic and Philosophic Manuscripts of 1844: "Estranged Labour"

SØREN KIERKEGAARD, *1813–1855*   194
   The Present Age, 1846: "The Individual and the Public"

HARRIET TAYLOR MILL, *1807–1858*   198
    "Enfranchisement of Women," 1851

ARTHUR SCHOPENHAUER, *1788–1860*   201
    Parerga and Paralipomena, vol. 2, 1851: "Character"
    "On the Wisdom of Life: Aphorisms"

HERBERT SPENCER, *1820–1903*   212
    Social Statics, 1851: "The Evanescence of Evil"
    The Man Versus the State, 1884: "The Coming Slavery"
    Principles of Sociology, 1896: "The Organic Analogy Reconsidered"
    The Proper Sphere of Government: "Letter XII," 1842

HARRIET MARTINEAU, *1802–1876*   218
    Autobiography, 1855 [1877]: "Single Life" | "The Woman Question" | "Women
       in Ireland," 1852 | "Brutality to Women," 1853

JOSEPH-ARTHUR GOBINEAU, COMTE DE, *1816–1882*   223
    Essay on the Inequality of Human Races, 1853–55: "The Inequality of Races" | "The
       Three Basic Races"

(PIERRE-GILLAUME-) FRÉDÉRIC LE PLAY, *1806–1882*   228
    Les Ouvriers europèens, 1855: "The Science of Society as a Theory of Social Reform"
    Social Reform, 1864: "Family Types: Patriarchal, Stem, Unstable"

JOHN RUSKIN, *1819–1900*   232
    "Modern Manufacture and Design," 1859
    Unto This Last, 1860: "The Roots of Honour"
    Sesame and Lilies, 1865: "Of Kings' Treasuries"
    Fors Clavigera, 1871–84: "Communism"

MATTHEW ARNOLD, *1822–1888*   237
    "Democracy," 1861
    Culture and Anarchy, 1869: "Doing as One Likes"
    "Equality," 1879

ALEKSANDR I. HERZEN, *1812–1870*   243
    My Past and Thoughts, 1861–67: "Second Thoughts on the Woman Question"

HENRY SUMNER MAINE, *1822–1888*   247
    Ancient Law, 1861: "Law of Nature and Equity"
    Lectures on the Early History of Institutions, 1875/88: "The Growth and Diffusion of
       Primitive Ideas"

NUMA DENIS FUSTEL DE COULANGES, *1830–1889*   250
    The Ancient City, 1864: "Marriage" | "Authority in the Family"

CHARLES DARWIN, *1809–1882*   253
   The Descent of Man, 1871: "Natural Selection" | "Conclusion"
   Expression of the Emotions in Man and Animals, 1872

EDWARD BURNETT TYLOR, *1832–1917*   258
   Primitive Culture, 1871: "The Development of Culture"

FRIEDRICH ENGELS, *1820–1895*   262
   Anti-Dühring, 1878: "On Morality"

part IV | THE CLASSICAL PERIOD OF MODERN SOCIAL THOUGHT

FRIEDRICH NIETZSCHE, *1844–1900*   266
   Human, All Too Human, 1878: "In Relations with Others"
   On the Genealogy of Morals, 1887: "What is the Meaning of Ascetic Ideals?"

WILHELM DILTHEY, *1833–1911*   272
   Introduction to the Human Sciences, 1883: "The Understanding of Others"

FERDINAND TÖNNIES, *1855–1936*   276
   Community and Society, 1887: "Relations Between Human Wills" | "Gemeinschaft
      by Blood"
   Custom: An Essay on Social Codes, 1909

GABRIEL TARDE, *1843–1904*   281
   The Laws of Imitation, 1890: "Universal Repetition"

WILLIAM JAMES, *1842–1910*   284
   "The Moral Philosopher and the Moral Life," 1891
   "What Makes a Life Significant?" 1899
   "The Moral Equivalent of War," 1910

EMILE DURKHEIM, *1858–1917*   290
   The Division of Labor in Society, 1893: "The Division of Labor and Happiness"
   "The Dualism of Human Nature and Its Social Conditions," 1914

GUSTAVE LE BON, *1841–1931*   295
   The Crowd, 1895: "The Mind of Crowds"

GAETANO MOSCA, *1858–1941*   299
   The Ruling Class, 1896: "The Rule of the Best"

CHARLOTTE ANNA PERKINS GILMAN, *1860–1935*   303
   Women and Economics, 1898: "The Eternal Feminine" | "Women as Persons" |
      "Masculine and Feminine"

MARCEL MAUSS, *1872–1950*   306
    Sacrifice: Its Nature and Function (with Henri Hubert), 1899: "Conclusion"
    A General Theory of Magic, 1902–03: "A Definition of Magic" | "Conclusion"

THORSTEIN VEBLEN, *1857–1929*   311
    The Theory of the Leisure Class, 1899: "Conspicuous Consumption"

VILFREDO PARETO, *1848–1923*   315
    Mind and Society, 1916: "Residues and Elites"

CHARLES HORTON COOLEY, *1864–1929*   319
    Human Nature and the Social Order, 1902: "The Meaning of 'I'"
    Social Organization, 1909: "Modern Communication: Superficiality and Strain" |
        "The Organization of the Ill-Paid Classes"

W. E. B. DU BOIS, *1868–1963*   325
    The Souls of Black Folk, 1903: "The Talented Tenth"
    "What is Civilization?—Africa's Answer," 1925

MAX WEBER, *1864–1920*   330
    Protestant Ethic and the Spirit of Capitalism, 1904/05: "Asceticism and the Spirit
        of Capitalism"
    "Religious Rejections of the World and Their Directions," 1913

WILLIAM GRAHAM SUMNER, *1840–1910*   336
    Folkways: A Study of the Sociological Importance of Usages, Manners, Customs,
        Mores, and Morals, 1907: "Fundamental Notions" | "Blacks and Whites
        in Southern Society"

LEON TROTSKY, *1879–1940*   340
    Results and Prospects, 1906: "What is the Permanent Revolution?"
    Literature and Revolution, 1924: "Proletarian Culture and Proletarian Art"

GEORG SIMMEL, *1858–1918*   346
    "Competition," 1908
    "The Social and the Individual Level"
    "Individual and Society in 18th and 19th Century Views of Life," 1917
    "On Love," 1921–22
    "Freedom and the Individual," 1957

GEORGES SOREL, *1847–1922*   357
    Reflections on Violence, 1908: "Political Myths"

LUCIEN LÉVY-BRUHL, *1857–1939*   361
    How Natives Think, 1910 [1926]: "Collective Representations in Primitives' Perceptions"
    Primitive Mentality, 1922

GYÖRGY LUKÁCS, *1885–1971*   365
  Aesthetic Culture, 1910
  History and Class Consciousness: "Reification and the Consciousness of the Proletariat,"
    1923

JAMES GEORGE FRAZER, *1854–1941*   371
  The Golden Bough: A Study in Magic and Religion, 1911–15: "Farewell to Nemi"

ROBERTO MICHELS, *1876–1936*   374
  Political Parties: A Sociological Study of the Oligarchical Tendencies of Modern
    Democracy, 1911: "Final Considerations"
  Sexual Ethics: A Study of Borderland Questions, 1911: "Conflict Between Profession
    and Motherhood"

ERNST TROELTSCH, *1866–1923*   380
  The Social Teaching of the Christian Churches, 1911: "Introduction and Preliminary
    Questions of Method" | "Sociological Effect of Luther's Thought: The New
    Conception of the Church"

SIGMUND FREUD, *1856–1939*   384
  Totem and Taboo, 1913: "Taboo and the Ambivalence of Emotions"
  Civilization and Its Discontents, 1930

MAX SCHELER, *1874–1928*   389
  Formalism in Ethics and Non-formal Ethics of Values, 1913/16: "The Structure of
    Values and Their Historical Variations"
  The Nature of Sympathy, 1931: "Classification of the Phenomena of Fellow-Feeling"

ANTONIO GRAMSCI, *1891–1937*   394
  "Socialism and Culture," 1916
  The Prison Notebooks, 1929–35: "What is Man?" | "Marxism and Modern Culture"

FERDINAND DE SAUSSURE, *1857–1913*   399
  Course in General Linguistics, 1916: "The Object of Linguistics" | "Graphic
    Representation of Language"

RUDOLF OTTO, *1869–1937*   403
  The Idea of the Holy: An Inquiry into the Non-rational Factor in the Idea of the Divine
    and Its Relation to the Rational, 1917: "The Rational and the Non-Rational"

W. I. THOMAS, *1863–1947*   406
  The Polish Peasant in Europe and America (with Florian Znaniecki), 1918–20: "Rational
    Control in Social Life"
  The Unadjusted Girl, 1923: "The Wishes"

part V | SOCIAL THEORY BETWEEN THE GREAT WARS

MOHANDAS GANDHI, *1869–1948*   412
"Gandhi's Message to All Men," 1920–27
"Advice to Negroes," 1924–36
"How to Enjoy Jail," 1932

WILLIAM FIELDING OGBURN, *1886–1959*   417
Social Change with Respect to Culture and Original Nature, 1922: "The Overemphasis
    of the Biological Factor"
"The Great Man Versus Social Forces," 1926
"Cultural Lag as Theory," 1957

JOHN DEWEY, *1859–1952*   423
Experience and Nature, 1925: "Communication and Communal Living"
The Public and Its Problems, 1927: "The Private and the Public"
Ethics, 1932: "Individual and Social Morality"

MAURICE HALBWACHS, *1877–1945*   428
The Social Frameworks of Memory, 1925: "Conclusion"
The Psychology of Social Class, 1955

KARL MANNHEIM, *1893–1947*   433
"The Ideological and Sociological Interpretation of Intellectual Phenomena," 1926
"The Meaning of Conservatism," 1927
Ideology and Utopia, 1929: "The Sociological Concept of Thought" | "The
    Contemporary Predicament of Thought"

BRONISLAW MALINOWSKI, *1884–1942*   442
Sex and Repression in Savage Society, 1927: "Motherhood and the Temptations of
    Incest" | "Culture and the 'Complex'"
Freedom and Civilization, 1944: "War Throughout the Ages"

MARTIN BUBER, *1878–1965*   448
Between Man and Man, 1929: "Community" | "Prospect" [for Humankind],
    (1938) 1965
"Society and the State," 1957

BERTRAND RUSSELL, *1872–1970*   454
Marriage and Morals, 1929: "Romantic Love"
Education and the Social Order, 1932: "The Herd in Education"
Authority and the Individual, 1949: "Individual and Social Ethics"

LUDWIG WITTGENSTEIN, *1889–1951*　　　460
　　Lectures on Ethics, Culture, and Value, 1966: "Ethics, Life, and Faith," 1929

GEORGE HERBERT MEAD, *1863–1931*　　　464
　　Mind, Self, and Society from the Standpoint of a Social Behaviorist, 1934:
　　　　"Meaning"　|　"The 'I' and the 'Me'," 1930

KARL JASPERS, *1883–1969*　　　469
　　Man in the Modern Age, 1931: "Mass-Rule"　|　"The Tension Between Technical
　　　　Mass-Order and Human Life"

OSWALD SPENGLER, *1880–1936*　　　474
　　Man and Technics: A Contribution to a Philosophy of Life, 1931

GEORGES BATAILLE, *1897–1962*　　　477
　　"The Psychological Structure of Fascism," 1933
　　"The Meaning of General Economy," 1949
　　"The Nature of Society: Social Bonding and Communication," 1947–48

ROBERT KING MERTON, *1910–2003*　　　485
　　"The Unanticipated Consequences of Social Action," 1936

NORBERT ELIAS, *1897–1990*　　　492
　　"An Outline of The Civilizing Process," 1936
　　"The Civilizing of Parents," 1980

TALCOTT PARSONS, *1902–1979*　　　500
　　The Structure of Social Action, 1937: "Hobbes and the Problem of Order"
　　"Death in the Western World," 1978

ERICH FROMM, *1900–1980*　　　508
　　Escape from Freedom, 1941: "Freedom and Democracy: The Illusion of
　　　　Individuality"　|　"Character and the Social Process"
　　The Sane Society, 1955: "Consumerism (as a Compensation for Anxiety and
　　　　Depression) versus the Joy of Life"

PITIRIM SOROKIN, *1889–1968*　　　514
　　The Crisis of Our Age, 1941: "Tragic Dualism, Chaotic Syncretism, Quantitative
　　　　Colossalism, and the Diminishing Creativeness of the Contemporary Sensate Culture"

JEAN-PAUL SARTRE, *1905–1980*　　　518
　　Being and Nothingness, 1943: "Freedom and Responsibility"
　　Anti-Semite and Jew, 1946
　　Critique of Dialectical Reason/Search for a Method, 1960: "Reification"

ERNST CASSIRER, *1874–1945*   523
   An Essay on Man, 1944: "The Definition of Man in Terms of Human Culture"
   The Myth of the State, 1946: "The Technique of the Modern Political Myths"

HENRI LEFEBVRE, *1901–1991*   530
   Critique of Everyday Life, 1991: "What is Possible," 1945

MAURICE MERLEAU-PONTY, *1908–1961*   534
   The Phenomenology of Perception, 1945: "Other Selves and the Human World"
   Signs, 1951/60: "Man and Adversity"

part VI | THEORIZING MASS CULTURE AND THE COLD WAR

MAX HORKHEIMER, *1895–1973*   542
   Eclipse of Reason, 1947: "Rise and Decline of the Individual"

KARL POPPER, *1902–1994*   547
   Conjectures and Refutations: The Growth of Scientific Knowledge, 1962: "Utopia and
      Violence," 1948 | "The History of Our Time: An Optimist's View," 1956

ARNOLD TOYNBEE, *1889–1975*   553
   Civilization on Trial, 1948: "The Meaning of History for the Soul"

CLAUDE LÉVI-STRAUSS, *1908–*   558
   Elementary Structures of Kinship, 1949: "The Principle of Reciprocity" | "The
      Transition to Complex Structures" | "The Principles of Kinship"

THEODOR ADORNO, *1903–1969*   564
   Minima Moralia, 1951: "Model of Virtue"
   The Culture Industry, 1991: "Free Time," 1954

GABRIEL (-HONORÉ) MARCEL, *1889–1973*   570
   Man Against Mass Society, 1951: "The Universal Against the Masses, I & II"
   The Existential Background of Human Dignity, 1963: "Mortality, Hope, and Freedom"

C. WRIGHT MILLS, *1916–1962*   576
   White Collar, 1951: "The Rhetoric of Competition" | "Work"

ROLAND BARTHES, *1915–1980*   581
   Mythologies, 1957: "Myth Today"
   Writing Degree Zero, 1953: "Political Modes of Writing"

ROBERT REDFIELD, *1897–1958*   587
    The Primitive World and Its Transformation, 1953: "Primitive World View" |
        "Changing Ethical Judgment"
    Peasant Society and Culture, 1956: "The Peasant View of the Good Life"

HERBERT MARCUSE, *1898–1979*   591
    Eros and Civilization, 1955: "The Transformation of Sexuality into Eros"
    One-Dimensional Man, 1964: "The Paralysis of Criticism: Society Without Opposition"

JACQUES (MARIE EMILE) LACAN, *1901–1981*   595
    The Language of the Self: The Function of Language in Psychoanalysis, 1956: "The
        Empty Word and the Full Word"

HANNAH ARENDT, *1906–1975*   599
    The Human Condition, 1958: "The Social and the Private" | "Reification"

ROGER CAILLOIS, *1913–1978*   605
    Man, Play, and Games, 1961: "The Definition of Play," 1958

HAROLD GARFINKEL, *1917–*   608
    Studies in Ethnomethodology, 1967: "Rational Behaviors," 1960

RAYMOND ARON, *1905–1983*   613
    The Dawn of Universal History, 1961

FRANTZ FANON, *1925–1961*   617
    The Wretched of the Earth, 1961: "Concerning Violence"

JÜRGEN HABERMAS, *1929-*   621
    "The Public Sphere," 1962/73
    Theory and Practice, 1971: "Dogmatism, Reason, and Decision"
    The Philosophical Discourse of Modernity: Twelve Lectures, 1987: "Modernity's
        Consciousness of Time and Its Need for Self-Reassurance"

MARY DOUGLAS, *1921–*   630
    Purity and Danger: An Analysis of the Concepts of Pollution and Taboo, 1966:
        "Introduction"
    Risk and Blame: Essays in Cultural Theory, 1992: "Risk and Danger"

SUSANNE LANGER, *1895–1985*   636
    Mind: An Essay on Human Feeling, 1967–82: "Idols of the Laboratory"

WALTER BENJAMIN, *1892–1940*   639
    Illuminations, 1968: "The Work of Art in the Age of Mechanical Reproduction"

part VII | POSTMODERNISM, GLOBALIZATION, AND THE NEW CENTURY

PIERRE BOURDIEU, *1930–2002*   644
  Outline of a Theory of Practice, 1972: "Structures, Habitus and Practices"
  Distinction: A Social Critique of the Judgement of Taste, 1979: "The Taste for Necessity
    and the Principle of Conformity" | "The 'Taste of Reflection' and the 'Taste of
    Sense'"

MICHEL FOUCAULT, *1926–1984*   653
  Discipline and Punish: The Birth of the Prison, 1975: "Panopticism"
  Politics, Philosophy, Culture: Interviews and Other Writings 1977–84: "The Minimalist
    Self"

MICHAEL OAKESHOTT, *1901–1990*   659
  On Human Conduct, 1975: "On the Understanding of Human Conduct"

JACQUES DERRIDA, *1930–*   663
  Writing and Difference, 1978: "Structure, Sign and Play in the Discourse of the Human
    Sciences"
  "Letter to a Japanese Friend," 1983
  "Geschlecht: Sexual Difference, Ontological Difference," 1987

CHRISTOPHER LASCH, *1932–1994*   672
  The Culture of Narcissism, 1978: "The Narcissistic Personality of Our Time"

ANTHONY GIDDENS, *1938–*   676
  Modernity and Self-Identity: Self and Society in the Late Modern Age, 1991:
    "Ontological Security and Existential Anxiety" | "Tribulations of the Self"

JEAN-FRANÇOIS LYOTARD, *1924–1998*   682
  The Postmodern Condition: A Report on Knowledge, 1979: "The Nature of the Social
    Bond: The Postmodern Perspective" | "Delegitimation"
  "One of the Things at Stake in Women's Struggles"

NIKLAS LUHMANN, *1927–1998*   689
  Political Theory in the Welfare State, 1990: "The Representation of Society Within
    Society," 1981
  Risk: A Sociological Theory, 1993: "The Concept of Risk"

LUCE IRIGARAY, *1930–*   694
  An Ethics of Sexual Difference, 1984: "Sexual Difference"
  Thinking the Difference: For a Peaceful Revolution, 1990: "Equal or Different?"

DOROTHY E. SMITH, *1926–*   700
  The Everyday World as Problematic: A Feminist Sociology, 1987
  Writing the Social: Critique, Theory, and Investigations, 1999: "The Ruling Relations"

JEAN BAUDRILLARD, *1929–*   706
    "Consumer Society," 1970
    "Simulacra and Simulations," 1981

LEWIS COSER, *1913–2003*   713
    A Handful of Thistles: Collected Papers in Moral Conviction, 1988: "The Notion of
        Civility in Contemporary Society"

DAVID HARVEY, *1935–*   718
    The Condition of Postmodernity: An Enquiry into the Origins of Cultural Change, 1989:
        "The Transformative and Speculative Logic of Capital" | "The Work of Art in
        an Age of Electronic Reproduction and Image Banks" | "Responses to
        Time-Space Compression"

JULIA KRISTEVA, *1941–*   724
    "Strangers to Ourselves," 1989

JUDITH BUTLER, *1956–*   729
    Gender Trouble, 1990: "Theorizing the Binary, the Unitary, and Beyond"
    Excitable Speech: A Politics of the Performative, 1997: "On Linguistic Vulnerability"

IMMANUEL WALLERSTEIN, *1930–*   734
    Unthinking Social Science: The Limits of Nineteenth-Century Paradigms, 1991: "World-
        Systems Analysis: The Second Phase"
    The End of the World as We Know It: Social Science for the Twenty-First Century,
        1999: "Ecology and Capitalist Costs of Production: No Exit"

ERNEST GELLNER, *1925–1995*   740
    Reason and Culture: The Historic Role of Rationality and Rationalism, 1992:
        "Rationality as a Way of Life" | "Recapitulation"

JOHN RAWLS, *1921–2002*   745
    Political Liberalism, 1993: "The Content of Public Reason"
    The Law of Peoples, 1999: "Public Reason and the Law of Peoples" | "Reconciliation
        to Our Social World"

RICHARD RORTY, *1931–*   751
    Philosophy and Social Hope, 1999: "Looking Backwards from the Year 2096," 1996

CHARLES TAYLOR, *1931–*   756
    Charles Taylor's Marianist Award Lecture, 1999: "A Catholic Modernity?"

ALASDAIR MACINTYRE, *1929–*   762
    "Rival Conceptions of the Common Good," 1997

Name Index   767
Subject Index   775

PREFACE

A child restricted to one candy bar for a week's pleasure will long consider the item from various angles before consuming and savoring it. But the same child let loose in a candy store without limits will likely gorge himself or herself in short order and lose the ability to distinguish the finest from the most mediocre sweets. Choices of this magnitude could become too much of a good thing. For some years the literate, privileged parts of the world have had access to electronic sources of social thought that were literally unimaginable only a decade before. If one wishes to read *The Anarchist's Cookbook,* for many years a scarce, "underground" text, one has only to enter the World Wide Web, and there it is, in multiple forms and versions. If one prefers the Greek and Latin foundational texts, one need not buy the Loeb Classics for thousands of dollars, but instead can go to various sites and print out whatever text is desired, in the original and in English translation. And if a reader still feels the need to read the work of Marx and Engels, the choice is to use the *Collected Works* in a 50-volume translation, or to read their writings on a screen in any of many sites dedicated to the Leftist tradition. So it goes.

We risk being drowned in social theory, social thought, political theory, cultural theory, multicultural theory, feminist theory, postcolonial theory, and so on—both in printed and electronic forms—so much so that if one wants only a sip of water, a torrent threatens to pour from the faucet. This book was designed to help the interested reader plunge into this vast debate about the nature of human life without risking fatal submersion beneath a wave of information that could not possibly be assimilated. I have tried to answer the question: which writers continue to speak to our age, and from which of their works might one take the most pertinent theorizing? From Kant, for instance, I have avoided the epistemological work for which he is famous, and gone instead to his ethics, not only because there he speaks more forcefully about the way life ought to be lived, but because his more formally philosophical works are impenetrable to most readers. Even with 140 authors represented, I have had to drop dozens of others for lack of space, and although other editors (from whom I hope to hear) might well make other selections, this set seems to me to cohere around the big questions: of what are human beings capable, and what kind of life should they lead? It was Tolstoy's question, and it is still the right one.

ACKNOWLEDGMENTS

My friends and colleagues, John McCarthy and Glenn Firebaugh, granted research assistance without which a project of this scale could not have been carried out. For help in toting about 800 books and photocopying, I must thank especially Erik Johnson, and also Phil Schwadel and Debbie Van Schyndel (now Kasper). And for extraordinary efforts in securing reprinting permissions, and for other indispensable research help over several years, deep thanks go to Julie Pelton. Jeff Lasser found a fine home for the book, acting not only as a masterful editor, but also becoming a friend. And if Won Jang is not the best at what she does, then who is?

Anne Sica once again selflessly helped me in various stages of the book's production, including indexing, and Paolo, Enzo, and Carlo provided the motivation to carry out the task.

Translation help came from my foreign agents, A. G. Sica and his accomplice, Hanna M. Meyer. Tina Burke inspired the selection of cover art. And none of this would have been imaginable without the intense labors of Paul Sica (1903–2002).

CREDITS

REFASHIONING THE
SOCIAL THOUGHT CANON

How and Why This Book Took Its Final Form

Assembling a book which attempts to convey to its readers a broad sense of what "social thought" has meant over centuries is a task taken up either by a fool or an imposter—so one might argue. A fool because the magnitude of the task is nearly boundless, and an imposter because defining a "canon" nowadays requires a mindset and a rack of organizing principles that, no matter how catholic in orientation, will likely offend or displease a sizeable portion of its potential audience. But scholarship has never spurned the improbable, even the Quixotic, especially when strong winds of change are at work in a given zone of thinking, as they have been within this area for the last couple of decades. It has seemed to me, after working with these texts for 30 years, that social thought has clumsily drifted away from the better features of its earlier incarnations, and toward a generalized forgetfulness of those informative observations that came before. I am therefore presenting a substantial body of readings which captures "the best of the best"—or, chastened by publishers' realism, at least as much of the best as could practically be contained within one volume. I have searched for those texts that would speak most forcibly to current interests, circumscribed as they might be when compared with the broader canvas of the past taken *in toto*.

What, precisely, is "social thought"? One can easily answer what it is not and then hope for the best by implication. It is not for the most part philosophy proper, since that discipline must take in logic, epistemology, aesthetics, some linguistics, and other subfields, none of which is exclusively or mainly concerned with social life in its larger sense. So, for instance, when including John Locke, most sections of his more formally philosophical writings (*An Essay Concerning Human Understanding*) might be left aside, while his essential commentaries on the best form of government warrant inclusion. Similarly with many other authors who appear here. Social thought is also not pure economics, though sociologically pertinent works by Adam Smith, Karl Marx, Vilfredo Pareto, and John Maynard Keynes—all very great economists—must be considered. The same could be said for psychology (of brain function, optical illusion, simple conditioning, and so on) or art theory (Clement Greenberg on modern art might be too technically aesthetic in nature, whereas Walter Benjamin's ideas about modern art speak more generally to the condition of Western civilization in the 20s and 30s).

There are some writers who seem to embody "social thought" in quintessential form: John Ruskin, Hannah Arendt, Isaiah Berlin, Herbert Marcuse, Matthew Arnold, Rousseau, Georg Simmel, among many others. They brought together in masterful form a range of observations from areas which we now define, as they did not, along academic disciplinary lines: literature, history, philosophy, social sciences, the arts, and so on. Ruskin is perhaps the best possible example, putting together whirling treatises that mix economics, art, social policy, literature, and social philosophy in a potion that is unlike any attempted today. Bright people who wrote insightfully about human relations in fairly direct terms—Heidegger did not, for instance, and so cannot properly be thought of as a social theorist, whereas some of his followers must be so considered, such as Arendt—are the ones whose texts I searched for material that could reasonably be included in this anthology. But I do not have any formal definition of "social thought," and generally regard eclectic catholicism the best guide. Which leads me to the vexed question of why some authors appear in the Contents and many others do not.

The first manuscript version of this book was subtitled *A Comprehensive Anthology,* was twice its current length and included selections from 185 authors, thus becoming too large to produce within one normal-sized volume. It began with Henku, an ancient Egyptian, writing circa 2900 BCE and culminated with Manuel Castells commenting on "informationalism" and globalization in 2001. In between were excerpts from Hammurabi (1700 BCE), Persian writers from the *Vendidad* and *Fargard IV* (630 BCE), Confucius (551–479 BCE), Plato (428–348 BCE), Aristotle (384–322 BCE), Epicurus (341–270 BCE), Hindu texts between 321 BCE and 200 CE, Mencius (4th century BCE), Lao Tzu (between 6th and 3rd centuries BCE), Polybius (204–122 BCE), plus three dozen others up to John Locke. I formulated this list through the pedestrian, empirical method of examining about fifty histories published during the last half-century on political and social theory, philosophy, and comparative religion, in an effort to identify those writers who have been most consistently regarded as essential to the ever-changing canon.

Anyone who has done similar excavations would not be surprised by the other theorists and sources whom I omitted from the present volume, including (in chronological order) Lucretius, Cicero, Epictetus, Marcus Aurelius, Augustine, *Koran,* Avicenna, John of Salisbury, Averrös, Aquinas, Dante, Marsilius of Padua, Ibn Khaldun, Christine de Pisan, Nicolas of Pusa, Pico della Mirandola, Machiavelli, Thomas More, Luther, Henricus Cornelius Agrippa, Erasmus, Calvin, Tullia d'Aragona, Veronica Franco, Moderata Fonte, Montaigne, Jean Bodin, Grotius, Arcangela Tarabotti, Anna Maria von Schurman, Hobbes, Spinoza, Cecilia Ferrazzi, and Pascal. It grieves my heart to have deleted them, my only solace being that perhaps in the future it will become feasible to issue a volume that complements this one and includes all these worthies. For the sad truth of Alfred North Whitehead's enduring quip (his most famous statement it now seems), that all philosophy is a series of footnotes to Plato, becomes quite plausible after one has read widely enough in premodern social, philosophical, religious, and political literature. For something to be utterly "new" and therefore absolutely foreign to Plato, Aristotle, Aquinas, Montaigne, or Hobbes, it must nearly by definition involve some invention—technological (e.g., the Web) or sociological (animal rights)—which could not have been anticipated by earlier thinkers because of the limitations imposed on them by their existential circumstances. Yet in terms of ordinary human interaction and political goings on, we must return to Terence's famous remark, much beloved by Marx and many others: *Homo sum; humani nihil a me alienum puto* ("I am human; and nothing human is foreign to me"), a sentiment from around 150 BCE. Or, slightly less elevated, but equally treasured among epigraph collectors: *Plus ça change, plus c'est la même chose* (the more things change, the more they stay the same).

Three thousand years of social thinking and analysis do not lend themselves to easily defensible categorization, so rather than trying to divide the book into subject headings, or some other typology of convenience, I stuck with sheer chronology. The authors I chose to excerpt represented every one I could identify from the dozens of volumes (all that I could find which were published since the turn of the 20th century) that attempted approximately the same task I had set before myself. To this I added a slew of women writers very recently "discovered," mostly from the European renaissance and early modern period, whose views of the male-dominating societies of their times provide a lively and prescient understanding of gender relations that continues to repay study these four and five centuries later. Alas, they were felled by the editor's axe for lack of space, because their "early modern" provenance could not be fitted within the temporal limits of the book that were established by the harsh financial forces that rule publishing today.

Equally disturbing were the authors who did indeed write during the prescribed period (since 1690), but who, according to the helpful sentiments of many reviewers whose opinions were solicited by another publisher, were not quite so central to the book's mission. These included Henri Bergson, Jean D'Alembert, Louis de Bonald, George Gissing, Lewis Morgan, Erich Remarque, Friedrich Schelling, Jonathan Swift, Alfred Wallace, and Florian Znaniecki. The selections from their works which I had chosen to include are wonderfully informative, and in some cases—Bergson, Gissing, Remarque, Znaniecki come to mind—quite unique as voices in the social thought choir. To have omitted them is yet another small injury to the proud but bloodied body of the book as it eventually came to stand. And lastly, by way of explaining why certain names do not appear in the Contents which one might well think ought to be there, consider this datum: when a dozen scholars who specialize in social thought were asked to evaluate still another version of the readings, they suggested that I delete some 26 writers, while at the same time urging me to add over 100 others, many of them from "developing countries." Their opinions were instructive to be sure, but fascinatingly frustrating as well, since it became quite clear that in this realm of scholarship, it is impossible to please everyone (perhaps anyone!). Particularly disturbing were the many suggestions of writers now working in Latin America, Africa, and Southeast Asia who have important things to say about social life at the macro-level, and whose work I could not fit into this book. Perhaps another book entirely should be given to them. Some of the authors who were nominated for inclusion (109 altogether) but whom I could not fit into this edition were Jane Addams, Louis Althusser, Mohammed Arkoun, Mikhail Bakunin, Ulrich Beck, Daniel Bell, Ruth Benedict, Harold Bloom, Robert Bly, and Jacob Burckhardt—just to list those within the first two letters of the alphabet. And whereas it is quite reasonable to include any or all of these authors into a newly constructed canon of social thought—some readers might even say they are indispensable to such a project—it was impossible, again, sheerly for reasons of expense and available pages.

Marx pointed out that "the real foundations" of all social life lie in political-economic relations, no matter how elaborate and obscuring the "superstructure" of beliefs and sentiments might be that are erected upon them. So, too, the subtle intellectual distinctions that might be drawn upon when selecting authors for a book such as this one amount to very little when confronted by the insistent demands from publishers for payment of reprint fees, a fact that has become the bane of anthologies and which makes creating another book like Parsons' huge *Theories of Society* out of the question. There are several authors whom I wanted badly to include in this edition of the book, but could not because of exorbitant reprint demands from their copyright owners, specifically Simone de Beauvoir (*The Second Sex*), Erving Goffman (*The Presentation of Self in Everyday Life*), Erik Erikson (*Childhood and Society*), and Manuel Castells (afterword to *The Hacker Ethic and the Spirit of the Information Age*). There are still others—Sartre,

Giddens, Marcuse, et cetera—from whose works I had intended to excerpt more than is here, but the same financial constraints imposed themselves. There is no good intellectual excuse for omitting these authors, needless to say, but larger forces are at work.

The Most Recent Canon Wars

In 1960 the Harvard doyen of social theorists, Talcott Parsons, and several associates edited *Theories of Society* (Free Press), the largest reader in social thought ever offered in English, coming to over one million words of print. Interestingly, it sold well enough to remain available for about 20 years, in a two-volume boxed set as well as a one-volume "student edition." Such a book today is inconceivable given extant market conditions and normal costs of college textbooks in the humanities and social sciences. And yet, with an ironical twist that Parsons might have appreciated, during the ensuing 44 years since his compendium appeared, social thought has experienced an unrivalled period of fabulous growth, not only in the U.S. and Europe, but all over the literate world. The Parsons volume, as one might expect, contained work by few women or people of color, not so much because Parsons and his distinguished co-editors chose to silence their voices out of chauvinist pride, but because they simply did not know of their existence. Today, of course, we are in an entirely different intellectual environment. Assembling a multicultural survey of social theory that would draw on (translated) texts from around the world, from many ethnic identifications, would surely prove to be a thrilling scholarly challenge, but would also likely eventuate in a volume several times as large as Parsons's huge book. The good news, as they say, is that we are awash in crackling social thought, yet the bad news is the same, for there is no reasonable way to bring these disparate writings together within one source.

This is not the place for a full scholarly treatment of "the canon wars" as they were dubbed a decade ago when they seemed to be raging at their fiercest. But a few remarks are in order, simply because a book such as this would seem to claim by its very existence, even if in muted tones, to offer a survey of readings in social thought which the naive reader might expect to be as nearly comprehensive as analytically possible. For all the reasons mentioned above, this has not been the case here, nor is it likely that any such book could be produced that is commercially viable in the anglophone world that might accomplish this highly desirable goal. Why? Principally because nobody any longer agrees on which authors or which sets of ideas are essential or even more or less worth knowing. It is nostalgia-mongering to believe there ever was a golden age for social thought during which solid consensus about these matters obtained for most interested parties.

Consider, for example, the place of Thomas Jefferson, who, prior to Fawn Brody's biography in the mid-70s, had been virtually above reproach as a social and political thinker. Her accusations about miscegenation at Monticello (a 175 year-old story she revived, but did not supplement) have since escalated into an industry of scholarship arguing over the details of DNA transmission along Jefferson's collateral line. This is the case even though the geneticists who broke the story in *Nature* some years ago refused on scientific grounds to name Jefferson as the indubitable father of Sally Hemings' children. Meanwhile, popular opinion, following popular media, has condemned him as an extraordinary hypocrite and libertine. For the time being it may seem no longer possible to put Jefferson forward as a first-rank political theorist because of these shadows on his memory.

Less salaciously, consider, too, the fate of Marxism and its many variants over the last thirty years. Social theory around 1970, first in Europe and eventually in the U.S., thrived on careful readings of Antonio Gramsci, Louis Althusser, Georg Lukács, Ernst Bloch, Henri Lefebvre, or the Frankfurt School. So many dissertations, books, articles, and conferences were held during the 70s on these thinkers that they seemed then to have entered "permanently" into the pantheon. And yet one is now hardpressed to find university courses which highlight their works, and except for the tragic figure of Walter Benjamin, only now fully coming into his own, none of these eminent thinkers from the Left is any longer considered worth extended analysis. There is an assumption, probably faulty, that today's readers literate in social thought should know something, however little, about these writers. But just as it is hard now to remember how many friendships were sundered because of conflicting enthusiasms for Althusser versus Gramsci, or Marcuse versus Lukács, so it seems improbable that at one point more than 25 volumes of Lukács's books had been translated into English, or that Gramsci's *Prison Notebooks* were treated like Biblical texts by the Left. When Dylan wrote "The Times They are A-Changing" in 1964, he neglected to mention (failing to read Hegel) that they were going to keep a-changing over and over, without rest.

Because all good ideas recirculate ad nauseam—Nietzsche's "eternal return" is the standard imagery—there is little doubt that some of these now neglected scholars will resurface, perhaps when the next global economic downturn or war of major proportion occurs. It is important that they, and others who are not presently fashionable (Spengler, Sorokin, Karen Horney, Gaetano Mosca, a long list) should be rehabilitated in due course because in some ways the social, political, and cultural worlds that press us on every side more and more begin to resemble that queasy time in European history prior to the First World War, when things seemed to have been going swimmingly for far too long. But such futuristic speculation aside, it is fairly easy to point to the beginnings of our current "culture" or "canon wars." The Stanford University Western culture course in 1987 came under attack and subsequent reconstruction, which made the national news and alerted non-intellectuals everywhere that the Ivory Tower was tilting off its axis.

Also in 1987 a little known philosophy professor and translator of Plato and Rousseau from the University of Chicago published *The Closing of the American Mind.* Allan Bloom fired a shot across the bow of everyone in the academy, and beyond it, who did not subscribe to Leo Strauss's conservatism, into which he had been indoctrinated as a graduate student during the 50s, and which the John M. Olin Foundation was continuing to sponsor there in the 80s. His bestseller was serialized in the *Kansas City Star* and other newspapers, an unheard-of event for an academic author's work, and very soon Allan Bloom was the best-known professor in the U.S. That book (and sister volumes, like E. D. Hirsch's *Cultural Literacy*), which harmonized well with the tone of Reagan's cultural politics, proved a boon to other serious works, even if for reasons Bloom never intended. His revulsion against campus violence in the 60s (specifically at Cornell, where he then worked) and his odd coupling of these events with the writings of Nietzsche, Max Weber, and others whom his teacher, Leo Strauss, had repudiated, set off an avalanche of popular and academic commentary that has not abated. It seemed then as it does now that everyone's ox was being gored by some interest group or other, so everyone was put on the defensive. Whereas for centuries one could have murmured "Plato" and met with solid agreement on the value of *The Republic* (a book Bloom translated), during the height of the culture wars, one might hear instead that Plato was a male and therefore irrelevant to women's experiences, Plato was homosexual (positively or negatively weighed), Plato's *Republic* exhibited proto-fascist tendencies and was also exclusively designed for men, Plato was a Westerner and therefore irrelevant to victims of "orientalism," or Plato was actually an African philosopher who had migrated to Greece unwillingly. And if "the father of Western philosophy" himself could be so pilloried in the "marketplace" (*sic*) of ideas, every writer and every text had become fair game for participants in those thousand battles, large or little, which determined reading lists for courses and clubs throughout the literate world.

The sheer volume of works that spoke to this debate quickly became overwhelming, particularly because the war was carried out with a new and highly effective tool—the introduction of the machine gun, the tank, and poison gas in WWI is perhaps analogous—the use of which did not hinge so much on standard scholarly discourse as on a loud anarchy of opinion. The world-wide-web allowed indiscretions and brilliant interventions, on equal footings, to be aired instantly by any interested viewer, which added to the heat of the mêlée, even if the cause of light suffered. Another Bloom, this one Harold, countered Allan Bloom's book with *The Western Canon: The Books and School of the Ages* (1994), in which he named and analyzed those works which he regarded as the backbone of Western intelligence and sensibility. None of the authors he chose is surprising, none very recent, and none fell under the sign of the "politically correct." One black female academic in Boston wrote in *The Chronicle of Higher Education* that Bloom's book was "bullshit" (she used the Spanish term). So it went.

Everyone seemed willing to try their hand at the canon-definition game. David Denby, a movie critic, returned to Columbia as a middle-aged student to reread their Western civilization survey books, *The Great Books: My Adventures with Homer, Rousseau, Woolf, and Other Indestructible Writers of the Western World* (1996) being the result. The notion of "indestructible writer" seemed to be whistling in the dark at that point, not only because of heated arguments about the value of one book versus another, but also because "the future of the book" had been called into question due to the apparent victory of screen-presented information versus the static printed page. Meanwhile, a Princeton critic, Alvin Kernan, published *The Death of Literature* (1990), then edited *What's Happened to the Humanities?* (1997), joining John Ellis's *Literature Lost: Social Agendas and the Corruption of the Humanities* (1997), in a swelling chorus of protest against wholesale repudiation of the books and authors whom older academics had been educated ("trained" is a word they resent) to honor and love.

Reclaiming the Classics (1998) by Herman Sinaiko sounded what became a familiar call to battle, as did a book with the similar title edited by Charles Camic, *Reclaiming the Sociological Classics* (1997). Jan Gorak's *The Making of the Modern Canon: Genesis and Crisis of a Literary Idea* (1991) took a measured, scholarly view, returning to antiquity to understand the mechanics of the process, whereas Carey Kaplan and Ellen C. Rose addressed more contemporary questions in *The Canon and the Common Reader* (1990), specifically focusing on women writers. It is enough for now to mention pertinent books by Robert von Hallberg (1984), Paul Lauter (1991), Albert S. Cook (1993), John Guillory (1993), Vassilis Lambropoulos (1993), Laura Ford (1994), William Casement

(1996), Lillian Robinson (1997), Gregory Jay (1997), and Anne Ferry (2001), all of which spoke directly to the debate over which books and authors ought to be most highly regarded, taught, quoted, and believed. "Cross-over" books written by scholars but aimed at "concerned citizens" also became a subgenre, e.g., Andrew Delbanco's *Required Reading: Why Our American Classics Matter Now* (1997) or, even more star-driven, Italo Calvino's *Why Read the Classics?* (1999). Even dissertations began to appear on the topic, e.g., Bethany Bryson's "Conflict and Cohesion: Why the Canon Wars Did not Destroy English Literature" (2000).

Besides dozens of books, scholarly and popular, articles appeared by the hundreds, since every discipline and subdiscipline which had anything to do with "sacred" texts felt the need to speak out unambiguously regarding the protection and proliferation of their heritage, however defined and redefined. Charles Altieri's "An Idea and Ideal of a Literary Canon" (1984), John Guillory's "Canonical and Non-Canonical: A Critique of the Current Debate" (1987), "Theorizing the Culture Wars" by J. Russell Perkin (1993; a review-essay covering Henry Gates' *Loose Canons,* Gerald Graff's *Beyond the Culture Wars,* and William Spanos's *The End of Education*), and William Calin's "Making a Canon" (1999) typify a very large mass of scholarly and "political" work that was done in the humanities and social sciences during this period. As with most large-scale academic feuds which inflame the public sphere, this one ran out of steam more from exhaustion than because "the issue," however defined, had been settled.

Whereas English literature and feminist philosophy seemed to inhabit the eye of the hurricane, social thought went through its own moments of self-discovery and reevaluation. After considering Steven Seidman's revisionist theory textbook, *Contested Knowledge,* and dozens of articles like Jo Eadie's "Boy Talk: Social Theory and Its Discontents," no-one who studies social thought seriously could ignore the enlarged terrain that had made itself visible over the last decade. *The Women Founders* by Patricia Lengermann and Jill Niebrugge-Brantley made room for Harriet Martineau, Jane Addams, Charlotte Perkins Gilman, Anna Julia Cooper, Marianne Weber, and others who to that point had not been treated as important theorists in any textbook. And yet, as I pointed out above, the joyful expansion of "the canon," with inclusion of queer theorists, feminists, post-colonialists, and others who have until recently been on the outside looking in, brings with it the sad truth that as ever more texts are added to "the list," fewer and fewer scholars can claim familiarity with the entirety. An era of a thousand flowers is also one of a thousand conversations, many of which are carried out oblivious to one another for sheer lack of time (e.g., see Seodial F. H. Deena, 2001). When Parsons' *The Structure of Social Action* (1937) was considered "the book" (roughly between 1950 and 1975) that every American social theorist had to read at some point, it supplied a common grounding to discussions, even when its readers took strong exception to Parsons' story of how classical theory had developed.

There is no such text that occupies an analogous position today—an "achievement" which postmodernists would doctrinally applaud. Enthusiastic supporters of "difference" and the fractured, fragmented epistemological zone of enterprise which antinomic differences create are not, I suspect, under the obligation to teach survey courses in social thought. For pedagogical purposes some coherence is required, some plausible narrative about the evolution and devolution of social theory, so that the novice can get hold of the arguments before taking on the more taxing question of which works deserve canonical status and which do not, which retained for the long haul, and which set aside. My predominant goal in this book has been to provide enough breadth to allow the energetic reader (with instructor, should there be one) to find something of interest, something on which to build their own discussions, whichever directions they eventually choose to take. One need not agree with everything one reads in order to learn. Yet if the Roman playwright Terence was right, that nothing human should be foreign to us, then working one's way through the history of social thought is a sound way to expand and enrich our humanity.

References

Altieri, Charles 1984: An Idea and Ideal of a Literary Canon. Pp. 41–64 in Robert Von Hallberg (ed), *Canons,* Chicago: University of Chicago Press.

Bloom, Allan 1987: *The Closing of the American Mind.* New York: Simon and Schuster.

Bloom, Harold 1994: *The Western Canon: The Books and School of the Ages.* New York: Harcourt, Brace, and Co.

Brody, Fawn 1974: *Thomas Jefferson: An Intimate History.* New York: W. W. Norton.

Bryson, Bethany Page 2000: Conflict and Cohesion: Why the Canon Wars Did Not Destroy English Literature. Doctoral dissertation, Princeton University.

Calin, William 1999: Making a Canon. *Philosophy and Literature,* 23:1, 1–16.

Calvino, Italo 1999: *Why Read the Classics?* New York: Pantheon Books.

Camic, Charles (ed) 1997: *Reclaiming the Sociological Classics: The State of the Scholarship.* Malden, MA: Blackwell Pubs.

Casement, William 1996: *The Great Canon Controversy: The Battle of the Books in Higher Education.* New Brunswick, NJ: Transaction Pubs.

Cook, Albert Spaulding 1993: *Canons and Wisdom.* Philadelphia: University of Pennsylvania Press.

Deena, Seodial F. H. 2001: *Canonization, Colonization, Decolonization: A Comparative Study of Political and Critical Works buy Minority Writers.* New York: Peter Lange.

Delbanco, Andrew 1997: *Required Reading: Why Our American Classics Matter Now.* New York: Farrar, Straus, and Giroux.

Eadie, Jo 2001: Boy Talk: Social Theory and Its Discontents [review essay]. *Sociology,* 35:2, 575–582.

Ferry, Anne 2001: *Tradition and the Individual Poem: An Inquiry into Anthologies.* Stanford: Stanford University Press.

Ford, Laura Christian 1994: *Liberal Education and the Canon: Five Great Texts Speak to Contemporary Social Issues.* Columbia, SC: Camden House.

Guillory, John 1987: Canonical and Non-Canonical: A Critique of the Current Debate. *ELH,* 54:3 (Autumn), 483–527.

———— 1993: *Cultural Capital: The Problem of Literary Canon Formation.* Chicago: University of Chicago Press.

Jay, Gregory S. 1997: *American Literature and the Culture Wars.* Ithaca: Cornell University Press.

Kaplan, Carey and Ellen Cronan Rose 1990: *The Canon and the Common Reader.* Knoxville: University of Tennessee Press.

Kernan, Alvin 1990: *The Death of Literature.* New Haven: Yale University Press.

Lambropoulos, Vassilis 1993: *The Rise of Eurocentrism: Anatomy of Interpretation.* Princeton: Princeton University Press.

Lauter, Paul 1991: *Canons and Contexts.* New York: Oxford University Press.

Lengermann, Patricia Madoo and Jill Niebrugge-Brantley 1998: *The Women Founders: Sociology and Social Theory 1830–1930: A Text/Reader.* New York: McGraw-Hill.

Perkin, J. Russell 1993: Theorizing the Culture Wars [review essay]. *Postmodern Culture,* 3:3.

Robinson, Lillian S. 1997: *In the Canon's Mouth: Dispatches from the Culture Wars.* Bloomington: Indiana University Press.

Seidman, Steven 1994: *Contested Knowledge: Social Theory in the Postmodern Era.* Oxford, UK: Blackwell.

Sinaiko, Herman L. 1998: *Reclaiming the Canon: Essays on Philosophy, Poetry, and History.* New Haven: Yale University Press.

von Hallberg, Robert (ed) 1984: *Canons* [articles from *Critical Inquiry*]. Chicago: University of Chicago Press.

part I

ORIGINS OF THE MODERN WORLDVIEW

John Locke   *1632–1704*

Mary Astell   *1668–1731*

Giambattista Vico   *1668–1744*

Voltaire   *1694–1778*

Montesquieu   *1689–1755*

Denis Diderot   *1713–1784*

Jean-Jacques Rousseau   *1712–1778*

Adam Smith   *1723–1790*

Adam Ferguson   *1723–1816*

John Millar   *1735–1801*

Immanuel Kant   *1724–1804*

Etienne de Condillac   *1715–1780*

David Hume   *1711–1776*

Thomas Jefferson   *1743–1826*

Johann G. Herder   *1744–1803*

Jeremy Bentham   *1748–1832*

JOHN LOCKE

1632–1704

Son of a country lawyer who fought with the Roundheads against the Crown, John Locke was born in Wrington, Somerset in England on August 29, 1632, was reared in Pensford, a few miles south of Bristol, remained a bachelor all his life, and died on October 28, 1704 at the age of 72 in Oates, Essex. Through his father's political connections, he was able to attend the Westminster School, where Locke chafed against the fierce discipline, then to Christ Church at Oxford University, receiving both a B.A. (1656) and M.A. (1658). He followed the traditional scholastic regimen (Greek, Latin, rhetoric, moral philosophy, geometry, and so on), but supplemented these uninspiring courses by studying science and medicine. As an elected fellow of Christ Church, Oxford, Locke was happy at the restoration of Charles II in 1660, and the next year he inherited part of his father's estate, relieving him from financial worry. After teaching undergraduates for four years, he refused to become ordained, was forced therefore to quit his post, and took up diplomatic work to Germany in 1665. He worked as household physician for Lord Ashley (later becoming Shaftesbury) despite having no medical degree, but served the much broader function of general advisor and friend. He later worked with Robert Boyle, a founder of modern chemistry, and Thomas Sydenham, a medical researcher. Interested primarily in natural science as well as investigating the ultimate grounding of moral and political philosophy, between 1675 and 1679 he lived in France and read Descartes in order to modernize his conception of philosophy. After a few years in England, he fled to Holland in 1683 due to Schaftesbury's arrest for treason, finally returning to Britain in 1689 with the Princess of Orange, soon to be Queen.

Locke loathed scholastic dogma but was also skeptical of Descartes' penchant for speculation, considering it a weakness in an otherwise important body of thought. Like Descartes, he much admired the growing strength of natural sciences, and even though he did not feel inclined to do original research in these areas, he was interested in their epistemological problems. This gave rise to his most important work, *An Essay Concerning Humane (sic) Understanding* (1690), published when he was 58. His *Two Treatises of Government* (1690) have remained fundamental works in political theory and continue to be studied avidly. The two selections offered here reflect Locke's broader concerns, the first with the practice of hermeneutics (theories and techniques of textual interpretation), particularly concerning the Biblical texts that fascinated him from a believer's viewpoint, and the second regarding the proper mode for educating young people, a favorite topic of early Enlightenment thinkers. (The following author, Mary Astell, opposed some of Locke's views about education.)

ESSAY CONCERNING HUMAN UNDERSTANDING, 1690

On Hermeneutics

I have heard sober Christians very much admire, why ordinary illiterate people, who were professors, that showed a concern for religion, seemed much more conversant in St. Paul's epistles than in the plainer, and (as it seemed to them) much more intelligible parts of the New Testament; they confessed, that, though they read St. Paul's epistles with their best attention, yet they generally found them too hard to be mastered; and they laboured in vain so far to reach the apostle's meaning, all along in the train of what he said, as to read them with that satisfaction that arises from a feeling that we understand and fully comprehend the force and reasoning of an author; and therefore they could not imagine what those saw in them, whose eyes they thought not much better than their own. But the case was plain; these sober inquisitive readers had a mind to see nothing in St Paul's epistles but just what he meant; whereas those others, of a quicker and gayer sight, could see in them what they pleased. Nothing is more acceptable to fancy than pliant terms, and expressions that are not obstinate; in such it can find its account with delight, and with them be illuminated, orthodox, infallible at pleasure, and in its own way. . . . Paul's meaning, to those of that way, in all those places where his thoughts and sense run counter to what any party has espoused for orthodox; as it must, unavoidably, to all but one of the different systems, in all those passages that any way relate to the points in controversy between them!

This is a mischief, which however frequent, and almost natural, reaches so far, that it would justly make all those who depend upon them wholly diffident of commentators, and let them see how little help was to be expected from them,

in relying on them for the true sense of the sacred Scripture, did they not take care to help to cozen themselves, by choosing to use and pin their faith on such expositors as explain the sacred Scripture in favour of those opinions that they beforehand have voted orthodox, and bring to the sacred Scripture, not for trial, but confirmation. . . .

In prosecution of this thought, I concluded it necessary, for the understanding of any one of St. Paul's epistles, to read it all through at one sitting; and to observe, as well as I could, the drift and design of his writing it. If the first reading gave me some light, the second gave me more; and so I persisted on, reading constantly the whole epistle over at once, till I came to have a good general view of the apostle's main purpose in writing the epistle, the chief branches of his discourse wherein he prosecuted it, the arguments he used, and the disposition of the whole.

This, I confess, is not to be obtained by one or two hasty readings; it must be repeated again and again, with a close attention to the tenour of the discourse, and a perfect neglect of the divisions into chapters and verses. On the contrary, the safest way is to suppose that the epistle has but one business, and one aim, until, by a frequent perusal of it, you are forced to see there are distinct independent matters in it, which will forwardly enough show themselves.

It requires so much more pains, judgment, and application, to find the coherence of obscure and abstruse writings, and makes them so much the more unfit to serve prejudice and pre-occupation, when found; that it is not to be wondered that St. Paul's epistles have, with many, passed rather for disjointed, loose, pious discourses, full of warmth and zeal and overflows of light, rather than for calm, strong, coherent reasonings, that carried a thread of argument and consistency all through them.

But this muttering of lazy or ill-disposed readers hindered me not from persisting in the course I had begun: I continued to read the same epistle over and over, and over again, until I came to discover, as appeared to me, what was the drift and aim of it, and by what steps and arguments St Paul prosecuted his purpose.

From *The Locke Reader,* John W. Yolton, Ed. Published by Cambridge University Press. Copyright © 1977.

⌒

"EDUCATION AS TRAINING FOR VIRTUE"

87. *Education sections 45, 70, 94, 99–100, 135, 159*

He that has not a mastery over his inclinations, he that knows not how to resist the importunity of present pleasure or pain, for the sake of what reason tells him is fit to be done, wants the true principle of virtue and industry, and is in danger never to be good for any thing. This temper, therefore, so contrary to unguided nature, is to be got betimes; and this habit, as the true foundation of future ability and happiness, is to be wrought into the mind, as early as may be, even from the first dawnings of any knowledge or apprehension in children; and so to be confirmed in them, by all the care and ways imaginable; by those who have the oversight of their education.

For you will be ready to say, "What shall I do with my son? If I keep him always at home, he will be in danger to be my young master; and if I send him abroad, how is it possible to keep him from the contagion of rudeness and vice, which is everywhere so in fashion? In my house he will perhaps be more innocent; but more ignorant too of the world: wanting there change of company, and being used constantly to the same faces, he will, when he comes abroad, be a sheepish or conceited creature."

I confess, both sides have their inconveniences. Being abroad, it is true, will make him bolder, and better able to bustle and shift amongst boys of his own age; and the emulation of schoolfellows often puts life and industry into young lads. But till you can find a school, wherein it is possible for the master to look after the manners of his scholars, and can show as great effects of his care of forming their minds to virtue, and their carriage to good breeding, as of forming their tongues to the learned languages; you must confess, that you have a strange value for words, when, preferring the languages of the ancient Greeks and Romans to that which made them

such brave men, you think it worth while to hazard your son's innocence and virtue, for a little Greek and Latin. For, as for that boldness and spirit, which lads get amongst their play fellows at school, it has ordinarily such a mixture of rudeness and an ill-turned confidence, that those misbecoming and disingenuous ways of shifting in the world must be unlearned, and all the tincture washed out again, to make way for better principles and such manners as make a truly worthy man. He that considers how diametrically opposite the skill of living well, and managing, as a man should do, his affairs in the world, is to that malapertness, tricking, or violence, learnt among schoolboys, will think the faults of a privater education infinitely to be preferred to such improvements; and will take care to preserve his child's innocence and modesty at home, as being nearer of kin, and more in the way of those qualities, which make an useful and able man. Nor does any one find, or so much as suspect, that the retirement and bashfulness, which their daughters are brought up in, makes them less knowing or less able women. Conversation, when they come into the world, soon gives them a becoming assurance; and whatsoever, beyond that, there is of rough and boisterous, may in men be very well spared too: for courage and steadiness, as I take it, he not in roughness and ill breeding.

Virtue is harder to be got, than a knowledge of the world; and, if lost in a young man, is seldom recovered. Sheepishness and ignorance of the world, the faults imputed to a private education, are neither the necessary consequences of being bred at home; nor, if they were, are they incurable evils. Vice is the more stubborn, as well as the more dangerous evil of the two; and therefore, in the first place, to be fenced against. If that sheepish softness, which often enervates those, who are bred like fondlings at home, be carefully to be avoided, it is principally so for virtue's sake; for fear lest such a yielding temper should be too susceptible of vicious impressions, and expose the novice too easily to be corrupted. A young man, before he leaves the shelter of his father's house, and the guard of a tutor, should be fortified with resolution, and made acquainted with men, to secure his virtue; lest he should be led into some ruinous course, or fatal precipice, before he is sufficiently acquainted with the dangers of conversation, and has steadiness enough not to yield to every temptation. Were it not for this, a young man's bashfulness, and ignorance of the world, would not so much need an early care. Conversation would cure it in a great measure; or, if that will not do it early enough, it is only a stronger reason for a good tutor at home. For, if pains be to be taken to give him a manly air and assurance betimes, it is chiefly as a fence to his virtue, when he goes into the world, under his own conduct. . . .

But fathers, observing that fortune is often most successfully courted by bold and bustling men, are glad to see their sons pert and forward betimes; take it for an happy omen, that they will be thriving men, and look on the tricks they play their school-fellows, or learn from them, as a proficiency in the art of living, and making their way through the world. But I must take the liberty to say, that he that lays the foundation of his son's fortune in virtue and good breeding, takes the only sure and warrantable way. And it is not the waggeries or cheats practised among school-boys, it is not their roughness one to another, nor the well-laid plots of robbing an orchard together, that makes an able man; but the principles of justice, generosity, and sobriety, joined with observation and industry, qualities which I judge school-boys do not learn much of one another. . . .

It is virtue then, direct virtue, which is the hard and valuable part to be aimed at in education; and not a forward pertness, or any little arts of shifting. All other considerations and accomplishments should give way, and be postponed, to this. This is the solid and substantial good, which tutors should not only read lectures, and talk of; but the labour and art of education should furnish the mind with, and fasten there, and never cease till the young man had a true relish of it, and placed his strength, his glory, and his pleasure in it. . . .

A governor should teach his scholar to guess at, and beware of, the designs of men he hath to do with, neither with too much suspicion, nor too much confidence; but, as the young man is by nature most inclined to either side, rectify him, and bend him the other way. He should accustom him to make, as much as is possible, a true judgment of men by those marks, which serve best to show what they are, and give a prospect into their inside; which often shows itself in little things, especially when they are not in parade, and upon their guard. He should acquaint him with the true state of the world, and dispose him to think no man better or worse, wiser or foolisher, than he really is. Thus, by safe and insensible degrees, he will pass from boy to a man; which is the most hazardous step in all the whole course of life. This therefore should be carefully watched, and a young man with great diligence handed over it; and not, as now usually is done, be taken from a governor's conduct, and all at once thrown into the world under his own, not without manifest danger of immediate spoiling; there being nothing more frequent, than instances of the great looseness, extravagancy, and debauchery, which young men have run into, as soon as they have been let loose from a severe and strict education: which, I think, may be chiefly imputed to their wrong way of breeding, especially in this part; for, having been bred up in a great ignorance of what the world truly is, and finding it quite another thing, when they come into it, than what they were taught it should be, and so imagined it was; are easily persuaded, by other kind of tutors, which they are sure to meet with, that the discipline they were kept under, and the lectures that were read to them, were but the formalities of education, and the restraints of childhood; that the freedom longing to men, is to take their swing in a full enjoyment of what was before forbidden them. . . .

The only fence against the world, is a thorough knowledge of it: into which a young gentleman should be entered by degrees, as, he can bear it; and the earlier the better, so he be in safe and skillful hands to guide him. The scene should be gently opened, and his entrance made step by step, and the dangers pointed out that attend him, from the several degrees, tempers, designs, and clubs of men. He should be prepared to be shocked by some, and caressed by others; warned who are like to oppose, who to mislead, who to undermine him, and who to serve him. He should be instructed how to know and distinguish men; where he should let them see, and when dissemble the knowledge of them, and their aims and workings. And if he be too forward to venture upon his own strength and skill, the perplexity and trouble of a misadventure now and then, that reaches not his innocence, his health, or reputation, may not be an ill way to teach him more caution.

MARY ASTELL

1668–1731

Mary Astell was born on November 12, 1666 in Newcastle-upon-Tyne in England, remained unmarried, and died on May 9, 1731 at Chelsea at the age of 64. Her uncle, a clergyman, taught her Latin, French, logic, mathematics, and natural philosophy, which surely put her in a very small minority of highly educated women at the time. At 20 she traveled to London and continued her studies there, finally moving to Chelsea. Astell opposed John Locke's views on education (see previous selection), and because of this heterodoxy, her own views were in turn attacked by some of her contemporaries.

Her most significant works include *A Serious Proposal to the Ladies, wherein a Method is offered for the Improvement of their Minds* (Part I, 1696; Part II, 1697), in which she urged women to study and meditate on religious subjects. She also proposed a scheme for a women's college which Queen Anne would have implemented had not Bishop Burnet objected. During her lifetime she was also known for *The Christian Religion, as professed by a Daughter of the Church of England* (1705), but today her most notable work is *Reflections on Marriage* (published anonymously in 1700, then reissued under her name in 1706). The last named work is interesting for many reasons, not least of which is the fact that it records the views of an unmarried woman at 40 about an institution in which she chose not to participate. As she explains in the excerpt reprinted here, Astell found it disturbing that "the sacred institution of marriage" could so often begin with high hopes and equally often tend toward a condition of miserable unhappiness, especially for the woman.

REFLECTIONS UPON MARRIAGE, 1700/06

. . . Is it the being ty'd to *One* that offends us? Why this ought rather to recommend Marriage to us, and would really do so, were we guided by Reason, and not by Humour or brutish Passion. He who does not make Friendship the chief inducement to his Choice, and prefer it before any other consideration, does not deserve a good Wife, and therefore should not complain if he goes without one. Now we can never grow weary of our Friends; the [10] longer we have had them the more they are endear'd to us; and if we have One well assur'd, we need seek no further, but are sufficiently happy in Her. The love of Variety in this and in other cases, shews only the ill Temper of our own Minds, in that we seek for *settled* Happiness in this present World, where it is not to be found, instead of being Content with a competent share, chearfully enjoying and being thankful for the Good that is afforded us, and patiently bearing with the Inconveniences that attend it.

The Christian Institution of Marriage provides the best that may be for Domestic Quiet and Content, and for the Education of Children; so that if we were not under the tye of Religion, even the Good of Society and civil Duty would oblige us to what that requires at our Hands. And since the very best of us are but poor frail Creatures, full of Ignorance and Infirmity, so that in justice we ought to tolerate each other, and exercise that Patience towards our Companions to Day, which we shall give them occasion to shew towards us to Morrow, the more we are accustom'd to any one's Conversation, the better shall we understand their Humour, be more able to comply with their Weakness and less offended at it. For he who would have every [11] one submit to his Humours and will not in his turn comply with them, tho' we should suppose him always in the Right, whereas a Man of this temper very seldom is so, he's not fit for a Husband, scarce fit for Society, but ought to be turn'd out of the Herd to live by himself.

There may indeed be inconveniences in a Married Life; but is there any Condition without them? And he who lives single that he may indulge Licentiousness and give up himself to the conduct of wild and ungovern'd Desires, or indeed out of any other inducement, than the Glory of God and the Good of his Soul, through the prospect he has of doing more Good, or because his frame and disposition of Mind are fitted for it, may rail as he pleases against Matrimony, but can never justifie his own Conduct, nor clear it from the imputation of Wickedness and Folly.

But if Marriage be such a blessed State, how comes it, may you say, that there are so few happy Marriages? Now in answer to this, it is not to be wonder'd that so few succeed, we should rather be surpriz'd to find so many do, considering how imprudently Men engage, the Motives they act by, and the very strange Conduct they observe throughout.

[12] For pray, what do Men propose to themselves in Marriage? What Qualifications do they look after in a Spouse? What will she bring is the first enquiry? How many Acres? Or how much ready Coin? Not that this is altogether an unnecessary Question, for Marriage without a Competency, that is, not only a bare Subsistence, but even a handsome and plentiful Provision, according to the Quality and Circumstances of the Parties, is no very comfortable Condition. They who marry for Love as they call it, find time enough to repent their rash Folly, and are not long in being convinc'd, that whatever fine Speeches might be made in the heat of Passion, there could be no *real Kindness* between those who can agree to make each other miserable. But as an Estate is to be consider'd, so it should not be the *Main,* much less the *Only* consideration, for Happiness does not depend on Wealth, *that* may be wanting, and too often is, where *this* abounds. He who Marries himself to a Fortune only, must expect no other satisfaction than that can bring him, but let him not say that Marriage but that his own Covetous or Prodigal Temper, has made him unhappy. What Joy has that Man in all his Plenty, who must either run from home to possess it, [13] contrary to all the Rules of Justice, to the Laws of God and Man, nay, even in opposition to Good nature, and Good breeding too, which some Men make more account of than all the rest; or else be forc'd to share

it with a Woman whose Person or Temper is disagreeable, whose presence is sufficient to sour all his Enjoyments, so that if he has any retrains of Religion, or Good manners, he must suffer the uneasiness of a continual watch, to force himself to a constrain'd Civility!

Few Men have so much Goodness as to bring themselves to a liking of what they loath'd, meerly because it is their Duty to like; on the contrary, when they Marry with an indifferency, to please their Friends or encrease their Fortune, the indifferency proceeds to an aversion, and perhaps even the kindness and complaisance of the poor abus'd Wife shall only serve to encrease it. What follows then? There is no content at home, so it is sought elsewhere, and the Fortune so unjustly got, is as carelessly squander'd. The Man takes a loose, what shou'd hinder him? He has all in his hands, and Custom has almost taken off that small Restraint Reputation us'd to lay. The Wife finds too late what was the Idol the Man adored [14] which her Vanity perhaps, or it may be the Commands and importunities of Relations, wou'd not let her see before; and now he has got *that* into his possession, she must make court to him for a little sorry Alimony out of her own Estate. If Discretion and Piety prevails upon her Passions she sits down quietly, contented with her lot, seeks no Consolation in the Multitude of Adorers, since he whom only she desir'd to please, because it was her duty to do so, will take no delight in her Wit or Beauty: She follows no Diversion to allay her Grief, uses no Cordials to support her Spirit, that may sully her Venue or bring a Cloud upon her Reputation, she makes no appeals to the misjudging Croud, hardly mentions her Misfortunes to her most intimate Acquaintance, nor lays a load on her Husband to ease her self, but wou'd if it were possible conceal his Crimes, tho' her Prudence and Vertue give him a thousand Reproaches without her Intention or knowledge; and retiring from the World, she seeks a more solid Comfort than it can give her, taking care to do nothing that Censoriousness or even Malice itself can misconstrue to her prejudice. Now she puts on all her Reserves, and thinks even innocent Liberties scarce [15] allowable in her Disconsolate State; she has other Business to mind: Nor does she in her Retirements reflect so much upon the hand that administers this bitter Cup, as con-

sider what is the best use she can make of it. And thus indeed Marriage, however unfortunate in other respects, becomes a very great Blessing to her. She might have been exposed to all the Temptations of a plentiful Fortune, have given up her self to Sloth and Luxury, and gone on at the common rate even of the better sort, in doing no hurt, and as little good: But now her kind Husband obliges her to *Consider*, and gives opportunity to exercise her Vertue; he makes it necessary to withdraw from those Gaities and Pleasures of Life, which do more mischief under the Shew of Innocency, than they cou'd if they appear'd attended with a Crime, discomposing and dissolving the Mind, and making it uncapable of any manner of good, to be sure of any thing Great and Excellent. Silence and Solitude, the being forc'd from the ordinary Entertainments of her Station, may perhaps seem a desolate condition at first, and we may allow her, poor weak Woman! to be somewhat shock'd at it, since even a wise and courageous Man perhaps would not keep his ground. We [16] would conceal if we could for the Honour of the Sex, Men's being baffled and dispirited by a smaller Matter, were not the Instances too frequent and too notorious.

But a little time wears off all the uneasiness, and puts her in possession of Pleasures, which till now she has unkindly been kept a stranger to. Affliction, the sincerest Friend, the frankest Monitor, the best Instructer, and indeed the only useful School that Women are ever put to, rouses her understanding, opens her Eyes, fixes her Attention, and diffuses such a Light, such a joy into her Mind, as not only Informs her better, but Entertains her more than ever her *Ruel* did tho', crouded by the Men of Wit. She now distinguishes between Truth and Appearances, between solid and apparent Good; has found out the instability of all Earthly Things, and won't any more be deceiv'd by relying on them; can discern who are the Flatterers of her Fortune, and who the Admirers and Encouragers of her Vertue; accounting it no little blessing to be rid of those Leeches, who only hung upon her for their own Advantage. Now sober Thoughts succeed to hurry and impertinence, to Forms and Ceremony, she can secure her Time, and knows how to [17] Improve it; never truly a Happy Woman till she came in the Eye of the World to be reckon'd Miserable.

Thus the Husband's Vices may become an occasion of the Wife's Vertues, and his Neglect do her a more real Good than his Kindness could. But all injur'd Wives don't behave themselves after this Fashion, nor can their Husbands justly expect it. With what Face can he blame her for following his Example, and being as extravagant on the one Hand, as he is on the other? Tho' she cannot justifie her Excesses to God, to the World, nor to her self, yet surely in respect of him they may admit of an excuse. For to all the rest of his Absurdities, (for Vice is always unreasonable) he adds one more, who expects that Vertue from another which he won't practise himself.

GIAMBATTISTA VICO

1668–1744

Giambattista (Giovanni Battista) Vico was born in Naples on June 23, 1668. He married Teresa Destito in December, 1699 when he was 31, and with her produced eight children. At the age of 75, he died on January 20, 1744, never having left his native city. Naples at the time of his birth and maturation was a hotbed of Enlightenment creativity, visited by the likes of Goethe and Leibniz, and filled with bookstores and salons where advanced ideas were discussed. Vico's education began early in his father's bookstore, where he perfected the audidacticism for which he became famous, and which accounted for his wide interests and peculiar manner of expression. Though he attended a range of schools, some run by Jesuits, he was largely self-taught, studying particularly Plato, Tacitus, Machiavelli, and attending to the salon discourse that highlighted Descartes, Spinoza, Locke, and other writers who at the time were upending the late medieval worldview. He served as a professor of rhetoric at the University of Naples from 1699 until 1741, but the pay was wholly inadequate to his needs, and when he did apply for a much better paying academic position, he was rebuffed.

We are fortunate to have from Vico's own hand in 1725 *The Autobiography* (added to in 1728 and 1731), written as part of what was to be a joint set of such works by various intellectuals in Italy, the only one to surface being Vico's. It is a great work in itself, and one wishes that we had similar documents for other scholars of this period. In encouraging this project, Leibniz had written in a letter of March 22, 1714, "I wish that authors would give us the history of their discoveries and the steps by which they have arrived at them." The hope then was to illustrate that "growth of knowledge" which is a foundational idea within the Enlightenment, and Vico's contribution well illustrates just how valuable such works can be. Yet the most important of Vico's work is his pathbreaking *The Principles of a New Science of the Common Nature of Nations,* commonly known as *The New Science,* published in 1725, with later, enlarged editions in 1730 and 1744. The lore about this difficult work—its influence on James Joyce's fiction, Jules Michelet's historiography, Marx's theory of revolution, and so on—has become itself an academic specialty, even as *The New Science* itself is seldom read with thorough understanding. The following selections come from this work of isolated genius and show how the evolution of language was for Vico as much an indicator of our humanness as any other cultural development. It is small wonder that his contemporaries thought he was a genius, a madman, or both, since his analyses of linguistic and historical change were unlike anything written up to that point.

THE NEW SCIENCE

Concerning the Course [of Human Things] Taken by the Nations, 1725

Three Kinds of Natures.   916. The first nature was a poetic or creative or, as we may even call it, divine nature. For, since the imagination is most powerful in those in whom reason is weakest, by weaving great illusions the first nature gave to bodies the being of substances animated by gods, and did so according to its own idea [of itself]. This was the nature of the theological poets, the most ancient sages in all the gentile nations, [of the times] when the gentile nations were founded upon the belief, possessed by each, in certain gods proper to each. It was, moreover, the wildest and most fearful of natures, but, through that same illusion of the imagination, they developed a terrifying fear of gods of their own invention. Whence endured these two eternal properties: that religion is the only potent means of controlling the wildness of peoples; and that religions prosper when those who preside over them themselves possess an inner reverence for them.

917. The second nature was heroic, which the heroes themselves took to be of divine origin, for since they believed that the gods created everything, they took themselves, as those generated under Jove's auspices, to be his children; and being of the human species, they located in this heroism, and did so with justice, the natural nobility through which they were the princes of the human race. This natural nobility they vaunted over those who repaired to their asylums in order to save themselves from the perils of their infamous bestial communion in which, coming without gods, they were taken to be beasts, in accordance with the two natures we reasoned out above.

918. The third nature was human, an intelligent and therefore modest, benign and reasonable nature, which recognises conscience (*coscienza*), reason and duty as laws.

From *Giambattista Vico: Selected Writings*, pp. 252-258. Translated and edited by Leon Pompa. Copyright © 1982. Reprinted with permission of Cambridge University Press.

Three Kinds of Customs

919. The first customs were steeped in religion and piety, like those narrated of Deucalion and Pyrrha, which sprang up immediately after the flood.

920. The second were choleric and punctilious, like those narrated by Achilles.

921. The third were dutiful, taught at the proper stage of civil duty.

Three Kinds of Natural Law

922. The first law was divine, for since men believed that the gods were everything or had made everything, they took themselves and everything connected therewith to be under the jurisdiction of the gods.

923. The second law was heroic or a law of force, moderated, however, by religion, which alone can confine force within [the limits of] duty when there are no laws or when those which exist are incapable of restraining it. Hence providence arranged that the first peoples, who were ferocious by nature, should be persuaded of [the truth of] their religion, in order that they should naturally become resigned to force and that, being still incapable of reason, they should judge the law by fortune, whence they sought advice through the divination of the auspices. This law of force is the law of Achilles who located the whole of justice at the point of his spear.

924. The third law is the human law which fully developed human reason dictates.

Three Kinds of Governments

925. The first governments were the divine governments which the Greeks called 'theocratic', in which man believed that the gods commanded everything. This was the age of the oracles, which are the most ancient things one reads of in history.

926. The second governments were the heroic or aristocratic governments, which is as much as to say, governments of the 'optimares', in the sense of 'the strongest'. In Greek [they were]

also the governments of the Heraclids, or men of the race of Hercules, in the sense of 'nobles', which were strewn throughout the whole of earliest Greece, of which the Spartan government later survived; and also the governments of 'Curetes' which, the Greeks noted, had spread into Saturnia or ancient Italy, Crete and Asia, and from which came the Romans' governments of the *Quirites,* that is governments of armed priests in public assembly. In these governments civil rights were wholly restricted to the ruling orders of the heroes themselves, because, as we mentioned above, the latter had the distinction of a nobler nature arising from their supposedly divine origin, while the plebs, as those of reputedly bestial origin, were allowed only the customary rights of life and natural liberty.

927. The third governments are the human governments in which, through that equality of intelligent nature which is the nature proper to man, all are equal in law. For either all are born free in their cities—the free popular cities, that is—in which the whole or the majority [of the people] constitute the just forces of the city, which thus makes them the lords of popular liberty; or [all are born free] in monarchies in which the monarchs make all their subjects equal in law and in which, by retaining in their hands alone the whole force of arms, the monarchs are themselves the only persons distinct in civil nature.

Three Kinds of Languages

928. Three kinds of languages.

929. The first of these was a divine mental language [operating] through mute religious acts or divine ceremonies, whence in their civil law the Romans retained the *actus legitimi* [lawful acts] with which they celebrated all affairs to do with civil utility. This language is appropriate to religions because of the following eternal property: that it is of greater importance to them that they be revered than reasoned; and it was necessary in those first times since the gentiles were as yet unable to articulate speech.

930. The second was a language [operating] through heroic emblems, the speech of [military] arms, which, as we pointed out earlier, survived in military discipline.

931. The third language is that of articulate speech which is used by all nations today.

Three Kinds of Characters

932. Three kinds of characters.

933. The first characters were the divine characters, properly called 'hieroglyphics', which, as we proved above, were employed by all nations in their origins. These were certain imaginative universals dictated [to man] naturally by that property, innate to the human mind, of finding pleasure in what is uniform (as we proposed in an axiom above); but since they were unable to create the uniform through genera [made] by abstraction, men did so through [ideal] images [made] by the imagination. All the particular species belonging to each genus were reduced to such poetic universals: everything, for example, to do with the auspices to Jove, everything to do with marriage to Juno, and, similarly, other [collections of related] things to other imaginative universals.

934. The second characters were the heroic characters, which were also imaginative universals, to which all the different kinds of heroic things were reduced: to Achilles, for example, all the deeds of mighty warriors, or to Ulysses all counsels of the wise. But, as the human mind later taught itself how to abstract forms and properties from their subjects, these imaginative genera gave way to intelligible genera, whence philosophers next arose; and later [still], the authors of the New Comedy, which appeared in the most human times of Greece, took these intelligible genera of human customs back from the philosophers and created [human] images of them in their comedies.

935. Finally came the vulgar characters whose development kept pace with that of the vulgar languages. And as the latter are genera, as it were, of the particulars in which the heroic languages had previously been spoken—in the way in which, as instanced earlier, 'I am angry' was created from the heroic expression 'the blood boils in my heart'—so, from the hundred and twenty thousand hieroglyphic characters still, for example, in use in China today, they made the few letters to which, as to genera, one can reduce the hundred and twenty thousand words of which

the articulate vulgar language of the Chinese is composed.

936. We asserted earlier that since such languages and letters were under the lordship of the vulgar [classes] of the peoples, both were called 'vulgar'. This lordship of language and letters must render the free peoples lords also of their laws, since the peoples give the laws those senses under which the powerful are drawn to observe them, [a thing] which, as we noted in the *Elements,* they would not [of themselves] desire. It is naturally denied to monarchs to take this lordship from the people, yet, in consequence of this denial in the nature of human civil things, this lordship which is inseparable from the peoples constitutes in large measure the power of the monarchs, so that the latter can command their royal laws, which hold over the powerful, in accordance with senses which the people have given them. Such lordship of vulgar letters and languages makes it necessary that, in the order of civil nature, the free popular states should have preceded the monarchies.

Three Kinds of Jurisprudence

937. Three kinds of jurisprudence or wisdom.

938. The first jurisprudence was a divine wisdom called, as we saw above, 'mystic theology', which means the science of the divine language or [the science] of understanding the divine mysteries of divination. It was thus a science of the divinity of the auspices and [of] vulgar wisdom, its first sages being the theological poets, who were the first sages of the gentile world. These theological poets were called *mystae* after this mystic theology, a word which Horace knowledgeably renders 'interpreters of the gods'. Hence to this first jurisprudence belonged the first and proper *interpreteri* [interpreting], pronounced like *interpatrari,* that is, 'to enter the fathers', the first name given to the gods, as we noted above. This is what Dante calls *indiarsi,* that is, to enter the mind of God (*Dio*). In such a jurisprudence, the just is decided solely by the solemnity of divine ceremonies, which explains why the Romans inherited so much superstition with their *actus legitimi* [lawful acts] and why the expressions *iustae nuptiae* and *iustum testamentum* for 'solemn' nuptials and testaments survived in their laws.

939. The second jurisprudence was the heroic jurisprudence, in which precautions were taken by means of certain proper words. This is the wisdom of Ulysses, whose talk in Homer is so guarded that he achieves the utility proposed to himself while preserving the propriety of his words. Hence the reputation of the ancient Roman jurists consisted entirely in their *cavere* [being on guard]; and their *de iure respondere* [replying in accordance with the law] was nothing other than their cautioning those who found it necessary to prove their rights in court to specify their exposition of the facts to the praetor in such way that they should fall under the formulae of action, to which the praetor would [then] be unable to deny them access. Similarly, in the recurrence of barbarism, the reputation of the doctors lay wholly in inventing clauses for safeguarding contracts and wills and in knowing how to formulate legal requests and articles: precisely the *cavere and de iure respondere* of the Roman jurists.

940. The third jurisprudence is the human jurisprudence which considers the truth of facts themselves and benignly shapes the justice of laws in accordance with whatever equity in cases requires. This is the jurisprudence celebrated in free popular states and even more in monarchies, which are both human governments.

941. Thus divine and heroic jurisprudence held to the certain in the times of crude nations, but human jurisprudence considers the true in the times of enlightened nations. And all this in consequence of our definitions of the certain and the true and of the relevant axioms laid down in the *Elements.*

Three Kinds of Authority

942. There were three kinds of authority. The first of these is that divine authority for which providence does not demand reason [in men]; the second is heroic authority, which resides entirely in the solemn formulae of the laws; and the third is human authority, which resides in esteeming people of experience, who are possessed of outstanding prudence in things practicable and sublime wisdom in things intelligible.

943. These three kinds of authority which jurisprudence adopts within the course traversed by the nations are a consequence of three kinds of

senatorial authorities which develop within the same course.

944. The first of these [senatorial authorities] was that authority of ownership from which those from whom we hold rights of ownership retained the title *auctores* and which is itself always called *auctoritas* in the Law of the Twelve Tables. This authority was rooted in the divine authority belonged quite properly to these governing senates. Hence the heroic senates gave their approval to that which the people had already discussed or, as Livy says, *eius, quod populus iussisset, deinde patres fierent autories* [the senators later became the authors of that which the people had ordered]. This did not, however, come about in Romulus' interregnum, as history recounts, but in the aristocracy's less elevated times when, according to our earlier reasoning, citizenship had been communicated to the plebs. Under this procedure, as Livy again says, *saepe spectabat ad vim*, that is, revolt often threatened, so that if the people wished to achieve success by it, they needed, for example, to nominate consuls towards whom the senate might be favourably inclined, just as with the nominations of magistrates by the peoples under the monarchies.

945. From the law of Publilius Philo onwards, when the Roman people was declared free and absolute master of sovereignty, as we noted above, the authority of the senate was that of guardianship, rather like that approval given by guardians to the business undertaken by their wards, when the latter are lords of their own patrimonies, which is called *autoritas tutorum*. The senate lent this authority to the people in a legal formula drawn up in advance by the senate, in which,

[again] rather like the authority which the guardian must lend to his ward, the senate would be present to the people, present in the great gatherings, present in the act of passing the law, if the people wanted it passed; otherwise the senate would 'antiquate' it and *probaret antiqua* [approve what already existed], which amounted to a declaration that the innovation was not required. All this was to ensure that in passing laws the people should not, as a result of unsound advice, do some public damage, and therefore that, in passing them, they should be regulated by the senate. Whence the formulae of the laws, which were brought by the senate to the people for the latter to pass, are knowledgeably defined by Cicero as *perscriptae autoritates*: not personal authorisations, like those of guardians who, by their presence, approve the acts of their wards, but authorisations written out in full (for this is the meaning of *perscribere*), as distinct from the formulae for actions which were written *per notas* [in abbreviations], which the people did not understand. This is what the Publilian Livy ordered: that from then on the authority of the senate, to speak with Livy, *valeret in incertum comitiorum eventum* [should be efficacious while the outcome of the public assembly was uncertain].

946. Finally, the state of popular liberty gave way to that of monarchy and the third kind of authority appeared, the authority of esteem or reputation for wisdom, and therefore that of advice, for which the jurists under the emperors were called *autores*. This must be the authority which belongs to senates under monarchs, who have full and absolute liberty to adopt or reject the advice of their senates.

VOLTAIRE

1694–1778

François-Marie Arouet (pseudonym, Voltaire) was born in Paris on November 21, 1694 (he claimed February 20th as his birthdate), later arguing that his mother's husband was not his father. He died 83 years later in the same city on May 30, 1778, owing to the excitement of being repatriated to France as a hero after a long exile. Voltaire was educated until he became 16 at the Jesuit college of Louis-le-Grand in Paris, studying literature, theater, satires, and social life. Though never married, he lived (as a paying guest) in the chateau of the Marquise Gabrielle-Émilie Châtalet for many years, and was her lover and companion from 1734 until 1749. They carried out enormously ambitious scientific and intellectual pursuits together and in their separate studies (she translated Newton's *Principia* from Latin into French, for example), while her husband busied himself with his regiment. She died in 1749, giving birth to still another man's child. Voltaire was exiled to England (about which he wrote brilliantly), Belgium, Germany (where he was the houseguest of Frederick the Great), and Switzerland, often because an arrest warrant had been issued for him by French government authorities at the behest of angry churchmen or insulted nobles. For writing an anti-government satire, he served 11 months in the Bastille when he was 23, and while there adopted his pen-name and wrote *Oedipus*, his first successful play.

He is said to have written an average of 15,000 words per day throughout his professional life, which accounts for the 90-volume set in French of his collected works, very little of which continues to be read. He wrote countless poems, plays, novels, histories, philosophical treatises, scientific works, travelogues, and political tracts. Voltaire is widely regarded as the most brilliant of all French writers, even if not the most profound or beloved. He wrote in a letter of 1741, "That which our eyes and mathematics demonstrate to us we must hold to be true. In all the rest we must say only, 'I don't know'." For this sort of observation he was regularly pilloried by the established orders and beloved by the growing audience for enlightened thought. In some important ways Voltaire more thoroughly embodied the ideals of the Enlightenment than any of his famous colleagues at the time, and surely influenced the framers of U.S. government as they were trying to fashion a nation based on liberty and empiricism. His major works include *Oedipe* (1718), *Philosophical Letters* (1734), the immortal *Candide* (1759), and the *Philosophical Dictionary* (1764). His heart lies in the national library of France, but the rest of his body was stolen from its sarcophagus by right-wing religious fanatics in 1814 and thrown into a refuse pile.

PHILOSOPHICAL LETTERS, 1733–34

On Persons of Rank Who Cultivate Learning

There was a time in France when the arts were cultivated by persons of the first importance in the state. Courtiers particularly took them up, in spite of dissipation, of the taste for trifles, of the passion for intrigue—all deities of the nation.

It seems to me that today the vogue at Court is not for learning. Perhaps in a while the fashion of thinking will return. All that is necessary is for a king to wish it; you can do what you please with this nation. In England people have a habit of thinking, and learning there is more highly honored than in France. This fortunate condition is a necessary consequence of their form of government. In London there are about eight hundred persons who have the right to speak in public and to support the interests of the nation. About five or six thousand claim the same honor in their turn; all the rest set themselves up as judges of these latter, and each man may publish what he thinks about public affairs. Thus the whole nation is under the necessity of educating itself. You are always hearing them talk of the governments of Athens and of Rome; in spite of themselves they think they had better read the authors who have treated of those governments; this study leads naturally to belles-lettres.

In general, men have the kind of mind that corresponds with their calling. Why as a rule have our magistrates, our lawyers, our doctors, and many of the clergy more learning, taste, and wit than one finds in all the other professions? The answer is that it's really their calling to have a cultivated mind, as it is that of a business man to know business.

PHILOSOPHICAL DICTIONARY, 1764

Ancients and Moderns

The great dispute between the ancients and the moderns is not yet settled; it has been on the table since the silver age succeeded the golden age. Mankind has always maintained that the good old times were much better than the present day. Nestor, in the *Iliad,* wishing to insinuate himself as a wise conciliator into the minds of Achilles and Agamemnon, starts by saying to them—"I lived formerly with better men than you; no, I have never seen and I shall never see such great personages as Dryas, Cenaeus, Exadius, Polyphemus, equals to the gods, etc."

Posterity has avenged Achilles for the poor compliment paid him by Nestor; now vainly praised by those who only praise antiquity. Nobody knows Dryas any longer; we have hardly heard of Exadius, or of Cenaeus; and as for Polyphemus, equal to the gods, he has not too good a reputation, unless the possession of a big eye in one's forehead, or the eating of men raw, partakes of divinity. . . .

It is not a matter knowing whether nature has been able to produce in our day as great geniuses and as good works as those of Greek and Latin antiquity; but to know whether we have them in fact. Without a doubt it is not impossible for there to be as big oaks in the forest of Chantilli as in the forest of Dodona; but supposing that the oaks of Dodona had spoken, it would be quite clear that they had a great advantage over ours, which in all probability will never speak.

Nature is not bizarre; but it is possible that she gave the Athenians a country and a sky more suitable than Westphalia and the Limousin for forming certain geniuses. Further, it is possible that the government of Athens, by seconding the climate, put into Demosthenes' head something

From *Philosophical Letters,* by Voltaire, Ernest Dilworth, Trans. Published by Bobbs-Merrill. Copyright © 1961.

From *The Portable Voltaire,* edited and with an Introduction by Ben Ray Redman. Published by The Viking Press (nineteenth printing). Copyright © 1969.

that the air of Climart and La Grenouillère and the government of Cardinal de Richelieu did not put into the heads of Omer Talon and Jerome Bignon.

This dispute is therefore a question of fact. Was antiquity more fecund in great monuments of all kinds, up to the time of Plutarch, than modern centuries have been from the century of the Medicis up to Louis XIV inclusive? . . .

There are therefore spheres in which the moderns are far superior to the ancients, and others, very few in number, in which we are their inferiors. It is to this that the whole dispute is reduced.

Equality

I. It is clear that men, in the enjoyment of their natural faculties, are equal: they are equal when they perform animal functions, and when they exercise their understanding. The King of China, the Great Mogul, the Padisha of Turkey, cannot say to the least of men: "I forbid you to digest, to go to the privy, or to think." All the animals of each species are equal among themselves. Animals, by nature, have over us the advantage of independence. If a bull which is wooing a heifer is driven away with the blows of the horns by a stronger bull, it goes in search of another mistress in another field, and lives free. A cock, beaten by a cock, consoles itself in another poultry-house. It is not so with us. A little vizier exiles a bostangi to Lemnos: the vizier Azem exiles the little vizier to Tenedos: the padisha exiles the vizier Azem to Rhodes: the Janissaries put the padisha in prison, and elect another who will exile good Mussulmans as he chooses; people will still be very obliged to him if he limits his sacred authority to this small exercise.

If this world were what it seems it should be, if man could find everywhere in it an easy subsistence, and a climate suitable to his nature, it is clear that it would be impossible for one man to enslave another. If this globe were covered with wholesome fruits; if the air, which should contribute to our life, gave us no diseases and no premature deaths; if man had no need of lodging and bed other than those of the buck and the deer; then the Gengis-Khans and the Tamerlanes would have no servants other than their children, who

would be decent enough to help them in their old age. . . .

All men then would be necessarily equal, if they were without needs. It is the poverty connected with our species which subordinates one man to another. It is not the inequality which is the real misfortune, it is the dependence. It matters very little that So-and-so calls himself "His Highness," and So-and-so "His Holiness"; but to serve the one or the other is hard.

A big family has cultivated fruitful soil; two little families nearby have thankless and rebellious fields; the two poor families have to serve the opulent family, or slaughter it. There is no difficulty in that. But one of the two indigent families offers its arms to the rich family in exchange for bread, while the other attacks and is defeated. The subservient family is the origin of the servants and the workmen; the beaten family is the origin of the slaves.

In our unhappy world it is impossible for men living in society not to be divided into two classes, the one the rich who command, the other the poor who serve; and these two classes are subdivided into a thousand; and these thousand still have different gradations. . . .

II. All the poor are not unhappy. The majority were born in that state, and continual work keeps them from feeling their position too keenly; but when they do feel it, then one sees wars, like that of the popular party against the senate party in Rome, like those of the peasants in Germany, England, and France. All these wars finish sooner or later with the subjection of the people, because the powerful have money, and money is master of everything in a state. I say in a state, for it is not the same between nations. The nation which makes the best use of the sword will always subjugate the nation which has more gold and less courage.

All men are born with a sufficiently violent liking for domination, wealth, and pleasure, and with a strong taste for idleness; consequently, all men covet the money, the wives, or the daughters of other men; they wish to be their master, to subject them to all their caprices, and to do nothing, or at least to do only very agreeable things. You see clearly that with these fine inclinations it is as impossible for men to be equal as it is impossible for two preachers or two professors of theology not to be jealous of each other.

The human race, such as it is, cannot subsist unless here is an infinity of useful men who possess nothing at all; for it is certain that a man who is well off will not leave his own land to come to till yours, and if you have need of a pair of shoes, it is not the Secretary to the Privy Council who will make them for you. Equality, therefore, is at once the most natural thing and the most fantastic.

~

"ESSAY ON THE MANNERS AND SPIRIT OF NATIONS"

Recapitulation

I have now gone through the immense scene of revolutions that the world has experienced since the time of Charlemagne; and to what have they all tended? To desolation, and the loss of millions of lives! Every great event has been a capital misfortune. History has kept no account of times of peace and tranquillity; it relates only ravages and disasters.

We have beheld our Europe overspread with barbarians after the fall of the Roman Empire; and these barbarians, after becoming Christians, continually at war with the Mohammedans or else destroying each other. . . .

What then have been the fruits of the blood of so many millions of men shed in battle, and the sacking of so many cities? Nothing great or considerable. The Christian powers have lost a great deal to the Turks, within these five centuries, and have gained scarcely anything from each other.

All history, then, in short, is little else than a long succession of useless cruelties; and if there happens any great revolution, it will bury the remembrance of all past disputes, wars, and fraudulent treaties, which have produced so many transitory miseries.

From *The Portable Voltaire,* edited and with an Introduction by Ben Ray Redman. Published by The Viking Press (nineteenth printing). Copyright © 1969.

MONTESQUIEU

1689–1755

Charles-Louis de Secondat, baron de La Brède et de Montesquieu was born on January 18, 1689 in the Château La Brède, near Bordeaux, France. He died in Paris on February 10, 1755, aged 66, succumbing to a fever. In 1700 he matriculated at the Collège de Juilly and in 1708 studied law in Bordeaux and Paris. When he was 26 he imitated his father by marrying a rich Protestant, Jeanne de Lartique, whose dowry was 100,000 livres. Their children included two daughters (one named Denise) and a son, Jean-Baptiste. In 1714 be became a judge in Bordeaux, and in 1716 he purchased a seat in the local parliament. With finances and social status thus secured, Montesquieu began studying Roman law carefully in order to advance his career, but also the natural sciences, in keeping with enlightened thought at the time. He also spent a great deal of time traveling in Europe, speaking with those political, cultural, and intellectual leaders from whom he thought he could learn, meanwhile leaving his estate in the capable hands of his wife.

His *Persian Letters* (1722) is in fact a satire of Parisian life, and has remained popular to this day, including such oddities as a discussion of Hobbes' political theory, the rudiments of demography, and a running comparison of Islamic and Christian civilizations. He also wrote a popular study of Rome's collapse (1734), but his masterpiece is *The Spirit of the Laws* (1748), for which he had been collecting information all his life, and which occupied 1,086 pages in two large volumes. In it he systematized all preceding theories of government and among other achievements, specified how the separation of powers ought to work, thereby much influencing the founders of the U.S. government. It is more the product of a leisurely provincial culture than the hectic Paris of the philosophes, but it has outlasted much of what was composed in the more exciting venues of the time. A foundational work in political theory, it continues to be studied and retranslated into every major language, recognized as the beginning point of the modern view of government based on a comparative examination of data, both historical and cross-cultural.

THE SPIRIT OF THE LAWS, 1748

Of the Laws in Relation to the Nature of a Despotic Government

From the nature of despotic power it follows that the single person, invested with this power, commits the execution of it also to a single person. A man whom his senses continually inform that he himself is everything and that his subjects are nothing, is naturally lazy, voluptuous, and ignorant. In consequence of this, he neglects the management of public affairs. But were he to commit the administration to many, there would be continual disputes among them; each would form intrigues to be his first slave; and he would be obliged to take the reins into his own hands. It is, therefore, more natural for him to resign it to a vizier, and to invest him with the same power as himself. The creation of a vizier is a fundamental law of this government. . . .

The same may be said of the princes of the East, who, being educated in a prison where eunuchs corrupt their hearts and debase their understandings, and where they are frequently kept ignorant even of their high rank, when drawn forth in order to be placed on the throne, are at first confounded: but as soon as they have chosen a vizier, and abandoned themselves in their seraglio to the most brutal passions, pursuing; in the midst of a prostituted court, every capricious extravagance, they would never have dreamed that they could find matters so easy.

The more extensive the empire, the larger the seraglio; and consequently the more voluptuous the prince. Hence the more nations such a sovereign has to rule, the less he attends to the cares of government; the more important his affairs, the less he makes them the subject of his deliberations.

In What Manner the Laws of Civil Slavery Relate to the Nature of the Climate

I.—Of civil Slavery   Slavery, properly so called, is the establishment of a right which gives to one man such a power over another as renders him absolute master of his life and fortune. The state of slavery is in its own nature bad. It is neither useful to the master nor to the slave; not to the slave, because he can do nothing through a motive of virtue; nor to the master, because by having an unlimited authority over his slaves he insensibly accustoms himself to the want of all moral virtues, and thence becomes fierce, hasty, severe, choleric, voluptuous, and cruel.

In despotic countries, where they are already in a state of political servitude, civil slavery is more tolerable than in other governments. Every one ought to be satisfied in those countries with necessaries and life. Hence the condition of a slave is hardly more burdensome than that of a subject.

But in a monarchical government, where it is of the utmost importance that human nature should not be debased or dispirited, there ought to be no slavery. In democracies, where they are all upon equality; and in aristocracies, where the laws ought to use their utmost endeavors to procure as great an equality as the nature of the government will permit, slavery is contrary to the spirit of the constitution: it only contributes to give a power and luxury to the citizens which they ought not to have. . . .

6.—The true Origin of the Right of Slavery   It is time to inquire into the true origin of the right of slavery. It ought to be founded on the nature of things; let us see if there be any cases where it can be derived thence.

In all despotic governments people make no difficulty in selling themselves; the political slavery in some measure annihilates the civil liberty.

According to Mr. Perry, the Muscovites sell themselves very readily: their reason for it is evident—their liberty is not worth keeping.

At Achim every one is for selling himself. Some of the chief lords have not less than a thousand slaves, all principal merchants, who have a great number of slaves themselves, and these also are not without their slaves. Their masters are their heirs, and put them into trade. In those states, the freemen being overpowered by the government, have no better resource than that of making themselves slaves to the tyrants in office.

This is the true and rational origin of that mild law of slavery which obtains in some countries: and mild it ought to be, as founded on the free choice a man makes of a master, for his own benefit; which forms a mutual convention between the two parties.

7.—Another Origin of the Right of Slavery There is another origin of the right of slavery, and even of the most cruel slavery which is to be seen among men. There are countries where the excess of heat enervates the body, and renders men so slothful and dispirited that nothing but the fear of chastisement can oblige them to perform any laborious duty: slavery is there more reconcilable to reason; and the master being as lazy with respect to his sovereign as his slave is with regard to him, this adds a political to a civil slavery.

Aristotle endeavors to prove that there are natural slaves; but what he says is far from proving it. If there be any such, I believe they are those of whom I have been speaking.

But as all men are born equal, slavery must be accounted unnatural, though in some countries it be founded on natural reason; and a wide difference ought to be made between such countries, and those in which even natural reason rejects it, as in Europe, where it has been so happily abolished.

Plutarch, in the "Life of Numa," says that in Saturn's time there was neither slave nor master. Christianity has restored that age in our climates.

8.—Inutility of Slavery among us Natural slavery, then, is to be limited to some particular parts of the world. In all other countries, even the most servile drudgeries may be performed by freemen.

Experience verifies my assertion. Before Christianity had abolished civil slavery in Europe, working in the mines was judged too toilsome for any but slaves or malefactors: at present there are men employed in them who are known to live comfortably. The magistrates have, by some small privileges, encouraged this profession: to an increase of labor they have joined an increase of gain; and have gone so far as to make those people better pleased with their condition than with any other which they could have embraced.

No labor is so heavy but it may be brought to a level with the workman's strength, when regulated by equity, and not by avarice. The violent fatigues which slaves are made to undergo in other parts may be supplied by a skilful use of ingenious machines. The Turkish mines in the Bannat of Temeswaer, though richer than those of Hungary, did not yield so much; because the working of them depended entirely on the strength of their slaves.

I know not whether this article be dictated by my understanding or by my heart. Possibly there is not that climate upon earth where the most laborious services might not with proper encouragement be performed by freemen. Bad laws having made lazy men, they have been reduced to slavery because of their laziness.

9.—Several Kinds of Slavery Slavery is of two kinds, real and personal. The real annexes the slave to the land, which Tacitus makes the condition of slaves among the Germans. They were not employed in the family: a stated tribute of corn, cattle, or other movables, paid to their master, was the whole of their servitude. And such a servitude still continues in Hungary, Bohemia, and several parts of Lower Germany.

Personal slavery consists in domestic services, and relates more to the master's person.

The worst degree of slavery is when it is at once both real and personal, as that of the Helotes among the Lacedaemonians. They underwent the fatigues of the field, and suffered all manner of insults at home. This helotism is contrary to the nature of things. Real slavery is to be found only among nations remarkable for their simplicity of life: all family business being done by the wives and children. Personal slavery is peculiar to voluptuous nations; luxury requiring the service of slaves in the house. But helotism joins in the same person the slavery established by voluptuous nations and that of the most simple.

10.—Regulations necessary in respect to Slavery But of whatsoever kind the slavery be, the civil laws should endeavor on the one hand to abolish the abuses of it, and on the other to guard against its dangers.

11.—Abuses of Slavery. In Mahommedan states, not only the life and goods of female slaves, but also what is called their virtue or honor, are at their master's disposal. One of the misfortunes of those countries is that the greatest part of the nation are born only to be subservient to the pleasures of the other. This servitude is alleviated by the laziness in which such slaves spend their days; which is an additional disadvantage to the state.

It is this indolence which renders the eastern seraglios so delightful to those very persons whom they were made to confine. People who dread nothing but labor may imagine themselves happy in those places of indolence and ease. But this shows how contrary they are to the very intent of the institution of slavery.

Reason requires that the master's power should not extend to what does not appertain to his service: slavery should be calculated for utility, and not for pleasure. The laws of chastity arise from those of nature, and ought in all nations to be respected.

If a law which preserves the chastity of slaves be good in those states where anarbitrary power bears down all before it, how much more will it be so in monarchies, and how much more still in republics?

The law of the Lombards has a regulation which ought to be adopted by all governments. "If a master debauches his slave's wife, the slave and his wife shall be restored to their freedom." An admirable expedient, which, without severity lays a powerful restraint on the incontinence of masters!

The Romans seem to have erred on this head. They allowed an unlimited scope to the master's lusts, and, in some measure denied their slaves the privilege of marrying. It is true, they were the lowest part of the nation; yet there should have been some care taken of their morals, especially as in prohibiting their marriage they corrupted the morals of the citizens.

12.—Danger from the Multitude of Slaves The multitude of slaves has different effects in different governments. It is no grievance in a despotic state, where the political servitude of the whole body takes away the sense of civil slavery. Those who are called freedmen in reality are little more so than they who do not come within that class; and

as the latter, in quality of eunuchs, freedmen, or slaves, have generally the management of all affairs, the condition of a freedman and that of a slave are very nearly allied. This makes it therefore almost a matter of indifference whether in such states the slaves be few or numerous.

But in moderate governments it is a point of the highest importance that there should not be a great number of slaves. The political liberty of those states adds to the value of civil liberty; and he who is deprived of the latter is also bereft of the former. He sees the happiness of a society, of which he is not so much as a member; he sees the security of others fenced by laws, himself without any protection. He perceives that his master has a soul, capable of enlarging itself; while his own labors under a continual depression. Nothing more assimilates a man to a beast than living among freedmen, himself a slave. Such people as these are natural enemies of society; and their number must be dangerous.

It is not therefore to be wondered at that moderate governments have been so frequently disturbed by the revolts of slaves, and that this so seldom happens in despotic states.

Of Laws in Relation to the Principles Which Form the General Spirit, the Morals, and Customs of a Nation

3.—Of Tyranny Where are two sorts of tyranny: one real, which arises from oppression; the other is seated in opinion; and is sure to be left whenever those who govern establish things shocking to the existing ideas of a nation.

Dio tells us that Augustus was desirous of being called Romulus; but having been informed that the people feared that he would cause himself to be crowned king, he changed his design. The old Romans were averse to a king, because they could not suffer any man to enjoy such power; these would not have a king, because they could not bear his manners. For though Caesar, the Triumvirs, and Augustus were really invested with regal power, they had preserved all the outward appearance of equality, while their private lives were a kind of contrast to the pomp and luxury of foreign monarchs; so that when the Romans were resolved to have no king, this only signified that they would preserve their customs, and not imitate those of the African and Eastern nations.

The same writer informs us that the Romans were exasperated against Augustus for making certain laws which were too severe; but as soon as he had recalled Pylades, the comedian, whom the jarring of different factions had driven out of the city, the discontent ceased. A people of this stamp have a more lively sense of tyranny when a player is banished than when they are deprived of their laws.

4.—Of the general Spirit of Mankind Mankind are influenced by various causes: by the climate, by the religion, by the laws, by the maxims of government, by precedents, morals, and customs; whence is formed a general spirit of nations.

In proportion as, in every country, any one of these causes acts with more force, the others in the same degree are weakened. Nature and the climate rule almost alone over the savages customs govern the Chinese; the laws tyrannize in Japan; morals had formerly all their influence at Sparta; maxims of government, and the ancient simplicity of manners once prevailed at Rome.

5.—How far we should be attentive lest the general Spirit of a Nation be changed Should there happen to be a country whose inhabitants were of a social temper, open-hearted, cheerful, endowed with taste and a facility in communicating their thoughts; who were sprightly and agreeable; sometimes imprudent, often indiscreet; and besides had courage, generosity, frankness, and a certain notion of honor, no one ought to endeavor to restrain their manners by laws, unless he would lay a constraint on their virtues. If in general the character be good, the little foibles that may be found in it are of small importance.

They might lay a restraint upon women, enact laws to reform their manners and to reduce their luxury, but who knows but that by these means they might lose that peculiar taste which would be the source of the wealth of the nation, and that politeness which would render the country frequented by strangers?

It is the business of the legislature to follow the spirit of the nation, when it is not contrary to the principles of government; for we do nothing

so well as when we act with freedom, and follow the bent of our natural genius.

If an air of pedantry be given to a nation that is naturally gay, the state will gain no advantage from it, either at home or abroad. Leave it to do frivolous things in the most serious manner, and with gayety the things most serious.

6.—That Everything ought not to be corrected Let them but leave us as we are, said a gentleman of a nation which had a very great resemblance to that we have been describing, and nature will repair whatever is amiss. She has given us vivacity capable of offending, and hurrying us beyond the bounds of respect: this same vivacity is corrected by the politeness it procures, inspiring us with a taste of the world, and, above all, for the conversation of the fair sex.

Let them leave us as we are; our indiscretions joined to our good nature would make the laws which should constrain our sociability not at all proper for us.

7.—Of the Athenians and Lacedaemonians The Athenians, this gentleman adds, were a nation that had some relation to ours. They mingled gayety with business; a stroke of raillery was as agreeable in the senate as in the theatre. This vivacity, which discovered itself in their councils, went along with them in the execution of their resolves. The character of the Spartans was one of gravity, seriousness, severity, and silence. It would have been as difficult to bring over an Athenian by teasing as it would a Spartan by diverting him.

8.—Effects of a sociable Temper The more communicative a people are the more easily they change their habits, because each is in a greater degree a spectacle to the other, and the singularities of individuals are better observed. The climate which influences one nation to take pleasure in being communicative, makes it also delight in change, and that which makes it delight in change forms its taste.

The society of the fair sex spoils the manners and forms the taste; the desire of giving greater pleasure than others establishes the embellishments of dress; and the desire of pleasing others more than ourselves gives rise to fashions. This fashion is a subject of importance; by encouraging a trifling turn of mind, it continually increases the branches of its commerce.

9.—Of the Vanity and Pride of Nations   Vanity is as advantageous to a government as pride is dangerous. To be convinced of this we need only represent, on the one hand, the numberless benefits which result from vanity, as industry, the arts, fashions, politeness, and taste; on the other, the infinite evils which spring from the pride of certain nations, as laziness, poverty, a total neglect of everything—in fine, the destruction of the nations which have happened to fall under their government, as well as of their own. Laziness is the effect of pride; labor, a consequence of vanity. The pride of a Spaniard leads him to decline labor; the vanity of a Frenchman to work better than others.

All lazy nations are grave; for those who do not labor regard themselves as the sovereigns of those who do.

If we search amongst all nations, we shall find that for the most part gravity, pride, and indolence go hand in hand.

The people of Achim are proud and lazy; those who have no slaves, hire one, if it be only to carry a quart of rice a hundred paces; they would be dishonored if they carried it themselves.

In many places people let their nails grow, that all may see they do not work.

Women in the Indies believe it shameful for them to learn to read: this is, they say, the business of their slaves, who sing canticles in the pagodas. In one tribe they do not spin; in another they make nothing but baskets and mats; they are not even to pound rice; and in others they must not go to fetch water. These rules are established by pride, and the same passion makes them followed. There is no necessity for mentioning that the moral qualities, according as they are blended with others, are productive of different effects; thus pride, joined to a vast ambition and notions of grandeur, produced such effects among the Romans as are known to all the world.

DENIS DIDEROT

1713–1784

Denis Diderot was born on October 4, 1713 in Langres, France, and his death came on July 31, 1784 when he was 70. At 30, in 1743, he secretly married Antoinette Champion, daughter of a linendraper, and they had three children, only one of whom—Angélique—survived. She eventually arranged her father's manuscripts after receiving an excellent education. He was educated by Jesuits at Langres, then spent 1729–1732 in Paris at the Collège d'Harcourt, the Lycée Louis-le-Grand, and the University of Paris, receiving an M.A. in 1732. He worked as a law clerk and developed a vital friendship with Rousseau that lasted from 1741 until 1756.

Needing money, he began his professional life in 1745 as a translator of Shaftesbury. In the same year a publisher asked him to translate a British encyclopedia into French, but instead Diderot asked the mathematician d'Alembert to work with him (and many others) to create the great *Encyclopédie,* the quintessential work of the French Enlightenment (and the source of the excerpts that follow). This unprecedented project was billed as a "rational dictionary," one in which dogmas of all kinds were to be banished, supplanted by the latest findings from the natural sciences and speculative, secular thought. In 1749 Diderot proposed a system for teaching the blind to read through touch, anticipating Louis Braille by a century. He was also imprisoned for three months after publishing a tract celebrating atheistic materialism. Nevertheless, the gigantic *Encyclopédie* was published between 1751 and 1772 through all manner of turmoil and hindrances, a testimony to Diderot's singlemindedness and dedication to this vital task, culminating in 17 volumes of text and 11 volumes of illustrations (several thousand plates of extraordinary beauty). Diderot managed to write a large collection of novels (especially *Jacques the Fatalist* and *Rameau's Nephew,* both published posthumously), plays, dialogues, and other works, even while editing the vast encyclopedia. Catharine the Great of Russia bought his library in 1772 since he was without income after the encyclopedia was finished, but she kindly allowed him to retain those books he needed for his scholarly work. He visited her for five months, wrote a plan for reorganizing her government, and then returned to Paris. Most of his intimate circle eventually disappeared, including his great friend, Sophie Volland in February, 1784. Their loving correspondence over 20 years is a significant work in its own right, and he died several months after she did, with these final words: "The first step toward philosophy is incredulity."

ENCYCLOPEDIÉ, 1751

Intolerance (Moral Sciences)

The word intolerance is generally understood to designate the savage passion that prompts us to hate and persecute those who are in error. But we should not confuse two very different things and must distinguish two types of intolerance, ecclesiastic and civil.

Ecclesiastic intolerance consists in considering as false all religions other than one's own, and in proclaiming this from the rooftops without being stopped by any form of terror, by worldly considerations, or even by the risk of losing one's life. Our article will not discuss this form of heroism which has produced so many martyrs throughout the centuries of the Church's existence.

Civil intolerance consists in breaking off all dealings with those whose opinions on God and his worship differ from ours, and in persecuting them violently in all sorts of ways.

A few lines taken from the Holy Scriptures, the Church fathers, and the decrees of the councils will suffice to show that whoever is intolerant in this second sense is an evil man, a bad Christian, a dangerous subject, a poor statesman, and a bad citizen.

Before we begin to treat this subject, however, we must say to the credit of our Catholic theologians that we have found several who agreed unreservedly with the ideas we shall set forth, ideas in which we follow the most respectable authorities. . . .

It is blasphemous to expose religion to the detestable accusation of being tyrannical, harsh, unjust, and antisocial, even if the object is to bring back into the faith those who have unfortunately strayed from it.

The mind can only acquiesce in what it accepts as true. The heart can only love what seems good to it. Violence will turn man into a hypocrite if he is weak, into a martyr if he is strong.

Whether he is weak or strong he will feel the injustice of being persecuted and will resent it.

Teaching, persuasion, and prayer, these are the only legitimate means of spreading the faith.

Whatever means provoke hate, indignation, and scorn, are blasphemous.

Whatever means awaken the passions and foster self-interest, are blasphemous.

Whatever means loosen natural bonds and estrange fathers from children, brothers from brothers, sisters from sisters, are blasphemous.

Whatever means would tend to incite men to rebellion, bring the nations under arms, and drench the earth with blood, are blasphemous.

It is blasphemous to coerce our conscience, the universal arbiter of our actions. Conscience must be enlightened, not constrained.

Men who err in good faith are to be pitied, never punished.

Neither men of good faith nor men of bad faith may be tormented; they must be left to the judgment of God.

If we break off dealings with those we call blasphemous, we will also break off with those we call miserly, indecent, ambitious, irascible, or depraved and will advise others to do the same. It will take only three or four intolerant men to tear apart the entire fabric of society.

If we may tear out one hair of anyone whose opinions differ from ours, we could also claim the whole head, for there is no limit to injustice. Our self-interest, our fanaticism, the occasion or the circumstances will then determine how far we will go in doing harm.

If an infidel prince asked the missionaries of an intolerant faith how their religion treats those who do not believe in it, they would either have to confess something odious, or lie, or keep a shameful silence.

When Christ sent his disciples to go among the nations, did he entreat them to kill or to die, to persecute or to suffer? . . .

You who are intolerant, is that what you do?

If your opinions give you the right to hate me, why should my opinions not give me the right to hate you also?

If you shout: "I have truth on my side," I shall shout just as loudly: "I have truth on my side," but I shall add: "What does it matter which one of us is wrong, as long as there is peace between us! If I am blind, do you have to strike a blind man in the face?"

If an intolerant man would clearly reveal what kind of a than he is, there would be no corner of the earth open to him, and no sensible man would dare set foot in the country where he lives. . . .

Saint Augustine: "Let those maltreat you who do not know under what difficulties truth is discovered and how hard it is to protect oneself against error. Let those maltreat you who do not know how rarely and under what exertions man overcomes the illusions of the flesh. Let those maltreat you who do not know how long one must sigh and groan before understanding anything of God. Let those maltreat you who have not fallen into error."

Saint Hilary: "You make use of compulsion in a cause that needs only reason; you use force where only light is needed."

Character (Moral Sciences)

It is that tendency of the soul that makes one inclined to perform certain actions rather than certain others. Thus a man who rarely or never forgives. anything has a vindictive character. I say "rarely" or "never"; for in fact a character is not formed by rigorous constancy but rather by the most usual disposition of the soul.

M. Duclos in his *Considérations sur les moeurs* is right in observing that most of the mistakes and follies committed by men come from the fact that their mind and their character are, so to speak, not in equilibrium. Cicero, for instance, had a great mind and a weak soul. That is why he was a great orator and a mediocre statesman. And this is true for many others as well.

Nothing is more dangerous to society than a man without character, that is, whose soul has no dominant disposition. We trust the virtuous man, we distrust the rogue. A man without character shifts from one to the other. It is impossible to guess what he is and we can consider him neither a friend nor an enemy. He is a sort of amphibian, if I can call him that, who can live in any element. This reminds me of Solon's fine law that declared infamous all those who did not take sides in an uprising. He felt that nothing was more to be feared than the undecided character of man.

Character of nations. The character of a nation consists in a certain propensity of the soul more commonly found in certain nations than in others, even though it may not be found in all the members of that *nation.* Thus the character of the French is to be lighthearted, gay, sociable, to love their king, and monarchy as such, etc.

In those nations that have a long history one can notice that there are certain basic traits in their character which have not changed. Thus the Athenians were avid for news in the time of Demosthenes; they were the same in the time of Saint Paul, and they still are so today. One can also read in Tacitus' admirable books observations about the customs of the Germans that are still true of their descendants.

It seems very likely that climate has a real influence on general character, for the character cannot be attributed to the form of government that always changes after a certain length of time. Still, one should not believe that the form of government, should it remain the same for a long time, is entirely without influence on the character of a nation. In a despotic state, for instance, the people will soon become lazy and vain, with excessive fondness for frivolities. The inclination toward the true and the beautiful is lost. They cannot be expected to think great thoughts or to perform great actions.

Character of societies and particular groups. Societies or particular groups within a people are to a certain extent little nations surrounded by a bigger one. They are like a graft, good or bad, implanted on the main trunk. Thus, these societies usually have a special quality, sometimes referred to as *esprit de corps.* In certain associations, for instance, the general character consists in the spirit of subordination; in others, and they are not the worst, the spirit of equality dominates. Some societies are attached to their customs, others believe they exist for the sake of change. What may be a fault in an individual can sometimes be a virtue in a group. According to the remark made by a wit, literary societies, for instance, would perforce have to be pedantic.

Often the character of a society is very different from the character of the nation in which it exists, like an alien shoot, so to speak.

Negroes (Commerce)

For the last few centuries the Europeans have carried on a trade in Negroes whom they obtain from Guinea and other coasts of Africa and whom they use to maintain the colonies established in various parts of America and in the West Indies. To justify this loathsome commerce, which is contrary to natural law, it is argued that ordinarily these slaves find the salvation of their souls in the loss of their liberty, and that the Christian teaching they receive, together with their indispensable role in the cultivation of sugar cane, tobacco, indigo, etc., softens the apparent inhumanity of a commerce where men buy and sell their fellow men as they would animals used in the cultivation of the land.

Trade in Negroes is carried on by all the nations which have settlements in the West Indies, and especially by the French, the English, the Portuguese, the Dutch, the Swedes, and the Danes. The Spaniards, in spite of the fact that they possess the greatest part of the Americas, have no direct way of acquiring slaves but have concluded treaties with other nations to furnish them with Negroes. For a long time this trade was carried on by the *Compagnie des grilles*, with headquarters in Genoa, and the Asiento in France. Since the Treaty of Utrecht in 1713 it is in the hands of the Southern Company in England. See *Assiente* and the article *Compagnie* [not in these selections]. . . .

These slaves are procured in various ways. Some, to escape famine and destitution, sell themselves, their children, and wives to the kings and the most powerful men among them, who have the means to feed them: for even though the Negroes in general have very modest needs, certain parts of Africa are at times so extraordinarily barren, particularly when, as is common, a cloud of locusts has passed through, that no crop of millet or rice can be harvested, nor any other vegetable that is their customary diet. Others are prisoners taken during wars or in the course of the raids these minor kings carry out on neighboring lands, often with no other object than to get slaves whom they bring back with them: the young, the old, women, girls, even babies at their mothers' breast.

There are Negroes who ambush each other while the European vessels are lying at anchor; and they bring those whom they have captured to the vessels to sell them and have them loaded on board against their wills. Thus one sees sons selling their fathers, fathers their children. Still more frequently one sees Negroes who are not linked by family ties put a price of a few bottles of brandy or bars of iron on each other's freedom.

Those who engage in this trade carry in their ships, besides the food for their crews, quantities of coarse meal, gray and white peas, beans, vinegar, and brandy, to feed the Negroes whom they hope to acquire during their trading expedition.

As soon as the trade is completed no time must be lost in setting sail. Experience has shown that as long as these unfortunates are still within sight of their homeland they are overcome by sorrow and gripped by despair. The former is the cause of many illnesses from which a large number perish during the crossing; the latter inclines them to suicide, which they effect either by refusing nourishment or by shutting off their breathing. This they do in a way they know of turning and twisting their tongues which unfailingly suffocates them. Others again shatter their head against the sides of the ship or throw themselves into the sea if the occasion presents itself.

This intense love of their homeland seems to diminish as they are carried farther away from it; their sadness gives way to gaiety. An almost infallible means of ridding them of this feeling and keeping them alive until they reach their destination is to play some musical instrument for them, even if it is only a hurdy-gurdy or a bagpipe.

When they arrive in the West Indies they are sold for three to five hundred livres, according to their age, their strength, and their health. Ordinarily they are not paid for in cash but in local products.

Negroes constitute the principal wealth of the inhabitants of the West Indies. Anyone who owns a dozen can be considered rich. Since they multiply a great deal in hot countries, their masters, provided they treat them kindly, can witness a steady increase in families who are born into slavery.

Their robust nature demands that they should be treated neither with excessive indulgence nor with excessive harshness. Moderate punishment renders them obedient and stimulates them to work, but excessive strictness makes them sullen and drives them to join the *négres marons,* or wild Negroes, who inhabit inaccessible regions of these islands, where they would rather put up with a most wretched life than return to slavery. . . .

Negro Slaves in the American Colonies. The excessive heat of the torrid zone, the change in food, and the constitutional weakness of white men makes it impossible for them to support hard physical labor in such a climate. Hence the regions of America which the Europeans have occupied would still not be under cultivation if it were not for the help of the Negroes who have been brought in from almost all parts of Guinea. These black men, who are by nature vigorous and who are accustomed to plain food, find a certain relief in America which renders their animal existence much better there than in their own country. This improvement makes it possible for them to withstand the work and to multiply abundantly. Their children are called "Creole Negroes," to distinguish them from the *négres dandas, bossals,* or foreign Negroes.

The majority of the Negroes who enrich the French colonies are taken directly from the African coast by the Company of the Indies (which has exclusive rights to the Senegal trade), or transported to the colonies on the ships of various French shipowners who have permission to trade with the other nations of the coast of Guinea. These Negroes were taken in war, or carried off by robbers, or sold for cash by unnatural relatives, or sold on orders of their king as punishment for some crime.

Of all the slaves those from Cape Verde, called Senegalese, are considered the finest in all of Africa. They are tall, well built, and have a smooth skin without any man-made marks: they have a well-proportioned nose, large eyes, white teeth, and their lower lip is darker than the rest of their face. This they bring about artfully by piercing the lip with thorns and introducing dust of crushed coal into the punctures.

These Negroes are idolaters. Their language is difficult to pronounce since most of the sounds are uttered with some effort deep in the throat. A considerable number speak Arabic and appear to follow the religion of Mohammed. All Senegalese, whether Moslem or not, are circumcised. They are employed in the plantations to take care of the horses and cattle, to work in the gardens, and as domestic servants.

The Aradas, the Fonds, the Foueda, and all the Negroes from the coast of Judah are idolaters and practice circumcision for reasons of cleanliness. These Negroes all speak more or less the same language although they live under different rulers. Their skin is reddish black. They have a flat nose, very white teeth, and rather fine faces. They practice incisions on their skin which leave ineradicable marks and serve to distinguish them from each other. The Aradas make these incisions in the fat of the cheeks just underneath the eyes; their marks look like warts the size of a pea. The Fonds scar their temples and the Foueda (especially the women) have their face, and even their whole body, incised to produce floral designs, arabesques, and regular patterns. They give the appearance of having a brown material embroidered in a Marseilles pattern (*piqûre de Marseille*) applied to their skin. These negroes are considered the best for work around the plantations: they often have an exact knowledge of the good and bad qualities of diverse plants that are unknown in Europe. The Aradas in particular concoct a poison with these plants and the poison of certain insects, against which no reliable remedy has yet been found. The effects of this poison are so unusual that those who use it are generally considered wizards by the inhabitants of that country.

The Mines Negroes are vigorous and easily learn the skills of a trade. Some of them work gold and silver and with a rough skill produce a kind of earring, rings for the fingers, and other types of small ornaments. They cut two or three long scars on their cheeks. They are courageous, but their pride leads them to self-destruction if they are aggrieved.

The coast of Angola, the kingdoms of Loango and Congo furnish an abundance of very fine Negroes who are fairly black and whose skin is not marked. The Congolese generally are pranksters, they are noisy and have a talent for mimicry that enables them to parody their fellows amusingly and to imitate very well the behavior and the cries of various animals. A single Congolese can put all the Negroes of a plantation in a good mood. Their penchant for pleasure makes them rather unsuitable for occupations that require hard work.

Moreover they are lazy, cowardly, and great gluttons, a characteristic that disposes them particularly to learning with ease all the details of the art of cooking. They are used as domestic servants since their looks are usually quite pleasing.

The Portuguese introduced some notions of Christianity into the kingdom of the Congo and did away with circumcision, which is practised widely among the other tribes of Africa.

The Bambara are the least valued of all the Negroes: they are rendered hideous by their dirtiness and by several big scars which they cut across their cheeks from their nose to their ears. They are lazy, drunkards, gluttons, and great thieves.

The Mandingues, the *Congres,* and *Mondongues* are not particularly valued. The last-named have their teeth filed to a point and among the other tribes have the reputation of being cannibals.

It is not possible to give detailed information in this article on the tribes of the Calbaris, Caplahons, Anans, Tiambas, Poulards and many others, several of whom live quite far inland, so that trade in them is difficult and not very plentiful.

Treatment of the Negroes when they arrive in the colonies.   The humanity and the self-interest of the owners do not permit them to have their slaves led to work as soon as they leave the ship. Usually these unfortunates have suffered during their voyage; they need to rest and to restore their health. Eight to ten days spent bathing morning and night in sea-water do them a great deal of good. One or two bleedings, a few treatments with laxatives, and above all good food soon put them in condition to serve their masters.

Their former compatriots feel drawn to them and adopt them: they bring them into their huts, care for them as they would for their own children, and instruct them in their duties, making them understand that they have been bought in order to work and not in order to be eaten, as

some of them imagined when they found that they were being well fed. Then their overseers take them to their work. The overseers punish them if they are not diligent, and these full-grown men submit to their fellows with great resignation.

Masters who have acquired new slaves are obliged to instruct them in the Catholic religion. It was on these grounds that Louis XIII was led to permit this trade in human flesh. . . .

General character of the Negroes.   Even if by chance one may meet upright men and women among the Negroes from Guinea (the majority are always depraved), most of them are disposed to immorality, vindictiveness, thievery, and lying. They are so obstinate that they never confess their faults, whatever chastisement they are made to undergo; even the fear of death does not move them. In spite of this kind of firmness, however, their natural bravado does not keep them from being afraid of wizards and spirits, which they call *zambys.*

As far as the Creole Negroes are concerned, their education has given them notions that make them somewhat better. Yet to a degree their original nature still shows through: they are vain, scornful, proud, and love finery, gambling, and women above all else. The women are in no way better than the men and follow the ardor of their temperament without any restraint. On the other hand they are capable of keen feelings, affection, and fidelity. The Negroes' faults do not affect all of them and one meets with some individuals who are very good. Several planters own entire families composed of very respectable individuals who are very attached to their masters and whose conduct would shame many a white man.

On the whole they are loyal, courageous, compassionate, charitable, obedient to their parents and especially their godfathers and godmothers, and very respectful of old people.

JEAN-JACQUES ROUSSEAU

1712–1778

Jean-Jacques Rousseau was born on June 28, 1712 in Geneva, Switzerland and died July 2, 1778 in Ermenonville, France at the age of 66. Between 1731 and 1741 he enjoyed the patronage of Baronne de Warnes in Savoy, during which time he studied philosophy, literature, and music. From there he went to Paris. When he was 56, he married Thérèse Le Vasseur, with whom since the 1740s he had had five children, all of whom were deposited into orphanages. We have unusually complete (though not entirely accurate) details about his life because he wrote his *Confessions* (1782–1789) which, along with *Reveries of a Solitary Walker* (1782), did a great deal to invent the modern autobiographical study of identity along philosophical lines.

Rousseau's ideas about political life and his forays into social theory, along with his indispensable autobiographies, keep him at the forefront of 18th century thinkers for today's readers. In the novel *Emile, or On Education* (1762), as well as the autobiographies, he perfected the ancient notion of "the noble savage" corrupted by civilization, which has ever since given rise to endless debate, even though he knew at the time such a creature never existed. His allied idea of "the general will" from *The Social Contract* (1761), plus his trenchant critique of law's protection of the status quo in *Discourse on the Origin of Inequality* (1755), have lodged him permanently in the pantheon of essential political and social thinkers. More than anything else, this is because Rousseau reminded his readers that the individual and the social order exist in permanent, necessary, and unavoidable conflict of the most fundamental kind. Even if Rousseau's solutions to the problem no longer seem so persuasive as they once did, his arguments remain the starting point for any discussions of the topic. He managed to transform the common appreciation of music and other arts, to advance a persuasive new notion of pedagogy, and to show through his own example the limits of propriety, social control, and rationality. His other important works include another novel, *Julie, or The New Heloise* (1761), *Letter to d'Alembert on the Theater* (1758), and *Discourse on the Sciences and the Arts* (1750). In 1761 alone he wrote three masterpieces, all of which continue to be read in renewed translations. Rousseau was unlike any other philosopher in his refusal to be tamed or bought off, and is as much read today because of his rebelliously creative personality as for his ideas.

A DISCOURSE ON A SUBJECT PROPOSED BY THE ACADEMY OF DIJON: WHAT IS THE ORIGIN OF INEQUALITY AMONG MEN, AND IS IT AUTHORIZED BY NATURAL LAW?, 1755

Preface

Of all human sciences the most useful and most imperfect appears to me to be that of mankind: and I will venture to say, the single inscription on the Temple of Delphi contained a precept more difficult and more important than is to be found in all the huge volumes that moralists have ever written. I consider the subject of the following discourse as one of the most interesting questions philosophy can propose, and unhappily for us, one of the most thorny that philosophers can have to solve. For how shall we know the source of inequality between men, if we do not begin by knowing mankind? And how shall man hope to see himself as nature made him, across all the changes which the succession of place, and time must have produced in his original constitution? How can he distinguish what is fundamental in his nature from the changes and additions which his circumstances and the advances he has made have introduced to modify his primitive condition? Like the statue of Glaucus, which was so disfigured by time, seas, and tempests, that it looked more like a wild beast than a god, the human soul, altered in society by a thousand causes perpetually recurring, by the acquisition of a multitude of truths and errors, by the changes happening to the constitution of the body, and by the continual jarring of the passions, has, so to speak, changed in appearance, so as to be hardly recognizable. Instead of a being, acting constantly from fixed and invariable principles, instead of that celestial and majestic simplicity, impressed on it by its divine Author, we find it only the frightful contrast of passion mistaking itself for reason, and of understanding grown delirious.

It is still more cruel that, as every advance made by the human species removes it still farther from its primitive state, the more discoveries we make, the more we deprive ourselves of the means of making the most important of all. Thus it is, in one sense, by our very study of man, that the knowledge of him is put out of our power.

It is easy to perceive that it is in these successive changes in the constitution of man that we must look for the origin of those differences which now distinguish men, who, it is allowed, are as equal among themselves as were the animals of every kind, before physical causes had introduced those varieties which are now observable among some of them.

It is, in fact, not to he conceived that these primary changes, however they may have arisen, could have altered, all at once and in the same manner, every individual of the species. It is natural to think that, while the condition of some of them grew better or worse, and they were acquiring various good or bad qualities not inherent in their nature, there were others who continued a longer time in their original condition. Such was doubtless the first source of the inequality of mankind, which it is much easier to point out thus in general terms, than to assign with precision to its actual causes. . . .

If we look at human society with a calm and disinterested eye, it seems, at first, to show us only the violence of the powerful and the oppression of the weak. The mind is shocked at the cruelty of the one, or is induced to lament the blindness of the other; and as nothing is less permanent in life than those external relations, which are more frequently produced by accident than wisdom, and which are called weakness or power, riches or poverty, all human institutions seem at first glance to be founded merely on banks of shifting sand. It is only by taking a closer look, and removing the dust and sand that surround the edifice, that we perceive the immovable basis on which it is raised, and learn to respect its foundations. Now, without a serious study of man, his natural faculties and their successive development, we shall never be able to make these necessary distinctions, or to separate, in the actual constitution of things, that which is the effect of the divine will, from the innovations attempted by human art. The political and moral investigations, therefore, to which the important question before us leads, are in even respect useful; while the hypothetical history of governments affords a lesson equally instructive to mankind.

In considering what we should have become, had we been left to ourselves, we should learn to bless Him, whose gracious hand, correcting our institutions, and giving them an immovable basis, has prevented those disorders which would otherwise have arisen from then, and caused our happiness to come from those very sources which seemed likely to involve us in misery.

A Dissertation On the Origin and Foundation of the Inequality of Mankind

It is of man that I have to speak; and the question I am investigating shows me that it is to men that I must address myself: for questions of this sort are not asked by those who are afraid to honour truth. I shall then confidently uphold the cause of humanity before the wise men who invite me to do so, and shall not be dissatisfied if I acquit myself in a manner worthy of my subject and of my judges.

I conceive that there are two kinds of inequality among the human species; one, which I call natural or physical, because it is established by nature, and consists in a difference of age, health, bodily strength, and the qualities of the mind or of the soul: and another, which may be called moral or political inequality, because it depends on a kind of convention, and is established, or at least authorized, by the consent of men. This latter consists of the different privileges which some men enjoy to the prejudice of others; such as that of being more rich, more honoured, more powerful, or even in a position to exact obedience.

It is useless to ask what is the source of natural inequality, because that question is answered by the simple definition of the word. Again, it is still more useless to inquire whether there is any essential connection between the two inequalities; for this would be only asking, in other words, whether those who command are necessarily better than those who obey, and if strength of body or of mind, wisdom, or virtue are always found in particular individuals, in proportion to their power or wealth: a question fit perhaps to be dis-

cussed by slaves in the hearing of their masters, but highly unbecoming to reasonable and free men in search of the truth.

The subject of the present discourse, therefore, is more precisely this. To mark, in the progress of things, the moment at which right took the place of violence and nature became subject to law, and to explain by what sequence of miracles the strong came to submit to serve the weak, and the people to purchase imaginary repose at the expense of real felicity. . . .

The first language of mankind, the most universal and vivid, in a word the only language man needed, before he had occasion to exert his eloquence to persuade assembled multitudes, was the simple cry of nature. But as this was excited only by a sort of instinct on urgent occasions, to implore assistance in case of danger, or relief in case of suffering, it could be of little use in the ordinary course of life, in which more moderate feelings prevail. When the ideas of men began to expand and multiply, and closer communication took place among them, they strove to invent more numerous signs and a more copious language. They multiplied the inflexions of the voice, and added gestures, which are in their own nature more expressive, and depend less for their meaning on a prior determination. Visible and movable objects were therefore expressed by gestures, and audible ones by imitative sounds: but, as hardly anything can be indicated by gestures, except objects actually present or easily described, and visible actions; as they are not universally useful—for darkness or the interposition of a material object destroys their efficacy—and as besides they rather request than secure our attention; men at length bethought themselves of substituting for them the articulate sounds of the voice, which, without bearing the same relation to any particular ideas, are better calculated to express them all, as conventional signs. Such an institution could only be made by common consent, and must have been effected in a manner not very easy for men whose gross organs had not been accustomed to any such exercise. It is also in itself still more difficult to conceive, since such a common agreement must have had motives, and speech seems to have been highly necessary to establish the use of it.

It is reasonable to suppose that the words first made use of by mankind had a much more extensive signification than those used in languages already formed, and that ignorant as they were of the division of discourse into its constituent parts, they at first gave every single word the sense of a whole proposition. When they began to distinguish subject and attribute, and noun and verb, which was itself no common effort of genius, substantives were at first only so many proper names; the present infinitive was the only tense of verbs; and the very idea of adjectives must have been developed with great difficulty; for every adjective is an abstract idea, and abstractions are painful and unnatural operations.

Every object at first received a particular name without regard to genus or species, which these primitive originators were not in a position to distinguish; every individual presented itself to their minds in isolation, as they are in the picture of nature. If one oak was called A, another was called B; for the primitive idea of two things is that they are not the same, and often takes a long time for what they have in common to be seen: so that, the narrower the limits of their knowledge of things, the more copious their dictionary must have been. The difficulty of using such a vocabulary could not be easily removed; for, to arrange beings under common and generic denominations, it became necessary to know their distinguishing properties: the need arose for observation and definition, that is to say, for natural history and metaphysics of a far more developed kind than men can at that time have possessed. . . .

But be the origins of language and society what they may, it may be at least inferred, from the little care which nature has taken to unite mankind by mutual wants, and to facilitate the use of speech, that she has contributed little to make them sociable, and has put little of her own into all they have done to create such bonds of union. It is in fact impossible to conceive why, in a state of nature, one man should stand more in need of the assistance of another, than a monkey or a wolf of the assistance of another of its kind: or, granting that he did, what motives could induce that other to assist him; or, even then, by what means they could agree about the conditions. I know it is incessantly repeated that man would in such state have been the most miserable of creatures; and indeed, if it be true, as I

think I have proved, that he must have lived many ages, before he could have either desire or an opportunity of emerging from it, this would be an accusation against nature, and not against the being which she had thus unhappily constituted. But as I understand the word "miserable," it either has no meaning at all, or else signifies only a painful privation of something, or a state of suffering either in body or soul I should be glad to have explained to me, what kind of misery a free being, whose heart is at ease and whose body is in health, can possibly suffer. I would ask also, whether a social or a natural life is most likely to become insupportable to those who enjoy it. We see around us hardly a creature in civil society, who does not lament his existence: we even see many deprive themselves of as much of it as they can, and laws human and divine together can hardly put a stop to the disorder. I ask, if it was ever known that a savage took it into his head, when at liberty, to complain of life or to make away with himself. Let us therefore judge, with less vanity, on which side the real misery is found. On the other hand, nothing could be more unhappy than savage man, dazzled by science, tormented by his passions, and reasoning about a state different from his own. It appears that providence most wisely determined that the faculties, which he potentially possessed, should develop themselves only as occasion offered to exercise them, in order that they might not be superfluous or perplexing to him, by appearing before their time, nor slow and useless when the need for them arose. In instinct alone, he had all he required for living in the state of nature; and with a developed understanding he has only just enough to support life in society.

It appears, at first view, that men in a state of nature, having no moral relations or determinate obligations one with another, could not be either good or bad, virtuous or vicious; unless we take these terms in a physical sense, and call, in an individual, those qualities vices which may be injurious to his preservation, and those virtues which contribute to it; in which case, he would have to be accounted most virtuous, who put least check on the pure impulses of nature. But without deviating from the ordinary sense of the words, it will be proper to suspend the judgment we might be led to form on such a state, and be on our guard against our prejudices, till we have weighed the matter in the scales of impartiality, and seen whether virtues or vices preponderate among civilized men: and whether their virtues do them more good than their vices do harm; till we have discovered whether the progress of the sciences sufficiently indemnifies them for the mischiefs they do one another, in proportion as they are better informed of the good they ought to do; or whether they would not be, on the whole, in a much happier condition if they had nothing to fear or to hope from any one, than as they are, subjected to universal dependence, and obliged to take everything from those who engage to give them nothing in return.

Above all, let us not conclude, with Hobbes, that because man has no idea of goodness, he must be naturally wicked; that he is vicious because he does not know virtue; that he always refuses to do his fellow-creatures services which he does not think they have a right to demand; or that by virtue of the right he truly claims everything he needs, he foolishly imagines himself the sole proprietor of the whole universe. Hobbes had seen clearly the defects of all the modern definitions of natural right: but the consequences which he deduces from his own show that he understands it in an equally false sense. In reasoning on the principles he lays down, he ought to have said that the state of nature, being that in which the care for our own preservation is the least prejudicial to that of others, was consequently the best calculated to promote peace, and the most suitable for mankind. He does say the exact opposite, in consequence of having improperly admitted, as a part of savage man's care for self-preservation, the gratification of a multitude of passions which are the work of society, and have made laws necessary. A bad man, he says, is a robust child. But it remains to be proved whether man in a state of nature is this robust child: and, should we grant that he is, what would he infer? Why truly, that if this man, when robust and strong, were dependent on others as he is when feeble, there is no extravagance he would not be guilty of; that he would beat his mother when she was too slow in giving him her breast; that he would strangle one of his younger brothers, if he should be troublesome to him, or bite the arm of another, if he put him to any inconvenience. But that man in the

state of nature is both strong and dependent involves two contrary suppositions. Man is weak when he is dependent, and is his own master before he comes to be strong. Hobbes did not reflect that the same cause, which prevents a savage from making use of his reason, as our jurists hold, prevents him also from abusing his faculties, as Hobbes himself allows: so that it may be justly said that savages are not bad merely because they do not know what it is to be good: for it is neither the development of the understanding nor the restraint of law that hinders them from doing ill; but the peacefulness of their passions, and their ignorance of vice: *tanto plus in illis proficit vitiorum ignoratio, quam in his cognitio virtutis.*[1] There is another principle which has escaped Hobbes; which, having been bestowed on mankind, to moderate, on certain occasions, the impetuosity of egoism, or, before its birth, the desire of self-preservation, tempers the ardour with which he pursues his own welfare, by an innate repugnance at seeing a fellow-creature suffer. I think I need not fear contradiction in holding man to be possessed of the only natural virtue, which could not be denied him by the most violent detractor of human virtue. I am speaking of compassion, which is a disposition suitable to creatures so weak and subject to so many evils as we certainly are: by so much the more universal and useful to mankind, as it comes before any kind of reflection; and at the same time so natural, that the very brutes themselves sometimes give evident proofs of it. Not to mention the tenderness of mothers for their offspring and the perils they encounter to save them from danger, it is well known that horses show a reluctance to trample on living bodies. One animal never passes by the dead body of another of its species: there are even some which give their fellows a sort of burial; while the mournful lowings of the cattle when they enter the slaughterhouse show the impression made on them by the horrible spectacle which meets them. We find, with pleasure, the author of *The Fable of the Bees* obliged to own that man is a compassionate and sensible being, and laying aside his cold subtlety of style, in the example he gives, to present us with the pathetic description of a man who, from a place of confinement, is compelled to behold a wild beast tear a child from the arms of its mother, grinding its tender limbs with its murderous teeth, and tearing its palpitating entrails with its claws. What horrid agitatation must not the eye-witness of such a scene experience, although he would not be personally concerned! What anxiety would he not suffer at not being able to give any assistance to the fainting mother and the dying infant! . . .

It is therefore quite certain that pity is a natural sentiment, which, by moderating in each individual the activity of the love of oneself, contributes to the mutual preservation of the entire species. Pity is what carries us without reflection to the aid of those we see suffering. Pity is what, in the state of nature, takes the place of laws, mores, and virtue, with the advantage that no one is tempted to disobey its sweet voice. Pity is what will prevent every robust savage from robbing a weak child or an infirm old man of his hard-earned subsistence, if he himself expects to be able to find his own someplace else. Instead of the sublime maxim of reasoned justice, *Do unto others as you would have them do unto you,* pity inspires all men with another maxim of natural goodness, much less perfect but perhaps more useful than the preceding one: *Do what is good for you with as little harm as possible to others.* In a word, it is in this natural sentiment, rather than in subtle arguments that one must search for the cause of the repugnance at doing evil that every man would experience, even independently of the maxims of education. Although it might be appropriate for Socrates and minds of his stature to acquire virtue through reason, the human race would long ago have ceased to exist, if its preservation had depended solely on the reasonings of its members.

Note

1. So much more does the ignorance of vice profit the one sort than the knowledge of virtue the other.

ADAM SMITH

1723–1790

Adam Smith was born on June 5, 1723 in Kirkcaldy, Fife, Scotland and died in Edinburgh at 67 years of age on July 17, 1790. At four he was kidnapped by gypsies, but was quickly abandoned by them. He never married, and seemed to have had such little success with women that the latest authority reads, "It is to be feared that the biographer can do little more with the topic of Smith's sex life than contribute a footnote to the history of sublimation" (Ian Simpson Ross, *The Life of Adam Smith,* Clarendon Press, 1995, p. 214). He attended the University of Glasgow, receiving the M.A. in 1740 when only 17, then proceeded on a scholarship to Balliol College, Oxford where he spent "about six years in self-education," since it was at that time an inferior intellectual setting to Glasgow. He became lecturer at Edinburgh from 1748–51, giving courses on literature, rhetoric, history, and economics. In 1751 he became Professor of Logic at Glasgow, then Professor of Moral Philosophy in 1752. He was happy there, mixing with the very bright members of what has since been called "the Scottish Enlightenment," not least of whom was his good friend David Hume. He served as a well-paid tutor in France in 1764 to a British duke (during which time he met Voltaire in Geneva), returned to Kilcaldy in 1767, on to London in 1773, and finally returned to Edinburgh in 1778 where he became the customs commissioner, a position his father had held in a much smaller town.

Smith's most important book in terms of social thought is his immortal *Theory of Moral Sentiments* (1759) in which he confronted the vexing question of how self-serving, egocentric people can learn to tame their passions in the interest of civility. He introduced the idea of an "inner man" which monitors and controls our behavior, and an "invisible hand" that guides social order, almost in spite of its centrifugal tendencies to disintegrate. Smith's magnum opus, *An Inquiry into the Nature and Causes of the Wealth of Nations* appeared in that auspicious year 1776 (along with Gibbon's *Decline and Fall of the Roman Empire*), and developed the "invisible hand" metaphor in so thorough a way that the book became the foundation of what Marx (who admired Smith) would later call "bourgeois political-economy."

THE THEORY OF MORAL SENTIMENTS, 1759

Of Sympathy

How selfish soever man may be supposed, there are evidently some principles in his nature which interest him in the fortune of others and render their happiness necessary to him, though he derives nothing from it except the pleasure of seeing it. Of this kind is pity or compassion, the emotion which we feel for the misery of others when we either see it or are made to conceive it in a very lively manner. That we often derive sorrow from the sorrow of others is a matter of fact too obvious to require any instances to prove it; for this sentiment, like all the other original passions of human nature, is by no means confined to the virtuous and humane, though they perhaps may feel it with the most exquisite sensibility. The greatest ruffian, the most hardened violator of the laws of society, is not altogether without it.

As we have no immediate experience of what other men feel, we can form no idea of the manner in which they are affected, but by conceiving what we ourselves should feel, in the like situation. Though our brother is upon the rack, as long as we ourselves are at our ease our senses will never inform us of what he suffers. They never did, and never can, carry us beyond our own person, and it is by the imagination only that we can form any conception of what are his sensations. Neither can that faculty help us to this any other way than by representing to us what would be our own if we were in his case. It is the impressions of our own senses only, not those of his, which our imaginations copy. By the imagination we place ourselves in his situation, we conceive ourselves enduring all the same torments, we enter, as it were, into his body and become in some measure the same person with him; and thence form some idea of his sensations, and even feel something which, though weaker in degree, is not altogether unlike them. His agonies, when they

are thus brought home to ourselves, when we have thus adopted and made them our own, begin at last to affect us, and we then tremble and shudder at the thought of what he feels. For as to be in pain or distress of any kind excites the most excessive sorrow, so to conceive or to imagine that we are in it excites some degree of the same emotion, in proportion to the vivacity or dulness of the conception.

That this is the source of our fellow-feeling for the misery of others, that it is by changing places in fancy with the sufferer, that we come either to conceive or to be affected by what he feels, may be demonstrated by many obvious observations, if it should not be thought sufficiently evident of itself. When we see a stroke aimed and just ready to fall upon the leg or arm of another person, we naturally shrink and draw back our own leg or our own arm; and when it does fall, we feel it in some measure, and are hurt by it as well as the sufferer. The mob, when they are gazing at a dancer on the slack rope, naturally writhe and twist and balance their own bodies, as they see him do, and as they feel that they themselves must do if in his situation. Persons of delicate fibres and a weak constitution of body complain that, in looking on the sores and ulcers which are exposed by beggars in the streets, they are apt to feel an itching or uneasy sensation in the corresponding part of their own bodies. The horror which they conceive at the misery of those wretches affects that particular part in themselves more than any other; because that horror arises from conceiving what they themselves would suffer, if they really were the wretches whom they are looking upon, and if that particular part in themselves was actually affected in the same miserable manner. The very force of this conception is sufficient, in their feeble frames, to produce that itching or uneasy sensation complained of. Men of the most robust make observe that in looking upon sore eyes they often feel a very sensible soreness in their own, which proceeds from the same reason; that organ being in the strongest man more delicate than any other part of the body is in the weakest.

Neither is it those circumstances only which create pain or sorrow that call forth our fellow-feeling. Whatever is the passion which arises from any object in the person principally concerned, an analogous emotion springs up at the thought of his situation, in the breast of every attentive spectator. Our joy for the deliverance of those heroes of tragedy or romance who interest us is as sincere as our grief for their distress, and our fellow-feeling with their misery is not more real than that with their happiness. We enter into their gratitude towards those faithful friends who did not desert them in their difficulties; and we heartily go along with their resentment against those perfidious traitors who injured, abandoned, or deceived them. In every passion of which the mind of man is susceptible, the emotions of the by-stander always correspond to what, by bringing the case home to himself, he imagines should be the sentiments of the sufferer.

Pity and compassion are words appropriated to signify our fellow-feeling with the sorrow of others. (Sympathy, though its meaning was, perhaps, originally the same, may now, however, without much impropriety, be made use of to denote our fellow-feeling with any passion whatever.)

Upon some occasions sympathy may seem to arise merely from the view of a certain emotion in another person. The passions, upon some occasions, may seem to be transfused from one man to another instantaneously, and antecedent to any knowledge of what excited them in the person principally concerned. Grief and joy, for example, strongly expressed in the look and gestures of any person, at once affect the spectator with some degree of a like painful or agreeable emotion. A smiling face is to everybody that sees it a cheerful object, as a sorrowful countenance, on the other hand, is a melancholy one.

This, however, does not hold universally or with regard to every passion. There are some passions of which the expressions excite no sort of sympathy, but, before we are acquainted with what gave occasion to them, serve rather to disgust and provoke us against them. The furious behaviour of an angry man is more likely to exasperate us against himself than against his enemies. As we are unacquainted with his provocation, we cannot bring his case home to ourselves, nor conceive anything like the passions which it excites. But we plainly see what is the situation of those with whom he is angry, and to what violence they may be exposed from so enraged an adversary. We readily, therefore, sympathize with their fear or resentment, and are immediately disposed to take part against the man from whom they appear to be in danger.

If the very appearances of grief and joy inspire us with some degree of the like emotions, it is because they suggest to us the general idea of some good or bad fortune that has befallen the person in whom we observe them; and in these passions this is sufficient to have some little influence upon us. The effects of grief and joy terminate in the person who feels those emotions, of which the expressions do not, like those of resentment, suggest to us the idea of any other person for whom we are concerned and whose interests are opposite to his. The general idea of good or bad fortune, therefore, creates some concern for the person who has met with it, but the general idea of provocation excites no sympathy with the anger of the man who has received it. Nature, it seems, teaches us to be more averse to enter into this passion, and, till informed of its cause, to be disposed rather to take part against it.

Even our sympathy with the grief or joy of another, before we are informed of the cause of either, is always extremely imperfect. General lamentations, which express nothing but the anguish of the sufferer, create rather a curiosity to inquire into his situation, along with some disposition to sympathize with him, than any actual sympathy that is very sensible. The first question which we ask is, what has befallen you? Till this be answered, though we are uneasy both from the vague idea of his misfortune, and still more from torturing ourselves with conjectures about what it may be, yet our fellow-feeling is not very considerable.

Sympathy, therefore, does not arise so much from the view of the passion as from that of the situation which excites it. We sometimes feel for another a passion of which he himself seems to be altogether incapable, because, when we put ourselves in his case, that passion arises in our breast from the imagination, though it does not in his from the reality. We blush for the impudence and rudeness of another, though he himself appears to have no sense of the impropriety of his own behaviour; because we cannot help feeling with what confusion we ourselves should be covered had we behaved in so absurd a manner.

Of Justice and Beneficence

Actions of a beneficent tendency, which proceed from proper motives, seem alone to require a reward, because such alone are the approved objects of gratitude, or excite the sympathetic gratitude of the spectator.

Actions of a hurtful tendency, which proceed from improper motives, seem alone to deserve punishment, because such alone are the approved objects of resentment, or excite the sympathetic resentment of the spectator.

Beneficence is always free; it cannot be extorted by force, the mere want of it exposes to no punishment, because the mere want of beneficence tends to do no real positive evil. It may disappoint of the good which might reasonably have been expected, and upon that account it may justly excite dislike and disapprobation; it cannot, however, provoke any resentment which mankind will go along with. The man who does not recompense his benefactor, when he has it in his power and when his benefactor needs his assistance, is, no doubt, guilty of the blackest ingratitude. The heart of every impartial spectator rejects all fellow-feeling with the selfishness of his motives, and he is the proper object of the highest disapprobation. But still he does no positive hurt to anybody. He only does not do that good which in propriety he ought to have done. He is the object of hatred, a passion which is naturally excited by impropriety of sentiment and behaviour; not of resentment, a passion which is never properly called forth but by actions which tend to do real and positive hurt to some particular persons. His want of gratitude, therefore, cannot be punished. To oblige him by force to perform what in gratitude he ought to perform, and what every impartial spectator would approve of him for performing, would, if possible, be still more improper than his neglecting to perform it. His benefactor would dishonour himself if he attempted by violence to constrain him to gratitude, and it would be impertinent for any third person, who was not the superior of either, to intermeddle. But of all the duties of beneficence, those which gratitude recommends to us approach nearest to what is called a perfect and complete obligation. What friendship, what generosity, what charity, would prompt us to do with universal approbation, is still

more free, and can still less be extorted by force than the duties of gratitude. We talk of the debt of gratitude, not of charity, or generosity, nor even of friendship, when friendship is mere esteem and has not been enhanced and complicated with gratitude for good offices.

Resentment seems to have been given us by nature for defense, and for defense only. It is the safeguard of justice and the security of innocence. It prompts us to beat off the mischief which is attempted to be done to us and to retaliate that which is already done, that the offender may be made to repent of his injustice, and that others, through fear of the like punishment, may be terrified from being guilty of the like offense. It must be reserved, therefore, for these purposes, nor can the spectator ever go along with it when it is exerted for any other. But the mere want of the beneficent virtues, though it may disappoint us of the good which might reasonably be expected, neither does, nor attempts to do, any mischief from which we can have occasion to defend ourselves.

There is, however, another virtue of which the observance is not left to the freedom of our own wills, which may be extorted by force, and of which the violation exposes to resentment and consequently to punishment. This virtue is justice: the violation of justice is injury; it does real and positive hurt to some particular persons, from motives which are naturally disapproved of. It is, therefore, the proper object of resentment, and of punishment which is the natural consequence of resentment. As mankind go along with, and approve of, the violence employed to avenge the hurt which is done by injustice, so they much more go along with, and approve of, that which is employed to prevent and beat off the injury, and to restrain the offender from hurting his neighbours. The person himself who meditates an injustice is sensible of this, and feels that force may, with the utmost propriety, be made use of, both by the person whom he is about to injure and by others, either to obstruct the execution of his crime or to punish him when he has executed it. And upon this is founded that remarkable distinction between justice and all the other social virtues, which has of late been particularly insisted upon by an author of very great and original genius, that we feel ourselves to be under a stricter obligation to act according to justice than agreeably to friendship, charity, or generosity; that the practice of these last mentioned virtues seems to be left in some measure to our own choice, but that, somehow or other, we feel ourselves to be in a peculiar manner tied, bound, and obliged to the observation of justice. We feel, that is to say, that force may with the utmost propriety, and with the approbation of all mankind, be made use of to constrain us to observe the rules of the one, but not to follow the precepts of the other. . . .

As every man doth, so it shall be done to him, and retaliation seems to be the great law which is dictated to us by nature. Beneficence and generosity we think due to the generous and beneficent. Those whose hearts never open to the feelings of humanity should, we think, be shut out in the same manner from the affections of all their fellow creatures, and be allowed to live in the midst of society as in a great desert where there is nobody to care for them or to inquire after them. The violator of the laws of justice ought to be made to feel himself that evil which he has done to another, and, since no regard to the sufferings of his brethren is capable of restraining him, he ought to be overawed by the fear of his own. The man who is barely innocent, who only observes the laws of justice with regard to others and merely abstains from hurting his neighbours, can merit only that his neighbours in their turn should respect his innocence, and that the same laws should be religiously observed with regard to him.

ADAM FERGUSON

1723–1816

Adam Ferguson was born on June 20, 1723 (15 days after Adam Smith), in Logie Rait, Perthshire, Scotland. He died 92 years later on February 22, 1816 in St. Andrews. In 1766, the year of his first major publication, he married "Miss Burnet, from Aberdeenshire, the amiable niece of the distinguished Professor Black of Edinburgh," and their family eventually included six children. He attended the Perth Grammar School, then the University of St. Andrews, receiving the M.A. in 1742 (after virtually teaching himself Greek in a very short time, memorizing 100 lines of Homer per day). His subsequent career was varied, serving as deputy chaplain of the 42nd Regiment (Black Watch) at the battle of Fontenoy in 1745, Professor of Natural Philosophy at the University of Edinburgh in 1759, then Professor and Chair of Mental Philosophy and Moral Philosophy from 1764, and also a member of the Carlisle Commission in 1778 to America for unsuccessful negotiations with the obstinate colonists. As a friend of Hume, Smith, Gibbon, and others in that galaxy of intellectuals, he interacted personally and textually with some of the most gifted thinkers of his era.

His *Essay on the History of Civil Society* (1767) gave Ferguson the opportunity to participate in a popular pastime of Enlightenment scholars, in trying to determine at what point and through what mechanisms humanity evolved from its "barbarian" past into its civilized present. It is from this book that the excerpt printed below originates, showing Ferguson's interest in the perennial issues facing all societies regarding happiness, luxury, and the pernicious influence of egotism. It also gives Ferguson a reasonable claim to being a founding father of sociology. This important study was followed by a related work, *Institutes of Moral Philosophy* (1769). In keeping with Gibbon's work, with whom he corresponded, he published *History of the Progress and Termination of the Roman Republic* (3 vols.) in 1783, then offered his *Principles of Moral and Political Science* (2 vols.) in 1792. Ferguson's strength lay in connecting ideas current at the time regarding the development of morality, and what we would call "the normative structure" of societies, with substantial historical and anthropological studies which gave his studies a validating cross-cultural dimension.

AN ESSAY ON THE HISTORY OF CIVIL SOCIETY, 1767

Of Moral Sentiment

Men assemble to deliberate on business; they separate from jealousies of interest; but in their several collisions, whether as friends or as enemies, a fire is struck out which the regards to interest or safety cannot confine. The value of a favour is not measured when sentiments of kindness are perceived; and the term *misfortune* has but a feeble meaning, when compared to that of *insult* and *wrong*.

As actors or spectators, we are perpetually made to feel the difference of human conduct, and from a bare recital of transactions which have passed in ages and countries remote from our own, are moved with admiration and pity, or transported with indignation and rage. Our sensibility on this subject gives their charm, in retirement, to the relations of history, and to the fictions of poetry; sends forth the tear of compassion, gives to the blood its briskest movement, and to the eye its liveliest glances of displeasure or joy. It turns human life into an interesting spectacle, and perpetually solicits even the indolent to mix, as opponents or friends, in the scenes which are acted before them. Joined to the powers of deliberation and reason, it constitutes the basis of a moral nature; and whilst it dictates the terms of praise and of blame, serves to class our fellow-creatures by the most admirable and engaging, or the most odious and contemptible, denominations.

It is pleasant to find men, who, in their speculations, deny the reality of moral distinctions, forget in detail the general positions they maintain, and give loose to ridicule, indignation, and scorn, as if any of these sentiments could have place, were the actions of men indifferent; and with acrimony pretend to detect the fraud by which moral restraints have been imposed, as if to censure a fraud were not already to take a part on the side of morality. . . .

Every peasant will tell us, that a man hath his rights; and that to trespass on those rights is injustice. If we ask him farther, what he means by the term *right*? we probably force him to substitute a less significant, or less proper term, in the place of this; or require him to account for what is an original mode of his mind, and a sentiment to which he ultimately refers, when he would explain himself upon any particular application of his language.

The rights of individuals may relate to a variety of subjects, and be comprehended under different heads. Prior to the establishment of property, and the distinction of ranks, men have a right to defend their persons, and to act with freedom; they have a right to maintain the apprehensions of reason, and the feelings of the heart; and they cannot for a moment converse with one another, without feeling that the part they maintain may be just or unjust. It is not, however, our business here to carry the notion of a right into its several applications, but to reason on the sentiment of favour with which that notion is entertained in the mind.

If it be true, that men are united by instinct, that they act in society from affections of kindness and friendship; if it be true, that even prior to acquaintance and habitude, men, as such, are commonly to one another objects of attention, and some degree of regard; that while their prosperity is beheld with indifference, their afflictions are considered with commiseration; if calamities be measured by the numbers and the qualities of men they involve; and if every suffering of a fellow-creature draws a crowd of attentive spectators; if even in the case of those to whom we do not habitually wish any positive good, we are still averse to be the instruments of harm; it should seem, that in these various appearances of an amicable disposition, the foundations of a moral apprehension are sufficiently laid, and the sense of a right which we maintain for ourselves, is by a movement of humanity and candour extended to our fellow creatures.

What is it that prompts the tongue when we censure an act of cruelty or oppression? What is it that constitutes our restraint from offences that tend to distress our fellow-creatures? It is probably, in both uses, a particular application of that principle, which, in presence of the sorrowful, sends forth the tear of compassion; and a combination of all those sentiments, which constitute a benevolent disposition; and if not a resolution to do good, at least an aversion to be the instrument of harm. . . .

To love, and even to hate, on the apprehension of moral qualities, to espouse one party from a sense of justice, to oppose another with indignation excited by iniquity, are the common indications of probity, and the operations of an animated, upright, and generous spirit. To guard against unjust partialities, and ill-grounded antipathies; to maintain that composure of mind, which, without impairing its sensibility or ardour, proceeds in every instance with discernment and penetration, are the marks of a vigorous and cultivated spirit. To be able to follow the dictates of such a spirit through all the varieties of human life, and with a mind always master of itself, in prosperity or adversity, and possessed of all its abilities, when the subjects in hazard are life, or freedom, as much as in treating simple questions of interest, are the triumphs of magnanimity, and true elevation of mind. 'The event of the day is decided. Draw this javelin from my body now,' said Epaminondas, 'and let me bleed.'

In what situation, or by what instruction, is this wonderful character to be formed? Is it found in the nurseries of affectation, pertness, and vanity, from which fashion is propagated, and the genteel is announced? in great and opulent cities, where men vie with one another in equipage, dress, and the reputation of fortune? Is it within the admired precincts of a court, where we may learn to smile without being pleased, to caress without affection, to wound with the secret weapons of envy and jealousy, and to rest our personal importance on circumstances which we cannot always with honour command? No: but in a situation where the great sentiments of the heart are awakened; where the characters of men, not their situations and fortunes, are the principal distinction; where the anxieties of interest, or vanity, perish in the blaze of more vigorous emotions; and where the human soul, having felt and recognised its objects, like an animal who has tasted the blood of his prey, cannot descend to pursuits that leave its talents and its force unemployed.

Of Happiness

Having had under our consideration the active powers and the moral qualities which distinguish the nature of man, is it still necessary that we should treat of his happiness apart? This significant term, the most frequent, and the most familiar, in our conversation, is, perhaps, on reflection, the least understood. It serves to express our satisfaction, when any desire is gratified: It is pronounced with a sigh, when our object is distant: It means what we wish to obtain, and what we seldom stay to examine. We estimate the value of every subject by its utility, and its influence on happiness; but we think that utility itself, and happiness, require no explanation.

Those men are commonly esteemed the happiest, whose desires are most frequently gratified. But if, in reality, the possession of what we desire, and a continued fruition, were requisite to happiness, mankind for the most part would have reason to complain of their lot. What they call their enjoyments, are generally momentary; and the object of sanguine expectation, when obtained, no longer continues to occupy the mind: A new passion succeeds, and the imagination, as before, is intent on a distant felicity.

How many reflections of this sort are suggested by melancholy, or by the effects of that very languor and inoccupation into which we would willingly sink, under the notion of freedom from care and trouble?

When we enter on a formal computation of the enjoyments or sufferings which are prepared for mankind, it is a chance but we find that pain, by its intenseness, its duration, or frequency, is greatly predominant. The activity and eagerness with which we press from one stage of life to another, our unwillingness to return on the paths we have trod, our aversion in age to renew the frolics of youth, or to repeat in manhood the amusements of children, have been accordingly stated as proofs, that our memory of the past, and our feeling of the present, are equal subjects of dislike and displeasure.

This conclusion, however, like many others, drawn from our supposed knowledge of causes, does not correspond with experience. In every street, in every village, in every field, the greater number of persons we meet, carry an aspect that is chearful or thoughtless, indifferent, composed, busy, or animated. The labourer whistles to his team, and the mechanic is at ease in his calling; the frolicsome and the gay feel a series of pleasures, of which we know not the source; even they who demonstrate the miseries of human life, when intent on their argument, escape from their sorrows, and find a tolerable pastime in proving that men are unhappy.

The very terms *pleasure* and *pain*, perhaps, are equivocal; but if they are confined, as they appear to be in many of our reasonings, to the mere sensations which have a reference to external objects, either in the memory of the past, the feeling of the present, or the apprehension of the future, it is a great error to suppose, that they comprehend all the constituents of happiness or misery; or that the good humour of an ordinary life is maintained by the prevalence of those pleasures which have their separate names, and are, on reflection, distinctly remembered.

The mind, during the greater part of its existence, is employed in active exertions, not in merely attending to its own feelings of pleasure or pain; and the list of its faculties, understanding, memory, foresight, sentiment, will, and intention, only contains the names of its different operations.

In the absence of every sensation to which we commonly give the names either of *enjoyment* or *suffering*, our very existence may have its opposite qualities of *happiness* or *misery*; and if what we call *pleasure* or *pain*, occupies but a small part of human life, compared to what passes in contrivance and execution, in pursuits and expectations, in conduct, reflection, and social engagements; it must appear, that our active pursuits, at least on account of their duration, deserve the greater part of our attention. When their occasions have failed, the demand is not for pleasure, but for something to do; and the very complaints of a sufferer are not so sure a mark of distress, as the stare of the languid. . . .

Every nation is a band of robbers, who prey without restraint, or remorse, on their neighbours. Cattle, says Achilles, may be seized in every field; and the coasts of the Aegean sea were accordingly pillaged by the heroes of Homer, for no other reason, than because those heroes chose to possess themselves of the brass and iron, the cattle, the slaves, and the women, which were found among the nations around them.

Of Luxury

We are far from being agreed on the application of the term *luxury*, or on that degree of its meaning which is consistent with national prosperity, or with the moral rectitude of our nature. It is sometimes employed to signify a manner of life which we think necessary to civilization, and even to happiness. It is, in our panegyric of polished ages, the parent of arts, the support of commerce, and the minister of national greatness, and of opulence. It is, in our censure of degenerate manners, the source of corruption, and the presage of national declension and ruin. It is admired, and it is blamed; it is treated as ornamental and useful; and it is proscribed as a vice. . . .

Luxury, therefore, considered as a predilection in favour of the objects of vanity, and the costly materials of pleasure, is ruinous to the human character; considered as the mere use of accommodations and conveniencies which the age has procured, rather depends on the progress which the mechanical arts have made, and on the degree in which the fortunes of men are unequally parcelled, than on the dispositions of particular men either to vice or to virtue.

Different measures of luxury are, however, variously suited to different constitutions of government. The advancement of arts supposes an unequal distribution of fortune; and the means of distinction they bring, serve to render the separation of ranks more sensible. Luxury is, upon this account, apart from all its moral effects, adverse to the form of democratical government; and in any state of society, can be safely admitted in that degree only in which the members of the community are supposed of unequal rank, and constitute public order by means of a regular subordination. High degrees of it appear salutary, and even necessary, in monarchical and mixed governments; where, besides the encouragement to arts and commerce, it serves to give lustre to those hereditary or constitutional dignities which have a place of importance in the political system.

JOHN MILLAR

1735–1801

John Millar was born on June 22, 1735 at Shotts, Lanarkshire in Scotland, and died of pleurisy on May 30, 1801 in Lanarkshire, almost having reached his 66th birthday. His happy marriage to Margaret Craig in 1760, lasting until her death 34 years later, produced four sons and six daughters (and two infant deaths); she miraculously found time to vet his manuscripts. He studied at the University of Glasgow, becoming friends with his professor, Adam Smith, and soon thereafter began a longterm relationship with David Hume, who helped him professionally. Though beginning a brilliant law career, after only sixteen months he gave it up in order to become a professor, owing to his marriage and the need for a more predictable, if modest, income. Thus he joined the small but powerful circle of Scottish thinkers who so much influenced readers far beyond the borders of their country during the late 18th century. He belonged to the Literary Club in Glasgow, wherein the leading lights of the day held weekly meetings to discuss scholarly and political manuscripts. During the forty years of his membership, he never failed to prepare properly, nor did he allow other events to block his attendance. He spent most of his life shuttling between the University, where he was Professor of Civil Law beginning in 1761, and a 30-acre farm of poor land near Kilbride called Whitemoss. There he would listen to criticism of his manuscripts offered by his growing family as they matured. He increased the enrollment of law students at Glasgow by tenfold by innovatively giving excellent lectures in English rather than Latin. He was widely known for a colloquial and entertaining approach to lecturing, which differed from the written lectures of his colleagues, and he was much admired for this style of communicating the quickly changing ideas that swirled through the Scottish universities at the time. Unlike the other members of the Scottish Enlightenment, he very seldom traveled. One favorite son emigrated to Pennsylvania and died there of heat stroke.

His major works include *The Origin of the Distinction of Ranks* (1771; 4th ed., 1806, with a long biographical sketch appended by John Craig) and *Historical View of the English Government* (1787). The former work supplies the excerpts for this book, illustrating that Millar developed an historically based theory of what is now called "social stratification," and as such was one of the earliest social theorists to do so. The particular passages pertain to the condition of women in various societies, the social costs of slavery, and the origins of "the division of labor," a term which became central to social and political-economic research in the late 19th century, more than a century after Millar wrote about it.

THE ORIGIN OF THE DISTINCTION OF RANKS, 1771/79

Of the Rank and Condition of Women in Different Ages

The elects of poverty and barbarism, with respect to the condition of women. Of all our passions, it should seem that those which unite the sexes are most easily affected by the peculiar circumstances in which we are placed, and most liable to be influenced by the power of habit and education. Upon this account they exhibit the most wonderful variety of appearances, and, in different ages and countries, have produced the greatest diversity of manners and customs.

The state of mankind in the rudest period of society, is extremely unfavourable to the improvement of these passions. A savage who earns his food by hunting and fishing, or by gathering the spontaneous fruits of the earth, is incapable of attaining any considerable refinement in his pleasures. He finds so much difficulty, and is exposed to so many hardships in procuring mere necessaries, that he has no leisure or encouragement to aim at the luxuries and conveniencies of life. His wants are few, in proportion to the narrowness of his circumstances. With him, the great object is to be able to satisfy his hunger, and, after the utmost exertions of labour and activity, to enjoy the relief of idleness and repose. He has no time for cultivating a correspondence with the other sex, nor for attending to those enjoyments which result from it; and his desires being neither cherished by affluence, nor inflamed by indulgence, are allowed to remain in that moderate state which renders them barely sufficient for the continuation of the species.

The facility with which he may commonly gratify these appetites, is another circumstance by which his situation is peculiarly distinguished. In the most rude and barbarous ages, little or no property can be acquired by particular persons; and, consequently, there are no differences of rank to interrupt the free intercourse of the sexes.

The pride of family, as well as the insolence of wealth, is unknown; and there are no distinctions among individuals, but those which arise from their age and experience, from their strength, courage, and other personal qualities. The members of different families, being all nearly upon a level, maintain the most familiar intercourse with one another, and, when impelled by natural instinct, give way to their mutual desires without hesitation or reluctance. They are unacquainted with those refinements which create a strong preference of particular objects, and with those artificial rules of decency and decorum which might lay a restraint upon their conduct.

It cannot be supposed, therefore, that the passions of sex will rise to any considerable height in the breast of a savage. He must have little regard for pleasures which he can purchase at so easy a rate. He meets with no difficulties nor disappointments to enhance the value of his enjoyment, or to rouse and animate him in the pursuit of it. He arrives at the end of his wishes, before they have sufficiently occupied his thoughts, or engaged him in those delightful anticipations of happiness which the imagination is apt to display in the most flattering colours. He is a stranger to that long continued solicitude, those alternate hopes and fears, which agitate and torment the lover, and which, by awakening the sensibility, while they relax the vigour of his mind, render his prevailing inclinations more irresistible.

The phlegmatic disposition of savages, in this particular, has accordingly been often remarked as a distinguishing part of their character. There is good reason to be that, in the state of simplicity which precedes all cultivation and improvement, the intercourse of the sexes, is chiefly regulated by the primary intention of nature; that it is of consequence totally interrupted by the periods of pregnancy; and that the same laws, with respect to the difference of seasons, which govern the constitution of inferior animals, have also an influence upon the desires of the human species.

The Usual Effect of Opulence and Civilized Manners

These institutions and customs are such as might be expected from the limited experience, as well as from the rude manners of an early age. By reducing his servants into a state of slavery, the

From *The Origin of the Distinction of Ranks or, An Inquiry Into the Circumstances Which Give Rise to Influence and Authority in the Different Members of Society,* Fourth Edition, by John Millar, Esq. Published for Longman, Hurst, Rees, and Orme, 1806.

master appears, at first sight, to reap the highest advantage from their future labour and service. But when a people become civilized, and when they have made considerable progress in commerce and manufactures, one would imagine they should entertain more liberal views, and be influenced by more extensive considerations of utility.

A slave, who receives no wages in return for his labour, can never be supposed to exert much vigour or activity in the exercise of any employment. He obtains a livelihood at any rate; and by his utmost assiduity he is able to procure no more. As he works merely in consequence of the terror in which he is held, it may be imagined that he will be idle as often as he can with impunity. This circumstance may easily be overlooked in a country where the inhabitants are strangers to improvement. But when the arts begin to flourish, when the wonderful effects of industry and skill in cheapening commodities, and in bringing them to perfection, become more and more conspicuous, it must be evident that little profit can be drawn from the labour of a slave, who has neither been encouraged to acquire that dexterity, nor those habits of application, which are essentially requisite in the finer and more difficult branches of manufacture. . . .

It is further to be observed, that, in a polished nation, the acquisition of slaves is commonly much more expensive than among a simple and barbarous people. . . .

When these circumstances are duly considered, it will be found that the work of a slave, who receives nothing but a bare subsistence, is really dearer than that of a free man, to whom constant wages are given in proportion to his industry.

Unhappily, men have seldom been in a condition to examine this point with proper attention, and with sufficient impartiality. The practice of slavery being introduced in an early age, is afterwards regarded with that blind prepossession which is commonly acquired in favour of ancient usages: its inconveniencies are overlooked, and every innovation, with respect to it, is considered as a dangerous measure. The possession of power is too agreeable to be easily relinquished. Few people will venture upon a new experiment; and, amidst the general prejudices of a country, fewer still are capable of making it with fairness. We

find, accordingly, that this institution, however inconsistent with the rights of humanity, however pernicious and contrary to the true interest of the master, has generally remained in those countries where it was once established, and has been handed down from one generation to another, during all the successive improvements of society, in knowledge, arts, and manufactures.

The advancement of a nation, in these particulars, is even frequently attended with greater severity in the treatment of the slaves. The simplicity of early ages admits of little distinction between the master and his servants, in their employments or manner of living; and though, from the impetuosity and violence of his temper, they may, on some occasions, be subjected to hardships, he enjoys no great superiority over them, in their dress, their lodging, or ordinary entertainment. By the introduction of wealth and luxury, this equality is gradually destroyed.

⌇

"SOCIAL CONSEQUENCES OF THE DIVISION OF LABOUR"

There can be no doubt that this division in the labours, both of art and of science, is calculated for promoting improvement. From the limited powers both of the mind and the body, the exertions of an individual are likely to be more vigorous and successful when confined to a particular channel, than when diffused over a boundless expanse. The athlete who limited his application to one of the gymnastic exercises, was commonly enabled to practice it with more dexterity than he who studied to become proficient in them all.

But though the separation of different trades and professions, together with the consequent division of labour and application in the exercise of them, has a tendency to improve every art or science, it has frequently an opposite effect upon the personal qualities of those individuals who are en-

From *John Millar of Glasgow, 1735-1801: His Life and Thought and His Contributions to Sociological Analysis*, by William C. Lehmann. Published by Cambridge University Press. Copyright © 1960.

gaged in such employments. In the sciences, indeed, and even in the liberal arts, the application of those who follow particular professions can seldom be so much limited as to prove destructive to general knowledge. . . . But the mechanical arts admit such minute divisions of labour, that the workmen belonging to a manufacture are each of them employed, for the most part, in a single manual operation, and have no concern in the result of their several productions. It is hardly possible that these mechanics should acquire extensive information or intelligence. In proportion as the operation which they perform is narrow, it will supply them with few ideas; and according as the necessity of obtaining a livelihood obliges them to double their industry, they have the less opportunity or leisure to procure the means of observation, or to find topics of reflection from other quarters. As their employment requires constant attention to an object which can afford no variety of occupation to their minds, they are apt to acquire an habitual vacancy of thought, unenlivened by any prospects, but such as are derived from the future wages of their labour, or from the grateful returns of bodily repose and sleep. They become, like machines, actuated by a regular weight, and performing certain movements with great celerity and exactness, but of small compass, and unfitted for any other use. In the intervals of their work, they can draw but little improvement from the society of companions, bred to similar employments, with whom, if they have much intercourse, they are most likely to seek amusement in drinking and dissipation. . . .

Even in the same country there is a sensible difference between different professions; and, according as every separate employment gives rise to a greater subdivision of workmen and artificers, it has a greater tendency to withdraw from them the means of intellectual improvement. The business of agriculture, for example, is less capable of a minute subdivision of labour than the greater part of mechanical employment. The same workman has often occasion to plough, to sow, and to reap; to cultivate the ground for different purposes, and to prepare its various productions for the market. He is obliged alternately to handle very opposite tools and instruments; to repair, and even sometimes, to make them for his own use; and always to accommodate the different parts of his labour to the change of the seasons and to the variations of the weather. He is employed, in the management and rearing of cattle, becomes frequently a grazier and a corn-merchant, and is unavoidably initiated in the mysteries of the horse-jockey. What an extent of knowledge, therefore, must he possess! What a diversity of talents must he exercise, in comparison with the mechanic, who employs his whole labour in sharpening the point, or in putting on the head of a pin? How different the education of those two persons! The pin-maker, who commonly lives in a town, will have more of the fashionable improvements of society than the peasant; he will undoubtedly be better dressed; he will, in all probability, have more book-learning, as well as less coarseness in the tone of his voice, and less uncouthness in his appearance and deportment. . . . But in a bargain, he would, assuredly, be no match for his rival. He would be greatly inferior in real intelligence and acuteness; much less qualified to converse with his superiors, to take advantage of their foibles, to give a plausible account of his measures, or to adapt his behaviour to any peculiar and unexpected emergency. . . .

As the circumstances of commercial society are unfavourable to the mental improvements of the populace, it ought to be the great aim of the public to counteract, in this respect, the natural tendency of mechanical employments, and by the institution of schools and seminaries of education, to communicate, as far as possible, to the most useful, but humble class of citizens, that knowledge which their way of life has, in some degree, prevented them from acquiring. It is needless to observe how imperfect such institutions have hitherto been. The principal schools and colleges of Europe have been intended for the benefit merely of the higher orders; and even for this purpose, the greater part of them are not very judiciously modelled. But men of rank and fortune, and in general those who are exempted from bodily labour, have little occasion, in this respect, for the aid of the public, and perhaps would be better supplied, if left, in a great measure, to their own exertions. The execution, however, of a liberal plan for the instruction of the lower orders, would be a valuable addition to those efforts for the maintenance of the poor, for the relief of the diseased and infirm, and for the correction of the malefactor, which have proceeded from the humanity and public spirit of the present age. The parish schools in Scotland, are the only extensive provisions of that nature hitherto known in the island; and though it must be confessed that they are but ill calculated for the purposes of general education, the advantages resulting from them, even in their present state, have been distinctly felt, and very universally acknowledged.

IMMANUEL KANT

1724–1804

Immanuel Kant, the son of a harness maker, was born on April 22, 1724 in Königsberg, Prussia (now Kaliningrad, Russia), a remote town in the provinces from where he seldom strayed throughout his nearly 80 years, dying there on February 12, 1804. He resolutely chose to remain a bachelor and was probably also celibate, so far as his biographers have been able to discern. He began at 8 in a Pietist school that conformed to his parents' faith, and he spent 8 years there, learning to love the Latin classics. In 1740 he matriculated at the University of Königsberg where he was diverted from theology by the more appealing natural sciences and math, and promptly began his first book, on kinetic energy. Forced to earn a living after the death of his father in 1746, he became a tutor and worked for several families over the next nine years by moving 60 miles from his hometown to Arnsdorf. He finished his delayed degree in 1755 at the age of 31, and took a poorly paid position at his alma mater in the same year. Probably inspired by teaching a huge array of courses over the next several years, he wrote on diverse topics, such as human racial differences, the source of fire, earthquake causation, and cosmology. Like many of his fellow philosophes, he was entirely uninhibited by what we now call "disciplinary boundaries," for he and his colleagues were at the time recreating these boundaries to suit their own catholic interests.

Kant is generally regarded as one of the finest Western philosophers, somewhat lower perhaps than Plato, but surely on an equal footing with anyone else, including Hegel, who has taken human cognition and valuation as his principal concern. His "three critiques"—of pure reason (1781), practical reason (1788), and judgment (1790)—redefined Western philosophy almost entirely, and continue to inspire countless commentaries and debates around the world. Recently new biographical studies and fresh translations of his major works have appeared in English, something which cannot be said for most 18th century thinkers. In terms of social thought, however, Kant is not noticeably more significant than many other writers whose works fill this volume. That is, he gave profound attention to the workings of the individual mind—to its ability to reason, to form morally correct decisions, and to shape a satisfying aesthetics—but he was much less concerned, than, say, Adam Smith, with the interpersonal dynamics of social life and the need to clarify what its parameters might be. For this reason a relatively minor work, and by far one of the easiest to read, provides selections for this book, his *Lectures on Ethics*. Very unlike his major philosophical treatises, this collection of talks shows Kant at his most human and endearing, far removed from the icy heights of "pure reason."

LECTURES ON ETHICS, 1775–80

Suicide

Suicide can be regarded in various lights; it might be held to be reprehensible, or permissible, or even heroic. In the first place we have the specious view that suicide can be allowed and tolerated. Its advocates argue thus. So long as he does not violate the proprietary rights of others, man is a free agent. With regard to his body there are various things he can properly do; he can have a boil lanced or a limb amputated, and disregard a scar; he is, in fact, free to do whatever he may consider useful and advisable. If then he comes to the conclusion that the most useful and advisable thing that he can do is to put an end to his life, why should he not be entitled to do so? Why not, if he sees that he can no longer go on living and that he will be ridding himself of misfortune, torment and disgrace? To be sure he robs himself of a full life, but he escapes once and for all from calamity and misfortune. The argument sounds most plausible. But let us, leaving aside religious considerations, examine the act itself. We may treat our body as we please, provided our motives are those of self-preservation. If, for instance, his foot is a hindrance to life, a man might have it amputated. To preserve his person he has the right of disposal over his body. But in taking his life he does not preserve his person; he disposes of his person and not of its attendant circumstances; he robs himself of his person. This is contrary to the highest duty we have towards ourselves, for it annuls the condition of all other duties; it goes beyond the limits of the use of free will, for this use is possible only through the existence of the Subject.

There is another set of considerations which make suicide seem plausible. A man might find himself so placed that he can continue living only under circumstances which deprive life of all value; in which he can no longer live conformably to virtue and prudence, so that he must from noble motives put an end to his life. The advocates of

this view quote in support of it the example of Cato. Cato knew that the entire Roman nation relied upon him in their resistance to Caesar, but he found that he could not prevent himself from falling into Caesar's hands. What was he to do? If he, the champion of freedom, submitted, every one would say, "If Cato himself submits, what else can we do?" If, on the other hand, he killed himself, his death might spur on the Romans to fight to the bitter end in defence of their freedom. So he killed himself. He thought that it was necessary for him to die. He thought that if he could not go on living as Cato, he could not go on living at all. It must certainly be admitted that in a case such as this, where suicide is a virtue, appearances are in its favour. But this is the only example which has given the world the opportunity of defending suicide. It is the only example of its kind and there has been no similar case since. Lucretia also killed herself, but on grounds of modesty and in a fury of vengeance. It is obviously our duty to preserve our honour, particularly in relation to the opposite sex, for whom it is a merit; but we must endeavour to save our honour only to this extent, that we ought not to surrender it for selfish and lustful purposes. To do what Lucretia did is to adopt a remedy which is not at our disposal; it would have been better had she defended her honour unto death; that would not have been suicide and would have been right; for it is no suicide to risk one's life against one's enemies, and even to sacrifice it, in order to observe one's duties towards oneself.

No one under the sun can bind me to commit suicide; no sovereign can do so. The sovereign can call upon his subjects to fight to the death for their country, and those who fall on the field of battle are not suicides, but the victims of fate. Not only is this not suicide; but the opposite, a faint heart and fear of the death which threatens by the necessity of fate, is no true self-preservation; for he who runs away to save his own life, and leaves his comrades in the lurch, is a coward; but he who defends himself and his fellows even unto death is no suicide, but noble and high-minded; for life is not to be highly regarded for its own sake. I should endeavour to preserve my own life only so far as I am worthy to live. We must draw a distinction between the suicide and the victim of fate. A man who shortens his life by intemperance is guilty of imprudence and indirectly of his own death; but his guilt is not direct; he did not intend to kill himself; his death was not premeditated. For all our offences are either *culpa* or *doles.* There is certainly no *doles* here, but there is *culpa;* and we can say of such a man that he was guilty of his own death, but we cannot say of him that he is a suicide. What constitutes suicide is the intention to destroy oneself. Intemperance and excess which shorten life ought not, therefore, to be called suicide; for if we raise intemperance to the level of suicide, we lower suicide to the level of intemperance. Imprudence, which does not imply a desire to cease to live, must, therefore, be distinguished from the intention to murder oneself. Serious violations of our duty towards ourselves produce an aversion accompanied either by horror or by disgust; suicide is of the horrible kind, *crimina carnis* of the disgusting. We shrink in horror from suicide because all nature seeks its own preservation; an injured tree, a living body, an animal does so; how then could man make of his freedom, which is the acme of life and constitutes its worth, a principle for his own destruction? Nothing more terrible can be imagined; for if man were on every occasion master of his own life, he would be master of the lives of others; and being ready to sacrifice his life at any and every time rather than be captured, he could perpetrate every conceivable crime and vice. We are, therefore, horrified at the very thought of suicide; by it man sinks lower than the beasts; we look upon a suicide as carrion, whilst our sympathy goes forth to the victim of fate.

Those who advocate suicide seek to give the widest interpretation to freedom. There is something flattering in the thought that we can take our own life if we are so minded; and so we find even right-thinking persons defending suicide in this respect. There are many circumstances under which life ought to be sacrificed. If I cannot preserve my life except by violating my duties towards myself, I am bound to sacrifice my life rather than violate these duties. But suicide is in no circumstances permissible. Humanity in one's own person is something inviolable; it is a holy trust; man is master of all else, but he must not lay hands upon himself. A being who existed of his own necessity could not possibly destroy himself; a being whose existence is not necessary must re-

gard life as the condition of everything else, and in the consciousness that life is a trust reposed in him, such a being recoils at the thought of committing a breach of his holy trust by turning his life against himself. Man can only dispose over things; beasts are things in this sense; but man is not a thing, not a beast. If he disposes over himself, he treats his value as that of a beast. He who so behaves, who has no respect for human nature and makes a thing of himself, becomes for everyone an Object of freewill. We are free to treat him as a beast, as a thing, and to use him for our sport as we do a horse or a dog, for he is no longer a human being; he has made a thing of himself, and, having himself discarded his humanity, he cannot expect that others should respect humanity in him. Yet humanity is worthy of esteem. Even when a man is a bad man, humanity in his person is worthy of esteem. Suicide is not abominable and inadmissible because life should be highly prized; were it so, we could each have our own opinion of how highly we should prize it, and the rule of prudence would often indicate suicide as the best means. But the rule of morality does not admit of it under any condition because it degrades human nature below the level of animal nature and so destroys it. Yet there is much in the world far more important than life. To observe morality is far more important. It is better to sacrifice one's life than one's morality. To live is not a necessity; but to live honourably while life lasts is a necessity. We can at all times go on living and doing our duty towards ourselves without having to do violence to ourselves. But he who is prepared to take his own life is no longer worthy to live at all. The pragmatic ground of impulse to live is happiness. Can I then take my own life because I cannot live happily? No! It is not necessary that whilst I live I should live happily; but it is necessary that so long as I live I should live honourably. Misery gives no right to any man to take his own life, for then we should all be entitled to take our lives for lack of pleasure. All our duties towards ourselves would then be directed towards pleasure; but the fulfillment of those duties may demand that we should even sacrifice our life.

Is suicide heroic or cowardly? Sophistication, even though well meant, is not a good thing. It is not good to defend either virtue or vice by splitting hairs. Even right-thinking people declaim against suicide on wrong lines. They say that it is arrant cowardice. But instances of suicide of great heroism exist. We cannot, for example, regard the suicides of Cato and of Atticus as cowardly. Rage, passion and insanity are the most frequent causes of suicide, and that is why persons who attempt suicide and are saved from it are so terrified at their own act that they do not dare to repeat the attempt. There was a time in Roman and in Greek history when suicide was regarded as honourable, so much so that the Romans forbade their slaves to commit suicide because they did not belong to themselves but to their masters and so were retarded as things, like all other animals. The Stoics said that suicide is the sage's peaceful death; he leaves the world as he might leave a smoky room for another, because it no longer pleases him; he leaves the world, not because he is no longer happy in it, but because he disdains it. . . .

But suicide is not inadmissible and abominable because God has forbidden it; God has forbidden it because it is abominable in that it degrades man's inner worth below that of the animal creation. Moral philosophers must, therefore, first and foremost show that suicide is abominable. We find, as a rule, that those who labour for their happiness are more liable to suicide; having tasted the refinements of pleasure, and being deprived of them, they give way to grief, sorrow, and melancholy.

Duties Towards the Body in Respect of Sexual Impulse

Amongst our inclinations there is one which is directed towards other human beings. They themselves, and not their work and services, are its Objects of enjoyment. It is true that man has no inclination to enjoy the flesh of another—except, perhaps, in the vengeance of war, and then it is hardly a desire—but none the less there does exist an inclination which we may call an appetite for enjoying another human being. We refer to sexual impulse. Man can, of course, use another human being as an instrument for his service; he can use his hands, his feet, and even all his powers; he can use him for his own purposes with the other's consent. But there is no way in which a human being can be made an Object of indulgence for another except through sexual impulse.

This is in the nature of a sense, which we can call the sixth sense; it is an appetite for another human being. We say that a man loves someone when he has an inclination towards another person. If by this love we mean true human love, then it admits of no distinction between types of persons, or between young and old. But a love that springs merely from sexual impulse cannot be love at all, but only appetite. Human love is goodwill, affection, promoting the happiness of others and finding joy in their happiness. But it is clear that, when a person loves another purely from sexual desire, none of these factors enter into the love. Far from there being any concern for the happiness of the loved one, the lover, in order to satisfy his desire and still his appetite, may even plunge the loved one into the depths of misery. Sexual love makes of the loved person an Object of appetite; as soon as that appetite has been stilled, the person is cast aside as one casts away a lemon which has been sucked dry. Sexual love can, of course, be combined with human love and so carry with it the characteristics of the latter, but taken by itself and for itself, it is nothing more than appetite. Taken by itself it is a degradation of human nature; for as soon as a person becomes an Object of appetite for another, all motives of moral relationship cease to function, because as an Object of appetite for another a person becomes a thing and can be treated and used as such by every one. This is the only case in which a human being, is designed by nature as the Object of another's enjoyment. Sexual desire is at the root of it; and that is why we are ashamed of it, and why all strict moralists, and those who had pretensions to be regarded as saints, sought to suppress and extirpate it. It is true that without it a man would be incomplete; he would rightly believe that he lacked the necessary organs, and this would make him imperfect as a human being; none the less men made pretence on this question and sought to suppress these inclinations because they degraded mankind.

Because sexuality is not an inclination which one human being has for another as such, but is an inclination for the sex of another, it is a principle of the degradation of human nature, in that it gives rise to the preference of one sex to the other, and to the dishonouring of that sex through the satisfaction of desire. The desire which a man has for a woman is not directed towards her because she is a human being, but because she is a woman; that she is a human being is of no concern to the man; only her sex is the object of his desires. Human nature is thus subordinated. Hence it comes that all men and women do their best to make not their human nature but their sex more alluring and direct their activities and lusts entirely towards sex. Human nature is thereby Sacrificed to sex. If then a man wishes to satisfy his desire, and a woman hers, they stimulate each other's desire; their inclinations meet, but their object is not human nature but sex, and each of them dishonours the human nature of the other. They make of humanity an instrument for the satisfaction of their lusts and inclinations, and dishonour it by placing it on a level with animal nature. Sexuality, therefore, exposes mankind to the danger of equality with the beasts. But as man has this desire from nature, the question arises how far he can properly make use of it without injury to his manhood. How far may persons allow one of the opposite sex to satisfy his or her desire upon them? Can they sell themselves, or let themselves out on hire, or by some other contract allow use to be made of their sexual faculties? Philosophers generally point out the harm done by this inclination and the ruin it brings to the body or to the commonwealth, and they believe that, except for the harm it does, there would be nothing contemptible in such conduct in itself. But if this were so, and if giving vent to this desire was not in itself abominable and did not involve immorality, then any one who could avoid being harmed by them could make whatever use he wanted of his sexual propensities. For the prohibitions of prudence are never unconditional; and the conduct would in itself be unobjectionable, and would only be harmful under certain conditions. But in point of fact, there is in the conduct itself something which is contemptible and contrary to the dictates of morality. It follows, therefore, that there must be certain conditions under which alone the use of the *facultates sexuales* would be in keeping with morality. There must be a basis for restraining our freedom in the use we make of our inclinations so that they conform to the principles of morality. We shall endeavour to discover these conditions and this basis. Man cannot dispose over himself because he is not a thing; he is

not his own property; to say that he is would be self-contradictory; for in so far as he is a person he is a Subject in whom the ownership of things can be vested, and if he were his own property, he would be a thing over which he could have ownership. But a person cannot be a property and so cannot be a thing which can be owned, for it is impossible to be a person and a thing, the proprietor and the property.

Accordingly, a man is not at his own disposal. He is not entitled to sell a limb, not even one of his teeth. But to allow one's person for profit to be used by another for the satisfaction of sexual desire, to make of oneself an Object of demand, is to dispose over oneself as over a thing and to make of oneself a thing on which another satisfies his appetite, just as he satisfies his hunger upon a steak. But since the inclination is directed towards one's sex and not towards one's humanity, it is clear that one thus partially sacrifices one's humanity and thereby runs a moral risk. Human beings are, therefore, not entitled to offer themselves, for profit, as things for the use of others in the satisfaction of their sexual propensities. In so doing they would run the risk of having their person used by all and sundry as an instrument for the satisfaction of inclination. This way of satisfying sexuality is *vaga libido*, in which one satisfies the inclinations of others for gain. It is possible for either sex. To let one's person out on hire and to surrender it to another for the satisfaction of his sexual desire in return for money is the depth of infamy. The underlying moral principle is that man is not his own property and cannot do with his body what he will. The body is part of the self; in its togetherness with the self it constitutes the person; a man cannot make of his person a thing, and this is exactly what happens in *vaga libido*. This manner of satisfying sexual desire is. therefore, not permitted by the rules of morality. . . .

But let us pursue this aspect further and examine the case of a man who takes two wives. In such a case each wife would have but half a man, although she would be giving herself wholly and ought in consequence to be entitled to the whole man. To sum up: *vaga libido* is ruled out on moral grounds; the same applies to concubinage; there only remains matrimony, and in matrimony polygamy is ruled out also for moral reasons; we, therefore, reach the conclusion that the only feasible arrangement is that of monogamous marriage. Only under that condition can I indulge my *facultas sexualis.* We cannot here pursue the subject further.

But one other question arises, that of incest. Incest consists in intercourse between the sexes in a form which, by reason of consanguinity, must be ruled out; but are there moral grounds on which incest, in all forms of sexual intercourse, must be ruled out? They are grounds which apply conditionally, except in one case, in which they have absolute validity. The sole case in which the moral grounds against incest apply absolutely is that of intercourse between parents and children. Between parents and children there must be a respect which should continue throughout life, and this rules out of court any question of equality. Moreover, in sexual intercourse each person submits to the other in the highest degree, whereas between parents and their children subjection is one-sided; the children must submit to the parents only; there can, therefore, be no equal union. This is the only case in which incest is absolutely forbidden by nature. In other cases incest forbids itself, but is not incest in the order of nature. The state prohibits incest, but at the beginning there must have been intermarriage between brothers and sisters. At the same time nature has implanted in our breasts a natural opposition to incest. She intended us to combine with other races and so to prevent too great a sameness in one society. Too close a connection, too intimate an acquaintance produces sexual indifference and repugnance. But this propensity must be restrained by modesty; otherwise it becomes commonplace, reduces the object of the desire to the commonplace and results in indifference. Sexual desire is very fastidious; nature has given it strength, but it must be restrained by modesty. It is on that account that savages, who go about stark-naked, are cold towards each other; for that reason, too, a person whom we have known from youth evokes no desire within us, but a strange person attracts us much more strongly. Thus nature has herself provided restraints upon any desire between brother and sister.

Wealth

A man whose possessions are sufficient for his needs is well-to-do; if he has sufficient not only for his needs but also for other purposes, he is a man of means; if he has sufficient for his needs and other purposes and then to spare he is a man of wealth; if he has so much as would enable him to make others also well-to-do, he is rich. Riches are a sufficiency for luxury. On the other hand, if a man has only sufficient for his barest necessities he is poor, and if he has not sufficient even for these he is needy. Not only the man who possesses wealth values it, but others do so too. A wealthy man is highly esteemed by his fellows because of his wealth; a needy man is less respected because of his straitened circumstances. We shall soon see the reasons for this. All wealth is means, in so far as it is a means for satisfying the owner's wants, free purposes and inclinations. Wealth in excess of this is a fortune; to have a fortune is more than to have means. A fortune has two advantages. In the first place it makes us independent of others. A man who has a fortune does not need others and does not require their help. In the second place, fortune is power; it has purchasing power; it enables us to procure all that can be produced by human powers. A fortune, in the literal sense, consists of money and goods; it makes a man independent, by putting him in a position where he need serve no one and beg of none, because he can buy what he wants. Money enables a man to bring others under his power; for reasons of self-interest they will labour for him and do his bidding. By dependence upon others man loses in worth, and so a man of independent means is an object of respect. It is in the nature of things that we should respect less a man who depends upon others; but if, like an officer, he in turn makes others dependent upon him he restores the balance. For that reason a common soldier and a man-servant are less respected than an officer and a master. Since, then, money makes one independent, one gains respect by the possession of it; one has worth, needs no one and depends on no one. But in making us independent of others, money in the long run makes us dependent upon itself; it frees us from others in order to enslave us. The worth which springs from independence is only negative; the positive value of wealth arises from the power which wealth gives us. Money gives me the power to use the powers of others in my service. The ancients held that riches are not noble because it is properly the disdain of riches that is noble. That is true. To the understanding the contempt of riches is noble, yet in the world of appearance riches themselves are noble. A rich man has great influence upon the social structure and on the general welfare; he provides occupation for many people. This does not, however, make his person noble; but the contempt for riches does. Riches ennoble a person's circumstances, but not himself.

ETIENNE DE CONDILLAC

1715–1780

From a family of lawyers, Étienne Bonnot was born on September 30, 1715 in Grenoble, France, took the name by which he is now known from the family's estate when his father died, and expired after 65 years on August 3, 1780 in Flux, near Beaugency. As the Abbé of Mureaux, he never married, having become a Catholic priest in 1740, though he spent much more time in scholarly pursuits than in carrying out clerical duties. That same year he moved to Paris and began a long friendship with the Encyclopedists, notably Diderot and Rousseau (who had tutored his older brother). Owing to a stream of early publications on scientific and philosophical topics, from 1758 until 1767 he lived in Parma as a tutor to Prince Ferdinand, grandson of Louis XV. Holding this position for 9 years, he capitalized on the opportunity by compiling a 16-volume summary of his pedagogy for the young prince, published in 1775. He was elected to the Berlin Academy in 1752 and the French Academy in 1768.

In addition to publishing works about human perception, animals, teaching, and a range of other issues (some of the ideas from which appeared in Diderot's *Encyclopedia*, though in articles written by others), he also found time to consider social and economic questions. It is from his *Commerce and Government Considered in Relation to Each Other* (1776) that the selection reprinted below comes. Here Condillac reconsiders the ancient question—which seemed to fascinate the Enlightenment more than it had writers from the preceding couple of centuries—of the proper balance between hedonistic consumption versus ascetic labor. It is interesting that he begins by considering the case of America, that "New World" where anything seemed possible, at least for a time.

COMMERCE AND GOVERNMENT CONSIDERED IN THEIR MUTUAL RELATIONSHIP, 1776

Of the Employment of Men in a Society which has Simple Tastes

In America, on the lands abandoned to their natural fertility and covered with forests, each savage needs the product of eighty or a hundred arpents for his subsistence; since the animals off which he chiefly feeds cannot increase their number much in the woods where they find little pasturage; and because, besides, the savages destroy more than they can consume.

With these huge, almost desert lands we can contrast those of our tribe, when the number of men was equal to the number of arpents. There you have the two extremes of population.

This tribe has the advantage over a horde of savages of finding abundance in the places where it is settled: but it needs many arts to leave the coarse condition in which it finds itself initially.

I shall not undertake to explain how it makes this discovery: that research is not my subject. I move to the time when it will know those arts which go back to remotest antiquity: the art of grinding wheat and making bread from it; the art of raising herds; the art of making cloth with the wool of animals, with their hair, with cotton, linen, etc., and finally, a beginning of architecture.

Then it finds in bread a more refined food than the corn which it previously ate in its harvested state. It has, in the milk of its herds and in their flesh, an additional food which lets it subsist with greater ease. The stuffs or materials with which it clothes itself protect it better from the elements than skins coarsely sewn together, and they are all the more suitable as they have a suppleness which gives the body freedom in all its movements. Finally, buildings, which are more solid and larger, are a better shelter for things the tribe wants to keep and it finds more commodities there.

From *Commerce and Government Considered in Their Mutual Relationship*, by Abbé de Condillac and translated by Shelagh Eltis. Published by permission of Edward Elgar Publishing Ltd. Copyright © 1997, 1976.

When materials are suitable and long-lasting, it is of little importance that they should be worked with more refinement: if food is plentiful and healthy, it would perhaps be dangerous for it to become more delicate: and when solid buildings are large enough to lodge a family and enclose all the things it needs, is it really essential to find in them all the commodities to which a less hardy people has become accustomed?

Between a coarse and an indulgent existence, I should like to mark out a simple life, and if possible, to fix the notion of it with some precision.

I picture to myself a coarse life in the original state our tribe was in: I picture to myself a soft life in those times when every kind of excess had corrupted behaviour. These extremes are easy to grasp. It is between the one and the other that we should find the simple life. But where does it begin and where does it end? There you have what one can only show roughly.

We pass from the coarse life to the simple life, and from the simple life to the soft life, by a succession of those things which custom makes essential to us and which for this reason I have called of *secondary need*. So the arts must make some progress to draw us from a coarse life; and they must halt after some progress, to prevent our falling into a soft existence. The movement from one to the other is imperceptible, and it is only ever more or less that the simple life distances itself from one of the extremes, as it is only ever more or less that it approaches the other. It is therefore not possible to speak of it with exact precision.

It is easy to picture to oneself what the simple life was, when men, before gathering together in towns, lived in the fields they cultivated. Then, whatever progress the arts had made, all concerned agriculture which was the prime art, the art prized above all.

Now, so long as agriculture was regarded as the first art, as that to which all others must refer back, far from being able to become soft, men were necessarily sober and hardworking. The government, which was simple then, required few laws, and did not involve itself in long discussions. Cases between individuals that were put to arbitration had as judges neighbours whose fairness was known. Matters of general import were dealt with in the assembly of heads of household or of the chiefs who represented them; and order, in some sense, maintained itself among a people who had few needs.

There you have the simple life: it is marked out in the work men do in an agricultural society which supports itself with few laws. This simplicity will last, so long as the citizens are only cultivators; and it will retain some vestiges in every period when agriculture is of some esteem among them. . . .

It is with reason that one judges that when a nation is not refined, in its food, or its dress, or its lodging, it is enough for it to live in plenty and comfort, if a quarter of its citizens are employed in the daily tasks of cultivation and the unrefined arts.

Another quarter, or thereabouts, are too young or too old to contribute by their work to the advantage of society. So that would leave half without a job. It is this half which withdraws to the towns. It includes the landowners who find themselves naturally entrusted with the main cares of government; the merchants who enable the greatest possible sale of all the necessities of life; and the artisans who work with greater skill on raw materials.

If the arts remain in this state, where the work of a quarter of the citizens is enough for everyone's subsistence, most of those who have no land in their ownership will be unable to subsist, since they will be without jobs, and that will be the majority.

One cannot fail to recognise that therein lay a source of disturbances. Now if it is important on the one hand that each citizen can live off his work, it is certain on the other that one will not be able to give everyone work, except when the arts have made fresh progress. It is therefore in society's interest that this progress should be made. . . .

What I call *refinement* can be found in the raw material and in the work. In the raw material, when people prefer those which are drawn from abroad, simply because they are rarer and without finding any other advantage from them; in the work, when people prefer a more finished article even though it is neither more solid nor more useful.

Now, as soon as there is less refinement in prime materials and work the artefacts will be less costly. Once the artefacts are less costly they will better adjusted to the citizens' means. . . .

Everyone works in competition in this society; and because each one has the choice of his occupation, and enjoys complete freedom, one person's work does not harm another's work. Competition, which distributes the jobs, puts each person in his place: all subsist, and the state is rich from the labours of all. There you have the point to which the arts should lead, and at which they should remain.

Indeed, if, to make further progress, they put too much refinement into customary goods; if they create in us the need for a multitude of things which are only for ostentation; if they give us another need for a mass of frivolities: it is then that the citizens, far from helping to raise and consolidate the structure of society by their work, seem on the contrary to sap its foundations. Luxury, which we shall discuss, will take artisans away from the most useful arts; it will take the ploughman from the plough; it will raise the price of the most basic necessities; and for the small number of citizens who will live in affluence, the mass will fall into wretchedness. . . .

Let us conclude that, since all citizens should be occupied in a society, it is beneficial or even necessary for the arts to make enough progress to provide work for all. It is the goods of which custom makes the need felt which should be the rule of men's employment, and procure for some the means of subsistence by working, without exposing others to a descent into softness.

Of Luxury

As soon as one writes on luxury, some excuse it, others satirise it, and one proves nothing. The fact is that people do not try to agree.

We speak of luxury as of something of which we have a perfect notion, and yet we only have a comparative notion of it. What is luxury for one people is not for another; and for the same people what used to be luxury can cease to be so.

Luxury in the original meaning of the word, is the same thing as excess; and when one uses it in that sense one begins to agree on it. But when we forget this first meaning, and so to speak rush to a host of associated ideas, without stopping at any one, we no longer know what we want to say. For the moment let us substitute the word *excess* for *luxury.*

The rough and ready life of our tribe, from the point of its settlement, would be an excess of refinement in the eyes of a savage, who, being accustomed to live from hunting and fishing, could not understand the purpose of the needs it had created for itself. Because the land, without being worked, provides for his subsistence, it seems to him that those who cultivate it are too fastidious about the means of subsistence.

There you have, in his judgement, an excess, which is not so in our judgement, or in that of our tribe.

But even among our tribe, each new comfort which custom will introduce can be seen as an excess of refinement by all those who do not yet feel the need for it. Is the tribe thus condemned to fall from excess to excess, according to its progress in the arts?

Men only differ in their judgement as to what all are agreed to call excess, because, as they do not all have the same needs, it is natural that what seems excess to one, does not seem so to another. There you probably have the reason why one has so much difficulty in knowing what one means when one speaks of luxury.

I distinguish two sorts of excess: those which are only so because they seem such in the eyes of a certain number; others which are so because they seem so in everyone's eyes. I make luxury consist of the latter. So then let us see what are the things which must appear a luxury in everyone's eyes.

However refined goods might have appeared at the beginning, they are in no way an excess when it is in their nature to become of common use. Then they are a consequence of the progress it is so important to make in the arts; and there will come a time when everyone will be agreed in considering them necessary. One can even see that they can be reconciled with simplicity.

When, on the other hand, goods of a kind that can never become plentiful are kept back for the smallest number to the exclusion of the majority, they must always be regarded as an excess: even those who have the greatest pleasure in their enjoyment could not disagree. Therefore luxury consists in the articles which appear an excess in the eyes of all, since by their nature they are reserved for the minority to the exclusion of the majority. . . .

So luxury can exist in the use of goods which one summons from afar: but that is not the only kind. There may be luxury in the use of goods which one draws from a neighbouring nation, and even in the use of goods which one finds in one's own country. . . .

It is a statement of fact that only the simple life can make a people rich, powerful and happy. See Greece at her zenith: she owes the power which astounds decadent nations to her residuum of simplicity. Even see the peoples of Asia before Cyrus. They had vices, they knew gorgeous display; but luxury had not yet spread its mortal poison over every part of society. If splendour was evident in the treasures amassed for future need, in great enterprises, in works as gargantuan as they were useful; if it was evident in movable goods, in clothes; at least they did not know all our comforts and they were even less familiar with all the frivolities which we are not ashamed to have made necessities for ourselves. Even the luxury of the table, such as it was, only occurred at state feasts. It consisted in plentifulness rather than in refinement. There was not twice daily a profusion of dishes, even in individuals' houses, prepared with elegance and spread out with luxury.

I would happily excuse the luxury of the ancient peoples of Asia. I see it reconciled with a residuum of simplicity, even in the palaces of kings. If it is great, I see it supported by even greater wealth, and I understand that it may have been of some use. But we who, in our wretchedness, have only resources which ruin us, and who to obtain these resources do not fear to dishonour ourselves, we want to live in luxury, and we expect our luxury to be useful!

DAVID HUME

1711–1776

The son of a minor nobleman and a judge's daughter, David Hume was born on May 7, 1711 in Edinburgh, Scotland while his mother was visiting there, but lived at Ninewells, the family estate, at Chinside, Berwick-upon-Tweed. He never married, and died 65 years later in the same city after doing a lot of traveling. He entered Edinburgh University at 12 and left several years later, which was typical at the time. Mostly, though, he educated himself, not in law which his family urged, but in a wide range of belles lettres. His intellectual ambition was fierce and because of over-exertion, he drove himself into a mental collapse at the age of 18 in 1729, from which it took him some time to recover. Having done so, though, he composed between the ages of 24 and 26 *A Treatise of Human Nature,* which, despite its youthful flaws, has proved to be the most read of his philosophical works. In later years he produced what he regarded as superior, mature works, such as *Enquiry Concerning Human Understanding* (1748) and a rewrite of the *Treatise* in part, which he renamed *Enquiry Concerning the Principles of Morals* (1751)—which is excerpted below—and repudiated his earlier book as embarrassingly juvenile. Meanwhile, he also wrote series of essays (e.g., *Essays Moral and Political* [1741–42], some of which became more popular and brought him more fame than his epistemological writings. He also wrote a monumental *History of England* (1754–1762) in six large volumes which continues to be read even today, despite its strong political viewpoint. Finally, his *Political Discourses* were published in 1752. In 1766 he returned to Britain from France with Rousseau in tow, but the latter's mental peculiarities led to an unfortunate break, which Hume chronicled in a book (1766) in an effort to demonstrate his innocence in the matter.

Taking Newton and Locke as his models for thought and writing, Hume clearly mixed the most rarefied examinations of consciousness and the cognitive process with easily digested ruminations about political and everyday events and conditions. Kant credited him with providing an entirely new and "undogmatic" way of viewing the world, and Adam Smith, his executor, considered him "a perfectly wise and virtuous man," or as close to same as humans are likely to be. He is still admired for lucid, entertaining prose, particularly in his mature works, and James Boswell, Samuel Johnson's biographer, simply called him "the greatest writer in Britain." The signature notion among Scots during this period—that "sympathy" lies at the base of all morality—reappears in Hume, and connects his social theory with that of Adam Smith and Adam Ferguson.

AN ENQUIRY CONCERNING THE PRINCIPLES OF MORALS, 1751

Concerning Moral Sentiment

If the foregoing hypothesis be received, it will now be easy for us to determine the question first started, concerning the general principles of morals; and though we postponed the decision of that question, lest it should then involve us in intricate speculations, which are unfit for moral discourses; we may resume it at present, and examine how far either *reason* or *sentiment* enters into all decisions of praise or censure.

One principal foundation of moral praise being supposed to lie in the usefulness of any quality or action, it is evident that *reason* must enter for a considerable share in all decisions of this kind; since nothing but that faculty can instruct us in the tendency of qualities and actions, and point out their beneficial consequences to society and to their possessor. In many cases this is an affair liable to great controversy: doubts may arise; opposite interests may occur; and a preference must be given to one side, from very nice views, and a small overbalance of utility. This is particularly remarkable in questions with regard to justice; as is, indeed, natural to suppose, from that species of utility which attends this virtue. Were every single instance of justice, like that of benevolence, useful to society; this would be a more simple state of the case, and seldom liable to great controversy. But as single instances of justice are often pernicious in their first and immediate tendency, and as the advantage to society results only from the observance of the general rule, and from the concurrence and combination of several persons in the same equitable conduct; the case here becomes more intricate and involved. The various circumstances of society; the various consequences of any practice; the various interests which may be proposed; these, on many occasions, are doubtful, and subject to great discussion and inquiry. The object of municipal laws is to fix all the questions with regard to justice: the debates of civilians; the

reflections of politicians; the precedents of history and public records, are all directed to the same purpose. And a very accurate *reason* or *judgement* is often requisite, to give the true determination, amidst such intricate doubts arising from obscure opposite utilities.

But though reason, when fully assisted and improved, be sufficient to instruct us in the pernicious or useful tendency of qualities and actions; it is not alone sufficient to produce any moral blame or approbation. Utility is only a tendency to a certain end; and were the end totally indifferent to us, we should feel the same indifference towards the means. It is requisite a *sentiment* should here display itself, in order to give a preference to the useful above the pernicious tendencies. This sentiment can be no other than a feeling for the happiness of mankind, and a resentment of their misery; since these are the different ends which virtue and vice have a tendency to promote. Here therefore *reason* instructs us in the several tendencies of actions, and *humanity* makes a distinction in favour of those which are useful and beneficial.

This partition between the faculties of understanding and sentiment, in all moral decisions, seems clear from the preceding hypothesis. But I shall suppose that hypothesis false: it will then be requisite to look out for some other theory that may be satisfactory; and I dare venture to affirm that none such will ever be found, so long as we suppose reason to be the sole source of morals. . . .

II. When a man, at any time, deliberates concerning his own conduct (as, whether he had better, in a particular emergence, assist a brother or a benefactor), he must consider these separate relations, with all the circumstances and situations of the persons, in order to determine the superior duty and obligation; and in order to determine the proportion of lines in any triangle, it is necessary to examine the nature of that figure, and the relation which its several parts bear to each other. But notwithstanding this appearing similarity in the two cases, there is, at bottom, an extreme difference between them. A speculative reasoner concerning triangles or circles considers the several known and given relations of the parts of these figures; and thence infers some unknown relation, which is dependent on the former. But in moral deliberations we must be acquainted beforehand with all the objects, and all their relations to each other and from a comparison of the whole, fix our choice nor approbation. No new fact to be ascertained; no new relation to be discovered. All the circumstances of the case are supposed to be laid before us, ere we can fix any sentence of blame or approbation. If any material circumstance be yet unknown or doubtful, we must first employ our inquiry or intellectual faculties to assure us of it; and must suspend for a time all moral decision or sentiment. While we are ignorant whether a man were aggressor or not, how can we determine whether the person who killed him be criminal or innocent? But after every circumstance, every relation is known, the understanding has no further room to operate, nor any object on which it could employ itself. The approbation or blame which then ensues, cannot be the work of the judgement, but of the heart; and is not a speculative proposition or affirmation, but an active feeling or sentiment. In the disquisitions of the understanding, from known circumstances and relations, we infer some new and unknown. In moral decisions, all the circumstances and relations must be previously known; and the mind, from the contemplation of the whole, feels some new impression of affection or disgust, esteem or contempt, approbation or blame.

Hence the great difference between a mistake of *fact* and one of *right*; and hence the reason why the one is commonly criminal and not the other.

❧

OF NATIONAL CHARACTERS

The vulgar are apt to carry all *national characters* to extremes; and having once established it as a principle, that any people are knavish, or cowardly, or ignorant, they will admit of no exception, but comprehend every individual under the same censure. Men of sense condemn these undistinguishing judgments: Though at the same time,

they allow, that each nation has a peculiar set of manners, and that some particular qualities are more frequently to be met with among one people than among their neighbours. The common people in SWITZERLAND have probably more honesty than those of the same rank in IRELAND; and every prudent man will, from that circumstance alone, make a difference in the trust which he reposes in each. We have reason to expect greater wit and gaiety in a *Frenchman* than in a SPANIARD; though CERVANTES was born in SPAIN. An ENGLISHMAN will naturally be supposed to have more knowledge than a DANE; though TYCHO BRAHE was a native of DENMARK.

Different reasons are assigned for these *national characters*; while some account for them from *moral,* others from *physical* causes. By moral causes, I mean all circumstances, which are fitted to work on the mind as motives or reasons, and which render a peculiar set of manners habitual to us. Of this kind are, the nature of the government, the revolutions of public affairs, the plenty or penury in which the people live, the situation of the nation with regard to its neighbours, and such like circumstances. By *physical* causes I mean those qualities of the air and climate, which are supposed to work insensibly on the temper, by altering the tone and habit of the body, and giving a particular complexion, which, though reflection and reason may sometimes overcome it, will yet prevail among the generality of mankind, and have an influence on their manners.

That the character of a nation will much depend on *moral* causes, must be evident to the most superficial observer; since a nation is nothing but a collection of individuals; and the manners of individuals are frequently determined by these causes. As poverty and hard labour debase the minds of the common people, and render them unfit for any science and ingenious profession; so where any government becomes very oppressive to all its subjects, it must have a proportional effect on their temper and genius, and must banish all the liberal arts from among them.

The same principle of moral causes fixes the character of different professions, and alters even that disposition, which the particular members receive from the hand of nature. A *soldier* and a *priest* are different characters, in all nations, and all ages; and this difference is founded on circumstances, whose operation is eternal and unalterable.

The uncertainty of their life makes soldiers lavish and generous, as well as brave: Their idleness, together with the large societies, which they form in camps or garrisons, inclines them to pleasure and gallantry: By their frequent change of company, they acquire good breeding and an openness of behaviour: Being employed only against a public and an open enemy, they become candid, honest, and undesigning: And as they use more the labour of the body than that of the mind, they are commonly thoughtless and ignorant.

It is a trite, but not altogether a false maxim, that *priests of all religions are the same,* and though the character of the profession will not, in every instance, prevail over the personal character, yet is it sure always to predominate with the greater number. For as chymists observe, that spirits, when raised to a certain height, are all the same, from whatever materials they be extracted; so these men, being elevated above humanity, acquire a uniform character, which is entirely their own, and which, in my opinion, is, generally speaking, not the most amiable that is to be met with in human society. It is, in most points, opposite to that of a soldier; as is the way of life, from which it is derived.

If we run over the globe, or revolve the annals of history, We shall discover every where signs of a sympathy or contagion of manners, none of the influence of air or climate.

First. We may observe, that, where a very extensive government has been established for many centuries, it spreads a national character over the whole empire, and communicates to every part a similarity of manners. Thus the CHINESE have the greatest uniformity of character imaginable: though the air and climate, in different parts of those vast dominions, admit of very considerable variations.

Secondly. In small governments, which are contiguous, the people have notwithstanding a different character, and are often as distinguishable in their manners as the most distant nations. ATHENS and THEBES were but a short day's journey from each other; though the ATHENIANS were as remarkable for ingenuity, politeness, and gaiety, as the THEBANS for dulness, rusticity, and a phlegmatic temper. PLUTARCH, discoursing of the effects of air on the minds of men, observes, that the inhabitants of the PIAERUM possessed very different tempers from those of the higher town in ATHENS, which was distant about four miles from the former: But I believe no one attributes the difference of manners in WAPPING and St. JAMES's, to a difference of air or climate.

Thirdly. The same national character commonly follows the authority of government to a precise boundary; and upon crossing a river or passing a mountain, one finds a new set of manners, with a new government. The LANGUEDOCIANS and GASCONS are the gayest people in FRANCE; but whenever you pass the PYRENEES, you are among SPANIARDS. Is it conceivable, that the qualities of the air should change exactly with the limits of an empire, which depend so much on the accidents of battles, negociations, and marriages?

Fourthly. Where any set of men, scattered over distant nations, maintain a close society or communication together, they acquire a similitude of manners, and have but little in common with the nations amongst whom they live. Thus the JEWS in EUROPE, and the ARSIENIANS in the east, have a peculiar character, and the former are as much noted for fraud, as the latter for probity. The *Jesuits,* in all *Roman-catholic* countries, are also observed to have a character peculiar to themselves.

Fifthly. Where any accident, as a difference in language or religion, keeps two nations, inhabiting the same country, from mixing with each other, they will preserve, during several centuries, a distinct and even opposite set of manners. The integrity, gravity, and bravery of the TURKS, form an exact contrast to the deceit, levity, and cowardice of the modern GREEKS.

Sixthly. The same set of manners will follow a nation, and adhere to them over the whole globe, as well as the same laws and language. The SPANISH, ENGLISH, FRENCH and DUTCH colonies are all distinguishable even between the tropics.

Seventhly. The manners of a people change very considerably from one age to another; either by great alterations in their government, by the mixtures of new people, or by that inconstancy, to which all human affairs are subject. The ingenuity, industry, and activity of the ancient GREEKS have nothing in common with the stupidity and indolence of the present inhabitants of those regions. Candour, bravery, and love of liberty formed the character of the ancient ROMANS; as subtilty, cowardice, and a slavish disposition do that of the modern. The old SPANIARDS were restless, turbulent, and so addicted to war, that many of them killed themselves, when deprived of their arms by the ROMANS. One would find an equal difficulty at present, (at least one would have found it fifty years ago) to rouze up the modern SPANIARDS to arms. The BATAVIANS were all soldiers of fortune, and hired themselves into the ROMAN armies. Their posterity make use of foreigners for the same purpose that the ROMANS did their ancestors. Though some few strokes of the FRENCH character be the same with that which CEASAR has ascribed to the GAULS; yet what comparison between the civility, humanity, and knowledge of the modern inhabitants of that country, and the ignorance, barbarity, and grossness of the ancient? Not to insist upon the great difference between the present possessors of BRITAIN, and those before the ROMAN conquest; we may observe that our ancestors, a few centuries ago, were sunk into the most abject superstition, last century they were inflamed with the most furious enthusiasm, and are now settled into the most cool indifference with regard to religious matters, that is to be found in any nation of the world.

Eighthly. Where several neighbouring nations have a very close communication together, either by policy, commerce, or travelling, they acquire a similitude of manners, proportioned to the communication. Thus all the FRANKS appear to have a uniform character to the eastern nations. The differences among them are like the peculiar accents of different provinces, which are not distinguishable, except by an ear accustomed to them, and which commonly escape a foreigner.

Ninthly. We may often remark a wonderful mixture of manners and characters in the same nation, speaking the same language, and subject to the same government: And in this particular the ENGLISH are the most remarkable of any people, that perhaps ever were in the world. Nor is this to be ascribed to the mutability and uncertainty of their climate, or to any other *physical* causes; since all these causes take place in the neighbouring country of SCOTLAND, without having the same effect. Where the government of a nation is altogether republican, it is apt to beget a peculiar set of manners. Where it is altogether monarchical, it is more apt to have the same effect; the imitation of superiors spreading the national manners faster among the people. If the governing part of a state consist altogether of merchants, as in HOLLAND, their uniform way of life will fix their character. If it consists chiefly of nobles and landed gentry, like GERMANY, FRANCE, and SPAIN, the same effect follows. The genius of a particular sect or religion is also apt to mould the manners of a people. But the ENGLISH government is a mixture of monarchy, aristocracy, and democracy. The people in authority are composed of gentry and merchants. All sects of religion are to be found among them. And the great liberty and independency, which every man enjoys, allows him to display the manners peculiar to him. Hence the ENGLISH, of any people in the universe, have the least of a national character, unless this very singularity may pass for such.

THOMAS JEFFERSON

1743–1826

Thomas Jefferson was born on April 13, 1743 at Shadwell in Albemarle County, Virginia. He was given an excellent education by his father, including a stint at the College of William and Mary from 1760–1763, where he became friends with notable intellectuals and politicians who aided him in his career. George Wythe tutored him in law for five years, and Jefferson entered the bar in 1767. He married Martha Wayles Skelton on January 1, 1772 when he was 28, and they produced six children, two of whom lived to maturity. She died shortly after giving birth on September 6, 1782 and Jefferson was inconsolably grief-stricken. He had retired from public life in order to preserve her health, but to no avail. He died nearly 44 years later at his famous home, Monticello, on July 4, 1826, having reached his 83rd year.

The third President of the U.S., governor of Virginia, founder of the Library of Congress, inventor, political theorist, historian, architect, violinist, and founder of the University of Virginia is too well known in all these roles to require much detailing here. In addition to authoring most of the Declaration of Independence and writing innumerable letters and papers as part of his government service, he also published *Notes on Virginia* in 1782. In this work Jefferson demonstrates his keen analytic ability in understanding the aboriginal peoples who were met with European colonization of the enormous landmass which was then known as Virginia. He also shows that his grasp of anthropological information was tied to political preoccupations, to the overriding question of how the "natives" could be included in the new American state. His letters are full of astute observations regarding the native populations, and from these several appear below which speak specifically to the critical differences between the British and Indian cultures. Along with slavery, this was the most pressing issue during his governmental service, as he pointed out in his letters. They portray him as insightful, reasonable, and sympathetic to the Indians' plight, unlike so many of his countrymen at the time.

NOTES ON THE STATE OF VIRGINIA, 1782

Query XVIII

Manners: The particular customs and manners that may happen to be received in that state?

It is difficult to determine on the standard by which the manners of a nation may be tried, whether *catholic,* or *particular.* It is more difficult for a native to bring to that standard the manners of his own nation, familiarized to him by habit. There must doubtless be an unhappy influence on the manners of our people produced by the existence of slavery among us. The whole commerce between master and slave is a perpetual exercise of the most boisterous passions, the most unremitting despotism on the one part, and degrading submissions on the other. Our children see this, and learn to imitate it; for man is an imitative animal. This quality is the germ of all education in him. From his cradle to his grave he is learning to do what he sees others do. If a parent could find no motive either in his philanthropy or his self-love, for restraining the intemperance of passion towards his slave, it should always be a sufficient one that his child is present. But generally it is not sufficient. The parent storms, the child looks on, catches the lineaments of wrath, puts on the same airs in the circle of smaller slaves, gives a loose to his worst of passions, and thus nursed, educated, and daily exercised in tyranny, cannot but be stamped by it with odious peculiarities. The man must be a prodigy who can retain his manners and morals undepraved by such circumstances. And with what execration should the statesman be loaded, who permitting one half the citizens thus to trample on the rights of the other, transforms those into despots, and these into enemies, destroys the morals of the one part, and the amor patriæ of the other. For if a slave can have a country in this world, it must be any other in preference to that in which he is born to live and labour for another: in which he must lock up the faculties of his nature, contribute as far as depends on his individual endeavours to the evanishment of the human race, or entail his own miserable condition on the endless generations proceeding from him. With the morals of the people, their industry also is destroyed. For in a warm climate, no man will labour for himself who can make another labour for him. This is so true, that of the proprietors of slaves a very small proportion indeed are ever seen to labour. And can the liberties of a nation be thought secure when we have removed their only firm basis, a conviction in the minds of the people at these liberties are of the gift of God? That they are not be violated but with his wrath? Indeed I tremble for my country when I reflect that God is just: that his justice cannot sleep for ever: that considering numbers, nature and natural means only, a revolution of the wheel of fortune, an exchange of situation, is among possible events: that it may become probable by supernatural interference! The Almighty has no attribute which can take side with us in such a contest.—But is impossible to be temperate and to pursue this subject through the various considerations of policy, of morals, of history natural and civil. We must be contented to hope they will force their way into every one's mind. I think a change already perceptible, since the origin of the present revolution. The spirit of the master is abating, that of the slave rising from the dust, his condition mollifying, the way I hope preparing, under the auspices of heaven, for a total emancipation, and that this is disposed, in the order of events, to be with the consent of the masters, rather than by their extirpation.

✎

INDIAN ADDRESSES

To Brother John Baptist de Coigne
Charlottesville, June 1781

Brother John Baptist de Coigne,—I am very much pleased with the visit you have made us, and particularly that it has happened when the wise men from all parts of our country were assembled together in council, and had an opportunity of hearing the friendly discourse you held to me. We are all sensible of your friendship, and of the services you have rendered, and I now, for my countrymen, return you thanks, and, most particularly, for your assistance to the garrison which was besieged by the hostile Indians. I hope it will please the great being above to continue you long in life, in health and in friendship to us; and that your son will afterwards succeed you in wisdom, in good disposition, and in power over your people. I consider the name you have given as particularly honorable to me, but I value it the more as it proves your attachment to my country. We, like you, are Americans, born in the same land, and having the same interests. I have carefully attended to the figures represented on the skins, and to their explanation, and shall always keep them hanging on the walls in remembrance of you and your nation. I have joined with you sincerely in smoking the pipe of peace; it is a good old custom handed down by your ancestors, and as such I respect and join in it with reverence. I hope we shall long continue to smoke in friendship together. You find us, brother, engaged in war with a powerful nation. Our forefathers were Englishmen, inhabitants of a little island beyond the great water, and, being distressed for land, they came and settled here. As long as we were young and weak, the English whom we had left behind, made us carry all our wealth to their country, to enrich them; and, not satisfied with this, to whatever length began to say we were their slaves, and should do whatever they ordered us. We were now grown up and felt ourselves strong, we knew we were free as they were, that we came here of our own accord and not at their biddance, and were determined to be free as long as we should exist. For this reason they made war on us. They have now waged that war six years, and have not yet won more land from us than will serve to bury the warriors they have lost. Your old father, the king of France, has joined us in the war, and done many good things for us. We are bound forever to love him and wish you to love him, brother, because he is a good and true friend to us. The Spaniards have also joined us, and other powerful nations are now entering into the war to punish the robberies and violences the English have committed on them. The English stand alone, without a friend to support them, hated by all mankind because they are proud and unjust. This quarrel, when it first began, was a family quarrel between us and the English, who were then our brothers. We, therefore, did not wish you to engage in it at all. We are strong enough of ourselves without wasting your blood in fighting our battles. The Eng-

lish, knowing this, have been always suing to the Indians to help them fight. We do not wish you to take up the hatchet. We love and esteem you. We wish you to multiply and be strong. The English, on the other hand, wish to set you and us to cutting one another's throats, that when we are dead they may take all our land. It is better for you not to join in this quarrel, unless the English have killed any of your warriors or done you any other injury. If they have, you have a right to go to war with them, and revenge the injury, and we have none to restrain you. Any free nation has a right to punish those who have done them an injury. I say the same, brother, as to the Indians who treat you ill. While I advise you, like an affectionate friend, to avoid unnecessary war, I do not assume the right of restraining you from punishing your enemies.

To the Brothers of the Choctaw Nation
December 17, 1803

Brothers of the Choctaw Nation:—

We have long heard of your nation as a numerous, peaceable, and friendly people; but this is the first visit we have had from its great men at the seat of our government. I welcome you here; am glad to take you by the hand, and to assure you, for your nation, that we are their friends. Born in the same land, we ought to live as brothers, doing to each other all the good we can, and not listening to wicked men, who may endeavor to make us enemies. By living in peace, we can help and prosper one another; by waging war, we can kill and destroy many on both sides; but those who survive will not be the happier for that. Then, brothers, let it forever be peace and good neighborhood between us. Our seventeen States compose a great and growing nation. Their children are as the leaves of the trees, which the winds are spreading over the forest. But we are just also. We take from no nation what belongs to it. Our growing numbers make us always willing to buy lands from our red brethren, when they are willing to sell. But be assured we never mean to disturb them in their possessions. On the contrary, the lines established between us by mutual consent, shall be sacredly preserved, and will protect your lands from all encroachments by our own people or any others. We will give you a copy of the law, made by our great Council, for punishing our people, who may encroach on your lands, or injure you otherwise. Carry it with you to your homes, and preserve it, as the shield which we spread over you, to protect your land, your property and persons.

It is at the request which you sent me in September, signed by Puckshanublee and other chiefs, and which you now repeat, that I listen to your proposition to sell us lands. You say you owe a great debt to your merchants, that you have nothing to pay it with but lands, and you pray us to take lands, and pay your debt. The sum you have occasion for, brothers, is a very great one. We have never yet paid as much to any our red brethren for the purchase of lands. You propose to us some on the Tombiabee, and some on the Mississippi. Those on the Mississippi suit us well. We wish to have establishments on that river, as resting places for our boats, to furnish them provisions, and to receive our people who fall sick on the way to or from New Orleans, which is now ours. In that quarter, therefore, we are willing to purchase as much as you will spare. But as to the manner in which the line shall be run, we are not judges of it here, nor qualified to make any bargain. But we will appoint persons hereafter to treat with you on the spot, who, knowing the country and quality of the lands, will be better able to agree with you on a line which will give us a just equivalent for the sum of money you want paid.

You have spoken, brothers, of the lands which your fathers formerly sold and marked off to the English, and which they ceded to us with the rest of the country they held here; and you say that, though you do not know whether your fathers were paid for them, you have marked the line over again for us, and do not ask repayment. It has always been the custom, brothers, when lands were bought of the red men, to pay for them immediately, and none of us have ever seen an example of such a debt remaining unpaid. It is to satisfy their immediate wants that the red men have usually sold lands; and in such a case, they would not let the debt be unpaid. The presumption from custom then is strong; so it is also from the great length of time since your fathers sold these lands. But we have, moreover, been informed by persons now living, and who assisted the English in making the purchase, that the price was paid at the time. Were it otherwise, as it was their contract, it would be their debt, not ours.

I rejoice, brothers, to hear you propose to become cultivators of the earth for the maintenance of your families. Be assured you will support them better and with less labor, by raising stock and bread, and by spinning and weaving clothes, than by hunting. A little land cultivated, and a little labor, will procure more provisions than the most successful hunt; and a woman will clothe more by spinning and weaving, than a man by hunting. Compared with you, we are but as of yesterday in this land. Yet see how much more we have multiplied by industry, and the exercise of that reason which you possess in common with us. Follow then our example, brethren, and we will aid you with great pleasure.

The clothes and other necessaries which we sent you the last year, were, as you supposed, a present from us. We never meant to ask land or any other payment for them; and the store which we sent on, was at your request also; and to accommodate you with necessaries at a reasonable price, you wished of course to have it on your land; but the land would continue yours, not ours.

As to the removal of the store, the interpreter, and the agent, and any other matters you may wish to speak about, the Secretary at War will enter into explanations with you, and whatever he says, you may consider as said by myself, and what he promises you will be faithfully performed.

I am glad, brothers, you are willing to go and visit some other parts of our country. Carriages shall be ready to convey you, and you shall be taken care of on your journey; and when you shall have returned here and rested yourselves to your own mind, you shall be sent home by land. We had provided for your coming by land, and were sorry for the mistake which carried you to Savannah instead of Augusta, and exposed you to the risks of a voyage by sea. Had any accident happened to you, though we could not help it, it would have been a cause of great mourning to us. But we thank the Great Spirit who took care of you on the ocean, and brought you safe and in good health to the seat of our great Council; and we hope His care will accompany and protect you, on your journey and return home; and that He will preserve and prosper your nation in all its just pursuits.

JOHANN G. HERDER

1744–1803

Johann Gottfried von Herder, gifted son of poor parents, was born in Mohrungen, East Prussia (now Morag, Poland) on August 25, 1744 and died in Weimar, Germany on December 18, 1803, at age 59. He wrote enough material to fill 45 volumes of collected works, issued posthumously by his wife, Caroline Flachsland, whom he married in 1773. The pivotal event of his youth, after studying in local schools and at the University of Königsberg (from 1762), was a trip by ship from Riga, where he'd gone to teach, to Nantes by way of Holland and England, about which he published a book (1769). Though only 25, these reflections about the nature of human life and the meaning of history anticipated later ideas of Goethe (whom he met in 1770), von Humboldt, the Schlegels, the Grimms, Hegel, Dilthey, and others. Five years Goethe's senior, he impressed his new friend so much that Goethe arranged for an administrative position for him at Weimar (following a five-year stint as court preacher in Bückeburg), where he remained after 1776, writing furiously. His main works include *Essay on the Origin of Language* (1772), often compared with Rousseau's contemporaneous reflections; *Another Philosophy of History Concerning the Development of Mankind* (1774), where the fateful conflict between the individual and the collectivity is first broached, soon becoming a major theme of the Romantic movement; *Ideas about the Philosophy of the History of Mankind* (1784–91), and *On German Character and Art* (1773). A conflict of egos and political vision with Goethe led to a break from his friend and benefactor after 1790, and he began to repudiate views of literature and philosophy which he himself had helped to found 20 years before. He also attacked Kant's philosophy in 1799 with his *Metacritique of the Critique of Pure Reason,* though with little longterm success.

Herder has been grouped with "the irrationalists," as they are sometimes called: philosophers of history and human action who refuse to celebrate human powers of rational thought and action along the lines of Newton, Descartes, or Berkeley. In place of an all-powerful capacity to think and behave along purely rational lines, he substituted "feeling" (*Gefühl*) which for Herder is what gives human cognition its fundamental nature. Our experience of the world, the natural and the social, rests most basically on our corporeal response to whatever resists its desire for expression and possession—an argument which anticipates Merleau-Ponty's ideas 200 years later. The selections offered here come from his principal work on the philosophy of history, and show Herder coming to terms with questions about historical change, the virtues of women, and the growing role of reason in history (which became Hegel's theme as well).

IDEAS FOR A PHILOSOPHY OF THE HISTORY OF MAN, 1784–91

National Genius and the Environment

The Feelings and Inclinations of Men are every where conformable to their Organization, and the Circumstances in which they live; but they are every where swayed by Custom and Opinion

Self-preservation is the first object of every existing being: from the grain of sand to the solar orb, every thing strives, to remain what it is: for this purpose instinct is impressed on the brute; for this, reason, the substitute of instinct, is given to man. In obedience to this law, he every where seeks food at the impulse of inexorable hunger: from his infancy, without knowing why or wherefore, he strives to exercise his powers, to be in motion. The weary does not call for sleep; but sleep comes, and renovates his existence: the vital powers relieve the sick, when they can, or at least strive to remove the disease. Man defends his life against every thing, that attacks it; and even without being sensible, that Nature has taken measures, both within and around him, for his support.

There have been philosophers, who, on account of this instinct of self-preservation, have classed man with the beasts of prey, and deemed his natural state a state of warfare. It is evident, there is much impropriety in this. Man, it is true, is a robber, in tearing the fruit from the tree; a murderer, in killing an animal; and the most cruel oppressor on the face of the Earth, while with his foot, and with his breath perhaps, he deprives of life innumerable multitudes of invisible creatures. Every man knows the attempts of the gentle Hindoo and extravagant Egyptian philosophy, to render man a perfectly harmless creature: but to the eye of the speculatist they appear to have been in vain. We cannot look into the chaos of the elements; and if we refrain from devouring any visible animal, we cannot avoid swallowing a number

of minute living creatures, in water, air, milk, and vegetables.

But away with these subtilties, and, considering man among his brethren, let us ask: is he by nature a beast of prey toward his fellows, is he an unsocial being? By his make he is not the former; and by his birth the latter still less. Conceived in the bosom of Love, and nourished at the breast of Affection, he is educated by men, and receives from them a thousand unearned benefits. Thus he is actually formed in and for society, without which be could neither have received his being, nor have become a man. Insociability commences with him, when violence is done to his nature, by his coming into collision with other men: but this is no exception, as here he acts conformably to the great universal law of self-preservation. Let us inquire what means Nature has invented, to satisfy and restrain him as much as possible even here, and prevent a state of general warfare among mankind

1. As man is the most artfully complicated of all creatures, so great a variety of genetic character occurs in no other. Blind imperious instinct is wanting to his delicate frame; but in him the varying currents of thoughts and desires flow into each other, in a manner peculiar to himself. Thus man, from his very nature, will clash but little in his pursuits with man; his dispositions, sensations, and propensities, being so infinitely diversified, and as it were individualized. What is a matter of indifference to one man, to another is an object of desire: and then each has a world of enjoyment in himself, each a creation of his own.

2. Nature has bestowed on this diverging species an ample space, the extensive fertile Earth, over which the most different climates and modes of life have room to spread. Here she has raised mountains, there she has placed deserts or rivers, which keep men separate: on the hunter she has bestowed the extensive forest, on the fisherman the ample sea, on the shepherd the spacious plain. It is not her fault, that birds, deceived by the fowler's art, fly into his net, where they fight over their food, peck out each other's eyes, and contaminate the air they breathe: for she has placed the bird in the air, and not in the net of the fowler. See those wild species, how tamely they live together! no one envies another; each procures and enjoys what he wants in peace. It is repugnant to the

truth of history, to set up the malicious discordant disposition of men crowded together, of rival artists, opposing politicians, envious authors, for the general character of the species: the rankling wounds of these malignant thorns are unknown to the greater part of mankind; to those who breathe the free air, not the pestilential atmosphere of towns. He who maintains laws are necessary, because otherwise men would live lawlessly, takes for granted, what it is incumbent on him to prove. If man were not thronged together in close prisons, they would need no ventilators to purify the air: were not their minds inflamed by artificial madness, they would not require the restraining hand of correlative art.

3. Nature, too, has shortened, as far as she could, the time, that men must remain together. Man requires a long time to educate; but then he is still weak: he is a child, quickly provoked, and as easily forgetting his anger; often displeased, but incapable of bearing malice. As soon as he arrives at years of maturity, a new instinct awakes in him, and he quits the house of his father. Nature acts in this instinct: she drives him out, to construct his own nest.

And with whom does he construct it? With a creature as dissimilarly similar to himself, and whose passions are as unlikely to come into collision with his, as is consistent with the end of their forming an union together. The nature of the woman is different from that of the man: she differs in her feelings, she differs in her actions. Miserable he, who is rivalled by his wife, or excelled by her in manly virtues! She was destined to rule him by kindness and condescension alone, which render the apple of discord the apple of love. . . .

Let us proceed to the virtues of women, as they display themselves in the history of mankind. Even among the most savage people the woman is distinguished from the man by more delicate civility, and love of ornament and decoration: and these qualities are discernible, even where the nation has to contend against an unfriendly climate, and the most distressing want. Every where the woman adorns herself, however scanty the materials she is able to procure. So in the early spring the Earth, rich in life, sends forth at least a few inodorous blossoms, to show what she is capable of effecting in other seasons.

Cleanliness is another female virtue, to which woman is impelled by nature, and excited by her desire to please. The regulations, may often supererogatory laws and customs, by which all unvitiated nations keep women when labouring under disease in a state of separation, that no injury may accrue from them, reflect disgrace on many civilized people. They are in consequence unacquainted with a great part of the weaknesses, which among us are both the effects, and again new causes, of that deep degeneracy, which licentious, diseased effeminacy transmits to a wretched offspring.

The gentle endurance, the indefatigable activity, for which the softer sex, when not corrupted by the abuses of civilization, are distinguished, deserve still greater commendation. They bear with resignation the yoke, that the rude superiority of strength in man, his love of idleness and inaction, and lastly the faults of their ancestors, have entailed on them as an hereditary custom; and the most perfect examples of this are often found among the most wretched people. It is not from dissimulation, that in many regions the marriageable females must be compelled by force to submit to the drudgery of the wedded state: they run from their hut, they flee into the desert: with tears they put on the bridal garland, the last flower of their freer, player youth. Most of the epithalamiums of such nations are meant to encourage and console the bride, and are composed in a melancholy strain, at which we are apt to laugh, because we are insensible of their innocence and truth. The bride takes a tender leave of all, that was dear to her youth, quits the house of her parents, as one dead to them for ever, loses her former name, and becomes the property of a stranger, who in all likelihood will treat her as a slave. She must sacrifice to him every thing, that is most dear to a human being, her person, her liberty, her will, nay probably her life and health; and all for the gratification of a passion, to which the modest virgin is yet a stranger, and which will soon be drowned in a sea of inconveniences. Happy is it, that Nature has endowed and adorned the female heart with an unspeakably affectionate and powerful sense of the personal worth of man. This enables her to bear also his severities: her mind willingly turns from them to the contemplation of whatever she considers as noble, great, valiant, and uncommon in him: with exalted feelings she participates in the manly deeds, the evening recital of which softens the fatigue of her toilsome day, and is proud, since she is destined to obedience, that she has such a husband to obey. Thus the love of the romantic in the female character is a benevolent gift of Nature; a balsam for the woman, and an animating reward for the man: for the most valuable prize of the youth was ever the love of a maiden.

Lastly must be mentioned that sweet maternal affection bestowed on woman by Nature; almost independent of cool reason, and far remote from the selfish desire of reward. The mother loves her child, not because he is amiable, but as a living part of herself, the child of her heart, the copy of her nature. Hence her bowels yearn with compassion for his sufferings; her heart beats higher at his happiness; her blood flows more placidly, while he receives the stream from her breast. These maternal feelings pervade every uncorrupted nation upon Earth: no climate, by which all other things are changed, could alter this: the most depraved customs of society alone can in time perhaps render enervating vices more pleasing than the tender pains of maternal love. The Greenlander suckles her son three or four years, because her climate affords no food proper for infants: she submits to all the perversities arising from the latent insolence of the future man with indulgent forbearance. The Negress displays more than manly strength, when a monster attacks her child: we read with astonishment instances of maternal magnanimity contemning life. Lastly, when the tender mother, whom we call a savage, is deprived of her chief consolation, the object of her care, and that for which she values life, her feelings surpass description: How then can these nations be deficient in sentiments of true female humanity, unless perhaps want and mournful necessity, or a false point of honour and some barbarous hereditary custom, occasionally lead them astray? The germs of every great and noble feeling not only exist in all places, but are universally unfolded, as much as the way of life, climate, tradition, or peculiarity of the nation will permit.

Humanity the End of Human Nature

From the Laws of their internal Nature, Reason and Justice must gain more Footing among Men in the Course of Time, and promote a more durable Humanity

All the doubts and complaints of men, respecting the uncertainty and little observable progress of good in history, arise from this, that the melancholy wanderer sees too little on his way. If he extended his view, and impartially compared with each other the times, that we most accurately know from history; farther, if he dived into the nature of man, and weighed what truth and reason are; he would doubt as little of their progress, as of the most indisputable physical truth. For thousands of years our sun and all the fixed stars were supposed to be immovable: a fortunate telescope now permits us no longer to doubt of their movement. So in some future age, a more accurate comparison of the periods exhibited in the history of our species will not merely give us a superficial view of this exhilarating truth, but, in spite of all apparent disorder, will enable us to calculate the laws, according to which this progress is effected by the power of human nature. Standing on the verge of ancient history, as on a central point, I shall do no more than cursorily note a few general principles, which will serve as leading stars, to guide us on our future way.

First. *Times connect themselves together, in virtue of their nature; and with them the child of Time, the race of mankind, with all its operations and productions.*

No sophistical argument can lead us to deny, that our Earth has grown older in the course of some thousands of years; and that this wanderer round the Sun is greatly altered since its origin. In its bowels we perceive how it once was constituted; and we need but look around us, to see its present constitution. The ocean foams no longer; it is subsided peaceably into its bed: the wandering streams have found their shores; and plants and animals have run through a progressive series of years in their different races. As not a sunbeam has been lost upon our Earth since its creation; so no falling leaf, no wasted seed, no carcase of a decaying animal, and still less an action of any living being, has been without effect. Vegetation, for example, has increased, and extended itself as far as it could: every living race has spread within the limits nature assigned it, through the means of others: and even the senseless devastations of man, as well as his industry, have been active implements in the hand of Time. Fresh harvests have waved over the ruins of the cities he has destroyed: the elements have strewed the dust oblivion upon them; and soon new generations have arisen, who have erected new buildings upon the old, and even with their ancient remains. Omnipotence itself cannot ordain, that effects shall not be effects: it cannot restore the Earth to what it was thousands of years ago, so that these thousands of years, with all their consequences, shall not have been.

Already therefore a certain progress of the human species is inseparable from the progress of Time, as far as man is included in the family of Time and Earth. Were the progenitor of man kind now to appear, and view his descendants, how would he be astonished! His body was formed for a youthful Earth; his frame, his ideas, and his way of life, must have been adapted to that constitution of the elements, which then prevailed; and considerable alteration in this must have taken place, in the course of six thousand years or upwards. In many parts America is no longer what it was when discovered: two thousand years hence, its ancient history will have the air of romance.

Secondly. *The habitations of mankind render the progress of the human species still more evident.*

Where are the times when people dwelled as troglodytes, dispersed about in caves, behind their walls, and every stranger was an enemy? Merely from the course of time no cave, no wall, afforded security: men must learn to know one another; for collectively they are but one family, on one planet of no great extent. It is a melancholy reflection, that every where they first learned to know one another as enemies, and beheld each other with astonishment as so many wolves: but such was the order of nature. The weak feared the strong; the deceived, the deceiver; he who had been expelled, him who could again expel him; the unexperienced child, every stranger. This infantile fear, however, and all its abuses, could not alter the course of nature: the bond of union between nations was knit, though, from the rude state of man, in a rough manner. Growing reason may burst the knots, but cannot untwist the band, and still less undo the discoveries, that have once been made. What are the geologies of Moses and Orpheus, Homer and Herodotus, Strabo and Pliny,

compared with ours? What was the commerce of the Phenicians, Greeks, and Romans, to the trade of Europe? Thus with what has hitherto been effected the clew to the labyrinth of what is to be done is given us. Man, while he continues man, will not cease from wandering over his planet, till it is completely known to him: from this neither storms nor shipwreck, nor those vast mountains of ice, nor all the perils of either pole, will deter him; no more than they have deterred him from the first most difficult attempts, even when navigation was very defective. The incentive to all these enterprizes lies in his own breast, lies in man's nature. Curiosity, and the insatiable desire of wealth, fame, discovery, and increase of strength, and even new wants and discontents, inseparable from the present course of things, will impel him; and they by whom dangers have been surmounted in former times, his celebrated and successful predecessors, will animate him. Thus the will of providence will be promoted both by good and bad incentives, till man knows and acts upon the whole of his species. To him the Earth is given; and he will not desist, till it is wholly his own, at least as far as regards knowledge and use. Are we not already ashamed, that one hemisphere of our planet remained for so long a time as unknown to us, as if had been the other side of the Moon?

Thirdly. *In consequence of the internal nature of the human mind, its activity has hitherto been employed solely on means of grounding more deeply the humanity and cultivation of our, species, and extending them farther.*

How vast the progress from the first raft that floated on the water to an European ship! Neither the inventor of the former, nor the many inventors of the various arts and sciences that contribute to navigation, ever formed the least conception of what would arise from the combination of their discoveries: each obeyed his particular impulse of want or curiosity: but it is inherent in the nature of the human intellect, and of the general connexion of all things, that no attempt; no discovery, can be made in vain. Those islanders, who had never seen an European vessel, beheld the monster with astonishment, some prodigy of another World; and were still more astonished when they found, that men like themselves could guide it, pleasure over the trackless ocean. Could their astonishment have been converted into rational reflection on every great purpose, and every little mean, of this floating world of art, how much higher would their admiration of the human mind have risen? Whither do not the hands of Europeans at present reach, by means of this single implement? Whither may they not reach thereafter?

Beside this art, others innumerable have been invented within the space of a few years by mankind, that extend their sway over air and water, over Earth and Heaven. And when we reflect, that but few nations were engaged in this contest of mental activity, while the greater part of the rest slumbered in the lap of ancient custom; when we reflect, that almost all our inventions were made at very early periods, and scarcely any trace, scarcely any ruin, of an ancient structure, or an ancient institution, exists, that is not connected with our early history; what a prospect does this historically demonstrated activity of the human mind give us for the infinity of future ages! In the few centuries during which Greece flourished, in the few centuries of modern improvement, how much has been conceived; invented, done, reduced to order, and preserved for future ages, in Europe, the least quarter of the Globe, and almost in its smallest parts! How prolific the seeds, that art and science have copiously shed, while one nourishes, one animates and excites the other! As when a string is touched, not only everything that has music resounds to it, but all its harmonious tones reecho the sound, till it becomes imperceptible; so the human mind has invented and created, when an harmonious point of its interiour has been hit. When a new concord was struck, in a creation where every thing is connected, innumerable new concatenations followed of course.

JEREMY BENTHAM

1748–1832

The son and grandson of lawyers (from whom he learned Enlightenment rationality) and of a pious mother and grandmothers (who infected him with superstitions), Jeremy Bentham was born on February 15, 1748 on Red Lion Street in Houndsditch, Spitalfields, London. He unsuccessfully proposed marriage to Caroline Fox in the 1780s, and died after 84 years on June 6, 1832 at The Heritage, Queen's Square Place, London, after enjoying what biographers have called "a happy life." By his orders, his body was preserved, with a wax head replacing his own, and is displayed in the main building of University College, London, an institution he founded. A prodigy, he began Latin at 4 and read voraciously even then, which made him a spectacle at Westminster School, after which he attended Queens College, Oxford, receiving the B.A. in 1763, at 15. Under the influence of his father, who hoped he would become Lord Chancellor, he was admitted to the bar, but refused to practice law, instead doing chemical experiments and writing sometimes eight to twelve hours per day. He decided against the law after hearing William Blackstone's lectures, instead choosing to reform law by writing criticisms of its practical and theoretical aspects. This he did religiously, usually producing between 10 and 20 sheets of manuscript per day. He traveled to Russia to visit his brother, Samuel, and while there (1785–1788) wrote unflaggingly, inventing the infamous "panopticon" prison design which he fruitlessly tried to sell to Catherine the Great and many others over the next 20 years. An inheritance from his father in 1796 freed him from any work but writing. He relentlessly tried to influence legal and political reform, and met with considerable success, often by influencing other notables such as George Grote, John Austin, and the Mills, father and son.

Yet the reason for Bentham's inclusion in the pantheon of social theorists lies in the root idea of Utilitarianisn (the greatest happiness of the greatest number), his attempt to quantify happiness through a "felicific calculus," and the related argument that people are by nature self-centered and rational, not given to genuine concern for others, nor truly interested in collective existence. Today's "rational choice theory," so much relied upon in economics, political science and in certain branches of sociology, has its roots in Bentham's doctrines, even if he is seldom acknowledged to be its progenitor. His main work along these lines appears in *An Introduction to the Principles of Morals and Legislation* (1789), which must have impressed the dignitaries of the new French nation since soon after their Revolution they made him an honorary citizen, in 1792. From this work the selections in this book have been chosen, on utility and the measurement of pleasure.

AN INTRODUCTION TO THE PRINCIPLES OF MORALS AND LEGISLATION, 1789

Of the Principle of Utility

Nature has placed mankind under the governance of two sovereign masters, *pain* and *pleasure.* It is for them alone to point out what we ought to do, as well as to determine what we shall do. On the one hand the standard of right and wrong, on the other the chain of causes and effects, are fastened to their throne. They govern us in all we do, in all we say, in all we think: every effort we can make to throw off our subjection, will serve but to demonstrate and confirm it. In words a man may pretend to abjure their empire: but in reality he will remain subject to it all the while. The *principle of utility* recognises this subjection, and assumes it for the foundation of that system, the object of which is to rear the fabric of felicity by the hands of reason and of law. Systems which this principle, without thinking of it: if not for the ordering of their own actions, yet for the trying of their own actions, as well as of those of other men. There have been, at the same time, not many, perhaps, even of the most intelligent, who have been disposed to embrace it purely and without reserve. There are even few who have not taken some occasion or other to quarrel with it, either on account of their not understanding always how to apply it, or on account of some prejudice or other which they were afraid to examine into, or could not bear to part with. For such is the stuff that man is made of: in principle and in practice, in a right track and in a wrong one, the rarest of all human qualities is consistency.

XIII. When a man attempts to combat the principle of utility, it is with reasons drawn, without his being aware of it, from that very principle itself. . . .

His arguments, if they prove any thing, prove not that the principle is *wrong,* but that, according to the applications he supposed to be made of it, it is *misapplied.* Is it possible for a man to move the

earth? Yes; but he must first find out another earth to stand upon.

Of the Four Sanctions or Sources of Pain and Pleasure

I. It has been shown that the happiness of the individuals, of whom a community is composed, that is, their pleasures and their security, is the end and the sole end which the legislator ought to have in view: the sole standard, in conformity to which each individual ought, as far as depends upon the legislator, to be *made* to fashion his behaviour. But whether it be this or any thing else that is to be *done,* there is nothing by which a man can ultimately be *made* to do it, but either pain or pleasure. Having taken a general view of these two grand objects (viz. pleasure, and what comes to the same thing, immunity from pain) in the character of final causes; it will be necessary to take a view of pleasure and pain itself, in the character of *efficient* causes or means.

II. There are four distinguishable sources from which pleasure and pain are in use to flow: considered separately, they may be termed the *physical,* the *political,* the *moral,* and the *religious:* and inasmuch as the pleasures and pains belonging to each of them are capable of giving a binding force to any law or rule of conduct, they may all of them be termed *sanctions.*

III. If it be in the present life, and from the ordinary course of nature, not purposely modified by the interposition of the will of any human being, nor by any extraordinary interposition of any superior invisible being, that the pleasure or pain takes place or is expected, it may be said to issue from, or to belong to, the *physical sanction.*

IV. If at the hands of a *particular* person or set of persons in the community, who under names correspondent to that of *judge,* are chosen for the particular purpose of dispensing it, according to the will of the sovereign or supreme ruling power in the state, it may be said to issue from the *political sanction.*

V. If at the hands of such *chance* persons in the community, as the party in question may happen in the course of his life to have concerns with, according to each man's spontaneous disposition, and not according to any settled or concerted rule, it may be said to issue from the *moral* or *popular sanction.*

VI. If from the immediate hand of a superior invisible being, either in the present life, or in a future, it may be said to issue from the *religious sanction.*

VII. Pleasures or pains which may be expected to issue from the *physical, political,* or *moral* sanctions, must all of them be expected to be experienced, if ever, in the *present* life: those which may be expected to issue from the religious sanction, may be expected to be experienced either in the *present* life or in a *future.* . . .

XI. Of these four sanctions, the physical is altogether, we may observe, the groundwork of the political and the moral: so is it also of the religious, in as far as the latter bears relation to the present life. It is included in each of these other three. This may operate in any case (that is, any of the pains or pleasures belonging to it may operate) independently of *them:* none of *them* can operate but by means of this. In a word, the powers of nature may operate of themselves; but neither the magistrate, nor men at large, *can* operate, nor is God in the case in question *supposed* to operate, but through the powers of nature.

XII. For these four objects, which in their nature have so much in common, it seemed of use to find a common name. It seemed of use, in the first place, for the convenience of giving a name to certain pleasures and pains, for which a name equally characteristic could hardly otherwise have been found: in the second place, for the sake of holding up the efficacy of certain moral forces, the influence of which is apt not to be sufficiently at-

tended to. Does the political sanction exert an influence over the conduct of mankind? The moral, the religious sanctions, do so too. In every inch of his career are the operations of the political magistrate liable to be aided or impeded by these two foreign powers: who, one or other of them, or both, are sure to be either his rivals or his allies. Does it happen to him to leave them out in his calculations? he will be sure almost to find himself mistaken in the result. Of all this we shall find abundant proofs in the sequel of this work. It behoves him, therefore, to have them continually before his eyes; and that under such a name as exhibits the relation they bear to his own purposes and designs.

Value of a Lot of Pleasure or Pain, How to be Measured

I. Pleasures then, and the avoidance of pains are the *ends* which the legislator has in view: it behoves him therefore to understand their *value.* Pleasures and pains are the *instruments* he has to work with: it behoves him therefore to understand their force, which is again, in another point of view, their value.

II. To a person considered by *himself,* the value of a pleasure or pain considered by *itself,* will be greater or less, according to the four following circumstances: . . .

1. Its *intensity.*
2. Its *duration.*
3. Its *certainty* or *uncertainty.*
4. Its *propinquity* or *remoteness.*

part II

REVOLUTION AND ROMANTICISM

Edmund Burke *1729–1797*

Mary Wollstonecraft *1759–1797*

Thomas Paine *1737–1809*

Friedrich Schiller *1759–1805*

Marquis de Condorcet *1743–1794*

Georg Wilhelm Friedrich Hegel *1770–1831*

Thomas Robert Malthus *1766–1834*

Friedrich Schleiermacher *1768–1834*

Jean-Charles-Leonard Simonde de Sismondi *1773–1842*

Johann Gottlieb Fichte *1762–1814*

Joseph de Maistre *1753–1821*

Henri Comte de Saint-Simon *1760–1825*

Thomas Carlyle *1795–1881*

Francois-Marie-Charles Fourier *1772–1837*

EDMUND BURKE

1729–1797

Edmund Burke, a lawyer's son, was born on January 12, 1729 in Dublin, Ireland. He married Jane Mary Nugent in 1757 and had one son, Richard, who, three years before Burke's own death, died suddenly in the prime of life, bringing enormous grief to both his parents. After 68 years he died at Beaconsfield, Buckingham County, England on July 9, 1797, never having recovered from his son's demise. He was schooled in Ballitore, Kildare County, then at Trinity College, Dublin from 1743–48. In 1750 he moved to London to study law, lost interest, and traveled for a half-dozen years, managing to write *A Vindication of Natural Society* (1756), and, quite unrelatedly, *A Philosophical Enquiry into the Origin of our Ideas of the Sublime and Beautiful* (1757), which was positively received by Kant, Diderot, and Lessing, and still bears study. He worked as Marquess of Rockingham's secretary from 1765 until 1782, became for six years a member of Parliament from Bristol in 1774, and after losing that seat, was given another by Rockingham, a "pocket borough" called Malton. He wrote and spoke about the proper relationship between the Crown and its subjects, and rejected pure democracy as the tyranny of numbers. He also wrote about the right of England to tax its American colonies, and concluded that governments should be cooperative ventures, in which tradition ought to mediate conflicts between the rulers and ruled. He also wrote about Ireland and India, not always with complete emotional control, and drafted the East India Bill of 1783. In all these writings, he deferred to the "law of nature," and urged his readers and auditors to heed nature's strictures on human caprice.

Burke's most famous and important study is his *Reflections on the Revolution in France* (1790), to which many responses were written, including Tom Paine's *The Rights of Man*. Burke was suspicious of revolutionary political and social changes because they tend toward fratricide and the total destruction of civility (what Durkheim would call "anomie" a century later). He thought the Revolution was entirely too rationalist, and its brutality was an outgrowth of having dashed too far from traditional social relations, and therefore into uncharted utopian and dystopian territory. These worries are recorded in the selections reprinted below, one from his observations about the French Revolution, where, he argued, individual liberty was in fact crushed just as it was allegedly being advanced, and the second from his early work on natural society. In both one quickly notes Burke's famously pungent writing style, one that has been the subject of scholarly comment even up to our own time. Studies of Burke's remarkably skillful rhetoric have become a cottage industry unto themselves.

REFLECTIONS ON THE REVOLUTION IN FRANCE, 1790

Dear Sir,

You are pleased to call again, and with some earnestness, for my thoughts on the late proceedings in France. I will not give you reason to imagine that I think my sentiments of such value as to wish myself to be solicited about them. They are of too little consequence to be very anxiously either communicated or withheld. It was from attention to you, and to you only, that I hesitated at the time when you first desired to receive them. In the first letter I had the honour to write to you, and which at length I send, I wrote neither for, nor from, any description of men; nor shall I in this. My errors, if any, are my own. My reputation alone is to answer for them.

You see, Sir, by the long letter I have transmitted to you, that though I do most heartily wish that France may be animated by a spirit of rational liberty, and that I think you bound, in all honest policy, to provide a permanent body in which that spirit may reside, and an effectual organ by which it may act, it is my misfortune to entertain great doubts concerning several material points in your late transactions. . . .

I flatter myself that I love a manly, moral, regulated liberty as well as any gentleman of that society, be he who he will; and perhaps I have given as good proofs of my attachment to that cause, in the whole course of my public conduct. I think I envy liberty as little as they do, to any other nation. But I cannot stand forward, and give praise or blame to anything which relates to human actions, and human concerns, on a simple view of the object, as it stands stripped of every relation, in all the nakedness and solitude of metaphysical abstraction. Circumstances (which with some gentlemen pass for nothing) give in reality to every political principle its distinguishing colour and discriminating effect. The circumstances are what render every civil and political scheme beneficial or noxious to mankind. Abstractedly speaking, government, as well as liberty, is good; yet could I, in common sense, ten years ago, have felicitated France on her enjoyment of a government (for she then had a government) without inquiry what the nature of that government was, or how it was administered? Can I now congratulate the same nation upon its freedom? Is it because liberty in the abstract may be classed amongst the blessings of mankind, that I am seriously to felicitate a mad-man, who has escaped from the protecting restraint and wholesome darkness of his cell, on his restoration to the enjoyment of light and liberty? Am I to congratulate a highwayman and murderer, who has broke prison, upon the recovery of his natural rights? This would be to act over again the scene of the criminals condemned to the galleys, and their heroic deliverer, the metaphysic knight of the sorrowful countenance.

When I see the spirit of liberty in action, I see a strong principle at work; and this, for a while, is all I can possibly know of it. The wild *gas*, the fixed air, is plainly broke loose: but we ought to suspend our judgment until the first effervescence is a little subsided, till the liquor is cleared, and until we see something deeper than the agitation of a troubled and frothy surface. I must be tolerably sure, before I venture publicly to congratulate men upon a blessing, that they have really received one. Flattery corrupts both the receiver and the giver; and adulation is not of more service to the people than to kings. I should therefore suspend my congratulations on the new liberty of France, until I was informed how it had been combined with government; with public force; with the discipline and obedience of armies; with the collection of an effective and well-distributed revenue; with morality and religion; with the solidity of property; with peace and order; with civil and social manners. All these (in their way) are good things too; and, without them, liberty is not a benefit whilst it lasts, and is not likely to continue long. The effect of liberty to individuals is, that they may do what they please: we ought to see what it will please them to do, before we risk congratulations, which may be soon turned into complaints. Prudence would dictate this in the case of separate, insulated, private men; but liberty, when men act in bodies, is *power*. Considerate people, before they declare themselves, will observe the use which is made of *power*; and particularly of so trying a thing as *new* power in *new* persons, of whose principles, tempers, and dispositions they have little or no experience, and in situations, where those who appear the most stirring in the scene may possibly not be the real movers. . . .

Compute your gains: see what is got by those extravagant and presumptuous speculations which have taught your leaders to despise all their predecessors, and all their contemporaries, and even to despise themselves, until the moment in which they became truly despicable. By following those false lights, France has bought undisguised calamities at a higher price than any nation has purchased the most unequivocal blessings! France has bought poverty by crime! France has not sacrificed her virtue to her interest, but she has abandoned her interest, that she might prostitute her virtue. All other nations have begun the fabric of a new government, or the reformation of an old, by establishing originally, or by enforcing with greater exactness, some rites or other of religion. All other people have laid the foundations of civil freedom in severer manners, and a system of a more austere and masculine morality. France, when she let loose the reins of regal authority, doubled the licence of a ferocious dissoluteness in manners, and of an insolent irreligion in opinions and practices; and has extended through all ranks of life, as if she were communicating some privilege, or laying open some secluded benefit, all the unhappy corruptions that usually were the disease of wealth and power. This is one of the new principles of equality in France.

France, by the perfidy of her leaders, has utterly disgraced the tone of lenient council in the cabinets of princes, and disarmed it of its most potent topics. She has sanctified the dark, suspicious maxims of tyrannous distrust; and taught kings to tremble at (what will hereafter be called) the delusive plausibilities of moral politicians. Sovereigns will consider those, who advise them to place an unlimited confidence in their people, as subverters of their thrones; as traitors who aim at their destruction, by leading their easy good-nature, under specious pretences, to admit combinations of bold and faithless men into a participation of their power. This alone (if there were nothing else) is an irreparable calamity to you and to mankind. Remember that your parliament of

Paris told your king, that, in calling the states together, he had nothing to fear but the prodigal excess of their zeal in providing for the support of the throne. It is right that these men should hide their heads. It is right that they should bear their part in the ruin which their counsel has brought on their sovereign and their country. Such sanguine declarations tend to lull authority asleep; to encourage it rashly to engage in perilous adventures of untried policy; to neglect those provisions, preparations, and precautions, which distinguished benevolence from imbecility; and without which no man can answer for the salutary effect of any abstract plan of government or of freedom. For want of these, they have seen the medicine of the state corrupted into its poison. They have seen the French rebel against a mild and lawful monarch, with more fury, outrage, and insult, than ever any people has been known to rise against the most illegal usurper, or the most sanguinary tyrant. Their resistance was made to concession; their revolt was from protection; their blow was aimed at a hand holding out graces, favours, and immunities.

This was unnatural. The rest is in order.

⌒

A VINDICATION OF NATURAL SOCIETY, 1756

Discontents in the Kingdom

. . . To complain of the age we live in, to murmur at the present possessors of power, to lament the past, to conceive extravagant hopes of the future, are the common dispositions of the greatest part of mankind; indeed the necessary effects of the ignorance and levity of the vulgar. Such complaints and humors have existed in all times; yet as all times have not been alike, true political sagacity manifests itself in distinguishing that complaint which only characterizes the general infirmity of

From *Burke's Politics: Selected Writings and Speeches of Edmund Burke on Reform, Revolution, and War*, Ross J.S. Hoffman and Paul Levack, Eds. Published by Alfred A. Knopf. Copyright © 1967.

human nature from those which are symptoms of the particular distemperature of our own air and season.

Nobody, I believe, will consider it merely as the language of spleen or disappointment if I say that there is something particularly alarming in the present conjuncture. There is hardly a man, in or out of power, who holds any other language. That government is at once dreaded and contemned; that the laws are despoiled of all their respected and salutary terrors; that their inaction is a subject of ridicule, and their exertion of abhorrence; that rank, and office and title, and all the solemn plausibilities of the world, have lost their reverence and effect; that our foreign politics are as much deranged as our domestic economy; that our dependencies are slackened in their affection, and loosened from their obedience; that we know neither how to yield nor how to enforce; that hardly anything above or below, abroad or at home, is sound and entire; but that disconnection and confusion, in offices, in parties, in families, in Parliament, in the nation, prevail beyond the disorders of any former time: these are facts universally admitted and lamented.

This state of things is the more extraordinary because the great parties which formerly divided and agitated the kingdom are known to be in a manner entirely dissolved. No great external calamity has visited the nation; no pestilence or famine. We do not labor at present under any scheme of taxation new or oppressive in the quantity or in the mode. Nor are we engaged in unsuccessful war; in which our misfortunes might easily pervert our judgment; and our minds, sore from the loss of national glory, might feel every blow of fortune as a crime in government.

It is impossible that the cause of this strange distemper should not sometimes become a subject of discourse. It is a compliment due, and which I willingly pay, to those who administer our affairs, to take notice in the first place of their speculation. Our ministers are of opinion that the increase of our trade and manufactures, that our growth by colonization, and by conquest, have concurred to accumulate immense wealth in the hands of some individuals; and this again being dispersed among the people has rendered them universally proud, ferocious, and ungovernable; that the insolences of some from their enormous wealth, and the boldness of others from a guilty poverty, have rendered them capable of the most atrophous attempts; so that they have trampled upon all subordination, and violently born down the unarmed laws of a free government; barriers too feeble against the fury of a populace so fierce and licentious as ours. They contend that no adequate protraction has been given for so spreading a discontent, our affairs having been conducted throughout with remarkable temper and consummate wisdom. The wicked industry of some libelers, joined to the intrigues of a few disappointed politicians, have, in their opinion, been able to produce this unnatural ferment in the nation.

Nothing indeed can be more unnatural than the present convulsions of this country, if the above account be a true one. I confess I shall assent to it with great reluctance, and only on the compulsion of the clearest and firmest proofs; because their account resolves itself into this short, but discouraging proposition, "That we have a very good ministry, but that we are a very bad people"; that we set ourselves to bite the hand that feeds us; that with a malignant insanity we oppose the measures, and ungratefully vilify the persons, of those whose sole object is our own peace and prosperity. If a few puny libelers, acting under a knot of factious politicians, without virtue, parts, or character (such they are constantly represented by these gentlemen), are sufficient to excite this disturbance, very perverse must be the disposition of that people amongst whom such a disturbance can be excited by such means. It is besides no small aggravation of the public misfortune that the disease, on this hypothesis, appears to be without remedy. If the wealth of the nation be the cause of its turbulence, I imagine it is not proposed to introduce poverty as a constable to keep the peace. If our dominions abroad are the roots which feed all this rank luxuriance of sedition, it is not intended to cut them off in order to famish the fruit. If our liberty has ensemble the executive power, there is no design, I hope, to call in the aid of despotism to fill up the deficiencies of law. Whatever may be intended, these things are not yet professed. We seem therefore to be driven to absolute despair; for we have no other materials to work upon but those out of which God has been pleased to form the inhabitants of this island. . . .

I am not one of those who think that the people are never in the wrong. They have been so, frequently and outrageously, both in other countries and in this. But I do say that in all disputes between them and their rulers, the presumption is at least upon a par in favor of the people. . . . When popular discontents have been very prevalent, it may well be affirmed and supported that there has been generally something found amiss in the constitution, or in the conduct of government. The people have no interest in disorder. When they do wrong, it is their error, and not their crime. But with the governing part of the state, it is far otherwise. They certainly may act ill by design, as well as by mistake. . . .

MARY WOLLSTONECRAFT

1759–1797

A farmer's daughter, Mary Wollstonecraft was born on April 27, 1759 in London. Finding herself pregnant, she married her lover, the political theorist William Godwin, on March 29, 1797 and died 11 days after giving birth to their daughter, Mary, on September 10, 1797 at the age of 38. (Her motherless daughter became Mary Wollstonecraft Shelley, the second wife of the poet, and author of Frankenstein.) In a short life she accomplished a great deal. She began her professional life as a teacher and governess, and capitalized on this experience with her first book, Thoughts on the Education of Daughters, in 1787 when she was 28. Her novel, Mary, appeared the following year, and she also meanwhile worked as a translator. Like so many intellectuals of her time, she was fascinated by the social experiment that was the French Revolution, and went to Paris in 1792 to study it firsthand. She took up residence with an American, Gilbert Imlay, and their daughter, Fanny, was born in 1794. When Captain Imlay refused to marry her, she attempted suicide in 1795, events which caused her to be written about in scandalous terms during the Victorian period. Only recently have her writings taken precedence over her biography among people interested in the history of feminist thought. Recovering from this personal debacle, she returned with her daughter to London and worked for James Johnson, a publisher, involving herself in a heady group of radical thinkers that included Thomas Paine, William Blake, William Wordsworth, and William Godwin, her future husband and father of her second daughter. Godwin wrote a first biography of his wife, many having appeared since.

Mary Wollstonecraft Godwin, by publishing *A Vindication of the Rights of Woman* in 1792 (following *A Vindication of the Rights of Man* two years prior), became the first and most important exponent of women's rights during the late Enlightenment period. She argued for a political and cultural agenda which at the time was extremely radical, that women ought to have access to the same rights as men in the realms of education, work, and the political-legal sphere. Women, she said, were not on earth simply to make men happy, also an outrageous notion for the time. The materials printed below are from these two important tracts and argue in clear and forceful terms for an equality of opportunity for both genders that is surprisingly modern, while at the same time portraying the fundamental differences between male and female in a way that is more recognizably a product of its time.

VINDICATION OF THE RIGHTS OF MEN, 1790

I know that a lively imagination renders a man particularly calculated to shine in conversation and in those desultory productions where method is disregarded; and the instantaneous applause which his eloquence extorts is at once a reward and a spur. Once a wit and always a wit, is an aphorism that has received the sanction of experience; yet I am apt to conclude that the man who with scrupulous anxiety endeavours to support that shining character, can never nourish by reflection any profound, or, if you please, metaphysical passion. Ambition becomes only the tool of vanity, and his reason, the weather-cock of unrestrained feelings, is only employed to varnish over the faults which it ought to have corrected.

Sacred, however, would the infirmities and errors of a good man be, in my eyes, if they were only displayed in a private circle; if the venial fault only rendered the wit anxious, like a celebrated beauty, to raise admiration on every occasion, and excite emotion, instead of the calm reciprocation of mutual esteem and unimpassioned respect. Such vanity enlivens social intercourse, and forces the little great man to be always on his guard to secure his throne; and an ingenious man, who is ever on the watch for conquest, will, in his eagerness to exhibit his whole store of knowledge, furnish an attentive observer with some useful information, calcined by fancy and formed by taste.

And though some dry reasoner might whisper that the arguments were superficial, and should even add, that the feelings which are thus ostentatiously displayed are often the cold declamation of the head, and not the effusions of the heart—what will these shrewd remarks avail, when the witty arguments and ornamental feelings are on a level with the comprehension of the fashionable world, and a book is found very amusing? Even the Ladies, Sir, may repeat your sprightly sallies, and retail in theatrical attitudes many of your sentimental exclamations. Sensibil-

ity is the *manie* of the day, and compassion the virtue which is to cover a multitude of vices, whilst justice is left to mourn in sullen silence, and balance truth in vain.

In life, an honest man with a confined understanding is frequently the slave of his habits and the dupe of his feelings, whilst the man with a clearer head and colder heart makes the passions of others bend to his interest; but truly sublime is the character that acts from principle, and governs the inferior springs of activity without slackening their vigour; whose feelings give vital heat to his resolves, but never hurry him into feverish eccentricities.

However, as you have informed us that respect chills love, it is natural to conclude, that all your pretty flights arise from your pampered sensibility; and that, vain of this fancied preeminence of organs, you foster every emotion till the fumes, mounting to your brain, dispel the sober suggestions of reason. It is not in this view surprising, that when you should argue you become impassioned, and that reflection inflames your imagination, instead of enlightening your understanding. . . .

The birthright of man, to give you, Sir, a short definition of this disputed right, is such a degree of liberty, civil and religious, as is compatible with the liberty of every other individual with whom he is united in a social compact, and the continued existence of that compact.

Liberty, in this simple, unsophisticated sense, I acknowledge, is a fair idea that has never yet received a form in the various governments that have been established on our beauteous globe; the demon of property has ever been at hand to encroach on the sacred rights of men, and to fence round with awful pomp laws that war with justice. But that it results from the eternal foundation of right—from immutable truth—who will presume to deny, that pretends to rationality—if reason has led them to build their morality and religion on an everlasting foundation—the attributes of God?

I glow with indignation when I attempt, methodically, to unravel your slavish paradoxes, in which I can find no fixed first principle to refute; I shall not, therefore, condescend to shew where you affirm in one page what you deny in another; and how frequently you draw conclusions with-

From *Mary Wollstonecraft: Political Writings*, Janet Todd, Ed. Published by the University of Toronto Press. Copyright © 1993.

out any previous premises:—it would be something like cowardice to fight with a man who had never exercised the weapons with which his opponent chose to combat, and irksome to refute sentence after sentence in which the latent spirit of tyranny appeared.

I perceive, from the whole tenor of your Reflections, that you have a mortal antipathy to reason; but, if there is any thing like argument, or first principles, in your wild declamation, behold the result:—that we are to reverence the rust of antiquity, and term the unnatural customs, which ignorance and mistaken self-interest have consolidated, the sage fruit of experience: nay, that, if we do discover some errors, our feelings should lead us to excuse, with blind love, or unprincipled filial affection, the venerable vestiges of ancient days. These are gothic notions of beauty—the ivy is beautiful, but, when it insidiously destroys the trunk from which it receives support, who would not grub it up?

Further, that we ought cautiously to remain for ever in frozen inactivity, because a thaw, whilst it nourishes the soil, spreads a temporary inundation; and the fear of risking any personal present convenience should prevent a struggle for the most estimable advantages. This is sound reasoning, I grant, in the mouth of the rich and short-sighted.

⟡

A VINDICATION OF THE RIGHTS OF WOMAN, 1792

Introduction

After considering the historic page, and viewing the living world with anxious solicitude, the most melancholy emotions of sorrowful indignation have depressed my spirits, and I have sighed when obliged to confess, that either nature has made a great difference between man and man, or that the civilization which has hitherto taken place in

the world has been very partial. I have turned over various books written on the subject of education, and patiently observed the conduct of parents and the management of schools; but what has been the result?—a profound conviction that the neglected education of my fellow-creatures is the grand source of the misery I deplore; and that women, in particular, are rendered weak and wretched by a variety of concurring causes, originating from one hasty conclusion. The conduct and manners of women, in fact, evidently prove that their minds are not in a healthy state; for, like the flowers which are planted in too rich a soil, strength and usefulness are sacrificed to beauty; and the flaunting leaves, after having pleased a fastidious eye, fade, disregarded on the stalk, long before the season when they ought to have arrived at maturity.—One cause of this barren blooming I attribute to a false system of education, gathered from the books written on this subject by men who, considering females rather as women than human creatures, have been more anxious to make them alluring mistresses than affectionate wives and rational mothers; and the understanding of the sex has been so bubbled by this specious homage, that the civilized women of the present century, with a few exceptions, are only anxious to inspire love, when they ought to cherish a nobler ambition, and by their abilities and virtues exact respect.

In a treatise, therefore, on female rights and manners, the works, which have been particularly written for their improvement must not be overlooked; especially when it is asserted, in direct terms, that the minds of women are enfeebled by false refinement; that the books of instruction, written by men of genius, have had the same tendency as more frivolous productions; and that, in the true style of Mahometanism, they are treated as a kind of subordinate beings, and not as a part of the human species, when improveable reason is allowed to be the dignified distinction which raises men above the brute creation, and puts a natural sceptre in a feeble hand.

Yet, because I am a woman, I would not lead my readers to suppose that I mean violently to agitate the contested question respecting the equality or inferiority of the sex; but as the subject lies in my way, and I cannot pass it over without subjecting the main tendency of my reasoning to misconstruction, I shall stop a moment to deliver, in a few words, my opinion.—In the government of the physical world it is observable that the female in point of strength is, in general, inferior to the male. This is the law of nature; and it does not appear to be suspended or abrogated in favour of woman. A degree of physical superiority cannot, therefore, be denied—and it is a noble prerogative! But not content with this natural preeminence, men endeavour to sink us still lower, merely to render us alluring objects for a moment; and women, intoxicated by the adoration which men, under the influence of their senses, pay them, do not seek to obtain a durable interest in their hearts, or to become the friends of the fellow creatures who find amusement in their society.

I am aware of an obvious inference:—from every quarter have I heard exclamations against masculine women; but where are they to be found? If by this appellation men mean to inveigh against their ardour in hunting, shooting, and gaming, I shall most cordially join in the cry; but if it be against the imitation of manly virtues, or, more properly speaking, the attainment of those talents and virtues, the exercise of which ennobles the human character, and which raise females in the scale of animal being, when they are comprehensively termed mankind;—all those who view them with a philosophic eye must, I should think, wish with me, that they may every day grow more and more masculine.

This discussion naturally divides the subject. I shall first consider women in the grand light of human creatures, who, in common with men, are placed on this earth to unfold their faculties; and afterwards I shall more particularly point out their peculiar designation.

I wish also to steer clear of an error which many respectable writers have fallen into; for the instruction which has hitherto been addressed to women, has rather been applicable to *ladies,* if the little indirect advice, that is scattered through Sandford and Merton, be excepted; but, addressing my sex in a firmer tone, I pay particular attention to those in the middle class, because they appear to be in the most natural state. Perhaps the seeds of false- refinement, immorality, and vanity, have ever been shed by the great. Weak, artificial beings, raised above the common wants and af-

fections of their race, in a premature unnatural manner, undermine the very foundation of virtue, and spread corruption through the whole mass of society! As a class of mankind they have the strongest claim to pity; the education of the rich tends to render them vain and helpless, and the unfolding mind is not strengthened by the practice of those duties which dignify the human character.—They only live to amuse themselves, and by the same law which in nature invariably produces certain effects, they soon only afford barren amusement.

But as I purpose taking a separate view of the different ranks of society, and of the moral character of women, in each, this hint is, for the present, sufficient; and I have only alluded to the subject, because it appears to me to be the very essence of an introduction to give a cursory account of the contents of the work it introduces.

My own sex, I hope, will excuse me, if I treat them like rational creatures, instead of flattering their *fascinating* graces, and viewing them as if they were in a state of perpetual childhood, unable to stand alone. I earnestly wish to point out in what true dignity and human happiness consists—I wish to persuade women to endeavour to acquire strength, both of mind and body, and to convince them that the soft phrases, susceptibility of heart, delicacy of sentiment, and refinement of taste, are almost synonymous with epithets of weakness, and that those beings who are only the objects of pity and that kind of love, which has been termed its sister, will soon become objects of contempt.

Dismissing then those pretty feminine phrases, which the men condescendingly use to soften our slavish dependence, and despising that weak elegancy of mind, exquisite sensibility, and sweet docility of manners, supposed to be the sexual characteristics of the weaker vessel, I wish to show that elegance is inferior to virtue, that the first object of laudable ambition is to obtain a character as a human being, regardless of the distinction of sex; and that secondary views should be brought to this simple touchstone. . . .

If then it can be fairly deduced from the present conduct of the sex, from the prevalent fondness for pleasure which takes place of ambition and those nobler passions that open and enlarge the soul; that the instruction which women have hitherto received has only tended, with the constitution of civil society, to render them insignificant objects of desire—mere propagators of fools!—if it can be proved that in aiming to accomplish them, without cultivating their understandings, they are taken out of their sphere of duties, and made ridiculous and useless when the short-lived bloom of beauty is over, I presume that *rational* men will excuse me for endeavouring to persuade them to become more masculine and respectable.

Indeed the word masculine is only a bugbear: there is little reason to fear that women will acquire too much courage or fortitude; for their apparent inferiority with respect to bodily strength, must render them, in some degree, dependent on men in the various relations of life; but why should it be increased by prejudices that give a sex to virtue, and confound simple truths with sensual reveries?

Women are, in fact, so much degraded by mistaken notions of female excellence, that I do not mean to add a paradox when I assert, that this artificial weakness produces a propensity to tyrannize, and gives birth to cunning, the natural opponent of strength, which leads them to play off those contemptible infantine airs that undermine esteem even whilst they excite desire. Let men become more chaste and modest, and if women do not grow wiser in the same ratio, it will be clear that they have weaker understandings. It seems scarcely necessary to say, that I now speak of the sex in general. Many individuals have more sense than their male relatives; and, as nothing preponderates where there is a constant struggle for an equilibrium, without it has naturally more gravity, some women govern their husbands without degrading themselves, because intellect will always govern.

THOMAS PAINE

1737–1809

Thomas Paine, son of a Quaker corset-maker, was born on January 29, 1737 in Thetford, Norfolk, England and died in New York City 72 years later on June 8, 1809. His first wife was Mary Lambert, whom he married on September 27, 1759, and who died in 1760 along with the infant during delivery, a shock which made it difficult henceforth for Paine to associate with women socially. Eventually he married the much younger Elizabeth Ollive in 1771, but they separated the following year. Because of the laws of the time regarding women and marriage (keenly analyzed by Mary Wollstonecraft), the remainder of her life was unpleasant since divorce was not allowed. Paine occasionally sent her money, but they never saw each other again, thus ending any domestic relations for both of them. He worked as a tax-collector from 1761 through 1774, but wrote about its inefficient aspects in a pamphlet (1772), which led to his dismissal. His personal and professional lives having collapsed, he met Ben Franklin in London in 1774 and with his help, found work as a writer in U.S., first in Philadelphia, then in New York. He fought for Washington in the Revolution for five months and did a range of work for the new government, for which he was handsomely repaid in land and sterling. Back in Europe from 1787 through 1802, he was imprisoned for 11 months by Robespierre for having voted against executing Louis XVI, escaped the guillotine by mere accident, and was released after intervention by James Monroe, minister to France. While in prison he wrote the second section of *The Age of Reason,* his most famous work in which, among other things, he attacked the Bible. He meanwhile had also published *The Rights of Man: Being an Answer to Mr. Burke's Attack on the French Revolution* in 1791, which is the source for the excerpt reprinted here.

Though poorly educated and crusty in his demeanor and view of the world, Paine was a world-class polemicist and passionately engaged in the most important political debates of his era. He was lionized and served as a bold inspiration for revolution both in France and the U.S. during his lifetime, although by the time he returned to the U.S. in 1802, he lamented that his fame had dissipated. He gaily threw off the shackles of religion, tradition, and social class and wrote unsparingly of what it would take to fashion a new political world in which men (*sic*) would be judged by their abilities rather than their religious beliefs or their station at birth. Though personally troubled through much of his life, and ending it surrounded by well-wishers who futilely begged him to repent and be saved, he nevertheless managed to compose bracing political tracts that seem as modern now in most of their prescriptions for change as they did then.

RIGHTS OF MAN, 1791/92

Conclusion

. . . From the revolutions of America and France, and the symptoms that have appeared in other countries, it is evident that the opinion of the world is changed with respect to systems of Government, and that revolutions are not within the compass of political calculations. The progress of time and circumstances, which men assign to the accomplishment of great changes, is too mechanical to measure the force of the mind, and the rapidity of reflection, by which revolutions are generated: All the old governments have received a shock from those that already appear, and which were once more improbable, and are a greater subject of wonder, than a general revolution in Europe would be now.

When we survey the wretched condition of man under the monarchical and hereditary systems of Government, dragged from his home by one power, driven by another, and impoverished by taxes more than by enemies, it becomes evident that those systems are bad, and that a general revolution in the principle and construction of Governments is necessary.

What is government more than the management of the affairs of a Nation? It is not, and from its nature cannot be, the property of any particular man or family, but of the whole community, at whose expense it is supported; and though by force or contrivance it has been usurped into an inheritance, the usurpation cannot alter the right of things. Sovereignty as a matter of right appertains to the Nation only, and not to any individual; and a Nation has at all times an inherent indefeasible right to abolish any form of Government it finds inconvenient, and establish such as accords with its interest, disposition, and happiness. The romantic and barbarous distinction of men into Kings and subjects, though it may suit the condition of courtiers, cannot that of citizens; and is exploded by the principle upon which Governments

are now founded. Every citizen is a member of the Sovereignty, and, as such, can acknowledge no personal subjection; and his obedience can be only to the laws.

When men think of what Government is, they must necessarily suppose it to possess a knowledge of all the objects and matters upon which its authority is to be exercised. In this view of Government, the republican system, as established by America and France, operates to embrace the whole of a Nation; and the knowledge necessary to the interest of all its parts, is to be found in the center, which the parts by representation form: But the old Governments are on a construction that excludes knowledge as well as happiness; Government by Monks, who know nothing of the world beyond the walls of a Convent, is as consistent as Government by Kings.

What were formerly called Revolutions were little more than a change of persons, or an alteration of local circumstances. They rose and fell like things of course, and had nothing in their existence or their fate that could influence beyond the spot that produced them. But what we now see in the world, from the Revolutions of America and France, is a renovation of the natural order of things, a system of principles as universal as truth and the existence of man, and combining moral with political happiness and national prosperity.

I. Men are born and always continue free and equal in respect of their rights. Civil distinctions, therefore, can be founded only on public utility.

II. The end of all political associations is the preservation of the natural and imprescriptible rights of man; and these rights are liberty, property, security, and resistance of oppression.

III. The Nation is essentially the source of all Sovereignty; nor can any INDIVIDUAL, *or,* ANY BODY OF MEN, *be entitled to any authority which is not expressly derived from it.*

In these principles, there is nothing to throw a Nation into confusion by inflaming ambition. They are calculated to call forth wisdom and abilities, and to exercise them for the public good, and not for the emolument or aggrandizement of particular descriptions of men or families. Monarchial sovereignty, the enemy of mankind, and the source of misery, is abolished; and sovereignty itself is restored to its natural and original place, the

From *Thomas Paine: Selections From His Writings,* with an Introduction by James S. Allen. Published by International Publishers. Copyright © 1937.

Nation: Were this the case throughout Europe, the cause of wars would be taken away. . . .

Whether the forms and maxims of Governments which are still in practice, were adapted to the condition of the world at the period they were established, is not in this case the question. The older they are, the less correspondence can they have with the present state of things. Time, and change of circumstances and opinions, have the same progressive effect in rendering modes of Government obsolete, as they have upon customs and manners. Agriculture, commerce, manufactures, and the tranquil arts, by which the prosperity of Nations is best promoted, require a different system of Government, and a different species of knowledge to direct its operations, than what might have been required in the former condition of the world.

As it is not difficult to perceive, from the enlightened state of mankind, that hereditary Governments are verging to their decline, and that Revolutions on the broad basis of national sovereignty, and Government by representation, are making their way in Europe, it would be an act of wisdom to anticipate their approach, and produce Revolutions by reason and accommodation, rather than commit them to the issue of convulsions.

From what we now see, nothing of reform on the political world ought to be held improbable. It is an age of Revolutions, in which every thing may be looked for. The intrigue of Courts, by which the system of war is kept up, may provoke a confederation of Nations to abolish it: and an European Congress, to patronize the progress of free Government, and promote the civilization of Nations with each other, is an event nearer in probability, than once were the Revolutions and alliance of France and America.

FRIEDRICH SCHILLER

1759–1805

Johann Christoph Friedrich von Schiller was born on November 10, 1759 in Marbach, Württenberg and died 45 years later in Weimar, Saxe-Weimar on May 9, 1805 from "catarrhal fever" after years of painful illnesses. In 1788 he married the youngest daughter of the von Lengefeld family of Rudolstadt, after pining pointlessly for the love of a married woman in Mannheim. His father was a retired military officer in charge of horticulture and gardens in a duke's estate, Ludwigsburg. The Duke insisted that Friedrich at 13 attend his own military school, and for eight years Schiller bore the harsh discipline common to such institutions, while learning medicine, having switched from law, and also disappointing his parents, who hoped he would choose the ministry. At 21 he was assigned to a Stuttgart regiment as a poorly paid assistant medical officer, and developed an intense dislike of robotic discipline. Such sentiments inspired his earliest poems and plays, particularly his first drama, *The Robbers,* in which the protagonist, Karl Moor (as Karl Marx was later known in his family circle, owing to his dark complexion) becomes a "sublime criminal" by refusing to be coerced into socially acceptable, though unjust, behavior. Though tempered in its revolutionary rhetoric by the conventions of the day, Schiller's intentions were clear to his audience at the first performance on January 13, 1782 (he'd finished the play four years before, when he was 19). The angry Duke promptly sentenced him to two week's detention and forbad him to write more plays. Schiller, naturally unwilling to accept this judgment, fled to Mannheim where he hoped for aid and understanding from the reigning nobleman, only to be disappointed. This did not prevent him from writing several other important plays in the next few years, relying meanwhile on the generosity of friends.

Schiller figures in the history of social thought because in 1794–95, under the influence of Kant and his friend, Goethe, he published *Letters on the Aesthetic Education of Man.* This slim book has influenced many theorists ever since, including Herbert Marcuse in the 1960s. Here Schiller explains that play is normal behavior for humans and that social arrangements which arbitrarily confine or constrain people so that they cannot freely enjoy themselves is a perversion of our fundamental nature. Needless to say, this sentiment has never sat well with authoritarians, whether from the monarchy, the clergy, or industry. Unnatural mechanization of life was anathema to Schiller, so he has ever since been a champion of the spontaneous and creative against the threatening forces of control and subordination that have grown up like weeds in the last two centuries. As one of his deepest admirers put it, "No one has stressed the moral necessity of maintaining spiritual independence in the face of destiny so strongly as Schiller; no one has experienced so deeply the fact that the tragic in human existence lends nobility and dignity to the human being" (Frederick Ungar in *Friedrich Schiller,* 1959, p. 19).

LETTERS ON THE AESTHETIC EDUCATION OF MAN, 1794–95

Third Letter

We must therefore search for some support for the continuation of society, to make it independent of the actual State which we want to abolish.

This support is not to be found in the natural character of Man, which, selfish and violent as it is, aims far more at the destruction than at the preservation of society; as little is it to be found in his moral character, which *ex hypothesi* has yet to be formed, and upon which, because it is free and because it is never apparent, the lawgiver can never operate and never with certainty depend. The important thing, therefore, is to dissociate caprice from the physical and freedom from the moral character; to make the first conformable with law, the second dependent on impressions; to remove the former somewhat further from matter in order to bring the latter somewhat nearer to it—so as to create a third character which, related to these other two, might pave the way for a transition from the realm of mere force to the rule of law, and, without impeding the development of the moral character, might serve rather as a sensible pledge of a morality as yet unseen.

Fourth Letter

This much is certain: only the predominance of such a character among a people can complete without harm the transformation of a State according to moral principles, and only such a character too can guarantee its perpetuation. In the establishment of a moral State the ethical law is reckoned upon as an active power, and free will is drawn into the realm of causes where everything coheres with strict necessity and stability. But we know that the dispositions of the human will always remain fortuitous, and that only with absolute Being does physical coincide with moral necessity. If therefore we are to count upon the

moral conduct of Man as upon *natural* consequences, it must *be* his nature, and Man must be led by his very impulses to such a mode of life as only a moral character can have for its result. But the will of Man stands completely free between duty and inclination, and no physical compulsion can or may encroach upon this sovereign right of his personality. If therefore he is to retain this capacity for choice and nevertheless be a reliable link in the causal concatenation of forces, this can only be achieved if the operations of both those motives in the realm of phenomena prove to be exactly similar, and if the subject matter of his volition remains the same through every variation of its form, so that his impulses are sufficiently consonant with his reason to have the value of a universal legislation.

Every individual man, it may be said, carries in disposition and determination a pure ideal man within himself, with whose unalterable unity it is the great task of his existence, throughout all his vicissitudes, to harmonize. This pure human being, who may be recognized more or less distinctly in every person, is represented by the *State,* the objective and, so to say, canonical form in which the diversity of persons endeavours to unite itself. But two different ways can be thought of, in which Man in time can be made to coincide with Man in idea, and consequently as many in which the State can affirm itself in individuals: either by the pure man suppressing the empirical—the State abrogating the individual—or by the individual *becoming* State—temporal Man being raised to the dignity of ideal Man. . . .

The statesman-artist must approach his material with a quite different respect from that which the fine artist feigns towards his; not merely subjectively, and for a delusive effect upon the senses, but objectively, for its inner being, he must pay careful heed to its idiosyncrasy and its personality.

But just for that very reason, because the State is to be an organization which is formed by itself and for itself, it can really become such only insofar as the parts have been severally attuned to the idea of the whole. Because the State serves as a representation of pure and objective humanity in the breast of its citizens, it will have to maintain towards those citizens the same relationship in which they stand to each other, and it can respect their subjective humanity only in such degree as this is exalted to objectivity. If the inner man is at one with himself; he will preserve his idiosyncrasy even in the widest universality of his conduct, and the State will be simply the interpreter of his fine instinct, the clearer expression of his inner legislation. On the other hand, if in the character of a people the subjective man is opposed to the objective in so contradictory a fashion that only the suppression of the former can secure the triumph of the latter, the State too will assume the full severity of the law against the citizen, and must ruthlessly trample underfoot any such hostile individuality in order not to be its victim.

But Man can be at odds with himself in a double fashion: either as savage if his feelings rule his principles, or as barbarian if his principles destroy his feelings. The savage despises Art and recognizes Nature as his sovereign mistress; the barbarian derides and dishonours Nature, but—more contemptible than the savage—he continues frequently enough to become the slave of his slave. The cultured man makes a friend of Nature and respects her freedom while merely curbing her caprice.

When therefore Reason introduces her moral unity into physical society, she must not injure the multiplicity of Nature. When Nature strives to maintain her multiplicity in the moral structure of society, there must be no rupture in its moral unity; the triumphant form rests equidistant from uniformity and confusion. *Totality* of character must therefore be found in a people that is capable and worthy of exchanging the State of need for the State of freedom.

MARIE-JEAN-ANTOINE-NICOLAS DE CARITAT, MARQUIS DE CONDORCET

1743–1794

Marie-Jean-Antoine-Nicolas de Caritat, marquis de Condorcet was born on September 17, 1743 in Ribemont, Picardy, France. He married a beauty of the age, Sofie de Grouchy in 1786, they had one daughter, and his widow published his complete works from 1801 to 1804. He died, either from exhaustion after being hunted, or from poison, at 50 in Bourg-la-Reine on March 29, 1794, a victim of the French Revolution for being a nobleman. He attended the Jesuit College in Reims and the College of Navarre in Paris. He became friends with most of the philosophes and contributed materially to the *Encyclopedia* of Diderot and d'Alembert. The latter also sponsored his scientific work, which included an innovative treatise on probability (1785). While living with his wife in her hotel suite, he served as inspector general of the mint. He wrote two biographies of friends which became best-sellers, one on Turgot (1786), the other on Voltaire (1789). After the Revolution, he served in the new government and pushed for reform of the education system. He voted not to behead Louis XVI, but was also among the first to demand a republic, for which he wrote a constitution that Robespierre did not like. He had to flee Paris given these events, and while in hiding the last two years of his life, he wrote *Sketch for a Historical Picture of the Progress of the Human Mind,* in order to take his mind off his dire straits (from which the excerpt here is taken).

According to Condorcet (and Turgot, in some ways his model), human history passes through definite stages (9 of them, plus one for the future), leading from simplicity and barbarism to complexity and perfection. Over time racism disappears, inequality between nations also diminishes, and members of advancing societies gain a chance to improve substantially, toward perfection. The phrase "equal opportunity" would easily fit within Condorcet's program for progressive politics. Condorcet, like Voltaire, disliked religion intensely, as well as its handmaiden, monarchy. If his work has a weakness, from our point of view, it lies in its exaggerated optimism about humanity's prospects, which must have seemed in the late 18th century much more sanguine than they do in the early 21st. We still read Condorcet because his writings are based on so many admirable Enlightenment virtues: religious freedom, denunciation of slavery, reform of education so that it can reach the masses, elimination of feudal economic restrictions, and a celebration of "reason" as the primary motive force behind human liberation and self-awareness. This cheery hopefulness for the human prospect is evident in the selection reprinted below.

SKETCH FOR A HISTORICAL PICTURE OF THE PROGRESS OF THE HUMAN MIND, 1795

Introduction

. . . If one studies this development as it manifests itself in the inhabitants of a certain area at a certain period of time and then traces it on from generation to generation, one has the picture of the progress of the human mind. This progress is subject to the same general laws that can be observed in the development of the faculties of the individual, and it is indeed no more than the sum of that development realized in a large number of individuals joined together in society. What happens at any particular moment is the result of what has happened at all previous moments, and itself has an influence on what will happen in the future.

So such a picture is historical, since it is a record of change and is based on the observation of human societies throughout the different stages of their development. It ought to reveal the order of this change and the influence that each moment exerts upon the subsequent moment, and so ought also to show, in the modifications that the human species has undergone, ceaselessly renewing itself through the immensity of the centuries, the path that it has followed, the steps that it has made towards truth or happiness.

Such observations upon what man has been and what he is today, will instruct us about the means we should employ to make certain and rapid the further progress that his nature allows him still to hope for.

Such is the aim of the work that I have undertaken, and its result will be to show by appeal to reason and fact that nature has set no term to the perfection of human faculties; that the perfectibility of man is truly indefinite; and that the progress of this perfectibility, from now onwards independent of any power that might wish to halt it, has no other limit than the duration of the globe upon which nature has cast us. This progress will doubtless vary in speed, but it will

never be reversed as long as the earth occupies its present place in the system of the universe, and as long as the general laws of this system produce neither a general cataclysm nor such changes as will deprive the human race of its present faculties and its present resources.

The first stage of civilization observed amongst human beings is that of a small society whose members live by hunting and fishing, and know only how to make rather crude weapons and household utensils and to build or dig for themselves a place in which to live, but are already in possession of a language with which to communicate their needs, and a small number of moral ideas which serve as common laws of conduct; living in families, conforming to general customs which take the place of laws, and even possessing a crude system of government.

The uncertainty of life, the difficulty man experiences in providing for his needs, and the necessary cycle of extreme activity and total idleness do not allow him the leisure in which he can indulge in thought and enrich his understanding with new combinations of ideas. The means of satisfying his needs are too dependent on chance and the seasons to encourage any occupation whose progress might be handed down to later generations, and so each man confines himself to perfecting his own individual skill and talent.

Thus the progress of the human species was necessarily very slow; it could move forward only from time to time when it was favoured by exceptional circumstances. . . .

A life that was less hazardous and more leisured gave opportunities for meditation or, at least, for sustained observation. Some people adopted the practice of exchanging part of their surplus for labour from which they would then be absolved. In consequence there arose a class of men whose time was not wholly taken up in manual labour and whose desires extended beyond their elementary needs. Industry was born; the arts that were already known, were spread and perfected; as men became more experienced and attentive, quite casual information suggested to them new arts; the population grew as the means of subsistence became less dangerous and precarious; agriculture, which could support a greater number of people on the same amount of land, replaced the other means of subsistence; it encouraged the growth of the population and this, in its turn, favoured progress; acquired ideas were communicated more quickly and were perpetuated more surely in a society that had become more sedentary, more accessible and more intimate. Already, the dawn of science had begun to break; man revealed himself to be distinct from the other species of animals and seemed no longer confined like them to a purely individual perfection.

As human relations increased in number, scope and complexity, it became necessary to have a method of communicating with those who were absent, of perpetuating the memory of an event with greater precision than that afforded by oral tradition, of fixing the terms of an agreement with greater certainty than that assured by the testimony of witnesses, and of registering in a more enduring manner those respected customs according to which the members of a single society had agreed to regulate their conduct. So the need for writing was felt, and writing was invented. It seems to have been at first a genuine system of representation, but this gave way to a more conventional representation which preserved merely the characteristic features of objects. Finally by a sort of metaphor analogous to that which had already been introduced into language, the image of a physical object came to express moral ideas. The origin of these signs, like that of words, was ultimately forgotten, and writing became the art of attaching a conventional sign to every idea, to every word, and so by extension, to every modification of ideas and words.

And so mankind had both a written and spoken language, both of which had to be learnt and between which an equivalence had to be established.

Certain men of genius, humanity's eternal benefactors, whose names and country are for ever buried in oblivion, observed that all the words of a language were nothing but the combinations of a very limited number of primary sounds, but that their number, though very limited, was enough to form an almost limitless number of different combinations. They devised the notion of using visible signs to designate not the ideas or the words that corresponded to ideas, but the simple elements of which words are composed. And here we have the origin of the alphabet; a small number of signs sufficed to write everything, just as a small number of sounds sufficed to say everything. The written language was the same as the spoken language; all that was necessary was to know how to recognize and reproduce these few signs, and this final step assured the progress of the human race for ever.

[Perhaps it would be useful today to invent a written language that, reserved exclusively for the sciences, expressing only the combinations of those simple ideas which are the same for every mind, and used only for the reasoning of strict logic, for the precise and calculated operations of the understanding, would be understood by the people of every country and could be translated into every vernacular and would not have to be altered, as happens now, when it passed into general use.]

[So by a strange revolution this type of writing, whose survival would only have helped to prolong ignorance, would now become, in the hands of philosophy, a useful tool for the swift propagation of enlightenment and for the perfection of scientific method.]

The Tenth Stage: The Future Progress of the Human Mind

If man can, with almost complete assurance, predict phenomena when he knows their laws, and if, even when he does not, he can still, with great expectation of success, forecast the future on the basis of his experience of the past, why, then, should it be regarded as a fantastic undertaking to sketch, with some pretence to truth, the future destiny of man on the basis of his history? The sole foundation for belief in the natural sciences is this idea, that the general laws directing the phenomena of the universe, known or unknown, are necessary and constant. Why should this principle be any less true for the development of the intellectual and moral faculties of man than for the other operations of nature? Since beliefs founded on past experience of like conditions provide the only rule of conduct for the wisest of men, why should the philosopher be forbidden to base his conjectures on these same foundations, so long as he does not attribute to them a certainty superior to that warranted by the number, the constancy, and the accuracy of his observations?

Our hopes for the future condition of the human race can be subsumed under three important heads: the abolition of inequality between nations, the progress of equality within each nation, and the true perfection of mankind. Will all nations one day attain state of civilization which the most enlightened, the freest and the least burdened by prejudices, such as the French and the Anglo-Americans, have attained already? Will the vast gulf that separates these peoples from the slavery of nations under the rule of monarchs, from the barbarism of African tribes, from the ignorance of savages, little by little disappear?

Is there on the face of the earth a nation whose inhabitants have been debarred by nature herself from the enjoyment of freedom and the exercise of reason?

Are those differences which have hitherto been seen in every civilized country in respect of the enlightenment, the resources, and the wealth enjoyed by the different classes into which it is divided, is that inequality between men which was aggravated or perhaps produced by the earliest progress of society, are these art of civilization itself, or are they due to the present imperfections of the social art? Will they necessarily decrease and ultimately make way for a real equality, the final end of the social art, in which even the effects of the natural differences between men will be mitigated and the only kind of inequality to persist will be that which is in the interests of all and which favours the progress of civilization, of education, and of industry, without entailing either poverty, humiliation, or dependence? In other words, will men approach a condition in which everyone will have the knowledge necessary to conduct himself in the ordinary affairs of life, according to the light of his own reason, to preserve his mind free from prejudice, to understand his rights and to exercise them in accordance with his conscience and his creed; in which everyone will become able, through the development of his faculties, to find the means of providing for his needs; and in which at last misery and folly will be the exception, and no longer the habitual lot of a section of society?

Is the human race to better itself, either by discoveries in the sciences and the arts, and so in the means to individual welfare and general prosperity; or by progress in the principles of conduct or practical morality; or by a true perfection of the intellectual, moral, or physical faculties of man, an improvement which may result from a perfection either of the instruments used to heighten the intensity of these faculties and to direct their use or of the natural constitution of man?

In answering these three questions we shall find in the experience of the past, in the observation of the progress that the sciences and civilization have already made, in the analysis of the progress of the human mind and of the development of its faculties, the strongest reasons for believing that nature has set no limit to the realization of our hopes.

GEORG WILHELM FRIEDRICH HEGEL

1770–1831

Georg Wilhelm Friedrich Hegel, son of a tax collector, was born on August 27, 1770 in Stuttgart, Württemberg, the same year as Beethoven. He married Marie von Tucher of Nürnberg in 1811, she being 22 years his junior, and in a happy marriage had with her two sons, Karl, an historian, and Immanuel, a minister. His illegitimate son, Ludwig, by his landlady in Jena some years before, was accepted into their household. Hegel's mother taught him rudimentary Latin before he entered grade school in Stuttgart. As a boy he already behaved in Hegelian fashion by making copious excerpts from books and periodicals, arranging them in alphabetical order, and thereby trying to make systematic sense of his enlarging world of knowledge. Graduating at 18, he then attended the University of Tübingen with the ministry in mind. But constraining orthodoxy snuffed out this vocational path, and instead he studied Greek philosophy and literature, and history. What most distinguished the other great idealist philosopher, Kant, from Hegel was principally the former's fascination with natural science methods and the latter's deep immersion in the history of thought and of institutions (he favored Gibbon). Always serious among his friends (a mighty crowd, which included the poet Hölderlin, the philosopher Schelling and the noble Goethe), though well liked, he could never speak well before groups, which made it hard for him to advance as a minister or professor. Instead, he worked in Berne as a tutor (1793–1796) where his schedule allowed for a great deal of reading and writing. While there he wrote an extraordinary essay that some say captures his lifelong project, "The Spirit of Christianity and Its Fate," yet oddly never published until 1907. He escaped from this exile to Frankfurt and a tutorship arranged by Hölderlin. His financial straits eased somewhat with his father's death and inheritance in 1799, and in 1801 he moved to Jena, where he taught logic to all of 11 students. Meanwhile, he worked on his masterpiece, *The Phenomenology of Spirit* (1807) which did not win for him any noticeable acclaim, despite its eventual profound influence until our own time. Hegel tried to explain in this book, among other things, how human consciousness came to be aware of itself, and how it connects with a larger world-consciousness that at times seems synonymous with the Christian God. Meanwhile, his career stalled, he tried editing a newspaper in Bamberg, which did not work, and then turned to being principal at a prep school in Nürnberg from December 1808 until August 1816. That a man who had written such a book was reduced to this sort of work—which he did well—is one of the many oddities in the history of thought.

He spent a year or so at Heidelberg University, then, finally, in 1818 was offered the best job in Germany for a philosopher, at Berlin. During the 1820s Hegel became the official philosopher of the realm, writing path-breaking works on art, the philosophy of religion, the history of philosophy, the philosophy of history, and so on. His place in the history of social thought was won not only from sections of the *Phenomenology* (from which the excerpt below originates), but also due to the *Philosophy of Right* (1821), an analysis of citizenship in the modern world, which involves the constant struggle to balance conscience with duty. Marx was influenced deeply by both these works, as were most later thinkers who concerned themselves with power and justice.

THE PHENOMENOLOGY OF THE SPIRIT, 1807

Master and Servant

Self-consciousness exists in itself and for itself, in that, and by the fact that it exists for another self-consciousness; that is to say, it is only by being acknowledged or "recognized." The conception of this, its unity in its duplication, of infinitude realizing itself in self-consciousness, has many sides to it and encloses within it elements of varied significance. Thus its moments must on the one hand be strictly kept apart in detailed distinctiveness, and, on the other, in this distinction must, at the same time, also be taken as not distinguished, or must always be accepted and understood in their opposite sense. This double meaning of what is distinguished lies in the nature of self-consciousness: of its being infinite, or directly the opposite of the determinateness in which it is fixed. The detailed exposition of the notion of this spiritual unity in its duplication will bring before us the process of Recognition.

I. [The double self-consciousness.]

Self-consciousness has before it another self-consciousness; it has come outside itself. This has

From *The Philosophy of Hegel*, Carl J. Friedrich, Ed. Published by The Modern Library. Copyright © 1953.

a double significance. First, it has lost its own self, since it finds itself as an *other* being; secondly, it has thereby sublimated that other, for it does not regard the other as essentially real, but sees its own self in the other.

It must suspend this its other self. To do so is to suspend and preserve that first double meaning, and is therefore a second double meaning. First, it must set itself to suspend the other independent being, in order thereby to become certain of itself as true being; secondly, it thereupon proceeds to suspend its own self, for this other is itself.

This suspension in a double sense of its otherness in a double sense is at the same time a return in a double sense into itself. For, firstly, through suspension, it gets back itself, because is becomes one with itself again through the canceling of its otherness; but secondly, it likewise gives otherness back again to the other self-consciousness, for it was aware of being in the other, it cancels this its own being in the other and thus lets the other again go free.

This process of self-consciousness in relation to another self-consciousness has in this manner been represented as the action of one alone. But this action on the part of the one has itself the double significance of being at once its own action and the action of that other as well. For the other is likewise independent, shut up within itself, and there is nothing in it which is not there through itself. The first does not have the object before it in the way that object primarily exists for desire, but as an object existing independently for itself, over which therefore it has no power to do anything for its own behoof, if that object does not *per se* do what the first does to it. The process then is absolutely the double process of both self-consciousness. Each sees the other do the same as itself; each itself does what it demands on the part of the other, and for that reason does what it does, only so far as the other does the same. Action from one side only would be useless, because what is to happen can only be brought about by means of both.

The action has then a *double meaning* not only in the sense that it is an act done to itself as well as to the other, but also inasmuch as it is in its undivided entirety the act of the one as well as of the other.

In this movement we see the process repeated which came before us as the play of forces; in the present case, however it is found in consciousness. What in the former had effect only for us (contemplating experience), holds here for the terms themselves. The middle term is self-consciousness which breaks itself up into the extremes; and each extreme is this interchange of its own determinateness, and complete transition into the opposite. While *qua* consciousness, it no doubt comes outside itself, still, in being outside itself it is at the same time restrained within itself, it exists for itself, and its self-externalization is for consciousness. *Consciousness* finds that it immediately is and is not another consciousness, as also that this other is for itself only when it cancels itself as existing for itself, and has self-existence only in the self-existence of the other. Each is the mediating term to the other, through which each mediates and unites itself with itself; and each is to itself and to the other an immediate self-existing reality, which, at the same time, exists thus for itself only through this mediation. They recognize themselves as mutually recognizing one another.

This pure conception of recognition, of duplication of self-consciousness within its unity, we must now consider in the way its process appears for self-consciousness. It will, in the first place, present the aspect of the disparity of the two, or the break-up of the middle term into the extremes, which *qua* extremes, are opposed to one

another, and of which one is merely recognized, while the other only recognizes.

2. [The conflict of the opposed self-consciousnesses.]

Self-consciousness is primarily simple being-by-itself, self-identity by exclusion of every other from itself. It takes its essential nature and absolute object to be Ego; and in this immediacy, in this bare fact of its self-existence, it is individual. That which for it is the other stands as unessential object, as object with the impress and character of negation. But the other is also a self-consciousness; an individual makes its appearance in antithesis to an individual. Appearing thus in their immediacy, they are for each other in the manner of ordinary objects. They are independent individual forms, modes of consciousness that have not risen above the bare level of life (for the existent object here has been determined as life). They are, moreover, forms of consciousness which have not yet accomplished for one another the process of absolute abstraction, of uprooting all immediate existence, and of being merely the bare, negative fact of self-identical consciousness; or, in other words, have not yet revealed themselves to each other as existing purely for themselves, i.e., as self-consciousness. Each is indeed certain of its own self, but not of the other, and hence its own certainty of itself is still without truth. For its truth would be merely that its own individual existence for itself would be shown to it to be an independent object, or, which is the same thing, that the object would be exhibited as this pure certainty of itself. By the notion of recognition, however, this is not possible, except in the form that as the other is for it, so it is for the other; each in its self through its own action and again through the action of the other achieves this pure abstraction of existence for self. . . .

3. [Master and Servant. (a) Rule of the master.]

The master is the consciousness that exists *for itself*; but no longer merely the general notion of existence for the self. Rather, it is consciousness which, while existing on its own account, is mediated with itself through another consciousness, viz., bound up with an independent being or with thinghood in general. The master brings himself into relation to both these moments, to a thing as such, the object of desire, and to the consciousness whose essential character is thinghood, and since the master, *qua* notion of self-consciousness, is (a) an immediate relation of self-existence, but is now moreover at the same time (b) mediation, or a being-for-self which is for itself only through an other—he (the master) stands in relation (a) immediately to both, (b) mediately to each through the other. The master relates himself to the servant mediately through independent existence, for that is precisely what keeps the servant in bond; it is his chain, from which he could not, in the struggle, get away, and for that reason he proves himself dependent, shows that his independence consists in his being a thing. The master, however, is the power controlling this state of existence, for he has shown in the struggle that he holds existence to be merely something negative. Since he is the power dominating the negative nature of existence, while this existence again is the power controlling the other (the servant), the master holds, as a consequence, this other in subordination. In the same way the master relates himself to the thing mediately through the servant. The servant being a self-consciousness in the broad sense, also takes up a negative attitude to things and cancels them; but the thing is, at the same time, independent for him, and, in consequence, he cannot, with all his negating, get so far as to annihilate it outright and be done with it; that is to say, he merely works on it. To the master, on the other hand, by means of this mediating process, belongs the immediate relation, in the sense of the pure negation of it; in other words he gets the enjoyment. What mere desire did not attain, he now succeeds in attaining, viz., to have done with the thing, and find satisfaction in enjoyment. Desire alone did not get the length of this, because of the independence of the thing. The master, however, who has interposed the servant between it and himself, thereby relates himself merely to the dependence of the thing, and enjoys it without qualification and without reserve. The aspect of its independence he leaves to the servant, who labors upon it.

In these two moments, the master gets his recognition through another consciousness, for in them the latter affirms itself as unessential, both by working upon the thing, and, on the other hand, by the fact of being dependent on a deter-minate existence; in neither case can this other get the mastery over existence, and succeed in absolutely negating it. We have thus here this moment of recognition, viz., that the other consciousness cancels itself as self-existent, and *ipso facto,* itself does what the first does to it. In the same way we have the other moment, that this action on the part of the second is the action proper of the first; for what is done by the servant is properly an action on the part of the master. The latter exists only for himself, that is his essential nature; he is the negative power without qualification, a power to which the thing is nothing, and his is thus the absolutely essential action in this situation, while the servant's is not so, his is an unessential activity. But for recognition proper there is needed the moment that what the master does to the other he should also do to himself, and what the servant does to himself, he should do to the other also. On that account a form of recognition has arisen that is one-sided and unequal.

In all this, the unessential consciousness is, for the master, the object which embodies the truth of his certainty of himself. But it is evident that this object does not correspond to its notion; for, just where the master has effectively achieved rule, he really finds that something has come about quite different from an independent consciousness. It is not an independent, but rather a dependent consciousness that he has achieved. He is thus not assured of self-existence as his truth; he finds that his truth is rather the unessential consciousness, and the fortuitous unessential action of that consciousness.

The truth of the independent consciousness is accordingly the consciousness of the servant. This doubtless appears in the first instance outside it, and not as the truth of self-consciousness. But just as the position, of master showed its essential nature to be the reverse of what it wants to be, so, too, the position of servant will, when completed, pass into the opposite of what it immediately is: being a consciousness repressed within itself, it will enter into itself, and change around into real and true independence.

[(b) Anxiety.]

We have seen what the position of servant is only in relation to that of the master. But it is a self-consciousness, and we have now to consider what it is, in this regard, in and for itself. In the first instance, the master is taken to be the essential reality for the state of the servant; hence, for it, the truth is the independent consciousness existing for itself, although this truth is not yet taken as inherent in the servant's position itself. Still, it does in fact contain within itself this truth of pure negativity and self-existence, because it has experienced this reality within it. For this self-consciousness was not in peril and fear for this element or that, nor for this or that moment of time, it was afraid for its entire being; it felt the fear of death, it was in mortal terror of its sovereign master. It has been through that experience melted to its inmost soul, has trembled throughout its every fiber, the stable foundations of its whole being have quaked within it. This complete perturbation of its entire substance, this absolute dissolution of all its stability into fluent continuity, is, however, the simple, ultimate nature of self-consciousness, absolute negativity, pure self-referrent existence, which consequently is involved in this type of consciousness. This moment of pure self-existence is moreover a fact for it; for in the master this moment is consciously his object. Further, this servant's consciousness is not only this total dissolution in a general way; in serving and toiling, the servant actually carries this out. By serving he cancels in every particular moment his dependence on and attachment to natural existence, and by his work removes this existence.

THOMAS ROBERT MALTHUS

1766–1834

Thomas Robert Malthus was born into a wealthy family on February 14 or 17, 1766 at the Rookery, near Dorking, Surrey in England. He married Harriet Eckersall in 1804 and they had three children. After 68 years, he died at St. Catherine, near Bath, Somerset. His father used his friend Rousseau's *Emile* as a guidebook for educating Malthus at home until 1784 when he went to Jesus College, Cambridge, graduating in 1788 and receiving an M.A. in 1791, and finally taking holy orders in 1797. He became a professor of modern history "and political economy" at East India Company's college in Haileybury, Hertfordshire, the first professorship so named in Britain.

Partly to refute, politely to be sure, his father's great optimism about the prospects for future society, Malthus published in 1798 the anonymous work, *An Essay on the Principle of Population as it Affects the Future Improvement of Society, with Remarks on the Speculations of Mr. Godwin, M. Condorcet, and other Writers.* He pointed out that humans reproduce geometrically, whereas food supplies increase arithmetically, which means that population must be controlled if poverty is to be averted. Although his mathematics were weak and his use of statistics primitive, his argument seemed strongly anchored in a mass of data, and began to influence legislation concerning poor workers, the way they were to be treated by the government as well as their employers. He doggedly insisted on this view with each new edition of the book, up to the 6th and last in 1826. It's obvious in the selection reprinted below that Malthus was very much the clergyman, invoking "Christian virtues" when it suited his argument, and viewing humankind's prodigious capacity for reproduction as an activity that needed to be quelled, not only for economic but for ethical reasons. Although universally known as a father of the astringent science of demography, as well as political-economy, in fact his ideas have as much to do with the "vices and virtues" of a Christian cleric as they do with purely scientific management of data. He invented important terms, like "effective demand," and wondered about how prices are established and what role luxuries ought to play in a capitalist economy. It's also said that he anticipated by a century some of Keynes' ideas when he wrote about "gluts," as they were called then (also a problem for Sismondi, as we will see), or the boom and bust cycles that everyone living within the capitalist world system has come to recognize as virtually unavoidable. He also anticipated deficit spending, both governmental and private, by noting that thrift, pushed too far, became literally counterproductive for capitalist acquisition and creativity.

AN ESSAY ON THE PRINCIPLE OF POPULATION, 1798

I think I may fairly make two postulata.

First, That food is necessary to the existence of man.

Secondly, That the passion between the sexes is necessary and will remain nearly in its present state.

These two laws, ever since we have had any knowledge of mankind, appear to have been fixed laws of our nature, and as we have not hitherto seen any alteration in them, we have no right to conclude that they will ever cease to be what they now, are, without, an immediate act of power in that Being who first arranged the system of the universe, and for the advantage of his creatures, still executes, according to fixed laws, all its various operations. . . .

Assuming then, my postulata as granted, I say, that the power of population is indefinitely greater than the power in the earth to produce subsistence for man.

Population, when unchecked, increases in a geometrical ratio. Subsistence increases only in an arithmetical ratio. A slight acquaintance with numbers will shew the immensity of the first power in comparison of the second.

By that law of our nature which makes food necessary to the life of man, the effects of these two unequal powers must be kept equal.

This implies a strong and constantly operating check on population from the difficulty of subsistence. This difficulty must fall some where and must necessarily be severely felt by a large portion of mankind. . . .

This natural inequality of the two powers of population and of production in the earth and that great law of our nature which must constantly keep their effects equal form the great difficulty that to me appears insurmountable in the way to the perfectibility of society. All other arguments are of slight and subordinate consideration in comparison of this. I see no way by which man can escape from the weight of this law which pervades all animated nature. No fancied equality, no agrarian regulations in their utmost extent, could remove the pressure of it even for a single century. And it appears, therefore, to be decisive against the possible existence of a society, all the members of which should live in ease, happiness, and comparative leisure; and feel no anxiety about providing the means of subsistence for themselves and families.

Consequently, if the premises are just, the argument is conclusive against the perfectibility of the mass of mankind. . . .

The sorrows and distresses of life form another class of excitements, which seem to be necessary, by a peculiar train of impressions, to soften and humanize the heart, to awaken social sympathy, to generate all the Christian virtues, and to afford scope for the ample exertion of benevolence. The general tendency of an uniform course of prosperity is rather to degrade than exalt the character. The heart that has never known sorrow itself will seldom be feelingly alive to the pains and pleasures, the wants and wishes, of its fellow beings. It will seldom be overflowing with that warmth of brotherly love, those kind and amiable affections, which dignify the human character even more than the possession of the highest talents. Talents, indeed, though undoubtedly a very prominent, and fine feature of mind, can by no means be considered as constituting the whole of it. There are many minds which have not been exposed to those excitements that usually form talents, that have yet been vivified to a high degree by the excitements of social sympathy. In every rank of life, in the lowest as frequently as in the highest, characters are to be found overflowing with the milk of human kindness, breathing love towards God and man, and though without those peculiar powers of mind called talents, evidently holding a higher rank in the scale of beings than many who possess them. Evangelical charity, meekness, piety, and all that class of virtues distinguished particularly by the name of Christian virtues do not seem necessarily to include abilities, yet a soul possessed of these amiable utilities, a soul awakened and vivified by these delightful sympathies, seems to hold a nearer commerce, with the skies than mere acuteness of intellect. . . .

From *On Population,* by Thomas Robert Malthus, Gertrude Himmelfarb, Ed. Published by The Modern Library. Copyright © 1960.

The greatest talents have been frequently misapplied and have produced evil proportionate to the extent of their powers. Both reason and revelation seem to assure us that such minds will be condemned to eternal death, but while on earth, these vicious instruments performed their part in the great mass of impressions, by the disgust and abhorrence which they excited. It seems highly probable, that moral evil is absolutely necessary to the production of moral excellence. A being with only good placed in view, may be justly said to be impelled by a blind necessity. The pursuit of good in this case can be no indication of virtuous propensities. It might be said, perhaps, that Infinite Wisdom cannot want such an indication as outward action, but would foreknow with certainty whether the being would chuse good or evil. This might be a plausible argument against a state of trial, but will not hold against the supposition that mind in this world is in a state of formation. Upon this idea, the being that has seen moral evil and has felt disapprobation and disgust at it is essentially different from the being that has seen only good. They are pieces of clay that have received distinct impressions: they must, therefore, necessarily be in different shapes; or, even if we allow them both to have the same lovely form of virtue, it must be acknowledged, that one has undergone the further process, necessary to give firmness and durability to its substance; while the other is still exposed to injury, and liable to be broken by every accidental impulse. An ardent love and admiration of virtue seems to imply the existence of something opposite to it, and it seems highly probable that the same beauty of form and substance, the same perfection of character, could not be generated without the impressions of disapprobation which arise from the spectacle of moral evil.

When the mind has been awakened into activity, by the passions, and the wants of the body, intellectual wants arise; and desire of knowledge, and the impatience under ignorance form a new and important class of excitements. Every part of nature seems peculiarly calculated to furnish stimulants to mental exertion of this kind, and to offer inexhaustible food for the most unremitted inquiry. Our immortal Bard says of Cleopatra—

Custom cannot stale
Her infinite variety

The expression, when applied to any one object, may be considered as a poetical amplification, but it is accurately true when applied to nature. Infinite variety, seems, indeed, eminently her characteristic feature. The shades that are here and there blended in the picture give spirit, life, and prominence to her exuberant beauties, and those roughnesses and inequalities, those inferior parts that support the superior, though they sometimes offend the fastidious microscopic eye of short sighted man, contribute to the symmetry, grace, and fair proportion of the whole. . . .

Our ideas of virtue and vice are not, perhaps, very accurate and well-defined; but few, I think, would call an action really virtuous which was well performed simply and solely from the dread of a very great punishment or the expectation of a very great reward. The fear of the Lord is very justly said to be the beginning of wisdom, but the end of wisdom is the love of the Lord and the admiration of moral good. The denunciation of future punishment contained in the scriptures seem to be well calculated to arrest the progress of the vicious and awaken the attention of the careless, but we see from repeated experience that they are not accompanied with evidence of such a nature as to overpower the human will and to make men lead virtuous lives with vicious dispositions, merely from a dread of hereafter. A genuine faith, by which I mean a faith that shews itself in all virtues of a truly christian life, may generally be considered as an indication of an amiable and virtuous disposition, operated upon more by love than by pure unmixed fear.

When we reflect on the temptations to which man must necessarily be exposed in this world, from the structure of his frame, and the operation of the laws of nature, and the consequent moral certainty that many vessels will come out of this mighty creative furnace in wrong shapes, it is perfectly impossible to conceive that any of these creatures of God's hand can be condemned to eternal suffering. Could we once admit such as idea, all our national conceptions of goodness and justice would be completely overthrown, and we could no longer look up to God as a merciful, and righteous Being. But the doctrine of life and immortality which was brought to light by the gospel, the doctrine that the end of righteousness is everlasting life, but that the wages of sin are death, is in every respect just and merciful, and worthy of the Great Creator. Nothing can appear more constant to our reason than that those beings what come out of the creative process of the world in lovely and beautiful forms, should be crowned with immortality, while those which come out misshapen, those whose minds are not suited to a purer and happier state of existence, should perish and be condemned to mix again with their original clay. Eternal condemnation of this kind may be considered as a species of eternal punishment, and it is not wonderful that it should be presented, sometimes under images of suffering. But life and death, salvation and destruction, are more frequently opposed to each other in the New Testament than happiness and misery. The Supreme Being would appear to us in a very different view if we were to consider him as pursuing the creatures that had offended him with eternal hate and torture, instead of merely condemning to their original insensibility those beings that, by the operation of general laws, had not been formed with qualities suited to a purer state of happiness.

Life is, generally speaking, a blessing independent of a future state. It is a gift which the vicious would not always be ready to throw away, even if they had no fear of death. The partial pain, therefore, that is inflicted by the Supreme Creator, while he is forming numberless beings to a capacity of the highest enjoyments, is but as the dust of the balance in comparison of the happiness that is communicated, and we have every reason to think that there is no more evil in the world than what is absolutely necessary as one of the ingredients in the mighty process.

FRIEDRICH SCHLEIERMACHER

1768–1834

Friedrich Daniel Ernst Schleiermacher was born on November 21, 1768 in Breslau, Silesia in Prussia (now Wrocław, Poland) and died 65 years later in Berlin (from inflammation of the lungs), his funeral procession drawing 25,000 people. He unsuccessfully tried for six years to win Eleanor Grunow away from her husband, giving up in 1802 and moving away from her when she decided to stay in her unhappy marriage to another pastor. Instead, he married Henriette von Willich, a friend's widow, in 1809; their one son died young. Schleiermacher, middle child of three, was the son of a Calvinist military chaplain and of a mother whose family was also filled with clergy. He attended a Moravian (Pietist) school between 1783 and 1787, but his critical attitude toward orthodox belief pitted him against his instructors, so against the wishes of his father, he then matriculated at the University of Halle from 1787 to 1789, living with his maternal uncle, a theology professor. He studied hard and became a lifelong Kantian. For two years he worked as a tutor in East Prussia, as did so many of his philosophically oriented peers at the time, then in 1796 as a chaplain in a Berlin hospital for the aged. There his roommate was Friedrich von Schlegel, an important Romantic writer. In 1802 he used an invitation to serve as minister to a congregation in Stolp, Pomerania to escape the torment of Mrs. Grunow. Two years later he became chaplain and assistant professor at his alma mater in Halle, and was promoted to professor of theology in 1805. Napoleon's army forced his to leave Halle in 1807 for Berlin, where he gave lectures on resisting the French invasion, and also help found the new University there. He became one of its first professors in 1810, while still serving as a pastor for Trinity Church. He was busy with a wide range of ministerial and political activities, publishing *A Brief Outline of the Study of Theology* in 1811 for guidance to those wishing to connect their church's activities with a specific theological doctrine. He was not popular with the Prussian king because of his unorthodox view of the proper relation between church and state, but an order for his banishment from the kingdom was not executed.

Schleiermacher's *On Religion: Speeches to Its Cultured Despisers* has been a favorite among sophisticated readers ever since its publication in 1799. It reflects his visceral response to the rejection of religious sentiments common to people he met in Berlin at the time, and to the link that he found between Romantic literature and religiosity of the kind he prescribed. It is from this work that the excerpt below comes, in which Schleiermacher skillfully shows the connection between rationality and religious belief, and illustrates that religious sentiment is best thought of in terms of feeling (*Gefühl*), or what today might be called "the rationality of emotion." He also argued that religious affiliation serves an essential function in helping societies cohere over time and changing circumstances.

ON RELIGION: SPEECHES TO ITS CULTURED DESPISERS

Religion and Reason

Now that we have some ground beneath us, we are in a better position to inquire about the source of this confusion. May there not be some reason for this constant connection of principles and ideas with religion? In the same way is there not a cause for the connection of action with religion? Without such an inquiry it would be vain to proceed farther. . . . But do not forget that this is scientific treatment of religion, knowledge about it, and not religion itself.

Nor can the description be equal to the thing described. The feeling may dwell in many sound and strong, as for example in almost all women, without ever having been specially a matter of contemplation. Nor may you say religion is lacking, but only knowledge about religion. Furthermore, do not forget what we have already established, that this contemplation presupposes the original activity. It depends entirely upon it. If the ideas and principles are not from reflection on a man's own feeling, they must be learned by rote and utterly void. Make sure of this, that no man is pious, however perfectly he understands these principles and conceptions, however much he believes he possesses them in clearest consciousness, who cannot show that they have originated in himself and, being the outcome of his own feeling, are peculiar to himself. Do not present him to me as pious, for he is not. His soul is barren in religious matters, and his ideas are merely supposititious children which he has adopted, in the secret feeling of his own weakness. As for those who parade religion and make a boast of it, I always characterize them as unholy and removed from all divine life. One has conceptions of the ordering of the world and formulas to express them, the other has prescriptions whereby to order himself and inner experiences to authenticate them.

The one weaves his formulas into a system of faith, and the other spins out of his prescriptions a scheme of salvation. It being observed that neither has any proper standing ground without feeling, strife ensues as to how many conceptions and declarations, how many precepts and exercises, how many emotions and sensations must be accepted in order to conglomerate a sound religion that shall be neither specially cold nor enthusiastic, dry nor shallow. O fools, and slow of heart! They do not know that all this is mere analysis of the religious sense, which they must have made for themselves, if it is to have any meaning. . . .

From within, in their original, characteristic form, the emotions of piety must issue. They must be indubitably your own feelings, and not mere stale descriptions of the feelings of others, which could at best issue in a wretched imitation.

Now the religious ideas which form those systems can and ought to be nothing else than such a description, for religion cannot and will not originate in the pure impulse to know. What we feel and are conscious of in religious emotions is not the nature of things, but their operation upon us. What you may know or believe about the nature of things is far beneath the sphere of religion. . . .

Now religion is to take up into our lives and to submit to be swayed by them, each of these influences and their consequent emotions, not by themselves but as a part of the Whole, not as limited and in opposition to other things, but as an exhibition of the Infinite in our life. Anything beyond this, any effort to penetrate into the nature and substance of things is no longer religion, but seeks to be a science of some sort.

On the other hand, to take what are meant as descriptions of our feelings for a science of the object, in some way the revealed product of religion, or to regard it as science and religion at the same time, necessarily leads to mysticism and vain mythology. . . . The sum total of religion is to feel that, in its highest unity, all that moves us in feeling is one; to feel that aught single and particular is only possible by means of this unity; to feel, that is to say, that our being and living is a being and living in and through God. But it is not necessary that the Deity should be presented as also one distinct object. To many this view is necessary, and to all it is welcome, yet it is always hazardous and

From *On Religion: Speeches to Its Cultured Despisers*, by Friedrich Schleiermacher, John Oman, Trans. Kegan Paul, Trench, Trubner & Co., 1893.

fruitful in difficulties. It is not easy to avoid the appearance of making Him susceptible of suffering like other objects. It is only one way of characterizing God, and, from the difficulties of it, common speech will probably never rid itself. But to treat this objective conception of God just as if it were a perception, as if apart from His operation upon us through the world the existence of God before the world, and outside of the world, though for the world, were either by or in religion exhibited as science is, so far as religion is concerned, vain mythology. What is only a help for presentation is treated as a reality. It is a misunderstanding very easily made, but it is quite outside the peculiar territory of religion.

From all this you will at once perceive how the question, whether religion is a system or not, is to be treated. It admits of an entire negative, and also of a direct affirmative, in a way that perhaps you scarce expected. Religion is certainly a system, if you mean that it is formed according to an inward and necessary connection. That the religious sense of one person is moved in one way, and that of another in another is not pure accident, as if the emotions formed no whole, as if any emotions might be caused in the same individual by the same object. Whatever occurs anywhere, whether among many or few as a peculiar and distinct kind of feeling is in itself complete, and by its nature necessary. What you find as religious emotions among Turks or Indians, cannot equally appear among Christians. The essential oneness of religiousness spreads itself out in a great variety of provinces, and again, in each province it contracts itself, and the narrower and smaller the province there is necessarily more excluded as incompatible and more included as characteristic. Christianity, for example, is a whole in itself, but so is any of the divisions that may at any time have appeared in it, down to Protestantism and Catholicism in modern times. Finally, the piety of each individual, whereby he is rooted in the greater unity, is a whole by itself. It is a rounded whole, based on his peculiarity, on what you call his character, of which it forms one side. Religion thus fashions itself with endless variety, down even to the single personality.

Each form again is a whole and capable of an endless number of characteristic manifestations.

Sociality and Religion

If there is religion at all, it must be social, for that is the nature of man, and it is quite peculiarly the nature of religion. You must confess that when an individual has produced and wrought out something in his own mind, it is morbid and in the highest degree unnatural to wish to reserve it to himself. He should express it in the indispensable fellowship and mutual dependence of action. And there is also a spiritual nature which he has in common with the rest of his species which demands that he express and communicate all that is in him. The more violently he is moved and the more deeply he is impressed, the stronger that social impulse works. And this is true even if we regard it only as the endeavour to find the feeling in others, and so to be sure that nothing has been encountered that is not human.

You see that this is not a case of endeavouring to make others like ourselves, nor of believing that what is in one man is indispensable for all. It is only the endeavour to become conscious of and to exhibit the true relation of our own life to the common nature of man.

But indisputably the proper subjects for this impulse to communicate are the conscious states and feelings in which originally man feels himself passive. He is urged on to learn whether it may not be an alien and unworthy power that has produced them. Those are the things which mankind from childhood are chiefly engaged in communicating. His ideas, about the origin of which he can have no doubts, he would rather leave in quiet. Still more easily he resolves to reserve his judgments. But of all that enters by the senses and stirs the feelings he will have witnesses and participators. How could he keep to himself the most comprehensive and general influences of the world when they appear to him the greatest and most irresistible? How should he wish to reserve what most strongly drives him out of himself and makes him conscious that he cannot know himself from himself alone? If a religious view become clear to him, or a pious feeling stir his soul, it is rather his first endeavour to direct others to the same subject and if possible transmit the impulse.

The same nature that makes it necessary for the pious person to speak, provides him also with an audience. No element of life, so much as religion, has implanted along with it so vivid a feeling of man's utter incapacity ever to exhaust it for himself alone. No sooner has he any sense for it than he feels its infinity and his own limits. He is conscious that he grasps but a small part of it, and what he cannot himself reach he will, at least, so far as he is able, know and enjoy from the representations of those who have obtained it. This urges him to give his religion full expression, and, seeking his own perfection, to listen to every note that he can recognize as religious. Thus mutual communication organizes itself, and speech and hearing are to all alike indispensable.

But the communication of religion is not like the communication of ideas and perceptions to be sought in books. In this medium, too much of the pure impression of the original production is lost. Like dark stuffs that absorb the greater part of the rays of light, so everything of the pious emotion that the inadequate signs do not embrace and give out again, is swallowed up. In the written communication of piety, everything needs to be twice or thrice repeated, the original medium requiring to be again exhibited, and still its effect on men in general in their great unity can only be badly copied by multiplied reflection. Only when it is chased from the society of the living, religion must hide its varied life in the dead letter.

JEAN-CHARLES-LEONARD SIMONDE DE SISMONDI

1773–1842

Jean-Charles-Leonard Simonde de Sismondi (real name: Simonde) was born in Geneva on May 9, 1773, married Jessy Allen (an Englishwoman) in April, 1819, and died of stomach cancer on June 25, 1842 in Chéne, near Geneva, aged 69. He was well educated in literature, but his family wanted him to become a banker's clerk in Lyon. The French Revolution imperiled his family's social status, so they moved first to England for 18 months (1793–94), and then, having liquidated their assets in Geneva, to a small farm in Pescia, near Lucca in Italy between 1794 and 1800. He worked hard as a writer and farmer, taking particular note of the deleterious effects that industrialization had upon its workers, and the odd fact that Smith's economics seemed to focus exclusively on the production of ever more wealth, but had nothing to say about the production of human happiness—a deficiency he tried to correct with his own work. Later economists, notably Marx and Keynes, prized some of Sismondi's observations about "the glut" problem (overproduction, underconsumption), and the socio-economic costs of unlimited, cutthroat competition in a capitalist environment. Around 1804 he had the great good fortune of becoming very close with Madame De Stael, by far the most important female intellectual of the era. He traveled with her and the German philosopher Schlegel (whom Sismondi did not like), and she immortalized them in her novel, *Corinne* (1804–05; retranslated into English in 1987).

Among many other works (he seems always to have worked at least eight hours a day at his writing), he published *Picture of Tuscan Agriculture* in 1801, *Treatise on Commercial Riches* (1802/03, 2 vols.), the famous *The History of the Italian Republics in the Middle Ages* (1809–1818) in 16 volumes (a work since little known in the English-speaking world), *New Principles of Political Economy* in 1819, and *History of the French* between 1818 and 1842 in 29 volumes. It is interesting, given these bibliographical facts, that now he is remembered principally as an economist and not as an historian. Though his enormous history of French civilization has been superseded, his history of the Italian city-states, emphasizing their allegiance to freedom, is still valuable, and gave an intellectual boost to those politicians who 40 years later were trying to shape modern Italy during the Risorgimento.

In the selection reprinted here, Sismondi explains why slave production is inefficient and inhumane, both from a purely economic point of view as well as on ethical grounds. Given that he wrote this before 1819, he clearly anticipated similar arguments that nonetheless could not prevent the great conflagration Americans call The Civil War.

NEW PRINCIPLES OF POLITICAL ECONOMY, 1819

Of Slave Cultivation

But the progress of wealth, of luxury, and idleness, in all the states of antiquity, substituted the servile for the patriarchal mode of cultivation. The population lost much in happiness and number by this change; the earth gained little in productiveness. The Roman proprietors extending their patrimonies by the confiscated territories of vanquished states, the Greeks by wealth acquired from trade,—first abandoned manual labour, and soon afterwards despised it. Fixing their residence in towns, they entrusted the management of their estates to stewards and inspectors of slaves; and from that period, the condition of most part of the country population became intolerable. Labour, which had once been a point of communion betwixt the two ranks of society, now became a barrier of separation; contempt and severity succeeded to affectionate care; punishments were multiplied as they came to be inflicted by inferiors, and as the death of one or several slaves did not lessen the steward's wealth. Slaves who were ill-fed, ill-treated, ill-recompensed, could not fail to lose all interest in their master's affairs, and almost all understanding. Far from attending to their business with affection, they felt a secret joy every time they saw their oppressor's wealth diminished, or his hopes deceived.

It is believed that great savings can be made if the man who is made to work is not paid; however, he must be fed, and all the greed of the masters does not prevent that the subsistence of the slave costs almost as much as that of a free man. If some of his needs are not met, he will, on his part, take great pleasure in squandering the possessions of his enemy, instead of saving them. Moreover,

he must be bought; and the interest on his purchase price should be compared, not to his hire, but to what could have been saved on the wages. Physiologists have noticed that the cheerfulness of the working man increases his powers, and makes him feel less fatigue. This one principle gives a great superiority to the work of a free man over that of a slave, even given equal strength. Columella, who wrote around the year A.D. 40, advised landowners to use slaves whenever they could supervise them themselves; but to stay with free cultivators, the colons, if their estates were distant, and they did not want to live in the country, at the head of their workers.

The study of science, accompanied with habits of observation, certainly advanced the theory of agriculture; but its practice, at the same time, rapidly declined; a fact which all the agricultural writers of antiquity lament. The cultivation of land was entirely divested of that intelligence, affection, and zeal, which had once hastened its success. The revenues were smaller, and the expenses greater; and from that period, it became an object to save labour, more than to augment its produce. Slaves, after having driven every free cultivator from the fields, were themselves rapidly decreasing in number. During the decline of the Roman empire, the population of Italy was not less reduced than that of the *Agra Romano* is in our days; while at the same time, it had sunk into the last degree of wretchedness and penury.

The slave war of the years 73 to 71 B.C. made Rome recognize the danger of letting the subsistence of the state depend on a population that was simultaneously reduced to misery and despair. Pompey defeated Spartacus; but innumerable slaves were killed, and the frightened masters preferred to give up a part of their harvests so as not to increase the number of their enemies on their estates. . . .

The cultivation of the colonies situated on the Mexican Gulf, was founded, in like manner, on the baneful system of slavery; it has, in like manner, consumed the population, debased the human species, and deteriorated the system of agriculture. The Negro trade has of course filled up those voids, which the barbarity of planters annually produced in the agricultural population; and doubtless under a system of culture, such that the man who labours is constantly reduced below

From *New Principle of Political Economy,* by Jean-Charles-Leonard Simonde de Sismondi, Richard Hyse, Trans. Copyright © 1991. Published by permission of Transaction Publishers.

the necessaries of life, and the man who does not labour keeps all for himself, the net produce has always been considerable; but the gross produce, with which alone the nation is concerned, has uniformly been inferior to what would have arisen from any other system of agriculture, while the condition of more than seven-eighths of the population has continued to be miserable.

Furthermore, today the net income as well as the gross revenue in the colonies has declined so much that one cannot be enough amazed at the obstinacy of the colonists in maintaining slave cultivation. The land is infinitely more fertile in the West Indies than in France; the stronger sun produces there a much richer vegetation; their products can only grow in a limited space while they are sought after in the whole world; the expense of government, and that of defense, is borne by the mother country; and yet, the colonies are able to save their plantations only because their sugar and their coffee have been given the monopoly of the entire French market; and even with such an advantage, as tremendous as it is unjust, the land is valueless, and the price of a plantation represents only the capital used in its cultivation. Thus, the disadvantages of slave cultivation were sufficient to offset all the advantages of fertility, climate, the absence of taxes, and monopoly.

Power over slaves is not a right, but only robbery which, in certain countries, and under certain circumstances, the law does not punish. The slavemasters, the planters, speak often of their rights, the guarantees the laws of their country owe to their property; but the silence of the laws would not be able to change the morality of deeds; the impunity guaranteed to him who takes away the welfare of another does not abolish the distinction between right and wrong. Land ownership is a grant of the law made for the advantage of all; but the ownership of one's own person, and in the fruits of one's own labor is prior to the law. The slave was not only robbed on the day he was sold into servitude, he is robbed every day, because he is deprived of the fruits of his daily labor without compensation. The punishments and tortures with which the master penalizes his resistance are again new offenses the laws neglect to punish, because it concerns only a slave. The European master can have no illusions about the criminality of his acts; they are as much against

natural law as they are against the civil law of his country. The legislator seems only to have refrained from punishing the violations too far from his oversight; if master and his slave return to France and England, the slave comes again under the protection of the common law, and everyone of the injustices the master committed against the slave is punished, as they would be with respect to another citizen. Because in the Antilles civil law has not ratified the clearest provisions of natural law, the master may well claim immunity for the previous crimes against his slave, but he has no right whatever to demand that the law in the future not extend its protection to all men, and not suppress all wrongs. It is his fault that he has acquired knowingly a stolen good, that he has paid for the right to commit an injustice which is repeated every hour, and on whose nature he can have no doubt. If there is anyone in this who should be indemnified by the public, it is the slave, for the long abuse to which the injustice of the law has exposed him.

The question of emancipation, the substitution of another cultivation for slave cultivation, presents without doubt difficulties; but that is above all relative to the vigorous protection owed to a race a long time oppressed, as against the consequences of moral degradation to which we have subjected it. The legislator, after having brutalized the Negroes, then having allowed that these dehumanized beings be introduced into civilized society, has assumed the obligation to raise them again to the rank of human beings before according them rights; he owes them education, he owes them a gradual emancipation, because too quick a transition can only be fatal to them. But he owes nothing to their masters; in law, because their property is only validated by a progression of offenses, it merits no guarantee whatsoever; in reality, because this property has today no value. Indeed, if the monopoly of the colonies were abrogated, if all the ports were opened to the coffee and sugar produced by free labor, in the Indies and on the American continent, the expensive slave cultivation would not be able to meet competition; if the European garrisons were withdrawn from the Antilles, if the Creoles were not anymore protected against the Negroes by a foreign force they do not pay, then the last Creole would hasten to depart before the last soldier. This very day the Negro is not an asset, he is a cause of loss and danger to the white. It is not the slave at all who creates an income for the planter; the income is taken entirely from the pocket of the European consumer, to whom the colonial products are sold at monopoly prices; and the same consumer pays again to his government taxes to maintain, by armed force, a cultivation method which is not only tainted with injustice and cruelty, but is also more expensive and more ruinous than any other.

Generous people have sought to alleviate the fate of the Negroes, by attacking with determination the hateful traffic by which they are procured. They have succeeded in prohibiting it; and they have thus halted, at least in the English colonies, the continuation of a monstrous crime, and the destruction of new multitudes of unfortunates. As to the relief of the Negroes already enslaved in Jamaica and in the English colonies, the remedy has proven ineffectual. It is said that the owners cannot desire the destruction of their human herds anymore than the destruction of their animal herds. But for the most part, these owners lived in Europe. Self-interest motivates only the farmer who himself watches over his teams; it has no influence on his servant who makes it his business to profit therefrom. . . .

If the plantations of the absent colonials were rented to farmers, and if the slaves were trade a part of the assets of the farmer, their suffering would undoubtedly be less severe. In no other system of cultivation does the owner oblige himself to furnish the machinery of a farm three thousand miles away from his home. However, in no other could such a trust be more deadly. European laws declare that Negro free who debarks in a European port; they would be more just if they would declare that Negro free whose master has gone to Europe.

JOHANN GOTTLIEB FICHTE

1762–1814

Son of a ribbon weaver, Johann Gottlieb Fichte was born on May 19, 1792 in Rammenau, Upper Lusatia, Germany. At 31 he married Johanna Maria Rahn in Zürich in October, 1793, and they had one son. He died on January 27, 1814 in Berlin, not yet 52, having contracted a hospital fever brought home by his wife, who was a volunteer nurse. He attended the Pforta school, Naumburg from 1774 through 1780, and Jena for college, and on to Leipzig from 1781 through 1784. As most of his intellectual peer group, he first worked as a tutor, from 1784 through 1787 in Saxony, then in Zurich, 1788–90. At long last he was offered a professorship at Jena, which he held from 1793 to 1798, finally landing in Berlin (1799–1806). As a young scholar, Fichte found his principal influence in Kant's ethical doctrine, particularly concerning the moral worth of the individual. His first work, *An Attempt at a Critique of All Revelation* (1792), was written expressly to impress Kant, and even though their actual meeting did not go well, the older philosopher thought highly of the work and found a publisher for it. Because the author's identity was omitted from the book and readers assumed it was Kant's work, Fichte suddenly became, at 30, a notable philosopher. In this work Fichte pointed out the need for divine legitimation of moral rules, and suggested that an occasional revelation would add to the strength of behavioral norms which might otherwise be less likely to be followed.

In 1793, the year of his marriage, he published an appreciative tract explaining the French Revolution to correct popular misconceptions, and to illustrate the necessary link between freedom and rationality. In the following year appeared *The Vocation of the Scholar* (cf. Max Weber's "Science as a Vocation"), followed by a series of important works, including *Foundation of the Complete Theory of Knowledge* (1794), *The Vocation of Man* (1800), *On the Notion of the Theory of Science* (1794), *Characteristics of the Present Age* (1804), and *Addresses to the German Nation* (1807–08), which is still read. Of these, *The Vocation of Man* is most carefully studied today, and the source of one of the excerpts reprinted below, the other coming from *Characteristics*. He was fired from his job at Jena because of remarks he made in a scholarly journal he edited, *Philosophisches Journal,* which were interpreted as atheistic, and he left for Berlin in 1799.

In the excerpts offered below, Fichte relates faith to freedom, one of his central themes. He viewed human agency as part of a larger scheme, not something wholly independent of a religious cosmology. The other selection concerns his ideas for a universal history, a topic as compelling to his era as it has become suspicious to ours.

THE VOCATION OF MAN, 1800

Faith

Our species still laboriously extorts the means of its subsistence and preservation from an opposing Nature. The larger portion of mankind is still condemned through life to severe toil in order to supply nourishment for itself and for the smaller portion which thinks for it; immortal spirits are compelled to fix their whole thoughts and endeavors on the earth that brings forth their food. It still frequently happens that, when the laborer has completed his toil and has promised himself in return a lasting endurance for himself and for his work, a hostile element will destroy in a moment that which it has cost him years of patient forethought and industry to accomplish, and the assiduous and careful man is undeservedly made the prey of hunger and misery; often do floods, storms, volcanoes desolate whole countries, and works which bear the impress of a rational soul are mingled with their authors in the wild chaos of destruction and death. Disease sweeps into an untimely grave men in the pride of their strength and children whose existence has yet borne no fruit; pestilence stalks through blooming lands, leaves the few who escape its ravages like lonely orphans bereaved of the accustomed support of their fellows, and does all that it can do to give back to the wilderness regions which the labor of man has reclaimed from thence as a possession to himself. Thus it is now, but thus it cannot remain forever. No work that bears the stamp of Reason, and has been undertaken to extend her power, can ever be wholly lost in the onward progress of the ages. The sacrifices which the irregular violence of Nature extorts from Reason must at last exhaust, satiate, and appease that violence. The same power which has burst out into lawless fury cannot again commit like excesses; it cannot be destined to renew its ravages; by its own outbreak its energies must henceforth and forever be exhausted. All those outbreaks of unregulated power before which human

strength vanishes into nothing, those desolating hurricanes, those earthquakes, those volcanoes can be nothing but the last struggles of the rude mass against the law of regular, progressive, living, and systematic activity to which it is compelled to submit in opposition to its own undirected impulses—nothing but the last shivering strokes by which the perfect formation of our globe has yet to be accomplished. The resistance must gradually become weaker and at length be worn out, since, in the regulated progress of things, there can be nothing to renew its strength; that formation must at length be achieved and our destined dwelling place be made complete. Nature must gradually be resolved into a condition in which her regular action may be calculated and safely relied upon, and her power bear a fixed and definite relation to that which is destined to govern it—that of man. . . .

But it is not Nature, it is Freedom itself, by which the greatest and most terrible disorders incident to our race, are produced; man is the cruelest enemy of man. Lawless hordes of savages still wander over vast wildernesses—they meet, and the victor devours his foe at the triumphal feast; or where culture has at length united these wild hordes under some social bond, they attack each other, as nations, with the power which law and union have given them. Defying toil and privation, their armies traverse peaceful plains and forests; they meet each other, and the sight of their brethren is the signal for slaughter. Equipped with the mightiest inventions of the human intellect, hostile fleets plow their way through the ocean; through storm and tempest man rushes to meet his fellow men upon the lonely inhospitable sea; they meet, and defy the fury of the elements that they may destroy each other with their own hands. Even in the interior of states, where men seem to be united in equality under the law, it is still for the most part only force and fraud which rule under that venerable name; and here the warfare is so much the more shameful that it is not openly declared to be war, and the party attacked is even deprived of the privilege of defending itself against unjust oppression. Combinations of the few rejoice aloud in the ignorance, the folly, the vice, and the misery in which the greater number of their fellow men are sunk, avowedly seek to retain them in this state of degradation, and even to plunge them deeper in it in order to perpetuate their slavery—nay, would destroy anyone who should venture to enlighten or improve them. No attempt at amelioration can anywhere be made without rousing up from slumber a host of selfish interests to war against it, and uniting even the most varied and opposite in a common hostility. The good cause is ever the weaker, for it is simple and can be loved only for itself. Evil attracts each individual by the promise which is most seductive to him; and its adherents, always at war among themselves, so soon as the good makes its appearance, conclude a truce that they may unite the whole powers of their wickedness against it. . . .

Thus do all good intentions among men appear to be lost in vain disputations, which leave behind them no trace of their existence, while in the meantime the world goes on as well, or as ill, as it can without human effort—by the blind mechanism of Nature—and so will go on forever.

And so go on forever? No! unless the whole existence of humanity is to be an idle game, without significance and without end. It cannot be intended that those savage tribes should always remain savage; no race can be born with all the capacities of perfect humanity and yet be destined never to develop these capacities, never to become more than that which a sagacious animal by its own proper nature might become.

It is the vocation of our species to unite itself into one single body, all the parts of which shall be thoroughly known to each other, and all possessed of similar culture. Nature and even the passions and vices of men have from the beginning tended toward this end; a great part of the way toward it is already passed, and we may surely calculate that this end, which is the condition of all further progress, will in time be attained. Let us not ask of history if man, on the whole, has yet become purely moral! To a more extended, comprehensive, and powerful freedom he has certainly attained; but hitherto it has been an almost necessary result of his position that this choice has been applied chiefly to evil purposes.

CHARACTERISTICS OF THE PRESENT AGE, 1804

Idea of Universal History

Every particular Epoch of Time, as we have already hinted above, is the fundamental Idea of a particular Age. These Epochs and fundamental Ideas of particular Ages, however, can only be thoroughly understood by and through each other, and by means of their relation, to Universal Time. Hence it is clear that the Philosopher, in order to be able rightly to characterize any individual Age—and, if he will, his own—must first have understood *a priori* and thoroughly penetrated into the signification of Universal Time and all its possible Epochs.

This comprehension of Universal Time, like all philosophical comprehension, again presupposes a fundamental Idea of Time; an Idea of a fore-ordered, although only gradually unfolding, accomplishment of Time, in which each successive period is determined by the preceding;—or, to express this more shortly and in more common phraseology,—it presupposes a *World-plan,* which, in its primitive unity, may be clearly comprehended, and from which may be correctly deduced all the great Epochs of human life on Earth, so that they may be distinctly understood both in their origin, and in their connexion with each other. The former,—the World-plan,—is the fundamental Idea of the entire life of Man on Earth; the latter,—the chief Epochs of this life,—are the fundamental Ideas of particular Ages of which we have spoken, from which again the phenomena of these Ages are to be deduced.

We have thus, in the first place, a fundamental Idea of the entire life of Man, dividing itself into different Epochs, which can only be understood by and through each other; each of which Epochs is again the fundamental Idea of a particular Age, and is revealed in manifold phenomena therein.

The life of Mankind *on this Earth* stands here in place of the *One Universal Life,* and *Earthly Time* in place of *Universal Time;*—such are the limits within which we are confined by the proposed popular character of our discourses, since it is impossible to speak at once profoundly and popularly of the Heavenly and Eternal. . . .

The Idea of a World-Plan is thus implied in our inquiry, which, however, I am not at this time to deduce from the fundamental Idea indicated above, but only to point out. I say therefore,—and so lay the foundation of our rising edifice,—*the End of the Life of Mankind on Earth is this,—that in this Life they may order all their relations with* FREE-DOM *according to* REASON.

With *Freedom,* I have said;—their own Freedom,—the Freedom of Mankind in their collective capacity,—*as a Race:*—and this Freedom is the first accessory condition of our fundamental principle which I intend at present to pursue, leaving the other conditions, which may likewise need explanation, to the subsequent lectures. This Freedom becomes apparent in the collective consciousness of the Race, and it appears there as the proper and peculiar Freedom of the Race;—as a true and real fact;—the product of the Race during its Life and proceeding from its Life, so that the absolute existence of the Race itself is necessarily implied in the existence of the fact and product thus attributed to it. . . .

The great Whole of Life is spread out into Ages, which sometimes seem to cross, sometimes to run parallel with each other:—1*st,* The Epoch of the unlimited dominion of Reason as Instinct:—*the State of Innocence of the Human Race.* 2*nd,* The Epoch in which Reason as Instinct is changed into an external ruling Authority;—the Age of positive Systems of life and doctrine, which never go back to their ultimate foundations, and hence have no power to convince but on the contrary merely desire to compel, and which demand blind faith and unconditional obedience:—*the State of progressive Sin.* 3*rd,* The Epoch of Liberation,—*directly* from the external ruling Authority—*indirectly* from the power of Reason as Instinct, and *generally* from Reason in any form;—the Age of absolute indifference towards all truth, and of entire and unrestrained licentiousness:—*the State of completed Sinfulness.* 4*th,* The Epoch of Reason as *Knowledge;*—the Age in which Truth is looked upon as the *highest,* and loved before all other things:—*the State of progressive Justification.* 5*th,* The Epoch of Reason as Art;—the Age in which Humanity with more sure and unerring hand builds itself up into a fitting image and representative of Reason:—*the State of completed Justification and Sanctifcation.* Thus, the whole progress which, upon this view, Humanity makes here below, is only a retrogression to the point on which it stood at first, and has nothing in view save that return to its original condition.

JOSEPH DE MAISTRE

1753–1821

Count Joseph de Maistre, son of a Senator in the Savoy legislature, was born on April 1, 1754 in Chambéry, France. He married Francoise de Morand in 1786 when he was 32, they had children, and he died in Turin, Italy on February 26, 1821 when 66 from "paralysis," thought by some to be a result of an unhappy domestic situation. Though he wrote in French, he was never a citizen of France, but instead a willing subject of the House of Savoy, and eventually assumed his father's role as a Senator in 1788. The Jesuits educated him before he attended the University of Turin, from which he took his law degree. In 1792 French troops in Chambéry sent him into exile, first in Lausanne for four years, then to St. Petersburg, Russia from 1803 until 1817. He later held important legal posts in Sardinia and Piedmont (until 1821). Though now infamously known as an arch-conservative and opponent to the ideological claims of the Revolutionists, he was not predisposed to this posture before August, 1789 when the French Revolution's ruling body began destroying through legislation the hierarchical society of Paris. He thought this and allied actions would prove disastrous for the progress of civilization, and conflicted with the more cosmopolitan notions he had accepted while a young man. Moreover, he challenged the reigning ideas of the philosophes, the celebration of reason's force in human relations which had been held throughout the 18th century. As a devout Catholic, he much preferred to emphasize the strength of tradition and ancient dogma to the newly minted notions then flowing through the capitals of Europe. One of his most famous books, *The Pope* (1817) held that the pope was infallible, and that atheism and immorality could only be curbed if his authority was recognized as such.

De Maistre was a learned man and immensely effective polemicist. His notebooks indicate that he was at home with French, Greek, Latin, English, Italian, Spanish, Portuguese, and probably Russian. He read very widely in contemporary philosophy, but also knew the Hebrew and Graeco-roman classics. He drew on all this material when attacking the main planks of the Enlightenment, also taking sustenance from Burke's more famous critique of the French Revolution (1790). Like most conservatives, he valued obedience over spontaneity and belief over skepticism. He also wrote as if he were a priest, fully in tune with Church doctrine. His rhetoric was powerful, but his logic was even more insistent, and his primary objective was to demonstrate the absolute need for societal order rather than rapid social change. The excerpts reprinted below come from his essays on the relationship between sovereign power and belief, between the relations of power that cement social networks versus the individual's private desires.

ON GOD AND SOCIETY, 1808–09

An anonymous writer who was much occupied with such speculations and who has strived to fathom the hidden foundations of the social edifice believed himself in the right when, nearly twenty years ago, he advanced the following propositions as so many incontestable axioms diametrically opposed to the theories of that time.*

1. No constitution arises from deliberation. The rights of the people are never written, except as simple restatements of previous, unwritten rights.
2. [In the formation of constitutions] human action is so far circumscribed that the men who act become only circumstances. [It is even very common that in pursuing a certain end they attain another.]
3. The rights of the PEOPLE, properly so called, proceed almost always from the concessions of sovereigns and thus may be definitely fixed in history, but no one can ascertain the date or the authors of the rights of the monarch and the aristocracy.
4. These concessions themselves have always been preceded by a state of things which rendered them necessary and for which the sovereign was not responsible.
5. Although written laws [*lois*] are merely the declarations of preexisting laws [*droits*], it is far from true that all these laws can be written.
6. The more of it one puts into writing, the weaker the institution becomes.
7. No nation can give itself liberty if it is not already free, for human influence extends only as far as existing rights have developed.
8. Legislators, strictly defined, are extraordinary men, belonging perhaps only to the world of antiquity and to the youth of nations.
9. Even these legislators, notwithstanding their marvelous power, have only combined parts of what already existed.
10. In a sense, liberty is the gift of kings, for nearly all free nations were established by kings.
11. There never existed a free nation which did not have seeds of liberty as old as itself in its natural constitution. Nor has any nation ever successfully attempted to develop, by its fundamental written laws, rights other than those which existed in its natural constitution.
12. No assembly of men whatsoever can form a nation. Indeed, such an enterprise should be ranked among the most memorable follies.

Since 1796, the date of the first edition of the work we quote, it does not appear that anything has happened in the world which might have induced the author to abandon his theory. . . .

It is written, BY ME PRINCES RULE. This is not a church phrase, a metaphor of the preacher. It is a literal truth, simple and palpable. It is a law of the political world. God literally makes kings. He prepares royal races, maturing them under a cloud which conceals their origin. At length they appear, crowned with glory and honor; they take their places; and this is the most certain sign of their legitimacy.

Royal families arise of themselves, as it were, unattended either by violence or marked deliberation but with a certain magnificent tranquillity which is difficult to express. LEGITIMATE USURPATION would seem the correct phrase (if not too bold) to characterize such origins, which time hastens to consecrate. . . .

The moral order has its laws, as does the physical, and their investigation is quite worthy of occupying a true philosopher's meditations.

~⌒⌒~

STUDY ON SOVEREIGNTY

The Weakness of Human Power

In all political or religious works, whatever their aim or importance, it is a general rule that there is never any proportion between cause and effect. The effect is always immense in relation to the cause, so that man may know that he is only an instrument and that alone he can create nothing. . . .

From *On God and Society,* by Joseph De Maistre, Elisha Greifer, Ed., Laurence M. Porter, Trans. Published by Henry Regnery Company, A Gateway Edition. Copyright © 1959.

Reprinted with the permission of Scribner, a Division of Simon & Schuster Adult Publishing Group, from *The Works of Joseph de Maistre,* translated by Jack Lively. Copyright © 1965 by Jack Lively. All rights reserved.

The more human reason trusts in itself and tries to rely on its own resources, the more absurd it is and the more it reveals its lack of power. This is why the world's greatest scourge has always been, in every age, what is called *philosophy,* for philosophy is nothing but the human reason acting alone, and the human reason reduced to its own resources is nothing but a brute whose power is restricted to destroying. . . .

The Best Species of Government

The best government for each nation is that which, in the territory occupied by this nation, is capable of producing the greatest possible sum of happiness and strength, for the greatest possible number of men, during the longest possible time. I venture to believe that the justice of this definition cannot be denied and that it is by following it that comparison between states from the point of view of their governments becomes possible. In fact, although it is impossible to ask *What is the best form of government?* nothing stops us asking, *Which nation is relatively the most numerous, the strongest, and the happiest, over the greatest period of time, through the influence of the government suitable to it?*

What peculiarity of mind prevents us from using in the study of politics the same methods of reasoning and the same general hypotheses which guide us in the study of other sciences?

In physical research, if there is a problem of estimating a variable force, we take the average quantity. In astronomy in particular we always talk of *average distance* and *average time.* To judge the merit of a government, the same method should be used.

Any government is a variable force that produces effects as variable as itself, within certain limits. To judge it, it should not be examined at a given moment, but over the whole of its existence. Then to judge the French monarchy properly, a sum of the virtues and vices of all the French kings should be made, and divided by sixty-six: the result is an *average king;* and the same is true of other monarchies.

Democracy has one brilliant moment, but it is a moment and it must pay dearly for it. The great days of Athens might, I agree, inspire desires in the subject of a monarchy, languishing in such and such a period under an inept or wicked king. Nevertheless, we would be greatly mistaken if we

claimed to establish the superiority of democracy over monarchy by comparing moment for moment, because, in this way of judging, we neglect among other things the consideration of duration, which is a necessary element of these sorts of calculation.

In general, all democratic governments are only transitory meteors, whose brilliance excludes duration. . . .

In discussing the different kinds of government, the general happiness is not sufficiently considered, although it should be our sole criterion. We should have the courage to face a glaring truth which would cool our enthusiasm for free constitutions a little; this is that, in every republic over a certain size, what is called *liberty* is only the total sacrifice of a great number of men for the independence and pride of a small number. . . .

Properly speaking, all governments are monarchies which differ only in whether the monarch is for life or for a term of years, hereditary or elective, individual or corporate; or, if you will (for it is the same idea in other terms), all governments are aristocratic, composed of a greater or smaller number of rulers, from democracy, in which this aristocracy is composed of as many men as the nature of things permits, to monarchy, in which the aristocracy, inevitable under every government, is headed by a single man topping the pyramid and which undoubtedly constitutes the most natural government for man.

On the Nature of Sovereignty

Monarchy   It can be said in general that all men are born for monarchy. This form of government is the most ancient and the most universal. . . . Monarchical government is so natural that, without realizing it, men identify it with sovereignty. They seem tacitly to agree that, wherever there is no king, there is no real *sovereign.* . . .

This is particularly striking in everything that has been said on both sides of the question that formed the subject of the first book of this work. The adversaries of divine origin always hold a grudge against *kings* and talk only of *kings.* They do not want to accept that the authority of kings comes from God: but it is not a question of *royalty* in particular but of *sovereignty* in general. Yes, all sovereignty derives from God; whatever form it takes, it is not the work of man. It is one, absolute and inviolable of its nature. Why, then, lay the blame on royalty, as though the inconveniences which are relied on to attack this system are not the same in any form of government? Once again, it is because royalty is *the natural government* and because in common discourse men confuse it with sovereignty by disregarding other governments, just as they neglect the exception when enunciating the general rule. . . .

Man must always be brought back to history, which is the first and indeed the only teacher in politics. Whoever says that man is born for liberty is speaking nonsense. If a being of a superior order undertook the *natural history* of man, surely he would seek his directions in the history of facts. When he knew what man is and has always been, what he does and has always done, he would write; and doubtless he would reject as foolish the notion that man is not what he should be and that his condition is contrary to the laws of creation. The very expression of this proposition is sufficient to refute it.

HENRI COMTE DE SAINT-SIMON

1760–1825

Comte de Claude Henri de Rouvroy Saint-Simon, impoverished noble, was born in Paris on October 17, 1760, married at 40 for less than a year after which it was annulled, and died 64 years later in the same city, having been rich and poor more than once. He worked under d'Alembert and after a spotty education, joined the military, ending up at Yorktown, Virginia as a captain of artillery under the rebels. After a short time in prison (1793–94) during the French Revolution, he emerged to discover that because of currency devaluation, he was suddenly rich. After 40 years as a soldier and speculator, he used the windfall for intellectual purposes, setting up a salon, traveling to Madame de Stael in Geneva, in England, and thereby educated himself at the feet of other learned people. He became fascinated with the opportunity to use industrialization to improve the condition of society at large, especially the working classes, and he pictured a society that would be run by an elite "priesthood" of scientists and philosophes. They would be guided in their behavior by a new sort of Christian-socialism, which over time came to be known as Saint-Simonism, and held considerable influence in Europe through the 1830 revolution in France. Napoleon III, Thomas Carlyle, Auguste Comte, Friedrich Engels (who called him a genius), and many other notable thinkers held Saint-Simon's ideas in high esteem, and tried to bring his ideas to life within the new social organization of Europe, England, and the United States in their writings and actions. He was so influential that after his death a peculiar sect tried to start a religion based on veneration of him and his ideas, but it seems to have died out fairly quickly.

The social sciences owe Saint-Simon a great deal. He was among the first to hypothesize that intellectuals, properly schooled, could study the social order the way natural scientists study flora and fauna, and armed with this new, systematic knowledge, they could then control social and economic development in favor of the general welfare (*On the Reorganization of European Society,* 1814). The deep animus against industrial capitalism which began to flourish in the mid-19th century was not evident in Saint-Simon's work a half-century before. For him the possibilities for diminishing human suffering through poverty and misgovernment were real and encouraging, which is probably why his name became synonymous with a religious cult after his death. He offered what all religions put forth: hope for a better tomorrow. In the final year of his life he published *The New Christianity* (1825) in which he made the then shocking suggestion that the goal of the new religiosity should be to use the powers of industrialization to lessen the miseries of the society's poor. For this he won perpetual esteem among the Left, and was considered quite mad by the Right.

"ESSAY ON THE SCIENCE OF MAN," 1813

If we consider the general ideas that educated men have derived from their education concerning the course which the human mind has followed from the beginnings of its development, particularly the course of its development since the fifteenth century, we find that:

(1) Since that time the tendency has been to base all reasoning on facts which have been observed and analysed. Already astronomy, physics and chemistry have been reorganized on this positive basis: these sciences are nowadays an essential part, the very foundation of education. It follows necessarily that physiology, of which the science of man is a part, will be brought under the same method as the other physical sciences, and that it will be introduced into education when it has been made positive.

(2) The particular sciences are the elements of universal science. Universal science, namely philosophy, was bound to be conjectural, as long as the particular sciences remained so; it was bound to be partly conjectural and partly positive, while some of the special sciences had become positive, and others were still conjectural. It will become wholly positive when all the special sciences have become positive. This state of affairs will be realized when psychology and physiology have become based on observed and analysed facts; for there are no phenomena which are not either astronomical, chemical, physiological, or psychological. We can therefore conceive of a time when the philosophy taught in the schools will be positive.

(3) Systems of religion, politics, ethics, and education, are simply applications of the system of ideas, or, in other words, of the system of thought, considered under different aspects. Thus, it is obvious that when the new scientific system has been constructed, a reorganization of the religious, political, ethical, and educational system will take place; and consequently a reorganization of the church.

From *Henri Comte De Saint-Simon: Selected Writings*, F.M.H. Markham, Ed./Trans. Copyright © 1991. Published by permission of Gibson Press.

(4) National communities are particular applications of general ideas about social organization. Hence the reorganization of the general European political system will lead to changes in the national organization of the various peoples who together compose this great community. . . .

The Christian religion civilized the peoples of the North, stopped the disorder in which Italy was plunged, put the land of Europe under cultivation, drained the marshes, and made the climate healthy. It caused roads and bridges to be built, established hospitals, educated the people in reading and writing, kept registers of births, deaths, and marriages, began the collection of historical records; it diminished and almost abolished slavery, and, above all, organized the largest political community which has ever existed. Having rendered these important services, the Christian religion became an institution which had fulfilled its function, and completed the useful part of its career: it had attained old age. This institution, in respect of the laws it laid down, the judges it appointed, the ethics which it taught, the preachers it sent forth, had become a burden on society.

Religion, for a man of the intelligence of Bacon, could not be anything but a general scientific theory. The purpose of a theory is to organize facts. Fifteen hundred years had passed since this theory was formulated, and it is not surprising that it became inadequate to organize the knowledge acquired by the human mind fifteen hundred years later, and to explain the facts which had only been discovered long after its foundation.

The Arabs had completely refashioned science by founding a new school of astronomy and a new theory of medicine. Many discoveries had already been made on the new lines which they had laid down, but many more were needed before the materials for a new scientific edifice could be assembled. Bacon felt keenly the need for the human mind to continue its search for knowledge, and he therefore attacked the old conceptions which had required immense force by assuming a religious form. At the same time, he pointed out the various methods by which the human intellect could make discoveries in every scientific field.

Thus Bacon, who was as great as he could be in thought, speech and action, considering the age in which he lived, deprecate *a priori* philosophy and favoured as much as possible an *a posteriori* philosophy. Gentlemen, do you believe that Bacon, if he rose from his grave to-day, would speak in the same way? Imagine this great man, restored to life, and attending a session of the Institute. What would be his astonishment at seeing that philosophy was not the subject of any section of the first class, nor in any class of this comprehensive scientific institution. In fact, if Bacon, who is its inspiration in all its studies, wished to enter the Institute, he could not be admitted at all in the first class; he could be received into the second class only on the score of his style, and into the third, as a learned scholar! . . .

What are the means of hastening the progress of the sciences?

Do you wish, gentlemen, to organize yourselves? Nothing is easier: select an idea to which all other ideas can be related, and from which all principles can be deduced as consequences—then you will have a philosophy. This philosophy will necessarily be founded on the idea of universal gravitation, and all your researches will from that moment become systematic. As for the means of organizing your society, it is equally simple since it is the same. Assign philosophy to one of your classes; instruct the members you admit to it to deduce or to relate, according as they proceed *a priori* or *a posteriori, from* or *to* the idea of universal gravitation, all known phenomena. You will then find that you are systematically organized from the active and the passive point of view— that is to say, intellectually as a corporate body: and your power, in both respects, will become incalculable. And then to the University, he will say.

Your society has only a mongrel and precarious existence; it will inevitably be very short if you do not promptly take steps to strengthen it. The only means to achieve this result will be:

(1) To keep as closely in touch as possible with the institute, and to link yourselves intimately with it; so intimately that you will together form a single corporation, the great scientific corporation of France. This body will then be divided into two sections with distinct functions; the Institute for the advancement of sciences and yourselves for the teaching of it.

(2) Never to lose sight of the fact that in your teaching you should always give preference to the a priori method over the a posteriori method.

(3) To consider how a course of philosophy, based on the idea of gravitation, can be organized as soon as possible in the educational system (which is your concern); the object of this philosophy being to deduce from this principle, as directly as possible, the explanation of every kind of phenomenon.

❧

"ON SOCIAL ORGANIZATION," 1825

The mechanism of social organization was inevitably very complicated so long as the majority of individuals remained in a state of ignorance and improvidence which rendered them incapable of administering their own affairs. In this state of incomplete intellectual development they were swayed by brutal passions which urged them to revolt and every kind of anarchy.

In such a situation, which was the necessary prelude to a better social order, it was necessary for the minority to be organized on military lines, to obtain a monopoly of legislation, and so to keep all power to itself, in order to hold the majority in tutelage and subject the nation to strong discipline. Thus the main energies of the community have till now been directed to maintaining itself as a community, and any efforts directed to improving the moral and physical welfare of the nation have necessarily been regarded as secondary.

To-day this state of affairs can and should be completely altered. The main effort should be directed to the improvement of our moral and physical welfare; only a small amount of force is now required to maintain public order, since the majority have become used to work (which eliminates disorder) and now consists of men who have recently proved that they are capable of administering property, whether in land or money.

From *Henri Comte De Saint-Simon: Selected Writings*, F.M.H. Markham, Ed./Trans. Copyright © 1991. Published by permission of Gibson Press.

As the minority no longer has need of force to keep the proletarian class in subordination, the course which it should adopt is as follows:

(1) A policy by which the proletariat will have the strongest interest in maintaining public order.

(2) A policy which aims at making the inheritance of landed property as easy as possible.

(3) A policy which aims at giving the highest political importance to the workers.

Such a policy is quite simple and obvious, if one takes the trouble to judge the situation by one's own intelligence, and to shake off the yoke enforced on our minds by the political principles of our ancestors— principles which were sound and useful in their own day, but are no longer applicable to present circumstances. The mass of the population is now composed of men (apart from exceptions which occur more or less equally in every class) who are capable of administering property whether in land or in money, and therefore we can and must work directly for the improvement of the moral and physical welfare of the community.

The most direct method of improving the moral and physical welfare of the majority of the population is to give priority in State expenditure to ensuring work for all fit men, to secure their physical existence; spreading throughout the proletarian class a knowledge of positive science; ensuring for this class forms of recreation and interests which will develop their intelligence.

We must add to this the measures necessary to ensure that the national wealth is administered by men most fitted for it, and most concerned in its administration, that is to say the most important industrialists.

Thus the community, by means of these fundamental arrangements, will be organized in a way which will completely satisfy reasonable men of every class.

There will no longer be a fear of insurrection, and consequently no longer a need to maintain large standing armies to suppress it; no longer a need to spend enormous sums on a police force; no longer a fear of foreign danger, for a body of thirty millions of men who are a contented community would easily repel attack, even if the whole human race combined against them.

We might add that neither princes nor peoples would be so mad as to attack a nation of thirty millions who displayed no aggressive intentions against their neighbours, and were united internally by mutual interests.

Furthermore, there would no longer be a need for a system of police-spying in a community in which the vast majority had an interest in maintaining the established order.

THOMAS CARLYLE

1795–1881

Thomas Carlyle, devoted son of a strict Calvinist mason and farmer, was born on December 4, 1795 in Ecclefechan, Dumfriesshire, Scotland, one of nine children. He married Jane Welsh, a well-off physician's daughter, on October 17, 1826 when he was 30 and she 25, a fruitful yet perplexing relationship that is astonishingly well documented through their letters and autobiographies. When she died 40 years later, he said the "light of his life has gone out," and in order to survive, he wrote a detailed memoir about her. Carlyle died on February 5, 1881 in London. After Annan Academy, he graduated from Edinburgh University in 1809 after an eclectic reading program of his own devising. Rather than pleasing his father by becoming a minister, he pursued mathematics, and taught it at Annan from 1814 to 1816, then to a Kirkcaldy school, where he met the mystic and famous Scottish preacher, Edward Irving. They became fast friends for life. Tiring of teaching, he returned to the University in 1819 to study law, but did not find it to his liking, either. He faced poverty, loneliness, and a lack of direction or meaning. He underwent a religious conversion, fictionalized in *Sartor Resartus* (a plan for spiritual renewal), and traveled about, teaching here and there, and becoming expert in German, the literature that became his favorite.

Carlyle supported himself by writing, and was one of the first British intellectuals to do so since a literate class of book and journal buyers was finally in place. J. S. Mill accidentally burned the manuscript of Carlyle's *French Revolution*, but he forgave him and rewrote it. It's been estimated that over the course of his career, he provided his family with an average of £150/annum, which was adequate for a solidly upper-middle class life most of the time. He translated Goethe's *Wilhelm Meister's Apprenticeship* in 1824 and also wrote many books, most became very famous and continue to be read, among them *The French Revolution* in 3 volumes (1837), *Sartor Resartus* (1833), *Life of Oliver Cromwell* (1845), *Frederick the Great* in 6 volumes, (1858–1865), *Heroes and Hero-Worship* (1841), and *Past and Present* (1843). Most of these works remain in print to this day; in fact, a "new and complete edition" of his *Reminiscences* was issued in 1997.

As revealed in the excerpt reprinted below, Carlyle appreciated the "new age" of industrial production, but was also concerned lest its coarser characteristics overshadow the more spiritually elevated achievements of bygone eras. He wondered if the likes of Mozart, Newton, or Raphael would very likely be seen again in an age of what he called "mechanism," a thought which is still being debated. His prose could be maddeningly overblown, but his sense of his own era is correctly valued even now.

"SIGNS OF THE TIMES," 1829

Were we required to characterise this age of ours by any single epithet, we should be tempted to call it, not an Heroical, Devotional, Philosophical, or Moral Age, but, above all others, the Mechanical Age. It is the Age of Machinery, in every outward and inward sense of that word; the age which, with its whole undivided might, forwards, teaches and practises the great art of adapting means to ends. Nothing is now done directly, or by hand; all is by rule and calculated contrivance. For the simplest operation, some helps and accompaniments, some cunning abbreviating process is in readiness. Our old modes of exertion are all discredited, and thrown aside. On every hand, the living artisan is driven from his workshop, to make room for a speedier, inanimate one. The shuttle drops from the fingers of the weaver, and falls into iron fingers that ply it faster. The sailor furls his sail, and lays down his oar; and bids a strong, unwearied servant, on vaporous wings, bear him through the waters. Men have crossed oceans by steam; the Birmingham Fire-king has visited the fabulous East; and the genius of the Cape, were there any Camoens now to sing it, has again been alarmed, and with far stranger thunders than Gamas. There is no end to machinery. Even the horse is stripped of his harness, and finds a fleet fire-horse yoked in his stead. Nay, we have an artist that hatches chickens by steam; the very brood-hen is to be superseded! For all earthly, and for some unearthly purposes, we have machines and mechanic furtherances; for mincing our cabbages; for casting us into magnetic sleep. We remove mountains, and make seas our smooth highway; nothing can resist us. We war with rude Nature; and, by our resistless engines, come off always victorious, and loaded with spoils.

What wonderful accessions have thus been made, and are still making, to the physical power of mankind; how much better fed, clothed, lodged and, in all outward respects, accommodated men now are, or might be, by a given quantity of labour, is a grateful reflection which forces itself on every one. What changes, too, this addition of power is introducing into the Social System; how wealth has more and more increased, and at the same time gathered itself more and more into masses, strangely altering the old relations, and increasing the distance between the rich and the poor, will be a question for Political Economists, and a much more complex and important one than any they have yet engaged with.

But leaving these matters for the present, let us observe how the mechanical genius of our time has diffused itself into quite other provinces. Not the external and physical alone is now managed by machinery, but the internal and spiritual also. Here too nothing follows its spontaneous course, nothing is left to be accomplished by old natural methods. Everything has its cunningly devised implements, its preëstablished apparatus; it is not done by hand, but by machinery. Thus we have machines for Education: Lancastrian machines; Hamiltonian machines; monitors, maps and emblems. Instruction, that mysterious communing of Wisdom with Ignorance, is no longer an indefinable tentative process, requiring a study of individual aptitudes, and a perpetual variation of means and methods, to attain the same end; but a secure, universal, straightforward business, to be conducted in the gross, by proper mechanism, with such intellect as comes to hand. Then, we have Religious machines, of all imaginable varieties; the Bible Society, professing a far higher and heavenly structure, is found, on inquiry, to be altogether an earthly contrivance: supported by collection of moneys, by fomenting of vanities, by puffing, intrigue and chicane; a machine for converting the Heathen. It is the same in all other departments. Has any man, or any society of men, a truth to speak, a piece of spiritual work to do; they can nowise proceed at once and with the mere natural organs, but must first call a public meeting, appoint committees, issue prospectuses, eat a public dinner; in a word, construct or borrow machinery, wherewith to speak it and do it. Without machinery they were hopeless, helpless; a colony of Hindoo weavers squatting in the heart of Lancashire. Mark, too, how every machine must have its moving power, in some of the great currents of society; every little sect among us, Unitarians,

From *A Carlyle Reader: Selections from the Writings of Thomas Carlyle*, G.B. Tennyson, Ed. Published by Cambridge University Press. Copyright © 1984.

Utilitarians, Anabaptists, Phrenologists, must have its Periodical, its monthly or quarterly Magazine;—hanging out, like its windmill, into the *popularis aura,* to grind meal for the society.

With individuals, in like manner, natural strength avails little. No individual now hopes to accomplish the poorest enterprise single-handed and without mechanical aids; he must make interest with some existing corporation, and till his field with their oxen. In these days, more emphatically than ever, 'to live signifies to unite with a party, or to make one.' Philosophy, Science, Art, Literature, all depend on machinery. No Newton, by silent meditation, now discovers the system of the world from the falling of an apple; but some quite other than Newton stands in his museum, his Scientific Institution, and behind whole batteries of retorts, digesters, and galvanic piles imperatively 'interrogates Nature,'—who, however, shows no haste to answer. In defect of Raphaels, and Angelos, and Mozarts, we have Royal Academies of Painting, Sculpture, Music; whereby the languishing spirit of Art may be strengthened, as by the more generous diet of a Public Kitchen. Literature, too, has its Paternoster-row mechanism, its Trade-dinners, its Editorial conclaves, and huge subterranean, puffing bellows; so that books are not only printed, but, in a great measure, written and sold, by machinery.

National culture, spiritual benefit of all sorts, is under the same management. No Queen Christina, in these times, needs to send for her Descartes; no King Frederick for his Voltaire, and painfully nourish him with pensions and flattery: Any sovereign of taste, who wishes to enlighten his people, has only to impose a new tax, and with the proceeds establish Philosophic Institutes. Hence the Royal and Imperial societies, the Bibliotèques, Glyptothèques, Technothèques, which front us in all capital cities; like so many well-finished hives, to which it is expected the stray agencies of Wisdom will swarm of their own accord, and hive and make honey. In like manner, among ourselves, when it is thought that religion is declining, we have only to vote half-a-million's worth of bricks and mortar, and build new churches. In Ireland it seems they have gone still farther, having actually established a 'Penny-a-week Purgatory-Society'! Thus does the Genius of Mechanism stand by to help us in all difficulties

and emergencies, and with his iron back bears all our burdens.

These things, which we state lightly enough here, are yet of deep import, and indicate a mighty change in our whole manner of existence. For the same habit regulates not our modes of action alone, but our modes of thought and feeling. Men are grown mechanical in head and in heart, as well as in hand. They have lost faith in individual endeavour, and in natural force, of any kind. Not for internal perfection, but for external combinations and arrangements, for institutions, constitutions,—for Mechanism of one sort or other, do they hope and struggle. Their whole efforts, attachments, opinions, turn on mechanism, and are of a mechanical character. . . .

These and the like facts are so familiar, the truths which they preach so obvious, and have in all past times been so universally believed and acted on, that we should almost feel ashamed for repeating them; were it not that, on every hand, the memory of them seems to have passed away, or at best died into a faint tradition, of no value as a practical principle. To judge by the loud clamour of our Constitution-builders, Statists, Economists, directors, creators, reformers of Public Societies; in a word, all manner of Mechanists, from the Cartwright up to the Code-maker; and by the nearly total silence of all Preachers and Teachers who should give a voice to Poetry, Religion and Morality, we might fancy either that man's Dynamical nature was, to all spiritual intents, extinct, or else so perfected that nothing more was to be made of it by the old means; and hence forth only in his Mechanical contrivances did any hope exist for him.

To define the limits of these two departments of man's activity, which work into one another, and by means of one another, so intricately and inseparably, were by its nature an impossible attempt. Their relative importance, even to the wisest mind, will vary in different times, according to the special wants and dispositions of those times. Mean while, it seems clear enough that only in the right coordination of the two, and the vigorous forwarding of both, does our true line of action lie. Undue cultivation of the inward or Dynamical province leads to idle, visionary, impracticable courses, and, especially in rude eras, to Superstition and Fanaticism, with their long train of baleful and well-known evils. Undue cultivation of the outward, again, though less immediately prejudicial, and even for the time productive of many palpable benefits, must, in the long-run, by destroying Moral Force, which is the parent of all other force, prove not less certainly, and perhaps still more hopelessly, pernicious. This, we take it, is the grand characteristic of our age. By our skill in Mechanism, it has come to pass, that in the management of external things we excel all other ages, while in whatever respects the pure moral nature, in true diginity of soul and character, we are perhaps inferior to most civilised ages.

FRANÇOIS-MARIE-CHARLES FOURIER

1772–1837

François-Marie-Charles Fourier, son of a prosperous draper, was born on April 7, 1772 in Besançon, France, did not marry, and died on October 10, 1837 in Paris at the age of 65. He was well-educated at local schools between 1781 and 1787, travelled in France, Germany, and Holland. Losing his inheritance because of adverse politics, he was forced by necessity to serve in the army for two years, then let go because of poor health. He then became a merchant in Lyon, participated in a social experiment at Rambouillet which was shortlived, and in 1812, after inheriting his mother's estate, was free to write. In 1829, however, he was again short of funds and chose to work for an American firm in Paris. He was known as "other-worldly" in his demeanor, very sensitive and in some ways quite out of touch with everyday reality.

He published *The Social Destiny of Man* in 1808 while still a bank clerk, and *The New Industrial World* in 1829–30. Like others of his period, Fourier wished to reform society along lines which he believed to be both rational and humane, for he thought that raw capitalism, rampant individualism, and endless competition were wasteful and full of destructive interpersonal hostility (an insight for which Marx valued him). He proposed that the social order be reorganized along communal lines, the key element being producer groups known as "phalanges" of 1600 people. Individuals would be rewarded proportionately in terms of their phalanges' productivity, and they would change work roles frequently so that power did not accrue to an elite. He believed that eight stages of evolutionary improvement existed (using Isaac Newton as his inspiration), the apex being "harmony," to which his proposed society would aspire. The drawback to modern civilization was its perpetual and, for Fourier, gratuitous repression of humanity's fundamental desire for untrammeled pleasure, and when this oppressive apparatus could be dismantled, humankind would "naturally" find its true identity and prosper. Conventional marriage arrangements would have to be abolished so that erotic interests might be pursued as individuals chose to do so. In some ways, he anticipated along these lines later thinkers such as Freud, Herbert Marcuse, and Norman O. Brown. It was also important for his plan that rich and poor share the same living quarters so that empathy could be engendered among everyone. This entire plan became known as Fourierism, and was tried in France and the U.S., most famously at Brook Farm, Massachusetts (1841–46) and in Red Bank, New Jersey. In France newspapers and journals were begun that propagated his ideas, the final one being suppressed by the government in 1843. Fourier waited in vain for wealthy capitalists to embrace his prescription for amiable social change.

"SOCIAL EVOLUTION," 1829

Humanity in its social career has thirty-six periods to pass through; I give below a table of the first, which will suffice for the matter contained in this volume:

LADDER OF THE FIRST AGE OF THE SOCIAL WORLD.

Periods anterior to industry.
- K. Bastard, without man.
- 1. Primitive, termed Eden.
- 2. Savage state or inertia.

Industry divided up, repulsive.
- 3. Patriarchism, small industry.
- 4. Barbarism, medium industry.
- 5. Civilisation, large industry.

Industry associative, attractive.
- 6. Guaranteeism, semi-association.
- 7. Sociantism, simple association.
- 8. Harmonism, composite association.

I make no mention of the ninth and the following periods because we are not able at present to elevate ourselves beyond the eighth which, itself, is an infinitely happy one when compared with the four existing states of society. It will spread suddenly and spontaneously over the whole of the human race, owing simply to the influence of profit, pleasure, and, above all, industrial attraction,—a mechanism with which our statesmen and moralists are quite unacquainted.—(N. M., 11.)

Each of these periods is subdivided into phases. The following are the phases of civilisation:

Ascending Vibration.

INFANCY OR FIRST PHASE.

Simple germ,	- Exclusive marriage or monogamy.
Composite ,,	- Patriarchal or aristocratic feudalism.
PIVOT,	- - *Civil rights of the wife.*
Counterpoise,	- - Great federated vassals.
Tone,	- - Chivalric illusions.

ADOLESCENCE OR SECOND PHASE.

Simple germ,	- Communal privileges.
Composite ,,	- Cultivation of arts and sciences.
PIVOT,	- - *Enfranchisement of labourers.*
Counterpoise,	- - Representative system.
Tone,	- - Illusions of liberty.

APOGEE OR PLENITUDE.

Germs: nautical art, experimental chemistry.
Characteristics: clearing of land, fiscal loans.

Descending Vibration.

VIRILITY OR THIRD PHASE.

Simple germ,	- Mercantile and fiscal spirit.
Composite ,,	- Joint-stock companies.
PIVOT,	- - *Maritime monopoly.*
Counterpoise,	- - Anarchical commerce.
Tone,	- - Economic illusions.

DECAY OR FOURTH PHASE.

Simple germ,	- Municipal pawn-shops.
Composite ,,	- Trade privileges, limited in number.
PIVOT,	- - *Industrial feudalism.*
Counterpoise,	- - Farmers of feudal monopolies.
Tone,	- - Illusions of association.

(N. M., 387.)

Our destiny is to advance; every social period must progress towards the one above it: it is Nature's wish that barbarism should tend towards

---

From *Selections From The Works of Fourier*, Julia Franklin, Trans. Published by Swan Sonnenschein & Co., 1901.

civilisation and attain to it by degrees; that civilisation should tend to guaranteeism, that guaranteeism should tend to simple association, and so of the other periods. The same is true of phases: the first must tend towards the second, this to the third, this again to the fourth, this to the transition state, and so on in succession. If a society lingers too long in a period or phase, it engenders corruption like stagnant water. (This rule is subject to certain exceptions for the periods inferior to civilisation.)

It is only during the past hundred years that we have been in the third phase of civilisation; but in this short space of time the phase has advanced very rapidly, owing to the colossal progress of industry; so that to-day the third phase exceeds its natural limits. We have too much material for a stage so little advanced; and, this material not finding its natural employment, there is a consequent overloading and discomfort in the social mechanism. This results in a fermentation which taints it; it develops a great number of malevolent characteristics, symptoms of lassitude, effects of the disproportion which exists between our industrial means and the inferior stage to which they are applied. We have too much industry for a civilisation so little advanced, detained in the third phase; it is besieged by the need of raising itself at least to the fourth; thence arise the properties of exuberance and deterioration, of which I shall enumerate the most salient.—(N. M., 418.)

We shall not follow the right path until we establish guaranteeism. It is a stratagem which ought to be employed to oppose liberalism, a stationery spirit which is incapable of advancing, and which is enamoured of a characteristic of the second phase, the *representative system,* a little scheme good in a small republic such as Sparta or Athens, but altogether illusory in a vast and opulent empire like France.—(N. M., 388.)

Every society has a greater or less admixture of characteristics taken from superior or inferior periods; the French, for instance have lately adopted the *unity of industrial and administrative relations;* this method, which is one of the characteristics of the sixth period, was introduced by the uniform metric system and the civil code of Napoleon, two institutions opposed to the civilised Order, one of whose characteristics is the *incoherence of industrial and administrative relations.* We have, then, on this point, *deviated from Civilisation and worked into the sixth period.* We have worked into it on other points also, notably by *religious toleration.* The English, who practise a degree of intolerance worthy of the twelfth century, are in this respect more civilised than we. The Germans likewise are more civilised than we as regards the incoherence of laws, customs, and industrial relations; in Germany one encounters at every turn different measures, sorts of money, laws, and usages, by which means a stranger is robbed and cheated far more easily than if there were but one kind of measure, money, code, etc. This chaos of relations is favourable to the mechanism of civilisation, which seeks, as its aim, to raise knavery to the highest point; and this would be attained by fully developing the sixteen special characteristics of civilisation.

Nevertheless philosophers maintain "that civilisation has been raised by the adoption of religious toleration, industrial and administrative unity." That is expressing one's self very poorly; they should have said that *the social Order has been raised and Civilisation lowered;* in reality, if all the sixteen characteristics of the sixth period were successively adopted it would result in the total annihilation of Civilisation,—it would be destroyed under the belief that it was being perfected. The social Order would be better organised, but the fifth would have been replaced by the sixth period. These distinctions of characteristics lead to an amusing conclusion: it is that *the little good to be found in the Civilised Order is due only to features that are contrary to Civilisation.*—(Q. M., 127.)

The associative Order will fulfil the wish of the nations, by securing to all progressive wealth, the object of everyone's desire: as for Civilisation, from which we are going to emerge, far from its being the industrial destiny of man, it is but a passing scourge with which most of the planets are afflicted during their first ages; it is for the human race a temporary malady, like teething for infants; it has been prolonged two thousand five hundred years too long through the inadventence or the pride of the sophists who have disdained all investigation of Association and Attraction; in fine, the Savage, Patriarchal, Barbarous, and Civilised forms of society are but the thorny paths, the ladders which are to lead us up to the social state which is the destiny of Man, and outside of which all the efforts of the best rulers are unable in any way to remedy the ills of mankind.

It is in vain, then, Philosophers, that you accumulate libraries to search for happiness, while the root of all the social ills has not been eradicated,— *industrial parcelling* or incoherent labour which is the antipodes of God's designs. You complain that Nature refuses you the knowledge of her laws: well! if you have, up to the present, been unable to discover them, why do you hesitate to recognise the insufficiency of your methods and to seek new ones? Either Nature does not desire the happiness of man, or your methods are reproved by her, since they have not been able to wrest from her the secret which you are endeavouring to obtain. Do you see her refractory to the efforts of physicists as she is to yours? No, for they study her laws instead of dictating laws to her; and you only study to stifle the voice of Nature, to stifle the Attraction which is the interpreter of her designs, since it leads on every hand to domestic-agricultural Association.

What a contrast, therefore, between your blunderings and the achievements of the exact sciences! Each day you add new errors to the old ones, while each day sees the physical sciences advancing upon the road of truth and shedding a lustre upon modern times equal to the opprobrium which has been cast upon them by the visions of regeneration of the sophists.—(U. U., ii., 128, 129.)

✧

"OF THE RÔLE OF THE PASSIONS," 1830

All those philosophical whims called duties have no relation whatever to Nature; duty proceeds from men, Attraction proceeds from God; now, if we desire to know the designs of God, we must study Attraction, Nature only, without any regard to duty, which varies with every age, while the nature of the passions has been and will remain invariable among all nations of men.—(Q. M., 107.)

The learned world is wholly imbued with a doctrine termed MORALITY, which is a mortal enemy of passional attraction.

Morality teaches man to be at war with himself to resist his passions, to repress them, to believe that God was incapable of organising our souls, our passions wisely; that he needed the teachings of Plato and Seneca in order to know how to distribute characteristics and instincts. Imbued with these prejudices regarding the impotence of God, the learned world was not qualified to estimate the natural impulses or passional attractions, which morality proscribes and relegates to the rank of vices.

It is true that these impulses entice us only to evil, if we yield to them individually; but we must calculate their effect upon a body of about two thousand persons socially combined, and not upon families or isolated individuals: this is what the learned world has not thought of; in studying it, it would have recognised that as soon as the number of associates (*sociétaires*) has reached 1600, the natural impulses, termed attractions, tend to form series of contrasting groups, in which everything incites to industry, become attractive, and to virtue, become lucrative.—(N. M., 125.)

The passions, believed to be the enemies of concord, in reality conduce to that unity from which we deem them so far removed. But outside of the mechanism termed *"exalted,"* emulatory, *interlocked (engrenées) Series*, they are but unchained tigers, incomprehensible enigmas. It is this which has caused philosophers to say that we ought to repress them; an opinion doubly absurd inasmuch as we can only repress our passions by *violence* or *absorbing replacement*, which replacement is no repression. On the other hand, should they be efficiently repressed, the civilised order would rapidly decline and relapse into the nomad state, where the passions would still be malevolent as with us. The virtue of shepherds is as doubtful as that of their apologists, and our utopia-makers, by thus attributing virtues to imaginary peoples, only succeed in proving the impossibility of introducing virtue into civilisation.—(U. U., iii., 33.)

From *Selections From The Works of Fourier,* Julia Franklin, Trans. Published by Swan Sonnenschein & Co., 1901.

We are quite familiar with the five *sensitive* passions tending to Luxury, the four *affective* ones tending to Groups; it only remains for us to learn about the three *distributive* ones whose combined impulse produces *Series,* a social method of which the secret has been lost since the age of primitive mankind, who were unable to maintain the Series more than about 300 years.—(Q. M., 118.)

The four *affective* passions tending to form the four groups of friendship, love, ambition, paternity or consanguinity are familiar enough; but no analyses, or parallels, or scales have been made of them.

The three others, termed distributive, are totally misunderstood, and bear only the title of VICES, although they are infinitely precious; for these three possess the property of forming and directing the series of groups, the mainspring of social harmony. Since these series are not formed in the civilised order, the three distributive passions cause disorder only. Let us define them.—(U. U., i., 145.) . . .

The principle which must be our starting-point is, *that a general perfection in industry will be attained by the universal demands and refinement of the consumers, regarding food and clothing, furniture and amusements.*—(N. M., 253.)

Of what service would the great perfection of culture in every variety of production be to the Harmonians if they had to deal with a public moral and uniform in its tastes, eating only to moderate their passions, and forbidding themselves all sensual refinement, for the benefit of repressive morality. In that case, the general perfection of products would decline from lack of appreciation, the cabalistic spirit would lose its activity among the groups of producers and preparers, agricultural industry would sink back into rudeness, such as we have to-day, when we find scarcely a hundredth part of the civilised capable of judging of the excellence of a commodity; as a consequence, a vendor who deals in false wares has ninety-nine chances of selling against one of rejection: that is why all provisions are so poor in civilisation.

To obviate this disorder, the associative state will train children to the cabalistic spirit in three directions: in consumption, preparation, and production. It will accustom them from an early age to develop and direct their taste in regard to every dish, every savour, and every form of preparing food; to exact in the most insignificant viands modes of cooking varied in accordance with the various tastes; to form, in short, the cabalistic scale in consumption, which will result in its being extended to the work of preparing, preserving, and producing.—(N. M., 71.)

In the civilised order, where labour is repugnant, where the people are too poor to participate in the consumption of choice foods, and where the epicure is not a cultivator, his epicurism lacks a *direct* bond with cultivation; it is nothing but sensuality, *simple* and ignoble, as is all else which does not attain to *composite* mechanism, or the influence of production and consumption acting upon the same individual.—(U. U., iii., 50.)

The argument would be the same for each of the passions which you term vices. You will recognise by the theory of the combined order that all our characteristics are good and judiciously distributed, that we ought to develop and not correct Nature.

Starting from this principle, we must conclude that the greater the number of pleasures and the more often they are varied, the less shall we be able to abuse them, for pleasures, like labour, become a pledge of health when practised in moderation. A dinner of an hour, diversified by animated conversation which precludes haste and gluttony, will necessarily be moderate, and serve to restore and augment our energies, which would be exhausted by a long repast, liable to be immoderate, such as our great dinners in civilisation.

Harmony, which will offer, particularly to the rich, a choice of pleasures every hour, nay, even every quarter of an hour, will prevent all excesses by the mere fact of the multiplicity of enjoyments; their frequent succession will be a guarantee of moderation and health. Thenceforth everyone will gain in vigour in proportion to the number of his amusements,—an effect contrary to that produced by them in the civilised mechanism, where the most voluptuous class is everywhere the one soonest deprived of vigour. We must not lay the blame of this upon pleasures but upon the *rarity of pleasures,* which gives rise to excesses which seem to justify the moralists in condemning an epicurean mode of life.

Sanitary order, or equilibrium and moderation in the use of our senses, will spring, then, from the very abundance of pleasures which today are so pernicious on account of the excesses provoked by their rarity.—(U. U., iii., 155.)

My theory confines itself to *utilising the passions now condemned, just as Nature has given them to us and without in any way changing them.* That is the whole mystery, the whole secret of the calculus of passionate Attraction. There is no arguing there whether God was right or wrong in giving mankind these or those passions; the associative order avails itself of them without changing them, and as God has given them to us.—(U. U., iv., 157.)

Its mechanism produces co-incidence in every respect between individual interest and collective interest, in civilisation always divergent.

It makes use of men as they are, utilising the discords arising from antipathies, and other motives accounted vicious, and vindicating the Creator from the reproach of a lacuna in providence, in the matter of general unity and individual foresight.

Finally, it in nowise disturbs the established order, limiting itself to trial on a small scale, which will incite to imitation by the double allurement of quadruple proceeds and attractive industry.—(F. L, 497.)

❧

"OF THE CONDITION OF WOMEN," 1808

Every period has a certain characteristic which forms the *pivot of mechanism,* and the absence or presence of which determines the change of periods. This characteristic is always derived from

From *Selections From The Works of Fourier,* Julia Franklin, Trans. Published by Swan Sonnenschein & Co., 1901.

love. In the fourth period it is the *absolute servitude of woman;* in the fifth period it is *exclusive marriage and civil liberties of the wife; in the sixth period it is the amorous corporation* which ensures women the privilege of which I have spoken above. If a barbarous people adopted *exclusive marriage,* they would in a short time become civilised through this innovation alone; if we adopted the *seclusion and sale of women,* we should in a short time become barbarous through this single innovation; and if we adopted the *amorous guarantees,* we should find in this single measure an exit from civilisation and an entrance into the sixth period.

If God has endowed amorous customs with such great influence upon the social mechanism and upon the metamorphoses which it is capable of undergoing, this must be a consequence of his horror of oppression and violence; he desired the well-being or the misery of human societies to be proportional to the constraint or freedom which they would allow. Now God recognises as freedom only that which is extended to both sexes and not to one alone; he desired, likewise, that all the seeds of social abominations such as savagery, barbarism, civilisation, should have as their sole pivot the subjection of women, and that all the seeds of social well-being such as the sixth, seventh, eighth periods should have no pivot but the progressive enfranchisement of the weak sex.—(Q. M., 131.)

As a general proposition: *Social advances and changes of periods are brought about by virtue of the progress of women towards liberty, and the decadences of the social order are brought about by virtue of the decrease of liberty of women.*

Other events influence these political vicissitudes; but there is no cause which so rapidly produces social progress or decline as a change in the condition of women. I have already said that the adoption of closed harems would of itself soon transform us into barbarians, and the opening of the harems would of itself cause a people to pass from barbarism to civilisation. To sum up, *the extension of privileges to women is the general principle of all social progress.*—(Q. M., 195.)

It is not always an advantage to introduce a characteristic of a higher period; it may in certain cases become perverted by this political transplanting, and produce evil consequences; witness *free divorce,* which is a characteristic of the sixth period, and which has produced so much disorder in civilisation that it has been necessary to assign to it the narrowest limits. Nevertheless, free divorce is a very salutary custom in the sixth period, and there contributes eminently to domestic harmony; for it is there combined with other characteristics which do not exist in civilisation. We may see by this, that discretion must be employed in introducing a characteristic of one period into another, just as in transporting a plant into a climate not its own. [1] It was a mistake to suppose that unlimited religious toleration could be fitted for the civilised; in the long run, it would produce in agricultural states more evil than good if it did not accept religions which are characterised by the morals of the fourth, third, and second periods, such as Mohammedanism, Judaism, and idolatry. As for the present, their admission is a matter of indifference, since civilisation is drawing to its close.—(Q. M., 129.)

I do not mean to criticise civilised education here, or to insinuate that we ought to inspire women with a spirit of liberty. Assuredly, it is necessary that each social period should fashion its youth to reverence the dominant absurdities; and if in the barbarous order it is necessary to brutalise women, to persuade them that they have no souls, so as to dispose them to allow themselves to be sold in the market or shut up in a harem, it is likewise necessary in the civilised order to stupefy women from their infancy, so as to make them fit the philosophic dogmas, the servitude of marriage, and the debasement of falling into the power of a husband whose character will perhaps be the opposite of theirs. Now, since I should blame a barbarian who trained his daughters for the usages of the civilised state in which they will never live, I should likewise blame a civilised man who trained his daughters in a spirit of liberty and right peculiar to the sixth and seventh periods, which we have not attained.[2]

If I accuse the prevailing education and the servile spirit with I which it inspires women, I speak in relation to other societies where it will be unnecessary to pervert their character by force of prejudices. I indicate to them the distinguished position they might attain, following the example of those who have overcome the influences of education and resisted the oppressive system which the conjugal tie necessitates. In pointing to those women who have succeeded in spreading their wings, from viragos like Maria Theresa to those of a milder shade, like the Ninons and the Sévignés, I am justified in saying that woman in a state of liberty will excel man in all function of the mind or the body which are not the attributes that of physical force.

Already does man seem to have a premonition of this; he becomes indignant and alarmed when women belie the prejudice which accuses them of inferiority. Masculine jealousy has burst forth above all against women writers; philosophy has eliminated them from academic honours and thrust them ignominiously back to household concerns.

Was not this affront the proper due of learned women? The slave who wishes to ape his master merits from him only a glance of contempt. What concern had they with the vulgar glory of composing a book, of adding a few volumes to the millions of useless ones already in existence? What women were called to produce was not writers but liberators, a political Spartacus, geniuses who would devise means for raising their sex from degradation.

It is upon women that civilisation weighs; it was for women to attack it. What is their existence to-day? They live only by privation, even in industry, where man has invaded everything down to the petty occupations of sewing and the pen, while women are to be seen drudging at the painful labours of the field. Is it not scandalous to see athletes of thirty stooping over a desk, or transporting a cup of coffee with their shaggy arms, as if women and children were lacking to attend to these trifling duties of the desk and the household?

What, then, are the means of subsistence for women without a fortune? The distaff or it may be their charms, if they possess any. Yes, prostitution more or less veiled is their sole resource, and philosophy denies them even that; this is the abject fate to which they are reduced by that civilisation, that conjugal slavery, which they have not even thought of attacking. That was the only problem worthy of engaging women writers; their indolence in regard to it is one of the causes which have increased man's contempt. Slavery is never more contemptible than when by a blind submission it convinces the oppressor that his victim is born for slavery.—(Q. M., 220, 221.)

Civilised love, in marriage, is, at the end of a few months, or perhaps the second day, often nothing but pure brutality, chance coupling, induced by the domestic tie, devoid of any illusion of the mind or of the heart: a result very common among the masses where husband and wife, surfeited, morose, quarrelling with each other during the day, become necessarily reconciled upon retiring, because they have not the means to purchase two beds, and contact, the brute spur of the senses, triumphs a moment over conjugal satiety. If this be love, it is a love most material and trivial.

And yet this is the snare upon which philosophy reckons to transform the most gracious of the passions into a source of political dupery, to excite the rapid growth of population, and stimulate the poor by the sight of their progeny in rags. What a noble *rôle* assigned to love, in exchange for the freedom ravished from her! She is made among the civilised a provider of food for cannon; and among barbarians, a persecutor of the weaker half of humanity: these are, under the names of harem and marriage, the honourable functions which are assigned to love by our pretended lovers of liberty!

Confounded by the vices of their love-polity, they repel every suggestion of estimating the properties of free love. Ignorant and deceitful as to the proper uses of liberty, they desire it to be unlimited in commerce, where crime and roguery everywhere require the curb of the law; and they deprive love of all liberty—love whose vast scope in the passionate series would lead to all virtues, to all wonders in social politics. What an unlucky

science they make, these civilised theories; what an instinct of opposition to all the desires of nature and of truth!—(U. U., iv., 462.)

Notes

1. "All these new regenerators, Owen, Saint-Simon, and others, are strongly inclined to speculate upon the emancipation of women; they do not understand that before making any changes in the established order regarding the relations of love, many years are needed to create guarantees which do not now exist. . . . On the other hand, modifications in the regulation of love will only be applicable to a polished generation, educated entirely in the New Order, and faithful to certain laws of honour and delicacy which the Civilised make a sport of violating. A man is applauded in France if he succeeds in deceiving women and husbands; the morals of the Civilised are a sink of vice and duplicity. A generation trained to such usages could not but abuse an extension of liberty in love. . . ."

"And when the admission of these liberties would be suitable as far as fortune and manners are concerned, they will be introduced only *by degrees* and not suddenly. . . . Each liberty will be admitted only after it shall have been voted for throughout the entire globe, by the fathers and husbands; then it may be believed to be useful. The effect of these liberties will be a powerful contribution to the charm of labour, the increase of production, and the reign of loyal morals; but in civilisation we should witness only the production of the three opposite effects." (1831, *Pièg et Charl. des deux sect S.-Sim. et Ow.,* p. 53).—(Q. M., 155.)

2. To speak plainly, the fathers play a vile *rôle* in civilisation when they have any daughters to marry off. I can conceive how paternal affection may blind them to the infamy of the manoeuvres and cajoleries to which they resort in order to entice marriageable men; but they can at least not blind themselves as to the anxieties and contemptibleness of such a *rôle*. How ardently ought those who are overburdened with daughters to desire the invention of a new domestic Order, where marriage no longer exists, and where one is relieved of the care of providing girls with husbands, and what fervent thanks do they owe him who brings them this invention!—(Q. M., 168.)

part III

THE INVENTION OF MODERN SOCIAL THEORY

Auguste Comte   *1798–1857*

John Stuart Mill   *1806–1873*

Adolphe Quetelet   *1796–1874*

Alexis Tocqueville   *1805–1859*

Frederick Douglass   *1817–1895*

Karl Marx   *1818–1883*

Søren Kierkegaard   *1813–1855*

Harriet Taylor Mill   *1807–1858*

Arthur Schopenhauer   *1788–1860*

Herbert Spencer   *1820–1903*

Harriet Martineau   *1802–1876*

Joseph-Arthur Gobineau, Comte de   *1816–1882*

(Pierre-Gillaume-) Frédéric Le Play   *1806–1882*

John Ruskin   *1819–1900*

Matthew Arnold   *1822–1888*

Aleksandr I. Herzen   *1812–1870*

Henry Sumner Maine   *1822–1888*

Numa Denis Fustel de Coulanges   *1830–1889*

Charles Darwin   *1809–1882*

Edward Burnett Tylor   *1832–1917*

Friedrich Engels   *1820–1895*

AUGUSTE COMTE

1798–1857

Son of Louis, a tax official, and Rosalie Boyer, both fiercely royalist and devout Catholics, Isidore-Auguste-Marie-François-Xavier Comte was born on January 19, 1798 in Montpellier, France. He married Caroline Massin (wrongly considered a prostitute) in 1825, but they separated in 1842 without offspring. He found love with Clotilde de Vaux in 1845, but before they could become disillusioned, she died of tuberculosis in 1846. His posthumous adoration of her prompted him to rethink the role of women generally. Comte died on September 5, 1857 in Paris of stomach cancer.

Comte's education, unlike most of the philosophes, revolved around mathematics, for which he showed a prodigy's aptitude, matriculating at the École Polytechnique at only 16. Two years later the school was closed for a time, and he cobbled together a small income by tutoring math and journalism. Meanwhile, he read deeply and widely, particularly among authors who catalogued patterns in historical change, e.g., Montesquieu, Condorcet, Turgot, and de Maistre. His single most important influence was Saint-Simon, for whom he worked as a research assistant and collaborator from 1818 through 1824 until disagreements over proprietary control of certain ideas led to a fissure in their close association. If one reads Turgot's theory of civilizational stages or Saint-Simon's notions about the effects of industrialization on society, the major lineaments of Comte's theories show through. In addition, Comte, as a trained scientist and technician, was much taken with positivism as devised by Hume and Kant, and carried further by his English admirer and financial sponsor, J. S. Mill.

For Comte the world is knowable by scientific methods of investigation, and anything not so known is not worth pursuing or simply beyond human cognitive reach. Writing in a spirit that is still quite prevalent among certain social scientists, he believed that the same procedures of study which had produced such stunning successes in the natural sciences could, if properly refashioned, enjoy the same in the human sciences. It was this notion that caused him in 1839 to invent the word "sociology," a barbarous neologism created from forcing together a Greek and a Latin root. Comte's immortalization in sociology stems not only from having invented the word, but also from proposing that all human societies move through three stages, from the theological to the metaphysical and culminating in the positive. The final stage he regarded as the best, though it required special handling by a "priesthood" of secularized sociologists, who would promulgate myths for the masses while discreetly organizing the social order along positivist lines. He explained his plan in *The Positive Philosophy* (6 volumes, 1830–1842) and *The System of Positive Polity* (4 volumes, 1851–54). Their English translations, by Harriet Martineau, created a cult of Comteans in Britain and the U.S. which included important thinkers and social actors. Though personally very difficult to deal with—spiteful, egocentric, and dark in mood—he worked tirelessly for decades in hopes of creating a new system of analysis and beliefs that could stem the tide of revolutionary destruction in Europe, and benefit humanity at large.

PLAN OF THE SCIENTIFIC OPERATIONS NECESSARY FOR REORGANIZING SOCIETY, 1822

Introduction

A social system in its decline, a new system arrived at maturity and approaching its completion—such is the fundamental character that the general progress of civilization has assigned to the present epoch. In conformity with this state of things, two movements, differing in their nature, agitate society—one a movement of disorganization, the other of reorganization. By the former, considered apart, society is hurried towards a profound moral and political anarchy, which appears to menace it with a near and inevitable dissolution. By the latter it is guided to the definitive social condition of the human race, that best suited to its nature, and in which all progressive movements should receive their completest development and most direct application. In the coexistence of these two opposed tendencies consists the grand crisis now experienced by the most civilized nations; and this can be understood only when viewed under both aspects.

From the moment when this crisis began to show itself to the present time, the tendency of the ancient system to disorganization has predominated, or rather it alone is still plainly manifested. It was in the nature of things that the crisis should begin thus, so that the old system might be sufficiently modified to permit the direct formation of the new social system.

But now that this condition has been fully satisfied and the Catholico-feudal system has lost its power, as far as is possible, until the new system has been inaugurated, the preponderance still maintained by the negative tendency constitutes the greatest obstacle to the progress of civilization and even to the abolition of the ancient system. Its persistence forms the first cause of those terrible and continually renewed shocks by which the crisis is accompanied.

The only way of ending this stormy situation, of staying the anarchy that day by day invades society—in a word, of reducing the crisis to a simple moral movement—consists in inducing the civilized nations to abandon the negative and to adopt an organic attitude; turning all their efforts towards the formation of the new social system as the definitive object of the crisis and that for the attainment of which everything hitherto accomplished is only a preparation.

Such is the prime necessity of the present epoch. Such also is the general scope of my labors and the special aim of this essay, the object of which is to set in motion the forces capable of bringing society into the track of the new system.

A brief examination of the causes that have hitherto hindered and still do hinder society from frankly assuming an organic attitude should naturally precede an exposition of the measures necessary for effecting this object.

The numerous and repeated attempts made by the people and kings to reorganize society prove that the need of such a reorganization is generally felt. But on both sides it is only felt in a vague and imperfect manner. These two kinds of attempts are, though for different reasons, equally vicious. To the present time they have not, nor could they have, produced any real organic result. Far from tending to terminate the crisis, these efforts only contribute to prolong it. Such is the true cause that, in spite of so many efforts, by keeping society in the negative track, leaves it a prey to revolutions.

To establish this fundamental proposition, it is sufficient to take a general view of the attempts at reorganization undertaken by kings and the people.

The error committed by kings is easier to understand. For them the reorganization of society means the re-establishment pure and simple of the feudal and theological system in all its integrity. In their eyes no other means exist of terminating the anarchy that results from the decline of this system.

It would be unphilosophical to regard this view as if it were dictated mainly by the special interests of the governing classes. Chimerical though it be, this idea naturally presented itself to minds seeking, in good faith, a remedy for the existing crisis. They feel in its entire extent the need for a reorganization; but they have not considered the general progress of civilization, and, viewing the present state of affairs under one aspect only, they do not perceive the tendency of society to establish a new system more perfect, and not less harmonious, than the ancient one. In a word, it is natural that this view should be taken by rulers, since from their position they must of necessity perceive more clearly the anarchic state of society and consequently experience more forcibly the necessity for applying a remedy.

This is not the place to insist on the manifest absurdity of such an opinion, which is now universally recognized by the majority of enlightened men. Doubtless kings, while seeking to reconstruct the ancient system, do not comprehend the nature of the present crisis and are far from having measured the magnitude of their enterprise.

The downfall of the feudal and theological system does not spring, as they believe, from recent, solitary, and in some sort accidental causes. Their downfall, in place of being the effect of the crisis, is, on the contrary, its source. The decline of this system has come to pass continuously during the preceding centuries, by reason of a series of modifications, independent of the human will, to which all classes of society contributed, and of which kings themselves have often been the first agents and most eager promoters. In a word, it was the necessary consequence of the progress of civilization.

In order then to re-establish the ancient system, it would not be sufficient to push society back to the epoch when the existing crisis began to reveal itself. For, even supposing this could be done, which it could not, we should have merely replaced the body politic in the situation that necessitated the crisis. Retracing past ages, it would be requisite to repair, one by one, all the losses suffered by the ancient system during six centuries in comparison with which all that it has lost for the last thirty years is of no importance.

No other mode of effecting this would be possible but to annihilate all the results of civilization that have caused this decline.

Thus, for example, it would be absurd to assume that the eighteenth-century philosophy—itself the direct cause of the downfall of the ancient system considered in its spiritual aspects—could be destroyed unless we also assumed the annihilation of the sixteenth century, of which the philosophy of the last century is only the consequence and development. But, as the Reformation of Luther is, in its turn, simply a necessary result of the progress of the sciences of observation introduced into Europe by the Arabs, the re-establishment of the ancient system would not have been secured unless the positive sciences had been also suppressed.

In like manner, under temporal aspects, we should be led, step by step, to the necessity for replacing the industrial classes in a state of servitude, since in the last resort the enfranchisement of the commons is the first and general cause of the decline of the feudal system. Finally such an enterprise is set in its true light by this reflection, that after overcoming so many difficulties, the least of which taken by itself surpasses the power of man, we should have gained nothing but the postponement of the definitive fall of the ancient system by thus obliging society to recommence its destruction, since the principle of progressive civilization inherent in human nature would not have been extinguished.

It is manifest that no person could entertain a project that is monstrous, whether we consider its magnitude or its absurdity. Man, in spite of himself, belongs to his epoch. Those who oppose, as they believe, the greatest resistance to the progress of civilization unconsciously obey its irresistible influence, nay themselves second it. . . .

The manner in which the people have hitherto understood the reorganization of society is no less erroneous than that adopted by kings, though in a different way. Their error, however, is more excusable, since it lies in a misconception of the new system towards which the progress of civilization transports them, though its nature has not, as yet, been clearly determined; while kings pursue an enterprise the entire absurdity of which is plainly demonstrable, even by a superficial study of the past. In a word, kings are at variance with facts, the people with principles, the last being always more difficult to grasp. But it is much more important to eradicate the misconception of the people than that of kings, because the former constitutes an essential obstacle to the progress of civilization, and alone gives some show of reason to the latter.

The characteristic view that predominates in the popular mind as to the mode of reorganizing society indicates a profound ignorance of the fundamental conditions necessary to give consistency to any social system.

It essentially consists in attributing an organic character to the negative principles that served to destroy the feudal and theological system: in other words, it mistakes mere modifications of the old system for the system that has to be established.

If we attentively examine the doctrines now accredited among the people as exhibited in the speeches of their ablest adherents and as expounded in the most systematic writings, considered in themselves and in their successive growth, we shall find that they are conceived in a purely critical spirit, incapable of affording any basis for reorganization.

The government, which in a regular state of affairs stands at the head of society as the guide and agent of general activity, is, by these doctrines, systematically despoiled of every active influence. Deprived of any important participation in the organic life of the body politic, it is reduced to an office of mere negation. It is even thought that the entire action of the body politic upon its members ought to be strictly limited to the maintenance of public tranquillity. But in no active society has this ever been other than a subordinate object, the importance of which has even been singularly diminished by the development of civilization, since this has made it easy to maintain order.

Government is, thus, no longer regarded as the head of society destined to bind together the component units and to direct their activity to a common end. It is represented as a natural enemy encamped in the midst of our social system against which society needs to fortify itself by the guarantees already obtained while maintaining a permanent attitude of mistrust and defensive hostility ready to break forth at the first symptom of attack.

CONCLUSION: THE RELIGION OF HUMANITY, 1854

Love, then, is our principle; order our basis; and progress our end. Such, as the preceding chapters have shown, is the essential character of the system of life that positivism offers for the definite acceptance of society, a system that regulates the whole course of our private and public existence by bringing feeling, reason, and activity into permanent harmony. In this final synthesis, all essential conditions are far more perfectly fulfilled than in any other. Each special element of our nature is more fully developed, and at the same time the general working of the whole is more coherent Greater distinctness is given to the truth that the affective element predominates in our nature. Life in all its actions and thoughts is brought under the control and inspiring charm of social sympathy. . . .

And while reason is admitted to its due share of influence on human life, imagination is also strengthened and called into constant exercise, assuming henceforth its proper function, the idealization of truth. For the external basis of our conceptions, scientific investigation is necessary. But this basis once obtained, the constitution of our mind is far better adapted to aesthetic than to scientific study, provided always that imagination recognizes the controlling influence of science so well calculated to restrain its extravagance. . . .

Originating in the first instance with practical life, positivism will return thither with increased force, now that its long period of scientific preparation is accomplished, and that it has occupied the field of moral truth, henceforth its principal domain. Its principle of sympathy, so far from relaxing our efforts, will stimulate all our faculties to universal activity by urging them onwards towards perfection of every kind. Scientific study of the natural order is inculcated solely with the view of directing all the forces of man and of

From *Auguste Comte and Positivism: The Essential Writings,* Gertrud Lenzer, Ed. Published by Harper Torchbooks. Copyright © 1975.

society to its improvement by artificial effort. . . . Our theoretical powers once concentrated on the moral problems that form their principal field, our practical energies will not fail to take the same direction, devoting themselves to that portion of the natural order that is most imperfect and at the same time most modifiable. With these larger and more systematic views of human life, its best efforts will be given to the improvement of the mind, and still more to the improvement of the character and to the increase of affection and courage. Public and private life are now brought into close relation by the identity of their principal aims, which, being kept constantly in sight, ennoble every action in both. Practical questions must ever continue to preponderate, as before, over questions of theory, but this condition, so far from being adverse to speculative power, concentrates it upon the most difficult of all problems, the discovery of moral and social laws, our knowledge of which will never be fully adequate to our practical requirements. . . .

This, then, is the shape in which the great human problem comes definitely before us. Its solution demands all the appliances of social art. The primary principle on which the solution rests is the separation of the two elementary powers of society: the moral power of counsel, and the political power of command. The necessary preponderance of the latter, which rests upon material force, corresponds to the fact that in our imperfect nature, where the coarser wants are the most pressing and the most continuously felt, the selfish instincts are naturally stronger than the unselfish. Without this compulsory pressure, even our individual action would be feeble and purposeless, and social life still more certainly would lose its character and its energy. Moral force, therefore, resting on conviction and persuasion, should remain simply a modifying influence, never assuming imperative authority.

Originating in feeling and in reason, it represents the social side of our nature, and to this its direct influence is limited. Indeed, by the very fact that it is the expression of our highest attributes, it is precluded from that practical ascendancy that is possessed by faculties of a lower but more energetic kind. Inferior to material force in power, though superior to it in dignity, it contrasts and opposes its own classification of men according to

the standard of moral and intellectual worth, to the classification by wealth and worldly position that actually prevails. True, the higher standard will never be adopted practically, but the effort to uphold it will react beneficially on the natural order of society. It will restore the breadth of view and the sense of duty that are so apt to be impaired by the ordinary course of daily life.

The means of effecting this important result, the need of which is so generally felt, will not be wanting when the moderating power enters upon its characteristic function of preparing us for practical life by a rational system of education, throughout which, even in its intellectual department, moral considerations will predominate. This power will therefore concentrate itself upon theoretical and moral questions, and it can only maintain its position as the recognized organ of social sympathy by invariable abstinence from political action. It will be its first duty to contend against the ambitious instincts of its own members. True, such instincts, in spite of the impurity of their source, may be of use in those names who are really destined for the indispensable business of government. But for a spiritual power formal renunciation of wealth and rank is at the very root of its influence; it is the first of the conditions that justify it in resisting the encroachments to which political power is always tempted. Hence the classes to whose natural sympathies it looks for support are those who, like itself, are excluded from political administration.

Women, from their strongly sympathetic nature, were the original source of all moral influence, and they are peculiarly qualified by the passive character of their life to assist the action of the spiritual power in the family. With its most essential function of education they are intimately connected. Private education is entrusted to their sole charge, and public education simply consists in giving a more systematic shape to what the mother has already inculcated in childhood. As wives they assume still more distinctly the spiritual function of counsel, softening by persuasion where the philosopher can only influence by conviction. In social meetings, again, the only mode of public life adapted to their nature, they assist the spiritual power in the formation of public opinion of which it is the systematic organ, by applying the principles that it inculcates to the case of particular actions or persons. In all these matters their influence will be far more effectual when men have done their duty to women by setting them free from the pressure of material necessity, and when women on their side have renounced both power and wealth, as we see so often exemplified among the working classes.

The affinity of the people with the philosophic power is less direct and less pure, but it will be an active agent in removing the obstacles that the temporal power will inevitably oppose. The working classes, having but little spare time and small individual influence, cannot, except on rare occasions, participate in the practical administration of government, since all efficient government involves concentration of power. Moral force, on the contrary, created as it is by free convergence of opinion, admits of, and indeed requires, the widest ramification. Workingmen, owing to their freedom from practical responsibilities and their unconcern for personal aggrandizement, are better disposed than their employers to broad views and to generous sympathies, and will therefore naturally associate themselves with the spiritual power. It is they who will supply the principal basis of true public opinion, as soon as they are enabled by positive education, which is specially framed with a view to their case, to give greater definiteness to their aspirations. Their wants and their sympathies will alike bring them into contact with the philosophic priesthood as the systematic guardian of their interests against the governing classes. In return for such protection they will bring the whole weight of their influence to assist the priesthood in its great social mission, the subordination of government to morality. In those exceptional cases where it becomes necessary for the moderating power to assume political functions, the popular element will of itself suffice for the emergency, thus exempting the philosophic element from participating in an anomaly from which its character would suffer almost as seriously as the feminine element.

The direct influence of reason over our imperfect nature is so feeble that the new priesthood could not of itself ensure such respect for its theories as would bring them to any practical result. But the sympathies of women and of the people, operating in every town and in every family, will be sufficient to ensure its efficacy in organizing that legitimate degree of moral pressure that the poor may bring to bear upon the rich. Moreover, it will be one of the results of our common system of education that additional aid will spring from the governing classes themselves, for some of their noblest members will volunteer their assistance to the spiritual power, forming a sort of new chivalry. And yet, comprehensive as our organization of moral force will be, so great is the innate strength of the selfish instincts that our success in solving the great human problem will always fall short of what we might legitimately desire. To this conclusion we must come, in whatever way we regard the destiny of man, but it should only encourage us to combine our efforts still more strongly in order to ameliorate the order of nature in its most important aspects—those which are at once the most modifiable and the most imperfect. . . .

The only cases in which the spiritual power has to interfere specially for the protection of material interests fall under two principles, which are very plainly indicated by the natural order of society. The first principle is that man should support woman; the second, that the active class should support the speculative class. The necessity of both these conditions is evident: without them the affective and speculative functions of humanity cannot be adequately performed. . . .As to the second principle, it is one that has been already admitted by former systems. . . .If temporal and spiritual power are really to be separated, philosophers should have as little to do with wealth as with government. Resembling women in their exclusion from political power, their position as to wealth should be like that of the working classes, proper regard being given to the requirements of their office. By following this course, they may be confident that the purity of their opinions and advice will never be called in question.

These two conditions, then, capitalists, as the normal administrators of the common fund of wealth, will be expected to satisfy. They must, that is, so regulate the distribution of wages that women shall be released from work, and they must see that proper remuneration is given for intellectual labor. To exact the performance of these conditions seems no easy task; yet until they are satisfied, the equilibrium of our social economy will remain unstable. The present holders of a position that is no longer tenable on the imaginary ground of personal right may probably decline to accept these principles. In that case, their functions will pass in one way or another to new organs, until humanity finds servants who will not shirk their fundamental duties, but who will recognize them as the first condition of their tenure of power. . . . Rich men will feel that principles like these, leaving as they do to the individual the merit of voluntary action, are the only method of escaping from the political oppression with which they are now threatened. The free concentration of capital will then be readily accepted as necessary to its social usefulness, for great duties imply great powers.

This, then, is the way in which the priests of humanity may hope to regenerate the material power of wealth and bring the nutritive functions of society into harmony with the other parts of the body politic. The contests for which as yet there are but too many motives will then cease. . . .

From this view of the practical side of the religion of humanity taken in connection with its intellectual and moral side, we may form a general conception of the final reorganization of political institutions, by which alone the great Revolution can be brought to a close. But the time for effecting this reconstruction has not yet come. There must be a previous reconstruction of opinions and habits of life upon the basis laid down by positivism, and for this at least one generation is required. In the interval, all political measures must retain their provisional character, although in framing them the final state is always to be taken into account. As yet nothing can be said to have been established, except the moral principle on which positivism rests—the subordination of politics to morals. For this is in fact implicitly involved in the proclamation of a republic in France, a step that cannot now be recalled, and that implies that each citizen is to devote all his faculties to the service of humanity. But as to the social organization by which alone this principle can be carried into effect, although its basis has been laid down by positivism, it has not yet received the sanction of the public. It may be hoped, however, that the motto that I have put forward as descriptive of the new political philosophy, *Order and Progress*, will soon be adopted spontaneously.

JOHN STUART MILL

1806–1873

John Stuart Mill was born on May 20, 1806 in Pentonville, London. He married the widow, Mrs. Harriet Hardy Taylor, in 1851 and together they wrote important works concerning women's rights. He died just shy of his 67th birthday on May 8, 1873 in Avignon, where Harriet had been buried 15 years before. As is widely known, he was phenomenally educated by his father, documented by Mill in his famous *Autobiography* (1873). By the age of eight, he knew enough Greek to read Aesop, Xenophon, Lucian, six dialogues of Plato, and Isocrates. He also read a great deal of history, and began Latin at eight, plus geometry and algebra. At ten he was reading Plato and Demosthenes easily, and had begun teaching other children in the home. At twelve be studied Aristotle's logic in Greek, then medieval logicians in Latin, and when 13 began a study of political-economy, including works of Adam Smith and David Ricardo. He traveled to France at 14 to study natural sciences and math, living with Jeremy Bentham's brother. He then studied Roman law with John Austin. After this the prodigy began work at the headquarters of the British East India Company, along with his father. Throughout this unique educational experiment, Mill was in constant contact with his ambitious and rigorous father, who became as much a companion to him as parent. Yet, as we would now know based on child research, even the most intelligent and willing youth subjected to this level of regimented learning will eventually suffer the consequences of an aborted childhood. Mill's nervous collapse finally came when he was 20, and from that experience he began to study the arts in place of only science and math. His newfound enthusiasm for poetry put him into conflict with his father, perhaps for the first time.

Mill also contributed mightily to the cause of Utilitarianism and Comteanism in the anglophone world. He started or worked for important journals and newspapers, edited Bentham's works, engaged notables in the London Debating Society, all the while working for the East India Company. He composed lasting essays on de Tocqueville, Bentham, Coleridge, and many others. His place in the history of social thought was guaranteed by two publications, *A System of Logic* (1843) and *Principles of Political Economy* (1848, 2 vols.), the former work providing in part an epistemological defense of the new social sciences, explaining their difference from natural science methods. Today Mill is as much known for his marriage to Harriet Taylor in 1851 as for his previously published works. He portrayed her as a co-genius and they wrote about women's issues together. (He also credited her as a virtual co-author for his *Political Economy,* but could not acknowledge her help while she was still married to John Taylor.) Her death after seven years of marriage was a terrible blow for Mill, partly because she had inspired him to think in new, more "human" ways than he had before, and his subsequent writings turned on notions they had discussed, e.g., *On Liberty* (1851), still widely read.

"THE SPIRIT OF THE AGE," 1831

The "spirit of the age" is in some measure a novel expression. I do not believe that it is to be met with in any work exceeding fifty years in antiquity. The idea of comparing one's own age with former ages, or with our notion of those which are yet to come, had occurred to philosophers; but it never before was itself the dominant idea of any age.

It is an idea essentially belonging to an age of change. Before men begin to think much and long on the peculiarities of their own times, they must have begun to think that those times are, or are destined to be, distinguished in a very remarkable manner from the times which preceded them. Mankind are then divided, into those who are still what they were, and those who have changed: into the men of the present age, and the men of the past. To the former, the spirit of the age is a subject of exultation; to the latter, of terror, to both, of eager and anxious interest. The wisdom of ancestors, and the march of intellect, are bandied from mouth to mouth; each phrase originally an expression of respect and homage, each ultimately usurped by the partisans of the opposite catch word, and in the bitterness of their spirit, turned into the sarcastic jibe of hatred and insult.

The present times possess this character. A change has taken place in the human mind; a change which, being effected by insensible gradations, and without noise, had already proceeded far before it was generally perceived. When the fact disclosed itself, thousands awoke as from a dream. They knew not what processes had been going on in the minds of others, or even in their own, until the change began to invade outward objects; and it became clear that those were indeed new men, who insisted upon being governed in a new way.

But mankind are now conscious of their new position. The conviction is already not far from being universal, that the times are pregnant with

change; and that the nineteenth century will be known to posterity as the era of one of the greatest revolutions of which history has preserved the remembrance, in the human mind, and in the whole constitution of human society. . . .

No man whose good qualities were mainly those of another age, ever had much influence on his own. And since every age contains in itself the germ of all future ages as surely as the acorn contains the future forest, a knowledge of our own age is the fountain of prophecy—the only key to the history of posterity. It is only in the present that we can know the future; it is only through the present that it is in our power to influence that which is to come.

The first of the leading peculiarities of the present age is, that it is an age of transition. Mankind have outgrown old institutions and old doctrines, and have not yet acquired new ones. When we say outgrown, we intend to prejudge nothing. A man may not be either better or happier at six-and-twenty, than he was at six years of age: but the same jacket which fitted him then, will not fit him now.

The prominent trait just indicated in the character of the present age, was obvious a few years ago only to the more discerning: at present it forces itself upon the most inobservant. Much might be said, and shall be said on a fitting occasion, of the mode in which the old order of things has become unsuited to the state of society and of the human mind. But when almost every nation on the continent of Europe has achieved, or is in the course of rapidly achieving, a change in its form of government, when our own country, at all former times the most attached in Europe to its old institutions, proclaims almost with one voice that they are vicious both in the outline and in the details, and that they *shall* be renovated, and purified, and made fit for civilized man, we may assume that a part of the effects of the cause just now pointed out, speak sufficiently loudly for themselves. To him who can reflect, even these are but indications which tell of a more vital and radical change. Not only, in the conviction of almost all men, things as they are, are wrong—but, according to that same conviction, it is not by remaining in the old ways that they can be set right. Society demands, and anticipates, not merely a new machine, but a machine constructed in another manner. Mankind will not be led by their old maxims, nor by their old guides; and they will not choose either their opinions or their guides as they have done heretofore. The ancient constitutional texts were formerly spells which would call forth or allay the spirit of the English people at pleasure: what has become of the charm? Who can hope to sway the minds of the public by the old maxims of law, or commerce, or foreign policy, or ecclesiastical policy? Whose feelings are now roused by the mottoes and watch-words of Whig and Tory? And what Whig or Tory could command ten followers in the warfare of politics, by the weight of his own personal authority? Nay, what landlord could call forth his tenants, or what manufacturer his men? Do the poor respect the rich, or adopt their sentiments? Do the young respect the old, or adopt their sentiments? Of the feelings of our ancestors it may almost be said that we retain only such as are the natural and necessary growth of a state of human society, however constituted; and I only adopt the energetic expression of a member of the House of Commons, less than two years ago, in saying of the young men, even of that rank in society, that they are ready to advertise for opinions.

Since the facts are so manifest, there is the more chance that a few reflections on their causes, and on their probable consequences, will receive whatever portion of the readers' attention they may happen to deserve.

With respect, then, to the discredit into which old institutions and old doctrines have fallen, I may premise, that this discredit is, in my opinion, perfectly deserved. Having said this, I may perhaps hope, that no perverse interpretation will be put upon the remainder of my observations, in case some of them should not be quite so conformable to the sentiments of the day as my commencement might give reason to expect. The best guide is not he who, when people are in the right path, merely praises it, but he who shows them the pitfalls and the precipices by which it is endangered; and of which, as long as they were in the wrong road, it was not so necessary that they should be warned.

There is one very easy, and very pleasant way of accounting for this general departure from the modes of thinking of our ancestors: so easy, indeed, and so pleasant, especially to the hearer, as to be very convenient to such writers for hire or for applause, as address themselves not to the men of the age that is gone by, but to the men of the age which has commenced. This explanation is that which ascribes the altered state of opinion and feeling to the growth of the human understanding. According to this doctrine, we reject the sophisms and prejudices which misled the uncultivated minds of our ancestors, because we have learnt too much, and have become too wise, to be imposed upon by such sophisms and such prejudices. It is our knowledge and our sagacity which keep us free from these gross errors. We have now risen to the capacity of perceiving our true interests; and it is no longer in the power of impostors and charlatans to deceive us.

I am unable to adopt this theory. Though a firm believer in the improvement of the age, I do not believe that its improvement has been of this kind. The grand achievement of the present age is the *diffusion* of *superficial* knowledge; and that surely is no trifle, to have been accomplished by a single generation. The persons who are in possession of knowledge adequate to the formation of sound opinions by their own lights, form also a constantly increasing number, but hitherto at all times a small one. It would be carrying the notion of the march of intellect too far, to suppose that an average man of the present day is superior to the greatest men of the beginning of the eighteenth century; yet they *held* many opinions which we are fast renouncing. The intellect of the age, therefore, is not the cause which we are in search of. I do not perceive that, in the mental training which has been received by the immense majority of the reading and thinking part of my countrymen, or in the kind of knowledge and other intellectual ailment which has been supplied to them, there is any thing likely to render them much less accessible to the influence of imposture and charlatanerie than there ever was. . . .

This is the deep-seated error, the inveterate prejudice, which the real reformer of English education has to struggle against. Is it astonishing that great minds are not produced in a country where the test of a great mind is, agreeing in the opinions of the small minds? where every institution or spiritual culture which the country has—the church, the universities, and almost every dissenting community—are constituted on the following as their avowed principle: that the object is, not that the individual should go forth determined and qualified to seek truth ardently, vigorously, and disinterestedly; *not* that he be furnished at setting out with the needful aids and facilities, the needful materials and instruments for that search, and then left to the unshackled use of them; *not* that, by a free communion with the thoughts and deeds of the great minds which preceded him, he be inspired at once with the courage to dare all which truth and his conscience require, and the modesty to weigh well the grounds of what others think, before adopting contrary opinions of his own: *not* this—no; but that the triumph of the system, the merit, the excellence in the sight of God which it possesses, or which it can impart to its pupil, is, that his speculations shall terminate in the adoption, in words, of a particular set of opinions. That provided he adhere to these opinions, it matters little whether to receive them from authority or from examination; and worse, that it matters little by what temptations of interest or vanity, by what voluntary or involuntary sophistication with his intellect, and deadening of his noblest feelings, that result is arrived at; that it even matters comparatively little whether to his mind the words are mere words, or the representatives of realities—in what sense he receives the favoured set of propositions, or whether he attaches to them any sense at all. Were ever great minds thus formed? Never!

❧

"THE SUBJECTION OF WOMEN," 1869

The object of this Essay is to explain as clearly as I am able, the grounds of an opinion which I have held from the very earliest period when I had

From *Essays on Sex Equality,* by John Stuart Mill and Harriet Taylor Mill, Alice S. Rossi, Ed. Published by The University of Chicago Press. Copyright © 1970.

formed any opinions at all on social or political matters, and which, instead of being weakened or modified, has been constantly growing stronger by the progress of reflection and the experience of life: That the principle which regulates the existing social relations between the two sexes—the legal subordination of one sex to the other—is wrong in itself, and now one of the chief hindrances to human improvement; and that it ought to be replaced by a principle of perfect equality, admitting no power or privilege on the one side, nor disability on the other.

The very words necessary to express the task I have undertaken, show how arduous it is. But it would be a mistake to suppose that the difficulty of the case must lie in the insufficiency or obscurity of the grounds of reason on which my conviction rests. The difficulty is that which exists in all cases in which there is a mass of feeling to be contended against. So long as an opinion is strongly rooted in the feelings, it gains rather than loses in stability by having a preponderating weight of argument against it. For if it were accepted as a result of argument, the refutation of the argument might shake the solidity of the conviction; but when it rests solely on feeling, the worse it fares in argumentative contest, the more persuaded its adherents are that their feeling must have some deeper ground, which the arguments do not reach; and while the feeling remains, it is always throwing up fresh intrenchments of argument to repair any breach made in the old. And there are so many causes tending to make the feelings connected with this subject the most intense and most deeply-rooted of all those which gather round and protect old institutions and customs, that we need not wonder to find them as yet less undermined and loosened than any of the rest by the progress of the great modern spiritual and social transition; nor suppose that the barbarisms to which men cling longest must be less barbarisms than those which they earlier shake off.

In every respect the burthen is hard on those who attack an almost universal opinion. They must be very fortunate as well as unusually capable if they obtain a hearing at all. They have more difficulty in obtaining a trial, than any other litigants have in getting a verdict. If they do extort a hearing, they are subjected to a set of logical requirements totally different from those exacted from other people. In all other cases, the burthen of proof is supposed to lie with the affirmative. If a person is charged with a murder, it rests with those who accuse him to give proof of his guilt, not with himself to prove his innocence. If there is a difference of opinion about the reality of any alleged historical event, in which the feelings of men in general are not much interested, as the Siege of Troy for example, those who maintain that the event took place are expected to produce their proofs, before those who take the other side can be required to say anything; and at no time are these required to do more than show that the evidence produced by the others is of no value. Again, in practical matters, the burthen of proof is supposed to be with those who are against liberty; who contend for any restriction or prohibition; either any limitation of the general freedom of human action, or any disqualification or disparity of privilege affecting one person or kind of persons, as compared with others. The *a priori* presumption is in favour of freedom and impartiality. It is held that there should be no restraint not required by the general good, and that the law should be no respecter of persons, but should treat all alike, save where dissimilarity of treatment is required by positive reasons, either of justice or of policy. But of none of these rules of evidence will the benefit be allowed to those who maintain the opinion I profess. It is useless for me to say that those who maintain the doctrine that men have a right to command and women are under an oblig-

ation to obey, or that men are fit for government and women unfit, are on the affirmative side of the question, and that they are bound to show positive evidence for the assertions, or submit to their rejection. It is equally unavailing for me to say that those who deny to women any freedom or privilege rightly allowed to men, having the double presumption against them that they are opposing freedom and recommending partiality, must be held to the strictest proof of their case, and unless their success be such as to exclude all doubt, the judgment ought to go against them. These would be thought good pleas in any common case; but they will not be thought so in this instance. Before I could hope to make any impression, I should be expected not only to answer all that has ever been said by those who take the other side of the question, but to imagine all that could be said by them—to find them in reasons, as well as answer all I find: and besides refuting all arguments for the affirmative, I shall be called upon for invincible positive arguments to prove a negative. And even if I could do all this, and leave the opposite party with a host of unanswered arguments against them, and not a single unrefuted one on their side, I should be thought to have done little; for a cause supported on the one hand by universal usage, and on the other by so great a preponderance of popular sentiment, is supposed to have a presumption in its favour, superior to any conviction which an appeal to reason has power to produce in any intellects but those of a high class.

ADOLPHE QUETELET

1796–1874

Lambert Adolphe Jacques Quetelet was born on February 22, 1796 in Ghent, Flanders, Belgium, was married and had a son named Ernest (who took over his father's job directing the Royal Observatory of Brussels), and died at nearly the age of 88 in Brussels on February 17, 1874. He received a sound lyceum education in Ghent, then in 1819 took a Ph.D. in math in Brussels with a dissertation on conic sections, and taught math at his alma mater. He then studied astronomy at the Observatory of Paris, and statistics and probability with Joseph Fourier and Pierre Laplace. The Belgian government asked him to found and direct a Royal Observatory in 1828, which he did until his death, writing papers on many topics, including meteor activity, to which he applied his knowledge of statistics.

Around 1830 he began compiling statistical data for the Belgian and Dutch governments, and was able to demonstrate that the bell shaped curve, or "normal distribution," could be used not only as it was in astronomy, under the "law of error," but also could be applied to human affairs. In the work which assured his place among social scientists, *A Treatise on Man and the Development of His Faculties: An Essay on Social Physics* (1835), he was the first to prove that most behavior, even criminal activity, could be predicted for any given population by reference to "the average man," a statistical construction. This gave fuel to the debate then raging in Europe regarding the extent to which free will characterizes human action versus economic or biological determinism, a set of arguments which have cropped up again during the last decade.

In 1846 Quetelet published a book, probably the first, which showed how probability theory could be used in social science. For this he could rightly be called the father of quantitative methods in sociology, political science, and other fields. (He also organized the first international statistics conference in 1853.) The "average man," construed as what Max Weber later called an "ideal-type," could then be compared across time and place in order to produce the "laws" of social behavior which Quetelet's "social physics" promised eventually to deliver. The search for these laws continues to this day, though few have stood the test of time or of the statistical procedures they inspired. Quetelet's name is also attached to the standard obesity index, the formula for which is QI = (weight in pound) × 703 / (height in inches)squared. The selection reprinted below is from an early work of demographic criminology—a field of burning interest in the mid-19th century—in which Quetelet lays out seventeen "principal observations" relating to the foundation of what he called *physique social,* but which is translated here as "social mechanics."

RESEARCH ON THE PROPENSITY FOR CRIME AT DIFFERENT AGES, 1833

Concerning the Possibility of Establishing the Foundations of a Social Mechanics

I have tried to indicate in a former *Mémoire* of what importance observations would be which would have as their aim the study of the several components relating to man, either as regards physical or mental and moral qualities, and of the laws which these components follow in their development from birth to the grave.

The man which I considered is in society the analogue of the center of gravity in matter. He is a fictional being in regard to which all things happen in accordance with average results obtained for society. If the *average* man were ascertained for one nation, he would present the type of that nation. If he could be ascertained according to the mass of men, he would present the type of the human species altogether.

In being restricted to ascertaining the average man for one nation and studying him in a consistent way, one can judge the changes which he experiences because of the times, and recognize if these changes result from nature or from man who, in the social state, reacts on himself by virtue of certain forces which he has at his command from his free will.

In admitting that these forces actually exist, as all observations appear to prove, I call them *disturbing forces* of man by analogy with the disturbing forces which scientists have considered in the system of the universe. One imagines that the effects which result from them act with such slowness that they could be called equally by analogy *secular disturbances*. The science which would have such a study as a goal would be a veritable *social mechanics*, which, no doubt, would present laws quite as admirable as the mechanics of inanimate objects, and would bring to light the conservative principles which perhaps would be only the analogies of those we already know.

This way of looking at the social system has something positive about it which must, at first, frighten certain minds. Some will see in it a tendency to materialism. Others, in interpreting my ideas badly, will find there an exaggerated pretention to aggrandize the domain of the exact sciences and to place the geometrician in an element which is not his own. They will reproach me for becoming involved in absurd speculations while being occupied with things which are not susceptible to being measured.

With regard to the accusation of materialism, it has been reproduced so often and so regularly every time that the sciences have tried a new step, and when the philosophical mind in flowing outside ancient ruts searched to open up new paths for itself, that it has become almost superfluous to respond to it—today, especially, when it has been stripped of the appearance of chains and torments. Who could say, moreover, that one insults the divinity in exercising the most noble faculty which He has placed in us, in turning one's meditations toward the most sublime laws of the universe, in trying to discover the wonderful economy, the infinite wisdom that presided at its composition? Who would dare to accuse of baseness the scholars who, for the narrow and shabby world of the ancients, have substituted the knowledge of our magnificent solar system, and who have pushed back so far the limits of our starry sky that genius no longer dare: to fathom the depths lest with a religious respect? Certainly the knowledge of the marvelous laws which rule the system of the world which we owe to the research of scholars offers a very great idea of the power of the divinity in a manner other than that of that world which wishes to impose on us a blind superstition. If the rough pride of man felt itself frustrated on seeing how small is the place which he occupies on the grain of dust of which he made his universe, how much must his intelligence he rejoiced in having carried his power so far and having plunged so in depth into the secrets of the heavens.

After having seen the progress which the sciences have pursued in regard to universes, are we not able to try to pursue it in regard to men? Would it not be absurd to believe that, while all happens according to such admirable law's, the human species alone remains blindly neglected by itself, and that it possesses no principle at all of conservation? We are not afraid to say that such a supposition would be more offensive to the divinity than the very research which we intend to do.

But here a second objection is presented: is there a possibility of realizing what we have in view? We have said that the first step to take would be to ascertain the average man of different nations, either in physical or moral and intellectual qualities. Perhaps one will accord us the possibility of such an appreciation for the physical qualities of man which allow measurement directly, but how will it be proper to grasp them for moral and intellectual qualities? How will one ever maintain without absurdity that the courage of one man is to that of another as five is to six, for example, pretty nearly as one would say of their height? Would not one laugh at the pretention of a geometrician who would maintain seriously that he has calculated that the genius of Homer to that of Virgil is as three is to two? Certainly such pretentions would be absurd and ridiculous, and the one who would maintain them would prove himself of little judgment. It is advisable before all to be well understood on the meaning of words and to examine if what we want is possible. I am not even speaking according to the present state of science, but a state where science will be able to be raised one day. We can, in fact, demand of those who are occupied with social mechanics no more than of those who would have seen imperfectly the possibilities of forming a celestial mechanics in an age where there existed only defective astronomical observations and void or false theories with insufficient means of calculation. The first step to take was to come to an agreement on the means of performance and on the possibility of obtaining them. It was then necessary to gather together with zeal and perseverance precise observations, to create and perfect methods for putting these to work, and thus to prepare all the necessary elements of the structure which it was a question of setting up. But it is the course which I believe will be proper to follow to form a social mechanics. I think therefore that it is a question of examining if there is a possibility of obtaining the means of performance, and first if there is a possibility of ascertaining the average man.

Conclusions

In summing up the principal observations which comprise our work, we are led to these conclusions:

1. *Age* is without contradiction the cause which acts with the most energy to develop or moderate the propensity for crime.

2. This fatal propensity seems to develop in proportion to the intensity of physical strength and passions in man. It attains its maximum around 25 years, a period where physical development is pretty nearly ended. Intellectual and moral development, which takes place with more slowness, then moderates the propensity for crime which diminishes still more slowly by the weakening of man's physical strength and passions.

3. Although it is around the age of 25 that the *maximum* number of crimes of different types appears, this *maximum* is found advanced or retarded by some years, however, for certain crimes according to more or less tardy development of some qualities which are in relationship with these crimes. Thus, man pushed by violence and his passions at first yields to rape and indecent assaults. He enters almost at the same time into a career of theft which he seems to follow as by instinct until his last breath. The development of his strength carries him finally to all the acts of violence, to homicide, rebellion, thefts on the public ways. Later, reflection turns manslaughter into murder and poisoning. Finally, man, advancing in his career of crime, substitutes more cunning for strength and becomes a forger more than at any other period of his life.

4. *The difference of the sexes* has also a great influence on the propensity for crime. One counts, in general, before the tribunals only one woman accused for four men.

5. The propensity for crime grows and diminishes pretty nearly by the same degrees in the two sexes; however, the period of *maximum* arrives a little later in women and takes place around the age of 30.

6. Woman, without doubt out of a sense of weakness, commits crimes against property

rather than against persons; and when she seeks to destroy her fellow creature, she employs of preference poison. Moreover, in yielding to homicide, it does not appear that she is stopped by the enormity of the crimes which, for frequency, are presented in the following order: infanticide, abortion, parricide, injuries to parents, murder, assault and battery, manslaughter—so that one can say that the number of the guilty diminishes the further and more openly they have to go searching for their victims. These differences depend, without doubt, on the habits and the more sedentary life of woman. She is able to conceive and execute guilty schemes only toward individuals with whom she is more related.

7. *The seasons* exercise in their turn a very marked influence on the propensity for crime. Thus, it is during summer that the most crimes against persons and the fewest crimes against property are committed. The contrary takes place during winter.

8. It is to be noted that age and the seasons exercise nearly the same influence in causing mental alienation and crimes against persons to grow or diminish.

9. *The climate* appears to have influence especially on the propensity for crime against persons. This observation is confirmed at least among the races of men of southern climates, like the Pelagian race spread out on the slope of the Mediterranean and Corsica, on the one hand, and the Italians mixed with Dalmatians and Tyroleans, on the other hand. Rigorous climates which give birth to the most needs also give birth to the most crimes against property.

10. The countries where frequent mixtures of people have taken place, those where industry and commerce join together many people and things and offer the most activity, those finally where inequality of fortunes makes itself most felt, give, all things being equal, birth to a greater number of crimes.

11. *The professions* have great influence on the nature of crimes. Individuals of an independent profession indulge rather in crimes against persons, and the working class and servants in crimes against property. Habits of dependence at the same time as the sedentary life and physical weakness produce the same results in women.

12. *Education is* far from having on the propensity for crime an influence as energetic as one commonly supposes. We confuse, moreover, too often moral education with instruction which consists only of reading and writing, and which becomes most of the time a new instrument of crime.

13. It is the same with *poverty*. Several of the departments of France reputed the most poor are at the same time the most moral. Man is not pushed into crime because he has less, but more generally because he passes in an abrupt way from a state of ease to misery and to insufficiency in satisfying all the needs which he had created.

14. The more one rises in the orders of society, and by consequence in the degrees of education, the less one finds women criminal compared to men. As we draw nearer to the lowest classes of people, the habits of both sexes tend, in fact, to resemble one another more and more.

15. Out of 1,129 manslaughters which were committed in France during the space of four years, 446 were because of quarrels and brawls in a bar— that which tends to show the fatal influence of *the use of drink.*

16. In France, as in the Low Countries, we have counted annually around 1 accused out of 4,300 inhabitants. But in the first country, 39 accused out of 100 are acquitted; and in the second, 15 only. However, on both sides the same code was used; but in the Low Countries, judges perform the functions of the jury. Before correctional tribunals and police courts, where the accused have to deal only with judges, repression has been pretty nearly the same in both kingdoms.

17. In France, crimes against persons made up around a third of the number of crimes against property; and in the Low Countries, a quarter only. It is to be noted that the first type of crime gives rise comparatively to fewer convictions than the second, perhaps because one is so much the more loath to apply penalties insofar as they are more serious.

I will not finish this *Mémoire* without express-ing anew my astonishment at the constancy which is observed in results present each year in the documents which are related to the adminis-tration of justice. Nothing, at first, would seem to have to be less regular than the progress of crime. Nothing, it would seem, should escape more from all human prevision than the number of man-slaughters, for example, since they are committed in general following brawls which arise without motive and in encounters the most fortuitous in appearance. However, experience proves that, not only are manslaughters annually pretty nearly in the same number, but even that the instruments which serve to commit them are used in the same proportions. What can one say, then, about crimes that are reflected on!

ALEXIS TOCQUEVILLE

1805–1859

A tiny, fragile man of slight physical capacity, Comte Alexis Charles Henri Maurice Clérel de Tocqueville was born in Verneuil, France on July 29, 1805, married Mary Mottely, an Englishwoman, in October 1835, with whom he had no children, and died in Cannes on April 16, 1859 at the age of 53. He was encouraged by his noble family to become a lawyer, but politics was in his blood. His father's royalist connections made it possible for Tocqueville to become an assistant magistrate in 1827, but the Revolution of 1830 made it opportune for him to leave France. He received permission to visit the U.S. for nine months in 1831–32 with his lifelong friend Gustave de Beaumont (who also wrote about the trip) in order to study prison reform there. The result was the first part of *Democracy in America* (1835), which, taken together with the more ambitious second part (1840) is the most important analysis of early American culture ever written; yet another English translation appeared in 2001. The public acclaim and sales from this book (with translations into many languages) enriched Tocqueville so that he was able to reconstruct his family's estate in Normandy and pursue a life of politics once again, entering the Chamber of Deputies in 1837. He was enormously popular among his constituency, and he prophesied the 1848 revolutions across Europe, but was ignored by his political colleagues. After two years of great political success, he refused to bow to the new emperor, Louis-Napoléon, and in 1849 was stripped of power, beginning an unwelcome period of isolation, which coincided with a physical collapse. Hoping to regain his political position, he wrote *The Old Regime and the Revolution* (1856), a book still widely studied, in which he showed why monarchy had been reinstituted in France, even after the Revolution, in ways it could not be in the U.S.

Tocqueville's aristocratic great-grandfather was destroyed by the Revolution in France, and served as the younger man's model of what a politician should be. Tocqueville therefore spent his life trying to understand the relationship between what seemed to him to be the inevitable growth of democratic representation in the governments of Europe on the one side, and established authority and experience on the other. He was much concerned with "the tyranny of the majority" (as explained in the excerpts reprinted below), but equally impressed with the tremendous vitality and creativity he witnessed in the U.S., so very different from the less rambunctious political culture of Europe. He was also perplexed, as were so many other observers, by the institution of slavery, and he wrote about its inevitably negative meaning for U.S. political life in a prescient manner that has been referred to endlessly since it was published 170 years ago.

DEMOCRACY IN AMERICA, 1835–40

How Equality Suggests to the Americans the Idea of the Indefinite Perfectibility of Man

Equality suggests to the human mind several ideas that would not have originated from any other source, and it modifies almost all those previously entertained. I take as an example the idea of human perfectibility, because it is one of the principal notions that the intellect can conceive and because it constitutes of itself a great philosophical theory, which is everywhere to be traced by its consequences in the conduct of human affairs.

Although man has many points of resemblance with the brutes, one trait is peculiar to himself: he improves; they are incapable of improvement. Mankind could not fail to discover this difference from the beginning. The idea of perfectibility is therefore as old as the world; equality did not give birth to it, but has imparted to it a new character.

When the citizens of a community are classed according to rank, profession, or birth and when all men are forced to follow the career which chance has opened before them, everyone thinks that the utmost limits of human power are to be discerned in proximity to himself, and no one seeks any longer to resist the inevitable law of his destiny. Not, indeed, that an aristocratic people absolutely deny man's faculty of self-improvement, but they do not hold it to be indefinite; they can conceive amelioration, but not change: they imagine that the future condition of society may be better, but not essentially different; and, while they admit that humanity has made progress and may still have some to make, they assign to it beforehand certain impassable limits.

Thus they do not presume that they have arrived at the supreme good or at absolute truth (what people or what man was ever wild enough to imagine it?), but they cherish an opinion that they have pretty nearly reached that degree of greatness and knowledge which our imperfect nature admits of; and as nothing moves about them,

From *Democracy in America, Volume II,* by Alexis De Tocqueville, Phillips Bradley, Ed. Published by Vintage Books, a Division of Random House. Copyright © 1981.

they are willing to fancy that everything is in its fit place. Then it is that the legislator affects to lay down eternal laws; that kings and nations will raise none but imperishable monuments; and that the present generation undertakes to spare generations to come the care of regulating their destinies.

In proportion as castes disappear and the classes of society draw together, as manners, customs, and laws vary, because of the tumultuous intercourse of men, as new facts arise, as new truths are brought to light, as ancient opinions are dissipated and others take their place, the image of an ideal but always fugitive perfection presents itself to the human mind. Continual changes are then every instant occurring under the observation of every man; the position of some is rendered worse, and he learns but too well that no people and no individual, however enlightened they may be, can lay claim to infallibility; the condition of others is improved, whence he infers that man is endowed with an indefinite faculty for improvement. His reverses teach him that none have discovered absolute good; his success stimulates him to the never ending pursuit of it. Thus, forever seeking, forever falling to rise again, often disappointed, but not discouraged, he tends unceasingly towards that unmeasured greatness so indistinctly visible at the end of the long track which humanity has yet to tread.

It can hardly be believed how many facts naturally flow from the philosophical theory of the indefinite perfectibility of man or how strong an influence it exercises even on those who, living entirely for the purposes of action and not of thought, seem to conform their actions to it without knowing anything about it.

I accost an American sailor and inquire why the ships of his country are built so as to last for only a short time; he answers without hesitation that the art of navigation is every day making such rapid progress that the finest vessel would become almost useless if it lasted beyond a few years. In these words, which fell accidentally, and on a particular subject, from an uninstructed man, I recognize the general and systematic idea upon which a great people direct all their concerns.

Aristocratic nations are naturally too liable to narrow the scope of human perfectibility; democratic nations, to expand it beyond reason.

Unlimited Power of the Majority in the United States, and Its Consequences

Natural strength of the majority in democracies—Most of the American constitutions have increased this strength by artificial means—How this has been done—Pledged delegates—Moral power of the majority—Opinion as to its in fallibility—Respect for its rights, how augmented in the United States.

The very essence of democratic government consists in the absolute sovereignty of the majority; for there is nothing in democratic states that is capable of resisting it. Most of the American constitutions have sought to increase this natural strength of the majority by artificial means.

Of all political institutions, the legislature is the one that is most easily swayed by the will of the majority. The Americans determined that the members of the legislature should be elected by the people *directly*, and for a *very brief term*, in order to subject them, not only to the general convictions, but even to the daily passions, of their constituents. The members of both houses are taken from the same classes in society and nominated in the same manner; so that the movements of the legislative bodies are almost as rapid, and quite as irresistible, as those of a single assembly. It is to a legislature thus constituted that almost all the authority of the government has been entrusted.

At the same time that the law increased the strength of those authorities which of themselves were strong, it enfeebled more and more those which were naturally weak. It deprived the representatives of the executive power of all stability and independence; and by subjecting them completely to the caprices of the legislature, it robbed them of the slender influence that the nature of a democratic government might have allowed them to exercise. In several states the judicial power was also submitted to the election of the majority; and in all of them its existence was made to depend on the pleasure of the legislative authority, since the representatives were empowered annually to regulate the stipend of the judges.

Custom has done even more than law. A proceeding is becoming more and more general in the United States which will, in the end, do away with the guarantees of representative government: it frequently happens that the voters, in electing a delegate, point out a certain line of conduct to him and impose upon him certain positive obligations that he is pledged to fulfill. With the exception of the tumult, this comes to the same thing as if the majority itself held its deliberations in the marketplace.

Several particular circumstances combine to render the power of the majority in America not only preponderant, but irresistible. The moral authority of the majority is partly based upon the notion that there is more intelligence and wisdom in a number of men united than in a single individual, and that the number of the legislators is more important than their quality. The theory of equality is thus applied to the intellects of men; and human pride is thus assailed in its last retreat by a doctrine which the minority hesitate to admit, and to which they will but slowly assent. Like all other powers, and perhaps more than any other, the authority of the many requires the sanction of time in order to appear legitimate. At first it enforces obedience by constraint; and its laws are not *respected* until they have been long maintained.

The right of governing society, which the majority supposes itself to derive from its superior intelligence, was introduced into the United States by the first settlers; and this idea, which of itself would be sufficient to create a free nation, has now been amalgamated with the customs of the people and the minor incidents of social life.

The French under the old monarchy held it for a maxim that the king could do no wrong; and if he did do wrong, the blame was imputed to his advisers. This notion made obedience very easy; it enabled the subject to complain of the law without ceasing to love and honor the lawgiver. The Americans entertain the same opinion with respect to the majority.

The moral power of the majority is founded upon yet another principle, which is that the interests of the many are to be preferred to those of the few. It will readily be perceived that the respect here professed for the rights of the greater number must naturally increase or diminish according to the state of parties. When a nation is divided into several great irreconcilable interests, the privilege of the majority is often overlooked, because it is intolerable to comply with its demands.

If there existed in America a class of citizens whom the legislating majority sought to deprive of exclusive privileges which they had possessed for ages and to bring down from an elevated station to the level of the multitude, it is probable that the minority would be less ready to submit to its laws. But as the United States was colonized by men holding equal rank, there is as yet no natural or permanent disagreement between the interests of its different inhabitants.

There are communities in which the members of the minority can never hope to draw the majority over to their side, because they must then give up the very point that is at issue between them. Thus an aristocracy can never become a majority while it retains its exclusive privileges, and it cannot cede its privileges without ceasing to be an aristocracy.

In the United States, political questions cannot be taken up in so general and absolute a manner; and all parties are willing to recognize the rights of the majority, because they all hope at some time to be able to exercise them to their own advantage. The majority in that country, therefore, exercise a prodigious actual authority, and a power of opinion which is nearly as great; no obstacles exist which can impede or even retard its progress, so as to make it heed the complaints of those whom it crushes upon its path. This state of things is harmful in itself and dangerous for the future.

How the omnipotence of the majority increases, in America, the instability of legislation and administration inherent in democracy. The Americans increase the mutability of law that is inherent in a democracy by changing the legislature every year, and investing it with almost unbounded authority—The same effect is produced upon the administration—In America the pressure for social improvements is vastly greater, but less continuous, than in Europe.

I have already spoken of the natural defects of democratic institutions; each one of them increases in the same ratio as do power of the majority. To begin with the most evident of them all, the mutability of the laws is an evil inherent in a democratic government, because it is natural to democracies to raise new men to power. But this evil is more or less perceptible in proportion to the authority and the means of action which the legislature possesses.

In America the authority exercised by the legislatures is supreme; nothing prevents them from accomplishing their wishes with celerity and with irresistible power, and they are supplied with new representatives every year. That is to say, the circumstances which contribute most powerfully to democratic instability, and which admit of the free application of caprice to the most important objects, are here in full operation. Hence America is, at the present day, the country beyond all others where laws last the shortest time. Almost all the American constitutions have been amended within thirty years; there is therefore not one American state which has not modified the principles of its legislation in that time. As for the laws themselves, a single glance at the archives of the different states of the Union suffices to convince one that in America the activity of the legislator ever slackens. Not that the American democracy is naturally less stable than any other, but it is allowed to follow, in the formation of the laws, the natural instability of its desires.

The omnipotence of the majority and the rapid as well as absolute manner in which its decisions are executed in the United States not only render the law unstable, but exercise the same influence upon the execution of the law and the conduct of the administration. As the majority is the only power that it is important to court, all its projects are taken up with the greatest ardor; but no sooner is its attention distracted than all this ardor ceases; while in the free states of Europe, where the administration is at once independent and secure, the projects of the legislature continue to be executed even when its attention is directed to other objects.

In America certain improvements are prosecuted with much more zeal and activity than elsewhere; in Europe the same ends are promoted by much less social effort more continuously applied.

Some years ago several pious individuals undertook to ameliorate the condition of the prisons. The public were moved by their statements, and the reform of criminals became a popular undertaking. New prisons were built; and for the first time the idea of reforming as well as punishing the delinquent formed a part of prison discipline.

But this happy change, in which the public had taken so hearty an interest and which the simultaneous exertions of the citizens rendered irresistible, could not be completed in a moment. While the new penitentiaries were being erected and the will of the majority was hastening the work, the old prisons still existed and contained a great number of offenders. These jails became more unwholesome and corrupt in proportion as the new establishments were reformed and improved, forming a contrast that may readily be understood. The majority was so eagerly employed in founding the new prisons that those which already existed were forgotten; and as the general attention was diverted to a novel object, the care which had hitherto been bestowed upon the others ceased. The salutary regulations of discipline were first relaxed and afterwards broken; so that in the immediate neighborhood of a prison that bore witness to the mild and enlightened spirit of our times, dungeons existed that reminded one of the barbarism of the Middle Ages.

Tyranny of the majority. How the principle of the sovereignty of the people is to be understood—Impossibility of conceiving a mixed government—The sovereign power must exist somewhere—Precautions to be taken to control its action—These precautions have not been taken in the United States—Consequences.

I hold it to be an impious and detestable maxim that, politically speaking, the people have a right to do anything; and yet I have asserted that all authority originates in the will of the majority. Am I, then, in contradiction with myself?

A general law, which bears the name of justice, has been made and sanctioned, not only by a majority of this or that people, but by a majority of mankind. The rights of every people are therefore confined within the limits of what is just. A nation may be considered as a jury which is empowered to represent society at large and to apply justice, which is its law. Ought such a jury, which represents society, to have more power than the society itself whose laws it executes?

When I refuse to obey an unjust law, I do not contest the right of the majority to command, but I simply appeal from the sovereignty of the people to the sovereignty of mankind. Some have not feared to assert that a people can never outstep the boundaries of justice and reason in those affairs which are peculiarly its own; and that consequently full power may be given to the majority by which it is represented. But this is the language of a slave.

A majority taken collectively is only an individual, whose opinions, and frequently whose interests, are opposed to those of another individual, who is styled a minority. If it be admitted that a man possessing absolute power may misuse that power by wronging his adversaries, why should not a majority be liable to the same reproach? Men do not change their characters by uniting with one another; nor does their patience in the presence of obstacles increase with their strength. For my own part, I cannot believe it; the power to do everything, which I should refuse to one of my equals, I will never grant to any number of them. . . .

The greatest dangers of the American republics proceed from the omnipotence of the majority. Democratic republics liable to perish from a misuse of their power, and not from impotence—The governments of the American republics are more centralized and more energetic than those of the monarchies of Europe—Dangers resulting from this—Opinions of Madison and Jefferson upon this point.

Governments usually perish from impotence or from tyranny. In the former case, their power escapes from them; it is wrested from their grasp in the latter. Many observers who have witnessed the anarchy of democratic states have imagined that the government of those states was naturally weak and impotent. The truth is that when war is once begun between parties, the government loses its control over society. But I do not think that a democratic power is naturally without force or resources; say, rather, that it is almost always by the abuse of its force and the misemployment of its resources that it becomes a failure. Anarchy is almost always produced by its tyranny or its mistakes, but not by its want of strength.

It is important not to confuse stability with force, or the greatness of a thing with its duration.

In democratic republics the power that directs society is not stable, for it often changes hands and assumes a new direction. But whichever way it turns, its force is almost irresistible. The governments of the American republics appear to me to be as much centralized as those of the absolute monarchies of Europe, and more energetic than they are. I do not, therefore, imagine that they will perish from weakness.

If ever the free institutions of America are destroyed, that event may be attributed to the omnipotence of the majority, which may at some future time urge the minorities to desperation and oblige them to have recourse to physical force. Anarchy will then be the result, but it will have been brought about by despotism.

Mr. Madison expresses the same opinion in *The Federalist*, No. 51. "It is of great importance in a republic, not only to guard the society against the oppression of its rulers, but to guard one part of the society against the injustice of the other part.

The Three Races in the United States

Situation of the black population in the United States, and dangers with which its presence threatens the whites. Why it is more difficult to abolish slavery, and to efface all vestiges of it among the moderns than it was among the ancients—In the United States the prejudices of the whites against the blacks seem to increase in proportion as slavery is abolished—Situation of the Negroes in the Northern and Southern states—Why the Americans abolish slavery—Servitude, which debases the slave, impoverishes the master—Contrast between the left and the right bank of the Ohio—To what attributable—The black race, as well as slavery, recedes towards the South—Explanation of this fact—Difficulties attendant upon the abolition of slavery in the South—Dangers to come—General anxiety—Foundation of a black colony in Africa—Why the Americans of the South increase the hardships of slavery while they are distressed at its continuance.

The Indians will perish in the same isolated condition in which they have lived, but the destiny of the Negroes is in some measure interwoven with that of the Europeans. These two races are fas-

tened to each other without intermingling; and they are alike unable to separate entirely or to combine. The most formidable of all the ills that threaten the future of the Union arises from the presence of a black population upon its territory; and in contemplating the cause of the present embarrassments, or the future dangers of the United States, the observer is invariably led to this as a primary fact.

Generally speaking, men must make great and unceasing efforts before permanent evils are created; but there is one calamity which penetrated furtively into the world, and which was at first scarcely distinguishable amid the ordinary abuses of power: it originated with an individual whose name history has not preserved; it was wafted like some accursed germ upon a portion of the soil; but it afterwards nurtured itself, grew without effort, and spread naturally with the society to which it belonged. This calamity is slavery. Christianity suppressed slavery, but the Christians of the sixteenth century re-established it, as an exception, indeed, to their social system, and restricted to one of the races of mankind; but the wound thus inflicted upon humanity, though less extensive, was far more difficult to cure.

It is important to make an accurate distinction between slavery itself and its consequences. The immediate evils produced by slavery were very nearly the same in antiquity as they are among the moderns, but the consequences of these evils were different. The slave among the ancients belonged to the same race as his master, and was often the superior of the two in education[31] and intelligence. Freedom was the only distinction between them; and when freedom was conferred, they were easily confounded together. The ancients, then, had a very simple means of ridding themselves of slavery and its consequences: that of enfranchisement; and they succeeded as soon as they adopted this measure generally. Not but that in ancient states the vestiges of servitude subsisted for some time after servitude itself was abolished. There is a natural prejudice that prompts men to despise whoever has been their inferior long after he has become their equal; and the real inequality that is produced by fortune or by law is always succeeded by

TO EVEN SPREADS 7 LINES TR'D FROM P.175 TO P.174, 13 LINES FROM P176 TO P175, 6 LINES FROM P177 TO P176, 48ll PER PAGE.

an imaginary inequality that is implanted in the manners of the people. But among the ancients this secondary consequence of slavery had a natural limit; for the freedman bore so entire a resemblance to those born free that it soon became impossible to distinguish him from them.

The greatest difficulty in antiquity was that of altering the law; among the moderns it is that of altering the customs, and as far as we are concerned, the real obstacles begin where those of the ancients left off. This arises from the circumstance that among the moderns the abstract and transient fact of slavery is fatally united with the physical and permanent fact of color. The tradition of slavery dishonors the race, and the peculiarity of the race perpetuates the tradition of slavery. No African has ever voluntarily emigrated to the shores of the New World, whence it follows that all the blacks who are now found there are either slaves or freedmen. Thus the Negro transmits the eternal mark of his ignominy to all his descendants; and although the law may abolish slavery, God alone can obliterate the traces of its existence.

The modern slave differs from his master not only in his condition but in his origin. You may set the Negro free, but you cannot make him otherwise than an alien to the European. Nor is this all; we scarcely acknowledge the common features of humanity in this stranger whom slavery has brought among us. His physiognomy is to our eyes hideous, his understanding weak, his tastes low; and we are almost inclined to look upon him as a being intermediate between man and the brutes.[32] The moderns, then, after they have abolished slavery, have three prejudices to contend against, which are less easy to attack and far less easy to conquer than the mere fact of servitude: the prejudice of the master, the prejudice of the race, and the prejudice of color.

It is difficult for us, who have had the good fortune to be born among men like ourselves by nature and our equals by law, to conceive the irreconcilable differences that separate the Negro from the European in America. But we may derive some faint notion of them from analogy. France was formerly a country in which numerous inequalities existed that had been created by law.

Nothing can be more fictitious than a purely legal inferiority, nothing more contrary to the instinct of mankind than these permanent divisions established between beings evidently similar. Yet these divisions existed for ages; they still exist in many places; and everywhere they have left imaginary vestiges, which time alone can efface. If it be so difficult to root out an inequality that originates solely in the law, how are those distinctions to be destroyed which seem to be based upon the immutable laws of Nature herself? When I remember the extreme difficulty with which aristocratic bodies, of whatever nature they may be, are commingled with the mass of the people, and the exceeding care which they take to preserve for ages the ideal boundaries of their caste inviolate, I despair of seeing an aristocracy disappear which is founded upon visible and indelible signs. Those who hope that the Europeans will ever be amalgamated with the Negroes appear to me to delude themselves. I am not led to any such conclusion by my reason or by the evidence of facts. Hitherto wherever the whites have been the most powerful, they have held the blacks in degradation or in slavery; wherever the Negroes have been strongest, they have destroyed the whites: this has been the only balance that has ever taken place between the two races.

I see that in a certain portion of the territory of the United States at the present day the legal barrier which separated the two races is falling away, but not that which exists in the manners of the country; slavery recedes, but the prejudice to which it has given birth is immovable. Whoever has inhabited the United States must have perceived that in those parts of the Union in which the Negroes are no longer slaves they have in no wise drawn nearer to the whites. On the contrary, the prejudice of race appears to be stronger in the states that have abolished slavery than in those where it still exists; and nowhere is it so intolerant as in those states where servitude has never been known.

It is true that in the North of the Union marriages may be legally contracted between Negroes and whites; but public opinion would stigmatize as infamous a man who should connect himself with a Negress, and it would be difficult to cite a single instance of such a union. The electoral franchise has been conferred upon the Negroes in almost all the states in which slavery has been abolished, but if they come forward to vote, their lives are in danger. If oppressed, they may bring an action at law, but they will find none but whites among their judges; and although they may legally serve as jurors, prejudice repels them from that office. The same schools do not receive the children of the black and of the European. In the theaters gold cannot procure a seat for the servile race beside their former masters; in the hospitals they lie apart; and although they are allowed to invoke the same God as the whites, it must be at a different altar and in their own churches, with their own clergy. The gates of heaven are not closed against them, but their inferiority is continued to the very confines of the other world. When the Negro dies, his bones are cast aside, and the distinction of condition prevails even in the equality of death. Thus the Negro is free, but he can share neither the rights, nor the pleasures, nor the labor, nor the afflictions, nor the tomb of him whose equal he has been declared to be; and he cannot meet him upon fair terms in life or in death.

In the South, where slavery still exists, the Negroes are less carefully kept apart; they sometimes share the labors and the recreations of the whites; the whites consent to intermix with them to a certain extent, and although legislation treats them more harshly, the habits of the people are more tolerant and compassionate. In the South the master is not afraid to raise his slave to his own standing, because he knows that he can in a moment reduce him to the dust at pleasure. In the North the white no longer distinctly perceives the barrier that separates him from the degraded race, and he shuns the Negro with the more pertinacity since he fears lest they should some day be confounded together.

Among the Americans of the South, Nature sometimes reasserts her rights and restores a transient equality between the blacks and the whites; but in the North pride restrains the most imperious of human passions. The American of the Northern states would perhaps allow the Negress to share his licentious pleasures if the laws of his country did not declare that she may aspire to be the legitimate partner of his bed, but he recoils with horror from her who might become his wife.

Thus it is in the United States that the prejudice which repels the Negroes seems to increase in proportion as they are emancipated, and inequality is sanctioned by the manners while it is effaced from the laws of the country. But if the relative position of the two races that inhabit the United States is such as I have described, why have the Americans abolished slavery in the North of the Union, why do they maintain it in the South, and why do they aggravate its hardships? The answer is easily given. It is not for the good of the Negroes, but for that of the whites, that measures are taken to abolish slavery in the United States.

⎯⚬⎯

THE OLD REGIME AND THE REVOLUTION, 1856

Why Feudalism Had Come to Be More Detested in France Than in Any Other Country

At first sight it may appear surprising that the Revolution, whose primary aim, as we have seen, was to destroy every vestige of the institutions of the Middle Ages, should not have broken out in countries where those institutions had the greatest hold and bore most heavily on the people instead of those in which their yoke was relatively light.

At the close of the eighteenth century serfdom had not yet been completely abolished anywhere in Germany; indeed, in most parts of that country the peasants were still literally bound to the land, as they had been in the Middle Ages. The armies of Frederick II and Maria Theresa were composed almost entirely of men who were serfs on the medieval pattern.

From *The Old Regime and the French Revolution*, by Alexis De Tocqueville, translated by Stuart Gilbert, © 1955 by Doubleday, a division of Random House, Inc. Used by permission of Doubleday, a division of Random House, Inc.

In most German states in 1788 the peasant was not allowed to quit his lord's estate; if he did so, he was liable to be tracked down wherever he was and brought back in custody. He was subject to the jurisdiction of his lord, who kept a close eye on his private life and could punish him for intemperance or idleness. He could neither better his social position, change his occupation, nor even marry without his master's consent, and a great number of his working hours had to be spent in his master's service. The system of compulsory labor, known in France as the *corvée*, was in full force in Germany, and in some districts entailed no less than three days' work a week. The peasant was expected to keep the buildings on his lord's estate in good repair and to carry the produce of the estate to market; he drove his lord's carriage and carried his messages. Also he had to spend some years of his youth in his lord's household as a member of the domestic staff. However, it was possible for the serf to become a landowner, though his tenure was always hedged round with restrictions. He had to cultivate his land in a prescribed manner, under his lord's supervision, and could neither alienate nor mortgage it without permission. In some cases he was compelled to sell its produce, in others forbidden to sell it; in any case he was bound to keep the land under cultivation. Moreover, his children did not inherit his entire estate, some part of it being usually withheld by his lord.

It must not be thought that I am describing ancient or obsolete laws; these provisions can be found even in the code drawn up by Frederick the Great and put in force by his successor at the very time when the French Revolution was getting under way.

In France such conditions had long since passed away; the peasants could move about, buy and sell, work, and enter into contracts as they liked. Only in one or two eastern provinces, recent annexations, some last vestiges of serfdom lingered on; everywhere else it had wholly disappeared. Indeed, the abolition of serfdom had taken place in times so remote that its very date had been forgotten. However, as a result of recent research work it is now known that as early as the thirteenth century serfdom had ceased to exist in Normandy.

Meanwhile another revolution, of a different order, had done much to improve the status of the French peasant; he had not merely ceased to be a serf, he had also become a landowner. Though this change had far-reaching consequences, it is apt to be overlooked, . . .

Why then did these selfsame feudal rights arouse such bitter hatred in the heart of the French people that it has persisted even after its object has long since ceased to exist? One of the reasons is that the French peasant had become a landowner, and another that he had been completely emancipated from the control of his lord. (No doubt there were other reasons, but these, I think, were the chief ones.)

If the peasant had not owned his land he would hardly have noticed many of the charges which the feudal system imposed on all real estate. What could the tithe matter to a man who had no land of his own? He could simply deduct it from the rent. And even restrictions hampering agriculture mean nothing to an agriculturist who is simply cultivating land for the benefit of someone else.

Moreover, if the French peasant had still been under his lord's control, the feudal rights would have seemed much less obnoxious, because he would have regarded them as basic to the constitution of his country.

When the nobles had real power as well as privileges, when they governed and administered, their rights could be at once greater and less open to attack. In fact, the nobility was regarded in the age of feudalism much as the government is regarded by everyone today; its exactions were tolerated in view of the protection and security it provided. True, the nobles enjoyed invidious privileges and rights that weighed heavily on the commoner, but in return for this they kept order, administered justice, saw to the execution of the laws, came to the rescue of the oppressed, and watched over the interests of all. The more these functions passed out of the hands of the nobility, the more uncalled-for did their privileges appear—until at last their mere existence seemed a meaningless anachronism.

I would ask you to picture to yourself the French peasant as he was in the eighteenth century—or, rather, the peasant you know today, for he has not changed at all. His status is different, but not his personality. See how he appears in the records from which I have been quoting: a man so passionately devoted to the soil that he spends all his earnings on buying land, no matter what it costs. To acquire it he must begin by paying certain dues, not to the government but to other landowners of the neighborhood, who are as far removed as he from the central administration and almost as powerless as he. When at long last he has gained possession of this land which means so much to him, it is hardly an exaggeration to say that he sinks his heart in it along with the grain he sows. The possession of this little plot of earth, a tiny part, his very own, of the wide world, fills him with pride and a sense of independence. But now the neighbors aforesaid put in an appearance, drag him away from his cherished fields, and bid him work elsewhere without payment. When he tries to protect his seedlings from the animals they hunt, they tell him to take down his fences, and they lie in wait for him at river crossings to exact a toll. At the market there they are again, to make him pay for the right of selling the produce of his land, and when on his return home he wants to use the wheat he has put aside for his daily needs, he has to take it to their mill to have it ground, and then to have his bread baked in the lord's oven. Thus part of the income from his small domain goes to supporting these men in the form of charges which are imprescriptible and irredeemable. Whatever he sets out to do, he finds these tiresome neighbors barring his path, interfering in his simple pleasures and his work, and consuming the produce of his toil. And when he has done with them, other fine gentlemen dressed in black step in and take the greater part of his harvest. When we remember the special temperament of the French peasant proprietor in the eighteenth century, his ruling interests and passions, and the treatment accorded him, we can well understand the rankling grievances that burst into a flame in the French Revolution.

For even after it had ceased to be a political institution, the feudal system remained basic to the economic organization of France. In this restricted form it was far more hated than in the heyday of feudalism, and we are fully justified in saying that the very destruction of some of the institutions of the Middle Ages made those which survived seem all the more detestable.

Notes

31. It is well known that several of the most distinguished authors of antiquity, and among them Æsop and Terence, were or had been, slaves. Slaves were not always taken from barbarous nations; the chances of war reduced highly civilized men to servitude.

32. To induce the whites to abandon the opinion they have conceived of the moral and intellectual inferiority of their former slaves, the Negroes must change; but as long as this opinion persists, they cannot change.

FREDERICK DOUGLASS

1817–1895

Frederick Augustus Washington Bailey was born a slave in February 1818 (not 1817 as Douglass himself wrote) at Tuckahoe near Easton in Talbot County, Maryland. His grandfather, a free black woodcutter, and his grandmother, a slave with unusual autonomy, took care of him. He never knew his mother, who died when he was seven. Different sets of white plantation owners and their relatives raised him, probably because he was fathered by one of them, never identified. Sophia Auld taught him to read while he lived at the Auld home in Baltimore, though against her husband's wishes. Eventually, after many altercations with whites, he escaped to New York and assumed the name of Douglass from a character in Walter Scott's *Lady of the Lake* (1810), adding an "s." His fiancé from Maryland, Anna Murray, a free black, joined him there and they were married in late 1838, producing Rosetta (1839), Lewis Henry (1840), Frederick, Jr. (1842), and Charles Remond (1844). In 1841 Douglass began giving speeches at abolition meetings and began to be noticed for his oratorical skill, and his extraordinary autobiographical tales. He became a symbol for the anti-slavery movement, though not without experiencing personal danger and intellectual ambivalence as his role as the "token" black among whites.

Wendell Phillips and others in the movement persuaded Douglass to write up his speeches about his life, which was published in 1845, a 125-page document that sold well in the U.S. and Britain. It was so skillfully written that attacks on its authenticity began at once, something which Douglass's defenders tried to defuse. Due to sales abroad and concern about his physical safety in the U.S., Douglass left for Britain in 1845, where he lectured his astonished British hosts on their need to dissolve their relationships with American slaveholders. His freedom was bought in 1846 from Thomas Auld, so he returned to safety in December of that year, moving his family to Rochester, New York in 1847. He published *My Bondage and My Freedom* in 1855 with the help of Julia Griffiths, a white woman he'd met in England. The next several decades saw Douglass carrying out endless tasks associated with improving the condition of blacks in the U.S., through speeches, newspapers, and books. His wife died in 1882, Douglass became ill and depressed, but startled his children by marrying his white secretary, Helen Pitts, 21 years his junior. They toured the world together in the following years, after which they served in Haiti for two years as representatives of the U.S. government. Yet none of these daring activities surpassed in importance Douglass's achievement in writing his two autobiographies. Their influence has been incalculable as the first "slave narratives" to win widespread sympathy for an oppressed people.

"THE CHURCH AND PREJUDICE," SPEECH DELIVERED AT THE PLYMOUTH CHURCH ANTI-SLAVERY SOCIETY, DECEMBER 23, 1841

At the South I was a member of the Methodist Church. When I came north, I thought one Sunday I would attend communion, at one of the churches of my denomination, in the town I was staying. The white people gathered round the altar, the blacks clustered by the door. After the good minister had served out the bread and wine to one portion of those near him, he said, "These may withdraw, and others come forward"; thus he proceeded till all the white members had been served. Then he drew a long breath, and looking out towards the door, exclaimed, "Come up, colored friends, come up! for you know *God is no respecter of persons!*" I haven't been there to see the sacraments taken since.

At New Bedford, where I live, there was a great revival of religion not long ago—many were converted and "received" as they said, "into the kingdom of heaven." But it seems, the kingdom of heaven is like a net; at least so it was according to the practice of these pious Christians; and when the net was drawn ashore, they had to set down and cull out the fish. Well, it happened now that some of the fish had rather black scales; so these were sorted out and packed by themselves. But among those who experienced religion at this time was a colored girl; she was baptised in the same water as the rest; so she thought she might sit at the Lord's table and partake of the same sacramental elements with the others. The deacon handed round the cup, and when he came to the black girl, he could not pass her, for there was the minister looking right at him, and as he was a kind of abolitionist, the deacon was rather afraid of giving him offence; so he handed the girl the cup, and she tasted. Now it so happened that next to her sat a young lady who had been converted at the same time, baptised in the same water, and put her trust in the same blessed Saviour; yet

when the cup, containing the precious blood which had been shed for all, came to her, she rose in disdain, and walked out of the church. Such was the religion *she* had experienced!

Another young lady fell into a trance. When she awoke, she declared she had been to heaven. Her friends were all anxious to know what and whom she had seen there; so she told the whole story. But there was one good old lady whose curiosity went beyond that of all the others—and she inquired of the girl that had the vision, if she saw any black folks in heaven? After some hesitation, the reply was, *"Oh! I didn't go into the kitchen!"*

Thus you see, my hearers, this prejudice goes even into the church of God. And there are those who carry it so far that it is disagreeable to them even to think of going to heaven, if colored people are going there too. And whence comes it? The grand cause is slavery; but there are others less prominent; one of them is the way in which children in this part of the country are instructed to regard the blacks.

"Yes!" exclaimed an old gentleman, interrupting him—"when they behave wrong, they are told, 'black man come catch you.' "

Yet people in general will say they like colored men as well as any other, *but in their proper place!* They assign us that place; they don't let us do it for ourselves, nor will they allow us a voice in the decision. They will not allow that we have a head to think, and a heart to feel, and a soul to aspire. They treat us not as men, but as dogs—they cry "Stu-boy!" and expect us to run and do their bidding. That's the way we are liked. You degrade us, and then ask why we are degraded—you shut our mouths, and then ask why we don't speak—you close your colleges and seminaries against us, and then ask why we don't know more.

But all this prejudice sinks into insignificance in *my* mind, when compared with the enormous iniquity of the system which is its cause—the system that sold my four sisters and my brothers into bondage—and which calls in its priests to defend it even from the Bible! The slaveholding ministers preach up the divine right of the slaveholders to property in their fellow-men. The southern preachers say to the poor slave, "Oh! if you wish to be happy in time, happy in eternity, you must be obedient to your masters; their interest is yours. God made one portion of men to do the working, and another to do the thinking; how good God is! Now, you have no trouble or anxiety; but ah! you can't imagine how perplexing it is to your masters and mistresses to have so much thinking to do in your behalf! You cannot appreciate your blessings; you know not how happy a thing it is for you, that you were born of that portion of the human family which has the working, instead of the thinking to do! Oh! how grateful and obedient you ought to be to your masters! How beautiful are the arrangements of Providence! Look at your hard, horny hands—see how nicely they are adapted to the labor you have to perform! Look at our delicate fingers, so exactly fitted for our station, and see how manifest it is that God designed us to be His thinkers, and you the workers—Oh! the wisdom of God!"—I used to attend a Methodist church, in which my master was a class-leader; he would talk most sanctimoniously about the dear Redeemer, who was sent "to preach deliverance to the captives, and set at liberty them that are bruised"—he could pray at morning, pray at noon, and pray at night; yet he could lash up my poor cousin by his two thumbs, and inflict stripes and blows upon his bare back, till the blood streamed to the ground! all the time quoting scripture, for his authority, and appealing to that passage of the Holy Bible which says, "He that knoweth his master's will, and doeth it not, shall be beaten with many stripes!" Such was the amount of this good Methodist's piety.

National Anti-Slavery Standard, December 23, 1841

⟶

"MY SLAVE EXPERIENCE IN MARYLAND," SPEECH BEFORE THE AMERICAN ANTI-SLAVERY SOCIETY, MAY 6, 1845

I do not know that I can say anything to the point. My habits and early life have done much to unfit me for public speaking, and I fear that your patience has already been wearied by the lengthened remarks of other speakers, more eloquent than I can possibly be, and better prepared to command the attention of the audience. And I can scarcely hope to get your attention even for a longer period than fifteen minutes.

Before coming to this meeting, I had a sort of desire—I don't know but it was vanity—to stand before a New-York audience in the Tabernacle. But when I came in this morning, and looked at those massive pillars, and saw the vast throng which had assembled, I got a little frightened, and was afraid that I could not speak; but now that the audience is not so large and I have recovered from my fright, I will venture to say a word on Slavery.

I ran away from the South seven years ago—passing through this city in no little hurry, I assure you—and lived about three years in New Bedford, Massachusetts, before I became publicly known to the anti-slavery people. Since then I have been engaged for three years in telling the people what I know of it. I have come to this meeting to throw in my mite, and since no fugitive slave has preceded me, I am encouraged to say a word about the sunny South. I thought, when the eloquent female who addressed this audience a while ago, was speaking of the horrors of Slavery, that many an honest man would doubt the truth of the picture which she drew; and I can unite with the gentleman from Kentucky in saying, that she came far short of describing them.

I can tell you what I have seen with my own eyes, felt on my own person, and know to have occurred in my own neighborhood. I am not from any of those States where the slaves are said to be in their most degraded condition; but from Maryland, where Slavery is said to exist in its mildest form; yet I can stand here and relate atrocities which would make your blood to boil at the statement of them. I lived on the plantation of Col. Lloyd, on the eastern shore of Maryland, and belonged to that gentleman's clerk. He owned, probably, not less than a thousand slaves.

I mention the name of this man, and also of the persons who perpetrated the deeds which I am about to relate, running the risk of being hurled back into interminable bondage—for I am yet a slave;—yet for the sake of the cause—for the sake of humanity, I will mention the names, and glory in running the risk. I have the gratification to know that if I fall by the utterance of truth in this matter, that if I shall be hurled back into bondage to gratify the slaveholder—to be killed by inches—that every drop of blood which I shall shed, every groan which I shall utter, every pain which shall rack my frame, every sob in which I shall induldge, shall be the instrument, under God, of tearing down the bloody pillar of Slavery, and of hastening the day of deliverance for three millions of my brethren in bondage.

I therefore tell the names of these bloody men, not because they are worse than other men would have been in their circumstances. No, they are bloody from necessity. Slavery makes it necessary for the slaveholder to commit all conceivable outrages upon the miserable slave. It is impossible to hold the slaves in bondage without this.

We had on the plantation an overseer, by the name of Austin Gore, a man who was highly respected as an overseer—proud, ambitious, cruel, artful, obdurate. Nearly every slave stood in the utmost dread and horror of that man. His eye flashed confusion amongst them. He never spoke but to command, nor commanded but to be obeyed. He was lavish with the whip, sparing with his word. I have seen that man tie up men by the two hands, and for two hours, at intervals, ply the lash. I have seen women stretched up on the limbs of trees, and their bare backs made bloody with the lash. One slave refused to be whipped by him—I need not tell you that he was a man, though black his features, degraded his condition. He had committed some trifling offence—for they whip for trifling offences—the slave refused to be whipped, and ran—he did not stand to and fight his master as I did once, and might do again— though I hope I shall not have occasion to do so— he ran and stood in a creek, and refused to come out. At length his master told him he would shoot him if he did not come out. Three calls were to be given him. The first, second, and third, were given, at each of which the slave stood his ground. Gore, equally determined and firm, raised his musket, and in an instant poor Derby was no more. He sank beneath the waves, and naught but the crimsoned waters marked the spot. Then a general outcry might be heard amongst us. Mr. Lloyd asked Gore why he had resorted to such a cruel measure. He replied, coolly, that he had

done it from necessity; that the slave was setting a dangerous example, and that if he was permitted to be corrected and yet save his life, that the slaves would effectually rise and be freemen, and their masters be slaves. His defence was satisfactory. He remained on the plantation, and his fame went abroad. He still lives in St. Michaels, Talbot county, Maryland, and is now, I presume, as much respected, as though his guilty soul had never been stained with his brother's blood.

I might go on and mention other facts if time would permit. My own wife had a dear cousin who was terribly mangled in her sleep, while nursing the child of a Mrs. Hicks. Finding the girl asleep, Mrs. Hicks beat her to death with a billet of wood, and the woman has never been brought to justice. It is not a crime to kill a negro in Talbot county, Maryland, farther than it is a deprivation of a man's property. I used to know of one who boasted that he had killed two slaves, and with an oath would say, "I'm the only benefactor in the country."

Now, my friends, pardon me for having detained you so long; but let me tell you with regard to the feelings of the slave. The people at the North say—"Why don't you rise? If we were thus treated we would rise and throw off the yoke. We would wade knee deep in blood before we would endure the bondage." You'd rise up! Who are these that are asking for manhood in the slave, and who say that he has it not, because he does not rise? The very men who are ready by the Constitution to bring the strength of the nation to put us down! You, the people of New-York, the people of Massachusetts, of New England, of the whole Northern States, have sworn under God that we shall be slaves or die! And shall we three millions be taunted with a want of the love of freedom, by the very men who stand upon us and say, submit, or be crushed?

We don't ask you to engage in any physical warfare against the slaveholder. We only ask that in Massachusetts, and the several non-slaveholding States which maintain a union with the slaveholder—who stand with your heavy heels on the quivering heart-strings of the slave, that you will stand off. Leave us to take care of our masters. But here you come up to our masters and tell them that they ought to shoot us—to take away our wives and little ones—to sell our mothers into interminable bondage, and sever the tenderest ties. You say to us, if you dare to carry out the principles of our fathers, we'll shoot you down. Others may tamely submit; not I. You may put the chains upon me and fetter me, but I am not a slave, for my master who puts the chains upon me, shall stand in as much dread of me as I do of him. I ask you in the name of my three millions of brethren at the South. We know that we are unable to cope with you in numbers; you are numerically stronger, politically stronger, than we are—but we ask you if you will rend asunder the heart and [crush] the body of the slave? If so, you must do it at your own expense.

While you continue in the Union, you are as bad as the slaveholder. If you have thus wronged the poor black man, by stripping him of his freedom, how are you going to give evidence of your repentance? Undo what you have done. Do you say that the slave ought not to be free? These hands—are they not mine? This body—is it not mine? Again, I am your brother, white as you are. I'm your blood-kin. You don't get rid of me so easily. I mean to hold on to you. And in this land of liberty, I'm a slave. The twenty-six States that blaze forth on your flag, proclaim a compact to return me to bondage if I run away, and keep me in bondage if I submit. Wherever I go, under the aegis of your liberty, there I'm a slave. If I go to Lexington or Bunker Hill, there I'm a slave, chained in perpetual servitude. I may go to your deepest valley, to your highest mountain, I'm still a slave, and the bloodhound may chase me down.

Now I ask you if you are willing to have your country the hunting-ground of the slave. God says thou shalt not oppress: the Constitution says oppress: which will you serve, God or man? The American Anti-Slavery Society says God, and I am thankful for it. In the name of my brethren, to you, Mr. President, and the noble band who cluster around you, to you, who are scouted on every hand by priest, people, politician, Church, and State, to you I bring a thankful heart, and in the name of three millions of slaves, I offer you their gratitude for your faithful advocacy in behalf of the slave.

National Anti-Slavery Standard, May 22, 1845

KARL MARX

1818–1883

Karl Heinrich Marx, son of a politically active, liberal German lawyer and of Henrietta Pressburg from Holland, was born into privilege on May 5, 1818 in Trier, Rhine Province, Prussia. On both sides his ancestors had been rabbis, but his father converted to Protestantism out of professional necessity. After a seven year courtship, he married Jenny von Westphalen, from a rich noble family, on June 19, 1843, and they produced seven children, only three of whom lived into maturity, all daughters, and all extremely close to both parents. He also sired an illegitimate son, Frederick, by the family's longterm housekeeper, Helene Demuth. Frequently ill and dispirited after Jenny's death, he died at 64 from a lung abscess in London on March 14, 1883 and is buried in Hyde Park cemetery. Marx was educated in the Trier high school (1830–35), studied at Bonn for a year, known for its radical politics, then at Berlin in 1836, but for political reasons was denied permission to submit his doctoral dissertation there. He had fallen under the influence of leftist professors and friends, and finally submitted his dissertation, on Democritus and Epicurus, to the University of Jena in April 1841. Following this, he took a variety of journalistic jobs, finally ending up in Britain in August, 1849, having been expelled from three other countries because of his publications in newspapers and books which encouraged the working class to revolt. He stayed in London for the rest of his professional life, ironically supported by Engels' textile mill in Manchester, composing his greatest work, *Capital,* only one of three volumes of which he saw into print. The *Collected Works of Marx and Engels* in English, now nearing completion, amount to 50 thick volumes of writing.

As everyone knows, Marx and Marxism became the most famous and notorious ingredients in the program of world socialism and communism from about the 1850s until the collapse of the Soviet Union in 1989. His name became a totem for rapid social change, even when the vast majority of people identified as "Marxists" had never read his work. With his lifelong comrade, co-author, and financial backer, Friedrich Engels, he wrote *The Manifesto of the Communist Party* (1848) in two months on behalf of the League of the Just, a craftsman's organization of refugee Germans in London who asked Marx to join them. By nature a scholar and not a politico, Marx had to be dragged from his writing to participate in party work, but he was persuaded to do so repeatedly over the next 35 years. *The German Ideology* (1845–46), unpublished until 1932, laid out the philosophical roots of Marxism. A related work, *The Early Economic and Philosophic Manuscripts* (1844), never saw print until the 1930s in German, then the 1950s in English. Both had tremendous influence on the global Marxist renaissance of the 1960s since the ideas enunciated in these works could easily be connected to currents in philosophy, psychiatry, psychology, literature, sociology, and other fields. It might reasonably be argued that the work of Marx on the page as opposed to the global phenomenon of political Marxism bear as little fundamental relation to each other as do Jefferson's writings about the early U.S. to the state of the nation today. It is important to read Marx with this caveat in mind.

"CONTRIBUTION TO THE CRITIQUE OF POLITICAL ECONOMY," 1859

The first work which I undertook for a solution of the doubts which assailed me was a critical review of the Hegelian philosophy of right, a work the introduction to which appeared in 1844 in the *Deutsch-Französische Jahrbücher,* published in Paris. My investigation led to the result that legal relations as well as forms of state are to be grasped neither from themselves nor from the so-called general development of the human mind, but rather have their roots in the material conditions of life, the sum total of which Hegel, following the example of the Engishmen and Frenchmen of the eighteenth century, combines under the name of "civil society," that, however, the anatomy of civil society is to be sought in political economy. The investigation of the latter, which I began in Paris, I continued in Brussels, whither I had emigrated in consequence of an expulsion order of M. Guizot. The general result at which I arrived and which, once won, served as a guiding thread for my studies, can be briefly formulated as follows: In the social production of their life, men enter into definite relations that are indispensable and independent of their will, relations of production which correspond to a definite stage of development of their material productive forces. The sum total of these relations of production constitutes the economic structure of society, the real foundation, on which rises a legal and political superstructure and to which correspond definite forms of social consciousness. The mode of production of material life conditions the social, political and intellectual life process in general. It is not the consciousness of men that determines their being, but, on the contrary, their social being that determines their consciousness. At a certain stage of their development, the material productive forces of society come in conflict with the existing relations of production, or—what is but a legal expression for the same thing—with the property relations within which they have been at work hitherto. From forms of development of the pro-

ductive forces these relations turn into their fetters. Then begins an epoch of social revolution. With the change of the economic foundation the entire immense superstructure is more or less rapidly transformed. In considering such transformations a distinction should always be made between the material transformation of the economic conditions of production, which can be determined with the precision of natural science, and the legal, political, religious, aesthetic or philosophic—in short, ideological forms in which men become conscious of this conflict and fight it out. Just as our opinion of an individual is not based on what he thinks of himself, so can we not judge of such a period of transformation by its own consciousness; on the contrary, this consciousness must be explained rather from the contradictions of material life, from the existing conflict between the social productive forces and the relations of production. No social order ever perishes before all the productive forces for which there is room in it have developed; and new, higher relations of production never appear before the material conditions of their existence have matured in the womb of the old society itself. Therefore mankind always sets itself only such tasks as it can solve: since, looking at the matter more closely, it will always be found that the task itself arises only when the material conditions for its solution already exist or are at least in the process of formation. In broad outlines Asiatic, ancient, feudal, and modern bourgeois modes of production can be designated as progressive epochs in the economic formation of society. The bourgeois relations of production are the last antagonistic form of the social process of production—antagonistic not in the sense of individual antagonism, but of one arising from the social conditions of life of the individuals: at the same time the productive forces developing in the womb of bourgeois society create the material conditions for the solution of that antagonism. This social formation brings, therefore, the prehistory of human society to a close.

Frederick Engels, with whom, since the appearance of his brilliant sketch on the criticism of the economic categories (in the *Deutsch-Französische Jahrbücher*), I maintained a constant exchange of ideas by correspondence, had by another road (compare his *The Condition of the Working Class in England in 1844*) arrived at the same result as I, and when in the spring of 1845 he also settled in Brussels, we resolved to work out in common the opposition of our view to the ideological view of German philosophy, in fact, to settle accounts with our erstwhile philosophical conscience. The resolve was carried out in the form of a criticism of post-Hegelian philosophy. The manuscript, two large octavo volumes, had long reached its place of publication in Westphalia when we received the news that altered circumstances did not allow of its being printed. We abandoned the manuscript to the gnawing criticism of the mice all the more willingly as we had achieved our main purpose—self-clarification. Of the scattered works in which we put our views before the public at that time, now from one aspect, now from another, I will mention only the *Manifesto of the Communist Party,* jointly written by Engels and myself, and *Discours sur le libre échange* published by me. The decisive points of our view were first scientifically, although only polemically, indicated in my work published in 1847 and directed against Proudhon: *Misère de la Philosophie,* etc. A dissertation written in German on *Wage Labour,* in which I put together my lectures on this subject delivered in the Brussels German Workers' Society, was interrupted, while being printed, by the February Revolution and my consequent forcible removal from Belgium.

❧

THE GERMAN IDEOLOGY, 1845–46

The fact is, therefore, that definite individuals who are productively active in a definite way enter into these definite social and political relations. Empirical observation must in each separate instance bring out empirically, and without any mystification and, speculation, the connection of the social and political structure with production. The social structure and the State are continually evolving out

From *The Marx-Engels Reader,* Second Edition, Robert C. Tucker, Ed. Published by W.W. Norton & Company. Copyright © 1978.

of the life process of definite individuals, but of individuals, not as they may appear in their own or other people's imagination, but as they *really* are; i.e., as they operate, produce materially, and hence as they work under definite material limits, presuppositions and conditions independent of their will.

The production of ideas, of conceptions, of consciousness, is at first directly interwoven with the material activity and the material intercourse of men, the language of real life. Conceiving, thinking, the mental intercourse of men, appear at this stage as the direct efflux of their material behaviour. The same applies to mental production as expressed in the language of politics, laws, morality, religion, metaphysics, etc., of a people. Men are the producers of their conceptions, ideas, etc.—real, active men, as they are conditioned by a definite development of their productive forces and of the intercourse corresponding to these, up to its furthest forms. Consciousness can never be anything else than conscious existence, and the existence of men is their actual life-process. If in all ideology men and their circumstances appear upside-down as in a *camera obscura,* this phenomenon arises just as much from their historical life-process as the inversion of objects on the retina does from their physical life-process.

In direct contrast to German philosophy which descends from heaven to earth, here we ascend from earth to heaven. That is to say, we do not set out from what men say, imagine, conceive, nor from men as narrated, thought of, imagined, conceived, in order to arrive at men in the flesh. We set out from real, active men, and on the basis of their real life-process we demonstrate the development of the ideological reflexes and echoes of this life-process. The phantoms formed in the human brain are also, necessarily, sublimates of their material life-process, which is empirically verifiable and bound to material premises. Morality, religion, metaphysics, all the rest of ideology and their corresponding forms of consciousness, thus no longer retain the semblance of independence. They have no history, no development; but men, developing their material production and their material intercourse, alter, along with this their real existence, their thinking and the products of their thinking. Life is not determined by consciousness, but consciousness by life. In the first method of approach the starting-point is consciousness taken as the living individual; in the second method, which conforms to real life, it is the real living individuals themselves, and consciousness is considered solely as *their* consciousness.

This method of approach is not devoid of premises. It starts out from the real premises and does not abandon them for a moment. Its premises are men, not in any fantastic isolation and rigidity, but in their actual, empirically perceptible process of development under definite conditions. As soon as this active life-process is described, history ceases to be a collection of dead facts as it is with the empiricists (themselves still abstract), or an imagined activity of imagined subjects, as with the idealist.

Where speculation ends—in real life—there real, positive science begins: the representation of the practical activity, of the practical process of development of men. Empty talk about consciousness ceases, and real knowledge has to take its place. When reality is depicted, philosophy as an independent branch of knowledge loses its medium of existence. At the best its place can only be taken by a summing-up of the most general results, abstractions which arise from the observation of the historical development of men. Viewed apart from real history, these abstractions have in themselves no value whatsoever. They can only serve to facilitate the arrangement of historical material, to indicate the sequence of its separate strata. But they by no means afford a recipe or schema, as does philosophy, for neatly trimming the epochs of history. On the contrary, our difficulties begin only when we set about the observation and the arrangement—the real depiction—of our historical material, whether of a past epoch or of the present. The removal of these difficulties is governed by premises which it is quite impossible to state here, but which only the study of the actual life-process and the activity of the individuals of each epoch will make evident. We shall select here some of these abstractions, which we use in contradistinction to the ideologists, and shall illustrate them by historical examples.

CONTRIBUTION TO THE CRITIQUE OF HEGEL'S *PHILOSOPHY OF RIGHT,* 1843

Up till now the *political constitution* has been the *religious sphere,* the *religion* of national life; the heaven of its generality over against the *earthy existence* of its actuality. The political (here has been the only state sphere in the state, the only sphere in which the content as well as the form has been species-content, the truly general; but in such a way that at the same time, because this sphere has confronted the others, its content has also become formal and particular. *Political life* in the modern sense is the *scholasticism* of national life. *Monarchy* is the perfect expression of this estrangement. The *republic* is the negation of this estrangement within its own sphere. It is obvious that the political constitution as such is brought into being only where the private spheres have won an independent existence. Where trade and landed property are not free and have not yet become independent, the political constitution too does not yet exist. The Middle Ages were the *democracy of unfreedom.*

The abstraction of the *state as such* belongs only to modern times, because the abstraction of private life belongs only to modern times. The abstraction of the *political state* is a modern product.

In the Middle Ages there were serfs, feudal estates, merchant and trade guilds, corporations of scholars, etc.: that is to say, in the Middle Ages property, trade, society, man are *political;* the material content of the state is given by its form; every private sphere has a political character or is a political sphere; that is, politics is a characteristic of the private spheres too. In the Middle Ages the political constitution is the constitution of private property, but only because the constitution of private property is a political constitution. In the Middle Ages the life of the nation and the life of the state are identical. Man is the actual principle of the state—but *unfree* man. It is thus the *democracy of unfreedom*—estrangement carried to completion.

From *The Marx-Engels Reader,* Second Edition, Robert C. Tucker, Ed. Published by W.W. Norton & Company. Copyright © 1978.

The abstract reflected antithesis belongs only to the modern world. The Middle Ages are the period of *actual* dualism; modern times, one of *abstract* dualism.

"We have already noted the stage at which the division of constitutions into democracy, aristocracy and monarchy has been made—the standpoint, that is, of that unity which is still *substantial, which still remains within itself and has not yet come to its process of infinite differentiation and inner deepening*: at that stage, the element of the *final self-determining resolution of the will* does not emerge explicitly into its *own proper actuality* as an *immanent* organic factor in the state." In the spontaneously evolved monarchy, democracy and aristocracy there is as yet no political constitution as distinct from the actual, material state or the other content of the life of the nation. The political state does not yet appear as the *form* of the material state. Either, as in Greece, the *res publica*[3] is the real private affair of the citizens, their real content, and the private individual is a slave; the political state, *qua* political state, being the true and only content of the life and will of the citizens; or, as in an Asiatic despotism, the political state is nothing but the personal caprice of a single individual; or the political state, like the material state, is a slave. What distinguishes the modern state from these states characterized by the substantial unity between people and state is not, as Hegel would have it, that the various elements of the constitution have been developed into *particular* actuality, but that the constitution itself has been developed into a *particular* actuality alongside the actual life of the people—that the political state has become the *constitution* of the rest of the state.

* * *

Bureaucracy The "state formalism" which bureaucracy is, is the "state as formalism"; and it is as a formalism of this kind that Hegel has described bureaucracy. Since this "state formalism" constitutes itself as an actual power and itself becomes its own *material* content, it goes without saying that the "bureaucracy" is a web of *practical* illusions, or the "illusion of the state." The bureau-

cratic spirit is a jesuitical, theological spirit through and through. The bureaucrats are the jesuits and theologians of the state. The bureaucracy is *la république prêtre*.

Since by its *very nature* the bureaucracy is the "state as formalism," it is this also as regards its *purpose*. The actual purpose of the state therefore appears to the bureaucracy as an objective *hostile* to the state. The spirit of the bureaucracy is the "formal state spirit." The bureaucracy therefore turns the "formal state spirit" or the *actual* spiritlessness of the state into a categorical imperative. The bureaucracy takes itself to be the ultimate purpose of the state. Because the bureaucracy turns its "formal" objectives into its content, it comes into conflict everywhere with "real" objectives. It is therefore obliged to pass off the form for the content and the content for the form. State objectives are transformed into objectives of the department, and department objectives into objectives of the state. The bureaucracy is a circle from which no one can escape. Its hierarchy is a *hierarchy of knowledge*. The top entrusts the understanding of detail to the lower levels, whilst the lower levels credit the top with understanding of the general, and so all are mutually deceived.

The bureaucracy is the imaginary state alongside the real state—the spiritualism of the state. Each thing has therefore a double meaning, a real and a bureaucratic meaning, just as knowledge (and also the will) is both real and bureaucratic. The really existing, however, is treated in the light of its bureaucratic nature, its other-worldly, spiritual essence. The bureaucracy has the state, the spiritual essence of society, in its possession, as its *private property*. The general spirit of the bureaucracy is the *secret*, the mystery, preserved within itself by the hierarchy and against the outside world by being a closed corporation. Avowed political spirit, as also political-mindedness, therefore appear to the bureaucracy as *treason* against its mystery. Hence, *authority* is the basis of its knowledge, and the deification of authority is its *conviction*. Within the bureaucracy itself, however, *spiritualism* becomes *crass materialism*, the materialism of passive obedience, of faith in authority, of the *mechanism* of fixed and formalistic behaviour, and of fixed principles, views and traditions. In the case of the individual bureaucrat, the state objective turns into his private objective, into a *chasing after higher posts*, the *making of a career*. In the first place, he looks on actual life as something *material*, for the *spirit of this life has its distinctly separate existence* in the bureaucracy. The bureaucracy must therefore proceed to make life as material as possible. Secondly, actual life is material for the bureaucrat himself, i.e., so far as it becomes an object of bureaucratic manipulation; for his spirit is prescribed for him, his aim lies beyond him, and his existence is the existence of the department. The state only continues to exist as various fixed bureaucratic minds, bound together in subordination and passive obedience. *Actual* knowledge seems devoid of content, just as actual life seems dead; for this imaginary knowledge and this imaginary life are taken for the real thing. The bureaucrat must therefore deal with the actual state jesuitically, whether this jesuitry is conscious or unconscious. However, once its antithesis is knowledge, this jesuitry is likewise bound to achieve self-consciousness and then become deliberate jesuitry.

Whilst the bureaucracy is on the one hand this crass materialism, it manifests its crass spiritualism in the fact that it wants to *do everything*, i.e., by making the *will* the *causa prima*. For it is purely an *active* form of existence and receives its content from without and can prove its existence, therefore, only by shaping and restricting this content. For the bureaucrat the world is a mere object to be manipulated by him.

When Hegel calls the executive the *objective* aspect of the sovereignty dwelling in the monarch, that is right in the same sense in which the Catholic Church was the *real presence* of the sovereignty, substance and spirit of the Holy Trinity. In the bureaucracy the identity of state interest and particular private aim is established in such a way that the state interest becomes a *particular* private aim over against other private aims.

The abolition of the bureaucracy is only possible by the general interest *actually*—and not, as with Hegel, merely in thought, in *abstraction*—becoming the particular interest, which in turn is only possible as a result of the *particular* actually becoming the *general* interest. Hegel starts from an unreal antithesis and therefore achieves only an imaginary identity which is in truth again a contradictory identity. The bureaucracy is just such an identity.

Note

3. I.e., state, republic; etymologically, "public affairs."

⟿

ECONOMIC AND PHILOSOPHIC MANUSCRIPTS OF 1844

Estranged Labour

We have proceeded from the premises of political economy. We have accepted its language and its laws. We presupposed private property, the separation of labour, capital and land, and of wages, profit of capital and rent of land—likewise division of labour, competition, the concept of exchange-value, etc. On the basis of political economy itself, in its own words, we have shown that the worker sinks to the level of a commodity and becomes indeed the most wretched of commodities; that the wretchedness of the worker is in inverse proportion to the power and magnitude of his production; that the necessary result of competition is the accumulation of capital in a few hands, and thus the restoration of monopoly in a more terrible form; that finally the distinction between capitalist and land-rentier, like that between the tiller of the soil and the factory-worker, disappears and that the whole of society must fall apart into the two classes—the property-*owners* and the propertyless *workers*.

Political economy proceeds from the fact of private property, but it does not explain it to us. It expresses in general, abstract formulae the *material* process through which private property actually passes, and these formulae it then takes for *laws*. It does not *comprehend* these laws—i.e., it does not demonstrate how they arise from the very nature of private property. Political economy does not disclose the source of the division between labour and capital, and between capital and land. When, for example, it defines the relationship of wages to profit, it takes the interest of the

From *The Marx-Engels Reader*, Second Edition, Robert C. Tucker, Ed. Published by W.W. Norton & Company. Copyright © 1978.

capitalists to be the ultimate cause; i.e., it takes for granted what it is supposed to evolve. Similarly, competition comes in everywhere. It is explained from external circumstances. As to how far these external and apparently fortuitous circumstances are but the expression of a necessary course of development, political economy teaches us nothing. We have seen how, to it, exchange itself appears to be a fortuitous fact. The only wheels which political economy sets in motion are avarice and the *war amongst the avaricious—competition.*

Precisely because political economy does not grasp the connections within the movement, it was possible to counterpose, for instance, the doctrine of competition to the doctrine of monopoly, the doctrine of craft-liberty to the doctrine of the corporation, the doctrine of the division of landed property to the doctrine of the big estate—for competition, craft-liberty and the division of landed property were explained and comprehended only as fortuitous, pre-meditated and violent consequences of monopoly, the corporation, and feudal property, not as their necessary, inevitable and natural consequences.

Now, therefore, we have to grasp the essential connection between private property, avarice, and the separation of labour, capital and landed. property; between exchange and competition, value and the devaluation of men, monopoly and competition, etc.; the connection between this whole estrangement and the *money*-system.

Do not let us go back to a fictitious primordial condition as the political economist does, when he tries to explain. Such a primordial condition explains nothing. He merely pushes the question away into a grey nebulous distance. He assumes in the form of fact, of an event, what he is supposed to deduce—namely, the necessary relationship between two things—between, for example, division of labour and exchange. Theology in the same way explains the origin of evil by the fall of man: that is, it assumes as a fact, in historical form, what has to be explained.

We proceed from an *actual* economic fact.

The worker becomes all the poorer the more wealth he produces, the more his production increases in power and range. The worker becomes an ever cheaper commodity the more commodities he creates. With the *increasing value* of the world of things proceeds in direct proportion the *devalua-*

tion of the world of men. Labour produces not only commodities; it produces itself and the worker as a *commodity*—and does so in the proportion in which it produces commodities generally.

This fact expresses merely that the object which labour produces—labour's product—confronts it as *something alien,* as a *power independent* of the producer. The product of labour is labour which has been congealed in an object, which has become material: it is the *objectification* of labour. Labour's realization is its objectification. In the conditions dealt with by political economy this realization of labour appears as *loss of reality* for the workers; objectification as *loss of the object* and *object-bondage;* appropriation as *estrangement, as alienation.*

So much does labour's realization appear as loss of reality that the worker loses reality to the point of starving to death. So much does objectification appear as loss of the object that the worker is robbed of the objects most necessary not only for his life but for his work. Indeed, labour itself becomes an object which he can get hold of only with the greatest effort and with the most irregular interruptions. So much does the appropriation of the object appear as estrangement that the more objects the worker produces the fewer can he possess and the more he falls under the dominion of his product, capital.

All these consequences are contained in the definition that the worker is related to the *product of his labour* as to an *alien* object. For on this premise it is clear that the more the worker spends himself, the more powerful the alien objective world becomes which he creates ever-against himself, the poorer he himself—his inner world—becomes, the less belongs to him as his own. It is the same in religion. The more man puts into God, the less he retains in himself. The worker puts his life into the object; but now his life no longer belongs to him but to the object. Hence, the greater this activity, the greater is the worker's lack of objects. Whatever the product of his labour is, he is not. Therefore the greater this product, the less is he himself. The *alienation* of the worker in his product means not only that his labour becomes an object, an *external* existence, but that it exists *outside him,* independently, as something alien to him, and that it becomes a power of its own confronting him; it means that the life which he has conferred on the object confronts him as something hostile and alien.

Let us now look more closely at the *objectification,* at the production of the worker; and therein at the *estrangement,* the *loss* of the object, his product.

The worker can create nothing without *nature,* without the *sensuous external world.* It is the material on which his labor is manifested, in which it is active, from which and by means of which it produces.

But just as nature provides labor with the *means of life* in the sense that labour cannot live without objects on which to operate, on the other hand, it also provides the *means of life* in the more restricted sense—i.e., the means for the physical subsistence of the *worker* himself.

Thus the more the worker by his labour *appropriates* the external world, sensuous nature, the more he deprives himself of *means of life* in the double respect: first, that the sensuous external world more and more ceases to be an object belonging to his labour—to be his labour's *means of life;* and secondly, that it more and more ceases to be *means of life* in the immediate sense, means for the physical subsistence of the worker.

Thus in this double respect the worker becomes a slave of his object, first, in that he receives an *object of labour,* i.e., in that he receives *work;* and secondly, in that he receives *means of subsistence.* Therefore, it enables him to exist, first, as a *worker;* and, second, as a *physical subject.* The extremity of this bondage is that it is only as a *worker* that he continues to maintain himself as a *physical subject,* and that it is only as a *physical subject* that he is a *worker.*

(The laws of political economy express the estrangement of the worker in his object thus: the more the worker produces, the less he has to consume; the more values he creates, the more valueless, the more unworthy he becomes; the better formed his product, the more deformed becomes the worker; the more civilized his object, the more barbarous becomes the worker, the mightier labour becomes, the more powerless becomes the worker; the more ingenious labour becomes, the duller becomes the worker and the more he becomes nature's bondsman.)

Political economy conceals the estrangement inherent in the nature of labour by not considering the direct relationship between the worker (labour) *and production.* It is true that labour produces for the rich wonderful things—but for the worker it produces privation. It produces palaces—but for the worker, hovels. It produces beauty—but for the worker, deformity. It replaces labour by machines—but some of the workers it throws back to a barbarous type of labour, and the other workers it turns into machines. It produces intelligence—but for the worker idiocy, cretinism.

The direct relationship of labour to its produce is the relationship of the worker to the objects of his production. The relationship of the man of means to the objects of production and to production itself is only a consequence of this first relationship—and confirms it. We shall consider this other aspect later.

When we ask, then, what is the essential relationship of labour we are asking about the relationship of the *worker* to production.

Till now we have been considering the estrangement, the alienation of the worker only in one of its aspects, i.e., the worker's *relationship to the products of his labour.* But the estrangement is manifested not only in the result but in the *act of production*—within the *producing activity* itself. How would the worker come to face the product of his activity as a stranger, were it not that in the very act of production he was estranging himself from himself? The product is after all but the summary of the activity of production. If then the product of labour is alienation, production itself must be active alienation, the alienation of activity, the activity of alienation. In the estrangement of the object of labour is merely summarized the estrangement, the alienation, in the activity of labour itself.

What, then, constitutes the alienation of labour?

First, the fact that labour is *external* to the worker, i.e., it does not belong to his essential being; that in his work, therefore, he does not affirm himself but denies himself, does not feel content but unhappy, does not develop freely his physical and mental energy but mortifies his body and ruins his mind. The worker therefore only feels himself outside his work, and in his work feels outside himself. He is at home when he is not working, and when he is working he is not at home. His labour is therefore not voluntary, but coerced; it is *forced labour.* It is therefore not the satisfaction of a need; it is merely a *means* to satisfy needs external to it. Its alien character emerges clearly in the fact that as soon as no physical or other compulsion exists, labour is shunned like the plague. External labour, labour in which man alienates himself, is a labour of self-sacrifice, of mortification. Lastly, the external character of labour for the worker appears in the fact that it is not his own, but someone else's, that it does not belong to him, that in it he belongs, not to himself, but to another. Just as in religion the spontaneous activity of the human imagination, of the human, brain and the human heart, operates independently of the individual—that is, operates on him as an alien, divine or diabolical activity—in the same way the worker's activity is not his spontaneous activity. It belongs to another; it is the loss of his self.

As a result, therefore, man (the worker) no longer feels himself to be freely active in any but his animal functions—eating, drinking, procreating, or at most in his dwelling and in dressing-up, etc.; and in his human functions he no longer feels himself to be anything but an animal. What is animal becomes human and what is human becomes animal.

Certainly eating, drinking, procreating, etc., are also genuinely human functions. But in the abstraction which separates them from the sphere of all other human activity and turns them into sole and ultimate ends, they are animal.

We have considered the act of estranging practical human activity, labour, in two of its aspects. (1) The relation of the worker to the *product of labour* as an alien object exercising power over him. This relation is at the same time the relation to the sensuous external world, to the objects of nature as an alien world antagonistically opposed to him. (2) The relation of labour to the *act of production* within the *labour* process. This relation is the relation of the worker to his own activity as an alien activity not belonging to him; it is activity as suffering, strength as weakness, begetting as emasculating, the worker's own physical and mental energy, his personal life or what is life other than activity—as an activity which is turned against him, neither depends on nor belongs to him. Here we have *self-estrangement*, as we had previously the estrangement of the *thing*.

We have yet a third aspect of *estranged labour* to deduce front the two already considered.

Man is a species being, not only because in practice and in theory he adopts the species as his object (his own as well as those of other things), but—and this is only another way of expressing it—but also because he treats himself as the actual, living species; because he treats himself as a *universal* and therefore a free being.

The life of the species, both in man and in animals, consists physically in the fact that man (like the animal) lives on inorganic nature; and the more universal man is compared with an animal, the more universal is the sphere of inorganic nature on which he lives. Just as plants, animals, stones, the air, light, etc., constitute a part of human consciousness in the realm of theory, partly as objects of natural science, partly as objects of art—his spiritual inorganic nature, spiritual nourishment which he must first prepare to make it palatable and digestible—so too in the realm of practice they constitute a part of human life and human activity. Physically man lives only on these products of nature, whether they appear in the form of food, heating, clothes, a dwelling, or whatever it may be. The universality of man is in practice manifested precisely in the universality which makes all nature his *inorganic* body—both inasmuch as nature is (1) his direct means of life, and (2) the material, the object, and the instrument of his life-activity. Nature is man's *inorganic* body—nature, that is, in so far as it is not itself the human body. Man *lives* on nature—means that nature is his *body,* with which he must remain in continuous intercourse if he is not to die. That man's physical and spiritual life is linked to nature means simply that nature is linked to itself, for man is a part of nature.

In estranging from man (1) nature, and (2) himself, his own active functions, his life-activity, estranged labour estranges the *species* from man. It turns for him the *life of the species* into a means of individual life. First it estranges the life of the species and individual life, and secondly it makes individual life in its abstract form the purpose of the life of the species, likewise in its abstract and estranged form. . . .

Estranged labour turns thus:

(3) *Man's species being*, both nature and his spiritual species property, into a being *alien* to him,

into *a means to his individual existence*. It estranges man's own body from him, as it does external nature and his spiritual essence, his *human* being.

(4) An immediate consequence of the fact that man is estranged from the product of his labour, from his life-activity, from his species being is the *estrangement of man from man*. If a man is confronted by himself, he is confronted by the *other* man. What applies to a man's relation to his work, to the product of his labour and to himself, also holds of a man's relation to the other man, and to the other man's labour and object of labour.

In fact, the proposition that man's species nature is estranged from him means that one man is estranged from the other, as each of them is from man's essential nature.

The estrangement of man, and in fact every relationship in which man stands to himself, is first realized and expressed in the relationship in which a man stands to other men.

Hence within the relationship of estranged labour each man views the other in accordance with the standard and the position in which he finds himself as a worker.

We took our departure from a fact of political economy—the estrangement of the worker and his production. We have formulated the concept of this fact–*estranged, alienated* labour. We have analysed this concept—hence analysing merely a fact of political economy.

SØREN KIERKEGAARD

1813–1855

Søren Aabye Kierkegaard was born in Copenhagen, Denmark on May 5, 1813, the attentive son of a stern, prosperous Lutheran merchant of peculiar religious seriousness, who had dramatically cursed God for his misery before his fortunes changed and he became rich. Kierkegaard was briefly engaged to Regine Olsen, but broke the engagement through a long and histrionic process, never married, and died in the same city on November 11, 1855 at the age of 42. He had become paralyzed from the waist down a few weeks before dying, and claimed his illness was connected to a youthful spinal injury but was mostly psychosomatic in nature. In 1838 he lost his dominating father, but gained a large fortune on which to live for the rest of his life while writing endlessly. He graduated from the University of Copenhagen in 1840 with a masters in theology, travelled in Germany for the next two years, and returned from Berlin in 1842 with the bulky manuscript of *Either/Or: A Fragment of Life*. In this seminal work he contrasted the aesthetic versus ethical or religious modes of existence between which one must choose. He recounted the events of his abortive relationship with Ms. Olsen, explaining that had no ethical choice but to dispense with her, even at great emotional cost to himself. It was this stubborn insistence upon the need to act upon ethical choices which connected Kierkegaard with existentialism in the 1950s and 60s, and gave him a much wider reputation than he had had before. The target of his passionate, quixotic works was always intellectual sterility and abstractness, for the proliferation of which he blamed Hegel. This came out particularly in the important and strangely titled *Concluding Unscientific Postscript to the Philosophical Fragment: A Mimic-Pathetic-Dialectic Composition, an Existential Contribution* (1946), wherein he attacks the Hegelianism that had become the philosophical tidal wave of the period. For Kierkegaard, Hegel's attempt to systematize all existence was doomed to failure because life is forever changing and truth is to be found in this change, not in static categories.

Kierkegaard's other important works, which continue to be read and debated, include *Fear and Trembling* (1843), *Philosophical Fragments* (1844), *The Concept of Dread* (1844), and *Stages on Life's Way* (1845). This torrent of scholarly productivity is astonishing by any standard, and Kierkegaard actually hid his achievement, though not too successfully, by publishing the books under various pseudonyms. The selection reprinted here comes from an essay, "The Present Age," in which a bitter Kierkegaard rails against the beginnings of what we now call "mass culture," its dullness, predictability, and lack of subtlety. It had treated him badly, of course.

THE PRESENT AGE, 1846

The Individual and the Public

Our age is essentially one of understanding and reflection, without passion, momentarily bursting into enthusiasm, and shrewdly relapsing into repose.

If we had statistical tables of the consumption of intelligence from generation to generation as we have for spirits, we should be astounded at the enormous amount of scruple and deliberation consumed by even small, well-to-do families living quietly, and at the amount which the young, and even children, use. For just as the children's crusade may be said to typify the Middle Ages, precocious children are typical of the present age. In fact one is tempted to ask whether there is a single man left who, for once, commits an outrageous folly.

Nowadays not even a suicide kills himself in desperation. Before taking the step he deliberates so long and so carefully that he literally chokes with thought. It is even questionable whether he ought to be called a suicide, since it is really thought which takes his life. He does not die *with* deliberation but *from* deliberation.

It would therefore be very difficult to prosecute the present generation because of its legal quibbles; in fact, all its ability, virtuosity and good sense consists in trying to get a judgement and a decision without ever getting as far as action. If one may say of the revolutionary period that it runs wild, one would have to say of the present that it runs badly. Between them, the individual and his generation always bring each other to a standstill, with the result that the prosecuting attorney would find it next to impossible to get any fact admitted—because nothing ever happens. To judge from innumerable indications one would conclude that something quite exceptional had either just happened or was just about to happen. Yet any such conclusion would be quite wrong. Indications are, indeed, the only achievements of the age; and its skill and inventiveness in constructing

fascinating illusions, or its burst of enthusiasm, using as a deceitful escape some projected change of form, must be rated as high in the scale of cleverness and of the negative use of strength as the passionate, creative energy of the revolution in the corresponding scale of energy. But the present generation, wearied by its chimerical efforts, relapses into complete indolence. Its condition is that of a man who has only fallen asleep towards morning: first of all come great dreams, then a feeling of laziness, and finally a witty or clever excuse for remaining in bed.

The world's deepest misfortune is the unhappy objectivity (in the sense of the absence of personality) characteristic of all speech and teaching, and that the one great mechanical discovery after the other has made it possible to expound doctrines impersonally in constantly increasing measure. There no longer exist human beings: there are no lovers, no thinkers, etc. By means of the press the human race has enveloped itself in an atmospheric what-not of thoughts, feelings, moods; even of resolutions and purposes, all of which are no one's property, since they belong to all and none. It is a torture to the soul to note the callous incorrigibility with which a human being can resort to wherever he thinks there is some truth to be had, for the sole purpose of learning to expound it, so that his music box may add this piece to its repertoire; but as for doing anything about it, the thing never even occurs to him.

If the jewel which every one desired to possess lay far out on a frozen lake where the ice was very thin, watched over by the danger of death, while closer in the ice was perfectly safe, then in a passionate age the crowds would applaud the courage of the man who ventured out, they would tremble for him and with him in the danger of his decisive action, they would grieve over him if he were drowned, they would make a god of him if he secured the prize. But in an age without passion, in a reflective age, it would be otherwise. People would think each other clever in agreeing that it was unreasonable and not even worth while to venture so far out. And in this way they would transform *daring and enthusiasm* into a *feat of skill*, so as to do something, for after all

From *The Living Thoughts of Kierkegaard,* presented by W.H. Auden. Published by David McKay Company, Inc. Copyright © 1952.

"something must be done." The crowds would go out to watch from a safe place, and with the eyes of connoisseurs appraise the accomplished skater who could skate almost to the very edge (i.e., as far as the ice was still safe and the danger had not begun) and then turn back. The most accomplished skater would manage to go out to the furthermost point and then do a still more dangerous-looking run, so as to make the spectators hold their breath and say: "Ye gods! He is mad, he is risking his life." But look, and you will see that his skill was so astonishing that he managed to turn back just time, while the ice was perfectly safe and there was still no danger. As at the theatre, the crowd would applaud and acclaim him, surging homeward with the heroic artist in their midst, to honour him with a magnificent banquet. For intelligence has got the upper hand to such an extent that it transforms the real task into an unreal trick, and reality into play. During the banquet admiration would reach its height. Now the proper relation between the admirer and the object of admiration is one in which the admirer is edified by the thought that he is a man like the hero, humbled by the thought that he is incapable of such great actions, yet morally encouraged to emulate him according to his powers; but where intelligence has got the upper hand the character of admiration is completely altered. Even at the height of the banquet, when the applause was loudest, the admiring guests would all have a shrewd notion that the action of the man who received all the honour was not really so extraordinary, and that only by chance was the gathering for him, since after all, with a little practice, every one could have done as much. Briefly, instead of being strengthened in their discernment and encouraged to do good the guests would more probably go home with an even stronger predisposition for the most dangerous, if also the most respectable, of all diseases: to admire in public what they consider important in private, since everything is made into a joke; and so, stimulated by the gush of admiration, they are comfortably agreed that they might just as well admire themselves.

A quality is no longer related to its contrary, instead the partners both stand and observe each other and *the state of tension thus produced is really the end of the relationship.* For example, the admirer no longer cheerfully and happily acknowledges greatness, promptly expressing his appreciation, and then rebelling against its pride and arrogance. Nor is the relationship in any sense the opposite. The admirer and the object of admiration stand like two polite equals and observe each other. A subject no longer freely honours his king or is angered at his ambition. To be a subject has come to mean something quite different; it means to be a *third party.* The subject ceases to have a position within the relationship; he has no direct relation to the king but simply becomes an observer and deliberately works out the problem: i.e., the relation of a subject to his king. For a time committee after committee is formed, so long, that is to say, as there are still people who passionately want to be what they ought to be; but in the end the whole age becomes a committee. A father no longer curses his son in anger, using all his parental authority, nor does a son defy his father, a conflict which might end in the inwardness of forgiveness; on the contrary, their relationship is irreproachable, for it is really in process of ceasing to exist, since they are no longer related to one another within the relationship. In fact it has become a problem in which the two partners observe each other as in a game, instead of having any relation to each other, and they note down each other's remarks instead of showing a firm devotion. More and more people renounce the quiet and modest tasks of life that are so important and pleasing to God in order to achieve something greater; in order to think over the relationships of life in a higher relationship till in the end the whole generation has become a representation, who represent . . . it is difficult to say *who*; and who think about these relationships . . . for *whose* sake it is not easy to discover. A disobedient youth is no longer in fear of his schoolmaster—the relation is rather one of indifference in which schoolmaster and pupil discuss how a good school should be run. To go to school no longer means to be in fear of the master, or merely to learn, but it rather implies being interested in the problem of education. Again the differentiating relation of man to woman is never broken in an audaciously licentious manner; decency is observed in such a way that one can only describe these innocent borderline flirtations as trivial.

The bourgeois mind is really the inability to rise above the absolute reality of time and space, and as such is therefore able to devote itself to the highest objects, e.g., prayer, at certain times and with certain words.

The opposite of the bourgeois mentality is really the Quaker religion (in its abstract significance), where it includes the uncertainty and chance which is found in the life of so many; altogether it is an annihilation of the historical process. . . .

If the natural sciences had been developed in Socrates' day as they are now, all the sophists would have been scientists. One would have hung a microscope outside his shop in order to attract custom, and then would have had a sign painted saying: "Learn and see through a giant microscope how a man thinks" (and on reading the advertisement Socrates would have said: "that is how men who do not think behave").

Every distinguished individual always has something one-sided about him, and this one-sidedness may be an indirect indication of his real greatness, but it is not that greatness itself. So far are we human beings from realizing the ideal, that the second rank, the powerful one-sidedness, is pretty much the highest ever attained; but it must never be forgotten that it is only the second rank. It might be urged that the present generation is, from this point of view, praiseworthy, in so one-sidedly aiming to express the intellectual and the scientific. My answer would be that the misfortune of the present age is not that it is one-sided, but that it is abstractly all-sided. A one-sided individual rejects, and definitely, what he does not wish to include; but the abstractly all-sided individual imagines that he has everything through the one-sidedness of the intellectual. A one-sided believer refuses to have anything to do with thought, and a one-sided man of action will have nothing to do with science; but the one-sidedness

of the intellectual creates the illusion of having everything. . . .

Levelling can be accomplished by one particular cast, e.g., the clergy, the bourgeois, the peasants, by the people themselves. But all that is only the first movement of an abstract power within the concreteness of individuality.

In order that everything should be reduced to the same level it is first of all necessary to procure a phantom, its spirit, a monstrous abstraction, an all-embracing something which is nothing, a mirage—and that phantom is *the public.* It is only in an age which is without passion, yet reflective, that such phantom can develop itself with the help of the press which itself becomes an abstraction. In times of passion and tumult and enthusiasm, even when a people desire to realize a fruitless idea and lay waste and destroy everything: even then there is no such thing as a public. There are parties and they are concrete. The press, in times such as those, takes on a concrete character according to the division of parties. But just as sedentary professional people are the first to take up any fantastic illusion which comes their way, so a passionless, sedentary, reflective age, in which only the press exhibits a vague sort of life, fosters this phantom. The public is, in fact, the real Levelling-Master rather than the actual leveller, for whenever levelling is only approximately accomplished it is done by something, but the public is a monstrous nothing. The public is a concept which could not have occurred in antiquity because the people *en masse, in corpore,* took part in any situation which arose and were responsible for the actions of the individual, and, moreover, the individual was personally present and had to submit at once to applause or disapproval for his decision. Only when the sense of association in society is no longer strong enough to give life to concrete realities is the press able to create that abstraction "the public," consisting of unreal individuals who never are and never can be united in an actual situation or organization—and yet are held together as a whole.

HARRIET TAYLOR MILL

1807–1858

Daughter of a surgeon, Harriet Hardy was born in London on October 8, 1807, married John Taylor on March 14, 1826 when 18, with him had three children, and following his death married John Stuart Mill in 1851. She died on November 3, 1858 in Avignon, France, at 51. It was by marrying Mill and writing with him (and because he wrote so enthusiastically about her) that she has entered the canon of social theorists. Harriet Taylor and her husband, John, worked in a radical wing of the Unitarian Church, and through these associations, Harriet met John Stuart Mill in 1830. Their mutual attraction, on both intellectual and personal grounds, led to her estrangement from her husband and separation in 1833. Even though she did not become Mill's lover, so they said, the norms of that time made them outcasts from "polite society." They nevertheless spent time together and worked on essays and Mill's books, which he later claimed she virtually co-authored. Scholars have debated her true input ever since Mill made these claims in his *Autobiography,* but it is clear that she had great influence on Mill's view of the world whether or not she actually wrote his works with him. She pushed for the equality and independence of women, and tried to bring Mill around to this extremely radical view, for the time. He accepted their equality, but balked at the notion of women's total independence.

Harriet Mill was much taken with the ideas of Robert Owen, author of *A New View of Society* (1814), an early version of socialism. From him she took the notion that women's true equality with men depended on their full economic participation in life, which at the time was unheard of. John Taylor died of cancer in 1849, but the couple waited two years for the sake of appearances before marrying. *The Westminster Review* published an article allegedly by J. S. Mill, "The Enfranchisement of Women," shortly after their marriage, but it was in fact the work of Harriet. It is from this article that the excerpt below originates. They also wrote articles concerning legal remedies for the physical abuse of women by their husbands.

Before Harriet's death from tuberculosis in 1858, she and Mill had been working on a book, *The Subjection of Women,* which Mill finished with the help of Harriet's daughter, Helen Taylor, who continued helping Mill for the next 15 years. Mill warmly credits both women for their aid and for having minds superior to his own. Although the ideas which appear in these works now seem unexceptional, at the time they were considered extraordinarily odd, so much so that Mill brought the question of women's suffrage before the House of Commons in 1867, it was voted down, 196 to 73.

"ENFRANCHISEMENT OF WOMEN," 1851

Most of our readers will probably learn from these pages for the first time, that there has arisen in the United States, and in the most civilized and enlightened portion of them, an organized agitation on a new question—new, not to thinkers, nor to any one by whom the principles of free and popular government are felt as well as acknowledged, but new, and even unheard-of, as a subject for public meetings and practical political action. This question is, the enfranchisement of women; their admission, in law and in fact, to equality in all rights, political, civil, and social, with the male citizens of the community.

It will add to the surprise with which many will receive this intelligence, that the agitation which has commenced is not a pleading by male writers and orators for women, those who are professedly to be benefited remaining either indifferent or ostensibly hostile. It is a political movement, practical in its objects, carried on in a form which denotes an intention to persevere. And it is a movement not merely *for* women, but *by* them. Its first public manifestation appears to have been a Convention of Women, held in the State of Ohio, in the spring of 1850. Of this meeting we have seen no report. On the 23rd and 24th of October last, a succession of public meetings was held at Worcester in Massachusetts, under the name of a "Women's Rights Convention," of which the president was a woman, and nearly all the chief speakers women: numerously reinforced, however, by men, among whom were some of the most distinguished leaders in the kindred cause of negro emancipation. A general and four special committees were nominated, for the purpose of carrying on the undertaking until the next annual meeting.

According to the report in the *New York Tribune*, above a thousand persons were present throughout, and "if a larger place could have been had, many thousands more would have attended." The place was described as "crowded

from the beginning with attentive and interested listeners." In regard to the quality of the speaking, the proceedings bear an advantageous comparison with those of any popular movement with which we are acquainted, either in this country or in America. Very rarely in the oratory of public meetings is the part of verbiage and declamation so small, that of calm good sense and reason so considerable. The result of the Convention was in every respect encouraging to those by whom it was summoned: and it is probably destined to inaugurate one of the most important of the movements towards political and social reform, which are the best characteristics of the present age.

That the promoters of this new agitation take their stand on principles, and do not fear to declare these in their widest extent, without time-serving or compromise, will be seen from the resolutions adopted by the Convention, part of which we transcribe.

Resolved—That every human being, of full age, and resident for a proper length of time on the soil of the nation, who is required to obey the law, is entitled to a voice in its enactment; that every such person, whose property or labour is taxed for the support of the government, is entitled to a direct share in such government; therefore,

Resolved—That women are entitled to the right of suffrage, and to be considered eligible to office, . . . and that every party which claims to represent the humanity, the civilization, and the progress of the age, is bound to inscribe on its banners equality before the law, without distinction of sex or colour.

Resolved—That civil and political rights acknowledge no sex, and therefore the word "male" should be struck from every State Constitution.

Resolved—That, since the prospect of honourable and useful employment in after-life is the best stimulus to the use of educational advantages, and since the best education is that we give ourselves, in the struggles, employments, and discipline of life; therefore it is impossible that women should make full use of the instruction already accorded to them, or that their career should do justice to their faculties, until the avenues to the various civil and professional employments are thrown open to them.

Resolved—That every effort to educate women, without according to them their rights, and arousing their conscience by the weight of their responsibilities, is futile, and a waste of labour.

Resolved—That the laws of property, as affecting married persons, demand a thorough revisal, so that

"Enfranchisement of Women," by Harriet Taylor. Originally published in *Westminster Review,* July 1851.

all rights be equal between them; that the wife have, during life, an equal control over the property gained by their mutual toil and sacrifices, and be heir to her husband precisely to that extent that he is heir to her, and entitled at her death to dispose by will of the same share of the joint property as he is.

The following is a brief summary of the principal demands.

1. *Education* in primary and high schools, universities, medical, legal, and theological institutions.
2. *Partnership* in the labours and gains, risks and remunerations, of productive industry.
3. *A coequal share* in the formation and administration of laws—municipal, state, and national—through legislative assemblies, courts, and executive offices.

It would be difficult to put so much true, just, and reasonable meaning into a style so little calculated to recommend it as that of some of the resolutions. But whatever objection may be made to some of the expressions, none, in our opinion, can be made to the demands themselves. As a question of justice, the case seems to us too clear for dispute. As one of expediency, the more thoroughly it is examined the stronger it will appear.

That women have as good a claim as men have, in point of personal right, to the suffrage, or to a place in the jurybox, it would be difficult for any one to deny. It cannot certainly be denied by

the United States of America, as a people or as a community. Their democratic institutions rest avowedly on the inherent right of every one to a voice in the government. Their Declaration of Independence, framed by the men who are still their great constitutional authorities—that document which has been from the first, and is now, the acknowledged basis of their polity, commences with this express statement:

> We hold these truths to be self-evident: that all men are created equal; that they are endowed by their Creator with certain inalienable rights; that among these are life, liberty, and the pursuit of happiness; that to secure these rights, governments are instituted among men, deriving their just powers from the consent of the governed.

We do not imagine that any American democrat will evade the force of these expressions by the dishonest or ignorant subterfuge, that "men," in this memorable document, does not stand for human beings, but for one sex only; that "life, liberty, and the pursuit of happiness" are "inalienable rights" of only one moiety of the human species; and that "the governed," whose consent is affirmed to be the only source of just power, are meant for that half of mankind only, who, in relation to the other, have hitherto assumed the character of governors. The contradiction between principle and practice cannot be explained away.

ARTHUR SCHOPENHAUER

1788–1860

Arthur Schopenhauer was born in Danzig, Prussia (now Gdansk, Poland) on February 22, 1788, the son of a rich merchant father and a successful writer mother, with whom he competed and quarreled. He never married and died suddenly at 72 on September 21, 1860 in Frankfurt-am-Main. Schopenhauer grew up in Hamburg, where he was well educated, attending a business school, but also becoming well acquainted with Enlightenment thought. When he was 15 he took the traditional "grand tour" of Europe with his parents. After his father's premature death in 1805, his mother and younger sister, Adele, moved to Weimar where she inserted herself into the salon culture built around Goethe and Christoph Wieland. He stayed behind in Hamburg, studying liberal arts courses in preparation for college. He finally moved to the University of Göttingen in 1807 and pursued a medical degree, having finished college prep courses in Weimar and Gotha. His enthusiasm for medicine waned, and instead he pursued Plato's and Kant's philosophies. He then attended the University of Berlin, where he heard Schleiermacher and Fichte lecture. As others before him, he submitted his dissertation to the more relaxed standards of the University of Jena, in 1813. The rest of his professional life was spent in a fruitless attempt to unseat Hegel from the position of top philosopher at Berlin by scheduling his lectures simultaneously with Hegel's. This hopeless strategy guaranteed him no students, so after one set of lectures, he retired from the field and wrote instead.

What makes Schopenhauer interesting—he has long been a favorite philosopher for non-philosophers, second only perhaps to Nietzsche—is his sharp wit combined with a violent hostility to Hegel (shared by Kierkegaard). A keen appreciation for Plato and Kant, and his unique mixing of Indian religio-philosophical ideas with Western thought, something that had not been done before by a major European philosopher, combined with a bold refusal to be cowed by contemporary norms, has always given Schopenhauer's topical essays their special appeal. These were collected in his so-called *Parerga* (1851), but were quite unlike his principal work, *The World as Will and Representation,* a long and complex work of Kantian ambitions and vocabulary. Schopenhauer strayed from the Enlightenment emphasis on reason's hegemony in human action by highlighting the irrational power of sheer will or desire, not only in humankind, but suffusing the entire ecosystem. But after the ceaseless demands of desire comes inevitable death, a viewpoint which has given Schopenhauer a reputation as a great pessimist. The selections reprinted below speak to his typical concerns: "character" and a small set of aphorisms of the type that made him famous.

PARERGA AND PARALIPOMENA, VOL. 2, 1851

Character

Men who aspire to a happy, a brilliant and a long life, instead of to a virtuous one, are like foolish actors who want to be always having the great parts,—the parts that are marked by splendour and triumph. They fail to see that the important thing is not *what* or *how much,* but *how* they act.

Since *a man does not alter,* and his *moral character* remains absolutely the same all through his life; since he must play out the part which he has received, without the least deviation from the character; since neither experience, nor philosophy, nor religion can effect any improvement in him, the question arises, What is the meaning of life at all? To what purpose is it played, this farce in which everything that is essential is irrevocably fixed and determined?

It is played that a man may come to understand himself, that he may see what it is that he seeks and has sought to be; what he wants, and what, therefore, he is. *This is a knowledge which must be imparted to him from without.* Life is to man, in other words, to will, what chemical re-agents are to the body: it is only by life that a man reveals what he is, and it is only in so far as he reveals himself that he exists at all. Life is the manifestation of character, of the something that we understand by that word; and it is not in life, but outside of it, and outside time, that character undergoes alteration, as a result of the self-knowledge which life gives. Life is only the mirror into which a man gazes not in order that he may get a reflection of himself, but that he may come to understand himself by that reflection; that he may see *what* it is that the mirror shows. Life is the proofsheet, in which the compositors' errors are brought to light. How they become visible, and whether the type is large or small, are matters of no consequence. Neither in the externals of life nor in the course of history is there any significance; for as it is all one whether an error occurs in the large type or in the small, so it is all one, as regards the essence of the

matter, whether an evil disposition is mirrored as a conqueror of the world or a common swindler or ill-natured egoist. In one case he is seen of all men; in the other, perhaps only of himself; but that he should see himself is what signifies.

Therefore if egoism has a firm hold of a man and masters him, whether it be in the form of joy, or triumph, or lust, or hope, or frantic grief, or annoyance, or anger, or fear, or suspicion, or passion of any kind—he is in the devil's clutches and how he got into them does not matter. What is needful is that he should make haste to get out of them; and here, again, it does not matter how.

I have described character as *theoretically* an act of will lying beyond time, of which life in time, or *character in action,* is the development. For matters of practical life we all possess the one as well as the other; for we are constituted of them both. Character modifies our life more than we think, and it is to a certain extent true that every man is the architect of his own fortune. No doubt it seems as if our lot were assigned to us almost entirely from without, and imparted to us in something of the same way in which a melody outside us reaches the ear. But on looking back over our past, we see at once that our life consists of mere variations on one and the same theme, namely, our character, and that the same fundamental bass sounds through it all. This is an experience which a man can and must make in and by himself.

Not only a man's life, but his intellect too, may be possessed of a clear and definite character, so far as his intellect is applied to matters of theory. It is not every man, however, who has an intellect of this kind; for any such definite individuality as I mean is genius—an original view of the world, which presupposes an absolutely exceptional individuality, which is the essence of genius. A man's intellectual character is the theme on which all his works are variations. In an essay which I wrote in Weimar I called it the knack by which every genius produces his works, however various. This intellectual character determines the physiognomy of men of genius—what I might call *the theoretical physiognomy*—and gives it that distinguished expression which is chiefly seen in the eyes and the forehead. In the case of ordinary men the physiognomy presents no more than a weak analogy with the physiognomy of genius. On the other hand, all men possess *the practical physiognomy,* the stamp of will, of practical character, of moral disposition; and it shows itself chiefly in the mouth.

Since character, so far as we understand its nature, is above and beyond time, it cannot undergo any change under the influence of life. But although it must necessarily remain the same always, it requires time to unfold itself and show the very diverse aspects which it may possess. For character consists of two factors: one, the will-to-live itself, blind impulse, so-called impetuosity; the other, the restraint which the will acquires when it comes to understand the world; and the world, again, is itself will. A man may begin by following the craving of desire, until he comes to see how hollow and unreal a thing is life, how deceitful are its pleasures, what horrible aspects it possesses; and this it is that makes people hermits, penitents, Magdalenes. Nevertheless it is to be observed that no such change from a life of great indulgence in pleasure to one of resignation is possible, except to the man who of his own accord renounces pleasure. A really bad life cannot be changed into a virtuous one. The most beautiful soul, before it comes to know life from its horrible side, may eagerly drink the sweets of life and remain innocent. But it cannot commit a bad action; it cannot cause others suffering to do a pleasure to itself, for in that case it would see clearly what it would be doing; and whatever be its youth and inexperience it perceives the sufferings of others as clearly as its own pleasures. That is, why one bad action is a guarantee that numberless others will be committed as soon as circumstances give occasion for them. Somebody once remarked to me, with entire justice, that every man had something very good and humane in his disposition, and also something very bad and malignant; and that according as he was moved one or the other of them made its appearance. The sight of others' suffering arouses, not only in different men, but in one and the same man, at one moment an inexhaustible sympathy, at another a certain satisfaction; and this satisfaction may increase until it becomes the cruellest delight in pain. I observe in myself that at one moment I regard all mankind with heartfelt pity, at another with the greatest indifference, on occasion with hatred, nay, with a positive enjoyment of their pain.

All this shows very clearly that we are possessed of two different, nay, absolutely contradictory, ways of regarding the world: one according to the principle of individuation, which exhibits all creatures as entire strangers to us, as definitely not ourselves. We can have no feelings for them but those of indifference, envy, hatred, and delight that they suffer. The other way of regarding the world is in accordance with what I may call the *Tat-twam-asi—this-is-thyself* principle. All creatures are exhibited as identical with ourselves; and so it is pity and love which the sight of them arouses.

The one method separates individuals by impassable barriers; the other removes the barrier and brings the individuals together. The one makes us feel, in regard to every man, *that is what I am;* the other, *that is not what I am.* But it is remarkable that while the sight of another's suffering makes us feel our identity with him, and arouses our pity, this is not so with the sight of another's happiness. Then we almost always feel some envy; and even though we may have no such feeling in certain cases,—as, for instance, when our friends are happy,—yet the interest which we take in their happiness is of a weak description, and cannot compare with the sympathy which we feel with their suffering. Is this because we recognise all happiness to be a delusion, or an impediment to true welfare? No! I am inclined to think that it is because the sight of the pleasure, or the possessions, which are denied to us, arouses envy; that is to say, the wish that we, and not the other, had that pleasure or those possessions. . . .

As regards the freedom of the will, if it were the case that the will manifested itself in a single act alone, it would be a free act. But the will manifests itself in a course of life, that is to say, in a series of acts. Every one of these acts, therefore, is determined as a part of a complete whole, and cannot happen otherwise than it does happen. On the other hand, the whole series is free; it is simply the manifestation of an individualised will.

If a man feels inclined to commit a bad action and refrains, he is kept back either (1) by fear of punishment or vengeance; or (2) by superstition, in other words, fear of punishment in a future life; or (3) by the feeling of sympathy, including general charity; or (4) by the feeling of honour, in other words, the fear of shame; or (5) by the feeling of justice, that is, an objective attachment to fidelity and good-faith, coupled with a resolve to hold them sacred, because they are the foundation of all free intercourse between man and man, and therefore often of advantage to himself as well. This last thought, not indeed as a thought, but as a mere feeling, influences people very frequently. It is this that often compels a man of honour, when some great but unjust advantage is offered him, to reject it with contempt and proudly exclaim: *I am an honourable man!* For otherwise how should a poor man, confronted with the property which chance or even some worse agency has bestowed on the rich, whose very existence it is that makes him poor, feel so much sincere respect for this property, that he refuses to touch it even in his need; and although he has a prospect of escaping punishment, what other thought is it that can be at the bottom of such a man's honesty? He is resolved not to separate himself from the great community of honourable people who have the earth in possession, and whose laws are recognised everywhere. He knows that a single dishonest act will ostracise and proscribe him from that society for ever. No! a man will spend money on any soil that yields him good fruit, and he will make sacrifices for it.

With a good action,—that, every action in which a man's own advantage is ostensibly subordinated to another's,—the motive is either (1) self-interest, kept in the background; or (2) superstition, in other words, self-interest in the form of reward in another life; or (3) sympathy; or (4) the desire to lend a helping hand, in other words, attachment to the maxim that we should assist one another in need, and the wish to maintain this maxim, in view of the presumption that some day we ourselves may find it serve our turn. For what Kant calls a good action done from motives of duty and for the sake of duty there is, as will be seen, no room at all. Kant himself declares it to be doubtful whether an action was ever determined by pure motives of duty alone. I affirm most certainly that no action was ever so done; it is mere babble; there is nothing in it that could really act as a motive to any man. When he shelters himself behind verbiage of that sort, he is always actuated by one of the four motives which I have described. Among these it is obviously sympathy alone which is quite genuine and sincere.

Good and *bad* apply to character only *à potiori*; that is to say, we prefer the good to the bad; but,

absolutely, there is no such distinction. The difference arises at the point which lies between subordinating one's own advantage to that of another, and not subordinating it. If a man keeps to the exact muddle, he is *just.* But most men go an inch in their regard for others' welfare to twenty yards in regard for their own.

The source of *good* and of *bad character,* so far as we have any real knowledge of it, lies in this, that with the bad character the thought of the external world, and especially of the living creatures in it, is accompanied—all the more, the greater the resemblance between them and the individual self—by a constant feeling of *not I, not I, not I.*

Contrarily, with the good character (both being assumed to exist in a high degree) the same thought has for its accompaniment, like a fundamental bass, a constant feeling of *I, I, I.* From this spring benevolence and a disposition to help all men, and at the same time a cheerful, confident and tranquil frame of mind, the opposite of that which accompanies the bad character.

The difference, however, is only phenomenal, although it is a difference which is radical. But now we come to *the hardest of all problems:* How is it that, while the will, as the thing-in-itself, is identical, and from a metaphysical point of view one and the same in all its manifestations, there is nevertheless such an enormous difference between one character and another?—the malicious, diabolical wickedness of the one, and set off against it, the goodness of the other, showing all the more conspicuously. How is it that we get a Tiberius, a Caligula, a Carcalla, a Domitian, a Nero; and on the other hand, the Antonines, Titus, Hadrian, Nerva? How is it that among the animals, nay, in a higher species, in individual animals, there is a like difference?—the malignity of the cat most strongly developed in the tiger; the spite of the monkey; on the other hand, goodness, fidelity and love in the dog and the elephant. It is obvious that the principle of wickedness in the brute is the same as in man.

We may to some extent modify the difficulty of the problem by observing that the whole difference is in the end only one of degree. In every living creature, the fundamental propensities and instincts all exist, but they exist in very different degrees and proportions. This, however, is not enough to explain the facts.

We must fall back upon the intellect and its relation to the will; it is the only explanation that remains. A man's intellect, however, by no means stands in any direct and obvious relation with the goodness of his character. We may, it is true, discriminate between two kinds of intellect: between understanding, as the apprehension of relation in accordance with the Principle of Sufficient Reason, and cognition, a faculty akin to genius, which acts more directly, is independent of this law, and passes beyond the Principle of Individuation. The latter is the faculty which apprehends Ideas, and it is the faculty which has to do with morality. But even this explanation leaves much to be desired. *Fine minds are seldom fine souls* was the correct observation of Jean Paul; although they are never the contrary. Lord Bacon, who, to be sure, was less a fine soul than a fine mind, was a scoundrel.

⌒

"ON THE WISDOM OF LIFE: APHORISMS"

What makes us almost inevitably ridiculous is our serious way of treating the passing moment, as though it necessarily had all the importance which it seems to have. It is only a few great minds that are above this weakness, and, instead of being laughed at, have come to laugh themselves.

* * *

The bright and good moments of our life ought to teach us how to act aright when we are melancholy and dull and stupid, by preserving the memory of their results; and the melancholy, dull, and stupid moments should teach us to be modest when we are bright. For we generally value ourselves according to our best and brightest moments; and those in which we are weak and dull and miserable, we regard as no proper part of us. To remember them will teach us to be modest, humble, and tolerant.

Mark my words once for all, my dear friend, and be clever. Men are entirely self-centred, and

incapable of looking at things objectively. If you had a dog and wanted to make him fond of you, and fancied that of your hundred rare and excellent characteristics the mongrel would be sure to perceive one, and that that would be sufficient to make him devoted to you body and soul—if, I say, you fancied that, you would be a fool. Pat him, give him something to eat; and for the rest, be what you please: he will not in the least rare, but will be your faithful and devoted dog. Now, believe me, it is just the same with men—exactly the same. . . .

* * *

Consider that chance, which, with error, its brother, and folly, its aunt, and malice, its grandmother, rules in this world; which every year and every day, by blows great and small, embitters the life of every son of earth, and yours too; consider, I say, that it is to this wicked power that you owe your prosperity and independence; for it gave you what it refused to many thousands, just to be able to give it to individuals like you. Remembering all this, you will not behave as though you had a right to the possession of its gifts; but you will perceive what a capricious mistress it is that gives you her favours; and therefore when she takes it into her head to deprive you of some or all of them, you will not make a great fuss about her injustice; but you will recognise that what chance gave, chance has taken away; if needs be, you will observe that this power is not quite so favourable to you as she seemed to be hitherto. Why, she might have disposed not only of what she gave you, but also of your honest and hard-earned gains.

But if chance still remains so favourable to you as to give you more than almost all others whose path in life you may care to examine, oh! be happy; do not struggle for the possession of her presents; employ them properly; look upon them as property held from a capricious lord; use them wisely and well. . . .

* * *

We often find that people of great experience are the most frank and cordial in their intercourse with complete strangers, in whom they have no interest whatever. The reason of this is that men of experience know that it is almost impossible for people who stand in any sort of mutual relation to

From *The Complete Essays of Arthur Schopenhauer*, T. Bailey Saunders, Trans. Published by Wiley Book Company. Copyright © 1942.

be sincere and open with one another; but that there is always more or less of a strain between them, due to the fact that they are looking after their own interests, whether immediate or remote. They regret the fact, but they know that it is so; hence they leave their own people, rush into the arms of a complete stranger, and in happy confidence open their hearts to him. Thus it is that monks and the like, who have given up the world and are strangers to it, are such good people to turn to for advice.

* * *

It is only by practising mutual restraint and self-denial that we can act and talk with other people; and, therefore, if we have to converse at all, it can only be with a feeling of resignation. For if we seek society, it is because we want fresh impressions: these come from without, and are therefore foreign to ourselves. If a man fails to perceive this, and, when he seeks the society of others, is unwilling to practise resignation, and absolutely refuses to deny himself, nay, demands that others, who are altogether different from himself, shall nevertheless be just what he wants them to be for the moment, according to the degree of education which he has reached, or according to his intellectual powers or his mood—the man, I say, who does this, is in contradiction with himself. For while he wants some one who shall be different from himself, and wants him just because he is different, for the sake of society and fresh influence, he nevertheless demands that this other individual shall precisely resemble the imaginary creature who accords with his mood, and have no thoughts but those which he has himself.

Women are very liable to subjectivity of this kind; but men are not free from it either.

I observed once to Goethe, in complaining of the illusion and vanity of life, that when a friend is with us we do not think the same of him as when he is away. He replied: "Yes! because the absent friend is yourself, and he exists only in your head; whereas the friend who is present has an individuality of his own, and moves according to laws of his own, which cannot always be in accordance with those which you form for yourself."

* * *

A good supply of resignation is of the first importance in providing for the journey of life. It is a supply which we shall have to extract from disappointed hopes; and the sooner we do it, the better for the rest of the journey.

* * *

How should a man be content so long as he fails to obtain complete unity in his inmost being? For as long as two voices alternately speak in him, what is right for one must be wrong for the other. Thus he is always complaining. But has any man ever been completely at one with himself? Nay, is not the very thought a contradiction? . . .

* * *

The clever man, when he converses, will think less of what he is saying than of the person with whom he is speaking; for then he is sure to say nothing which he will afterwards regret; he is sure not to lay himself open, nor to commit an indiscretion. But his conversation will never be particularly interesting.

An intellectual man readily does the opposite, and with him the person with whom he converses is often no more than the mere occasion of a monologue; and it often happens that the other then makes up for his subordinate *rôle* by lying in wait for the man of intellect, and drawing his secrets out of him.

* * *

Nothing betrays less knowledge of humanity than to suppose that, if a man has a great many friends, it is a proof of merit and intrinsic value: as though men gave their friendship according to value and merit! as though they were not, rather, just like dogs, which love the person that pats them and gives them bits of meat, and never trouble themselves about anything else! The man who understands how to pat his fellows best, though they be the nastiest brutes,—that's the man who has many friends.

It is the converse that is true. Men of great intellectual worth, or, still more, men of genius, can bare only very few friends; for their clear eye soon discovers all defects, and their sense of rectitude is always being outraged afresh by the extent and the horror of them. It is only extreme necessity that can compel such men not to betray their feelings, or even to stroke the defects as if they were beautiful additions. Personal love (for we are not speaking of the reverence which is gained by authority) cannot be won by a man of genius, unless the gods have endowed him with an indestructible cheerfulness of temper, a glance that makes the world look beautiful, or unless he has succeeded by degrees in taking men exactly as they are; that is to say, in making a fool of the fools, as is right and proper. On the heights we must expect to be solitary.

* * *

Our constant discontent is for the most part rooted in the impulse of self-preservation. This passes into a kind of selfishness, and makes a duty out of the maxim that we should always fix our minds upon what we lack, so that we may endeavour to procure it. Thus it is that we are always intent on finding out what we want, and on thinking of it; but that maxim allows us to overlook undisturbed the things which we already possess; and so, as soon as we have obtained anything, we give it much less attention than before. We seldom think of what we have, but always of what we lack.

This maxim of egoism, which has, indeed, its advantages in procuring the means to the end in view, itself concurrently destroys the ultimate end, namely, contentment; like the bear in the fable that throws a stone at the hermit to kill the fly on his nose. We ought to wait until need and privation announce themselves, instead of looking for them. Minds that are naturally content do this, while hypochondrists do the reverse.

* * *

A man's nature is in harmony with itself when he desires to be nothing but what he is; that is to say, when he has attained by experience a knowledge of his strength and of his weakness, and makes use of the one and conceals the other, instead of playing with false coin, and trying to show a strength which he does not possess. It is a harmony which produces an agreeable and rational character; and for the simple reason that everything which makes the man and gives him his mental arid physical qualities is nothing but the manifestation of his will; is, in fact, what he

wills. Therefore it is the greatest of all inconsistencies to wish to be other than we are.

* * *

People of a strange and curious temperament can be happy only under strange circumstances, such as suit their nature, in the same way as ordinary circumstances suit the ordinary man; and such circumstances can arise only if, in some extraordinary way, they happen to meet with strange people of a character different indeed, but still exactly suited to their own. That is why men of rare or strange qualities are seldom happy.

* * *

All this pleasure is derived from the use and consciousness of power; and the greatest of pains that a man can feel is to perceive that his powers fail just when he wants to use them. Therefore it will be advantageous for every man to discover what powers he possesses, and what powers he lacks. Let him, then, develop the powers in which he is pre-eminent, and make a strong use of them; let him pursue the path where they will avail him; and even though he has to conquer his inclinations, let him avoid the path where such powers are requisite as he possesses only in a low degree. In this way he will often have a pleasant consciousness of strength, and seldom a painful consciousness of weakness; and it will go well with him. But if he lets himself be drawn into efforts demanding a kind of strength quite different from that in which he is preeminent, he will experience humiliation; and this is perhaps the most painful feeling with which a man can be afflicted.

Yet there are two sides to everything. The man who has insufficient self-confidence in a sphere where he has little power, and is never ready to make a venture, will on the one hand not even learn how to use the little power that he has; and on the other, in a sphere in which he would at least be able to achieve something, there will be a complete absence of effort, and consequently of pleasure. This is always hard to bear; for a man can never draw a complete blank in any department of human welfare without feeling some pain.

* * *

As a child, one has no conception of the inexorable character of the laws of nature, and of the stubborn way in which everything persists in remaining what it is. The child believes that even lifeless things are disposed to yield to it; perhaps because it feels itself one with nature, or, from mere unacquaintance with the world, believes that nature is disposed to be friendly. Thus it was that when I was a child, and had thrown my shoe into a large vessel full of milk, I was discovered entreating the shoe to jump out. Nor is a child on its guard against animals until it learns that they are ill-natured and spiteful. But not before we have gained mature experience do we recognise that human character is unalterable; that no entreaty, or representation, or example, or benefit, will bring a man to give up his ways; but that, on the contrary, every man is compelled to follow his own mode of acting and thinking, with the necessity of a law of nature; and that, however we take him, he always remains the same. It is only after we have obtained a clear and profound knowledge of this fact that we give up trying to persuade people, or to alter them and bring them round to our way of thinking. We try to accommodate ourselves to theirs instead, so far as they are indispensable to us, and to keep away from them so far as we cannot possibly agree.

Ultimately we come to perceive that even in matters of mere intellect—although its laws are the same for all, and the subject as opposed to the object of thought does not really enter into individuality—there is, nevertheless, no certainty that the whole truth of any matter can be communicated to any one, or that any one can be persuaded or compelled to assent to it; because, as Bacon says, *intellectus humanus luminis sicci non est:* the light of the human intellect is coloured by interest and passion.

* * *

It is just because *all happiness is of a negative character* that, when we succeed in being perfectly at our ease, we are not properly conscious of it. Everything seems to pass us softly and gently, and hardly to touch us until the moment is over; and then it is the positive feeling of something lacking that tells us of the happiness which has vanished; it is then that we observe that we have failed to hold it fast, and we suffer the pangs of self-reproach as well as of privation.

* * *

Every happiness that a man enjoys, and almost every friendship that he cherishes, rest upon illusion; for, as a rule, with increase of knowledge they are bound to vanish. Nevertheless, here as elsewhere, a man should courageously pursue truth, and never weary of striving to settle accounts with himself and the world. No matter what happens to the right or to the left of him,—be it a chimæra or fancy that makes him happy, let him take heart and go on, with no fear of the desert which widens to his view. Of one thing only must he be quite certain: that under no circumstances will he discover any lack of worth in himself when the veil is raised; the sight of it would be the Gorgon that would kill him. Therefore, if he wants to remain undeceived, let him in his inmost being feel his own worth. For to feel the lack of it is not merely the greatest, but also the only true affliction; all other sufferings of the mind may not only be healed, but may be immediately relieved, by the secure consciousness of worth. The man who is assured of it can sit down quietly under sufferings that would otherwise bring him to despair; and though he has no pleasures, no joys and no friends, he can rest in and on himself; so powerful is the comfort to be derived from a vivid consciousness of this advantage; a comfort to be preferred to every other earthly blessing. Contrarily, nothing in the world can relieve a man who knows his own worthlessness; all that he can do is to conceal it by deceiving people or deafening them with his noise; but neither expedient will serve him very long.

* * *

We must always try to preserve large views. If we are arrested by details we shall get confused, and see things awry. The success or the failure of the moment, and the impression that they make, should count for nothing.[1]

* * *

How difficult it is to learn to understand oneself, and clearly to recognise what it is that one wants before anything else; what it is, therefore, that is most immediately necessary to our happiness; then what comes next; and what takes the third and the fourth place, and so on.

Yet, without this knowledge, our life is planless, like a captain without a compass.

* * *

The sublime melancholy which leads us to cherish a lively conviction of the worthlessness of everything of all pleasures and of all mankind, and therefore to long for nothing, but to feel that life is merely a burden which must be borne to an end that cannot be very distant, is a much happier state of mind than any condition of desire, which, be it never so cheerful, would have us place a value on the illusions of the world, and strive to attain them.

This is a fact which we learn from experience; and it is clear, *á priori,* that one of these is a condition of illusion, and the other of knowledge.

Whether it is better to marry or not to marry is a question which in very many cases amounts to this: Are the cares of love more endurable than the anxieties of a livelihood?

* * *

Marriage is a trap which nature sets for us.[2]

* * *

Poets and philosophers who are married men incur by that very fact the suspicion that they are looking to their own welfare, and not to the interests of science and art.

* * *

Habit is everything. Hence to be calm and unruffled is merely to anticipate a habit; and it is a great advantage not to need to form it.

* * *

"Personality is the element of the greatest happiness." Since *pain* and *boredom* are the two chief enemies of human happiness, nature has provided our personality with a protection against both. We can ward off pain, which is more often of the mind than of the body, by *cheerfulness;* and boredom by *intelligence.* But neither of these is akin to the other; nay, in any high degree they are perhaps incompatible. As Aristotle remarks, genius is allied to melancholy; and people of very cheerful disposition are only intelligent on the surface. The better, therefore, anyone is by nature armed against one of these evils, the worse, as a rule, is he armed against the other.

There is no human life that is free from pain and boredom; and it is a special favour on the part of fate if a man is chiefly exposed to the evil against which nature has armed him the better; if fate, that is, sends a great deal of pain where there is a very cheerful temper in which to bear it, and much leisure where there is much intelligence, but not *vice versâ.* For if a man is intelligent, he feels pain doubly or trebly; and a cheerful but unintellectual temper finds solitude and unoccupied leisure altogether unendurable.

* * *

In the sphere of thought, absurdity and perversity remain the masters of this world, and their dominion is suspended only for brief periods. Nor is it otherwise in art; for there genuine work, seldom found and still more seldom appreciated, is again and again driven out by dullness, insipidity, and affectation.

It is just the same in the sphere of action. Most men, says Bias, are bad. Virtue is a stranger in this world; and boundless egoism, cunning and malice, are always the order of the day. It is wrong to deceive the young on this point, for it will only make them feel later on that their teachers were the first to deceive them. If the object is to render the pupil a better man by telling him that others are excellent, it fails; and it would be more to the purpose to say: Most men are bad, it is for you to be better. In this way he would, at least, he sent out into the world armed with a shrewd foresight, instead of having to be convinced by bitter experience that his teachers were wrong.

All ignorance is dangerous, and most errors must be dearly paid. And good luck must he have that carries unchastised an error in his head unto his death.[3]

* * *

Every piece of success has a doubly beneficial effect upon us when, apart from the special and material advantage which it brings it is accompanied by the enlivening assurance that the world, fate, or the dæmon within, does not mean so badly with us, nor is so opposed to our prosperity as we had fancied; when, in fine, it restores our courage to live.

Similarly, every misfortune or defeat has, in the contrary sense, an effect that is doubly depressing.

* * *

If we were not all of us exaggeratedly interested in ourselves, life would be so uninteresting that no one could endure it.

* * *

Everywhere in the world, and under all circumstances, it is only by force that anything can be done; but power is mostly in bad hands, because baseness is everywhere in a fearful majority.

* * *

Why should it be folly to be always intent on getting the greatest possible enjoyment out of the moment, which is our only sure possession? Our whole life is no more than a magnified present, and in itself as fleeting.

* * *

As a consequence of his individuality and the position in which he is placed, everyone without exception lives in a certain state of limitation, both as regards his ideas and the opinions which he forms. Another man is also limited, though not in the same way; but should he succeed in comprehending the other's limitation he can confuse and abash him, and put him to shame, by making him feel what his limitation is, even though the other be far and away his superior. Shrewd people often employ this circumstance to obtain a false and momentary advantage.

* * *

The only genuine superiority is that of the mind and character; all other kinds are fictitious,

affected, false; and it is good to make them feel that it is so when they try to show off before the superiority that is true.[4]

> All the world's a stage,
> And all the men and women merely players.

Exactly! Independently of what a man really is in himself, he has a part to play, which fate has imposed upon him from without, by determining his rank, education, and circumstances. The most immediate application of this truth appears to me to be that in life, as on the stage, we must distinguish between the actor and his part; distinguish, that is, the man in himself from his position and reputation—from the part which rank and circumstances have imposed upon him. How often it is that the worst actor plays the king, and the best the beggar! This may happen in life, too; and a man must be very *crude* to confuse the actor with his part.

* * *

Our life is so poor that none of the treasures of the world can make it rich; for the sources of enjoyment are soon found to be all very scanty, and it is in vain that we look for one that will always flow. Therefore, as regards our own welfare, there are only two ways in which we can use wealth. We can either spend it in ostentatious pomp, and feed on the cheap respect which our imaginary glory will bring us from the infatuated crowd; or, by avoiding all expenditure that will do us no good, we can let our wealth grow, so that we may have a bulwark against misfortune and want that shall be stronger and better every day; in view of the fact that life, though it has few delights, is rich in evils.

* * *

It is just because our real and inmost being is *will* that it is only by its exercise that we can attain a vivid consciousness of existence, although this is almost always attended by pain. Hence it is that existence is essentially painful, and that many persons for whose wants full provision is made arrange their day in accordance with extremely regular, monotonous, and definite habits. By this means they avoid all the pain which the movement of the will produces; but, on the other hand, their whole existence becomes a series of scenes and pictures that mean nothing. They are hardly aware that they exist. Nevertheless, it is the best way of settling accounts with life, so long as there is sufficient change to prevent an excessive feeling of boredom. It is much better still if the Muses give a man some worthy occupation, so that the pictures which fill his consciousness have some meaning, and yet not a meaning that can be brought into any relation with his will.

* * *

A man is *wise* only on condition of living in a world full of fools.

Notes

1. Translator's Note.—Schopenhauer, for some reason that is not apparent, wrote this remark in French.

2. Translator's Note.—Also in French.

3. Translator's Note.—This, again, is Schopenhauer's own English.

4. Translator's Note.—In the original this also is in French.

HERBERT SPENCER

1820–1903

Herbert Spencer, son of a Dissenter schoolmaster, was born on April 27, 1820 in Derby, Derbyshire, England, the only surviving child out of nine who were born to his parents. He never married, though may have been tempted to do so after getting to know Marian Evans (George Eliot, the novelist) in 1850. He seems to have regretted missing the opportunity when he was quite old, as recorded in his *Autobiography* (1904). He died in Brighton, Sussex on December 8, 1903, aged 83. Electing not to attend Cambridge, he educated himself, reading natural sciences. Giving up teaching after a short time, he served as a railway civil engineer from 1837 until 1841. Spencer believed all his life that "individuation" was the key to understanding organic life. Anything that blocked or tried to control the unfettered development of the growing uniqueness of the individual, surrounded by suffocating sameness, was not only very bad politics, but virtually a crime against nature. Though always attributed to Darwin, the expression "survival of the fittest" is Spencer's, and he coined it long before his more famous peer published his *Origin of Species*. As with so many other theorists of this era, he relied on a fortunate inheritance (from an uncle, when he was 33) to emancipate himself from ordinary work, committing himself whole-heartedly to the construction of an extremely elaborate, all-encompassing intellectual system he called *the Synthetic Philosophy*. Never the least bit uncertain of his importance as a thinker, he circulated a flyer in 1860 asking for subscriptions for this multi-volume work, having already published a synopsis of his grand undertaking in *Social Statics* (1851) and *Principles of Psychology* (1855).

Spencer is a unique figure in the history of modern social thought because he seldom consulted previous writers (and was therefore ignorant of the parallels, for instance, between his metaphysics and those of both Spinoza and Leibniz), he was primarily a natural scientist, not a litterateur, and he tried to write about everything which he believed fell under the domain of his system: biology, education, sociology (analytic and descriptive), psychology, and political science. There was a time in the nineteenth century when he was regularly referred to as "the Aristotle of the modern world," though this opinion faded very quickly after his death. Nevertheless, his contributions to all these fields were immense at the time, and his penchant for a thorough-going laissez-faire approach to social and political life was undeniably significant in Britain and the U.S. The selections below come from his first book and concern "evil," and on the role of government in managing industrial civilization—which, in contradistinction to Marx, he believed worked well if left undisturbed.

SOCIAL STATICS, 1851

The Evanescence of Evil

All evil results from the non-adaptation of constitution to conditions. This is true of everything that lives. Does a shrub dwindle in poor soil, or become sickly when deprived of light, or die outright if removed to a cold climate? it is because the harmony between its organization and its circumstances has been destroyed. These experiences of the farmyard and the menagerie which show that pain, disease, and death, are entailed upon animals by certain kinds of treatment, may all be generalised under the same law. Every suffering incident to the human body, from a headache up to a fatal illness—from a burn or a sprain, to accidental loss of life, is similarly traceable to the having placed that body in a situation for which its powers did not fit it. Nor is the expression confined in its application to physical evil; it comprehends moral evil also. Is the kindhearted man distressed by the sight of misery? is the bachelor unhappy because his means will not permit him to marry? does the mother mourn over her lost child? does the emigrant lament leaving his fatherland? are some made uncomfortable by having to pass their lives in distasteful occupations, and others from having no occupation at all? the explanation is still the same. No matter what the special nature of the evil, it is invariably referable to the one generic cause—want of congruity between the faculties and their spheres of action. . . .

Progress therefore, is not an accident, but a necessity. Instead of civilization being artificial, it is a part of nature; all of a piece with the development of the embryo or the unfolding of a flower. The modifications mankind have undergone, and are still undergoing, result from a law underlying the whole organic creation: and provided the human race continues, and the constitution of things remains the same, those modifications must end in completeness. As surely as the tree becomes bulky when it stands alone and slender if one of a group; as surely as the same creature assumes the different forms of carthorse and race-horse, according as its habits demand strength or speed; as surely as a blacksmith's arm grows large, and the skin of a labourer's hand thick; as surely as the eye tends to become long-sighted in the sailor, and short-sighted in the student; as surely as the blind attain a more delicate sense of touch; as surely as a clerk acquires rapidity in writing and calculation; as surely as the musician learns to detect an error of a semitone amidst what seems to others a very babel of sounds; as surely as a passion grows by indulgence and diminishes when restrained; as surely as a disregarded conscience becomes inert, and one that is obeyed active; as surely as there is any efficacy in educational culture, or any meaning in such terms as habit, custom, practice;—so surely must the human faculties be moulded into complete fitness for the social state; so surely must the things we call evil and immorality disappear; so surely must man become perfect.

THE MAN VERSUS THE STATE, 1884

The Coming Slavery

And now when there has been compassed this desired ideal, which "practical" politicians are helping Socialists to reach, and which is so tempting on that bright side which Socialists contemplate, what must be the accompanying shady side which they do not contemplate? It is a matter of common remark, often made when a marriage is impending, that those possessed by strong hopes habitually dwell on the promised pleasures and think nothing of the accompanying pains. A further exemplification of this truth is supplied by these political enthusiasts and fanatical revolutionists. Impressed with the miseries existing under our present social arrangements, and not regarding these miseries as caused by the ill-working of a human nature but partially adapted to the social state, they imagine them to be forthwith curable by this or that re-arrangement. Yet, even did their plans succeed it could only be by substituting one kind of evil for another. A little deliberate thought would show that under their proposed arrangements, their liberties must be surrendered in proportion as their material welfares were cared for.

For no form of co-operation, small or great, can be carried on without regulation, and an implied submission to the regulating agencies. Even one of their own organizations for effecting social changes yields them proof. It is compelled to have its councils, its local and general officers, its authoritative leaders, who must be obeyed under penalty of confusion and failure. And the experience of those who are loudest in their advocacy of a new social order under the paternal control of a Government, shows that even in private voluntarily-formed societies, the power of the regulative organization becomes great, if not irresistible; often, indeed, causing grumbling and restiveness among those controlled. Trades Unions which carry on a kind of industrial war in defence of workers' interests *versus* employers' interests, find that subordination almost military in its strictness is needful to secure efficient action; for divided councils prove fatal to success. And even in bodies of co-operators, formed for carrying on manufacturing or distributing businesses, and not needing that obedience to leaders which is required where the aims are offensive or defensive, it is still found that the administrative agency gains such supremacy that there arise complaints about "the tyranny of organization." Judge then what must happen when, instead of relatively small combinations, to which men may belong or not as they please, we have a national combination in which each citizen finds himself incorporated, and from which he cannot separate himself without leaving the country. Judge what must under such conditions become the despotism of a graduated and centralized officialism, holding in its hands the resources of the community, and having behind it whatever amount of force it finds requisite to carry out its decrees and maintain what it calls order. Well may Prince Bismarck display leanings towards State-socialism.

And then after recognizing, as they must if they think out their scheme, the power possessed by the regulative agency in the new social system so temptingly pictured, let its advocates ask themselves to what end this power must be used. Not dwelling exclusively, as they habitually do, on the material well-being and the mental gratifications to be provided for them by a beneficent administration, let them dwell a little on the price to be paid. The officials cannot create the needful supplies: they can but distribute among individuals that which the individuals have joined to produce. If the public agency is required to provide for them, it must reciprocally require them to furnish the means. There cannot be, as under our existing system, agreement between employer and employed—this the scheme excludes. There must in place of it be command by local authorities over workers, and acceptance by the workers of that which the authorities assign to them. And this, indeed, is the arrangement distinctly, but as it would seem inadvertently, pointed to by the members of the Democratic Federation. For they propose that production should be carried on by "agricultural and industrial *armies* under State-control:" apparently not remembering that armies pre-suppose grades of officers, by whom obedience would have to be insisted upon; since otherwise neither order nor efficient work could be ensured. So that each would stand toward the governing agency in the relation of slave to master.

"But the governing agency would be a master which he and others made and kept constantly in check; and one which therefore would not control him or others more than was needful for the benefit of each and all."

To which reply the first rejoinder is that, even if so, each member of the community as an individual would be a slave to the community as a whole. Such a relation has habitually existed in militant communities, even under quasi-popular forms of government. In ancient Greece the accepted principle was that the citizen belonged neither to himself nor to his family, but belonged to his city—the city being with the Greek equivalent to the community. And this doctrine, proper to a state of constant warfare, is a doctrine which socialism unawares re-introduces into a state intended to be purely industrial. The services of each will belong to the aggregate of all; and for these services, such returns will be given as the authorities think proper. So that even if the administration is of the beneficent kind intended to be secured, slavery, however mild, must be the outcome of the arrangement.

A second rejoinder is that the administration will presently become not of the intended kind, and that the slavery will not be mild. The socialist speculation is vitiated by an assumption like that which vitiates the speculations of the "practical" politician. It is assumed that officialism will work as it is intended to work, which it never does. The machinery of Communism, like existing social machinery, has to be framed out of existing human nature; and the defects of existing human nature will generate in the one the same evils as in the other. The love of power, the selfishness, the injustice, the untruthfulness, which often in comparatively short times bring private organizations to disaster, will inevitably, where their effects accumulate from generation to generation, work evils far greater and less remediable; since, vast and complex and possessed of all the resources, the administrative organization once developed and consolidated, must become irresistible. And if there needs proof that the periodic exercise of electoral power would fail to prevent this, it suffices to instance the French Government, which, purely popular in origin, and subject at short intervals to popular judgment, nevertheless tramples on the freedom of citizens to an extent which the English delegates to the late Trades Unions Congress say "is a disgrace to, and an anomaly in, a Republican nation."

The final result would be a revival of despotism. . . .

❧

PRINCIPLES OF SOCIOLOGY, 1896

The Organic Analogy Reconsidered

Here let it once more be pointed out that there exist no analogies between the body politic and a living body, save those necessitated by that mutual dependence of parts which they display in common. Though, in foregoing chapters, comparisons of social structures and functions to structures and functions in the human body, have in many cases been made, they have been made only because structures and functions in the human body furnish the most familiar illustrations of structures and functions in general. The social organism, discrete instead of concrete, asymmetrical instead of symmetrical, sensitive in all its units instead of having a single sensitive centre, is not comparable to any particular type of individual organism, animal or vegetal. All kinds of creatures are alike in so far as each shows us co-operation among its components for the benefit of the whole; and this trait, common to them, is a trait common also to communities. Further, among the many types of individual organisms, the degree of this co-operation measures the degree of evolution; and this general truth, too, is exhibited among social organisms. Once more, to effect increasing co-operation, creatures of every order show us increasingly-complex appliances for transfer and mutual influence; and to this general characteristic, societies of every order furnish a corresponding characteristic. Community in the fundamental principles of organization is thus the only community asserted.

But now let us drop this alleged parallelism between individual organizations and social organizations. I have used the analogies elaborated, but as a scaffolding to help in building up a coherent body of sociological inductions. Let us take away the scaffolding: the inductions will stand by themselves.

We saw that societies are aggregates which grow; that in various types of them there are great varieties in the degrees of growth reached; that types of successively larger sizes result from the aggregation and re-aggregation of those of smaller sizes; and that this increase by coalescence, joined with interstitial increase, is the process through which have been formed the vast civilized nations.

Along with increase of size in societies goes increase of structure. Primitive wandering hordes are without established unlikenesses of parts. With growth of them into tribes habitually come some differences; both in the powers and occupations of their members. Unions of tribes are followed by more differences, governmental and industrial—social grades running through the whole mass, and contrasts between the differently-occupied parts in different localities. Such differentiations multiply as the compounding progresses. They proceed from the general to the special: first the broad division between ruling and ruled; then within the ruling part divisions into political, religious, military, and within the ruled part divisions into food-producing classes and handi-craftsmen; then within each of these divisions minor ones, and so on.

⌇

THE PROPER SPHERE OF GOVERNMENT, 1842

Letter XII

A brief review of the arguments that have been set forth in the foregoing letters many serve to place the general question more distinctly before the mind.

Having shown that the proposed definition of state duties was in exact accordance with the primitive requirements of society—was, in fact, theoretically derived from them, and that its derivation did not countenance the universal interference now permitted; an attempt was made to exhibit some of the chief advantages that would arise out of the restoration of our various social institutions to their original freedom from legislative control; in the course of which it was argued:—

1. That all commercial restrictions have been proved, both by past and present experience, to be eminently inimical to social prosperity; that necessity is fast forcing us towards free trade, and that we must ultimately return to the perfect commercial liberty dictated by nature, from which we should never have diverged, had there been a proper limitation of state power.

From *Herbert Spencer: Political Writings*, John Offer, Ed. Published by Cambridge University Press. Copyright © 1994.

2. That a national church is to be deprecated, not only as being unnecessary to the spread of religion, but as opposing, by its worldliness, corruption, and uncharitableness, a barrier to its progress; that, on the showing of its own ministers, it is totally incapable of Christianising the nation, seeing that by the vital importance they attach to a state-paid priesthood, they practically admit that they have themselves imbibed so little Christian spirit that their own ministry would cease were it not for its emoluments; and hence in so far as the definition involves the disseverment of church and state, it is advantageous.

3. That a poor law, though apparently a boon to the working classes, is in reality a burden to them; that it delays the rectification of social abuses; that it discourages the exercise of genuine benevolence; that compulsory relief is degrading alike to the giver and to the receiver; that voluntaryism is equally applicable in the practice of religion as in its ministry; and that the blessings of charity would be secured unaccompanied by the evils of pauperism were the legislature prevented from meddling.

4. That war is universally admitted to be a great evil; that it is our duty as Christians to adopt all feasible means of putting an end to it; and that restricting governments, to the fulfilment of their primitive functions, and thereby depriving them of the power of invasion, would be the most effectual means of preventing it.

5. That artificial colonisation is injurious in each of its several influences; that colonial trade has always been turned into a monopoly for the benefit of the aristocracy; that the pretended protection given to the settlers has generally proved a great curse to them; that the original possessors of the soil have ever been cruelly persecuted in state-established colonies; and that the case of Pennsylvania affords satisfactory evidence of the superiority of that voluntary, unprotected, emigration, that must follow from the recognition of the proposed principle.

6. That a national education would tend to destroy that variety and originality of mind so essential to social progress; that it would dis-

courage improvement by annihilating healthy competition, and by placing in the way of reform the difficulties of institutional changes, in addition to the obstacles arising from natural prejudice in favour of existing modes of instruction; that we have no guarantee for its future efficiency, and have every reason to believe that it would ultimately become as corrupt as a national religion: that the mode of its support, involving as it must, the taxation of the whole community, consentients and dissentients, would be manifestly unjust; and that a constitution which necessarily excludes it, thereby commends itself to our adoption.

7. That the zealous advocacy, by certain medical men, of enactments for the preservation of the public health, arises from interested motives; that the health of the people is no more a subject for legislation than their religion; that no man can reasonably require the state to take that care of his body which he will not take himself; and that in this case as in every other, to do for the people what the Almighty has intended them to do for themselves, is infallibly to lower them in the scale of creation.

8. That by confining the attention of government to the preservation of order, and the protection of person and property, we should not only avoid the many injuries inflicted on us by its officious interferences, but should likewise secure the proper performance of its all-important, though now neglected duties.

Such are the evidences which have been adduced in favour of the theorem, that the administration of justice is the sole duty of the state. Others might be added, did it seem desirable. It is hoped, however, that those already set forth, if not of themselves sufficient to create in candid minds the conviction of its truth, will at least so far serve to exhibit its probability, as to beget for it a serious examination.

In conclusion, it will be well to remind the reader, that whatever may be the result of his deliberations upon this momentous question—whether he agrees with the arguments that have been brought forward, or dissents from them—whether he acknowledges the legitimacy of the deductions, or decides against them—one thing is certain. A definition of the duty of the state there must be. It needs no argument to prove that there is a boundary beyond which no legislative control should pass—that there are individual and social requirements whose fulfilment will be better secured by moral stimulus and voluntary exertion, than by any artificial regulations—that between the two extremes of its possible power, the *everything* and the *nothing* with which a government might be entrusted, there must be some point which both principle and policy indicate as its proper limitation. This point, this boundary, it behoves every man to fix for himself; and if he disagrees with the definition, as above expressed, consistency demands that he should make one for himself. If he wishes to avoid the imputation of political empiricism, he must ascertain the nature and intent of that national organ called the legislature, ere he seeks to prescribe its actions. Before he ventures to entertain another opinion upon what a government should *do*, he must first settle for himself the question—What is a government *for*?

HARRIET MARTINEAU

1802–1876

Daughter of a Huguenot textile manufacturer who eventually lost his business due to rapid technological change, Harriet Martineau, the sixth of eight children, was born in Norwich, Norfolk, England on June 12, 1802. She was briefly engaged to John Hugh Worthington, but after he went insane, she did not have to marry him and was apparently relieved. After 74 years she died in a house of her own design near Ambleside, Westmorland on June 27, 1876. She was a remarkably hardworking woman of letters, and despite enduring deafness and heart disease, her output was astonishing. It was also necessary following her father's death in 1826, because she needed to support herself and her mother. She could have relied on needlework, which was reliable, but she chose instead to become a writer, since she had been reading a great deal ever since going deaf at 12, and therefore knew much more than other people her age. In 1830 alone she turned out 52 pieces for a Unitarian periodical, a novel, a religious history, and other essays. Martineau's talent shone as she popularized economic ideas, about which she wrote brilliantly even without knowing Adam Smith's or David Ricardo's ideas. Her *Illustrations of Political Economy* (1832–34) became a best-seller, making it possible for her to take a two-year vacation to the U.S., which in turn gave rise to her immortal *Society in America* (1837), a key anti-slavery document. One of its chapters is called "The Political Non-existence of Women." In addition to her illustrative tales that explained political-economy to the literate masses, she also produced columns for newspapers and periodicals, both learned and popular, novels (some are still in print), travel books, and a valuable autobiography (1877), published in 3 volumes after her death. Also typical in her time among public intellectuals, she wrote thousands of letters.

Her most important contribution to social thought is probably her free translation from French of Comte's two major works (1830–1842, 6 vols., 1853, 2 vols.), which went through many printings in the nineteenth century, contributing vitally to Comte's posthumous importance in the anglophone sphere. Until recently she was known primarily as Comte's translator and interpreter, but during the last decade or so, she has begun to be seen as a social scientist in her own right, particularly through her *How to Observe Manners and Morals* (1838). The three selections reprinted below all concern women—the virtues of being single, physical abuse of wives, and the victimization of Irish women—about which she wrote with great passion and intelligence. These excerpts capture well her outspoken defense of those who during her period of history most needed and deserved her able assistance.

AUTOBIOGRAPHY, 1855 [1877]

Single Life

I am, in truth very thankful for not having married at all. I have never since been tempted, nor have suffered any thing at all in relation to that matter which is held to be all-important to woman,—love and marriage. Nothing, I mean, beyond occasional annoyance, presently disposed of. Every literary woman, no doubt, has plenty of importunity of that sort to deal with; but freedom of mind and coolness of manner dispose of it very easily: and since the time I have been speaking of, my mind has been wholly free from all idea of love-affairs. My subsequent literary life in London was clear from all difficulty and embarrassment,— no doubt because I was evidently too busy, and too full of interest of other kinds to feel any awkwardness,—to say nothing of my being then thirty years of age; an age at which, if ever, a woman is certainly qualified to take care of herself. I can easily conceive how I might have been tempted,— how some deep springs in my nature might have been touched, then as earlier; but, as a matter of fact, they never were; and I consider the immunity a great blessing, under the liabilities of a moral condition such as mine was in the olden time. If I had had a husband dependent on me for his happiness, the responsibility would have made me wretched. I had not faith enough in myself to endure avoidable responsibility. If my husband had not depended on me for his happiness, I should have been jealous. So also with children. The care would have so overpowered the joy, the love would have so exceeded the ordinary chances of life, the fear on my part would have so impaired the freedom on theirs, that I rejoice not to have been involved in a relation for which I was, or believed myself unfit. The veneration in which 1 hold domestic life has always shown me that life was not for those whose self-respect had been early broken down, or had never grown. Happily, the majority are free from this disability. Those who suffer under it had better be as I,—as my observation of married, as well as single life assures me. Then I see what conjugal love is, in the extremely rare cases in which it is seen in its perfection, I feel that there is a power of attachment in me that has never been touched. When I am among little children, it frightens me to think what my idolatry of my own children would have been. But, through it all, I have ever been thankful to be alone. My strong will, combined with anxiety of conscience, makes me fit only to live alone; and my taste and liking are for living alone. The older I have grown, the more serious and irremediable have seemed to me the evils and disadvantages of married life, as it exists among us at this time: and I am provided with what it is the bane of single life in ordinary cases to want—substantial, laborious and serious occupation. My business in life has been to think and learn, and to speak out with absolute freedom what I have thought and learned. The freedom is itself a positive and never-failing enjoyment to me, after the bondage of my early life. My work and I have been fitted to each other, as is proved by the success of my work and my own happiness in it. The simplicity and independence of this vocation first suited my infirm and ill-developed nature, and then sufficed for my needs, together with family ties and domestic duties, such as I have been blessed with, and as every woman's heart requires. Thus, I am not only entirely satisfied with my lot, but think it the very best for me,—under my constitution and circumstances: and I long ago came to the conclusion that, without meddling with the case of the wives and mothers, I am probably the happiest single woman in England. Who could have believed, in that awful year 1826, that such would be my conclusion a quarter of a century afterwards!

The Woman Question

. . . For, with all the aid from the admiration with which her memory was regarded in my childhood, and from my own disposition to honour all promoters of the welfare and in improvement of Woman, I never could reconcile my mind to Mary Wollstonecraft's writings, or to whatever I heard of her. It seemed to me, from the earliest time when I could think on the subject of Woman's Rights and condition, that the first requisite to advancement is the self-reliance which results from self-discipline. Women who would improve the condition and chances of their sex must, I am certain, be not only affectionate and devoted, but rational and dispassionate, with the devotedness of benevolence, and not merely of personal love. But Mary Wollstonecraft was, with all her powers, a poor victim of passion, with no control over her own peace, and no calmness or content except when the needs of her individual nature were satisfied. I felt, forty years ago, in regard to her, just what I feel now in regard to some of the most conspicuous denouncers of the wrongs of women at this day;—that their advocacy of Woman's cause becomes mere detriment, precisely in proportion to their personal reasons for unhappiness, unless they have fortitude enough (which loud complainants usually have not) to get their own troubles under their feet, and leave them wholly out of the account in stating the state of their sex. Nobody can be further than I am from being satisfied with the condition of my own sex, under the law and custom of my own country; but I decline all fellow-ship and co-operation with women of genius or otherwise favourable position, who injure the cause by their personal tendencies. When I see an eloquent writer insinuating to every body who comes across her that she is the victim of her husband's carelessness and cruelty, while he never spoke in his own defence: when I see her violating all good taste by her obtrusiveness in society, and oppressing every body about her by her epicurean selfishness every day, while raising in print an eloquent cry on behalf of the oppressed; I feel, to the bottom of my heart, that she is the worst enemy of the cause she professes to plead. The best friends of that cause are women who are morally as well as intellectually competent to the most serious business of life, and who must be clearly seen to speak from conviction of the truth, and not from personal unhappiness. The best friends of the cause are the happy wives and the busy,

cheerful, satisfied single women, who have no injuries of their own to avenge, and no painful vacuity or mortification to relieve. The best advocates are yet to come,—in the persons of women who are obtaining access to real social business,—the female physicians and other professors in America, the women of business and the female artists of France; and the hospital administrators, the nurses, the educators and substantially successful authors of our own country. Often as I am appealed to speak, or otherwise assist in the promotion of the cause of Woman, my answer is always the same:—that women, like men, can obtain whatever they show themselves fit for. Let them be educated,—let their powers be cultivated to the extent for which the means are already provided, and all that is wanted or ought to be desired will follow of course. Whatever a woman proves herself able to do, society will be thankful to see her do,—just as if she were a man. If she is scientific, science will welcome her, as it has welcomed every woman so qualified. I believe no scientific woman complains of wrongs. If capable of political thought and action, women will obtain even that. I judge by my own case. The time has not come which certainly will come, when women who are practically concerned in political life will have a voice in making the laws which they have to obey; but every woman who can think and speak wisely, and bring up her children soundly, in regard to the rights and duties of society, is advancing the time when the interests of women will be represented, as well as those of men. I have no vote at elections, though I am a tax-paying housekeeper and responsible citizen; and I regard the disability as an absurdity, seeing that I have for a long course of years influenced public affairs to an extent not professed or attempted by many men. But I do not see that I could do much good by personal complaints, which always have some suspicion or reality of passion in them. I think the better way is for us all to learn and to try to the utmost what we can do, and thus to win for ourselves the consideration which alone can secure us rational treatment. The Wollstonecraft order set to work at the other end, and, as I think, do infinite mischief; and, for my part, I do not wish to have any thing to do with them. Every allowance must be made for Mary Wollstonecraft herself, from the constitution and singular environment which determined her course: but I have never regarded her as a safe example, nor as a successful champion of Woman and her Rights.

Women in Ireland

August 27, 1852

Considering that women's labour is universally underpaid, in comparison with that of men, there is something very impressive to the traveller in Ireland in the conviction which grows upon him, from stage to stage, that it is the industry of women which is in great part sustaining the country. Though, in one view, there is moral beauty in the case, the symptom is a bad one. First, the men's wages are reduced to the lowest point; and then, capital turns to a lower-paid class, to the exclusion of the men, wherever the women can be employed in their stead. We should be sorry to draw any hasty conclusions on a matter of so much importance; but, recalling what we have seen since we landed, we cannot but declare that we have observed women not only diligently at work on their own branches of industry, but sharing the labours of the men in almost every employment that we happen to have witnessed. As an economical symptom, the employment of the least in the place of the most able-bodied is one of the peculiarities which marks the anomalous condition of Ireland. The famine time was, to be sure, an exception to all rules; but the same tendency was witnessed before, and is witnessed still. At that time, one of the London Companies sent directions to their agent to expend money to a certain amount, and on no account to allow anybody on their estates to starve. The agent determined to have a great piece of "slob" land dug,—employing for this purpose one boy out of every family of a certain number, with a staff of aged men for overseers, to superintend and measure the work. Spades, from a moderate to a very small size, were ordered; and a mighty provision of wheaten cakes was carried down to the place every day at noon. The boys were earnest and eager and conscien-

tious about their engagement. They were paid by the piece, and they worked well. Some little fellows, who were so small that they had to be lifted up to take their wages, earned 5s. a week. They grew fat upon their wheaten food, and their families were able to live on their earnings; and if the Company did not gain, they did not lose. But it must have been a piteous sight to see households supported by their children and grannies, instead of by the strong arm of him who stood between. The women were at work at the same time. The women of Ireland so learned to work then that it will be very long indeed before they get a holiday, or find their natural place as housewives.

We do not say recover their place as housewives; for there is abundance of evidence that they have not sunk from that position, but rather risen from a lower one than they now fill. . . .

So much for proper "women's work." But we observe women working almost everywhere. In the flax-fields there are more women than men pulling and steeping. In the potato fields it is often the women who are saving the remnant of the crop. In the harvest-fields there are as many women as men reaping and binding. In the bog, it is the women who, at half wages, set up, and turn, and help to stack the peat, not only for household use, but for sale, and in the service of the Irish Peat Company. In Belfast, the warehouses we saw were more than half peopled with women, engaged about the linens and muslins. And at the flax-works, near the city, not only were women employed in the spreading and drying, but in the rolling, roughing, and finishing, which had always till now been done by men. The men had struck for wages; and their work was given to girls, at 8d. per day.

Amidst facts like these, which accumulate as we go, one cannot but speculate on what is to be the end; or whether the men are to turn nurses and cooks, and to abide beside the hearth, while the women are earning the family bread. Perhaps the most consolatory way of viewing the case is that which we are quite willing to adopt,—that, practically, the condition of women, and therefore of their households, is rising. If there is something painful in seeing so undue a share of the burdens of life thrown upon the weaker sex; and if we cannot but remember that such a distribution of labour is an adopted symptom of barbarism; still, if the cabins are more decent, and the women more womanlike, it seems as if the process of change must be, on the whole, an advance. As to the way out of such a state of things, it seems as if it must be by that path to so many other benefits—agricultural improvement. The need of masculine labour, and the due regard of it, must both arise out of an improved cultivation of the soil; and it is not easy to see how they can arise in any other way.

Brutality to Women, 1853

One domestic subject is again exciting universal remark and must surely lead to action of one kind or another. Everybody is talking about the continued revelation of the brutality with which women of the working classes are treated, as disclosed by the reports of the police courts. Not a week passes without a report of some dreadful case of husbands, drunk or sober, ill-using their wives to a degree which, if practised upon brute, would be followed up by the Society for the Prevention of Cruelty to Animals. One fellow cooks his steak and eats it in the presence of wife and children who are famishing for bread. One, two, three, half a dozen, drag their wives about by the hair, knock their heads against the floor—and, even when pregnant, kick them about the body till they are insensible. Here a woman rushes into the street in the middle of the night, followed by her scared and naked children. Another is thrown down stairs, and is found by fellow lodgers half dead at the bottom. It is painful to write these things; but they are constantly being written by police reporters: and they engaged, as we know, so much notice from Parliament, whilst it was sitting, as to cause the passage of a new law for the punishment of brutality to women. This law, however, seems to avail little or nothing. It is observable that the culprits are often "amazed," "astounded," and so forth, at the severity of the sentences: but such a law can scarcely suffice to keep in check men who can be

so amazed, and who thereby show how insensible they are to the seriousness of their crime.

To the thoughtful observer, a most painful, and by far the most pathetic, part of the business is the unwillingness of the wives to prosecute. The avowal of "who did it," which is the first natural impulse, is retracted when public justice takes up the sinner. The reason of the reluctance is only too mournfully obvious. One poor creature recently exclaimed, when her husband was committed to prison, "Thank God! I shall have quietness for two months!" But for one such there are a dozen who know not how their children are to be fed in the interval, and who look forward with evident horror to the day which shall bring their husbands home again, exasperated by vengeance, full of the hatred which men feel towards those whom they have injured, to inflict a slower and more concealed torture—penalties which the law cannot take hold—of a gradual murder, which can never be brought home. We need not enlarge on this. What such a home must be, every one can imagine for himself.

One obvious feature of this class of cases amongst the lowest ranks of society is that the mistress is in a better condition than the wife. The mistress can free herself from her tyrant at any moment, while the wife has no escape. What say our moralists to this? Could human wit devise a more effectual way of discouraging marriage amongst certain classes, and countenancing illicit connexion? And what is the actual effect, at this moment, in our moral and Christian England? If what we have to tell shocks the moral reader, and strikes alarm into the hearts of all who truly and wisely believe that the institution of the Family is the only basis of public and private morality, it can only be said that it is time such men were shocked and grieved, for it is truth which strikes the blow to their feelings. All such should be called upon, by all their veneration for the institution of the Family, by all their interest in the national morality, by all the principles and prepossessions which fortify and endear their interest in Home, to take heed of a sign of the times.

What must be done?

JOSEPH-ARTHUR GOBINEAU, COMTE DE

1816–1882

Comte Joseph-Arthur de Gobineau was born on July 14, 1816 in Ville-d'Avray, France and died 66 years later in Turin, Italy. From an aristocratic, royalist lineage, Gobineau became famous as a theorist of racialist doctrine which held that the Aryans (Germanic peoples) were superior to all other skin tones or cultural types. Yet he wrote many other works which have nothing to do with this troubling line of thought, which has for many years given his name an unhappy connection to Nazism and other destructively racist political programs. But whereas the Nazis and other racist politicians have turned to Gobineau for inspiration, their plans included wholesale slaughter of "substandard" peoples, whereas for Gobineau, the question of racial superiority was strictly academic. This may seem unconscionable today, but it was "mainstream science" in his time. He had the good fortune of being a diplomat who was sent to Newfoundland, Brazil, Turkey, Germany, Iran (1855–58), Sweden, and Switzerland. Additionally, he served as Tocqueville's assistant when the former was a foreign diplomat in 1849. It was thus possible for Gobineau to collect data on different races by simply watching what went on around him. In addition, then, to writing novels, travel books, *A History of the Persians* (1869, 2 vols.), *The Religion and Philosophy of Central Asia* (1865), *The Renaissance* (1877), and other works, he put enormous effort into what he regarded as his masterpiece, *Essay on the Inequality of Human Races* (1853–55, 4 vols.). In his magnum opus he put forth a set of ideas which have ever since been associated with ignorant and dangerous racism, for which there is no longer any room in polite company, or among cosmopolitan thinkers and social actors. Gobineau argued that the Germanic races were the highest and most perfected, and that their interbreeding with either black or yellow races would lead to their degeneration. "Miscegenation" for Gobineau was not just a political matter, but also a biological concern, since based on his reading of the anthropological record, the human products of mixed race breeding endangered the longterm prospects of the whites, whose cultural achievements he most valued. Not only did a long list of political operatives seize on his theory, but Nietzsche, Hitler, Houston Stewart Chamberlain, and other notables thought highly of his formulations as well.

The excerpt reprinted below shows Gobineau at his most insistent and unenlightened. He explains in clear language why he believes there is a hierarchy to the races, and that each should stay clear of the others. What makes it interesting is not its anthropological or biological accuracy, since it lacks both, but rather the nature of his argument as a rhetorical performance. His opinions influenced many people, and one today must wonder why.

ESSAY ON THE INEQUALITY OF HUMAN RACES, 1853–55

The Inequality of Races

It is in the manner described in the last chapter that the secondary types, from which are descended the existing races, could have come into being. As to the type of man first created, the Adamite, we will leave him out of the argument altogether; for it is impossible to know anything of his specific character, or how far each of the later families has kept or lost its likeness to him. Our investigation will not take us further back than the races of the second stage.

I find these races naturally divided into three, and three only—the white, the black and the yellow. If I use a basis of division suggested by the colour of the skin, it is not that I consider it either correct or happy, for the three categories of which I speak are not distinguished exactly by colour, which is a very complex and variable thing; I have already said that certain facts in the conformation of the skeleton are far more important. But in default of inventing new names—which I do not consider myself justified in doing—I must make my choice from the vocabulary already in use. The terms may not be very good, but they are at any rate less open to objection than any others, especially if they are carefully defined. I certainly prefer them to all the designations taken from geography or history, for these have thrown an already confused subject into further confusion. So I may say, once for all, that I understand by *white* men the members of those races which are also called Caucasian, Semitic or Japhetic. By *black* men I mean the Hamites; by *yellow* the Altaic, Mongol, Finnish and Tartar branches. These are the three primitive elements of mankind. There is no more reason to admit Blumenbach's twenty-eight varieties than Prichard's seven; for both these schemes include notorious hybrids. It is probable that none of the three original types was ever found in absolute simplicity. The great cosmic agents had not merely brought into being the three clear-cut varieties; they had also, in the course of their action, caused many sub-species to appear. These were distinguished by some peculiar features, quite apart from the general character which they had in common with the whole branch. Racial crossing was not necessary to create these specific modifications; they existed before any interbreeding took place at all. It would be fruitless to try to identify them today in the hybrid agglomeration that constitutes what we call the white race. It would be equally impossible with regard to the yellow race. Perhaps the black type has to some extent kept itself pure; at any rate it has remained nearer its original form, and thus shows at first sight what, in the case of the other great human divisions, is not given by the testimony of our senses, but may be admitted on the strength of historical proof.

The Negroes have always perpetuated the original forms their race, such as the prognathous type with woolly air, the Hindu type of the Kamaun and the Deccan, and the Pelagian of Polynesia. New varieties have certainly been created from their intermixture; this is the origin of what we may call the 'tertiary types', which are seen in the White and yellow races, as well as the black.

Much has been made of a noteworthy fact, which is used today as a sure criterion for determining the racial purity of a nation. This fact is the resemblance of face, shape and general constitution, including gesture and carriage. The further these resemblances go, the less mixture of blood is there supposed to be in the whole people. On the other hand, the more crossing there has been, the greater differences we shall find in the features, stature, walk and general appearance of the individuals . . .

We must mention another law before going further. Crossing of blood does not merely imply the fusion of the two varieties, but also creates new characteristics, which henceforth furnish the most important standpoint from which to consider any particular subspecies. . . .

In order to appreciate the intellectual differences between races, we ought first to ascertain the degree of stupidity to which mankind can descend. We know already the highest point that it can reach, namely civilization.

Most scientific observers up to now have been very prone to make out the lowest types as worse than they really are.

Nearly all the early accounts of a savage tribe paint it in hideous colours, far more hideous than the reality. They give it so little power of reason and understanding, that it seems to be on a level with the monkey and below the elephant. It is true that we find the contrary opinion. If a captain is well received in an island, if he meets, as he believes, with a kind and hospitable welcome, and succeeds in making a few natives do a small amount of work with his sailors, then praises are showered on the happy people. They are declared to be fit for anything and capable of everything; and sometimes the enthusiasm bursts all bounds, and swears it has found among them some higher intelligences.

Even in the most hideous cannibal there is a spark of the divine fire, and to some extent the flame of understanding can always be kindled in him. There are no tribes so low that they do not pass some judgments, true or false, just or unjust, on the things around them; the mere existence of such judgments is enough to show that in every branch of mankind some ray of intelligence is kept alive. It is this that makes the most degraded savages accessible to the teachings of religion and distinguishes them in a special manner, of which they are themselves conscious, from even the most intelligent beasts.

Are however these moral possibilities, which lie at the back of every man's consciousness, capable of infinite extension? Do all men possess in an equal degree an unlimited power of intellectual development? In other words, has every human race the capacity for becoming equal to every other? The question is ultimately concerned with the infinite capacity for improvement possessed by the species as a whole, and with the equality of races. I deny both points. . . .

If the human races were equal, the course of history would form an affecting, glorious and magnificent picture. The races would all have been equally intelligent, with a keen eye for their true interests and the same aptitude for conquest and domination. Early in the world's history, they would have gladdened the face of the earth with a crowd of civilizations, all flourishing at the same time, and all exactly alike. At the moment when the most ancient Sanskrit peoples were founding their empire, and, by means of religion and the sword, were covering northern India with har-

vests, towns, palaces and temples; at the moment when the first Assyrian Empire was crowning the plains of the Tigris and Euphrates with its splendid buildings, and the chariots and horsemen of Nimrod were defying the four winds, we should have seen, on the African coast, among the tribes of the prognathous Negroes, the rise of an enlightened and cultured social state, skilful in adapting means to ends, and in possession of great wealth and power. . . .

Then the nations of the earth, equally enlightened and equally rich, some by the commerce of their seething maritime cities, some by the agriculture of their vast and flourishing prairies, others by the industries of a mountainous district, others again by the facilities for transport afforded them by their central position—all these, in spite of the temporary quarrels, civil wars and seditions inseparable from our condition as men, might soon have devised some system of balancing their conflicting interests. Civilizations identical in origin would, by a long process of give and take, have ended by being almost exactly alike; one might then have seen established that federation of the world which has been the dream of so many centuries, and which would inevitably be realized if all races were actually gifted, in the same degree, with the same powers.

But we know that such a picture is purely fantastic. The first peoples worthy of the name came together under the inspiration of an idea of union which the barbarians who lived more or less near them not only failed to conceive so quickly, but never conceived at all. The early peoples emigrated from their first home and came across other peoples, whom they conquered; but these again neither understood nor ever adopted with any intelligence the main ideas in the civilization which had been imposed on them. Far from showing that all the tribes of mankind are intellectually alike, the nations capable of civilization have always proved the contrary, first by the absolutely different foundations on which they based their states, and secondly by the marked antipathy which they showed to each other. The force of example has never awakened any instinct, in any people, which did not spring from their own nature. Spain and the Gauls saw the Phoenicians, the Greeks and the Carthaginians set up flourishing towns, one after the other, on their coasts. But both Spain and the Gauls refused to copy the manners and the government of these great trading powers. When the Romans came as conquerors, they only succeeded in introducing a different spirit by filling their new dominions with Roman colonies. Thus the case of the Celts and the Iberians shows that civilization cannot be acquired without the crossing of blood.

Consider the position of the American Indians at the present day. They live side by side with a people which always wishes to increase in numbers, to strengthen its power. They see thousands of ships passing up and down their waterways. They know that the strength of their masters is irresistible. They have no hope whatever of seeing their native land one day delivered from the conqueror; their whole continent is henceforth, as they all know, the inheritance of the European. A glance is enough to convince them of the tenacity of those foreign institutions under which human life ceases to depend, for its continuance, on the abundance of game or fish. From their purchases of brandy, guns, and blankets, they know that even their own coarse tastes would be more easily satisfied in the midst of such a society, which is always inviting them to come in, and which seeks, by bribes and flattery, to obtain their consent. It is always refused. They prefer to flee from one lonely spot to another; they bury themselves more and more in the heart of the country, abandoning all, even the bones of their fathers. They will die out, as they know well; but they are kept, by a mysterious feeling of horror, under the yoke of their unconquerable repulsion from the white race, and although they admire its strength and general superiority, their conscience and their whole nature, in a word, their blood, revolts from the mere thought of having anything in common with it. . . .

The preceding argument has established the following facts:

(i) The tribes which are savage at the present day have always been so, and always will be, however high the civilizations with which they are brought into contact.

(ii) For a savage people even to go on living in the midst of civilization, the nation which created the civilization must be a nobler branch of the same race.

(iii) This is also necessary if two distinct civilizations are to affect each other to any extent, by an exchange of qualities, and give birth to other civilizations compounded from their elements. That they should ever be fused together is of course out of the question.

(iv) The civilizations that proceed from two completely foreign races can only touch on the surface. They never coalesce, and the one will always exclude the other . . .

The irreconcilable antagonism between different races and cultures is clearly established by history, and such innate repulsion must imply unlikeness and inequality. If it is admitted that the European cannot hope to civilize the Negro, and manages to transmit to the mulatto only a very few of his own characteristics; if the children of a mulatto and a white woman cannot really understand anything better than a hybrid culture, a little nearer than their father's to the ideas of the white race—in that case, I am right in saying that the different races are unequal in intelligence.

The Three Basic Races

I have shown the unique place in the organic world occupied by the human species, the profound physical, as well as moral, differences separating it from all other kinds of living creatures. Considering it by itself, I have been able to distinguish, on physiological grounds alone, three great and clearly marked types, the black, the yellow and the white. However uncertain the aims of physiology may be, however meagre its resources, however defective its methods, it can proceed thus far with absolute certainty.

The negroid variety is the lowest, and stands at the foot of the ladder. The animal character, that appears in the shape of the pelvis, is stamped on the Negro from birth, and foreshadows his destiny. His intellect will always move within a very narrow circle. He is not however a mere brute, for behind his low receding brow, in the middle of his skull, we can see signs of a powerful energy, however crude its objects. If his mental faculties are dull or even non-existent, he often has an intensity of desire, and so of will, which may be called terrible. Many of his senses, especially taste and smell, are developed to an extent unknown to the other two races.

The very strength of his sensations is the most striking proof of his inferiority. All food is good in his eyes, nothing disgusts or repels him. What he desires is to eat, to eat furiously, and to excess; no carrion is too revolting to be swallowed by him. It is the same with odours; his inordinate desires are satisfied with all, however coarse, or even horrible. To these qualities may be added an instability and capriciousness of feeling, that cannot be tied down to any single object, and which, so far as he is concerned, do away with all distinctions of good and evil. We might even say that the violence with which he pursues the object that has aroused his senses and inflamed his desires is a guarantee of the desires being soon satisfied and the object forgotten. Finally, he is equally careless of his own life and that of others: he kills willingly, for the sake of killing; and this human machine, in whom it is so easy to arouse emotion, shows, in face of suffering, either a monstrous indifference or a cowardice that seeks a voluntary refuge in death.

The yellow race is the exact opposite of this type. The skull points forward, not backward. The forehead is wide and bony, often high and projecting. . . .

The great human civilizations are but ten in number and all of them have been produced upon the initiative of the white race. I should list them as follows:

1. The Indian civilization, which reached its highest point round the Indian Ocean, and in the north and east of the Indian continent, southeast of the Brahmaputra. It arose from a branch of a white people, the Aryans.

2. The Egyptians, round whom collected the Ethiopians, the Nubians, and a few smaller peoples to the west of the oasis of Ammon. This society was created by an Aryan colony from India, that settled in the upper valley of the Nile.

3. The Assyrians, with whom may be classed the Jews, the Phoenicians, the Lydians, the Carthaginians and the Hymiarites. They owed their civilizing qualities to the great white invasions which may be grouped under the name of the descendants of Shem and Ham. The Zoroastrian Iranians who ruled part of Central Asia under the names of Medes, Persians and Bactrians, were a branch of the Aryan family.

4. The Greeks, who came from the same Aryan stock, as modified by Semitic elements.

5. The Chinese civilization, arising from a cause similar to that operating in Egypt. An Aryan colony from India brought the light of civilization to China also. Instead however of becoming mixed with black peoples, as on the Nile, the colony became absorbed in Malay and yellow races, and was reinforced, from the northwest, by a fair number of white elements, equally Aryan but no longer Hindu.

6. The ancient civilizations of the Italian peninsula, the cradle of Roman culture. This was produced by a mixture of Celts, Iberians, Aryans and Semites.

7. The Germanic races, which in the fifth century transformed the Western mind. These were Aryans.

8, 9, 10. The three civilizations of America, the Alleghanian, the Mexican and the Peruvian.

Of the first seven civilizations, which are those of the Old World, six belong, at least in part, to the Aryan race, and the seventh, that of Assyria, owes to this race the Iranian renaissance, which is, historically, its best title to fame. Almost the whole of the continent of Europe is inhabited at the present time by groups of which the basis is white, but in which the non-Aryan elements are the most numerous. There is no true civilization, among the European peoples, where the Aryan branch is not predominant.

In the above list no Negro race is seen as the initiator of a civilization. Only when it is mixed with some other can it even be initiated into one.

Similarly, no spontaneous civilization is to be found among the yellow races; and when the Aryan blood is exhausted stagnation supervenes.

(PIERRE-GILLAUME-) FRÉDÉRIC LE PLAY

1806–1882

Son of a custom-house official, Pierre-Guillaume-Frédéric Le Play was born on April 11, 1806 in La Riviére-Saint-Sauveur, France, lived when young with his widowed mother, married, and a few days shy of his 76th birthday, died in Paris on April 5, 1882. He studied at the École Polytechnique and upon graduation worked for the State Department of Mines. Le Play took an important walking tour through Germany with a good friend, the philosopher Jean Reynaud, when he was 23 in order to study mines and the social conditions of workers. When he returned, he ruined his hands for life in a chemistry accident, enduring pain for over a year. But this did not deter him from carrying out prodigious amounts of social research, for he arranged his schedule so that he could travel half the year, collecting his own data from working families in Spain, Belgium, Great Britain, Russia, Denmark, Sweden, Norway, Germany, Austria, Hungary, and northern Italy. When in Russia the Czar gave him management of precious metal mines in the Urals which employed 45,000 men. Due to these peregrinations he learned to speak five languages and understood eight, which, although not unique at the time for intellectuals, separates him definitively from today's experts on family dynamics in industrial society. He became chief engineer and professor of metallurgy at the École des Mines from 1840 and the school's inspector from 1848. Always an amateur sociologist, he gave up engineering and administration in 1855 and turned full-time to social research, compiling a vast catalogue of family ethnographies. By using the case-method, which he helped develop, he was able in 1855 to publish *Les Oeuviers européenes*, an unprecedented set of 36 monographs concerning family budgets and related data from workers who were employed in various industries, for which he won an important prize from the Académie des Sciences. He was widely recognized for inventing and perfecting ethnographic research methods, so much so that Napoléon III asked him to organize the Exhibition of 1855, made him a state counsellor, senator of the empire, among other honors. He gave up politics only after the defeat of France in 1870 by Germany.

Le Play's *Social Reform* (1864, 2 vols.) and a scholarly journal allied with this work, plus his *The Organization of the Family* (1871), made him in essence the founder of what is now called "family sociology." By collecting and analyzing his own cross-national data, he set a high standard for subsequent researchers. The excerpts offered below come from his early work on European workers (1855), connecting social research with the reform efforts Le Play valued, and another piece is from his delineation of family types, published near the end of his very active life.

LES OUVRIERS EUROPÈENS, 1855

The Science of Society as a Theory of Social Reform

A few general considerations will enable us to establish the principles which underlie the observations revealed by comparative study of the workers of Europe. We will now present those observations which are particularly relevant to the reforms necessitated by the present situation in the West.

The diversity of proclivities and aptitudes in Europe is part of human nature; but it is also linked to the spirit of initiative and freedom fostered by Christianity which has so strongly marked the European character. In effect, European civilizations differ from Asian societies (those which survive today or merely remain in name alone) by the fact that European society was not bound by a single social system. Like all primitive entities, European society provided ample ground for human failings; but at the same time, it was ever ready to draw profit and glory from the great potential of the human mind. This has been an outstanding characteristic of Europe for centuries, and it becomes more pronounced every day. Because of this tendency, the peoples of Europe were able to firmly maintain order and stability without falling into the excesses of despotism or a caste system. They raised religious feeling to greater heights than had any other people without bowing to a theocratic regime or hampering freedom of thought; while preserving the concepts of governmental authority and collective action, they granted much more individual freedom than had any other race. By favoring the development of democracy, they accelerated the progress of the popular classes and affirmed the influence of the middle classes without stifling the sources of greatness which flow from an aristocracy. Finally, today more than ever, the peoples of Europe are clearly continuing their long-time progress toward unity of thought and action without forsaking the processes of emulation and achievement which are fostered by nationalism. History clearly teaches that no member of the European family has remained constantly faithful to these trends; nearly all have succumbed to some accidental deviation and have exaggerated the development of one of these principles, thus momentarily disrupting the harmony which is an indispensable condition of progress; but these states immediately entered a period of decadence, and the ascendance of other nations, together with their trying ordeals, quickly brought them back to the true path of civilization. . . .

There is no doubt as to the choice of which societies to honor with the role of guide. Notwithstanding national rivalries over secondary issues, public opinion unanimously recognizes a gradual amelioration of men and things from the far reaches of Europe to the territory of the richest provinces of Germany, France, and England. Several nations located outside the center of European civilization, although justifiably conscious of their own grandeur, nevertheless recognize the superiority of Europe's innovative peoples and follow their lead in the sciences, arts, industry, and even in the smallest details of social life. European superiority is revealed in all the forms and manifestations of human activity; it is evident in the classes of the population specifically studied in this work; to contest this fact would be paradoxical. Terms of comparison and the approximate rank of each nation can be established without a lengthy investigation; one would surely comply with standard measures of civilization—either certain purely physical facts, such as the extent of means of communication in each country, or elements of intellectual activity, such as the importance of schools or the number of books published each year.

◡

SOCIAL REFORM, 1864

Family Types Patriarchal, Stem, Unstable

The family is an everlasting institution, along with religion and property; and as in the case of these

From *Frédéric Le Play: On Family, Work, and Social Change*, Catherine Bodard Silver, Ed./Trans. University of Chicago Press. Copyright © 1982. Reprinted by permission.

From *Frédéric Le Play: On Family, Work, and Social Change*, Catherine Bodard Silver, Ed./Trans. University of Chicago Press. Copyright © 1982. Reprinted by permission.

other institutions, the family undergoes in its form considerable modifications. Combined with religion and property, the family provides the salient characteristic of each social organization. From a general point of view, families can be divided into two extreme types: the patriarchal family and the unstable family. The stem family provides an intermediate type.

The first kind of family is common among Eastern nomads, Russian peasants, and the Slavs of Central Europe. In this kind of family all the married sons remain near the father, who exercises extensive authority over them and their children. With the exception of a few household objects, property remains undivided among members of the family group. The father directs the labor and accumulates the products not required for the family's daily needs in the form of savings. Among nomadic shepherds, this community lasts throughout the father's lifetime. Among sedentary farmers, the group divides when the productivity of the ancestral land is no longer proportional to the size of the family and, depending on the availability of free land, the "swarm" which leaves the paternal household either settles nearby or emigrates to another area. When this division takes place, the father—thanks to the economy and labor of all—presides at the creation of the new household or the endowing of the emigrants. It is he, too, who designates the member of the family who will be charged with exercising the new patriarchal authority. The tendency for new households to desire independence is neutralized among the nomads by the necessities of life, which do not allow them to exist in isolation, and among sedentary farmers by the feudal organization of property. In both groups, independence is checked by traditional moral influences. This frame of mind is based on firm religious beliefs. It insures respect for the established order in the areas of work and social habits rather than developing a spirit of initiative. In this state of physical and moral restraint, the community hinders the development which outstanding individuals in the family might achieve in an independent situation. But, on the other hand, the community allows less diligent, less skilled, and morally delinquent individuals to share in the common well-being.

The second type, the unstable family, prevails today among the working-class populations sub-ject to the new manufacturing system of Western Europe. Moreover, this type of family is multiplying among the wealthier classes in France due to a number of influences, chief among them the forced division of property. The family unit starts with the union of husband and wife. At first it expands as children are born; but the family later shrinks as these children, who are completely devoid of any obligation toward their parents and relatives, leave home as bachelors to support themselves or start a new family. The family is finally dissolved when the parents die or, in the case of their premature death, with the dispersion of the minor children. Each child disposes freely of the dowry he receives when he leaves the paternal household; and in all cases he has complete control over the product of his labor. The precocious use of reason, encouraged by teaching in the schools, parental advice, or the example of the upper classes, leads the new generation to do good or evil according to its moral predisposition. This reliance on reasoning often results in an excessive propensity for innovation rather than a spirit of tradition. In this system, a single or married individual is no longer responsible for the needs of his relatives and rapidly rises to a higher situation if he possesses outstanding aptitudes. But in contrast, if he is unskilled or morally delinquent, he falls even faster to a wretched condition, unable to claim any assistance. Unfortunately, this latter state tends to perpetuate itself once it occurs, either because parents can no longer contribute through savings to the establishment of their children, as they do in the first system, or, above all, because the children are left without supervision and succumb to their evil inclinations or are perverted by bad examples at an early age. Thus we are witness to this peculiar social state—a condition unparalled in the annals of history—which has caused us to coin the term "pauperism."

The third type, the stem family, develops spontaneously among those peoples who, having reaped the benefits of agricultural work and sedentary life, have the good sense to defend their private lives against the domination of lawyers, the inroads of bureaucracy, and the excesses of the modern manufacturing system. In this type of social organization, only one married child remains with the parents. All the others receive a dowry and enjoy an independence which is impossible in the patriarchal family. This system perpetuates work habits, moral influences, and ancestral traditions in the paternal home. The family is a permanent source of protection on which all the members can rely throughout life's trials. This system thus offers individuals a security they could never find in the unstable family. The stem family sometimes arises from the traditional influences of patriarchal life, but it is never truly established without the beneficial influence of individual property. This system satisfies both those who are content in the situation in which they were born and those who boldly wish to rise in the social hierarchy through their own initiative. Lastly, it strikes a just balance between paternal authority and the freedom of the children, between stability and the improvement of social conditions. In order to demonstate the superiority of this system, one need only point out that it

comes into being wherever the family is free, and that it maintains itself despite events of serious magnitude which may disturb the established order. Thus, should the heir-associate happen to die prematurely, none of his siblings hesitates to give up a promising future, and all would be honored to return home and fill the sudden void.

In summary, as the peoples of Europe become freer and more prosperous, they modify the patriarchal family, which relies too heavily on the cult of tradition, while at the same time rejecting the unstable family, which is constantly undermined by the spirit of innovation. Firmly adhering to their religious beliefs and the principle of individual property, they tend more and more to organize in stem families, which satisfy both of these tendencies—tradition and innovation—and reconcile two equally imperious needs: a respect for good traditions and the search for useful changes.

JOHN RUSKIN

1819–1900

John Ruskin, the protected son of a rich wine merchant and a very attentive mother, was born on February 8, 1819 on Hunter Street, Brunswick Square, London, married Euphemia (Effie) Chalmers Gray on April 10, 1848 (unconsummated and annulled, 1854, after which she married the artist John Millais), and died on January 29, 1900 in Coniston, Lancashire at nearly 81 after a dozen years of silent mental illness. Ruskin seems to have been born an aesthete in the most profoundly creative and disturbing sense, which his wealthy parents understood when he was quite young. They therefore protected him from much intercourse with the troubling social world, and provided him with tutoring and other artistic opportunities. Beginning at 14 he took regular trips to Europe with them, and the Alpine elevations in particular seemed to relieve his anxieties. Eventually he began regular visits to the Dulwich College Picture Gallery near their new home when he reached 20, which served as a source of his aesthetic ideas ever after. An unrequited love for his father's Spanish partner's daughter when he was 17 seems to have blocked his further emotional development, and the energy which ordinary people invest in interpersonal life he shunted instead into an extremely refined sense of aesthetic evaluation. When he was 17 he matriculated at Christ Church, Oxford and developed important friendships, did not study very hard the assigned materials, and avoided the intervention of his doting mother, who had taken an apartment nearby. His father provided money with which he began collecting paintings by J. M. W. Turner. Tubercular hemorrhages interrupted his schooling, and he was taken to Italy and the Alps to recover. In 1843, when he was 24, the first of five volumes called Modern Painters appeared, and his reputation as an art critic was established. In 1858 he fell in love with Rose La Touche, an Irish girl much younger than he who eventually went mad, dying in 1875 with the relationship still unresolved.

Ruskin's work in art history and criticism continues to live, but for social thought, he is known for having given lectures and written books that were intended to bring social justice to working people, those who, unlike himself, had not inherited £120,000 from their fathers. Like other wealthy people of conscience, he thought that great art could liberate the masses, so he set up the Company of St. George in 1871, donated 10% of his income annually to it, using it as a platform from which to launch cultural initiatives aimed at the underprivileged. Meanwhile, he wrote articles on socialist economics which so infuriated the readers of *Cornhill Magazine,* where they were published, that the editor, William Thackeray, had to stop publishing them. They then appeared in Ruskin's *Unto This Last* (1862).

"MODERN MANUFACTURE AND DESIGN," 1859

Delivered at the Mechanics' Institute, Bradford, March 1, 1859.

The changes in the state of this country are now so rapid, that it would be wholly absurd to endeavour to lay down laws of art education for it under its present aspect and circumstances; and therefore I must necessarily ask, how much of it do you seriously intend within the next fifty years to be coal-pit, brick-field, or quarry? For the sake of distinctness of conclusion, I will suppose your success absolute: that from shore to shore the whole of the island is to be set as thick with chimneys as the masts stand in the docks of Liverpool: that there shall be no meadows in it; no trees; no gardens; only a little corn grown upon the house-tops, reaped and threshed by steam: that you do not leave even room for roads, but travel either over the roofs of your mills, on viaducts; or under their floors, in tunnels: that, the smoke having rendered the light of the sun unserviceable, you work always by the light of your own gas: that no acre of English ground shall be without its shaft and its engine; and therefore, no spot of English ground left, on which it shall be possible to stand, without a definite and calculable chance of being blown off it, at any moment, into small pieces.

Under these circumstances, (if this is to be the future of England,) no designing or any other development of beautiful art will be possible. Do not vex your minds, nor waste your money with any thought or effort in the matter. Beautiful art can only be produced by people who have beautiful things about them, and leisure to look at them; and unless you provide some elements of beauty for your workmen to be surrounded by, you will find that no elements of beauty can be invented by them. . . .

The great lesson of history is, that all the fine arts hitherto—having been supported by the selfish power of the noblesse, and never having extended their range to the comfort or the relief of the mass of the people—the arts, I say, thus practised, and thus matured, have only accelerated

the ruin of the States they adorned; and at the moment when, in any kingdom, you point to the triumphs of its greatest artists, you point also to the determined hour of the kingdom's decline. The names of great painters are like passing bells: in the name of Velasquez, you hear sounded the fall of Spain; in the name of Titian, that of Venice; in the name of Leonardo, that of Milan; in the name of Raphael, that of Rome. And there is profound justice in this; for in proportion to the nobleness of the power is the guilt of its use for purposes vain or vile; and hitherto the greater the art, the more surely has it been used, and used solely, for the decoration of pride, or the provoking of sensuality. Another course lies open to us. We may abandon the hope—or if you like the words better—we may disdain the temptation, of the pomp and grace of Italy in her youth. For us there can be no more the throne of marble—for us no more the vault of gold—but for us there is the loftier and lovelier privilege of bringing the power and charm of art within the reach of the humble and the poor; and as the magnificence of past ages failed by its narrowness and its pride, ours may prevail and continue, by its universality and its lowliness. . . .

And you must remember always that your business, as manufacturers, is to form the market, as much as to supply it. If, in short-sighted and reckless eagerness for wealth, you catch at every humour of the populace as it shapes itself into momentary demand—if, in jealous rivalry with neighbouring States, or with other producers, you try to attract attention by singularities, novelties, and gaudinesses—to make every design an advertisement, and pilfer every idea of a successful neighbour's, that you may insidiously imitate it, or pompously eclipse—no good design will ever be possible to you, or perceived by you. You may, by accident, snatch the market; or, by energy, command it; you may obtain the confidence of the public, and cause the ruin of opponent houses; or you may, with equal justice of fortune, be ruined by them. But whatever happens to you, this, at least, is certain, that the whole of your life will have been spent in corrupting public taste and encouraging public extravagances. Every preference you have won by gaudiness must have been based on the purchaser's vanity; every demand you have created by novelty has fostered in the consumer a habit of discontent; and when you retire into inactive life, you may, as a subject of consolation for your declining years, reflect that precisely according to the extent of your past operations, your life has been successful in retarding the arts, tarnishing the virtues, and confusing the manners of your country.

<hr>

UNTO THIS LAST, 1860

The Roots of Honour

The first question is, I say, how far it may be possible to fix the rate of wages, irrespectively of the demand for labour. Perhaps one of the most curious facts in the history of human error is the denial by the common political economist of the possibility of thus regulating wages; while, for all the important, and much of the unimportant, labour, on the earth, wages are already so regulated.

We do not sell our prime-ministership by Dutch auction; nor, on the decease of a bishop, whatever may be the general advantages of simony, do we (yet) offer his diocese to the clergyman who will take the episcopacy at the lowest contract. We (with exquisite sagacity of political economy!) do indeed sell commissions; but not openly, generalships: sick, we do not inquire for a physician who takes less than a guinea; litigious, we never think of reducing six-and-eight-pence to four-and-sixpence; caught in a shower, we do not canvass the cabmen, to find one who values his driving at less than sixpence a mile.

It is true that in all these cases there is, and in every conceivable case there must be, ultimate reference to the presumed difficulty of the work, or number of candidates for the office. If it were thought that the labour necessary to make a good physician would be gone through by a sufficient number of students with the prospect of only half-guinea fees, public consent would soon withdraw the unnecessary half-guinea. In this ultimate sense, the price of labour is indeed always regulated by the demand for it; but, so far as the prac-

tical and immediate administration of the matter is regarded, the best labour always has been, and is, as *all* labour ought to be, paid by an invariable standard.

"What!" the reader perhaps answers amazedly: "pay good and bad workmen alike?"

Certainly. The difference between one prelate's sermons and his successors—or between one physician's opinion and another's—is far greater, as respects the qualities of mind involved, and far more important in result to you personally, than the difference between good and bad laying of bricks (though that is greater than most people suppose). Yet you pay with equal fee, contentedly, the good and bad workmen upon your soul, and the good and bad workmen upon your body; much more may you pay, contentedly, with equal fees, the good and bad workmen upon your house.

"Nay, but I choose my physician and (?) my clergyman, thus indicating my sense of the quality of their work." By all means, also, choose your bricklayer; that is the proper reward of the good workman, to be "chosen." The natural and right system respecting all labour is, that it should be paid at a fixed rate, but the good workman employed, and the bad workman unemployed. The false, unnatural, and destructive system is when the bad workman is allowed to offer his work at half-price, and either take the place of the good, or force him by his competition to work for an inadequate sum.

This equality of wages, then, being the first object toward which we have to discover the directest available road; the second is, as above stated, that of maintaining constant numbers of workmen in employment, whatever may be the accidental demand for the article they produce.

<hr>

SESAME AND LILIES, 1865

Of Kings' Treasuries

No nation can last, which has made a mob of itself, however generous at heart. It must discipline its passions, and direct them, or they will discipline *it*, one day, with scorpion whips. Above all, a nation cannot last as a money-making mob: it cannot with impunity,—it cannot with existence,—go on despising literature, despising science, despising art, despising nature, despising compassion, and concentrating its soul on Pence. Do you think these are harsh or wild words? Have patience with me but a little longer. I will prove their truth to you, clause by clause.

(I.) I say first we have despised literature. What do we, as a nation, care about books? How much do you think we spend altogether on our libraries, public or private, as compared with what we spend on our horses? If a man spends lavishly on his library, you call him mad—bibliomaniac.

⌁

FORS CLAVIGERA, 1871–1884

Communism

Will you be at the pains, now, however, to learn rightly, and once for all, what Communism is? First, it means that everybody must work in common, and do common or simple work for his dinner; and that if any man will not do it, he must not have his dinner. That much, perhaps, you thought you knew?—but you did not think we Communists of the old school knew it also? You shall have it, then, in the words of the Chelsea farmer and stout Catholic, I was telling you of in our last number. He was born in Milk Street, London, three hundred and ninety-one years ago, and he planned a Commune flowing with milk and honey, and otherwise Elysian; and he called it the "Place of Wellbeing," or Utopia; which is a word you perhaps have occasionally used before now, like others, without understanding it;—(in the article of the Liverpool *Daily Post* before referred to, it occurs felicitously seven times). You shall use it in that stupid way no more, if I can

help it. Listen how matters really are managed there.

The chief, and almost the only business of the government, is to take care that no man may live idle, but that every one may follow his trade diligently: yet they do not wear themselves out with perpetual toil from morning to night, as if they were beasts of burden, which, as it is indeed a heavy slavery, so it is everywhere the common course of life amongst all mechanics except the Utopians: but they, dividing the day and night into twenty-four hours, appoint six of these for work, three of which are before dinner and three after; they then sup, and, at eight o'clock, counting from noon, go to bed and sleep eight hours; the rest of their time, besides that taken up in work, eating, and sleeping, is left to every man's discretion; yet they are not to abuse that interval of luxury and idleness, but must employ it in some proper exercise, according to their various inclinations, which is, for the most part, reading. . . .

XI.—The End of the Whole Matter

The following series of aphorisms contain the gist of *Fors Clavigera*, and may serve to facilitate the arrangement of its incidental matter.

1. Any form of government will work, provided the governors are real, and the people obey them; and none will work, if the governors are unreal, or the people disobedient. If you mean to have logs for kings, no quantity of liberty in choice of the wood will be of any profit to you:—nor will the wisest or best governor be able to serve you, if you mean to discuss his orders instead of obeying them.

2. The first duty of government is to see that the people have food, fuel, and clothes. The second, that they have means of moral and intellectual education.

3. Food, fuel, and clothes can only be got out of the ground, or sea, by muscular labor; and no man has any business to have any, unless he has done, if able, the muscular work necessary to produce his portion, or to render (as the labor of a surgeon or physician renders), equivalent benefit to life. It indeed saves both toil and time that one man should dig, another bake, and another tan; but the digger,

From *The Communism of John Ruskin*, W.D. Bliss, Ed. The Humboldt Publishing Co., 1891.

baker, and tanner are alike bound to do their equal day's duty; and the business of the government is to see that they have done it, before it gives any one of them their dinner.

4. While the daily teaching of God's truth, doing of His justice, and heroic bearing of His sword, are to be required of every human soul according to its ability, the mercenary professions of preaching, law-giving, and fighting must be entirely abolished.

5. Scholars, painters, and musicians, may be advisedly kept, on due pittance, to instruct or amuse the laborer after, or at, his work; provided the duty be severely restricted to those who have high special gifts of voice, touch, and imagination; and that the possessors of these melodious lips, light-fingered hands, and lively brains, do resolutely undergo the normal discipline necessary to insure their skill; the people whom they are to please, understanding, always, that they cannot employ these tricksy artists without working double-tides themselves, to provide them with beef and ale.

6. The duty of the government, as regards the distribution of its work, is to attend first to the wants of the most necessitous; therefore, to take particular charge of the back streets of every town; leaving the fine ones, more or less, according to their finery, to take care of themselves. And it is the duty of magistrates, and other persons in authority, but especially of all bishops, to know thoroughly the numbers, means of subsistence, and modes of life of the poorest persons in the community, and to be sure that *they* at least are virtuous and comfortable; for if poor persons be not virtuous, after all the wholesome discipline of povery, what must be the state of the rich, under their perilous trials and temptations?—but, on the other hand, if the poor are made comfortable and good, the rich have a fair chance of entering the kingdom of heaven also, if they choose to live honorably and decently.

MATTHEW ARNOLD

1822–1888

Matthew Arnold was born on December 24, 1822 in Laleham, Staines, Middlesex, England, married Frances Lucy Wightman in June, 1851, and died in Liverpool on April 15, 1888, the father of three sons who predeceased him, and one daughter, Lucy. He suffered a heart attack after leaping over a fence at the joyful prospect of retrieving his wife and daughter at the docks, returning from the U.S. His father was the famous Thomas Arnold, headmaster of Rugby School since 1828, where Arnold matriculated in 1837 after a year at Winchester. From there he went to Balliol College, Oxford (1840–44), where he won in 1843 the coveted Newdigate Prize (as had Ruskin) for the poem, *Cromwell*. He became a fellow of Oriel College, then a private secretary to Lord Lansdowne from 1847 through 1851, and finally, in need of more income due to marriage, used Lansdowne's power to become the inspector of schools for England at 29. This lifelong, strenuous job caused him to travel all over Britain examining pedagogical arrangements, sometimes forcing him to read 800 student bluebooks at a time. He also visited France, Belgium, Holland, and Switzerland as a British official, studying their school systems. His annual reports on the state of education were much appreciated as books, since they were written in his sharp style. In 1857, with help from friends, he was offered the Oxford chair of poetry, which he held for 10 years and thereby changed by writing a series of essays on criticism that fused his understanding of history with a keen awareness of England's modern cultural shortcomings, based no doubt on his travels.

Although still regarded as a master of Victorian poetry and prose, and studied as such, Arnold's place in the history of social thought comes from his unique volume, *Culture and Anarchy* (1869), in print ever since. Arnold argued that the philistinism of British commercial culture had very nearly extinguished those mental capacities which make an understanding of artistic and poetic truth possible, and that as such, it was in grave danger of being turned into nothing more than a "nation of shopkeepers," to use a common phrase of the time and since. Between "the barbarians" (the aristocracy) and "the philistines" (Marx's "bourgeoisie"), there was little space left for the cultivation of sensibilities which Arnold thought to be essential to civilized life. He did not mean by this a sort of foppish powdered-wig sort of drawing room "culture," but rather a sensitivity which can embrace "the best that has been known and thought in the world," to quote his most famous summary remark. The excerpts below include his observations about the meaning of democracy, equality, and "doing as one likes," in a style of thought and exposition which is uniquely his own.

"DEMOCRACY," 1861

In modern epochs the part of a high reason, of ideas, acquires constantly increasing importance in the conduct of the world's affairs. A fine culture is the complement of a high reason, and it is in the conjunction of both with character, with energy, that the ideal for men and nations is to be placed. It is common to hear remarks on the frequent divorce between culture and character, and to infer from this that culture is a mere varnish, and that character only deserves any serious attention. No error can be more fatal. Culture without character is, no doubt, something frivolous, vain, and weak; but character without culture is, on the other hand, something raw, blind, and dangerous. The most interesting, the most truly glorious peoples, are those in which the alliance of the two has been effected most successfully, and its result spread most widely. This is why the spectacle of ancient Athens has such profound interest for a rational man; that it is the spectacle of the culture of a *people*. It is not an aristocracy, leavening with its own high spirit the multitude which it wields, but leaving it the unformed multitude still; it is not a democracy, acute and energetic, but tasteless, narrow-minded, and ignoble; it is the middle and lower classes in the highest development of their humanity that these classes have yet reached. It was the *many* who relished those arts who were not satisfied with less than those monuments. In the conversations recorded by Plato, or even by the matter-of-fact Xenophon, which for the free yet refined discussion of ideas have set the tone for the whole cultivated world, shopkeepers and tradesmen of Athens mingle as speakers. For any one but a pedant, this is why a handful of Athenians of two thousand years ago are more interesting than the millions of most nations our contemporaries. Surely, if they knew this, those friends of progress, who have confidently pronounced the remains of the ancient world to be so much lumber, and a classical education an aristocratic impertinence, might be inclined to reconsider their sentence.

⌒

CULTURE AND ANARCHY, 1869

Doing as One Likes

I have been trying to show that culture is, or ought to be, the study and pursuit of perfection; and that of perfection, as pursued by culture, beauty and intelligence, or, in other words, sweetness and light, are the main characters. But hitherto I have been insisting chiefly on beauty, or sweetness, as a character of perfection. To complete rightly my design, it evidently remains to speak also of intelligence, or light, as a character of perfection.

First, however, I ought perhaps to notice that, both here and on the other side of the Atlantic, all sorts of objections are raised against the "religion of culture," as the objectors mockingly call it, which I am supposed to be promulgating. It is said to be a religion proposing parmaceti, or some scented salve or other, as a cure for human miseries; a religion breathing a spirit of cultivated inaction, making its believer refuse to lend a hand at uprooting the definite evils on all sides of us, and filling him with antipathy against the reforms and reformers which try to extirpate them. In general, it is summed up as being not practical, or,—as some critics familiarly put it,—all moonshine. . . .

It is said that a man with my theories of sweetness and light is full of antipathy against the rougher or coarser movements going on around him, that he will not lend a hand to the humble operation of uprooting evil by their means, and that therefore the believers in action grow impatient with them. But what if rough and coarse action, ill-calculated action, action with insufficient light, is, and has for a long time been, our bane? What if our urgent want now is, not to act at any price, but rather to lay in a stock of light for our difficulties? In that case, to refuse to lend a hand to

---

the rougher and coarser movements going on round us, to make the primary need, both for oneself and others, to consist in enlightening ourselves and qualifying ourselves to act less at random, is surely the best and in real truth the most practical line our endeavours can take. So that if I can show what my opponents call rough or coarse action, but what I would rather call random and ill-regulated action,—action with insufficient light, action pursued because we like to be doing something and doing it as we please, and do not like the trouble of thinking and the severe constraint of any kind of rule,—if I can show this to be, at the present moment, a practical mischief and dangerous to us, then I have found a practical use for light in correcting this state of things, and have only to exemplify how, in cases which fall under everybody's observation, it may deal with it.

When I began to speak of culture, I insisted on our bondage to machinery, on our proneness to value machinery as an end in itself, without looking beyond it to the end for which alone, in truth, it is valuable. Freedom, I said, was one of those things which we thus worshipped in itself, without enough regarding the ends for which freedom is to be desired. In our common notions and talk about freedom, we eminently show our idolatry of machinery. Our prevalent notion is,— and I quoted a number of instances to prove it,— that it is a most happy and important thing for a man merely to be able to do as he likes. On what he is to do when he is thus free to do as he likes, we do not lay so much stress. . . . Our middle class, the great representative of trade and Dissent, with its maxims of every man for himself in business, every man for himself in religion, dreads a powerful administration which might somehow interfere with it; and besides, it has its own decorative inutilities of vestrymanship and guardianship, which are to this class what lord-lieutenancy and the county magistracy are to the aristocratic class, and a stringent administration might either take these functions out of its hands, or prevent its exercising them in its own comfortable, independent manner, as at present.

Then as to our working class. This class, pressed constantly by the hard daily compulsion of material wants, is naturally the very centre and stronghold of our national idea, that it is man's ideal right and felicity to do as he likes. I think I

have somewhere related how M. Michelet said to me of the people of France, that it was "a nation of barbarians civilised by the conscription." He meant that through their military service the idea of public duty and of discipline was brought to the mind of these masses, in other respects so raw and uncultivated. Our masses are quite as raw and uncultivated as the French; and so far from their having the idea of public duty and of discipline, superior to the individual's self-will, brought to their mind by a universal obligation of military service, such as that of the conscription,—so far from their having this, the very idea of a conscription is so at variance with our English notion of the prime right and blessedness of doing as one likes, that I remember the manager of the Clay Cross works in Derbyshire told me during the Crimean war, when our want of soldiers was much felt and some people were talking of a conscription, that sooner than submit to a conscription the population of that district would flee to the mines, and lead a sort of Robin Hood life under ground.

For a long time, as I have said, the strong feudal habits of subordination and deference continued to tell upon the working class. The modern spirit has now almost entirely dissolved those habits, and the anarchical tendency of our worship of freedom in and for itself, of our superstitious faith, as I say, in machinery, is becoming very manifest. More and more, because of this our blind faith in machinery, because of our want of light to enable us to look beyond machinery to the end for which machinery is valuable, this and that man, and this and that body of men, all over the country, are beginning to assert and put in practice an Englishman's right to do what he likes; his right to march where he likes, meet where he likes, enter where he likes, hoot as he likes, threaten as he likes, smash as he likes. All this, I say, tends to anarchy; and though a number of excellent people, and particularly my friends of the Liberal or progressive party, as they call themselves, are kind enough to reassure us by saying that these are trifles, that a few transient outbreaks of rowdyism signify nothing, that our system of liberty is one which itself cures all the evils which it works, that the educated and intelligent classes stand in overwhelming strength and majestic repose, ready, like our military force in riots, to act at a moment's notice,—yet one finds that one's Liberal friends generally say this because they have such faith in themselves and their nostrums, when they shall return, as the public welfare requires, to place and power. But this faith of theirs one cannot exactly share, when one has so long had them and their nostrums at work, and sees that they have not prevented our coming to our present embarrassed condition. And one finds, also, that the outbreaks of rowdyism tend to become less and less of trifles, to become more frequent rather than less frequent; and that meanwhile our educated and intelligent classes remain in their majestic repose, and somehow or other, whatever happens, their overwhelming strength, like our military force in riots, never does act. . . .

Every one with anything like an adequate idea of human perfection has distinctly marked this subordination to higher and spiritual ends of the cultivation of bodily vigour and activity. "Bodily exercise profiteth little; but godliness is profitable unto all things," says the author of the Epistle to Timothy. And the utilitarian Franklin says just as explicitly:—"Eat and drink such an exact quantity as suits the constitution of thy body, *in reference to the services of the mind."* But the point of view of culture, keeping the mark of human perfection simply and broadly in view, and not assigning to this perfection, as religion or utilitarianism assigns to it, a special and limited character, this point of view, I say, of culture is best given by these words of Epictetus:—"It is a sign of ἀφυΐα," says he,—that is, of a nature not finely tempered,—"to give yourselves up to things which relate to the body; to make, for instance, a great fuss about exercise, a great fuss about eating, a great fuss about drinking, a great fuss about walking, a great fuss about riding. All these things ought to be done merely by the way: the formation of the spirit and character must be our real concern." This is admirable; and, indeed, the Greek—word εὐφυΐα, a finely tempered nature, gives exactly the notion of perfection as culture brings us to conceive it: a harmonious perfection, a perfection in which the characters of beauty and intelligence are both present, which unites "the two noblest of things," as Swift, who of one of the two, at any rate, had himself all too little, most happily calls them in his *Battle of the Books,*—"the two noblest of things, *sweetness and light."*. . .

But Greece did not err in having the idea of beauty, harmony, and complete human perfection, so present and paramount. It is impossible to have this idea too present and paramount; only, the moral fibre must be braced too. And we, because we have braced the moral fibre, are not on that account in the right way, if at the same time the idea of beauty, harmony, and complete human perfection, is wanting or misapprehended amongst us; and evidently it *is* wanting or misapprehended at present. And when we rely as we do on our religious organisations, which in themselves do not and cannot give us this idea, and think we have done enough if we make them spread and prevail, then, I say, we fall into our common fault of overvaluing machinery.

Nothing is more common than for people to confound the inward peace and satisfaction which follows the subduing of the obvious faults of our animality with what I may call absolute inward peace and satisfaction,—the peace and satisfaction which are reached as we draw near to complete spiritual perfection, and not merely to moral perfection, or rather to relative moral perfection. No people in the world have done more and struggled more to attain this relative moral perfection than our English race has. For no people in the world has the command to *resist the devil, to overcome the wicked one,* in the nearest and most obvious sense of those words, bad such a pressing force and reality. And we have had our reward, not only in the great worldly prosperity which our obedience to this command has brought us, but also, and far more, in great inward peace and satisfaction. But to me few things are more pathetic than to see people, on the strength of the inward peace and satisfaction which their rudimentary efforts towards perfection have brought them, employ, concerning their incomplete perfection and the religious organisations within which they have found it, language which properly applies only to complete perfection, and is a far-off echo of the human soul's prophecy of it. Religion itself, I need hardly say, supplies them in abundance with this grand language. And very freely do they use it; yet it is really the severest possible criticism of such an incomplete perfection as alone we have yet reached through our religious organisations.

The impulse of the English race towards moral development and self-conquest has nowhere so powerfully manifested itself as in Puritanism.

⟶

"EQUALITY," 1879

Heaven forbid that I should speak in dispraise of that unique and most English class which Mr. Charles Sumner extols—the large class of gentlemen, not of the landed class or of the nobility, but cultivated and refined. They are a seemly product of the energy and of the power to rise in our race. Without, in general, rank and splendour and wealth and luxury to polish them, they have made their own the high standard of life and manners of an aristocratic and refined class. Not having all the dissipations and distractions of this class, they are much more seriously alive to the power of intellect and knowledge, to the power of beauty. The sense of conduct, too, meets with fewer trials in this class. To some extent, however, their contiguousness to the aristocratic class has now the effect of materialising them, as it does the class of newly enriched people. The most palpable action is on the young amongst them, and on their standard of life and enjoyment. But in general, for this whole class, established facts, the materialism which they see regnant, too much block their mental horizon, and limit the possibilities of things to them. They are deficient in openness and flexibility of mind, in free play of ideas, in faith and ardour. Civilised they are, but they are not much of a civilising force; they are somehow bounded and ineffective.

So on the middle class they produce singularly little effect. What the middle class sees is that splendid piece of materialism, the aristocratic class, with a wealth and luxury utterly out of their reach, with a standard of social life and manners, the offspring of that wealth and luxury, seeming utterly out of their reach also. And thus they are thrown back upon themselves—upon a defective

From *Matthew Arnold: Selected Essays*, edited with an Introduction by Noel Annan. Published by Oxford University Press. Copyright © 1964.

type of religion, a narrow range of intellect and knowledge, a stunted sense of beauty, a low standard of manners. And the lower class see before them the aristocratic class, and its civilisation, such as it is, even infinitely more out of *their* reach than out of that of the middle class; while the life of the middle class, with its unlovely types of religion, thought, beauty, and manners, has naturally, in general, no great attractions for them either. And so they too are thrown back upon themselves; upon their beer, their gin, and their *fun.* Now, then, you will understand what I meant by saying that our inequality materialises our upper class, vulgarises our middle class, brutalises our lower.

And the greater the inequality the more marked is its bad action upon the middle and lower classes. . . .

What a strange religion, then, is our religion of inequality! Romance often helps a religion to hold its ground, and romance is good in its way; but ours is not even a romantic religion. No doubt our aristocracy is an object of very strong public interest. The *Times* itself bestows a leading article by way of epithalamium on the Duke of Norfolk's marriage. And those journals of a new type, full of talent, and which interest me particularly because they seem as if they were written by the young lion of our youth,—the young lion grown mellow and, as the French say, *viveur,* arrived at his full and ripe knowledge of the world, and minded to enjoy the smooth evenings of his days,—those journals, in the main a sort of social gazette of the aristocracy, are apparently not read by that class only which they most concern, but are read with great avidity by other classes also. And the common people too have undoubtedly, as Mr. Gladstone says, a wonderful preference for a lord. Yet our aristocracy, from the action upon it of the Wars of the Roses, the Tudors, and the political necessities of George the Third, is for the imagination a singularly modern and uninteresting one. Its splendour of station, its wealth, show, and luxury, is then what the other classes really admire in it; and this is not an elevating admiration. Such an admiration will never lift us out of our vulgarity and brutality, if we chance to be vulgar and brutal to start with; it will rather feed them and be fed by them. So that when Mr. Gladstone invites us to call our love of inequality 'the complement of the love of freedom or its negative pole, or the shadow which the love of freedom casts, or the reverberation of its voice in the halls of the constitution', we must surely answer that all this mystical eloquence is not in the least necessary to explain so simple a matter; that our love of inequality is really the vulgarity in us, and the brutality, admiring and worshipping the splendid materiality.

Our present social organisation, however, will and must endure until our middle class is provided with some better ideal of life than it has now. Our present organisation has been an appointed stage in our growth; it has been of good use, and has enabled us to do great things. But the use is at an end, and the stage is over.

ALEKSANDR I. HERZEN

1812–1870

Aleksandr Ivanovich Herzen (Hertzen or Gertsen), the bastard son of Ivan A. Yakovlev, a very rich Russian nobleman, and the commoner Luiza Haag of Stuttgart, was born in Moscow on April 6, 1812 (new style), married his cousin, Natalya Zakharina, in 1838, and died in Paris after 57 years. His father (at 42) had married his mother (a 16 year-old daughter of a minor official) in Germany, but their son was not recognized as such in Russia, so his father named him "Herzen" ("heart" in German) since he was what we now call a "love-child." He was raised in his father's palatial home and taught there by a platoon of tutors, from France, Germany, and Russia. Yet his stigmatized mixed parentage gave him an existential remove from his luxurious surroundings. Because of this he developed sympathies for the Decembrists and similar groups whose aim was to topple Russian serfdom and with it the aristocratic lifestyle into which his father had been born. A failed coup attempt in 1825 inspired Herzen to dedicate his life to social change when he was merely 13. While at the University of Moscow (1829–33) he rediscovered his maternal roots by becoming expert in the "nature philosophy" of Friedrich Schelling. He and a few intimate friends managed to combine pantheism from this source with utopianism from Saint-Simon so that their personal taste for freedom became an ideology that seemed ideally suited for the downtrodden in Russia at large. Even his father's high status could not protect him and his friends from arrest in 1834, and he spent the next eight years in internal exile in Kirov and Novgorod. This toughened him, and he thereafter dispensed with the fuzzy romanticism of Schelling, substituting for it more rigid notions from Hegel and Feuerbach, thus becoming what was widely known then as a "left-wing Hegelian" (about whom Marx wrote very critically). He and his colleagues had to take solace in revolutionary philosophy because genuinely revolutionary acts were impossible under Czar Nicholas I. Moving progressively further to the left, Herzen finally embraced Proudhon's anarchism, and left Russia for good in 1846 with his father's legacy. He went to Paris, where the Revolution of 1848 was about to begin, yet the actual events proved anticlimactic and ineffective to him. He was hoping for a cataclysmic collapse of the status quo, and realized it would not happen.

Herzen's place in social thought has been guaranteed by his memoir, *My Past and Thoughts* (1861–67), which is as highly esteemed in Russia as is *War and Peace,* but has not gained an equal reputation in the West. This multi-volume work is a superb portrait of 19th century radicalism, and also includes digressions on many topics, including the one reprinted here on the place of women in the Europe of his time.

MY PAST AND THOUGHTS, 1861–67

Second Thoughts on the Woman Question

I

. . . On one hand we have Proudhon's family, submissively welded and tightly clinched together, indissoluble marriage, indivisible paternal authority—a family in which for the sake of the community the persons perish, *except one,* the ferocious marriage in which is accepted the unchangeability of feelings and the abracadabra of a vow; on the other hand we have the doctrines that are springing up in which marriage and the family are unbound from each other, the irresistible force of passion is recognised, the non-liability of the past and the independence of the individual.

On one hand we have woman almost stoned for infidelity; on the other jealousy itself put *hors la loi* as a morbid, monstrous feeling of egoism and proprietorship and the romantic subversion of natural, healthy ideas.

Where is the truth . . . where is the middle line? Twenty-three years ago I was already seeking a way out of this forest of contradictions.

We are bold in denial and always ready to fling any of our Peruns into the river, but the Peruns of home and family life are somehow 'waterproof,' they always bob up. Perhaps there is no sense left in them—but life is left; evidently the weapons used against them simply glided over their snaky scales, have felled them, stunned them . . . but have not killed them.

Jealousy . . . Fidelity . . . Infidelity . . . Purity. . . . Dark forces, menacing words, thanks to which rivers of tears have flowed, and rivers of blood-words that set us shuddering like the memory of the Inquisition, of torture, of the plague . . . and yet they are the words under the shadow of which, as under the sword of Damocles, the family has lived and is living.

There is no turning them out of doors by abuse or by denial. They remain round the corner, slumbering, ready on the slightest occasion to destroy everything near and far, to destroy us ourselves. . . .

Clearly we must abandon our honourable intention of utterly extinguishing these smouldering flames and modestly confine ourselves to humanely guiding and subduing the consuming fire. You can no more bridle passions with logic than you can justify them in the lawcourts. Passions are facts and not dogmas.

Jealousy, moreover, has always enjoyed special privileges. In itself a violent and *perfectly natural* passion, which hitherto, instead of being muzzled and kept under, has only been stimulated. The Christian doctrine which, through hatred of the body, sets everything fleshly on an extraordinary height, and the aristocratic worship of blood and purity of race, have developed to the point of absurdity the conception of a mortal affront, a blot that cannot be washed off. Jealousy has received the *jus gladii,* the right of judgment and revenge. It has become a duty of *honour,* almost a virtue. All this will not stand a moment's criticism—but yet there still remains at the bottom of the heart a very real, insurmountable feeling of pain, of unhappiness, called jealousy, a feeling as elementary as the feeling of love itself, resisting every effort to deny it, an 'irreducible' feeling.

. . . Here again are the everlasting limits, the Caudine Forks under which history drives us. On both sides there is truth, on both there is falsehood. A brusque *entweder–oder* will lead you nowhere. At the moment of the complete negation of one of the terms it comes back, just as after the last quarter of the moon the first appears on the other side.

Hegel removed these boundary-posts of human reason, by rising to the *absolute spirit;* in it they did not vanish but were *transmuted, fulfilled,* as German theological science expressed it: this is mysticism, philosophical theodicy, allegory and reality purposely mixed up. All religious reconciliations of the irreconcilable are won by means of *redemptions,* that is, by sacred transmutation, sacred deception, a solution which solves nothing but is taken on trust. What can be more antithetical than free-will and necessity? Yet by faith even they are easily reconciled. Man will accept without a murmur the justice of punishment for an action which was pre-ordained.

Proudhon himself, in a different range of questions, was far more humane than German philosophy. From economic contradictions he escapes by the recognition of both sides under the restraint of a higher principle. Property as a right and property as theft are set side by side in everlasting balance, everlastingly complementary, under the ever-growing *Weltherrschaft of justice*. It is clear that the argument and the contradictions are transferred to another sphere, and that it is the conception of justice we have to call to account rather than the right of property.

The simpler, the less mystical and the less one-sided, the more real and practically applicable the higher principle is, the more completely it brings the contradictory terms to their lowest denomination.

The absolute, 'all-embracing' spirit of Hegel is replaced in Proudhon by the menacing idea of justice.

But the problem of the passions is not likely to be solved by that either. Passion is intrinsically unjust; justice is abstracted from the personal, it is 'interpersonal'—passion is only individual.

The solution here lies not in the lawcourt but in the humane development of individual character, in its removal from emotional self-centredness into the light of day, in the development of common interests.

The radical elimination of jealousy implies eliminating love for the individual, replacing it by love for woman or for man, by love of the sex in general. But it is just the personal, the individual, that pleases; it is just that which gives colouring, tone, sensuality to the whole of our life. Our emotion is personal, our happiness and unhappiness are personal happiness and unhappiness.

Doctrinairianism with all its logic is of as little comfort in personal sorrow as the consolations of the Romans with their rhetoric. Neither the tears of loss nor the tears of jealousy can be wiped away, nor should they be, but it is right and possible that they should flow humanely . . . and that they should be equally free from monastic poison, the ferocity of the beast, and the wail of the wounded owner of property.

To reduce the relationships of man and woman to a casual sexual encounter is just as impossible as to exalt and bolt them together in marriage which is indissoluble before the planks of the coffin. Both the one and the other may be met with at the extremes of sexual and marital relationships, as a special case, as an exception, but not as a general rule. The sexual relationship will be broken off or will continually tend towards a closer and firmer union, just as the indissoluble marriage will tend towards liberation from external bonds.

People have continually protested against both extremes. Indissoluble marriage has been accepted by them hypocritically, or in the heat of the moment. Casual intimacy has never had complete recognition; it has always been concealed, just as marriage has been a subject of boasting. All attempts at the official regulation of brothels, although aiming at their restriction, are offensive to the moral sense of society, which in organisation sees acceptance. The scheme of a gentleman in Paris, in the days of the Directorate, for establishing privileged brothels with their own hierarchy and so on, was even in those days received with hisses and overwhelmed by a story of laughter and contempt.

The healthy, normal life of man avoids the monastery just as much as the cattle-yard; the sexlessness of the monk, which the Church esteems above marriage, as much as the childless gratification of the passions. . . .

Marriage is for Christianity a concession, an inconsistency, a weakness. Christianity regards marriage as society regards concubinage.

The monk and the Catholic priest are condemned to perpetual celibacy by way of reward for their foolish triumph over human nature.

Christian marriage on the whole is sombre and unjust; it establishes inequality, which the Gospel preaches against, and delivers the wife into slavery to the husband. The wife is sacrificed, love (hateful to the Church) is sacrificed; after the Church ceremony it becomes a superfluity, and is replaced by duty and obligation. Of the brightest and most joyous of feelings Christianity has made a pain, a weariness, and a sin. The human race had either to die out or be inconsistent. Outraged nature protested.

It protested not only by acts followed by repentance and the gnawing of conscience, but by sympathy, by rehabilitation. The protest began in the very heyday of Catholicism and chivalry.

The threatening husband, Raoul, the Bluebeard in armour with the sword, tyrannical, jealous, and merciless; the barefoot monk, sullen, senseless, superstitious, ready to avenge himself for his privations, for his unnecessary struggle; jailers, hangmen, spies, . . . and in some cellar or turret a sobbing woman, a page in chains, for whom no one will intercede. All is darkness, savagery, blood, bigotry, violence, and Latin prayers chanted through the nose.

But behind the monk, the confessor and the jailer who, with the threatening husband, the father and the brother stand guard over the marriage, the folk-legend is forming in the stillness, the ballad is heard and is carried from place to place, from castle to castle, by troubadour and minnesinger—it champions the unhappy woman. The court smites, the song emancipates. The Church hurls its anathema at love outside marriage, the ballad curses marriage without love. It defends the love-sick page, the fallen wife, the oppressed daughter, not by reasoning but with sympathy, with pity, with tears, lamentation. The song is for the people its secular prayer, its other escape from the cold and hunger of life, from suffocating misery and heavy toil. . . .

Marriage without the intervention of the Church became a contract for the bodily enslavement of each to the other for life. The legislator has nothing to do with faith, with mystic ravings, so long as the contract is fulfilled, and if it is not he will find means of punishment and enforcement. And why not punish it? In England, the traditional country of juridical development, a boy of sixteen, made drunk by ales and gin and enrolled in a regiment by an old recruiting sergeant with ribbons on his hat, is subjected to the most fearful tortures. Why not punish a girl? Why not punish with shame, ruin, and forcible restoration to her master the girl who, with no clear understanding of what she is about, has contracted to love for life, and has admitted an *extra,* forgetting that the 'season-ticket' is not transferable. But these 'blue-chins' too have been attacked by the *trouvres* and novelists. Against the marriage of legal contract a psychiatrical, physiological dogma has been set up, the dogma of *the absolute infallibility of the passions and the incapacity of man to struggle against them.*

Those who were yesterday the slaves of marriage are now becoming the slaves of love. There is no law for love, there is no strength that can resist it.

After this, all rational control, all responsibility, every form of self-restraint is effaced. That man is in subjection to irresistible and ungovernable forces is a theory utterly opposed to that freedom of reason and by reason, to that formation of the character of a free man which all social theories aim at attaining by different paths.

Imaginary forces, if men take them for real, are just as powerful as real ones; and this is so because the substance generated by a human being is the same whatever the force that acts upon him. The man who is afraid of ghosts is afraid in exactly the same way as the man who is afraid of mad dogs, and may as easily die of fright. The difference is that in one case the man can be shown that his fears are nonsensical, and in the other be cannot.

I refuse to admit the sovereign position given to *love* in life; I deny it autocratic power and protest against the pusillanimous excuse of having been carried away by it.

HENRY SUMNER MAINE

1822–1888

Sir Henry James Sumner Maine, a physician's son, was born on August 15, 1822 in Kelso, Roxburghshire, Scotland, he married and had two sons, and on February 3, 1888 died at Cannes, after 65 years. His early education was at Christ's Hospital, after which he attended Pembroke College, Cambridge in 1840, graduating four years later as one of the best classical scholars of the period. He worked as a tutor, then as professor from 1847, and was called to the bar in 1850 and became a Reader in Jurisprudence and Civil Law at the Middle Temple, then Regius Professor of the Civil Law at Cambridge (1847–1854). Unlike most of his contemporaries, he became expert in Roman law at a time when it was not considered important to legal training. The lecture material he worked up for his early teaching positions became his greatest book, *Ancient Law* (1861), for which he instantly became well-known. He then traveled to India and stayed from 1863–69 as a Member of the Supreme Council, obtained the new chair in comparative and historical jurisprudence at Oxford in 1869, was elected master of Trinity Hall at Cambridge in 1877, finally became Whewell Professor of International Law.

While in India—where he went hoping to improve his health—he proved to be remarkably useful to the British and Indian authorities, particularly on questions of converting traditional understandings of suitable behavior into laws which could be prescribed and enforced in the modern fashion. He was so good at assimilating tradition into new legal forms that he was asked to extend his stay beyond the normal five year term. The question of civil marriage for unorthodox Hindus, for example, is one that he skillfully worked out to everyone's satisfaction. While in India he also served as vice-chancellor of the University of Calcutta, and from all these contacts he was able to bring to his later work a depth and breadth of cross-cultural comparison which very few of his contemporaries could match.

His other writings include *Early History of Institutions* (1875), *Early Law and Custom* (1883), and *Popular Government* (1885). The last named book argued the heterodox point that democracy is inherently unstable as a form of government and that it bears no necessary connection to societal progress. The book, like *Ancient Law*, is still in print and especially prized by libertarians. Maine studied many legal systems (Hindu, Hebrew, Germanic, Anglo-Saxon, and others) in order to establish his arguments about the fundamental nature of early law. He was particularly curious about the developmental differences between common and Roman law. The catch-phrase which defines Maine's interest—"from status to contract"—has graced every work in basic sociology since the field came into its own.

ANCIENT LAW, 1861

Law of Nature and Equity

The Romans described their legal system as consisting of two ingredients. "All nations," says the Institutional Treatise published under the authority of the Emperor Justinian, "who are ruled by laws and customs, are governed partly by their own particular laws, and partly by those laws which are common to all mankind. The law which a people enacts is called the Civil Law of that people, but that which natural reason appoints for all mankind is called the Law of Nations, because all nations use it." The part of the law "which natural reason appoints for all mankind" was the element which the Edict of the Prætor was supposed to have worked into Roman jurisprudence. Elsewhere it is styled more simply Jus Naturale, or the Law of Nature; and its ordinances are said to be directed by Natural Equity (*naturalis aequitas*) as well as by natural reason. I shall attempt to discover the origin of these famous phrases, Law of Nations, Law of Nature, Equity, and to determine how the conception which they indicate are related to one another.

The most superficial student of Roman history must be struck by the extraordinary degree in which the fortunes of the republic were affected by the presence of foreigners, under different names, on her soil. The causes of this immigration are discernible enough at a later period, for we can readily understand why men of all races should flock to the mistress of the world; but the same phenomenon of a large population of foreigners and denizens meets us in the very earliest records of the Roman State. No doubt, the instability of society in ancient Italy, composed as it was in great measure of robber tribes, gave men considerable inducement to locate themselves in the territory of any community strong enough to protect itself and them from external attack, even though protection should be purchased at the cost of heavy taxation, political disfranchisement, and much social humiliation. It is probable, however, that this explanation is imperfect, and that it could only be

From *Ancient Law: Its Connection with the Early History of Society, and Its Relation to Modern Ideas,* by Henry Sumner Maine. Published by Charles Scribner & Co., 1867.

completed by taking into account those active commercial relations which, though they little reflected in the military traditions of the republic, Rome appears certainly to have had with Carthage and with the interior of Italy in pre-historic times. Whatever were the circumstances to which it was attributable, the foreign element in the commonwealth determined the whole course of its history, which, at all its stages, is little more than a narrative of conflicts between a stubborn nationality and an alien population. Nothing like this has been seen in modern times; on the one hand, because modern European communities have seldom or never received any accession of foreign immigrants which was large enough to make itself felt by the bulk of the native citizens, and on the other, because modern states, being held together by allegiance to a king or political superior, absorb considerable bodies of immigrant settlers with a quickness unknown to the ancient world, where the original citizens of a commonwealth always believed themselves to be united by kinship in blood, and resented a claim to equality of privilege as a usurpation of their birth right. In the early Roman republic the principle of the absolute exclusion of foreigners pervaded the Civil Law no less than the constitution. The alien or denizen could have no share in any institution supposed to be coeval with the State. He could not have the benefit of Quiritarian law. He could not be a party to the *nexum* which was at once the conveyance and the contract of the primitive Romans. He could not sue by the Sacramental Action, a mode of litigation of which the origin mounts up to the very infancy of civilisation. Still, neither the interest nor the security of Rome permitted him to be quite outlawed. All ancient communities ran the risk of being overthrown by a very slight disturbance of equilibrium, and the mere instinct of self-preservation would force the Romans to devise some method of adjusting the rights and duties of foreigners, who might otherwise—and this was a danger of real importance in the ancient world—have decided their controversies by armed strife. Moreover, at no period of Roman history was foreign trade entirely neglected. It was therefore probably half as a measure of police and half in furtherance of commerce that jurisdiction was first assumed in disputes to which the parties were either foreigners or a native and a foreigner. . . . The expedient to which they reported was that of selecting the rules of law common to Rome and to the different Italian communities in which the immigrants were born. In other words, they set themselves to form a system answering to the primitive and literal meaning of Jus Gentium that is, Law common to all Nations. Jus Gentium was, in fact, the sum of the common ingredients in the customs of the old Italian tribes, for they were *all the nations* whom the Romans had the means of observing, and who sent successive swarms of immigrants to Roman soil. Whenever a particular usage was seen to be practised by a large number of separate races in common it was set down as part of the Law common to all Nations, or Gentium.

~◦~➔

LECTURES ON THE EARLY HISTORY OF INSTITUTIONS, 1875/1888

The Growth and Diffusion of Primitive Ideas

Mr. Tylor has justly observed that the true lesson of the new science of Comparative Mythology is the barrenness in primitive times of the faculty which we most associate with mental fertility, the Imagination. Comparative Jurisprudence, as might be expected from the natural stability of law and custom, yet more strongly suggests the same inference, and points to the fewness of ideas and the slowness of additions to the mental stock as among the most general characteristics of mankind in its infancy.

The fact that the generation of new ideas does not proceed in all states of society as rapidly as in that to which we belong, is only not familiar to us through our inveterate habit of confining our observation of human nature to a small portion of its phenomena. When we undertake to examine it, we are very apt to look exclusively at a part of Western Europe and perhaps of the American Continent. We constantly leave aside India, China, and the whole Mahometan East. This limitation of our field of vision is perfectly justifiable when we

From *Lectures on the Early History of Institutions,* by Sir Henry Sumner Maine. Published by Henry Holt and Company, 1888.

are occupied with the investigation of the laws of Progress. Progress is, in fact, the same thing as the continued production of new ideas, and we can only discover the law of this production by examining sequences of ideas where they are frequent and of considerable length. But the primitive condition of the progressive societies is best ascertained from the observable condition of those which are non-progressive; and thus we leave a serious gap in our knowledge when we put aside the mental state of the millions upon millions of men who fill what we vaguely call the East as a phenomenon of little interest and of no instructiveness. The fact is not unknown to most of us that, among these multitudes, Literature, Religion, and Art—or what corresponds to them—move always within a distinctly drawn circle of unchanging notions; but the fact that this condition of thought is rather the infancy of the human mind prolonged than a different maturity from that most familiar to us, is very seldom brought home to us with a clearness rendering it fruitful of instruction.

I do not, indeed, deny that the difference between the East and the West, in respect of the different speed at which new ideas are produced, is only a difference of degree. There were new ideas produced in India even during the disastrous period just before the English entered it, and in the earlier ages this production must have been rapid. There must have been a series of ages during which the progress of China was very steadily maintained, and doubtless our assumption of the absolute immobility of the Chinese and other societies is in part the expression of our ignorance. Conversely, I question whether new ideas come into being in the West as rapidly as modern literature and conversation sometimes suggest. It cannot, indeed, be doubted that causes, unknown to the ancient world, lead among us to the multiplication of ideas. Among them are the never-ceasing discovery of new facts of nature, inventions changing the circumstances and material conditions of life, and new rules of social conduct; the chief of this last class, and certainly the most powerful in the domain of law proper, I take to be the famous maxim that all institutions should be adapted to produce the greatest happiness of the greatest number. Nevertheless, there are not a few signs that even conscious efforts to increase the number of ideas have a very limited success.

NUMA DENIS FUSTEL DE COULANGES

1830–1889

Numa Denis Fustel de Coulanges was born in Paris on March 18, 1830, seems not to have married, and died in Massy (Seine-et-Oise) on September 13, 1889 at the age of 59. He was educated at the École Normale Superieure and at the French School in Athens, graduating in 1853 after directing archaeological excavations in Greece. His two dissertations that came out of this work (1858) reveal his lifelong penchant for detailed investigation of original sources, and his low opinion of contemporary historiography which relied on second-hand reports. His zeal for research of this rigorous style served as a guiding light for other historians, and mostly accounts for his work continuing to be read today. From 1860 through 1870 he taught history at Strassburg in brilliant fashion, but was fired after the Germans took over the city as a consequence of the Franco-Prussian War. He switched from ancient to medieval history at this point, and eventually completed a 6-volume work, *History of the Political Institutions of Medieval France* (1888–1892) in which he demonstrated that European feudal social structure originated in Roman times, and was not an invention of the German peoples, as had been argued by his colleagues across the Rhine. He also proved to his satisfaction that the "conquest of Gaul by the Germans" never occurred as such. Even when he was making implausible arguments, he did it with informed zeal and grace. Thus refusing to submit to German historical orthodoxy, he returned to his alma mater in Paris in 1870 and in 1878 assumed a chair at the Sorbonne in medieval history which had been created for him. Late in life he reluctantly accepted administrative posts, but his passionate devotion to learning left him little time for mundane affairs.

Fustel de Coulanges' place in the history of social thought is firmly anchored by his essential work, *The Ancient City: A Study of the Religion, Laws, and Institutions of Greece and Rome* (1864), new editions of which continue to be produced and read by historians the world over, even if the details of his research have of course been superseded. Not only is the book beautifully and subtly written, but its author put forward the then shocking thesis that it was religion which gave Rome its essential character, an argument he backed with careful attention to available documents of the era. Even though this flew in the face of most historians' views, the book had tremendous impact through the sheer virtuosity of its stated position. The selections reprinted below concern conceptions of marriage in the ancient family, and the sources of authority within it, extending therefore to the society at large.

THE ANCIENT CITY, 1864

Marriage

The first institution that the domestic religion established, probably, was marriage.

We must remark that this worship of the sacred fire and of ancestors, which was transmitted from male to male, did not belong, after all, exclusively to man; woman had a part in it. As a daughter, she took part in the religious acts of her father; as a wife, in those of her husband.

From this alone we see the essential character of the conjugal union among the ancients. Two families live side by side; but they have different gods. In one, a young daughter takes a part, from her infancy, in the religion of her father; she invokes his sacred fire; every day she offers it libations. She surrounds it with flowers and garlands on festal days. She asks its protection, and returns thanks for its favors. This paternal fire is her god. Let a young man of the neighboring family ask her in marriage, and something more is at stake than to pass from one house to the other. She must abandon the paternal fire, and henceforth invoke that of the husband. She must abandon her religion, practise other rites, and pronounce other prayers. She must give up the god of her infancy, and put herself under the protection of a god whom she knows not. Let her not hope to remain faithful to the one while honoring the other; for in this religion it is an immutable principle that the same person cannot invoke two sacred fires or two series of ancestors. "From the hour of marriage," says one of the ancients, "the wife has no longer anything in common with the domestic religion of her fathers; she sacrifices at the hearth of her husband."[1]

Marriage is, therefore, a grave step for the young girl, and not less grave for the husband; for this religion requires that one shall have been born near the sacred fire, in order to have the right to sacrifice to it. And yet he is now about to bring a stranger to this hearth; with her he will perform the mysterious ceremonies of his worship; he will reveal the rites and formulas which are the patrimony of his family. There is nothing more precious than this heritage; these gods, these rites, these hymns which he has received from his fathers, are what protect him in this life, and promise him riches, happiness, and virtue. And yet, instead of keeping to himself this tutelary power, as the savage keeps his idol or his amulet, he is going to admit a woman to share it with him.

Thus, when we penetrate the thoughts of these ancient men, we see of how great importance to them was the conjugal union, and how necessary to it was the intervention of religion. Was it not quite necessary that the young girl should be initiated into the religion that she was henceforth to follow by some sacred ceremony? Was not a sort of ordination or adoption necessary for her to become a priestess of this sacred fire, to which she was not attached by birth? . . .

Now, the religion that created marriage was not that of Jupiter, of Juno, or of the other gods of Olympus. The ceremony did not take place in a temple; it was performed in a house, and the domestic god presided. When the religion of the gods of the sky became preponderant, men could not help invoking them also in the prayers of marriage, it is true; it even became habitual to go to the temple before the marriage, and offer sacrifices to these gods. These sacrifices were called the preludes of marriage; but the principal and essential part of the ceremony always took place before the domestic hearth. . . .

We can understand, too, that such a marriage was indissoluble, and that divorce was almost impossible. The Roman law did indeed permit the dissolution of the marriage by *coemptio*, or by *usus*. But the dissolution of the religious marriage was very difficult. For that, a new sacred ceremony was necessary, as religion alone could separate what religion had united. The effect of the *confarreatio* could be destroyed only by the *difarreatio*. The husband and wife who wished to separate appeared for the last time before the common hearth; a priest and witnesses were present. As on the day of marriage, a cake of wheaten flour was presented to the husband and wife. But, instead of sharing it between them, they rejected it. Then, instead of prayers,

From *The Ancient City: A Study on the Religion, Laws, and Institutions of Greece and Rome,* by Numa Denis Fustel De Coulanges. Published by Doubleday & Company, Inc., 1901.

they pronounced formulas of a strange, severe, spiteful, frightful character, a sort of malediction, by which the wife renounced the worship and gods of the husband. From that moment the religious bond was broken. The community of worship having ceased, every other common interest ceased to exist, and the marriage was dissolved.

Authority in the Family

I. The Principle and Nature of the Paternal Power among the Ancients. The family did not receive its laws from the city. If the city had established private law, that law would probably have been different from what we have seen. It would have established the right of property and the right of succession on different principles; for it was not for the interest of the city that land should be inalienable and the patrimony indivisible. The law that permitted a father to sell or even to kill his son—a law that we find both in Greece and in Rome—was not established by a city. The city would rather have said to the father, "Your wife's and your son's life does not belong to you any more than their liberty does. I will protect them, even against you; you are not the one to judge them, or to kill them, if they have committed a crime; I will be their judge." If the city did not speak thus, it is evident that it could not. Private law existed before the city. When the city began to write its laws, it found this law already established, living, rooted in the customs, strong by universal observance. The city accepted it, because it could not do otherwise, and dared not modify it, except by degrees. Ancient law was not the work of a legislator; it was, on the contrary, imposed upon the legislator. It had its birth in the family. It sprang up spontaneously from the ancient principles which gave it root. It flowed from the religious belief which was universally admitted in the primitive age of these peoples, which exercised its empire over their intelligence and their wills.

A family was composed of a father, a mother, children, and slaves. This group, small as it was, required discipline. To whom, then, belonged the chief authority? To the father? No. There is in every house something that is above the father himself. It is the domestic religion; it is that god

whom the Greeks called the hearth-master,—'estia despoiua,—whom the Romans called *Lar familiaris*. This divinity of the interior, or, what amounts to the same thing, the belief that is in the human soul, is the least doubtful authority. This is what fixed rank in the family.

The father ranks first in presence of the sacred fire. He lights it, and supports it; he is its priest. In all religious acts his functions are the highest; he slays the victim, his mouth pronounces the formula of prayer which is to draw upon him and his the protection of the gods. The family and the worship are perpetuated through him; he represents, himself alone, the whole series of ancestors, and from him are to proceed the entire series of descendants. Upon him rests the domestic worship; he can almost say, like the Hindu, "I am the god." When death shall come, he will be a divine being whom his descendants will invoke.

This religion did not place woman in so high a rank. The wife takes part in the religious acts, indeed, but she is not the mistress of the hearth. She does not derive her religion from her birth. She was initiated into it at her marriage. . . .

The laws of Manu says, "Woman, during her infancy, depends upon her father; during her youth, upon her husband; when her husband is dead, upon her sons; if she has no son, on the nearest relative of her husband; for a woman ought never to govern herself according to her own will." The Greek laws and those of Rome are to the same effect. As a girl, she is under her father's control; if her father dies, she is governed by her brothers; married, she is under the guardianship of her husband; if the husband dies, she does not return to her own family, for she has renounced that forever by the sacred marriage; the widow remains subject to the guardianship of her husband's agnates—that is to say, of her own sons, if she has any, or, in default of sons, of the nearest kindred. So complete is her husband's authority over her, that he can, upon his death, designate a guardian for her, and even choose her a second husband.

Note

1. Stephen of Byzantium, patra.

CHARLES DARWIN

1809–1882

Son of a very successful physician, Charles Robert Darwin was born on February 12, 1809 at The Mount, Shrewsbury, Shropshire, England, and after making up a cost/benefit table regarding matrimony, he married his first cousin, Emma Wedgwood, on January 29, 1839 and with her had ten children, seven of whom lived into adulthood (three sons became noted scientists). He died on April 19, 1882 at Down House, Downe, Kent at the age of 73, and was interred at Westminster Abbey as dictated by a vote in Parliament. Darwin came from a scientific family (one grandfather, Erasmus Darwin, was a noted author of medical treatises, while the other, Josiah Wedgwood, was famous for porcelain manufacture). Darwin's childhood was one of privilege and comfort except for his mother's death when he was eight, and after some unenthusiastic schooling, he was sent to the University of Edinburgh to pursue medicine. Witnessing surgery he found repulsive, he shifted to the study of marine animals and to geology. His father then sent him to Cambridge for divinity training, but Darwin spent his time with sporting lads rather than studying theology. He did, though, continue to meet scientists and to learn from them. The pivotal event in his life occurred when he was nearly 23. Against his father's wishes, he set sail as an unpaid naturalist on the *Beagle*, a former warship refitted for scientific duties, a trip to the coastal islands of South America and the Pacific that lasted five years and provided Darwin with a lifetime's supply of zoological and biological samples. It also gave Darwin material for his book about the trip (1839), modeled on others he'd read before leaving.

An inheritance from his father allowed him to work exclusively at home in his laboratory about 16 miles from London, yet quite remote from the city's bustle. He suffered an odd assortment of ailments (sleeplessness, pounding heart, nausea, and so on), which are now thought to be psychosomatic in origin, probably due to the conflict he felt between his scientific discoveries and those around him who were devout Christians and would find his ideas objectionable, his wife among them. Darwin enjoyed his place in Victorian society and tried not to give offence to those whose good opinion he valued, yet he could not conceal his scientific discoveries forever, and paid a dear price when they became public. Darwin is extremely well known but little read beyond historians of science, not unlike Einstein in this respect. In social thought his ideas have given rise to a multitude of notions, many of them strongly at variance with what Darwin actually wrote and believed. "Social Darwinism," for example, ought better be called "Biological Spencerianism" for all the relation it bears to Darwin's actual scientific labors. The selections reprinted below come from his *Descent of Man* (1871) regarding the process of natural selection as it pertains to humans, and *The Expression of the Emotions in Man and Animals* (1872), where he gives his three principles that explain humankind's emotional responses.

THE DESCENT OF MAN, 1871

Natural Selection

We have now seen that man is variable in body and mind: and that the variations are induced, either directly or indirectly, by the same general causes, and obey the same general laws, as with the lower animals. Man has spread widely over the face of the earth, and must have been exposed, during his incessant migration, to the most diversified conditions. The inhabitants of Tierra del Fuego, the Cape of Good Hope, and Tasmania in the one hemisphere, and of the Arctic regions in the other, must have passed through many climates, and changed their habits many times, before they reached their present home. The early progenitors of man must also have tended, like all other animals, to have increased beyond their means of subsistence; they must, therefore, occasionally have been exposed to a struggle for existense, and consequently to the rigid law of natural selection. Beneficial variations of all kinds will thus, either occasionally or habitually, have been preserved and injurious one, eliminated. I do not refer to strongly-marked deviations of structure, which occur only at long intervals of time, but to mere individual differences. We know, for instance, that the muscle of our hands and feet, which determine our powers of movement, are liable, like those of the lower animals, to incessant variability. If then the progenitors of man inhabiting any district, especially one undergoing some change in its conditions, were divided into two equal bodies, the one half which included all the individuals best adapted by their powers of movement for gaining subsistence, or for defending themselves, would on an average survive in greater numbers, and procreate more offspring than the other and less well endowed half.

Man in the rudest state in which he now exists is the most dominant animal that has ever appeared on this earth. He has spread more widely than any other highly organised form: and all others have yielded before him. He manifestly owes this immense superiority to his intellectual faculties, to his social habits, which lead him to aid and defend his fellows, and to his corporeal structure. The supreme importance of these characters has been proved by the final arbitrament of the battle for life. Through his powers of intellect, articulate language has been evolved; and on this his wonderful advancement has mainly depended. As Mr. Chauncey Wright remarks: "a psychological analysis of the faculty of language stews, that even the smallest proficiency in it might require more brain power than the greatest proficiency in any other direction." He has invented and is able to use various weapons, tools, traps, &c. with which he defends himself, kills or catches prey, and otherwise obtains food. He has made rafts or canoes for fishing or crossing over to neighbouring fertile islands. He has discovered the art of making fire, by which hard and stringy roots can be rendered digestible, and poisonous roots or herbs innocuous. This discovery of fire, probably the greatest ever made by man, excepting language, dates from before the dawn of history. These several inventions, by which man in the rudest state has become so pre-eminent, are the direct results of the development of his powers of observation, memory, curiosity, imagination, and reason. I cannot, therefore, understand how it is that Mr. Wallace maintains that "natural selection could only have endowed the savage with a brain a little superior to that of an ape."

Although the intellectual powers and social habits of man are of paramount importance to him, we must not underrate the importance of his bodily structure. . . .

Archeologists are convinced that in enormous interval of time elapsed before our ancestors thought of grinding chipped flint into smooth tools. One can hardly doubt, that a man-like animal who possessed hand and arm sufficiently perfect to throw a stone with precision, or to form a flint into a rude tool, could, with sufficient practice, as far as mechanical skill alone is concerned, make almost anything which a civilised man can make. The structure of the hand in this respect may be compared with that of the vocal organs, which in the apes are used for uttering various cries, or, as in one genus, musical cadences; but in man the closely similar vocal organs have become adapted through the inherited effects of use for the utterance of articulate language.

Conclusion

In this chapter we have seen that as man at the present day is liable, like every other animal, to multiform individual differences or slight variations, so no doubt were the early progenitors of man; the variations being formerly induced by the same general causes, and governed by the same general and complex laws as at present. As all animals tend to multiply beyond their means of subsistence, so it must have been with the progenitors of man; and this would inevitably lead to a struggle for existence and to natural selection. The latter process would be greatly aided by the inherited effects of the increased use of parts, and these two processes would incessantly react on each other. It appears, also, as we shall hereafter see, that various unimportant characters have been acquired by man through sexual selection. An unexplained residuum of change must be left to the assumed uniform action of those unknown agencies, which occasionally induce strongly marked and abrupt deviations of structure in our domestic productions.

Judging from the habits of savages and of the greater number of the Quadrumana, primeval men, and even their ape-like progenitors, probably lived in society. With strictly social animals, natural selection sometimes acts on the individual, through the preservation of variations which are beneficial to the community. A community which includes a large number of well-endowed individuals increases in number, and is victorious over other less favoured ones; even although each separate member gains no advantage over the others of the same community. Associated insects have thus acquired many remarkable structures, which are of little or no service to the individual, such as the pollen-collecting apparatus, or the sting of the worker-bee, or the great jaws of soldier-ants. With the higher social animals, I am not aware that any structure has been modified solely for the good of the community, though some are of secondary service to it. For instance, the horns of ruminants and the great canine teeth of baboons appear to have been acquired by the males as weapons for sexual strife, but they are used in defence of the herd or troop. In regard to certain mental powers the case is wholly different; for these faculties have been chiefly, or even exclusively, gained for the benefit of the community, and the individuals thereof have at the same time gained an advantage indirectly.

In regard to bodily size or strength, we do not know whether man is descended from some small species, like the chimpanzee, or from one as powerful as the gorilla; and, therefore, we cannot say whether man has become larger and stronger, or smaller and weaker, than his ancestors. We should, however, bear in mind that all animal possessing great size, strength, and ferocity, and which, like the gorilla, could defend itself from all enemies, would not perhaps have become social: and this would most effectually have checked the acquirement of the higher mental qualities, such as sympathy and the love of his fellows. Hence it might have been an immense advantage to man to have sprung from some comparatively weak creature.

The small strength and speed of man, his want of natural weapons, &c., are more than counterbalanced, firstly, by his intellectual powers, through which he has formed for himself weapons, tools, &c., though still remaining in a barbarous state, and, secondly, by his social qualities which lead him to give and receive aid from his fellow-men. No country in the world abounds in a greater degree with dangerous beasts than Southern Africa; no country presents more fearful physical hardships than the Arctic regions; yet one of the puniest of races, that of the Bushmen, maintains itself in Southern Africa, as do the dwarfed Esquimaux in the Arctic regions. The ancestors of man were, no doubt, inferior in intellect, and probably in social disposition, to the lowest existing savages; but it is quite conceivable that they might have existed, or even flourished, if they had advanced in intellect, whilst gradually losing their brute-like powers, such as that of climbing trees, &c. But these ancestors would not have been exposed to any special danger, even if far more helpless and defenceless than any existing, savages, had they inhabited some warm continent or large island, such as Australia, New Guinea, or Borneo, which is now the home of the orang. And natural selection arising from the competition of tribe with tribe, in some such large area as one of these, together with the inherited effects of habit, would, under favourable conditions, have sufficed to raise man to his present high position in the organic scale.

EXPRESSION OF THE EMOTIONS IN MAN AND ANIMALS, 1872

I will begin by giving the three Principles, which appear to me to account for most of the expressions and gestures involuntarily used by man and the lower animals, under the influence of various emotions and sensations. I arrived, however, at these three Principles only at the close of my observations. They will be discussed in the present and two following chapters in a general manner. Facts observed both with man and the lower animals will here be made use of; but the latter facts are preferable, as less likely to deceive us. In the fourth and fifth chapters, I will describe the special expressions of some of the lower animals; and in the succeeding chapters those of man. Everyone will thus be able to judge for himself, how far my three principles throw light on the theory of the subject. It appears to me that so many expressions are thus explained in a fairly satisfactory manner, that probably all will hereafter be found to come under the same or closely analogous heads. I need hardly premise that movements or changes in any part of the body,—as the wagging of a dog's tail, the drawing back of a horse's ears, the shrugging of a man's shoulders, or the dilatation of the capillary vessels of the skin,—may all equally well serve for expression. The three Principles are as follows.

From *Human Nature: Darwin's View*, by Alexander Alland, Jr. Published by the Columbia University Press. Copyright © 1985.

I. *The principle of serviceable associated Habits.*—Certain complex actions are of direct or indirect service under certain states of the mind, in order to relieve or gratify certain sensations, desires, &c.; and whenever the same state of mind is induced, however feebly, there is a tendency through the force of habit and association for the same movements to be performed, though they may not then be of the least use. Some actions ordinarily associated through habit with certain states of the mind may be partially repressed through the will, and in such cases the muscles which are least under the separate control of the will are the most liable still to act, causing movements which we recognize as expressive. In certain other cases the checking of one habitual movement requires other slight movements; and these are like-wise expressive.

II. *The principle of Antithesis.*—Certain states of the mind lead to certain habitual actions, which are of service, as under our first principle. Now when a directly opposite state of mind is induced, there is a strong and involuntary tendency to the performance of movements of a directly opposite nature, though these are of no use; and such movements are in some cases highly expressive.

III. *The principle of actions due to the constitution of the Nervous System, independently from the first of the Will, and independently to a certain extent of Habit.*—When the sensorium is strongly excited, nerve-force is generated in excess, and is transmitted in certain definite directions, depending on the connection of the nerve-cells, and partly on habit: or the supply of nerve-force may, as it appears, be interrupted. Effects are thus produced which we recognize as expressive. This third principle may, for the sake of brevity, be called that of the direct action of the nervous system. . . .

To sum up this chapter, weeping is probably the result of some such chain of events as follows. Children, when wanting food or suffering in any way, cry out loudly, like the young of most other animals, partly as a call to their parents for aid, and partly from any great exertion serving as a relief. Prolonged screaming inevitably leads to the gorging of the blood-vessels of the eye; and this will have led, at first consciously and at last habitually, to the contraction of the muscles round the eyes in order to protect them. At the same time the spasmodic pressure on the surface of the eye, and the distension of the vessels within the eye, without necessarily entailing any conscious sensation, will have affected, through reflex action, the lacrymal glands. Finally, through the three principles of nerve-force readily passing along accustomed channels—of association, which is so widely extended in its power—and of certain actions, being more under the control of the will than others—it has come to pass that suffering readily causes the secretion of tears, without being necessarily accompanied by any other action.

Although in accordance with this view we must look at weeping as an incidental result, as purposeless as the secretion of tears from a blow outside the eye, or as a sneeze from the retina being affected by a bright light, yet this does not present any difficulty in our understanding how the secretion of tears serves as a relief to suffering. And by as much as the weeping is more violent or hysterical, by so much will the relief be greater,—on the same principle that the writhing of the whole body, the grinding of the teeth, and the uttering of piercing shrieks, all give relief under an agony of pain.

EDWARD BURNETT TYLOR

1832–1917

Sir Edward Burnett Tylor, son of a Quaker brass foundry owner, was born on October 2, 1832 in London, married Anna Fox of Somerset in 1858 with whom he lived for almost 60 years, but without children (which they regretted), and died aged 84 in Wellington, Somerset on January 2, 1917. After Quaker schooling at Tottenham, he was prevented by his religion from continuing his education, so at 16 began work in the family firm, dutifully taking a desk job for the next seven years, at which point he developed lung disease and was urged to travel to regain his health. He used his family's money for anthropological fieldwork in Cuba and then, for six arduous and dangerous months, in Mexico. His writings from this fieldtrip (undertaken at the invitation of Henry Christy, whom he met in Havana, another Quaker who worked in archaeology and ethnology) made his reputation in 1865 when he was 33. In 1881 he published *Anthropology*, which was the standard work for some time, a comprehensive catalogue of what was known at the time in the discipline he helped perfect. Tylor was the Gifford Lecturer in 1888, becoming the first Oxford anthropology professor in 1896.

But it was the publication of *Primitive Culture* in 1871 that established Tylor as the father of cultural anthropology, a book which has remained in print ever since. Influenced by Darwin (as was practically everyone at the time who worked in the human sciences), he argued in this book that humans have slowly progressed from a "savage" state of mind to one which would be more easily recognized by Victorians as "civilized." Using a fairly idealistic mode of explanation (as opposed to the materialism, say, of Marx in his ethnographic notebooks), Tylor hypothesized that "primitive" humans, confronted by the puzzles of the natural world, and fearful of them, invented "animism" to explain these quandaries to themselves. This form of thought holds that both creatures and inanimate objects are saturated with a living spirit which lends them their peculiar characteristics. He thought that animism may have arisen when "savages" tried to comprehend the difference between "soul" (what we would call "consciousness") and corporeal existence. Yet he also understood the importance of material culture, and tried to plot the development of technology against intellectual change over time. He was keen to prove that humans were one unified species no matter how different they might have appeared in 1871 when one considered Europe versus the other continents. Tylor also intrigued his readers of the day by pointing out what later came to be called "adumbrations" in culture: practices in allegedly primitive culture which have their parallels in modern life, similarities which become obvious only when pointed out as such. The selections reprinted below illustrate some of these ideas.

PRIMITIVE CULTURE, 1871

The Development of Culture

In taking up the problem of the development of culture as a branch of ethnological research, a first proceeding is to obtain a means of measurement. Seeking something like a definite line along which to reckon progression and retrogression in civilization, we may apparently find it best in the classification of real tribes and nations, past and present. Civilization actually existing among mankind in different grades, we are enabled to estimate and compare it by positive examples. The educated world of Europe and America practically settles a standard by simply placing its own nations at one end of the social series and savage tribes at the other, arranging the rest of mankind between these limits according as they correspond more closely to savage or to cultured life. The principal criteria of classification are the absence or presence, high or low development, of the industrial arts, especially metal-working, manufacture of implements and vessels, agriculture, architecture, &c., the extent of scientific knowledge, the definiteness of moral principles, the condition of religious belief and ceremony, the degree of social and political organization, and so forth. Thus, on the definite basis of compared facts, ethnographers are able to set up at least a rough scale of civilization. Few would dispute that the following races are arranged rightly in order of culture:—Australian, Tahitian, Aztec, Chinese, Italian. By treating the development of civilization on this—plain ethnographic basis, many difficulties may be avoided which have embarrassed its discussion. This may be seen by a glance at the relation which theoretical principles of civilization bear to the transitions to be observed as matter of fact between the extremes of savage and cultured life.

From an ideal point of view, civilization may be looked upon as the general improvement of mankind by higher organization of the individual and of society, to the end of promoting at once man's goodness, power, and happiness. This theoretical civilization does in no small measure correspond with actual civilization, as traced by comparing savagery with barbarism, and barbarism with modern educated life. So far as we take into account only material and intellectual culture, this is especially true. Acquaintance with the physical laws of the world, and the accompanying power of adapting nature to man's own ends, are, on the whole, lowest among savages, mean among barbarians, and highest among modern educated nations. Thus a transition from the savage state to our own would be, practically, that very progress of art and knowledge which is one main element in the development of culture.

But even those students who hold most strongly that the general course of civilization, as measured along the scale of races from savages to ourselves, is progress towards the benefit of mankind, must admit many and manifold exceptions. Industrial and intellectual culture by no mean advances uniformly in all its branches, and in fact excellence in various of its details is often obtained under conditions which keep back culture as a whole. It is true that these exceptions seldom swamp the general rule; and the Englishman, admitting that he does not climb trees like the wild Australian, nor track game like the savage of the Brazilian forest, nor compete with the ancient Etruscan and the modern Chinese in delicacy of goldsmith's work and ivory carving, nor reach the classic Greek level of oratory and sculpture, may yet claim for himself a general condition above any of these races. But there actually have to be taken into account developments of science and art which tend directly against culture. To have learnt to give poison secretly and effectually, to have raised a corrupt literature to pestilent perfection, to have organized a successful scheme to arrest free enquiry and proscribe free expression, are works of knowledge and skill whose progress toward their goal has hardly conduced to the general good. Thus, even in comparing mental and artistic culture among several peoples, the balance of good and ill is not quite easy to strike.

If not only knowledge and art, but at the same time moral and political excellence, be taken into consideration, it becomes yet harder to reckon on an ideal scale the advance or decline from stage to stage of culture. In fact, a combined

From *Primitive Culture: Researches into the Development of Mythology, Philosophy, Religion, Language, Art, and Custom,* by Edward B. Tylor. Brentano's Publishers, 1924.

intellectual and moral measure of human condition is an instrument which no student has as yet learnt properly to handle. Even granting that intellectual, moral, and political life may, on a broad view, be seen to progress together, it is obvious that they are far from advancing with equal steps. It may be taken as man's rule of duty in the world, that he shall strive to know as well as he can find out, and to do as well as he knows how. But the parting asunder of these two great principles, that separation of intelligence from virtue which accounts for so much of the wrong-doing of mankind, is continually seen to happen in the great movements of civilization. As one conspicuous instance of what all history stands to prove, if we study the early ages of Christianity, we may see men with minds pervaded by the new religion of duty, holiness, and love, yet at the same time actually falling away in intellectual life, thus at once vigorously grasping one half of civilization, and contemptuously casting off the other. Whether in high ranges or in low of human life, it may be seen that advance of culture seldom results at once in unmixed good. Courage, honesty, generosity, are virtues which may suffer, at least for a time, by the development of a sense of value of life and property. The savage who adopts something of foreign civilization too often loses his ruder virtues without gaining an equivalent. The white invader or colonist, though representing on the whole a higher moral standard than the savage he improves or destroys, often represents his standard very ill, and at best can hardly claim to substitute a life stronger, nobler, and purer at every point than that which he supersedes. The onward movement from barbarism has dropped behind it more than one quality of barbaric character which cultured modern men look back on with regret, and will even strive to regain by futile attempts to stop the course of history, and to restore the past in the midst of the present. So it is with social institutions. The slavery recognised by savage and barbarous races is preferable in kind to that which existed for centuries in late European colonies. The relation of the sexes among many savage tribes is more healthy than among the richer classes of the Mohammedan world. As a supreme authority of government, the savage councils of chiefs and elders compare favourably with the unbridled despotism under which so many cultured races have groaned. The Creek Indians, asked concerning their religion, replied that where agreement was not to be had, it was best to 'let every man paddle his canoe his own way:' and after long ages of theological strife and persecution, the modern world seems coming to think these savages not far wrong.

So when we read descriptions of the hospitality, the gentleness, the bravery, the deep religious feeling of the North American Indians, we admit their claims to our sincere admiration; but we must not forget that they were hospitable literally to a fault, that their gentleness would pass with a flash of anger into frenzy, that their bravery was stained with cruel and treacherous malignity, that their religion expressed itself in absurd belief and useless ceremony. The ideal savage of the 18th century may be held up as a living reproof to vicious and frivolous London; but in sober fact, a Londoner who should attempt to lead the atrocious life which the real savage may lead with impunity and even respect, would be a criminal only allowed to follow his savage models during his short intervals out of gaol. Savage moral standards are real enough, but they are far looser and weaker than ours. We may, I think, apply the often-repeated comparison of savages to children as fairly to their moral as to their intellectual condition. The better savage social life seems in but unstable equilibrium, liable to be easily upset by a touch of distress, temptation, or violence, and then it becomes the worse savage life, which we know by so many dismal and hideous examples. Altogether, it may be admitted that some rude tribes lead a life to be envied by some barbarous races, and even by the outcasts of higher nations. But that any known savage tribe would not be improved by judicious civilization, is a proposition which no moralist would dare to make; while the general tenour of the evidence goes far to justify the view that on the whole the civilized man is not only wiser and more capable than the savage, but also better and happier, and that the barbarian stands between. . . .

In fact, much of the labour spent investigating the progress and decline of civilization has been mis-spent, in premature attempts to treat that as a whole which is as yet only susceptible of divided study. The present comparatively narrow argument on the development of culture at any rate avoids this greatest perplexity. It takes cognizance principally of knowledge, art, and custom, and indeed only very partial cognizance within this field, the vast range of physical, political, social, and ethical considerations being left all but untouched. Its standard of reckoning progress and decline is not that of ideal good and evil, but of movement along a measured line from grade to grade of actual savagery, barbarism, and civilization. The thesis which I venture to sustain, within limits, is simply this, that the savage state in some measure represents an early condition of mankind, out of which the higher culture has gradually been developed or evolved, by processes still in regular operation as of old, the result showing that, on the whole, progress has far prevailed over relapse.

On this proposition, the main tendency of human society during its long term of existence has been to pass from a savage to a civilized state. Now all must admit a great part of this assertion to be not only truth, but truism. Referred to direct history, a great section of it proves to belong not to the domain of speculation, but to that of positive knowledge. It is mere matter of chronicle that modern civilization is a development of mediaeval civilization, which again is a development from civilization of the order represented in Greece, Assyria, or Egypt. Thus the higher culture being clearly traced back to what may be called the middle culture, the question which remains is whether this middle culture may be traced back to the lower culture, that is, to savagery. To affirm this, is merely to assert that the same kind of development in culture which has gone on inside our range of knowledge has also gone on outside it, its course of proceeding being unaffected by our having or not having reporters present. If any one holds that human thought and action were worked out in primaeval times according to laws essentially other than those of the modem world, it is for him to prove by valid evidence this anomalous state of things, otherwise the doctrine of permanent principle will hold good, as in astronomy or geology. That the tendency of culture has been similar throughout the existence of human society, and that we may fairly judge from its known historic course what its prehistoric course may have been, is a theory clearly entitled to precedence as a fundamental principle of ethnographic research.

FRIEDRICH ENGELS

1820–1895

Friedrich Engels, son of a forgiving mother and a successful Protestant textile manufacturer with mills in Germany and England, was born in Barmen, Rhine Province, Prussia on November 28, 1820 (two years after Marx) and died on August 5, 1895 in London after 74 years. He lived with an Irish woman, Mary Burns, from 1845 until her death in 1863, then lived with her sister Lizzy, also as wife, until she died in 1878, marrying her on her deathbed. With neither did he have children (though to aid his confederate, Marx, he claimed the paternity for Freddy Demuth, the illegitimate son by the lifelong Marx family servant, Helene Demuth). Engels dropped out of college preparatory school (so-called *Gymnasium*) the year before graduation, and under pressure from his father went to Bremen (1838–41) to learn business techniques during a time when textile factories were expanding. Yet during afterhours he sang in a choral society, wrote poems and political articles (as "Friedrich Oswald"), became expert in riding and fencing, and learned, so he claimed, 24 languages for the pleasure of it. More importantly, he began reading works of the Left Hegelians, joined the movement, and adopted a radical atheism wholly at odds with his family's beliefs. He served admirably for a year in an artillery unit while in Berlin, but also while there joined the "Doctor's Club" for philosophical debate, of which Marx was also a member. Moses Hess sold Engels on communism in 1842, a system of thought which "proved" that world history would gravitate inexorably toward a communist system.

Engels moved to Manchester, England (1842–44) to oversee his father's business interests, but also because it was a center of working class radicalism. His *The Condition of the Working Class in England* (1845) is a classic still avidly read for its historical information. In the preceding year, Engels submitted two articles to a journal which Marx was editing in Paris, the two became friends, and for the next 39 years until Marx's death they were inseparable intellectual partners. Marx's other friends early on recommended that he distance himself from the hot-tempered Engels, but to no avail. Debates over the extent to which Engels contributed to the invention of Marxism have largely been laid to rest, for a close examination of their huge correspondence shows that they worked hand-in-glove in developing all the principal notions that Marx eventually worked into *Capital* (the final two volumes of which Engels assembled after Marx's death in 1883). Engels' efficiently run mill in Manchester supplied Marx with a constant income (though variable in size), so that he could commit himself entirely to research. The selection below shows Engels as a social philosopher, something he did as a subsidiary interest to his main writings.

ANTI-DÜHRING, 1878

On Morality

If, then, we have not made much progress with truth and error, we can make even less with good and evil. This opposition manifests itself exclusively in the domain of morals, that is, a domain belonging to the history of mankind, and it is precisely in this field that final and ultimate truths are most sparsely sown. The conceptions of good and evil have varied so much from nation to nation and from age to age that they have often been in direct contradiction to each other.

But all the same, someone may object, good is not evil and evil is not good; if good is confused with evil there is an end to all morality, and everyone can do as he pleases. This is also, stripped of all oracular phrases, Herr Dühring's opinion. But the matter cannot be so simply disposed of. If it were such an easy business there would certainly be no dispute at all over good and evil; everyone would know what was good and what was bad. But how do things stand today? What morality is preached to us today? There is first Christian-feudal morality, inherited from earlier religious times; and this is divided, essentially, into a Catholic and a Protestant morality, each of which has no lack of subdivisions, from the Jesuit-Catholic and Orthodox-Protestant to loose "enlightened" moralities. Alongside these we find the modern-bourgeois morality and beside it also the proletarian morality of the future, so that in the most advanced European countries alone the past, present and future provide three great groups of moral theories which are in force simultaneously and alongside each other. Which, then, is the true one? Not one of them, in the sense of absolute finality; but certainly that morality contains the maximum elements promising permanence which, in the present, represents the overthrow of the present, represents the future, and that is proletarian morality.

But when we see that the three classes of modern society, the feudal aristocracy, the bourgeoisie and the proletariat, each have a morality of

From *The Marx-Engels Reader,* Second Edition, Robert C. Tucker, Ed. Published by W.W. Norton & Company. Copyright © 1978.

their own, we can only draw the one conclusion: that men, consciously or unconsciously, derive their ethical ideas in the last resort from the practical relations on which their class position is based—from the economic relations in which they carry on production and exchange.

But nevertheless there is quite a lot which the three moral theories mentioned above have in common—is this not at least a portion of a morality which is fixed once and for all? These moral theories represent three different stages of the same historical development, have therefore a common historical background, and for that reason alone they necessarily have much in common. Even more. At similar or approximately similar stages of economic development moral theories must of necessity be more or less in agreement. From the moment when private ownership of movable property developed, all societies in which this private ownership existed had to have this moral injunction in common: Thou shalt not steal. Does this injunction thereby become an eternal moral injunction? By no means. In a society in which all motives for stealing have been done away with, in which therefore at the very most only lunatics would ever steal, how the preacher of morals would be laughed at who tried solemnly to proclaim the eternal truth: Thou shalt not steal!

We therefore reject every attempt to impose on us any moral dogma whatsoever as an eternal, ultimate and forever immutable ethical law on the pretext that the moral world, too, has its permanent principles which stand above history and the differences between nations. We maintain on the contrary that all moral theories have been hitherto the product, in the last analysis, of the economic conditions of society obtaining at the time. And as society has hitherto moved in class antagonisms, morality has always been class morality; it has either justified the domination and the interests of the ruling class, or, ever since the oppressed class became powerful enough, it has represented its indignation against this domination and the future interests of the oppressed. That in this process there has on the whole been progress in morality, as in all other branches of human knowledge, no one will doubt. But we have not yet passed beyond class morality. A really human morality which stands above class antagonisms and above any recollection of them becomes possible only at a stage of society which has not only overcome class antagonisms but has even forgotten them in practical life. And now one can gauge Herr Dühring's presumption in advancing his claim, from the midst of the old class society and on the eve of a social revolution, to impose on the future classless society an eternal morality independent of time and changes in reality. Even assuming—what we do not know up to now—that he understands the structure of the society of the future at least in its main outlines.

part IV
THE CLASSICAL PERIOD
OF MODERN SOCIAL THOUGHT

Friedrich Nietzsche   *1844–1900*

Wilhelm Dilthey   *1833–1911*

Ferdinand Tönnies   *1855–1936*

Gabriel Tarde   *1843–1904*

William James   *1842–1910*

Emile Durkheim   *1858–1917*

Gustave Le Bon   *1841–1931*

Gaetano Mosca   *1858–1941*

Charlotte Anna Perkins Gilman   *1860–1935*

Marcel Mauss   *1872–1950*

Thorstein Veblen   *1857–1929*

Vilfredo Pareto   *1848–1923*

Charles Horton Cooley   *1864–1929*

W.E.B. Du Bois   *1868–1963*

Max Weber   *1864–1920*

William Graham Sumner   *1840–1910*

Leon Trotsky   *1879–1940*

Georg Simmel   *1858–1918*

Georges Sorel   *1847–1922*

Lucien Lévy-Bruhl   *1857–1939*

György Lukács   *1885–1971*

James George Frazer   *1854–1941*

Roberto Michels   *1876–1936*

Ernst Troeltsch   *1866–1923*

Sigmund Freud   *1856–1939*

Max Scheler   *1874–1928*

Antonio Gramsci   *1891–1937*

Ferdinand de Saussure   *1857–1913*

Rudolf Otto   *1869–1937*

W. I. Thomas   *1863–1947*

FRIEDRICH NIETZSCHE

1844–1900

Coming from a family filled with dedicated Lutheran pastors, Friedrich Wilhelm Nietzsche was born on October 15, 1844 in Röcken, near Leipzig, Germany, never married, and died at the age of 55 on August 25, 1900 in Weimar. Nietzsche's paternal grandfather was a well-known author of Protestant apologetics, his maternal grandfather was also a minister, and his father's position as pastor at Röcken came directly from King Friedrich Wilhelm IV, after whom Nietzsche was named. After his father died when he was five, Nietzsche grew up in a household made up of five women. His pre-university education was excellent, and he won a scholarship to a top Protestant boardingschool where his scholarly abilities were quickly recognized. From there he went to the University of Bonn for theology and classical philology but left after two years owing to disputes between his two favorite professors. Nietzsche turned to composing music, in the mode of Robert Schumann, as solace from this unpleasant situation. At 21 he followed a professor to the University of Leipzig, and in 1869 was granted a terminal degree even without the two dissertations expected of him, largely on the strength of his professor's extremely flattering appraisal of his prospects. He served in the military for a year, enduring a serious non-combat injury in March, 1868, and while on extended sick leave returned to Leipzig, making the crucial acquaintance of Wagner and studying Schopenhauer's philosophy, which he much admired. With help from friends, he became professor of philology at the University of Basel in 1869, reentered the military due to the Franco-Prussian War in 1870, and while helping to transport the wounded contracted both the diphtheria and dysentery that made him forever after physically frail. He was pensioned off in 1879 with 3,000 Swiss francs per annum for six years, time he put to great creative use.

Among his astonishing books are *The Birth of Tragedy* (1872), *Untimely Meditations* (1873), *Human, All Too Human* (1878), *The Gay Science* (1887), his masterpiece, *Thus Spake Zarathustra* (1883–85), *On the Genealogy of Morals* (1887), and *The Twilight of the Idols* (1888). His last 11 years were spent in asylums and in the homecare of his mother and then his sister, during which he was mentally incompetent probably owing to tertiary syphilis, a very common 19th century disease, especially among single men. Thus he created a unique philosophical legacy in only fifteen years of lucid creativity, 1873–1888, with the final year being his annus mirabilis during which he wrote no fewer than five books. In his lifetime his works were ignored beyond a small circle of friends. Only after his death did they attract the kind of sustained attention, often adulation, which they have enjoyed ever since. The selections reprinted below exhibit Nietzsche's penchant for the aphorism, a style of philosophizing he borrowed from the French, in addition to his comments on the meaning of asceticism. This portion of *On the Genealogy of Morals* has intrigued many social theorists, most notably Max Weber, who adapted this mode of thought to a sociological explanation of how religion affects economic behavior. It would be a much shorter task to list the thinkers whom Nietzsche did *not* influence in the century since his death than to name those he did. Heidegger's four-volume study of Nietzsche is just one instance of the theoretical weight he carries even into our own day.

HUMAN, ALL TOO HUMAN, 1878

In Relations with Others

293

Benevolent dissimulation.—In our relations with other people, a benevolent dissimulation is frequently required, as if we did not see through the motives for their actions.

294

Copies.—Not infrequently, we encounter copies of important people; and as with paintings, here too, most people are better pleased with the copies than with the originals.

295

The speaker.—We can speak very much to the point and yet in such a way that everyone in the world shouts the opposite: when, that is, we are not speaking to everyone in the world.

296

Lack of intimacy.—A lack of intimacy among friends is a mistake that cannot be censured without becoming irreparable.

297

On the art of giving.—Having to refuse a gift simply because it was not offered in the right way embitters us against the giver.

298

The most dangerous party member.—In every party there is someone whose far too credulous expression of the party's principles provokes the others to defect.

299

Adviser to the sick.—Whoever gives advice to someone who is sick acquires for himself a feeling of superiority over that person, whether the advice is taken or rejected. Hence, sick people who are sensitive and proud hate those who give advice even more than their sickness.

300

Two sorts of equality.—The passion for equality can express itself by someone either wanting to pull everyone else down to his level (by disparaging them, keeping secrets from them, or tripping them up) or wanting to pull himself up along with everyone else (by giving them recognition, helping them, taking pleasure in their success).

301

Against embarrassment.—The best means of coming to the assistance of people who are extremely embarrassed and of reassuring them consists in praising them with conviction.

302

Preference for particular virtues.—We do not put any special value upon possessing a virtue until we perceive its complete absence in our opponent.

303

Why we contradict.—We often contradict an opinion even though it is really only the tone in which it was expressed that we find disagreeable.

304

Trust and intimacy.—Whoever zealously seeks to force another person to be intimate with him is generally not certain whether he possesses that person's trust. Whoever is certain that he is trusted puts little value upon intimacy.

305

Equilibrium of friendship.—In our relationship with another person, we sometimes recover the appropriate equilibrium of friendship if we place a few grains of fault on our own side of the scale.

306

The most dangerous physicians.—The most dangerous physicians are those who, as born actors, have perfected the art of deception by which they imitate the born physician.

307

When paradoxes are in order.—To gain the assent of clever people to some proposition, we sometimes need only to present it in form of a tremendous paradox.

308

How courageous people are won over.—We persuade courageous people to undertake some action by representing it as more dangerous than it is.

309

Courtesies.—We count the courtesies shown to us by people whom we do not like as offenses.

310

Making people wait.—A sure way to provoke people and to put malicious thoughts in their heads is to make them wait for a long time. This makes people immoral.

311

Against trusting people.—People who grant us their complete trust believe that they thereby gain a right to ours. This is a false conclusion; we acquire no rights by making gifts.

312

Means of compensation.—Giving to someone whom we have injured the opportunity for a wit-ticism at our expense is often enough to provide satisfaction for him personally, or even to make him well-disposed toward us.

313

Vanity of the tongue.—Whether someone conceals his bad qualities and vices or admits them openly, what his vanity desires in both cases is to gain an advantage thereby: just observe how acutely he distinguishes between those from whom he conceals these qualities and those toward whom he is honest and sincere.

314

Considerate.—Wanting to offend nobody, to cause nobody harm, can as easily be the mark of a just disposition as of a fearful one.

315

Requisite for disputing.—Anyone who does not know how to put his thoughts on ice should not head into the heat of battle.

316

Association and arrogance.—We forget arrogance when we know that we are always among deserving people; being alone breeds presumption. Young people are arrogant because they associate with others like themselves, all of whom are nothing, but would like to be something important.

317

Motive of attack.—We often attack not only in order to do someone harm, to overcome him, but perhaps only in order to become conscious of our strength.

318

Flattery.—People who wish to use flattery to deaden our caution in dealing with them are employing a dangerous means, a sleeping potion, as it were, which if it does not put us to sleep, only keeps us all the more awake.

319

Good letter writers.—Someone who does not write any books, thinks a lot, and has insufficient society about him will generally be a good letter writer.

320

What is ugliest.—It is doubtful whether a much-traveled person will have found any parts of the world uglier than those in the human face.

321

Sympathetic people.—Natures that are sympathetic and always helpful in misfortune are rarely as likely to share in joy: when others are fortunate, they have nothing to do, are superfluous, feel as if they no longer possess their superior position, and hence easily manifest discontent.

322

Relatives of a suicide.—The relatives of a suicide hold it against him that he did not remain alive out of concern for their reputations.

323

Foreseeing ingratitude.—Someone who gives a large gift does not get any gratitude; for the recipient has already been burdened too much by accepting it.

324

In dull society.—Nobody thanks a clever person for his politeness in putting himself on their level in a social circle where it is not polite to show one's cleverness.

325

Presence of witnesses.—We leap all the more readily after someone who has fallen into the water if people are present who do not dare to do so.

326

Keeping silence.—For both parties involved, the most unpleasant way to respond to a polemic is to get annoyed and keep silent: for the attacker generally interprets silence as a sign of contempt.

327

The secret of a friend.—There are few people who, when they are at a loss for subject matter in conversation, will not reveal the secret affairs of their friends.

328

Humanity.—The humanity of famous people consists in graciously putting themselves in the wrong when they are among people who are not well known.

329

The self-conscious person.—People who do not feel sure of themselves in society use every opportunity for publicly displaying their superiority to anyone near at hand who is inferior to them, through teasing, for example.

330

Thanks.—A refined soul is oppressed by knowing anyone is under obligation to it; a coarse soul, by knowing itself under obligation to anyone.

331

Mark of alienation.—The strongest sign of alienation in the views that two people hold is when both speak ironically to the other, but neither senses the irony therein.

332

Arrogance of the meritorious.—Arrogance in those with merit gives even more offense than arrogance in those without merit: for the merit already gives offense by itself.

333

Danger in the voice.—Sometimes in conversation the sound of our own voice disconcerts us and misleads us into making assertions that do not correspond at all to our opinion.

334

In conversation.—In conversation, whether we tend to agree or disagree with the other person is completely a question of habit: the one makes as much sense as the other.

335

Fear of our neighbor.—We fear the hostile disposition of our neighbor because we are afraid that this disposition will enable him to penetrate our secrets.

⌐‿⌐

ON THE GENEOLOGY OF MORALS, 1887

What Is the Meaning of Ascetic Ideals?

"Careless, mocking, forceful—so does wisdom wish us: she is a woman, and never loves any one but a warrior." —Thus Spake Zarathustra.

1. What is the meaning of ascetic ideals? In artists, nothing, or too much; in philosophers and scholars, a kind of "flair" and instinct for the conditions most favourable to advanced intellectualism; in women, at best an *additional* seductive fascination, a little *morbidezza* on a fine piece of flesh; the angelhood of a fat, pretty animal; in physiological failures and whiners (in the *majority* of mortals), an attempt to pose as "too good" for this world, a holy form of debauchery, their chief weapon in the battle with lingering pain and ennui; in priests, the actual priestly faith, their best engine of power, and also the supreme authority for power; in saints, finally a pretext for hibernation, their *novissima gloriæ cupido,* their peace in nothingness ("God"), their form of madness.

But in the very fact that the ascetic ideal has meant so much to man, lies expressed the fundamental feature of man's will, his *horror vacui: he needs a goal*—and he will sooner will nothingness than not will at all.—Am I not understood?—Have I not been understood?—"Certainly not, sir?"—Well, let us begin at the beginning.

2. What is the meaning of ascetic ideals? . . . For there is no necessary antithesis between chastity and sensuality: every good marriage, every authentic heart-felt love transcends this antithesis. Wagner would, it seems to me, have done well to have brought this *pleasing* reality home once again to his Germans, by means of a bold and graceful " Luther Comedy," for there were and are among

From *The Complete Works of Friedrich Nietzsche,* Volume Thirteen, Dr. Oscar Levy, Ed. Published by Gordon Press. Copyright © 1974.

the Germans many revilers of sensuality; and perhaps Luther's greatest merit lies just in the fact of his having had the courage of his *sensuality* (it used to be called, prettily enough, "evangelistic freedom"). But even in those cases where that antithesis between chastity and sensuality does exist, there has fortunately been for some time no necessity for it to be in any way a tragic antithesis. This should, at any rate, be the case with all beings who are sound in mind and body, who are far from reckoning their delicate balance between "animal" and "angel," as being on the face of it one of the principles opposed to existence—the most subtle and brilliant spirits, such as Goethe, such as Hafiz, have even seen in this a *further* charm of life. Such "conflicts" actually allure one to life. On the other hand, it is only too clear that when once these ruined swine are reduced to worshipping chastity—and there are such swine—they only see and worship in it the antithesis to themselves, the antithesis to ruined swine. Oh what a tragic grunting and eagerness! . . .

5. What, then, is the meaning of ascetic ideals? In the case of an artist we are getting to understand their meaning: *Nothing at all . . . or so much* that it is as good as nothing at all. Indeed, what is the use of them? Our artists have for a long time past not taken up a sufficiently independent attitude, either in the world or against it, to warrant their valuations and the changes in these valuations exciting interest. At all times they have played the valet of some morality, philosophy, or religion, quite apart from the fact that unfortunately they have often enough been the inordinately supple courtiers of their clients and patrons, and the inquisitive toadies of the powers that are existing, or even of the new powers to come. To put it at the lowest, they always need a rampart, a support, an already constituted authority: artists never stand by themselves, standing alone is opposed to their deepest instincts. So, for example, did *Richard Wagner* take, "when the time had come," the philosopher Schopenhauer for his covering man in front, for his rampart. Who would consider it even thinkable, that he would have had the *courage* for an ascetic ideal, without the support afforded him by the philosophy of Schopenhauer, without the authority of Schopenhauer, which *dominated* Europe in the seventies? (This is without consideration of the question whether an artist without the milk* of an orthodoxy would have been possible at all.) This brings us to the more serious question: What is the meaning of a real *philosopher* paying homage to the ascetic ideal, a really self-dependent intellect like Schopenhauer, a man and knight with a glance of bronze, who has the courage to be himself, who knows how to stand alone without first waiting for men who cover him in front, and the nods of his superiors?

Note

*An allusion to the celebrated monologue in William Tell.

WILHELM DILTHEY

1833–1911

A theologian's son, Wilhelm Dilthey was born on November 19, 1833 in Biebrich, near Wiesbaden, Germany. He was briefly engaged in 1870, but then married another woman, Katharine Püttman on March 21, 1874, and their family was comprised of three children. At nearly 78 he died in Seis am Schlern, near Bozen in the Southern Tyrol, Austria-Hungary on October 1, 1911. After public school in Wiesbaden, he studied theology at Heidelberg, then Berlin, switching to philosophy. After some teaching he sequestered himself in his study and attended with unflagging zeal to the entire range of the humanities and early forms of social science. After a doctorate in Berlin in 1864, he assumed professorships at Basel (1866), Kiel (1868), Breslau (1871), finally ascending the academic thrown at Berlin in 1882, where he stayed. Dilthey's life was not one of great outward excitement, but his intellectual life was as compelling as any of the great 19th century polymaths around whom he worked, and from whom many others (like Simmel and Weber) learned a great deal about their own crafts.

Dilthey's synthetic scholarship combined elements from philosophy, history, aesthetics, and what we now call psychology, though that field was quite different from today's version as he was forming his own method of study. He knew from reading J. S. Mill's epistemology that a distinction had to be made between the natural sciences (*Naturwissenschaften*) and the human or social sciences (*Geisteswissenschaften*), so he fashioned a hermeneutic approach to socio-historical and biographical data that highlighted this difference. He first wrote about this in his *Introduction to the Human Sciences* (1883), which was finally translated into English during the last 15 years. His point (shared by other notables of the time, particularly the philosopher Wilhelm Windelband) was that when a scientist enters a lab to do an experiment, he does not, formally speaking, "interact" with the materials he or she is investigating. Relative to human action, the materials are inert, even though invasive experimental procedures can indeed affect the ultimate outcome of the experiment (a broad redefinition of Heisenberg's principle of indeterminacy). By contrast, when a social scientist or humanist investigates a record of human action through historical records or directly observes people interacting, he or she must empathize or intuit their motivations and responses to events in order to tell a story, to construct a narrative, that seems plausible to readers. This is the root of Dilthey's demand that practitioners of the *Geisteswissenschaften,* as opposed to natural scientists, perfect their capacity for *Verstehen,* the German term for "understanding." They must "understand" and "interpret," and not just "explain" how a given phenomenon operates.

INTRODUCTION TO THE HUMAN SCIENCES, 1883

The Understanding of Others and Their Expressions of Life

Understanding and interpretation is the method used through-out the human studies and all functions unite in it. It contains all the truths of the human studies. Everywhere understanding opens up a world.

On the basis of experience and self-understanding and the constant interaction between them, understanding of other people and their expressions of life is developed. Here, too, it is not a matter of logical construction or psychological analysis but of an epistemological analysis. We must now establish what understanding can contribute to historical knowledge.

What is given are always expressions of life; occurring in the world of the senses they are always expressions of a mind which they help us to understand. I include here not only expressions of life which mean or signify something but also those which, without intending to signify anything, make the mind of which they are expressions comprehensible to us. The kind and amount of understanding is different according to the classes of expressions of life.

The first of these classes is formed by concepts, judgements and larger thought structures. As constituent parts of science, separated from the experience in which they occurred, they have a common fundamental character in their conformity to logical norms. They retain their identity, therefore, independently of the position in which they occur in the context of thought. Judgement asserts the validity of a thought content independently of the varied situations in which it occurs, the difference of time and of people involved. This is the meaning of the law of identity. Thus the judgement is the same for the man who makes it and the one who understands it; it passes, as if transported, from the speaker into the possession of the one who understands it. This determines the kind of understanding for all logically perfect thought content which remains identical in every context and thus understanding is more complete here than in relation to any other expression of life. At the same time it does not express anything about its relations to the obscure and abundant life of the mind to the man who understands it. There is no hint of the peculiarities of the life from which it arose and it follows from its nature that it does not require us to go back to its psychological context.

Actions form another class of expressions of life. An action does not arise from the intention to communicate; however, because of the relation in which it stands to a purpose, the latter is contained in it. The relation of the action to the mind which it thus expresses is regular and so we can make assumptions about it. But it is certainly necessary to distinguish the state of mind conditioned by the circumstances which produces the action it expresses, from the context in life on which this state is based. Action, through the power of a decisive motive, steps from the plenitude of life into one-sidedness. However much it may have been considered it expresses only a part of our nature. It annihilates potentialities which lie in that nature. So action, too separates itself from the background of the content of life; and, unless accompanied by an explanation of how circumstances, purpose, means and context of life are linked together in it, it allows no comprehensive determination of the inner life from which it arose.

It is quite different with emotive expressions (*Erlebnisausdruck*). A special relation exists between them, the life from which they arise and the understanding which they produce. For expressions can contain more of the psychological context than any introspection can discover. They lift it from depths which consciousness does not illuminate. But it is part of the nature of expressions that the relations between them and the mind which is expressed in them can provide only a limited basis for understanding. They are not subject to the judgement of true or false, but to that of truthful or untruthful. For dissimulation, lie, or deception can break the relation between expression and the mental content which is expressed.

Here an important distinction asserts itself and is the source of the highest significance to which expression can rise in the human studies.

From *Meaning in History*, by Wilhelm Dilthey, H.P. Rickman, Ed. Published by George Allen & Unwin. Copyright © 1984.

What springs from the life of the day is subject to the power of its interests. The interpretation of what is transitory is also determined by the moment. It is terrible that in the struggle of practical interests every expression can be deceptive and its interpretation changed with the change in our situation. But, in great works, because some content of the mind separates itself from its creator, the poet, artist, or writer, we enter a sphere in which deception ends. No truly great work of art can, according to the conditions which hold good and are to be developed later, wish to give the illusion of a mental content foreign to its author; indeed, it does not want to say anything about its author. Truthful in itself it stands—fixed, visible, permanent; and, because of this, a skilled and certain understanding of it is possible. Thus there arises in the confines between science and action a circle in which life discloses itself at a depth inaccessible to observation, reflection and theory.

Understanding arises, first of all, from the interests of practical life where people are dependent on communicating with each other. They must make themselves mutually understood. The one must know what the other wants. Thus, first of all, the elementary forms of understanding arise. They are like letters of the alphabet which, joined together, make higher forms of understanding possible. By such an elementary form I mean the interpretation of a single expression of life. Logically it can be represented as an argument from analogy. The regular relation between the expression and what is expressed forms the link in the argument. In each of the classes listed individual expressions can be interpreted in this way. A series of letters combined into words which form a sentence is the expression of an assertion. A facial expression signifies pleasure or pain. The elementary acts of which continuous activities are composed, such as the picking up of an object, the dropping of a hammer, the cutting of wood with a saw, indicate the presence of certain purposes. In this elementary understanding we do not go back to the whole context of life which forms the permanent subject of the expressions of life. We are also not conscious of any deduction from which this understanding could have arisen.

The fundamental relationship on which the process of elementary understanding rests, is that of the expression to what it expresses. Elementary understanding is not an inference from an effect to a cause. Nor must we, with greater caution, grasp it as a procedure which goes back from the given reality to some part of the context of life which made the effect possible. Certainly the latter relation is contained in the circumstances themselves and thus the transition from one to the other is, as it were, always at the door; but it need not enter.

What is thus related is linked in a peculiar way. The relation between expressions of life and the world of mind, which governs all understanding, asserts itself here in its most elementary form; according to this, understanding tends towards articulate mental content which becomes its goal; yet the sensually given expressions are not submerged in that content. How, for instance, both the gesture and the terror are not two separate things but a unity, is based on this fundamental relation of expression to mental content. To this must be added the generic character of all the elementary forms of understanding which are to be discussed next.

I have shown how significant the objective mind is for the possibility of knowledge in the human studies. By this I mean the manifold forms in which what individuals hold in common have objectified themselves in the world of the senses. In this objective mind the past is a permanently enduring present for us. Its realm extends from the style of life and the forms of social intercourse, to the system of purposes which society has created for itself, to custom, law, state, religion, art, science and philosophy. For even the work of genius represents ideas, feelings and ideals commonly held in an age and environment. From this world of objective mind the self receives sustenance from earliest childhood. It is the medium in which the understanding of other people and their expressions takes place. For everything in which the mind has objectified itself contains something held in common by the I and the Thou. Every square planted with trees, every room in which seats are arranged, is intelligible to us from our infancy because human planning, arranging and valuing—common to us all—have assigned its place to every square and every object in the room. The child grows up within the order and customs of the family which it shares with the other members and its mother's orders are accepted in this context. Before it learns to talk it is already wholly immersed in that common medium. It learns to understand the gestures and facial expressions, movements and exclamations, words and sentences, only because it encounters them always in the same form and in the same relation to what they mean and express. Thus the individual orientates himself in the world of objective mind.

From this there follows a consequence important for the process of understanding. The expression of life which the individual grasps is, as a rule, not simply an isolated expression but filled with a knowledge of what is held in common and of a relation to the mental content.

This placing of the individual expressions of life into a common context is facilitated by the articulated order in the objective mind. It embraces particular homogenous systems like law or religion, and these have a firm regular structure. Thus, in civil law, the imperatives enunciated in legal clauses designed to secure what degree of perfection is possible in the conduct of certain human affairs, are related to court room procedures, law courts and the machinery for carrying out what they decide. Within such a context many

kinds of typical differences exist. Thus, the individual expressions of life which confront the understanding subject can be considered as belonging to a common sphere, to a type; and the relationship between the expression of life and the world of mind within that sphere not only places the expression into its context but also supplements the mental content which belongs to it. A sentence is intelligible because a language, the meaning of words and of inflexions, as well as the significance of syntactical arrangements, is common to a community. The fixed order of behaviour within a culture makes it possible for greetings or bows to signify by their nuances a certain mental attitude to other people and to be understood as doing so. In different countries the crafts developed particular procedures and particular instruments for special purposes; when, therefore, the craftsman uses a hammer or saw, his purpose is intelligible to us. In this sphere the relation between expressions of life and mental content is fixed everywhere by a common order. This explains why this relation is present in the grasping of an individual expression and why both links of the process are fused into a unity in the process of understanding, on the basis of the relation between expression and what is expressed, without a conscious reasoning process taking place.

FERDINAND TÖNNIES

1855–1936

The son of a hotel proprietor, Ferdinand Julius Tönnies was born on July 26, 1855 at Die Riep in Kirchspiel Oldenswort, Landschaft Eiderstedt, Herzogtum Schleswig, Germany, with a great-grandfather holding an important municipal government position, and a grandfather being a minister with doctoral degree, all part of the independent Frisian population. He married Marie Sieck and with her produced three sons and two daughters. After 80 years, he died in Kiel on April 9, 1936, three years after being dismissed from his professorship by the Nazis. After local schooling, his father's wealth made it possible for Tönnies to study history, archaeology, philology, and classics at the universities of Jena, Leipzig, Bonn, Berlin, and Tübingen, where he finished the doctorate in 1877 in classical philology (as had Nietzsche). In order to become a professor, he wrote the first draft of what eventually became his most famous work, *Gemeinschaft and Gesellschaft* (1987), and on the strength of a first draft, he began to teach at Kiel. He taught a little but preferred to do research, and also had troubled relations with the head administrator of Prussian universities because of his membership in the Ethical Culture Society, his socialism, his support of the working class, consumer cooperatives, adult education, and related "radical" causes. Such conflicts prevented him from achieving the rank of full professor until 1913 (in economics) when he was 58, and three years later he formally retired, though continued teaching until relieved by the fascists in 1933. He visited the U.S. in 1904 (along with Max Weber and many other German intellectuals) to attend the St. Louis Exposition, helped found the German Sociological Society in 1909 along with Weber and Simmel, he edited scholarly journals, brought out an English edition of Hobbes' works on political theory, and meanwhile wrote a dozen books and many articles on a range of topics, including appreciative studies of Karl Marx and Friedrich Schiller, Comte and Spinoza. He was a close student of Herbert Spencer and Henry Sumner Maine, and his own creativity was tied to some of their central notions, and he also wrote a study of popular opinion and the press long before these topics became ordinary. One of his key works is *Custom* (1909) in a series edited by Martin Buber.

Every student of introductory sociology has heard the dichotomy "Gemeinschaft versus Gesellschaft" early in the course, with the implication that Tönnies found the former (small communities) more humanly suitable to the latter (metropolitan societies), in the same way that he much preferred living in Kiel to life in Berlin. This is not quite accurate, since Tönnies' opposition between these social states includes both negative and positive characteristics of both, as is illustrated in the excerpts printed below.

COMMUNITY AND SOCIETY, 1887

Relations Between Human Wills

. . . All intimate, private, and exclusive living together, so we discover, is understood as life is Gemeinschaft (community). Gesellschaft (society) is public life—it is the world itself. In Gemeinschaft with one's family, one lives from birth on, bound to it in weal and woe. One goes into Gesellschaft as one goes into a strange country. A young man is warned against bad Gesellschaft, but the expression bad Gemeinschaft violates the meaning of the word. Lawyers may speak of domestic (*hausliche*) Gesellschaft, thinking only of the legalistic concept of social association; but the domestic Gemeinschaft, or home life with its immeasurable influence upon the human soul, has been felt by everyone who ever shared it. Likewise, a bride or groom knows that he or she goes into marriage as a complete Gemeinschaft of life (*communio totius vitae*). A Gesellschaft of life would be a contradiction in and of itself. One keeps or enjoys another's Gesellschaft, but not his Gemeinschaft in this sense. One becomes a part of a religious Gemeinschaft; religious Gesellschaften (associations or societies), like any other groups formed for given purposes, exist only in so far as they, viewed from without, take their places among the institutions of a political body or as they represent conceptual elements of a theory; they do not touch upon the religious Gemeinschaft as such. There exists a Gemeinschaft of language, of folkways or mores, or of beliefs; but by way of contrast, Gesellschaft exists in the realm of business, travel, or sciences. So of special importance are the commercial Gesellschaften; whereas, even though a certain familiarity and Gemeinschaft may exist among business partners, one could indeed hardly speak of commercial Gemeinschaft. To make the word combination "joint-stock Gemeinschaft" would be abominable. On the other hand, there exists a Gemeinschaft of ownership in fields, forest, and pasture. The Gemeinschaft of property between man and wife cannot be called Gesellschaft of property. Thus many differences become apparent.

In the most general way, one could speak of a Gemeinschaft comprising the whole of mankind, such as the Church wishes to be regarded. But human Gesellschaft is conceived as mere coexistence of people independent of each other. Recently, the concept of Gesellschaft as opposed to and distinct from the state has been developed. This term will also be used in this book, but can only derive its adequate explanation from the underlying contrast to the Gemeinschaft of the people.

Gemeinschaft is old; Gesellschaft is new as a name as well as a phenomenon. This has been recognized by an author who otherwise taught political science in all its aspects without penetrating to its fundamentals. "The entire concept of Gesellschaft (society) in a social and political sense," says Bluntschli (*Staatswörterbuch IV*), "finds its natural foundation in the folkways, mores, and ideas of the third estate. It is not really the concept of a people (*Volks-Begriff*) but the concept of the third estate . . . Its Gesellschaft has become the origin and expression of common opinion and tendencies . . . Wherever urban culture blossoms and bears fruits, Gesellschaft appears as its indispensable organ. The rural people know little of it." On the other hand, all praise of rural life has pointed out that the Gemeinschaft among people is stronger there and more alive; it is the lasting and genuine form of living together. In contrast to Gemeinschaft, Gesellschaft is transitory and superficial. Accordingly, Gemeinschaft should be understood as a living organism, Gesellschaft as a mechanical aggregate and artifact.

Gemeinschaft by Blood

The Gemeinschaft by blood, denoting unity of being, is developed and differentiated into Gemeinschaft of locality, which is based on a common

From *Community & Society,* by Ferdinand Tönnies, Charles P. Loomis, Trans./Ed. Published by Ryerson Press. Copyright 1940.

habitat. A further differentiation leads to the Gemeinschaft of mind, which implies only cooperation and coordinated action for a common goal. Gemeinschaft of locality may be conceived as a community of physical life, just as Gemeinschaft of mind expresses the community of mental life. In conjunction with the others, this last type of Gemeinschaft represents the truly human and supreme form of community. Kinship Gemeinschaft signifies a common relation to, and share in, human beings themselves, while in Gemeinschaft of locality such a common relation is established through collective ownership of land; and, in Gemeinschaft of mind, the common bond is represented by sacred places and worshiped deities. All three types of Gemeinschaft are closely interrelated in space as well as in time. They are, therefore, also related in all such single phenomena and in their development, as well as in general human culture and its history. Wherever human beings are related through their wills in an organic manner and affirm each other, we find one or another of the three types of Gemeinschaft. Either the earlier type involves the later one, or the later type has developed to relative independence, from some earlier one. It is, therefore, possible to deal with (1) kinship, (2) neighborhood, and (3) friendship as definite and meaningful derivations of these original categories.

The house constitutes the realm and, as it were, the body of kinship. Here people live together under one protecting roof. Here they share their possessions and their pleasures; they feed from the same supply, they sit at the same table. The dead are venerated here as invisible spirits, as if they were still powerful and held a protecting hand over their family. Thus, common fear and common honor ensure peaceful living and cooperation with greater certainty. The will and spirit of kinship is not confined within the walls of the house nor bound up with physical proximity; but, where it is strong and alive in the closest and most intimate relationship, it can live on itself, thrive on memory alone, and overcome any distance by its feeling and its imagination of nearness and common activity. Nevertheless, it seeks all the more for physical proximity and is loath to give it up, because such nearness alone will fulfill the desire for love. The ordinary human being, there-fore—in the long run and for the average of cases—feels best and most cheerful if he is surrounded by his family and relatives. He is among his own (*chez sot*).

Neighborhood describes the general character of living together in the rural village. The proximity of dwellings, the communal fields, and even the mere contiguity of holdings necessitate many contacts of human beings and cause inurement to and intimate knowledge of one another. They also necessitate cooperation in labor, order, and management, and lead to common supplication for grace and mercy to the gods and spirits of land and water who bring blessing or menace with disaster. Although essentially based upon proximity of habitation, this neighborhood type of Gemeinschaft can nevertheless persist during separation from the locality, but it then needs to be supported still more than ever by well-defined habits of reunion and sacred customs.

Friendship is independent of kinship and neighborhood, being conditioned by and resulting from similarity of work and intellectual attitude. It comes most easily into existence when crafts or callings are the same or of similar nature. Such a tie, however, must be made and maintained through easy and frequent meetings, which are most likely to take place in a town. A worshiped deity, created out of common mentality, has an immediate significance for the preservation of such a bond, since only, or at least mainly, this deity is able to give it living and lasting form. Such good spirit, therefore, is not bound to any place but lives in the conscience of its worshipers and accompanies them on their travels to foreign countries. Thus, those who are brethren of such a common faith feel, like members of the same craft or rank, everywhere united by a spiritual bond and the cooperation in a common task. Urban community of life may be classified as neighborhood, as is also the case with a community of domestic life in which nonrelated members or servants participate. In contradistinction, spiritual friendship forms a kind of invisible scene or meeting which has to be kept alive by artistic intuition and creative will. The relations between human beings themselves as friends and comrades have the least organic and intrinsically necessary character. They are the least instinctive and are based less upon habit than are the relationships of neighborhood. They are of a mental nature and seem to be founded, therefore, as compared with the earlier relationships, upon chance or free choice.

⌒

CUSTOM: AN ESSAY ON SOCIAL CODES, 1909

. . . Society, as the subject and supporter of fashion, stands in a certain contrast to custom. It is modern, cultured, cosmopolitan. It represents new principles throughout; it desires progress. Trade, the production of goods—the workshop, and the factory—are the elements by which it extends its network over the whole populated earth. It desires movement and *quick* movement; it must dissolve custom in order to develop a taste for the new and for imported goods. It figures on individual motives, especially on young people's curiosity and love of finery, and on the desire to barter and to trade in desired goods. Affection and fidelity to tradition, to one's own, to one's heritage, must necessarily give way. Commerce has ever a disintegrating effect.

Trade and commerce, urban life, the growth of big cities, the power of money, capitalism, class differentiation, and the striving for middle-class status and education—all these are facets of the same development of civilization, which favors fashion and is injurious to custom. Even the country folk soon find their old customs peculiar and absurd. Cheap, glittering wares impress them more than the old-fashioned household wares with the beautiful if quaint designs. And so it is in everything. The pattern of the metropolis is imitated. Goods quickly manufactured with mechanized techniques are often ugly and not durable, like the fashion from which they spring. All *gesellschaftliche* civilization has a quality utterly opposed to the artistic spirit which is rooted in tradition and in integrity. It is superficial and external.

From *Custom: An Essay on Social Codes,* by Ferdinand Tönnies, A. Farrell Borenstein, Trans. Published by The Free Press of Glencoe, A Division of the Crowell-Collier Publishing Company. Copyright © 1961.

The items of mass production are flimsy, uniform, monotonous; they lack genuineness.

Thus an age in which fashion and *gesellschaftliche* civilization predominate becomes powerful over against an age which underlies it and is yet retained within it: an age in which custom predominates, as an age of peasant-townsmen culture and the culture of the clergy and the nobility resting upon it. The former is pervaded with haste, unrest, continual novelty, fluidity and a persistence only in incessant change. Hence it is inclined to idealize its opposite; the antique becomes the style. One longs to return to nature; old castoffs are resurrected; old forms of life and old customs are valued and preserved.

A taste for religion is reactivated, and the simplicity, the homespun nature of genuine style and artistically correct forms are "discovered." This cycle recurs in rhythmic waves from time to time. Industry capitalizes on this fashion as it does on others. The spirit of *Gesellschaft* remains the same: it cannot jump over its own shadow. But in its forward movement lies the possibility of surmounting it. This lies in the reorganization of the economic foundations. If the natural interchange of production and consumption were to replace the predominance of the movable capital of trade and commerce, then, too, life would again become more stable, more quiet and more healthy. Consciously-nurtured custom and the fostering of art would again be possible.

Even religion would find new life as a *Weltanschauung* in the spirit of truth; or better, the idea of religion would be reawakened in the struggle for the spirit of truth and reverence. A society that unanimously pursues such a course, and with a clear and strong consciousness, would manifest an abandonment of the whims of fashion and an ability to produce a rational will. The growth of its rationality is that which in general distinguishes it. It is that which lies in the developmental lines of custom and civilization, and as such in its ennoblement and refinement.

These developmental lines have been repeatedly stressed: emancipation from superstition, spiritism and magic, the joy in intellectual pursuit, which itself can become an appreciation of art, and a striving for artistic naiveté and creativity. The present contains such elements and moments, although only in the form of a few scattered grains of seed. It can rather be said that the future *ought* to *be* developed in such a direction than that it *will* be.

The state, too, in its empirical appearance the other expression of society, exerts an effect on custom wholly analogous to that which society exerts on it. Custom is concrete, particularizing, rural, provincial-urban. The state represents an individual-abstract will which regulates—that is, wills to establish uniformity. Through ordinances and laws it fights custom where it seems noxious or only dangerous to it. The esteem of custom is diminished everywhere due to the state's absolute authority. The state serves progress, the development of independent personalities, but always at the expense of the folk and their *gemeinschaftlich* cooperative life.

It is futile, as many thinkers and scholars might be tempted to do, to lament this. The more one understands the inner necessity of the process, the more his lament will be silenced. But he does not need to suppress a sense of the tragic in the course of things. Precisely because—the progress is so immense, the collapse of tradition is highly charged with emotion. For the expectation that progress will restore or reestablish the good of the old life is linked with progress itself; and this it is not able to do. It can only achieve its own objective. It gives men the opportunity of livelihood and, in what time is left, the opportunity for education as well.

Everything native, genial and homely disappears. The individual is thrown on his own resources.

GABRIEL TARDE

1843–1904

Jean-Gabriel de Tarde was born on March 12, 1843 at Sarlat-la-Canéda, France, married Marthe Bardy-Delisle in 1877, had three sons with her, and died at 61 on May 13, 1904 in Paris. He attended Jesuit schools and then, forswearing his first love, philosophy, for needed income, he switched to law at the universities of Toulouse and Paris, finishing in 1866. He was a magistrate in Dordogne for 15 years, and was then invited to oversee criminal statistics at the Ministry of Justice in Paris beginning in 1894. At 57 he became professor of modern philosophy at the Collége de France, dying shortly thereafter. His important works are *Comparative Criminology* (1886), *The Laws of Imitation* (1890, translated by the noted American anthropologist, Elsie Clews Parsons), *Social Laws* (1898), and *Economic Psychology* (1902, 2 vols.). There are those who see Tarde as the most versatile social scientist of his era.

Following the lead of the economist Augustin Cournot (to whom *Laws of Imitation* is dedicated), and based on 15 years of listening to criminal cases as a judge, Tarde argued that about 1% of the population is capable of true innovation or invention, and that the rest imitate the new practices or ideas which regularly crop up. This accounts for waves of criminal activity in a given locale. Plotting the cycles of "imitation, opposition, and adaptation," which he regarded as the fundaments of social life, Tarde had identified his philosophy of history as well as the framework for his own version of social-psychology. He wrote in opposition to Durkheim, the younger doyen of French sociology during Tarde's lifetime, since for the former, individuality as such is essentially a fiction created by people who do not understand just how determined, even "over-determined," by social structure their chosen way of life is. Tarde by contrast gave precedence to genuine individuality, implying that a sociological determinism of the kind Durkheim espoused obscured more than it illuminated, for it covered up the fundamental character of social action. Tarde saw that people are easily bored, that they "naturally" rebel against established behaviors and norms, and therefore become agents of "invention" by incorporating extant practices into some fresh form or other which intrigues them. The next wave of inventors comes along, sure as clockwork, which gives social life its demonstrably cyclical nature. The selection reprinted below gives a sense of Tarde's style of thought, typical of his period (and reminiscent of Durkheim, too) in believing that "Science" could triumph over lapses in social order. Then social "dysfunctions" (as they were later named) would be identified as such, and could eventually be mitigated in their effects if scientists, like himself, alerted the public to its unknowing drift into social calamity.

THE LAWS OF IMITATION, 1890

Universal Repetition

Can we have a science or only a history, or, at most, a philosophy of social phenomena? This question is always open. And yet, if social facts are closely observed from a certain point of view, they can be reduced, like other facts, to series of minute and homogeneous phenomena and to the formulas, or laws, which sum up these series. Why, then, is the science of society still unborn, or born but recently, among all its adult and vigorous sister sciences? The chief reason is, I think, that we have thrown away the substance for its shadow and substituted words for things. We have thought it impossible to give a scientific look to *sociology* except by giving it a biological or, better still, a mechanical air. This is an attempt to light up the known by the unknown. It is transforming a solar system into a non-resolvable nebula in order to understand it better. In social subjects we are exceptionally privileged in having veritable causes, positive and specific acts, at first hand; this condition is wholly lacking in every other subject of investigation. It is unnecessary, therefore, to rely for an explanation of social facts upon those so-called general causes which physicists and naturalists are obliged to create under the name of force, energy, conditions of existence, and other verbal palliatives of their ignorance of the real groundwork of things.

But are we to consider that human acts are the sole factors of history? Surely this is too simple! And so we bind ourselves to contrive other causes on the type of those useful fictions which are elsewhere imposed upon us, and we congratulate ourselves upon being able at times to give an entirely impersonal colour to human phenomena by reason of our lofty, but, truly speaking, obscure, point of view. Let us ward off this vague idealism. Let us likewise ward off the vapid individualism which consists in explaining social changes as the caprices of certain great men. On the other hand, let us explain these changes through the more or less fortuitous appearance, as to time and place, of certain great ideas, or rather, of a considerable number of both major and minor ideas, of ideas which are generally anonymous and usually of obscure birth; which are simple or abstruse; which are seldom illustrious, but which are always novel. Because of this latter attribute, I shall take the liberty of baptising them collectively *inventions* or *discoveries*. By these two terms I mean any kind of an innovation or improvement, however slight, which is made in any previous innovation throughout the range of social phenomena—language, religion, politics, law, industry, or art. At the moment when this novel thing, big or little as it may be, is conceived of, or determined by, an individual, nothing appears to change in the social body,—just as nothing changes in the physical appearance of an organism which a harmful or beneficent microbe has just invaded,—and the gradual changes caused by the introduction of the new element seem to follow, without visible break, upon the anterior social changes into whose current they have glided. Hence arises the illusion which leads philosophers of history into affirming that there is a real and fundamental continuity in historic metamorphoses. The true causes can be reduced to a chain of ideas which are, to be sure, very numerous, but which are in themselves distinct and discontinuous, although they are connected by the much more numerous acts of imitation which are modelled upon them.

Our starting-point lies here in the re-inspiring initiatives which bring new wants, together with new satisfactions, into the world, and which then, through spontaneous and unconscious or artificial and deliberate imitation, propagate or tend to propagate, themselves, at a more or less rapid, but regular, rate, like a wave of light, or like a family of termites. The regularity to which I refer is not in the least apparent in social things until they are resolved into their several elements, when it is found to lie in the simplest of them, in combinations of distinct inventions, in flashes of genius which have been accumulated and changed into commonplace lights. I confess that this is an extremely difficult analysis. Socially, everything is either invention or imitation. And invention bears the same relation to imitation as a mountain to a

From *The Laws of Imitation*, by Gabriel Tarde, Elsie Clews Parsons, Trans. Published by Peter Smith. Copyright © 1962.

river. There is certainly nothing less subtle than this point of view; but in holding to it boldly and unreservedly, in exploiting it from the most trivial detail to the most complete synthesis of facts, we may, perhaps, notice how well fitted it is to bring into relief all the picturesqueness and, at the same time, all the simplicity of history, and to reveal historic perspectives which may be characterised by the freakishness of a rock-bound landscape, or by the conventionality of a park walk. This is idealism also, if you choose to call it so; but it is the idealism which consists in explaining history through the ideas of its actors, not through those of the historian.

If we consider the science of society from this point of view, we shall at once see that human sociology is related to animal sociologies, as a species to its genus, so to speak. That it is an extraordinary and infinitely superior species, I admit, but it is allied to the others, nevertheless. M. Espinas expressly states in his admirable work on *Sociétés animales,* a work which was written long before the first edition of this book, that the labours of ants may be very well explained on the principle *"of individual initiative followed by imitation."* This initiative is always an innovation or invention that is equal to one of our own in boldness of spirit. . . .

This is the essential point. Knowledge of causes is sometimes sufficient for foresight; but knowledge of resemblances always allows of enumeration and measurement, and science depends primarily upon number and measure. More than this is, of course, necessary. As soon as a new science has staked out its field of characteristic resemblances and repetitions, it must compare them and note the bond of solidarity which unites their concomitant variations. But, as a matter of fact, the mind does not fully understand nor clearly recognise the relation of cause and effect, except in as much as the effect resembles or repeats the cause, as, for example, when a sound wave produces another sound wave, or a cell, another cell. There is nothing more mysterious, one may say, than such reproductions. I admit this; but when we have once accepted this mystery, there is nothing clearer than the resulting series. Whereas, every time that *production* does not mean *reproduction of self,* we are entirely in the dark. . . .

Repetition exists, then, for the sake of variation. Otherwise, the necessity of death (a problem which M. Delbœuf considers in his book upon animate and inanimate matter, almost impossible of solution), would be incomprehensible; for why should not the top of life spin on, after it was wound up, forever? But under the hypothesis that repetitions exist only to embody all the phases of a certain unique originality which seeks expression, death must inevitably supervene after all these variations have been fully effected. I may note in this connection, in passing, that the relation of universal to particular, a relation which fed the entire philosophic controversy of the Middle Ages upon nominalism and realism, is precisely that of repetition to variation. *Nominalism* is the doctrine in accordance with which individual characteristics or idiosyncrasies are the only significant realities. *Realism,* on the other hand, considers only those traits worthy of attention and of the name of reality through which a given individual resembles other individuals and tends to reproduce himself in them. The interest of this kind of speculation is apparent when we consider that in politics individualism is a special kind of nominalism, and socialism, a special kind of realism.

All repetition, social, vital, or physical, *i.e., imitative, hereditary,* or *vibratory* repetition (to consider only the most salient and typical forms of universal repetition), springs from some innovation, just as every light radiates from some central point, and thus throughout science the normal appears to originate from the accidental.

WILLIAM JAMES

1842–1910

Son of the iconoclastic Swedenborgian, Henry James, Sr., brother of the great novelist, Henry James, and of the diarist Alice James, William James was born on January 11, 1842 in New York City. He married Alice Howe Gibbens on July 10, 1878 and their family included four sons and a daughter (for whom George Herbert Mead was hired as a tutor while he was a graduate student at Harvard). James died at Chocorua, New Hampshire, after a life filled with mental and physical infirmity on August 26, 1910, when he was 68. After an expedition to the Amazon assisting Louis Agassiz, he unenthusiastically studied medicine at Harvard, receiving the M.D. in 1869, but was unable to practice for several years as a psychological invalid given to fits of panic. His self-analysis of the problem and desperate attachment to Charles Renouvier's neo-Kantian notions of free will laid the basis for his later discoveries in psychology and moral philosophy. From 1872 through 1876, James was a physiology instructor at Harvard, but his earlier studies in Germany under several leading psychologists would not let go of his imagination. He formulated a new psychological "science" that brought psychophysics and brain physiology into contagion with more traditional topics within the field, wresting this new discipline away from the purely idealist conception of mind that was prevalent among the theologically inclined. With marriage, his ordeal with neurasthenia was over, for during his honeymoon he and his wife began working on a textbook for which James had signed a contract, due to the publisher within one year. In fact, he worked on it for twelve years, and succeeded in writing one of the most important introductory textbooks to any field ever composed by an American, *Principles of Psychology* (1890–92; 2 vols.), the abridged version of which was referred to by Harvard undergraduates for many years as "the Jimmy." Both versions have been continuously in print ever since, and even though by now many of the physiological details about brain functioning and perception which James believed have been cast aside, his book continues to be read for his analysis of consciousness, his use of language, and his ability to connect the "science" of psychology with a humanistic portrayal of psychological properties. James's work vacillated between psychology proper and pragmatic philosophy (so termed by James's friend, C. S. Peirce), and it is as much today for the latter work as the former that James is remembered and read. His other important works include *Pragmatism* (1907), *The Meaning of Truth* (1909), and, perhaps most importantly, *The Varieties of Religious Experience*, his Gifford Lectures (1902), widely regarded as the soundest general exposition of religiosity written in modern times. The excerpts below offer in condensed form James's views of the relation between morality and philosophy, the qualities which make up a meaningful life, and a famous observation about the nature of war as a moral problem.

"THE MORAL PHILOSOPHER AND THE MORAL LIFE," 1891

The main purpose of this paper is to show that there is no such thing possible as an ethical philosophy dogmatically made up in advance. We all help to determine the content of ethical philosophy so far as we contribute to the race's moral life. In other words, there can be no final truth in ethics any more than in physics, until the last man has had his experience and said his say. In the one case as in the other, however, the hypotheses which we now make while waiting, and the acts to which they prompt us, are among the indispensable conditions which determine what that 'say' shall be.

IV

. . . On the whole, then, we must conclude that no philosophy of ethics is possible in the old-fashioned absolute sense of the term. Everywhere the ethical philosopher must wait on facts. The thinkers who create the ideals come he knows not whence, their sensibilities are evolved he knows not how; and the question as to which of two conflicting ideals will give the best universe then and there, can be answered by him only through the aid of the experience of other men. I said some time ago, in treating of the 'first' question, that the intuitional moralists deserve credit for keeping most clearly to the psychological facts. They do much to spoil this merit on the whole, however, by mixing with it that dogmatic temper which, by absolute distinctions and unconditional 'thou shalt nots,' changes a growing, elastic, and continuous life into a superstitious system of relics and dead bones. In point of fact, there are no absolute evils, and there are no non-moral goods; and the *highest* ethical life—however few may be called to bear its burdens—consists at all times in the breaking of rules which have grown too narrow for the actual case. There is but one unconditional commandment, which is that we should seek incessantly, with fear and trembling, so to vote and to act as to bring about the very largest total universe of good which we can see. Abstract rules indeed can help; but they help the less in proportion as our intuitions are more piercing, and our vocation is the stronger for the moral life. For every real dilemma is in literal strictness a unique situation; and the exact combination of ideals realized and ideals disappointed which each decision creates is always a universe without a precedent, and for which no adequate previous rule exists. The philosopher, then, *qua* philosopher, is no better able to determine the best universe in the concrete emergency than other men. He sees, indeed, somewhat better than most men what the question always is—not a question of this good or that good simply taken, but of the two total universes with which these goods respectively belong. He knows that he must vote always for the richer universe, for the good which seems most organizable, most fit to enter into complex combinations, most apt to be a member of a more inclusive whole. But which particular universe this is he cannot know for certain in advance; he only knows that if he makes a bad mistake the cries of the wounded will soon inform him of the fact. In all this the philosopher is just like the rest of us non-philosophers, so far as we are just and sympathetic instinctively, and so far as we are open to the voice of complaint. His function is in fact indistinguishable from that of the best kind of statesman at the present day. His books upon ethics, therefore, themselves with a literature which is confessedly tentative and suggestive rather than dogmatic—I mean with novels and dramas of the deeper sort, with sermons, with books on statecraft and philanthropy and social and economical reform. Treated in this way ethical treatises may be voluminous and luminous as well; but they never can be *final*, except in their abstractest and vaguest features; and they must more and more abandon the old-fashioned, clear-cut, and would-be 'scientific' form.

V

The chief of all the reasons why concrete ethics cannot be final is that they have to wait on metaphysical and theological beliefs. I said some time back that real ethical relations existed in a purely human world. They would exist even in what we called a moral solitude if the thinker had various ideals which took hold of him in turn. His self of one day would make demands on his self of another; and some of the demands might be urgent and tyrannical, while others were gentle and easily put aside. We call the tyrannical demands *imperatives*. If we ignore these we do not hear the last of it. The good which we have wounded returns to plague us with interminable crops of consequential damages, compunctions, and regrets. Obligation can thus exist inside a single thinker's consciousness; and perfect peace can abide with him only so far as he lives according to some sort of a casuistic scale which keeps his more imperative goods on top. It is the nature of these goods to be cruel to their rivals. Nothing shall avail when weighed in the balance against them. They call out all the mercilessness in our disposition, and do not easily forgive us if we are so soft-hearted as to shrink from sacrifice in their behalf.

The deepest difference, practically, in the moral life of man is the difference between the easy-going and the strenuous mood. When in the easy-going mood the shrinking from present ill is our ruling consideration. The strenuous mood, on the contrary, makes us quite indifferent to present ill, if only the greater ideal be attained. The capacity for the strenuous mood probably lies slumbering in every man, but it has more difficulty in some than in others in waking up. It needs the wilder passions to arouse it, the big fears, loves, and indignations; or else the deeply penetrating appeal of some one of the higher fidelities, like justice, truth, or freedom. Strong relief is a necessity of its vision; and a world where all the mountains are brought down and all the valleys are exalted is no congenial place for its habitation. This is why in a solitary thinker this mood might slumber on forever without waking. His various ideals, known to him to be mere preferences of his own, are too nearly of the same denominational value: he can play fast or loose with them at will. . . .

The capacity of the strenuous mood lies so deep down among our natural human possibilities that even if there were no meta-physical or traditional grounds for believing in a God, men would postulate one simply as a pretext for living hard, and getting out of the game of existence its keenest possibilities of zest. Our attitude towards concrete evils is entirely different in a world where we believe there are none but finite demanders, from what it is in one where we joyously face tragedy for an infinite demander's sake. Every sort of energy and endurance, of courage and capacity for handling life's evils, is set free in those who have religious faith. For this reason the strenuous type of character will on the battle-field of human history always outwear the easy-going type, and religion will drive irreligion to the wall.

It would seem, too—and this is my final conclusion—that the stable and systematic moral universe for which the ethical philosopher asks is fully possible only in a world where there is a divine thinker with all-enveloping demands. If such a thinker existed, his way of subordinating the demands to one another would be the finally valid casuistic scale; his claims would be the most appealing; his ideal universe would be the most inclusive realizable whole. If he now exist, then actualized in his thought already must be that ethical philosophy which we seek as the pattern which our own must evermore approach. In the interests of our own ideal of systematically unified moral truth, therefore, we, as would-be philosophers, must postulate a divine thinker, and pray for the victory of the religious cause. Meanwhile, exactly what the thought of the infinite thinker may be is hidden from us even were we sure of his existence; so that our postulation of him after all serves only to let loose in us the strenuous mood. But this is what it does in all men, even those who have no interest in philosophy. The ethical philosopher, therefore, whenever he ventures to say which course of action is the best, is on no essentially different level from the common man. "See, I have set before thee this day life and good, and death and evil; therefore, choose life that thou and thy seed may live"—when this challenge comes to us, it is simply our total character and personal genius that are on trial; and if we invoke any so-called philosophy, our choice and use of that also are but revelations of our personal aptitude or incapacity for moral life. From this unsparing practical ordeal no professor's lectures and no array of books can save us. The solving word, for the learned and the unlearned man alike, lies in the last resort in the dumb willingnesses and unwillingnesses of their interior characters, and nowhere else. It is not in heaven, neither is it beyond the sea; but the word is very nigh unto thee, in thy mouth and in thy heart, that thou mayest do it.

⟶

"WHAT MAKES A LIFE SIGNIFICANT?" 1899

In my previous talk, 'On a Certain Blindness,' I tried to make you feel how soaked and shot-through life is with values and meanings which we fail to realize because of our external and insensible point of view. The meanings are there for the others, but they are not there for us. There lies more than a mere interest of curious speculation in understanding this. It has the most tremendous practical importance. I wish that I could convince you of it as I feel it myself. It is the basis of all our tolerance, social, religious, and political. The forgetting of it lies at the root of every stupid and sanguinary mistake that rulers over subject-peoples make. The first thing to learn in intercourse with others is non-interference with their own peculiar ways of being happy, provided those ways do not assume to interfere by violence with ours. No one has insight into all the ideals. No one should presume to judge them off-hand. The pretension to dogmatize about them in each other is the root of most human injustices and cruelties, and the trait in human character most likely to make the angels weep.

Every Jack sees in his own particular Jill charms and perfections to the enchantment of which we stolid onlookers are stone-cold. And which has the superior view of the absolute truth, he or we? Which has the more vital insight into the nature of Jill's existence, as a fact? Is he in excess, being in this matter a maniac? or are we in defect, being victims of a pathological anaesthesia as regards Jill's magical importance? Surely the latter; surely to Jack are the profounder truths revealed; surely poor Jill's palpitating little life-throbs *are* among the wonders of creation, *are*

worthy of this sympathetic interest; and it is to our shame that the rest of us cannot feel like Jack. For Jack realizes Jill concretely, and we do not. He struggles toward a union with her inner life, divining her feelings, anticipating her desires, understanding her limits as manfully as he can, and yet inadequately, too; for he is also afflicted with some blindness, even here. Whilst we, dead clods that we are, do not even seek after these things, but are contented that that portion of eternal fact named Jill should be for us as if it were not. Jill, who knows her inner life, knows that Jack's way of taking it—so importantly—is the true and serious way; and she responds to the truth in him by taking him truly and seriously, too. May the ancient blindness never wrap its clouds about either of them again! Where would any of *us* be, were there no one willing to know us as we really are or ready to repay us for *our* insight by making recognizant return? We ought, all of us, to realize each other in this intense, pathetic, and important way.

If you say that this is absurd, and that we cannot be in love with everyone at once, I merely point out to you that, as a matter of fact, certain persons do exist with an enormous capacity for friendship and for taking delight in other people's lives; and that such persons know more of truth than if their hearts were not so big. The vice of ordinary Jack and Jill affection is not its intensity, but its exclusions and its jealousies. Leave those out, and you see that the ideal I am holding up before you, however impracticable to-day, yet contains nothing intrinsically absurd.

We have unquestionably a great cloud-bank of ancestral blindness weighing down upon us, only transiently riven here and there by fitful revelations of the truth. It is vain to hope for this state of things to alter much. Our inner secrets must remain for the most part impenetrable by others, for beings as essentially practical as we are are necessarily short of sight. But, if we cannot gain much positive insight into one another, cannot we at least use our sense of our own blindness to make us more cautious in going over the dark places? Cannot we escape some of those hideous ancestral intolerances and cruelties, and positive reversals of the truth? . . .

In this solid and tridimensional sense, so to call it, those philosophers are right who contend

From *The Writings of William James: A Comprehensive Edition*, John J. McDermott, Ed. Published by Random House. Copyright © 1967.

that the world is a standing thing, with no progress, no real history. The changing conditions of history touch only the surface of the show. The altered equilibriums and redistributions only diversify our opportunities and open chances to us for new ideals. But, with each new ideal that comes into life, the chance for a life based on some old ideal will vanish; and he would needs be a presumptuous calculator who should with confidence say that the total sum of significances is positively and absolutely greater at any one epoch than at any other of the world.

I am speaking broadly, I know, and omitting to consider certain qualifications in which I myself believe. But one can only make one point in one lecture, and I shall be well content if I have brought my point home to you this evening in even a slight degree. *There are compensations:* and no outward changes of condition in life can keep the nightingale of its eternal meaning from singing in all sorts of different men's hearts. That is the main fact to remember. If we could not only admit it with our lips, but really and truly believe it, how our convulsive insistencies, how our antipathies and dreads of each other, would soften down! If the poor and the rich could look at each other in this way, *sub specie æternitatis,* how gentle would grow their disputes! what tolerance and good humor, what willingness to live and let live, would come into the world!

∾

"THE MORAL EQUIVALENT OF WAR," 1910

The war against war is going to be no holiday excursion or camping party. The military feelings are too deeply grounded to abdicate their place among our ideals until better substitutes are offered than the glory and shame that come to nations as well as to individuals from the ups and downs of politics and the vicissitudes of trade. There is something highly paradoxical in the mod-

ern man's relation to war. Ask all our millions, north and south, whether they would vote now (were such a thing possible) to have our war for the Union expunged from history, and the record of a peaceful transition to the present time substituted for that of its marches and battles, and probably hardly a handful of eccentrics would say yes. Those ancestors, those efforts, those memories and legends, are the most ideal part of what we now own together, a sacred spiritual possession worth more than all the blood poured out. Yet ask those same people whether they would be willing in cold blood to start another civil war now to gain another similar possession, and not one man or woman would vote for the proposition. In modern eyes, precious though wars may be, they must not be waged solely for the sake of the ideal harvest. Only when forced upon one, only when an enemy's injustice leaves us no alternative, is a war now thought permissible.

It was not thus in ancient times. The earlier men were hunting men, and to hunt a neighboring tribe, kill the males, loot the village and possess the females, was the most profitable, as well as the most exciting, way of living. Thus were the more martial tribes selected, and in chiefs and peoples a pure pugnacity and love of glory came to mingle with the more fundamental appetite for plunder.

Modern war is so expensive that we feel trade to be a better avenue to plunder; but modern man inherits all the innate pugnacity and all the love of glory of his ancestors. Showing war's irrationality and horror is of no effect upon him. The horrors make the fascination. War is the *strong* life; it is life *in extremis;* war-taxes are the only ones men never hesitate to pay, as the budgets of all nations show us.

History is a bath of blood. The Iliad is one long recital of how Diomedes and Ajax, Sarpedon and Hector *killed.* No detail of the wounds they made is spared us, and the Greek mind fed upon the story. Greek history is a panorama of jingoism and imperialism—war for war's sake, all the citizens being warriors. It is horrible reading, because of the irrationality of it all—save for the purpose of making "history"—and the history is that of the utter ruin of a civilization in intellectual respects perhaps the highest the earth has ever seen.

From *The Writings of William James: A Comprehensive Edition,* John J. McDermott, Ed. Published by Random House. Copyright © 1967.

It is plain that on this subject civilized man has developed a sort of double personality. If we take European nations, no legitimate interest of any one of them would seem to justify the tremendous destructions which a war to compass it would necessarily entail. It would seem as though common sense and reason ought to find a way to reach agreement in every conflict of honest interests. I myself think it our bounden duty to believe in such international rationality as possible. But, as things stand, I see how desperately hard it is to bring the peace-party and the war-party together, and I believe that the difficulty is due to certain deficiencies in the program of pacificism which set the militarist imagination strongly, and to a certain extent justifiably, against it. In the whole discussion both sides are on imaginative and sentimental ground. It is but one utopia against another, and everything one says must be abstract and hypothetical. Subject to this criticism and caution, I will try to characterize in abstract strokes the opposite imaginative forces, and point out what to my own very fallible mind seems the best utopian hypothesis, the most promising line of conciliation.

In my remarks, pacificist though I am, I will refuse to speak of the bestial side of the war-*régime* (already done justice to by many writers) and consider the higher aspects of militaristic sentiment. Patriotism no one thinks discreditable; nor does any one deny that war is the romance of history. But inordinate ambitions are the soul of every patriotism, and the possibility of violent death the soul of all romance. The militarily patri-

otic and romantic-minded everywhere, and especially the professional military class, refuse to admit for a moment that war may be a transitory phenomenon in social evolution. The notion of a sheep's paradise like that revolts, they say, our higher imagination. Where then would be the steeps of life? If war had ever stopped, we should have to re-invent it, on this view, to redeem life from flat degeneration. . . .

Wells adds that he thinks that the conceptions of order and discipline, the tradition of service and devotion, of physical fitness, unstinted exertion, and universal responsibility, which universal military duty is now teaching European nations, will remain a permanent acquisition, when the last ammunition has been used in the fireworks that celebrate the final peace. I believe as he does. It would be simply preposterous if the only force that could work ideals of honor and standards of efficiency into English or American natures should be the fear of being killed by the Germans or the Japanese. Great indeed is Fear; but it is not, as our military enthusiasts believe and try to make us believe, the only stimulus known for awakening the higher ranges of men's spiritual energy. The amount of alteration in public opinion which my utopia postulates is vastly less than the difference between the mentality of those black warriors who pursued Stanley's party on the Congo with their cannibal war-cry of "Meat! Meat!" and that of the "general-staff" of any civilized nation. History has seen the latter interval bridged over: the former one can be bridged over much more easily.

EMILE DURKHEIM

1858–1917

David-Émile Durkheim, the son and grandson of rabbis, was born in the Alsatian town of Épinal, Vosges, France on April 15, 1858. In 1887 he married Louise Julie Drey-fus, and their children were Marie and Andri, the latter killed in WWI in 1916. Durkheim's only son's death hastened his own on November 15, 1917 in Paris, where for many years he had been an essential fixture in the academic and pedagogical firma-ment. When Durkheim was 12, German troops occupied his town and his home, a memory which seemed to haunt him in that he suddenly was forced to comprehend what it meant to endure a normless, anomic social condition, and to lose the benefits of collective well-being which were fostered through proper social control and commonly held beliefs. As a youth he was schooled in the traditional education of Jewish students, but when still young found himself attracted to Catholic mysticism, and eventually dis-pensed with religion altogether in formal terms. A deeply religious sensibility, however, affected virtually all his scholarship, though recast in secular terms. He attended the École Normale Superieure (1879–82), France's best teacher's college. An early friend-ship with Jean Jaurés, later a leading socialist, broadened Durkheim's academic and po-litical interests to include philosophy and political action. He became a philosophy teacher at high schools in Sens and elsewhere (1882–87), then professor at the Univer-sity of Bordeaux (1887), becoming the first professor to teach social sciences in France, promoted to Professor of Social Science at Bordeaux in 1896, and then ascended to the University of Paris in 1902 where he specialized in the history and contemporary prac-tices of pedagogy, yet always in tandem with sociological research and writing.

Durkheim's central argument, which extends from his earliest to his final works, holds that a scientifically crafted theory of societal morality could prevent the sort of "anomie" which he thought afflicted citizens within The Third Republic, and that ex-tended as well to all rapidly industrializing nations. He treated this topic in his dissertation, *The Division of Labor in Society* (1893), a book that has almost biblical significance within so-ciology even today. Durkheim posed the question of how morally binding norms could be promulgated within a secularized and diversified society, and answered that it would have to be shaped through professional groups, each of which would be responsible for guiding and monitoring the behavior of its members. His other important works, all of them still very much alive and in print, include *Suicide* (1897), which demonstrates that killing one-self is as much a sociological as a psychological phenomenon, *The Rules of Sociological Method* (1895), pointing to the "social fact" as the foundation of social research, thus separating it from the work of the other social sciences, and the book which he regarded as his mas-terpiece, *The Elementary Forms of the Religious Life* (1915), an exhaustive study of aboriginal religious practices compared with their modern residues. He also co-authored with his nephew, Marcel Mauss, *Primitive Classification* (1903), an innovative study in what came to be called "the sociology of knowledge." Here the two authors demonstrated that the contrasting ways different societies arrange knowledge—they highlighted the Australian aboriginals, the Zuni, Sioux, and Chinese—is a direct reflection of their particular forms of social organization. This was a sharp attack on conventional epistemology, which held that all humans comprehend and analyze their environment in roughly the same way. Durkheim thus demonstrated how "sociologism" worked.

Durkheim also established the first scholarly journal of sociology in France, trained an entire generation of anthropologists and sociologists (many of them, including his son, being slaughtered in the First World War), and wrote a history of education in France (1938, posthumous) that remains a standard work. Given all these scholarly achievements, many argue that Durkheim is the father of modern sociology and the first to lay out in exact terms how the sociological viewpoint differs from those of the other social sciences.

THE DIVISION OF LABOUR IN SOCIETY, 1893

The Division of Labour and Happiness

But is it true that the happiness of men increases in proportion as men progress? Nothing is more doubtful.

There are certainly many pleasures open to us today that more simple natures are unaware of. Yet on the other hand we are prone to much suffering that is spared them, and it is by no means sure that the balance is in our favour. Thought is undoubtedly a source of enjoyment, one that can be very acute. On the other hand, however, how many joys are disturbed by it! For one problem resolved, how many questions are raised to which there is no answer! For one doubt cleared up, how many mysteries do we perceive that disconcert us! Likewise, although the savage does not know the pleasures that a very active life procures for us, his compensation is that he is not a prey to boredom, that tor-

ment of the cultured mind. He lets his life flow gently by without continually feeling the need to fill its too fleeting moments with great but hasty activity. Moreover, let us not forget that work is still only for the majority of men a toil and a burden.

The objection will be made that among civilised peoples life is more varied, and that variety is necessary for pleasure. But accompanying a greater mobility, civilisation brings in its train greater uniformity, for it has imposed upon mankind monotonous and unceasing labour. The savage goes from one occupation to another, according to the circumstances and the needs that impel him. Civilised man gives himself entirely over to his task, always the same, and one that offers less variety the more restricted it is. Organisation necessarily implies an absolute regularity in habits, for a change cannot occur in the mode of functioning of an organ without its having repercussions upon the whole organism. In this sense our life offers us a lesser share of the unexpected, whilst at the same time, by its greater instability, it takes away from enjoyment some of the security that it needs.

It is true that our nervous system, which has become more delicate, is open to feeble stimuli that did not affect our forefathers, because they were of a coarser grain. Yet also many stimuli that were agreeable have become too strong for us, and are in consequence painful. If we are sensitive to more pleasures, we are also sensitive to more sorrows. Moreover, if it is true that, other things being equal, suffering produces in the organism greater repercussions than does joy, that an unpleasant stimulus has a more painful effect upon us than a pleasant stimulus of the same intensity causes us pleasure, this greater sensibility might well be more contrary than favourable to happiness. In fact, very highly strung nervous systems live in pain and even end up by becoming attached to it. Is it not very remarkable that the fundamental cult of the most civilised religions is that of human suffering? Doubtless, for life to continue today, as in former times, on average the amount of pleasure should exceed the sorrow. Yet it is not certain that this excess of pleasure is very considerable.

Finally, above all it is not proved that this excess ever gives the measure of happiness. Doubtless such obscure questions as yet have hardly been studied, and nothing can be affirmed with certainty. However, it does really seem that happiness is something different from the sum total of pleasure. It is a general and constant state that accompanies the regular activity of all our organic and psychological functions. Thus continuous activities such as respiration and circulation procure no positive enjoyment. Yet it is above all upon these that depend our good humour and vitality. Every pleasure is a sort of crisis; it is born, lasts for a moment, and dies. Life, on the other hand, goes on. What causes its basic charm must be continuous, just as it is. Pleasure is local; it is an affective sentiment limited to one spot in the organism or the consciousness. Life resides in neither, but is everywhere present. Our attachment to it must therefore depend on some cause that is likewise of a general nature. In short, what happiness expresses is not the momentary state of this or that particular function, but the healthiness of physical and moral life as a whole. As pleasure accompanies the normal exercise of intermittent functions, it is indeed an element in happiness, and the greater place these functions have in one's life the more important it is. But it is not happiness. Pleasure cannot vary the level of happiness save within restricted limits, for it relates to ephemeral causes, whereas happiness consists of permanent attitudes. For local events to be able to affect pro-

foundly this fundamental basis of our sensibility, they must be repeated with exceptional frequency and have exceptional consequences. Most often, on the contrary, it is pleasure that depends upon happiness: according to whether we are happy or unhappy, everything appears to smile upon us or make us sad. It has been very rightly asserted that we carry our happiness within ourselves. . . .

Thus there is no connection between the variations in happiness and the progress of the division of labour.

This is an extremely important proposition. The upshot is that, in order to explain the transformations through which society has passed, we should not investigate what influence they exert upon men's happiness, since it is not that influence which has brought them about. Social science must resolutely renounce the utilitarian comparisons to which it has too often assented. Moreover, such considerations are necessarily subjective, for every time that we compare pleasures or interests, since all objective criteria are lacking, we cannot help throwing into the scales our own ideas and preferences, and we proclaim as scientific truth what is personal opinion.

~

"THE DUALISM OF HUMAN NATURE AND ITS SOCIAL CONDITIONS," 1914

Although sociology is defined as the science of societies, it cannot, in reality, deal with the human groups that are the immediate object of its investigation without eventually touching on the individual who is the basic element of which these groups are composed. For society can exist only if it penetrates the consciousness of individuals and fashions it in "its image and resemblance." We can say, therefore, with assurance and without being

From "The Dualism of Human Nature and Its Social Condition," by Emile Durkheim. Published in *Emile Durkheim, 1858-1917,* Kurt H. Wolff, Ed. Published by Arno Press. Copyright © 1960, 1980.

excessively dogmatic, that a great number of our mental states, including some of the most important ones, are of social origin. In this case, then, it is the whole that, in a large measure, produces the part; consequently, it is impossible to attempt to explain the whole without explaining the part—without explaining, at least, the part as a result of the whole. The supreme product of collective activity is that ensemble of intellectual and moral goods that we call civilization; it is for this reason that Auguste Comte referred to sociology as the science of civilization. However, it is civilization that has made man what he is; it is what distinguishes him from the animal: man is man only because he is civilized. To look for the causes and conditions upon which civilization depends is, therefore, to seek out also the causes and conditions of what is most specifically human in man. And so sociology, which draws on psychology and could not do without it, brings to it, in a just return, a contribution that equals and surpasses in importance the services that it receives from it. It is only by historical analysis that we can discover what makes up man, since it is only in the course of history that he is formed. . . .

The peculiarity referred to is the constitutional duality of human nature. In every age, man has been intensely aware of this duality. He has, in fact, everywhere conceived of himself as being formed of two radically heterogeneous beings: the body and the soul. Even when the soul is represented in a material form, its substance is not thought of as being of the same nature as the body. It is said that it is more ethereal, more subtle, more plastic, that it does not affect the senses as do the other objects to which they react, that it is not subject to the same laws as these objects, and so on. And not only are these two beings substantially different, they are in a large measure independent of each other, and are often even in conflict. For centuries it was believed that after this life the soul could escape from the body and lead an autonomous existence far from it. This independence was made manifest at the time of death when the body dissolved and disappeared and the soul survived and continued to follow, under new conditions and for varying lengths of time, the path of its own destiny. It can even be said that although the body and the soul are closely associated, they do not belong to the same world. The body is an integral part of the material universe, as it is made known to us by sensory experience; the abode of the soul is elsewhere, and the soul tends ceaselessly to return to it. This abode is the world of the sacred. Therefore, the soul is invested with a dignity that has always been denied the body, which is considered essentially profane, and it inspires those feelings that are everywhere reserved for that which is divine. It is made of the same substance as are the sacred beings: it differs from them only in degree.

A belief that is as universal and permanent as this cannot be purely illusory. There must be something in man that gives rise to this feeling that his nature is dual, a feeling that men in all known civilizations have experienced. Psychological analysis has, in fact, confirmed the existence of this duality: it finds it at the very heart of our inner life. . . .

Because they are held in common, concepts are the supreme instrument of all intellectual exchange. By means of them minds communicate. Doubtless when one thinks through the concepts that he receives from the community, he individualizes them and marks them with his personal imprint, but there is nothing personal that is not susceptible to this type of individualization.

These two aspects of our psychic life are, therefore, opposed to each other as are the personal and the impersonal. There is in us a being that represents everything in relation to itself and from its own point of view; in everything that it does, this being has no other object but itself. There is another being in us, however, which knows things *sub specie aeternitatis,* as if it were participating in some thought other than its own, and which, in its acts, tends to accomplish ends that surpass its own. The old formula *homo duplex* is therefore verified by the facts. Far from being simple, our inner life has something that is like a double center of gravity. On the one hand is our individuality—and, more particularly, our body in which it is based; on the other is everything in us that expresses something other than ourselves.

Not only are these two groups of states of consciousness different in their origins and their properties, but there is a true antagonism between them. They mutually contradict and deny each other. We cannot pursue moral ends without causing a split within ourselves, without offending the instincts and the penchants that are the most deeply rooted in our bodies. There is no moral act that does not imply a sacrifice, for, as Kant has shown, the law of duty cannot be obeyed without humiliating our individual, or, as he calls it, our "empirical" sensitivity. We can accept this sacrifice without resistance and even with enthusiasm, but even when it is accomplished in a surge of joy, the sacrifice is no less real. The pain that the ascetic seeks is pain nonetheless, and this antinomy is so deep and so radical that it can never be completely resolved. How can we belong entirely to ourselves, and entirely to others at one and the same time? . . .

It is this disagreement, this perpetual division against ourselves, that produces both our grandeur and our misery; our misery because we are thus condemned to live in suffering; and our grandeur because it is this division that distinguishes us from all other beings. The animal proceeds to his pleasure in a single and exclusive movement; man alone is normally obliged to make a place for suffering in his life.

Thus the traditional antithesis of the body and soul is not a vain mythological concept that is without foundation in reality. It is true that we are double, that we are the realization of an antinomy. In connection with this truth, however, a question arises that philosophy and even positive psychology cannot avoid: Where do this duality and this antinomy come from? How is it that each of us is, to quote another of Pascal's phrases, a "monster of contradictions" that can never completely satisfy itself? And, certainly, if this odd condition is one of the distinctive traits of humanity, the science of man must try to account for it.

GUSTAVE LE BON

1841–1931

Gustave Le Bon was born on May 7, 1841 in Nogent-le-Rotrou, France and died 90 years later at Marnes-la-Coquette. He received a medical degree in 1866 from the University of Paris, but never practiced formally. Instead he followed a typical 19th century pattern for intellectuals, traveling in Asia, Europe, and North Africa, then writing books recounting his experiences, mixed with anthropological and archaeological findings. Exhausting this vein, he shifted to early social psychology, considering it a "science" more than a branch of philosophy as had been the case earlier. This new interest explains the scientistic title of his next book, *The Psychological Laws of the Evolution of Peoples* (1894), mercifully translated as *The Psychology of Peoples*. Just as Comte and others had pursued "social physics" and the "laws" of behavior which were to illuminate societal change in precise fashion, Le Bon likewise harnessed his intellectual commitment to the belief that predictable patterns of individual behavior were discoverable. Also following Comte and Saint-Simon, he argued that societal development needed to be guided by a scientific elite, since most people's behavior was driven by thoughtless responses to their emotions rather than to rational faculties. He also followed precedent by invoking "national character" and matters of race to explain evolutionary changes in various cultures, probably recalling his days as a world traveler.

The work, however, for which he is widely remembered among experts in collective behavior and social psychology he entitled *The Psychology of the Crowd* (1895), translated as *The Crowd* (about which Benito Mussolini wrote that it was "one of the books that interested me most"). It is this work for which he is remembered today, especially because of an edition from 1960 to which Robert K. Merton wrote a laudatory introduction. There he recalls that in 1954, the dean of American psychology, Gordon Allport, referred to *The Crowd* as "perhaps the most influential book ever written in social psychology," an astonishing verdict about a work which Merton said "it might have been fairly described as a vogue book." Given that *The Lonely Crowd* had become an enormous best seller in the early 50s, and that "mass culture" was just beginning to be studied carefully, it was no wonder that Le Bon's ideas once again found an audience. He believed that once people submerse themselves in a mob or crowd, their behavior and "thought" becomes enslaved to the forces of this entity, much larger and more powerful than they. Le Bon pointed out the well-known fact that an individual's intelligence means nothing in a crowd, and that the "crowd's sentiment" replaces any given person's judgment. This is what makes collective action so appealing and so dangerous, as we now know too well.

THE CROWD, 1895

The Mind of Crowds

In its ordinary sense the word "crowd" means a gathering of individuals of whatever nationality, profession, or sex, and whatever be the chances that have brought them together. From the psychological point of view the expression "crowd" assumes quite a different signification. Under certain given circumstances, and only under those circumstances, an agglomeration of men presents new characteristics very different from those of the individuals composing it. The sentiments and ideas of all the persons in the gathering take one and the same direction, and their conscious personality vanishes. A collective mind is formed, doubtless transitory, but presenting very clearly defined characteristics. The gathering has thus become what, in the absence of a better expression, I will call an organised crowd, or, if the term is considered preferable, a psychological crowd. It forms a single being, and is subjected to the *law of the mental unity of crowds.*

It is evident that it is not by the mere fact of a number of individuals finding themselves accidentally side by side that they acquire the character of an organised crowd. A thousand individuals accidentally gathered in a public place without any determined object in no way constitute a crowd from the psychological point of view. To acquire the special characteristics of such a crowd, the influence is necessary of certain predisposing causes, of which we shall have to determine the nature.

The disappearance of conscious personality and the turning of feelings and thoughts in a different direction, which are the primary characteristics of a crowd about to become organised, do not always involve the simultaneous presence of a number of individuals on one spot. Thousands of isolated individuals may acquire at certain moments, and under the influence of certain violent emotions—such, for example, as a great national event—the characteristics of a psychological crowd. It will be sufficient in that case that a mere

chance should bring them together for their acts to at once assume the characteristics peculiar to the acts of a crowd. At certain moments half a dozen men might constitute a psychological crowd, which may not happen in the case of hundreds of men gathered together by accident. On the other hand, an entire nation, though there may be no visible agglomeration, may become a crowd under the action of certain influences.

A psychological crowd once constituted, it acquires certain provisional but determinable general characteristics. To these general characteristics there are adjoined particular characteristics which vary according to the elements of which the crowd is composed, and may modify its mental constitution. Psychological crowds, then, are susceptible of classification; and when we come to occupy ourselves with this matter, we shall see that a heterogeneous crowd—that is, a crowd composed of dissimilar elements—presents certain characteristics in common with homogeneous crowds—that is, with crowds composed of elements more or less akin (sects, castes, and classes)—and side by side with these common characteristics particularities which permit of the two kinds of crowds being differentiated.

But before occupying ourselves with the different categories of crowds, we must first of all examine the characteristics common to them all. We shall set to work like the naturalist, who begins by describing the general characteristics common to all the members of a family, before concerning himself with the particular characteristics which allow the differentiation of the genera and species that the family includes.

It is not easy to describe the mind of crowds with exactness, because its organisation varies not only according to race and composition, but also according to the nature and intensity of the exciting causes to which crowds are subjected. The same difficulty, however, presents itself in the psychological study of an individual. It is only in novels that individuals are found to traverse their whole life with an unvarying character. It is only the uniformity of the environment that creates the apparent uniformity of characters. I have shown elsewhere that all mental constitutions contain possibilities of character which may be manifested in consequence of a sudden change of environment. This explains how it was that among the most savage members of the French Convention were to be found inoffensive citizens who, under ordinary circumstances, would have been peaceable notaries or virtuous magistrates. The storm past, they resumed their normal character of quiet, law-abiding citizens. Napoleon found amongst them his most docile servants.

It being impossible to study here all the successive degrees of organisation of crowds, we shall concern ourselves more especially with such crowds as have attained to the phase of complete organisation. In this way we shall see what crowds may become, but not what they invariably are. It is only in this advanced phase of organisation that certain new and special characteristics are superimposed on the unvarying and dominant character of the race; then takes place that turning already alluded to of all the feelings and thoughts of the collectivity in an identical direction. It is only under such circumstances too, that what I have called above the *psychological law of the mental unity of crowds* comes into play.

Among the psychological characteristics of crowds there are some that they may present in common with isolated individuals, and others, on the contrary, which are absolutely peculiar to them and are only to be met with in collectivities. It is these special characteristics that we shall study, first of all, in order to show their importance.

The most striking peculiarity presented by a psychological crowd is the following: Whoever be the individuals that compose it, however like or unlike be their mode of life, their occupations, their character, or their intelligence, the fact that they have been transformed into a crowd puts them in possession of a sort of collective mind which makes them feel, think, and act in a manner quite different from that in which each individual of them would feel, think, and act were he in a state of isolation. There are certain ideas and feelings which do not come into being, or do not transform themselves into acts except in the case of individuals forming a crowd. The psychological crowd is a provisional being formed of heterogeneous elements, which for a moment are combined, exactly as the cells which constitute a living body form by their reunion a new being which displays characteristics very different from those possessed by each of the cells singly.

Contrary to an opinion which one is astonished to find coming from the pen of so acute a philosopher as Herbert Spencer, in the aggregate which constitutes a crowd there is in no sort a summing-up of or an average struck between its elements. What really takes place is a combination followed by the creation of new characteristics, just as in chemistry certain elements, when brought into contact—bases and acids, for example—combine to form a new body possessing properties quite different from those of the bodies that have served to form it.

It is easy to prove how much the individual forming part of a crowd differs from the isolated individual, but it is less easy to discover the causes of this difference.

To obtain at any rate a glimpse of them it is necessary in the first place to call to mind the truth established by modern psychology, that unconscious phenomena play an altogether preponderating part not only in organic life, but also in the operations of the intelligence. The conscious life of the mind is of small importance in comparison with its unconscious life. The most subtle analyst, the most acute observer, is scarcely successful in discovering more than a very small number of the unconscious motives that determine his conduct. Our conscious acts are the outcome of an unconscious substratum created in the mind in the main by hereditary influences. This substratum consists of the innumerable common characteristics handed down from generation to generation, which constitute the genius of a race. Behind the avowed causes of our acts there undoubtedly lie secret causes that we do not avow, but behind these secret causes there are many others more secret still which we ourselves ignore. The greater part of our daily actions are the result of hidden motives which escape our observation.

It is more especially with respect to those unconscious elements which constitute the genius of a race that all the individuals belonging to it resemble each other, while it is principally in respect to the conscious elements of their character—the fruit of education, and yet more of exceptional hereditary conditions—that they differ from each other. Men the most unlike in the matter of their intelligence possess instincts, passions, and feelings that are very similar. In the case of everything that belongs to the realm of sentiment—religion, politics, morality, the affections and antipathies, etc.—the most eminent men seldom surpass the standard of the most ordinary individuals. From the intellectual point of view an abyss may exist between a great mathematician and his bootmaker, but from the point of view of character the difference is most often slight or non-existent.

It is precisely these general qualities of character, governed by forces of which we are unconscious, and possessed by the majority of the normal individuals of a race in much the same degree—it is precisely these qualities, I say, that in crowds become common property. In the collective mind the intellectual aptitudes of the individuals, and in consequence their individuality, are weakened. The heterogeneous is swamped by the homogeneous, and the unconscious qualities obtain the upper hand.

GAETANO MOSCA

1858–1941

Gaetano Mosca was born on April 1, 1858 in Palermo, Sicily, he married Maria Guiseppa Salemi on February 11, 1888, and he died 83 years later on November 8, 1941 in Rome. Biographical information is scarce except for a short statement he incorporated into a preface to an early work in 1884, his *Teorica*. He came from a respectable Piedmontese family which had migrated south. He took at law degree at the University of Palermo in 1881 at 23, just four years after beginning university studies. His published thesis, "The Factors of Nationality," presaged the style of thinking that would characterize all his subsequent scholarship: refusal to accept ideologies at face value, political and historical realism, and the hope of emulating Machiavelli's skeptical mode of analysis. He was particularly put off by the unsavory connection that had suffused the nineteenth century between nationalism and Romanticism, a semi-mystical (and necessarily mystifying) union which he believed obscured the actual operation of governments. His experience as a political journalist, begun when he was 21, surely abetted his impatience with fuzzy or wishful thinking when it came to understanding the appropriation and dispensation of power in European societies. After his Sicilian law studies, he went to Rome and studied there with several leading lights in constitutional law, electoral systems, economic and financial issues, while keeping abreast of political journalism (a field of influence which many Italian intellectuals considered part of their natural terrain).

On the strength of his important *Teorica* (*Theory of Governments and Parliamentary Government*, 1884), wherein he offered the first modern interpretation of political classes, he was asked to teach constitutional law at his alma mater at 26. But following his marriage two years later, he left for Rome permanently, where he not only taught but also was editor of government proceedings, a rich source of data for his masterpiece. He meanwhile also became intimate friends with a Prime Minister, which caused him to apportion more of his time to practical rather than scholarly matters. In 1896 he published his most important work, *Elementi di scienza politica* (oddly reentitled *The Ruling Class*), and by means of it won a professorship at Turin. It is well known that the fascist government creatively misinterpreted Mosca's teachings in this book in order to further its own cause, but had they properly interpreted his work they would have found that he was an enemy of the far right. Mosca was unusual as social theorists go in that he served in the Italian parliament while teaching, even serving as Under-Secretary of State. In Turin he made many intellectual friends, none more important than with Roberto Michels, whose book, *Political Parties* (1911), is a companion-piece to Mosca's. The message of *The Ruling Class* is that elites perpetuate themselves, clothe themselves in deceptive ideological trappings, but in the end are always most interested in their own survival and control of power, no matter what their professed aims. He condemned fascism, democracy, and monarchy alike, believing that the best form of government would combine an aristocratic elite with the constant renewal of its ranks from other classes, based on merit.

THE RULING CLASS, 1896

Rule of the Best

. . . Beginning with Morelly, Mably and Babeuf, and coming down to Louis Blanc, Proudhon and Lassalle, most writers who have tried to sketch a complete plan for human regeneration have included in their programs, now a partial and gradual, now a complete and immediate, inauguration of communism and abolition of private property. These results were regarded, of course, as desirable results, which were to be achieved by the majority will because they were desirable. Following, roughly, some hints of Pierre Leroux, Marx simplifies all that. He dispenses with the individual will and has the desired results achieved by the fatal course of history. Without any doubt at all his method has its advantages. If a reform is inevitable, there is not much that one can do about it. It cannot be criticized and demolished, the way one can criticize and demolish a fundamental reform that rests upon the authority, or the desire, of a mere individual. Not only that. Among all the arguments in favor of a doctrine, the most convincing will always be the one that represents its triumph as inevitable in a more or less immediate future.

4. Another notion that has troubled the minds of people who have pondered political problems since the day when Plato wrote his dialogues is that "the best people" ought to be the ones to govern a country. The consequence of that aspiration has been, and perhaps still is, that good souls go looking for a political system that will make the concept a reality, or at least point the way to doing so. During the last decades of the eighteenth century and the first half of the nineteenth and, indeed, for a decade or two longer, that yearning has been intensified because it has found nourishment in the optimistic conception of human nature to which we have so often alluded. That opinion made it easy to imagine that if one could change institutions all the less noble instincts that ravage our poor humanity would automatically be suppressed or become atrophied.

In order to determine just how much truth and error there may be in that outlook, we ought first to decide just what sort of people deserve to be called "the best."

Evidently, in ordinary language, the word "best," as the superlative of the adjective "good," should serve to designate persons who are distinguished from the average of men by exceptional "goodness." The "best" on that basis would be the most altruistic people, those who are most inclined to sacrifice themselves for others rather than to sacrifice others to themselves, those who in life give much and receive little, those who are—to use a phrase of Dora Melegari—*faiseurs de joie* rather than *faiseurs de peines*. They would be people in whom the instinct to surmount or remove any obstacle to the satisfaction of their passions or interests is better restrained and controlled than it is in the average run of men.

But surely it must have become apparent by this day and age that "goodness," taken in such a literal sense, is a quality that is of great service to others but of very little service, as a rule, to those who possess it. At best, it does fairly little harm to people who are born to a social position, or who by chance achieve a social position, that is so high as to cure all temptation in any one who might be inclined to take advantage of them. But even in such a case, the individual to whom the adjective "good" might legitimately be applied must be able to renounce the prospect of rising as high in the social scale as he might be entitled to rise in view of his other qualities. For to rise in the social scale, even in calm and normal times, the prime requisite, beyond any question, is a capacity for hard work; but the requisite next in importance is ambition, a firm resolve to get on in the world, to outstrip one's fellows. Now those traits hardly go with extreme sensitiveness or, to be quite frank, with "goodness" either. For "goodness" cannot remain indifferent to the hurts of those who must be thrust behind if one is to step ahead of them; and when goodness is deep and sincere, one is loath to appraise the merits, rights, and feelings of others at an infinitely less value than one's own.

It may seem strange at first glance that, in general, people should insist that their rulers have the loftiest and most delicate moral qualities and

From *The Ruling Class*, by Gaetano Mosca, Hannah D. Kahn, Trans., Arthur Liningston, Ed. Published by McGraw-Hill Book Company. Copyright 1939.

think much of the public interest and little of their own, but that when they themselves are in question, and especially when they are trying to get ahead and reach the highest positions, they are at no pains whatever to observe the precepts which they insist should be the unfailing guides of their superiors. As a matter of fact, all that we can justly ask of our superiors is that they should not fall below the average moral level of the society they govern, that they should harmonize their interests *to a certain extent* with the public interest and that they should not do anything that is too base, too cheap, too repulsive—anything, in short, that would disqualify the man who does it in the environment in which he lives.

But the expression "best," when applied to political life, may also mean, and indeed ordinarily does mean, that the "best" man is the man who possesses the requisites that make him best fitted to govern his fellow men. Understood in that sense, the adjective may always be applied to ruling classes in normal times, because the fact that they are ruling classes shows that, at the given time, in the given country, they contain the individuals who are best fitted to govern—and such fitness by no means implies that they are the "best" individuals intellectually, much less the "best" individuals morally. For if one is to govern men, more useful than a sense of justice—and much more useful than altruism, or even than extent of knowledge or broadness of view—are perspicacity, a ready intuition of individual and mass psychology, strength of will and, especially, confidence in oneself. With good reason did Machiavelli put into the mouth of Cosimo de' Medici the much quoted remark, that states are not ruled with prayer-books.

In our day the distinction between the statesman and the politician is beginning to make its way into the plain man's thinking. The statesman is a man who, by the breadth of his knowledge and the depth of his insight, acquires a clear and accurate awareness of the needs of the society in which he lives, and who knows how to find the best means for leading that society with the least possible shock and suffering to the goal which it should, or at least can, attain. Statesmen in that sense were Cavour and Bismarck. A statesman was Stolypin, the Russian minister of 1906, who saw that in Russia, what with a growth in popula-

tion and a necessary intensification of agriculture, a system of collective property without division among the peasants could not last, and who therefore put forward measures which would have created a class of private peasant landowners and a true rural bourgeoisie in Russia in about half a century. It was not Stolypin's fault if the measures that he promoted did not have time to show their full effects. He died a premature death in 1911, murdered by fanatical idiots.

The politician, on the other hand, is a man who has the qualifications that are required for reaching the highest posts in the governmental system and knows how to stay there. It is a great good fortune for a people when it can find leaders who combine the eminent and rare qualities of the statesman with the secondary qualities of the politician; and it is no mean stroke of luck for a nation when its politicians have at their elbows statesmen by whose views they can profit. . . .

As we have already suggested, therefore, we can afford to be satisfied if the politicians who are in power do not fall below the average for the ruling class in their brains and in their morals. When the intellectual and moral level of the ruling class is high enough for its members to understand and appreciate the ideas of thinkers who study political problems intensively, it is not necessary for the latter to attain power in order to have their programs carried out. The intellectual pressure that the ruling class as a whole exerts—what is commonly called "public opinion"—will force the politicians to suit their policies more or less to the views of those who represent the best that the political intelligence of a people can produce. . . .

5. The fact that, as a rule, those who occupy high office are almost never the "best" in an absolute sense, but rather individuals who possess the qualities that are best suited to directing and dominating men, shows how hard, and indeed how impossible, it is under ordinary circumstances to apply absolute justice, as man is able to conceive of that ideal, to a political system. But to achieve absolute justice has been the dream of noble spirits and lofty minds from Plato on. We might even say that it has been a convenient pretext for many ambitious and more or less vulgar men to use in trying to replace those who are at the top.

Absolute justice in a political system can only mean that the success of every individual, the rank he occupies in the political scale, should correspond exactly with the actual utility of the service which he has rendered, or is rendering, to society. At bottom, it is a question of applying a concept which was definitely formulated for the first time by Saint-Simon and which furnished the famous formula in which the Saint-Simonians summed up their program: "To each according to his ability, to each ability according to its results."

CHARLOTTE ANNA PERKINS GILMAN

1860–1935

Charlotte Anna Perkins Stetson Gilman was born in Hartford, Connecticut on July 3, 1860, the daughter of Frederick Beecher Perkins, the black sheep of a famous family, sometime head librarian in both Boston and San Francisco, a member of the noted Beecher clan. But he abandoned his family when Charlotte was an infant, so it was her mother, Mary A. Fitch Westcott, who raised her and her brother, Thomas, moving from place to place, always short of funds and never receiving aid from the famous father. Charlotte tried to establish contact with him as she aged, but was rebuffed. She married Charles W. Stetson in 1884, had one daughter in 1885, was divorced in 1894, then married George Houghton Gilman in 1900. Her most passionate letters, however, are not addressed to men, but to women, and in these she wished she could have been born male. She died by suicide owing to the misery of cancer in Pasadena, California on August 17, 1935, having reached 75 years. Always the poor relation with a notable name, Perkins studied at the Rhode Island School of Design from 1881–83, moved to California with her husband and became clinically depressed after her daughter's birth, living with her mother in California from 1888–1891. In January, 1892, she published "The Yellow Wallpaper," one of the best descriptions of the onset of mental imbalance ever composed by man or woman. It terrifyingly chronicled her own debilitating ailment during the preceding half-dozen years (as she notes in an appendix to the story, published later), and readers of the time found it extremely disturbing. Meanwhile, in trying to construct her own version of life, she made money by sewing, teaching, painting, ran a boardinghouse, and, like her mother, moved a great deal. In 1892 she published "The Right to Earn Money," which, like much of her work, represents her own desires and needs as an independent woman, now separated from her husband.

Of her 2000 published pieces made up of journalism, poetry, satires, and so on, it was *Women and Economics: A Study of the Economic Relation Between Men and Women as a Factor in Social Evolution* (1898), that landed her in the small pantheon of female social theorists. Other pertinent works—*Concerning Children* (1900), *The Home* (1903), *Human Work* (1904), *The Man-Made World, or Our Androcentric Culture* (1911), and *His Religion and Hers* (1923)—won her a reputation at the time as a significant social analyst, but her work on women's economic dependency on men has been reprinted ever since. Although much of her argument is taken from what was common to many theorists and reformers of her time, her particular focus on the basic inequality of socio-economic standing between men and women has made the book a classic in its field.

WOMEN AND ECONOMICS, 1898

The Eternal Feminine

. . . We, for economic uses, have artificially developed the cow's capacity for producing milk. She has become a walking milk-machine, bred and tended to that express end, her value measured in quarts. The secretion of milk is a maternal function,—a sex-function. The cow is over-sexed. Turn her loose in natural conditions, and, if she survive the change, she would revert in a very few generations to the plain cow, with her energies used in the general activities of her race, and not all running to milk.

Physically, woman belongs to a tall, vigorous, beautiful animal species, capable of great and varied exertion. In every race and time when she has opportunity for racial activity, she develops accordingly, and is no less a woman for being a healthy human creature. In every race and time where she is denied this opportunity,—and few, indeed, have been her years of freedom,—she has developed in the lines of action to which she was confined; and those were always lines of sex-activity. In consequence the body of woman, speaking in the largest generalization, manifests sex-distinction predominantly.

Woman's femininity—and "the eternal feminine" means simply the eternal sexual—is more apparent in proportion to her humanity than the femininity of other animals in proportion to their caninity or felinity or equinity. "A feminine hand" or "a feminine foot" is distinguishable anywhere. We do not hear of "a feminine paw" or "a feminine hoof." A hand is an organ of prehension, a foot an organ of locomotion: they are not secondary sexual characteristics. The comparative smallness and feebleness of woman is a sex-distinction. We have carried it to such an excess that women are commonly known as "the weaker sex." There is no such glaring difference between male and female in other advanced species. In the long migrations of birds, in the ceaseless motion of the grazing herds that used to swing up and down over the continent each year, in the wild, steep journeys of the breeding salmon, nothing is heard of the weaker sex. And among the higher carnivora, where longer maintenance of the young brings their condition nearer ours, the hunter dreads the attack of the female more than that of the male. The disproportionate weakness is an excessive sex-distinction. Its injurious effect may be broadly shown in the Oriental nations, where the female in curtained harems is confined most exclusively to sex-functions and denied most fully the exercise of race-functions. In such peoples the weakness, the tendency to small bones and adipose tissue of the over-sexed female, is transmitted to the male, with a retarding effect on the development of the race. Conversely, in early Germanic tribes the comparatively free and humanly developed women—tall, strong, and brave—transmitted to their sons a greater proportion of human power and much less of morbid sex-tendency.

The degree of feebleness and clumsiness common to women, the comparative inability to stand, walk, run, jump, climb, and perform other race-functions common to both sexes, is an excessive sex-distinction; and the ensuing transmission of this relative feebleness to their children, boys and girls alike, retards human development. Strong, free, active women, the sturdy, field-working peasant, the burden-bearing savage, are no less good mothers for their human strength. But our civilized "feminine delicacy," which appears somewhat less delicate when recognized as an expression of sexuality in excess,—makes us no better mothers, but worse. The relative weakness of women is a sex-distinction. It is apparent in her to a degree that injures motherhood, that injures wifehood, that injures the individual. The sex-usefulness and the human usefulness of women, their general duty to their kind, are greatly injured by this degree of distinction. In every way the over-sexed condition of the human female reacts unfavorably upon herself, her husband, her children, and the race.

In its psychic manifestation this intense sex-distinction is equally apparent. The primal instinct of sex-attraction has developed under social forces into a conscious passion of enormous power, a deep and lifelong devotion, overwhelming in its force. This is excessive in both sexes, but more so in women than in men,—not so commonly in its simple physical form, but in the unreasoning intensity of emotion that refuses all guidance, and drives those possessed by it to risk every other good for this one end. It is not at first sight easy, and it may seem an irreverent and thankless task, to discriminate here between what is good in the "master passion" and what is evil, and especially to claim for one sex more of this feeling than for the other; but such discrimination can be made.

It is good for the individual and for the race to have developed such a degree of passionate and permanent love as shall best promote the happiness of individuals and the reproduction of species. It is not good for the race or for the individual that this feeling should have become so intense as to override all other human faculties, to make a mock of the accumulated wisdom of the ages, the stored power of the will; to drive the individual—against his own plain conviction—into a union sure to result in evil, or to hold the individual helpless in such an evil union, when made.

Women as Persons

From the time our children are born, we use every means known to accentuate sex-distinction in both boy and girl; and the reason that the boy is not so hopelessly marked by it as the girl is that he has the whole field of human expression open to him besides. In our steady insistence on proclaiming sex-distinction we have grown to consider most human attributes as masculine attributes, for the simple reason that they were allowed to men and forbidden to women.

A clear and definite understanding of the difference between race-attributes and sex-attributes should be established. Life consists of action. The action of a living thing is along two main lines,—self-preservation and race-preservation. The processes that keep the individual alive, from the involuntary action of his internal organs to the voluntary action of his external organs,—every act, from breathing to hunting his food, which contributes to the maintenance of the individual life,—these are the processes of self-preservation. Whatever activities tend to keep the race alive, to reproduce the individual, from the involuntary action of the internal organs to the voluntary action of the external organs; every act from the development of germ-cells to the taking care of children, which contributes to the maintenance of the racial life,—these are the processes of race-preservation. In race-preservation, male and female have distinctive organs, distinctive functions, distinctive lines of action. In self-preservation, male and female have the same organs, the same functions, the same lines of action. In the human species our processes of race-preservation have reached a certain degree of elaboration; but our processes of self-preservation have gone farther, much farther.

Masculine and Feminine

Little by little, very slowly, and with most unjust and cruel opposition, at cost of all life holds most dear, it is being gradually established by many martyrdoms that human work is woman's as well as man's. Harriet Martineau must conceal her writing under her sewing when callers came, because "to sew" was a feminine verb, and "to write" a masculine one. Mary Somerville[3] must struggle to hide her work from even relatives, because mathematics was a "masculine" pursuit. Sex has been made to dominate the whole human world,—all the main avenues of life marked "male," and the female left to be a female, and nothing else.

MARCEL MAUSS

1872–1950

Marcel Mauss, nephew of Émile Durkheim, was born in Durkheim's hometown, Épinal, in the eastern border region of France on May 10, 1872, married Marthe-Rose Dupret in 1934, did not reproduce, and at 77 died February 10, 1950 in Paris. He graduated from the Lycée in Épinal in 1890, then studied where his uncle taught, the University of Bordeaux, pursuing philosophy, psychology, law, and sociology, graduating in 1892. Besides helping Durkheim with *Suicide,* Mauss began in the 1890s a lifelong study of linguistics, Indology, Sanskrit, Hebrew, and the history of religions at the École Pratique des Hautes Études, and from 1895 through 1897 at the Sorbonne. He won the right to teach in 1895 with a dissertation on *The Gift,* but it was not ready for publication until 1909. During the 1890s he was also very active politically in a number of socialist parties, and took part in defending Alfred Dreyfus against the fabricated government case against him. In addition to scholarly travels, he also co-edited the *L'Année sociologique,* which his uncle had begun, taking it over entirely when his uncle died in 1917. Like so many academics of the time, he served in the French army during WWI from 1914–1919, but unlike so many others, he survived. Between 1925 and 1929 he co-founded the Ethnological Institute at the University of Paris along with Lucien Lévy-Bruhl and Paul Rivet. He served as Professor of Sociology at the Collége de France from 1931–1940, a position he lost on October 12, 1940, but was reinstated on November 21, 1944. Although he did not carry out the fieldwork which has for decades been the *rite de passage* for all anthropologists, his studies of sacrifice, magic, gift relations, forms of exchange in pre-industrial societies, and related themes gave his work a functionalist coherence which continues to make it fundamental to anthropological reasoning.

Mauss's work has always been appreciated by anthropologists, and influenced Lévi-Strauss, Radcliffe-Brown, Evans-Pritchard, and others. But only during the last 15 years or so has it gained more widespread attention among other social scientists. The selections reprinted below hint at reasons for this newfound attention. In his work on sacrifice, Mauss contends that every sacrificial act must be considered as part of a multilayered set of social rituals, the goals of which are always the same: to aid in the integration of the society and to ease difficult conditions or events for the participants. Very much in his uncle's vein, Mauss was always alert to modes of premodern interaction which highlight group continuity and cohesiveness over individual celebration of ego. "Community" becomes the pivotal term, and not "the individual" as such. Also, in his discussion of magic he once again uses a Durkheimian gambit to prove its "unmagical," mundane nature.

SACRIFICE: ITS NATURE AND FUNCTION, 1899

Conclusion

. . . Every sacrifice takes place in certain given circumstances and with a view to certain determined ends. From the diversity of the ends which may be pursued in this way arise varying procedures, of which we have given a few examples. Now there is no religion in which these procedures do not coexist in greater or lesser number; all the sacrificial rituals we know of display a great complexity. Moreover, there is no special rite that is not complex in itself, for either it pursues several ends at the same time, or, to attain one end, it sets in motion several forces. We have seen that sacrifices of desacralization and even expiatory sacrifices proper become entangled with communion sacrifices. But many other examples of complexity might be given. The Amazulu, to bring on rain, assemble a herd of black bullocks, kill one and eat it in silence, and then burn its bones outside the village; which constitutes three different themes in one operation. . . .

But if sacrifice is so complex, whence comes its unity? It is because, fundamentally, beneath the diverse forms it takes, it always consists in one same procedure, which maybe used for the most widely differing purposes. *This procedure consists in establishing a means of communication between the sacred and the profane worlds through the mediation of a victim, that is, of a thing that in the course of the ceremony is destroyed.* Now, contrary to what Smith believed, the victim does not necessarily come to the sacrifice with a religious nature already perfected and clearly defined: it is the sacrifice itself that confers this upon it. Sacrifice can therefore impart to the victim most varied powers and thereby make it suitable for fulfilling the most varied functions, either by different rites or during the same rite. The victim can also pass on a sacred character of the religious world to the profane world, or vice versa. It remains indifferent to the direction of the current that passes through it. At the same time the spirit that has been released from the victim can be entrusted with the task of bearing a prayer to the heavenly powers, it can be used to foretell the future, to redeem oneself from the wrath of the gods by making over one's portion of the victim to them, and, lastly, enjoying the sacred flesh that remains. On the other hand, once the victim has been set apart, it has a certain autonomy, no matter what may be done. It is a focus of energy from which are released effects that surpass the narrow purpose that the sacrifier has assigned to the rite. An animal is sacrificed to redeem a *dikshita;* an immediate consequence is that the freed spirit departs to nourish the eternal life of the species. Thus sacrifice naturally exceeds the narrow aims that the most elementary theologies assign to it. This is because it is not made up solely of a series of individual actions. The rite sets in motion the whole complex of sacred things to which it is addressed. From the very beginning of this study sacrifice has appeared as a particular ramification of the system of consecration. . . .

On the one hand, this personal renunciation of their property by individuals or groups nourishes social forces. Not, doubtless, that society has need of the things which are the materials of sacrifice. Here everything occurs in the world of ideas, and it is mental and moral energies that are in question. But the act of abnegation implicit in every sacrifice, by recalling frequently to the consciousness of the individual the presence of collective forces, in fact sustains their ideal existence. These expiations and general purifications, communions and sacralizations of groups, these creations of the spirits of the cities give—or renew periodically for the community, represented by its gods—that character, good, strong, grave, and terrible, which is one of the essential traits of any social entity. Moreover, individuals find their own advantage in this same act. They confer upon each other, upon themselves, and upon those things they hold dear, the whole strength of society. They invest with the authority of society their vows, their oaths, their marriages. They surround, as if with a protective sanctity, the fields they have ploughed and the houses they have built. At the same time they find in sacrifice the means of redressing equilibriums that have been upset: by expiation they redeem themselves from social obloquy, the consequence of error, and re-enter the community; by the apportionments they make of those things whose use society has reserved for itself, they acquire the right to enjoy them. The social norm is thus maintained without danger to themselves, without diminution for the group. Thus the social function of sacrifice is fulfilled, both for individuals and for the community. And as society is made up not only of men, but also of things and events, we perceive how sacrifice can follow and at the same time reproduce the rhythms of human life and of nature; how it has been able to become both periodical by the use of natural phenomena, and occasional, as are the momentary needs of men, and in short to adapt itself to a thousand purposes.

A GENERAL THEORY OF MAGIC, 1902–03

A Definition of Magic

We suggest, provisionally, that magic has been sufficiently distinguished in various societies from other systems of social facts. This being the case we have reason to believe that magic not only forms a distinct class of phenomena but that it is also susceptible to clear definition. We shall have to provide this definition for ourselves, since we cannot be content to accept facts as 'magical' simply because they have been so called by the actors themselves or observers. The points of view of such people are subjective, hence not necessarily scientific. A religion designates the remnants of former cults as 'magical' even when the rites are still being performed in a religious manner; this way of looking at things has even been followed by scholars—a folklorist as distinguished as Skeat considers the old agrarian rites of the Malays as magical. As far as we are concerned, magic should

From *A General Theory of Magic,* by Marcel Mauss, Robert Bain, Trans. Published by Routledge. Copyright © 2001, 1975. Used by permission of Routledge, an imprint of Taylor & Francis Books Ltd.

be used to refer to those things which society as a whole considers magical and not those qualified as such by a single segment of society only. However we are also aware that some societies are not very coherent in their notions of magic and, even if they are, this has only come about gradually. Consequently, we are not very optimistic about suddenly discovering an ideal definition of our subject; this must await the conclusion of our analysis of the relations between magic and religion.

In magic we have officers, actions and representations: we call a person who accomplishes magical actions a *magician,* even if he is not a professional; *magical representations* are those ideas and beliefs which correspond to magical actions; as for these actions, with regard to which we have defined the other elements of magic, we shall call them *magical rites.* At this stage it is important to distinguish between these activities and other social practices with which they might be confused.

In the first place, magic and magical rites, as a whole, are traditional facts. Actions which are never repeated cannot be called magical. If the whole community does not believe in the efficacy of a group of actions, they cannot be magical. The form of the ritual is eminently transmissible and this is sanctioned by public opinion. It follows from this that strictly individual actions, such as the private superstitions of gamblers, cannot be called magical.

The kind of traditional practices which might be confused with magical activities include legal actions, techniques and religious ritual. Magic has been linked with a system of jural obligations, since in many places there are words and gestures which are binding sanctions. It is true that legal actions may often acquire a ritual character and that contracts, oaths and trials by ordeal are to a certain extent sacramental. Nevertheless, the fact remains that although they contain ritual elements they are not magical rites in themselves. If they assume a special kind of efficacy or if they do more than merely establish contractual relations between persons, they cease to be legal actions and do become magical or religious rites. Ritual acts, on the contrary, are essentially thought to be able to produce much more than a contract: rites are eminently effective; they are creative; they *do* things. It is through these qualities that magical ritual is recognizable as such. In some cases even, ritual derives its name from a reference to these effective characteristics: in India the word which best corresponds to our word ritual is *karman*, action; sympathetic magic is the *factum, krtyá*, par excellence. The German word *Zauber* has the same etymological meaning; in other languages the words for magic contain the root *to do*. . . .

Isolation and secrecy are two almost perfect signs of the intimate character of a magical rite. They are always features of a person or persons working in a private capacity; both the act and the actor are shrouded in mystery.

In fact, however, the various characteristics we have so far revealed only reflect the irreligiosity of magical rites. They are anti-religious and it is desired that they be so. In any case, they do not belong to those organized systems which we call cults. Religious practices, on the contrary, even fortuitous and voluntary ones, are always predictable, prescribed and official. They *do* form part of a cult. Gifts presented to gods on the occasion of a vow, or an expiatory sacrifice offered during illness, are regular kinds of homage. Although performed in each case voluntarily, they are really obligatory and inevitable actions. Magical rites, on the other hand, while they may occur regularly (as in the case of agricultural magic) and fulfil a need when they are performed for specific ends (such as a cure), are always considered unauthorized, abnormal and, at the very least, not highly estimable. Medical rites, however useful and licit they may be made to appear, do not involve the same degree of solemnity, nor the same idea of an accomplished duty, as do expiatory sacrifices or vows made to a curative divinity. When somebody has recourse to a medicine man, the owner of a spirit-fetish, a bone-mender or a magician, there is certainly a need, but no moral obligation is involved. . . .

We have thus arrived at a provisionally adequate definition of magical phenomena. A magical rite is *any rite which does not play a part in organized cults*—it is private, secret, mysterious and approaches the limit of a prohibited rite. With this definition, and taking into consideration the other elements of magic which we have mentioned, we have the first hint of its special qualities. It will be noticed that we do not define magic in terms of the structure of its rites, but by the circumstances in which these rites occur, which in turn determine the place they occupy in the totality of social customs.

Conclusion

Magic is, therefore, a social phenomenon. It only remains for us to show what place it holds among the other social phenomena, religion excepted, since we shall return to that later. Its relationships with law and custom, with economy and aesthetics, and also with language, however fascinating they may be, do not concern us here. Between these types of facts and magic we have a mere exchange of influences. Magic has no genuine kinship with anything apart from religion on the one hand and science and technology on the other.

We have said that magic tends to resemble technology, as it becomes more individualistic and specialized in the pursuit of its varied aims. Nevertheless, these two series of facts contain more than an external similarity: there is a functional identity, since, as we pointed out in our definition, both have the same aims. While religion is directed towards more metaphysical ends and is involved in the creation of idealistic images, magic has found a thousand fissures in the mystical world from whence it draws its forces, and is continually leaving it in order to take part in everyday life and play a practical role there. It has a taste for the concrete. Religion, on the other hand, tends to be abstract. Magic works in the same way as do our techniques, crafts, medicine, chemistry, industry, etc. Magic is essentially the art of doing things, and magicians have always taken advantage of their know-how, their dexterity, their manual skill. Magic is the domain of pure production, *ex nihilo*. With words and gestures it does what techniques achieve by labour. Fortunately, the magical art has not always been characterized by gesticulations into thin air. It has dealt with material things, carried out real experiments and even made its own discoveries. . . .

Though we may feel ourselves to be very far removed from magic, we are still very much bound up with it. Our ideas of good and bad luck, of quintessence, which are still familiar to us, are very close to the idea of magic itself. Neither technology, science, nor the directing principles of our reason are quite free from their original taint. We are not being daring, I think, if we suggest that a good part of all those non-positive mystical and poetical elements in our notions of force, causation, effect and substance could be traced back to the old habits of mind in which magic was born and which the human mind is slow to throw off.

THORSTEIN VEBLEN

1857–1929

Thorstein Bunde Veblen, son of recent Norwegian immigrants who produced 12 children (one of whom became a physics professor in Iowa), was born on July 30, 1857 in Manitowoc County, Wisconsin, ten years after his parents' arrival in the U.S. He married the wealthy Ellen Rolfe in 1888, they divorced, and then married Anne Fessenden "Babe" Bradley in 1914, who brought two daughters into the marriage. Veblen died on August 3, 1929 at 72 near Menlo Park, California—a wonderful irony in that his new notion of "conspicuous consumption" and the site of the 1990s Silicon Valley boom a hundred years later illuminate each other handily. Veblen studied at Carleton College, graduating in 1880 after only three years, then went to Johns Hopkins and Yale for graduate studies, taking the doctorate in philosophy at Yale in 1884. Unable to find a professorial job, he returned to his father's farm and read for seven years. Already he had established a penchant for mocking received wisdom and angering authorities by writing brilliant critiques, while speaking English with a strong Norwegian accent. He reentered graduate school to study economics at Cornell in 1891, then joined a flock of the nation's most talented academics by moving to the newly founded University of Chicago in 1893 with a supporting professor. Forced to leave there for failure to conform to rules of marital and academic propriety, he became associate professor at Stanford from 1906 until 1909 when, so the story goes, he was fired by Mrs. Leland Stanford in a telegram sent from Paris after she'd read an article in which Veblen supported the rights of Chinese "coolie" laborers in California. He then went to the University of Missouri as a mere "lecturer" from 1911 until 1917, at times living in what amounted to a shed behind another professor's home, yet producing there some of his best work. He ended his career at the New School in New York (1918–1926), but found it hard to lecture and was supported materially by former students and friends.

The crusty, cynical, brilliant Veblen is surely one of a very small number of bona fide American geniuses in the social sciences who matured during the 19th century. His *Theory of the Leisure Class: An Economic Study of Institutions* (1899) made him a name to reckon with among the literate public, but did nothing to advance his career in economics. He argued that making money in order to spend it lavishly—a pattern of both the 1890s and the 1990s in the U.S.—undercut productivity, and was a perversion of humanity's ability to create new processes and items. He elaborated this insight, along with originating what came to be called "institutional economics," in *The Theory of Business Enterprise* (1904), *The Instinct of Workmanship and the State of the Industrial Arts* (1914), *Imperial Germany and the Industrial Revolution* (1915), and *The Vested Interests and the State of the Industrial Arts* (1919). He also attacked the businessmen who ran America's universities in *The Higher Learning in America* (1918), which has been reprinted a number of times, as have his others. Whenever the political-economic ship of state runs aground, people remember Veblen and read him. Few American economists can claim this distinction.

THE THEORY OF THE LEISURE CLASS, 1899

Conspicuous Consumption

. . . Conspicuous consumption of valuable goods is a means of reputability to the gentleman of leisure. As wealth accumulates on his hands, his own unaided effort will not avail to sufficiently put his opulence in evidence by this method. The aid of friends and competitors is therefore brought in by resorting to the giving of valuable presents and expensive feasts and entertainments. Presents and feasts had probably another origin than that of naive ostentation, but they acquired their utility for this purpose very early, and they have retained that character to the present; so that their utility in this respect has now long been the substantial ground on which these usages rest. Costly entertainments, such as the potlatch or the ball, are peculiarly adapted to serve this end. The competitor with whom the entertainer wishes to institute a comparison is, by this method, made to serve as a means to the end. He consumes vicariously for his host at the same time that he is a witness to the consumption of that excess of good things which his host is unable to dispose of single-handed, and he is also made to witness his host's facility in etiquette.

In the giving of costly entertainments other motives, of a more genial kind, are of course also present. The custom of festive gatherings probably originated in motives of conviviality and religion; these motives are also present in the later development, but they do not continue to be the sole motives. The latter-day leisure-class festivities and entertainments may continue in some slight degree to serve the religious need and in a higher degree the needs of recreation and conviviality, but they also serve an invidious purpose; and they serve it none the less effectually for having a colourable noninvidious ground in these more avowable motives. But the economic effect of these social amenities is not therefore lessened, either in the vicarious consumption of goods or in the exhibition of difficult and costly achievements in etiquette.

As wealth accumulates, the leisure class develops further in function and structure, and there arises a differentiation within the class. There is a more or less elaborate system of rank and grades. This differentiation is furthered by the inheritance of wealth and the consequent inheritance of gentility. With the inheritance of gentility goes the inheritance of obligatory leisure; and gentility of a sufficient potency to entail a life of leisure may be inherited without the complement of wealth required to maintain a dignified leisure. Gentle blood may be transmitted without goods enough to afford a reputably free consumption at one's ease. Hence results a class of impecunious gentlemen of leisure, incidentally referred to already. These half-caste gentlemen of leisure fall into a system of hierarchical gradations. Those who stand near the higher and the highest grades of the wealthy leisure class, in point of birth, or in point of wealth, or both, outrank the remoter-born and the pecuniarily weaker. These lower grades, especially the impecunious, or marginal, gentlemen of leisure, affiliate themselves by a system of dependence or fealty to the great ones; by so doing they gain an increment of repute, or of the means with which to lead a life of leisure, from their patron. They become his courtiers or retainers, servants; and being fed and countenanced by their patron they are indices of his rank and vicarious consumers of his superfluous wealth. Many of these affiliated gentlemen of leisure are at the same time lesser men of substance in their own right; so that some of them are scarcely at all, others only partially, to be rated as vicarious consumers. So many of them, however, as make up the retainers and hangers-on of the patron may be classed as vicarious consumers without qualification. Many of these again, and also many of the other aristocracy of less degree, have in turn attached to their persons a more or less comprehensive group of vicarious consumers in the persons of their wives and children, their servants, retainers, etc.

Throughout this graduated scheme of vicarious leisure and vicarious consumption the rule holds that these offices must be performed in some such manner, or under some such circumstance or insignia, as shall point plainly to the master to whom this leisure or consumption pertains, and to whom therefore the resulting increment of good repute of right inures. The consumption and leisure executed by these persons for their master or patron represents an investment on his part with a view to an increase of good fame. As regards feasts and largesses this is obvious enough, and the imputation of repute to the host or patron here takes place immediately, on the ground of common notoriety. Where leisure and consumption is performed vicariously by henchmen and retainers, imputation of the resulting repute to the patron is effected by their residing near his person so that it may be plain to all men from what source they draw. As the group whose good esteem is to be secured in this way grows larger, more patent means are required to indicate the imputation of merit for the leisure performed, and to this end uniforms, badges, and liveries come into vogue. The wearing of uniforms or liveries implies a considerable degree of dependence, and may even be said to be a mark of servitude, real or ostensible. The wearers of uniforms and liveries may be roughly divided into two classes—the free and the servile, or the noble and the ignoble. The services performed by them are likewise divisible into noble and ignoble. Of course the distinction is not observed with strict consistency in practice; the less debasing of the base services and the less honorific of the noble functions are not infrequently merged in the same person. But the general distinction is not on that account to be overlooked. What may add some perplexity is the fact that this fundamental distinction between noble and ignoble, which rests on the nature of the ostensible service performed, is traversed by a secondary distinction into honorific and humiliating, resting on the rank of the person for whom the service is performed or whose livery is worn. So, those offices which are by right the proper employment of the leisure class are noble; such are government, fighting, hunting, the care of arms and accoutrements, and the like,—in short, those which may be classed as ostensibly predatory employments. On the other hand, those employments which properly fall to the industrious class are ignoble; such as handicraft or other productive labour, menial services, and the like. But a base service performed for a person of very high degree may become a very honorific office; as for instance the office of a Maid of Honour or of a Lady in Waiting to the Queen,

or the King's Master of the Horse or his Keeper of the Hounds. The two offices last named suggest a principle of some general bearing. Whenever, as in these cases, the menial service in question has to do directly with the primary leisure employments of fighting and hunting, it easily acquires a reflected honorific character. In this way great honour may come to attach to an employment which in its own nature belongs to the baser sort.

In the later development of peaceable industry, the usage of employing an idle corps of uniformed men-at-arms gradually lapses. Vicarious consumption by dependents bearing the insignia of their patron or master narrows down to a corps of liveried menials. In a heightened degree, therefore, the livery comes to be a badge of servitude, or rather of servility. Something of a honorific character always attached to the livery of the armed retainer, but this honorific character disappears when the livery becomes the exclusive badge of the menial. The livery becomes obnoxious to nearly all who are required to wear it. We are yet so little removed from a state of effective slavery as still to be fully sensitive to the sting of any imputation of servility. This antipathy asserts itself even in the case of the liveries or uniforms which some corporations prescribe as the distinctive dress of their employees. In this country the aversion even goes the length of discrediting—in a mild and uncertain way—those government employments, military and civil, which require the wearing of a livery or uniform.

With the disappearance of servitude, the number of vicarious consumers attached to any one gentleman tends, on the whole, to decrease. The like is of course true, and perhaps in a still higher degree, of the number of dependents who perform vicarious leisure for him. In a general way, though not wholly nor consistently, these two groups coincide. The dependent who was first delegated for these duties was the wife, or the chief wife; and, as would be expected, in the later development of the institution, when the number of persons by whom these duties are customarily performed gradually narrows, the wife remains the last. In the higher grades of society a large volume of both these kinds of service is required; and here the wife is of course still assisted in the work by a more or less numerous corps of menials. But as we descend the social scale, the point is presently reached where the duties of vicarious leisure and consumption devolve upon the wife alone. In the communities of the Western culture, this point is at present found among the lower middle class.

And here occurs a curious inversion. It is a fact of common observation that in this lower middle class there is no pretence of leisure on the part of the head of the household. Through force of circumstances it has fallen into disuse. But the middle-class wife still carries on the business of vicarious leisure, for the good name of the household and its master. In descending the social scale in any modern industrial community, the primary fact—the conspicuous leisure of the master of the household—disappears at a relatively high point. The head of the middle-class household has been reduced by economic circumstances to turn his hand to gaining a livelihood by occupations which often partake largely of the character of industry, as in the case of the ordinary business man of to-day. But the derivative fact—the vicarious leisure and consumption rendered by the wife, and the auxiliary vicarious performance of leisure by menials—remains in vogue as a conventionality which the demands of reputability will not suffer to be slighted. It is by no means an uncommon spectacle to find a man applying himself to work with the utmost assiduity, in order that his wife may in due form render for him that degree of vicarious leisure which the common sense of the time demands.

The leisure rendered by the wife in such cases is, of course, not a simple manifestation of idleness or indolence. It almost invariably occurs disguised under some form of work or household duties or social amenities, which prove on analysis to serve little or no ulterior end beyond showing that she does not and need not occupy herself with anything that is gainful or that is of substantial use. As has already been noticed under the head of manners, the greater part of the customary round of domestic cares to which the middle-class housewife gives her time and effort is of this character. Not that the results of her attention to household matters, of a decorative and mundificatory character, are not pleasing to the sense of men trained in middle-class proprieties; but the taste to which these effects of household adornment and tidiness appeal is a taste which has been formed under the selective guidance of a canon of propriety that demands just these evidences of wasted effort. The effects are pleasing to us chiefly because we have been taught to find them pleasing. There goes into these domestic duties much solicitude for a proper combination of form and colour, and for other ends that are to be classed as aesthetic in the proper sense of the terra; and it is not denied that effects having some substantial aesthetic value are sometimes attained. Pretty much all that is here insisted on is that, as regards these amenities of life, the housewife's efforts are under the guidance of traditions that have been shaped by the law of conspicuously wasteful expenditure of time and substance. If beauty or comfort is achieved,—and it is a more or less fortuitous circumstance if they are,—they must be achieved by means and methods that commend themselves to the great economic law of wasted effort. The more reputable, "presentable" portion of middle-class household paraphernalia are, on the other hand, items of conspicuous consumption, and on the other hand, apparatus for putting in evidence the vicarious leisure rendered by the housewife.

The requirement of vicarious consumption at the hands of the wife continues in force even at a lower point in the pecuniary scale than the requirement of vicarious leisure. At a point below which little if any pretence of wasted effort, in ceremonial cleanness and the like, is observable, and where there is assuredly no conscious attempt at ostensible leisure, decency still requires the wife to consume some goods conspicuously for the reputability of the household and its head. So that, as the latter-day-outcome of this evolution of an archaic institution, the wife, who was at the outset the drudge and chattel of the man, both in fact and in theory,—the producer of goods for him to consume, has become the ceremonial consumer of goods which he produces. But she still quite unmistakably remains his chattel in theory; for the habitual rendering of vicarious leisure and consumption is the abiding mark of the unfree servant.

VILFREDO PARETO

1848–1923

The son of Raffaele Pareto (a civil engineer, professor, and then government minister) and Marie Metenier, a Frenchwoman, Fritz Wilfred Pareto, later named Vilfredo Frederico Damaso Pareto (from 1882), the Marchese of Parigi, was born on July 15, 1848 (year of Europe's revolutions) in Paris. He married Alessandrina "Dina" Bakounine (Bakunin) in 1889, separated in 1903, began cohabiting with Jeanne Régis in 1906, and married her in 1923 (after moving in order to divorce Bakunin), adopting her daughter, Marguerita Antoinette Régis, as his own. After 75 years, on August 19, 1923, he died in Céligny, Geneva, Switzerland, where he had lived since 1900. His father was an Italian political refugee from the 1830 revolutions, a Republican, and Pareto began life in Paris in a bilingual household, then moved to Genova, Liguria, Italy (1852–59), several years in Casale Monferrato, Piedmont so his father could improve his professional position as a government administrator of mines and industry, then to Turin, and finally to Florence. Meanwhile, Pareto followed his father in taking degrees in math, physics, and engineering, finishing his doctorate in 1870 with a dissertation on the then new applications of differential equations to the question of elasticity and equilibrium in solid bodies. It was this extraordinary proficiency in applied math (relative to everybody else then working in the social sciences) which made it possible for Pareto to contribute mightily to the development of econometrics, to equilibrium and systems theory in sociology, and, by establishing cyclical patterns to rulership, to political science. From 1873 until 1893 he lived in Toscany. In 1892 he wrote 160 articles for newspapers and magazines in an attempt to win a seat in the Italian government, but failed, so took Léon Walras's vacated chair in political-economics at Lausanne in 1893. With his uncle's bequest, he was free of money worries after 1898 and committed himself wholly to research, but this time in history and social sciences, and not in the natural sciences or engineering.

Pareto is a neglected genius of the modern period. Living coterminously with Weber, Durkheim, Simmel, and Freud, he has shared none of their posthumous fame except for a brief period in the 1930s when he was widely lionized, especially among U.S. intellectuals at Harvard. This is probably more a quirk of history than a valid judgment on the quality of his ideas and research. In his autobiography, Mussolini claimed to have attended Pareto's lectures on political-economy at Lausanne (along with hundreds of other students), and a link was forged in the popular mind between fascism and Pareto's theory of "the circulation of elites." The connection is artificial, for Pareto made no secret of his aversion to any form of authoritarian rule, including fascism. Nevertheless, his ideas have suffered as a consequence of this unsavory historical connection. Yet the arguments of Pareto's *Manual of Political Economy* (1906)—which features "the Pareto optimality or ophelimity principle" that is in every economics textbook—and his four-volume *Treatise on General Sociology* (1916; Eng. tr. *Mind and Society*) have not been seriously reconsidered, except in Italy, in the entire post-WWII period. Pareto's unique analysis of the role of nonrational, nonlogical, or irrational behaviors ("residues" and "derivations," as he called them) in individuals and social groups has not been equalled in scope and depth. Yet the pessimistic conclusions he drew from his dogged historical and cultural research repels most readers today who are, understandably given recent history, more interested in ameliorative than in denunciative social theory.

THE MIND AND SOCIETY, 1916

"Residues and Elites"

2025. Heterogeneousness of Society and Circulation Among its Various Elements. We have more than once found ourselves called upon to consider the heterogeneous character of society, and we shall have to consider it all the more closely now that we are coming to our investigation of the conditions that determine the social equilibrium. To have a clear road ahead of us, it would be wise to go into that matter somewhat thoroughly at this point.

Whether certain theorists like it or not, the fact is that human society is not a homogeneous thing, that individuals are physically, morally, and intellectually different. Here we are interested in things as they actually are. Of that fact, therefore, we have to take account. And we must also take account of another fact: that the social classes are not entirely distinct, even in countries where a caste system prevails; and that in modern civilized countries circulation among the various classes is exceedingly rapid. To consider at all exhaustively here this matter of the diversity of the vastly numerous social groups and the numberless ways in which they mix is out of the question. As usual, therefore, since we cannot have the more, we

must rest content with the less and try to make the problem easier in order to have it the more manageable. That is a first step along a path that others may go on following. We shall consider the problem only in its bearing on the social equilibrium and try to reduce as far as possible the numbers of the groups and the modes of circulation, putting under one head phenomena that prove to be roughly and after a fashion similar. . . .

2034. So we get two strata in a population: (I) A lower stratum, the *non-élite*, with whose possible influence on government we are not just here concerned; then (2) a higher stratum, the *élite*, which is divided into two: (a) a governing *élite*; (b) a non-governing *elite*. . . .

2037. In societies where the social unit is the family the label worn by the head of the family also benefits all other members. In Rome, the man who became Emperor generally raised his freedmen to the higher class, and oftentimes, in fact, to the governing *élite*. For that matter, now more, now fewer, of the freedmen taking part in the Roman government possessed qualities good or bad that justified their wearing the labels which they had won through imperial bounty. In our societies, the social unit is the individual; but the place that the individual occupies in society also benefits his wife, his children, his connexions, his friends. . . .

2042. To this mixing, in the particular case in which only two groups, the *élite* and the non-*élite*, are envisaged, the term "circulation of élites" has

From *The Mind and Society: A Treatise on General Sociology*, by Vilfredo Pareto, Andrew Bongiorno and Arthur Livingston, Eds., Arthur Livingston, Trans. Originally published by Harcourt & Brace, New York, 1935.

been applied—in French, *circulation des élites* [or in more general terms "class-circulation"].

2043. In conclusion we must pay special attention (I), in the case of one single group, to the proportions between the total of the group and the number of individuals who are nominally members of it but do not possess the qualities requisite for effective membership; and then (2), in the case of various groups, to the ways in which transitions from one group to the other occur, and to the intensity of that movement—that is to say, to the velocity of the circulation.

2044. Velocity in circulation has to be considered not only absolutely but also in relation to the supply of and the demand for certain social elements. A country that is always at peace does not require many soldiers in its governing class, and the production of generals may be overexuberant as compared with the demand. But when a country is in a state of continuous warfare many soldiers are necessary, and though production remains at the same level it may not meet the demand. That, we might note in passing, has been one of the causes for the collapse of many aristocracies. . . .

2046. We must not confuse the state of law with the state of fact. The latter alone, or almost alone, has a bearing on the social equilibrium. There are many examples of castes that are legally closed, but into which, in point of fact, newcomers make their way, and often in large numbers. On the other hand, what difference does it make if a caste is legally open, but conditions *de facto* prevent new accessions to it? If a person who acquires wealth thereby becomes a member of the governing class, but no one gets rich, it is as if the class were closed; and if only a few get rich, it is as if the law erected serious barriers against access to the caste. Something of that sort was observable towards the end of the Roman Empire. People who acquired wealth entered the order of the curials. But only a few individuals made any money. Theoretically we might examine any number of groups. Practically we have to confine ourselves to the more important. We shall proceed by successive approximations, starting with the simple and going on to the complex.

2047. *Higher Class and Lower Class in General.* The least we can do is to divide society into two strata: a higher stratum, which usually contains the rulers, and a lower stratum, which usually contains the ruled. That fact is so obvious that it has always forced itself even upon the most casual observation, and so for the circulation of individuals between the two strata. Even Plato had an inkling of class-circulation and tried to regulate it artificially (§ 278). The "new man," the upstart, the *parvenu*, has always been a subject of interest, and literature has analyzed him unendingly. Here, then, we are merely giving a more exact form to things that have long been perceived more or less vaguely. Above, in §§ 1723 f., we noted a varying distribution of residues in the various social groupings, and chiefly in the higher and the lower class. Such heterogeneousness is a fact perceived by the most superficial glance.

2053. Aristocracies do not last. Whatever the causes, it is an incontestable fact that after a certain length of time they pass away. History is a graveyard of aristocracies. The Athenian "People" was an aristocracy as compared with the remainder of a population of resident aliens and slaves. It vanished without leaving any descent. The various aristocracies of Rome vanished in their time. So did the aristocracies of the Barbarians. Where, in France, are the descendants of the Frankish conquerors? The genealogies of the English nobility have been very exactly kept; and they show that very few families still remain to claim descent from the comrades of William the Conqueror. The rest have vanished. In Germany the aristocracy of the present day is very largely made up of descendants of vassals of the lords of old. The populations of European countries have increased enormously during the past few centuries. It is as certain as certain can be that the aristocracies have not increased in proportion.

2054. They decay not in numbers only. They decay also in quality, in the sense that they lose their vigour, that there is a decline in the proportions of the residues which enabled them to win their power and hold it. The governing class is restored not only in numbers, but—and that is the more important thing—in quality, by families rising from the lower classes and bringing with them the vigour and the proportions of residues necessary for keeping themselves in power. It is also restored by the loss of its more degenerate members.

2055. If one of those movements comes to an end, or worse still, if they both come to an end, the governing class crashes to ruin and often sweeps the whole of a nation along with it. Potent cause of disturbance in the equilibrium is the accumulation of superior elements in the lower classes and, conversely, of inferior elements in the higher classes. If human aristocracies were like thorough-breds among animals, which reproduce themselves over long periods of time with approximately the same traits, the history of the human race would be something altogether different from the history we know.

2056. In virtue of class-circulation, the governing *élite* is always in a state of slow and continuous transformation. It flows on like a river, never being today what it was yesterday. From time to time sudden and violent disturbances occur. There is a flood—the river overflows its banks. Afterwards, the new governing *élite* again resumes its slow transformation. The flood has subsided, the river is again flowing normally in its wonted bed.

CHARLES HORTON COOLEY

1864–1929

Charles Horton Cooley, the sickly son of a judge on the Supreme Court of Michigan, was born on August 17, 1864 in Ann Arbor, Michigan, the fourth of six children. He married Elsie Jones (a medical school professor's daughter) in 1890, with whom he produced two daughters and one son, and died from cancer at 64 on May 8, 1929. He entered the University of Michigan in 1880, took a B.A. in 1887, traveled to Europe, and then earned a doctorate in 1894 in political-economy with a dissertation called "The Theory of Transportation." There being no sociology department at Michigan, some doctoral examination questions relating to Cooley's interests were sent from the department at Columbia University, founded by Franklin Giddings in 1889. He then spent three years in Washington, D.C. as a statistician for the Interstate Commerce Commission, began teaching sociology at his alma mater in 1892 and never left, moving from the departments of political science to political-economy to sociology (in 1907). His principal books are *Human Nature and the Social Order* (1902), *Social Organization* (1909), and *Social Process* (1918). He treated both macro and micro dimensions of social life, though is better known for the latter.

Cooley is usually considered the helping theorist behind the more important work of George Herbert Mead, and to some extent, John Dewey, both of whom he knew at the University of Michigan in the early 1890s. Cooley studied the developmental behavior of his own children (like Piaget), using this informal method to create an elementary social psychology that is quintessentially American. It is very unlike Freud, for there is no mention of a subconscious, nor is there any emphasis on "the family drama" tied to conflict and inevitable intergenerational resolution of friction. For Cooley, the site of theoretical interest is always "the I," which develops through what he called "the looking glass self," the only idea to which his name is firmly anchored. He believed that creating the self is a collective project, worked out between the social actor and the other members of his or her "primary group." By monitoring the responses one receives to behavior, especially in the essential settings of family and community, the developing person begins to understand the nature of his or her own "self," its possibilities for growth as well as the constraints which constitute social control. However, for Cooley there was no necessarily dark consequence of being raised in a family setting, as there was for Freud and many of his followers. He thought that "sympathetic introspection" made it possible for people to comprehend more or less what others in their social circle were experiencing, and thereby to modulate their own behavior to suit group norms—a notion which is strongy related to the *verstehende* method of Dilthey. Cooley was thus anti-behavioristic and optimistic, at least when considering the exclusively social-psychological. As is shown in the excerpts below, he also had larger scholarly interests, like the role of the then developing mass media on the collective identity, as well as the role of unionization in improving the lives of the working class.

HUMAN NATURE AND THE SOCIAL ORDER, 1902

The Meaning of "I"

... The distinctive thing in the idea for which the pronouns of the first person are names is apparently a characteristic kind of feeling which may be called the my feeling or sense of appropriation. Almost any sort of ideas may be associated with this feeling, and so come to be named "I" or "mine," but the feeling, and that alone it would seem, is the determining factor in the matter. As Professor James says in his admirable discussion of the self, the words "me" and "self" designate "all the things which have the power to produce in a stream of consciousness excitement of a certain peculiar sort" This view is very fully set forth by Professor Hiram M. Stanley, whose work, "The Evolutionary Psychology of Feeling," has an extremely suggestive chapter on self-feeling.

I do not mean that the feeling aspect of the self is necessarily more important than any other, but that it is the immediate and decisive sign and proof of what "I" is; there is no appeal from it; if we go behind it it must be to study its history and conditions, not to question its authority. But, of course, this study of history and conditions may be quite as profitable as the direct on of self-feeling. What I would wish to do is to present each aspect in its proper light.

The emotion or feeling of self may be regarded as instinctive, and was doubtless evolved in connection with its important function in stimulating and unifying the special activities of individuals. It is thus very profoundly rooted in the history of the human race and apparently indispensable to any plan of life at all similar to ours. It seems to exist in a vague though vigorous form at the birth of each individual, and, like other instinctive ideas or germs of ideas, to be defined and developed by experience, becoming associated, or rather incorporated, with muscular, visual, and other sensations; with perceptions, apperceptions, and conceptions of every degree of complexity and

of infinite variety of content; and, especially, with personal ideas. Meantime the feeling itself does not remain unaltered, but undergoes differentiation and refinement just as does any other sort of crude innate feeling. Thus, while retaining under every phase its characteristic tone or flavor, it breaks up into innumerable self-sentiments. And concrete self-feeling, as it exists in mature persons, is a whole made up of these various sentiments, along with a good deal of primitive emotion not thus broken up. It partakes fully of the general development of the mind, but never loses that peculiar gusto of appropriation that causes us to name a thought with a first-personal pronoun. The other contents of the self-idea are of little use, apparently, in defining it, because they are so extremely various. It would be no more futile, it seems to me, to attempt to define fear by enumerating the things that people are afraid of, than to attempt to define "I" by enumerating the objects with which the word is associated. Very much as fear means primarily a state of feeling, or its expression, and not darkness, fire, lions, snakes, or other things that excite it, so "I" means primarily self-feeling, or its expression, and not body, clothes, treasures, ambition, honors, and the like, with which this feeling may be connected. In either ease it is possible and useful to go behind the feeling and inquire what ideas arouse it and why they do so, but this is in a sense a secondary investigation. ...

But perhaps the best way to realise the naive meaning of "I" is to listen to the talk of children playing together, especially if they do not agree very well. They use the first person with none of the conventional self-repression of their elders, but with much emphasis and variety of inflection, so that its emotional animus is unmistakable.

Self-feeling of a reflective and agreeable sort, an appropriative seat of contemplation, is strongly suggested by the word "gloating." To gloat, in this sense, is as much as to think "mine, mine, mine," with a pleasant warmth of feeling. Thus a boy gloats over something he has made with his scroll-saw, over the bird he has brought down with his gun, or over his collection of stamps or eggs; a girl gloats over her new clothes, and over the approving words or looks of others; a farmer over his fields and his stock; a business man over his trade and his bank account; a mother over her child; the poet over a successful quatrain; the self-right-

From *Human Nature and the Social Order,* by Charles Horton Cooley. Published by Schocken Books. Copyright © 1964.

eous man over the state of his soul; and in like manner every one gloats over the prosperity of any cherished idea.

I would not be understood as saying that self-feeling is clearly marked off in experience from other kinds of feeling; but it is, perhaps, as definite in this regard as anger, fear, grief, and the likes. To quote Professor James, "The emotions themselves of self-satisfaction and abasement are of a unique sort, each as worthy to be classed as a primitive emotional species as are, for example, rage or pain." It is true here, as wherever mental facts are distinguished, that there are no fences, but that one thing merges by degrees into another. Yet if "I" did not denote an idea much the same in all minds and fairly distinguishable from other ideas, it could not be used freely and universally as a means of communication. . . .

The social self is simply any idea, or system of ideas, drawn from the communicative life, that the mind cherishes as its own. Self-feeling has its chief scope within the general life, not outside of it; the special endeavor or tendency of which it is the emotional aspect finds its principal field of exercise in a world of personal forces, reflected in the mind by a world of personal impressions.

SOCIAL ORGANIZATION, 1909

Modern Communication: Superficiality and Strain

The action of the new communication is essentially stimulating, and so may, in some of its phases, be injurious. It costs the individual more in the way of mental function to take a normal part in the new order of things than it did in the old. Not only is his outlook broader, so that he is incited to think and feel about a wider range of matters, but he is required to be a more thorough-going specialist in the mastery of his particular function; both extension and intension have grown. General culture and technical training are alike more exigent than they used to be, and their demands visibly increase from year to year, not only in the schools but in life at large. The man who does not meet them falls behind the procession, and becomes in some sense a failure: either unable to make a living, or narrow and out of touch with generous movements.

Fortunately, from this point of view, our mental functions are as a rule rather sluggish, so that the spur of modern intercourse is for the most part wholesome, awakening the mind, abating sensuality, and giving men idea and purpose. Such ill effect as may be ascribed to it seems to fall chiefly under the two heads, superficiality and strain, which the reader will perceive to be another view of that enlargement and animation discussed in the last chapter but one.

There is a rather general agreement among observers that, outside of his specialty, the man of our somewhat hurried civilization is apt to have an impatient, touch-and-go habit of mind as regards both thought and feeling. We are trying to do many and various things, and are driven to versatility and short cuts at some expense to truth and depth. "The habit of inattention," said De Tocqueville about 1835, "must be considered as the greatest defect of the democratic character"; and recently his judgment has been confirmed by Ostrogorski, who thinks that deliverance from the bonds of space and time has made the American a man of short views, wedded to the present, accustomed to getting quick returns, and with no deep root anywhere. We have reduced *ennui* considerably; but a moderate *ennui* is justly reckoned by Comte and others as one of the springs of progress, and it is no unmixed good that we are too busy to be unhappy.

In this matter, as in so many others, we should discriminate, so far as we can, between permanent conditions of modern life and what is due merely to change, between democracy and confusion. There is nothing in the nature of democracy to prevent its attaining, when transition has somewhat abated, a diverse and stable organization of its own sort, with great advantage to our spiritual composure and productivity.

In the meanwhile it is beyond doubt that the constant and varied stimulus of a confused time makes sustained attention difficult. Certainly our popular literature is written for those who run as they read, and carries the principle of economy of attention beyond anything previously imagined. And in feeling it seems to be true that we tend toward a somewhat superficial kindliness and adaptability, rather than sustained passion of any kind. Generally speaking, mind is spread out very thin over our civilization; a good sort of mind, no doubt, but quite thin.

All this may be counteracted in various ways, especially by thoroughness in education, and is perhaps to be regarded as lack of maturity rather than as incurable defect.

Mental strain, in spite of the alarming opinions sometimes expressed, is by no means a general condition in modern society, nor likely to become so; it is confined to a relatively small number, in whom individual weakness, or unusual stress, or both, has rendered life too much for the spirit. Yet this number includes a great part of those who perform the more exacting intellectual functions in business and the professions, as well as peculiarly weak, or sensitive, or unfortunate individuals in all walks of life. In general there is an increase of self-consciousness and choice; there is more opportunity, more responsibility, more complexity, a greater burden upon intelligence, will and character. The individual not only can but must deal with a flood of urgent suggestions, or be swamped by them. "This age that blots out life with question marks" forces us to think and choose whether we are ready or not.

Worse, probably, than anything in the way of work—though that is often destructive—is the anxious insecurity in which our changing life keeps a large part of the population, the well-to-do as well as the poor. And an educated and imaginative people feels such anxieties more than one deadened by ignorance. "In America," said De Tocqueville, "I saw the freest and most enlightened men placed in the happiest circumstances which the world affords; it seemed to me as if a cloud habitually hung upon their brows, and I thought them serious and almost sad, even in their pleasures."

Not long ago Mr. H. D. Sedgwick contributed to a magazine a study of what he called "The New American Type," based on an exhibition of English and American portraits, some recent, some a century old. He found that the more recent were conspicuously marked by the signs of unrest and strain. Speaking of Mr. Sargent's subjects he says, "The obvious qualities in his portraits are disquiet, lack of equilibrium, absence of principle, . . . a mind unoccupied by the rightful heirs, as if the home of principle and dogma had been transformed into an inn for wayfarers. Sargent's women are more marked than his men; women, as physically more delicate, are the first to reveal the strain of physical and psychical maladjustment. The thin spirit of life shivers pathetically in its 'fleshly dress'; in the intensity of its eagerness it is all unconscious of its spiritual fidgeting on finding itself astray—no path, no blazings, the old forgotten, the new not formed." The early Americans, he says, "were not limber minded men, not readily agnostic, not nicely sceptical; they were . . . eighteenth century Englishmen." Of Reynolds' women he observes, "These ladies led lives unvexed; natural affections, a few brief saws, a half-dozen principles, kept their brows smooth, their cheeks ripe, their lips most wooable." People had "a stable physique and a well-ordered, logical, dogmatic philosophy." The older portraits "chant a chorus of praise for national character, for class distinctions, for dogma and belief, for character, for good manners, for honor, for contemplation, for vision to look upon life as a whole, for appreciation that the world is to be enjoyed, for freedom from democracy, for capacity in lighter mood to treat existence as a comedy told by Goldoni."*

This may or may not be dispassionately just, but it sets forth one side of the case—a side the more pertinent for being unpopular—and suggests a very real though intangible difference between the people of our time and those of a century ago—one which all students must have felt. It is what we feel in literature when we compare the people of Jane Austen with those, let us say, of the author of The House of Mirth.

I do not propose to inquire how far the effects of strain may be seen in an increase of certain distinctly pathological phenomena, such as neurasthenia, the use of drugs, insanity and suicide. That it has an important working in this way—difficult, however, to separate from that of other factors— is generally conceded. In the growth of suicide we seem to have a statistical demonstration of the destructive effect of social stress at its worst; and of general paralysis, which is rapidly increasing and has been called the disease of the century, we are told that "it is the disease of excess, of vice, of overwork, of prolonged worry; it is especially the disease of great urban centres, and its existence usually seems to show that the organism has entered upon a competitive race for which it is not fully equipped."

The Organization of the Ill-Paid Classes

. . . It is quite apparent that an organized and intelligent class-consciousness in the hand-working people is one of the primary needs of a democratic society. In so far as this part of the people is lacking in a knowledge of its situation and in the practice of orderly self-assertion, a real freedom will also be lacking, and we shall have some kind of subjection in its place; freedom being impossible without group organization. That industrial classes exist—in the sense already explained— cannot well be denied, and existing they ought to be conscious and self-directing.

The most obvious need of class-consciousness is for self-assertion against the pressure of other classes, and this is both most necessary and most difficult with those who lack wealth and the command over organized forces which it implies. In a free society, especially, the Lord helps those who help themselves; and those who are weak in money must be strong in union, and must also exert themselves to make good any deficiency in leadership that comes from ability deserting to more favored classes.

That the dominant power of wealth has an oppressive action, for the most part involuntary,

upon the people below, will hardly be denied by any competent student. The industrial progress of our time is accompanied by sufferings that are involved with the progress. These sufferings—at least in their more tangible forms—fall almost wholly upon the poorer classes, while the richer get a larger share of the increased product which the progress brings. By sufferings I mean not only the physical hardship and liability to disease, early decay, and mutilation or death by accident, which fell to the hand-worker; but also the debasement of children by premature and stunting labor, the comparative lack of intellectual and social opportunities, the ugly and discouraging surroundings, and the insecurity of employment, to which he and his are subject. There is no purpose to inflict these things; but they are inflicted, and the only remedy is a public consciousness, especially in the classes who suffer from them, of their causes and the means by which they can be done away with.

The principal expressions of class-consciousness in the hand-working classes in our day are labor unions and that wider, vaguer, more philosophical or religious movement, too various for definition, which is known as socialism. Regarding the latter I will only say at present that it includes much of what is most vital in the contemporary working of the democratic spirit; the large problems with which its doctrines deal I prefer to discuss in my own way.

Labor unions are a simpler matter. They have arisen out of the urgent need of self-defence, not so much against deliberate aggression as against brutal confusion and neglect. The industrial population has been tossed about on the swirl of economic change like so much sawdust on a river, sometimes prosperous, sometimes miserable, never secure, and living largely under degrading, inhuman conditions. Against this state of things the higher class of artisans—as measured by skill, wages and general intelligence—have made a partly successful struggle through coöperation in associations, which, however, include much less than half of those who might be expected to take advantage of them. That they are an effective means of class self-assertion is evident from the antagonism they have aroused. . . .

Thus, if unions should never raise wages or shorten hours, they would yet be invaluable to the manhood of their members. At worst, they ensure the joy of an open fight and of companionship in defeat. Self-assertion through voluntary organization is of the essence of democracy, and if any part of the people proves incapable of it it is a bad sign for the country. On this ground alone it would seem that patriots should desire to see organization of this sort extend throughout the industrial population.

Note

*The Atlantic Monthly, April, 1904.

W.E.B. DU BOIS

1868–1963

William Edward Burghardt Du Bois was born on February 23, 1868 in Great Barrington, Massachusetts, married Nina Gomer on May 12, 1896, their son died at 18 months of dysentery, and their daughter survived. After Nina's death Du Bois married Shirley Graham in 1951, and adopted her son. Disgusted with the condition of African Americans, and after being accused of serving as a foreign agent by the U.S., he joined the communist party, moved to Ghana and became a citizen there, dying in Accra on August 27, 1963 when he was 95. Du Bois was fortunate in growing up in a city of 5000 with only about 40 black residents. He was therefore shielded in part from the more blatant racism typical in other parts of the country. He began his lifelong journalism while in high school, serving as correspondent to the *New York Globe*. Despite his intellectual and political precocity, he was financially unable to follow his most capable classmates to Harvard, but was pleased to win a scholarship to Fisk College in Nashville. There he encountered racism typical in the U.S. in 1885, and it sharpened his resolve to fight it. In summers he taught in a county school, experiencing dire poverty first hand. Graduating from Fisk in 1888, he took another B.A. in 1890, M.A. in 1891, and the doctorate in 1895, all from Harvard. His dissertation, *The Suppression of the African Slave-Trade to the United States of America, 1638–1860,* was published in 1896 and is still in print, immediately establishing Du Bois as a voice to be reckoned with among black intellectuals. The list of Du Bois's subsequent publications and achievements fills many pages. Suffice it to say that he wrote some of the most influential works by any black American, and that he took political positions that have infuriated his enemies while endearing him to comrades.

From the point of view of social thought, Du Bois's major achievement is not his historiography, such as the dissertation and *Black Reconstruction* (1935), but instead two principal works, *The Philadelphia Negro* (1899) and, far more importantly, an essay collection called *The Souls of Black Folk* (1903). In the latter work he introduced the notion of the black "double consciousness" and "the talented tenth," and by so doing separated himself from the accommodationist strategy of Booker T. Washington, the other indispensable black intellectual of the time. The former work is equally astonishing, for which Du Bois interviewed 5000 Philadelphians, drew a comprehensive demographic map of the city, and thus wrote a sociological classic. He also, interestingly, met with Max Weber in 1904, and Weber promised to have his *Souls* translated into German. Du Bois's work is as indispensable to black intellectualism as is Weber's to the European variant.

THE SOULS OF BLACK FOLK, 1903

The Talented Tenth

The Negro race, like all races, is going to be saved by its exceptional men. The problem of education, then, among Negroes must first of all deal with the Talented Tenth; it is the problem of developing the Best of this race that they may guide the Mass away from the contamination and death of the Worst, in their own and other races. Now the training of men is a difficult and intricate task. Its technique is a matter for educational experts, but its object is for the vision of seers. If we make money the object of man-training, we shall develop money-makers but not necessarily men; if we make technical skill the object of education, we may possess artisans but not, in nature, men. Men we shall have only as we make manhood the object of the work of the schools—intelligence, broad sympathy, knowledge of the world that was and is, and of the relation of men to it—this is the curriculum of that Higher Education which must underlie true life. On this foundation we may build bread winning, skill of hand and quickness of brain, with never a fear lest the child and man mistake the means of living for the object of life.

If this be true—and who can deny it—three tasks lay before me; first to show from the past that the Talented Tenth as they have risen among American Negroes have been worthy of leadership; secondly, to show how these men may be educated and developed; and thirdly, to show their relation to the Negro problem.

You misjudge us because you do not know us. From the very first it has been the educated and intelligent of the Negro people that have led and elevated the mass, and the sole obstacles that nullified and retarded their efforts were slavery and race prejudice; for what is slavery but the legalized survival of the unfit and the nullification of the work of natural internal leadership? Negro leadership, therefore, sought from the first to rid the race of this awful incubus that it might make way for natural selection and the survival of the fittest. In colonial days came Phillis Wheatley and

From *Black Folk–Then and Now*, by W.E.B. Du Bois. Published by Holt, Rinehart and Winston. Copyright © 1939.

Paul Cuffe striving against the bars of prejudice; and Benjamin Banneker, the almanac maker, voiced their longings when he said to Thomas Jefferson, "I freely and cheerfully acknowledge that I am of the African Race, and in colour which is natural to them, of the deepest dye; and it is under a sense of the most profound gratitude to the Supreme Ruler of the Universe, that I now confess to you that I am not under that state of tyrannical thraldom and inhuman captivity to which too many of my brethren are doomed, but that I have abundantly tasted of the fruition of those blessings which proceed from that free and unequalled liberty with which you are favored, and which I hope you will willingly allow, you have mercifully received from the immediate hand of that Being from whom proceedeth every good and perfect gift.

"Suffer me to recall to your mind that time, in which the arms of the British crown were exerted with every powerful effort, in order to reduce you to a state of servitude; look back, I entreat you, on the variety of dangers to which you were exposed; reflect on that period in which every human aid appeared unavailable, and in which even hope and fortitude wore the aspect of inability to the conflict, and you cannot but be led to a serious and grateful sense of your miraculous and providential preservation, you cannot but acknowledge, that the present freedom and tranquility which you enjoy, you have mercifully received, and that a peculiar blessing of heaven.

"This, sir, was a time when you clearly saw into the injustice of a state of Slavery, and in which you had just apprehensions of the horrors of its condition. It was then that your abhorrence thereof was so excited, that you publicly held forth this true and invaluable doctrine, which is worthy to be recorded and remembered in all succeeding ages: 'We hold these truths to be self evident, that all men are created equal; that they are endowed with certain inalienable rights, and that among these are life, liberty and the pursuit of happiness.'". . .

And so now we come to the present—a day of cowardice and vacillation, of strident wide voiced wrong and faint hearted compromise; of double-faced dallying with Truth and Right. Who are today guiding the work of the Negro people? The "exceptions" of course. And yet so sure as this

Talented Tenth is pointed out, the blind worshippers of the Average cry out in alarm: "These are the exceptions, look here at death, disease and crime—these are the happy rule. Of course they are the rule, because a silly nation made them the rule: Because for three long centuries this people lynched Negroes who dared to be brave, raped black women who dared to be virtuous, crushed dark-hued youth who dared to be ambitious, and encouraged and made to flourish servility and lewdness and apathy. But not even this was able to crush all manhood and chastity and aspiration from black folk. A saving remnant continually survives and persists, continually aspires, continually shows itself in thrift and ability and character. Exceptional it is to be sure, but this is its chiefest promise; it shows the capability of Negro blood, the promise of black men. Do Americans ever stop to reflect that there are in this land a million men of Negro blood, well-educated, owners of homes, against the honor of whose womanhood no breath was ever raised, whose men occupy position's of trust and usefulness, and who, judged by any standard, have reached the full measure of the best type of modern European culture? Is it fair, is it decent, is it Christian to ignore these facts of the Negro problem, to belittle such aspiration, to nullify such leadership and seek to crush these people back into the mass out of which by toil and travail, they and their fathers have raised themselves?

Can the masses of the Negro people be in any possible way more quickly raised than by the effort and example of this aristocracy of talent and character? Was there ever a nation on God's fair earth civilized from the bottom upward? Never; it is, ever was and ever will be from the top downward that culture filters. The Talented Tenth rises and pulls all that are worth the saving up to their vantage ground. This is the history of human progress; and two historic mistakes which have hindered that progress were the thinking first that no more could ever rise save the few already risen; or second, that it would better the unrisen to pull the risen down.

How then shall the leaders of a struggling people be trained and the hands of the risen few be strengthened? There can be but one answer: The best and most capable of their youth must be schooled in the colleges and universities of the land. We will not quarrel as to just what the university of the Negro should teach or how it should teach it—I willingly admit that each soul and each race-soul needs its own peculiar curriculum. But this is true: A university is a human invention for the transmission of knowledge and culture from generation to generation, through the training of quick minds and pure hearts, and for this work no other human invention will suffice, not even trade and industrial schools.

All men cannot go to college but some men must; every isolated group or nation must have its yeast, must have for the talented few centers of training where men are not so mystified and befuddled by the hard necessary toil of earning a living, as to have no aims higher than their bellies, and no God greater than Gold. This is true training, and thus in the beginning were the favored sons of the freedmen trained.

⌐◆⌐

"WHAT IS CIVILIZATION?—AFRICA'S ANSWER," 1925

Three things Africa has given the world, and they form the essence of African culture: Beginnings, the village unit, and Art in sculpture and music.

Long before the last two thousand years, which we call the years of modern civilization, lay the beginnings of human culture. For ten thousand years—perhaps fifty thousand years and more—mankind struggled with the first steps of advance; struggled and wavered, forged forward, retreated, fell, and rose again. This was a period fateful for all mankind—for all culture. It was far more tremendous in its ultimate significance than anything that has happened since.

It was during these years that the black race, in its own land, Africa, and in all the paths by which it wended its way thither, seems always to have been first. Wherever one sees the first faint steps of human culture, the first successful fight

From *A W.E.B. Du Bois Reader,* Andrew G. Paschal, Ed. Published by Collier Books. Copyright © 1971.

against wild beasts, the striving against weather and disease, there one sees black men. To be sure, they were not the only beginners, but they seem to have been the successful and persistent ones. Thus Africa appears as the Father of man-kind, and the people who eventually settled there, wherever they have wandered before or since—along the Ganges, the Euphrates, and the Nile, in Cyprus and about the Mediterranean shores—form the largest and often the only group of human beings successfully advancing from animal savagery toward primitive civilization. The ancient world looked upon them continually as creators of human culture and rang with their tributes. Hammurabi, the law giver of Babylonia, is called "to go forth like the sun over the Black race." The Greeks sent Zeus and Poseidon to feast annually with the "Blameless Blacks," and the Roman historians tell us that the Blacks "conceive themselves to be of greater antiquity than any other nation. They suppose themselves also to be the inventors of divine worship, of festivals, of solemn assemblies, of sacrifices, and every religious practice. They affirm that the Egyptians are one of their colonies."

Out of many things that these beginnings emphasize we may select one: the discovery of the use of iron. Probably the properties of iron have been discovered in the world many times and in many places, but it seems likely that while Europe was still in its stone age and while neither Egypt nor Western Asia nor ancient China knew iron, the black Africans had invented the art of smelting. It was a moment big with promise for the uplift of the human race. No effective industry, no sure defense was possible for mankind with laboriously chipped stone tools. Copper and bronze made great advance over stone, but only hard iron founded modern industry; and this marvelous discovery was made by African Negroes.

The second thing that came out of the early strife of black folk was the village unit. I shall never forget my first glimpse of an African village. The night before, we had ridden the bar in the moonlight with the curious singing of lithe black boys. Above on the great headland twinkled Monrovia; below lay the black and silent forests beside a sombre sea. But this morning down by the sea and down by the forests suddenly we walked out into a little town. It was a town of the Vais. It was

a thing of clay, colored cream and purple; clean, quiet, small, with perhaps a dozen or more homes. Authority was here and religion, industry and trade, education and art. It was not a complete thing from a modern point of view. It had little or no machinery; it lay almost defenseless against surrounding malaria. Of news service with the greater world, there was none. Though its whole inner being had been changed and in some respects upset by the new surrounding and invading economy, this little village was a mighty thing; it had come down from a mighty past. Its beginning stretched back in time thousands and thousands of years; it gathered to itself traditions and customs springing almost from the birth of the world. In space alone it stretched back along a path leading from the low thunder of the sea on the black West Coast to the great central plateau of Africa with forest, lake, and sand, two hundred miles away. . . .

No matter whence the African village came and how it is to-day distorted and changed, and has been in the past glorified and degraded, it is a singularly persistent and eternal thing. Again and again this village with its conical huts, its central fire, its grassy streets, its fields of grain and fruit, and its cattle has been reborn in Africa and has spread itself over the endless miles of the continent. Even the African city as it rose time and time again was a city of villages. Ancient Jenne, whence comes our modern word Guinea, "had seven thousand villages so near to one another that the chief of Jentu had no need of messengers," but cried his messages from gate to gate and village to village until within a few moments they had gone a hundred miles to Lake Dibo.

We know the village unit the world over and among all people, but among most folk the village early lost itself in some larger unit, and civilization became a matter of city and state and nation. But the African village, because of geography and climate, because perhaps of some curious inner tenacity and strength of tradition, persisted and did on a small scale what the world has continually attempted on a wider scale and never satisfactorily accomplished. The African village socialized the individual completely, and yet because the village was small this socialization did not submerge and kill individuality. When the city socializes the modern man he becomes mechanical, and cities tend to be all alike. When the nation attempts to socialize the modern man the result is often a soulless Leviathan. The African village attempted a small part of the task of the modern city and state, and accomplished that part more successfully. It lost thereby breadth and power, it failed to integrate into a larger permanent imperialism. It never succumbed wholly to a militarism of its own but for that very reason it tasted slavery of every sort to others. But it was and is and perhaps will long be in its limited way a perfect human thing. . . .

The second and more terrible way in which Africa paid for her individualistic village culture was by the slave trade; Christian Europe traded in human beings for four hundred years. The slave trade alone cost Africa in dead and stolen nearly one hundred million souls. And yet people to-day ask the cause of the stagnation of culture in that land since 1600!

Nevertheless for all this there was compensation, and this compensation was African art. The sense of beauty is the last and best gift of Africa to the world and the true essence of the black man's soul. African art is the offspring of the climate and the Negro soul. The sunshine of central Africa cloaks you like a golden blanket; it hangs heavy about your shoulders; it envelops you; it smothers you in a soft but mighty embrace. The rain of Africa is a consuming flood, a river pouring out of heaven, without banks or current. In Africa the swift, the energetic are the dead. In Africa the "lazy" survive and live. This African laziness is several things; it is shelter from the penetrating rain; it is defense from malaria. And it brings with it leisure and dreams and human intercourse.

Deep in the forest fastness and by the banks of low, vast rivers; in the deep tense quiet of the endless jungle, the human soul whispered its folk tales, carved its pictures, sang its rhythmic songs, and danced and danced. The languages of Africa grew and developed for their unique work, "so simple and clear in their phonology, so logical in their syntax." From these has descended one of the richest masses of oral tradition of poetry and folk lore which the world knows. To this was early added the art of sculpture.

MAX WEBER

1864–1920

Max Weber, Jr., son of an important Prussian lawyer/politician and a pious mother, was the eldest of six children, born on April 21, 1864 in Erfurt, Prussia. (His brother, Alfred, also became a famous sociologist and cultural analyst.) Max married his cousin, Marianne Schnitger, in 1893, they had no children, and he died unexpectedly, a victim of the global influenza pandemic on June 14, 1920, at 56. Weber was raised in a wealthy suburb of Berlin, and because of childhood illnesses was often bedridden and therefore bookish. His father's large home served as a salon for the political and intellectual elite of Prussia, and conversations among these distinguished guests drew Weber into a realm of cultural awareness that today is impossible to reproduce. Given his enormous hunger for knowledge, he began writing essays on ponderous topics when still in middle school, and had begun to join in on adult discussions before he neared college age. He never took formal schooling very seriously, but educated himself to an extraordinary degree through reading and interaction with academic relatives and houseguests. He pursued law, economics, and philosophy at Heidelberg, Strassburg, Berlin, and Göttingen (1882–86), served in the army reserve for two years during college, returned home and studied law at Berlin, graduating in 1889. He then won academic appointments at Berlin and Freiburg, but was forced to retire from teaching after a massive nervous breakdown that immobilized him from between 1897 and 1903, but became well enough to take an extended trip to the U.S. in 1904. Freed of teaching duties by an inheritance, he spent the next 16 years or so producing an unrivalled body of socio-cultural, economic, and sociological analysis that is second to none in the history of modern social science.

Weber's common fame rests on his *Protestant Ethic and the Spirit of Capitalism,* originally two articles in a scholarly journal (1904/05). Here he demonstrated why northern European Protestant behavior was more conducive to the formation of early capitalism than were southern European Catholic beliefs and practices, an hypothesis which has given rise to thousands of commentaries and critiques. But he also contributed fundamental works to the sociology of law (which he virtually invented), the sociology of music (also a first), the sociology of the economy, the philosophy of social science method, the comparative sociology of religion (also his creation), social stratification, the sociology of bureaucracy and of power and "charisma" (his term), and so on. His major work is *Economy and Society* (1922), a massive study assembled posthumously from his papers by his wife, an important intellectual and feminist leader in Germany, and translated into English in 1968 for the first time. Weber's importance grows with time, and he is the only classic social theorist for whom today an entire scholarly journal is named. A recent bibliography of works in English concerning Weber numbers over 4900 items, and as Marx and Freud become increasingly less tenable as the major analysts of the modern world, Weber's ideas become ever more pertinent and revealing.

PROTESTANT ETHIC AND THE SPIRIT OF CAPITALISM, 1904/05

Asceticism and the Spirit of Capitalism

. . . This worldly Protestant asceticism, as we may recapitulate up to this point, acted powerfully against the spontaneous enjoyment of possessions; it restricted consumption, especially of luxuries. On the other hand, it had the psychological effect of freeing the acquisition of goods from the inhibitions of traditionalistic ethics. It broke the bonds of the impulse of acquisition in that it not only legalized it, but (in the sense discussed) looked upon it as directly willed by God. The campaign against the temptations of the flesh, and the dependence on external things, was, as besides the Puritans, the great Quaker apologist Barclay expressly says, not a struggle against the rational acquisition, but against the irrational use of wealth.

But this irrational use was exemplified in the outward forms of luxury which their code condemned as idolatry of the flesh, however natural they had appeared to the feudal mind. On the other hand, they approved the rational and utilitarian uses of wealth which were willed by God for the needs of the individual and the community. They did not wish to impose mortification on the man of wealth, but the use of his means for necessary and practical things. The idea of comfort characteristically limits the extent of ethically permissible expenditures. It is naturally no accident that the development of a manner of living consistent with that idea may be observed earliest and most clearly among the most consistent representatives of this whole attitude toward life. Over against the glitter and ostentation of feudal magnificence which, resting on an unsound economic basis, prefers a sordid elegance to a sober simplicity, they set the clean and solid comfort of the middle-class home as an ideal. . . .

When the limitation of consumption is combined with this release of acquisitive activity, the inevitable practical result is obvious: accumulation of capital through ascetic compulsion to save. The restraints which were imposed upon the consumption of wealth naturally served to increase it by making possible the productive investment of capital. How strong this influence was is not, unfortunately, susceptible of exact statistical demonstration. In New England the connection is so evident that it did not escape the eye of so discerning a historian as Doyle. But also in Holland, which was really only dominated by strict Calvinism for seven years, the greater simplicity of life in the more seriously religious circles, in combination with great wealth, led to an excessive propensity to accumulations. . . .

One of the fundamental elements of the spirit of modern capitalism, and not only of that but of all modern culture: rational conduct on the basis of the idea of the calling, was born—that is what this discussion has sought to demonstrate—from the spirit of Christian asceticism. One has only to re-read the passage from Franklin, quoted at the beginning of this essay, in order to see that the essential elements of the attitude which was there called the spirit of capitalism are the same as what we have just shown to be the content of the Puritan worldly asceticism, only without the religious basis, which by Franklin's time had died away. The idea that modern labour has an ascetic character is of course not new. Limitation to specialized work, with a renunciation of the Faustian universality of man which it involves, is a condition of any valuable work in the modern world; hence deeds and renunciation inevitably condition each other today. This fundamentally ascetic trait of middle-class life, if it attempts to be a way of life at all, and not simply the absence of any, was what Goethe wanted to teach, at the height of his wisdom, in the *Wander-jahren,* and in the end which he gave to the life of his *Faust.* For him the realization meant a renunciation, a departure from an age of full and beautiful humanity, which can no more be repeated in the course of our cultural development than can the flower of the Athenian culture of antiquity.

The Puritan wanted to work in a calling; we are forced to do so. For when asceticism was carried out of monastic cells into everyday life, and began to dominate worldly morality, it did its part in building the tremendous cosmos of the modern economic order. This order is now bound to the technical and economic conditions of machine production which to-day determine the lives of all the individuals who are born into this mechanism, not only those directly concerned with economic acquisition, with irresistible force. Perhaps it will so determine them until the last ton of fossilized coal is burnt. In Baxter's view the care for external goods should only lie on the shoulders of the "saint like a light cloak, which can be thrown aside at any moment." But fate decreed that the cloak should become an iron cage.

Since asceticism undertook to remodel the world and to work out its ideals in the world, material goods have gained an increasing and finally an inexorable power over the lives of men as at no previous period in history. To-day the spirit of religious asceticism—whether finally, who knows?—has escaped from the cage. But victorious capitalism, since it rests on mechanical foundations, needs its support no longer. The rosy blush of its laughing heir, the Enlightenment, seems also to be irretrievably fading, and the idea of duty in one's calling prowls about in our lives like the ghost of dead religious beliefs. Where the fulfilment of the calling cannot directly be related to the highest spiritual and cultural values, or when, on the other hand, it need not be felt simply as economic compulsion, the individual generally abandons the attempt to justify it at all. In the field of its highest development, in the United States, the pursuit of wealth, stripped of its religious and ethical meaning, tends to become associated with purely mundane passions, which often actually give it the character of sport."

No one knows who will live in this cage in the future, or whether at the end of this tremendous development entirely new prophets will arise, or there will be a great rebirth of old ideas and ideals, or, if neither, mechanized petrification, embellished with a sort of convulsive self-importance. For of the last stage of this cultural development, it might well be truly said: "Specialists without spirit, sensualists without heart; this nullity imagines that it has attained a level of civilization never before achieved."

"RELIGIOUS REJECTIONS OF THE WORLD AND THEIR DIRECTIONS," 1913

The most irrational form of religious behavior, the mystic experience, is in its innermost being not only alien but hostile to all form. Form is unfortunate and inexpressible to the mystic because he believes precisely in the experience of exploding all forms, and hopes by this to be absorbed into the 'All-oneness' which lies beyond any kind of determination and form. For him the indubitable psychological affinity of profoundly shaking experiences in art and religion can only be a symptom of the diabolical nature of art. Especially music, the most 'inward' of all the arts, can appear in its purest form of instrumental music as an irresponsible *Ersatz* for primary religious experience. The internal logic of instrumental music as a realm not living 'within' appears as a deceptive pretension to religious experience. The well-known stand of the Council of Trent may in part have stemmed from this sentiment. Art becomes an 'idolatry,' a competing power, and a deceptive bedazzlement; and the images and the allegory of religious subjects appear as blasphemy.

In empirical, historical reality, this psychological affinity between art and religion has led to ever-renewed alliances, which have been quite significant for the evolution of art. The great majority of religions have in some manner entered such alliances. The more they wished to be universalist mass religions and were thus directed to emotional propaganda and mass appeals, the more systematic were their alliances with art. But all genuine virtuoso religions have remained very coy when confronting art, as a consequence of the inner structure of the contradiction between religion and art. This holds true for virtuoso religiosity in its active asceticist bent as well as in its mystical turn. The more religion has emphasized either the supra-worldliness of its God or the other-worldliness of salvation, the more harshly has art been refuted.

7: The Erotic Sphere

The brotherly ethic of salvation religion is in profound tension with the greatest irrational force of

From *Max Weber: Essays in Sociology*, H.H. Gerth and C. Wright Mills, Eds./Trans. Copyright © 1958, 1946 by H.H. Gerth and C. Wright Mills. Used by permission of Oxford University Press, Inc.

life: sexual love. The more sublimated sexuality is, and the more principled and relentlessly consistent the salvation ethic of brotherhood is, the sharper is the tension between sex and religion.

Originally the relation of sex and religion was very intimate. Sexual intercourse was very frequently part of magic orgiasticism or was an unintended result of orgiastic excitement. The foundation of the Skoptsy (Castrators) sect in Russia evolved from an attempt to do away with the sexual result of the orgiastic dance (radjeny) of the *Chlyst,* which was evaluated as sinful. Sacred harlotry has had nothing whatsoever to do with an alleged 'primitive promiscuity'; it has usually been a survival of magical orgiasticism in which every ecstasy was considered 'holy.' And profane heterosexual, as well as homosexual, prostitution is very ancient and often rather sophisticated. (The training of tribades occurs among so-called *aborigines.*)

The transition from such prostitution to legally constituted marriage is full of all sorts of intermediary forms. Conceptions of marriage as an economic arrangement for providing security for the wife and legal inheritance for the child; as an institution which is important (because of the death sacrifices of the descendants) for destiny in the beyond; and as important for the begetting of children—these conceptions of marriage are pre-prophetic and universal. They therefore have had nothing to do with asceticism as such. And sexual life, *per se,* has had its ghosts and gods as has every other function.

A certain tension between religion and sex came to *the* fore only with the temporary cultic chastity of priests. This rather ancient chastity may well have been determined by the fact that from the point of view of the strictly stereotyped ritual of the regulated community cult, sexuality was readily considered to be specifically dominated by demons. Furthermore, it was no accident that subsequently the prophetic religions, as well as the priest-controlled life orders, have, almost without significant exception, regulated sexual intercourse in favor of *marriage.* The contrast of all rational regulation of life with magical orgiasticism and all sorts of irrational frenzies is expressed in this fact.

The tension of religion and sex has been augmented by evolutionary factors on both sides. On the side of sexuality the tension has led through sublimation into 'eroticism,' and therewith into a consciously cultivated, and hence, a non-routinized sphere. Sex has been non-routinized not solely or necessarily in the sense of being estranged from conventions, for eroticism is a contrast to the sober naturalism of the peasant. And it was precisely eroticism which the conventions of knighthood usually made the object of regulation. These conventions, however, characteristically regulated eroticism by veiling the natural and organic basis of sexuality.

The extraordinary quality of eroticism has consisted precisely in a gradual turning away from the naive naturalism of sex. The reason and significance of this evolution, however, involve the universal rationalization and intellectualization of culture. We wish to present, in a few sketches, the phases of this development. We shall proceed with examples from the Occident.

The total being of man has now been alienated from the organic cycle of peasant life; life has been increasingly enriched in cultural content, whether this content is evaluated as intellectually or otherwise supra-individual. All this has worked, through the estrangement of life value from that which is merely naturally given, toward a further enhancement of the special position of eroticism. Eroticism was raised into the sphere of conscious enjoyment (in the most sublime sense of the term). Nevertheless, indeed because of this elevation, eroticism appeared to be like a gate into the most irrational and thereby real kernel of life, as compared with the mechanisms of rationalization. The degree and the manner in which a value-emphasis was thus placed upon eroticism as such has varied enormously throughout history.

To the unrestrained feelings of a warriordom, the possession of and the fight for women has ranked about equally with the fight for treasure and the conquest of power. At the time of pre-classic Hellenism, in the period of knighthood romance, an erotic disappointment could be considered by Archilochos as a significant experience of lasting relevance, and the capture of a woman could be considered the incomparable incident of a heroic war.

The tragedians knew sexual love as a genuine power of destiny, and their lore incorporated lingering echoes of the myths. On the whole, however, a woman, Sappho, remained unequalled by man in the capacity for erotic feeling. The classic Hellenic period, the period of the Hoplite army, conceived of erotic matters in a relatively and unusually sober manner. As all their self-revelations prove, these men were even more sober than the educated stratum of the Chinese. Yet it is not true that this period did not know the deadly earnestness of sexual love. Rather, the contrary was characteristic of Hellenic love. We should remind ourselves—despite Aspasia—of Pericles' speech and finally of the well-known statement of Demosthenes.

To the exclusively masculine character of this epoch of 'democracy,' the treatment of erotic experience with women as 'life-fate'—to speak in our vocabulary—would have appeared as almost sophomoric and sentimental. The 'comrade,' the boy, was the object demanded with all the ceremony of love, and this fact stood precisely in the center of Hellenic culture. Thus, with all its magnificence, Plato's eros is nevertheless a strongly tempered feeling. The beauty of Bacchian passion as such was not an official component of this relation.

The possibility of problems and of tragedy of a principled character came about in the erotical sphere, at first, through certain demands for responsibility, which, in the Occident, stem from Christianity. However, the value-accentuation of the erotic sensation as such evolved primarily and before all else under the cultural conditioning of feudal notions of honor. This happened by a carrying over of the symbols of knightly vassalship into the erotically sublimated sexual relation. Eroticism was given a value-accent most frequently when, during the fusion of vassalship and erotic relations, there occurred a combination with crypto-erotic religiosity, or directly with asceticism as during the Middle Ages. The troubadour love of the Christian Middle Ages is known to have been an erotic service of vassals. It was not oriented towards girls, but exclusively towards the wives of other men; it involved (in theory!) abstentious love nights and a casuistic code of duties. Therewith began the 'probation' of the man, not before his equals but in the face of the erotic interest of the 'lady.'

The conception of the 'lady' was constituted solely and precisely by virtue of her judging func-

tion. The masculinity of Hellenism is in strict contrast to this relation of the vassal to the 'lady.'

A further enhancement of the specifically sensational character of eroticism developed with the transition from the conventions of the Renaissance to the increasingly nonmilitary intellectualism of salon culture. Despite the great differences between the conventions of Antiquity and the Renaissance, the latter were essentially masculine and agonistic; in this respect, they were closely related to antiquity. This was due to the fact that by the time of the Cortegiano and of Shakespeare, the Renaissance conventions had cast off the asceticism of Christian knighthood.

Salon culture rested upon the conviction that inter-sexual conversation is valuable as a creative power. The overt or latent erotic sensation and the agonistic probation of the cavalier before the lady became an indispensable means of stimulating this conversation. Since the *Lettres Portugaises,* the actual love problems of women became a specific intellectual market value, and feminine love correspondence became 'literature.'

The last accentuation of the erotical sphere occurred in terms of intellectualist cultures. It occurred where this sphere collided with the unavoidably ascetic trait of the vocational specialist type of man. Under this tension between the erotic sphere and rational everyday life, specifically extramarital sexual life, which had been removed from everyday affairs, could appear as the only tie which still linked man with the natural fountain of all life. For man had now been completely emancipated from the cycle of the old, simple, and organic existence of the peasant. . . .

Under these conditions, the erotic relation seems to offer the unsurpassable peak of the fulfilment of the request for love in the direct fusion of the souls of one to the other. This boundless giving of oneself is as radical as possible in its opposition to all functionality, rationality, and generality. It is displayed here as the unique meaning which one creature in his irrationality has for another, and only for this specific other. However, from the point of view of eroticism, this meaning, and with it the value-content of the relation itself, rests upon the possibility of a communion which is felt as a complete unification, as a fading of the 'thou.' It is so overpowering that it is interpreted 'symbolically': as a sacrament. The lover realizes himself to be rooted in the kernel of the truly living, which is eternally inaccessible to any rational endeavor. He knows himself to be freed from the cold skeleton hands of rational orders, just as completely as from the banality of everyday routine. This consciousness of the lover rests upon the ineffaceability and inexhaustibleness of his own experience. The experience is by no means communicable and in this respect it is equivalent to the 'having' of the mystic. This is not only due to the intensity of the lover's experience, but to the immediacy of the possessed reality. Knowing 'life itself' joined to him, the lover stands opposite what is for him the objectless experiences of the mystic, as if he were facing the fading light of an unreal sphere.

As the knowing love of the mature man stands to the passionate enthusiasm of the youth, so stands the deadly earnestness of this eroticism of intellectualism to chivalrous love. In contrast to chivalrous love, this mature love of intellectualism reaffirms the natural quality of the sexual sphere, but it does so consciously, as an embodied creative power.

WILLIAM GRAHAM SUMNER

1840–1910

The son of British parents, William Graham Sumner was born in Paterson, New Jersey on October 30, 1840, grew up in New Haven and Hartford, Connecticut, married Jeannie Elliott in April, 1871, and died on April 10, 1910 in Englewood, New Jersey at 69. Sumner's father was a mechanic from Lancashire who became the victim of the business cycle in the U.S., arriving in time for the 1837 depression and never being able to attain financial security despite hard work. He lost an eye in an industrial accident and died poor in 1881, becoming for Sumner the "forgotten man" whom he memorialized in his most famous political essay. Sumner's mother died when he was eight, and he and his younger brother (who eventually split over political issues) were raised by a stingy stepmother whom they planned to murder. Through these turmoils Sumner learned to contain his emotions and was famous in adulthood for an aloof sternness, which developed into a love for Baconian, inductive science and not grand theories, a deep passion for details. After public school in Hartford, Sumner went to Yale in 1859 on the basis of his father's rare financial success, there enduring the rigid curriculum in place since 1828, becoming a classicist by necessity. Despite his lack of wealth or social standing, he was elected to the Skull and Bones fraternity, a connection which helped him throughout his career. He graduated in 1863, and like most of his classmates, his draft notice for the Civil War was "sold" to a poorer man, so he did not serve. He went abroad for more study, tutored at Yale for several more in classics, worked as a minister, and finally returned to Yale in 1873 to become a beginning professor, from which he never left except for a European hiatus in 1890–92 to recover from a mental breakdown. His teaching became legendary at Yale, summarized by one student as "everything about society that a gentleman ought to know." He and the President of Yale feuded publicly over Sumner's use of Herbert Spencer's introduction to sociology, one of many polemical disputes in which he was engaged, usually on financial or political topics.

Sumner wrote biographies of political leaders, a history of currency, a history of finance in the American Revolution, and a history of protection, plus hundreds of articles for popular and scholarly journals. But the works for which he is now remembered regarding social thought are *What Social Classes Owe to Each Other* (1883) and, more substantially, *Folkways: A Study of the Sociological Importance of Usages, Manners, Customs, Mores, and Morals* (1906). Sumner argued in this timeless volume that people are driven by the four basic instincts of fear, vanity, hunger, and the need for love. (W. I. Thomas resuscitated this notion as "the four wishes" in 1918.) To fulfill them societies create customary norms (folkways) that guide behavior, and some of these over time, and upon reflection, gain an ethical weight, thus becoming moral norms (mores, singular "mos"). *Folkways* is the largest catalogue of such behavior ever assembled, and was meant to be part of a much larger enterprise, *The Science of Society* (4 vols), which Sumner never lived to complete. It was assembled posthumously by his colleague and apostle, Albert Keller.

FOLKWAYS, 1907

Fundamental Notions

1. Definition and mode of origin of the folkways. If we put together all that we have learned from anthropology and ethnography about primitive men and primitive society, we perceive that the first task of life is to live. Men begin with acts, not with thoughts. Every moment brings necessities which must be satisfied at once. Need was the first experience, and it was followed at once by a blundering effort to satisfy it. It is generally taken for granted that men inherited some guiding instincts from their beast ancestry, and it may be true, although it has never been proved. If there were such inheritances, they controlled and aided the first efforts to satisfy needs. Analogy makes it easy to assume that the ways of beasts had produced channels of habit and predisposition along which dexterities and other psychophysical activities would run easily. Experiments with newborn animals show that in the absence of any experience of the relation of means to ends, efforts to satisfy needs are clumsy and blundering. The method is that of trial and failure, which produces repeated pain, loss, and disappointments. Nevertheless, it is a method of rude experiment and selection. The earliest efforts of men were of this kind. Need was the impelling force. Pleasure and pain, on the one side and the other, were the rude constraints which defined the line on which efforts must proceed. The ability to distinguish between pleasure and pain is the only psychical power which is to be assumed. Thus ways of doing things were selected, which were expedient. They answered the purpose better than other ways, or with less toil and pain. Along the course on which efforts were compelled to go, habit, routine, and skill were developed. The struggle to maintain existence was carried on, not individually, but in groups. Each profited by the other's experience; hence there was concurrence towards that which proved to be most expedient. All at last adopted the same way

for the same purpose; hence the ways turned into customs and became mass phenomena. Instincts were developed in connection with them. In this way folkways arise. The young learn them by tradition, imitation, and authority. The folkways, at a time, provide for all the needs of life then and there. They are uniform, universal in the group, imperative, and invariable. As time goes on, the folkways become more and more arbitrary, positive, and imperative. If asked why they act in a certain way in certain cases, primitive people always answer that it is because they and their ancestors always have done so. A sanction also arises from ghost fear. The ghosts of ancestors would be angry if the living should change the ancient folkways (see sec. 6).

2. The folkways are a societal force. The operation by which folkways are produced consists in the frequent repetition of petty acts, often by great numbers acting in concert or, at least, acting in the same way when face to face with the same need. The immediate motive is interest. It produces habit in the individual and custom in the group. It is, therefore, in the highest degree original and primitive. By habit and custom it exerts a strain on every individual within its range; therefore it rises to a societal force to which great classes of societal phenomena are due. Its earliest stages, its course, and laws may be studied; also its influence on individuals and their reaction on it. It is our present purpose so to study it. We have to recognize it as one of the chief forces by which a society is made to be what it is. Out of the unconscious experiment which every repetition of the ways includes, there issues pleasure or pain, and then, so far as the men are capable of reflection, convictions that the ways are conducive to societal welfare. These two experiences are not the same. The most uncivilized men, both in the food quest and in war, do things which are painful, but which have been found to be expedient. Perhaps these cases teach the sense of social welfare better than those which are pleasurable and favorable to welfare. The former cases call for some intelligent reflection on experience. When this conviction as to the relation to welfare is added to the folkways they are converted into mores, and, by virtue of the philosophical and ethical element added to

From *Folkways: A Study of the Sociological Importance of Usages, Manners, Customs, Mores, and Morals,* by William Graham Sumner. Published by Ginn and Company, 1906.

them, they win utility and importance and become the source of the science and the art of living.

3. Folkways are made unconsciously. It is of the first importance to notice that, from the first acts by which men try to satisfy needs, each act stands by itself, and looks no further than the immediate satisfaction. From recurrent needs arise habits for the individual and customs for the group, but these results are consequences which were never conscious, and never foreseen or intended. They are not noticed until they have long existed, and it is still longer before they are appreciated. Another long time must pass, and a higher stage of mental development must be reached, before they can be used as a basis from which to deduce rules for meeting, in the future, problems whose pressure can be foreseen. The folkways, therefore, are not creations of human purpose and wit. They are like products of natural forces which men unconsciously set in operation, or they are like the instinctive ways of animals, which are developed out of experience, which reach a final form of maximum adaptation to an interest, which are handed down by tradition and admit of no exception or variation, yet change to meet new conditions, still within the same limited methods, and without rational reflection or purpose. From this it results that all the life of human beings, in all ages and stages of culture, is primarily controlled by a vast mass of folkways handed down from the earliest existence of the race, having the nature of the ways of other animals, only the top-most layers of which are subject to change and control, and have been somewhat modified by human philosophy, ethics, and religion, or by other acts of intelligent reflection. We are told of savages that "It is difficult to exhaust the customs and small ceremonial usages of a savage people. Custom regulates the whole of a man's actions,—his bathing, washing, cutting his hair, eating, drinking, and fasting. From his cradle to his grave he is the slave of ancient usage. In his life there is nothing free, nothing original, nothing spontaneous, no progress towards a higher and better life, and no attempt to improve his condition, mentally, morally, or spiritually." All

men act in this way with only a little wider margin of voluntary variation. . . .

6. The aleatory interest. If we should try to find a specimen society in which expedient ways of satisfying needs and interest were found by trial and failure, and by long selection from experience, as broadly described in sec. I above, it might be impossible to find one. Such a practical and utilitarian mode of procedure, even when mixed with ghost sanction, is rationalistic. It would not be suited to the ways and temper of primitive men. There was an element in the most elementary experience which was irrational and defied all expedient methods. One might use the best known means with the greatest care, yet fail of the result. On the other hand, one might get a great result with no effort at all. One might also incur a calamity without any fault of his own. This was the aleatory element in life, the element of risk and loss, good or bad fortune. This element is never absent from the affairs of men. It has greatly influenced their life philosophy and policy. On one aide, good luck may mean something for nothing, the extreme case of prosperity and felicity. On the other side, ill luck may mean failure, loss, calamity, and disappointment, in spite of the most earnest and well-planned endeavor. The minds of men always dwell more on bad luck. They accept ordinary prosperity as a matter of course. Misfortunes arrest their attention and remain in their memory. Hence the ills of life are the mode of manifestation of the aleatory element which has most affected life policy. Primitive men ascribed all incidents to the agency of men or of ghosts and spirits. Good and ill luck were attributed to the superior powers, and were supposed to be due to their pleasure or displeasure at the conduct of men. This group of notions constitutes goblinism. It furnishes a complete world philosophy. The element of luck is always present in the struggle for existence. That is why primitive men never could carry on the struggle for existence, disregarding the aleatory element and employing a utilitarian method only. The aleatory element has always been the connecting link between the struggle for existence and religion. It was only by religious rites that the aleatory element in the struggle for existence could be controlled. The notions of ghosts, demons, another world, etc., were all fantastic. They lacked all connection with facts, and were arbitrary constructions put upon experience. They were poetic and developed by poetic construction and imaginative deduction. The nexus between them and events was not cause and effect, but magic. They therefore led to delusive deductions in regard to life and its meaning, which entered into subsequent action as guiding faiths, and imperative notions about the conditions of success. The authority of religion and that of custom coalesced into one indivisible obligation. Therefore the simple statement of experiment and expediency in the first paragraph above is not derived directly from actual cases, but is a product of analysis and inference. It must also be added that vanity and ghost fear produced needs which was as eager to satisfy as those of hunger of the family.

Blacks and Whites in Southern Society

In our southern states, before the civil war, whites and blacks had formed habits of action and feeling towards each other. They lived in peace and concord, and each one grew up in the ways which were traditional and customary. The civil war abolished legal rights and left the two races to learn how to live together under other relations than before. The whites have never been converted from the old mores. Those who still survive look back with regret and affection to the old social usages and customary sentiments and feelings. The two races have not yet made new mores. Vain attempts have been made to control the new order by legislation. The only result is the proof that legislation cannot make mores. We see also that mores do not form under social convulsion and discord. It is only just now that the new society seems to be taking shape. There is a trend in the mores now as they begin to form under the new state of things. It is not at all what the humanitarians hoped and expected. The two races are separating more than ever before. The strongest point in the new code seems to be that any white man is boycotted and despised if he "associates with negroes." Some are anxious to interfere and try to control. They take their stand on ethical views of what is going on. It is evidently impossible for any one to interfere. We are like spectators at a great natural convulsion. The results will be such as the facts and forces call for. We cannot foresee them. They do not depend on ethical views any more than the volcanic eruption on Martinique contained an ethical element. All the faiths, hopes, energies, and sacrifices of both whites and blacks are components in the new construction of folkways by which the two races will learn how to live together. As we go along with the constructive process it is very plain that what once was, or what any one thinks ought to be, but slightly affects what, at any moment, is. The mores which once were are a memory. Those which any one thinks ought to be are a dream. The only thing with which we can deal are those which are.

LEON TROTSKY

1879–1940

The son of a Jewish colonist farmer in the steppe, who was as stubborn as his revolutionary son, and of an educated middle-class mother, Lev Davidovich Bronshtein was born in Yanovka, Ukraine, near Elizavetgrad on November 7, 1879, and married Aleksandra Sokolovskaya (in spring or summer, 1900), with whom he had two daughters. He then married Natalya Sedova in 1903, and their family included two sons, all the while maintaining cordial relations with his first wife, a co-revolutionary who was initially far more radical than her future husband. Bronshtein was murdered by one of Stalin's assassins at his exile home in Coyoacan, Mexico City on August 20, 1940, struck in the head with a pickaxe as he worked at his desk. He attended school in Odessa, went to the university there briefly, but left in 1897, involving himself in revolutionary groups from a young age and thereby infuriating his father, who believed that the czarist system could never be removed. In 1898 he was exiled to Siberia, and Sokolovskaya accompanied him. Their marriage may have been in part a political convenience, but his affection for her seemed genuine to observers. Taking Trotsky as his name, he escaped to England in 1902, and returned to Russia in 1917 to participate in the Revolution with Lenin. He became a successful commander of the red forces in the civil war that followed the Bolshevik accession to power in 1918, a conflict that involved troops and supplies from a number of European nations, and the U.S., in an effort to remove the communists. After Lenin's death, Trotsky was forced from power by Stalin and exiled in 1929, going to France (1933), Norway (1935), and Mexico (1936).

Trotsky was without doubt the most brilliant writer and propagandist of the Bolshevik contingent, even though Lenin was surely the more effective politician, perhaps because he was not so patently superior to the rank and file to incite discord among them in the way Trotsky did. Bernard Shaw gave Trotsky high praise for his political prose, despite reading his work in translation. From the point of view of social theory, only a few of his many books have stood the test of time, specifically *Permanent Revolution* (1931) and *Literature and Revolution* (1924). His autobiography, *My Life* (1930), is a masterpiece of the genre and remains for many readers their favorite of all Trotsky's books. And his enormous *History of the Russian Revolution* is indispensable to the topic, showing Trotsky at his best as a politically engaged intellectual who could dispassionately tell a vexed story in which he played a leading role. The idea of "permanent revolution" dates back to the 1905 revolution in Russia, and argues that the struggle between the bourgeoisie and the proletariat is perpetual and global, and that revolution confined to one country is impossible and politically pointless. Stalin, of course, took the opposite view, which is one reason why he exiled Trotsky.

RESULTS AND PROSPECTS, 1906

What Is the Permanent Revolution?

Basic Postulates

I hope that the reader will not object if, to end this book, I attempt, without fear of repetition, to formulate succinctly my principal conclusions.

1. The theory of the permanent revolution now demands the greatest attention from every Marxist, for the course of the class and ideological struggle has fully and finally raised this question from the realm of reminiscences over old differences of opinion among Russian Marxists, and converted it into a question of the character, the inner connexions and methods of the international revolution in general.

2. With regard to countries with a belated bourgeois development, especially the colonial and semi-colonial countries, the theory of the permanent revolution signifies that the complete and genuine solution of their tasks of achieving *democracy and national emancipation* is conceivable only through the dictatorship of the proletariat as the leader of the subjugated nation, above all of its peasant masses.

3. Not only the agrarian, but also the national question assigns to the peasantry—the overwhelming majority of the population in backward countries—an exceptional place in the democratic revolution. Without as alliance of the proletariat with the peasantry the tasks of the democratic revolution cannot be solved, nor even seriously posed. But the alliance of these two classes can be realized in no other way than through an irreconcilable struggle against the influence of the national-liberal bourgeoisie.

4. No matter what the first episodic stages of the revolution may be in the individual countries, the realization of the revolutionary alliance between the proletariat and the peasantry is conceivable only under the political leadership of the proletarian vanguard, organized in the Communist Party. This in turn means that the victory of the democratic revolution is conceivable only through the dictatorship of the proletariat which bases itself upon the alliance with the peasantry and solves first of all the tasks of the democratic revolution.

5. Assessed historically, the old slogan of Bolshevism— 'the democratic dictatorship of the proletariat and peasantry'—expressed primly the above-characterized relationship of the proletariat, the peasantry and the liberal bourgeoisie. This has been confirmed by the experience of October. But Lenin's old formula did not settle in advance the problem of what the reciprocal relations would be between the proletariat and the peasantry within the revolutionary bloc. In other words, the formula deliberately retained a certain algebraic quality, which had to make way for more precise arithmetical quantities in the process of historical experience. However, the latter showed, and under circumstances that exclude any kind of misinterpretation, that no matter how great the revolutionary role of the peasantry may be, it nevertheless cannot be an independent role and even less a leading one. The peasant follows either the worker or the bourgeois. This means that the 'democratic dictatorship of the proletariat and peasantry' is only conceivable as a *dictatorship of the proletariat that leads the peasant masses behind it.*

6. A democratic dictatorship of the proletariat and peasantry, as a regime that is distinguished from the dictatorship of the proletariat by its class content, might be realized only in a case where an *independent* revolutionary party could be constituted, expressing the interests of the peasants and in general of petty-bourgeois democracy—a party capable of conquering power with this or that degree of aid from the proletariat, and of determining its revolutionary programme. . . .

7. The Comintern's endeavour to foist upon the Eastern countries the slogan of the democratic dictatorship of the proletariat and peasantry, finally and long ago exhausted by history, can have only a reactionary effect.

From *The Permanent Revolution and Results and Prospects*, by Leon Trotsky. Published by Merit Publishers. Copyright © 1969.

Insofar as this slogan is counterposed to the slogan of the dictatorship of the proletariat, it contributes politically to the dissolution of the proletariat in the petty-bourgeois masses and thus creates the most favourable conditions for the hegemony of the national bourgeoisie and consequently for the collapse of the democratic revolution. The introduction of this slogan into the programme of the Comintern is a direct betrayal of Marxism and of the October tradition of Bolshevism.

8. The dictatorship of the proletariat which has risen to power as the leader of the democratic revolution is inevitably and very quickly confronted with tasks, the fulfilment of which is bound up with deep inroads into the rights of bourgeois property. The democratic revolution grows over directly into the socialist revolution and thereby becomes a *permanent* revolution.

9. The conquest of power by the proletariat does not complete the revolution, but only opens it. Socialist construction is conceivable only on the foundation of the class struggle, on a national and international scale. This under the conditions of an overwhelming predominance of capitalist relationships on the world arena, must inevitably lead to explosions, that is, internally to civil wars and externally to revolutionary wars. Therein lies the permanent character of the socialist revolution as such, regardless of whether it is a backward country that is involved, which only yesterday accomplished its democratic revolution, or an old capitalist country which already has behind it a long epoch of democracy and parliamentarism.

10. The completion of the socialist revolution within national limits is unthinkable. One of the basic reasons for the crisis in bourgeois society is the fact that the productive forces created by it can no longer be reconciled with the framework of the national state. From this follow, on the one hand, imperialist wars, on the other, the utopia of a bourgeois United States of Europe. The socialist revolution begins on the national arena, it unfolds on the international arena, and is completed on the world arena. Thus, the socialist revolution becomes a permanent revolution in a newer

and broader sense of the word: it attains completion only in the final victory of the new society on our entire planet.

11. The above-outlined sketch of the development of the world revolution eliminates the question of countries that are 'mature' or 'immature' for socialism in the spirit of that pedantic, lifeless classification given by the present programme of the Comintern. Insofar as capitalism has created a world market, a world division of labour and world productive forces, it has also prepared world economy as—a whole for socialist transformation.

Different countries will go through this process at different tempos. Backward countries may, under certain conditions, arrive at the dictatorship of the proletariat sooner than advanced countries, but they will come later than the latter to socialism. . . .

12. The theory of socialism in one country, which rose on the yeast of the reaction against October, is the only theory that consistently and to the very end opposes the theory of the permanent revolution.

The attempt of the epigones, under the lash of our criticism, to confine the application of the theory of socialism in one country exclusively to Russia, because of its specific characteristics (its vastness and its natural resources), does not improve matters but only makes them worse. The break with the internationalist position always and invariably leads to national *messianism*, that is, to attributing special superiorities and qualities to ones own country, which allegedly permit it to play a rôle to which other countries cannot attain.

The world division of labour, the dependence of Soviet industry upon foreign technology, the dependence of the productive forces of the advanced countries of Europe upon Asiatic raw materials, etc., etc., make the construction of an independent socialist society in any single country in the world impossible.

13. The theory of Stalin and Bukharin, running counter to the entire experience of the Russian revolution, not only sets up the democratic revolution mechanically in contrast to the socialist revolution, but also makes a breach

between the national revolution and the international revolution.

This theory imposes upon revolutions in backward countries the task of establishing an unrealizable régime of democratic dictatorship, which it counterposes to the dictatorship of the proletariat. Thereby this theory introduces illusions and fictions into politics, paralyses the struggle for power of the proletariat in the East, and hampers the victory of the colonial revolution. . . .

14. The programme of the Comintern created by Bukharin is eclectic through and through. It makes the hopeless attempt to reconcile the theory of socialism in one country with Marxist internationalism, which is, however, inseparable from the permanent character of the world revolution. The struggle of the Communist Left Opposition for a correct policy and a healthy regime in the Communist International is inseparably bound up with the struggle for the Marxist programme. The question of the programme is in turn inseparable from the question of the two mutually exclusive theories: the theory of permanent revolution and the theory of socialism in one country. The problem of the permanent revolution has long ago outgrown the episodic differences of opinion between Lenin and Trotsky, which were completely exhausted by history. The struggle is between the basic ideas of Marx and Lenin on the one side and the eclecticism of the centrists on the other.

⌁

LITERATURE AND REVOLUTION, 1924

Proletarian Culture and Proletarian Art

Every ruling class creates its own culture, and consequently, its own art. History has known the slave-owning cultures of the East and of classic antiquity, the feudal culture of medieval Europe

and the bourgeois culture which now rules the world. It would follow from this, that the proletariat has also to create its own culture and its own art.

The question, however, is not as simple as it seems at first glance. Society in which slave-owners were the ruling class, existed for many and many centuries. The same is true of Feudalism. Bourgeois culture, if one were to count only from the time of its open and turbulent manifestation, that is, from the period of the Renaissance, has existed five centuries, but it did not reach its greatest flowering until the Nineteenth Century, or, more correctly, the second half of it. History shows that the formation of a new culture which centers around a ruling class demands considerable time and reaches completion only at the period preceding the political decadence of that class.

Will the proletariat have enough time to create a "proletarian" culture? In contrast to the regime of the slave-owners and of the feudal lords and of the bourgeoisie, the proletariat regards its dictatorship as a brief period of transition. When we wish to denounce the all-too-optimistic views about the transition to Socialism, we point out that the period of the social revolution, on a world scale, will last not months and not years, but decades—decades, but not centuries, and certainly not thousands of years. Can the proletariat in this time create a new culture? It is legitimate to doubt this, because the years of social revolution will be years of fierce class struggles in which destruction will occupy more room than new construction. At any rate, the energy of the proletariat itself will be spent mainly in conquering power, in retaining and strengthening it and in applying it to the most urgent needs of existence and of further struggle. The proletariat, however, will reach its highest tension and the fullest manifestation of its class character during this revolutionary period and it will be within such narrow limits that the possibility of planful, cultural reconstruction will be confined. On the other hand, as the new régime will be more and more protected from political and military surprises and as the conditions for cultural creation will become more favorable, the proletariat will be more and more dissolved into a Socialist community and will free itself from its class characteristics and thus cease to be a proletariat. In other words, there can be no question of

From *Literature and Revolution,* by Leon Trotsky, Rose Strunsky, Trans. Published by International Publishers, 1925.

the creation of a new culture, that is, of construction on a large historic scale during the period of dictatorship. The cultural reconstruction which will begin when the need of the iron clutch of a dictatorship unparalleled in history will have disappeared, will not have a class character. This seems to lead to the conclusion that there is no proletarian culture and that there never will be any and in fact there is no reason to regret this. The proletariat acquires power for the purpose of doing away forever with class culture and to make way for human culture. We frequently seem to forget this.

The formless talk about proletarian culture, in antithesis to bourgeois culture, feeds on the extremely uncritical identification of the historic destinies of the proletariat with those of the bourgeoisie. A shallow and purely liberal method of making analogies of historic forms has nothing in common with Marxism. There is no real analogy between the historic development of the bourgeoisie and of the working-class.

The development of bourgeois culture began several centuries before the bourgeoisie took into its own hands the power of the state by means of a series of revolutions. Even when the bourgeoisie was a third estate, almost deprived of its rights, it played a great and continually growing part in all the fields of culture. This is especially clear in the case of architecture. The Gothic churches were not built suddenly, under the impulse of a religious inspiration. The construction of the Cologne cathedral, its architecture and its sculpture, sum up the architectural experience of mankind from the time of the cave and combine the elements of this experience in a new style which expresses the culture of its own epoch which is, in the final analysis, the social structure and technique of this epoch. The old prebourgeoisie of the guilds was the factual builder of the Gothic. When it grew and waxed strong, that is, when it became richer, the bourgeoisie passed through the Gothic stage consciously and actively and created its own architectural style, not for the church, however, but for its own palaces. With its basis on the Gothic, it turned to antiquity, especially to Roman architecture and the Moorish, and applied all these to the conditions and needs of the new city community, thus creating the Renaissance (Italy at the end of the first quarter of the Fifteenth Century). Specialists may count the elements which the Renaissance owes to antiquity and those it owes to the Gothic and may argue as to which side is the stronger. But the Renaissance only begins when the new social class, already culturally satiated, feels itself strong enough to come out from under the yoke of the Gothic arch, to look at Gothic art and on all that preceded it as material for its own disposal, and to use the technique of the past for its own artistic aims. This refers also to all the other arts, but with this difference, that because of their greater flexibility, that is, of their lesser dependence upon utilitarian aims and materials, the "free" arts do not reveal the dialectics of successive styles with such firm logic as does architecture.

From the time of the Renaissance and of the Reformation which created more favorable intellectual and political conditions for the bourgeoisie in feudal society, to the time of the Revolution which transferred power to the bourgeoisie (in France), there passed three or four centuries of growth in the material and intellectual force of the bourgeoisie. The great French Revolution and the wars which grew out of it temporarily lowered the material level of culture. But later the capitalist régime became established as the "natural" and the "eternal".

Thus the fundamental processes of the growth of bourgeois culture and of its crystallization into style were determined by the characteristics of the bourgeoisie as a possessing and exploiting class. The bourgeoisie not only developed materially within feudal society, entwining itself in various ways with the latter and attracting wealth into his own hands, but it weaned the intelligentsia to its side and created its cultural foundation (schools, universities, academies, newspapers, magazines) long before it openly took possession of the state. It is sufficient to remember that the German bourgeoisie, with its incomparable technology, philosophy, science and art, allowed the power of the state to lie in the hands of a feudal bureaucratic class as late as 1918 and decided, or, more correctly, was forced to take power into its own hands only when the material foundations of German culture began to fall to pieces.

But one may answer: It took thousands of years to create the slave-owning art and only hundreds of years for the bourgeois art. Why, then, could not proletarian art be created in tens of years? The technical bases of life are not at all the same at present and therefore the tempo is also different. This objection, which at first sight seems convincing, in reality misses the crux of the question. Undoubtedly, in the development of the new society, the time will come when economics, cultural life and art will receive the greatest impulse forward. At the present time we can only create fancies about their tempo. In a society which will have thrown off the pinching and stulifying worry about one's daily bread in which community restaurants will prepare good, wholesome and tasteful food for all to choose, in which communal laundries will wash clean everyone's good linen, in which children, all the children, will be well fed and strong and gay, and in which they will absorb the fundamental elements of science and art as they absorb albumen and air and the warmth of the sun, in a society in which electricity and the radio will not be the crafts they are today, but will come from inexhaustible sources of super-power at the call of a central button, in which there will be no "useless mouths", in which the liberated egotism of man—a mighty force!—will be directed wholly towards the understanding, the transformation and the betterment of the universe—in such a society the dynamic development of culture will be incomparable with anything that went on in the past. But all this will come only after a climb, prolonged and difficult, which is still ahead of us. And we are speaking only about the period of the climb.

GEORG SIMMEL

1858–1918

Georg Simmel was born on March 1, 1858 in Berlin, the son of the "Felix and Sarotti" chocolate factory owner, the youngest of seven children in this family of assimilated Jews. He married the noted feminist and author Gertrud Kinel (pseudonym: Marie Luise Enckendorff) in 1890 and with her had one son in 1891, Hans, who became a physician. (After being liberated from the Holocaust camp at Dachau, Hans emigrated to the U.S.) In 1904 Simmel also had an illegitimate daughter, Angela, with one of his students, Gertrud Kantorowicz, poet and art historian. He attended the Friedrich-Werder-Gymnasiums, graduating in 1876, then studied history and philosophy (particularly Kant) at the University of Berlin. His first important writing in graduate school concerned the psychological-ethnological dimensions of music, and his first dissertation pertained to Kant's theory of material reality (1881). His habilitation also treated Kant (1885). He taught at Berlin at a lowly rank due mostly to anti-Semitism from 1885–1890, but was promoted slightly and stayed there until 1914, when he was finally offered a full professorship in philosophy at the minor university at Strassburg. Only there four years, he died of cancer on September 26, 1918 at the age of 60. During the first ten years of his career, he lectured to important American sociologists, including George Herbert Mead and Albion Small, the latter founding the sociology department at Chicago, and the *American Journal of Sociology,* which published many translations of Simmel's work in its first decade (1894–1904). Simmel also co-founded the German Sociological Society with Weber and Tönnies in 1909.

Difficult to pigeonhole, Simmel wrote books about Goethe, Rembrandt, Nietzsche, and Schopenhauer, the effect of money and commodification on interpersonal relations, sex roles, the sociology of religion, and one of the first and best introductory textbooks for sociology (1908). Although he inherited substantial funds, it has recently been argued by a leading Simmel authority that he taught out of financial necessity, not simply to keep himself occupied, as had long been thought. This meant, according to the German system, that his salary rose or fell strictly based upon the number of students who elected to enroll in his lecture courses, which tended therefore to be quite large. He was famous as a brilliant speaker, but because he needed to insure a steady stream of students, he created lectures on a bewildering array of topics, far broader than those delivered by his colleagues. He addressed the nature of love, fashion, the role of the stranger, the nobility, the prostitute, the poor, the role of women, the question of how urban life affected mental health, and scores of other topics designed to entrance a paying audience of mature students. Along the way he also created a "formal" sociology that emphasized the shape, the morphology of social relations, rather than the content, thus carving out a place for sociology among its sister disciplines. In his *Philosophy of Money* (1900) he also offered the single most important elaboration of Marx's *Capital* by any social theorist until Weber's *Economy and Society* appeared 22 years later. Simmel was a unique figure in the history of theory, and has found an entirely new audience as postmodern studies have grown in volume and quality over the last two decades. More than the "modernists" Durkheim, Marx, or Weber, Simmel's interest in the fragmentary nature of modern culture and its affects on the individual, positive and negative, is more in keeping the postmodernist sensibility than those of his famous peers.

"COMPETITION," 1908

Particular kinds of such a synthesis are found in the phenomena lumped together under the name of competition. The foremost sociological characteristic of competition is the fact that conflict in it is indirect. In so far as one gets rid of an adversary or damages him directly, one does not compete with him. In general, linguistic usage reserves the term only for conflicts which consist in parallel efforts by both parties concerning the same prize. The difference of this from other kinds of conflict can perhaps be described in more detail as follows.

The Socializing and Civilizing Function of Competition

Yet the progress of its content which competition achieves by means of its peculiarly interwoven form of interaction is not so important here as is its immediately sociological process. The aim for which competition occurs within a society is presumably always the favor of one or more third persons. Each of the competing parties therefore tries to come as close to that third one as possible. Usually, the poisonous, divisive, destructive effects of competition are stressed, and for the rest it is merely admitted that it creates certain values as its product. But in addition, it has, after all, this immense sociating effect. Competition compels the

From *Conflict and the Web of Group-Affiliations*, by Georg Simmel, Kurt H. Wolff, Ed./Trans. Copyright © 1955. Published by The Free Press; copyright renewed 1983 by Kurt H. Wolff. Reprinted with the permission of The Free Press, a Division of Simon & Schuster Adult Publishing Group.

wooer who has a co-wooer, and often in this way alone comes to be a wooer properly speaking, to go out to the wooed, come close to him, establish ties with him, find his strengths and weaknesses and adjust to them, find all bridges, or cast new ones, which might connect the competitor's own being and doing with his.

To be sure, this often happens at the price of the competitor's own dignity and of the objective value of his product. Competition, above all competition among the makers of the highest intellectual products, makes those who are destined to guide the mass subordinate themselves to it. In order to permit the effective exercise of their function as teachers, party leaders, artists, or journalists, they must obey the instincts or moods of the mass once the mass can choose among them, which it can because of their competition. As far as *content* is concerned, this certainly makes for a reversal of the hierarchy of social life-values; but this does not detract from the *formal* significance of competition for the synthesis of society. Innumerable times, it achieves what usually only love can do: the divination of the innermost wishes of the other, even before he himself becomes aware of them. Antagonistic tension with his competitor sharpens the businessman's sensitivity to the tendencies of the public, even to the point of clairvoyance, in respect to future changes in the public's tastes, fashions, interests—not only the businessman's, but also the journalist's, artist's, bookseller's, parliamentarian's. Modern competition is described as the fight of all against all, but at the same time it is the fight of all *for* all. Nobody will deny the tragedy of social elements working against one another, instead of for; of the squandering of innumerable forces in the struggle against the competitor—forces which could be used for positive achievements; or, finally, of the discarding of the positive and valuable achievement, unused and unrewarded, as soon as a more valuable or at least a more appealing one competes with it.

But all these liabilities of competition in the social balance sheet must only be added to the immense synthetic force of the fact that, in society, competition is competition for man, a wrestling for applause and effort, exemption and devotion of all kinds, a wrestling of the few for the many, as well as of the many for the few. In short, it is a web of a thousand sociological threads by means of conscious concentration on the will and feeling and thinking of fellowmen, of the adaptation of the producers to the consumers, of the delicately multiplied possibilities of gaining favor and connection. Once the narrow and naive solidarity of primitive social conditions yielded to decentralization (which was bound to have been the immediate result of the quantitative enlargement of the group), man's effort toward man, his adaptation to the other, seems possible only at the price of competition, that is, of the simultaneous fight *against* a fellowman *for* a third one—against whom, for that matter, he may well compete in some other relationship for the former. Given the breadth and individualization of society, many kinds of interest, which eventually hold the group together throughout its members, seem to come alive and stay alive only when the urgency and requirements of the competitive struggle force them upon the individual.

Man's most valuable object is man, directly and indirectly. Indirectly, because in him are stored the energies of sub-human nature, as in the animal we eat or make work for us, are stored those of the vegetable kingdom; and in plants, those of sun and earth, air and water. Man is the most condensed, most fruitfully exploitable phenomenon; and the necessity of psychologically winning him over grows in the measure in which slavery, that is, his mechanical appropriation, weakens. The fight against man, which was a fight for him and his enslavement, thus changes into the more complex phenomenon of competition. To be sure, in it too, a man fights another man, but *for* a third one. And the winning over of that third one can be achieved in a thousand ways

only through the sociological means of persuasion or conviction, surpassing or underselling, suggestion or threat, in short, through psychological connection. But just as often, this winning over also means in its effect such a psychological connection, the founding of a relationship—from the momentary relation established by a purchase in a store to marriage. As the intensity and condensation of life-contents increases culturally, the straggle for the most condensed of all goods, the human soul, must take on ever larger proportions and must multiply and deepen interactions which bring men together and which are both the means and the ends of that struggle.

❧

"THE SOCIAL AND THE INDIVIDUAL LEVEL"

An Example of General Sociology

There was a time when the only topic of social investigation was the historical fate or the practical politics of particular groups. During the last decades, however, *sociation,* or the life of groups as units, has become such a topic. Attention thus was attracted by what is common to *all* groups inasmuch as they are societies. This presently led to the examination of a closely related problem—of the characteristics which distinguish social from individual life. At first glance, the differences seem obvious. For instance, there is the basic immortality of the group, as against the mortality of the individual. There is the possibility of the group eliminating even its most important elements without collapsing—an elimination which, applied to the individual, would annihilate him. But the problem was of a more subtle, perhaps psychological, nature. No matter whether one considers the group that exists irrespective of its individual members a fiction or a reality, in order to understand certain facts one must treat it as if it actually did have its own life, and laws, and other characteristics. And if one is to justify the sociological standpoint, it is precisely the differences between these characteristics and those of the individual existence that one must clarify.

§ 1. The Determinateness of the Group and the Vacillation of the Individual

A clue for the ascertainment of these differences lies in the suggestion that societal actions have incomparably greater purposiveness and to-the-pointness than individual actions. The individual, the argument goes, is torn by conflicting feelings, impulses, and considerations. In his conduct, he is not always certain subjectively, much less correct objectively, in his knowledge of alternatives. Although it often changes its line of action, the social group is, by contrast, nevertheless determined at any one moment to follow, without reservation, the line of that moment. Above all, it always knows whom to consider its enemy and whom its friend. Furthermore, it shows less discrepancy than the individual between will and deed, and between means and ends. Individual actions, therefore, strike us as "free," and mass actions impress us as if they were determined by natural laws.

This whole formulation is highly questionable. Nevertheless, it merely exaggerates a real and highly significant difference between group and individual. The difference results from the fact that the aims of the public spirit, as of any collective, are those that usually strike the individual as if they were his own fundamentally simple and primitive aims. There are two reasons why this fact is so often not realized. One is the power that public aims have gained with the expansion of their range. The other is the highly complex techniques with which especially *modern* public life appeals to the individual intelligence when trying to put these aims into practice. The social group does not vacillate or err in *all* its aims, just as the individual does not in only his most *primitive* ones. The insurance of his existence, the acquisition of new property, the pleasure derived from the maintenance and expansion of his power, and the protection of his possessions are fundamental drives of the individual. In pursuing their satisfaction, he associates with an indefinite number of

other individuals. It is because he does not choose these aspirations nor vacillate in their pursuit that the social aspiration, which unites him with others, knows no choice or vacillation either. Furthermore, just as the individual proceeds with clarity, determination, and certainty of aim in his purely egoistic actions, so the mass in regard to all of its aims. The mass does not know the dualism of egoistic and altruistic impulses, a dualism that often renders the individual helpless and makes him embrace a vacuum. Law, the first and essential condition of the life of groups, large and small, has aptly been called the "ethical minimum." As a matter of fact, the norms adequate to secure the continuation of the group (even if only precariously), constitute a bare minimum for the external existence of the individual as a social being. If he observed only them, without tying himself to a large number of additional laws, he would be an ethical abnormality, an utterly impossible being.

§ 2. Individual vs. Group Member

This consideration hints at the nature of the difference in level between the mass and the individual. The difference becomes clearly visible, and can be understood, on the basis of only one fact. This fact is the possibility of separating, in the individual himself, the qualities and behaviors by which he "forms" the "mass" and which he contributes to the collective spirit, on the one hand; and, on the other, different qualities which constitute his private property, as it were, and which lift him out of everything he may have in common with others. The first part of his nature can evidently consist only in more primitive elements, that are inferior in terms of finesse and intellectuality. This is so, above all, because it is the existence of these elements alone that we can be relatively sure of in all individuals. If the organic world gradually develops from lower to higher forms, the lower and more primitive ones, obviously, are the oldest. But thus, they are also the most widely diffused: the heredity of the species is the more certainly transmitted to the individual, the longer it has been in existence and has become fixed. By contrast, more recently acquired organs—such as the higher and more complex organs are to a much greater extent—always are more variable; and it is impossible to be sure whether all members of a given species already possess them. Thus the length of time during which a given trait has been inherited constitutes the real relation that exists between its primitive character and its diffusion. But we must consider not only biological heredity. There also are intellectual traits that manifest themselves in word and knowledge, in orientation of feeling, and in norms of will and judgment. As traditions, both conscious and unconscious, they permeate the individual; and the more so, the more generally, firmly, and unquestionably they have become parts of the intellectual life of his society—that is, the older they are. To this same extent, however, they are also less complex; they are coarser and closer to the immediate manifestations and necessities of life. As they become more refined and differentiated, they lose the probability of being the property of all. Rather, they become more or less individual, and are only accidentally shared with others. . . .

§ 4. The Sociological Significance of Individual Similarity and Dissimilarity

It is above all the practical significance of men for one another that is determined by both similarities and differences among them. Similarity, as fact or as tendency, is no less important than difference. In the most varied forms, both are the great principles of all external and internal development. In fact, the cultural history of mankind can be conceived as the history of the struggles and conciliatory attempts between the two. For the actions of the individual, his difference from others is of far greater interest than is his similarity with them. It largely is differentiation from others that challenges and determines our activity. We depend on the observation of their differences if we want to use them and adopt the right attitude toward them. Our practical interest concentrates on what gives us advantages and disadvantages in our dealings with them, not on that in which we coincide. Similarity, rather, provides the indispensable condition for any developing action whatever. Darwin reports that in his many contacts with animal breeders he never met one who believed in the common origin of species. The interest in the slight variation that characterized the particular stock which he happened to breed and which consti-

tuted a practical value for him, so occupied his consciousness that it left no room for noting the basic similarity of this stock with other races and species. It is understandable that such an interest in the differentiae of his property should extend to all other possessions and relations of the individual. In general, we may say that if something is objectively of equal importance in terms of both similarity with a type and differentiation from it, we will be more conscious of the differentiation. In regard to the similarity, organic purposiveness perhaps proceeds without consciousness, because in practical life it needs all the consciousness there is for the awareness of differences. The interest in differentiation in fact is so great that in practice it produces differences where there is no objective basis for them. We note, for instance, that organizations, whether they be legislative bodies or committees in charge of "social functions," in spite of their outspoken and unifying positions and aims, are apt, in the course of time, to split up into factions; and these factions stand in relations to one another that are similar to those between the original organization as a whole and another organization with a totally different character. It is as if each individual largely felt his own significance only by contrasting himself with others. As a matter of fact, where such a contrast does not exist, he may even artificially create it. He may do so even when the whole solidarity and unity he now scans in his search for a contrast, derive from the existence of a united front that he and others have formed in opposition to another similar united front.

§ 5. The Individual's Superiority over the Mass

Countless additional examples from cultural and social history testify to the fact that the new, the rare, and the individual (merely three aspects, evidently, of the same fundamental phenomenon) are rated as the valuationally preferred. This discussion, however, only has the purpose of throwing light on the inverse phenomenon, the fact, that is, that the qualities and behaviors with which the individual forms a mass, because he shares them with others, are rated valuationally inferior. Here we deal with what might be called the sociological tragedy as such. The more refined, highly developed, articulated the qualities of an individual are, the more unlikely are they to make him similar to other individuals and to form a unit with corresponding qualities in others. Rather, they tend to become incomparable; and the elements, in terms of which the individual can count on adapting himself to others and on forming a homogeneous mass with them, are increasingly reduced to lower and primitively more sensuous levels. This explains how it is possible for the "folk" or the "mass" to be spoken of with contempt, without there being any need for the individual to feel himself referred to by this usage, which actually does not refer to any individual. As soon as the individual is considered in his entirety, he appears to possess much higher qualities than those he contributes to the collective unit. This situation has found its classical formulation in Schiller: "Seen singly, everybody is passably intelligent and reasonable; but united into a body, they are block-heads." The fact that individuals, in all their divergencies, leave only the lowest parts of their personalities to form a common denominator, is stressed by Heine: "You have rarely understood me, and rarely did I understand you. Only when we met in the mire did we understand each other at once."

This difference between the individual and the mass level is so profoundly characteristic of social existence and is of such important consequences that it is worthwhile quoting additional observations. They come from authorities of extremely different historical positions who are similar, however, in the sense that these positions gave them exceptional insight into collective phenomena. Solon is supposed to have said that each of his Athenians is a shrewd fox; but that, if assembled on the Pnyx, they amount to a herd of sheep. The Cardinal Retz, when describing the procedure of the Parisian parliament at the time of the *Fronde,* notes in his memoirs that numerous bodies, even if their members include many high-stationed and cultivated individuals, in common discussion and procedure always act as a mob, reverting to the conceptions and passions of the common people. Frederick the Great, in a remark that is very similar to that of Solon, says that his generals are the most reasonable people as long as

he talks to them as individuals, but that they are "sheepheads" when assembled in war council. Evidently something comparable is suggested by the English historian Freeman, who observes that the House of Commons, though an aristocratic body in terms of the ranks of its members, nevertheless, when assembled, behaves like a democratic rabble. The best authority on British trade unions notes that their mass assemblies often result in very stupid and pernicious resolutions, so that most of such meetings have been given up in favor of assemblies of delegates. This is confirmed by observations that are insignificant in their contents but are sociologically relevant, not only because of their frequency, but also because they symbolize historically very important situations and events. I shall give only a few examples. Eating and drinking, the oldest and intellectually most negligible functions, can form a tie, often the only one, among very heterogeneous persons and groups. Stag parties may be attended by highly cultivated individuals who, nevertheless, have the tendency to pass the time by telling off-color jokes. Among younger people, the peak of gaiety and harmony is always attained by means of the most primitive and intellectually least pretentious social games.

The difference between the individual and collective levels accounts for the fact that the necessity to oblige the masses, or even habitually to expose oneself to them, easily corrupts the character. It pulls the individual away from his individuality and down to a level with all and sundry. To consider it a questionable virtue of the journalist, the actor, and the demagogue to "seek the favor of the masses" would not be altogether justified if these masses consisted of the sum of the total personal existences of their members. For there is no reason whatever to despise *them.* But actually, the mass is no such sum. It is a new phenomenon made up, not of the total individualities of its members, but only of those fragments of each of them in which he coincides with all others. These fragments, therefore, can be nothing but the lowest and most primitive. It is *this* mass, and the level that must always remain accessible to each of its members, that these intellectually and morally endangered persons serve—and not each of its members in its entirety.

"INDIVIDUAL AND SOCIETY IN EIGHTEENTH- AND NINETEENTH-CENTURY VIEWS OF LIFE," 1917

An Example of Philosophical Sociology

§ 1. Individual Life as the Basis of the Conflict between Individual and Society

The really practical problem of society is the relation between its forces and forms and the individual's own life. The question is not whether society exists only in the individuals or also outside of them. For even if we attribute "life," properly speaking, only to individuals, and identify the life of society with that of its individual members, we must admit the existence of conflict between the two. One reason for this conflict is the fact that in the individuals themselves, social elements fuse into the particular phenomenon called "society." "Society" develops its own vehicles and organs by whose claims and commands the individual is confronted as by an alien party. A second reason results from another aspect of the inherency of society in the individual. For man has the capacity to decompose himself into parts and to feel any one of these as his proper self. Yet each part may collide with any other and may struggle for the dominion over the individual's actions. . . .

§ 2. Individual Egoism vs. Individual Self-Perfection as an Objective Value

The formulation presented seems to me to describe the contrast between the two parties much more comprehensively than does its customary reduction to the egoism-altruism dichotomy. On the one hand, the individual's striving for wholeness appears as egoism, which is contrasted with the altruism of his ordering himself into society as a selectivity formed social member of it. Yet on the other hand, the very quest of society is an egoism that does violence to the individual for the benefit

and utility of the many, and that often makes for an extremely one-sided individual specialization, and even atrophy. Finally, the individual's urge toward self-perfection is not necessarily an expression of egoism. It may also be an objective ideal whose goal is by no means success in terms of happiness and narrowly personal interests but a super-personal value realized in the personality.

What has just been suggested—and what will be elaborated presently—appears to me to exemplify a very significant stage in the development of cultural-philosophical consciousness. It also throws new light on the ethics of the individual and, indirectly, on the ethics of society. It is popularly held that all intentions which do not break through the orbit of the individual existence and interest are of an egoistic nature, and that egoism is overcome only when concern shifts toward the welfare of the Thou or of society. Yet it is already some time that a deeper reflection on the values of life has ascertained a third alternative, most impressively perhaps in the figures of Goethe and Nietzsche (though not in any abstract formula). It is the possibility that the perfection of the individual as such constitutes an objective value, quite irrespective of its significance for any other individuals, or in merely accidental connection with it. This value, moreover, may exist in utter disregard for the happiness or unhappiness of this individual himself, or may even be in conflict with them. What a person represents in terms of strength, nobility of character, achievement, or harmony of life, is very often quite unrelated to what he or others "get out" of these qualities. All that can be said about them is that the world is enriched by the existence in it of a valuable human being who is perfect in himself. Certainly, his value often consists in his practical devotion to other individuals or groups; but to limit it to this would be to proceed by an arbitrary moralistic dogma. For, beauty and perfection of life, the working upon oneself, the passionate efforts to obtain ideal goods, do not always result in happiness. These efforts and aims are inspired by certain *world* values, and may have no other effect than to create and maintain a particular attitude in the individual consciousness.

Countless times, the individual craves situations, events, insights, achievements, in whose particular existence or general nature he simply sees ultimately satisfactory aims. Occasionally the content of such cravings may be the improvement or well-being of others. But not necessarily: the aim is striven after for the sake of its own realization; and, therefore, to sacrifice others or even oneself may not be too high a price. *"Fiat justitia, pereat mundus;"* the fulfillment of divine will merely because it is divine; the fanaticism of the artist, completion of whose work makes him forget any other consideration, altruistic or egoistic; the political idealist's enthusiasm for a constitutional reform that renders him entirely indifferent to the question of how the citizens would fare under it—these are examples of purely objective valuations that permeate even the most trivial contents. The acting individual feels himself to be only the object or executor—who at bottom is accidental—of the task his cause puts to him. The passion for this cause is as little concerned with the I, Thou, or society as the value of the state of the world can be measured in terms of the world's pleasure or suffering (although it can, of course, be partly so measured). Yet, evidently, the claims made by individuals or groups, insofar as they, too, are agents of ultimate values, do not necessarily coincide with the individual's striving after such objective values. Particularly if he tries to realize a value either in himself or in an accomplishment that is unappreciated socially, the super-egoistic nature of his procedure is not rewarded by society. Society claims the individual for itself. It wants to make of him a form that it can incorporate into its own structure. And this societal claim is often so incompatible with the claim imposed on the individual by his striving after an objective value, as only a purely egoistic claim can be incompatible with a purely social one.

～

"ON LOVE," 1921–22

Between the I and the Thou, the first conflict arises for the human consciousness, and the first consolidation as well. The temporal priority of this relationship has the consequence that it subsequently qualifies as what might be called the absolute material on which, in the final analysis, our decisions and valuations, the justice and injustice of our

praxis, and the claims upon us are made good. Ultimately, every intention of our conduct is exhausted in the alternation between egoism and altruism, which assume countless modifications and means, guises and consequences. Even when it is subordinated to objective ideals—as in Plato, Thomas Aquinas, Kant, and socialism—egoism is still more or less clearly designated as the immanent counterprinciple. The immediate concrete demand, however, even if not the abstract demand, always has a Thou, personal or trans-individual, as its content. It is the general opinion that the choice between egoism and altruism is made on the level of eudaemonism as the source of its content. Aside from the fact that there is no sense in which this level comprises all the dimensions in which these concepts can be extended, even the most complete extension ascribed to them is incapable of adequately expressing our real ultimate motivations.

At this point, I shall only take note of an argument that lies off the path of our present inquiry. There are countless occasions in which our will is concerned with objective formations of existence in such a way that a state, an event, or an aspect of things is simply supposed to exist, without giving any consideration at all to the result that the realization of this intention has for an I or a Thou. This thoroughly objective intention, which lies beyond every I and Thou and their unreconciled or reconciled dualism, seems to me to be an undeniable and quite distinctively human fact. And in the sense that this fact lies above that dualism, another fact lies beneath it: purely impulsive behavior. If we call it egoistic when someone follows his impulses in an unconstrained fashion, then we elevate his behavior above its own sphere into another, in which an altruistic claim is raised. Because his behavior does not, of course, satisfy this demand, it appears as egoistic. In itself, however, it has this property no more than the growth of a plant or the falling of a stone, both of which follow their own purely distinctive laws, can be called egoistic. Quite rightly, egoism always signifies a teleological orientation—to some sort of reaction of the Ego. In calling an action egoistic, we implicitly presuppose such an orientation, which, however, it is precisely the nature of the impulse to resist. And yet its content can be directly linked with the well-being of a Thou, the destruction of the I, or with something that is teleologically completely senseless; for the claim that impulses signify adaptations that are of use only to the subject does not even hold true physiologically, much less psychologically.

Suppose that on the basis of these simple cases we have grasped the possible independence of our conduct from the alternative of egoism and altruism. In that event we shall also be able to penetrate that more complicated relationship—whose reductive power, however, is no less severe—in which conduct is motivated "out of love." If we call an action altruistic in the strict sense when it is for the benefit of a person whom we find quite indifferent or unsympathetic, even hostile, then action out of love cannot properly be characterized in the same way. Our own impulse is too narrow and our own satisfaction too closely interwoven with it to simply transpose its *Telos* onto the Thou. For the same reason, the concept of egoism will not work here either. Aside from all the selflessness that lies in the material content of action out of love, the concept of egoism would not conform to its nobility and value. Finally, from the perspective of its ultimate source, action out of love is too integral and continuous to qualify as some sort of mechanical composite of both motivations.

Thus the only remaining possibility is to regard motivation on the basis of love as distinctive and primary, unaffected by that usual reduction. The fact that the question concerning this reduction is inappropriate in this context follows from the consideration that a rationalistic psychology can either enthrone action out of love as altruistic or degrade it as fundamentally egoistic with apparently the same justification. It is also relevant that in this context the relationship between purpose and impulse is quite distinctive. Suppose that I accede to the wishes of another person because I regard them as worthy and just. In that case, action in accordance with the justice of these wishes is my ultimate purpose, and the realization of this justice is my own decisive motive. Suppose I do the same thing because I love the person. As regards the phenomenon in question, the condition of this person which is to be brought about is still my ultimate purpose. And yet it is not my real motive. On the contrary, my real motive is my love, the motive force of which is only transformed into this *Telos*—however, as this might be expressed, by itself alone. In all other cases our

action, regardless of whether its basis invariably has a positive value, is separated from its ultimate motive by a certain distance. This does not hold true for love, for which the following differentiating factor is decisive: Love for another person as what might be called the general motive for a particular action is more indivisibly connected with its content and permeates it much more directly than holds true for any other motivation with the possible exception of hate.

There is a sense in which we come from a greater distance when we do someone a good turn because of morality or inner acquiescence, religion, or social solidarity than when we do this because of love. The character of the good deed, with its tension between the I and the Thou, simply does not appear in the same clearcut fashion here. That is because the I has felt its way across the hiatus to the Thou. The existential will of the I flows to the Thou with complete intimacy. It does not need a bridge, which separates just as it connects.

❧

"FREEDOM AND THE INDIVIDUAL," 1957

The general European consensus is that the era of the Italian Renaissance created what we call individuality. By this is it meant a state of inner and external liberation of the individual from the communal forms of the Middle Ages, forms which had constricted the pattern of his life, his activities, and his fundamental impulses through homogenizing groups. These had, as it were, allowed the boundaries of the individual to become blurred, suppressing the development of personal freedom, of intrinsic uniqueness, and of the sense of responsibility for one's self. I will set aside the question whether the Middle Ages lacked all traces of individuality. The conscious emphasis on individuality as a matter of principle certainly does seem to have been the original accomplishment of the Renaissance. This took place in such a way the

From *Georg Simmel: On Individuality and Social Forms*, D. Levine, Ed./Trans. Copyright © 1972. Reprinted with permission of the University of Chicago Press.

will to power, to distinction, and to becoming honored and famous was diffused among men to a degree never before known. If for a time in Florence at the beginning of this period, as has been reported, there was no pervasive fashion in masculine attire since each man wished to deport himself in a manner peculiar to himself, it was not a matter of simple distinctiveness, of being different. The individual wanted to be *conspicuous;* he wanted to present himself more propitiously and more remarkably than was possible by means of the established forms. This is the behavioral reality of the individualism of distinction, which is associated with the ambition of Renaissance man, with his ruthless self-aggrandizement, with his value emphasis on being unique.

It is self-evident that such yearning and realization as this cannot remain a constant condition of men and society, but must pass away like an intoxication. Appearing here as a striving for aggrandizement, individualism still left behind in the lowlands and commonplaces of existence so many restrictions, so many impossibilities for the individual to develop his powers, to live out his life freely, to sense the self-sufficiency of his person—so many of these that the accumulation of this pressure led once again to an explosion in the eighteenth century. But this occurred from a different direction; it was led by a different ideal of individuality, one whose innermost impulse was not to distinction, but to freedom.

Freedom becomes for the eighteenth century the universal demand which the individual uses to cover his manifold grievances and self-assertions against society. This is readily observable in a variety of contexts. One sees it under the garb of political economy among the physiocrats, who extol the free competition of individual interests as the natural order of things; in its sentimental elaboration by Rousseau, for whom the ravaging of man by historical society is the source of all atrophy and all evil; in its political manifestation in the French Revolution, which elevated the idea of an individual freedom to the point of forbidding workers to form unions even for the protection of their own interests; and in its philosophical sublimation by Kant and Fichte, who conceived the ego as the bearer of the knowable world and made its absolute autonomy *the* moral value.

The inadequacy of the socially sanctioned forms of life in the eighteenth century, compared with the material and intellectual productivity of the period, struck the consciousness of individuals as an unbearable restriction of their energies. Those restrictive forms included the privileges of the higher estates as well as the despotic control of commerce; the still powerful survivals of the guild system as well as to the intolerant pressure of the church; the corvée expected from the peasant population as well paternalism in the life of the state and the restrictions imposed on municipal constitutions. The oppressiveness of such institutions, which had lost their intrinsic justification, gave rise to the ideal of pure freedom for the individual. If only these restraints would collapse and cease forcing the powers of the personality into their own unnatural channels, then all the internal and external values that were already in full vigor, but which were politically, religiously, and economically crippled, would unfold, leading society out of the era of historical unreason and into the era of natural rationality.

The individualism that sought its realization in this way was based on the notion of the *natural equality* of individuals, on the conception that all the restrictions just mentioned were artificially produced inequalities and that once these had been banished along with their historical fortuitousness, their injustice, and their burdensomeness, perfected man would emerge. And since he was perfect, perfect in morality, in beauty, and in happiness, he could show no differences. The deep cultural-historical movement that generated this conception flows out of the eighteenth century's concept of nature, which is entirely mechanistic and scientific in orientation. In that concept, nothing exists except the general law, and every phenomenon, be it a human being or a nebula in the Milky Way, is merely a single instance of some law or laws. Even if the form of an individual phenomenon is absolutely unrepeatable, it is still a mere crosspoint and a resolvable constellation of universal laws. This is why it is man in general, universal man, who occupies the center of interest for this period instead of historically given, particular, and differentiated man. The latter is in principle reduced to the former; in each individual person, man in general lives as his essence, just as every piece of matter, peculiar as its configuration may be, exhibits in its essence the pervasive laws of matter in general.

It is at this point that freedom and equality can be seen to belong together by right from the very outset. For if universal humanity—as it were—exists as the essential core of every man, who is individualized by empirical traits, social position, and accidental configuration, all one need do is *free* him from all these historical influences and diversions that ravage his deepest essence, and then what is common to all, man as such can emerge in him as this essence.

Here lies the pivotal point of this concept of individuality, which is one of the great conceptions of intellectual history: when man is freed from everything that is not wholly himself, what remains as the actual substance of his being is man in general, mankind, which lives in him and in everyone else, the ever identical fundamental essence that is merely empiricohistorically disguised, diminished, and distorted. It is this signifi-

cance of the universal which makes the literature of the Revolutionary period continually speak about the "people," the "tyrant," and "freedom" in such general terms. It is for this reason that "natural religion" has a providence in general, a justness in general, a divine education in general, but does not recognize the right of any particular manifestatins of this generality. It is for this reason that "natural law" is based on the fiction of isolated and identical individuals. And this is why Frederick the Great can call the prince "the first judge, the first man of finance, the first minister of society," but then in the same breath, call him "a *man* like the least of his subjects."

The basic metaphysical motif that finds expression during the eighteenth century in the practical demand for "freedom and equality" is this: the worth of each individual's configuration is based, to be sure, on him alone, on his personal responsibility, but along with that it is based on what the individual has in common with all others.

GEORGES SOREL

1847–1922

Georges Sorel, was born in Cherbourg, France on November 2, 1847, to a business-man and his wife, the daughter of the mayor of Barfleur. Much to the horror of his bourgeois family, Sorel lived without benefit of marriage with Marie-Euphasie David, an illiterate proletarian, to whom he was immensely attached until her death in 1897, af-ter which he dedicated his work to her memory. His rigid Catholic ethics, so unlike those of many other radical thinkers of the era, seem to have been inspired by this woman. He died in Boulogne-sur-Seine on August 30, 1922 at 74. Sorel's father went bankrupt, which may have shaken his class identity, but he nevertheless spent a comfortable youth, including contact with his cousin, Albert Sorel, later a famed historian and politi-cian. After graduating in 1864 with distinction from the College of Cherbourg, he stud-ied in Paris at the École Polytechnique, the finest school of its kind in France. He afterward joined the Bureau of Bridges and Highways and worked for 25 years as a civil engineer for the French government in Corsica, the Alps, Algeria, settling in the Pyre-nees, then retired at 45 on his pension and his mother's small inheritance in order to write. Over the succeeding three decades, he produced an idiosyncratic but fascinating stream of books on a range of topics, including Marxism, social theory, the philosophy of science, and anarchism. In this pattern—being trained as an engineer and then shift-ing to social theory—he enlarged the Gallic tradition of both Comte and Pareto. Other than writing inflammatory books, his life was strictly bourgeois except for his unmarried living arrangements. Sorel is puzzling in that his background and behavior was solidly conventional, yet his social thought is anything but.

Early in his writing career he produced monographs on the Bible, Socrates, Roman ruins, state power, a critique of Marxism, a history of Renan in 4 volumes, and so on. But when he published *Reflection on Violence* in 1908 (English translation, 1914), he be-came world famous. Like other writers of the time (most notably Roberto Michels, Gaetano Mosca, and Pareto), he was intrigued by the motivating forces behind social movements, particularly those that are violent and seek wholesale societal transforma-tion. He focused on the "heroic" type of political actor (usually a male) and on the need for a "myth" that would propel his followers into self-abnegating, sometimes suicidal dedication to a cause. With an engineer's remove from the passionate political stance and the distance from the fray that his unpolitical life assured him, Sorel was able to dis-sect the workings of mass movements typical of his time in a way that nobody else had done. His book continues to serve as a basic analysis of these phenomena.

REFLECTIONS ON VIOLENCE, 1908

Political Myths

. . . In the course of this study one thing has always been present in my mind, which seemed to me so evident that I did not think it worth while to lay much stress on it—that men who are participating in a great social movement always picture their coming action as a battle in which their cause is certain to triumph. These constructions, knowledge of which is so important for historians, I propose to call myths; the syndicalist "general strike" and Marx's catastrophic revolution are such myths. As remarkable examples of such myths, I have given those which were constructed by primitive Christianity, by the Reformation, by the Revolution and by the followers of Mazzini. I now wish to show that we should not attempt to analyse such groups of images in the way that we analyse a thing into its elements, but that they must be taken as a whole, as historical forces, and that we should be especially careful not to make any comparison between accomplished fact and the picture people had formed for themselves before action.

I could have given one more example which is perhaps still more striking: Catholics have never been discouraged even in the hardest trials, because they have always pictured the history of the Church as a series of battles between Satan and the hierarchy supported by Christ; every new difficulty which arises is only an episode in a war which must finally end in the victory of Catholicism.

At the beginning of the nineteenth century the revolutionary persecutions revived this myth of the struggle with Satan, which inspired so many of the eloquent pages in Joseph de Maistre; this rejuvenation explains to a large extent the religious renascence which took place at that epoch. If Catholicism is in danger at the present time, it is to a great extent owing to the fact that the myth of the Church militant tends to disappear. Ecclesiastical literature has greatly contributed to rendering it ridiculous; thus in 1872, a Belgian writer

recommended a revival of exorcisms, as they seemed to him an efficacious means of combating the revolutionaries. Many educated Catholics are horrified when they discover that the ideas of Joseph de Maistre have helped to encourage the ignorance of the clergy, which did not attempt to acquire an adequate knowledge of a science which it held to be accursed; to these educated Catholics the myth of the struggle with Satan then appears dangerous, and they point out its ridiculous aspects; but they do not in the least understand its historical bearing. The gentle, sceptical, and, above all, pacific, habits of the present generation are, moreover, unfavourable to its continued existence; and the enemies of the Church loudly proclaim that they do not wish to return to a regime of persecution which might restore their former power to warlike images.

In employing the term myth I believed that I had made a happy choice, because I thus put myself in a position to refuse any discussion whatever with the people who wish to submit the idea of a general strike to a detailed criticism, and who accumulate objections against its practical possibility. It appears, on the contrary, that I had made a most unfortunate choice, for while some told me that myths were only suitable to a primitive state of society, others imagined that I thought the modern world might be moved by illusions analogous in nature to those which Renan thought might usefully replace religion. But there has been a worse misunderstanding than this even; for it has been asserted that my theory of myths was only a kind of lawyer's plea, a falsification of the real opinions of the revolutionaries, the *sophistry of an intellectualist.*

If this were true, I should not have been exactly fortunate, for I have always tried to escape the influence of that intellectualist philosophy, which seems to me a great hindrance to the historian who allows himself to be dominated by it. The contradiction that exists between this philosophy and the true understanding of events has often struck the readers of Renan. Renan is continually wavering between his own intuition, which was nearly always admirable, and a philosophy which cannot touch history without falling into platitudes; but, alas, he too often believed himself bound to think in accordance with the *scientific opinions* of his day.

From *Reflections on Violence*, by Georges Sorel, T.E. Hulme and J. Roth, Trans. Published by The Free Press. Copyright © 1950.

The intellectualist philosophy finds itself unable to explain phenomena like the following—the sacrifice of his life which the soldier of Napoleon made in order to have had the honour of taking part in "immortal deeds" and of living in the glory of France, knowing all the time that "he would always be a poor man"; then, again, the extraordinary virtues shown by the Romans who resigned themselves to a frightful inequality and who suffered so much to conquer the world; "the belief in glory (which was) a value without equal," created by Greece, and as a result of which "a selection was made from the swarming masses of humanity, life acquired an incentive and there was a recompense here for those who had pursued the good and the beautiful." The intellectualist philosophy, far from being able to explain these things, leads, on the contrary, to an admiration for the fifty-first chapter of Jeremiah, "the lofty though profoundly sad feeling with which the peaceful man contemplates these falls of empires, and the pity excited in the heart of the wise man by the spectacle of the nations *labouring for vanity*, victims of the arrogance of the few." Greece, according to Renan, did not experience anything of that kind, and I do not think that we need complain about that. Moreover, he himself praises the Romans for not having acted in accordance with the conceptions of the Jewish thinker. "They laboured, they wore themselves out for nothing, said the Jewish thinker—yes, doubtless, but those are the virtues that history rewards."

Religions constitute a very troublesome problem for the intellectualists, for they can neither regard them as being with-out historical importance nor can they explain them. Renan, for example, has written some very strange sentences on this subject. "Religion is a necessary imposture. Even the most obvious ways of throwing dust in people's eyes cannot be neglected when you are dealing with a race as stupid as the human species, a race created for error, which, when it does admit the truth, never does so for the right reasons. It is necessary then to give it the wrong ones."

Comparing Giordano Bruno, who "allowed himself to be burnt at Champ-de-Flore" with Galileo, who submitted to the Holy See, Renan sides with the second, because, according to him, the scientist need not bring anything to support his discoveries beyond good arguments. He considered that the Italian philosopher wished to supplement his inadequate proofs by his sacrifice, and he puts forward this scornful maxim: "A man suffers martyrdom only for the sake of things about which he is not certain." Renan here confuses *conviction*, which must have been very powerful in Bruno's case, with that particular kind of *certitude* about the accepted theories of science, which instruction ultimately produces; it would be difficult to give a more misleading idea of the forces which really move men.

The whole of this philosophy can be summed up in the following phrase of Renan's: "Human affairs are always an approximation lacking gravity and precision"; and as a matter of fact, for an intellectualist, what lacks precision must also lack gravity. But in Renan the conscientious historian was never entirely asleep, and he at once adds as a corrective: "To have realised this truth is a great result obtained by philosophy; but it is an abdication of any active role. The future lies in the hands of those who are not disillusioned." From this we may conclude that the intellectualist philosophy is entirely unable to explain the great movements of history.

The intellectualist philosophy would have vainly endeavoured to convince the ardent Catholics, who for so long struggled successfully against the revolutionary traditions, that the myth of the Church militant was not in harmony with the scientific theories formulated by the most learned authors according to the best rules of criticism; it would never have succeeded in persuading them. It would not have been possible to shake the faith that these men had in the promises made to the Church by any argument; and so long as this faith remained, the myth was, in their eyes, incontestable. Similarly, the objections urged by philosophy against the revolutionary myths would have made an impression only on those men who were anxious to find a pretext for abandoning any active rôle, for remaining revolutionary in words only.

I can understand the fear that this myth of the general strike inspires in many *worthy progressives*, on account of its character of *infinity*; the world of to-day is very much inclined to return to the opinions of the ancients and to subordinate ethics to the smooth working of public affairs, which results in a definition of virtue as the golden mean; as long as socialism remains a *doctrine expressed only in words,* it is very easy to deflect it towards this doctrine of the golden mean; but this transformation is manifestly impossible when the myth of the "general strike" is introduced, as this implies an absolute revolution. You know as well as I do that all that is best in the modern mind is derived from this "torment of the infinite"; you are not one of those people who look upon the tricks by means of which readers can be deceived by words, as happy discoveries. That is why you will not condemn me for having attached great worth to a myth which gives to socialism such high moral value and such great sincerity. It is because the theory of myths tends to produce such fine results that so many seek to dispute it.

LUCIEN LÉVY-BRUHL

1857–1939

Lucien Lévy-Bruhl was born in Paris on April 19, 1857, married the daughter of a diamond merchant and had three children with her, one of whom, Henri (b. 1884), became a famous sociologist of law. He died nearly 82 years later in the same city on March 13, 1939. His first schooling at the lycée Charlemagne proved that he was an extraordinary student, and in the annual national tests, he and a friend took all the top awards. His passions and abilities were strong in philosophy and music, and he weighed whether to pursue conducting or a professorial career. His professor at l'École normale supérieure, none other than Fustel de Coulanges, tried unsuccessfully to push him into history, but he pursued philosophy instead, taking a degree in 1879. In addition, he studied psychopathology and took clinical courses at Sainte-Anne. His first teaching jobs were at Poitiers and Amiens (1879–1883), where he married. Lévy-Bruhl completed his doctoral dissertations in 1884, one concerning responsibility, while the Latin thesis was about Seneca and God. He held a professorship at Paris in Higher Rhetoric at the lycée Louis-le-Grand between 1885 and 1895, moving to the Sorbonne in 1896 where he was titular professor of the history of modern philosophy from 1904, also designated as professor at l'École libre des Sciences politiques, where he specialized in the history of political ideas and public opinion in Germany after 1815. During the rest of his professional career, Lévy-Bruhl wrote about a dizzying array of topics, including Flaubert's philosophy, Comte's social theory, Rousseau's influence on Germany, Heine's politics, Leibniz's philosophy, and so on. He also worked for the French government during WWI for free, helping a former student run the Ministry of Munitions. Late in life he traveled worldwide giving lectures and inaugurating ethnological institutes. He was friends with Durkheim and met Einstein in Greece.

His principal books include *Ethics and Moral Science* (1903), *How Natives Think* (1910), and *Primitive Mentality* (1922). Contrary to much that has been written in the last generation, Lévy-Bruhl did not in any way wish to demean the thought processes of premodern peoples, nor to regard their thinking as a stage on the way toward Western syllogistic reasoning. His argument, borrowed from Durkheim and Marcel Mauss, was that people think according to their society's intellectual and perceptual norms, and that premodern thought processes do not concern themselves as much with the problem of contradiction as do modern Western logicians. His knowing appreciation for cultural differences was famous among his students and colleagues, which led to a worldwide reputation as a thoughtful and sensitive ethnologist, something that his current reputation completely belies.

HOW NATIVES THINK, 1910 [1926]

Collective Representations in Primitives' Perceptions

II.   The very considerable part played by collective representations in the primitives' perceptions does not result alone in impressing a mystic character upon them. The same cause leads to another consequence, and these perceptions are accordingly *oriented* differently from our own. In that which our perceptions retain, as well as in that which is disregarded, the chief determining factor is the amount of reliance that we can place upon the unvarying reappearance of phenomena in the same given conditions. They conduce to effect the maximum "objective" validity, and, as a result, to eliminate everything prejudicial or merely unnecessary to this objectivity. From this standpoint, too, primitives do not perceive as we do. In certain cases where direct practical interest are at stake, we undoubtedly find that they pay great attention to, and are often very skilful in detecting differences in impressions which are very similar, and in recognizing external signs of objects or phenomena, upon which their subsistence and possibly even their lives, depend. (The shrewdness of the Australian aborigines in finding and profiting by the dew which has fallen during the night, and other similar facts, are an example of this.) But, even setting aside that which these fine perceptions owe to training and memory, we still find that in most cases primitives' perceptive powers, instead of tending to reject whatever would lesson objectivity, lay special stress upon the mystic properties, the occult forces of beings and phenomena, and are thus oriented upon factors which, to us, appear subjective, although to primitives they are at least as real as the others. This characteristic of their perceptions enables them to account for certain phenomena, the "explanation" of which, when based solely upon mental or logical processes in the individual, does not appear adequate. . . .

From *How Natives Think*, by Lucien Lévy-Bruhl, Lilian A. Clare, Trans. Published by Washington Square Press. Copyright © 1966.

I shall therefore refer it to the same theory. If we ask ourselves: how has the primitive come to associate with the idea of his shadow beliefs which we find to be almost universal? we might reply by an ingenious explanation, and one which would be psychologically probable, but it would be unsound, because the problem cannot be propounded in such terms as these. To enunciate it thus would be to imply that the idea of his shadow to the primitive is the same as to us, and the rest is superimposed. Now it really is nothing like that. The perception of the shadow, as of the body itself, like that of the image or the name, is a mystic perception, in which that which we properly call the shadow,—the design upon the ground of a figure which recalls the form of a being or object lighted from the opposite side—is only one element among many. We have not to discover how the perception of the shadow has been placed in juxtaposition or united with such and such a representation: these indeed form an integral part of the perception, so far as we can trace it in past observations. For this reason I should be prepared to take up a counter-position to that of De Groot. "The Chinese," he says, "are even to these days without ideas; the physical causation of shadows. . . . They must needs see in a shadow something more than a negation of light." I, on the contrary, should say: the Chinese, having a mystic perception of the shadow, as participating in the life and all the properties of the tangible body, cannot represent it as mere "negation of light." To be able to see a purely physic phenomenon in the production of the shadow, it would be necessary to have an idea of such a phenomenon, and we know that such an idea is lacking to the primitive. In undeveloped communities, there is no perception unaccompanied by mystic qualities and occult properties, and why should the shadow be any exception?

Finally, the same considerations apply equally to another class of phenomena—dreams which occupy an important place in the primitive mind. To primitives the dream is not, as it is to us, simply a manifestation of mental activity which occurs during sleep, a more or less orderly series of representations to which, when awake, the dreamer would give no credence, because they lack the conditions essential to object validity. This last characteristic, though it does not escape primitives, seems to interest them but slightly. On the other hand, the dream, to them, is of far greater significance than to us. It is first a percept as real as those of the waking state, but above all it is a provision of the future, a communication and intercourse with spirits, souls, divinities, a means of establishing a relation with their own special guardian angel, and even of discovering who this may be. Their confidence in the reality of that which the dreams makes known to them is very profound.

~⟶

PRIMITIVE MENTALITY, 1922

Introduction

I. Among the differences which distinguish the mentality of primitive communities from our own, there is one which has attracted the attention of many of those who have observed such peoples under the most favourable conditions—that is, before their ideas have been modified by prolonged association with white races. These observers have maintained that primitives manifest a decided distaste for reasoning, for what logicians call the "discursive operations of thought"; at the same time they have remarked that this distaste did not arise out of any radical incapability or any inherent defect in their understanding, but was rather to be accounted for by their general methods of thought.

In short, the entire mental habit which rules out abstract thought and reasoning, properly so-called, seems to be met with in a large number of uncivilized communities, and constitutes a characteristic and essential trait of primitive mentality.

II. Why is it that primitive mentality shows such indifference to, one might almost say such dislike of, the discursive operations of thought, of reasoning, and reflection, when to us they are the

From *Primitive Mentality,* by Lucien Lévy-Bruhl, Lilian A. Clare, Trans. Published by George Allen & Unwin Ltd., 1923.

natural and almost continuous occupation of the human mind?

It is due neither to incapacity nor inaptitude, since those who have drawn our attention to this feature of primitive mentality expressly state that among them are "minds quite as capable of scientific thought as those of Europeans," and we have seen that Australian and Melanesian children learn what the missionary teaches them quite as readily as French or English children would do. Neither is it the result of profound intellectual torpor, of enervation and unconquerable weariness, for these same natives who find an insuperable difficulty in the very slightest abstract thought, and who never seem to take the trouble to reason, show themselves on the contrary, observant, wise, skilfull, clever, even subtle, when an object interests them, especially when it is a case of obtaining something they very much desire.

The observer who recently remarked on their "stupidity" goes into ecstasies over their ingenuity and their taste. We must therefore not take the word "stupidity" literally. Or rather, we must ask ourselves whence this apparent stupidity arises, and what are its determining features.

As we have seen above, it has been explained by the very missionaries who have testified to the primitives' dislike of the very simplest logical process. The explanation they give has been derived from the fact that the primitives whom they have studied never thought, and never wanted to think, of more than a very few things—those necessary to their subsistence, their flocks and herds, their game, fish, etc. The mental habits they would thus acquire would become so pronounced that all other things, especially if abstract in their nature, would be powerless to arrest their attention. "They only believe what the see; their ideas go no further than the regions of sense: what is not directly perceived is not thought," and so on.

But this statement does not settle the question. If the observations reported are correct, as they seem to be, it tends rather to complicate it. Firstly, we do not see why the pursuit of interests which are entirely material, or even why the limited number of the ordinary objects of thought, should necessarily result in the incapability of reflection and the distaste for reasoning. On the contrary, such specialization, and the concentration of the mental powers and the attention on a small number of things to the exclusion of others, ought rather to bring about a kind of definite and precise adaptation, mental as well as physical, to the pursuit of them; and this adaptation, being partly intellectual, would involve a certain development of ingenuity, reflection, and skill in arriving at the means best calculated to attain the desired end. This is in fact what often happens.

That, side by side with this adaptation, primitives manifest an almost insuperable indifference with regard to matters bearing no visible relation to those which interest them, is frequently matter of painful experience to the missionary. But the incapability of understanding the Gospel message, and even the refusal to listen to it, are not of themselves sufficient proof of the primitives' distaste for logical thought, specially when we remember that these same primitives exhibit considerable mental activity when the subject of thought interests them, when it deals with their cattle or their wives, for instance.

Moreover, is it not rash to account for this dislike by their exclusive attachment to the objects of sense, since the missionaries show us that, in other respects, primitives are the most fervent believers one can find? We cannot rid their minds of the belief that an infinite number of invisible beings and actions are actually real. . . . The primitive makes no distinction between this world and the other, between what is actually preset to sense, and what is beyond. He actually dwells with invisible spirits and intangible forces. To him it is these that are the real and actual. His faith is expressed in his most insignificant as well as in his most important act. It impregnates his whole life and conduct.

If then, primitive mentality avoids and ignores logical thought, if it refrains from reasoning and reflecting, it is not from incapacity to surmount what is evident to sense, nor is it because such mentality is exclusively attached to a very small number of objects, and these of a material kind only. The very witnesses who insist upon this trait of the primitive mind also authorize and even

oblige us to reject such explanations. We must therefore look elsewhere. And if our search is to meet with any success we must present the problem in term which render an exact solution possible.

Instead of imagining the primitives whom we are studying to be like ourselves and making them think as we shout do in their places—a proceeding which can only lead to hypotheses, at most merely probable, and nearly always false—let us on the contrary endeavour to guard against our own mental habits, and try to discover, by analysing their collective representations and the connections between these, what the primitives' way of thinking would be.

As long as we assume that their minds are orientated like our own, that they react as ours do to the impressions made upon them, we assume, by implication, that they *should* reason and reflect as ours do with regard to the phenomena and entities of the known world. But we agree that as a matter of fact they neither reason nor reflect thus, and to explain this apparent anomaly we make use of a number of different hypotheses, such as the feebleness and torpidity of their minds, their perplexity, childlike ignorance, stupidity, etc., none of which take the facts sufficiently into account.

Let us abandon this position and rid our minds of all preconceived ideas in entering upon an objective study of primitive mentality, in the way in which it manifests itself in the institutions of uncivilized races or in the collective ideas from which these institutions are derived. Then we shall no longer define the mental activity of primitives beforehand as a rudimentary form of our own, and consider it childish and almost pathological. On the contrary, it will appear to be normal under the conditions in which it is employed, to be both complex and developed in its own way. By ceasing to connect it with a type which is not its own, and trying to determine its functioning solely according to the manifestations peculiar to it, we may hope that our description and analysis of it will not misrepresent its nature.

GYÖRGY LUKÁCS

1885–1971

György von Lukács (universally known as "Georg"), the second son of a wealthy banker (who had changed his name from Löwinger) and a Viennese mother named Wertheimer, was born in Budapest, Hungary in a German-speaking home on April 13, 1885. He married Ljena Grabenko on May 14, 1914, and died on June 4, 1971 in his hometown at the age of 86. Lukács studied law from 1902 through 1906, all the while writing literary criticism, culminating in a history of modern drama in Hungarian (1906–07). He moved to Berlin and studied with Simmel (1909–10). Around 1910 he wrote *The Soul and the Forms,* a quasi-mystical investigation of literature, based on articles he'd written for a local journal. This work eventually impressed Max Weber and won Lukács a regular invitation to the Webers' famous Sunday afternoon salon in Heidelberg between 1912 and 1915. His studies with Weber and Simmel influenced his social theory of the 1920s, but late in life he would dismiss them both as bourgeois apologists in his most uneven work, *The Destruction of Reason* (1962). Lukács threw off the traces of his class origins and joined the communist party in 1918, served as minister of culture in a short-lived leftwing government in Budapest, moved to Vienna in 1919, and then to Berlin from 1929–1933, after which his Jewish heritage made it necessary for him to leave, this time for Moscow (1933–45). He served Hungary in the Parliament and became Professor of the Philosophy of Culture at the University of Budapest in 1956. He did some of his best work late in life, including his massive, unfinished *Aesthetics* (1963) and *The Young Hegel* (1967).

Lukács repudiated his heritage and his noble name in order to pursue Marxist theory and practice, becoming the most brilliant theoretician and literary critic of the movement following WWI. His *History and Class Consciousness* (1923) set a new standard for creative theorizing among Marxists, matched only at times by Trotsky, and in a different way entirely by the Frankfurt School Germans, with whom he was acquainted. In that book he explored the meaning of reification, commodity fetishization, and blind obedience of legal formalism, all of which he thought could be eliminated in a communist state. Lukács never gave up his love of literature, even while being denounced by communist hardliners, and he wrote entire books on Goethe, Thomas Mann, fictional realism, the historical novel, Solzhenitsyn, and so on. The selections reprinted below treat "aesthetic culture," so-called, for which Lukács simultaneously felt attraction and repulsion, in that the products of this frame of mind were inspiring, but were built on the backs of the proletariat. His very famous definition of "reification" is also included, in brief.

AESTHETIC CULTURE, 1910

> The world is full of armies, But that is not what will kill us.   —Beta Balázs

If there is culture today, it can only be an aesthetic culture. If one wants to raise seriously the question whether there is a centre to man's self-alienation and egocentrism, that question should be raised here. If one is critically disposed towards modern life, one must critique the aesthete in the same way that the Sophist would have done in Socrates' Athens, as the Pope and the robber knights in the bright days of medieval times, the warbling troubadour and the mystic in the waning Middle Ages, as the petty tyrant and militant philosopher in the eighteenth century.

There are of course those who hold a different view—but their talk merely confirms our own perception. There are those who, when the topic turns to culture, prefer to talk about aeroplanes and railways, the speed and efficiency of telegraphs. They discuss the rise of literacy in modern 'democracy' (as if modern man's soul really craved to read) and point out the number of people whose rights are denied in a democracy (even if they phrase it differently). But let us never forget one thing: all these manifestations—even in the best of circumstances—are merely roads to a culture; they merely provide an opportunity, enhance the potential, and lend substance to the formative power of culture.

But culture can impart substance to anything, provided it possesses the innate power of creativity. Culture: the unifier of life; a unity strong enough to intensify and enrich life. And yet, can we claim that travel means more to us just because we reach our destination in a day, rather than a month? Have our letters gained in depth and become more soulful on account of a faster mail service? Did human responses to life become stronger and more homogeneous only because a larger number of people get closer to things and to more things?

Indisputably, modern culture has produced two pure types: the expert and the aesthete. They are incompatible and mutually exclusive—and yet each needs the other to complement himself. The life of the expert: the sacrifice of one's whole life so that one segment of 'the' life becomes more manageable; the external aspects of life define its inner content, where means turn into ends. And the life of the aesthete? What else, but exclusively an inner life? What else, but the complete disappearance of all 'secondary' things from a genuine and real life? What else, but life in the realms of the soul, confined, as Maeterlinck put it, exclusively there?

It is by no means pure chance that placed the expert and aesthete side by side as mutually exclusive. For I could just as easily describe their respective essences as follows. The expert embraces the *l'art pour l'art* of professionalism; the goodness of 'accomplishing' things as man's primary goal, irrespective of what is being said or accomplished. The aesthete embraces sensation as an occupation, a profession. But a sensation which conceals from man life itself. Therefore, the deep solidarity of the two types (which lends real content to their seemingly formal contrast) is that their respective roads, whose meaning and significance lies in the goals to which they lead, become self-serving. In both, their respective purity as types is the result of inner impoverishment. The unity of the two types is due to their one-sided lives, and the one-dimensionality of their soul. The souls of aesthete and expert are devoid of that richness and strength that can relate everything to the centre of one's being, because it knows everything does in fact relate to it. . . .

Every culture denotes the conquest of life. Culture signifies a powerful unity of all aspects of life (this is never a conceptual unity of course), so that no matter what perspective we choose on life, we see essentially the same thing everywhere. In an authentic culture everything is symbolic, because everything expresses—and expresses it equally—what is of paramount importance: how the individual reacts to life, how his whole being responds to and confronts life as a whole.

The centre of aesthetic culture is: the mood. The mood is the most common mediator (though hardly the most important or profound) of an artwork. The essence of mood is its accidental, nonanalysable nature and, in fact, its conscious distance from the non-analytical approach is due to the transient relation which obtains between the observer and the object of observation. Aesthetic culture owes its birth to the very moment when man's spiritual activity expands and encompasses the whole of life, in other words, the moment when life itself is seen as an endless sequence of transient moods. It was born when objects ceased to exist, because everything was merely an occasion for the mood; when all that was permanent disappeared from life, because the mood proved intolerant of what was permanent and recurrent. It was born when life was stripped of all values, and it now values the products of moods, that is to say, the products of fortuitous circumstances devoid of any necessary correlation with values.

In a sense the unity of aesthetic culture does exist: as a lack of unity. Aesthetic culture has a central tenet: the peripheral nature of all things. This culture also has a symbol for everything: namely that nothing is symbolic, that everything is what it appears to be in the very moment we experience it, nor is there anything anywhere that amounts to more than this. What enables aesthetic culture to transcend the purely individual (for man's heritage forms an essential part of culture) is that only the particular individual moods are regarded as transcendent. Aesthetic culture also has its own concept of human relations: the total loneliness of man, the complete negation of human contacts.

Aesthetic culture becomes the art of life; the elevation of life into an art. In the hands of the sovereign artist everything becomes a substance. It matters not whether he paints, composes a sonnet, or just lives.

But we now know better. It was a lie that the art of life is a genuine art for, in essence, it merely imposed the dominant powers and directions of art on life itself. No. The art of life is merely the enjoyment of life; not artistic creativity. The art of life in reality applied the theories of artistic gratification (more correctly: some theories) against life itself.

The fundamental lie of aesthetic culture or (in some of its serious representatives) its tragic paradox is that it has proscribed all real spiritual activity, and equated all manifestations of life with an affectionate surrender to transient moments. And precisely because everything comes from within, nothing really comes from without. It is only the external world and its objects that induce moods, and if someone elects to enjoy the manifestation of his soul as a beautiful moment, even then he remains a passive observer of something that chance brought in his way. For absolute freedom is the most terrifying of unfreedoms. 'Everything is only a mood', even the beautiful, majestic freedom of the soul, whose sovereignty lies in its ability to absorb all that exists in the dynamic, active soul. 'Everything is only a mood': so nothing counts more than mood, the most confining form of slavery, the most horrifying self-mutilation of the soul. Complete passivity can never constitute the principle of life (only in the formal sense that death and life, health and sickness can be one—in a definition), nor can anarchy be the cornerstone of its foundation.

The 'aesthetic culture', the 'art of life' glorifies the soul's debasement, its inability to create and to act, and pronounces the soul's surrender to moods as the very principle of life. Aesthetic culture amounts to an admission, conscious or unconscious, compounded by a lie, of its own inability to know how to live (to rule over life or form it). The 'art of life': it amounts to no more than dilettantism in life; to being stone-blind about true creativity and its real essence.

~

HISTORY AND CLASS CONSCIOUSNESS

Reification and the Consciousness of the Proletariat, 1923

> To be radical is to go to the root of the matter. For man, however, the root is man himself. —Marx: *Critique of Hegel's Philosophy of Right.*

The Phenomenon of Reification

1. The essence of commodity-structure has often been pointed out. Its basis is that a relation

---

between people takes on the character of a thing and thus acquires a 'phantom objectivity', an autonomy that seems so strictly rational and all-embracing as to conceal every trace of its fundamental nature: the relation between people. It is beyond the scope of this essay to discuss the central importance of this problem for economics itself. Nor shall we consider its implications for the economic doctrines of the vulgar Marxists which follow from their abandonment of this starting-point.

Our intention here is to *base* ourselves on Marx's economic analyses and to proceed from there to a discusssion of the problems growing out of the fetish character of commodities, both as an objective form and also as a subjective stance corresponding to it. Only by understanding this can we obtain a clear insight into the ideological problems of capitalism and its downfall.

Before tackling the problem itself we must be quite clear in our minds that commodity fetishism is a *specific* problem of our age, the age of modern capitalism. Commodity exchange and the corresponding subjective and objective commodity relations existed, as we know, when society was still very primitive. What is at issue here, however, is the question: how far is commodity exchange together with its structural consequences able to influence the total outer and inner life of society? Thus the extent to which such exchange is the dominant form of metabolic change in a society cannot simply be treated in quantitative terms—as would harmonise with the modern modes of thought already eroded by the reifying effects of the dominant commodity form. The distinction, between a society where this form is dominant, permeating every expression of life, and a society where it only makes an episodic appearance is essentially one of quality. For depending on which is the case, all the subjective and objective phenomena in the societies concerned are objectified in qualitatively different ways.

Marx lays great stress on the essentially episodic appearance of the commodity form in primitive societies: "Direct barter, the original natural form of exchange, represents rather the beginning of the transformation of use-values into commodities, than that of commodities into money. Exchange value has as yet no form of its own, but is still directly bound up with use-value.

This is manifested in two ways. Production, in its entire organisation, aims at the creation of use-values and not of exchange values, and it is only when their supply exceeds the measure of consumption that use-values cease to be use-values, and become means of exchange, i.e. commodities. At the same time, they become commodities only within the limits of being direct use-values distributed at opposite poles, so that the commodities to be exchanged by their possessors must be use-values to both—each commodity to its non-possessor. As a matter of fact, the exchange of commodities originates not within the primitive communities, but where they end, on their borders at the few points where they come in contact with other communities. That is where barter begins, and from here it strikes back into the interior of the community, decomposing it." We note that the observation about the disintegrating effect of a commodity exchange directed in upon itself clearly shows the qualitative change engendered by the dominance of commodities.

However, even when commodities have this impact on the internal structure of a society, this does not suffice to make them constitutive of that society. To achieve that it would be necessary—as we emphasized above for the commodity structure to penetrate society in all its aspects and to remould it in its own image. It is not enough merely to establish an external link with independent processes concerned with the production of exchange values. The qualitative difference between the commodity as one form among many regulating the metabolism of human society and the commodity as the universal structuring principle has effects over and above the fact that the commodity relation as an isolated phenomenon exerts a negative influence at best on the structure and organisation of society. The distinction also has repercussions upon the nature and validity of the category itself. Where the commodity is universal it manifests itself differently from the commodity as a particular, isolated, non-dominant phenomenon.

The fact that the boundaries lack sharp definition must not be allowed to blur the qualitative nature of the decisive distinction. The situation where commodity exchange is not dominant has been defined by Marx as follows: "The quantitative ratio in which products are exchanged is at first quite arbitrary. They assume the form of commodities inasmuch as they are exchangeables, i.e. expressions of one and the same thing. Continued exchange and more regular reproduction for exchange reduces this arbitrariness more and more. But at first not for the producer and consumer, but for their go-between, the merchant, who compares money-prices and pockets the difference. It is through his own movements that he establishes equivalence. Merchant's capital is originally merely the intervening movement between extremes which it does not control and between premises which it does not create."

And *this* development of the commodity to the point where it becomes the dominant form in society did not take place until the advent of modern capitalism. Hence it is not to be wondered that the personal nature of economic relations was still understood clearly on occasion at the start of capitalist development, but that as the process advanced and forms became more complex and less direct, it became increasingly difficult and rare to find anyone penetrating the veil of reification. Marx sees the matter in this way: "In preceding forms of society this economic mystification arose principally with respect to money and interest-bearing capital. In the nature of things it is excluded, in the first place, where production for the use-value, for immediate personal requirements, predominates; and secondly, where slavery or serfdom form the broad foundation of social production, as in antiquity and during the Middle Ages. Here, the domination of the producers by the conditions of production is concealed by the relations of dominion and servitude which appear and are evident as the direct motive power of the process of production."

The commodity can only be understood in its undistorted essence when it becomes the universal category of society as a whole. Only in this context does the reification produced by commodity relations assume decisive importance both for the objective evolution of society and for the stance adopted by men towards it. Only then does the commodity become crucial for the subjugation of men's consciousness to the forms in which this reification finds expression and for their attempts to comprehend the process or to rebel against its disastrous effects and liberate themselves from servitude to the 'second natures' so created.

Marx describes the basic phenomenon of reification as follows: "A commodity is therefore a mysterious thing, simply because in it the social character of men's labour appears to them as an objective character stamped upon the product of that labour; because the relation of the producers to the sum total of their own labour is presented to them as a social relation, existing not between themselves, but between the products of their labour. This is the reason why the products of labour become commodities, social things whose qualities are at the same time perceptible and imperceptible by the senses. . . .It is only a definite social relation between men that assumes, in their eyes, the fantastic form of a relation between things.

What is of central importance here is that because of this situation a man's own activity, his own labour becomes something objective and independent of him, something that controls him by virtue of an autonomy alien to man. There is both an objective and a subjective side to this phenomenon. *Objectively* a world of objects and relations between things springs into being (the world of commodities and their movements on the market). The laws governing these objects are indeed gradually discovered by man, but even so they confront him as invisible forces that generate their own power. The individual can use his knowledge of these laws to his own advantage, but he is not able to modify the process by his own activity. *Subjective* where the market economy has been fully developed—a man's activity becomes estranged from himself, it turns into a commodity which, subject to the non-human objectivity of the natural laws of society, must go its own way independently of man just like any consumer article. "What is characteristic of the capitalist age," says Marx, "is that in the eyes of the labourer himself labour-power assumes the form of a commodity belonging to him. On the other hand it is only at this moment that the commodity form of the products of labour becomes general."

Thus the universality of the commodity form is responsible both objectively and subjectively for the abstraction of the human labour incorporated in commodities. (On the other hand, this universality becomes historically possible because this process of abstraction has been completed.) *Objectively,* in so far as the commodity form facilitates the equal exchange of qualitatively different objects, it can only exist if that formal equality is in fact recognised—at any rate in this relation, which indeed confers upon them their commodity nature. *Subjectively,* this formal equality of human labour in the abstract is not only the common factor to which the various commodities are reduced; it also becomes the real principle governing the actual production of commodities. . . .

We are concerned above all with the *principle* at work here: the principle of rationalisation based on-what is and *can be calculated.* The chief changes undergone by the subject and object of the economic process are as follows: (1) in the first place, the mathematical analysis of work-processes denotes a break with the organic, irrational and qualitatively determined unity of the product. Rationalisation in the sense of being able to predict with ever greater precision all the results to be achieved is only to be acquired by the exact breakdown of every complex into its elements and by the study of the special laws governing production. Accordingly it must declare war on the organic manufacture of whole products based on the *traditional amalgam of empirical experiences of work:* rationalisation is unthinkable without specialisation.

The finished article ceases to be the object of the work-process. The latter turns into the objective synthesis of rationalised special systems whose unity is determined by pure calculation and which must therefore seem to be arbitrarily connected with each other. This destroys the organic necessity with which inter-related special operations are unified in the end-product. The unity of a product as a *commodity* no longer coincides with its unity as a use-value: as society becomes more radically capitalistic the increasing technical autonomy of the special operations involved in production is expressed also as an economic autonomy, as the growing relativisation of the commodity character of a product at the various stages of production. It is thus possible to separate forcibly the production of a use-value in time and space. This goes hand in hand with the union in time and space of special operations that are related to a set of heterogeneous use-values.

(2) In the second place, this fragmentation of the object of production necessarily entails the fragmentation of its subject. In consequence of the rationalisation of the work-process the human qualities and idiosyncrasies of the worker appear increasingly as *mere sources of error* when contrasted with these abstract special laws functioning according to rational predictions. Neither objectively nor in his relation to his work does man appear as the authentic master of the process; on the contrary, he is a mechanical part incorporated into a mechanical system. He finds it already pre-existing and self-sufficient, it functions independently of him and he has to conform to its laws whether he likes it or not. As labour is progressively rationalised and mechanised his lack of will is reinforced by the way in which his activity becomes less and less active and more and more *contemplative.* The contemplative stance adopted towards a process mechanically conforming to fixed laws and enacted independently of man's consciousness and impervious to human intervention, i.e. a perfectly closed system, must likewise transform the basic categories of man's immediate attitude to the world: it reduces space and time to a common denominator and degrades time to the dimension of space.

JAMES GEORGE FRAZER

1854–1941

Sir James George Frazer (knighted in 1914) was born in Glasgow, Scotland on January 1, 1854 and died at the age of 87 on May 7, 1941. Bronislaw Malinowski reported in an extended obituary that "His mundane glory was largely due to the activities of Lady Frazer, who took upon herself the management of his worldly career . . . a somewhat redoubtable life companion." Frazer's biographer reports that Lady Frazer was born in Alsace as Elizabeth Adelsdörfer, perhaps a Jew, who married Charles Grove, a mariner, and had two daughters with him. When he died she moved to Cambridge to make money by writing an encyclopedia of dance. There she met the committed bachelor, Frazer, and *mirabile dictu,* they were married, after which she ran his life and his writing like "a dragon." Frazer attended Hellensburgh academy in Dumbarton, then went to Glasgow University in 1869, moving from there to Trinity College, Cambridge, became a fellow there in 1879, and was called to the Bar in the same year. In 1907 he was made professor of social anthropology at Liverpool, but returned almost immediately to Cambridge, teaching until 1922. His books include *Totemism* (1887), *Totemism and Exogamy* (1910), *Man, God, and Immortality* (1927), and *Creation and Evolution in Primitive Cosmogonies* (1935).

Frazer became world famous for his multivolume work (either 12 or 15 depending on source volumes counted), *The Golden Bough* (1890–1915). After he abridged it in 1922, the book attained a vast audience in the one-volume edition which it still enjoys today. Although he did no field work himself, he was sent information by missionaries, travelers, and anthropologists from all over the world, which he dutifully entered into his scheme. Frazer showed through his vast comparative anthropological study that myths and rituals were connected in preliterate societies, and that Christian myths could be linked with many originating in other cultures. Magic for Frazer (as defined by Tylor) meant technically precise acts thought to influence physical reality, whereas religion was a plea for help from some higher power, a distinction that became fundamental to subsequent anthropology. He distinguished "the law of similarity" and "the law of contact or contagion" to explain magical practices. Following others in the Darwinian/Spencerian camp, he believed that human thought evolved from the magical to religious to scientific stages (which also parallels Comte's tripartite division of human history). Poets (notably T. S. Eliot) and other creative writers, social scientists, and philosophers became fascinated with Frazer's compendium, since it seemed to provide the first comprehensive view of what might be termed humankind's "cultural subconscious." It was this new element to comparative mythology that so excited thinkers like Freud (whom Frazer refused to read or believe), Carl Jung, Geza Roheim, and many others. It seemed to promise a view of humanity at its most basic, illustrating both great diversity and significant similarity across cultures in terms of fundamental beliefs. Naturally, over the succeeding century, some of Frazer's scholarly claims and his psychological theory of ritualistic behavior have had to be rectified, yet the work lives on, not least for its documentation of what a Victorian scholarly polymath could accomplish given enough time. It remains a monument to a single scholar's energy.

THE GOLDEN BOUGH, 1911–15

Farewell to Nemi

. . . If then we consider, on the one hand, the essential similarity of man's chief wants everywhere and at all times, and on the other hand, the wide difference between the means he has adopted to satisfy them in different ages, we shall perhaps be disposed to conclude that the movement of the higher thought, so far as we can trace it, has on the whole been from magic through religion to science. In magic man depends on his own strength to meet the difficulties and dangers that beset him on every side. He believes in a certain established order of nature on which he can surely count, and which he can manipulate for his own ends. When he discovers his mistake, when he recognises sadly that both the order of nature which he had assumed and the control which he had believed himself to exercise over it were purely imaginary, he ceases to rely on his own intelligence and his own unaided efforts, and throws himself humbly on the mercy of certain great invisible beings behind the veil of nature, to whom he now ascribes all those far-reaching powers which he once arrogated to himself. Thus in the acuter minds magic is gradually superseded by religion, which explains the succession of natural phenomena as regulated by the will, the passion, or the caprice of spiritual beings like man in kind, though vastly superior to him in power.

But as time goes on this explanation in its turn proves to be unsatisfactory. For it assumes

that the succession of natural events is not determined by immutable laws, but is to some extent variable and irregular, and this assumption is not borne out by closer observation. On the contrary, the more we scrutinise that succession the more we are struck by the rigid uniformity, the punctual precision with which, wherever we can follow them, the operations of nature are carried on. Every great advance in knowledge has extended the sphere of order and correspondingly restricted the sphere of apparent disorder in the world, till now we are ready to anticipate that even in regions where chance and confusion appear still to reign, a fuller knowledge would everywhere reduce the seeming chaos to cosmos. Thus the keener minds, still pressing forward to a deeper solution of the mysteries of the universe, come to reject the religious theory of nature as inadequate, and to revert in a measure to the older standpoint of magic by postulating explicitly, what in magic had only been implicitly assumed, to wit, an inflexible regularity) in the order of natural events, which, if carefully observed, enables us to foresee their course with certainty and to act accordingly. In short, religion, regarded as an explanation of nature, is displaced by science.

But while science has this much in common with magic that both rest on a faith in order as the underlying principle of all things, readers of this work will hardly need to be reminded that the order presupposed by magic differs widely from that which forms the basis of science. The difference flows naturally from the different modes in which the two orders have been reached. For whereas— the order on which magic reckons is merely an extension, by false analogy, of the order in which ideas present themselves to our minds, the order laid down by science is derived from patient and

From *The Golden Bough: A Study in Magic and Religion,* by Sir James George Frazer. Published by The Macmillan Company, 1922.

exact observation of the phenomena themselves. The abundance, the solidity, and the splendour of the results already achieved by science are well fitted to inspire us with a cheerful confidence in the soundness of its method. Here at last, after groping about in the dark for countless ages, man has hit upon a clue to the labyrinth, a golden key that opens many locks in the treasury of nature. It is probably not too much to say that the hope of progress—moral and intellectual as well as material—in the future is bound up with the fortunes of science, and that every obstacle placed in the way of scientific discovery is a wrong to humanity.

Yet the history of thought should warn us against concluding that because the scientific theory of the world is the best that has yet been formulated, it is necessarily complete and final. We must remember that at bottom the generalisations of science or, in common parlance, the laws of nature are merely hypotheses devised to explain that ever-shifting phantasmagoria of thought which we dignify with the high-sounding names of the world and the universe. In the last analysis magic, religion, and science are nothing but theories of thought; and as science has supplanted its predecessors, so it may hereafter be itself superseded by some more perfect hypothesis, perhaps by some totally different way of looking at the phenomena—of registering the shadows on the screen of which we in this generation can form no idea. The advance of knowledge is an infinite progression towards a goal that for ever recedes. We need not murmur at the endless pursuit:

Fatti non foste a viver come bruti
Ma per seguir virtute e conoscenza.

Great things will come of that pursuit, though we may not enjoy them. Brighter stars will rise on some voyager of the future—some great Ulysses of the realms of thought—than shine on us. The dreams of magic may one day be the waking realities of science. But a dark shadow lies athwart the far end of this fair prospect. For however vast the increase of knowledge and of power which the future may have in store for man, he can scarcely hope to stay the sweep of those great forces which seem to be making silently but relentlessly for the destruction of all this starry universe in which our earth swims as a speck or mote. In the ages to come man may be able to predict, perhaps even to control, the wayward courses of the winds and clouds, but hardly will his puny hands have strength to speed afresh our slackening planet in its orbit or rekindle the dying fire of the sun. Yet the philosopher who trembles at the idea of such distant catastrophes may console himself by reflecting that these gloomy apprehensions, like the earth and the sun themselves, are only parts of that unsubstantial world which thought has conjured up out of the void, and that the phantoms which the subtle enchantress has evoked to-day she may ban to-morrow: They too, like so much that to common eyes seems solid, may melt into air, into thin air.

Without dipping so far into the future, we may illustrate the course which thought has hitherto run by likening it to a web woven of three different threads—the black thread of magic, the red thread of religion, and the white thread of science, if under science we may include those simple truths, drawn from observation, of nature, of which men in all ages have possessed a store. Could we then survey the web of thought from the beginning, we should probably perceive it to be at fast a chequer of black and whine, a patchwork of true and false notions, hardly tinged as yet by the red thread of religion. But carry your eye farther along the fabric and you will remark that, while the black and white chequer still runs through it, there rests on the middle portico of the web, where religion has entered most deeply into its texture, a dark crimson stain, which shades off insensibly into a lighter tint as the white thread of science is woven more and more into the tissue. To a web thus chequered and stained, thus shot with threads of diverse hues, but gradually changing colour the farther it is unrolled, the state of modern thought, with all its divergent aims and conflicting tendencies, may be compared. Will the great movement which for centuries has been slowly altering the complexion of thought be continued in the near future? or will a reaction set in which may arrest progress and even undo much that has been done? To keep up our parable, what will be the colour of the web which the Fates are now weaving on the humming loom of time? will it be white or red? We cannot tell. A faint glimmering light illumines the backward portion of the web. Clouds and thick darkness hide the other end.

ROBERTO MICHELS

1876–1936

The only child of a rich merchant father, Roberto Michels was born in Cologne, Germany on January 9, 1876, married Gisela Lindner in 1900, made with her a family of three children, and died on May 2 or 3, 1936 in Rome. He was privately tutored and then entered the French College in Berlin between 1885 and 1889. For the next five years he enrolled in the Carl Friedrich Gymnasium in Eisenach, Thüringen, graduating in 1894. He served his compulsory year in the military (1895–96) in Hannover and Weimar, then studied history and national economics at the Sorbonne, the universities of Munich, Leipzig, and Halle, receiving his doctorate in 1900 in history from the latter. He also became active that year in the socialist movement. His habilitation was finished at the Universities of Marburg and Jena in 1907. His attempt to find a suitable academic job met with frustration due to his politics, and despite the friendly intervention of Max Weber. He wrote a second habilitation in political-economy under Achille Loria at the University of Turin in 1907, and held a modest academic appointment there until 1928. From 1914 until 1928 he lived in Basel, Switzerland, finally achieving the rank of Professor of Political Economy and Statistics, where he developed a friendship with Vilfredo Pareto. Joining the National Fascist Party of Italy in 1923, he was guest lecturer at the universities of Messina and Rome. Interestingly, he also was a visiting professor at the University of Chicago and at Williams College in 1927. He spent the last eight years of his life in Perugia, Umbria, and Rome. He was personally supported by Mussolini and worked as a propagandist until his death, though not without reservations.

Michels will always be remembered for having stated the "iron law of oligarchy" in *Political Parties: A Sociological Study of the Oligarchical Tendencies of Modern Democracy* (1911), from which one selection below comes. Michels argued that no matter what political orientation an organization might have, it will shortly be run by a self-perpetuating oligarchy that refuses to cede power without being deposed. He based this argument in part on his own experience in the Social Democratic Party in Germany before his conversion to fascism—that is, from far left to far right. Michels also wrote *First Lectures in Political Sociology* and *Sexual Ethics: A Study of Borderland Questions* (1911). The latter is particularly interesting today given the attention that changing gender roles have received, and Michels' late Victorian notions, mixed with a socialist predisposition, are worth review.

POLITICAL PARTIES: A SOCIOLOGICAL STUDY OF THE OLIGARCHICAL TENDENCIES OF MODERN DEMOCRACY, 1911

Final Considerations

Leadership is a necessary phenomenon in every form of social life. Consequently it is not the task of science to inquire whether this phenomenon is good or evil, or predominantly one or the other. But there is great scientific value in the demonstration that every system of leadership is incompatible with the most essential postulates of democracy. We are now aware that the law of the historic necessity of oligarchy is primarily based upon a series of facts of experience. Like all other scientific laws, sociological laws are derived from empirical observation. In order, however, to deprive our axiom of its purely descriptive character, and to confer upon it that status of analytical explanation which can alone transform a formula into a law, it does not suffice to contemplate from a unitary outlook those phenomena which may be empirically established; we must also study the determining causes of these phenomena. Such has been our task.

Now, if we leave out of consideration the tendency of the leaders to organize themselves and to consolidate their interests, and if we leave also out of consideration the gratitude of the led towards the leaders, and the general immobility and passivity of the masses, we are led to conclude that the principal cause of oligarchy in the democratic parties is to be found in the technical indispensability of leadership.

The process which *has* begun in consequence of the differentiation of functions in the party is completed by a complex of qualities which the leaders acquire through their detachment from the mass. At the outset, leaders arise spontaneously; their functions are accessory and gratuitous. Soon, however, they become professional leaders, and in this second stage of development they are stable and irremovable.

It follows that the explanation of the oligarchical phenomenon which thus results is partly psychological; oligarchy derives, that is to say, from the psychical transformations which the leading personalities in the parties undergo in the course of their lives. But also, and still more, oligarchy depends upon what we may term the psychology of organization itself, that is to say, upon the tactical and technical necessities which result from the consolidation of every disciplined political aggregate. Reduced to its most concise expression, the fundamental sociological law of political parties (the term "political" being here used in its most comprehensive significance) may be formulated in the following terms: "It is organization which gives birth to the dominion of the elected over the electors, of the mandataries over the mandators, of the delegates over the delegators. Who says organization, says oligarchy."

Every party organization represents an oligarchical power grounded upon a democratic basis. We find everywhere electors and elected. Also we find everywhere that the power of the elected leaders over the electing masses is almost unlimited. The oligarchical structure of the building suffocates the basic democratic principle. That which is oppresses that which ought to be. For the masses, this essential difference between the reality and the ideal remains a mystery. Socialists often cherish a sincere belief that a new *élite* of politicians will keep faith better than did the old. The notion of the representation of popular interests, a notion to which the great majority of democrats, and in especial the working-class masses of the German-speaking lands, cleave with so much tenacity and confidence, is an illusion engendered by a false illumination, is an effect of mirage. . . .

The socialist parties, like the trade unions, are living forms of social life. As such they react with the utmost energy against any attempt to analyse their structure or their nature, as if it were a method of vivisection. When science attains to results which conflict with their apriorist ideology, they revolt with all their power. Yet their defence is extremely feeble. Those among the representatives of such organizations whose scientific earnestness and personal good faith make it impossible for them to deny outright the existence of oligarchical tendencies in every form

From *Political Parties: A Sociological Study of the Oligarchical Tendencies of Modern Democracy,* by Roberto Michels, Eden and Cedar Paul, Trans. Published by Hearst's International Library Co., 1915.

of democracy, endeavour to explain these tendencies as the outcomes of a kind of atavism in the mentality of the masses, characteristic of the youth of the movement. The masses, they assure us, are still infected by the oligarchic virus simply because they have been oppressed during long centuries of slavery, and have never yet enjoyed an autonomous existence. The socialist regime, however, will soon restore them to health, and will furnish them with all the capacity necessary for self-government. Nothing could be more anti-scientific—than the supposition that as soon as socialists have gained possession of governmental power it will suffice for the masses to exercise a little control over their leaders to secure that the interests of these leaders shall coincide perfectly with the interests of the led. . . .

The objective immaturity of the mass is not a mere transitory phenomenon which will disappear with the progress of democratization *au lendemain du socialisme*. On the contrary, it derives from the very nature of the mass as mass, for this, even when organized, suffers from an incurable incompetence for the solution of the diverse problems which present themselves for solution—because the mass *per se* is amorphous, and therefore needs division of labour, specialization, and guidance. . . .

It is, in fact, a general characteristic of democracy, and hence also of the labour movement, to stimulate and to strengthen in the individual the intellectual aptitudes for criticism and control. We have seen how the progressive bureaucratization of the democratic organism tends to neutralize the beneficial effects of such criticism and such control. None the less it is true that the labour movement, in virtue of the theoretical postulates it proclaims, is apt to bring into existence (in opposition to the will of the leaders) a certain number of free spirits who, moved by principle, by instinct, or by both, desire to revise the base upon which authority is established. Urged on by conviction or by temperament, they are never weary of asking an eternal "Why?" about every human institution. Now this predisposition towards free inquiry, in which we cannot fad to recognize one of the most precious factors of civilization, will gradually increase in proportion as the economic status of the masses undergoes improvement and becomes more stable, and in proportion as they are admitted more effec-

tively to the advantages of civilization. A wider education involves an increasing capacity for exercising control. Can we not observe every day that among the well-to-do the authority of the leaders over the led, extensive though it be, is never so unrestricted as in the case of the leaders of the poor? Taking in the mass, the poor are powerless and disarmed vis-à-vis their leaders. Their intellectual and cultural inferiority makes it impossible for them to see whither the leader is going, or to estimate in advance the significance of his actions. It is, consequently, the great task of social education to raise the intellectual level of the masses, so that they may be enabled, within the limits of what is possible, to counteract the oligarchical tendencies of the working-class movement.

In view of the perennial incompetence of the masses, we have to recognize the existence of two regulative principles:—

1. The *ideological* tendency of democracy towards criticism and control;
2. The *effective* counter-tendency of democracy towards the creation of parties ever more complex and ever more differentiated—parties, that is to say, which are increasingly based upon the competence of the few.

To the idealist, the analysis of the forms of contemporary democracy cannot fail to be a source of bitter deceptions and profound discouragement. Those alone, perhaps, are in a position to pass a fair judgment upon democracy who, without lapsing into dilettantist sentimentalism, recognize that all scientific and human ideals have relative values. If we wish to estimate the value of democracy, we must do so in comparison with its converse, pure aristocracy. The defects inherent in democracy are obvious. It is none the less true that as a form of social life we must choose democracy as the least of evils. The ideal government would doubtless be that of an aristocracy of persons at once morally good and technically efficient, But where shall we discover such an aristocracy? We may find it sometimes, though very rarely, as the outcome of deliberate selection; but we shall never find it where the hereditary principle remains in operation. Thus monarchy in its pristine purity must be considered as imperfection incarnate, as the most incurable of ills; from the moral point of view it is inferior even to the most revolting of demagogic dictatorships, for the corrupt organism of the latter at least contains a healthy principle upon whose working we may continue to base hopes of social resanation. It may be said, therefore, that the more humanity comes to recognize the advantages which democracy, however imperfect, presents over aristocracy, even at its best, the less likely is it that a recognition of the defects of democracy will provoke a return to aristocracy. Apart from certain formal differences and from the qualities which can be acquired only by good education and inheritance (qualities in which aristocracy will always have the advantage over democracy—qualities which democracy either neglects altogether, or, attempting to imitate them, falsifies them to the point of caricature), the defects of democracy will be found to inhere in its inability to get rid of its aristocratic scorns. On the other hand, nothing but a serene and frank examination of the oligarchical dangers of democracy will enable us to minimize these dangers, even though they can never be entirely avoided.

The democratic currents of history resemble successive waves. They break ever on the same shoal. They are ever renewed. This enduring spectacle is simultaneously encouraging and depressing. When democracies have gained a certain stage of development, they undergo a gradual transformation, adopting the artistocratic spirit, and in many uses also the aristocratic forms, against which at the outset they straggled so fiercely. Now new accusers arise to denounce the traitors; after an era of glorious combats and of inglorious power, they end by fusing with the old dominant clan; whereupon once more they are in their turn attacked by fresh opponents who appeal to the name of democracy. It is probable that this, cruel game will continue without end.

⌒

SEXUAL ETHICS, 1911

Conflict between Profession and Motherhood

A woman can give no higher praise to her husband than to say that he has never failed to provide help and encouragement in the development of her natural gifts, and that he has been by her side, not only in the troubles of child-bearing—a companionship rare enough, as every one knows—but to aid her, whenever requisite, in the cultivation of her intelligence. The rarity of the instances in which husbands thus encourage the mental development of their wives, and even of those in which they fail to put obstacles in the way of their wives' aspirations in this direction, is due to the general prevalence among the middle class of every country in the world of a peculiar conception of the duties of the married woman as housewife and mother. Speaking generally, men regard feminine culture with a certain disfavour, so that they are apt to prefer a woman who, although a good housewife, is intellectually a little goose, to a cultivated woman, even though the latter too has all the domestic virtues. In eighteenth-century Naples it was considered dangerous to teach women to read and write, the fear being that this would give them more liberty than was good for them. The talent of a Genovesi was required to demonstrate, from the example of the women of France and Holland, the practical utility of feminine instruction, and the lack of any danger therein to morality.' With very rare exceptions, the intellectual development of the wife in certain situations which we shall now consider in detail, is rendered impossible by the prepotent egoism of the husband.

1. The first of these situations is that in which independent activities on the part of the wife would involve more work for the husband, forcing him to undertake a share of the

From *A Study of Borderland Questions: Sexual Ethics*, by Roberto Michels. Published by Transaction Publishers. Copyright © 2002.

domestic duties, in order to leave the woman free for intellectual and social work. This will be obstinately resisted by the husband even when he is altogether inferior in capacity to his wife, and when the proposed new division of labour would entail social and even economic advantages for the family as a whole.

2. The second case is that in which the wife's inclinations are towards politics and public life, and her views on these questions differ from those of her husband. A man will sometimes forgive his wife for public activities carried on by his own side; but he can hardly endure that she should have political views different from his own, at any rate he cannot endure the open expression of such views. The most modern of men, if he consents that his wife should take a part, even restricted, in public life, will not be easy if she advocates views that differ in any respect from his own. The public advertisement of such differences would be regarded by him as a scandal, and would probably wreck the family life. In the history of modern party politics, we find numerous instances in which wives have played a prominent part, and have played it with force, knowledge, and skill, in the advocacy of the husband's political tendencies. On the other hand, cases are frequent enough in which sons have shaken off the political views of the family, and have actively worked on behalf of political tendencies diametrically opposed to those of their fathers—though it must be admitted that in such a case the father is apt to consider the son's action in the light of a personal offence. But as far as I know, we cannot find a single example in which the wife has completely discarded the political ideas of the husband and has publicly advocated those of some opposed tendency, without a complete rupture of conjugal relationships. We may infer from these facts that the dependence of the wife upon the husband is far more complete than the dependence of the son upon the father. This consideration forces upon our attention one of the gravest difficulties facing the honest and unrestricted application of women's right to the suffrage. Will the husband, we have to ask ourselves, permit his wife to give practical effect in this matter to views divergent from his own; will he permit the like liberty to his unmarried daughters?

3. The third case is that in which the special development of the wife's faculties is in the same field as that in which the husband is engaged in his life-work, and the wife exhibits more ability than the husband. The man will gladly accept his wife's support and assistance in his professional occupation. The medical man will find something for his wife to do as nurse or dispenser; the protestant clergyman will an occasions entrust to his wife the care of souls; the man of science will permit his wife to perform for him all kinds of preparatory work, will entrust to her the correction of his proofs or the preparation of indexes and tables of contents. Sometimes he will agree to her undertaking more advanced and more independent work in his own specialty, above all if this course should prove lucrative. Medical practitioners of different sexes may be associated in marriage; the actor and the actress may be husband and wife. But in such cases it is always presupposed that the wife's endowments must not be so great as to put into the shade those of the husband, as to under-mine his social authority and professional value. A man cannot endure to be eclipsed by his wife in his own chosen field. A typical recent example is that of the Viennese tenor who, jealous of the popularity of his wife, also a celebrated singer, paid a number of persons to attend the Opera in order to hiss her off the stage.

Thus masculine egoism imposes limits in many cases to the possibility of women's intellectual development.

In all social classes, the highest not excepted, intellectual women are scarce even to-day. Some women have too much to do; others have too little; and the members of a third section pass their time in the unwholesome environment of luxury and amusement, in all kinds of frivolity and worldly trivialities. It is true that in certain circles and in certain countries women exhibit a veritable mania for culture. But this applies to marriageable women and not to those already married. Even in the case of the former, higher education is apt to serve only as a means to an end, to enable them to attain more readily to marriage. Once they find themselves in this haven, they throw away their hard-gained intellectuality as so much useless lumber. Intellectual women—by which term I do not mean to refer merely to the bluestocking nor to the wealthy woman who coquets with knowledge in her odd moments, but to the woman with a true breadth of view and a sound understanding of the great problems of mankind—are to-day but rarely encountered. This scarcity is by no means to be explained by the suggestion that science is beyond the capacity of the feminine brain, and still less can it be affirmed, as certain male pedants contend, that higher education is destructive to womanliness and renders women incapable of fulfilling their true mission in life. The sources of the trouble lie far deeper than this.

ERNST TROELTSCH

1866–1923

Ernst Troeltsch, a physician's son, was born in Haunstetten, near Augsburg, Bavaria on February 17, 1865, married Marta Fick of the landed gentry, on May 13, 1901, with whom he had one son in 1913, Eberhard, when Troeltsch was 48. He died in Berlin on February 1, 1923 just shy of his 58th birthday. Encouraged by his father to approach intellectual matters via a strongly scientific frame of mind, he also learned the classics thoroughly while attending the Augsburg Gymnasium prior to studies at the universities of Erlangen (1884–88), Berlin, and Göttingen. He became an ordained Lutheran minister at the Munich seminary in 1888, claiming in his autobiography that theology allowed him to bring together disparate intellectual interests in a unique fashion. After academic positions at Göttingen and Bonn, he achieved a full professorship at Heidelberg in 1894, and between 1910 and 1915 enjoyed the rare distinction of being Max Weber's tenant in a large house on the Neckar River in Heidelberg which is now owned by the University. Troeltsch's family occupied the top floor of this spacious home at 17 Ziegelhäuser Landstrasse, and the interaction between Weber and his colleague regarding the history of religion was daily and intense, as they were both working on these matters at the same time (between 1900 and 1920). He switched from theology to philosophy at Berlin in 1915, realizing that his scholarly preferences lay more with the latter than the former, moving from believer to analyst.

Troeltsch will always be known for his single large book, *The Social Teaching of the Christian Churches* (1912, 2 vols.), despite having written others and many articles. In writing this book, he joined Weber in creating the "sociology of religion." Troeltsch wrote as an intellectual and cultural historian, illustrating the connections between different social groups, denominations, and sects and the ideas which they chose to embrace at various points in the church's history. Troeltsch was also deeply involved in what came to be called "the historicist controversy." Those who believed church dogma in absolutist terms could not tolerate a view which weighed the teachings of various churches throughout history, noting the similarities and differences among sets of ideas in rather dispassionate terms. This was precisely the historicist viewpoint, which Troeltsch adopted and practiced. However, he recognized the limits of historicist thinking, since he did believe that a core of truth existed within Christian dogma, which had to be reinterpreted by each succeeding generation on its own historical terms. Additionally, his distinction between church and sect was one that Weber made great use of in his own *Sociology of Religion* (1922).

THE SOCIAL TEACHING OF THE CHRISTIAN CHURCHES, 1911

Introduction and Preliminary Questions of Method

. . . This, then, is the question: What is the basis of the social teaching of the churches? From the point of view of their essential nature in principle what is their attitude towards the modern social problem? And what should be their attitude?

This question is all the more important since one of the special advantages of ecclesiastical social science is that it possesses meta-physical convictions based on principle. In this the churches are one with the Social Democrats, and for that reason the political party of the Centre, the Conservatives with their "patriarchal" ideas, and the revolutionary Social Democrats have the strongest power of influencing other people, whereas Liberalism, which by its relative tendency is split up into individual peculiarities, practical compromises, and middle-class learning, either does not possess this power, or it possesses it no longer, since for the present, at least, its fundamental individualistic idea has become exhausted. . . .

In the current sense, the idea of the "Social" means a definite, clearly defined section of the general sociological phenomena—that is, the sociological relations which are not regulated by the State, nor by political interest, save in so far as they are indirectly influenced by them. This sociological section is composed of the various questions which arise out of economic life, the sociological tension between various groups with different customs and aims, division of labour, class organization, and some other interests which cannot be directly characterized as political, but which actually have a great influence on the collective life of the State; since the development of the modern constitutional State, however, these interests have definitely separated themselves from it. The "social problem", therefore, really consists in the relation

between the political community and these sociological phenomena, which, although they are essentially non-political, are yet of outstanding importance from the political point of view. Thus Lorenz von Stein, for instance, from his observation of the development of France, set the conception of "Society" alongside that of the State, and heralded the social problem of the present day. Rodbertus, the other prophet of the social problem, has defined Society as the "personified total content of the peripheral life-activities, which express themselves in the lower strata of social life, through individual multiplicities, in those sections of social life which the State does not control". It is, however, essential to retain this narrower significance of the words "society" and "social" as they are particularly accentuated by the present situation. For it is impossible to speak of Society as the total sum of varying grades of sociological groups, with their mutual complexities and interactions. It is not an entity which can be surveyed scientifically. Because of the infinitude of its groupings and the manifold ways we may choose for the linking up of sociological phenomena. Society is something inconceivable—an abstraction like civilization, or history in general, about which only dilettanti speak as a whole. In truth, all thought of it involves a seizing and relating of some particular factor which interests us, and by means of which the sociological phenomena which are related to it come into the field of vision at the same time. Even the keenest thinker, who is capable of looking at things from the broadest point of view and in abstract terms, if he tries to think about Society as a whole, finds his ideas dispersing in all directions, into the infinitude of sociological classifications which emerge from any other possible point of view.

There is no "natural-science" conception of Society such as there is of mechanics, which will cover all particular phenomena. The conception of Society is an historical conception, and out of an infinite wealth of individual sociological developments it is always only able to seize upon certain phenomena and to study them in their various connections; even when this conception seizes upon those aspects which are most important for life—and in so doing naturally touches an extremely widespread complication of sociological groups—it never exhausts the universal conception of Society in general. This means, however, that in this instance "Society" type, precisely because it possesses this faculty, it is equally inconsistent to use the terms "society" and the "social element" with which Christianity is contrasted to indicate Society as a whole. Indeed, even Stein's conception of Society, which includes everything which does not come under the scope of the modern constitutional State, is still too broad. By "Society" modern science means, and rightly, primarily the social relationships which result from the economic phenomena. That is to say, it is the Society composed of all who labour, who are divided up into various classes and professional groups according to the work they do, which produces and exchanges goods, a Society organized upon the basis of the economic needs of existence, with all its manifold complications. . . .

Thus it is an actual fact of history that from the beginning all the social doctrines of Christianity have been likewise doctrines both of the State and of Society. At the same time, owing to the emphasis of Christian thought upon personality, the Family is always regarded as the basis both of the State and of Society, and is thus bound up with all Christian social doctrine. Once more, therefore, the conception of the "Social" widens out, since in the development of a religious doctrine of fellowship the Family, the State, and the economic order of Society are combined as closely related sociological formations. They do not exhaust the meaning of Society in general, but they are the great objects which the religious structure of Society must seek to assimilate, whereas it can leave the other elements to look after themselves. Christian social doctrine, therefore is a doctrine of the most important non-religious sociological structures which are erected upon an independent foundation, or, to use its own language, of its relation with the most powerful social forces of the "world". If we admit that the State and Society, together with innumerable other forces, are still the main formative powers of civilization, then the ultimate problem may be stated thus: How can the Church harmonize with these main forces in such a way that together they will form a unity of civilization?

Sociological Effect of Luther's Thought: The New Conception of the Church

We now come to our second main question: What were the sociological results of this religious transformation of Christianity? . . .

In this connection the decisive element is not the peculiar juridical form of the Lutheran conception of the Church (with, which the next section will deal), but, primarily, it is the fundamental fact that, from the very outset, this whole intellectual outlook belongs, essentially, to the Church-type. This means that the new conception of the Church fundamentally determines the sociological outlook of all the Protestant groups and gives to them its peculiar difficulties.

In spite of the fact that this school of thought has many affinities with the sect-type, in spite of its individualism, its lay religion, its appeal to the authority of the Bible, its emphasis upon the subjective realization of salvation in personal and inward Christian piety, and on the restriction of the true Church to real Christians, who have been truly "born again"—in spite of all this, in its inmost being it reveals no tendency whatever towards the sect-type; indeed, it regards the Church-type, in the most natural way, as the only Christian type of ecclesiastical organization.

From the very outset this is what Luther intended: (1) the reform of the ecclesiastical organ of grace and of redemption, so that its true basis of grace may be revealed in the Word, in the knowledge of Christ, and in the assurance of the forgiveness of Sins which springs from Christ; (2) the reform of the priesthood, in order to restore it to its true office, instituted by Christ Himself, of the proclamation of the Word, or "preaching Christ"; (3) the reform of the sacraments—that is, from rites which impart the "Substance of grace", they are to be transformed into rites appointed by Christ as "means of grace" which seal the assurance of the Gospel of the forgiveness of sins.

Luther took for granted that, along with these demands for reform, all baptized Christians, however immature or nominal; they might be, were included in the Church; that Infant Baptism should be retained and universally practised, and that the efficacy of the means of grace is independent of the subjective state both of the celebrant and of the soul which receives these mysteries. Luther had no desire to found a new Church; he simply wished to introduce an *instauratio catholica*, that is, to lead the One Catholic Apostolic Church, founded by Christ and endowed by Him with ministry, Word, and Sacrament, back to its purely spiritual activity of proclaiming the Word which creates faith.

The Word itself, however, its foundation in the Bible, its manifestation in the Sacrament, and its proclamation in the sermon, is to him an objective and precious endowment, intended for the benefit of all the individuals in the world, which the Church (as an institution) appropriates, and which is to be administered in an orderly manner by officials appointed for that purpose. Where officials of this kind do not exist laymen may officiate in their stead. The layman who discharges this duty, however, is thereby entitled to that precise share in the objective treasury of grace. In this respect, in the significance of a *Depositum* which the organ of grace established by Christ appropriates, and in the complete independence of the organ of grace from any standard of subjective realization, Luther's conception of grace is precisely the same as that of Catholicism. The differences lie only in the conception of the content of grace. From that point of view, however, both the nature and the method of influence of the ecclesiastical institution are considerably different.

The hierarchical sacramental Church is replaced by the Church which lays the main emphasis upon the Word of Scripture and its proclamation by the preachers. This Church, however, is also an institution set over its members as their supernatural source, instituted and directed by God Himself. This Church is entirely unaffected by the occurrence or non-occurrence of the subjective effects of conversion in particular individuals: in itself it is holy and Divine, through the converting power inherent in the "Word"; its position as a Divine institution is still supreme, even when very few are actually "converted" souls, while as a united body it extends its influence through all its special developments in the form of a national church, or in other ways. For, where there is the Word and the Sacrament, there is the Church, and the supernatural source of all experiences of salvation; and faith is certain that "the Word of God never returns unto Him void", that is, but finally its dwelling miraculous power will yet overcome all obstacles, and that in the end it must also inwardly convert humanity to Christ. This will certainly never be a comprehensive conversion including the whole of humanity. The Devil and sin are too strong for that, and the confusions of the present Church point to the End of the World, in which the great conflict between Christ and Antichrist will bring the struggle to a conclusion.

This conception of the Church is extremely spiritual and idealistic, making the essence of the Church to consist in the Word, the Sacrament, and the office of the ministry, and restricting it to a purely spiritual sphere of influence.

SIGMUND FREUD

1856–1939

Sigmund (Sigismund) Schlomo Freud, the son of a remote, 40-year old Jewish wool merchant and a younger, second wife, was born in Freiberg, Moravia, in Austria on May 6, 1856, and in 1886 married Martha Bernays (whose ancestors included Heinrich Heine), with whom he had six children. One of them, Anna Freud, became an important analyst and carefully tended her father's legacy. Freud died after a long and torturous war with cancer on September 23, 1939 in London at 83. His two older half-brothers were not so important to his childhood as was his nephew, John, one year older. Freud's theorizing about sibling rivalry, domestic power struggles, and the roots of neuroses seem to have grown out of his own "family drama," plus the special dynamics of Victorian, patriarchal Vienna at the fin de siècle, a city that was his home for 78 years (1860–1938). Freud attended the Sperl Gymnasium, was inspired by Goethe's works to pursue science (even though he was extremely gifted as a German prose writer), and became a physiologist, doing research on the brain and the medicinal properties of cocaine. During the early 1880s Freud accepted the materialist explanations for consciousness then prevalent among physicians, but in 1885, after studying for 19 weeks with Charcot in Paris, and seeing what could be done with "hysterics" under hypnosis, he realized that "mind" and "brain" are not synonymous. From that time on he slowly developed his psychoanalytic theories of the neuroses, and in so doing added a glossary of terms and new notions to every educated person's vocabulary, up to our own day. His early professional friendships with William Fliess and Josef Breuer helped Freud refine the basic psychoanalytic view of human sexuality, aggression, and the "talking cure" which he practiced at Berggasse 19 in Vienna for almost 50 years.

Freud wrote so much, his colleagues and students wrote much more, and the entire psychoanalytic industry has proven so prolific and contentious that it is impossible to summarize his (or their) achievement in a few words. Luckily, though, there is a fairly clean distinction that exists between Freud's massive clinical work on mentally ill patients on the one hand, and on the other his anthropological, cultural, and historical ruminations about the troubling dialectical relationship that has always obtained between individuals and the requirements of social order. Whereas many theorists (like Cooley, Mead, or James) thought this relationship to be tricky, but in general non-corrosive, for Freud it was filled with dire consequences. His denunciation of religious beliefs, in *The Future of an Illusion* (1927), is one of the bitterest of its genre. Similarly, in *Civilization and Its Discontents* (1930; *Unbehagen in der Kultur,* literally, "the uneasy/disquieting feeling in culture"), the old, cancer-ridden man, with the barbaric European politics of his day clearly in mind, states that civilization thrives in precise opposition to the repression of the individual's most powerful desires. He studied Leonardo da Vinci (1910), works of Michelangelo, and popular novels, all with the aim of illustrating how difficult it is for the creative individual to bear up under the repressive weight of social structure and control. From these works we get the essential concept of "sublimation," which for social thought is probably the most significant of Freud's neologisms. His other works which pertain to the social world beyond the psychiatrist's couch include *Totem and Taboo* (1913), *Group Psychology and the Analysis of the Ego* (1921), and *Moses and Monotheism* (1938). The further Freud got from his clinical findings, the more adventurously captious he became, which is perhaps why these very books are the ones that are still today most often reconsidered, long after many of his purely psychoanalytic texts have become less persuasive. The selections below come from these more speculative works which, although less important to Freud himself than his clinical discoveries, might well outlast them in cultural importance.

TOTEM AND TABOO, 1913

Taboo and the Ambivalence of Emotions

Taboo is a Polynesian word, the translation of which provides difficulties for us because we no longer possess the idea which it connotes. It was still current with the ancient Romans: their word "sacer" was the same as the taboo of the Polynesians. The αγoζ of the Greeks and the Kodaush of the Hebrews must also have signified the same thing which the Polynesians express through their word taboo and what many races in America, Africa (Madagascar), North and Central Asia express through analogous designations.

For us the meaning of taboo branches off into two opposite directions. On the one hand it means to us, sacred, consecrated: but on the other and it means, uncanny, dangerous, forbidden, and unclean. The opposite for taboo is designated in Polynesian by the word *noa* and signifies something ordinary and generally accessible. Thus something like the concept of reserve inheres in taboo; taboo expresses itself essentially in prohibitions and restrictions. Our combination of "holy dread" would often express the meaning of taboo.

The taboo restrictions are different from religious or moral prohibitions. They are not traced to a commandment of a god, but really they themselves impose their own prohibitions; they are differentiated from moral ambitions by failing to be included in a system which declares abstinences in general to be necessary and gives reasons for this necessity. The taboo prohibitions lack all justification and are of unknown origin. Though incomprehensible to us they are taken as a matter of course by those who are under their dominance.

Wundt calls taboo the oldest unwritten code of law of humanity. It is generally assumed that taboo is older than the gods and goes back to the pre-religious age. . . .

We may say, however, that we deal with a series of restrictions which these primitive races impose upon themselves; this and that is forbidden without any apparent reason; nor does it occur to them to question this matter, for they subject themselves to these restrictions as a matter of course and are convinced that any transgression will be punished automatically in the most severe manner. There are reliable reports that innocent transgressions of such prohibitions have actually been punished automatically. For instance, the innocent offender who, had eaten from a forbidden animal became deeply depressed, expected his death and then actually died. The prohibitions mostly concern matters which are capable of enjoyment such as freedom of movement and

From *The Basic Writings of Sigmund Freud,* Dr. A. A. Brill, Ed./Trans. Published by The Modern Library. Copyright © 1938.

unstrained intercourse; in some cases they appear very ingenious, evidently representing obstinences and renunciations; in other cases their content is quite incomprehensible, they seem to concern themselves with trifles and give the impression of ceremonials. Something like a theory seems to underlie all these prohibitions, it seems as if these prohibitions are necessary because some persons and objects possess a dangerous power which is transmitted by contact with the object so charged, almost like a contagion. The quantity of this dangerous property is also taken into consideration; Some persons or things have more of it than others and the danger is precisely in accordance with the charge. The most peculiar part of it is that any one who has violated such a prohibition assumes the nature of the forbidden object as if he had absorbed the whole dangerous charge. This power is inherent in all persons who are more or less prominent, such as kings, priests and the newly born, in all exceptional physical states such as menstruation, puberty and birth, in everything sinister like illness and death and in everything connected with these conditions by virtue of contagion or dissemination.

However, the term "taboo" includes all persons, localities, objects and temporary conditions which are carriers or sources of this mysterious attribute. The prohibition derived from this attribute is also designated as taboo, and lastly taboo, in the literal sense, includes everything that is sacred, above the ordinary, and at the same time dangerous, unclean and mysterious.

Both this word and the system corresponding to it express a fragment of psychic life which really is not comprehensible to us. And indeed it would seem that no understanding of it could be possible without entering into the study of the beliefs in spirits and demons which is so characteristic of these low grades of culture.

Now why should we take any interest at all in the riddle of taboo? Not only, I think, because every psychological problem is well worth that effort of investigation for its own sake, but for other reasons as well. It may be surmised that the taboo of Polynesian savages is after all not so remote from us as we were at first inclined to believe; the moral and customary prohibitions which we ourselves obey may have some the relation to this primitive taboo the explanation of which may in the end throw light upon the dark origin of our own "categorical imperative.". . .

But the real sources of taboo lie deeper than in the interests of the privileged classes: "They begin where the most primitive and at the same time the most enduring human impulses have their origin, namely, *in the fear of the effect of demonic powers.* "The taboo, which originally was nothing more than the objectified fear of the demonic power thought to be concealed in the tabooed object, forbids the irritation of this power and demands the placation of the demon whenever the taboo has been knowingly or unknowingly violated."

The taboo then gradually became an autonomous power which has attached itself from demonism. It becomes the compulsion of custom and tradition and finally the law. "But the commandment concealed behind taboo prohibitions which differ materially according to place and time, had originally the meaning. Beware of the wrath of the demons."

CIVILIZATION AND ITS DISCONTENTS, 1930

Why do our relatives, the animals, not exhibit any such cultural struggle? We do not know. Very probably some of them—the bees, the ants, the termites—strove for thousands of years before they arrived at the State institutions, the distribution of functions and the restrictions on the individual, for which we admire them to-day. It is a mark of our present condition that we know from our own feelings that we should not think ourselves happy in any of these animal States or in any of the roles assigned in them to the individual. In the case of other animal species it may be that a temporary balance has been reached between the influences of their environment and the mutually contending instincts within them, and that thus a cessation of development has come about. It may be that in primitive man a fresh access of libido kindled a renewed burst of activity on the part of the destructive instinct. There are a great many questions here to which as yet there is no answer.

Another question concerns us more nearly. What means does civilization employ in order to inhibit the aggressiveness which opposes it, to make it harmless, to get rid of it, perhaps? We have already become acquainted with a few of these methods, but not yet with the one that appears to be the most important. This we can study in the history of the development of the individual. What happens in him to render his desire for aggression innocuous? Something very remarkable, which we should never have guessed and which is nevertheless quite obvious. His aggressiveness is introjected, internalized; it is, in point of fact, sent back to where it came from—that is, it is directed towards his own ego. There it is taken over by a portion of the ego, which sets itself over against the rest of the ego as super-ego, and which now, in the form of 'conscience', is ready to put into action against the ego the same harsh aggressiveness that the ego would have liked to satisfy upon other, extraneous individuals. The tension between the harsh super-ego and the ego that is subjected to it, is called by us the sense of guilt; it expresses itself as a need for punishment. Civilization, therefore, obtains mastery over the individual's dangerous desire for aggression by weakening and disarming it and by setting up an agency within him to watch over it, like a garrison in a conquered city.

As to the origin of the sense of guilt, the analyst has different views from other psychologists; but even he does not find it easy to give an account of it. To begin with, if we ask how a person comes to have a sense of guilt, we arrive at an answer which cannot be disputed: a person feels guilty (devout people would say 'sinful') when he has done something which he knows to be 'bad'. But then we notice how little this answer tells us. Perhaps, after some hesitation, we shall add that even when a person has not actually done the bad thing but has only recognized in himself an intention to do it, he may regard himself as guilty; and the question then arises of why the intention is regarded as equal to the deed. Both cases, however, presuppose that one had already recognized that what is bad is reprehensible, is something that

must not be carried out. How is this judgement arrived at? We may reject the existence of an original, as it were natural, capacity to distinguish good from bad. What is bad is often not at all what is injurious or dangerous to the ego; on the contrary, it may be something which is desirable and enjoyable to the ego. Here, therefore, there is an extraneous influence at work, and it is this that decides what is to be called good or bad. Since a person's own feelings would not have led him along this path, he must have had a motive for submitting to this extraneous influence. Such a motive is easily discovered in his helplessness and his dependence on other people, and it can best be designated as fear of loss of love. If he loses the love of another person upon whom he is dependent, he also ceases to be protected from a variety of dangers. Above all, he is exposed to the danger that this stronger person will show his superiority in the form of punishment. At the beginning, therefore, what is bad is whatever causes one to be threatened with loss of love. For fear of that loss, one must avoid it. This, too, is the reason why it makes little difference whether one has already done the bad thing or only intends to do it. In either case the danger only sets in if and when the authority discovers it, and in either case the authority would behave in the same way.

This state of mind is called a 'bad conscience'; but actually it does not deserve this name, for at this stage the sense of guilt is clearly only a fear of loss of love, 'social' anxiety. In small children it can never be anything else, but in many adults, too, it has only changed to the extent that the place of the father or the two parents is taken by the larger human community. Consequently, such people habitually allow themselves to do any bad thing which promises them enjoyment, so long as they are sure that the authority will not know anything about it or cannot blame them for it; they are afraid only of being found out. Present-day society has to reckon in general with this state of mind.

A great change takes place only when the authority is internalized through the establishment of a super-ego. The phenomena of conscience then reach a higher stage. Actually, it is not until now that we should speak of conscience or a sense of guilt. At this point, too, the fear of being found out comes to an end; the distinction, moreover, between doing something bad and wishing to do it disappears entirely, since nothing can be hidden from the super-ego, not even thoughts. It is true that the seriousness of the situation from a real point of view has passed away, for the new authority, the super-ego, has no motive that we know of for ill-treating the ego, with which it is intimately bound up; but genetic influence, which leads to the survival of what is past and has been surmounted, makes itself felt in the fact that fundamentally things remain as they were at the beginning. The super-ego torments the sinful ego with the same feeling of anxiety and is on the watch for opportunities of getting it punished by the external world.

At this second stage of development, the conscience exhibits a peculiarity which was absent from the first stage and which is no longer easy to account for. For the more virtuous a man is, the more severe and distrustful is its behaviour, so that ultimately it is precisely those people who have carried saintliness furthest who reproach themselves with the worst sinfulness. This means that virtue forfeits some part of its promised reward; the docile and continent ego does not enjoy the trust of its mentor, and strives in vain, it would seem, to acquire it. The objection will at once be made that these difficulties are artificial ones, and it will be said that a stricter and more vigilant conscience is precisely the hallmark of a moral man. Moreover, when saints call themselves sinners, they are not so wrong, considering the temptations to instinctual satisfaction to which they are exposed in a specially high degree—since, as is well known, temptations are merely increased by constant frustration, whereas an occasional satisfaction of them causes them to diminish, at least for the time being. The field of ethics, which is so full of problems, presents us with another fact: namely that ill-luck—that is, external frustration—so greatly enhances the power of the conscience in the super-ego. As long as things go well with a man, his conscience is lenient and lets the ego do all sorts of things; but when misfortune befalls him, he searches his soul, acknowledges his sinfulness, heightens the demands of his conscience, imposes abstinences on himself and punishes himself with penances. Whole peoples have behaved in this way, and still do. This, however, is easily explained by the original infantile stage of conscience, which, as we see, is not given up after

the introjection into the super-ego, but persists alongside of it and behind it. Fate is regarded as a substitute for the parental agency. If a man is unfortunate it means that he is no longer loved by this highest power; and, threatened by such a loss of love, he once more bows to the parental representative in his super-ego—a representative whom, in his days of good fortune, he was ready to neglect. This becomes especially clear where Fate is looked upon in the strictly religious sense of being nothing else than an expression of the Divine Will. The people of Israel had believed themselves to be the favourite child of God, and when the great Father caused misfortune after misfortune to rain down upon this people of his, they were shaken in their belief in his relationship to them or questioned his power or righteousness. Instead, they produced the prophets, who held up their sinfulness before them; and out of their sense of guilt they created the over-strict commandments of their priestly religion. It is remarkable how differently a primitive man behaves. If he has met with a misfortune, he does not throw the blame on himself but on his fetish, which has obviously not done its duty, and he gives it a thrashing instead of punishing himself.

Thus we know of two origins of the sense of guilt: one arising from fear of an authority, and the other, later on, arising from fear of the super-ego. The first insists upon a renunciation of instinctual satisfactions; the second, as well as doing this, presses for punishment, since the continuance of the forbidden wishes cannot be concealed from the super-ego. . . .

These interrelations are so complicated and at the same time so important that, at the risk of repeating myself, I shall approach them from yet another angle. The chronological sequence, then, would be as follows. First comes renunciation of instinct owing to fear of aggression by the *external* authority. (This is, of course, what fear of the loss of love amounts to, for love is a protection against this punitive aggression.) After that comes the erection of an *internal* authority, and renunciation of instinct owing to fear of it—owing to fear of conscience. In this second situation bad intentions are equated with bad actions, and hence come a sense of guilt and a need for punishment. The aggressiveness of conscience keeps up the aggressiveness of the authority.

MAX SCHELER

1874–1928

Max Scheler, son of a Jewish mother and Protestant father, was born on August 22, 1874 in Munich. He was married three times, first to Amalie von Dewitz-Krebs, with whom he had two sons, one of whom died young, the other killed in a Nazi concentration camp between 1938 and 1940 after being designated as a sociopath. Scheler himself said that this son inherited all the negative characteristics residing in both his parents. His first marriage ended in 1911, and the next year he then married Maerit Fürtwangler, 17 years his junior. They were unable to reproduce, but were strongly attached to each other until Scheler met Maria Scheu in 1919, who became his assistant and mistress at the University of Cologne. Maerit could not tolerate the menage after a while, so divorced him in 1924, despite the fact that Scheler tried to maintain good relations with both women. Maria was 18 years his junior, they had one son, and she lived until 1969, 41 years longer than Scheler, and spent her life editing and publishing his works in a uniform edition. Scheler died of a second heart attack on May 19, 1928 in Frankfurt am Main, aged 53. He worked at Jena in 1901, learned from Edmund Husserl about phenomenology, worked as a diplomat in Geneva and the Hague during WWI, ended in Cologne as a professor, converting to Catholicism and pacifism. Because of his politics and marital fiasco, he was fired in 1910 from Catholic University in Munich, and moved to Göttingen where he gave lectures on a subscription basis in hotel rooms rented by a friend. He was, by all accounts, a thrilling speaker, and more than one auditor regarded him as an almost prototypical genius of expression, combining a precise philosophical vocabulary based on phenomenology with broad human concerns about love, sympathy, war, capitalism, and literature.

Scheler's first important work was *Formalism in Ethics and Non-Formal Ethics of Values* (1913–16) in which he criticized Kant, showing that normatively or ethically correct behavior originates in one of five value types anchored in the individual's *ordo amoris* ("order" or "logic" of the heart, a notion borrowed from Blaise Pascal). Thus it is not reason which dictates ethics, but a pre-rational sense of correctness that is energized in concrete social actions, a notion not too distant from American pragmatism, which Scheler studied and admired. His place in social theory was established by his speculations regarding "philosophical anthropology," including *Man's Place in the Universe* (1928), *On the Eternal in Man* (1921), and *Phenomenology and Theory of Feeling of Sympathy and of Love and Hatred*. His work was suppressed by the Nazis, and even though he has never been accorded much fame in Germany, his works are translated and read throughout the rest of the world.

FORMALISM IN ETHICS AND NON-FORMAL ETHICS OF VALUES, 1913/16

The Structure of Values and Their Historical Variations

In order to *compare* peoples or other groups in terms of their moral values, it is first necessary to *reduce* such peoples or groups to the *same* conditions in terms of their intellectual culture, their techniques of action, the levels of expression of their value estimations and their extra-moral estimations, their degrees and types of solidarity of interest, their ability to suffer, etc. For the variations and developments of moral value estimations are in principle never direct consequences of all the other variations; and, more particularly, they are not consequences of the level of intellectual culture. A very highly developed, differentiated intellectual culture can have very primitive moral feeling, and vice versa; the increased dovetailing of interests, which is the driving wheel of civilization, with the resulting security of life, property, and commerce, can go hand in hand with a very low level of moral culture.

It is necessary to get behind all the costumes and disguises in which the moral value sphere appears to us in history in order to find the material of problems concerning the dimensions of the relativity of morals.

Within this material, however, there are five strata which must be sharply differentiated for all historical considerations of moral affairs.

First, there are variations in *feeling* (i.e., "cognizing") values themselves, as well as in the *structure* of *preferring* values and *loving* and *hating.* Let us take the liberty of calling these variations as a whole variations in the "*ethos.*"

Second, there are variations which occur in the sphere of *judgment* and the sphere of rules of the *assessment* of values and value ranks given in these functions and acts. These are variations in "*ethics*" (in the broadest sense of the term).

Third, there are variations in *types* of unity of *institutions, goods,* and *actions,* i.e., the quintessences of institutions, goods, and actions, the uni-

ties of which are founded in moral value complexes, e.g., "marriage," "monogamy," "murder," "theft," "lying," etc. These types must be clearly differentiated from the (positive) definitions that are valid on the basis of mores and positive law, i.e., what shall *obtain* as "marriage," "monogamy," "murder," or "theft." Yet these types lie behind these changing definitions as the foundation of the definability of these things. They represent unities of *states of affairs,* but as such they can be distinguished only on the basis of certain *value complexes* as these or other . . . unities. Thus murder never = killing . . . a man (or killing with intent and deliberation), a lie never = conscious statement of an untruth, etc. The essence of such unities of states of affairs is such that in each case a peculiar, morally negative value complex which is basic to each case must be given if such an action is to become a lie or murder. Variations of this kind can be called variations in existing *morals,* to which a science of morals corresponds.

Fourth, and very different from all of these variations, are variations in *practical morality.* Practical morality pertains to the value of the factual comportment of men, that is, comportment on the basis of norms which belong to the relations of value ranks recognized by *these men,* and which correspond to *their own* structures of preferring. The value of such practical comportment is completely relative to its "*ethos*" and can never be measured by an ethos of another epoch or that of another people. Only *after* we take possession of an ethos of a certain age can we judge the actions and types of comportment of the people of that age; such judgment also requires preliminary knowledge of their unities of moral *types.* On the other hand, we can assess historical being and action *itself* (in terms of a refeeling understanding of the *ethos* of the epoch). In so doing, we can disregard the principles of the ethics of this age, as well as the factual assessments made by people in this age and the instances which they regarded as authoritative. On the other hand, an action that is "bad" in relation to the ethos of its age can nevertheless be absolutely "good" if the acting person surpasses, in his ethos, the ethos of his time. Indeed, according to the nature of the relation between morality and ethos, and not according to the fortuitous immorality of contemporaries or their insufficient ethics, the *moral genius,* who is superior to the ethos of his time, i.e., who has

From *Formalism in Ethics and Non-Formal Ethics of Values,* by Max Scheler, Manfred S. Frings and Robert L. Funk, Trans. Copyright © 1973. Reprinted by permission of The Northwestern University Press.

made a new advance into the realm of extant values by being the first to comprehend a higher value, is assessed and judged as morally inferior by the extant ethos, "legitimately" and *without* deception or error. The broad transitions in the history of an ethos are therefore replete with individuals who are necessarily victimized by this *tragedy* which is essentially immanent to moral development itself, but not because they are subject to the moral disapproval of a historian.

Fifth, and finally, it is necessary to distinguish the variations in moralities from variations belonging to the areas of *mores* and *customs*, i.e., forms of action and expression whose validity and practice are rooted solely in (genuine) traditions, and whose nature is such that a deviation from them presupposes an act of willing. Mores and customs *themselves* can be morally good and evil, and their origins can almost always be found in morally immediate and relevant acts and actions. They can "transmit" what is morally of positive and negative value. An action against mores, insofar as it is without reason, i.e., without insight into their moral deficiency, is practically immoral because the ethos is already coeffective in the very *selection* of actions within a tradition and is also the measure of practical morality. With this insight, however, it becomes moral. . . .

❧

THE NATURE OF SYMPATHY, 1931

Classification of the Phenomena of Fellow-Feeling

We must first distinguish from true fellow-feeling all such attitudes as merely contribute to our *apprehending, understanding*, and, in general, *reproducing* (emotionally) the experiences of others, including their states of feeling. Such acts have often, and quite mistakenly, been assimilated to fellow-feeling. This has come about chiefly through

the theory of projective 'empathy' which attempted to explain both at the same time. . . .

The reproduction of feeling or experience must therefore be sharply distinguished from fellow-feeling. It is indeed a case of feeling the other's feeling, not just knowing of it, nor judging that the other has it; but it is not the same as going through the experience itself. In reproduced feeling we sense the quality of the other's feeling, without it being transmitted to us, or evoking a similar real emotion in us. The other's feeling is given exactly like a landscape which we 'see' subjectively in memory, or a melody which we 'hear' in similar fashion—a state of affairs quite different from the fact that we remember the landscape or the melody (possibly with an accompanying recollection of the fact 'that it was seen, or heard'). In the present case there is a real seeing or hearing, yet without the object seen or heard being perceived and accepted as really present; the past is simply 're-presented'. Equally little does the reproduction of feeling of experience imply any sort of 'participation' in the other's experience. Throughout our visualizing of the experience we can remain quite indifferent to whatever has evoked it. . . .

Thus neither 'projective empathy' nor 'imitation' is necessary in order to explain the primary components of fellow-feeling, viz. understanding, and the vicarious reproduction of feeling or experience. Indeed so far as the first-mentioned acts come into it, It is not understanding they produce, but the possibility of *delusive* understanding.

Let us now turn to *fellow-feeling*, which is primarily based upon those constituents of 'vicarious' understanding already dealt with. Here there are *four* quite different relationships to be distinguished. I call them:

(1) Immediate community of feeling, e.g. of one and the same sorrow, 'with someone'.
(2) Fellow feeling 'about something'; rejoicing in his joy and commiseration with his sorrow.
(3) Mere emotional infection.
(4) True emotional identification.

(1) Community of Feeling. Two parents stand beside the dead body of a beloved child. They feel in common the 'same sorrow, the 'same' anguish. It is not that A feels this sorrow and B feels it also, and moreover that they both know they are

feeling it. No, it is a *feeling-in-common.* A's sorrow is in no way an 'external'. matter for B here, as it is, e.g. for their friend C, who joins them, and commiserates 'with them' or 'upon their sorrow'. On the contrary, they feel it together, in the sense that they feel and experience in common, not only the self-same value-situation, but also the same keenness of emotion in regard to it. The sorrow, as value-content, and the grief, as characterizing the functional relation thereto, are here *one and identical.* It will be evident that we can only feel mental suffering in this fashion, not physical pain or sensory feelings. There is no such thing as a 'common pain'. Sensory types of feeling ('feeling-sensations' as Stumpf calls them), are by nature not susceptible of this highest form of fellow-feeling. They are inevitably 'external' to us in some respect, inspiring only commiseration 'with' and 'upon' the suffering of pain by the other person. By the same token, there is certainly such a thing as rejoicing at another's sensory pleasure, but never mutual enjoyment of it (as a common feeling-sensation). It may, however, be the case that A first feels sorrow by himself and is then joined by B in a common feeling. But this, as will be seen, presupposes the higher emotion of love.

(2) Fellow-Feeling. The second case is quite different. Here also, the one person's sorrow is not simply the motivating cause of the other's. *All* fellow-feeling involves *intentional reference* of the feeling of joy or sorrow to the other person's experience. It points this way simply *qua* feeling—there is no need of any prior judgement or intimation 'that the other person is in trouble'; nor does it arise only upon sight of the other's grief, for it can also 'envisage' such grief, and does so, indeed, in its very capacity as a feeling. But here A's suffering is first presented *as* A's in an act of understanding or 'vicarious' feeling experienced as such, and it is to this material that B's primary commiseration is directed. That is, *my* commiseration and *his* suffering are phenomenologically *two different facts,* not *one* fact, as in the first case. While in the first case the functions of vicarious experience and feeling are so interwo-

ven with the very fellow feeling itself as to be indistinguishable from it, in the second case the two functions are plainly distinguished even *while* experiencing them. Fellow-feeling proper, actual 'participation', presents itself in the very phenomenon as a *re-action* to the state and value of the other's feelings—as these are 'visualized' in vicariously feeling. Thus in this case the two functions of *vicariously visualized* feeling, and *participation* in feeling are separately given and must be sharply distinguished. Very many descriptions of fellow-feeling suffer from failure to make this distinction.

Nothing shows the fundamental diversity of the two functions more plainly, than the fact that the first of them can not only be given without the second, but is also present as a basis for the very *opposite* of an (associated) act of fellow-feeling. This happens, for instance, where there is specific pleasure in cruelty, and to a lesser extent in brutality. The *cruel* man owes his awareness of the pain or sorrow he causes entirely to a capacity for visualizing feeling! His joy lies in 'torturing' and in the agony of his victim. As he feels, vicariously, the increasing pain or suffering of his victim, so his own primary pleasure and enjoyment at the other's pain also increases. Cruelty consists not at all in the cruel man's being simply 'insensitive' to other peoples' suffering. Such 'insensitivity' is therefore a quite different defect in man to lack of fellow-feeling. It is chiefly found in pathological cases (e.g. in melancholia), where it arises as a result of the patient's exclusive preoccupation in his own feelings, which altogether prevents him from giving emotional acceptance to the experience of other people. In contrast to cruelty, *'brutality'* is merely a disregard of other peoples' experience, despite the apprehension of it in feeling. Thus, to regard a human being as a mere log of wood and to treat the object accordingly, is not to be 'brutal' towards him. On the other hand, it is characteristic of brutality, that, given merely a sense of life, undifferentiated, as yet, into separate experiences, given even the fact of an enhanced appearance of life or a tendency towards it, any violent interruption of this tendency (as in vandalism towards plants and trees, to which one cannot be 'cruel'), is enough to mark it as brutal.

(3) Emotional Infection. Quite different again from these, is the case where there is no true appearance of fellow-feeling at all, although it is very frequently confused with this. Such confusion has given rise to the mistaken theories of positivism concerning the evolution of fellow-feeling (Herbert Spencer) and, moreover, to a quite false appreciation of values, particularly in connection with pity. I have in mind the case of mere *emotional infection*. We all know how the cheerful atmosphere in a 'pub' or at a party may 'infect' the newcomers, who may even have been depressed beforehand, so that they are 'swept up' into the prevailing gaiety. Of course such people are equally remote from a rejoicing of either the first or the second type. It is the same when laughter proves 'catching', as can happen especially with children, and to a still greater extent among girls, who have less sensitivity, but react more readily. The same thing occurs when a group is infected by the mournful tone of one of its members, as so often happens among old women, where one recounts her woes while the others grow more and more tearful. Naturally, this has nothing whatever to do with pity. Here there is neither a *directing* of feeling towards the other's joy or suffering, nor any participation in her experience. On the contrary, it is characteristic of emotional infection that it occurs only as a transference of the *state* of feeling, and does *not* presuppose any sort of *knowledge* of the joy which others feel. Thus one may only notice afterwards that a mournful feeling, encountered in oneself, is traceable to infection from a group one has visited some hours before. There is nothing in the mournful feeling itself to point to this origin; only by inference from causal consideration does it become clear where it came from. For such contagion it is by no means necessary that any *emotional* experiences should have occurred in the other person. Even the *objective* aspects of such feelings, which attach to natural objects, or are discerned in an 'atmosphere'—such as the serenity of a spring landscape, the melancholy of a rainy day, the wretchedness of a room—can work infectiously in this way on the state of our emotions.

ANTONIO GRAMSCI

1891–1937

The fourth of seven children, Antonio Gramsci was born on January 23, 1891 in Ales, Sardinia, to a distanced father and an adoring mother whose liveliness and humor were carried on by her famous son. When young he was dropped by a maid, and the injuries stunted him so that he never reached five feet in height. His older brother Gennaro's socialist allegiance influenced Antonio's politics. His youth was marred by poverty when his father lost his job and was imprisoned for malfeasance in 1897, which caused Gramsci to quit school at 11 and work in a tax office for two years before returning to graduate in Ghilarza. More years of grueling poverty, hunger, and physical discomfort took their toll on Gramsci and very likely contributed to his early death. Despite these hindrances, his native intelligence impressed his teachers, and he won a scholarship to the University of Turin, where he became an active leftist. Leaving the university prematurely in 1915, he became a noted journalist for *Avanti!*, and his name became known throughout Italy. He and several friends founded *The New Order*, a radical weekly in 1919. In 1922–23, he traveled to Russia and married the violinist Julka Schucht, with whom he had two sons (Delio and Giuliano, who lives in Moscow). On the evening of November 8, 1926, Gramsci was arrested and spent the rest of his life behind bars or in hospital confinement by order of the fascists. His sister-in-law, Tania Schucht, was his main support while there, and he wrote her and others letters which have become famous documents in the history of the European Left. Beaten down by his imprisonment, he died at a hospital in Rome from a cerebral hemorrhage on April 27, 1937, at the age of 46. It was while imprisoned that he wrote his most famous works of Marxist analysis, *Prison Notebooks* and the *Letters from Prison*, which are touching even for readers uninterested in his politics. All these were published long after his death and became globally important only in the 1970s.

Gramsci has become famous for several terms which have become standard analytic tools within the Marxist lexicon: "hegemony," "organic intellectual," "historical bloc," to name a few. In his *Notebooks* he considered a wide range of issues that were pressing at the time for the worldwide Left, including what relationship fascism had to Marxism, how a leftist government could put to use the "Fordist" technology of the U.S. without losing its principles, the proper role of literature in socialist revolution, and so on. The selections reprinted below focus on the issue of "culture" for the Marxist intellectual, and in analyzing this troubling relationship, Gramsci shares the rhetorical landscape with Walter Benjamin, with whom he is often compared.

"SOCIALISM AND CULTURE," 1916

We must break the habit of thinking that culture is encyclopedic knowledge whereby man is viewed as a mere container in which to pour and conserve empirical data or brute disconnected facts which he will have to subsequently pigeonhole in his brain as in the columns of a dictionary so as to be able to eventually respond to the varied stimuli of the external world. This form of culture is truly harmful, especially to the proletariat. It only serves to create misfits, people who believe themselves superior to the rest of humanity because they have accumulated in their memory a certain quantity of facts and dates which they cough up at every opportunity to almost raise a barrier between themselves and others. This form of culture serves to create that pale and broken-winded intellectualism (so well devastated by Romain Rolland) which has produced a whole crowd of boasters and day-dreamers more harmful to a healthy social life than tuberculosis or syphillis microbes are to the body's beauty and health. The average student who knows a little Latin and a little history and the mediocre lawyer who has succeeded in tearing from his sloth a scrap of diploma and in getting himself passed by professors, will believe themselves different from and superior to even the best, skilled worker who performs in life a very definite, indispensable task and who is worth in his activity a hundred times more than the others may be worth in theirs. But this is not culture, it is pedantry. This is not intelligence, but mere intellect. And against these there is good reason to react.

Culture is something entirely different. It is the organization, the disciplining of one's inner self; it is the appropriation of one's own personality; it is the conquest of a superior consciousness whereby it becomes possible to understand one's own historical value, function in life, rights and duties. But all of this cannot happen through spontaneous evolution, through the independent actions and reactions of one's own will as in the animal and vegetable worlds where each individual selects and unconsciously specifies its own organs according to the inevitable law of things. Man is above all spirit, i.e., a creation of history and not of nature. Otherwise, it would be impossible to explain why to the extent that there have always been exploiters and exploited, and producers and selfish consumers of wealth, socialism has not yet been achieved. It is only because humanity has gradually become aware of its own value and has acquired the right to live independently of the schemes and rights of historically previously-established minorities. And this consciousness has been formed not under the ugly goad of physiological necessities, but through intelligent reflection, first on the part of a few and then by a whole class, reflecting on the reasons for certain conditions and on how best to convert them from causes of servitude into symbols of rebellion and social reconstruction. What this means is that every revolution has been preceded by an intense critical effort of cultural penetration, of the infusion of ideas through groups of men who were initially unresponsive and thought only of resolving day by day, hour by hour, their own political and social problems, without creating links of solidarity with others who found themselves under the same conditions.

THE PRISON NOTEBOOKS, 1929–35

What Is Man?

This is the primary and main question in philosophy. How can it he answered? The definition is to be found in man himself, and therefore in each single man. But is this correct? In each single man, we will discover what each "single man" is. But we are not interested in what each single man is, which, after all, signifies what each single man is at each single moment. When we consider it, we find that by putting the question "What is man?" we really mean; "What can man become?", that is, whether or not man can control his own destiny, can "make himself", can create a life for himself. Therefore we say that man is a process, and precisely the process of his actions. When we consider it, the question "what is man?" is not an abstract or "objective" question. It stems from what we have thought about ourselves and others, and, relative to what we have thought and seen, we seek to know what we are and what we can become, whether it is true and within what limits that we do "make ourselves", create our own lives and our own destinies. We want to know this "now", in the given conditions of the present and of our "daily" life, and not about any life and about any man.

The question arises and derives its content from special, or rather, determined patterns of considering the life of man; the most important of these patterns is the "religious" one and a given religious one—Catholicism. Actually when we ask ourselves "what is man, how important is his will and his concrete activity in the creation of himself and the life he lives?" what we mean is: "Is Catholicism a true concept of man and of life? In being a Catholic, in making Catholicism a way of life, are we mistaken or right?" Everyone has the vague intuition that to make Catholicism a way of life is a mistake, because no one completely embraces Catholicism as a way of life even while declaring himself a Catholic. A strict Catholic who applied Catholic rules to every act of his life would appear as a monster; and this, when one thinks about it, is the strongest, most irrefutable criticism of Catholicism itself.

Catholics will reply by saying that no concepts are rigidly followed, and they are right. But this only proves that there does not in fact exist historically one rule and no other for thinking and functioning that applies equally to all men. It is no argument for Catholicism, even though this way of thinking and acting has for centuries been organised to this end—something which has not yet happened with any other religion with the same means at its disposal, the same spirit of system, the same continuity and centralisation. From the "philosophical" point of view, Catholicism's failure to satisfy rests in the fact that despite everything, it roots the cause of all evil in man himself,

that is, it conceives of man as a clearly defined and limited individual. It can be said that all philosophies up to the present repeat this position taken by the Catholics; man is conceived of as limited by his individuality, and his spirit as well. It is precisely on this point that a change in the conception of man is required. That is, it is essential to conceive of man as a series of active relationships (a process) in which individuality, while of the greatest importance, is not the sole element to be considered. The humanity reflected in every individual consists of various elements: (1) the individual, (2) other men, (3) nature. The second and third elements are not as simple as they seem. The individual does not enter into relations with other men in opposition to them but through an organic unity with them, because he becomes part of social organisms of all kinds from the simplest to the most complex. Thus man does not enter into relationship with native simply because he is himself part of nature, but actively, through work and through techniques. More. These relationships are not mechanical. They are active and conscious, and they correspond to the lesser or greater intelligence which the individual man possesses; therefore one can say that man changes himself, modifies himself, to the same extent that he changes and modifies the whole complex of relationships of which he is the nexus. In this sense the true philosopher is, and cannot avoid being political—that is, man active, who changes his environment—environment being understood to include the relationships into which each individual enters. If individuality is the whole mass of these relationships, the acquiring of a personality means the acquiring of consciousness of these relationships, and changing the personality means changing the whole mass of these relationships.

But, as stated earlier, these relationships are not simple. Moreover, some are involuntary and some voluntary. Furthermore, the very fact of being more or less profoundly conscious (knowing more or less of the way in which these relationships can be modified) already modifies them. Once recognised as necessary, these same necessary relationships change in aspect and importance. In this sense, recognition is power. But this problem is complicated in still another aspect; it is not enough to know the totality of the relations as they exist in a given moment within a given pattern; it is important to know their genesis, the impulse of their formation, because each individual is not only the synthesis of existing relations but also the history of these relations, the sum of all of the past. It will be said that what each individual is able to change is very little indeed. But considering that each individual is able to associate himself with all others who desire the same changes as himself, and provided the change is a rational one, the single individual is able to multiply himself by an impressive number and can thus obtain a far more radical change than would first appear. . . .

Thus the problem of what man is is always posed as the problem of so-called "human nature", or of "man in general", the attempt to create a science of man (a philosophy) whose point of departure is primarily based on a "unitary" idea, on an abstraction designed to contain all that is "human". But is "humanity", as a reality and as an idea, a point of departure—or a point of arrival? Or isn't it rather that when posed as a point of departure, the attempt is reduced to a survival of theology and metaphysics? Philosophy cannot be reduced to naturalistic anthropology; unity in mankind is not a quality of man's biological nature; the differences in man which matter in history are not the biological differences (of race, skull formation, skin colour, etc.), from which is deduced the theory that man is what he eats. In Europe man eats grain, in Asia, rice, etc.—which can then be reduced to the other statement: "Man is the country he inhabits", because diet is generally related to the country inhabited. And not even "biological unity" has counted for much in history (man is the animal who devoured his own kind when he was closest to the "natural state", before he was able "artificially" to multiply production of natural benefits). Nor did the "faculty of reasoning" or "spirit" create unity; it cannot be recognised as a "unifying" fact because it is a categorical formal concept. It is not "thought" but what is actually thought which unites and differentiates men.

The most satisfying answer is that "human nature" is a "complex of human relations", be-

cause this answer includes the idea of "becoming" (man becomes, changes himself continually with the changing of social relations), and because it denies "man in general". In reality social relations are expressed by diverse groups of men which are presupposed and the unity of which is dialectical and not formal. Man is aristocratic because he is the servant of the soil, etc. It can also be said that man's nature is "history" (and in this sense, history equals spirit, the nature of man is the spirit), if history is given the meaning of "becoming" in a *concordia discors* which does not destroy unity but contains within itself grounds for a possible unity. Therefore "human nature" is not to be found in any one particular man but in the whole history of mankind (and the fact that we naturally use the word "kind" is significant), while in each single individual are found characteristics made distinct through their difference from the characteristics of other individuals. The concept of "spirit" in traditional philosophy and the concept of "human nature" in biology also, should be defined as "scientific utopias" which are substitutes for the greater utopia "human nature" sought for in God (and in man, the son of God), and which indicate the travail of history, rational and emotional hopes, etc. It is true, of course, that the religions which preached the equality of men as the sons of God, as well as those philosophies which affirmed Man's equality on the basis of his reasoning faculty, were the expressions of complex revolutionary movements (the transformation of the classical world, the transformation of the mediaeval world), and that these forged the strongest links in the chain of historical development.

Marxism and Modern Culture

Marxism has been a potent force in modern culture and, to a certain extent, has determined and fertilised a number of currents of thought within it. The study of this most significant fact has been either neglected or ignored outright by the so-called orthodox (Marxists) and for the following reasons: the most significant philosophical combination that occurred was that in which Marxism was blended with various idealist tendencies, and was regarded by the orthodox, who were necessarily bound to the cultural currents of the last century (positivism, scientism), as an absurdity if not sheer charlatanism. . . .

Why did Marxism suffer the fate of having its principal elements absorbed by both idealism and philosophical materialism? Investigation into this question is sure to be complex and delicate, requiring much subtlety of analysis and intellectual caution. It is very easy to be taken in by outward appearances and to miss the hidden similarities and the necessary but disguised links. The identification of the concepts which Marxism "ceded" to traditional philosophies, and for which they temporarily provided a new lease of life, must be made with careful criticism and means nothing more nor less than rewriting the history of modern thought from the time when Marxism was founded. . . .

Marxism was confronted with two tasks: to combat modern ideologies in their most refined form in order to create its own core of dependent intellectuals; and to educate the masses of the people whose level of culture was mediaeval. Given the nature of the new philosophy the second and basic task absorbed all its strength, both, quantitatively and qualitatively. For "didactic" reasons the new philosophy developed in a cultural form only slightly higher than the popular average (which was very low), and as such was absolutely inadequate for overcoming the ideology of the educated classes, despite the fact that the new philosophy had been expressly created to supersede the highest cultural manifestation of the period, classical German philosophy, and in order to recruit into the new social class whose world view it was a group of intellectuals of its own. On the other hand modern culture, particularly the idealist, has been unable to elaborate a popular culture and has failed to provide a moral and scientific content to its own educational programmes, which still remain abstract and theoretical schemes. It is still the culture of a narrow intellectual aristocracy which is able to attract the youth only when it becomes immediately and topically political. . . .

Marxism assumes this whole cultural past— the Renaissance and the Reformation, German Philosophy, the French Revolution, Calvinism and English classical political economy, lay liberalism and the historical "linking which rests at the foun-

dation of the whole modern conception of life. Marxism crowns the whole movement for intellectual and moral reform dialecticised in the contrast between popular and higher culture. It corresponds to the nexus of Protestant Reformation plus French Revolution. It is philosophy which is also politics, and it is politics which is also philosophy. It is still passing through its popularising stage; to develop a core of independent intellectuals is no simple task but a long process with actions and reactions, agreements and dissolutions and new formations, both numerous and complex; it is the creation of a subordinate social group, without historical initiative, which is constantly growing but in a disorganised manner, never being able to pass beyond a qualitative stage which always lies this side of the possession of State power, of real hegemony over all of society which alone permits a certain organic equilibrium in the development of the intellectual group. Marxism itself has become "prejudice" and "superstition"; as it is, it is the popular aspect of modern historical thinking, but it contains within itself the principle for overcoming this. In the history of culture, which is broader by far than that of philosophy, whenever popular culture has flowered because there was a period of revolt and the metal of a new class was being selected out of the popular mass, there has always been a flowering of "materialism", while conversely the traditional classes have clung to spiritualism. Hegel, astride the French revolution and the Restoration, dialecticised the two streams in the history of thought: materialism and spiritualism, but his synthesis was "a man standing on his head". Those who followed after Hegel destroyed this unity and a return was made to materialist systems of thought on the one hand and on the other, to the spiritual. Marxism, through its founder, relived this whole experience from Hegel to Feuerbach and French materialism in order to reconstitute the synthesis of the dialectical unity—"man on his feet". The mutilation suffered by Hegelian thought was also inflicted on Marxism; on the one hand there has been a return to philosophical materialism and on the other, modern idealist thought has tried to incorporate into itself elements from Marxism which were indispensable to it in its search for a new elixir.

FERDINAND DE SAUSSURE

1857–1913

Ferdinand de Saussure was born in Geneva, Switzerland on November 26, 1857 and died there on February 22, 1913 at the age of 55. Known as a founder of what came to be called "structural linguistics," he wrote a brilliant student paper in 1879, "Memoir on the Original System of Vowels in the Indo-European Languages," explaining how the "a" sound is alternated in Indo-European languages. He never published another monograph, and his total scholarly output came to only 600 pages, probably a paucity record for an influential Victorian scholar. He taught at the School of Advanced Studies in Paris (1881–91) and was professor of Sanskrit and linguistics at the University of Geneva (1901–1913). His most important work, which initiated modern linguistics, was assembled posthumously from several sets of students' notes (as was the case with George Herbert Mead 30 years later), some of them of professional stenographic quality, and was entitled by his editors *Course in General Linguistics* (1916).

Many social theorists are known for contributing a few key terms or phrases to the intellectual sphere, and Saussure is one of them. In trying to establish a new science of linguistics, he wanted to distance himself from those theorists (like Gottlob Frege) who thought that language's meaning could be understood only if connected with objects in the perceivable world. Instead, Saussure argued that language is a contained system made up of "synchronic" (stable) and "diachronic" (changing) dimensions, and that understanding verbal expressions had to take into consideration both dimensions, but with separate sets of analytic tools. He also distinguished sharply between the speech that people utter (*parole*) and the language rules which govern speech, but are not thought about by practiced speakers once they internalize these rules (*langue*). Thus, for the structural linguist of the earlier sort, people move into a language-world, adopt its ways of doing business unconsciously, express themselves as best they can with the available sounds, and pass out of this world without ever having had much impact on, or awareness of, the underlying structure. As the German philosopher, Hans-Georg Gadamer, expressed it, "People do not speak language; language speaks them." The great anthropologist, Claude Levi-Strauss, openly acknowledged his indebtedness to Saussure's form of structuralism when he applied these ideas to the study of premodern societies in the 1940s. During the 1960s Saussure's ideas became de rigueur to cite and reflect upon in France, and then elsewhere, when they were adopted by Roland Barthes, Louis Althusser, Michel Foucault, and their many followers and imitators, even though each of them used the rules of "structural transformation" differently depending on their substantive analytic interests.

COURSE IN GENERAL LINGUISTICS, 1916

The Object of Linguistics

. . . But what is language [*langue*]? It is not to be confused with human speech [*langage*], of which it is only a definite part, though certainly an essential one. It is both a social product of the faculty of speech and a collection of necessary conventions that have been adopted by a social body to permit individuals to exercise that faculty. Taken as a whole, speech is many-sided and heterogeneous; straddling several areas simultaneously—physical, physiological, and psychological—it belongs both to the individual and to society; we cannot put it into any category of human facts, for we cannot discover its unity.

Language, on the contrary, is a self-contained whole and a principle of classification. As soon as we give language first place among the facts of speech, we introduce a natural order into a mass that lends itself to no other classification. . . .

How does the social crystallization of language come about? Which parts of the circuit are involved? For all parts probably do not participate equally in it.

The nonpsychological part can be rejected from the outset. When we hear people speaking a language that we do not know, we perceive the sounds but remain outside the social fact because we do not understand them.

Neither is the psychological part of the circuit wholly responsible: the executive side is missing, for execution is never carried out by the collectivity. Execution is always individual, and the individual is always its master: I shall call the executive side *speaking* [*parole*].

Through the functioning of the receptive and co-ordinating faculties, impressions that are perceptibly the same for all are made on the minds of speakers. How can that social product be pictured is such a way that language will stand apart from

everything else? If we could embrace the sum of word-images stored in the minds of all individuals, we could identify the social bond that constitutes language. It is a storehouse filled by the members of a given community through their active use of speaking, a grammatical system that has a potential existence in each brain, or, more specifically, in the brains of a group of individuals. For language is not complete in any speaker; it exists perfectly only within a collectivity.

In separating language from speaking we are at the same time separating: (1) what is social from what is individual; and (2) what is essential from what is accessory and more or less accidental.

Language is not a function of the speaker; it is a product that is passively assimilated by the individual. It never requires premeditation, and reflection enters in only for the purpose of classification, which we shall take up later (pp. 122 ff.).

Speaking, on the contrary, is an individual act. It is wilful and intellectual. Within the act, we should distinguish between: (1) the combinations by which the speaker uses the language code for expressing his own thought; and (2) the psychophysical mechanism that allows him to exteriorize those combinations.

Note that I have defined things rather than words; these definitions are not endangered by certain ambiguous words that do not have identical meanings in different languages. For instance, German *Sprache* means both "language" and "speech"; *Rede* almost corresponds to "speaking" but adds the special connotation of "discourse." Latin *sermo* designates both "speech" and "speaking," while *lingua* means "language," etc. No word corresponds exactly to any of the notions specified above; that is why all definitions of words are made in vain; starting from words in defining things is a bad procedure.

To summarize, these are the characteristics of language:

1. Language is a well-defined object in the heterogeneous mass of speech facts. It can be localized in the limited segment of the speaking-circuit where an auditory image becomes associated with a concept. It is the social side of speech, outside the individual who can

never create nor modify it by himself; it exists only by virtue of a sort of contract signed by the members of a community. Moreover, the individual must always serve an apprenticeship in order to learn the functioning of language; a child assimilates it only gradually. It is such a distinct thing that a man deprived of the use of speaking retains it provided that he understands the vocal signs that he hears.

2. Language, unlike speaking, is something that we can study separately. Although dead languages are no longer spoken, we can easily assimilate their linguistic organisms. We can dispense with the other elements of speech; indeed, the science of language is possible only if the other elements are excluded.

3. Whereas speech is heterogeneous, language, as defined, is homogeneous. It is a system of signs in which the only essential thing is the union of meanings and sound-images, and in which both parts of the sign are psychological.

4. Language is concrete, no less so than speaking; and this is a help in our study of it. Linguistic signs, though basically psychological, are not abstractions; associations which bear the stamp of collective approval—and which added together constitute language—are realities that have their seat in the brain. Besides, linguistic signs are tangible; it is possible to reduce them to conventional written symbols, whereas it would be impossible to provide detailed photographs of acts of speaking [*actes de parole*]; the pronunciation of even the smallest word represents an infinite number of muscular movements that could be identified and put into graphic form only with great difficulty. In language, on the contrary, there is only the sound-image, and the latter can be translated into a fixed visual image. . . .

Language is a system of signs that express ideas, and is therefore comparable to a system of writing, the alphabet of deaf-mutes, symbolic rites, polite formulas, military signals, etc. But it is the most important of all these systems.

A science that studies the life of signs within society is conceivable; it would be a part of social psychology and consequently of general psychology; I shall call it *semiology* (from Greek *sēmeîon* 'sign'). Semiology would show what *constitutes signs,* what laws govern them. Since the science does not yet exist, no one can say what it would be; but it has a right to existence, a place staked out in advance. Linguistics is only a part of the general science of semiology; the laws discovered by semiology will be applicable to linguistics, and the latter will circumscribe a well-defined area within the mass of anthropological facts.

Graphic Representation of Language

Influence of Writing; Reasons for Its
Ascendance, over the Spoken Form

Language and writing are two distinct systems of signs; the second exists for the sole purpose of representing the first. The linguistic object is not both the written and the spoken forms of words; the spoken forms alone constitute the object. But the spoken word is so intimately bound to its written image that the latter manages to usurp the main role. People attach even more importance to the written image of a vocal sign than to the sign itself. A similar mistake would be in thinking that more can be learned about someone by looking at his photograph than by viewing him directly.

This illusion, which has always existed, is reflected in many of the notions that are currently bandied about on the subject of language. Take the notion that an idiom changes more rapidly when writing does not exist. Nothing could be further from the truth. Writing may retard the process of change under certain conditions, but its absence in no way jeopardizes the preservation of language. The oldest written texts of Lithuanian, which is still spoken in eastern Prussia and in a part of Russia, date from 1540; but the language of even that late period offers a more faithful picture of Proto-Indo-European than does Latin of 300 B.C. This one example is enough to show the extent to which languages are independent of writing. . . .

But how is the influence of writing to be explained?

1. First, the graphic form of words strikes us as being something permanent and stable, better suited than sound to account for the unity of language throughout time. Though it creates a purely fictitious unity, the superficial bond of writing is much easier to grasp than the only true bond, the bond of sound.

2. Most people pay more attention to visual impressions simply because these are sharper and more lasting than aural impressions; that is why they show a preference for the former. The graphic force manages to force itself upon them at the expense of sound.

3. The literary language adds to the undeserved importance of writing. It has its dictionaries and grammars; in school, children are taught from and by means of books; language is apparently governed by a code; the code itself consists of a written set of strict rules of usage, orthography; and that is why writing acquires primary importance. The result is that people forget that they learn to speak before they learn to write, and the natural sequence is reversed.

4. Finally, when there is a disagreement between language and orthography, settlement of the dispute is difficult for everyone except the linguist; and since he is given no voice in the matter, the written form almost inevitably wins out, for any solution supported by it is easier; thus writing assumes undeserved importance.

RUDOLF OTTO

1869–1937

Karl Louis Rudolf Otto was born on September 25, 1969 in the village of Peine, Hannover in Prussia, where his father owned a malt factory. Always of poor health, Otto fell from a tower in Stauffenberg near Marburg in 1936 (whether by choice or not is unclear) and died at 67 of pneumonia while recuperating from this event on March 6, 1937 in Marburg. His family moved to Hildesheim in 1882 when he was 13, his father died, and he entered the Gymnasium Andreanum. In May 1888 he matriculated at the very conservative University of Erlangen, studying theology, then moved to the more liberal and historically oriented University of Göttingen in 1891. He passed his two theology exams, studying under noted scholars in this area, and received the "Licentiate" in theology (Ph.D.) in 1895, having written a dissertation on the meaning of the "Holy Spirit" in Martin Luther's work. After eight years of teaching as an instructor, he became an associate professor at Göttingen in 1906, and then professor of systematic theology at Breslau (1915) and Marburg (1917). Meanwhile, he joined a group of like-minded theologians called "The Friends of *Die Christliche Welt,*" named for an influential liberal periodical of the time. Otto also served politically in the Prussian legislature between 1913 and 1918, and worked on the revised Prussian constitution in 1919. He helped form a "religious league for humanity" during the Weimar Period (1920s) in Germany, hoping that renewed religiosity could alter the course of history away from violent and political solutions to those based on Christian beliefs and behavior. Otto's interest in world religious experience was greatly enhanced by two long tours he took, one in 1911–12 to Africa and Asia, the other from 1927–28 to the Middle East and South Asia. He also gave lectures at Oberlin College in Ohio in 1924, and at Uppsala, Sweden in 1926. These travels and lectures gave rise to his *Mysticism East and West* (1926) and *India's Religion of Grace and Christianity* (1930).

Otto is widely remembered today for his *The Idea of the Holy* (1917), a book that has influenced thinkers far beyond the circles of Protestant theology in which he worked. Particularly interesting from the social theory viewpoint is Otto's notion of non-rationality or irrationality when compared with similar notions in the work of Max Weber, Vilfredo Pareto, Freud, and others. Building on Friedrich Schleiermacher's ideas from a century before, and disagreeing with his eminent colleague at Göttingen, Ernst Troeltsch, Otto held that religious experience (more mystically defined than by William James) originated in awe, in a desire for "the numinous," a term he coined. He wanted to explain what religiosity "felt like" to the believer, and in describing it this way, he advanced beyond his famous predecessors.

THE IDEA OF THE HOLY, 1917

The Rational and the Non-Rational

It is essential to every theistic conception of God, and most of all to the Christian, that it designates and precisely characterizes deity by the attributes spirit, reason, purpose, good will, supreme power, unity, selfhood. The nature of God is thus thought of by analogy with our human nature of reason and personality; only, whereas in ourselves we are aware of this as qualified by restriction and limitation, as applied to God the attributes we use are 'completed', i.e. thought as absolute and unqualified. Now all these attributes constitute clear and definite *concepts*: they can be grasped by the intellect; they can be analysed by thought; they even admit of definition. An object that can thus be thought conceptually may be termed *rational*. The nature of deity described in the attributes above mentioned is, then, a rational nature; and a religion which recognizes and maintains such a view of God is in so far a 'rational' religion. Only on such terms is *belief* possible in contrast to mere *feeling*. And of Christianity at least it is false that 'feeling is all, the name but sound and smoke'; where 'name' stands for conception or thought. Rather we count this the very mark and criterion of a religion's high rank and superior value—that it should have no lack of conceptions about God; that it should admit knowledge—the knowledge that comes by faith—of the transcendent in terms of conceptual thought, whether those already mentioned or others which continue and develop them. Christianity not only possesses such *conceptions* but possesses them in unique clarity and abundance, and this is, though not the sole or even the chief, yet a very real sign of its superiority over religions of other forms and at other levels. This must be asserted at the outset and with the most positive emphasis.

But, when this is granted, we have to be on our guard against an error which would lead to a wrong and one-sided interpretation of religion. This is the view that the essence of deity can be given completely and exhaustively in such 'rational' attributions as have been referred to above and in others like them. It is not an unnatural misconception. We are prompted to it by the traditional language of edification, with its characteristic phraseology and ideas; by the learned treatment of religious themes in sermon and theological instruction; and further even by our Holy Scriptures themselves. In all these cases the 'rational' element occupies the foreground, and often nothing else seems to be present at all. But this is after all to be expected. All language, in so far as it consists of words, purports to convey ideas or concepts;—that is what language means;—and the more clearly and unequivocally it does so, the better the language. And hence expositions of religious truth in language inevitably tend to stress the 'rational' attributes of God.

But though the above mistake is thus a natural one enough, it is none the less seriously misleading. For so far are these 'rational' attributes from exhausting the idea of deity, that they in fact imply a non-rational or supra-rational Subject of which they are predicates. They are 'essential' (and not merely 'accidental') attributes of that subject, but they are also, it is important to notice, *synthetic* essential attributes. That is to say, we have to predicate them of a subject which they qualify, but which in its deeper essence is not, nor indeed can be, comprehended in them; which rather requires comprehension of a quite different kind. Yet, though it eludes the conceptual way of understanding, it must be in some way or other within our grasp, else absolutely nothing could be asserted of it. And even mysticism, in speaking of it as tò arrhton, the ineffable, does not really mean to imply that absolutely nothing can be asserted of the object of the religious consciousness; otherwise, mysticism could exist only in unbroken silence, whereas what has generally been a characteristic of the mystics is their copious eloquence.

Here for the first time we come up against the contrast between rationalism and profounder religion, and with this contrast and its signs we shall be repeatedly concerned in what follows. We have here in fact the first and most distinctive mark of rationalism, with which all the rest are bound up.

It is not that which is commonly asserted, that rationalism is the denial, and its opposite the affirmation, of the miraculous. That is manifestly a wrong or at least a very superficial distinction. For the traditional theory of the miraculous as the occasional breach in the causal nexus in nature by a Being who himself instituted and must therefore be master of it this—theory is itself as massively 'rational' as it is possible to be. Rationalists have often enough acquiesced in the possibility of the miraculous in this sense; they have even themselves contributed to frame a theory of it;—whereas anti-rationalists have been often indifferent to the whole controversy about miracles. The difference between rationalism and its opposite is to be found elsewhere. It resolves itself rather into a peculiar difference of *quality* in the mental attitude and emotional content of the religious life itself. All depends upon this: in our idea of God is the non-rational overborne, even perhaps wholly excluded, by the rational? Or conversely, does the *non-rational* itself preponderate over the rational? Looking at the matter thus, we see that the common dictum, that orthodoxy itself has been the mother of rationalism, is in some measure well founded. It is not simply that orthodoxy was preoccupied with doctrine and the framing of dogma, for these have been no less a concern of the wildest mystics. It is rather that orthodoxy found in the construction of dogma and doctrine no way to do justice to the non-rational aspect of its subject. So far from keeping the non-rational element in religion alive in the heart of the religious experience, orthodox Christianity manifestly failed to recognize its value, and by this failure gave to the idea of God a one-sidedly intellectualistic and rationalistic interpretation.

This bias to rationalization still prevails, not only in theology but in the science of comparative religion in general, and from top to bottom of it. The modern students of mythology, and those who pursue research into the religion of 'primitive man' and attempt to reconstruct the 'bases' or 'sources' of religion, are all victims to it. Men do not, of course, in these cases employ those lofty 'rational' concepts which we took as our point of departure; but they tend to take these concepts and their gradual 'evolution' as setting the main problem of their inquiry, and fashion ideas and notions of lower value, which they regard as paving the way for them. It is always in terms of concepts and ideas that the subject is pursued, 'natural' ones, moreover, such as have a place in the general sphere of man's ideational life, and are not specifically 'religious'. And then with a resolution and cunning which one can hardly help admiring, men shut their eyes to that which is quite unique in the religious experience, even in its most primitive manifestations. But it is rather a matter for astonishment than for admiration! For if there be any single domain of human experience that presents us with something unmistakably specific and unique, peculiar to itself, assuredly it is that of the religious life. In truth the enemy has often a keener vision in this matter than either the champion of religion or the neutral and professedly impartial theorist. For the adversaries on their side know very well that the entire 'pother about mysticism' has nothing to do with 'reason' and 'rationality'.

And so it is salutary that we should be incited to notice that religion is not exclusively contained and exhaustively comprised in any series of 'rational' assertions; and it is well worth while to attempt to bring the relation of the different 'moments' of religion to one another clearly before the mind, so that its nature may become more manifest.

W. I. THOMAS

1863–1947

One of six children of a poor farmer and Methodist preacher, William Isaac Thomas was born on August 13, 1863 in Russell County, Virginia, grew up in Knoxville, Tennessee, where his father had moved the family so the children could be well educated. He married Harriet Park in 1888, they were divorced without children, and in 1935 he married Dorothy Swaine, a sociologist and demographer thirty-six years younger than he, again without reproducing. He died in Berkeley, California on May 12, 1947 at 83. Thomas studied literature and classics at the University of Tennessee in Knoxville, graduating in 1884, and in 1888–89 went to Berlin and Göttingen (as did many aspiring U.S. intellectuals at the time) to study language and classics. From 1889 to 1895 he was professor of English and then sociology at Oberlin College, moving to pursue the novice fields of sociology and anthropology at the newly founded University of Chicago, from which he received the first doctorate ever granted by that program in 1896 with a dissertation called "On a Difference in the Metabolism of the Sexes." He began teaching at Chicago almost immediately upon arrival and rose through the ranks to Full Professor by 1910, meanwhile helping to found the *American Journal of Sociology.* A philanthropist named Helen Culver backed Thomas's research with the enormous sum of $50,000 between 1908 and 1918, and he directed the Culver Fund for Race Psychology in order to study immigration issues. Having met the noted Polish intellectual Florian Znaniecki in 1913, Thomas and his co-author produced the first great work from the "Chicago school of sociology," *The Polish Peasant in America* (1918–1920, 5 vols), still considered an unrivalled classic of its kind. In 1918 Thomas was accused of an impropriety at a Chicago hotel with a woman not his wife and summarily fired from his professorship, then left for New York where he found work directing a research project for the Carnegie Foundation on "Old World Traits Transplanted." From 1923–28 he taught at the New School (where he met Veblen, also a refugee from scandal). Pitirim Sorokin invited Thomas to Harvard (1936–37), and from there he returned to New York as a private researcher and teacher, also working for the Social Science Research Council.

In 1907 Thomas published *Sex and Society,* the first "objective" study by a sociologist of the topic. He was interested in Freudianism and other unfashionable topics, which cost him later in unexpected ways. His *Source-Book for Social Origins* (1909) is also a major contribution, to ethnology. However, he remains most famous for the "four wishes" that he argued all humans require for happiness, which he described in *The Unadjusted Girl* (1923): new experience, security, response, and recognition.

THE POLISH PEASANT IN EUROPE AND AMERICA, 1918–20

Rational Control in Social Life

One of the most significant features of social evolution is the growing importance which a conscious and rational technique tends, to assume in social life. We are less and less ready to let any social processes go on without our active interference and we feel more and more dissatisfied with any active interference based upon a mere whim of an individual or a social body, or upon preconceived philosophical, religious, or moral generalizations.

The marvelous results attained by a rational technique in the sphere of material reality invite us to apply some analogous procedure to social reality. Our success in controlling nature gives us confidence that we shall eventually be able to control the social world in the same measure. Our actual inefficiency in this line is due, not to any fundamental limitation of our reason, but simply to the historical fact that the objective attitude toward social reality is a recent acquisition.

While our realization that nature can be controlled only by treating it as independent of any immediate act of our will or reason is four centuries old, our confidence in "legislation" and in "moral suasion" shows that this idea is not yet generally realized with regard to the social world. But the tendency to rational control is growing in this field also and constitutes at present an insistent demand on the social sciences.

This demand for a rational control results from the increasing rapidity of social evolution. The old forms of control were based upon the assumption of an essential stability of the whole social framework and were effective only in so far as this stability was real. In a stable social organization there is time enough to develop in a purely empirical way, through innumerable experiments and failures, approximately sufficient means of control with regard to the ordinary and frequent social phenomena, while the errors made in treating the uncommon and rare phenomena seldom affect social life in such a manner as to imperil the existence of the group; if they do, then the catastrophe is accepted as incomprehensible and inevitable. Thus—to take an example—the Polish peasant community has developed during many centuries complicated systems of beliefs and rules of behavior sufficient to control social life under ordinary circumstances, and the cohesion of the group and the persistence of its membership are strong enough to withstand passively the influence of eventual extraordinary occurrences, although there is no adequate method of meeting them. And if the crisis is too serious and the old unity or prosperity of the group breaks down, this is usually treated at first as a result of superior forces against which no fight is possible.

But when, owing to the breakdown of the isolation of the group and its contact with a more complex and fluid world, the social evolution becomes more rapid and the crises more frequent and varied, there is no time for the same gradual, empirical, unmethodical elaboration of approximately adequate means of control, and no crisis can be passively borne, but every one must be met in a more or less adequate way, for they are too various and frequent not to imperil social life unless controlled in time. The substitution of a conscious technique for a half-conscious routine has become, therefore, a social necessity, though it is evident that the development of this technique could be only gradual, and that even now we find in it many implicit or explicit ideas and methods corresponding to stages of human thought passed hundreds or even thousands of years ago.

~

THE UNADJUSTED GIRL, 1923

The Wishes

It is impossible to understand completely any human being or any single act of his behavior, just as it is impossible to understand completely why a particular wild rose bloomed under a particular hedge at a particular moment. A complete understanding in either case would imply an understanding of all cosmic processes, of their interrelations and sequences. But it is not harder to comprehend the behavior of the "unadjusted" or "delinquent" person, say the vagabond or the prostitute, than that of the normally adjusted person, say the business man or the housewife.

In either case we realize that certain influences have been at work throughout life and that these are partly inborn, representing the original nature of man, the so-called instincts, and partly the claims, appeals, rewards, and punishments of society,—the influences of his social environment. But if we attempt to determine why the call of the wild prevails in the one case and the call of home, regular work, and "duty" in the other, we do not have different problems but aspects of the same general problem. It is only as we understand behavior as a whole that we can appreciate the failure of certain individuals to conform to the usual standards. And similarly, the unrest and maladjustment of the girl can be treated only as specifications of the general unrest and maladjustment.

In this connection students of psychology and education have been particularly interested in determining, what the inborn tendencies really are. . . .

We understand of course that these expressions of emotion mean a preparation for action which will be useful in preserving life (anger), avoiding death (fear), and in reproducing the species (love), but even if our knowledge of the nervous system of man were complete we could not read out of it all the concrete varieties of human experience. The variety of expressions of behavior is as great as the variety of situations arising in the external world, while the nervous system represents only a general mechanism for action. We can however approach the problem of behavior through the study of the forces which impel to action, namely, the wishes, and we shall see that these correspond in general with the nervous mechanism.

The human wishes have a great variety of concrete forms but are capable of the following general classification:

1. The desire for new experience.
2. The desire for security.

3. The desire for response.
4. The desire for recognition.

1. The Desire for New Experience. Men crave excitement, and all experiences are exciting which have in them some resemblance to the pursuit, flight, capture, escape, death which characterized the earlier life of mankind. Behavior is an adaptation to environment, and the nervous system itself is a developmental adaptation. It represents, among other things, a hunting pattern of interest. "Adventure" is what the young boy wants, and stories of adventure. Hunting trips are enticing; they are the survival of natural life. All sports are of the hunting pattern; there is a contest of skill, daring, and cunning. It is impossible not to admire the nerve of a daring burglar or highwayman. A fight, even a dog fight, will draw a crowd. In gambling or dice throwing you have the thrill of success or the chagrin of defeat. The organism craves stimulation and seeks expansion and shock even through alcohol and drugs. "Sensations" occupy a large part of the space in newspapers. Courtship has in it an element of "pursuit." Novels, theaters, motion pictures, etc., are partly an adaptation to this desire, and their popularity is a sign of its elemental force. . . .

2. The Desire for Security. The desire for security is opposed to the desire for new experience. The desire for new experience is, as we have seen, emotionally related to anger, which tends to invite death, and expresses itself in courage, advance, attack, pursuit. The desire for new experience implies, therefore, motion, change, danger, instability, social irresponsibility. The individual dominated by it shows a tendency to disregard prevailing standards and group interests. He may be a social failure on account of his instability, or a social success if he converts his experiences into social values,—puts them into the form of a poem, makes of them a contribution to science. The desire for security, on the other hand, is based on fear, which tends to avoid death and expresses itself in timidity, avoidance, and flight. The individual dominated by it is cautious, conservative, and apprehensive, tending also to regular habits, systematic work, and the accumulation of property.

The social types known as "bohemian" and "philistine" are determined respectively by the domination of the desire for new experience and the desire for security. The miser represents a case where the means of security has become an end in itself. . . .

3. The Desire for Response. Up to this point I have described the types of mental impressionability connected with the pursuit of food and the avoidance of death, which are closely connected with the emotions of anger and fear. The desire for response, on the other hand, is primarily related to the instinct of love, and shows itself in the tendency to seek and to give signs of appreciation in connection with other individuals.

There is first of all the devotion of the mother to the child and the response of the child, indicated in the passage from Watson above, and in the following passage from Thorndike. . . .

4. The Desire for Recognition. This wish is expressed in the general struggle of men for position in their social group, in—devices for securing a recognized, enviable, and advantageous social status. Among girls dress is now perhaps the favorite means of securing distinction and showing class. A Bohemian immigrant girl expressed her philosophy in a word: "After all, life is mostly what you wear." Veblen's volume, *Theory of the Leisure Class*, points out that the status of men is established partly through the show of wealth made by their wives. Distinction is sought also in connection with skillful and hazardous activities, as in sports, war, and exploration. Playwriters and sculptors consciously strive for public favor and "fame." In the "achievement" of Pasteur (case 6) and of similar scientific work there is not only the pleasure of the "pursuit" itself, but the pleasure of public recognition. Boasting, bullying, cruelty, tyranny, "the will to power" have in them a sadistic element allied to the emotion of anger and are efforts to compel a recognition of the personality. The frailty of women, their illness, and even feigned illness, is often used as a power-device, as well as a device to provoke response. On the other hand, humility, selfsacrifice, saintliness, and martyrdom may lead to distinction. The showy motives connected with the appeal for recognition we define as "vanity"; the creative activities we call "ambition."

The importance of recognition and status for the individual and for society is very great. The individual not only wants them but he needs them for the development of his personality. The lack of them and the fear of never obtaining them are probably the main source of those psychopathic disturbances which the Freudians treat as sexual in origin.

On the other hand society alone is able to confer status on the individual and in seeking to obtain it he makes himself responsible to society and is forced to regulate the expression of his wishes. His dependence on public opinion is perhaps the strongest factor impelling him to conform to the highest demands which society makes upon him. . . .

From the foregoing description it will be seen that wishes of the same general class—those which tend to arise from the same emotional background—may be totally different in moral quality. The moral good or evil of a wish depends on the social meaning or value of the activity which results from it. Thus the vagabond, the adventurer, the spendthrift, the bohemian are dominated by the desire for new experience, but so are the inventor and the scientist; adventures with women and the tendency to domesticity are both expressions of the desire for response; vain ostentation and creative artistic work both are designed to provoke recognition; avarice and business enterprise are actuated by the desire for security.

Moreover, when a concrete wish of any general class arises it may be accompanied and qualified by any or all of the other classes of wishes. Thus when Pasteur undertook the quest described above we do not know what wish was uppermost. Certainly the love of the work was very strong, the ardor of pursuit, the new experience; the anticipation of the recognition of the public, the scientific fame involved in the achievement was surely present; he invited response from his wife and colleagues, and he possibly had the wish also to put his future professional and material life on a secure basis. The immigrant who comes to America may wish to see the new world (new experience), make a fortune (security), have a higher standing on his return (recognition), and induce a certain person to marry him (response).

The general pattern of behavior which a given individual tends to follow is the basis of our judgment of his character. Our appreciation (positive or negative) of the character of the individual is based on his display of certain wishes as against others and on his modes of seeking their realization. Whether given wishes tend to predominate in this or that person is dependent primarily on what is called temperament, and apparently this is a chemical matter, dependent on the secretions of the glandular systems. Individuals are certainly temperamentally predisposed toward certain classes of the wishes. But we know also, and I shall illustrate presently, that the expression of the wishes is profoundly influenced by the approval of the man's immediate circle and of the general public. The conversions of wild young men to stable ways, from new experience to security,

through marriage, religion, and business responsibility, are examples of this. We may therefore define character as an expression of the organization of the wishes resulting from temperament and experience, understanding by "organization" the general pattern which the wishes as a whole tend to assume among themselves.

The significant point about the wishes as related to the study of behavior is that they are the motor element, the starting point of activity. Any influences which may be brought to bear must be exercised on the wishes.

We may assume also that an individual life cannot be called normal in which, all the four types of wishes are not satisfied in some measure and in some form.

part V

SOCIAL THEORY
BETWEEN THE GREAT WARS

Mohandas Gandhi   *1869–1948*

William Fielding Ogburn   *1886–1959*

John Dewey   *1859–1952*

Maurice Halbwachs   *1877–1945*

Karl Mannheim   *1893–1947*

Bronislaw Malinowski   *1884–1942*

Martin Buber   *1878–1965*

Bertrand Russell   *1872–1970*

Ludwig Wittgenstein   *1889–1951*

George Herbert Mead   *1863–1931*

Karl Jaspers   *1883–1969*

Oswald Spengler   *1880–1936*

Georges Bataille   *1897–1962*

Robert King Merton   *1910–2003*

Norbert Elias   *1897–1990*

Talcott Parsons   *1902–1979*

Erich Fromm   *1900–1980*

Pitirim Sorokin   *1889–1968*

Jean-Paul Sartre   *1905–1980*

Ernst Cassirer   *1874–1945*

Henri Lefebvre   *1901–1991*

Maurice Merleau-Ponty   *1908–1961*

MOHANDAS GANDHI

1869–1948

Son of a poorly educated but effective government administrator under the British suzerainty, Mohandas Karamchand Gandhi was born on October 2, 1869 in Porbandar, western India, at 13 was married to Kasturbai (1882) with whom he had children, and was murdered for political reasons in Delhi on January 20, 1948, aged 78. He was the youngest son of his father's fourth wife, a woman of virtuosic dedication to religious ritual, fasting, and her familial duties. Gandhi's life has been thoroughly documented, not least by himself in an *Autobiography* (1925), which relates his political and spiritual "experiments with truth," as he called them, not because of his great intellectual achievements (he was a poor student when young), but because he set a standard for interpersonal and political decency that had not been seen before on the global stage. He left India in 1888 for legal training in England, and while there read fundamental works of Western and Eastern thought, also associating with the London Vegetarian Society. Returning to India in 1891, he learned his mother had died, and he failed miserably as a lawyer, being too shy for the work. He accepted a mediocre assignment from an Indian firm to move to South Africa in 1893, surely the pivotal moment of his political self-awareness, for there he felt racism for the first time, and rebelled. Overcoming pathological shyness and stage fright, he organized a fight against a new bill which would deprive Indians in Natal from voting. At 25, the Gandhi the world came to know seemed to be born out of nothing. His petitions and articles began to be noticed even in England, and he was persuaded to stay in Natal. He brought his wife and children out of India in 1897, and was nearly lynched by a white mob, but refused to prosecute them as a matter of principle. The rest of Gandhi's political tale is well known, focusing on India and the removal of British hegemony, and along the way he created a new brand of passive resistance which has been imitated worldwide ever since by aggrieved groups.

Gandhi's position in the history of social thought (despite his 90-volumes of published works) hinges on a few very simple principles that he cobbled together, partly from Indian religion, and partly from odd sources, like John Ruskin's *Unto This Last,* an anti-capitalist screed that he read in 1904 and which inspired him to set up communal farms. Gandhi's "message" was to insist at all costs on fundamental human dignity, never to play political games for short-term advantage, always to take the moral high road, and to insist on equal rights. On the other hand, he lived a life of self-abnegation and asceticism, with one foot in this world and another well into a post-corporeal existence. It is probably this "saintly" combination that has given his name its lasting importance for the last century.

"GANDHI'S MESSAGE TO ALL MEN," 1920–27

. . . The more efficient a force is, the more silent and the more subtle it is. Love is the subtlest force in the world . . . [1]

[The] force of love . . . truly comes into play only when it meets with causes of hatred. True Non-violence does not ignore or blind itself to causes of hatred, but in spite of the knowledge of their existence, operates upon the person setting those causes in motion. . . . The law of Non-violence—returning good for evil, loving one's enemy, involves a knowledge of the blemishes of the "enemy." Hence do the Scriptures say . . . "Forgiveness is an attribute of the brave."[2]

. . . I can no more preach Non-violence to a coward than I can tempt a blind man to enjoy healthy scenes. Non-violence is the summit of bravery. . . .[3]

. . . Suffering in one's own person is . . . the essence of non-violence and is the chosen substitute for violence to others. It is not because I value life low that I can countenance with joy thousands voluntarily losing their lives for Satyagraha, but because I know that it results in the long run in the least loss of life, and what is more, it ennobles those who lose their lives . . . [Unless] Europe is to commit suicide, some nation will have to dare to disarm herself and take large risks. The level of non-violence in that nation . . . will naturally have risen so high as to command universal respect. Her judgments will be unerring, her decisions will be firm, her capacity for heroic self-sacrifice will be great; and she will want to live as much for other nations as for herself. . . .[4]

. . . They say "means are after all [just] means." I would say "means are after all everything." As the means, so the end. Violent means will give violent Swaraj. . . . There is no wall of separation between means and end. . . . I have been endeavoring to keep the country to means that are purely peaceful and legitimate.[5]

. . . If we take care of the means we are bound to reach the end sooner or later. . . .[6]

. . . Truth is my God. Non-violence is the means of realizing Him. . . .[7]

I am not a "statesman in the garb of a saint." But since Truth is the highest wisdom, sometimes my acts appear to be consistent with the highest statesmanship. But I hope I have no policy in me save the policy of Truth and Non-violence . . . [8]

[To] me . . . there is no way to find Truth except the way of Non-violence. . . . For I know that a man who forsakes Truth can forsake his country and his nearest and dearest ones . . . [9]

. . . I will not sacrifice Truth and Non-violence even for the deliverance of my country or religion . . . [10]

. . . The movement of non-violent non-cooperation has nothing in common with the historical struggles for freedom in the West. It is not based on brute force or hatred. It does not aim at destroying the tyrant. It is a movement of self-purification. It therefore seeks to convert the tyrant. . . .[11]

. . . A revolutionary murders or robs not for the good of his victims, whom he often considers to be fit only to be injured, but for the supposed good of society.[12]

. . . Conscience is the ripe fruit of strictest discipline. . . . There is no such thing, therefore, as mass conscience . . .

. . . The introduction of conscience into our public life is welcome . . . if it has taught a few of us to stand up for human dignity and rights in the face of the heaviest odds. . . .[13]

. . . I have no secret methods. I know no diplomacy save that of truth. I have no weapon but non-violence. I may be unconsciously led astray for a while but not for all time. I have therefore well-defined limitations. . . .

There is no principle worth the name if it is not wholly good. I swear by non-violence because I know that it alone conduces to the highest good of mankind, not merely in, the next world, but in this also. I object to violence because, when it appears to do good, the good is only temporary, the evil it does is permanent. . . .[15]

. . . Terrorism set up by reformers may be just as bad as Government terrorism, and it is often worse because it draws a certain amount of false sympathy. . . .[16]

. . . I invite the revolutionaries not to commit suicide and drag with them unwilling victims.

From *The Essential Gandhi*, by Mahatma Gandhi, Louis Fischer, Trans. Copyright © 1962 by Louis Fischer. Copyright renewed 1990 by Victor Fischer and George Fischer. Preface by Eknath Easwaran. Copyright © 2002 by The Blue Mountain Center of Meditation. Used by permission of Random House, Inc.

India's way is not Europe's. India is not Calcutta and Bombay. India lives in her seven hundred thousand villages. If the revolutionaries are as many let them spread out into these villages and try to bring sunshine into the dark dungeons of the millions of their countrymen. That would be worthier of their ambition and love of the land than the exciting and unquenchable thirst for the blood of English officials and those who are assisting them. It is nobler to try to change their spirit than to take their lives.[17]

[A friend] says that non-violence cannot be attained by the mass of people. And yet, we find the general work of mankind is being carried on from day to day by the mass of people acting in harmony as if by instinct. If they were instinctively violent, the world would end in no time. They remain peaceful. . . . It is when the mass mind is unnaturally influenced by wicked men that the mass of mankind commit violence. But they forget it as quickly as they commit it because they return to their peaceful nature immediately the evil influence of the directing mind has been removed.[18]

. . . I hope to demonstrate that real Swaraj [Self-Rule] will come not by the acquisition of authority by a few but by the acquisition of the capacity by all to resist authority when abused. In other words, Swaraj is to be attained by educating the masses to a sense of their capacity to regulate and control authority.[19]

. . . If we all discharge our duties, rights will not be far to seek. If leaving duties unperformed, we run after rights, they will escape us like a will o' the wisp. . . . The same teaching has been embodied by Krishna in the immortal words: "Action alone is thine. Leave thou the fruit severely alone." Action is duty, fruit is the right.

. . . He who understands the doctrine of self-help blames himself for failure. It is on this ground that I object to violence. If we blame others where we should blame ourselves, and wish for or bring about their destruction, [it] does not remove the root cause of the disease, which, on the contrary sinks all the deeper for . . . ignorance . . .[20]

[It] is necessary for workers to become self-reliant and dare to prosecute their plans if they so desire, without hankering after the backing of . . . persons supposed to be great and influential. Let them rely upon the strength of their own conviction and the cause they seek to espouse. Mistakes

there will be. Suffering, even avoidable, there must be. But nations are not easily made . . .[21]

. . . The way of peace insures internal growth and stability. We reject it because we fancy that it involves submission to the will of the ruler who has imposed himself upon us. . . . The suffering to be undergone. . . . will be nothing compared to the physical suffering and the moral loss we must incur in trying the way of war. And the suffering in following the way of peace must benefit both. It will be like the pleasurable travail of a new birth.[22]

[He] alone is truly non-violent who remains non-violent even though he has the ability to strike. . . . I have had in my life many an opportunity of shooting my opponents and earning the crown of martyrdom but I had not the heart to shoot any of them. For I did not want them to shoot me, however much they disliked my methods. I wanted them to convince me of my error as I was trying to convince them of theirs. "Do unto others as you would that they should do unto you."[23]

Most people do not understand the complicated machinery of the government. They do not realize every citizen silently but none the less certainly sustains the government of the day in ways of which he has no knowledge. Every citizen therefore renders himself responsible for every act of his government. And it is quite proper to support it so long as the actions of the government are bearable. But when they hurt him and his nation it becomes his duty to withdraw his support.[24]

. . . I cannot satisfy myself with false cooperation—anything inferior to twenty-four carats gold. . . . [My non-coöperation] harms no one, it is non-coöperation with evil, with an evil system, and not with the evil-doer. My religion teaches me to love even an evil-doer . . .[25]

Notes

1. *Young India*, December 4, 1924.

2. *Young India*, September 29, 1927.

3. *Young India*, May 29, 1924.

4. *Young India*, October 8, 1925.

5. *Young India*, July 17, 1924.

6. *M. K. Gandi, From Yeravda Mandir* (Ahmedabad: Navajivan Press, 1937), Chapter 3, p. 13.

7. *Young India*, January 8, 1925.

8. *Young India*, January 20, 1927.

9. *Speech at Wardha on Hindu-Moslem riots, December, 1920, in D. G. Tendulkar, Mahatma: The Life of Mohandas Karamchand Gandi*, Volume II, p. 312.

10. *Young India*, January 20, 1927.

11. *Young India*, February 11, 1926.

12. *Young India*, May 21, 1925.

13. *Young India*, August 21, 1924.

15. *Young India*, May 21, 1925.

16. *Young India*, December 18, 1924.

17. *Young India*, March 12, 1925.

18. *Young India*, July 8, 1926.

19. *Young India*, January 29, 1925.

20. *Young India*, January 8, 1925.

21. *Young India*, May 19, 1927.

22. *Young India*, May 20, 1925.

23. *Young India*, May 7, 1925.

24. *Young India*, July 28, 1920.

25. Speech for an "at home" given by the Indian Association, printed in *Young India*, August 25, 1925.

～⌒～

"ADVICE TO NEGROES," 1924–36

[Gandhi usually asked his American visitors about the treatment of Negroes in the United States. American Negroes were among his visitors and correspondents.]

A civilization is to be judged by its treatment of minorities.[1]

[A group of American Negroes sent Gandhi a telegram of encouragement, to which he replied in *Young India*:]

Theirs is perhaps a task more difficult than ours. But they have some very fine workers among them. Many students of history consider that the future is with them. They have a fine physique. They have a glorious imagination. They are as simple as they are brave. Monsieur Finot has shown by his scientific researches that there is in them no inherent inferiority. . . . All they need is opportunity. I know that if they have caught the spirit of the Indian movement [the spirit of non-violence] their progress must be rapid?"]

[It] may be through the Negroes that the unadulterated message of Non-violence will be delivered to the world.

[Discussing Non-violence with Gandhi, Dr. Howard Thurman, a Negro minister and writer, asked him, "How are we to train individuals or communities in this difficult art?"]

There is no royal road, except through living the creed in your life. . . . If for mastering of the physical sciences you have to devote a whole lifetime, how many lifetimes may be needed for mastering the greatest spiritual force that mankind has known? But why worry even if it means several lifetimes? For, if this is the only permanent thing in life, if this is the only thing that counts, then whatever effort you bestow on mastering it is well-spent . . .

If you feel humiliated [by a bully, for example] you will be justified in slapping [him] in the face or taking whatever action you might deem necessary to vindicate your self-respect. The use of force, in the circumstance, would be the natural consequence if you are not a coward. But if you have assimilated the non-violent spirit, there should be no feeling of humiliation in you. Your non-violent behavior should then either make the bully feel ashamed of himself and prevent the insult, or make you proof against it, so that the insult would remain . . . in the bully's mouth and not touch you at all.

. . . Non-violence . . . is not a mechanical thing. You do not become non-violent by merely saying, "I shall not use force." It must be felt in the heart. . . . When there is that feeling it will express itself through some action. It may be a sign, a glance, even silence. But, such as it is, it will melt the heart of the wrong-doer and check the wrong.

. . . Supposing I was a Negro and my sister was ravished by a white or lynched by a whole community, what would be my duty?—I ask myself. And the answer comes to me: I must not wish ill to these but neither must I cooperate with them. It may be that ordinarily I depend on the lynching community for my livelihood. I refuse to coöperate with them, refuse even to touch the food that comes from them and I refuse to coöperate with even my brother Negroes who tolerate the wrong. . . .

[Persecution of the Indians and Negroes in South Africa by the whites never ceased to arouse Gandhi's indignation.]

. . . South Africa has many wise men and women. . . . It will be a tragedy for the world if they do not rise superior to their debilitating surroundings and give a proper lead to their country on this vexed and vexing problem of White supremacy. Is it not by this time a played out game? . . .

To see the universal and all-pervading Spirit of Truth face to face one must be able to love the meanest of creation as oneself. And a man who aspires after that cannot afford to keep out of any field of life. That is why my devotion to Truth has drawn me into the field of politics; and I can say without the slightest hesitation, and yet in all humility, that those who say that religion has nothing to do with politics do not know what religion means.

Identification with everything that lives is impossible without self-purification; without self-purification the observance of the law of Ahimsa must remain an empty dream; God can never be realized by one who is not pure of heart. Self-purification therefore must mean purification in all the walks of life. And purification being highly infectious, purification of oneself necessarily leads to the purification of one's surroundings.

But the path of self-purification is hard and steep. To attain to perfect purity one has to become absolutely passion-free in thought, speech and action; to rise above the opposing currents of love and hatred, attachment and repulsion. I know that I have not in me as yet that triple purity, in spite of constant ceaseless striving for it. That is why the world's praise fails to move me, indeed it very often stings me. To conquer the subtle passions seems to me to be harder far than the physical conquest of the world by the force of arms. Ever since my return to India I have had experiences of the dormant passions lying hidden within me. The knowledge of them has made me feel humiliated though not defeated. The experiences and experiments have sustained me and given me great joy. But I know that I have still before me a difficult path to traverse. I must reduce myself to zero. So long as a man does not of his own free will put himself last among his fellow creatures, there is no salvation for him. Ahimsa is the farthest limit of humility.

Notes

1. Louis Fischer, *The Life of Mahatma Gandhi*, Part II, Chapter 43, p. 425.

"HOW TO ENJOY JAIL," 1932

. . . We must make the best possible use of the invaluable leisure in jail. Perhaps the best of uses would be to cultivate the power of independent thought. We are often thoughtless and therefore like only to read books or, worse still, to talk. . . . As a matter of fact, there is an art of thinking just as there is an art of reading. We should be able to think the right thought at the right time and not indulge in thinking useless thoughts as well as in reading useless books. . . . It is my experience daring every incarceration that it affords us a fine opportunity of thinking . . . to some purpose. . . .

. . . My own reading is quite odd. I am doing some Urdu at present. I am also trying to get some idea of currency and exchange, as ignorance of it would be in excusable. There is the desire to render service at the back of these studies. The same desire impels me to deepen my knowledge of Tamil as well as Bengali and Marathi. If we have to stay in jail for a pretty long time, I may recommence the study of all these languages. . . .

[Never] write a bad hand whether there is hurry or not: This lesson everyone should learn from my misfortune. Bad writing and bad everything is truly [violence]. We have a rare opportunity of learning the virtue of patience in prison life.

. . . The word "criminal" should be taboo from our dictionary. Or we are all criminals. "Those of you that are without sin cast the first stone." And no one was found to dare cast the stone at the sinning harlot. As a jailer once said, all are criminals in secret. . . . Let them therefore be good companions. I know this is easier said than done. And that is exactly what the *Gita* and as a matter of fact all religions enjoin upon us to do.

WILLIAM FIELDING OGBURN

1886–1959

Son of a planter/merchant, William Fielding Ogburn was born on June 29, 1886 in Butler, Georgia, married Rubyn (or "Ruben") Reynolds on September 15, 1910, had two sons with her, and died on April 27, 1959 in Tallahassee, Florida at 72. Ogburn attended Mercer University, then went to Chicago for the masters (1909) and doctorate (1912), also taking a law degree. After teaching at Reed College and the University of Washington, he became professor of sociology at Columbia University (1919–1927), then moved to the University of Chicago and worked there until retirement in 1951, followed by visiting academic positions worldwide. He also served as research director for Herbert Hoover's committee on "recent social trends," which eventuated into two large volumes of studies under the same title (1928–33). He was also president of the American Sociological Association in 1929 and of the American Statistical Association in 1931.

His most important book was *Social Change, with Respect to Culture and Original Nature* (1922; revised in 1950). Other works included *The Social Sciences and Their Interrelationships* (edited with A. A. Goldenweiser; 1927), *Sociology,* a textbook, with M. F. Nimkoff (1940–1964 various editions), and *On Culture and Social Change: Selected Papers,* edited by Otis Dudley Duncan (1964). Like so many social theorists, a single term always recalls Ogburn's name, "cultural lag," which he used as the basis of his argument in *Social Change.* Ogburn was committed to statistical and methodological refinements in his effort to advance sociology into a truly scientific posture, yet oddly enough, he is now remembered principally as the theorist of change. He argued that social change results from invention, (which, properly viewed, is an artful rearrangement of already existing cultural elements or traits into some fresh pattern that serves some new function), accumulation, diffusion, and adjustment. When a revolutionary invention or cultural innovation is introduced into a society's operations, a "lag" ensues between the ideas and emotional responses to it and the actual functioning of the invention itself. Also, the lag is felt differentially throughout various institutions of the social order, some adjusting more rapidly to the innovation than others. Recalling his Marxist youth, Ogburn argued for a subtle form of materialistic or mechanical determinism, and he insisted on the precise measurement of these effects, thereby elevating sociology, so he thought, above the philosophical and ethical concerns from which it had arisen in the 19th century. The selections below allow Ogburn to confront common understandings of gender roles, "the great man" in history, and social change, and through rigorous reasoning, to deflate and readjust each of them to suit his own vision.

SOCIAL CHANGE WITH RESPECT TO CULTURE AND ORIGINAL NATURE, 1922

The Overemphasis of the Biological Factor

Popular tendency to confuse the cultural and the psychological or, as Kroeber phrases it, the social and the mental, probably results in an overemphasis of the psychological and an underemphasis of the cultural. This is particularly noticeable in accounting for the traits of the sexes. Women, for instance, are supposed to have an absorbing interest in purely personal affairs and relationships while men are more interested in objective discussions of movements and events. This difference is frequently commented upon in considering the entrance of women into politics and into business. The somewhat intimate relationship between women and children is supposed to account for this difference on biological grounds. As a biological explanation it is a bit mystical. It seems more plausible to seek the explanation in the differences in daily activities of men and women. The work of men takes them more into the world of events, social movements and business. Whereas woman's restricted sphere of the family, centring around husband and children and social friendships, seems more personal. So that while women may be more interested in the personal than men, this difference is either wholly due to culture or else is greatly accentuated by culture. Women are said also not to be averse to methods involving slight deceptions, at least apparently they resort more readily than men to subterfuge or other less direct but ingenious ways of obtaining their ends. This observation, if true, may be intended to apply to the fields of the more purely personal relationships and not for instance to the spheres of business activity. This is popularly supposed to be a feminine trait, meaning a hereditary biological it, yet close observers have attributed its origin to a cultural situation where men hold economic and social power. Men are thus more direct and frank in their actions, while with women there is a more or less variable pressure to be indirect in the pursuit of their aims. And even such a trait as modesty which

seems so closely identified with the distinctive biological characteristics of women is certainly greatly emphasized by social conditions.

A great many of these so-called feminine traits are analyzed and their cultural aspects explained by Mrs. Coolidge in her most interesting book, *Why Women are So.* Such a study as Mrs. Coolidge has made, while it does not segregate and measure the influence of original nature and of culture, certainly does demonstrate quite satisfactorily that there is a popular tendency to attribute much that is cultural to hereditary biological factors. Popular opinion describes a large assortment of traits as feminine, perhaps a slightly smaller number as masculine, and a more or less vague list as common to both the sexes. If these traits were considered from the purely biological point of view, the list of feminine and of masculine traits would probably be much smaller and certainly much less prominent, or if plotted in curves there would be great overlapping of the curves. The great division of labor along sex lines found all through society, while perhaps in part occasioned by biological differences, certainly results in an exaggeration in the popular mind of the biological differences between the sexes. The point under consideration is not an inquiry as to what biological differences do exist, There are morphological differences, quite probably emotional differences, and there may be indeed some intellectual differences. But what should be pointed out is that these emotional and intellectual differences are popularly exaggerated by reading the psychological into the cultural influences, a confusion of the two factors.

There are several reasons why cultural traits tend to be popularly interpreted as biological traits. The effect of culture on an individual is carried around by that individual in the forms of habit, training, education, technique, conditioned reflexes. These acquired ways of doing things are seen as part of an individual as truly as his physiognomy is. The association is almost as close. They become a part of his psychological self and are generally more or less permanently descriptive of the personality. The concept of the original nature of man does not frequently appear in the ordinary judgments of life. It takes some special training and imagination to see the original nature of man beneath his cultural exterior, for it is only in special situations in life where such penetrating observation is called for. Man as nature plus nurture is thus popularly seen as nature. Acquired characteristics are thought to be so integral a part of an individual as to be hereditary. Indeed it required special research to disprove this. So it seems very natural to interpret cultural traits as psychological traits.

        * *

"THE GREAT MAN VERSUS SOCIAL FORCES," 1926

A question of long standing in sociology is the relative influence of the individual in social change. How important is the great man in history; how important is genius in science and invention; how important the outstanding personality in religion and art and leadership in social movements? The traditional point of view has been to attribute much importance to the great individual in all those achievements and social processes. However with the rise of the idea of determinism as against the freedom of the will, of economic history in contrast to the exploits of kings and military chieftains, and of the studies of the relation of the group to the individual, the importance of factors in history other than the individual has been more and more appreciated. The purpose of the following paper is to add to the analysis of this ever-interesting question some ideas coming from recent researches in sociology, psychology, and statistics.

    The analysis of this problem is often confused by the mixing of two different conceptions of greatness, the greatness that is attributable to heredity and the greatness of the developed personality, which is the product of both environment and heredity. For instance, if one wishes to inquire as to, say, Abraham Lincoln's influence as a great man on the course of history, one may not be particularly interested in dissecting Lincoln into two parts, heredity and environment. But if one wishes to contrast Lincoln as a great man with the

social forces of his times, one must remember that Lincoln, the adult man, represents a part of the social forces (since they helped to produce him) with which it is desired to contrast him. And the fact that Lincoln differed from other men of his times cannot wholly be attributed to heredity, since the forces of the environment do not play upon all in the same degree and manner. Our need then, in order to make the analysis of the general problem sharp, is to consider the greatness which is attributable to heredity. And the first task is to learn something of the frequency of the hereditary elements of greatness. . . .

    It would appear from the foregoing that high orders of greatness, in so far as they are biologically determined, are fairly plentiful. That is, the potentialities of greatness are common. One may, however, guess that greatness is a biological mutation, in which case, it is without the range of normal variations and hence rare. But mutations are probably so rare indeed, judging from the extensive observations for mutations on *Drosophila,* that the great in human society could in general hardly be biological mutations.

    Furthermore, the biological elements of greatness are probably not only plentiful but fairly constant over time. For race is notably stable, and in large civilized groups selection probably operates on large numbers of persons. We should therefore certainly expect constancy within the short space of a few centuries. It is important to consider the point of variation, for our understanding of cause, such as we work with practically in science, is that it is only the phenomena that vary that we term causes. Then if inherited abilities of a high order are probably fairly constant and plentiful in very large groups of civilized peoples, it seems questionable whether one is right in attributing so much weight to inherited greatness as a cause of progress and also in explaining the absence of achievement to the scarcity of inherited abilities.

    Yet all of us who have studied history or observed social movements have felt the scarcity and need of great men, of great leaders. Does not this observed rarity of great men invalidate the somewhat theoretical arguments of the preceding statements? This apparent discrepancy is partly due to confusing the two conceptions of greatness, commented on previously, the inherited bases of greatness and the great man as a developed

From *Social Change with Respect to Culture and Original Nature,* by William Fielding Ogburn. Published by B. W. Huebsch, Inc. Copyright 1922.

personality. The latter, great men of history with developed personalities, are, it will be claimed later, more likely to vary and hence be scarce than men with the inherited elements of greatness which, alone, have just been under consideration.

There are various ways by which social conditions make greatness rare or frequent. The original material of heredity is subjected to what the psychologists call the learning process, that is, the original impulses are conditioned into habits, so that they operate through a somewhat complex organization of habits. Personalities are thus formed and become fairly fixed by the time adult life is reached. These personalities become varied one from another, for the social conditions setting habits are greatly varied. . . .

The inference to be drawn from such data is, for instance, that the discovery of the calculus was not dependent upon Newton; for if Newton had died, it would have been discovered by Leibnitz. And we think that if neither Leibnitz nor Newton had lived, it would still have been discovered by some other mathematician. So also the theory of evolution by variation and natural selection would have been developed even if Wallace and Darwin had never lived.

The reason we think this relatively great role of culture is over-looked in popular thought regarding inventions is because the essential dependence of a particular invention on the existence of other inventions is not appreciated. Our devotion to hero-worship obscures the fact. But an airplane is just as dependent for its origin on the light engine as it is upon a great inventor. The steamboat is similarly dependent upon the steam engine; calculus, on analytical geometry; and each special invention in electricity, on a number of other subsidiary inventions. The existence of such necessary subsidiary inventions for the achievement of a particular invention is extremely variable, so specialized is the relationship, and is much more variable than the existence of inherited mental ability of a high order. . . .

These three factors—mental ability, cultural material, and social valuations—which have been deduced from a study of invention, are also factors in various kinds of great achievement as well as in mechanical invention. Sometimes some one of these factors plays a more important role than the others. . . .

The role of the exceptional individual in the social process and the relative dependence of social change and achievement on social forces or on the great man will no doubt be a subject of debate for some time to come. But these results of recent researches do seem to clarify the analysis. Our conclusions are that greatness must be conceived in terms of inherited qualities and environmental traits. The distribution of inherited qualities appears to be such that the inherited abilities of greatness should be plentiful and constant, facts which minimize the importance of the great man, biologically conceived. On the social-forces side, there are two important factors that affect great achievement—the existing cultural materials and the social valuations. These two factors vary greatly over time and by place and hence may be called causes of great achievement. They are of the nature of social forces. Great men are thus the product of their times. They in turn influence their times; that is, their achievements influence the times. The great man is thus a medium in social change. The phenomenon of the great man varies in the different kinds of social activities, and each situation should be separately analyzed as to the relative strength of the different factors. In some cases psychological traits of personality are more important than others. These factors at the present time are only with great difficulty susceptible of precise measurement. But certain extended observations indicate that the production of great men and their influence are strongly conditioned and determined by the particular existing stage of the historical development. The great man and his work appear therefore as only a step in a process, largely dependent upon other factors.

❧

"CULTURAL LAG AS THEORY," 1957

I shall begin with a definition. A cultural lag occurs when one of two parts of culture which are correlated changes before or in greater degree than the other part does, thereby causing less adjustment between the two parts than existed previously.

An illustration is the lag in the construction of highways for automobile traffic. The two parts in this illustration are the automobile and the highway. These two parts of culture were in good adjustment in, say, 1910, when the automobile was slow and the highways were narrow country roads with curves and bends over which had been laid a hard surface. The automobile traveled at not a great rate of speed and could take the turns without too much trouble or danger. It was essentially for local transportation. But as time went on, this first part, the automobile, which is called an "independent variable," underwent many changes, particularly the engine, which developed speeds capable of sixty, seventy, eighty miles an hour, with brakes that could stop the car relatively quickly. But the narrow highways with sharp bends did not change as soon as did the automobile. On these roads the driver must slow up or have accidents. A decade or more later we are building a few broad highways with no sharp curves, which will make the automobile a vehicle for long-distance travel. The old highways, the dependent variable, are not adapted to the new automobiles, so that there is a maladjustment between the highways and the automobile. The adjustment, as measured by speeds, was better for local travel around 1910 than it is for long-distance travel on these roads at present. The adjustment will be better on the new express highways. Since the adjustment is made by the dependent variable, it is that part of culture which adapts and is called "adaptive culture."

The concept of cultural lag, just defined and illustrated, was first published in 1922 in a chapter of a book on social change which carried this title, "The Hypothesis of Cultural Lag.". . .

I first used the term in 1914, when I was a professor of economics and sociology at Reed College. I had for a long time been impressed with the economic interpretation of history, though as a user of partial correlation techniques I was appreciative of its limitations. The economic interpretation of history may be illustrated by the claim that the Crusades in the Middle Ages for the recovery of the Holy Land from the possession of the infi-

dels were not a product of religious motives but resulted from the search for trade routes to the East. This economic drive utilized the religious fervor for purposes of enlistment. I do not wish to discuss the validity of the economic interpretation in this particular instance but rather to note that there was an economic factor in the Crusades and that it was obscured or disguised.

This word, "disguised," was widely current in the early part of the twentieth century because of the influence of Freud, all of whose writings I had read at the time. In his book *The Interpretation of Dreams,* he called the dream, as first remembered, the "manifest content," and the interpretation of the dream, the "latent content." Thus, if a person dreamed that a steam roller was about to crush him, that would be the manifest content, but if the interpretation showed that the steam roller was a symbol for a dominating father, that would be the latent content. The latent content was disguised. About this time, I read before the American Economic Association a paper stressing this point and entitled "The Psychological Basis for the Economic Interpretation of History," claiming that the economic factor was often disguised. But as I thought more about it, the disguise factor in social causation seemed less important—than the time factor. . . .

I did attempt to generalize the theory. It is this: A cultural lag is independent of the nature of the initiating part or of the lagging part, provided that they are interconnected. The independent variable may be technological, economic, political, ideological, or anything else. But when the unequal time or degree of change produces a strain on the interconnected parts or is expressed differently when the correlation is lessened, then it is called a cultural lag. The extent of the generalized applicability of the theory rests on how much interconnection exists among the parts of culture. That many connections exist is obvious. Religion is interrelated with science. Family is correlated with education. Education and industry have connections. Highways are necessary for automobiles. On the other hand, some interrelations are slight or do not exist at all between other parts. Painting is not related to the production of gasoline. And I was about to say that writing poetry is unrelated to aviation. But I recall seeing a sizable book of collected poems on aviation. To the extent that culture is like a machine with parts that fit, cultural lag is widespread. If, however, cultural parts are no more related than pebbles strewn on the beach, then cultural lags are rare. There must, of course, be change occurring at unequal time intervals. An indication that cultural lags are common phenomena is suggested by the incorporation of the theory in books on general sociology. . . .

If there were time, dozens of cultural lags causing very serious problems could be listed, lags which arise largely because inventions and technology have increased in volume and rapidity faster than we are making adaptations to them. The great need of our time is to reduce this lag. Cultural lags are one characteristic of the process of social evolution, which occurs in a closely integrated society in periods of rapid change. In the long perspective of history, though, lags are not visible because they have been caught up. They are visible phenomena largely at the present time.

JOHN DEWEY

1859–1952

The third of four sons born to a grocer's wife, John Dewey was born on October 20, 1859 in Burlington, Vermont, and married Harriet Alice Chipman on July 28, 1886, an orphan who'd been raised in Dodge City, Kansas by a judge and his wife. Dewey took from her family and herself some of his interest in social justice and the publicly defined nature of truth. He and his wife produced six children between 1887 and 1900, 3 of each gender. Dewey died at 92 in New York City on June 20 or 21, 1952. He graduated from the University of Vermont in 1879, taught high school for two years in Oil City, Pennsylvania, then entered Johns Hopkins for graduate study in 1882 (the first doctoral program in the U.S., and modeled after the German system), receiving his Ph.D. in 1884 with a dissertation (now lost) on Kant's psychology. He studied with Charles Peirce, G. Stanley Hall, and more importantly, with the Hegelian, G. S. Morris. He followed his mentor to the University of Michigan, staying there from 1884 until 1894 (where he knew Cooley and Mead), headed to the newly founded University of Chicago in 1894, where he started the world-famous "Lab School" for educational research, still operating as such, and finally, after a dispute about the School with Chicago's president, moved to Columbia University where he taught throngs of students until retirement in 1930.

Dewey was one of the founding members of the American pragmatist school, along with Peirce, William James, Mead, and Josiah Royce. He was also a "public intellectual" of mighty stature, writing elaborate and sometimes arcane metaphysical works in philosophy, while also able to convey his ideas about education to the literate masses. He published *Psychology* (1887), *Leibniz's New Essays Concerning the Human Understanding* (1888; cf. Bertrand Russell's *The Philosophy of Leibniz*, 1900, his rival), and his famous paper, "The Reflex Arc Concept in Psychology," viewed as the beginning of "functional psychology." Yet after moving to Chicago he gave up his Hegelian epistemology and values, and, influenced by the behaviorism then in the air, began to fashion a Chicago-style pragmatism (what he called "instrumentalism"), which brought him much closer to earth. At the turn of the century he also began to write lucid studies of educational theory and practice, which remain the bedrock of theorizing in pedagogy to this day. When he was 78 he traveled to Mexico to oversee hearings during which Trotsky defended himself against Stalin's charges, just one of Dewey's many public roles. Dewey's ability to communicate complex ideas in relatively simple English is on display in the selections reprinted below, concerning the nature of sociation as the human condition, the dialectical need for privacy in the public setting, and the nature of morality. He was for 50 years or more the nation's favorite philosopher, something akin to Bertrand Russell in England, but without the biting satire and distancing from the common man.

EXPERIENCE AND NATURE, 1925

Communication and Communal Living

Of all affairs, communication is the most wonderful. That things should be able to pass from the plane of external pushing and pulling to that of revealing themselves to man, and thereby to themselves; and that the fruit of communication should be participation, sharing, is a wonder by the side of which transubstantiation pales. When communication occurs, all natural events are subject to reconsideration and revision; they are readapted to meet the requirements of conversation, whether it be public discourse or that preliminary discourse termed thinking. Events turn into objects, things with meaning. They may be referred to when they do not exist, and thus be operative among things distant in space and time, through vicarious presence in a new medium.

Brute efficiencies and inarticulate consummations as soon as they can be spoken of are liberated from local and accidental contexts, and are eager for naturalization in any non-insulated, communicating part of the world. Events when once they are named lead an independent and double life. In addition to their original existence, they are subject to ideal experimentation: their meanings may be infinitely combined and rearranged in imagination, and the outcome of this inner experimentation—which is thought—may issue forth in interaction with crude or raw events. Meanings having been deflected from the rapid and roaring stream of events into a calm and traversable canal, rejoin the main stream, and color, temper and compose its course. Where communication exists, things in acquiring meaning thereby acquire representatives, surrogates, signs and implicates, which are infinitely more amenable to management, more permanent and accommodating than events in their first estate.

By this fashion, qualitative immediacies cease to be dumbly rapturous, a possession that is obsessive and an incorporation that involves submergence; conditions found in sensations and passions. They become capable of survey, contemplation,

From *Intelligence in the Modern World: John Dewey's Philosophy*, Joseph Ratner, Ed. Published by The Modern Library. Copyright 1939.

and ideal or logical elaboration: when something can be said of qualities they are purveyors of instruction. Learning and teaching come into being, and there is no event which may not yield information. A directly enjoyed thing adds to itself meaning, and enjoyment is thereby idealized. Even the dumb pang of an ache achieves a significant existence when it can be designated and descanted upon: it ceases to be merely oppressive and becomes important; it gains importance because it becomes representative. It has the dignity of an office.

Associated or joint activity is a condition of the creation of a community. But association itself is physical and organic, while communal life is moral, that is emotionally, intellectually, consciously sustained. Human beings combine in behavior as directly and unconsciously as do atoms, stellar masses and cells; as directly and unknowingly as they divide and repel. They do so in virtue of their own structure, as man and woman unite, as the baby seeks the breast and the breast is there to supply its need. They do so from external circumstances, pressure from without, as atoms combine or separate in presence of an electric charge, or as sheep huddle together from the cold. Associated activity needs no explanation; things are made that way. But no amount of aggregated collective action of itself constitutes a community. For beings who observe and think, and whose ideas are absorbed by impulses and become sentiments and interests, "we" is as inevitable as "I." But "we" and "our" exist only when the consequences of combined action are perceived and become an object of desire and effort, just as "I" and "mine" appear on the scene only when a distinctive share in mutual action is consciously asserted or claimed. Human associations may be ever so organic in origin and firm in operation, but they develop into societies in a human sense only as their consequences, being known, are esteemed and sought for. Even if "society" were as much an organism as some writers have held, it would not on that account be society. Interactions, transactions, occur *de facto* and the results of interdependence follow. But participation in activities and sharing in results are additive concerns. They demand *communication* as a prerequisite. . . .

To learn to be human is to develop through the give-and-take of communication an effective sense of being an individually distinctive member of a community; one who understands and appreciates its beliefs, desires and methods, and who contributes to a further conversion of organic powers into human resources and values. But this translation is never finished. The old Adam, the unregenerate element in human nature, persists. It shows itself wherever the method obtains of attaining results by use of force instead of by the method of communication and enlightenment. It manifests itself more subtly, pervasively and effectually when knowledge and the instrumentalities of skill which are the product of communal life are employed in the service of wants and impulses—which have not themselves been modified by reference to a shared interest. To the doctrine of "natural" economy which held that commercial exchange would bring about such an interdependence that harmony would automatically result, Rousseau gave an adequate answer in advance. He pointed out that interdependence provides just the situation which makes it possible and worth while for the stronger and abler to exploit others for their own ends, to keep others in a state of subjection where they can be utilized as animated tools. The remedy he suggested, a return to a condition of independence based on isolation, was hardly seriously meant. But its desperateness is evidence of the urgency of the problem. Its negative character was equivalent to surrender of any hope of solution. By contrast it indicates the nature of the only possible solution: the perfecting of the means and ways of communication of meanings so that genuinely shared interest in the consequences of interdependent activities may inform desire and effort and thereby direct action.

⌒

THE PUBLIC AND ITS PROBLEMS, 1927

The Private and the Public

There is, however, an intelligible question about human association: Not the question how individuals or singular beings come to be connected, but how they come to be connected in just those ways which give human communities traits so different from those which mark assemblies of electrons, unions of trees in forests, swarms of insects, herds of sheep, and constellations of stars. When we consider the difference we at once come upon the fact that the consequences of conjoint action take on a new value when they are observed. For notice of the effects of connected action forces men to reflect upon the connection itself; it makes it an object of attention and interest. Each acts, in so far as the connection is known, in view of the connection. Individuals still do the thinking, desiring and purposing, but what they think of is the consequences of their behavior upon that of others and that of others upon themselves. . . .

The distinction between private and public is thus in no sense equivalent to the distinction between individual and social, even if we suppose that the latter distinction has a definite meaning. Many private acts are social; their consequences contribute to the welfare of the community or affect its status and prospects. In the broad sense any transaction deliberately carried on between two or more persons is social in quality. It is a form of associated behavior and its consequences may influence further associations. A man may serve others, even in the community at large, in carrying on a private business. To some extent it is true, as Adam Smith asserted, that our breakfast table is better supplied by the convergent outcome of activities of farmers, grocers and butchers carrying on private affairs with a view to private profit than it would be if we were served on a basis of philanthropy or public spirit. Communities have been supplied with works of art, with scientific discoveries, because of the personal delight found by private persons in engaging in these activities. There are private philanthropists who act so that needy persons or the community as a whole profit by the endowment of libraries, hospitals and educational institutions. In short, private acts may be socially valuable both by indirect consequences and by direct intention.

There is therefore no necessary connection between the private character of an act and its non-social or anti-social character. The public, moreover, cannot be identified with the socially useful. One of the most regular activities of the politically organized community has been waging war. Even the most bellicose of militarists will hardly contend that all wars have been socially helpful, or deny that some have been so destructive of social values that it would have been infinitely better if they had not been waged. The argument for the non-equivalence of the public and the social, in any praiseworthy sense of social, does not rest upon the case of war alone. There is no one, I suppose, so enamored of political action as to hold that it has never been short-sighted, foolish and harmful. There are even those who hold that the presumption is always that social loss will result from agents of the public doing anything which could be done by persons in their private capacity. There are many more who protest that some special public activity, whether prohibition, a protective tariff or the expanded meaning given the Monroe Doctrine, is baleful to society. Indeed every serious political dispute turns upon the question whether a given political act is socially beneficial or harmful.

Just as behavior is not anti-social or non-social because privately undertaken, it is not necessarily socially valuable because carried on in the name of the public by public agents. The argument has not carried us far, but at least it has warned us against identifying the community and its interests with the state or the politically organized community. And the differentiation may dispose us to look with more favor upon the proposition already advanced: namely, that the line between private and public is to be drawn on the basis of the extent and scope of the consequences of acts which are so important as to need control, whether by inhibition or by promotion. We distinguish private and public buildings, private and public schools, private baths and public highways, private assets and public funds, private persons and public officials. It is our thesis that in this distinction we find the key to the nature and office of the state. It is not without significance that etymologically "private" is defined in opposition to "official," a private person being one deprived of public position. The public consists of all those who are affected by the indirect consequences of transactions to such an extent that it is deemed necessary to have those consequences systematically cared for. Officials are those who look out for and take care of the interests thus af-

fected. Since those who are indirectly affected are not direct participants in the transactions in question, it is necessary that certain persons be set apart to represent them, and see to it that their interests are conserved and protected. The buildings, property, funds, and other physical resources involved in the performance of this office are *res publica,* the common-wealth. The public as far as organized by means of officials and material agencies to care for the extensive and enduring indirect consequences of transactions between persons is the *Populus.*

❧

ETHICS, 1932

Individual and Social Morality

When social life is stable, when custom rules, the problems of morals have to do with the adjustments which individuals make to the institutions in which they live, rather than with the moral quality of the institutions themselves. Men take their social relations for granted; they are what they are and, in being that, are what they should be. If anything is wrong it is due to the failure of individuals to do what social customs tell them to do. Only a few daring persons criticize ancestral habits, and then only guardedly. When social life is in a state of flux, moral issues cease to gather exclusively about personal conformity and deviation. They center in the value of social arrangements, of laws, of inherited traditions that have crystallized into institutions, in changes that are desirable. Institutions lose their quasi-sacredness and are the objects of moral questioning. We now live in such a period. Ever since the latter half of the eighteenth century the interesting and stirring human problems for intellectual inquiry as well as for practical application have arisen out of criticism of existing social arrangements and traditions, in State, government, law, church, family, industry, business, international relations. So far as moral theories have kept aloof from perplexi-

From *Intelligence in the Modern World: John Dewey's Philosophy,* Joseph Ratner, Ed. Published by The Modern Library. Copyright 1939.

ties about social policies in these fields, so far as they have merely repeated commonplaces about personal conduct in isolation from social issues, they have become anemic and sterile.

Indeed, one of the chief values, from the standpoint of theory, of considering the moral bearing of social problems is that we are then confronted with live issues in which vital choices still have to be made, and with situations where principles are still in process of forming. We are thus saved from the "moralistic" narrowing down of morals; we appreciate that morals are as wide as the area of everything which affects the values of human living. These values are involved on the widest scale in social issues. Hence critical questioning of existing institutions and critical discussion of changes, proposed on the theory that they will produce social betterment, are the best means of enforcing the fact that moral theory is more than a remote exercise in conceptual analysis or than a mere mode of preaching and exhortation. When we take the social point of view we are compelled to realize the extent to which our moral beliefs are a product of the social environment and also the extent to which *thinking*, new ideas, can change this environment.

MAURICE HALBWACHS

1877–1945

Son of a professor of German, Maurice Halbwachs was born on March 11, 1877 in Reims, Marne, France, married Yvonne Basch (daughter of the philosopher Victor Basch) in 1913 and had two sons with her, and at 68 was killed by the Nazis at Buchenwald concentration camp in Thüringen on March 16, 1945, just days before liberation by the Allies. He attended the Lycée Michelet and the Lycée Henri-Quartre in Paris, then matriculated at the elite École Normale Supérieure in Paris, graduating in 1898, then taking his "aggrégation" in 1901 in philosophy. He taught at lycées in Nancy and in Tours (1901–04), lectured at the University of Göttingen (1904–05), and from 1905–09 he studied economics, law, and math at the Sorbonne. A pivotal event occurred in 1905 when he got to know Émile Durkheim, with whom he worked on the *Année Sociologique,* while also co-editing several other scholarly and political journals. For his law degree in 1909 he wrote a thesis concerning Parisian land prices between 1860 and 1900, then became a teacher at another lycée, this time in Reims. Moving to Berlin in 1909, he became a foreign correspondent for *L'Humanité* (Paris) and studied the German economy and Marxism. Eventually he was deported for political reasons, returning to the Sorbonne to finish his habilitation in 1912. His dissertation concerned hierarchy and class relationships in contemporary societies. During WWI he worked in the war department, and finally in 1919 became a professor (sociology and pedagogy, Durkheim's specialty) at Strassburg. He was visiting professor at the University of Chicago in 1932, and from 1934 through 1944 was sociology professor at the Sorbonne, working with Durkheim's nephew, Marcel Mauss. The Gestapo arrested him on July 23, 1944, only two months after becoming professor of collective psychology at the Collège de France.

Halbwachs only recently became an important figure in the history of social thought outside the francophone world. His *Collective Memory* appeared in 1925 but was not translated until 1980, and his *Les causes du suicide* (1930) is still not in English. Lewis Coser's collection, *Maurice Halbwachs on Collective Memory* (1992), has gone a long way toward filling this gap in the history of Durkheimian social analysis. The reason for Halbwachs' recent fame relates to the desire, during the postmodern period, to understand how national identities are created and negotiated now that most of the verities which gave rise to the imperialist nation-states of the 19th century have disappeared. This became especially intriguing for social analysts after the collapse of the U.S.S.R. in 1989 and the reemergence of collective identities that had for decades been suppressed. Halbwachs was one of the first recent theorists to address these issues systematically.

THE SOCIAL FRAMEWORKS OF MEMORY, 1925

Conclusion

. . . The individual calls recollections to mind by relying on the frameworks of social memory. In other words, the various groups that compose society are capable, at every moment of reconstructing their past. But, as we have seen, they most frequently distort that past in the act of reconstructing it. There are surely many facts, and many details of certain facts, that the individual would forget if others did not keep their memory alive for him. But, on the other hand, society can live only if there is a sufficient unity of outlooks among the individuals and groups comprising it. The multiplicity and diversity of human groups result from an increase in needs as well as from the intellectual and organizational faculties of the society. Society accommodates itself to these conditions, just as it must accept the limited duration of individual life. It remains nevertheless true that the necessity by which people must enclose themselves in limited groups (families, religious groups, and social classes, just to mention these)—though less ineluctable and less irrevocable than the necessity to be enclosed in a determined duration of life—is opposed to the social need for unity, in the same way that the latter may be opposed to the social need for continuity. This is why society tends to erase from its memory all that might separate individuals, or that might distance groups from each other. It is also why society, in each period, rearranges its recollections in such a way as to adjust them to the variable conditions of its equilibrium.

If we limited ourselves to the consciousness of individuals, this is what would seem to be the case. Recollections which have not been thought about for a long time are reproduced without change. But when reflection begins to operate, when instead of letting the past recur, we reconstruct it through an effort of reasoning, what happens is that we distort that past, because we wish

to introduce greater coherence. It is then reason or intelligence that chooses among the store of recollections, eliminates some of them, and arranges the others according to an order conforming with our ideas of the moment. From this comes many alterations. But I have shown that memory is a collective function. Let us then place ourselves in the perspective of the group. If recollections reappear, this is because at each moment society possesses the necessary means to reproduce them. We might perhaps be led to distinguish two kinds of activities within social thought: on the one hand a memory, that is, a framework made out of notions that serve as landmarks for us and that refer exclusively to the past; on the other hand a rational activity that takes its point of departure in the conditions in which the society at the moment finds itself, in other words, in the present. This memory functions only when under the control of this reason. When a society abandons or modifies its traditions, is it not in order to satisfy rational needs, and at the very moment in which they appear?

But why is it that traditions yield? Why do recollections defer to the ideas and reflections that society opposes to them? These ideas represent, if you will, the consciousness that society has of itself in its present situation. They result from a collective reflection detached from any set of opinions that takes into account only what exists, not what has once been. It is the present. It is undoubtedly difficult to modify the present, but is it not much more difficult in certain respects to transform the image of the past that is also—at least virtually—in the present, since society always carries within its thought the frameworks of memory? After all, the present, if we consider the area of collective thought that it occupies, weighs very little in comparison to the past. Ancient representations are imposed on us with all the force acquired from the ancient societies in which they assumed collective form. The older they are, the stronger they will be; the greater the number of people and the more widespread the groups that have adopted them, the more potent these representations become. Even greater collective forces would be needed to oppose these collective forces. But present-day ideas extend over a much shorter duration. Whence do such ideas gain the energy and the collective substance needed to resist traditions?

There is only one possible explanation. If the ideas of today are capable of being opposed to recollections and of prevailing over them to the extent of transforming them, this is because such ideas correspond to a collective experience, if not as ancient, at least much larger. Such ideas are (like traditions) held in common not only by the members of the group under consideration, but also by other contemporary groups. Reason is opposed to tradition as an extended society is to a narrow one. In addition, present-day ideas are truly new only for the members of the group which they permeate. Wherever they do not clash with traditions, such ideas have been able to develop freely and to take the form of traditions themselves. What a group opposes to its past is not its present; it is rather the past (perhaps the more recent past, but no matter) of other groups with whom it tends to identify itself.

To sum up: social beliefs, whatever their origin, have a double character. They are collective traditions or recollections, but they are also ideas or conventions that result from a knowledge of the present. Were it purely conventional (in this sense), social thought would be purely logical. It would allow only that which is serviceable under its present conditions. It would succeed in extinguishing, in all members of the group, all the recollections that hold them back, be it even slightly, and which would permit them to be both part of the society of yesterday and part of the society of today. Were society purely traditional, it would not allow itself to be permeated by any idea—or even by any fact—that was in disagreement, however slight, with its oldest beliefs. Hence, in both cases, society would not allow any compromise between consciousness of present conditions and attachment to traditional beliefs. Society would be based entirely on the one or the other. But social thought is not abstract. Even when they correspond to and express the present, the ideas of society are always embodied in persons or groups. Behind a title, a virtue, or a quality, society immediately perceives those who possess them. Those groups and persons exist in the passage of time and leave their traces in the memory of people. In this sense, there is no social idea that would not at the same time be a recollection of the society. But, on the other hand, society would labor in vain if it

attempted to recapture in a purely concrete form a particular figure or event that has left a strong imprint in its memory. As soon as each person and each historical fact has permeated this memory, it is transposed into a teaching, a notion, or a symbol and takes on a meaning. It becomes an element of the society's system of ideas. This explains why traditions and present-day ideas can exist side by side. In reality present-day ideas are also traditions, and both refer at the same time and with the same right to an ancient or recent social life from which they in some way took their point of departure. Just as the Pantheon of imperial Rome gave shelter to all cults—provided that these were indeed cults—society admits all traditions (even the most recent), provided that they are indeed traditions. In the same way, society admits all ideas (even the most ancient), provided that they are ideas, that is, that they have a place in its thought and that they still interest present-day people who understand them. From this it follows that social thought is essentially a memory and that its entire content consists only of collective recollections or remembrances. But it also follows that, among them, only those recollections subsist that in every period society, working within its present-day frameworks, can reconstruct.

~

THE PSYCHOLOGY OF SOCIAL CLASS, 1955

Why is it that in general we think of the people of the past, and particularly the distant past, as being so entirely different from ourselves? We cannot, of course, go back in time; society no more than the individual can travel over again the way it has come. But this is not the only reason for our feeling that the figures of the past are alien to us. They seem distant not only in time but in the scale of evolution, as though they were of another species, outwardly like us but dwelling in an atmosphere in which the very air was different, and the ideas and feelings and even the sensations cannot have been the same as to-day's. This is much what we feel when we read history books or historical novels, or visit old buildings and places where things have stood still for half a century; we feel it even more strongly when we try to evoke the inhabitants of such places, who went about their lives inside these walls and seem now as inaccessible as ghosts or the unknown dwellers on some far-off planet.

Such feelings would be easy to explain if man himself (i.e., the human race) were subject to evolution quite apart from all changes in social environment. Then we should not think of ourselves as beings of the same substance with similar organs, capable of identical reactions to impressions from the world around us. Each generation could be considered as a new phase in organic evolution. . . .

Men, then, have been basically the same ever since the species first appeared with its fundamental characteristics, distinct from all other living things. Take a small child during the first two years of its life, or even later—it is not only a matter of its physical appearance but of its impressions, the ill-defined and shapeless realm of its concepts, its appetites, desires and emotions and its attitude towards objects and people. Where, in this respect, is the difference between a small child of the twentieth century in a peasant or working-class or *bourgeois* environment, and a small child in one of the tribes we call primitive, but which is in fact only slightly nearer the point of departure and so less far advanced? Throughout the time when its social environment has not yet affected its nature it is the same being, subject to the same forces in both cases, as Kipling's Mowgli. If this action of society were not felt from the moment the child first acquires habits, and especially when he begins to speak, we should still be in the same state as the earliest savages and our actions would have no motivations other than theirs. . . .

* * *

Have we now considered all the determinants of individual behaviour in social life? Moralists may reproach us for not having given central place to the sense of duty. And indeed we have not spoken of duty pure and simple, of the categorical imperative, the moral law, because it concerns man's interior life. As for social morality and social duties, their content is determined by the different social groups to which we belong: there is class morality, professional morality, civic morality, religious morality and the scientist's and artist's morality too; the object of this whole study has not been to construct a theory but to examine what men believe, that is, what they do.

True, we have discussed neither justice nor charity; so we might recall Spencer's definition of these two virtues and the distinction he drew between them. Justice consists in obeying established laws, and is founded on the idea that these laws are the condition of order, that is of the maintenance of society at the stage it has reached. It is negative, since for the most part it counsels us to abstain from doing things; it is collective, because it applies equally to all members of the group under its sway. Charity consists of everything done to better social conditions, or rather to do away with the evil produced by strict justice wherever in particular cases it fails to eliminate social inequalities and extreme hardship. It is positive since it demands initiative, effort, a sort of offering up of ourselves; it is individual, since every single person can practise it in his milieu and as far as his influence is felt.

These are two types of behaviour, and two types of men represent them who complement as well as being opposed to each other. But somewhere between them a wider justice can be imagined, what we might call social justice, going beyond strictly legal justice and differing from charity in that it is collective. It could be called solidarity, as it is found within certain social groups: a morality of collaboration and mutual help, taking shape within the framework of modern social life. There is in such an idea a whole programme, one which is inspiring more and more members of our societies.

But to conclude a study which has been concerned for the most part with the economic aspect of social life we should insist rather on another distinction, concerned with more immediate issues: that which can be drawn between the morality of producers and that of consumers.[1]

Every individual is of course both. But economic evolution as it has taken place for more than a century under the capitalist system seems to have been tending principally towards an increase, indeed an unlimited increase in production. Things are produced not for consumption but for the sake of producing, and consumers are expected to ensure markets for production at its own price because the development of production depends on this. Of course this is the condition of a certain economic progress, but it brings with it the paradoxical result that, with ever more products, there are still whole sections of the populace who lack commodities—even necessities—that modern techniques should ensure for them. It should be possible to reconcile economic progress with a more equitable distribution of total wealth, and thus allow the living standards of the lower classes to rise. Such is the principle behind the morality of the consumer, subordinating all mankind's activities to the satisfaction of the needs of the greatest number. The whole problem of the economic system lies here.

Stendhal's chief interest in life lay in observing how men go about "the pursuit of happiness." And there indeed lies—or should lie—the essential determinant of human conduct. Individuals succeed more or less as chance or their temperament, their skill or experience allows. They pursue happiness singly, in broken ranks. But let us consider not individuals but groups. Urban civilization has led, as we have seen, to a sharp division into two areas; productive activity and consumption. But while there has been a drawing together and combination of all forms of work in accordance with rules that answer to nothing but production or professional necessities; and while every social group bends its efforts to this end, we may well ask whether they have succeeded in organizing the other half of life so efficiently—that part which is devoted to satisfying needs, in short, the most important part? For we must take the word consumption to imply not only destruction but also achievement. It is for man a matter of realizing himself to the full within the framework and opportunities of collective life; and while it holds out very rich possibilities in this respect, as yet they have been neither exploited nor even explored.

Men are well aware of this; hence the passionate interest now taken in every form of association and every institution inspired by community feeling. They have understood that collective effort is necessary to organize the pursuit of happiness socially in something so complex as modern civilization. Happiness, in fact, is not in these circumstances the automatic result of increasing wealth and productivity. Perhaps even, as Bergson suggested, austerity, restrictions and even a certain asceticism is a necessary element in material satisfaction. In short, this is a determinant as yet unclear, but beginning to take shape. Certainly, if it is to grow and increase in strength, more and more attention must be paid to our experience of life as a social phenomenon, and a science of man must at last be established. Here again it is up to society to find within itself those who are best fitted to carry out such investigations; and at the same time it must create an environment favourable to the progress of these studies.

Note

1. Horace M. Kallen, *The Decline and the Rise of the Consumer, a Philosophy of Consumer Cooperation,* New York, 1936.

KARL MANNHEIM

1893–1947

Károly (Karl) Mannheim was born in Budapest, Hungary on March 27, 1893, the only child of a textile manufacturer. He married "Juliska" Károlyné Julia Láng (known professionally as Julia Lang), a psychologist, in 1921, and they had no children. She collaborated with him as an unacknowledged author on a number of his works, and gave his writings a self/society depth they would probably otherwise have lacked. Mannheim's high school and college education was accomplished in Budapest, where he specialized in philosophy and in comparative literature at the Péter Pázmány University of the Human Sciences. In May 1918 he passed the state exam in German and French speech and literature, and in November graduated summa cum laude with a dissertation in philosophy called "The Structural Analysis of Epistemology" (translated as *Structures of Thinking* in 1982). Soon he was involved in regular discussion groups with Georg Lukács (an older relative) and other notable intellectuals in Budapest. Due to political upheaval in Hungary following WWI (in which Lukács played an official role), Mannheim emigrated to Vienna in 1919, then to Germany in 1920, to Freiburg and then Heidelberg. From 1922 through 1925 he worked on his second dissertation under the direction of Alfred Weber (Max's brother), a brilliant work on "Conservative Thought: A study in the sociology of knowledge" (translated as *Conservative Thought* in 1953). This was one of the first scholarly works ever to use the term "*Wissenssoziologie*" in its title, and prepared Mannheim for a leading role as an innovator in this new field. Between 1926 and 1930 Mannheim taught in Heidelberg, then was promoted and moved to Frankfurt as professor of sociology and political-economy. His assistant there was Norbert Elias, later himself a world-class social theorist and cultural historian. Mannheim fled the Nazis in 1933 and ended up in England, where he taught at the University of London and the London School of Economics, also editing the influential "International Library of Sociology and Social Reconstruction," until his premature death (of a congenitally weak heart) on January 9, 1947, at the age of 53.

Surely one of the most gifted social theorists post-Weber, Mannheim wrote a series of articles in the mid 1920s (perhaps competing with his cousin, Lukács) which were assembled as *Ideology and Utopia* in 1929 (soon translated by the young Edward Shils at Louis Wirth's suggestion), and became one of the most influential social science books of the century. It remains in print today. Mannheim believed that arguments over truth which stayed within conventional boundaries of epistemology missed an essential social ingredient and were therefore false, because no-one could claim absolute knowledge inasmuch as everyone's *Weltanschauungen* (worldviews) reflected the limitations of their position in the social order. These positions he called "ideologies," and in his essays, following the recently deceased Weber, he went through a number of groups and religious organizations in history, showing how their intellectual arguments turned on mundane characteristics of their lives and political-economic roles. Equally persuasive was Mannheim's ingenious essay on "Conservative Thought," wherein he connected 20th century authoritarianism with 18th century philosophy and cultural history. The "conservative mindset" for Mannheim had a long and interesting lineage, but one that culminated in perverse tendencies during his own lifetime. Mannheim's other important books included *Man and Society in an Age of Reconstruction* (1940), *Freedom, Power, and Democratic Planning* (1950) and *Essays in the Sociology of Knowledge* (1952). As with Weber, most of Mannheim's works were published posthumously, assembled by devoted students and his wife.

"THE IDEOLOGICAL AND THE SOCIOLOGICAL INTERPRETATION OF INTELLECTUAL PHENOMENA," 1926

. . . One of the meanings of 'ideological' is a way of looking at ideas, in contrast to the sociological. Such a formulation emphasizes the possibility of two manners of viewing the same phenomenon and suggests that the difference between idea and ideology may be in the difference between two ways of looking, two attitudes. The same idea (in the sense of any intellectual-psychological content whatever toward which there is a conscious orientation) appears as 'idea' as long as one attempts to grasp and interpret it 'from within', but as 'ideology' when one considers it from points of view that lie outside of it, particularly from 'social existence'. In this sense, every idea (whether intrinsically true or false) may be considered both 'from within' and from 'existence'. . . .

Types of Interpretation

We now wish to locate the sociological among other kinds of interpretation. Since, as far as we know, no typology of them exists, we must try to construct one which, it should be noted, is bound to be preliminary, rather than complete. A com-

plete one can be established only once the different kinds of interpretation have been explored by means of numerous concrete studies in various areas of intellectual endeavor.

In order to find the most comprehensive principle of classification, we begin with the contrast that we found sketched by Marx as that between the ideological and the sociological consideration of cultural phenomena and that we have called, in an enlarged sense, their intrinsic and their extrinsic interpretation.

We have seen that intrinsic interpretation includes several types (of which more presently), just as we have observed several types of extrinsic interpretation. The first group in our list, then, contains *intrinsic interpretations*.

(1) Interpretations that try to ascertain *intended meaning*. We recall that by intrinsic interpretations we understand those ways of grasping intellectual phenomena that for this purpose do not leave the realm of the 'ideological'. Simplest among them is the type that limits itself to the clearest possible grasp of what Max Weber called the 'subjectively intended meaning'. It is distinguished from the ordinary understanding of meaning only in so far as it tries to locate and critically ascertain it by comparing different passages and documents of a work. Its aim is to comprehend the 'sense' of that work, or to present a doctrine in the sense in which the author himself intended it and wanted it understood.

(2) A second kind of interpretation may be called *objective*. Like all intrinsic interpretations, it

does not leave the ideological level. It does not ask, however, how the author himself intended his meaning but, starting from the author's own premises, tries to draw correct conclusions from them. (Example: 'To understand Kant better than he understood himself.')

(3) A third kind of intrinsic interpretation aims at understanding an author in terms of *another system,* or other axioms, than his own. (Example: the various interpretations of Plato on the basis of modern philosophical systems—see, e.g., [Paul] Natorp's book on Plato.) Ahistorically oriented interpreters will always claim this kind of interpretation to be absolute, that is, oriented toward a system of absolute truths. Since we do not wish to enter into an epistemological discussion, we only observe that, whereas from a non-historicist standpoint, there does exist this challenge of an 'absolute interpretation', for the historicist, 'absolute interpretation' can only mean interpreting a system in terms of another.

The kinds of interpretation mentioned thus far may be contrasted as *systematic* with those that are *genetic* and to which we now turn. We distinguish two general types of genetic interpretation: those undertaken with an immanent (ideological) attitude, and those presupposing a consideration 'from without'. We begin with the first type.

(4) Interpretations that try to ascertain the *genesis of a meaning.* This is one of the oldest kinds of interpretation; but in the course of intellectual history it has undergone the most varied changes. It is directed, not at the factual genesis of a given meaning, but at its origin. It is attempted in cosmogonies and mythologies and lives on, though in modified form, in the various justifications, of natural right. Illustrations are Robinsonades in economic theory or contract theories in political philosophy which, properly understood, are theories concerning the genesis of meanings, not concerning origins in positive history. The same kind of interpretation obtains in the field of logic, in the attempt, for instance, at a typological derivation of all possible classes of epistemological or metaphysical theories and at the understanding of the intellectual phenomenon under analysis in terms of its 'logical locus'. The same kind of interpretation, however, is possible not only in the theoretical sphere but also in art. Here an illustration

is the effort to understand, say, a gate or a cupola in reference to all possible artistic solutions of the relevant, ultimately technical, tasks, and to determine a given solution by reference to its aesthetic locus within all possible types.

(5) Distinct from the preceding class of interpretations is that which aims at genesis in the manner of the *history of ideas.* In its crude form, it is mere history of motifs; in its more complex version, history of problems. Non-theoretical fields, too, may be studied from this point of view. This interpretation in terms of the history of problems is distinguished from that of the genesis of meaning in so far as the factual historical genesis is wholly irrelevant for the former, whereas the latter, by contrast, largely follows positive historical developments. It tries to account for the various elements of the system to be interpreted by taking them out of the unique and systematic context by virtue of which they are imbedded in that system, and relating them to a problem unfolding in history. The answer to the question toward which problems such an approach is oriented depends, of course, on the concerns of the individual student taking this approach. In short, this interpretation, too, is genetic, but is still 'from within'.

(6) A particular transition between genetic and systematic interpretations, as well as between intrinsic and extrinsic interpretations, is made by those types of interpretation that we should like to call interpretations in terms of immanent, or *ideological, totality.* While not leaving the ideological plane, they do leave the specific sphere in which the intellectual phenomenon under analysis is located. Thus, a given philosophy is not understood in terms of philosophy alone, nor a given art in terms of art alone, but by reference to the ideological totality of the age concerned. These interpretations try to understand phenomena by reference to the relevant total world views. We wish to distinguish two types.

(a) One we have called *documentary interpretation* (in our essay 'On the Interpretation of *Weltanschauung').* Its characteristic features are the reconstruction of the totality by means adjusted to handling the sphere of the irrational and the attempt thereby to understand and interpret the phenomenon under analysis. Spengler's morphology may serve as an example.

(b) The *rationalizing method* interprets phenomena by reference to the total intellectual process. It differs from the preceding type by creating an overall synthesis through a rationalization so rigorous as to do violence, usually, to the specific character of concrete phenomena. In view of his method of synthesizing history that is patterned after the model of logic, Hegel might be cited as an example; in other respects, however, his work must be identified as idealistic extrinsic interpretation.

All interpretations discussed thus far have in common the attempt at grasping the phenomenon to be interpreted from within the ideological sphere itself. Those which remain to be dealt with have been more thoroughly analyzed in the preceding chapter. We have found them to be characterized by the interpretation of the intellectual phenomenon in terms of an *existence* postulated *outside* the sphere of the intrinsic meaning of that phenomenon.

We again wish to distinguish two types. The first tries to explain intellectual contents by reference to un-meaning existence. The other functionalizes them by reference to an existence outside them but conceives of this existence as a context of meaning.

(7) The first group—purely *causal explanations*—is listed here only because of the clear contrast with the second. For causal explanations are not, properly speaking, interpretations, but determinations of un-meaning causal nexuses. They are concerned with the ascertainment of all those processes which, in themselves un-meaning, that is, not understandable, can merely be observed in their regularity; while they are preconditions, they are not presuppositions of the context of meaning to be interpreted. Here belong the efforts of explanatory psychology, biology, etc.

(8) In contrast to this group of extrinsic interpretations that try to grasp meaning by reference to un-meaning existence, there are those that we have identified as interpretations by reference to *meaningful existence*. We have distinguished the two types of them as, (a) the idealistic, (b) the positivistic, functionalization of phenomena. Sociological interpretation is a certain variant of the second of these. Among intrinsic interpretations, we have singled out those that proceed in terms of immanent, or ideological, totality. The last classes

of interpretations now under analysis likewise proceed in terms of a totality, but the totality is existential. They take the entire ideological sphere, together with the social existence that ties behind it, as a unit, and thus represent the highest stage of total interpretation as such.

Here we ought also to discuss those kinds of interpretation that try to understand and interpret a given phenomenon by reference to the context of life and experience of, (a) an individual (biographical method), and (b) a historical social group. But it would lead too far to relate 'understanding' individual and collective psychology to (for instance) economic and sociological extrinsic interpretation and to tackle the general problem of the relationship between 'understanding' psychology and 'understanding' sociology.

Instead, we now wish to group the kinds of interpretation discussed in tabular form.

I. Interpretations Based on an 'Intrinsic Consideration' (Ideological Interpretations)
  A. Systematic Interpretations
    (1) Interpretations of subjectively intended meaning
    (2) Objective interpretations
    (3) Interpretations in terms of other systems
  B. Genetic Interpretations
    (a) Genetic Interpretations that Trace Meaning to Meaning
      (4) Interpretations in terms of the genesis of meaning
      (5) History of ideas
      (6) Interpretations in terms of immanent ideological totality
        1. Documentary interpretations
        2. Rationalizing reconstructions of totality
II. Interpretations Based on an 'Extrinsic Consideration'
    (b) Interpretations that Trace Meaning to UnMeaning Existence (Causal Explanations)
      (7) Various types of causal explanation (not properly interpretations)
    (c) Interpretations that Trace Meaning to Meaningful Existence
      (8) Interpretations in terms of meaningful total existence

1. Idealistic
2. Positivistic (sociological)
   a. In the substructure the concept of society
   b. In the substructure drives, etc.
3. Interpretations in 'understanding'-individual and 'understanding' collective psychology

Even this inventory of the most important kinds of interpretation shows the peculiarity of intellectual phenomena, which is that they can be approached from many different angles. It also shows that the kinds listed, of which the most modern is the sociological, cannot be fixed for all time. For they rise and change along with the historical development of consciousness and thus offer the possibility of an ever increasing and transforming penetration of the intellectual world.

~

"THE MEANING OF CONSERVATISM," 1927

I. Traditionalism and conservatism

Let us begin by analysing more exactly what we mean by 'conservatism.' Is conservatism a phenomenon universal to all mankind, or is it an entirely new product of the historical and sociological conditions of our own time? The answer is that both sorts of conservatism exist. On the one hand, there is the definitely modern sort which is the product of particular historical and social circumstances, and which has its own peculiar traditions, form and structure. We could call the first sort 'natural conservatism',[1] and the second sort 'modern conservatism', were it not that the word 'natural' is already heavily burdened with many different meanings. It will perhaps be better therefore if we adopt Max Weber's term *'traditionalism'* to denote the first type; so that when we speak of 'conservatism' we shall always

mean 'modern' conservatism—something essentially different from mere 'traditionalism.'

Traditionalism signifies a tendency to cling to vegetative patterns, to old ways of life which we may well consider as fairly ubiquitous and universal. This 'instinctive' traditionalism may be seen as the original reaction to deliberate reforming tendencies. In its original form it was bound up with magical elements in consciousness; conversely, among primitive peoples, respect for traditional ways of life is strongly linked with the fear of magical evils attendant on change. Traditionalism of this kind also exists today, and is often similarly connected with magical hang-overs from the old consciousness. Traditionalism is not therefore necessarily bound up, even today, with political or other sorts of conservatism. 'Progressive' people for instance, regardless of their political convictions, may often act 'traditionalistically' to a very large extent in many other spheres of their lives.

Thus, we do not intend the term 'conservatism' to be understood in a general psychological sense. The progressive who acts 'traditionalistically' in private or business life, or the conservative who acts 'progressively' outside politics, should make the point clear.

The word 'traditionalist' describes what, to a greater or less degree, is a formal psychological characteristic of every individual's mind. 'Conservative' action, however, is always dependent on *a concrete set of circumstances*. There is no means of knowing in advance what form a 'conservative' action in the political sense will take, whereas the general attitude implied in the term 'traditionalist' enables us to calculate more or less accurately what a 'traditionalist' action will be like. There is no doubt, for instance, what the traditionalist reaction to the introduction of the railway will be. But how a conservative will react can only be determined approximately *if we know a good deal about the conservative movement* in the period and in the country under discussion. We are not concerned here to enumerate all the different factors which go to produce a particular type of conservatism in a particular country at a particular period. This much is clear, however, that acting along conservative lines (at any rate in the political sphere) involves more than automatic responses of a certain type; it means that the individual is consciously or unconsciously guided by a way of thinking and acting which has its own history behind it, before it comes into contact with the individual. This contact with the individual may under certain circumstances change to some extent the form and development of this way of thinking and acting, but even when the particular individual is no longer there to participate in it, it will still have its own history and development apart from him. Political conservatism is therefore an *objective mental structure,* as opposed to the 'subjectivity' of the isolated individual. It is *not* objective in the sense of being eternally and universally valid. No *a priori* deductions can be made from the 'principles' of conservatism. Nor does it exist apart from the individuals who realize it in practice and embody it in their actions. It is not an immanent principle with a given law of development which the individual members of the movement merely unfold—possibly in unconscious fashion—without adding anything of their own. In one word, conservatism is not an objective entity in any rightly or wrongly understood Platonist sense of the pre-existence of ideas. But as compared with the *hic et nunc* experience of the particular individual it has a certain very definite objectivity. . . .

Conservatism is just such an historically developed, dynamic, objective structural configuration. People experience, and act, in a 'conservative' way (as distinct from a merely 'traditionalist' way) in so far, and only in so far, as they *incorporate* themselves into one of the phases of development of this objective mental structure (usually into the contemporary phase), and behave in terms of the structure, either by simply reproducing it in whole or in part, or by developing it further by adapting it to a particular concrete situation.

Only when the peculiar nature of the objectivity of a dynamic structural configuration has been grasped can one be in a position to distinguish 'conservative' from 'traditionalist' behaviour.

Traditionalist behaviour is almost purely reactive. Conservative behaviour is meaningful, and moreover is meaningful in relation to circumstances which change from epoch to epoch. It is therefore clear why there is no necessary contradiction in the fact that a politically progressive man can react in an entirely traditionalist way in his everyday life. In the political sphere, he lets himself be guided more or less consciously by an objective, structural configuration; in his everyday life, his behaviour is merely reactive. Two points now arise. Firstly the term 'conservatism' must not be, assumed to be a purely political one, although on the whole, as we shall see, its political aspect is perhaps the rather more important one. Conservatism also implies a general philosophical and emotional complex which may even constitute a definite style of thought. Secondly, conservatism as an objective historical structural configuration must not be assumed to include no traditionalist elements within itself. Quite the contrary. We shall see, in fact, that conservatism takes a particular historical form of traditionalism and develops it to its logical conclusions.

Nevertheless, in spite of this apparent overlapping of the two phenomena, or maybe even because of it, the distinction between merely traditionalist and conservative behaviour is a very clear one. Precisely because of its purely formal, semi-reactive nature, traditionalist behaviour has practically no traceable history, whereas conservatism, on the other hand, is an entity with a clear historical and social continuity, which has arisen and developed in a particular historical and social situation, as the best of all guides to history—language—clearly demonstrates; the very word 'conservatism' is a new one of comparatively recent origin.

It was Chateaubriand who first lent the word its peculiar meaning when he called the periodical he issued to propagate the ideas of the clerical and political Restoration, *The Conservative.* The word entered into general use in Germany in the thirties, and was officially adopted in England in 1835. We can take the emergence of a new terminology to indicate the emergence of a new social phenomenon, although of course it tells us little about the latter's actual nature.

IDEOLOGY AND UTOPIA, 1929

The Sociological Concept of Thought

. . . The principal thesis of the sociology of knowledge is that there are modes of thought which cannot be adequately understood as long as their social origins are obscured. It is indeed true that only the individual is capable of thinking. There is no such metaphysical entity as a group mind which thinks over and above the heads of individuals, or whose ideas the individual merely reproduces. Nevertheless it would be false to deduce from this that all the ideas and sentiments which motivate an individual have their origin in him alone, and can be adequately explained solely on the basis of his own life-experience.

Just as it would be incorrect to attempt to derive a language merely from observing a single individual, who speaks not a language of his own but rather that of his contemporaries and predecessors who have prepared the path for him, so it is incorrect to explain the totality of an outlook only with reference to its genesis in the mind of the individual. Only in a quite limited sense does the single individual create out of himself the mode of speech and of thought we attribute to him. He speaks the language of his group; he thinks in the manner in which his group thinks. He finds at his disposal only certain words and their meanings. These not only determine to a large extent the avenues of approach to the surrounding world, but they also show at the same time from which angle and in which context of activity objects have hitherto been perceptible and accessible to the group or the individual.

The first point which we now have to emphasize is that the approach of the sociology of knowledge intentionally does not start with the single individual and his thinking in order then to proceed directly in the manner of the philosopher to the abstract heights of "thought as such." Rather, the sociology of knowledge seeks to comprehend thought in the concrete setting of an historical-social situation out of which individually differentiated thought only very gradually emerges. Thus, it is not men in general who think, or even isolated individuals who do the thinking, but men in certain groups who have developed a particular style of thought in an endless series of responses to certain typical situations characterizing their common position.

Strictly speaking it is incorrect to say that the single individual thinks. Rather it is more correct to insist that he participates in thinking further what other men have thought before him. He finds himself in an inherited situation with patterns of thought which are appropriate to this situation and attempts to elaborate further the inherited modes of response or to substitute others for them in order to deal more adequately with the new challenges which have arisen out of the shifts and changes in his situation. Every individual is therefore in a two-fold sense, predetermined by the fact of growing up in a society: on the one hand he finds a ready-made situation and on the other he finds in that situation preformed patterns of thought and of conduct.

The second feature characterizing the method of the sociology of knowledge is that it does not sever the concretely existing modes of thought from the context of collective action through which we first discover the world in an intellectual sense. Men living in groups do not merely coexist physically as discrete individuals. They do not confront the objects of the world from the abstract levels of a contemplating mind as such, nor do they do so exclusively as solitary beings. On the contrary they are with and against one another in diversely organized groups, and while doing so they think with and against one another. Then persons, bound together into groups, strive in accordance with the character and position of the groups to which they belong to change the surrounding world of nature and society or attempt to maintain it in a given condition. It is the direction of this will to change or to maintain, of this collective activity, which produces the guiding thread for the emergence of their problems, their concepts, and their forms of thought. In accord with the particular context of collective activity in which they participate, men always tend to see the world which surrounds them differently. Just as pure logical analysis has severed individual thought from its group situation, so it also separated thought from action: It did this on the tacit assumption that those inherent connections which always exist in reality between thought on the one hand, and group and activity on the other, are either insignificant for "correct" thinking or can be detached from these foundations without any resultant difficulties. But the fact that one ignores something by no means puts an end to its existence. Nor can anyone who has not first given himself whole-heartedly to the exact observation of the wealth of forms in which men really think decide *a priori* whether this severance from the social situation and context of activity is always realizable. Nor indeed can it be determined offhand that such a complete dichotomy is fully desirable precisely in the interest of objective factual knowledge.

It may be that, in certain spheres of knowledge, it is the impulse to act which first makes the objects of the world accessible to the acting subject, and it may be further that it is this factor which determines the selection of those elements of reality which enter into thought. And it is not inconceivable that if this volitional factor were entirely excluded (in so far as such a thing is possible), the concrete content would completely disappear from the concepts, and the organizing principle which first makes possible an intelligent statement of the problem would be lost.

But this is not to say that in those domains where attachment to the group and orientation towards action seem to be an essential element in the situation, every possibility of intellectual, critical self-control is futile. Perhaps it is precisely when the hitherto concealed dependence of thought on group existence and its rootedness in action becomes visible that it really becomes possible for the first time, through becoming aware of them, to attain a new mode of control over previously uncontrolled factors in thought.

This brings us to the central problem of the book. These remarks should make it clear that a preoccupation with these problems and their solution will furnish a foundation for the social sciences and answer the question as to the possibility of the scientific guidance of political life. It is, of course, true that in the social sciences, as else-where, the ultimate criterion of truth or falsity is to be found in the investigation of the object, and the sociology of knowledge is no substitute for this. But the examination of the object is not an isolated act; it takes place in a context which is coloured by values and collective-unconscious, volitional impulses. In the social sciences it is this intellectual interest, oriented in a matrix of collective activity, which provides not only the general questions, but the concrete hypotheses for research and the thought-models for the ordering of experience. Only as we succeed in bringing into the area of conscious and explicit observation the various points of departure and of approach to the facts which are current in scientific as well as popular discussion, can we hope, in the course of time, to control the unconscious motivations and presuppositions which, in the last analysis, have brought these modes of thought into existence. A new type of objectivity in the social sciences is attainable not through the exclusion of evaluations but through the critical awareness and control of them.

The Contemporary Predicament of Thought

It is by no means an accident that the problem of the social and activistic roots of thinking has emerged in our generation. Nor is it accidental that the unconscious, which has hitherto motivated our thought and activity, has been gradually raised to the level of awareness and thereby made accessible to control. It would be a failure to recognize its relevance to our own plight if we did not see that it is a specific social situation which has impelled us to reflect about the social roots of our knowledge. It is one of the fundamental insights of the sociology of knowledge that the process by which collective-unconscious motives become conscious cannot operate in every epoch, but only in a quite specific situation. This situation is sociologically determinable. One can point out with relative precision the factors which are inevitably forcing more and more persons to reflect not merely about the things of the world, but about thinking itself and even here not so much about truth in itself, as about the alarming fact that the same world can appear differently to different observers.

It is clear that such problems can become general only in an age in which disagreement is more conspicuous than agreement. One turns from the direct observation of things to the consideration of ways of thinking only when the possibility of the direct and continuous elaboration of concepts concerning things and situations has collapsed in the face of a multiplicity of fundamentally divergent definitions. Now we are enabled to designate more precisely than a general and formal analysis makes possible exactly in which social and intellectual situation such as a show of attention from things to divergent opinions and from them to the unconscious motives of thought must necessarily occur. In what follows we wish to point out only a few of the most significant social factors which are operating in this direction.

Above all, the multiplicity of ways of thinking cannot become a problem in periods when social stability underlies and guarantees the internal unity of a world-view. As long as the same meanings of words, the same ways of deducing ideas, are inculcated from childhood on into every member of the group, divergent thought-processes cannot exist in that society. Even a gradual modification in ways of thinking (where it should happen to arise), does not become perceptible to the members of a group who live in a stable situation as long as the tempo in the adaptations of ways of thinking to new problems is so slow that it extends over several generations. In such a case, one and the same generation in the course of its own life span can scarcely become aware that a change is taking place.

But in addition to the general dynamics of the historical process, factors of quite another sort must enter before the multiplicity of the ways of thinking will become noticeable and emerge as a theme for reflection. Thus it is primarily the intensification of social mobility which destroys the earlier illusion, prevalent in a static society, that all things can change, but thought remains eternally the same. And what is more, the two forms of social mobility, horizontal and vertical, operate in different ways to reveal this multiplicity of styles of thought. Horizontal mobility (movement from one position to another or from one country to another without changing social status) shows us that different peoples think differently. As long, however, as the traditions of one's national and local group remain unbroken, one remains so attached to its customary ways of thinking that the ways of thinking which are perceived in other groups are regarded as curiosities, errors, ambiguities, or heresies. At this stage one does not doubt either the correctness of one's own traditions of thought or the unity and uniformity of thought in general.

Only when horizontal mobility is accompanied by intensive vertical mobility, i.e. rapid movement between strata in the sense of social ascent and descent, is the belief in the general and eternal validity of one's own thought-forms shaken.

BRONISLAW MALINOWSKI

1884–1942

Son of a linguistics professor (Slavic philology) and learned, linguistically gifted mother from rich landowners, Bronislaw Kasper Malinowski was born in Krakow, Poland on April 7, 1884 when it was part of the Austro-Hungarian Empire. He married Elsie Rosaline Masson, a chemistry professor's daughter from Melbourne, in 1919 and with her had three daughters. In 1940 he married the artist Anna Valetta Hayman-Joyce, who published some of his work posthumously. He died at 58 in New Haven, Connecticut on May 16, 1942. Malinowski, always sickly, was home-schooled, eventually received a doctorate in philosophy, physics, and math from his father's workplace, the University of Krakow (Jagiellonian University) in 1908, and also studied at Leipzig. He read James Frazer's *Golden Bough*, and ever after acknowledged it as the source of his earliest enthusiasm for anthropology. His affectionate, lengthy obituary for Frazer (in *A Scientific Theory of Culture*, 1944) is one of the most sympathetic treatments Frazer received. After traveling considerably with his widowed mother, in 1910 he went to the London School of Economics. There he wrote persuasive syntheses of anthropological material concerning the Australian aborigines (also the basis of Emile Durkheim's masterpiece, *Elementary Forms of the Religious Life*, a work important to Malinowski), and began to develop a reputation for his anthropological perspicacity. Carrying out the mandatory rite de passage for all aspiring anthropologists, he spent six months in New Guinea in 1914, the written results of which earned him a D. Sc. in 1916 from the University of London. Next he visited the Trobriand Islands for two years, 1917–18, making them in the process one of the most famous of all anthropological sites. He learned the language, lived in a tent, kept a journal in Polish that revealed the deep difficulties of fieldwork, studied ceremonies, sexual relations, agricultural practices, legal systems, and kept a close eye on the gap that inevitably arises in any culture between desirable norms versus actual behaviors. As the founder of social anthropology, he traveled a great deal, influencing a broad range of intellectuals, and became a reader at the University of London in 1924, and professor from 1927, ending up at Yale because of WWII, where he soon died.

Malinowski's "anthropology" article in the *Britannica* (13th edition) explains that "functionalism" is the only proper way to interpret cultural data. His bestselling books which illustrated this concept included *Argonauts of the Western Pacific* (1922), *Sex and Repression in Savage Society* (1927), *The Sexual Life of Savages in North-Western Melanesia* (1929), and *Magic, Science and Religion and Other Essays* (1948).

SEX AND REPRESSION IN SAVAGE SOCIETY, 1927

Motherhood and the Temptations of Incest

The subject of the "origins" of incest prohibitions is one of the most discussed and vexed questions of anthropology. It is associated with the problem of exogamy or of primitive forms of marriage, with hypotheses of former promiscuity and so on. There is not the slightest doubt that exogamy is correlated with the prohibition of incest, that it is merely an extension of this taboo, exactly as the institution of the clan with its classificatory terms of relationship is simply an extension of the family and its mode of kinship nomenclature. We shall not enter into this problem, especially because in this we are in agreement with such anthropologists as Westermarck and Lowie.

To clear the ground it will be well to remember that biologists are in agreement on the point that there is no detrimental effect produced upon the species by incestuous unions. Whether incest in the state of nature might be detrimental if it occurred regularly is an academic question. In the state of nature the young animals leave the parental group at maturity and mate at random with any females encountered during rut. Incest at best can be but a sporadic occurrence. In animal incest, then, there is no biological harm nor obviously is there any moral harm. Moreover, there is no reason to suppose that in animals there is any special temptation.

While with the animal then there is neither biological danger nor temptation and in consequence no instinctive barriers against incest, with man, on the contrary, we find in all societies that the strongest barrier and the most fundamental prohibition are those against incest. This we shall try to explain not by any hypotheses about a primitive act of legislation nor by any assumptions of special aversion to sexual intercourse with inmates of the same household, but as the result of two phenomena which spring up under culture. In the first place, under the mechanisms which constitute the human family serious temptations

From *Sex and Repression in Savage Society,* by Bronislaw Malinowski. Published by Harcourt, Brace and Company. Copyright 1927.

to incest arise. In the second place, side by side with the sex temptations, specific perils come into being for the human family, due to the existence of the incestuous tendencies. On the first point, therefore, we have to agree with Freud and disagree with the well-known theory of Westermarck, who assumes innate disinclination to mate between members of the same household. In assuming, however, a temptation to incest under culture, we do not follow the psycho-analytic theory which regards the infantile attachment to the mother as essentially sexual.

This is perhaps the main thesis which Freud has attempted to establish in his three contributions to sexual theory. He tries to prove that the relations between a small child and its mother, above all in the act of suckling, are essentially sexual. From this it results that the first sexual attachment of a male towards the mother is, in other words, normally an incestuous attachment. "This fixation of libido," to use a psycho-analytic phrase, remains throughout life, and it is the source of the constant incestuous temptations which have to be repressed and as such form one of the two components of the Œdipus complex.

This theory it is impossible to adopt. The relation between an infant and its mother is essentially different from a sexual attitude. Instincts must be defined not simply by introspective methods, not merely by analysis of the feeling tones such as pain and pleasure, but above all by their function. An instinct is a more or less definite innate mechanism by which the individual responds to a specific situation by a definite form of behaviour in satisfaction of definite organic wants. The relation of the suckling to its mother is first of all induced by the desire for nutrition. The bodily clinging of a child to its mother again satisfies its bodily wants of warmth, protection and guidance. The child is not fit to cope with the environment by its own forces alone, and as the only medium through which it can act is the maternal organism it clings instinctively to the mother. In sexual relations the aim of bodily attraction and clinging is that union which leads to impregnation. Each of these two innate tendencies—the mother-to-child behaviour and the process of mating—cover a big range of preparatory and consummatory actions which present certain similarities. The line of division, however, is clear, because one set of acts, tendencies and feelings serves to complete the infant's unripe organism, to nourish, to protect and warm it; the other set of acts subserves the union of sexual organs and the production of a new individual.

We cannot therefore accept the simple solution that the temptation of incest is due to sexual relation between the infant and mother. The sensuous pleasure which is common to both relations is a component of every successful instinctive behaviour. The pleasure index cannot serve to differentiate instincts, since it is a general character of them all. But although we have to postulate different instincts for each emotional attitude yet there is one element common to them both. It is not merely that they are endowed with the general pleasure tone of all instincts, but there is also a sensuous pleasure derived from bodily contact. The active exercise of the drive which a child feels towards its mother's organism consists in the permanent clinging to the mother's body in the fullest possible epidermic contact, above all in the contact of the child's lips with the mother's nipple. The analogy between the preparatory actions of the sexual drive and the consummatory actions of the infantile impulse are remarkable. The two are to be distinguished mainly by their function and by the essential difference between the consummatory actions in each case. . . .

The father and the mother are training the child into independence and into cultural maturity; their physiological rôle is already over.

Now into such a situation the inclination towards incest would enter as a destructive element. Any approach of the mother with sensual or erotic temptations would involve the disruption of the relationship so laboriously constructed. Mating with her would have to be, as all mating must be, preceded by courtship and a type of behaviour completely incompatible with submission, independence and reverence. The mother, moreover, is not alone. She is married to another male. Any sensual temptation would not only upset completely the relation between son and mother but also, indirectly, that between son and father. Active hostile rivalry would replace the harmonious relationship which is the type of complete dependence and thorough submission to leadership. If,

therefore, we agree with the psycho-analysts that incest must be a universal temptation, we see that its dangers are not merely psychological nor can they be explained by any such hypotheses as that of Freud's primeval crime. Incest must be forbidden because, if our analysis of the family and its rôle in the formation of culture be correct, incest is incompatible with the establishment of the first foundations of culture. In any type of civilization in which custom, morals, and law would allow incest, the family could not continue to exist. At maturity we would witness the breaking up of the family, hence complete social chaos and an impossibility of continuing cultural tradition. Incest would mean the upsetting of age distinctions, the mixing up of generations, the disorganization of sentiments and a violent exchange of rôles at a time when the family is the most important educational medium. No society could exist under such conditions. The alternative type of culture under which incest is excluded, is the only one consistent with the existence of social organization and culture.

Culture and the "Complex"

. . . The process of elimination of certain attitudes and impulses from the relation between father and child and mother and child present a considerable range of possibilities. The systematic organization of impulses and emotions may be carried out by a gradual drawing off and waning from certain attitudes, by dramatic shocks, by organized ideals, as in the ceremonials, by ridicule, and public opinion. By such mechanisms we find, for instance, that sensuality is gradually eliminated from the child's relation to its mother, while often tenderness between father and child is replaced by a stern and coercive relation. The way in which these mechanisms operate does not lead to exactly the same results. And many maladjustments within the mind and in society can be traced back to the faulty cultural mechanism by which sexuality is suppressed and regulated or by which authority is imposed. This we have presented with great detail in a small number of concrete cases in the first two parts of the book. This again has been theoretically justified in this last part.

Thus the building up of the sentiments, the conflicts and maladjustments which this implies, depend largely upon the sociological mechanism which works in a given society. The main aspects of this mechanism are the regulation of infantile sexuality, the incest taboos, exogamy, the apportionment of authority and the type of household organization. In this perhaps lies the main contribution of the present memoir. We have been able to indicate the relation between biological, psychological and sociological factors. We have developed a theory of the plasticity of instincts under culture and of the transformation of instinctive response into cultural adjustment. On its psychological side our theory suggests a line of approach which, while giving full due to the influence of social factors, does away with the hypotheses of "group mind", the "collective unconscious", "gregarious instinct", and similar metaphysical conceptions.

In all this we are constantly dealing with the central problems of psycho-analysis, the problems of incest, of paternal authority, of the sexual taboo and of the ripening of the instinct. In fact the results of my argument confirm the general teachings of psycho-analysts on several points, though they imply the need of serious revision on others. Even on the concrete question of the influence of mother-right and its function, the results which I have published previously and the conclusions of this book are not entirely subversive of psycho-analytic doctrine. Mother-right, as has been remarked, possesses an additional advantage over father-right in that it "splits the Œdipus complex", dividing the authority between two males, while on the other hand it introduces a consistent scheme of incest prohibition in which exogamy follows directly from the sexual taboo within the household. We had to recognize, however, that mother-right is not altogether dependent upon the complex, that it is a wider phenomenon determined by a variety of causes. These I have tried to state concretely in order to meet Dr. Jones's objection that I assume this appearance for unknown sociological and economic reasons. I have tried to show that mother-right can be made intelligible as the more useful of the two alternative forms of reckoning kinship. The real point, as we

saw, is that the unilateral mode of counting relationship is adopted in almost all cultures but that among peoples of low cultural level the maternal line shows distinct advantage over the paternal one. Among these signal characteristic advantages of mother-right we find its power to modify and split the "complex".

~~~

FREEDOM AND CIVILIZATION, 1944

War Throughout the Ages

The real difference between free cultures and cultures pervaded by the principle of servitude and bondage is determined by whether they are constituted for the avoidance of crises, their prevention, and their alleviation; or whether their charter aims at the preparation of crises. Such latter communities at times thrive through such self-prepared crises, and use them as the means to the end of establishing more power for the rulers through discipline, bondage and slavery.

There is only one type of crisis which, starting late in evolution, has lasted throughout recorded historical times and has now plunged humanity into the worst universal calamity ever known. This is war. . . .

The anthropologist is in a position to trace the phenomena of human strife and fighting throughout the ages; from the beginnings of civilization to that new type of savagery against which we are now fighting in the hope of abolishing war forever. . . .

One or two important conclusions can be drawn. If war were really due to an innate biological urge, it would certainly occur at the earliest stages of development. For at these stages the biological needs of man are most clearly manifested in an outspoken undisguised manner. Such biological forces as hunger, sex appetite, even individual or personal pugnacity, manifest themselves most definitely at this stage. But pugnacity, as a natural reaction of anger, is directed only towards the individual guilty of violence or malice. It does not engender any collective organized fighting.

The simplest analysis of human behavior shows that aggression or pugnacity is a derived impulse. It arises from the thwarting of one of the basic physiological drives, or else from interference with culturally determined interests, appetites of desires. When sex, hunger, ambition or wealth are threatened, aggression occurs. Culture is an adaptive instrumentality which transforms and redefines even such biological imperatives as sex, hunger or the need of protection. The derived impulse of aggression is even more subject to redefinition in an infinite variety of ways. Human beings fight, not because they are biologically impelled, but because they are culturally induced, by trophies as in head-hunting, by wealth as in looting, by revenge as in primitive wars.

The ethnographer has first to register a striking fact. Aggressiveness, like charity, begins at home. At the lowest levels, we find quarrels, brawls and fighting only and exclusively among members of small, institutionally organized groups. The closer the bonds of co-operation, the greater the community of interests, the more opportunity there will be for disagreement, opposition, and hence, aggressiveness. At the same time, culture steps in at this point and produces an indispensable remedy by means of legally defined avoidance between strangers, or else by strictly determined rules of intertribal intercourse, which are typical of primitive foreign relations. If we insist that war is a fight between two independent and politically organized groups, war does not occur at a primitive level.

We see thus that there is a complete disjunction at the beginnings of human civilization between the psychological fact of aggression and the cultural fact of feuds and fights. The raw material of pugnacity certainly does exist. It is to be found primarily within the component institutions of every society. It is never a biologically determined link between an impulse of aggression and an act of organized violence.*

Hence war is not just fighting; it is not the direct expression of anger, the passion of violence, or man-to-man aggression. Fighting under the impulse of anger occurs at all levels of development in face-to-face relations, as the eternal argument by force. This aggressiveness is definitely tamed by the law of organized life.

We conclude therefore that primitive man, past or present, never used fighting or combat as an instrument of intertribal policy. He never knew genuine war. He was not, however, without virility or even pugnacity. Thus we see that war is not the original or natural state of mankind. . . .

Thus the main positive function of war is its unifying, cross-fertilizing effects and the creation of larger sized units, which thus have a greater scope for development. Conquest under such conditions leads to a natural division of functions within the larger unit. After fusion between the two groups we find a new culture, a new nation, and a new state. From one of its components this new entity receives the elements of military and political efficiency; from the other its economic qualities, its wealth and its technological development. The impact of two cultures and the process of fusion invariably promote the clearer formulation of both tribal systems of customary law. We would be safe in assuming that it is through conquest that the earliest systems of formulated codes, of established courts, and of organized police force were established. In economic organization also the conquerors, by establishing roads and communication, safeguarding safety, and policing the whole empire, stimulate commerce and the interchange of goods, the need of which is brought about by the divergence in the productive abilities of the two groups. Religious and scientific ideas are exchanged and cross-fertilize each other.

We must emphasize that when war functions creatively, the centralized political organization resumes once more its positive role as protector of the people. It is in the measure that national or tribal unity, which is established by conquest, can show a higher cultural development and political, legal and administrative efficiency that conquest becomes of real evolutionary importance. In the general appraisal of the cultural effects of war, that is, its function in the widest connotation of this word, we can say that a war which in its results produces through conquest, federation, or amalgamation a wider cultural framework may play a constructive part in human evolution. In its results, therefore, it can create a wider scope for collective and individual freedom within the new culture or the new commonwealth through this abrogation of freedom.

Note

*For a fuller analysis of pugnacity and aggressiveness, see my article, "An Anthropological Analysis of War," *American Journal of Sociology,* Vol. XLVI, No. 4, January 1941.

MARTIN BUBER

1878–1965

Son of an agronomist and a mother who was also an assimilated Jew, Martin Buber
was born in Vienna on February 8, 1878, married Paula Winckler, a non-Jewish writer
who converted, in 1901, and died in Jerusalem on June 13, 1965 at the age of 87. His
mother abandoned him and his father when he was three, so part of his search for "dialogue" and meeting of minds is perhaps an attempt to recover this lost bond. His grand-
parents raised him in Lemberg (Lviv), Ukraine, his grandfather Solomon Buber being a
monied philanthropist and amateur scholar of Jewish texts and rabbinical lore. Buber's
grandmother was committed to modernizing Judaism along Enlightenment lines.
Though immersed in Jewish culture, Buber became more entranced by Schiller's German poetry than the Talmud. Partly because of his excellent education in classics when
young, he stopped observing Jewish services during adolescence. Between 1896 and
1900, he attended the Universities of Vienna, Berlin, Leipzig, and Zürich, receiving his
doctorate from the former in 1904 with a dissertation concerning two mystics, Nicholas
of Cusa and Jakob Böhme, and their theories of the individual. Yet like so many young
thinkers of the period, he was most taken with Nietzsche's ideas, especially concerning
nihilism and the failure of modern culture.

Theodor Herzl invited him in 1910 to deal in concrete terms with his Zionism by
editing *Die Welt* (The World), the leading Zionist weekly, but political differences ended
the relationship quickly. Instead, he founded the monthly, *Der Jude*, in 1916 and ran it
until 1924, a periodical which became required reading for Jewish intellectuals. About
the same time he became a student of Hasidism, an 18th century Jewish fundamental-
ism which Buber thought could serve as a platform from which the religion could save
itself in the modern world. In 1923 he became professor at the University of Frankfurt,
and the next year he headed adult Jewish education in the city. His speeches about Judaism and politics were shut down by the Gestapo, so he fled in 1938, removing to
Palestine, where he became professor at Hebrew University until 1951, and where he
loudly opposed any policies which would separate Arab from Jew and set up an antagonistic state for either group. His most influential book is *I and Thou* (1923), a perennial
bestseller of 20th century religiosity, and also *Between Man and Man* (1947). He also
edited *Tales of the Hasidim* (1947–48), and wrote *Paths in Utopia* (1949) concerning the
successes and failures of the Israeli kibbutz movement. At his death both Jews and
Arabs mourned, for no-one else had insisted on the need for genuine dialogue and
openness between competing groups of believers in the way he had.

BETWEEN MAN AND MAN, 1929

Community

In the view customary today, which is defined by politics, the only important thing in groups, in the present as in history, is what they aim at and what they accomplish. Significance is ascribed to what goes on within them only in so far as it influences the group's action with regard to its aim. Thus it is conceded to a band conspiring to conquer the state power that the comradeship which fills it is of value, just because it strengthens the band's reliable assault power. Precise obedience will do as well, if enthusiastic drill makes up for the associates remaining strangers to one another; there are indeed good grounds for preferring the rigid system. If the group is striving even to reach a higher form of society then it can seem dangerous if in the life of the group itself something of this higher form begins to be realized in embryo. For from such a premature seriousness a suppression of the "effective" impetus is feared. The opinion apparently is that the man who whiles away his time as a guest on an oasis may be accounted lost for the project of irrigating the Sahara.

By this simplified mode of valuation the real and individual worth of a group remains as uncomprehended as when we judge a person by his effect alone and not by his qualities. The perversion of thought grows when chatter is added about sacrifice of being, about renunciation of self-realization, where possible with a reference to the favourite metaphor of the dung. Happiness, possession, power, authority, life can be renounced, but sacrifice of being is a sublime absurdity. And no moment, if it has to vouch for its relation to reality, can call upon any kind of later, future moments for whose sake, in order to make them fat, it has remained so lean.

The feeling of community does not reign where the desired change of institutions is wrested in common, but without community, from a resisting world. It reigns where the fight that is fought takes place from the position of a community struggling for its own reality as a community. But the future too is decided here at the same time; all political "achievements" are at best auxiliary troops to the effect which changes the very core, and which is wrought on the unsurveyable ways of secret history by the moment of realization. No way leads to any other goal but to that which is like it.

But who in all these massed, mingled, marching collectivities still perceives what that is for which he supposes he is striving—what community is? They have all surrendered to its counterpart. Collectivity is not a binding but a bundling together: individuals packed together, armed and equipped in common, with only as much life from man to man as will inflame the marching step. But community, growing community (which is all we have known so far) is the being no longer side by side but *with* one another of a multitude of persons. And this multitude, though it also moves towards one goal, yet experiences everywhere a turning to, a dynamic facing of, the other, a flowing from *I* to *Thou*. Community is where community happens. Collectivity is based on an organized atrophy of personal existence, community on its increase and confirmation in life lived towards one other. The modern zeal for collectivity is a flight from community's testing and consecration of the person. . . . The man of the youth movement, pondering his problems, was concerned (whatever the particular matter at different times) with his very own share in it, he "experienced" his *I* without pledging a self—in order not to have to pledge a self in response and responsibility. The man of the collective undertaking, striding to action, succeeded beforehand in getting rid of himself and thus radically escaping the question of pledging a self. Progress is nevertheless to be recorded. With the former monologue presented itself as dialogue. With the latter it is considerably simpler, for the life of monologue is by their desire driven out from most men, or they are broken of the habit; and the others, who give the orders, have at least no need to feign any dialogic.

Dialogue and monologue are silenced. Bundled together, men march without *Thou* and without *I*, those of the left who want to abolish memory, and those of the right who want to regulate it: hostile and separated hosts, they march into the common abyss. . . .

A man in the crowd is a stick stuck in a bundle moving through the water, abandoned to the current or being pushed by a pole from the bank in this or that direction. Even if it seems to the stick at times that it is moving by its own motion it has in fact none of its own; and the bundle, too, in which it drifts has only an illusion of self-propulsion. I do not know if Kierkegaard is right when he says that the crowd is untruth—I should rather describe it as non-truth since (in distinction from some of its masters) it is not on the same plane as the truth, it is not in the least opposed to it. But it is certainly "un-freedom". In what un-freedom consists cannot be adequately learned under the pressure of fate, whether it is the compulsion of need or of men; for there still remains the rebellion of the inmost heart, the tacit appeal to the secrecy of eternity. It can be adequately learned only when you are tied up in the bundle of the crowd, sharing its opinions and desires, and only dully perceiving that you are in this condition.

The man who is living with the body politic is quite different. He is not bundled, but bound. He is bound up in relation to it, betrothed to it, married to it, therefore suffering his destiny along with it; rather, simply suffering it, always willing and ready to suffer it, but not abandoning himself blindly to any of its movements, rather confronting each movement watchfully and carefully that it does not miss truth and loyalty.

Prospect, (1938) 1965

. . . The fundamental fact of human existence is neither the individual as such nor the aggregate as such. Each, considered by itself, is a mighty abstraction. The individual is a fact of existence in so far as he steps into a living relation with other individuals. The aggregate is a fact of existence in so far as it is built up of living units of relation. The fundamental fact of human existence is man with man. What is peculiarly characteristic of the human world is above all that something takes place between one being and another the like of which can be found nowhere in nature. Language is only a sign and a means for it, all

achievement of the spirit has been incited by it. Man is made man by it; but on its way it does not merely unfold, it also decays and withers away. It is rooted in one being turning to another as another, as this particular other being, in order to communicate with it in a sphere which is common to them but which reaches out beyond the special sphere of each. I call this sphere, which is established with the existence of man as man but which is conceptually still uncomprehended, the sphere of "between." Though being realized in very different degrees, it is a primal category of human reality. This is where the genuine third alternative must begin.

The view which establishes the concept of "between" is to be acquired by no longer localizing the relation between human beings, as is customary, either within individual souls or in a general world which embraces and determines them, but in actual fact *between* them.

"Between" is not an auxiliary construction, but the real place and bearer of what happens between men; it has received no specific attention because, in distinction from the individual soul and its context, it does not exhibit a smooth continuity, but is ever and again reconstituted in accordance with men's meetings with one another; hence what is experience has been annexed naturally to the continuous elements, the soul and its world. . . .

On the far side of the subjective, on this side of the objective, on the narrow ridge, where *I* and *Thou* meet, there is the realm of "between."

This reality, whose disclosure has begun in our time, shows the way, leading beyond individualism and collectivism, for the life decision of future generations. Here the genuine third alternative is indicated, the knowledge of which will help to bring about the genuine person again and to establish genuine community.

This reality provides the starting-point for the philosophical science of man; and from this point an advance may be made on the one hand to a transformed understanding of the person and on the other to a transformed understanding of community. The central subject of this science is neither the individual nor the collective but man with man. That essence of man which is special to him can be directly known only in a living relation. The gorilla, too, is an individual; a termitary, too, is a collective; but *I* and *Thou* exist only in our world, because man exists, and the *I*, moreover, exists only through the relation to the *Thou*. The philosophical science of man, which includes anthropology and sociology, must take as its starting-point the consideration of this subject, "man with man." If you consider the individual by himself, then you see of man just as much as you see of the moon; only man with man provides a full image. If you consider the aggregate by itself, then you see of man just as much as we see of the Milky Way; only man with man is a completely outlined form. Consider man with man, and you see human life, dynamic, twofold, the giver and the receiver, he who does and he who endures, the attacking force and the defending force, the nature which investigates and the nature which supplies information, the request begged and granted—and always both together, completing one another in mutual contribution, together showing forth man. Now you can turn to the individual and you recognize him as man according to the possibility of relation which he shows; you can turn to the aggregate and you recognize it as man according to the fullness of relation which he shows. We may come nearer the answer to the question what man is when we come to see him as the eternal meeting of the One with the Other.

⌒

"SOCIETY AND THE STATE," 1957

In Bertrand Russell's book on *Power*, which appeared late in 1938—the author calls it a "new social analysis"—power is defined as "the fundamental concept in social science, in the same sense in which energy is the fundamental concept in

physics." This bold concept on the part of a distinguished logician, which reminds us of Nietzsche's doctrine that he attacked so vigorously, is a typical example of the confusion between the social principle and the political principle even in our time, one hundred years after the rise of scientific sociology. It has long been recognized that all social structures have a certain measure of power, authority, and dominion, without which they could not exist; in none of the non-political structures, however, is this the essential element. But it is inherent in all social structures that men either find themselves already linked with one another in an association based on a common need or a common interest, or that they band themselves together for such a purpose, whether in an existing or a newly-formed society. The primary element must not be superseded by the secondary element—association by subordination, fellowship by domination or, schematically speaking, the horizontal structure by the vertical. The American political scientist, MacIver, has rightly said that "to identify the social with the political is to be guilty of the grossest of all confusions, which completely bars any understanding of either society or the state."

The defective differentiation between the social and the political principles, upon which the more or less problematical cooperation of all human group-existence rests, goes back to very ancient times. A classic example of mistaking the one principle for the other, though, to be sure, of a very different kind, is the well-known chapter in the *Politeia*, where Plato begins by tracing the origin of the *polis* directly from the primeval social fact of division of labour, and then, almost imperceptibly, goes on to include among the essential occupations that of the rulers, so that we suddenly find the population split up into two pre-eminently political sections: those who give orders and those who obey them; rulers and ruled; those who possess the instruments of coercion and those who are subject to them—all this under the harmless guise of the mere division of labour. We should take careful note of what Plato does here. He has his Socrates set his interlocutors the task of "seeing with their mind's eye a *polis* in the making." The readers of this dialogue naturally thought in terms of the contemporary Athens as it had emerged from the reforms of Kleisthenes—in other words, in terms of a society of free citizens who were hardly aware of the difference between the rulers and the ruled because of the constant interchange between the former and the latter within the citizenry, whereby the constituents of today became the representatives of tomorrow; and because, furthermore, the fact that the officials could be elected and dismissed obviated any feeling that an irksome bureaucracy might arise. This community, in which a firm foundation of slavery made it theoretically possible for every citizen to participate in the business of the Council while engaged in his private concerns, could, indeed, be deduced from an evolution of the division of labour—an evolution in which the vocation of politics was not specialized. However, the class—or rather the caste of the guardians—which Plato introduces into this discussion comes not within the scope of the historical *polis* but of that of his Utopia, where this caste, which has been represented to us as one vocation among others, actually stands in a political relationship to the rest of the community: that of a ruling society over against a society of the ruled. The term "society" and not a mere "group" is used here advisedly inasmuch as, in liberating its members from private property and private marriage, Plato raises it above the general community and constitutes it as a separate society.

This confusion of the social principle with the political is typical of by far the greater part of the thinking of ancient times. . . .

With Saint-Simon and Hegel we find ourselves on the threshold of modern sociology. But the society known to this sociology has become something different, namely, the society of the modern class struggle. Two men at that time undertook, each after his own fashion, to create a synthesis between Hegel and Saint-Simon. One was Lorenz von Stein, the founder of scientific sociology, and the other Karl Marx, the father of scientific socialism. The thinking of both men was so deeply rooted in the new situation that, on the crucial issue of the relationship between the social and the political principle, they were unable to take over the heritage either of Saint-Simon or of Hegel. Stein, who was a disciple of Saint-Simon's,

could not share his belief that control of the State should be taken over by the leaders of social production because he regarded society only as the main arena of human conflict. He tried to hold fast to Hegel's views concerning the overmastering and unifying function of the perfect State, but did not really succeed. Marx, who adopted Hegel's mode of thought, objected to such a function on the part of the State because, as a "superstructure," the latter was necessarily a tool in the hands of the ruling class of society, and he strove to set up in its stead a State that would pave the way for a classless society by means of a dictatorship of the lowest social order, which would then be absorbed into the classless society. Stein, who held that "the movement of opposition between the State and society was the content of the whole inner history of all the peoples," attributes supremacy to the State in terms of philosophical abstraction; but in dealing with the concrete reality he affirms society, which is shaken through and through by conflicts; his concern is with that society. Hence the science of social reality begins with Stein (and not with Comte, as some think, because the latter lags behind his master Saint-Simon in distinguishing between the social and the political principle). Marx, who evinced no particular interest in the State in his theoretical thinking, could suggest nothing but a highly centralized all-embracing and all-disposing revolutionary State which leaves no room for the social principle and so thoroughly absorbs the free society that only in a messianic vision can it be merged in it. That is why a socialist movement began with Marx in which the social principle is found only as an ultimate aim, but not in the practical scheme.

Even nowadays, in the midst of wide-ranging and extremely detailed social knowledge and planning, sociology is faced ever and again with the problem of the relationship between the social and the political principle. This relationship must not be confused with that between Society and the State because, as Tarde rightly says, there is no form of social activity which cannot, on some side or at some moment, become political; we must realize that social forms, on the one hand, and State institutions, on the other, are crystallizations of the two principles. But it is most essential that we recognize the structural difference between the two spheres in regard to the relationship between unity and multiformity.

The society of a nation is composed not of individuals but of societies, and not, as Comte thought, of families alone but of societies, groups, circles, unions, co-operative bodies, and communities varying very widely in type, form, scope, and dynamics. Society (with a capital S) is not only their collectivity and setting, but also their substance and essence; they are contained within it, but it is also within them all, and none of them, in their innermost being, can withdraw from it. In so far as the mere proximity of the societies tends to change into union, in so far as all kinds of leagues and alliances develop among them—in the social-federative sphere, that is to say—Society achieves its object. Just as Society keeps individuals together in their way of life by force of habit and custom and holds them close to one another and, by public opinion, in the sense of continuity, keeps them together in their way of thinking, so it influences the contacts and the mutual relations between the societies. Society cannot, however, quell the conflicts between the different groups; it is powerless to unite the divergent and clashing groups; it can develop what they have in common, but cannot force it upon them. The State alone can do that. The means

which it employs for this purpose are not social but definitely political. But all the facilities at the disposal of the State, whether punitive or propagandistic, would not enable even a State not dominated by a single social group (that is to say, by one relatively independent of social divarications) to control the areas of conflict if it were not for the fundamental political fact of general instability. The fact that every people feels itself threatened by the others gives the State its definitive unifying power; it depends upon the instinct of self-preservation of society itself; the latent external crisis enables it when necessary to get the upper hand in internal crises. A permanent state of true, positive, and creative peace between the peoples would greatly diminish the supremacy of the political principle over the social. This does not, however, in the least signify that in that event the power to control the internal situation of conflict would necessarily be lessened thereby. Rather is it to be assumed that if, instead of the prevailing anarchical relationships among the nations, there were co-operation in the control of raw materials, agreement on methods of manufacture of such materials, and regulation of the world market, Society would be in a position, for the first time, to constitute itself as such.

BERTRAND RUSSELL

1872–1970

Bertrand Arthur William Russell, son of Lord John (Viscount Amberley) and Katherine Stanley Russell, was born on May 18, 1872 in Trelleck, Monmouthshire, England, becoming Third Earl of Russell, Viscount Amberley in 1931. He married Alys Whitall Pearsall Smith (sister of the wit and critic Logan Pearsall Smith) of Pennsylvania in 1894, divorced 1921; Dora Winifred Black, 1921, divorced 1935, one son, one daughter; Patricia Helen Spence, 1936, divorced 1952, one son; Edith Finch, 1952. He died in Wales on February 2, 1970, not quite 98. Russell attended Trinity College, Cambridge and took first class honors toward his M.A. in 1894, where he lectured until 1916, and was fired for opposing WWI, spending 4.5 months in prison. He taught briefly at Harvard in 1914, and in Peking 1920–21. He and his wife, Dora, founded an experimental school, Beacon Hill, in Sussex (1927–32), after which he again taught at Universities of Chicago, California, Harvard, and City College of New York (though lost that job due to his heterodox beliefs). He finally worked at the Barnes Foundation in Merion, Pennsylvania (1941–42). More importantly, Russell became a voice of reason in a maddened world for most of the 20th century, even becoming an iconic figure among the youth who protested the Viet Nam War, when he was in his 90s. He was jailed at 89 while protesting the proliferation of nuclear weapons. Philosophically, he was an inventor of modern mathematical logic (with Alfred North Whitehead), an expert on Leibniz, and a popularizer of philosophical ideas in his history of Western philosophy and other books aimed at novices. He also wrote dozens of studies on marriage, politics, nuclear warfare, 19th century political and intellectual history, three volumes of autobiography, war, China, relativity, educational theory and practice, matter, divorce, power, Christianity, John Stuart Mill, war crimes in Viet Nam, two volumes of his parents' letters, and so on. He was probably the most brilliant conversationalist of his age.

In terms of social thought, Russell's contributions are many, though some are by now dated by the predominant beliefs of his era—which he fought his entire life. His ideas about private life are instructive even now, as spelled out in books like *Marriage and Morals* (1929), and his dim view of organized religion (*Why I Am Not a Christian*, 1927) and support for atheism are still read with interest. He also gave a full-dress treatment to the question of politics in *Power: A Social Analysis* (1938) and supplemented this with *Authority and the Individual* (1949). His pedagogical theorizing (which irked John Dewey) was spelled out in *Education and the Social Order* (1932). The selections below, from these books, show Russell at his characteristic best, insisting on individual rights against "the herd."

MARRIAGE AND MORALS, 1929

Romantic Love

With the victory of Christianity and the barbarians, the relations of men and women sank to a pitch of brutality which had been unknown in the ancient world for many centuries. The ancient world was vicious, but not brutal. In the Dark Ages religion and barbarism combined to degrade the sexual side of life. In marriage, the wife had no rights; outside marriage, since all was sin, there was no object in curbing the natural beastliness of the uncivilized male. The immorality of the Middle Ages was widespread and disgusting; bishops lived in open sin with their own daughters, and archbishops promoted their male favourites to neighbouring sees. There was a growing belief in the celibacy of the clergy, but practice did not keep pace with precept. Pope Gregory VII made immense exertions to cause priests to put away their concubines, yet so late as the time of Abélard we find him regarding it as possible, though scandalous, for him to marry Héloïse. It was only towards the end of the thirteenth century that the celibacy of the clergy was rigidly enforced. The clergy, of course, continued to have illicit relations with women, though they could not give any dignity or beauty to these relations owing to the fact that they themselves considered them immoral and impure. Nor could the Church, in view of its ascetic outlook on sex, do anything whatever to beautify the conception of love. To do this was necessarily the work of the laity.

> "It was not surprising that, having once broken their vows and begun to live what they deemed a life of habitual sin, the clergy should soon have sunk far below the level of the laity. We may not lay much stress on such isolated instances of depravity as that of Pope John XXIII, who was condemned for incest, among many other crimes, and for adultery; or the abbot-elect of St. Augustine, at Canterbury, who in 1171 was found, on investigation, to have seventeen illegitimate children in a single village; or an abbot of St. Pelayo, in Spain, who in 1130 was proved to have kept not less

than seventy concubines; or Henry III, Bishop of Liége, who was deposed in 1274 for having sixty-five illegitimate children; but it is impossible to resist the evidence of a long chain of Councils and ecclesiastical writers, who conspire in depicting far greater evils than simple concubinage. It was observed, that when the priests actually took wives, the knowledge that these connections were illegal was peculiarly fatal to their fidelity, and bigamy and extreme mobility of attachments were especially common among them. The writers of the middle ages are full of accounts of nunneries that were like brothels, of the vast multitude of infanticides within their walls, and of that inveterate prevalence of incest among the clergy, which rendered it necessary again and again to issue the most stringent enactments that priests should not be permitted to live with their mothers or sisters. Unnatural love, which it had been one of the great services of Christianity almost to eradicate from the world, is more than once spoken of as lingering in the monasteries; and shortly before the Reformation, complaints became loud and frequent of the employment of the confessional for the purposes of debauchery.". . .

To say that romantic love was unknown before the Middle Ages would not be correct, but it was only in the Middle Ages that it became a commonly recognized form of passion. The essential of romantic love is that it regards the beloved object as very difficult to possess and as very precious. It makes, therefore, great efforts of many kinds to win the love of the beloved object, by poetry, by song, by feats of arms, or by whatever other method may be thought most pleasing to the lady. The belief in the immense value of the lady is a psychological effect of the difficulty of obtaining her, and I think it may be laid down that when a man has no difficulty in obtaining a woman, his feeling towards her does not take the form of romantic love. Romantic love, as it appears in the Middle Ages, was not directed at first towards women with whom the lover could have either legitimate or illegitimate sexual relations; it was directed towards women of the highest respectability, who were separated, from their romantic lovers by insuperable barriers of morality and convention. So thoroughly had the Church performed its task of making men feel sex inherently impure, that it had become impossible to feel any poetic sentiment towards a lady unless she was regarded as unattainable. Accordingly love, if it was to have any beauty, had to be Platonic. It is very difficult for the modern to feel in imagination the psychology of the poet lovers in the Middle Ages. They profess ardent devotion without any desire for intimacy, and this seems to a modern so curious that he is apt to regard their love as no more than a literary convention. Doubtless on occasion it was no more than this, and doubtless its literary expression was dominated by conventions. But the love of Dante for Beatrice, as expressed in the "Vita Nuova,"is certainly not merely conventional: I should say, on the contrary, that it is an emotion more passionate than any known to most moderns. The nobler spirits of the Middle Ages thought ill of this terrestrial life; our human instincts were to them the products of corruption and original sin; they hated the body and its lusts; pure joy was to them only possible in ecstatic contemplation of a kind which seemed to them free from all sexual alloy. In the sphere of love, this outlook could not but produce the kind of attitude which we find in Dante. A man who deeply loved and respected a woman would find it impossible to associate with her the idea of sexual intercourse, since all sexual intercourse would be to him more or less impure; his love would therefore take poetic and imaginative forms, and would naturally become filled with symbolism. . . .

In quite modern times, that is to say since about the period of the French Revolution, an idea has grown up that marriage should be the outcome of romantic love. Most moderns, at any rate in English-speaking countries, take this for granted, and have no idea that not long ago it was a revolutionary innovation. The novels and plays of a hundred years ago deal largely with the struggle of the younger generation to establish this new basis for marriage as opposed to the traditional marriage of parental choice. Whether the effect has been as good as the innovators hoped may be doubted. There is something to be said for Mrs. Malaprop's principle, that love and aversion both wear off in matrimony so that it is better to begin with a little aversion. Certain it is that when people marry without previous sexual knowledge of each other and under the influence of romantic love, each imagines the other to be possessed of more than mortal perfections, and conceives that marriage is going to be one long dream of bliss. This is especially liable to be the case with the woman if she has been brought up ignorant and

pure, and therefore incapable of sex hunger from congeniality.

❧

EDUCATION AND THE SOCIAL ORDER, 1932

The Herd in Education

One of the most important factors in the formation of character is the influence of the herd upon the individual during childhood and youth. Many failures of integration in personality result from the conflict between two different herds to both of which a child belongs, while others arise from conflicts between the herd and individual tastes. It should be an important consideration in education to secure that the influence of the herd is not excessive, and that its operations are beneficial rather than harmful.

Most young people are subject to the operation of two different kinds of herd, which may be called respectively the great herd and the small herd. The great herd is one composed not exclusively of young people, but of the whole society to which the child belongs. This is determined in the main by the child's home, except where there is a very definite conflict between home and school, as happens, for example, with the children of immigrants in the United States. During the time that a boy or girl spends at school, the great herd is, however, of less importance than the small herd consisting of school-fellows. Every collection of human beings in habitual close proximity develops a herd feeling, which is shown in a certain instinctive uniformity of behaviour, and in hostility to any individual having the same proximity but not felt as one of the group. Every new boy at school has to submit to a certain period during which he is regarded with unfriendly suspicion by those who are already incorporated in the school herd. If the boy is in no way peculiar, he is presently accepted as one of the group, and comes to act as the others act, to feel as they feel, and to think as they think. If, on the other hand, he is in any way unusual, one of two things may happen: he may become the leader of the herd, or he may remain a persecuted oddity. Some very few, by combining unusual good-nature with eccentricity, may become licensed lunatics, like 'mad Shelley' at Eton.

Conventional men acquire, during their school years, that quick and almost instinctive realization of what is demanded in order to be a conventional member of the herd, which is needed for common-place respectability in later life. If a fellow-member of a club does anything which is not entirely correct, a man will remember from his boyhood the kind of treatment which was meted out to queer boys; and, while modifying his behaviour to suit the code of adult civilization, he will still keep it, in its essential pattern, what it became in those early years. This constitutes the really effective moral code to which men are subjected. A man may do things which are immoral; he may do things which are illegal; he may be callous, or brutal, or, on a suitable occasion, rude; but he must not do any of those things for which his class will cold-shoulder him. What these things are depends, of course, upon the country and the age and the social class concerned. But in every country, in every age, and in every social class, there are such things.

Fear of the herd is very deeply rooted in almost all men and women. And this fear is first implanted at school. It becomes, therefore, a matter of great importance in moral education that the things punished by the school herd shall be, as far as possible, undesirable things which it is within the boy's power to alter. But to secure this is extremely difficult. The natural code for a herd of boys is, as a rule, not a very exalted one. And among the things which they are most likely to punish are things which do not lie within the power of their victims. A boy who has a birthmark on his face, or whose breath is offensive, is likely to endure agonies at school, and not one boy in a hundred will consider that he deserves any mercy. I do not think this is inevitable. I think it is possible to teach boys a more merciful attitude, but the matter is difficult, and schoolmasters who like what is called manliness are not likely to do much in this direction.

More serious, from a social, though not from an individual, point of view, is the case of those boys whose larger herd is in some way in opposition to the smaller herd of the school, such as Jews in a school composed mainly of Gentiles. Most Jews, even in the most liberal societies, have been subjected during boyhood to insults on account of their race, and these insults remain in their memory, colouring their whole outlook upon life and society. A boy may be taught at home to be proud of being a Jew: he may know with his intellect that Jewish civilization is older than that of most Western nations, and that the contribution of Jews has been, in proportion to their numbers, incomparably greater than that of Gentiles. Nevertheless, when he hears other boys shout 'Sheeney!' or 'Ike!' after him in tones of derision, he finds it difficult to remember that it is a fine thing to be a Jew; and if he does remember it, he remembers it defiantly. In this way a discord is planted in his soul between the standards of home and the standards of school. This discord is a cause of great nervous tension, and also of a profound instinctive fear. Apart from Jewish nationalism, there are two typical reactions to this situation: one that of the revolutionary, the other that of the toady. We may take Karl Marx and Disraeli as two extreme examples of these reactions. The hatred which Karl Marx felt for the existing order it is likely he would not have felt if he had been a Gentile. But having too much intelligence to hate Gentiles as such, he transferred his hatred from Gentiles as a whole to capitalists. And since capitalists were, in fact, largely hateful, he succeeded, by viewing them with the eyes of hatred, in inventing a largely true theory of their place in the social order. Disraeli, who was a Jew in race but a Christian in religion, met the situation in another way. He admired, with the profoundest sincerity, the splendours of aristocracy and the magnificence of monarchy. There, he felt in his bones, was stability. There was safety from persecution. There was immunity from pogroms. The same fear of the hostile herd which, in Karl Marx, turned to revolution, turned in Disraeli to protective imitation. With amazing skill he made himself one of the admired herd, rose to supremacy within it, became the leader of a proud aristocracy, and the favourite of his sovereign. The keynote of his life is contained in his exclamation when the House of Commons laughed down his maiden speech: 'The time will come when you *shall* hear me!' How different is the attitude of the born aristocrat in the face of laughter is illustrated by the story of the elder Pitt, who once began a speech in the House with the words: 'Sugar, Sir—,' which caused a titter. Looking round, he repeated in louder tones: 'Sugar, Sir—,' and again there was a titter. A third time, with looks of wrath, and in a voice of thunder, he repeated: 'Sugar, Sir—.' And this time not the faintest titter was to be heard. . . .

The above illustrations are designed to suggest that the school herd is one of the most important factors in determining character, especially when it conflicts with some individual or social characteristic in a boy of exceptional talents. The man who wishes to found a good school must think more about the character of the herd which he is creating than about any other single element. If the himself is kindly and tolerant, but permits the school herd to be cruel and intolerant, the boys under his care will experience a painful environment in spite of his excellences. I think that in some modern schools the doctrine of non-interference is carried to a point where this sort of thing may easily occur. If the children are never interfered with by the adults, the bigger children are likely to establish a tyranny over the smaller ones, so that the liberty which is supposed to be the watchword of the school will exist only for an aristocracy of the physically strong. It is, however, extremely difficult to prevent the tyranny of older children by means of direct disciplinary measures. If the grown-ups exercise force in their dealings with the older children, the older children will, in turn, exercise force in their dealings with the smaller ones. The thing to be aimed at is to have as little pressure of the herd as possible, and as little dominance of physical strength as is compatible with juvenile human nature. While it is well for boys and girls to learn the lesson of social dealings with their contemporaries, it is not well for them to be subjected to too intense a herd pressure. Herd pressure is to be judged by two things: first, its intensity, and second, its direction. If it is very intense, it produces adults who are timid and conventional, except in a few rare instances. This is regrettable, however excellent may be the moral standards by which the herd is actuated.

AUTHORITY AND THE INDIVIDUAL, 1949

Individual and Social Ethics

. . . Broadly speaking, we have distinguished two main purposes of social activities: on the one hand, security and justice require centralized governmental control, which must extend to the creation of a world government if it is to be effective. Progress, on the contrary, requires the utmost scope for personal initiative that is compatible with social order.

The method of securing as much as possible of both these aims is *devolution*. The world government must leave national governments free in everything not involved in the prevention of war; national governments, in their turn, must leave as much scope as possible to local authorities. In industry, it must not be thought that all problems are solved when there is nationalization. A large industry—e.g. railways—should have a large measure of self-government; the relation of employees to the state in a nationalized industry should not be a mere reproduction of their former relation to private employers. Everything concerned with opinion, such as newspapers, books, and political propaganda, must be left to genuine competition, and carefully safeguarded from governmental control, as well as from every other form of monopoly. But the competition must be cultural and intellectual, not economic, and still less military or by means of the criminal law.

In cultural matters, diversity is a condition of progress. Bodies that have a certain independence of the state, such as universities and learned societies, have great value in this respect. It is deplorable to see, as in present-day Russia, men of science compelled to subscribe to obscurantist nonsense at the behest of scientifically ignorant politicians who are able and willing to enforce their ridiculous decisions by the use of economic and police power. Such pitiful spectacles can only be prevented by limiting the activities of politicians to the sphere in which they may be supposed competent. They should not presume to decide what is good music, or good biology, or good philosophy. I should not wish such matters to be decided in this country by the personal taste of any Prime Minister, past, present, or future, even if, by good luck, his taste were impeccable.

I come now to the question of personal ethics, as opposed to the question of social and political institutions. No man is wholly free, and no man is wholly a slave. To the extent to which a man has freedom, he needs a personal morality to guide his conduct. There are some who would say that a man need only obey the accepted moral code of his community. But I do not think any student of anthropology could be content with this answer. Such practices as cannibalism, human sacrifice, and head hunting have died out as a result of moral protests against conventional moral opinion. If a man seriously desires to live the best life that is open to him, he must learn to be critical of the tribal customs and tribal beliefs that are generally accepted among his neighbors.

But in regard to departures, on conscientious grounds, from what is thought right by the society to which a man belongs, we must distinguish between the authority of custom and the authority of law. Very much stronger grounds are needed to justify an action which is illegal than to justify one which only contravenes conventional morality. The reason is that respect for law is an indispensable condition for the existence of any tolerable social order. When a man considers a certain law to be bad, he has a right, and may have a duty, to try to get it changed, but it is only in rare cases that he does right to break it. I do not deny that there are situations in which law-breaking becomes a duty: it is a duty when a man profoundly believes that it would be a sin to obey. This covers the case of the conscientious objector. Even if you are quite convinced that he is mistaken, you cannot say that he ought not to act as his conscience dictates. When legislators are wise, they avoid, as far as possible, framing laws in such a way as to compel conscientious men to choose between sin and what is legally a crime.

I think it must also be admitted that there are cases in which revolution is justifiable. There are cases where the legal government is so bad that it is worth while to overthrow it by force in spite of the risk of anarchy that is involved. This risk is very real. It is noteworthy that the most successful revolutions—that of England in 1688 and that of America in 1776—were carried out by men who were deeply imbued with a respect for law. Where this is absent, revolution is apt to lead to either anarchy or dictatorship. Obedience to the law, therefore, though not an *absolute* principle, is one to which great weight must be attached, and to which exceptions should only be admitted in rare cases after mature consideration.

We are led by such problems to a deep duality in ethics, which, however perplexing, demands recognition.

Throughout recorded history, ethical beliefs have had two very different sources, one political, the other concerned with personal religious and moral convictions. In the Old Testament the two appear quite separately, one as the Law, the other as the Prophets. In the Middle Ages there was the same kind of distinction between the official morality inculcated by the hierarchy and the personal holiness that was taught and practiced by the great mystics. This duality of personal and civic morality, which still persists, is one of which any adequate ethical theory must take account. Without civic morality communities perish; without personal morality their survival has no value. Therefore civic and personal morality are equally necessary to a good world.

Ethics is not concerned *solely* with duty to my neighbor, however rightly such duty may be conceived. The performance of public duty is not the whole of what makes a good life; there is also the pursuit of private excellence. For Man, though partly social, is not wholly so. He has thoughts and feelings and impulses which may be wise or foolish, noble or base, filled with love or inspired by hate. And for the better among these thoughts and feelings and impulses, if his life is to be tolerable, there must be scope. For although few men can be happy in solitude, still fewer can be happy in a community which allows no freedom of individual action.

LUDWIG WITTGENSTEIN

1889–1951

Ludwig Josef Johann Wittgenstein, the youngest of eight children in a wealthy and highly cultured family, was born on April 26, 1889 in Vienna, did not marry nor reproduce (probably being homosexual), and died just after his 62nd birthday on April 29, 1951 in Cambridge, England. His father ran the largest iron and steel industry in Austria, and Johannes Brahms was a family friend, often visiting their "palace." Wittgenstein was tutored at home, attended a scientifically oriented boarding school in Linz, Austria from 14 through 17, then studied engineering at the Technical High School (a college) in Charlottenburg (Berlin) from 1906–1908. He worked as a researcher on aircraft engine design at the University of Manchester, 1908–11, and difficulties in applying math to design problems persuaded him to pursue "pure" mathematics at Trinity College, Cambridge University (1912–13). Having read Bertrand Russell's *Principles of Mathematics* (1903), he went to Cambridge to study with him. Russell, not easily impressed, regarded him as having a nonpareil mind, and the student soon exhausted the teacher's supply of information and ideas through long discussions. From there he went into seclusion in Skjolden, Norway for work on logic.

He volunteered for the Austrian Army during WWI (during which his brother, a concert pianist, lost an arm), and was decorated for bravery working in an artillery unit (1914–1918). During the war he kept a notebook of ideas, and after being captured by the Italians, he sent the manuscript to Russell. Only through Russell's help was Wittgenstein able to find a publisher for *Tractatus Logico-Philosophicus* (1922), which has long been regarded as a fundamental source in contemporary philosophy, reshaping the way everyone understands the way language works. In 1913 he had inherited a fortune from his deceased father, but in 1919 he gave it away, retired from philosophy, and became a village school teacher in Austria (1920–25). Eventually this life palled and he returned to Vienna to design his sister's mansion. Rediscovering his philosophical fire, he returned to Cambridge in 1929 and lectured there for the rest of his days when he was not in his Norwegian hut. His influence was spread by word of mouth and his students' notes, for his major work of the second period is *Philosophical Investigations* (1953), published posthumously. As revealed in the selection below, Wittgenstein was extremely concerned with ethically correct behavior (surely partly a result of his war service, and which accounts for his refusal to live as a rich man), and he turned his gargantuan intellect to problems of social life with the same passionate dedication with which he had reconstructed logic and linguistics.

LECTURES ON ETHICS, CULTURE, AND VALUE, 1966

Ethics, Life, and Faith, 1929

My subject, as you know, is Ethics and I will adopt the explanation of that term which Professor Moore has given in his book *Principia Ethica*. He says: 'Ethics is the general enquiry into what is good.' Now I am going to use the term Ethics in a slightly wider sense, in a sense in fact which includes what I believe to be the most essential part of what is generally called Aesthetics. And to make you see as clearly as possible what I take to be the subject matter of Ethics I will put before you a number of more or less synonymous expressions each of which could be substituted for the above definition, and by enumerating them I want to produce the same sort of effect which Galton produced when he took a number of photos of different faces on the same photographic plate in order to get the picture of the typical features they all had in common. And as by showing to you such a collective photo I could make you see what is the typical—say—Chinese face; so if you look through the row of synonyms which I will put before you, you will, I hope, be able to see the characteristic features they all have in common and these are the characteristic features of Ethics. Now instead of saying 'Ethics is the enquiry into what is good' I could have said Ethics is the enquiry into what is valuable, or, into what is really important, or I could have said Ethics is the enquiry into the meaning of life, or into what makes life worth living, or into the right way of living. I believe if you look at all these phrases you will get a rough idea as to what it is that Ethics is concerned with. Now the first thing that strikes one about all these expressions is that each of them is actually used in two very different senses. I will call them the trivial or relative sense on the one hand and the ethical or absolute sense on the other. If for instance I say that this is a good chair this means that the chair serves a certain predetermined purpose and the word good here has only meaning so far as this purpose has been pre-

viously fixed upon. In fact the word good in the relative sense simply means coming up to a certain predetermined standard. Thus when we say that this man is a good pianist we mean that he can play pieces of a certain degree of difficulty with a certain degree of dexterity. And similarly if I say that it is *important* for me not to catch cold I mean that catching a cold produces certain describable disturbances in my life and if I say that this is the *right* road I mean that it's the right road relative to a certain goal. Used in this way these expressions don't present any difficult or deep problems. But this is not how Ethics uses them. Supposing that I could play tennis and one of you saw me playing and said 'Well, you play pretty badly' and suppose I answered 'I know, I'm playing badly but I don't want to play any better,' all the other man could say would be 'Ah then that's all right.' But suppose I had told one of you a preposterous lie and he came up to me and said 'You're behaving like a beast' and then I were to say 'I know I behave badly, but then I don't want to behave any better,' could he then say 'Ah, then that's all right'? Certainly not; he would say 'Well, you *ought* to want to behave better.' Here you have an absolute judgment of value, whereas the first instance was one of a relative judgment. The essence of this difference seems to be obviously this: Every judgment of relative value is a mere statement of facts and can therefore be put in such a form that it loses all the appearance of a judgment of value: Instead of saying 'This is the right way to Granchester,' I could equally well have said, 'This is the right way you have to go if you want to get to Granchester in the shortest time'; 'This man is a good runner' simply means that he runs a certain number of miles in a certain number of minutes, etc. Now what I wish to contend is that, although all judgments of relative value can be shown to be mere statements of facts, no statement of fact can ever be, or imply, a judgment of absolute value. Let me explain this: Suppose one of you were an omniscient person and therefore knew all the movements of all the bodies in the world dead or alive and that he also knew all the states of mind of all human beings that ever lived, and suppose this man wrote all he knew in a big book, then this book would contain the whole description of the world; and what I want to say is, that this book would contain nothing that we would call an *ethical* judgment or anything that would logically imply such a judgment. It would of course contain all relative judgments of value and all true scientific propositions and in fact all true propositions that can be made. But all the facts described would, as it were, stand on the same level and in the same way all propositions stand on the same level. There are no propositions which, in any absolute sense, are sublime, important, or trivial. Now perhaps some of you will agree to that and be reminded of Hamlet's words: 'Nothing is either good or bad, but thinking makes it so.' But this again could lead to a misunderstanding. What Hamlet says seems to imply that good and bad, though not qualities of the world outside us, are attributes to our states of mind. But what I mean is that a state of mind, so far as we mean by that a fact which we can describe, is in no ethical sense good or bad. If for instance in our world-book we read the description of a murder with all its details physical and psychological, the mere description of these facts will contain nothing which we could call an *ethical* proposition. The murder will be on exactly the same level as any other event, for instance the falling of a stone. Certainly the reading of this description might cause us pain or rage or any other emotion, or we might read about the pain or rage caused by this murder in other people when they heard of it, but there will simply be facts, facts, and facts but no Ethics. And now I must say that if I contemplate what Ethics really would have to be if there were such a science, this result seems to me quite obvious. It seems to me obvious that nothing we could ever think or say should be *the* thing. That we cannot write a scientific book, the subject matter of which could be intrinsically sublime and above all other subject matters. I can only describe my feeling by the metaphor, that, if a man could write a book on Ethics which really was a book on Ethics, this book would, with an explosion, destroy all the other books in the world. Our words used as we use them in science, are vessels capable only of containing and conveying meaning and sense, *natural* meaning and sense. Ethics, if it is anything, is supernatural and our words will only express facts; as a teacup will only hold a teacup full of water and if I were to pour out a gallon over it. I said that so far as facts and propositions are concerned there is only relative value and relative good, right, etc. And let

me, before I go on, illustrate this by a rather obvious example. The right road is the road which leads to an arbitrarily predetermined end and it is quite clear to us all that there is no sense in talking about the right road apart from such a predetermined goal. Now let us see what we could possibly mean by the expression, '*the* absolutely right road.' I think it would be the road which *everybody* on seeing it would, *with logical necessity*, have to go, or be ashamed for not going. And similarly the *absolute good*, if it is a describable state of affairs, would be one which everybody, independent of his tastes and inclinations, would *necessarily* bring about or feel guilty for not bringing about. And I want to say that such a state of affairs is a chimera. No state of affairs has, in itself, what I would like to call the coercive power of an absolute judge. Then what have all of us who, like myself, are still tempted to use such expressions as 'absolute good,' 'absolute value,' etc., what have we in mind and what do we try to express? Now whenever I try to make this clear to myself it is natural that I should recall cases in which I would certainly use these expressions and I am then in the situation in which you would be if, for instance, I were to give you a lecture on the psychology of pleasure. What you would do then would be to try and recall some typical situation in which you always felt pleasure. For, bearing this situation in mind, all I should say to you would become concrete and, as it were, controllable. One man would perhaps choose as his stock example the sensation when taking a walk on a fine summer's day. Now in this situation I am, if I want to fix my mind on what I mean by absolute or ethical value. And there, in my case, it always happens that the idea of one particular experience presents itself to me which therefore is, in a sense, my experience *par excellence* and this is the reason why, in talking to you now, I will use this experience as my first and foremost example. (As I have said before, this is an entirely personal matter and others would find other examples more striking.) I will describe this experience in order, if possible, to make you recall the same or similar experiences, so that we may have a common ground for our investigation. I believe the best way of describing it is to say that when I have it *I wonder at the existence of the world*. And I am then inclined to use such phrases as 'how extraordinary that anything should exist' or 'how extraordinary that the world should exist.'. . . .

And I will now describe the experience of wondering at the existence of the world by saying: it is the experience of seeing the world as a miracle. Now I am tempted to say that the right expression in language for the miracle of the existence of the world, though it is not any proposition *in* language, is the existence of language itself. But what then does it mean to be aware of this miracle at some times and not at other times? For all I have said by shifting the expression of the miraculous from an expression *by means of* language to the expression *by the existence* of language, all I have said is again that we cannot express what we want to express and that all we *say* about the absolute miraculous remains nonsense. Now the answer to all this will seem perfectly clear to many of you. You will say: Well, if certain experiences constantly tempt us to attribute a quality to them which we call absolute or ethical value and importance, this simply shows that by these words we *don't* mean nonsense, that after all what we mean by saying that an experience has absolute value *is just a fact like other facts* and that all it comes to is that we have not yet succeeded in finding the correct logical analysis of what we mean by our ethical and religious expressions. Now when this is urged against me I at once see clearly, as it were in a flash of light, not only that no description that I can think of would do to describe what I mean by absolute value, but that I would reject every significant description that anybody could possibly suggest, *ab initio,* on the ground of its significance. That is to say: I see now that these nonsensical expressions were not nonsensical because I had not yet found the correct expressions, but that their nonsensicality was their very essence. For all I wanted to do with them was just *to go beyond* the world and that is to say beyond significant language. My whole tendency and I believe the tendency of all men who ever tried to write or talk Ethics or Religion was to run against the boundaries of language. This running against the walls of our cage is perfectly, absolutely hopeless. Ethics so far as it springs from the desire to say something about the ultimate meaning of life, the absolute good, the absolute valuable, can be no science. What it says does not add to our knowledge in any sense. But it is a document of a tendency in the human mind which I personally cannot help respecting deeply and I would not for my life ridicule it.

* * *

Christianity is not a doctrine, not, I mean, a theory about what has happened and will happen to the human soul, but a description of something that actually takes place in human life. For 'consciousness of sin' is a real event and so are despair and salvation through faith. Those who speak of such things (Bunyan for instance) are simply describing what has happened to them, whatever gloss anyone may want to put on it.

GEORGE HERBERT MEAD

1863–1931

His father being a theology professor and his mother late in life President of Mount Holyoke College, George Herbert Mead, was born near the campus of Mount Holyoke in South Hadley, Massachusetts on February 27, 1863. He married Helen Kingsbury Castle in 1891 and they had one son, Henry, an artist, born in 1892. At 68 Mead died in Chicago on April 26, 1931. Mead grew up in New Hampshire and Oberlin, Ohio, where he went to college, despite his father's untimely death when he was 18. He edited the *Oberlin Review* with Henry N. Castle, his future brother-in-law, and then taught public school for four months in 1883. The next year he worked as a surveyor in Minnesota for a railroad company, and then as a tutor in Minneapolis (1885–87). Mead then went to Harvard to study philosophy and psychology, took a B.A. in philosophy in 1888 with the thesis, "How Large a Share has the Subject in the Object World?" He also tutored William James's children and lived with the James family for a time. For the next two years he studied philosophy, psychology, and economics at Leipzig and Berlin (where he heard Simmel lecture), but left in 1891 without finishing his doctorate, having a job offer in the U.S. With Dewey and Cooley as colleagues, he taught philosophy and psychology at the University of Michigan until being called to the University of Chicago, just opened, in 1894, along with Dewey. He stayed there, making his way to Full Professor by 1907, meanwhile helping to create the early "Chicago School" of sociology, as well as working vigorously on Chicago area social welfare boards. Thus, he worked with W. I. Thomas and Robert Park at the University, and Jane Addams of Hull House and many others in trying to shape the vast immigrant population into a workable Chicago citizenry. He also edited *The Elementary School Teacher and Course of Study.* He was physically unable to accept Dewey's invitation to teach at Columbia University for 1931/32, a tribute to his importance in Dewey's thought.

Mead remains the most highly regarded American social theorist of the early 20th century, and because of the forceful proselytizing of his student, Herbert Blumer, the field of "symbolic interaction" that is based on Mead's ideas has thrived for a half-century. Mead wrote many professional articles but no books, so his fame rests entirely upon stenographic records of his lectures during the 20s that were dutifully transcribed and published shortly after his death. The most important is *Mind, Self, and Society* (1934), although his history of philosophy, *Movements of Thought in the Nineteenth Century* (1936) remains highly regarded, and his more properly speculative works—*Philosophy of the Present* (1932) and *Philosophy of the Act* (1938)—have given him an essential place in the history of pragmatism. For social theorists Mead's strongest contribution lies in his dialectical understanding of "the self" as it develops through interaction in the social field. The child monitors his or her behavior, adjusting it to suit the social environment, and in so doing begins to comprehend how the "I," the "me," and the larger world ("generalized other") fit together into some semblance of workable normalcy. This is closely allied to Cooley's ideas of childhood socialization, which is hardly surprising given their longterm friendship. For Mead the social world is always "emergent," as are the selves which must navigate it.

MIND, SELF, AND SOCIETY FROM THE STANDPOINT OF A SOCIAL BEHAVIORIST, 1934

Meaning

We are particularly concerned with intelligence on the human level, that is, with the adjustment to one another of the acts of different human individuals within the human social process; an adjustment which takes place through communication: by gestures on the lower planes of human evolution, and by significant symbols (gestures which possess meanings and are hence more than mere substitute stimuli) on the higher planes of human evolution.

The central factor in such adjustment is "meaning." Meaning arises and lies within the field of the relation between the gesture of a given human organism and the subsequent behavior of this organism as indicated to another human organism by that gesture. If that gesture does so indicate to another organism the subsequent (or resultant) behavior of the given organism, then it has meaning. In other words, the relationship between a given stimulus—as a gesture—and the later phases of the social act of which it is an early (if not the initial) phase constitutes the field within which meaning originates and exists. Meaning is thus a development of something objectively there as a relation between certain phases of the social act; it is not a psychical addition to that act and it is not an "idea" as traditionally conceived. A gesture by one organism, the

resultant of the social act in which the gesture is an early phase, and the response of another organism to the gesture, are the relata in a triple or threefold relationship of gesture to first organism, of gesture to second organism, and of gesture to subsequent phases of the given social act; and this threefold relationship constitutes the matrix within which meaning arises, or which develops into the field of meaning. The gesture stands for a certain resultant of the social act, a resultant to which there is a definite response on the part of the individuals involved therein; so that meaning is given or stated in terms of response. Meaning is implicit—if not always explicit—in the relationship among the various phases of the social act to which it refers, and out of which it develops. And its development takes place in terms of symbolization at the human evolutionary level.

We have been concerning ourselves, in general, with the social process of experience and behavior as it appears in the calling out by the act of one organism of an adjustment to that act in the responsive act of another organism. We have seen that the nature of meaning is intimately associated with the social process as it thus appears, that meaning involves this three-fold relation among phases of the social act as the context in which it arises and develops: this relation of the gesture of one organism to the adjustive response of another organism (also implicated in the given act), and to the completion of the given act—a relation such that the second organism responds to the gesture of the first as indicating or referring to the completion of the given act. For example, the chick's response to the cluck of the mother hen is a response to the meaning of the cluck; the cluck refers to danger or to food, as the case may be, and has this meaning or connotation for the chick.

The social process, as involving communication, is in a sense responsible for the appearance of new objects in the field of experience of the individual organisms implicated in that process. Organic processes or responses in a sense constitute the objects to which they are responses; that is to say, any given biological organism is in a way responsible for the existence (in the sense of the meanings they have for it) of the objects to which it physiologically and chemically responds. There would, for example, be no food—no edible objects—if there were no organisms which could digest it. And similarly, the social process in a sense constitutes the objects to which it responds, or to which it is an adjustment. That is to say, objects are constituted in terms of meanings within the social process of experience and behavior through the mutual adjustment to one another of the responses or actions of the various individual organisms involved in that process, an adjustment made possible by means of a communication which takes the form of a conversation of gestures in the earlier evolutionary stages of that process, and of language in its later stages.

Awareness or consciousness is not necessary to the presence of meaning in the process of social experience. A gesture on the part of one organism in any given social act calls out a response on the part of another organism which is directly related to the action of the first organism and its outcome; and a gesture is a symbol of the result of the given social act of one organism (the organism making it) in so far as it is responded to by another organism (thereby also involved in that act) as indicating that result. The mechanism of meaning is thus present in the social act before the emergence of consciousness or awareness of meaning occurs. The act or adjustive response of the second organism gives to the gesture of the first organism the meaning which it has.

Symbolization constitutes objects not constituted before, objects which would not exist except for the context of social relationships wherein symbolization occurs. Language does not simply symbolize a situation or object which is already there in advance; it makes possible the existence or the appearance of that situation or object, for it is a part of the mechanism whereby that situation or object is created. The social process relates the responses of one individual to the gestures of another, as the meanings of the latter, and is thus responsible for the rise and existence of new objects in the social situation, objects dependent upon or constituted by these meanings. Meaning is thus not to be conceived, fundamentally, as a state of consciousness, or as a set of organized relations existing or subsisting mentally outside the field of experience into which they enter; on the contrary, it should be conceived objectively, as having its existence entirely within this field itself.[13] The response of one organism to the gesture of another in any given social act is the meaning of that gesture, and also is in a sense responsible for the appearance or coming into being of the new object—or new content of an old object—to which that gesture refers through the outcome of the given social act in which it is an early phase. For, to repeat, objects are in a genuine sense constituted within the social process of experience, by the communication and mutual adjustment of behavior among the individual organisms which are involved in that process and which carry it on. Just as in fencing the parry is an interpretation of the thrust, so, in the social act, the adjustive response of one organism to the gesture of another is the interpretation of that gesture by that organism—it is the meaning of that gesture.

At the level of self-consciousness such a gesture becomes a symbol, a significant symbol. But the interpretation of gestures is not, basically, a process going on in a mind as such, or one necessarily involving a mind; it is an external, overt, physical, or physiological process going on in the actual field of social experience. Meaning can be described, accounted for, or stated in terms of symbols or language at its highest and most complex stage of development (the stage it reaches in human experience), but language simply lifts out of the social process a situation which is logically or implicitly there already. The language symbol is simply a significant or conscious gesture.

Two main points are being made here: (1) that the social process, through the communication which it makes possible among the individuals implicated in it, is responsible for the appearance of a whole set of new objects in nature, which exist in relation to it (objects, namely, of "common sense"); and (2) that the gesture of one organism and the adjustive response of another organism to that gesture within any given social act bring out the relationship that exists between the gesture as the beginning of the given act and the completion or resultant of the given act, to which the gesture refers. These are the two basic and complementary logical aspects of the social process.

The result of any given social act is definitely separated from the gesture indicating it by the response of another organism to that gesture, a response which points to the result of that act as indicated by that gesture. This situation is all there—is completely given—on the non-mental, non-conscious level, before the analysis of it on the mental or conscious level. Dewey says that meaning arises through communication.[14] It is to the content to which the social process gives rise that this statement refers; not to bare ideas or printed words as such, but to the social process which has been so largely responsible for the objects constituting the daily environment in which we live: a process in which communication plays the main part. That process can give rise to these new objects in nature only in so far as it makes possible communication among the individual organisms involved in it. And the sense in which it is responsible for their existence—indeed for the existence of the whole world of common-sense objects—is the sense in which it determines, conditions, and makes possible their abstraction from the total structure of events, as identities which are relevant for everyday social behavior; and in that sense, or as having that meaning, they are existent only relative to that behavior.

The "I" and the "Me"

We have discussed at length the social foundations of the self, and hinted that the self does not consist simply in the bare organization of social attitudes. We may now explicitly raise the question as to the nature of the "I" which is aware of the social "me." I do not mean to raise the metaphysical question of how a person can be both "I" and "me," but to ask for the significance of this distinction from the point of view of conduct itself. Where in conduct does the "I" come in as over against the "me"? If

one determines what his position is in society and feels himself as having a certain function and privilege, these are all defined with reference to an "I," but the "I" is not a "me" and cannot become a "me." We may have a better self and a worse self, but that again is not the "I" as over against the "me," because they are both selves. We approve of one and disapprove of the other, but when we bring up one or the other they are there for such approval as "me's." The "I" does not get into the limelight; we talk to ourselves, but do not see ourselves. The "I" reacts to the self which arises through the taking of the attitudes of others. Through taking those attitudes we have introduced the "me" and we react to it as an "I."

The simplest way of handling the problem would be in terms of memory. I talk to myself, and I remember what I said and perhaps the emotional content that went with it. The "I" of this moment is present in the "me" of the next moment. There again I cannot turn around quick enough to catch myself. I become a "me" in so far as I remember what I said. The "I" can be given, however, this functional relationship. It is because of the "I" that we say that we are never fully aware of what we are, that we surprise ourselves by our own action. It is as we act that we are aware of ourselves. It is in memory that the "I" is constantly present in experience. We can go back directly a few moments in our experience, and then we are dependent upon memory images for the rest. So that the "I" in memory is there as the spokesman of the self of the second, or minute, or day ago. As given, it is a "me," but it is a "me" which was the "I" at the earlier time. If you ask, then, where directly in your own experience the "I" comes in, the answer is that it comes in as a historical figure. It is what you were a second ago that is the "I" of the "me." It is another "me" that has to take that rôle. You cannot get the immediate response of the "I" in the process.[11] The "I" is in a certain sense that with which we do identify ourselves. The getting of it into experience constitutes one of the problems of most of our conscious experience; it is not directly given in experience.

The "I" is the response of the organism to the attitudes of the others; the "me" is the organized set of attitudes of others which one himself assumes. The attitudes of the others constitute the organized "me," and then one reacts toward that as an "I." I now wish to examine these concepts in greater detail.

There is neither "I" nor "me" in the conversation of gestures; the whole act is not yet carried out, but the preparation takes place in this field of gesture. Now, in so far as the individual arouses in himself the attitudes of the others, there arises an organized group of responses. And it is due to the individual's ability to take the attitudes of these others in so far as they can be organized that he gets self-consciousness. The taking of all of those organized sets of attitudes gives him his "me"; that is the self he is aware of. He can throw the ball to some other member because of the demand made upon him from other members of the team. That is the self that immediately exists for him in his consciousness. He has their attitudes, knows what they want and what the consequence of any act of his will be, and he has assumed responsibility for the situation. Now, it is the presence of those organized sets of attitudes that constitutes that "me" to which he as an "I" is responding. But what that response will be he does not know and nobody else knows. Perhaps he will make a brilliant play or an error. The response to that situation as it appears in his immediate experience is uncertain, and it is that which constitutes the "I."

The "I" is his action over against that social situation within his own conduct, and it gets into his experience only after he has carried out the act. Then he is aware of it. He had to do such a thing and he did it. He fulfils his duty and he may look with pride at the throw which he made. The "me" arises to do that duty—that is the way in which it arises in his experience. He had in him all the attitudes of others, calling for a certain response; that was the "me" of that situation, and his response is the "I.". . .

The "I," then, in this relation of the "I" and the "me," is something that is, so to speak, responding to a social situation which is within the experience of the individual. It is the answer which the individual makes to the attitude which others take toward him when he assumes an attitude toward them. Now, the attitudes he is taking toward them are present in his own experience, but his response to them will contain a novel element. The "I" gives the sense of freedom, of initiative. The situation is there for us to act in a self-conscious fashion. We are aware of ourselves, and of what the situation is, but exactly how we will act never gets into experience until after the action takes place.

Such is the basis for the fact that the "I" does not appear in the same sense in experience as does the "me." The "me" represents a definite organization of the community there in our own attitudes, and calling for a response, but the response that takes place is something that just happens. There is no certainty in regard to it. There is a moral necessity but no mechanical necessity for the act. When it does take place then we find what has been done. The above account gives us, I think, the relative position of the "I" and "me" in the situation, and the grounds for the separation of the two in behavior. The two are separated in the process but they belong together in the sense of being parts of a whole. They are separated and yet they belong together. The separation of the "I" and the "me" is not fictitious. They are not identical, for, as I have said, the "I" is something that is never entirely calculable. The "me" does call for a certain sort of an "I" in so far as we meet the obligations that are given in conduct itself, but the "I" is always something different from what the situation itself calls for. So there is always that distinction, if you like, between the "I" and the "me." The "I" both calls out the "me" and responds to it. Taken together they constitute a personality as it appears in social experience. The self is essentially a social process going on with these two distinguishable phases. If it did not have these two phases there could not be conscious responsibility, and there would be nothing novel in experience.

Notes

13. Nature has meaning and implication but not indication by symbols. The symbol is distinguishable from the meaning it refers to. Meanings are in nature, but symbols are the heritage of man (1924).

14. [See *Experience and Nature,* chap. v.]

11. The sensitivity of the organism brings parts of itself into the environment. It does not, however, bring the life-process itself into the environment, and the complete imaginative presentation of the organism is unable to present the living of the organism. It can conceivably present the conditions under which living takes place but not the unitary life-process. The physical organism in the environment always remains a thing (MS).

KARL JASPERS

1883–1969

The son of a lawyer/bank director, Karl Theodor Jaspers was born in Oldenburg, near Bremen, Germany on February 23, 1883. He married Gertrud Mayer in 1910, a gifted Jewish intellectual who was linguistically and philosophically capable of being her husband's most trusted debater and colleague. Jaspers died from a stroke in Basel, Switzerland on February 26, 1969, having reached his 86th birthday. He came from a long line of farmers and merchants who valued Kantian morality but were not necessarily attuned to organized religion. In high school he alone resisted the principal's pressure to join a fraternity based on social class distinctions rather than true friendship. In his 19th year he learned that he suffered from bronchiectasis leading to cardiac decompensation, which made physically strenuous activity or sleepless nights of scholarship impossible, for he expected to die from this incurable malady at middle age. He therefore rigorously controlled his output of energy and worked with extreme efficiency. Unhappy with legal fictions and philosophers' pretensions (at the universities of Heidelberg, Munich, Göttingen, and Berlin), he decided to learn something concrete and took a medical degree at Berlin in 1909. He then worked for four years at the Heidelberg psychiatric hospital as a researcher, and published *General Psychopathology* in 1913, which went through seven editions. He became friends at Heidelberg with Max Weber, "the greatest German of our age," as Jaspers called him, enemies of Heinrich Rickert and others, and generally went his own way. Despite this fiercely independent posture, he won a professorship at Heidelberg over the philosophy department's objections, but then published nothing from 1923 to 1931. Suddenly he published two masterpieces, *Man in the Modern Age* (1931), which inspired a Habermas response 50 years later, and his three-volume *Philosophy* (1932). He was prevented from teaching by the Nazis because his wife was Jewish and because of his resistance to fascism. While housebound, he wrote a four-volume history of philosophy that is still read, and they were both saved from the Holocaust when Americans entered Heidelberg in 1945, two weeks before he and his wife were to be sent to a camp. After the war he taught in Basel, and became the universally admired "good German," while his books on atomic warfare, global peace, German war guilt, and existential philosophy became world-wide bestsellers.

Jasper's *Existenzphilosophie* is famously difficult because of a special jargon he invented, a mixture of Husserl's phenomenology and his own formulations. Yet when he turned to social issues, as he did increasingly as he aged, he wrote lucidly and persuasively. The selection below on the politics of "the masses" and loss of individual autonomy is a case in point.

MAN IN THE MODERN AGE, 1931

Mass-Rule

The technical life-order and the masses are closely interrelated. The huge machinery of social provision must be adapted to the peculiarities of the masses; its functioning, to the amount of labour power available; its output, to the demands of the consumers. We infer, therefore, that the masses must rule, and yet we find that they cannot rule.

Peculiarities of the Masses. The term 'masses' is ambiguous. If we mean an undifferentiated aggregate of contemporary persons in a particular situation and forming a unity because they are all under the stress of the same affects, it is plain that such an aggregate can only exist for a brief space of time. If we use the word 'masses' as a synonym for the 'public', this denotes a group of persons mentally interlinked by their common reception of certain opinions, but a group vague in its limits and its stratification, though at times a typical historical product. The 'masses', however, as an aggregate of persons who are articulated in some apparatus of the life-order in such a manner that the will and the peculiarities of the majority among them are decisive, constitute the unceasingly operative and effective power in our world—the power which manifests itself no more than transiently in the 'public' or in a 'mob'.

The peculiarities of the masses as the fleeting unity of a mob or crowd have been ably analysed by Gustav le Bon as impulsiveness, suggestibility, intolerance, and mutability. The 'public' is a phantom, the phantom of an opinion supposed to exist in a vast number of persons who have no effective interrelation and though the opinion is not effectively present in the units. Such an opinion is spoken of as 'public opinion', a fiction which is appealed to by individuals and by groups as supporting their special views. It is impalpable, illusory, transient; ''tis here, 'tis there, 'tis gone'; a nullity which can nevertheless for a moment

endow the multitude with power to uplift or to destroy.

The peculiarities of the masses articulated in an apparatus are not uniform. The manual worker, the salaried employee, the doctor, the lawyer, do not as such combine to form the masses; each is a potential individual; but the proletariat, the general body of the medical profession, the teaching staff of a university—these respectively combine to form an articulated 'mass' insofar as in actual fact the majority of the corporation decides the nature, the actions, the resolves of all its members. One might expect that the average qualities of human nature would everywhere prevail. What the 'mass-man' on the average is, is disclosed in what most people do; in what is usually bought and consumed; in what one can generally expect when one has to deal with people 'in the mass'—as apart from the 'fads' of individuals, just as the budget of a private household throws light upon the tastes of the members of that household, so does the budget of a State (to the extent that the majority decides) disclose the tastes of the bulk of its citizens. If we know how much money an individual has to spend, we can infer his peculiarities when he tells us 'I cannot afford this, but I can afford that'. Contact with many persons teaches us what, on the average, we can expect from them. For millenniums, judgments in these respects have been remarkably similar. People 'in the mass' would seem to be guided by the search for pleasure and to work only under the crack of the whip or when impelled by a craving for bread and for dainties; yet they are bored when they have nothing to do, and have a perpetual craving for novelty.

An articulated mass, however, has other qualities than these. In that sense there is no 'mass' of all mankind; there are only diverse masses which form, dissolve, and reform. The corporations which, by tranquil efficiency or by organised voting, decide what shall happen, are articulated masses when within each of them the individual counts only as a unit among many having like powers. Yet these articulated masses are mutable, diversified, transitory expressions of some specific historical outcome of human existence. Articulated masses can, however, express themselves at times in other than average ways, showing themselves capable on these occasions of the unusual. Although as a rule the mass is stupider and less cultivated than the individual, in exceptional instances it may excel the individual in shrewdness and profundity.

Importance of the Masses. Man as member of a mass is no longer his isolated self. The individual is merged in the mass, to become something other than he is when he stands alone. On the other hand in the mass the individual becomes an isolated atom whose individual craving to exist has been sacrificed, since the fiction of a general equality prevails. Yet each individual continues to say to himself: 'What another has, I also want; what another can do, I also can do.' In secret, therefore, envy persists, and so does the longing to enjoy by having more and being of more importance than others.

This inevitable mass-effect is intensified today by the complicated articulations of a modern economic society. The rule of the masses affects the activities and habits of the individual. It has become obligatory to fulfill a function which shall in some way be regarded as useful to the masses. The masses and their apparatus are the object of our most vital interest. The masses are our masters; and for every one who looks facts in the face his existence has become dependent on them, so that the thought of them must control his doings, his cares, and his duties. He may despise them in their average aspects; or he may feel that the solidarity of all mankind is destined some day to become a reality; or he may, while not denying the responsibility which each man has for all, still hold more or less aloof, but it remains a responsibility he can never evade. He belongs to the masses, though they threaten to let him founder amid rhetoric and the commotions of the multitude. Even an articulated mass always tends to become unspiritual and inhuman. It is life without existence, superstition without faith. It may stamp all flat; it is disinclined to tolerate independence and greatness, but prone to constrain people to become as automatic as ants.

When the titanic apparatus of the mass-order has been consolidated, the individual has to serve it, and must from time to time combine with his fellows in order to renovate it. If he wants to make his livelihood by intellectual activity, he will find it very difficult to do this except by satisfying the needs of the many. He must give currency to something that will please the crowd. They seek satisfaction in the pleasures of the table, eroticism, self-assertion; they find no joy in life if one of these gratifications be curtailed. They also desire some means of self-knowledge. They desire to be led in such a way that they can fancy themselves leaders. Without wishing to be free, they would fain be accounted free. One who would please their taste must produce what is really average and commonplace, though not frankly styled such; must glorify or at least justify something as universally human. Whatever is beyond their understanding is uncongenial to them.

One who would influence the masses must have recourse to the art of advertisement. The clamour of puffery is to-day requisite even for an intellectual movement. The days of quiet and unpretentious activity seem over and done with. You must keep yourself in the public eye, give lectures, make speeches, arouse a sensation. Yet the mass-apparatus lacks true greatness of representation, lacks solemnity. No one believes in festal celebrations, not even the participants. In the Middle Ages, the Pope sometimes made a quasi-royal progress through Europe; but we can hardly conceive such a thing today in (let us suppose) the United States, the present chief centre of world-power. The Americans would not take the successor of St. Peter seriously!

The Tension Between Technical Mass-Order and Human Life

Limits are imposed upon the life-order by a specifically modern conflict. The mass-order brings into being a universal life-apparatus, which proves destructive to the world of a truly human life.

Man lives as part of a social environment to which he is bound by remembered and prospective ties. Men do not exist as isolated units, but as members of a family in the home; as friends in a group; as parts of this, that, or the other 'herd' with well-known historical origins. He has become what he is thanks to a tradition which enables him to look back into the obscurity of his beginnings and makes him responsible for his own future and that of his associates. Only in virtue of a long view before and after does he acquire a substantial tenure in that world which he constructs out of his heritage from the past. His daily life is permeated by the spirit of a perceptibly present world which, however small, is still something other than himself. His inviolable property is a narrow space, the ownership of which enables him to share in the totality of human history.

The technical life-order which came into being for the supply of the needs of the masses did at the outset preserve these real worlds of human creatures, by furnishing them with commodities. But when at length the time arrived when nothing in the individual's immediate and real environing world was any longer made, shaped, or fashioned by that individual for his own purposes; when everything that came, came merely as the gratification of momentary need, to be used up and cast aside; when the very dwelling-place was machine-made, when the environment had become despiritualised, when the day's work grew sufficient to itself and ceased to be built up into a constituent of the worker's life—then man was, as it were, bereft of his world. Cast adrift in this way, lacking all sense of historical continuity with past or future, man cannot remain man. The universalisation of the life-order threatens to reduce the life of the real man in a real world to mere functioning.

But man as individual refuses to allow himself to be absorbed into a life-order which would only leave him in being as a function for the maintenance of the whole. True, he can live in the apparatus with the aid of a thousand relationships on which he is dependent and in which he collaborates; but since he has become a mere replaceable cog in a wheelwork regardless of his individuality, he rebels if there is no other way in which he can manifest his selfhood. . . .

These tendencies towards the break-up of the home are all the more menacing since they arise, through an inevitable development, out of the very being of the individuals who are to be found in family groups, those islands which still stand firm against the stream of the universal life-order. Marriage is one of the most thorny problems which contemporary man has to handle. It is impossible to foresee how many persons will be found constitutionally incompetent for the task. Numerous, beyond question, will be those who, losing that contact with the public and authorita-

tive spirit which is necessary to their selfhood, will plunge into fathomless waters. It has further to be remembered that marriage has of late been rendered more difficult by the emancipation of woman and the growth of her economic independence, so that there is now an enormous supply of unmarried women ready and willing to gratify the sexual desires of the male. In many instances marriage is at best a contract, a breach of which on the part of the husband will entail only the conventional punishment of alimony. Increasing licence is attended by a demand for the facilitation of divorce. A sign of the disruption of connubial ties is the multiplication of books on marriage.

In view of this disorder, it has become the aim of the universal life-order to re-establish order in a domain where order can only be achieved by the individual through freedom and in consequence of the essential worth of his being, enlightened by education. Because erotic indulgence has been tending to loosen all ties, the rationalised life-order has endeavoured to master this perilous nonrationality. Even the sexual life is being technicised by the prescriptions of hygiene and all kinds of regulations for its skillful management, that it may become as pleasurable and free from conflicts as possible. Such a book as Van de Velde's *Ideal Marriage*, aiming as it does at the sexualisation of the conjugal union, is symptomatic of our time and of the attempt to rob the nonrational of its sting. We cannot but regard as significant the fact that in the prospectus of this work even Catholic theologians are found to recommend it. Both by the religious degradation of marriage to a life of the second order (a life which only by ecclesiastical sanction can be saved from the stigma of unchastity), and by the technicisation of love as a dangerous non-rationality, is the unconditionality that realises itself in marriage involuntarily but radically denied. Religion and technique here join forces unaware, in a campaign against love as the foundation of marriage. Thus regarded, marriage has no need of legitimation, for, being of existential origin, it has the unconditionality of life-determining fidelity—which will perhaps only ensure erotic happiness for casual moments. Love which is assured of itself solely through the freedom of existence has absorbed eroticism into itself, without degrading it and without recognising its lustful demands.

He who has jettisoned the ties of family and selfhood instead of developing them from their roots into an aggregate, can only live in the anticipated but ever-elusive spirit of the mass. If I do this, I fix my eyes on the universal life-order in the endeavour to attain everything thereby, while betraying my own true world and abandoning my claim to it. The home crumbles when I no longer confide in it, living only as class and as community of interests and as function in an enterprise, and pushing whithersoever I think that power inheres. What is only attainable through the whole does not absolve me from the demand that I should also effectively undertake such things as are primarily attainable through my own initiative.

The limit to the universal life-order is, therefore, imposed by the freedom of the individual who must (if human beings are to remain human beings) evoke from his own self that which no other can evoke from him.

Dread of Life. In the rationalisation and universalisation of the life-order there has grown contemporaneously with its fantastic success an awareness of imminent ruin tantamount to a dread of the approaching end of all that makes life worth living. Not only does the apparatus seem, by its perfectionment, to threaten the annihilation of everything, even the apparatus itself is menaced. A paradox results. Man's life has become dependent upon the apparatus which proves ruinous to mankind at one and the same time by its perfectionment and by its breakdown.

OSWALD SPENGLER

1880–1936

Eldest of four children and the only boy, Oswald Spengler was born on May 29, 1880 in Blankenburg, Germany, did not marry, and died on May 8, 1936 in Munich, not quite 56. His father was trained in mining technology, but provided for the family through a position in the German postal system. Spengler's mother came from an artistic family. In addition to anxiety attacks, he began to suffer migraines when young which troubled him lifelong. At ten his family moved to Halle, where he took the conventional *gymnasium* curriculum of Greek, Latin, science, and math, then went to the local University before moving to Munich and Berlin where he fell under the influence of Goethe and Nietzsche. Despite his father's death when he was 21, he was able to attend college through the kindness of an aunt. His doctorate was from Halle in 1904, with a dissertation on Heraclitus. Failing his comprehensive exams for lack of sufficiently detailed bibliographical references in his work, he passed on the second attempt in 1904. His habilitation, permitting him to teach, was "The Development of the Organ of Sight in the Higher Realms of the Animal Kingdom." He worked as a schoolmaster from 1904–11 in Saarbrücken, Düsseldorf, and Hamburg, teaching German literature, science, math, and history. But he did not care for the work, so when his inheritance became available in 1911, he quit teaching and worked independently in Munich. At first he wrote about topical political matters focusing on the Great Powers' arms competition, and quickly understood that Europe was on the road to self-destruction, a notion proved right by The Great War, so he thought. Having invested his inheritance in foreign securities, by 1917 he was penniless, but he was ready to publish the first volume of his great work in 1918, finally finding a willing publisher. Everyone was shocked at its success, very much the right message at the right time: *The Decline of the West: Form and Actuality.* He became a celebrity, even visiting and debating with Max Weber, the leading social scientist of the era. He theorized the reasons for alleged cultural decline, and the public accepted his tale. Academic historians, however, dismissed his work as more poetry and spiritualism than bona fide historical research. In 1922 a revised version of Volume 1 appeared, and in 1923, Volume 2, *Perspectives of World History.*

Spengler rejected linear explanations of history in favor of cycles. He believed that history revealed eight periods during which "high culture" predominated, each one characterized by a "prime symbol," which he explained in detail. The West's symbol was "the Faustian Soul" (from Goethe's *Faustus*), which led to its inevitable collapse—followed by rebirth and rematuration over time. Spengler also wrote *Man and Technics* (1932), from which the selection reprinted below comes, where he restated in simplified form, and free of the stupendous documentation offered in his major work, his principal arguments about the likely prospects for modern societies. His work resonated perfectly with the dark public mood of the interwar years in Europe, as well as in the U.S., where the book became a bestseller, even in an expensive two-volume edition. In 1959 it was abridged to a single volume in German, then offered in English in 1961.

MAN AND TECHNICS: A CONTRIBUTION TO A PHILOSOPHY OF LIFE, 1931

. . . Every high Culture *is* a tragedy. The history of mankind *as a whole* is tragic. But the sacrilege and the catastrophe of the Faustian are greater than all others, greater than anything Æschylus or Shakespeare ever imagined. The creature is rising up against its creator. As once the microcosm Man against Nature, so now the microcosm Machine is revolting against Nordic Man. The lord of the World is becoming the slave of the Machine, which is forcing him—forcing us all, whether we are aware of it or not—to follow its course. The victor, crashed, is dragged to death by the team.

At the commencement of the twentieth century the aspect of the "world" on this small planet is somewhat of this sort. A group of nations of Nordic blood under the leadership of British, Germans, French, and Americans commands the situation. Their political power depends on their *wealth*, and their wealth consists in their *industrial* strength. . . .

But it is of the tragedy of the time that this unfettered human thought can no longer grasp its own consequences. Technics has become as esoteric as the higher mathematics which it uses, while physical theory has refined its intellectual abstractions from phenomena to such a pitch that (without clearly perceiving the fact) it has reached the pure foundations of human knowing.[1] *The mechanization of the world* has entered on a phase of highly dangerous over-tension. The picture of the earth, with its plants, animals, and men, has altered. In a few decades most of the great forests have gone, to be turned into news-print, and climatic changes have been thereby set afoot which imperil the land-economy of whole populations. Innumerable animal species have been extinguished, or nearly so, like the bison; whole races of humanity have been brought almost to vanishing-point, like the North American Indian and the Australian.

From *Man and Technics: A Contribution to a Philosophy of Life*, by Oswald Spengler, Charles Francis Atkinson, Trans. Published by Alfred A. Knopf, Inc. Copyright 1932.

All things organic are dying in the grip of organization. An artificial world is permeating and poisoning the natural. The Civilization itself has become a machine that does, or tries to do, everything in mechanical fashion. We think only in horse-power now; we cannot look, at a waterfall without mentally turning it into electric power; we cannot survey a countryside full of pasturing cattle without thinking of its exploitation as a source of meat-supply; we cannot look at the beautiful old handwork of an unspoilt primitive people without wishing to replace it by a modern technical process. Our technical thinking *must* have its actualization, sensible or senseless. The luxury of the machine is the consequence of a necessity of thought. In last analysis, the machine is a *symbol*, like its secret ideal, perpetual motion—a spiritual and intellectual, but no vital necessity. . . .

But *how long* will it stay on these heights? Even on the present scale our technical processes and installations, if they are to be maintained, require, let us say a hundred thousand outstanding brains, as organizers and discoverers and engineers. These must be strong—nay, even creative—talents, enthusiasts for their work, and formed for it by a steeling of years' duration at great expense. Actually, it is just this calling that has for the last fifty years irresistibly attracted the strongest and ablest of the white youth. Even the children play with technical things. In the urban classes and families, whose sons chiefly come into consideration in this connexion, there was already a tradition of comfort and culture, so that the normal preconditions were already provided for that mature and autumnal product, technical intellectuality.

But all this is changing in the last decades, in all the countries where large-scale industry is of old standing. The Faustian thought begins to be sick of machines. A weariness is spreading, a sort of pacifism of the battle with Nature. Men are returning to forms of life simpler and nearer to Nature; they are spending their time in sport instead of technical experiments. The great cities are becoming hateful to them, and they would fain get away from the pressure of soulless facts and the clear cold atmosphere of technical organization. And it is precisely the strong and creative talents that are turning away from practical problems and sciences and towards pure speculation. Occultism and Spiritualism, Hindu philosophies, metaphysical inquisitiveness under Christian or pagan colouring, all of which were despised in the Darwinian period, are coming up again. It is the spirit of Rome in the Age of Augustus. Out of satiety of life, men take refuge from civilization in the more primitive parts of the earth, in vagabondage, in suicide. *The flight of the born leader from the Machine is beginning.* Every big entrepreneur has occasion to observe a falling off in the intellectual qualities of his recruits. But the grand technical development of the nineteenth century had been possible only because the intellectual level was constantly becoming higher. Even a stationary condition, short of an actual falling-off, is dangerous and points to an ending, however numerous and however well schooled may be the hands ready for work.

And how is it with them? The tension between work of leadership and work of execution has reached the level of a catastrophe. The importance of the former, the economic value of every real personality in it, has become so great that it is invisible and incomprehensible to the majority of the underlings. In the latter, the work of the hands, the individual is now *entirely* without significance. Only numbers matter. In the consciousness of this unalterable state of things, aggravated, poisoned, and financially exploited by egoistic orators and journalists, men are so forlorn that it is mere human nature to revolt against the rôle for which the machine (not, as they imagine, its pos-

sessors) ear-marks most of them. There is beginning, in numberless forms—from sabotage, by way of strike, to suicide—*the mutiny of the Hands against their destiny,* against the machine, against the organized life, against anything and everything. The organization of work, as it has existed for thousands of years, based on the idea of "collective doing" and the consequent division of labour between leaders and led, heads and hands, is being disintegrated from below. But "mass" is no more than a negation (specifically, a negation of the concept of organization) and not something viable in itself. An army without officers is only a superfluous and forlorn herd of men. A chaos of brickbats and scrap-iron is a building no more. This mutiny, world-wide, threatens to put an end to the *possibility* of technical economic work. The leaders may take to flight, but the led, become superfluous, are lost. Their numbers are their death. . . .

We are born into this time and must bravely follow the path to the destined end. There is no other way. Our duty is to hold on to the lost position, without hope, without rescue, like that Roman soldier whose bones were found in front of a door in Pompeii, who, during the eruption of Vesuvius, died at his post because they forgot to relieve him. That is greatness. That is what it means to be a thoroughbred. The honourable end is the one thing that can not be taken from a man.

Notes

1. *Decline of the West,* English edition, Vol. 1, pp. 420 et seq.

GEORGES BATAILLE

1897–1962

Son of a blind, syphilitic father who became paralyzed from the disease when his son was only three, Georges Bataille (pseudonyms: Lord Auch, Pierre Angélique, Louis Trente) was born on September 10, 1897 in Billom, Puy-de-Dôme, France, married the actress Silvia Maklès (divorced, 1934) (who later married Jacques Lacan), then married Diane de Beauharnais in 1946, with whom he had one daughter. In between the two he had a relationship with Colette Peignot, who died in 1938. After 64 years he died in Paris on July 8, 1962, probably from tuberculosis. Bataille's parents were atheists, so he decided to join the Catholic priesthood when young, but then withdrew from its ranks. Tuberculosis kept him out of combat during WWI, after which he studied medieval history at the École des Chartes, graduating in 1922 with a thesis on thirteenth-century verse. He then went to Madrid on a research fellowship, and while there saw a bullfighter's death in the ring which caused him to begin thinking about the connection between violence and eroticism. Returning to Paris, he worked at the Bibliothèque Nationale for the next 20 years, rising in the ranks to deputy keeper and editor of *Documents*. After flirting with surrealism and considering the cultural implications of psychoanalysis, Bataille "began to write seriously" in 1927 with the erotic novel, *Story of the Eye* (1928; English tr., 1967). Meanwhile, he also founded a range of scholarly and political/cultural journals, along with which he and others began the so-called Collège de Sociologie in 1939. In 1946 he founded the influential journal *Critique,* and edited it until his death. In his various editorial capacities, he was the first to publish Foucault, Derrida, Barthes, and others.

He began to pursue his primary interest, the connection of the erotic, the obscene, orgiastic enthusiasms, and the accompanying annihilation of the "rational" self in a paroxysm of lived experience. After his "day-job" as librarian was concluded, he made regular use of female whores, as much for the erotic experience as for material about which to write, an activity which caused him professional troubles at the Bibliotèque and led, along with his tuberculosis, to his leaving that post in 1944. He took other library jobs, but was always short of funds, which led Picasso, Miro, and Max Ernst to sell some of their works in 1961 to benefit him. His final book, *The Tears of Eros* (1961), was banned in France by André Malraux in his role of culture minister because of graphic representation of torture in China. Bataille was writing with thoughts of his daughter's arrest on political charges in Algeria. His *The Accursed Share* (1947; tr. 1988, 3 vols) and *Theory of Religion* (tr. 1988) fit well with the mindset of the 1980s and 90s and have influenced a range of social theorists.

"THE PSYCHOLOGICAL STRUCTURE OF FASCISM," 1933

The Homogeneous Part of Society

A psychological description of society must begin with that segment which is most accessible to understanding—and apparently the most fundamental—whose significant trait is tendential homogeneity. *Homogeneity* signifies here the commensurability of elements and the awareness of this commensurability: human relations are sustained by a reduction to fixed rules based on the consciousness of the possible identity of delineable persons and situations; in principle, all violence is excluded from this course of existence.

Production is the basis of social *homogeneity*. *Homogeneous* society is productive society, namely useful society. Every useless element is excluded, not from all of society, but from its *homogeneous* part. In this part, each element must be useful to another without the homogeneous activity ever being able to attain the form of activity *valid in itself*. A useful activity has a common measure with another useful activity, but not with activity *for itself*.

The common measure, the foundation of social *homogeneity* and of the activity arising from it, is money, namely the calculable equivalent of the different products of collective activity. Money serves to measure all work, and makes man a function of measurable products. According to the judgment of *homogeneous* society, each man is worth what he produces; in other words, he stops being an existence *for itself*. He is no more than a function, arranged within measurable limits, of collective production (which makes him an existence *for something other than itself*).

But the *homogeneous* individual is truly a function of his personal products only in artisanal production, where the means of production are relatively inexpensive and can be owned by the artisan. In industrial civilization, the producer is distinguished from the owner of the means of pro-

duction, and it is the latter who appropriates the products for himself: consequently, it is he who, in modern society, is the function of the products; it is he—and not the producer—who founds social *homogeneity*.

Thus in the present order of things, the *homogeneous* part of society is made up of those men who own the means of production or the money *destined for their upkeep or purchase*. It is exactly in the middle segment of the so-called capitalist or bourgeois class that the tendential reduction of human character takes place, making it an abstract and interchangeable entity: a reflection of the *homogeneous things* the individual owns.

This reduction is then extended as much as possible to the so-called middle classes that variously benefit from realized profit. But the industrial proletariat remains for the most part irreducible. It maintains a double relation to homogeneous activity: the latter excludes it—not from work but from profit. As agents of production, the workers fall within the framework of the social organization, but the homogeneous reduction as a rule only affects their wage-earning activity; they are integrated into the psychological *homogeneity* in terms of their behaviour on the job, but not generally as men. Outside of the factory, and even beyond its technical operations, a labourer is, with regard to a *homogeneous* person (boss, bureaucrat, etc.), a stranger, a man of another nature, of a non-reduced, non-subjugated nature.

The Fundamental Conditions of Fascism

As has already been indicated, *heterogeneous* processes as a whole can only enter into play once the fundamental *homogeneity* of society (the apparatus of production) has become dissociated because of its internal contradictions. Further, it can be stated that, even though it generally occurs in he blindest fashion, the development of heterogeneity necessarily comes to signify a solution to the problem posed by the contradictions of *homogeneity*. Once in power, developed *heterogeneous* forces dispose of the means of coercion necessary to resolve the differences that had arisen between previously irreconcilable elements. But it goes without saying that, at the end of a movement that excludes all subversion, the thrust of these resolutions will have been consistent with the general direction of the existing homogeneity, namely, with the interests of the capitalists.

The change resides in the fact that, having had recourse to fascist *heterogeneity*, these interests, from the moment of crisis on, are those of a group opposed to privately owned enterprises. As a result, the very structure of capitalism—the principle of which had been that of a spontaneous *homogeneity* of production based on competition, a de facto coincidence of the interests of the group of producers with the absolute freedom of each enterprise—finds itself profoundly altered. The awareness, developed in some German capitalists, of the peril to which this freedom subjected them in a critical period, must naturally be placed at the origin of the effervescence and triumph of National-Socialism. However, it is evident that this awareness did not yet exist for Italian capitalists who, from the moment of the march on Rome, were exclusively preoccupied with the irresolvability of their conflicts with the workers. It thus appears that the unity of fascism is located in its actual psychological structure and not in the economic conditions that serves as its base. (This does not contradict the fact that a general logical development of the economy retroactively provides the different fascisms with a common economic signification that they share, to be sure, with the political activity—absolutely foreign to fascism in the strictest sense—of the current government of the United States.)

Whatever the economic danger to which fascism responded, the awareness of this danger and the need to avoid it actually represent an as yet empty desire, which could be propped up by money. The realization of the force able to respond to the desire and to utilize the available monies takes place only in the heterogeneous region, and its possibility depends upon the actual structure of that region: on the whole, it is possible to consider this structure as variable depending on whether the society is democratic or monarchical.

Truly monarchical societies (as distinct from the adapted or bastardized political forms represented by England today or pre-fascist Italy) are characterized by the fact that a sovereign agency, having an ancient origin and an absolute form, is connected to the existing *homogeneity*. The constant evolution of the constitutive elements of this *homogeneity* can necessitate fundamental changes, but the need for change can become represented internally only in an alerted minority: the whole of the homogeneous elements and the immediate principle of *homogeneity* remain committed to upholding the juridical forms and the existing administrative framework guaranteed by the authority of the king; the authority of the king coincides reciprocally with the upholding of these forms and this framework. Thus the upper part of the *heterogeneous* region is both immobilized and immobilizing, and only the lower part formed by the impoverished and oppressed classes is capable of entering into movement. But, for the latter, passive and oppressed by definition, the fact of entering into movement represents a profound alteration of their nature: in order to take part in a struggle against the sovereign agency and the legal homogeneity oppressing them, the lower classes must pass from a passive and diffuse state to a form of conscious activity; in Marxist terms, these classes must become aware of themselves as a revolutionary proletariat. This proletariat cannot actually be limited to itself it is in fact only a point of concentration for every dissociated social element that has been banished to *heterogeneity*. It is even possible to say that such a point of concentration exists in a sense prior to the formation of what must be called the 'conscious proletariat': the general description of the heterogeneous region actually implies that it be posited as a constitutive element of the structure of a whole that includes not only imperative forms and impoverished forms but also *subversive forms*. These subversive forms are none other than the lower forms transformed with a view to the struggle against the sovereign forms. The necessity inherent to subversive forms requires that what is low become high, that what is high become low; this is the requirement in which the nature of subversion is expressed. In the case where the sovereign forms of a society are immobilized and bound, the diverse elements that have been banished to *heterogeneity* as a result of social decomposition can only ally themselves with the formations which result when the oppressed class become active: they are necessarily dedicated to subversion. The fraction of the bourgeoisie that has become aware of the incompatibility with established social frameworks becomes united against figures of authority and blends in with the effervescent masses in revolt; and even in the period immediately following the destruction of the monarchy, social movements continued to be governed by the initial anti-authoritarian character of the revolution.

But in a democratic society (at least when such a society is not galvanized by the necessity of going to war) the *heterogeneous* imperative agency (nation in republican forms, king in constitutional monarchies) is reduced to an atrophied existence, so that its destruction no longer appears to be a necessary condition of change. In such a situation, the imperative forms can even be considered as a free field, open to all possibilities of effervescence and movement, just as subversive forms are in a democracy. And when homogeneous society undergoes a critical disintegration, the dissociated elements no longer necessarily enter the orbit of subversive attraction: in addition there forms at the top an imperative attraction that no longer immobilizes those who are subjected to it. As a rule, until just recently, this imperative attraction only exerted itself in the direction of restoration. It was thus limited before hand by the prior nature of the disappeared sovereignty which most often implied a prohibitive loss of contact between the sovereign agency and the lower classes (the only spontaneous historical restoration, that of Bonapartism, must be put into relation with the manifest popular sources of Bonapartist power). In France, it is true, some of the constitutive forms of fascism were able to be elaborated in the formation—but especially in the difficulties of the formation—of an imperative attraction aimed at a dynastic restoration. The possibility of fascism nonetheless depended upon the fact that a reversion to vanished sovereign forms was out of the question in Italy, where the monarchy subsisted in a reduced state. Added to this subsistence, it was precisely the insufficiency of the royal formation that necessitated the formation of—and left the field open for—an entirely renewed imperative attraction with a popular base. Under these new conditions (with regard to the classical revolutionary dissociations in monarchical societies) the lower classes no longer exclusively experience the attraction represented by socialist subversion, and a military type of organization has in part begun

to draw them into the orbit of sovereignty. Likewise, the dissociated elements (belonging to the middle or dominating classes) have found a new outlet for their effervescence, and it is not surprising that, given the choice between subversive or imperative solutions, the majority opted for the imperative.

⌐∿⌐

"THE MEANING OF GENERAL ECONOMY," 1949

The Dependence of the Economy on the Circulation of Energy on the Earth

When it is necessary to change an automobile tyre, open an abscess or plough a vineyard it is easy to manage a quite limited operation. The elements on which the action is brought to bear are not completely isolated from the rest of the world, but it is possible to act on them as if they were: one can complete the operation without once needing to consider the whole, of which the tyre, the abscess or the vineyard is nevertheless an integral part. The changes brought about do not perceptibly alter the other things, nor does the ceaseless action from without have an appreciable effect on the conduct of the operation. But things are different when we consider a substantial economic activity such as the production of automobiles in the United States, or, *a fortiori,* when it is a question of economic activity in general.

Between the production of automobiles and the *general* movement of the economy, the interdependence is rather clear, but the economy taken as a whole is usually studied as if it were a matter of an isolatable system of operation. Production and consumption are linked together, but, considered jointly, it does not seem difficult to study them as one might study an elementary operation relatively independent of that which it is not.

This method is legitimate, and science never proceeds differently. However, economic science

From *The Bataille Reader,* Fred Botting and Scott Wilson, Eds. Copyright © 1997. Reprinted by permission of Blackwell Publishers Ltd.

does not give results of the same order as physics studying, first, a precise phenomenon, then all studiable phenomena as a co-ordinated whole. Economic phenomena are not easy to isolate, and their general co-ordination is not easy to establish. So it is possible to raise this question concerning them: shouldn't productive activity as a whole be considered in terms of the modifications it receives from its surroundings or brings about in its surroundings? In other words, isn't there a need to study the system of human production and consumption within a much larger framework?

In the sciences such problems ordinarily have an academic character, but economic activity is so far reaching that no one will be surprised if a first question is followed by other, less abstract ones: In overall industrial development, are there not social conflicts and planetary wars? In the global activity of men, in short, are there not causes and effects that will appear only provided that *the general data of the economy* are studied? Will we be able to make ourselves the masters of such a dangerous activity (and one that we could not abandon in any case) without having grasped its *general* consequences? Should we not, given the constant development of economic forces, pose the general problems that are linked to the movement of energy on the globe?

These questions allow one to glimpse both the theoretical meaning and the practical importance of the principles they introduce.

The Necessity of Losing the Excess Energy that Cannot be Used for a System's Growth

At first sight, it is easy to recognize in the economy—*in the production and use of wealth*—a particular aspect of terrestrial activity regarded as a cosmic phenomenon. A movement is produced on the surface of the globe that results from the circulation of energy at this point in the universe. The economic activity of men appropriates this movement, making use of the resulting possibilities for certain ends. But this movement has a pattern and laws with which, as a rule, those who use them and depend on them are unacquainted. Thus the question arises: is the general determination of energy circulating in the biosphere altered by man's activity? Or rather, isn't the latter's

intention vitiated by a determination of which it is ignorant, which it overlooks and cannot change?

Without waiting, I will give an inescapable answer.

Man's disregard for the material basis of his life still causes him to err in a serious way. Humanity exploits given material resources, but by restricting them as it does to a resolution of the immediate difficulties it encounters (a resolution which it has hastily had to define as an ideal), it assigns to the forces it employs an end which they cannot have. Beyond our immediate ends, man's activity in fact pursues the useless and infinite fulfillment of the universe.

Of course, the error that results from so complete a disregard does not just concern man's claim to lucidity. It is not easy to realize one's own ends if one must, in trying to do so, carry out a movement that surpasses them. No doubt these ends and this movement may not be entirely irreconcilable; but if these two terms are to be reconciled we must cease to ignore one of them; otherwise, our works quickly turn to catastrophe.

I will begin with a basic fact: the living organism, in a situation determined by the play of energy on the surface of the globe, ordinarily receives more energy than is necessary for maintaining life; the excess energy (wealth) can be used for the growth of a system (e.g., an organism); if the system can no longer grow, or if the excess cannot be completely absorbed in its growth, it must necessarily be lost without profit; it must be spent, willingly or not, gloriously or catastrophically.

The Poverty of Organisms or Limited Systems and the Excess Wealth of Living Nature

Minds accustomed to seeing the development of productive forces as the ideal end of activity refuse to recognize that energy, which constitutes wealth, must ultimately be spent lavishly (without return), and that a series of profitable operations has absolutely no other effect than the squandering of profits. To affirm that it is necessary to dissipate a substantial portion of energy produced, sending it up in smoke, is to go against judgements that form the basis of a rational economy. We know cases where wealth has had to be destroyed (coffee thrown into the sea), but these scandals cannot reasonably be offered as examples to follow. They are the acknowledgement of an impotence, and no one could find in them the image and essence of wealth. Indeed, involuntary destruction (such as the disposal of coffee overboard) has in every case the meaning of failure; it is experienced as a misfortune; in no way can it be presented as desirable. And yet it is the type of operation without which there is no solution. When one considers the *totality* of productive wealth on the surface of the globe, it is evident that the products of this wealth can be employed for productive ends only insofar as the living organism that is economic mankind can increase its equipment. This is not entirely—neither always nor indefinitely—possible. A surplus must be dissipated through deficit operations: the final dissipation cannot fail to carry out the movement that animates terrestrial energy.

The contrary usually appears for the reason that the economy is never considered *in general*. The human mind reduces operations, in science as in life, to an entity based on typical *particular* systems (organisms or enterprises). Economic activity, considered as a whole, is conceived in terms of particular operations with limited ends. The mind generalizes by composing the aggregate of these operations. Economic science merely generalizes the isolated situation; it restricts its object to operations carried out with a view to a limited end, that of economic man. It does not take into consideration a play of energy that no particular end limits: the play of *living matter in general*, involved in the movement of light of which it is the result. On the surface of the globe, for *living matter in general*, energy is always in excess; the question is always posed in terms of extravagance. The choice is limited to how the wealth is to be squandered. It is to the *particular* living being, or to limited populations of living beings, that the problem of necessity presents itself. But man is not just the separate being that contends with the living world and with other men for his share of resources. The general movement of exudation (of waste) of living matter impels him, and he cannot stop it; moreover, being at the summit, his sovereignty in the living world identifies him with this movement; it destines him, in a privileged way, to that glorious opera-

tion, to useless consumption. If he denies this, as he is constantly urged to do by the consciousness of a *necessity*, of an indigence inherent in separate beings (which are constantly short of resources, which are nothing but eternally *needy* individuals), his denial does not alter the global movement of energy in the least: the latter cannot accumulate limitlessly in the productive forces; eventually, like a river into the sea, it is bound to escape us and be lost to us.

✎

"THE NATURE OF SOCIETY: SOCIAL BONDING AND COMMUNICATION," 1947–48

> There exists at the basis of human life a principle of insufficiency. On his own, each man imagines others to be incapable or unworthy of 'being'. —*Inner Experience*, p. 81

> I would like to simplify, to brave the feeling of insufficiency. I myself am not sufficient and only maintain my 'pretence' by means of the shadow in which I find myself. —*Inner Experience*, p. 82

There is no transcendence from an animal that eats to an animal which is eaten. Equally there is no distinction, since an animal does not eat another because it thinks it is different from it.

Against this idea, we could point to the fact that animals do not eat one another but first determine which species they do eat and which they don't.

However, I shall not pause at this objection, because I believe it has a value that is less important than the position of similitude I will argue.

The similitude is linked, I would say, to a distinction based upon the fact that the animal which eats the other does not distinguish what it eats in the way we distinguish an object. The distinction is possible from the position of an object, but does not exist in so far as the object has not been established. The animal which is eaten by another animal does not yet exist in this sense as an object. This is why we cannot say that it is subordinated to the one which eats.

Between the eaten animal and the one which eats there is no relation of subordination. It cannot be said, in spite of the human custom of calling the lion the king of the beasts, that there exists anything in animal life which might be ruled in this way. Animals eat one another without there being any subordination other than what results from force.

In humanity it is quite the opposite. The object is established as such and the animal we eat establishes a relation of subordination between us and it.

The eaten animal is killed, then cooked; in other words it is treated as a separate being, as a very distinct thing which we can prepare in any way we like. Man treats the animal as a range of possibilities which are subordinated to him.

He only eats it when it is dead; it is the dead animal which is esteemed by him and it is esteemed as a thing.

The eaten animal is not the only thing which exists for man. The tool which has served to kill the animal is no less a thing than the animal itself, to the extent that right from the start a world of things, a plan of things is defined by the human situation, and finally mankind itself is added to it, situated in it by means of the way it looks at itself.

Chronologically, this is perhaps, in relation to the primitive situation I have described, an anticipation, but the only thing one can say about this is that it is a matter for discussion and that it is very difficult to speak with chronological precision of the moment mankind created a plan of things and situated itself in this plan.

This situation of things, of objects, in relation to the subject, is that of transcendence.

In relation to the subject, things are transcendent; in other words, the sphere of internal life which extends to the sphere of communication between different subjects is entirely different from the sphere of things as much for the earliest people as for those today. Although not entirely different, there is one difference for the earliest people in the same way as there is for us.

This attitude of transcendence, this response of a world into which mankind does not penetrate and with which it has no communication, which is subordinated to it, created a sort of fundamental difficulty.

From that moment a life is introduced in which immediacy has vanished and which is placed under the sway of the subordination of one part of the world to the other part.

This subordination can also be considered by the man who dominates as a limitation, in the sense that from the moment that an object is subordinated to it, it no longer enters into the domain defined by the object, but is situated outside it and can feel, at any moment, the desire to push domination to the point of communication. It is only by regaining communication with the object that domination can appear entire, in other words domination can appear entire only from the moment it is suppressed.

It appears that in the facts themselves this double movement from the desire to dominate and communicate is translated into the destruction of the object.

The destruction of the object takes place, not exactly as a sacrifice (at least in the most apparently primitive situations) but at the very least, when the object is an animal, under the form of putting the object to death.

It is striking that, in putting an animal to death as an object, the concern of primitive people was not so much to hurt the animal as, on the contrary, to look after it. In the same way, to the extent that the animal was considered to be an object, man considered that he had offended the animal and it is through ceasing to consider it as an object (that is, by killing it) that he repaired the offence he had committed.

In fact the destruction of the animal is, in primitive rituals, a crucial moment, a moment to which no other can be compared. It is through the destruction of the animal that the profane world, the world of transcendence, the inaccessible world, is overcome and that, by so doing, this world which created limits for the earliest active people is overcome and, through this surmounting, the world of immanence, that is, of violence and immediacy, is located.

The festival is connected with the destruction of the animal.

The festival begins at the moment when activity has ceased to have a goal. Through the destruction of the animal, the goal is equally surmounted at the same time as the object. This is translated into primitive forms by the frequent fact that the destroyed animal is not eaten by the one who has destroyed it. The destroyed animal being the totem, the totem of the clan, in a given situation it is the clan which kills the animal, but it is the neighbouring clan which eats it.

The animal is so situated outside the goal (in other words outside self-interest) that it is given to others to eat, in order that it be clear that it is lost, that the one who has killed it has done so to lose and not to gain.

Besides, it is this which introduces the surge of emancipation, the surge of relaxation, the surge of violence of the festival, as a moment of rupture.

From the moment that the world of things is denied, where the interest which exists in the primacy of activity has ceased to dominate, at that moment, what I first called 'animality' would be introduced, but not as animality, as an unloosening of a situation which had been closed.

In the productive activity of things, this violence had been compressed, had been reserved, had been limited to a certain number of actions all linked to goals. Once the festival is unleashed, actions cease to be linked to goals.

However, we should not fail to notice that, in this unleashing, a certain limit remains, which is not opposed to the unleashing but defines its meaning in relation to a given constraint.

The unleashing of the festival is an unleashing of man in the world. Yet this unleashing is linked to the group, to the closed community within which it takes place.

Naturally this is determined by a geographical situation, but it no less has meaning because it is within this limited geographical framework that the very adversary itself is connected, in primitive belief, to self-interest.

When the animal is killed, the Primitive imagines that it facilitates the fecundity of the species. In general, the animal is eaten and so finds itself fecundated, and can therefore ensure the prosperity of a community.

ROBERT KING MERTON

1910–2003

Robert King Merton was born in the Jewish slums of Philadelphia as Meyer Robert Skolnick on July 4 or 5, 1910, around midnight, the son of a Russian immigrant carpenter/truck driver and a mother with great ambitions for her two children. He married Suzanne Carhart on September 8, 1934 and with her had two daughters and a son, Robert Carhart Merton, who won the Nobel Prize for Economics in 1997. He separated from his first wife in 1968 and began living with Harriet Zuckerman, whom he married in 1993. Merton died in New York City on February 23, 2003 at the age of 92. Merton changed his name from Skolnick when an adolescent in order to enhance his career as a magician, at first adopting "Merlin," but being persuaded by a wise brother-in-law to use something less hackneyed. Merton's tall patrician good looks and the name change made it easier for him to "blend" with the New England culture of anti-Semitic Harvard in the 30s, and for most of his career his ethnic origins were unknown to the thousands of his professional admirers around the world. After public school in Philadelphia, Merton attended Temple University on a scholarship where he attracted the attention of a sociologist who in turn introduced him to Pitirim Sorokin, brilliant founder of the sociology department at Harvard. On the basis of a conversation at a professional meeting, Sorokin invited Merton to Harvard for graduate study in 1931, where he worked principally with George Sarton, doyen of studies in the history of science. Merton's dissertation, *Science, Technology and Society in Seventeenth Century England* was published in Sarton's journal, *Osiris*, and was reissued in 1968 in a revised version. It is regarded as the founding document in the American school of the sociology of science. Merton put what he had learned writing this work to semi-political use in 1942 when he wrote "Science and Democratic Social Structure," a provocative piece in which "communism" is shown to be the preferred mode of scientific work and cumulative progress. He identified the "ethos of science" as being made up of "universalism, communism, disinterestedness, and organized skepticism," a model that held sway for two decades until upended somewhat by Merton's younger friend, Thomas Kuhn in *The Structure of Scientific Revolutions* (1962).

After teaching briefly at Tulane, Merton moved to Columbia in the early 40s and stayed there, shaping the sociology department in his own image during the 50s and 60s. He wrote a series of articles between 1936 and the early 50s which eventually comprised *Social Theory and Social Structure* (1949; 1968 enl.ed.), surely the most important essay collection from a U.S. sociologist in the postwar period. He also wrote a virtuosic intellectual history, *On the Shoulders of Giants* (1965; several editions) that became a favorite across the humanities and social sciences. Using a prose style second to none among sociologists,

Merton bequeathed to the social sciences a number of ideas and phrases (focus groups, reference group, status set, self-fulfilling prophecy, unanticipated consequences of social action, the Matthew Effect, and so on), none of which he claimed to have invented ab novo, but each of which he sharpened and put to creative scholarly use. His longterm collaboration with Paul Lazarsfeld at Columbia University (1941–1976) is perhaps the most famous and fruitful linking of "theory and method" to have been fully realized in any one sociology department in the U.S., and has been much celebrated in memoirs of the period. It was often stated as a matter of undebatable fact that had the Nobel Prize been awarded to sociology, Merton would have been its first recipient.

"THE UNANTICIPATED CONSEQUENCES OF SOCIAL ACTION," 1936

In some one of its numerous forms, the problem of the unanticipated consequences of purposive action has been touched upon by virtually every substantial contributor to the long history of social thought.[1] The diversity of context[2] and variety of terms[3] by which this problem has been known, however, have tended to obscure any continuity in its consideration. In fact, this diversity of context—ranging from theology to technology—has been so pronounced that not only has the substantial identity of the problem been overlooked, but no systematic, scientific analysis of it has as yet been made. The failure to subject the problem to thorough-going investigation has perhaps resulted in part from its having been linked historically with transcendental and ethical considerations. Obviously, the ready solution provided by ascribing uncontemplated consequences of action to the inscrutable will of God or Providence or Fate precludes, in the mind of the believer, any need for scientific analysis. Whatever the actual reasons, the fact remains that although the process has been widely recognized and its importance appreciated, it still awaits systematic treatment.

From *Social Thought and Social Structure*, by Robert K. Merton. Published by ASR. Copyright 1936.

Formulation of the Problem

Although the phrase, unanticipated consequences of purposive social action, is in a measure self-explanatory, the setting of the problem demands further specification. In the first place, the greater part of this paper deals with isolated purposive acts rather than with their integration into a coherent system of action (though some reference will be made to the latter). This limitation is prescribed by expediency; a treatment of systems of action would introduce further unmanageable complications. Furthermore, *unforeseen* consequences should not be identified with consequences which are necessarily *undesirable* (from the standpoint of the actor). For though these results are unintended, they are not upon their occurrence always deemed axiologically negative. In short, undesired effects are not always undesirable effects. The intended and anticipated outcomes of purposive action, however, are always, in the very nature of the case, relatively desirable to the actor, though they may seem axiologically negative to an outside observer. This is true even in the polar instance where the intended result is "the lesser of two evils" or in such cases as suicide, ascetic mortification and self-torture which, in given situations, are deemed desirable relative to other possible alternatives.

Rigorously speaking, the *consequences* of purposive action are limited to those elements in the resulting situation that are exclusively the outcome of the action, that is, that would not have occurred had the action not taken place. Concretely, however, the consequences result from the interplay of the action and the objective situation, the conditions of actions.[4] We shall be primarily concerned with a pattern of results of action under certain conditions. This still involves the problems of causal imputation (of which more later) though to a less pressing degree than consequences in the rigorous sense. These relatively concrete consequences may be differentiated into (a) consequences to the actor(s), (b) consequences to other persons mediated through the social structure, the culture, and the civilization.[5]

In considering *purposive* action, we are concerned with "conduct" as distinct from "behavior," that is, with action that involves motives and consequently a choice between alternatives.[6] For the time being, we take purposes as given, so that any theories that "reduce" purpose to conditioned reflexes or tropisms, which assert that motives are simply compounded of instinctual drives, may be considered as irrelevant. Psychological considerations of the source or origin of motives, although undoubtedly important for a more complete understanding of the mechanisms involved in the development of unexpected consequences of conduct, will be ignored.

Moreover, it is not assumed that social action always involves clearcut, explicit purpose. Such awareness of purpose may be unusual, the aim of action more often than not being nebulous and hazy. This is certainly the case with habitual action which, though it may originally have been induced by conscious purpose, is characteristically performed without such awareness. The significance of habitual action will be discussed later.

Above all, it must not be inferred that purposive action implies "rationality" of human action (that persons always use the objectively most adequate means for the attainment of their end).[7] In fact, part of my analysis is devoted to identifying those elements which account for concrete deviations from rationality of action. Moreover, rationality and irrationality are not to be identified with the success and failure of action, respectively. For in a situation where the number of *possible* actions for attaining a given end is severely limited, one acts rationally by selecting the means

which, on the basis of the available evidence, has the greatest probability of attaining this goal[8] even though the goal may actually *not* be attained.[9] Contrariwise, an end may be attained by action that, on the basis of the knowledge available to the actor, is irrational (as in the case of "hunches").

Turning now to *action,* we differentiate this into two kinds: unorganized and formally organized. The first refers to actions of individuals considered distributively out of which may grow the second when like-minded individuals form an association in order to achieve a common purpose. Unanticipated consequences follow both types of action, although the second type seems to afford a better opportunity for sociological analysis since the processes of formal organization more often make for explicit statements of purpose and procedure. . . .

Sources of Unanticipated Consequences

The most obvious limitation to a correct anticipation of consequences of action is provided by the existing state of knowledge. The extent of this limitation can be best appreciated by assuming the simplest case where the lack of adequate knowledge is the *sole* barrier to a correct anticipation.[11] Obviously, a very large number of concrete reasons for inadequate knowledge may be found, but it is also possible to summarize several classes of factors that are most important.

Ignorance. The first class derives from the type of knowledge—usually, perhaps exclusively—attained in the sciences of human behavior. The social scientist usually finds stochastic, not functional relationships.[12] This is to say, in the study of human behavior, there is found a set of different values of one variable associated with each value of the other variable(s), or in less formal language, the set of consequences of any repeated act is not constant but there is a range of possible consequences, *any one of which may follow the act in a given case.* In some instances, we have sufficient knowledge of the limits of the range of possible consequences, and even adequate knowledge for ascertaining the statistical (empirical) probabilities of the various possible consequences, but it is impossible to predict with certainty the results in any particular case. Our classifications of acts and situations never involve completely homogeneous categories nor even categories whose approximate degree of homogeneity is sufficient for the prediction of particular events.[13] We have here the paradox that whereas past experiences are the guide to our expectations on the assumption that certain past, present and future acts are sufficiently alike to be grouped in the same category, these experiences are in fact different. To the extent that these differences are pertinent to the outcome of the action and appropriate corrections for these differences are not adopted, the actual results will differ from the expected. As Poincare has put it, " . . . small differences in the initial conditions produce very great ones in the final phenomena. . . . Prediction becomes impossible, and we have the fortuitous phenomenon."[14]

However, deviations from the usual consequences of an act can be anticipated by the actor who recognizes in the given situation some differences from previous similar situations. But insofar as these differences can themselves not be subsumed under general rules, the direction and extent of these deviations cannot be anticipated.[15] It is clear, then, that the partial knowledge in the light of which action is commonly carried on permits a varying range of unexpected outcomes of conduct.

Error.   A second major factor in unexpected consequences of conduct, perhaps as pervasive as ignorance, is error. Error may intrude itself, of course, in any phase of purposive action: we may err in our appraisal of the present situation, in our inference from this to the future objective situation, in our selection of a course of action, or finally in the execution of the action chosen. A common fallacy is frequently involved in the too-ready assumption that actions which have in the past led to the desired outcome will continue to do so. This assumption is often fixed in the mechanism of habit and there often finds pragmatic justification. But precisely because habit is a mode of activity that has previously led to the attainment of certain ends, it tends to become automatic and undeliberative through continued repetition so that the actor fails to recognize that procedures

which have been successful *in certain circumstances* need not be so *under any and all conditions.*[18] Just as rigidities in social organization often balk and block the satisfaction of new wants, so rigidities in individual behavior block the satisfaction of old wants in a changing social environment.

Error may also be involved in instances where the actor attends to only one or some of the pertinent aspects of the situation that influence the outcome of the action. This may range from the case of simple neglect (lack of thoroughness in examining the situation) to pathological obsession where there is a determined refusal or inability to consider certain elements of the problem. This last type has been extensively dealt with in the psychiatric literature. In cases of wish-fulfilment, emotional involvements lead to a distortion of the objective situation and of the probable future course of events; action predicated upon imaginary conditions must have unexpected consequences.

Imperious Immediacy of Interest.   A third general type of factor, the "imperious immediacy of interest," refers to instances where the actor's paramount concern with the foreseen immediate consequences excludes consideration of further or other consequences of the same act. The most prominent elements in such immediacy of interest range from physiological needs to basic cultural values. Thus, Vico's imaginative example of the "origin of the family," which derived from the practice of men carrying their mates into caves to satisfy their sex drive out of the sight of God, might serve as a somewhat fantastic illustration of the first. Another kind of example is provided by that doctrine of classical economics in which the individual endeavoring to employ his capital where most profitable to him and thus tending to render the annual revenue of society as great as possible is, in the words of Adam Smith, led "by an invisible hand to promote an end which was no part of his intention."

However, after the acute analysis by Max Weber, it goes without saying that action motivated by interest is not antithetical to an intensive investigation of the conditions and means of successful action. On the contrary, it would seem that interest, if it is to be satisfied, requires objective analysis of situation and instrumentality, as is assumed to be characteristic of "economic man." The irony is that intense interest often tends to preclude such analysis precisely because strong concern with the satisfaction of the immediate interest is a psychological generator of emotional bias, with consequent lopsidedness or failure to engage in the required calculations. It is as much a fallacious assumption to hold that interested action necessarily entails a rational calculation of the elements in the situation[19] as to deny rationality any and all influence over such conduct. Moreover, action in which the element of immediacy of interest is involved may be rational in terms of the values basic to that interest but irrational in terms of the life organization of the individual. Rational, in the sense that it is an action which may be expected to lead to the attainment of the specific goal; irrational, in the sense that it may defeat the pursuit or attainment of other values, not, at the moment, paramount but which nonetheless form an integral part of the individual's scale of values. Thus, *precisely because a particular action is not carried out in a psychological or social vacuum, its effects will ramify into outer spheres of value and interest.* For example, the practice of birth control for "economic reasons" influences the age-composition and size of sibships with profound consequences of a psychological and social character and, in larger aggregations, of course, affects the rate of population growth.

Basic Values.   Superficially similar to the factor of immediacy of interest, but differing from it in a significant theoretical sense, is that of basic values. This refers to instances where further consequences of action are not considered because of the felt necessity of the action enjoined by fundamental values. The classical analysis is Weber's study of the Protestant Ethic and the spirit of capitalism. He has properly generalized this case, saying that active asceticism paradoxically leads to its own decline through the accumulation of wealth and possessions entailed by the conjunction of intense productive activity and decreased consumption.

The process contributes much to the dynamic of social and cultural change, as has been recognized with varying degrees of cogency by Hegel, Marx, Wundt, and many others. The empirical observation is incontestable: activities oriented toward certain values release processes that so react as to change the very scale of values which precipitated them. This process can come about when a system of basic values enjoins certain *specific* actions, and adherents are concerned not with the objective consequences of these actions but with the subjective satisfaction of duty well performed. Or, action in accordance with a dominant set of values tends to be focused upon that particular value-area. But with the complex interaction that constitutes society, action ramifies. Its consequences are not restricted to the specific area in which they are intended to center and occur in interrelated fields explicitly ignored at the time of action. Yet it is because these fields are in fact interrelated that the further consequences in adjacent areas tend to *react* upon the fundamental value-system. It is this usually unlooked-for reaction that constitutes a most important element in the process of secularization, of the transformation or breakdown of basic value-systems. Here is the essential paradox of social action—the "realization" of values may lead to their renunciation. We may paraphrase Goethe and speak of "Die Kraft, die stets das Gute will, und stets das Böse schafft."

Self-Defeating Predictions.   There is one other circumstance, peculiar to human conduct, that stands in the way of successful social prediction and planning. Public predictions of future social developments are frequently not sustained precisely because the prediction has become a new element in the concrete situation, thus tending to change the initial course of developments. This is not true of prediction in fields that do not pertain to human conduct. Thus, the prediction of the return of Halley's comet does not in any way influence the orbit of that comet; but, to take a concrete social example, Marx's prediction of the progressive concentration of wealth and increasing misery of the masses did influence the very process predicted. For at least one of the consequences of socialist preaching in the nineteenth century was the spread of organization of labor, which, made conscious of its unfavorable bargaining position in cases of individual contract, organized to enjoy the advantages of collective bargaining, thus slowing up, if not eliminating, the developments that Marx had predicted.[20]

Thus, to the extent that the predictions of social scientists are made public and action proceeds with full cognizance of these predictions, the "other-things-being-equal" condition tacitly assumed in all forecasting is not fulfilled. Other things will not be equal just because the scientist has introduced a new "other thing"—his prediction.[21] This contingency may often account for social movements developing in utterly unanticipated directions, and it hence assumes considerable importance for social planning.

The foregoing discussion represents no more than the briefest exposition of the major elements involved in one fundamental social process. It would take us too far afield, and certainly beyond the compass of this paper, to examine exhaustively the implications of this analysis for social prediction, control, and planning. We may maintain, however, even at this preliminary juncture, that no blanket statement categorically affirming or denying the practical feasibility of *all* social planning is warranted. Before we may indulge in such generalizations, we must examine and classify the *types* of social action and organization with reference to the elements here discussed and then refer our generalizations to these essentially different types. If the present analysis has served to set the problem, even in only its paramount aspects, and to direct attention toward the need for a systematic and objective study of the elements involved in the development of unanticipated consequences of purposive social action, the treatment of which has for much too long been consigned to the realm of theology and speculative philosophy, then it has achieved its avowed purpose.

Notes

1. Some of the theorists, though their contributions are by no means of equal importance, are: Machiavelli, Vico, Adam Smith (and some later classical economists), Marx, Engels, Wundt, Pareto, Max Weber, Graham Wallas, Cooley, Sorokin, Gini, Chapin, von Schelting.

2. This problem has been related to such heterogeneous subjects as: the problem of evil (theodicy), moral responsibility, free will, predestination, deism, teleology, fatalism, logical, illogical and nonlogical behavior, social prediction, planning and control, social cycles, the pleasure- and reality principles, and historical "accidents."

3. Some of the terms by which the whole or certain aspects of the process have been known are: Providence (imma-

nent or transcendental), Moira, *Paradoxie der Folgen, Schicksal,* social forces, heterogony of ends, immanent causation, dialectical movement, principle of emergence and creative synthesis.

4. Cf. Frank H. Knight, *Risk, Uncertainty and Profit* (Boston and New York: Houghton Mifflin Co., 1921), pp. 201–2. Professor Knight's doctoral dissertation represents by far the most searching treatment of certain phases of this problem that I have yet seen.

5. For the distinction between society, culture and civilization, see Alfred Weber, "Prinzipielles zur Kultursoziologie: Gesellschaftsprozess, Civilisationsprozess und Kulturbewegung," *Archiv für Sozialwissenschalt und Sozialpolitik,* 47, 1920, pp. 1–49; R. K. Merton, "Civilization and Culture," *Sociology and Social Research* 21 (1936), pp. 103–13.

6. Knight, *op. cit,* p. 52.

7. Max Weber, *Wirtschalt und Gesellschaft* (Tbingen: J. C. B. Mohr, 1925), pp. 3 ff.

8. See J. Bertrand, *Calcul des probabilités* (Paris, 1889), pp. 90 ff.; J. M. Keynes, *A Treatise on Probability* (London: The Macmillan Co., 1921), Chap. XXVI.

9. [For a specific application of this general observation, see the discussion of "discrepant appraisals of role-performance" on pp. 28–30 of this volume.]

11. Most discussions of unanticipated consequences limit the explanation of unanticipated consequences to this one factor of ignorance. Such a view either reduces itself to a sheer tautology or exaggerates the role of only one of many factors. In the first instance, the argument runs in this fashion: "if we had only known enough, we could have anticipated the consequences which, as it happens, were unforeseen." The evident fallacy in this *post mortem* argument rests in the word "enough" which is implicitly taken to mean "enough knowledge to foresee" the consequences of our action. It is then no difficult matter to uphold the contention. This viewpoint is basic to several schools of educational theory, just as it was to Comte's dictum, *savoir pour prevoir, prevoir pour pouvoir.* This intellectualist stand has gained credence partly because of its implicit optimism and because of the indubitable fact that sheer ignorance does actually account for the occurrence of some unforeseen consequences in some cases.

12. Cf. A. A. Tschuprow, *Grundbegriffe und Grundprobleme der Korrelations-theorie* (Leipzig: B. G. Teubner, 1925), pp. 20 ff., where he introduces the term "stochastic." It is apparent that stochastic associations are obtained because we have not ascertained, or having ascertained, have not controlled the other variables in the situation that influence the final result.

13. A classification into completely homogeneous categories would, of course, lead to functional associations and would permit successful prediction, but the aspects of social action which are of practical importance are too varied and numerous to permit such homogeneous classification.

14. Henri Poincaré, *Calcul des probabilités* (Paris, 1912), p. 2.

15. The actor's awareness of his ignorance and its implications is perhaps most acute in the type of conduct which Thomas and Znaniecki attribute to the wish for "new ex-

perience." This is the case where unforeseen consequences actually constitute the purpose of action, but there is always the tacit assumption that the consequences will be desirable.

18. Similar fallacies in the field of thought have been variously designated as "the philosophical fallacy" (Dewey), the "principle of limits" (Sorokin, Bridgman) and, with a somewhat different emphasis, "the fallacy of misplaced concreteness" (Whitehead). [For an application of the general idea to the case of organizations, see pp. 74–75 of this volume and "Bureaucratic Structure and Personality," in Merton, *Social Theory and Social Structure* (New York: The Free Press, 1968, enlarged ed.), pp. 249–60.]

19. The assumption is tenable only in a normative sense. Obviously such calculation, within the limits specified in our previous discussion, *should* be made if the probability of satisfying the interest is to be at a maximum. The error lies in confusing norm with actuality.

20. Corrado Gini, *Prime lineé di patologia economica* (Milan: A. Giuffrè, 1935), pp. 72–75. John Venn uses the picturesque term "suicidal prophecies" to refer to this process and properly observes that it represents a class of considerations which have been much neglected by the various sciences of human conduct. See his *Logic of Chance* (London, 1888), pp. 225–26.

21. [For the correlative process, see the paper, "The Self-Fulfilling Prophecy" first published a dozen years after this one, and reprinted in Merton, *op.cit.*, 1968, pp. 475–90.]

NORBERT ELIAS

1897–1990

Only child of a textile manufacturer, Norbert Elias was born in Breslau, Schlesien (now Wroclaw, Poland) on June 22, 1897, never married nor reproduced, and died in Amsterdam on August 1, 1990, age 93. His mother, Sophie, was killed in a concentration camp in 1941 due to being Jewish. Elias studied in the *gymnasium* in Breslau until 1915, served as a telegraph operator during WWI on both Eastern and Western fronts, suffered a nervous breakdown in 1917 and was reassigned away from combat. Elias studied physics, then medicine, at Breslau, and took summer courses at Heidelberg (1919) and Freiburg im Breisgau (1920). Due to the economic crisis following WWI, Elias's father's firm collapsed and he had to work in an export business from 1922 through 1924, finally taking his doctorate in philosophy at Breslau with the dissertation, "Idea and Individualism." For the next six years he lived in Heidelberg, working under Max Weber's younger brother, Alfred, culminating in an habilitation called "The Meaning of Florentine Society and Culture in the Origins of Science." Following this he lived in Frankfurt for three years, and worked as Karl Mannheim's research assistant. He wrote a second habilitation, "Court Society," which was never accepted due to the Nazi regime's closing of the Institute for Sociology; the study was finally published in 1969. At this point Elias undertook an extraordinary task: with practically no funds and no contacts, he moved to France (1933–35) and then to Britain (1935–1990), where he tutored and lived on tiny stipends from Jewish refugee organizations. Meanwhile, he wrote a work destined to make him famous 40 years later, *The Civilizing Process* (1939, 2 vols.; Eng. tr. 1978/82). After WWII, Elias struggled to make ends meet, but finally at 57 was offered a post at the University of Leicester, a minor British institution (where he influenced his young colleague, Anthony Giddens), and remained there until he retired to Holland.

In his major work Elias tried to use some of Freud's notions, while not accepting his orthodoxy, and also posited himself in opposition to Talcott Parsons's structural functionalism, all in an effort to generate a new grand theory of social change over the preceding five centuries, which he called "figurational" or "process sociology." He wished to overcome the traditional and to his mind unnecessarily confining bifurcation of social reality with the individual to one side, the collectivity on the other. For Elias, neither need necessarily be privileged over the other, so long as "figurations" could be isolated and studied as they developed historically. He did this by charting the growth of manners and civil behavior since the Renaissance, principally by examining (in the British Museum) textbooks written for the nobility on how to behave at court (Erasmus wrote a famous one, for instance, which went through hundreds of printings). By telling this story—and also by showing how courtly behavior influenced the growth of the state and accompanying macro changes, Elias thought he could bypass the shortcomings of other theories which tended to favor either the isolated ego (Freud, Simmel to some extent, Mead, James) or the collectivity (Marx, Durkheim, Weber to some extent, Le Bon). He regarded this as his major theoretical achievement, and the world finally caught up with him in the 1980s as he entered the last decade of his long life.

"AN OUTLINE OF *THE CIVILIZING PROCESS*," 1936

. . . Central to this study are modes of behaviour considered typical of people who are civilized in a Western way. The problem they pose is simple enough. Western people have not always behaved in the manner we are accustomed to regard as typical or as the hallmark of 'civilized' people. If a member of present-day Western civilized society were to find himself suddenly transported into a past epoch of his own society, such as the medieval-feudal period, he would find there much that he esteems 'uncivilized' in other societies today. His reaction would scarcely differ from that produced in him at present by the behaviour of people in feudal societies outside the Western world. He would, depending on his situation and inclinations, be either attracted by the wilder, more unrestrained and adventurous life of the upper classes in this society, or repulsed by the 'barbaric' customs, the squalour and coarseness that he encountered there. And whatever he understands by his own 'civilization', he would at any rate feel quite unequivocally that society in this past period of Western history was not 'civilized' in the same sense and to the same degree as Western society today.

This state of affairs may seem obvious to many people, and it might appear unnecessary to refer to it here. But it necessarily gives rise to questions which cannot with equal justice be said to be clearly present in the consciousness of living generations, although these questions are not

without importance for an understanding of ourselves. How did this change, this 'civilizing' of the West, actually happen? Of what did it consist? And what were its causes or motive forces? It is to the solution of these main questions that this study attempts to contribute.

To facilitate understanding of this book, and thus as an introduction to the questions themselves, it seems necessary to examine the different meanings and evaluations assigned to the concept of 'civilization' in Germany and France. This inquiry makes up the first chapter. It may help the reader to see the concepts of *Kultur* and *civilisation* as somewhat less rigidly and self-evidently opposed. And it may also make a small contribution toward improving the German historical understanding of the behaviour of Frenchmen and Englishmen, and the French and English understanding of the behaviour of Germans. But in the end it will also serve to clarify certain typical features of the civilizing process.

To gain access to the main questions, it is necessary first to obtain a clearer picture of how the behaviour and affective life of Western peoples slowly changed after the Middle Ages. To show this is the task of the second chapter. It attempts as simply and clearly as possible to open the way to an understanding of the *psychical* process of civilization. It may be that the idea of a psychical process extending over many generations appears hazardous and dubious to present-day historical thinking. But it is not possible to decide in a purely theoretical, speculative way whether the changes in psychical makeup observable in the course of Western history took place in a particular order and direction. Only a scrutiny of documents of historical experience can show what is correct and what is incorrect in such theories.

From "An Outline of the Civilizing Process," as seen in *The Norbert Elias Reader: A Biographical Selection*, Johan Goudsblom and Stephen Mennell, Eds. Published by Blackwell Publishers Ltd. Copyright © 1998.

That is why it is not possible here, when knowledge of this documentary material cannot be presupposed, to give a brief preliminary sketch of the structure and central ideas of the whole book. They themselves take on a firmer form only gradually, in a continuous observation of historical facts and a constant checking and revision of what has been seen previously through what entered later into the field of observation. And thus the individual parts of this study, its structure and method, will probably be completely intelligible only when they are perceived in their entirety. It must suffice here, to facilitate the reader's understanding, to pick out a few problems.

The second chapter contains a number of series of examples. They serve to show development in an accelerated fashion. In a few pages we see how in the course of centuries the standard of human behaviour on the same occasion very gradually shifts in a specific direction. We see people at table, we see them going to bed or in hostile clashes. In these and other elementary activities the manner in which the individual behaves and feels slowly changes. This change is in the direction of a gradual 'civilization', but only historical experience makes clearer what this word actually means. It shows, for example, the decisive role played in this civilizing process by a very specific change in the feelings of shame and delicacy. The standard of what society demands and prohibits changes; in conjunction with this, the threshold of socially instilled displeasure and fear moves; and the question of sociogenic fears thus emerges as one of the central problems of the civilizing process.

Very closely related to this is a further range of questions. The distance in behaviour and whole psychical structure between children and adults increases in the course of the civilizing process. Here, for example, lies the key to the question of why some peoples or groups of peoples appear to us as 'younger' or 'more childlike', others as 'older' or 'more grown-up'. What we are trying to express in this way are differences in the kind and stage of the civilizing process that these societies have attained; but that is a separate question which cannot be included within the framework of this study. The series of examples and the interpretations of them in the second chapter show one thing very clearly: the specific process of psychological 'growing up' in Western societies, which frequently occupies the minds of psychologists and pedagogues today, is nothing other than the individual civilizing process to which each young person, as a result of the social civilizing process over many centuries, is automatically subjected from earliest childhood, to a greater or lesser degree and with greater or lesser success. The psychogenesis of the adult makeup in civilized society cannot, therefore, be understood if considered independently of the sociogenesis of our 'civilization'. By a kind of basic 'sociogenetic law' the individual, in his short history, passes once more through some of the processes that his society has traversed in its long history.

It is the purpose of the third chapter, which constitutes the greater part of the second volume, to make certain processes in this long history of society more accessible to understanding. It attempts, within a number of precisely defined areas, to clarify how and why in the course of its history the structure of Western society continuously changes, and points at the same time to an answer to the question of why, in the same areas, the standard of behaviour and the psychical makeup of Western peoples change.

We see, for example, the social landscape of the early Middle Ages. There is a multitude of greater and smaller castles; even the town settlements of earlier times have become feudalized. Their centres too are formed by the castles and estates of lords from the warrior class. The question is: What are the sets of social relationships that press toward the development of what we call the 'feudal system'? The attempt is made to demonstrate some of these 'mechanisms of feudalization'. We see further how, from the castle landscape, together with a number of free, urban craft and commercial settlements, a number of larger and richer feudal estates slowly emerge. Within the warrior class itself a kind of upper stratum forms more and more distinctly; their dwelling places are the real centres of *Minnesang* and the lyrics of the troubadors, on the one hand, and of *courtois* forms of behaviour on the other. If earlier in the book the *courtois* standard of conduct is placed at the starting point of a number of sequences of examples giving a picture of the subsequent change of psychical makeup, here we gain access to the sociogenesis of these *courtois* forms of behaviour themselves.

Or we see, for example, how the early form of what we call a 'state' develops. In the age of absolutism, under the watchword of *civilité*, behaviour moves very perceptibly toward the standard that we denote today by a derivative of the word *civilité* as 'civilized' behaviour. It therefore seems necessary, in elucidating this civilizing process, to obtain a clearer picture of what gave rise to the absolutist regimes and therefore to the absolutist state. It is not only the observation of the past that points in this direction; a wealth of contemporary observations suggest strongly that the structure of civilized behaviour is closely interrelated with the organization of Western societies in the form of states. The question, in other words, is: How did the extremely decentralized society of the early Middle Ages, in which numerous greater and smaller warriors were the real rulers of Western territory, become one of the internally more or less pacified but outwardly embattled societies that we call states? Which dynamics of human interdependencies push toward the integration of ever larger areas under a relatively stable and centralized government apparatus?

It may perhaps seem at first sight an unnecessary complication to investigate the genesis of each historical formation. But since every historical phenomenon, human attitudes as much as social institutions, did actually once 'develop', how can modes of thought prove either simple or adequate in explaining these phenomena if, by a kind of artificial abstraction, they isolate the phenomena from their natural, historical flow, deprive them of their character as movement and process, and try to understand them as static formations without regard to the way in which they have come into being and change? It is not theoretical prejudice but experience itself which urges us to seek intellectual ways and means of steering a course between the Scylla of this 'statism', which tends to express all historical movement as something motionless and without evolution, and the Charybdis of the 'historical relativism' which sees in history only constant transformation, without penetrating to the order underlying this transformation and to the laws governing the formation of historical structures. That is what is attempted here. The sociogenetic and psychogenetic investi-

gation sets out to reveal the *order* underlying historical *changes*, their mechanics and their concrete mechanisms; and it seems that in this way a large number of questions that appear complicated or even beyond understanding today can be given fairly simple and precise answers.

For this reason, this study also inquires into the sociogenesis of the state. There is, to take one aspect of the history of the state's formation and structure, the problem of the 'monopoly of force'. Max Weber pointed out, mainly for the sake of definition, that one of the constitutive institutions required by the social organization we call a state is a monopoly in the exercise of physical force. Here the attempt is made to reveal something of the concrete historical processes that, from the time when the exercise of force was the privilege of a host of rival warriors, gradually impelled society towards this centralization and monopolization of the use of physical violence and its instruments. It can be shown that the tendency to form such monopolies in this past epoch of our history is neither easier nor more difficult to understand than, for example, the strong tendency toward monopolization in our own epoch. And it is then not difficult to understand that with this monopolization of physical violence as the point of intersection of a multitude of social interconnections, the whole apparatus which shapes the individual, the mode of operation of the social demands and prohibitions which mould his social makeup, and above all the kinds of fear that play a part in his life are decisively changed.

Finally, the concluding 'Sketch of a Theory of Civilization' underlines once more the connections between changes in the structure of society and changes in the structure of behaviour and psychical makeup. Much of what could only be hinted at earlier, in depicting concrete historical processes, is now stated explicitly. We find here, for example, a short sketch of the structure of the fears experienced as shame and delicacy, as a kind of theoretical summing-up of what previously emerged of itself from the study of historical documents; we find an explanation of precisely why fears of this kind play an especially important role in the advance of the civilizing process; and at the same time, some light is shed on the formation of the 'superego' and on the relation of the conscious and unconscious impulses in the psyche of civilized people. Here an answer is given to the question of historical processes; the question of how all these processes, consisting of nothing but the actions of individual people, nevertheless give rise to institutions and formations which were neither intended nor planned by any single individual in the form they actually take. And finally, in a broad survey, these insights from the past are combined into a single picture with experiences from the present.

⌒

"THE CIVILIZING OF PARENTS," 1980

. . . I would like to reconstruct, as far as possible in the limited space, the broad contours of the civilizing process of the parent–child relationship. Only when one has a picture of this developmental trend in view does one gain a more vivid understanding of the particularity and the problems of the parent–child figuration in the developed industrial nations of our time. In reconstructing this aspect of the civilizing process, I will make use, as I have already done in other cases, of a series of snapshots. In themselves, each of them can be misunderstood as a description of a state. But if one sees them as 'stills' in a movie, as fragments of a process, then with their help it is not difficult to see the broad line of the development.

Today the treatment of children in earlier times, especially infants, is in many respects difficult to imagine. There is an abundance of evidence for it, but the facts which it refers to are unwelcome today. Our feelings bristle, our consciences resist the insight. At first glance the facts can also appear contradictory. One sees no order in them; and this is also how they are usually written about, as if it concerns a heap of facts without their own order.

Nevertheless, there is a clear order in the sequence. The model of the civilizing process can serve as a guide. What is decisive is how one conceives the functions children have for parents. There are social relations in which it is an advantage for parents to have many children. For farmers with sufficient land, for example, children usually represent cheap labour power. In such cases, they often begin early to help with work, and they may produce more than they consume.

Particularly in urban societies, although not only in these, simple families often have no use for more and more children. Everywhere in the history of urban societies, from antiquity to the European eighteenth century, and perhaps still further, we thus encounter accepted methods of infanticide. Children came, they cried, they generated work, and the parents had no use for them, often enough no food. Eliminating little children is easy. In ancient Greece and Rome we hear time and time again of infants thrown onto dungheaps or in rivers. Exposing children was part of everyday life. People were used to it. Until the late nineteenth century there was no law against infanticide. Public opinion in antiquity also regarded the killing of infants or the sale of children—if they were pretty, to brothels, otherwise as slaves—as self-evident. The threshold of sensibility among people in antiquity—like those of Europeans in the Middle Ages and the early modern period—was quite different from that of the present day, particularly in relation to the use of physical violence. People assumed that they were violent to each other, they were attuned to it. No one noticed that children required special treatment. In a recent study it was said:

> Infanticide during antiquity has usually been played down despite literally hundreds of clear references by ancient writers that it was an accepted, everyday occurrence. Children were thrown into rivers, flung into dung-heaps and cess trenches, 'potted' in jars to starve to death, and exposed on every hill and roadside, 'a prey for birds, food for wilds beasts to rend' (Euripides, *Ion*, 504). To begin with, any child that was not perfect in shape and size, or cried too little or too much, or was otherwise than is described in the gynaecological writings on 'How to Recognize the Newborn that is Worth Rearing,' was generally killed. Beyond this, the first-born was usually allowed to live, especially if it was a boy. Girls were, of course, valued little and the instructions of Hilarion to his wife Alis (1 BC) are typical of the way these things were discussed: 'If, as may happen, you give birth to a child, if it is a boy let it live, if it is a girl, expose it.'

The result was a large imbalance of males over females which was typical of the West until well into the Middle Ages . . .

It was similar regarding the role of drives in the relations between parents and children. Whether it concerned feelings of love or hate, tenderness or aggression, they all used to play a far greater and more open role in interactions between parents and children, they were far more untamed and spontaneous, not only on the part of children, but also that of parents—corresponding to the prevailing standard of civilization—than is the case today.

Today it can happen that a mother experiences a sort of shock—a baby shock—when she finds herself confronted by the untamed animalism of her young child. Only the child's smallness and relative weakness conceals the intensity of infants' greed and the strength of their desire from parents. The fact that children have quite strong instinctual needs, prefigurative forms of sexuality, was only brought to adult consciousness in the twentieth century through Freud's scientific discoveries. For many people this has remained an unwelcome message to the present day. The preceding great spurt in rationalization had largely hidden this fact from people's consciousness. Particularly in the eighteenth and nineteenth centuries, but also before that, among adults human sexuality was increasingly placed behind the scenes of social life. The growing reserve which adults had to impose on interaction with each other, worked into their interiors—it became a self-constraint, and also rose like an invisible wall between parents and children. Corresponding to this unarticulated shame among adults concerning their own sexuality, the notion spread that children are human beings who are still free of the sin of sexuality, who in this respect are as innocent as angels. Because in reality no child lived up to these ideal expectations, parents in the seclusion of their own homes always had to ask themselves why precisely their children had characteristics which did not measure up to the angelic character which was supposed to be normal for all children. Perhaps it is because of this discrepancy between a socially accepted, but completely fantastic ideal image of children and children's thoroughly nonangelic, more animalistic, at least passionate and wild nature, that the punishments

which people in this period regarded as necessary disciplinary measures were particularly harsh. This sequence in the reflective shifts—the first, in the course of which adults tried to conceal the passionate and strongly animalistic character of children's nature in connection with the stronger control over their own animalistic impulses, and the second, in the course of which, with the help of scientific reflection, the particularity of children and, as an aspect of that, their initially weakly domesticated animalistic drives, was rediscovered—has to be kept in sight, if we wish to understand why in earlier epochs the relationship between parents and children in many respects took a different form from more recent times.

IV

For a long time, the relation between parents and children was determined to a large extent by traditional customs, which left a great deal of room for spontaneous drive-impulses among both parents and children. Rules which were based on scientific or scientifically-presented reflection played hardly any role in the formation of the relationship between parents and children. Today it is not entirely easy for us to put ourselves in a situation in which parents are almost completely uninfluenced by knowledge about the particular nature of their children, that is, about the differences between the personality structures of children and adults. Parents in ancient Greece and Rome, or in the Middle Ages, did not ask themselves, as is increasingly the case today: Am I making any mistakes in my relationship with my child? Will I damage them, if I do this or that? They conducted themselves spontaneously to a far greater degree, and were generally more influenced by what they felt themselves than by attempts to empathize with children, more influenced by what children meant to them than by thoughts on what they and their actions meant to children.

In this situation a circumstance came to light, which today is often concealed from view, namely the fact that the relation between parents and children is a relation of domination, one with a highly unequal balance of power. Children are initially as good as completely in the power of their parents; more precisely, the parents' power chances—compared with those of their children, particularly young children—are very great. In societies like ours there is hardly any other form of relationship in which the power differential between interdependent people is as great as that in the parent–child relation. Nonetheless, in this case, too, there is a reciprocity of power chances. It is not only that parents have power over children—normally children, and even new-born children, also have power over parents. They can call their parents to their aid by crying. In many cases, the birth of a child forces parents to re-arrange their lifestyle. If one asks why it is that children have considerable power over adults, one encounters again a situation referred to earlier: children have a function for parents. They represent the fulfilment of particular parental needs and wishes. I do not want to enter here into which parental needs the presence of children fulfils. It is sufficient to pose the question: what form does the parent–child relation take when children fulfil no needs or wishes for their parents? Today, thanks to a specific technological development, parents are able to decide whether and how many children they want to have. But in earlier societies parents usually produced children blindly, without any wish or need for a child or a further child. They had children, who had no function for them. These children, accordingly, also had limited power chances in relation to their parents; all power lay with the latter.

Earlier societies were generally more set up than industrial ones so that the people composing them would try to exploit their power chances to the last, relatively unconcerned about the destiny of subordinate people. They were then prepared to accept the same when fate turned against them.

We need to keep this relatively greater harshness of social life in view if we wish to understand the structure of the parent–child relation in societies like ancient Greece and Rome or the Middle Ages. What strike us as atrocities and inhumanity in the relations between parents and children in earlier times does not exclude the presence of parental love and affection for their children. But today a legend has become established which makes it look as if parental love and affection for their children is something more or less natural and, beyond that, an always stable, permanent and life-long feeling. In this case, too, a social

'should' is transformed into the notion of a natural 'is'. The exposure and killing of infants in earlier times was basically nothing other than a barbaric form of birth control. Particularly for the poorer strata in ancient, medieval and even early-modern urban societies, a high birth rate was a great burden. No wonder that in London one still found dying infants on dungheaps in the eighteenth century. Adults also imposed fewer restraints on their own drives in relation to children than is the case today. Mothers playing with their children's sexual organs is also today in some countries a wide-spread custom. That children witnessed their parents' sexual activity was self-evident in the enclosed quarters of the poorer groups in the population. That sexual games, whether it be children among each other—such as siblings who slept in the same bed—or between children and adults, often occurred, just as in ancient society, is easy to understand if we consider that for a long time the state did not concern itself with such occurrences, and that the participants developed no guilty consciences because of such acts. Contemporary historians often speak in this context of the 'abuse' of children in earlier times. But that, too, is a projection of current standards onto societies which did not have the same living conditions. Children had a strong and quite physically expressed need for love. Today we cannot establish how far children in, say, antiquity, were willing, how far unwilling partners in adults' sexual games. That they often were involved, can hardly be doubted.

By nature children are so constituted that they can awaken delight and love in adults. How chubby, how coquettish they can be, how fiery their tenderness and their displays of love! But then they often change quite suddenly. They are fickle, they cry, are filthy, refuse cuddles, thrash about and fight like little wild animals. A contemporary poet has written:

> I cried
> half dead
> the neighbours
> rang
> why
> does the child cry?
> end
> of the blows

(G. Kalow, *erdgaleere*, Munich, 1969.)

But it is doubtful whether neighbours in earlier societies were always concerned when a child cried. For a long time, too, state authorities had neither laws nor executive organs to mobilize in the protection of children. What would prevent adults from allowing children to die when they got on their nerves or when they had insufficient food to eat; I will refrain from listing all the other aspects of childhood which used to be possible and which are no longer possible today.

TALCOTT PARSONS

1902–1979

Talcott Parsons, the son of the minister who was President of Marietta College, and whose mother was an early feminist, was born on December 13, 1902 in Colorado Springs, Colorado, married Helen Bancroft Walker on April 30, 1927, and with her produced three children, Anne (an anthropologist of Italian culture), Charles (an economist), and Susan. At 76 he died while on a trip to Heidelberg, on May 8, 1979, celebrating his early academic success in that town fifty years before. Parsons attended the Horace Mann High School in New York City, graduating in 1920, then studied biology at Amherst College, but ended up with interests in political economy. He studied political-economy at the London School of Economics in 1924–25, then moved to Heidelberg for more study along similar lines, receiving his doctorate there with the dissertation " 'Capitalism' in Recent German Literature: Sombart and Weber." He taught at Amherst for one year, then moved to Harvard where he remained from 1927 until 1973, becoming Full Professor in 1944, over the objection of the department's founder, Pitirim Sorokin. While there he formed a new department, Social Relations, which brought together anthropology, political science, social psychology, and sociology, thereby isolating Sorokin in sociology proper. He taught a galaxy of sociologists who would carry his structural-functionalist scheme around the country and the world, particularly during the 40s and 50s, and he was President of the American Sociological Association in 1949. His leadership of the theory wing of American sociology began to wane with C. Wright Mills' famous attack on "grand theory" in *The Sociological Imagination* (1959) and was over with Alvin Gouldner's *The Coming Crisis of Western Sociology* (1970). He spent his retirement years at the University of Pennsylvania, where about 500 of his books are on display in the main library.

Parsons wrote one brilliant book, *The Structure of Social Action* (1937), a large study of Weber, Durkheim, Pareto, and Alfred Marshall, the economist, in which Parsons claimed to have discovered a "convergence" of ideas among these four geniuses which, interestingly, seem to culminate in Parsons' own ideas about the nature of social order. Parsons was especially intrigued by how societies deal with the "Hobbesian problem of order," which is understandable given the history of the 20th century during Parson's lifetime to that point. Fascinated with normative "consensus" and the avoidance of unwieldy societal conflict, he created his own sociological glossary, including the terms voluntarism, the AGIL scheme of action, universalistic versus particularistic norms, and a large assortment of two-by-two tables into which he cast the personality/social structure dialectic.

THE STRUCTURE OF SOCIAL ACTION, 1937

Hobbes and the Problem of Order

For present purposes the basis of Hobbes' social thinking lies in his famous concept of the state of nature as the war of all against all. Hobbes is almost entirely devoid of normative thinking. He sets up no ideal of what conduct should be, but merely investigates the ultimate conditions of social life. Man, he says, is guided by a plurality of passions. The good is simply that which any man desires. But unfortunately there are very severe limitations on the extent to which these desires can be realized, limitations which according to Hobbes lie primarily in the nature of the relations of man to man.

Man is not devoid of reason. But reason is essentially a servant of the passions—it is the faculty of devising ways and means to secure what one desires. Desires are random, there is "no common rule of good and evil to be taken from the nature of the objects themselves." Hence since the passions, the ultimate ends of action, are diverse there is nothing to prevent their pursuit resulting in conflict.

In Hobbes' thinking, the reason for this danger of conflict is to be found in the part played by power. Since all men are seeking to realize their desires they must necessarily seek command over means to this realization. The power a man has is in Hobbes' own words simply "his present means to obtain some future apparent good." One very large element of power is the ability to command the recognition and services of other men. To Hobbes this is the most important among those means which, in the nature of things, are limited. The consequence is that what means to his ends one man commands another is necessarily shut off from. Hence power as a proximate end is inherently a source of division between men.

> Nature hath made men so equal in the faculties of body and mind, that though there be found one man sometimes manifestly stronger in body or of quicker mind than another, yet when all is reckoned together the difference between man and man is not so considerable as that one man can thereupon claim to himself any benefit, to which another may not pretend as well as he.... From this equality of ability ariseth equality of hope in the attaining of our ends. And therefore if any two men desire the same thing which nevertheless they cannot both enjoy, they become enemies; and in the way to their end endeavor to destroy or subdue one another.

In the absence of any restraining control men will adopt to this immediate end the most efficient available means. These means are found in the last analysis to be force and fraud. Hence a situation where every man is the enemy of every other, endeavoring to destroy or subdue him by force or fraud or both. This is nothing but a state of war.

But such a state is even less in conformity with human desires than what most of us know. It is in Hobbes' famous words a state where the life of man is "solitary, poor, nasty, brutish and short." The fear of such a state of things calls into action, as a servant of the most fundamental of all the passions, that of self-preservation, at least a modicum of reason which finds a solution if the difficulty in the social contract. By its terms men agreed to give up their natural liberty to a sovereign authority which in turn guarantees them security, that is immunity from aggression by the force or fraud of others. It is only through the authority of this sovereign that the war of all against all is held in check and order and security maintained.

Hobbes' system of social theory is almost a pure case of utilitarianism. The basis of human action lies in the "passions." These are discrete, randomly variant ends of action, "There is no common rule of good and evil to be taken from the nature of the objects themselves." In the pursuit of these ends men act rationally, choosing, within the limitations of the situation, the most efficient means. But this rationality is strictly limited, reason is the "servant of the passions," it is concerned only with questions of ways and means.

But Hobbes went much farther than merely defining with extraordinary precision the basic units of a utilitarian system of action. He went on to deduce the character of the concrete system which would result if its units were in fact as defined. And in so doing he became involved in an empirical problem which has not yet been encountered, as the present discussion so far has been confined to defining units and noting merely their logical relations in utilitarian thought—the problem of *order*. This problem, in the sense in which Hobbes posed it, constitutes the most fundamental empirical difficulty of utilitarian thought. It will form the main thread of the historical discussion of the utilitarian system and its outcome.

Before taking up his experience with it, two meanings of the term which may easily become confused should be distinguished. They may be called normative order and factual order respectively. The antithesis of the latter is randomness or chance in the strict sense of phenomena conforming to the statistical laws of probability. Factual order, then, connotes essentially accessibility to understanding in terms of logical theory, especially of science. Chance variations are in these terms impossible to understand or to reduce to law. Chance or randomness is the name for that which is incomprehensible, not capable of intelligible analysis.

Normative order, on the other hand, is always relative to a given system of norms or normative elements, whether ends, rules or other norms. . . .

Before leaving Hobbes it is important to elaborate a little further the reasons for the precariousness of order so far as the utilitarian elements actually dominate action. This precariousness rests, in the last analysis, on the existence of classes of things which are scarce, relative to the demand for them, which, as Hobbes says, "two [or more] men desire" but "which nevertheless they cannot both enjoy." Reflection will show that there are many such things desired by men either as ends in themselves or as means to other ends. But Hobbes, with his characteristic penetration, saw that it was not necessary to enumerate and catalogue them and to rest the argument on such a detailed consideration, but that their crucial importance was inherent in the very existence of social relations themselves. For it is inherent in the latter that the actions of men should be potential means to each other's ends. Hence as a proximate end it is a direct corollary of the postulate of rationality that all men should desire and seek power over one another. Thus the concept of power

comes to occupy a central position in the, analysis of the problem of order. A purely utilitarian society is chaotic and unstable, because in the absence of limitations on the use of means, particularly force and fraud, it must, in the nature of the case, resolve itself into an unlimited struggle for power; and in the struggle for the immediate end, power, all prospect of attainment of the ultimate, of what Hobbes called the diverse passions, is irreparably lost.

If the above analysis is correct one might suppose that Hobbes' early experiments with logical thinking on a utilitarian basis would have brought that type of social thought to a rapid and deserved demise. But such was very far from being the case, indeed in the eighteenth and nineteenth centuries it enjoyed a period of such vogue as to be considered almost among the eternal verities themselves. But this was not because the Hobbesian problem was satisfactorily solved. On the contrary, as so often happens in the history of thought, it was blithely ignored and covered up by implicit assumptions. How did this happen?

It is significant that the immediate practical animus of Hobbes' social thought lay in the defense of political authority on a secular basis. A strong government, justified by the social contract, was a necessary bulwark of the security of the commonwealth, threatened as it was by the imminent danger of the resurgence of force and fraud. It has already been remarked that in the argument over political obligation those who defend individual liberty tend to make use of normative rather than factual arguments. It is largely in this context that what later came to be the dominant stream of utilitarian thought developed, so that Hobbes was virtually forgotten. In the process of development there took place a subtle, change. What started as normative arguments about what ought to be, became embodied in the assumptions of what was predominantly considered a factual, scientific theory of human action as it was. By some this theory was looked upon as literally descriptive of the existing social order; by others, more skeptically as, though not the whole truth, at least justified for heuristic, purposes; and above all in either case as constituting the working conceptual tools of a great tradition of thought. Hence for present purposes it matters little which of the two positions was taken since the empirical qualifications of utilitarian theory were embodied in residual categories which played no positive part in the theoretical system itself, at least until the time of its incipient breakdown.

⌒

"DEATH IN THE WESTERN WORLD," 1978

That the death of every known human individual has been one of the central facts of life so long as there has been any human awareness of the human condition does not mean that, being so well known, it is not problematical. On the contrary, like history, it has needed to be redefined and newly analyzed, virtually with every generation. However, as has also been the case with history, with the advancement of knowledge later reinterpretations may have some advantages over earlier.

I start from the proposition that if we are to speak of the death of individuals, we need some conceptualization, beyond common sense, of what a human individual, or "person," is. First, I do not propose to discuss the meaning of the deaths of members of other species, insects, elephants, or dogs, but only of human individuals. Second, I propose to confine discussion to individual persons and not to examine societies, civilizations, or races in this sense.

I

Within these limitations I should like to start with the statement that the human individual is a synthesized *combination* of a living organism and a "personality system," conceived and analyzed at the level of "action" in the sense in which I had and various others have used that term. In older terminology, he is a combination of a "body" and a "mind." The concept of a personality as *analytically* distinguished from an organism is no more mystical than is that of a "culture" as distinguished

from the human population (of organisms) who are its "bearers." The primary criterion of personality as distinguished from the organism, is an organization in terms of symbols and their meaningful relations to each other and to persons. In the process of evolution, personalities should be regarded as emergent from the organic level, as are cultural systems in a different, though related way.

Human individuals, seen in their organic aspect, come into being through bisexual reproduction—and birth—as do all the higher organisms. They then go through a more or less well defined life course and eventually die. The most important single difference among such individual organisms is the duration of their lives, but for each species there is a maximum span: for humans, it is somewhere between ninety and one hundred years. In this sense death is universal, the only question being "at what age?" Within these limits the circumstances of both life and death vary enormously.

It seems that these considerations have an immediate bearing on one of the current controversies about death, namely, the frequent allegation that American society—and some say others—attempts to "deny death." Insofar as this is the case (and I am skeptical), the contention has to be in the face of a vast body of biological knowledge. If any biological proposition can be regarded as firmly established, it is that, for sexually reproducing species, the mortality of individual, "phenotypical" organisms is completely normal. Indeed, mortality could not have evolved if it did not have positive survival value *for the species,* unless evolutionary theory is completely wrong. This fact will be a baseline for our whole analysis.

The human individual is not only a living organism but also a special kind of organism who uses symbols, notably linguistic ones. He learns symbolic meanings, communicates with others and with himself through them as media, and regulates his behaviour, his thought, and his feelings in symbolic terms. I call the individual in this aspect an *actor.* Is an actor "born"? Clearly not in the sense in which an organism is. However, part of the development of the human child is a gradual and complicated process, which has sometimes been called *socialization,* whereby the personality becomes formed. The learning of patterns of relation to others, of language, and of structured ways of handling one's own action in relation to the environment is the center of this process.

Does a personality, then, also die? Because the symbiosis between organism and personality is so close, just as no personality in the human sense can be conceived to develop independently of a living child organism, so it is reasonable to believe that no human personality can be conceived as such to survive the death of the same organism, in the organic sense of death. With respect to causation, however, if the personality is an empirical reality, it certainly influences what happens to the organism, the person's "body," as well as vice versa. The extreme case is suicide, which surely can seldom be explained by purely somatic processes, without any "motives" being involved, as often can a death from cancer. But more generally there is every reason to believe that there are "psychic" factors in many deaths, all manner of illnesses, and various other organic events.

It is firmly established that the viability of the individual organism, human and nonhuman, is self-limiting. Thus, even in the absence of unfavorable environmental conditions, in the course of the "aging" process, there will occur gradual impairment of various organic capacities, until some combination of these impairments proves fatal. Organic death can be staved off by medical measures but cannot be totally prevented. There seems every reason to believe, but there is less clear-cut evidence on this point, that the same is in principle true of the action-personality component of the individual. This means that, with aging, various components of that complex entity lose the necessary capacities to maintain its balances, which eventually will lead to a breakdown. The cases in which there is virtual cessation of personality function without organic death are suggestive in this sense. More generally, if, as I strongly believe, the phenomena of mental illness are real and not merely epiphenomena of organic processes, then it stands to reason that some of them can be severe enough to eventuate in personality death, partly independent of organic death.

We have already noted that at the organic level the human individual does not stand alone but is part of an intergenerational chain of indefinite, though not infinite, durability, most notably the species. The individual organism dies, but if he/she reproduces, the "line" continues into future generations. This intergenerational continuity is as much a fact of life as are individual births and deaths.

There is a direct parallel on the action side: An individual personality is "generated" in symbiosis with a growing individual human organism and dies with that organism. But the individual personality is embedded in transindividual action systems, at two levels, social systems (most notably, whole societies) and cultural systems. There is a close analogy between these two and the relation between somatoplasm and germ plasm on the organic side, both of which are "carried" by the individual organism. Thus, the sociocultural "matrix" in which the individual personality is embedded is in an important sense the counterpart of the population-species matrix in which the individual organism is embedded.

At the organic level the individual organism dies, but the species continues, "life goes on." Also, the individual personality dies, but the society and cultural system, of which in life he was a part, also "goes on." I strongly suspect that this parallel is more than simple analogy.

What is organic death? It is of course a many-faceted thing, but as Freud and many others have said, it is in one principal aspect the "return to the inorganic" state. At this level the human body, as that of other organisms, is made up of inorganic materials but *organized* in quite special ways. When that organization breaks down, the constituent materials are no longer part of a living organism but come to be assimilated to the inorganic environment. In a certain sense this insight has been ancient religious lore; witness the Gospel, "Dust thou art, to dust thou shalt return."

Is the death of a personality to be simply assimilated to this organic paradigm? Most positivists and materialists would say, yes. This answer however, has not been accepted by the majority in most human societies and cultures. From such very primitive peoples as the Australian aborigines, especially as their religion was analyzed by Durkheim, to the most sophisticated of the world religions, there have persisted beliefs in the existence of an individual soul, which can be conceived both to antedate and to survive the individual organism or body, though the ideas of preexistence and of survival have not always co-existed in any given culture. The literature of cultural anthropology and of comparative religion can supply many instances. The issue of the individuality of this nonorganic component of the human individual, outside its symbiosis with the living organism, is also a basis of variability. . . .

VII

So far as it is accessible to cognitive understanding at all, the meaning of death for individual human beings must be approached in the framework of the human condition as a whole. It must include both the relevant scientific and philosophical understanding and must attempt to synthesize them. Finally, it must, as clearly as possible, recognize and take account of the limits of our scientific as well as our philosophical understanding.

We have contended that the development of modern science has so changed the picture as to require revision of many of the received features of Christian tradition, both Catholic and Protestant. This development of science took place in three great stages marked by the synthesis of physical science and the seventeenth century, that of biological science in the nineteenth, and that of the action sciences in the nineteenth to twentieth.

The most important generalizations seem to be the following. First the human individual constitutes a unique symbiotic synthesis of two main components, a living organism and a living personality. Second, both components seem to be *inherently* limited in duration of life, and we have no knowledge which indicates that their symbiosis can be in any radical sense dissociated. Third, the individualized entity *both* is embedded in and derives in some sense from a transgenerational matrix which, seen in relation to individual mortality, has indefinite but not infinite durability.

From this point of view, death, or the limited temporal duration of the individual life course, must be regarded as one of the facts of life that is as inexorable as the need to eat and breathe in order to live. In this sense, death is completely normal, to the point that its "denial" must be regarded as pathological. Moreover, this normality includes the consideration that from an evolutionary point of view, which we have contended is basic to *all* modern science, death must be regarded as having high survival value organically at least to the species, actionwise to the future of the sociocultural system. These scientific considerations are not trivial, or conventional, or culture-bound but are *fundamental*.

There is a parallel set of considerations on the philosophical side. For purpose of elucidating this aspect of the problem complex I have used Kant's framework as presented in his three critiques. On the one hand, this orientation is critical in that it challenges the contention that absolute knowledge is demonstrable in *any* of the three aspects of the human condition. Thus, any conception like that of the ontological essence of nature, the idea of God, or the notion of the eternal life of the human soul are categorized as *Dinge an sich*, which in principle are not demonstrable by rational cognitive procedures.

At the same time, Kant insisted, and I follow him here, on the cognitive necessity of assuming a transcendental component, a set of categories in each of the three realms, that is not reducible to the status of humanly available inputs from either the empirical or the absolute telic references of the human condition. We have interpreted this to mean that human orientation must be relativized to the human condition not treated as dogmatically fixed in the nature of things.

The consequence of this revitalization that we have particularly emphasized is that it creates a new openness for orientations, which men are free to exploit by speculation and to commit themselves in faith but with reference to which they cannot claim what Kant called apodictic certainty. At the same time, we again insist with Kant that this openness must be qualified by the continuing subjection of human life to the constraints of the transcendental aspects of the human condition, which presumably cannot be altered by human action.

If this is a correct account of the situation, it is not surprising that there is a great deal of bafflement, anxiety, and indeed downright confusion in the contemporary attitudes and opinions in this area. I think that in its broad lines what I have presented is indeed an accurate diagnosis of the situation, but it would certainly be too much to claim that such an orientation is fully institutionalized.

It can be said to be most firmly established at philosophical levels and those of rather abstract scientific theory. Even there, however, there is still much controversy and anything like full consensus seems to be far off. Yet I still maintain that the development, say, from the medieval Catholic synthesis, is the *main line*. The grounds for this belief rest on the conviction that no equally basic alternative is available in the main cultural tradition and that this broad orientation is the most congenial to "reasonable men" in our situation. So far as fundamentals are concerned, I am afraid that, within the limitations of this essay, it will be necessary to leave it at that.

It may help, however, to mitigate the impression of extreme abstractness if in closing I very briefly discuss three empirical points. First, though scientific evidence has established the fact of the inevitability of death with increasing clarity, this does not mean that the *experience* of death by human populations may not change with changing circumstances. Thus, Victor Lidz and I have distinguished between inevitable death and "adventitious" death—that is "premature" relative to the full life span and in principle preventable by human action. Within the last century and a half or so, this latter category of deaths has decreased enormously. The proportion of persons in modern populations over sixty-five has thus increased greatly, as has the expectancy of life at birth to seventy-two in 1975 in the United States. This clearly means that a greatly increased proportion of modern humans live out a full life course. Perhaps precisely because of this change, premature deaths from diseases, wars, accidents, or natural disasters like earthquakes have become more, rather than less disturbing events than they were previously.

Moreover, persons who live to a ripe old age will experience an inevitably larger number of deaths of persons important to them. These will be in decreasing number the deaths of persons younger than themselves notably their own children, but increasingly those of their parents and whole ranges of persons of an older generation such as teachers, senior occupational associates, and public figures. (During this writing, for example, I learned of the death of Mao Tse-tung, certainly a figure of worldwide significance.) Quite clearly, these demographic changes have a strong effect on the balance of experience and expecta-

tion of the deaths of significant others and anticipation of one's own death.

Second, one of the centrally important aspects of a process of change in orientation of the sort described should be the appearance of signs of the differentiation of attitudes and conceptions in the relevant area. As Fox, Lidz, and I have pointed out, there has indeed been such a process of differentiation, which seems not yet to be completed, with respect to both ends of the life cycle. With respect to the beginning, there is the controversy over abortion. However this controversy may eventually be resolved, it seems unlikely that public attitudes will go back to the traditional positions of either no abortions in any circumstances or only abortions that are strictly necessary to save the life of the mother. The interesting feature of this controversy is that it has entailed attempts to specify the point at which the life of a human *person,* as distinct from the human *organism* at conception, begins.

Concomitant with this has been an attempt at redefinition of death. So far the most important approach has been to draw a line *within* the organic sector between what has been called "brain death," in which irreversible changes have taken place, destroying the functioning of the central nervous system, and what has been called "metabolic death," in which above all heartbeat and respiration have ceased. The problem has been highlighted by the capacity of "artificial" measures, say, mechanical respirations, to keep persons "alive" for long periods despite the fact that brain function has irreversibly ceased. The point of major interest here is the connection of brain function with the personality level of individuality. Hence, an organism that continues to "live" at *only* the metabolic level may be said to be dead as a person. We would expect still further elaborations of these themes in the future.

Third, we may make a few remarks about the significance for our problem of Freud's most mature theoretical statement. It will be remembered that in his last major theoretical work, Freud rather drastically revised his views on the nature of anxiety, coming to focus on the expectation of the loss of an "object." By "object" Freud meant a human individual standing in an emotionally significant relation to the person of reference. To the child, of course, his parents become "lost objects" as he grows up in that their significance to him as growing child is inevitably "lost." The ultimate loss of a concrete human person as object (of cathexis, Freud said) is the death of that person. To have "grown away" from one's parents is one thing but to experience their actual deaths is another. Freud's own account of the impact on him of his father's death is a particularly relevant case in point.

Equally clearly, an individual's own death, in anticipation, can be subsumed under the category of object loss, particularly in view of Freud's theory of narcissism, by which he meant the individual's cathexis of his own self as a love object.

Anxiety, however, is neither the actual experience of object loss nor is it, according to Freud, the fear of it. It is an anticipatory orientation in which the actor's own emotional security is particularly involved. It is a field of rather free play of fantasy as to what might be the consequences of an anticipated or merely possible event.

Given the hypothesis, to which I subscribe, that in our scientifically oriented civilization there is widespread acceptance of death—meant as the antithesis of its denial—I see no reason why this should eliminate or even substantially reduce *anxiety* about death, both that of others and one's own. Indeed, in speaking earlier about the impact of demographic changes in the incidence of death, I suggested that in certain circumstances the level of anxiety may be expected to increase rather than the reverse.

It seems that the frequent assertions that our society is characterized by pervasive denial of death may often be interpreted as calling attention to widespread anxiety about death, which I submit is *not* the same thing. There can be no doubt that in most cases death is, in experience and in anticipation, a traumatic event. Fantasies, in such circumstances, are often marked by unrealism. But the prevalence of such phenomena does not constitute a distortion of the basic cultural framework within which we moderns orient ourselves to the meaning of death.

Indeed, in my opinion, this and the two preceding illustrations serve to enhance the importance of clarification at the theoretical and philosophical levels, to which the bulk of this essay has been devoted. Clarification is essential if we are to understand such problems as the shifts in attitudes toward various age groups in modern society, particularly older persons, the relatively sudden eruption of dissatisfaction with traditional modes of conceptualizing the beginning and the termination of human lives, and allegations about the pervasive denial of death, which is often interpreted as a kind of failure of "intestinal fortitude." However important recent movements for increasing expression of emotional interests and the like, ours remains a culture to which its cognitive framework is of paramount significance. It is a contribution to the understanding of this framework and its meaning, in an area that is emotionally highly sensitive, that I would like this essay to be evaluated.

ERICH FROMM

1900–1980

Erich Pinchas Fromm, only child of an orthodox Jewish wine merchant, was born in Frankfurt on March 23, 1900. He referred to his parents and himself as "neurotic," and took his Judaism very seriously until he was about 26. He married Frieda Reichmann (a psychoanalyst) on June 16, 1926, and separated in 1931, then married Henny Gurland in 1944, who died in 1952, finally marrying Annis Freeman in 1953. A few days before his 80th birthday, he died in Muralto, Switzerland from his fourth heart attack (earlier ones in 1966, 1977, and 1978). He graduated from the Wöler-Schule in Frankfurt in 1918, was despondent over the "irrationality" that had produced WWI, and then spent a year studying law at the local University. But in his search for the meaning of aggression and civilizational collapse, he migrated to sociology, where he, like Norbert Elias, studied under Alfred Weber, Max's brother, along with Heinrich Rickert and Karl Jaspers. Fromm finished his doctorate in 1922 with a dissertation on the sociopsychological structures of Jewish diaspora communities. In Munich he studied psychiatry and psychology, then in 1928 moved to Berlin for a didactic analysis with Hans Sachs, plus more psychoanalytical studies at the Karl Abraham Institute. In 1929 he co-founded the South German Institute for Psychoanalysis in Frankfurt, and the next year joined a group that would become the famous "Frankfurt School" of critical sociology. In 1931 he contracted TB, separated from his first wife, and lived part time in Davos until April, 1934. He began publishing psychoanalytic works in 1932, and in 1933 was invited to Chicago by Karen Horney, the noted American analyst, with whom he became friends. This prompted him to emigrate to the U.S. in May, 1934, and despite continued health problems, worked once again with the Frankfurt School colleagues based at Columbia. He got to know Harry Stack Sullivan, and published on the "authoritarian personality" in 1936. In 1937 he left orthodox Freudianism and took an explanatory path more toward relatedness and less toward sexual drives. In 1938 he relapsed with TB and spent six months at a Davos sanatorium.

In 1941 Fromm made himself internationally famous with *Escape from Freedom,* often regarded as his most important book (see the excerpt below), an intellectual feat which also got him a position at the New School in New York City. Later he published *The Sane Society* (1955), after moving to Mexico in 1950, showing how the anti-social tendencies of modern people are more a function of crushing social structure and its demands than of primordial drives of the kind Freud and his followers posited. He also returned to his youthful enthusiasm in *Marx's Concept of Man* (1961) in which he analyzed the early philosophical works of Marx, and connected them with contemporary interests in alienation. He also wrote popular works about Mexican peasants, religion, psychoanalytic doctrine, consumerism, and an excellent late work, *The Anatomy of Human Destructiveness* (1973) which is the best of that genre. He was immensely famous and influential in the mid-60s, even though he spent most of his time in Mexico. His political action in the U.S. ended when Eugene McCarthy was defeated by Nixon in 1968. Fromm was by all counts the most popular psychoanalytic Marxist of his era, far overshadowing his former colleagues in the Frankfurt School, who seemed to resent his fame and diminished his role in their official histories. Yet his star has faded just as theirs has become brighter in the ensuing 20 years since his death. Now his answers seem somehow too pat for our troubled times of "postmodernity" and globalization.

ESCAPE FROM FREEDOM, 1941

Freedom and Democracy: The Illusion of Individuality

Our aim will be to show that the structure of modern society affects man in two ways simultaneously: he becomes more independent, self-reliant, and critical, and he becomes more isolated, alone and afraid.

. . . In discussing the two aspects of freedom for modern man, we have pointed out the economic conditions that make for increasing isolation and powerlessness of the individual in our era; in discussing the psychological results we have shown that this powerlessness leads either to the kind of escape that we find in the authoritarian character, or else to a compulsive conforming in the process of which the isolated individual becomes an automaton, loses his self, and yet at the same time consciously conceives of himself as free and subject only to himself. . . .

In our society emotions in general are discouraged. While there can be no doubt that any creative thinking—as well as any other creative activity—is inseparably linked with emotion, it has become an ideal to think and to live without emotions. To be "emotional" has become synonymous with being unsound or unbalanced. By the acceptance of this standard the individual has become greatly weakened; his thinking is impoverished and flattened. On the other hand, since

emotions cannot be completely killed, they must have their existence totally apart from the intellectual side of the personality; the result is the cheap and insincere sentimentality with which movies and popular songs feed millions of emotion-starved customers.

There is one tabooed emotion that I want to mention in particular, because its suppression touches deeply on the roots of personality: the sense of tragedy. As we saw in an earlier chapter, the awareness of death and of the tragic aspect of life, whether dim or clear, is one of the basic characteristics of man. Each culture has its own way of coping with the problem of death. For those societies in which the process of individuation has progressed but little, the end of individual existence is less of a problem since the experience of individual existence itself is less developed. Death is not yet conceived as being basically different from life. Cultures in which we find a higher development of individuation have treated death according to their social and psychological structure. . . .

Character and the Social Process

While it is true that man is molded by the necessities of the economic and social structure of society, he is not infinitely adaptable. Not only are there certain physiological needs that imperatively call for satisfaction, but there are also certain psychological qualities inherent in man that need to be satisfied and that result in certain reactions if they are frustrated. What are these qualities? The most important seems to be the tendency to grow, to develop and realize potentialities which man has developed in the course of history—as, for instance, the faculty of creative and critical thinking and of having differentiated emotional and sensuous experiences. Each of these potentialities has a dynamism of its own. Once they have developed in the process of evolution they tend to be expressed. This tendency can be suppressed and frustrated, but such suppression results in new reactions, particularly in the formation of destructive and symbiotic impulses. It also seems that this general tendency to grow—which is the psychological equivalent of the identical biological tendency—results in such specific tendencies as the desire for freedom and the hatred against oppression, since freedom is the fundamental condition for any growth. Again, the desire for freedom can be repressed, it can disappear from the awareness of the individual; but even then it does not cease to exist as a potentiality, and indicates its existence by the conscious or unconscious hatred by which such suppression is always accompanied.

We find then that for everybody who is powerless, justice and truth are the most important weapons in the fight for his freedom and growth. Aside from the fact that the majority of mankind throughout its history has had to defend itself against more powerful groups which could oppress and exploit it, every individual in childhood goes through a period which is characterized by powerlessness. It seems to us that in this state of powerlessness traits like the sense of justice and truth develop and become potentialities common to man as such. We arrive therefore at the fact that, *although character development is shaped by the basic conditions of life and although there is no biologically fixed human nature, human nature has a dynamism of its own that constitutes an active factor in the evolution of the social process.* Even if we are not yet able to state clearly in psychological terms what the exact nature of this human dynamism is, we must recognize its existence. In trying to avoid the errors of biological and metaphysical concepts we must not succumb to an equally grave error, that of a sociological relativism in which man is nothing but a puppet, directed by the strings of social circumstances. Man's inalienable rights of freedom and happiness are founded in inherent human qualities: his striving lo live, to expand and to express the potentialities that have developed in him in the process of historical evolution. . . .

The third important point of difference is closely linked up with the previous ones. Freud, on the basis of his instinctivistic orientation and also of a profound conviction of the wickedness of human nature, is prone to interpret all "ideal" motives in man as the result of something "mean"; a case in point is his explanation of the sense of justice as the outcome of the original envy a child has for anybody who has more than he. As has been pointed out before, we believe that ideals like truth, justice, freedom, although they are frequently mere phrases or rationalizations, can be genuine strivings, and that any analysis which does not deal with these strivings as dynamic factors is fallacious. These ideals have no metaphysical character but are rooted in the conditions of human life and can be analyzed as such. The fear of falling back into metaphysical or idealistic concepts should not stand in the way of such analysis. It is the task of psychology as an empirical science to study motivation by ideals as well as the moral problems connected with them, and thereby to free our thinking on such matters from the unempirical and metaphysical elements that befog the issues in their traditional treatment. . . .

What is the principle of interpretation that this book has applied to the understanding of the human basis of culture? Before answering this question it may be useful to recall the main trends of interpretation with which our own differs.

1. The "psychologistic" approach which characterizes Freud's thinking, according to which cultural phenomena are rooted in psychological factors that result from instinctual drives which in themselves are influenced by society only through some measure of suppression. Following this line of interpretation Freudian authors have explained capitalism as the outcome of anal eroticism and the development of early Christianity as the result of the ambivalence toward the father image.

2. The "economistic" approach, as it is presented in the misapplication of Marx's interpretation of history. According to this view, subjective economic interests are the cause of cultural phenomena, such as religion and political ideas. From such a pseudo-Marxian viewpoint, one might try to explain Protestantism as no more than the answer to certain economic needs of the bourgeoisie.

3. Finally there is the "idealistic" position, which is represented by Max Weber s analysis, *The Protestant Ethic and the Spirit of Capitalism.* He holds that new religious ideas are responsible for the development of a new type of economic behavior and a new spirit of culture, although he emphasizes that this behavior is never *exclusively* determined by religious doctrines.

In contrast to these explanations, we have assumed that ideologies and culture in general are rooted in the social character; that the social character itself is molded by the mode of existence of a given society; and that in their turn the dominant character traits become productive forces shaping the social process. With regard to the problem of the spirit of Protestantism and capitalism, I have tried to show that the collapse of medieval society threatened the middle class; that this threat resulted in a feeling of powerless isolation and doubt; that this psychological change was responsible for the appeal of Luther's and Calvin's doctrines; that these doctrines intensified and stabilized the characterological changes; and that the character traits that thus developed then became productive forces in the development of capitalism which in itself resulted from economic and political changes. . . .

Economic forces are effective, but they must be understood not as psychological motivations but as objective conditions; psychological forces are effective, but they must be understood as historically conditioned themselves; ideas are effective, but they must be understood as being rooted in the whole of the character structure of members of a social group. In spite of this interdependence of economic, psychological, and ideological forces, however, each of them has also a certain independence. This is particularly true of the economic development which, being dependent on objective factors, such as the natural productive forces, technique, geographical factors, takes place according to its own laws. As to the psychological forces, we have indicated that the same holds true; they are molded by the external conditions of life, but they also have a dynamism of their own; that is, they are the expression of human needs which, although they can be molded, cannot be uprooted. In the ideological sphere we find a similar autonomy rooted in logical laws and in the tradition of the body of knowledge acquired in the course of history.

We can restate the principle in terms of social character: The social character results from the dynamic adaptation of human nature to the structure of society. Changing social conditions result in changes of the social character, that is, in new needs and anxieties. These new needs give rise to new ideas and, as it were, make men susceptible to them; these new ideas in their turn tend to stabilize and intensify the new social character and to determine man's actions. In other words, social conditions influence ideological phenomena through the medium of character; character, on the other hand, is not the result of passive adaptation to social conditions but of a dynamic adaptation on the basis of elements that either are biological, inherent in human nature or have become inherent as the result of historic evolution.

❧

THE SANE SOCIETY, 1955

Consumerism (as a Compensation of Anxiety and Depression) versus the Joy of Life

Man is in the process of becoming a *homo consumens,* total consumer. This image of man almost has the character of a new religious vision in which heaven is just a big warehouse where everyone can buy something new every day, indeed, where he can buy everything that he wants and even a little more than his neighbor. This vision of the total consumer is indeed a new image of man that is conquering the world, quite regardless of differences of political organization and ideology.

To begin with, I would like to describe this *homo consumens* as a psychological phenomenon, as a new type of social character, which has its own dynamic. This dynamic can be understood only in the sense of the Freudian character dynamic if one distinguishes between what a person is aware of and the unconscious forces that drive him. *Homo consumens* is the person for whom everything becomes an object of consumption: cigarettes and beer, liquor, books, love and sexuality, lectures and picture galleries. There is nothing whatsoever that could not become an object of consumption for this person. Even certain drugs from which one can derive immediate enlightenment are consumed.

The question arises: Is not man by his nature someone who must consume in order to stay alive? Indeed, man must consume things just like any other living creature. Yet the novel phenomenon consists in the fact that a character structure develops for which even things that were acquired in an entirely different manner, i. e, the rich world of human invention and culture, become, without exception, objects of consumption.

From a psychological point of view, what does this manner of consumption consist in [and what is used to compensate for it]? Unconsciously, this new type of person is a passive, empty, anxious, isolated person for whom life has no meaning and who is profoundly alienated and bored. If one asks these people who are today consuming liquor, travel vacations, and books whether they feel unhappy and bored, then they answer, "Not at all, we're completely happy. We go on trips, we drink, we eat, we buy more and more for ourselves. You aren't bored doing that!"

Consciously, then, these people are not bored. At this point, one must indeed ask analytically whether it is possible that these people are perhaps unconsciously empty, bored, and alienated and whether it is possible that they are passive people unconsciously—the eternal infant who does not only wait for his bottle, but for whom everything is a bottle and who never develops an activity by his own powers.

In fact, the anxious, bored, alienated person compensates for his anxiety by a compulsive consumption that, as a general illness—or, more precisely, as a symptom of the "pathology of normalcy"—no one thinks is an illness. Indeed, one thinks of the idea of "illness" only when someone is sicker than other people. When, however everyone suffers from the same illness, the idea of illness does not at all arise in people's minds. Thus, this inner void, this inner anxiety is symbolically cured by compulsive consumption.

Compulsive eating disorder is the paradigm of this mechanism. If one looks into why certain people suffer from compulsive eating disorders, then one indeed finds that, behind this disorder, which is acknowledged as such, there is something unconscious, namely, depression or anxiety. A person feels empty, and in order simultaneously to fill this void symbolically, he fills himself up with other things, with things that come from the outside, in order to overcome the feeling of inner emptiness and inner weakness. Many people notice in themselves that, when they are anxious or feel depressed, they have a certain tendency to buy something or to go to the refrigerator or to eat a little more than usual and that they then feel somewhat less depressed and somewhat less anxious.

On the other hand, the problem is very closely tied up with the economic structure of modern western society, which is economically based on the reality of complete, absolute and ever-growing consumption. What the economy needs most of all for its own operation is that people buy, buy, and buy again, since there is otherwise no constantly growing demand for goods that industry can produce and must produce to an ever-growing degree if it wants to multiply its capital. For that reason, industry compels people by all means of temptation to consume more.

In the nineteenth century, it was immoral to buy something for which one did not have the money. In the twentieth century, it is considered to be immoral not to buy something for which one does not have the money, since people buy and travel even on installment payments. By means of an enormously refined advertising mechanism, the economy seduces people into buying more and more.

People become anxious and alienated by the capitalist system's method of production: because this system produces larger and larger economic and bureaucratic giants vis-à-vis which the individual person feels small and helpless; because the individual person can participate less and less actively in the events within society; because there is an enormous fear in many social circles of not moving up, of losing the position that one has attained, the fear that one's own wife and friends will judge one as a "failure" if one does not reach what the others reach.

In reality, we are dealing with a *circulus vitiosus:* the person who becomes anxious in this system consumes. But also the person who is lured to consumption becomes anxious, because he becomes a passive person, because he always only takes things in, because he does not actively experience anything in the world. The more anxious he becomes, the more he must consume, and the more he consumes, the more anxious he becomes. Thus, there arises the circle in which man feels all the more powerless as his machines become more powerful, that is, as what he produces becomes more powerful. And he compensates for all this by constant and never-ending consumption.

The problem of *pseudo freedom* is tied up with the problem of consumption. In the nineteenth century, the idea of freedom was essentially connected with having property at one's disposal and with the freedom of commercial enterprise. Today, private property is only a very small part of the means of production in the advanced capitalist countries. General Motors and the Ford Company, the two largest automobile giants in America, for example, are in the hands of a self-perpetuating bureaucracy, and the hundreds of thousands of owners of the actual property do not have a crucial influence on the companies. (The freedom of property is a concept that was really meaningful only in the nineteenth century. That is why Marx was wrong when he believed that one could change something essential through the socialization of the means of production. Marx oriented himself to the nineteenth century's concept of property and did not foresee that property as a means of production would no longer be a basic notion in the twentieth century.)

Today's pseudo-freedom lies in the sphere of consumption. The consumer comes to the supermarket and sees ten different brands of cigarettes that have already been trumpeted on the radio, on television, and in the newspapers. They all are vying for his favor, as if they wanted to say, "Please, choose me!" Now, it is true that the buyer basically knows that all these are actually the same brands, whether they be cigarettes or the soaps that are praised with pretty girls or even just with girls' legs. Purely intellectually, the buyer is aware that all of that is completely irrational. Nevertheless, it gives him a feeling of freedom to be able to choose what he wants. So he grants his favor to Chesterfield cigarettes instead of Marlboro or to Marlboro instead of Chesterfield.

By exactly this means, though, he becomes a pseudo-personality. When he defines himself by smoking Marlboro, he determines his being by having this object of consumption. That is his self, his personality. In the act of choosing, he experiences his power, while, in reality, he is experiencing his powerlessness, because his choosing is only the result of influences that are at work behind his back. He believes that he is consciously making his choice, while, in reality, he is prompted into choosing between two different products that are suggested to him. It is important that people smoke and that, in making this choice, they have the experience of freedom and of power.

PITIRIM SOROKIN

1889–1968

Pitirim Aleksandrovic Sorokin, the second of three sons of an icon maker and artist, was born in Tur'ja, Russia on January 21, 1889, married Elena Baratinskaya in 1917 (who received her Ph.D. in botany at the University of Minnesota in 1925), and had two sons with her, Peter (scientist) and Sergei (engineer). He died in Winchester, Massachusetts on February 10, 1968, age 75. Sorokin's mother died in 1892 and the youngest son was sent to live with an aunt while Pitirim and his brother, Vassily, traveled with his father in search of work. Injured in his upper lip with a hammer by his drunken father, and after a year of healing, Pitirim and his brother fled in 1899. He received a church-sponsored scholarship in 1903, and shortly thereafter began consorting with anti-czarist political groups, which eventually got him jailed for two months in 1907. For the next two years he tutored and fraternized with artists and intellectuals, also meeting his future wife. He studied psychology at the Psychoneurological Institute in St Petersburg in 1909–10, followed by his first publication (1911), a bout with TB, and a developing reputation as a revolutionary thinker. He took his undergraduate degree at the University of St. Petersburg (1914), and after writing two dissertations, became the first professor of sociology there (1919–1922). He fled the new Soviet Union after being labeled an enemy of the state for having served as Kerensky's secretary in the transitional Menshevik government (1917), and by crossing Siberia at great personal risk, emigrated to the U.S. in 1922. He recounts this harrowing episode in one of his two autobiographies, *A Long Journey* (1963). Sorokin quickly became the most distinguished sociologist at the University of Minnesota after 1924, where he wrote a pioneering textbook on rural sociology with a colleague, and also delineated the modern study of social classes with his now classic study, *Social Mobility* (1927). He was asked to found the sociology department at Harvard in 1930, which he did brilliantly, bringing in graduate students like Robert Merton and George Homans. Using Merton and others as research assistants, Sorokin compiled a monumental comparative study of cultures across time and space, *Social and Cultural Dynamics* (4 vols., 1937–41), which for a time was widely read and discussed, even by those who opposed his general theory. Later it was abridged into a single volume. Sorokin's attempt to systematize sociology for undergraduates was called *Society, Culture, and Personality* (1947), but was much too difficult and comprehensive for its intended audience. It did, however, well summarize Sorokin's general sociology to that point. Shifting focus, he published *Altruistic Love* in 1950, and with money from the Lilly Foundation, he began a series of studies at his Center for Creative Altruism which he hoped would help divert global civilization from its apparent collision course with atomic war and self-destruction.

Sorokin remains famous for a distinction he made in popularization, *The Crisis of Our Age* (1941), and elsewhere between "sensate" and "ideational" societies, the first given to brute empiricism and, behaviorally, tending toward the hedonistic, the latter more prone to mysticism and religious experience, naturally developing restraint and obedience. Sorokin claimed that societies vacillate between these poles over time, but he was extremely concerned about the likely future of Western culture, because it had entered a period of what seemed to him uninhibited sensate practices which, when linked with atomic weapons, spelled disaster. In ways his argument recalls that of Spengler, but Sorokin was much more sociological and systematic in gathering and presenting data.

THE CRISIS OF OUR AGE, 1941

Tragic Dualism, Chaotic Syncretism, Quantitative Colossalism, and Diminishing Creativeness of the Contemporary Sensate Culture

The Culture of Man's Glorification and Degradation. When any socio-cultural system enters the stage of its disintegration, the following four symptoms of the disintegration appear and grow in it: first, the inner self-contradictions of an irreconcilable dualism in such a culture; second, its formlessness—a chaotic syncretism of undigested elements taken from different cultures; third a quantitative colossalism—mere size and quantity at the cost of quality; and fourth, a progressive exhaustion of its creativeness in the field of great and perennial values. In addition to all the signs of disintegration discussed previously, these four symptoms of disintegration have already emerged and are rampant in this contemporary sensate culture of ours.

Our culture in its present sensate phase is full of irreconcilable contradictions. It proclaims equality of all human beings; and it practices an enormous number of intellectual, moral, mental, economic, political, and other inequalities. It proclaims "the equality of opportunity" in theory; in

practice it provides practically none. It proclaims "government of the people, for the people, and by the people"; in practice it tends to be more and more an oligarchy or a plutocracy or a dictatorship of this or that faction. It stimulates an expansion of wishes and wants, and it inhibits their satisfaction. It proclaims social security and a decent minimum of living conditions for everyone, even as it is progressively destroying security for all and showing itself incapable of eliminating unemployment or of giving decent conditions to the masses. It strives to achieve the maximum of happiness for the maximum number of human beings, but it increasingly fails in that purpose. It advertises the elimination of group hatreds, while in fact it increasingly seethes with group antagonism of every kind—racial, national, state, religious, class and others. The unprecedented explosion of internal disturbances and wars of the twentieth century is an incontrovertible evidence of that failure. Our culture condemns egotisms of all kinds and boasts of the socialization and humanization of everything and everybody; in reality, it displays unbridled greed, cruelty, and egotism of individuals as well as of groups, beginning with innumerable lobbying and pressure groups and continuing throughout economic, political, occupational, religious, state, family, and other groups. And so on, and so on.

Without attempting to enumerate all the self-contradictions of this culture of ours, let us take, instead, what appears to be its central self-contradiction. This consists in the fact that *our culture simultaneously is a culture of man's glorification and of man's degradation.* On the one hand, it boundlessly glorifies man and extols man-made culture and society. On the other, it utterly degrades the human being and all his cultural and social values. We live in an age which exalts man as the supreme end, and, at the same time, an age which vilifies man and his cultural values endlessly. The "World of Tomorrow" in the New York World's Fair is a flat symbol of one aspect of this tragic dualism; the catastrophe of the present war is a sign of the other.

Never before has man displayed such a genius for scientific discoveries and technological inventions. No previous period can rival the power of contemporary man in the modification of cosmic and biological conditions to suit his needs. At no time before has man been the molder of his own destiny to such an extent as he is now. We live, indeed, in an age of the greatest triumph of human genius.

No wonder, therefore, that we are proud of man. It is not strange that our culture has become homo-centric, humanitarian, and humanistic *par excellence*. Man is its glorious center. It makes him "the measure of all things." It exalts him as the hero and the greatest value, not by virtue of his creation by God in God's own image, but in his own right, by virtue of man's own marvelous achievements. It substitutes the religion of humanity for the religions of superhuman deities. It professes a firm belief in the possibility of limitless progress based on man's ability to control his own destiny, to eradicate all social and cultural evils, and to create an even better and finer world, free from war and bloody strife, from crime, poverty, insanity, stupidity, and vulgarity. In all these respects we live, indeed, in an era of a truly great glorification of man and his culture.

Unfortunately, this dazzling façade is not the only aspect of our cultural and social edifice. Like the mythical double-faced Janus, it has another—and more sinister—face, the face of a great degradation and de-humanization of man; of debasement, distortion, and desecration of all social and cultural values. If the dazzling façade glorifies man as a divine hero, the second face strips him of anything divine and heroic. If one face of our culture shows it as a creative flame of human genius rising higher and higher—*per aspera ad astra*—to the eternal world of absolute values, its second face sneers at such a self-delusion and drags it down to the level of a mere reflexological ant hill, to the mere "adjustment mechanism" of human ants and bees.

We do not like to parade this sinister face of our culture; it is not exhibited at any World's Fair; and yet it is as certain as any solid fact can be. Even more, in the course of time, as we have seen, it is appearing more and more frequently, and progressively tends to overshadow the sunny aspect of our cultural world. A mere glance at the main compartments of our culture will be sufficient to show this fact.

To begin with, take *contemporary science* and ask how it defines man. The current answers are, as we have seen, that man is a variety of electron-proton complex; or an animal closely related to the ape or monkey; or a reflex mechanism; or a variety of stimulus-response relationships; or a psychoanalytical bag filled either by libido or basic physiological drives; or a mechanism controlled mainly by digestive and economic needs. Such are the current physico-chemical, biological, and psycho-social conceptions of man. No doubt man *is* all these things. But do any or all of these conceptions completely explain the essential nature of man? Do they touch his most fundamental properties which make him a creature unique in the world? Most of the definitions which pretend to be especially scientific rarely, if ever, raise such questions. They pass them by.

We are so accustomed to such views that we often fail to see the utter depreciation of man and his culture implied in them. Instead of depicting man as a child of God, and a bearer of the highest values in this empirical world, and for this reason sacred, they strip him of anything divine and great and reduce him to a mere inorganic or organic complex. Thus is contemporary science permeated by the tragic dualism discussed earlier. With one hand it creates all the real values that increase man's *summum bonum;* With the other it invents cannon and bombers, poisonous gas and tanks, that kill man and destroy his culture.

Like science, *contemporary philosophy* has also contributed its share to the degradation of man and his culture: first, in the form of the growth of mechanistic materialism for the last few centuries;

second, in th debasement of the truth itself either to a mere matter of convenience (Mach, Poincaré, Petzold, Richard Avenarius, K. Pearson, William James, John Dewey, and other representatives of positivism, neo-positivism, pragmatism, operationalism, instrumentalism, logical positivism, and other similar philosophical movements), or to a mere fictional and arbitrary "convention" (the philosophies of *also ob* or "as if"); or to a mere "ideology," "derivation," or "rationalization" as a by-product of economic, sensual, or other drives and residues (Marxianism, Paretianism, Freudianism); and third, in making the organs of the senses the main and often the only criterion of truth. Materialism identifies man and cultural values with matter; for this reason it cannot help stripping man and his values of any exceptional and unique position in the world. Truth reduced to a mere convenience or convention destroys itself. In the maze of contradictory conveniences and conventions, thousands of contradictory "truths" appear, each as valid as the others. For this reason the very difference between the true and the false disappears.

With the degradation of truth, man is debased from the sublime seeker after truth as an absolute value to that of the hypocrite who uses "truth" as a beautiful smoke screen for the justification of his impulses and lust, profit and greed. In so far as modern philosophy propagated these conceptions, it has its own poisonous aspect and contributes to the depreciation of man and of truth itself. . . .

Similar dualism pervades our minds, our conduct, and our social relationships. We aspire for happiness; and prepare wretchedness for ourselves. The more we try to improve our well-being, the more we lose our peace of mind, without which no happiness is possible. Instead of being serene, at peace with God, the world and his fellow men, contemporary man is a boiling pot of desires that are at war with one another, and with those of his fellows. He is torn between them, cannot control them, and is in a state of perpetual dissatisfaction and restlessness. We aspire for the maximum of material comfort; and we condone privation and misery. We eulogize love, and cultivate hatred. We proclaim man sacred, and slaughter him pitilessly. We proclaim peace, and wage war. We believe in cooperation and solidarity, and multiply competition, rivalry, antagonism, and conflicts. We stand for order, and plot revolutions. We boast of the guaranteed rights of man, of the sanctity of constitutions and covenants; and we deprive man of all rights and break all constitutions and pacts. And so on, endlessly. The tragic dualism of our culture is indisputable and is widening from day to day. Its soul is hopelessly split. It is a house divided against itself. The dark Demon in it is at relentless war with its Good Genius. And the Demon of Destruction has been progressively rising over its creative Angel. Hence the spread of the sinister blackout of our culture.

JEAN-PAUL SARTRE

1905–1980

Jean-Paul Sartre, whose father (naval officer) died shortly after his birth, was born on June 21, 1905 in Paris, lived for decades with the feminist theorist and novelist Simone de Beauvoir, never reproduced, and died on April 15, 1980 in his hometown at 74. De Beauvoir's multi-volume autobiography provides detailed information about their lives and writings, even including one entire volume concerning Sartre's final battle with lung disease. Sartre's substitute father was his maternal grandfather, Carl Schweitzer, a German professor at the Sorbonne and also uncle of the world-famous musicologist and colonial physician, Albert Schweitzer. In *The Words* (1963), an elegantly concise autobiography, Sartre explained that his ocular peculiarity and small size made him persona non grata among other children, and that despite his mother's efforts to find him playmates, he was mostly left to his own devices. Luckily for the world of literature and philosophy, he hid from a painful social world in his family's 6th floor apartment, and wrote himself into a happier frame of mind. His output was torrential and lifelong (e.g., his four-volume, 3000-page study of Flaubert is almost unreadably prolix, as is his screenplay for the life of Freud). Sartre went to the Lycée Henri IV in Paris and then to another school in La Rochelle after acquiring a stepfather. From there he took the traditional route of the French intellectual elite by graduating from the École Normale Supérieure (1929). He was blessed not only with an unmarried lifelong mate of extraordinary gifts, but also with a circle of friends and rivals that at the time would have been hard to beat for sheer brilliance, including Raymond Aron, Merleau-Ponty, Simone Weil, Jean Hyppolite, and Levi-Strauss. He also spent a year studying philosophy in Berlin with both Heidegger and Husserl, from whom he adopted a syntactically challenged style of philosophizing that is quite removed from the clarity of his novels and plays. From 1929–31 he served in a military meteorological unit, rejoined in 1940, was a prisoner for nine months until 1941, and then worked in the Resistance until 1944. He founded *Les Temps modernes* in 1944, taught at a number of lycées, rejected the Nobel Prize in 1964, and during the 60s was a globally recognized spokesman against war and nuclear proliferation. He and Bertrand Russell were the philosophical grandfathers of the worldwide anti-war movements.

Sartre's writings about social matters suffuse all his works, but his specific comments on the nature of human freedom, on the deleterious effects of reified thought, and on the corrosiveness of anti-Semitism are among the best known of his bounteous writings. His novels are more pleasant to read, but his discourses about freedom are equally important.

BEING AND NOTHINGNESS, 1943

Freedom and Responsibility

Although the considerations which are about to follow are of interest primarily to the ethicist, it may nevertheless be worthwhile after these descriptions and arguments to return to the freedom of the for-itself and to try to understand what the fact of this freedom represents for human destiny.

The essential consequence of our earlier remarks is that man being condemned to be free carries the weight of the whole world on his shoulders; he is responsible for the world and for himself as a way of being. We are taking the word "responsibility" in its ordinary sense as "consciousness (of) being the incontestable author of an event or of an object." In this sense the responsibility of the for-itself is overwhelming since he is the one by whom it happens that *there is* a world; since he is also the one who makes himself be, then whatever may be the situation in which he finds himself, the for-itself must wholly assume this situation with its peculiar coefficient of adversity, even though it be insupportable. He must assume the situation with the proud consciousness of being the author of it, for the very worst disadvantages or the worst threats which can endanger my person have meaning only in and through my project; and it is on the ground of the engagement which I am that they appear. It is therefore senseless to think of complaining since nothing foreign has decided what we feel, what we live, or what we are.

Furthermore this absolute responsibility is not resignation; it is simply the logical requirement of the consequences of our freedom. What happens to me happens through me, and I can neither affect myself with it nor revolt against it nor resign myself to it. Moreover everything which happens to me is *mine*. By this we must understand first of all that I am always equal to what happens to me *qua* man, for what happens to a

From *Being and Nothingness*, by Jean-Paul Sartre. English translation copyright © 1956 by Philosophical Library. Originally appeared in French as *L'Etre et le Néant*, copyright © 1943 By Editions Gallimard. Reprinted by permission of Georges Borchardt, Inc., for Éditions Gallimard.

man through other men and through himself can be only human. The most terrible situations of war, the worst tortures do not create a non-human state of things; there is no non-human situation. It is only through fear, flight, and recourse to magical types of conduct that I shall decide on the non-human, but this decision is human, and I shall carry the entire responsibility for it. But in addition the situation is *mine* because it is the image of my free choice of myself, and everything which it presents to me is *mine* in that this represents me and symbolizes me. Is it not I who decide the coefficient of adversity in things and even their unpredictability by deciding myself?

Thus there are no *accidents* in a life; a community event which suddenly bursts forth and involves me in it does not come from the outside. If I am mobilized in a war, this war is *my* war; it is in my image and I deserve it. I deserve it first because I could always get out of it by suicide or by desertion; these ultimate possibles are those *which* must always be present for us when there is a question of envisaging a situation. For lack of getting out of it, I have *chosen* it. This can be due to inertia, to cowardice in the face of public opinion, or because I prefer certain other values to the value of the refusal to join in the war (the good opinion of my relatives, the honor of my family, *etc.*). Anyway you look at it, it is a matter of a choice. This choice will be repeated later on again and again without a break until the end of the war. Therefore we must agree with the statement by J. Romains, "In war there are no innocent victims." If therefore I have preferred war to death or to dishonor, everything takes place as if I bore the entire responsibility for this war. Of course others have declared it, and one might be tempted perhaps to consider me as a simple accomplice. But this notion of complicity has only a juridical sense, and it does not hold here. For it depended on me, that for me and by me this war should not exist, and I have decided that it does exist. There was no compulsion here, for the compulsion could have got no hold on a freedom. I did not have any excuse; for as we have said repeatedly in this book, the peculiar character of human-reality is that it is without excuse. Therefore it remains for me only to lay claim to this war.

ANTI-SEMITE AND JEW, 1946

The preceding remarks of course make no pretense at providing a solution to the Jewish problem. But perhaps they do give us a basis for stating the conditions on which a solution might be envisaged.

In effect, we have just seen that, contrary to a widespread opinion, it is not the Jewish character that provokes anti-Semitism but, rather, that it is the anti-Semite who creates the Jew. The primary phenomenon, therefore, is anti-Semitism, a regressive social force and a conception deriving from the prelogical world. With the problem thus stated, what are we to do about it? Clearly, the solution of the problem involves a definition both of the goal to be attained and of the means for its attainment. All too often people discuss means when they are still uncertain of their goal.

In short, what can we seek? Assimilation? That is a dream; the true opponent of assimilation is not the Jew but the anti-Semite, as we have already demonstrated. Since his emancipation—that is, for about a century and a half—the Jew has tried to gain acceptance in a society that rejects him. It is pointless to ask him to hasten this integration, which always recedes before him; so long as there is anti-Semitism, assimilation cannot be realized.

It is true that some people advocate the employment of drastic means. There are even Jews who suggest that all Jews be forced to change their names. But this measure would be inadequate; it would be necessary to supplement it with a policy of mixed marriages and a rigorous interdiction against Jewish religious practices—in particular, circumcision. I say quite simply: these measures would be inhumane. Possibly Napoleon might have thought of such measures, but what Napoleon sought was precisely the sacrifice of the person to the community. No democracy can seek the integration of the Jews at such a cost.

Moreover, such a procedure could be advocated only by inauthentic Jews who are a prey to a crisis of anti-Semitism; it aims at nothing less than the liquidation of the Jewish race. It represents an extreme form of the tendency we have noticed in the democrat, a tendency purely and simply to suppress the Jew for the sake of *the man.* But *the man* does not exist; there are Jews, Protestants, Catholics; there are Frenchmen, Englishmen, Germans; there are whites, blacks, yellows. In short, these drastic measures of coercion would mean the annihilation of a spiritual community, founded on custom and affection, to the advantage of the national community. Most conscious Jews would refuse assimilation if it were presented to them under this aspect. Certainly they wish to integrate themselves in the nation, but *as Jews,* and who would dare to reproach them for that? We have forced them to think of themselves as Jews, we have made them conscious of their solidarity with other Jews. Should we be astonished that they now reject a policy that would destroy Israel?

CRITIQUE OF DIALECTICAL REASON/SEARCH FOR A METHOD, 1960

Reification

We must clearly understand here that the rediscovery of scarcity in experience does not claim at all to contradict the Marxist theory, nor to complete it. It is of another order. The essential discovery of Marxism is that labor, as historical reality and as the utilization of determined tools in an already determined social and material sphere, is the real basis of the organization of social relations. This discovery *can no longer* be challenged. What *we* are showing is this: the possibility that these social relations become contradictory itself proceeds from an inert and material negation, which is re-interiorized by man. We are also showing that *violence,* as the negative relation of one *praxis* to another, characterizes the immediate relation of all men, not as real action but as the inorganic structure re-interiorized by organisms; also, that the possibility of reification is given in all human relations—even in a pre-capitalist period, even in relations between family members or friends. As for scarcity itself, it has a formal dialectic that we have sketched out: the scarcity of the product, the scarcity of the tool, the scarcity of the worker, the scarcity of the consumer; also, it has an historical and concrete dialectic, of which we have nothing to say, since it is for the historians to retrace these stages. In fact, it would be necessary to show a double transition under the influence of production itself. On the one hand, there is a transition from scarcity as the expendable character of each person with respect to all, to scarcity as society's designation of groups of underconsuming producers. (At this moment the relation becomes *violence* between the groups, not because it has been necessarily established by violence—Engels is right—but because it is in itself a relation of violence, between violent men.) On the other hand, there is a transition from the absolute scarcity, as a certain impossibility of existing together in certain material conditions determined for all the members of the group, to relative scarcity as the impossibility, in given circumstances, for the group to grow beyond a certain limit without the mode or relations of production changing (*i.e.,* scarcity re-assumed as the discreet liquidation of the unproductive, within a given society and according to certain rules *at the same time as* the choosing of undernourished producers). This relative scarcity which itself has an historical dialectic (that is, an intelligible history) passes into the rank of *institution,* in societies divided into classes. The analytic study of the relations of scarcity is called political economy. All this is tantamount to saying that in restoring to scarcity its importance, one does not revert to some pre-Marxist theory asserting the supremacy of the "consumption" factor; rather, one brings out negativity, as the implicit motive of the historical dialectic, and gives it its intelligibility. In the *environment of scarcity,* all the structures of a determined society rest upon its mode of production. . . .

Praxis is above all the instrumentalization of material reality. It envelops the inanimate thing in a totalizing project which imposes a pseudo-organic unity upon it. By this I mean that this unity is indeed that of a whole, but that it remains social and

human, it does not attain *in itself* the structures of exteriority which constitute the molecular world. If, on the other hand, the unity persists, it is *through material inertia.* But since this unity is nothing but the passive reflection of the *praxis*—that is, of a human undertaking carried out under determined conditions, with well-defined tools and within an historical society at a certain stage of its development—the object produced reflects the entire collectivity. Only it reflects the collectivity in the dimension of passivity. Let us take the example of the act of *sealing:* it is done on the occasion of certain ceremonies (treaties, contracts, etc.), by means of a certain tool. The wax *reproduces* [*retourne*] this act; its inertia reflects the action as pure *being-there.* At this level, the practice absorbed by its "material" becomes the material caricature of the human. The manufactured object proposes to, and imposes upon, men. It designates them and indicates to them how it is to be used. This complex of signs could be introduced into a general theory of meaning, by saying that the tool is meaningful [*significant*] and that man is here a *meant* [*signifié*]. In actual fact, the meaning came to the tool through the labor of man, and man can mean only what he knows. In a sense, then, it seems that the tool reflects for individuals only their own knowledge. This can be seen in the routine of the artisan, who grasps, through the tool he himself has made, the eternal recurrence of the same gestures that define a permanent status within the corporation or the town, with respect to an unvarying clientele.

But precisely because the meaning has taken on the character of materiality, it enters into relation with the entire universe. This means that an infinity of unpredictable relations is established, through the intermediary of social practice, between the matter that absorbs the *praxis* and the other materialized meanings.

The inert *praxis* permeating matter transforms natural forces without meaning into quasi-human practices—that is, into passified actions. Grousset correctly notes that the Chinese peasants are colonists: for four thousand years they have conquered the arable soil at the borders of the country, at the expense of nature and the nomads. One aspect of their activity is the de-forestation which has gone on, century after century. This *praxis* is living and real, and retains a traditional aspect: even recently, the peasant was ripping out bushes to clear a place for millet. But at the same time, the *praxis* leave its mark upon nature, both positively and negatively. Its positive aspect is that of the soil and its apportionment to cultivation. Its negative aspect is a meaning not grasped by the peasants themselves, precisely because it is an absence: *the absence of trees*. This characteristic immediately strikes any European who *today* flies over China in an airplane: the present government has become aware of it and knows the seriousness of the danger. But the traditionalist Chinese of past centuries could not grasp it, for their goal was the conquest of the soil; they saw the plenty represented by the harvest, and were not alert to *that lack* which was for them, at the most, only a liberation—the elimination of an obstacle. From this viewpoint, deforestation—as passified practice that has become *characteristic* of the mountains, in particular of those that dominate Szechwan—transforms the physico-chemical sector that might be called "wild" because it starts where human practice ends. To begin with, this wild sector is human to the exact extent to which it reveals, for society, its historical limit at a determined moment. But above all, deforestation as the elimination of obstacles becomes, negatively, the absence of protection: since the loess of mountains and of peneplains is not held by the trees, it fills the rivers, raises them above the level of the plain and, in the lower parts of their courses, blocks them up like a cork so that they overflow. Thus, the whole process of the terrible Chinese floods appears as a deliberately constructed mechanism. If some enemy of man-kind had wanted to persecute the workers of Great China, he would have ordered mercenary troops systematically to deforest the mountains. The positive system of cultivation is transformed into an infernal machine. Now, the enemy who brought the loess, the river, the gravity, the whole hydro-dynamics, into this destructive apparatus—is the peasant himself. But his activity, taken in the moment of its living development, does not warrant, by intention or in reality, this reversal: in *this* place, for *this* man who is farming, there exists only an organic link between the negative (elimination of the obstacle) and the positive (enlargement of the arable sector). For counter-finality to exist, it is necessary above all that a sort of *disposition* of matter (here, the geological and hydrographic structure of China) adumbrate it in advance. . . .

Matter alone carries meanings. It retains them in itself, like engravings, and gives them their real effectiveness: in losing their human properties, man's projects are engraved in Being—their translucency becomes opacity, their superficiality becomes density, their volatile lightness becomes permanence; they *come into Being* as they lose their character of lived event. Insofar as they are Being, they refuse—even if they are deciphered and known—to be dissolved themselves into knowledge. Only matter itself, knocking against matter, can disintegrate them. The meaning of human labor is that man reduces himself to inorganic materiality, in order to act materially upon matter and to change his material life. Through tran-substantiation, the project that our bodies engrave in the thing assumes the substantial characteristics of that thing, without entirely losing its original qualities. Thus it comes to possess an inert future, within which we shall have to determine our own future. The future comes to man through things, to the extent that it has come to things through man. Meanings as passive impenetrability become, in the human universe, the surrogates for man: to them he delegates his powers. By contact, and by passive action *at a distance,* they modify the whole of the material universe. This means both that they have been engraved into Being, and that Being has been poured into the world of meanings. But in addition, this means that these heavy and inert objects are situated at the base of a community whose relations are *from one side* relations of interiority. It is through this interiority that a material element can modify, at a distance, another material element (for example, the reduction in the output of the mines in the Americas checked inflation in the Mediterranean countries in the mid-seventeenth century). But by this very modification, it helps to break the link of interiority that unites men among themselves. From this point of view, one can accept both Durkheim's formula: "Treat social facts as things," and the answer of Weber and of contemporaries: "Social facts are not things." Or, if you prefer, social facts are things to the extent that *all things,* directly or indirectly, are social facts.

Critique de la raison dialectique,
224–225, 231–233, 245–246.

ERNST CASSIRER

1874–1945

Ernst Cassirer was born in Breslau, Silesia, Germany (now Poland) on July 28, 1874, son of a rich Jewish merchant and a doting mother, who favored Ernst over her other eight children perhaps because of his sunny disposition. He married Toni Bondy, his first cousin, in 1902, producing with her during a happy marriage Heinz, another son, and one daughter, dying at the age of 70 in New York City on April 13, 1945. As a boy Cassirer was unusually concerned with issues of justice, was talented physically (swimming the broad Oder River regularly), and adored everything musical. He was initially a substandard student, more interested in sibling play than in study. But his maternal grandfather's cultured ways and large library attracted him to scholarly pursuits during his summer visits outside of Breslau. By the age of 12 he had read many classics, including all of Shakespeare, but only discovered *Hamlet* when it was given to him for his 13th birthday, since it had been missing from his grandfather's library. He graduated at the top of his class from high school, and set off to study law, at his father's request, but quickly switched to German philosophy and literature, then art history. He matriculated at the universities of Berlin, Leipzig, Heidelberg, Marburg, and Munich, moving about probably because of a certain dissatisfaction with the courses offered.

The pivotal moment of his schooling took place in the summer of 1894 when in Berlin he took Georg Simmel's course on Kant. Hearing praise from Simmel about Hermann Cohen's knowledge of Kant, Cassirer moved to Marburg to study with the man himself. Cohen and other neo-Kantians were fighting against the nativist mysticism that had typified German culture since the Middle Ages, recalling instead the Enlightenment's disdain for the irrational. Cassirer was caught up in this wave of clearheadedness, and presented himself to Cohen as a fully formed philosopher, owing in part to his phenomenal memory for texts. Finishing a dissertation on Leibniz in just two years (1899), he taught in Berlin, was a drafted civil servant during WWI, and eventually became professor of philosophy at Hamburg from 1919–1933, at Oxford (1933–35), Göteborg (1935–41), Yale (1941–44), and Columbia (1944–45). Cassirer during the 40s through the 60s was one of the most influential philosophers in the Western world. His *Philosophy of Symbolic Forms* (3 vols, 1923–29) made his reputation initially, but just as important in terms of social thought are *An Essay on Man* (1944), *The Myth of the State* (1946), *The Philosophy of the Enlightenment* (1932), and *The Problem of Knowledge* (1950). His biography of Kant is also a standard, though difficult, work. He influenced Susanne Langer, but like Vico, who inspired Cassirer's interest in myth, he has had few true followers.

AN ESSAY ON MAN, 1944

The Definition of Man in Terms of Human Culture

It was a turning point in Greek culture and Greek thought when Plato interpreted the maxim "Know thyself" in an entirely new sense. This interpretation introduced a problem which was not only alien to pre-Socratic thought but also went far beyond the limits of the Socratic method. In order to obey the demand of the Delphic god, in order to fulfill the religious duty of self-examination and self-knowledge, Socrates had approached the individual man. Plato recognized the limitations of the Socratic way of inquiry. In order to solve the problem, he declared, we must project it upon a larger plan. The phenomena we encounter in our individual experience are so various, so complicated and contradictory that we can scarcely disentangle them. Man is to be studied not in his individual life but in his political and social life. Human nature, according to Plato, is like a difficult text, the meaning of which has to be deciphered by philosophy. But in our personal experience this text is written in such small characters that it becomes illegible. The first labor of philosophy must be to enlarge these characters. Philosophy cannot give us a satisfactory theory of man until it has developed a theory of the state. The nature of man is written in capital letters in the nature of the state. Here the hidden meaning of the text suddenly emerges, and what seemed obscure and confused becomes clear and legible.

But political life is not the only form of a communal human existence. In the history of mankind the state, in its present form, is a late product of the civilizing process. Long before man had discovered this form of social organization he had made other attempts to organize his feelings, desires, and thoughts. Such organizations and systematizations are contained in language, in myth, in religion, and in art. We must accept this broader basis if we wish to develop a theory of man. The

state, however important, is not all. It cannot express or absorb all the other activities of man. To be sure these activities in their historical evolution are closely connected with the development of the state; in many respects they are dependent upon the forms of political life. But, while not possessing a separate historical existence, they have nevertheless a purport and value of their own.

In modern philosophy Comte was one of the first to approach this problem and to formulate it in a clear and systematic way. It is something of a paradox that in this respect we must regard the positivism of Comte as a modern parallel to the Platonic theory of man. Comte was of course never a Platonist. He could not accept the logical and metaphysical presuppositions upon which Plato's theory of ideas is based. Yet, on the other hand, he was strongly opposed to the views of the French ideologists. In his hierarchy of human knowledge two new sciences, the science of social ethics and that of social dynamics, occupy the highest rank. From this sociological viewpoint Comte attacks the psychologism of his age. One of the fundamental maxims of his philosophy is that our method of studying man must, indeed, be subjective, but that it cannot be individual. For the subject we wish to know is not the individual consciousness but the universal subject. If we refer to this subject by the term "humanity," then we must affirm that humanity is not to be explained by man, but man by humanity. The problem must be reformulated and re-examined; it must be put on a broader and sounder basis. Such a basis we have discovered in sociological and historical thought. "To know yourself," says Comte, "know history." Henceforth historical psychology supplements and supersedes all previous forms of individual psychology. "The so-called observations made on the mind, considered in itself and *a priori*,", wrote Comte in a letter, "are pure illusions. All that we call *logic, metaphysics, ideology,* is an idle fancy and a dream when it is not an absurdity."[1]

In Comte's *Cours de philosophie positive* we can trace step by step the nineteenth-century transition in methodological ideals. Comte began merely as a scientist, his interest being apparently wholly absorbed in mathematical, physical, and chemical problems. In his hierarchy of human knowledge the scale goes from astronomy

---

From *An Essay on Man: An Introduction to a Philosophy of Human Culture*, by Ernst Cassirer. Published by Yale University Press. Copyright © 1944, 1992. Reprinted by permission.

through mathematics, physics, and chemistry to biology. Then comes what looks like a sudden reversal of this order. As we approach the human world the principles of mathematics or of the natural sciences do not become invalid, but they are no longer sufficient. Social phenomena are subject to the same rules as physical phenomena, yet they are of a different and much more complicated character. They are not to be 'described merely in terms of physics, chemistry, and biology. "In all social phenomena," says Comte,

> we perceive the working of the physiological laws of the individual; and moreover something which modifies their effects, and which belongs to the influence of individuals over each other—singularly complicated in the case of the human race by the influence of generations on their successors. Thus it is clear that our social science must issue from that which relates to the life of the individual. On the other hand, there is no occasion to suppose, as some eminent physiologists have done, that Social Physics is only an appendage to Physiology. The phenomena of the two are not identical, though they are homogeneous: and it is of high importance to hold the two sciences separate. As social conditions modify the operation of physiological laws, Social Physics must have a set of observations of its own.[2]

The disciples and followers of Comte were not, however, inclined to accept this distinction. They denied the difference between physiology and sociology because they feared that acknowledging it would lead back to a metaphysical dualism. Their ambition was to establish a purely naturalistic theory of the social and cultural world. To this end they found it necessary to negate and destroy all those barriers which seem to separate the human from the animal world. The theory of evolution had evidently effaced all these differences. Even before Darwin the progress of natural history had frustrated all attempts at such differentiation. In the earlier stages of empirical observation it was still possible for the scientist to cherish the hope of finding eventually an anatomical character reserved for man. As late as the eighteenth century it was still a generally accepted theory that there is a marked difference, in some respects a sharp contrast, between the anatomical structure of man and that of the other animals. It was one of Goethe's great merits in the

field of comparative anatomy that he vigorously combated this theory. The same homogeneity, not merely in the anatomical and physiological but also in the mental structure of man, remained to be demonstrated. For this purpose all the attacks on the older way of thinking had to be concentrated upon one point. The thing to be proved was that what we call the intelligence of man is by no means a self-dependent, original faculty. Proponents of the naturalistic theories could appeal for proof to the principles of psychology established by the older schools of sensationalism. Taine developed the psychological basis for his general theory of human culture in a work on the intelligence of man.[3] According to Taine, what we call "intelligent behavior" is not a special principle or privilege of human nature; it is only a more refined and complicated play of the same associative mechanism and automatism which we find in all animal reactions. If we accept this explanation the difference between intelligence and instinct becomes negligible; it is a mere difference of degree, not of quality. Intelligence itself becomes a useless and scientifically meaningless term.

The most surprising and paradoxical feature of the theories of this type is the striking contrast between what they promise and what they actually give us. The thinkers who built up these theories were very severe with respect to their methodological principles. They were not content to speak of human nature in terms of our common experience, for they were striving after a much higher ideal, an ideal of absolute scientific exactness. But if we compare their results with this standard we cannot help being greatly disappointed. "Instinct" is a very vague term. It may have a certain descriptive value but it has obviously no explanatory value. By reducing some classes of organic or human phenomena to certain fundamental instincts, we have not alleged a new cause; we have only introduced a new name. We have put a question, not answered one. The term "instinct" gives us at best as *idem per idem*, and in most cases it is an *obscurum per obscurius*. Even in the description of animal behavior most modern biologists and psycho-biologists have become very cautious about using it. They warn us against the fallacies which appear to be inextricably connected with it. They try rather to avoid or to abandon "the error freighted concept of instinct and the oversimple concept of intelligence" In one of his most recent publications Robert M. Yerkes declares that the terms "instinct" and "intelligence" are outmoded and that the concepts for which they stand are sadly in need of redefining.[4] But in the field of anthropological philosophy we are still, apparently, far from any such redefinition. Here these terms are very often accepted quite naively without critical analysis. When used in this way the concept of instinct becomes an example of that typical methodological error which was described by William James as the psychologist's fallacy. The word "instinct," which may be useful for the description of animal or human behavior, is hypostatized into a sort, of natural power. Curiously enough this error was often committed by thinkers who, in all other respects, felt secure against relapses into scholastic realism or "faculty-psychology." A very clear and impressive criticism of this mode of thinking is contained in John Dewey's *Human Nature and Conduct.* "It is unscientific," writes Dewey,

> to try to restrict original activities to a definite number of sharply demarcated classes of instincts. And the practical result of this attempt is injurious. To classify is, indeed, as useful as it is natural. The indefinite multitude of particular and changing events is met by the mind with acts of defining, inventorying, and listing, reducing to common heads and tying up in bunches. . . . But when we assume that our lists and bunches represent fixed separations and collections *in rerum natura,* we obstruct rather than aid our transactions with things. We are guilty of a presumption which nature promptly punishes. We are rendered incompetent to deal effectively with the delicacies and novelties of nature and life. . . . The tendency to forget the office of distinctions and classifications, and to take them as marking things in themselves is the current fallacy of scientific specialism. . . . This attitude which once flourished in physical science now governs theorizing about human nature. Man has been resolved into a definite collection of primary instincts which may be numbered, catalogued and exhaustively described one by one. Theorists differ only or chiefly as to their number and ranking. Some say one, self-love; some two, egoism and altruism; some three, greed, fear and glory; while today writers of a more empirical turn run the number up to fifty and sixty. But in fact there are as many specific reactions to differing stimulating conditions

as there is time for, and our lists are only classifications for a purpose.[5]

After this brief survey of the different methods that have hitherto been employed in answering the question: What is man? we now come to our central issue. Are these methods sufficient and exhaustive? Or is there still another approach to an anthropological philosophy? Is any other way left open besides that of psychological introspection, biological observation and experiment, and of historical investigation? I have endeavored to discover such an alternative approach in my *Philosophy of Symbolic Forms.*[6] The method of this work is by no means a radical innovation. It is not designed to abrogate but to complement former views. The philosophy of symbolic forms starts from the presupposition that, if there is any definition of the nature or "essence" of man, this definition can only be understood as a functional one, not a substantial one. We cannot define man by any inherent principle which constitutes his metaphysical essence—nor calm we define him by any inborn faculty or instinct that may be ascertained by empirical observation. Man's outstanding characteristic, his distinguishing mark, is not his metaphysical or physical nature—but his work. It is this work, it is the system of human activities, which defines and determines the circle of "humanity." Language, myth, religion, art, science, history are the constituents, the various sectors of this circle. A "philosophy of man" would therefore be a philosophy which would give us insight into the fundamental structure of each of these human activities, and which at the same time would enable us to understand them as an organic whole. Language, art, myth, religion are no isolated, random creations. They are held together by a common bond. But this bond is not a *vinculum substantiale,* as it was conceived and described in scholastic thought; it is rather a *vinculum functionale.* It is the basic function of speech, of myth, of art, of religion that we must seek far behind their innumerable shapes and utterances, and that in the last analysis we must attempt to trace back to a common origin.

It is obvious that in the performance of this task we cannot neglect any possible source of information. We must examine all the available empirical evidence, and utilize all the methods of introspection, biological observation, and historical inquiry. These older methods are not to be eliminated but referred to a new intellectual center, and hence seen from a new angle. In describing the structure of language, myth, religion, art, and science, we feel the constant need of a psychological terminology. We speak of religious "feeling," of artistic or mythical "imagination," of logical or rational thought. And we cannot enter into all these worlds without a sound scientific psychological method. Child psychology gives us valuable clues for the study of the general development of human speech. Even more valuable seems to be the help we get from the study of general sociology. We cannot understand the form of primitive mythical thought without taking into consideration the forms of primitive society. And more urgent still is the use of historical methods. The question as to what language myth, and religion "are" cannot be answered without a penetrating study of their historical development.

Notes

1. Comte, *Lettres à Valat*, p. 89; cited from L. Lévy-Bruhl, *La philosophie d'Auguste Comte*. For further details see Lévy-Bruhl, *op. cit.* English trans., *The Philosophy Of Comte* (New York and London, 1903), pp. 247 ff.

2. Comte, *Cours de philosophie positive*. English trans. by Harriet Martineau, *Positive Philosophy* (New York, 1855), Intro., chap. ii, 45 f.

3. *De l'intelligence* (Paris, 1870). 2 vols.

4. *Chimpanzees*, p. 110.

5. John Dewey, *Human Nature and Conduct* (New York, Holt & Co., 1922), Pt. II, sec. 5, p. 131.

6. *Philosophie der symbolischen Formen*. Vol. I, *Die Sprache* (1923); Vol. II, *Das sythische Denken* (1925); Vol. III, *Phaenomenologie der Erkenntnis* (1929).

THE MYTH OF THE STATE, 1946

The Technique of the Modern Political Myths

If we try to resolve our contemporary political myths into their elements we find that they contain no entirely new feature. All the elements were already well known. Carlyle's theory of hero worship and Gobineau's thesis of the fundamental moral and intellectual diversity of races had been discussed over and over again. But all these discussions remained in a sense merely academic. To change the old ideas into strong and powerful political weapons something more was needed. They had to be accommodated to the understanding of a different audience. For this purpose a fresh instrument was required—not only an instrument of thought but also of action. A new technique had to be developed. This was the last and decisive factor. To put it into scientific terminology we may say that this technique had a catalytical effect. It accelerated all reactions and gave them their full effect. While the soil for the Myth of the Twentieth Century had been prepared long before, it could not have home its fruit without the skilful use of the new technical tool.

The general conditions which favored this development and contributed to its final victory appeared in the period after the first World War. At this time all the nations which had been engaged in the war encountered the same fundamental difficulties. They began to realize that, even for the victorious nations, the war had, in no field, brought a real solution. On all sides new questions arose. The international, the social, and the human conflicts became more and more intense. They were felt everywhere. But in England, France, and North America there remained always some prospect of solving these conflicts by ordinary and normal means. In Germany, however, the case was different. From one day to the next the problem became more acute and more complicated. The leaders of the Weimar Republic had done their best to cope with these problems by diplomatic transactions or legislative measures. But all their efforts seemed to have been made in vain. In the times of inflation and unemployment Germany's whole social and economic system was threatened with a complete collapse. The normal resources seemed to have been exhausted. This was the natural soil upon which the political myths could grow up and in which they found ample nourishment. . . .

In desperate situations man will always have recourse to desperate means—and our present-day political myths have been such desperate means. If reason has failed us, there remains always the *ultima ratio,* the power of the miraculous and mysterious. Primitive societies are not ruled by written laws, statutes, institutions or constitutions, bills of right or political charters. Nevertheless even the most primitive forms of social life show us a very clear and a very strict organization. The members of these societies are by no means living in a state of anarchy or confusion. Perhaps the most primitive societies we know of are those totemistic societies that we find among the American aboriginal tribes and among the native tribes of northern and central Australia, that have been carefully studied and described in the works of Spencer and Gillen. In these totemistic societies we find no complex and elaborate mythology, comparable to Greek, Indian, or Egyptian mythologies; we find no worship of personal gods and no personification of the great powers of nature. But they are held together by another, and even stronger, force; by a definite ritual based upon mythical conceptions—their beliefs in the animal ancestors. Every member of the group belongs to a special totemistic clan; and thereby he is bound in the chain of fixed tradition. He has to abstain from certain kinds of food; he has to observe very strict rules of exogamy or endogamy; and he has to perform, at certain times, in regular intervals and in a rigid and unchangeable order the same rituals which are a dramatic representation of the life of the totemistic ancestors. All this is imposed upon the members of the tribe not by force but by their fundamental and mythical conceptions, and the binding power of these conceptions is irresistible; it is never called into question.

Later on there appear other political and social forces. The mythical organization of society seems to be superseded by a rational organization. In quiet and peaceful times, in periods of relative stability and security, this rational organization is easily *ben;* it is not a gift with which human nature is endowed; it is rather a task, and the most arduous task that man can set himself. It is no datum, but a demand; an ethical imperative. To fulfil this demand becomes especially hard in times of a severe and dangerous social crisis when the breakdown of the whole public life seems to be imminent. At these times the individual begins to feel a deep mistrust in his own powers. Freedom is not a natural inheritance of man. In order to possess it we have to create it. If man were simply to follow his natural instincts he would not strive for freedom; he would rather choose dependence. Obviously it is much easier to depend upon others than to think, to judge, and to decide for himself. That accounts for the fact that both in individual and in political life freedom is so often regarded much more as a burden than a privilege. Under extremely difficult conditions man tries to cast off this burden. Here the totalitarian state and the political myths step in. The new political parties promise, at least, an escape from the dilemma. They suppress and destroy the very sense of freedom; but, at the same time, they relieve men from all personal responsibility. . . .

Curiously enough this new art of divination first made its appearance not in German politics but in German philosophy. In 1918 there appeared Oswald Spengler's *Decline of the West.* Perhaps never before had a philosophical book such a sensational success. It was translated into almost every language and read by all sorts of readers—philosophers and scientists, historians and politicians, students and scholars, tradesmen and the man in the street. What was the reason for this unprecedented success, what was the magic spell that this book exerted over its readers? It seems to be a paradox; but to my mind the cause of Spengler's success is to be sought rather in the title of his book than in its contents. The title *Der Untergang des Abendlandes* was an electric spark that set the imagination of Spengler's readers aflame. The book was published in July, 1918, at the end of the first World War. At this time many, if not most of us, had realized that something was rotten in the state of our highly praised Western civilization. Spengler's book expressed, in a sharp and trenchant way, this general uneasiness. It was not at all a scientific book. Spengler despised and openly challenged all methods of science. "Nature," he declared, "is to be handled scientifically, history poetically." Yet even this is not the real meaning of Spengler's work. A poet lives in the world of his imagination; and a great religious poet, like Dante or Milton, also lives in a world of prophetic vision. But he does not take these visions for realities; nor does he make of them a philosophy of history. This, however, was precisely the case of Spengler. He boasted of having found a new method by which historical and cultural events could be predicted in the same way and with the same exactness as an astronomer predicts an eclipse of the sun or the moon. "In this book is attempted for the first time the venture of predetermining history, of following the still unraveled stages in the destiny of a culture, and specifically of the only culture of our times and our planet which is actually in the phase of fulfilment—the West European-American."

These words give us a clue to Spengler's book and its enormous influence. If it be possible not only to relate the story of human civilization but to predetermine its future course, a great step in advance has, indeed, been made. Obviously the man who spoke in this way was no mere scientist nor was he a historian or philosopher. According to Spengler the rise, decline, and fall of civilizations do not depend upon the so-called laws of nature. They are determined by a higher power, the power of destiny. Destiny not causality is the moving force in human history. The birth of a cultural world, says Spengler, is always a mystical act, a decree of destiny. Such acts are entirely impenetrable to our poor, abstract, scientific, or philosophical concepts.

HENRI LEFEBVRE

1901–1991

Son of a Ministry of Finance bureaucrat, Henri Lefebvre ("Smith" in French) was born on June 16, 1901 in Hagetmau, Landes, France, was the father of six children with his first wife, remarried in 1981, and died during the night of June 28/29 in 1991 at the age of 90. He graduated from the Lycée Louis le Grand in 1917, took a philosophy degree in 1919 at Provence, and a second philosophy degree from the Sorbonne in 1920. During the 20s he worked with other young intellectuals who had embraced extracurricular Marxism (Paul Nizan, Georges Politzer, and others) by establishing a number of short-lived journals from which to expound this "new" viewpoint on the French scene, and by joining the Communist Party in 1928. He was a professor during the 30s, fought in the Resistance (1940–43), worked for the French radio network after WWII, and became a research director of the Centre National de la Recherche Scientifique in Paris (1949–1961). He then taught at Strasbourg for several years, finishing at the University of Paris-Nanterre (1965–73). He eventually broke with the Party because of his heterodox, semi-"bourgeois" worldview and writings.

Lefebvre came to the attention of English-language readers with two books, *The Sociology of Marx* (1968) and *Everyday Life in the Modern World* (1971) in the aftermath of the revolutionary "events of May '68," as they were then called. He was hailed by the New Left as the grand old man of French Marxism, but with an extremely cultured and urbane face, very far removed from the rougher version then in power in the USSR and the Soviet Bloc countries. He was in some ways to French Marxism what Lukács had become to Central European leftist thought. His *Survival of Capitalism* (1976) was also noted for its timely consideration of what was then known as "late capitalism." After his death his importance increased among urbanists with *The Production of Space* (1991) and *Writings on Cities* (1996). In French he also wrote books on Nietzsche, Lukács, Descartes, modernity, capitalism, dialectical materialism, existentialism, Hegel, Diderot, Rabelais, aesthetics, rural sociology, the Pyrenees, structuralism, and a four-volume study of the state. The selection excerpted below is from his best-known work in English in an enlarged version (*Critique of Everyday Life,* 1947/1991), where Lefebvre shows how the utopian dimension of Marxism serves continued uses even as the economic foibles of planned economies have been fully exposed by recent history. Given his almost unique combination of practical political activity for decades, mixed with the higher reaches of Gallic intellectuality, Lefebvre's voice remains essential among those on the Left, and will probably be reappropriated in due course as the global economy goes through another of its inevitable cycles.

CRITIQUE OF EVERYDAY LIFE, 1991

What Is Possible, 1945

. . . Human life has progressed: material progress, 'moral' progress—but that is only part of the truth. The deprivation, the alienation of life is its other aspect.

In reply to the naïve theoreticians of complete, continuous progress we must demonstrate in particular the decline of everyday life since the community of Antiquity, and man's growing alienation. We must present a firm answer to the Robinson Crusoe-esque idyllists who denigrate the present and theorize the 'good old days', by demonstrating the progress that has been accomplished: in knowledge and in consciousness, in power over nature. Above all we must demonstrate the breadth and magnificence of the *possibilities* which are opening out for man; and which are so really possible, so near, so rationally achievable (once the *political* obstacles are shattered) that this proximity of what is possible can be taken for *one of the meanings* (painfully and frighteningly unconscious) of the famous 'modern disquiet', the anguish caused by 'existence' as it still is! . . .

Now the simplest, most mundane events can show how economic and technical 'progress' has worked.

Several years ago a world-wide firm which was trying to extend the market and put a rival firm out of business decided to distribute paraffin lamps to Chinese peasants free of charge, while its rivals, less 'generous' or less shrewd, went on selling them. And now in several million poverty-stricken Chinese households artificial light (an immense progress) shines down on muddy floors and rotten matting—because even peasants who cannot afford to buy a lamp can afford to buy paraffin. . . . The 'progress' capitalism brings, like its 'generosity', is just a means to an end: profit.

To take an example from much nearer home: in France, in the Pyrenees, just a stone's throw from dams and powerful ultra-modern hydro-electric installations, there are many hamlets, thousands of houses where peasants live almost as 'primitive' a life as the Chinese. They have no electric light either. Elsewhere, more or less everywhere, in town and country alike, electric light illuminates the peeling plaster of slums and the sordid walls of hovels. (Although even in Paris there are still houses and flats without modern lighting.)

Mundane, without literary interest, and picked at random from an infinity of possible equally significant examples, these facts show that up until now 'progress' has affected existing social realities only secondarily, modifying them as little as possible, according to the strict dictates of capitalist profitability. The important thing is that human beings be profitable, not that their lives be changed. As far as is possible, capitalism respects the pre-existing shape and contours of people's lives. Only grudgingly, so to speak, does it bring about any change. Criticism of capitalism as a contradictory 'mode of production' which is dying as a result of its contradictions is strengthened by criticism of capitalism as the distributor of the wealth and 'progress' it has produced.

And so, constantly staring us in the face, mundane and therefore generally unnoticed—whereas in the future it will be seen as a characteristic and scandalous trait of our era, the era of the decadent bourgeoisie—is this fact: that *life is lagging behind what is possible*, that it is retarded. What incredible backwardness. This has up until now been constantly increasing; it parallels the growing disparity between the knowledge of the contemporary physicist and that of the 'average' man, or between that of the Marxist sociologist and that of the bourgeois politician.

Once pointed out, the contrast becomes staggeringly obvious, blinding; it is to be found everywhere, whichever way we turn, and never ceases to amaze. . . .

Everything great and splendid is founded on power and wealth. They are the basis of beauty. This is why the rebel and the anarchic protester who decries all of history and all the works of past centuries because he sees in them only the skills and the threat of domination is making a mistake. He sees alienated forms, but not the greatness within. The rebel can only see to the end of his own 'private' consciousness, which he levels against *everything* human, confusing the oppressors with the oppressed masses, who were nevertheless the basis and the meaning of history and past works. Castles, palaces, cathedrals, fortresses, all speak in their various ways of the greatness and the strength of the people who built them and against whom they were built. This real greatness shines through the fake grandeur of rulers and endows these buildings with a lasting 'beauty'. The bourgeoisie is alone in having given its buildings a single, over-obvious meaning, impoverished, deprived of reality: that meaning is abstract wealth and brutal domination; that is why it has succeeded in producing perfect ugliness and perfect vulgarity. The man who denigrates the past, and who nearly always denigrates the present and the possible as well, cannot understand this dialectic of art, this dual character of works and of history. He does not even sense it. Protesting against bourgeois stupidity and oppression, the anarchic individualist is enclosed in 'private' consciousness, itself a product of the bourgeois era, and no longer understands human power and the community upon which that power is founded. The historical forms of this community, from the village to the nation, escape him. He is, and only wants to be, a human atom (in the scientifically archaic sense of the word, where 'atom' meant the lowest isolatable reality). By following alienation to its very extremes he is merely playing into the hands of the bourgeoisie. Embryonic or unconscious, this kind of anarchism is very widespread. There is a kind of revolt, a kind of criticism of life, that implies and results in the acceptance of this life *as the only one possible*. As a direct consequence this attitude precludes any understanding of *what is humanly possible*. . . .

Dialectical method applies its criticism to its own efforts as well. The 'vision' of the world it strives for, a vision it first glimpses at certain 'moments' of thought—the total conception of the world, the possibility of the *total man*—will only make sense once it stops being a 'vision' and a 'conception': once it penetrates life and transforms it. This 'philosophy' wants to be serious without taking itself seriously.

The truly human man will not be a man of a few dazzling moments, a drunken man, a man who feeds upon himself. There have been and will always be visionaries, geniuses or heroes who have their 'moments', moments which may be extraordinarily important and effective. But man

will appropriate nature, and will make the world 'the joy man gives himself', for the days, for the centuries yet to come.

The programme we have sketched for a critique of everyday life can be summed up as follows:

(a) It will involve a methodical confrontation of so-called 'modern' life on the one hand, with the past, and on the other—and above all—with *the possible*, so that the points or sectors where a 'decadence' or a withdrawal from life have occurred—the points of backwardness in terms of what is possible—the points where new forms are appearing, rich in possibilities—can be determined.

(b) Studied from this point of view, human reality appears as an opposition and 'contrast' between a certain number of terms: everyday life and festival—mass moments and exceptional moments—triviality and splendour—seriousness and play—reality and dreams, etc.

The critique of everyday life involves an investigation of the exact relations between these terms. It implies criticism of the trivial by the exceptional—*but at the same time* criticism of the exceptional by the trivial, of the 'elite' by the mass—of festival, dreams, art and poetry, by reality.

(c) Equally, the critique of everyday life implies a confrontation of effective human reality with its 'expressions': moral doctrines, psychology, philosophy, religion, literature.

From this point of view, religion is nothing but a direct, immediate, negative, destructive, incessant and skillful criticism of life—skillful enough even to give itself the appearance of not being what it really is.

Philosophy was an *indirect* criticism of life by an external (meta-physical) 'truth'. It is now appropriate to examine the philosophy of the past from this perspective—and that is the task facing 'today's' philosopher. To study philosophy as an indirect criticism of life is to perceive (everyday) life as a direct critique of philosophy.

(d) The relations between groups and individuals in everyday life interact in a manner which in part escapes the specialized sciences. By a process of abstraction these sciences infer certain relations, certain essential aspects, from the extraordinary complexities of human reality. But have they completed this task? It seems that once the relations identified by history, political economy or biology have been extracted from human reality, a kind of enormous, shapeless, ill-defined mass remains. This is the murky background from which known relations and superior activities (scientific, political, aesthetic) are picked out.

It is this 'human raw material' that the study of everyday life takes as its proper object. It studies it both in itself and in its relation with the differentiated, superior forms that it underpins. In this way it will help to grasp the 'total content' of consciousness; this will be its contribution towards the attempt to achieve unity, totality—the realization of the total man.

Going beyond the emotional attempts by philanthropists and sentimental (petty-bourgeois) humanists to 'magnify' humble gestures, and beyond that allegedly superior irony which has systematically devalued life, seeing it merely as back-stage activity or comic relief in a tragedy, the critique of everyday life—critical and positive—must clear the way for a genuine humanism, for a humanism which believes in the human because it knows it.

MAURICE MERLEAU-PONTY

1908–1961

Maurice Merleau-Ponty was born on March 14, 1908 in Rockefort-sur-Mer, Charente-Maritime, France, was married to a psychiatrist and had one daughter, and died at 53 in Paris, May 4, 1961 from coronary thrombosis. He shared the fate of many of his generation in that his father was killed in WWI. And like many intellectuals of his period, he studied at the École Normale Supérieure, finishing in 1931, then taught at various lycées, became an officer during WWII, a professor at Lyon in 1945, moving to the Sorbonne in 1949, and to the Collège de France in 1952. Before being called to his chair at the Collège (the youngest person so named), he was in charge of child psychology. His relationship with Sartre is legendary, in that he was introduced to Husserl's work by his friend, they both began *Les Temps modernes,* served as its co-editors, and finally broke when Sartre's insistent Marxism seemed to Merleau-Ponty a philosophically indefensible position. It has been argued that his thought was created in more or less constant dialectical tension with Sartre's (and others in their close intellectual circle, including de Beauvoir).

His principal works include *The Phenomenology of Perception* (1945), *Sense and Non-Sense* (1948), and *Signs* (1960). In the former work, which is usually considered his masterpiece, he argued that standard mind/body dualism no longer makes sense when considered against the backdrop of what is now known about the physiology and psychology of perception. Moreover, the conceit that the mind and the body are separate entities seems to Merleau-Ponty is an outmoded notion and makes neither physiological nor psychological sense. We are not minds who unreflectively order our bodies to accommodate our whims, as if the master/slave dialectic familiar from Hegel's *Phenomenology* applied as well to the brain and the corpus that carries it about. Merleau-Ponty instead insists that the mind in the body—the "body-subject" is his term—be regarded as a coherent perceptual organ, which is how he accounts phenomenologically for habit, ambiguity, reversibility, and other practices and performances which have, since Descartes, so troubled the Western philosophical tradition. Where most philosophers have seen a break or rupture, he sees unity, if not union, between the mind and body. The body can "know" as readily as can the mind, if only observers are able to reorganize their categories to understand it as doing so. He did not interpret the body as static and the mind as dynamic, but understood them to be in dialectical tension regarding what he called "centers of meaning." Differently, in *Humanism and Terror* (1947), Merleau-Ponty tried to explain the "necessary" violence of the Moscow show trials in terms of communism's mortal battle with German fascism.

THE PHENOMENOLOGY OF PERCEPTION, 1945

Other Selves and the Human World

. . . Our relationship to the social is like our relationship to the word, deeper than any express perception or any judgement. It is as false to place ourselves in society as an object among other objects, as it is to place society within ourselves as a object of thought, and in both cases the mistake lies in treating the social as an object. We must return to the social with which we are in contact by the mere fact of existing, and which we carry about inseparably with us before any objectification. Objective and scientific consciousness of the past and of civilizations would be impossible had I not, through the intermediary of my society, my cultural world and their horizons, at least a possible communication with them, and if the place of the Athenian Republic or the Roman Empire were not somewhere marked out on the borders of my own history, and if they were not there as so many individuals to be known, indeterminate but pre-existing, and if I did not find in my own life the basic structures of history. The social is already there when we come to know or judge it. An individualistic or sociological philosophy is a certain perception of co-existence systematized and made explicit. Prior to the process of becoming aware, the social exists obscurely and as a summons. At the end of *Notre Patrie* Péguy finds once again a buried voice which had never ceased to speak, much as we realize on waking that objects have not, during the night, ceased to be, or that someone has been knocking for some time at our door. Despite cultural, moral, occupational and ideological differences, the Russian peasants of 1917 joined the workers of Petrograd and Moscow in the struggle, because they felt that they shared the same fate, class was experienced in concrete terms before becoming the object of a deliberate volition. Primarily the social does not exist as a third person object. It is the mistake of the investigator, the 'great man' and the historian to try to treat it

as an object. Fabrice would have liked to see the Battle of Waterloo as one sees a landscape, but found nothing but confused episodes. Does the Emperor really see it on his map? It reduces itself in his eyes to a general plan by no means free from gaps; why is this regiment not making headway; why don't the reserves come up? The historian who is not engaged in the battle and who sees it from all angles, who brings together a mass of evidence, and who knows what the result was, thinks he has grasped it in its essential truth. But what he gives us is no more than a representation; he does not bring before us the battle itself since the issue was, at the time, contingent, and is no longer so when the historian recounts it, since the deeper causes of defeat and the fortuitous incidents which brought them into play were, in that singular event called Waterloo, equally determining factors, and since the historian assigns to the said singular event its place in the general process of decline of the Empire. The true Waterloo resides neither in what Fabrice, nor the Emperor, nor the historian sees, it is not a determinable object, it is what *comes about* on the fringes of all perspectives, and on which they are all erected. The historian and the philosopher are in search of an objective definition of class or nation: is the nation based on common language or on conceptions of life; is class based on income statistics or on its place in the process of production? It is well known that none of these criteria enables us to decide whether an individual belongs to a nation or a class. In all revolutions there are members of the privileged class who make common cause with the revolutionaries, and members of the oppressed class who remain faithful to the privileged. And every nation has its traitors. This is because the nation and class are neither versions of fate which hold the individual in subjection from the outside nor values which he posits from within. They are modes of coexistence which are a call upon him. Under conditions of calm, the nation and the class are there as stimuli to which I respond only absent-mindedly or confusedly; they are merely latent. A revolutionary situation, or one of national danger, transforms those preconscious relationships with class and nation, hitherto merely lived through, into the definite taking of a stand; the tacit commitment becomes explicit. But it appears to itself as anterior to decision.

The problem of the existential modality of the social is here at one with all problems of transcendence. Whether we are concerned with my body, the natural world, the past, birth or death, the question is always how I can be open to phenomena which transcend me, and which nevertheless exist only to the extent that I take them up and live them; *how the presence to myself (Urpräsenz) which establishes my own limits and conditions every alien presence is at the same time depresentation (Entgegenwärtigung) and throws me outside myself.* Both idealism and realism, the former by making the external world immanent in me, the latter by subjecting me to a causal action, falsify the motivational relations existing between the external and internal worlds, and make this relationship unintelligible. Our individual past, for example, cannot be given to us either on the one hand by the actual survival of states of consciousness or paths traced in the brain, or on the other by a consciousness of the past which constitutes it and immediately arrives at it: in either case we should lack any sense of the past, for the past would, strictly speaking, be present. If anything of the past is to exist for us, it can be only in an ambiguous presence, anterior to any express evocation, like a field upon which we have an opening. It must exist for us even though we may not be thinking of it, and all our recollections must have their substance in and be drawn from this opaque mass. Similarly, if the world were to me merely a collection of things, and the thing merely a collection of properties, I should have no certainties, but merely probabilities, no unchallengeable reality, but merely conditional truths. If the past and the world exist, they must be theoretically immanent—they can be only what I see behind and around me—and factually transcendent—they exist in my life before appearing as objects of my explicit acts. Similarly, moreover, my birth and death cannot be objects of thought for me. Being established in my life, buttressed by my thinking nature, fastened down in this transcendental field which was opened for me by my first perception, and in which all absence is merely the obverse of a presence, all silence a modality of the being of sound, I enjoy a sort of ubiquity and theoretical eternity, I feel destined to move in a flow of endless life, neither the beginning nor the end of which I can experience in thought, since it is my

living self who think of them, and since thus, my life always forestalls and survives itself. Yet this same thinking nature which produces in me a superabundance of being opens the world to me through a perspective, along with which there comes to me the feeling of my contingency, the dread of being outstripped, so that, although I do not manage to encompass my death in thought, I nevertheless live in an atmosphere of death in general, and there is a kind of essence of death always on the horizon of my thinking. In short, just as the instant of my death is a future to which I have not access, so I am necessarily destined never to experience the presence of another person to himself. And yet each other person does exist for me as an unchallengeable style or setting of co-existence, and my life has a social atmosphere just as it has a flavour of mortality.

We have discovered, with the natural and social worlds, the truly transcendental, which is not the totality of constituting operations whereby a transparent world, free from obscurity and impenetrable solidity, is spread out before an impartial spectator, but that ambiguous life in which the forms of transcendence have their *Ursprung,* and which, through a fundamental contradiction, puts me in communication with them, and on this basis makes knowledge possible. It will perhaps be maintained that a philosophy cannot be centred round a contradiction, and that all our descriptions, since they ultimately defy thought, are quite meaningless. The objection would be valid if we were content to lay bare, under the term phenomenon or phenomenal field, a layer of prelogical or magical experiences. For in that case we should have to choose between believing the descriptions and abandoning thought, or knowing what we are talking about and abandoning our descriptions. These descriptions must become an opportunity for defining a variety of comprehension and reflection altogether more radical than objective thought. To phenomenology understood as direct description needs to be added a phenomenology of phenomenology. We must return to the *cogito,* in search of a more fundamental *Logos* than that of objective thought, one which endows the latter with its relative validity, and at the same time assigns to it its place. At the level of being it will never be intelligible that the subject should be both *naturans* and *naturatus,* infinite and finite.

But if we rediscover time beneath the subject, and if we relate to the paradox of time those of the body, the world, the thing, and other people, we shall understand that beyond these there is nothing to understand.

⤙⤚

SIGNS, 1951/60

Man and Adversity

. . . We men who have lived as our problem the development of communism and the War, and who have read Gide and Valéry and Proust and Husserl and Heidegger and Freud are the same. Whatever our responses have been, there should be a way to circumscribe perceptible zones of our experience and formulate, if not ideas about man that we hold in common, at least a new experience of our condition.

With these reservations, we propose to acknowledge that our century is distinguished by a completely new association of "materialism" and "idealism," of pessimism and optimism, or rather by the fact that it has gone beyond these antitheses. Our contemporaries have no difficulty thinking both that human life is the demand for an original order and that this order could not possibly endure or even truly exist except under certain very precise and very concrete conditions which can fail to materialize, no natural arrangement of things and the world predestining them to make a human life possible.

It is true that there were philosophers and scientists in 1900 who set certain biological and material conditions for human existence. But they were ordinarily "materialists" in the sense the term had at the end of the last century. They made humanity an episode of evolution, civilizations a particular case of adaptation, and even resolved life into its physical and chemical components. For them the properly human perspective on the world was a superfluous phenomenon; and those

who saw the contingency of humanity ordinarily treated values, institutions, works of art, and words as a system of signs referring in the last analysis to the elementary needs and desires of all organisms.

It is true, on the other hand, that there were "idealist" authors who assumed other motive forces than these in humanity; but when they did not derive them from some supernatural source, they related them to a human nature which guaranteed their unconditional efficacy. *Human nature* had truth and justice for attributes, as other species have fins or wings. The epoch was full of these absolutes and these divided notions. There was the absolute of the State pervading all events; and a State which did not reimburse its lenders was considered dishonest, even if it was in the midst of a revolution. The value of money was an absolute, and men scarcely dreamed of treating it as simply an aid to economic and social functioning. There was also a moral gold-standard: family and marriage were the good, even if they secreted hatred and rebellion. "Things of the spirit" were intrinsically noble, even if books (like so many works in 1900) translated only morose reveries. There were values and, on the other hand, realities, there was mind and, on the other hand, body; there was the interior and, on the other hand, the exterior. But what if it were precisely the case that the order of facts invaded that of values, if it were recognized that dichotomies are tenable only this side of a certain point of misery and danger? Even those among us today who are taking up the word "humanism" again no longer maintain the *shameless humanism* of our elders. What is perhaps proper to our time is to disassociate humanism from the idea of a humanity fully guaranteed by natural law, and not only reconcile consciousness of human values and consciousness of the infrastructures which keep them in existence, but insist upon their inseparability.

If we were asked in concluding to give our remarks a philosophical formulation, we would say that our times have experienced and are experiencing, more perhaps than any other, contingency. The contingency of evil to begin with: there is not a force at the beginning of human life which guides it toward its ruin or toward chaos. On the contrary, each gesture of our body or our language, each act of political life, as we have seen, spontaneously takes account of the other person and goes beyond itself in its singular aspects toward a universal meaning. When our initiatives get bogged down in the paste of the body, of language, or of that world beyond measure which is given to us to finish, it is not that a *malin génie* sets his will against us; it is only a matter of a sort of inertia, a passive resistance, a dying fall of meaning—an anonymous *adversity*. But good is contingent too. We do not guide the body by repressing it, nor language by putting it in thought, nor history by dint of value judgments; we must always espouse each one of these situations, and when they go beyond themselves they do so spontaneously. Progress is not necessary with a metaphysical necessity; we can only say that experience will very likely end up by eliminating false solutions and working its way out of impasses. But at what price, by how many detours? We cannot even exclude in principle the possibility that humanity, like a sentence which does not succeed in drawing to a close, will suffer shipwreck on its way.

It is true that the totality of beings known by the name of men and defined by the commonly known physical characteristics also have in common a natural light or opening to being which makes cultural acquisitions communicable to all men and to them alone. But this lightning flash we find in every glance called human is just as visible in the most cruel forms of sadism as it is in Italian painting. It is precisely this flash which makes everything possible on man's part, and right up to the end. Man is absolutely distinct from animal species, but precisely in the respect that he has no original equipment and is the place of contingency, which sometimes takes the form of a kind of miracle (in the sense in which men have spoken of the *miracle of Greece*), and sometimes the form of an unintentional adversity. Our age is as far from explaining man by the lower as it is by the higher, and for the same reasons. To explain the *Mona Lisa* by the sexual history of Leonardo da Vinci or to explain it by some divine motion Leonardo da Vinci was the instrument of or by some human nature capable of beauty still involves giving way to the retrospective illusion, realizing the valuable in advance—misunderstanding the human moment *par excellence* in

which a life woven out of chance events turns back upon, regrasps, and expresses itself. . . .

In short, fear of contingency is everywhere, even in the doctrines which helped reveal it. Whereas Marxism is based entirely upon going beyond nature through human *praxis*, today's Marxists veil the risk such a transformation of the world implies. Whereas Catholicism, particularly in France, is being crossed by a vigorous movement of inquiry next to which the Modernism of the beginning of the century seems sentimental and vague, the heirarchy reaffirms the most worn-out forms of theological explanation with the Syllabus. Its position is understandable: it is indeed true that a man cannot seriously think about the contingency of existence and hold to the Syllabus. It is even true that religion is bound up with a minimum of explanatory thought. In a recent article Francois Mauriac implied that atheism could receive an honorable meaning if it took issue only with the God of philosophers and scientists, God in idea. But without God in idea, without the infinite thought which created the world, Christ is a man and his birth and Passion cease to be acts of God and become symbols of the human condition. It would not be reasonable to expect a religion to conceive of humanity, according to Giraudoux's beautiful phrase, as the "caryatid of the void." But the return to an explanatory theology and the compulsive reaffirmation of the *Ens realissimum* drag back all the consequences of a massive transcendence that religious reflection was trying to escape. Once again the Church, its sacred depository, its unverifiable secret beyond the visible, separates itself from actual society. Once more the Heaven of principles and the earth of existence are sundered. Once more philosophic doubt is only a formality. Once more adversity is called Satan and the war against it is already won. Occult thought scores a point.

Once again, between Christians and non-Christians, as between Marxists and non-Marxists, conversation is becoming difficult. How could there possibly be any real exchange between the man who knows and the man who does not know? What can a man say if he sees no relationship, not even a dialectical one, between state communism and the withering away of the state, when another man says that he does? If a man sees no relationship between the Gospels and the clergy's role in Spain, when another says they are not irreconcilable? Sometimes one starts to dream about what culture, literary life, and teaching could be if all those who participate, having for once rejected idols, would give themselves up to the happiness of reflecting together. But this dream is not reasonable. The discussions of our time are so convulsive only because it is resisting a truth which is right at hand, and because in recognizing—without any intervening veil—the menace of adversity, it is closer perhaps than any other to recognizing the metamorphoses of Fortune.

part VI

THEORIZING MASS CULTURE AND THE COLD WAR

Max Horkheimer *1895–1973*

Karl Popper *1902–1994*

Arnold Toynbee *1889–1975*

Claude Lévi-Strauss *1908–*

Theodor Adorno *1903–1969*

Gabriel (-Honoré) Marcel *1889–1973*

C. Wright Mills *1916–1962*

Roland Barthes *1915–1980*

Robert Redfield *1897–1958*

Herbert Marcuse *1898–1979*

Jacques (Marie Emile) Lacan *1901–1981*

Hannah Arendt *1906–1975*

Roger Caillois *1913–1978*

Harold Garfinkel *1917–*

Raymond Aron *1905–1983*

Frantz Fanon *1925–1961*

Jürgen Habermas *1929–*

Mary Douglas *1921–*

Susanne Langer *1895–1985*

Walter Benjamin *1892–1940*

MAX HORKHEIMER

1895–1973

Son of a Jewish factory owner, Max Horkheimer was born in Stuttgart, Germany on February 14, 1895, married Rosa Riekher in 1926 (d. 1969), and died in Nürnberg on July 7, 1973 at 76. He graduated from prep school in 1911 and began vocational training, also becoming friends with his future colleague, Friedrich Pollock. He worked for his father and participated in the war effort from 1917–1918, and graduated from college in 1919. He pursued graduate studies in psychology and philosophy, then attended the universities at Munich, Freiburg, and Frankfurt, taking his degree at the latter in 1925. There he studied with Hans Cornelius and wrote a 78-page dissertation called "Antinomies of Teleological Judgement." His lifelong creative friendship with Theodor Adorno began at this time. His habilitation thesis was "Kant's *Critique of Judgement* as Link Between Theoretical and Practical Philosophy" (64 pp., 1925). He was an unsalaried lecturer in Frankfurt in 1926, was promoted to professor of philosophy in 1930 and the next year, by means of an endowment from a wealthy businessman, he became director of the new Institute for Social Research, now famous worldwide as "the Frankfurt School of Critical Theory." Joining him in this effort were young men who later became enormously famous, including Erich Fromm, Herbert Marcuse, Adorno, Walter Benjamin, Pollock, Leo Löwenthal, and others. One of the most important features of the Institute was its new journal, *Zeitschrift für Sozialforschung,* which Horkheimer edited. He and his colleagues began a multi-volume study of the family under fascism, which was later in the U.S. transmogrified into the famous *Authoritarian Personality* (1950) by Adorno and others as part of the "Studies in Prejudice" series. Horkheimer was forced to emigrate with most of his colleagues, who were Jewish, to New York in 1934, where the Institute for Social Research was reestablished at Columbia University during the war years, becomes a U.S. citizen (1940), moved to Pacific Palisades, California where he wrote the famous *Dialectic of Enlightenment* (1944) with Adorno. He returned to Frankfurt as professor of social philosophy in 1949, and reopened the famed Institute. Except for lectures in Chicago from 1954 through 1959, he remained in Germany until his death, where he became progressively pessimistic and anti-revolutionary just as his ideas, especially due to his "Traditional and Critical Theory" essay (1970), had become influential among the global New Left, peopled by scholars 50 years his junior. His final aphoristic works are more attuned to those of Schopenhauer and Nietzsche than to Marx or Marcuse, which may account for his less significant stature today among Frankfurt School aficionados than is the case with either Adorno or Walter Benjamin.

ECLIPSE OF REASON, 1947

Rise and Decline of the Individual

The crisis of reason is manifested in the crisis of the individual, as whose agency it has developed. The illusion that traditional philosophy has cherished about the individual and about reason—the illusion of their eternity—is being dispelled. The individual once conceived of reason exclusively as an instrument of the self. Now he experiences the reverse of this self-deification. The machine has dropped the driver; it is racing blindly into space. At the moment of consummation, reason has become irrational and stultified. The theme of this time is self-preservation, while there is no self to preserve. In view of this situation, it behooves us to reflect upon the concept of the individual.

When we speak of the individual as a historical entity, we mean not merely the space-time and the sense existence of a particular member of the human race, but, in addition, his awareness of his own individuality as a conscious human being, including recognition of his own identity. This perception of the identity of the self is not equally strong in all persons. It is more clearly defined in adults than in children, who must learn to call themselves 'I'—the most elementary affirmation of identity. It is likewise weaker among primitive than among civilized men; indeed, the aborigine who has only recently been exposed to the dynamic of Western civilization often seems very uncertain of his identity. Living in the gratifications and frustrations of the moment, he seems but dimly aware that as an individual he must go on to face the hazards of tomorrow. This lag, it need hardly be said, partly accounts for the common belief that these people are lazy or that they are liars—a reproach that presupposes in the accused the very sense of identity they lack. The qualities found in extreme form among oppressed peoples, such as the Negroes, are also manifested, as a tendency, in persons of oppressed social classes that lack the economic fundament of inherited property. Thus, stunted individuality is found also among the poor white population of the American South. If these submerged people were not conditioned to imitation of their superiors, blatant advertising or educational appeals exhorting them to cultivation of personality would inevitably seem to them condescending, not to say hypocritical—an effort to lull them into a state of delusional contentment.

Individuality presupposes the voluntary sacrifice of immediate satisfaction for the sake of security, material and spiritual maintenance of one's own existence. When the roads to such a life are blocked, one has little incentive to deny oneself momentary pleasures. Hence, individuality among the masses is far less integrated and enduring than among the so-called elite. On the other hand, the elite have always been more preoccupied with the strategies of gaining and holding power. Social power is today more than ever mediated by power over things. The more intense an individual's concern with power over things, the more will things dominate him, the more will he lack any genuine individual traits, and the more will his mind be transformed into an automaton of formalized reason.

The story of the individual, even in ancient Greece, which not only created the concept of individuality but set the patterns for Western culture, is still largely unwritten. The model of the emerging individual is the Greek hero. Daring and self-reliant, he triumphs in the struggle for survival and emancipates himself from tradition as well as from the tribe. To historians like Jacob Burckhardt, such a hero is the incarnation of an unbridled and naive egoism. Nevertheless, while his boundless ego radiates the spirit of domination and intensifies the antagonism of the individual to the community and its mores, he remains unclear about the nature of the conflict between his ego and the world, and hence repeatedly falls prey to all kinds of intrigue. His awe-inspiring deeds do not spring from some personally motivated trait, such as malice or cruelty, but rather from a desire to avenge a crime or ward off a curse. The concept of heroism is inseparable from that of sacrifice. The tragic hero originates in the conflict between the tribe and its members, a conflict in which the individual is always defeated. One may say that the life of the hero is not so much a manifestation of individuality as a prelude to its birth, through the marriage of self-preservation and self-sacrifice.

The only one of Homer's heroes who strikes us as having individuality, a mind of his own, is Ulysses, and he is too wily to seem truly heroic.

The typical Greek individual came to flower in the age of the polis, or city-state, with the crystallization of a burgher class. In Athenian ideology the state was both superior and antecedent to its citizens. But this predominance of the polis facilitated rather than hindered the rise of the individual: it effected a balance between the state and its members, between individual freedom and communal welfare, as nowhere more eloquently depicted than in the Funeral Oration of Pericles. In a famous passage of the *Politics*,[1] Aristotle describes the Greek burgher as a type of individual who, in possessing both the courage of the European and the intelligence of the Asiatic, that is, combining the capacity for self-preservation with reflection, acquired the ability to dominate others without losing his freedom. The Hellenic race, he says, 'if it could be formed into one state, would be able to rule the world.'[2] Time and again when urban culture was at its peak, for instance in Florence during the fifteenth century, a similar balance of psychological forces was achieved. The fortunes of the individual have always been bound up with the development of urban society. The city dweller is the individual par excellence. The great individualists who were critical of city life, such as Rousseau and Tolstoi, had their intellectual roots in urban traditions; Thoreau's escape to the woods was conceived by a student of the Greek polis rather than by a peasant. In these men the individualistic dread of civilization was nourished by its fruits. The antagonism between individuality and the economic and social conditions of its existence, as expressed by these authors, is an essential element in individuality itself. Today, this antagonism is supplanted in the conscious minds of individuals by the desire to adapt themselves to reality. . . .

The deification of industrial activity knows no limits. Relaxation comes to be regarded as a kind of vice so far as it is not necessary to assure fitness for further activity. 'American philosophy,' says Moses F. Aronson, 'postulates the reality of an open and dynamic universe. A fluid universe is not a place to rest in, nor does it encourage the esthetic delight of passive contemplation. A world in constant process of unfolding stimulates the active imagination and invites the exercise of muscular intelligence.'[5] He feels that pragmatism 'reflects the characteristics of a frontier-nurtured, athletic mentality grappling with the perplexities engendered by the rising tide of industrialism swirling against the background of a rural economy.'[6]

However, the difference between the 'frontier-nurtured mentality' of the actual American pioneers and that of its modern propagators seems a glaring one. The pioneers themselves did not hypostatize means as ends. They embraced hard toil in their immediate struggle for survival; in their dreams they may well have fantasied about the pleasures of a less dynamic and much more restful universe. They probably made a value of the esthetic delight of passive contemplation in their concepts of beatitude or in their ideal of a culture to be achieved.

Their latest epigoni, when they adopt an intellectual profession in the modern division of labor, extol the obverse values. By speaking of theoretical endeavors as 'muscular' and 'athletic,' and as in this sense a 'spontaneous native growth,' they are trying, as though with a twinge of bad conscience, to hold on to their heritage of the 'strenuous life' from the frontiersmen and also to assimilate their language to the activistic vocabulary of manual occupations, particularly of agricultural and industrial labor. They glorify co-ordination and uniformity even in the realm of ideas. . . .

If modern society tends to negate all the attributes of individuality, are its members not compensated, it may be asked, by the rationality of its organization? The technocrats often maintain that when their theories are put into practice, depressions will become a thing of the past and basic economic disproportions will disappear; the whole productive mechanism will work smoothly according to blueprints. Actually, modern society is not so far from having realized the technocratic dream. The needs of the consumers as well as of the producers, which under the liberal market system made themselves felt in distorted and irrational forms, in a process culminating in depressions, can now to a great extent be forecast and satisfied or negated in accordance with the policies of economic and political leaders. The expression of human needs is no longer distorted by the dubious economic indicators of the market; instead; these needs are determined by statistics, and all kinds of engineers—industrial technical, political—struggle to keep them under control. But if this new rationality is in one way closer to the idea of reason than the market system, it is in another way farther from it.

Dealings between the members of different social groups under the older system were really determined not by the market but by the unequal distribution of economic power, yet the transformation of human relations into objective economic mechanisms gave the individual, at least in principle, a certain independence. When unsuccessful competitors went to the wall or backward groups were reduced to misery under the liberalistic economy, they could preserve a sense of human dignity even though they were economically cast down, because responsibility for their plight could be thrown upon anonymous economic processes. Today individuals or entire groups may still suffer ruin through blind economic forces; but these are represented by better organized, more powerful elites. Although the interrelations of these dominant groups are subject to vicissitudes, they understand each other well in many respects. When concentration and centralization of industrial forces extinguish political liberalism in its turn, the victims are doomed in their entirety. Under totalitarianism, when an individual or group is singled out by the elite for discrimination, it is not only deprived of the means of livelihood, but its very human essence is attacked. American society may take a different course. However, the dwindling away of individual thinking and resistance, as it is brought about by the economic and cultural mechanisms of modem industrialism, will render evolution toward the humane increasingly difficult.

By making the watchword of production a kind of religious creed by professing technocratic ideas and branding as 'unproductive' such groups as do not have access to the big industrial bastions; industry causes itself and society to forget that production has become to an ever greater extent a means in the struggle for power. The policies of economic leaders, on which society in its present stage more and more directly depends, are dogged and particularistic, and therefore perhaps even blinder with respect to the real needs of society than were the automatic trends that once determined the market. Irrationality still molds the fate of men. . . .

Every instrumentality of mass culture serves to reinforce the social pressures upon individuality, precluding all possibility that the individual will somehow preserve himself in the face of all the atomizing machinery of modern society. The accent on individual heroism and on the self-made man in popular biographies and pseudo-romantic novels and films does not invalidate this observation.[8] These machine-made incentives to self-preservation actually accelerate the dissolution of individuality. Just as the slogans of rugged individualism are politically useful to large trusts in seeking exemption from social control, so in mass culture the rhetoric of individualism, by imposing patterns for collective imitation, disavows the very principle to which it gives lip service. If, in the words of Huey Long, every man can be a king, why cannot every girl be a movie queen, whose uniqueness consists in being typical?

The individual no longer has a personal history. Though everything changes, nothing moves. . . .

The feudal appearance of the bourgeois world is vanishing; many factors converge here to remove the aureole of magic from developments that have long since been described by the sociologists. At a time when the perfection of observational instruments of every kind is causing language itself to lose its expressive quality and to take on more and more exclusively the character of a set of signs, even the notion of the infinite meaning and value of every individual soul has become outmoded. Religion itself is in the process of adapting to these new circumstances. The customer's loss of his regal status is part of the same process that we see in the resigned attitude of Christianity: the process of being struck dumb amid endless noise. It is clear that the improved material position of wide strata of the population is connected with, and indeed largely conditions, the loss of the individual's illusion that he is a free subject. Yet in today's individual, for all that he is more modest and malleable, bourgeois subjectivity does not disappear, as feudal self-awareness did at an earlier time. The fact is rather that self-awareness in contemporary society is directly connected with belonging to some collectivity: to an age group or vocational group, and ultimately to the nation. The divergence between individual and group that is now disappearing continues to show up among stunted individuals, criminals, and people who can assert themselves only by opposition to everything else.

Notes

1. *Politica*, vii, 7, 1327 b.

2. Transl. by Benjamin Jowett, in *The Works of Aristotle*, ed. by W. D. Ross, Oxford, 1921, v. x.

5. Cf. Charles Beard, *The American Spirit*, p. 666.

6. Ibid. p. 665.

8. Cf. Leo Lowenthal: 'Biographies in Popular Magazines,' in *Radio Research*, 1942–43, New York, 1944, pp. 507–48.

KARL POPPER

1902–1994

Sir Karl Raimund Popper was born in Vienna, July 28, 1902, the third child and only son of a Jewish lawyer with a "bookish" nature, keenly interested in the classics and philosophy, and a mother from whom he acquired a passionate devotion to music, so much so that he once considered pursuing music professionally. It is also suggested that his view of knowledge and his animus against historicism could both be linked in broad terms to his appreciation for changes in musical forms over time. Popper married Josephine Henninger in 1930 (d. 1985), reaching the age of 92 before dying in London on September 17, 1994. After attending the local *Realgymnasium* (an unhappy experience, partly because Popper disliked its testing procedures, and because he was too ill to attend school for some months), in 1918 he began studying at the University of Vienna, but without formal matriculation procedures. He was in 1919 swept up in the postwar enthusiasm for Marxism, joining the Association of Socialist School Students, and also paid careful attention to the new theories of Freud and Adler, as part of doing social work with poor children. Yet the orthodox, doctrinaire qualities that typified both streams of thought put off the young Popper, insinuating in him a dislike of dogmatic thinking that he made his philosophical calling card over the next 75 years. He began to contrast Einstein's comfort with what Popper later called "falsifiability" against what he thought were the insulated theories of Marx and Freud that made them unscientific. He became certified to teach elementary school in 1925, received the doctorate in 1928 in philosophy, and was granted permission to teach high school math and physics in 1929. Herbert Feigl, a member of the Vienna Circle of logical positivism, persuaded Popper to put his objections to the Circle's main arguments into book form, which gave rise to his first and most famous work, *Logik der Forschung* (1934). The book's success took him to England in 1935 to lecture, but fascism in Europe prompted him to move to New Zealand in 1937 to teach at the University of Canterbury. With the *Anschluss* of his homeland by Hitler, he began to write about social and political topics, then relocated to the London School of Economics in 1946, then to the University of London, from which he retired in 1969. His *Logic of Scientific Discovery* (1959) had made him famous, and he was knighted in 1965 and received the Insignia of a Companion of Honor in 1982.

Popper believed that knowledge should be discovered and validated collectively, in the full light of day, and that any body of ideas which is not susceptible to such an investigation loses the designation of science and instead must be viewed as merely a myth. His other major works are *The Open Society and Its Enemies* (1945), *The Poverty of Historicism* (1944), and *Conjectures and Refutations* (essays) (1962). His "falsifiability thesis" has entered every textbook in the philosophy of science, and his notorious and in some ways amateurish attacks on Plato, Hegel, and Marx in *The Open Society* inspired George Soros, the billionaire financier, to fund a think-tank which aims to put Popper's ideas to practical use in shaping the global economy.

CONJECTURES AND REFUTATIONS, 1962

Utopia and Violence, 1948

There are many people who hate violence and are convinced that it is one of their foremost and at the same time one of their most hopeful tasks to work for its reduction and, if possible, for its elimination from human life. I am among these hopeful enemies of violence. I not only hate violence, but I firmly believe that the fight against it is not at all hopeless. I realize that the task is difficult. I realize that, only too often in the course of history, it has happened that what appeared at first to be a great success in the fight against violence was followed by defeat. I do not overlook the fact that the new age of violence which was opened by the two World wars is by no means at an end. Nazism and Fascism are thoroughly beaten, but I must admit that their defeat does not mean that barbarism and brutality have been defeated. On the contrary, it is no use closing our eyes to the fact that these hateful ideas achieved something like victory in defeat. I have to admit that Hitler succeeded in degrading the moral standards of our Western world, and that in the world of today there is more violence and brutal force than would have been tolerated even in the decade after the first World war. And we must face the possibility that our civilization may ultimately be destroyed by those new weapons which Hitlerism wished upon us, perhaps even within the first decades after the second World war; for no doubt the spirit of Hitlerism won its greatest victory over us when, after its defeat, we used the weapons which the threat of Nazism had induced us to develop. But in spite of all this I am today no less hopeful than I have ever been that violence can be defeated. It is our only hope; and long stretches in the history of Western as well as of Eastern civilizations prove that it need not be a vain hope—that violence can be reduced, and brought under the control of reason.

This is perhaps why I, like many others, believe in reason; why I call myself a rationalist. I am

Excerpts from Chapters 18 and 19, in *Conjectures and Refutations*, by Karl Popper. Copyright Karl Popper 1963, and the estate of Karl Popper, 1994. Used by permission of the estate of Karl Popper.

a rationalist because I see in the attitude of reasonableness the only alternative to violence.

When two men disagree, they do so either because their opinions differ, or because their interests differ, or both. There are many kinds of disagreement in social life which must be decided one way or another. The question may be one which must be settled, because failure to settle it may create new difficulties whose cumulative effects may cause an intolerable strain, such as a state of continual and intense preparation for deciding the issue. (An armaments race is an example.) To reach a decision may be a necessity.

How can a decision be reached? There are, in the main, only two possible ways: argument (including arguments submitted to arbitration, for example to some international court of justice) and violence. Or, if it is interests that clash, the two alternatives are a reasonable compromise or an attempt to destroy the opposing interest.

A rationalist, as I use the word, is a man who attempts to reach decisions by argument and perhaps, in certain cases, by compromise, rather than by violence. He is a man who would rather be unsuccessful in convincing another man by argument than successful in crushing him by force, by intimidation and threats, or even by persuasive propaganda.

We shall understand better what I mean by reasonableness if we consider the difference between trying to convince a man by argument and trying to persuade him by propaganda.

The difference does not lie so much in the use of argument. Propaganda often uses argument too. Nor does the difference lie in our conviction that our arguments are conclusive, and must be admitted to be conclusive by any reasonable man. It lies rather in an attitude of give and take, in a readiness not only to convince the other man but also possibly to be convinced by him. What I call the attitude of reasonableness may be characterized by a remark like this: 'I think I am right, but I may be wrong and you may be right, and in any case let us discuss it, for in this way we are likely to get nearer to a true understanding than if we each merely insist that we are right.'

It will be realized that what I call the attitude of reasonableness or the rationalistic attitude presupposes a certain amount of intellectual humility. Perhaps only those can take it up who are aware that they are sometimes wrong, and who do not habitually forget their mistakes. It is born of the realization that we are not omniscient, and that we owe most of our knowledge to others. It is an attitude which tries as far as possible to transfer to the field of opinions in general the two rules of every legal proceeding: first, that one should always hear both sides, and secondly, that one does not make a good judge if one is a party to the case.

I believe that we can avoid violence only in so far as we practise this attitude of reasonableness when dealing with one another in social life; and that any other attitude is likely to produce violence—even a one-sided attempt to deal with others by gentle persuasion, and to convince them by argument and example of those insights we are proud of possessing, and of whose truth we are absolutely certain. We all remember how many religious wars were fought for a religion of love and gentleness; how many bodies were burned alive with the genuinely kind intention of saving souls from the eternal fire of hell. Only if we give up our authoritarian attitude in the realm of opinion, only if we establish the attitude of give and take, of readiness to learn from other people, can we hope to control acts of violence inspired by piety and duty.

There are many difficulties impeding the rapid spread of reasonableness. One of the main difficulties is that it always takes two to make a discussion reasonable. Each of the parties must be ready to learn from the other. You cannot have a rational discussion with a man who prefers shooting you to being convinced by you. In other words, there are limits to the attitude of reasonableness. It is the same with tolerance. You must not, without qualification, accept the principle of tolerating all those who are intolerant; if you do, you will destroy not only yourself, but also the attitude of tolerance. (All this is indicated in the remark I made before—that reasonableness must be an attitude of *give and take*.)

An important consequence of all this is that we must not allow the distinction between attack and defence to become blurred. We must insist upon this distinction, and support and develop social institutions (national as well as international) whose function it is to discriminate between aggression and resistance to aggression.

I think I have said enough to make clear what I intend to convey by calling myself a rationalist. My rationalism is not dogmatic. I fully admit that I cannot rationally prove it. I frankly confess that I choose rationalism because I hate violence, and I do not deceive myself into believing that this hatred has any rational grounds. Or to put it another way, my rationalism is not self-contained, but rests on an irrational faith in the attitude of reasonableness. I do not see that we can go beyond this. One could say, perhaps, that my irrational faith in equal and reciprocal rights to convince others and be convinced by them is a faith in human reason; or simply, that I believe in man.

The History of Our Time: An Optimist's View, 1956

I have chosen as the title of my lecture 'The History of Our Time: An Optimist's View', and I feel that I should begin by explaining this title.

When I say 'History', I wish to refer particularly to our social and political history, but also to our moral and intellectual history. By the word 'our', I mean the free world of the Atlantic Community—especially England, the United States, the Scandinavian countries and Switzerland, and the outposts of this world in the Pacific, Australia and New Zealand. By 'our time' I mean, in particular, the period since 1914. But I also mean the last fifty or sixty years—that is to say the time since the Boer War, or the age of Winston Churchill, as one might call it; the last hundred years—that is, in the main, the time since the abolition of slavery and since John Stuart Mill; the last two hundred years—that is, in the main, the time since the American Revolution, since Hume, Voltaire, Kant, and Burke; and to a lesser extent, the last three hundred years—the time since the

Reformation; since Locke, and since Newton. So much for the phrase 'The History of Our Time'.

Now I come to the word 'Optimist'. First let me make it quite clear that if I call myself an optimist, I do not wish to suggest that I know anything about the future. I do not wish to pose as a prophet, least of all as a historical prophet. On the contrary, I have for many years tried to defend the view that historical prophecy is a kind of quackery.[1] I do not believe in historical laws, and I disbelieve especially in anything like a law of progress. In fact, I believe that it is much easier for us to regress than to progress.

Though I believe all this, I think that I may fairly describe myself as an optimist. For my optimism lies entirely in my interpretation of the present and the immediate past. It lies in my strongly appreciative view of our own time. And whatever you might think about this optimism you will have to admit that it has a scarcity value. In fact the wailings of the pessimists have become somewhat monotonous. No doubt there is much in our world about which we can rightly complain if only we give our mind to it; and no doubt it is sometimes most important to find out what is wrong with us. But I think that the other side of the story might also get a hearing.

Thus it is with respect to the immediate past and to our own time that I hold optimistic views. And this brings me finally to the word 'view' which is the last word of my title. What I shall be aiming at in this lecture is to sketch, in a few strokes, a kind of bird's-eye view of our time. It will no doubt be a very personal view—an interpretation rather than a description. But I shall try to support it by argument. And although pessimists will feel that my view is superficial, I shall at least try to present it in a way that may challenge them.

And so I begin with a challenge. I will challenge a certain belief which seems to be widely held, and held in widely different quarters; not only by many Churchmen whose sincerity is beyond doubt, but also by some rationalists such as Bertrand Russell, whom I greatly admire as a man and as a philosopher.

Russell has more than once expressed the belief I wish to challenge. He has complained that

our intellectual development has outrun our moral development.

We have become very clever, according to Russell, indeed too clever. We can make lots of wonderful gadgets, including television, high-speed rockets, and an atom bomb, or a thermonuclear bomb, if you prefer. But we have not been able to achieve that moral and political growth and maturity which alone could safely direct and control the uses to which we put our tremendous intellectual powers. This is why we now find ourselves in mortal danger. Our evil national pride has prevented us from achieving the world-state in time.

To put this view in a nutshell: we are clever, perhaps too clever, but we are also wicked; and this mixture of cleverness and wickedness lies at the root of our troubles.

As against this, I shall maintain precisely the opposite. My *first thesis* is this.

We are good, perhaps a little too good, but we are also a little stupid; and it is this mixture of goodness and stupidity which lies at the root of our troubles.

To avoid misunderstandings, I should stress that when I use the word 'we' in this thesis, I include myself.

You may perhaps ask me why my first thesis should be part of an optimist's view. There are various reasons. One is that wickedness is even more difficult to combat than a limited measure of stupidity, because good men who are not very clever are usually very anxious to learn.

Another reason is that I do not think that we are hopelessly stupid, and this is surely an optimist's view. What is wrong with us is that we so easily mislead ourselves, and that we are so easily 'led by the nose' by others, as Samuel Butler says in *Erewhon*. I hope you will let me quote from one of my favourite passages: 'It will be seen', Butler writes, ' . . . that the Erewhonians are a meek and long-suffering people, easily led by the nose, and quick to offer up common sense at the shrine of logic, when a philosopher arises among them, who carries them away . . . by convincing them that their existing institutions are not based on the strictest principles of morality.'. . .

But let us turn to larger problems. Our free world has very nearly, if not completely, succeeded in abolishing the greatest evils which have hitherto beset the social life of man.

Let me give you a list of what I believe to be some of the greatest of those evils which can be remedied, or relieved, by social co-operation: They are:

Poverty
Unemployment and some similar forms of
    Social Insecurity
Sickness and Pain
Penal Cruelty
Slavery and other forms of Serfdom
Religious and Racial Discrimination
Lack of Educational Opportunities
Rigid Class Differences
War

Let us see what has been achieved; not only here in Great Britain, through the Welfare State, but by one method or another everywhere in the free world.

Abject poverty has been practically abolished. Instead of being a mass phenomenon, the problem has almost become one of detecting the isolated cases which still persist.

The problems of unemployment and of some other forms of insecurity have changed completely. We are now faced with new problems brought into being by the fact that the problem of mass-unemployment has largely been solved.

Fairly continuous progress is being made in dealing with the problems of sickness and pain.

Penal reform has largely abolished cruelty in this field.

The story of the successful fight against slavery has become the everlasting pride of this country and of the United States.

Religious discrimination has practically disappeared. Racial discrimination has diminished to an extent surpassing the hopes of the most hopeful. What makes these two achievements even more astonishing is the fact that religious prejudices, and even more so racial prejudices, are probably as widespread as they were fifty years ago, or very nearly so.

The problem of educational opportunities is still very serious, but it is being tackled sincerely and with energy.

Class differences have diminished enormously everywhere. In Scandinavia, the United States, Canada, Australia and New Zealand, we have, in fact, something approaching classless societies.

My eighth point was war. This point I must discuss more fully. It may be best to formulate what I have to say here as my *third thesis.*

My third thesis is that since the time of the Boer War, none of the democratic governments of the free world has been in a position to wage a war of aggression. No democratic government would be united upon the issue, because they would not have the nation united behind them. Aggressive war has become almost a moral impossibility. . . .

The war of ideas is a Greek invention. It is one of the most important inventions ever made. Indeed, the possibility of fighting with words instead of fighting with swords is the very basis of our civilization, and especially of all its legal and parliamentary institutions. And this habit of fighting with words and ideas is one of the few things which still unite the worlds on the two sides of the Iron Curtain (although on the other side, words have only inadequately replaced swords, and are sometimes used to prepare for the kill). To see how powerful ideas have become since the days of the Greeks, we only need to remember that all religious wars were wars of ideas, and that all revolutions were revolutions of ideas. Although these ideas were more often false and pernicious than true and beneficial there is perhaps a certain tendency for some of the better ones to survive, provided they find sufficiently powerful and intelligent support.

All this may be formulated in my *fourth thesis.* It is as follows.

The power of ideas, and especially of moral and religious ideas, is at least as important as that of physical resources.

I am well aware of the fact that some students of politics are strongly opposed to this thesis; that there is an influential school of so-called political realists who declare that 'ideologies', as they call them, have little influence upon political reality, and that whatever influence they have must be pernicious. But I do not think that this is a tenable view. Were it true, Christianity would have had no influence on history; and the United States would be inexplicable, or merely the result of a pernicious mistake.

My fourth thesis, the doctrine of the power of ideas, is characteristic of the liberal and rationalist thought of the eighteenth and nineteenth centuries.

But the liberal movement did not believe only in the power of ideas. It also upheld a view which I consider mistaken. It believed that there was little need for competing ideas to join battle. This was because it supposed that truth, once put forward, would always be recognized. It believed in the theory that truth is manifest—that it cannot be missed once the powers which are interested in its suppression and perversion are destroyed.

This important and influential idea—that truth is manifest—is one form of optimism which I cannot support. I am convinced that it is mistaken, and that, on the contrary, truth is hard, and often painful, to come by. This, then, is my *fifth thesis.*

Truth is hard to come by.

This thesis explains to some extent the wars of religion. And although it is a piece of epistemology, it can throw much light upon the history of Europe since the Renaissance, and even since classical antiquity.

Note

1. See my *Poverty of Historicism,* 1957; and ch. 16.

ARNOLD TOYNBEE

1889–1975

Son of Harry Valpy Toynbee, a social worker, and Sarah Marshall Toynbee (one of very few Victorian British women to hold a college degree), Arnold Joseph Toynbee was born into a family of scholars on April 14, 1889 in London, married Rosalind Murray in September, 1912 (divorced, 1945), with whom he had two sons, and then married Veronica Marjorie Boulter (a writer) in 1946. At 86 he died in York, North Yorkshire, on October 22, 1975. Intending from an early age to imitate his mother's ability as an historian, and carefully coached by her to be one, he attended Winchester College (1902–07), then Balliol College, Oxford (1907–11), taking high honors and becoming so fluent in Greek and Latin that he sometimes preferred communicating in those languages rather than English. He also traveled to the British Archaeological School in Athens, Greece (1911–12) and explored Greece looking for historical data. His experiences in Greece and in the library convinced him that a holistic view of human history was the only truly useful kind, and that it was his job as historian to escape the imaginative limitations of his own culture and century of birth. He was a fellow and tutor at Balliol College from 1912–1915, then became Koraes Professor of Byzantine and Modern Greek Language, Literature and History at the University of London (1919–24), then a research professor until 1955. Because of illness, he did noncombatant war work for the British during WWI, finally working in the Foreign Office's Intelligence Department in 1918, and (like Max Weber) he served his government by being part of the delegation attending the Peace Conference in Paris (1919) and again after WWII (1946).

Toynbee was for much of the 20th century the world's most recognized historian of the huge scale by publishing *The Study of History* (12 vols) between 1934 and 1961. In addition, he also wrote or edited several dozen other books beginning with *Greek Policy since 1882* in 1914 and ending with *Constantine Porphyrogenitus and His World* (1973), followed by a half-dozen posthumous volumes. Toynbee's philosophy of history irritated most professional historians no end because he tried, by means of gargantuan solo erudition, to explain the rise and fall of civilizations that made for excellent socio-religious speculation but for poor attention to the details of historical factuality. Like many before him, he thought he discerned a pattern to civilizational history, from genesis to growth, then breakdown and disintegration, then reconstruction as reflected in the records of the 21 societies he regarded as most important. He mixed his historiography with sustained attention to contemporary politics, viewing the latter through lenses ground in the workshop of the former, and giving the world his special view through the annual publication, *Survey of International Affairs*. With one foot in ancient times, one in modern, he gave the world a unique vision.

CIVILIZATION ON TRIAL, 1948

The Meaning of History for the Soul

Let us start our inquiry by examining successively two points of view which lie at opposite extremes of the historico-theological gamut, but which, if respectively tenable, would each solve the problem of the meaning of history for the soul in fairly simple terms. In the writer's opinion (he may as well declare in advance) both points of view are in truth untenable, though each does contain an element of truth which it invalidates through the exaggeration of pushing it to extremes.

A Purely This-Worldly View

The first of these two extreme views is that, for the soul, the whole meaning of its existence is contained in history.

On this view, the individual human being is nothing but a part of the society of which he is a member. The individual exists for society, not society for the individual. Therefore the significant and important thing in human life is not the spiritual development of souls but the social development of communities. In the writer's opinion, this thesis is not true, and, when it has been taken as true and has been put into action, it has produced moral enormities.

The proposition that the individual is a mere part of a social whole may be the truth about social insects—bees, ants, and termites—but it is not the truth about any human beings of whom we have any knowledge. An early twentieth-century school of anthropologists, of which Durkheim was the leading representative, drew a picture of primitive man which portrayed him as being almost of a different mental and spiritual breed from our allegedly rational selves. Drawing its evidence from descriptions of surviving primitive societies, this

school represented primitive man as being governed not by the rational operation of the individual intellect, but by the collective emotion of the human herd. This sharp distinction between an "uncivilized" and a "civilized" breed of man has, however, to be radically revised and toned down in the light of the illuminating psychological discoveries that have been made since Durkheim's day. Psychological research has shown us that the so-called savage has no monopoly of the emotionally governed life of the collective unconscious. Though it happens to have been first laid bare in the soul of primitive man by anthropological observation, psychological research has made it clear that, in our comparatively sophisticated souls too, the collective unconscious underlies a consciousness that rides on it like a cockleshell floating precariously on a bottomless and shoreless ocean. Whatever the constitution of the human psyche may prove to be, we can already be more or less certain that it is substantially the same in human beings like ourselves, who are in the act of attempting to climb from the level of primitive human life to the ledge of civilization, and in ex-primitives, like the Papuans of New Guinea and the Negritos of Central Africa, who have been played upon, within the last few thousand years, by the radiation of societies that have been in process of civilization within that period. The psychic make-up of all extant human beings, in all extant types of society, appears to be substantially identical, and we have no ground for believing it to have been different in the earliest representatives of the species *sapiens* of the genus *homo* that are known to us, not from the anthropologist's personal intercourse with living people, but from the archaeologist's and the physiologist's deciphering of the revealing evidence of artifacts and skeletons. In the *most* primitive as well as in the least primitive state in which *homo sapiens* is in any way known to us, we may conclude that the individual human being possesses some measure of self-conscious personality that raises his soul above the level of the water of the collective unconscious, and this means that the individual soul does have a genuine life of its own which is distinct from the life of society. We may also conclude that individuality is a pearl of great moral price, when we observe the moral enormities that occur when this pearl is trampled in the mire.

A Solely Other-Worldly View

Let us now take a flying leap to the opposite pole and examine the antithetical view that, for the soul, the whole meaning of its existence lies outside history.

On this view, this world is wholly meaningless and evil. The task of the soul in this world is to endure it, to detach itself from it, to get out of it. This is the view of the Buddhist, Stoic and Epicurean schools of philosophy (whatever the Buddha's own personal outlook may have been). There is a strong vein of it in Platonism. And it has been one of the historic interpretations (in the writer's belief, a mistaken one) of Christianity.

According to the extreme Buddhist view, the soul itself is part and parcel of the phenomenal world, so that, in order to get rid of the phenomenal world, the soul has to extinguish itself. At any rate, it has to extinguish elements in itself which, to the Christian mind, are essential for the soul's existence: for example, above all, the feelings of love and pity. This is unmistakably evident in the Hinayana interpretation of Buddhism, but it is also implicit in the Mahayana, however reluctant the followers of the Mahayana school may be to dwell on the ultimate implications of their own tenets. The Mahayanian Bodhisattva may be moved, by his love and pity for his fellow sentient beings, to postpone his own entry into Nirvana for aeons upon aeons for the sake of helping his fellows to follow the path that he has found for himself. Yet this path is, after all, the orthodox one that leads to salvation through *self-extinction*, and the Bodhisattva's sacrifice, though immense, is not irrevocable or everlasting. At long last, he is going to take that final step into the Nirvana on whose threshold he already stands, and, in the act, he will extinguish, with himself, the love and pity that have won for him the answering love and gratitude of mankind.

The Stoic might be described (perhaps too unkindly) as a would-be Buddhist who has not had quite the full courage of his convictions. As for the Epicurean, be regards this world as an accidental, meaningless, and evil product of the mechanical interplay of atoms, and—since the probable duration of the particular ephemeral world in which he happens to find himself may be drearily long by comparison with a human being's expectation of life—he must look forward to, or expedite, his own dissolution as the only way out for himself.

The Christian of the extreme other-worldly school does, of course, believe that God exists and that this world has been created by Him for a purpose, but this purpose, as he sees it, is the negative one of training the soul, by suffering, for life in another world with which this world has nothing positive in common.

This view that the whole meaning of the soul's existence lies outside history seems to the writer to present difficulties, even in its attenuated Christian version, that are insurmountable from the Christian standpoint. . . .

The view that, for the soul, the whole meaning of its existence lies outside history thus proves to be no less repellent than the antithetical view which we examined first; yet, in this case, as in that, there is an element of truth underlying the mistaken belief. While it is not true that man's social life and human relations in this world are merely a means towards a personal spiritual end, the underlying truths are that in this world we do learn by suffering; that life in this world is not an end in itself and by itself; that it is only a fragment (even if an authentic one) of some larger whole; and that, in this larger whole, the central and dominant (though not the only) feature in the soul's spiritual landscape is its relation to God.

*A Third View: the World a Province
of the Kingdom of God*

We have now rejected two views, both of which offer an answer to our question: What is the meaning of history for the soul? We have refused to admit that, for the soul, the meaning of its existence lies either wholly in history or wholly outside history. And this pair of negative conclusions confronts us with a dilemma.

In rejecting the view that the meaning of the soul's existence lies wholly in history, we have vindicated the primacy—as a fact, as a right, and as a duty—of each individual soul's relation to God. But if every soul, at any time or place, and in any social or historical situation in this world, is in a position to know and love God—or, in traditional theological terms, in a position to find salvation—this truth might seem to empty history of significance. If the most primitive people, in the most rudimentary conditions of social and spiritual life in this world, can achieve the true end of man in man's relation to God, then why should we strive to make this world a better place? Indeed, what intelligible meaning could be attached to those words? On the other hand, in rejecting the view that the meaning of the soul's existence lies wholly outside history, we have vindicated the primacy of God's love in His relation to His creatures. But, if this world has the positive value that it must have if God loves it and has become incarnate in it, then His attempts, and our attempts under His inspiration and on His behalf, to make this world a better place must be right and significant in some sense.

Can we resolve this apparent contradiction? We might perhaps resolve it for practical purposes if we could find an answer to the question: In what sense can there be progress in this world?

The progress with which we are here concerned is a progressive improvement, continuous and cumulative from generation to generation, in our social heritage. By progress, we must mean this; for there is no warrant for supposing that, within "historical times," there has been any progress in the evolution of human nature itself, either physical or spiritual. Even if we push our historical horizon back to the date of the first emergence of *homo sapiens,* the period is infinitesimally short on the time scale of the evolution of life on this planet. Western man, at the present high level of his intellectual powers and technological aptitudes, has not sloughed off Adam's heirloom of original sin, and, to the best of our knowledge, *homo aurignacius,* a hundred thousand years ago, must have been endowed, for good or evil, with the self-same spiritual, as well as physical, characteristics that we find in ourselves. Progress then, if discernible within "historical times," must have been progress in the improvement of our social heritage and not progress in the improvement of our breed, and the evidence for social progress is, of course, impressive in the field of scientific knowledge and its application to technology: in everything, that is to say, which has to do with man's command over non-human nature. This, however, is a side issue; for the impressiveness of the evidence for progress in this particular field is matched by the obviousness of the fact that man is relatively good at dealing with non-human nature. What he is bad at is his dealing with human nature in himself and in his fellow human beings. *A fortiori,* he has proved to be very bad indeed at getting into the right relation with God. Man has been a dazzling success in the field of intellect and "know-how" and a dismal failure in the things of the spirit, and it has been the great tragedy of human life on Earth that this sensational inequality of man's respective achievements in the non-human and in the spiritual sphere should, so far at any rate, have been this way round; for the spiritual side of man's life is of vastly greater importance for man's well-being (even for his material well-being, in the last resort) than is his command over non-human nature.

What is the position, then, in terms of this spiritual side of life which matters so much to man and in which he has so far been so backward? Can there be cumulative progress in the improvement of our social heritage in terms of the spiritual life of mankind—which means the spiritual life of individual souls, since man's relation to God is personal and not collective? A conceivable kind of progress in these spiritual terms—a kind that would give significance to history and would, so to speak, justify God's love for this world and His incarnation in it—would be a cumulative increase in the means of Grace at the disposal of each soul in this world. There are, of course, elements, and very important elements, in man's spiritual situation in this world which would not be affected by such an increase in the means of Grace available. It would not affect either man's innate tendency to original sin or his capacity for obtaining salvation in this world. Every child would be born in the bondage of original sin under the new and the old spiritual dispensation alike, though the child born under the new dispensation might be far better armed and aided than his predecessors were for obtaining his liberation. Again, under the old and the new dispensation alike, the opportunity for obtaining salvation in this world would be open to every soul, since every soul always and everywhere has within its reach the possibility of knowing and loving God. The actual—and momentous—effect of a cumulative increase in the means of Grace at man's disposal in this world would be to make it possible for human souls, while still in this world, to come to know God better and come to love Him more nearly in his own way.

On such a view, this world would not be a spiritual exercise ground beyond the pale of the Kingdom of God; it would be a province of the Kingdom—one province only, and not the most important one, yet one which had the same absolute value as the rest, and therefore one in which spiritual action could, and would, be fully significant and worth while; the one thing of manifest and abiding value in a world in which all other things are vanity.

CLAUDE LÉVI-STRAUSS

1908–

Son of a painter and member of an intellectual Jewish extended family, Claude Lévi-Strauss was born in Brussels, Belgium on November 28, 1908, married Dina Dreyfus in 1932 (divorced), then married Rosemarie Ullmo in 1946 (divorced, one son), then Monique Roman on April 5, 1954 (one son). He studied law and philosophy at the University of Paris (1927–32) and taught at various lycées in France while becoming affiliated with Sartre's circle of young intellectuals. He moved to Sao Paolo, Brazil in 1934 to become professor of sociology, did fieldwork about which he wrote at length for decades, left in 1937, and became visiting professor at the New School in New York City during WWII, and while there began to study the structuralist linguistic theory of Roman Jakobson. For 24 years he directed the École Pratique des Hautes Études (Univ. of Paris), 1950–74, was elected to the chair of social anthropology at the Collège de France in 1959, the highest such position in France, and retired from it in 1982.

With his first and perhaps most important book, *The Elementary Structures of Kinship* (1949), Lévi-Strauss showed how to analyze human relations by means of a structuralist apparatus which brought to the surface forms of social organization, and the myths which support them, that were not previously available for examination along the lines he proposed. Over the next twenty years he put to use his particular model of work in a range of books, including *Structural Anthropology* (Vol. 1, 1958; 1964) and *Mythologiques* (4 vols., 1964–71), translated as *The Raw and the Cooked* (1969), *From Honey to Ashes* (1973), *The Origin of Table Manners* (1978), and *The Naked Man* (1981). However, his most widely read books and those which will probably outlast his elaborate structuralist analyses are two: his autobiography of his Brazilian fieldwork, *Tristes Tropiques* (1955; Eng. tr. 1973), which is novel-like in its self-analytic style and readability, posing the question of why and how Westerners alone have carried out anthropological work among "The Other;" and *The Savage Mind* (1966), now a classic in modern anthropological theorizing that summarizes Lévi-Strauss's notion of how to understand premodern thought and behavior. Lévi-Strauss's coordinating idea—that a perceivable pattern exists beneath all the confusing surface reality of "primitive" mythology and ritual—has been embraced not only by cultural anthropologists, but also by literary critics, philosophers of language, and sociologists. Coinciding in time if not in origin with Noam Chomsky's and Roman Jakobson's structural linguistics, plus analogous tendencies in Foucault, Lacan, Althusser, and Barthes, Lévi-Strauss became the standard-bearer of the school, partly because he based his ideas on data he had collected among the Brazilian Indians.

ELEMENTARY STRUCTURES OF KINSHIP, 1949

The Principle of Reciprocity

The conclusions of the famous *Essai sur le Don* are well known. In this study, which today is regarded as a classic, Mauss sought to show that exchange in primitive societies consists not so much in economic transactions as in reciprocal gifts, that these reciprocal gifts have a far more important function in these societies than in our own, and that this primitive form of exchange is not merely nor essentially of an economic nature but is what he aptly calls 'a total social fact', that is, an event which has a significance that is at once social and religious, magic and economic, utilitarian and sentimental, jural and moral. It is well known that in many primitive societies, particularly those of the Pacific Islands and the North-west Pacific coast of Canada and Alaska, every ceremony celebrating an important event is accompanied by a distribution of wealth. Thus in New Zealand the ceremonial offering of clothes, jewelery, arms, food and various goods was a common feature of Maori social life. These gifts were made on the occasions of births, marriages, deaths, exhumations, peace treaties, crimes and misdemeanours and many other things too numerous to mention. Similarly, Firth includes among ceremonial exchanges in Polynesia 'birth, initiation, marriage, sickness, death and other social events, as well as much religious ritual'. In a more limited section of the region, another observer cites betrothal, marriage, pregnancy, birth and death, and describes presents offered by the young man's father at a betrothal feast, viz., ten baskets of dried fish, thousand ripe and six thousand green coconuts, the young man himself receiving in exchange two cakes four feet square and six inches thick.

These gifts are either exchanged immediately for equivalent gifts or are received by the beneficiaries on condition that at a later date they will give counter-gifts often exceeding the original goods in value, but which in their turn bring about a subsequent right to receive new gifts surpassing the original ones in sumptuousness. The most characteristic of these institutions is the *potlatch* of the Indians of Alaska and the Vancouver region. During the *potlatch* considerable valuables are transferred in this way, sometimes mounting to several tens of thousands of rugs handed over in kind, or in the Symbolical form of copper plaques whose face value increases in terms of the importance of the transactions in which they have figured. These ceremonies have a triple purpose, viz., to return gifts previously received, together with an appropriate amount of interest, sometimes as much as 100 per cent; to establish publicly the claim of a family or social group to a title or prerogative, or to announce officially a change of status; finally, to surpass a rival in generosity, to crush him if possible with future obligations which it is hoped he cannot meet, so as to take from him his prerogatives, titles, rank, authority and prestige. Doubtless the system of reciprocal gifts only reaches such vast proportions among the Indians of the Northwest Pacific coast, virtuosi who display a genius and an exceptional aptitude for the treatment of the fundamental themes of primitive culture. But Mauss has been able to establish the existence of analogous institutions in Melanesia and Polynesia. For example, it is certain that the main purpose of the feasts of several New Guinea tribes is to obtain recognition of a new *pangua* by an assembly of witnesses, that is, the same function which, according to Barnett, is the fundamental basis of the Alaskan *potlatch*. The same author sees the desire to go one better than anyone else as a characteristic peculiar to Kwakiutl ceremonies, and regards the interest-bearing loan as a preliminary transaction to the potlatch, rather than as one of its modalities. Doubtless there are local variations, but the various aspects of the institution form a whole found in a more or less systematized way in North and South America, Asia and Africa. It is a question of a universal mode of culture, although not everywhere equally developed.

From *Elementary Structures of Kinship*, by Claude Lévi-Strauss. Published first in France under the title *Les Structures Elementaires de la Parente*, in 1949. A revised edition was published under the same title in France in 1967. Translation ©1969 by Beacon Press. Reprinted by permission of Beacon Press, Boston.

But it should also be stressed that this attitude of primitive thought towards the exchange of goods is not only expressed in clearly defined and localized institutions. It permeates every transaction, ritual or profane, in which objects or produce are given or received. Implicitly or explicitly, the double assumption is found everywhere that reciprocal gifts constitute a means—normal or privileged, depending on the group—of transferring goods, or certain goods, and that these gifts are not offered principally or essentially with the idea of receiving a profit or advantage of an economic nature. 'On birth ceremonies,' writes Turner of the refined Samoan culture, 'after receiving the *oloa* and the *tonga,* the "masculine" and "feminine" property, the husband and wife were left no richer than they were.'. . .

The idea that a mysterious advantage is attached to the acquisition of commodities, or at least certain commodities, by means of reciprocal gifts, rather than by individual production or acquisition, is not confined to primitive society. The Alaskan Indians distinguish objects of consumption or provisions which do not go beyond the circle of production and family consumption, and wealth—property *par excellence*—which the Kwakiutl call 'the rich food'. The latter includes painted rugs, horn spoons, bowls and other ceremonial containers, ceremonial clothes, and so on, any object whose symbolical value infinitely outweighs the value of the labour or raw material, and which alone can enter into ritual cycles of tribal and intertribal exchange. But a similar distinction still operates in modern society. There are certain types of object which are especially appropriate for presents, precisely because of their non-utilitarian nature. In some Latin countries these objects can only be found, in all their luxury and diversity, in stores set up especially for this purpose, such as 'casas de regalias' or 'casas de presentes', and which are similar to Anglo-Saxon 'gift shops'. It is hardly necessary to note that these gifts, like invitations (which, though not exclusively, are also free distributions of food and drink), are 'returned'. This is an example of reciprocity in our society. . . .

The Transition to Complex Structures

One conclusion immediately emerges from the study of simple forms of generalized exchange: that, kept in the simple state, they are not viable. Generalized exchange leads to hypergamy, i.e., the participants in the great cycle of exchange, gradually gaining differences in status from the very fact of the formula of exchange, can only receive spouses from partners occupying a superior or an inferior position in the hierarchy. It will be recalled that the appearance of this critical phase is still attested to for ancient India. Let us take the most common case in which the rule prescribes marriage with a woman of an immediately inferior status. How do women of the highest class get married? In a system of generalized exchange, the continuity of the link is ensured by a single cycle of exchange which connects all constituent elements of the group as partners. No interruption can occur at any point in the cycle without the total structure, which is the basis of social order and individual security, being in danger of collapse. The Kachin system reveals generalized exchange at the precise moment when this dramatic problem makes its appearance.

There must be a solution to this problem. We have already encountered one, in which groups united by a cycle of generalized exchange are subdivided, often two by two, into more restricted formations, pairs of which commence to exchange. The evolution of the Assamese and Chinese systems and the Tungus and Manchu systems, give varied illustrations of this process. Local systems of restricted exchange begin to function within a total system of generalized exchange, and gradually replace it. The group gives up a *simple* form of generalized exchange for an equally *simple* form of restricted exchange. But it can also preserve the principle of generalized exchange by renouncing a *simple* form for a *complex* form. This is the European development.

Firstly, let us consider the case in which the contradiction inherent in the hypergamous rule in some way rigidifies the cycle of generalized exchange. The cycle is interrupted, the indefinite chain of prestations and counter-prestations seizes up. The partners mark time, and, placed in a position where it is impossible for them to fulfil their prestations, keep their daughters by marrying them to their sons, until a miracle sets the whole machine going again. Needless to say, such a process is contagious. It must gradually reach every member of the body social, and change hypergamy to endogamy. Only India has systematically and durably adopted this solution. However, the whole area provides rough and provisional skeletal forms of this solution. Such is the eclectic attitude of Iran, which associates a quite supple class endogamy with sporadic marriage between near relatives, or the Egyptian practice of consanguineal marriages. However, if our interpretation of the latter is correct, it is echoed in Iran and even in Greece, in the custom of the daughter-heir, who, in the absence of a male heir, marries a close relative. In fact, the Egyptian or Polynesian marriage with the older sister, to the exclusion of the younger sister, seems merely an extreme form of female inheritance. In western Europe, patristic literature and, later, Elizabethan drama, reveal the extent and duration of the vacillations of the public conscience on the question of consanguineal marriages.

However, another solution is equally possible, and it is this which has ultimately left its mark on the European system. Since generalized exchange engenders hypergamy, and hypergamy leads either to regressive solutions (restricted exchange or endogamy), or to the complete paralysis of the body social, an arbitrary element will be introduced into the system, a sort of sociological *clinamen*, which, whenever the subtle mechanism of exchange is obstructed, will, like a *Deus ex machina*, give the necessary push for a new impetus. India clearly conceived the idea of this *clinamen*, although it finally took a different path and left the task of developing and systematizing the formula of it to others. This is the *swayamvara* marriage, to which a whole action of the Mahabharata is devoted. It consists, for a person occupying a high social rank, in the privilege of giving his daughter in marriage to a man of any status, who

has performed some extraordinary feat, or better still, has been chosen by the girl herself. How else would she proceed, since, as a king's daughter in any hypergamous system she would be denied any spouse of the social rule were strictly observed? Undoubtedly, *swayamvara* marriage as described in epic poetry and folklore, from Assam to central and western Europe, is largely a myth. Yet the transfiguration into mythological form conceals a real problem, and probably positive institutions as well. Even in the Middle Ages, Welsh law distinguished between two forms of marriage, *rod o cenedl, 'gift by kindred'* and *lladrut*, 'stolen, secret or furtive', the former being the surrender of the woman by her family, the latter, the gift of the woman by herself. Can we not recognize here, in their probable juxtaposition over a long period, the logical and perhaps historical starting point and point of arrival of the evolution of generalized exchange? . . .

The Principles of Kinship

The multiple rules prohibiting or prescribing certain types of spouse, and the prohibition of incest, which embodies them all, become clear as soon as one grants that society must exist. But society might not have been. Have we therefore resolved one problem, as we thought, only to see its whole importance shifted to another problem, the solution to which appears even more hypothetical than that to which we have devoted all our attention? In actual fact, let us note, we are not faced with two problems but with only one. If our proposed interpretation is correct, the rules of kinship and marriage are not made necessary by the social state. They are the social state itself, reshaping biological relationships and natural sentiments, forcing them into structures implying them as well as others, and compelling them to rise above their original characteristics. The natural state recognizes only indivision and appropriation, and their chance admixture. However, as Proudhon has already observed in connexion with another problem, these notions can only be transcended on a new and different level: 'Property is non-reciprocity, and non-reciprocity is theft. . . . But common ownership is also non-reciprocity, since it is the negation of opposing terms; it is still theft. Between property and common ownership I could construct a whole world.' What is this world, unless it is that to which social life ceaselessly bends itself in a never wholly successful attempt to construct and reconstruct an approximate image of it, that world of reciprocity which the laws of kinship and marriage, in their own sphere of interest, laboriously derive from relationships which are otherwise condemned to remain either sterile or immoderate?

However, the progress of contemporary social anthropology would be of small account if we had to be content with an act of faith—fruitful no doubt, and in its time, legitimate—in the dialectic process ineluctably giving rise to the world of reciprocity, as the synthesis of two contradictory characteristics inherent in the natural order. Experimental study of the facts can join with the philosophers' presentiments, not only in attesting that this is what happened, but in describing, or beginning to describe, how things happened.

In this regard, Freud's work is an example and a lesson. The moment the claim was made that certain extant features of the human mind could be explained by an historically certain and logically necessary event, it was permissible, and even prescribed, to attempt a scrupulous restoration of the sequence. The failure of *Totem and Taboo,* far from being inherent in the author's proposed design, results rather from his hesitation to avail himself of the ultimate consequences implied in his premises. He ought to have seen that phenomena involving the most fundamental structure of the human mind could not have appeared once and for all. They are repeated in their entirety within each consciousness, and the relevant explanation falls within an order which transcends both historical successions and contemporary correlations. Ontogenesis does not reproduce phylogenesis, or the contrary. Both hypotheses lead to the same contradictions. One can speak of explanations only when the past of the species constantly recurs in

the indefinitely multiplied drama of each individual thought, because it is itself only the retrospective projection of a transition which has occurred, because it occurs continually.

As far as Freud's work is concerned, this timidity leads to a strange and double paradox. Freud successfully accounts, not for the beginning of civilization but for its present state; and setting out to explain the origin of a prohibition, he succeeds in explaining, certainly not why incest is consciously condemned, but how it happens to be unconsciously desired. It has been stated and restated that what makes *Totem and Taboo* unacceptable, as an interpretation of the prohibition of incest and its origins, is the gratuitousness of the hypothesis of the male horde and of primitive murder, a vicious circle deriving the social state from events which presuppose it. However, like all myths, the one presented in *Totem and Taboo* with such great dramatic force admits of two interpretations. The desire for the mother or the sister, the murder of the father and the sons' repentance, undoubtedly do not correspond to any fact or group of facts occupying a given place in history. But perhaps they symbolically express an ancient and lasting dream. The magic of this dream, its power to mould men's thoughts unbeknown to them, arises precisely from the fact that the acts it evokes have never been committed, because culture has opposed them at all times and in all places. Symbolic gratifications in which the incest urge finds its expression, according to Freud, do not therefore commemorate an actual event. They are something else, and more, the permanent expression of a desire for disorder, or rather counter-order. Festivals turn social life topsy-turvy, not because it was once like this but because it has never been, and can never be, any different. Past characteristics have explanatory value only in so far as they coincide with present and future characteristics.

Freud has sometimes suggested that certain basic phenomena find their explanation in the permanent structure of the human mind, rather than in its history. For example, anxiety would result from a contradiction between what the situation demands and the means at the individual's disposal to deal with it, for example, by the help-lessness of the new-born child before the afflux of external stimuli. Anxiety would thus appear before the differentiation of the super-ego: 'It is highly probable that the immediate precipitating causes of primal regression are quantitative factors such as an excessive degree of excitation and the breaking through of the protective shield against stimuli.' Indeed, the severity of the super-ego is in no way related to the degree of severity experienced. Inhibition thus gives proof of an internal and not an external origin. To us these views alone seem capable of giving an answer to a question posed very disturbingly by the psycho-analytic study of children, namely that among young children 'the feeling of sin' appears more precise, and better formed, than the individual history of each case would suggest. This would be explained if, as Freud supposed, it were possible for inhibitions in the broadest sense (disgust shame, moral and aesthetic demands) to be 'organically determined and . . . occasionally . . . produced without the help of education'. There would be two forms of sublimation, one delivered from education and purely cultural, the other 'a lower form', proceeding by an autonomous reac-

tion and appearing at the beginning of the latency period. It might even be that in these exceptionally favourable cases it would continue throughout life.

These bold assumptions concerning the thesis of *Totem and Taboo*, and the accompanying hesitations, are revealing. They show a social science like psychoanalysis—for it is one—still wavering between the tradition of an historical sociology, looking, as Rivers did, to the distant past for the reason for the present-day situation—and a more modem and scientifically more solid attitude, which expects a knowledge of its future and past from an analysis of the present. Moreover, the latter is clearly the practitioner's point of view. But it cannot be overemphasized that the path followed in delving into the structure of the conflicts to which a sick man is prone, in order to recreate its history and so arrive at the initial situation around which all subsequent developments took place, is contrary to that of the theory as presented in *Totem and Taboo*. In the one case, the progression is from experience to myths, and from myths to structure. In the other, a myth is invented to explain the facts, in other words, one behaves like the sick man instead of diagnosing him.

THEODOR ADORNO

1903–1969

Theodor Ludwig Wiesengrund (a.k.a., Theodor W. Adorno, Hektor Rottweiler, Teddie Wiesengrund, Theodor Wiesengrund-Adorno, Castor Zwieback), was the only child of a Jewish wine merchant and a Corsican opera singer (Maria Cavelli-Adorno della Piana Wiesengrund), born in Frankfurt, Germany on September 11, 1903. He married Margarete "Gretel" Karplus, a chemist, in 1937, they had no children, and Adorno died in Visp, Switzerland, not quite 66, on August 6, 1969. Adorno's father switched from Judaism to Protestantism when his son was born, to which was added his mother's native Catholicism, making for an unusual household. While maturing in Frankfurt, it was to his mother's musicality (and his aunt's, a pianist) that he was naturally drawn, and which affected his view of life and his way of theorizing. While at the Kaiser Wilhelms-Gynmasium in Frankfurt, he became friends with the future theorist of film, Siegfried Kracauer. In 1919 he began music composition instruction with Bernard Sekles, and adopted his first pseudonym, Teddie Wiesengrund. From 1921 through 1923 he studied musicology, philosophy, sociology, and psychology at the University of Frankfurt. Under Hans Cornelius's direction, he wrote a dissertation, "The Transcendence of the Material and the Noetic in Husserl's Phenomenology" (1924), though withdrew it. In this pivotal year he became friends with Max Horkheimer and Walter Benjamin, forming the core of what would become "The Frankfurt School." He began to publish music criticism in newspapers, and also published his first musical composition. He began living five months each year in Vienna in order to study composition with Alban Berg and piano with Eduard Steuermann. His habilitation, again with Cornelius, was "The Concept of the Unconscious in Transcendental Psychology" (1927), and a philosophy habilitation, written for Paul Tillich, was "Kierkegaard: Construction of an Aesthetic" (1931), recently translated into English. After two years of teaching, he was fired for being Jewish and left for London (1934–38) and then New York and California, where he waited out the war and worked with Horkheimer and his colleagues. He and Horkheimer wrote a pathbreaking book in 1944, *The Dialectic of Enlightenment,* which when translated into English 30 years later made a huge impact among young leftist intellectuals. He also advised Thomas Mann on technical musical matters when the former was writing *Doctor Faustus* (1947) while they both resided in Pacific Palisades, California. He returned to Frankfurt after WWII (where Habermas was his teaching assistant), and eventually became an iconic figure among the New Left, but with whom he found himself in conflict due to what he perceived as their "fascist" tendencies for authoritarian control of consciousness. It was stress caused by student interactions that probably hastened his premature death.

Adorno's principal idea in the realm of social theory is embodied in his book *Negative Dialectics* (1966). Though difficult to summarize, Adorno's insight (inspired in part by work with Horkheimer and Benjamin) revolves around the realization that Kantian philosophy, particularly of ethics, contains a dangerous underside which enthusiasts of the Enlightenment had missed. "Reason" is not always friendly to civilizational survival, particularly when taken to irrational ends, as in the machinery of the Holocaust. And when ethics are formally stated, but free of any content, they can be used to justify a range of actions, some of which have consequences far removed from the intentions of their framers. Like his friend, Marcuse, Adorno also wondered if a genuinely negative dialectical moment (in Hegel's terms) could any longer be found in Western society, since the "culture industry" applied a strangling uniformity to ideas and creations which almost immediately undercut any genuinely critical inspiration before it could take hold and effect change.

MINIMA MORALIA, 1951

Model of Virtue

Everyone has heard of the connection between repression and morality as instinctual renunciation. But moral ideas not only suppress the rest, they are directly derived from the existence of the suppressors. Since Homer Greek linguistic usage has intertwined the concepts of goodness and wealth. *Kalokagathia*, held up by the humanists to modem society as a model of aesthetico-moral harmony, always laid heavy stress on possessions, and Aristotle's *Politics* openly admits the fusion of inner worth with status in its definition of nobility as 'inherited wealth, combined with excellence'. The conception of the *polis* in the classical age, embracing both inward and outward existence, the individual's position in the city state and his self as a unity, made it possible to attribute moral rank to riches without arousing the crude suspicions even at that time befitting the doctrine. If visible influence in the existing state is the measure of a man, then it is only consistent to accredit the material wealth which tangibly underwrites his influence to his character, since moral substance itself is

seen, no differently than in Hegel's philosophy of later years, as constituted by his participation in objective social reality. It was the advent of Christianity that first negated this identification, with its proposition that a camel could pass more easily through a needle's eye than a rich man enter heaven. But the special theological premium on poverty indicates how deeply the general consciousness was stamped by the morality of possessions. Fixed property was a means of differentiation from nomadic disorder, against which all norms were directed; to be good and to have goods coincided from the beginning. The good man is he who rules himself as he does his own property: his autonomous being is modelled on material power. The rich should therefore not be accused of immorality—the reproach has ever been part of the armature of political repression—but rather made aware that, to the others, they represent morality. In it goods are reflected. Wealth as goodness is an element in the world's mortar: the tenacious illusion of their identity prevents the confrontation of moral ideas with the order in which the rich are right, while at the same time it has been impossible to conceive concrete definitions of morality other than those derived from wealth. The further the individual and society diverge in later periods through the competition of interests, and the more the individual is thrown back on himself, the more doggedly he clings to the notion of the moral nature of wealth.

Wealth shall vouch for the possibility of reuniting what is sundered, the inward and the outward. Such is the secret of intramundane asceticism, the businessman's boundless exertion—falsely hypostasized by Max Weber—*ad maiorem dei gloriam.* Material success joins individual and society not merely in the comfortable and by now questionable sense that the rich man can escape solitude, but far more radically: if blind, isolated self-interest is pursued far enough it turns, as economic power, into social predominance and manifests itself as an incarnation of the all-uniting principle. He who is rich or attains riches, feels that he has accomplished 'on his own initiative, as a self, what the objective spirit, the truly irrational predestination of a society held together by brutal economic inequality, intends. So the rich man can claim as goodness what really only betokens its absence. He himself and others perceive him as the realization of the general principle. Because this is one of injustice, the unjust man regularly becomes just, and not merely in illusion, but supported by the supreme might of the law by which society reproduces itself. The wealth of individuals is inseparable from the progress of society in 'prehistory'. The rich control the means of production. Technical advances in which society as a whole participates are therefore put down primarily to 'their'—today industry's—progress, and the Fords necessarily seem benefactors to the extent that they actually are so within the framework of the existing relations of production. Their pre-established privilege makes it appear as if they are relinquishing something belonging to them—that is, the increase of use-values, while they are really, in the blessings they administer, only letting a part of the profit flow back where it came from. Hence the delusive character of the moral hierarchy. Certainly, poverty has always been glorified as asceticism, the social condition for gaining the very riches in which morality becomes manifest; nevertheless, as is known, 'what a man is worth' means his bank balance, and in German commercial jargon to say 'the man is good' means that he can pay. However, what the reason of state of an omnipotent economy confesses so cynically, extends unavowed to the behaviour of individuals. The private generosity that the rich can supposedly afford, the aura of happiness surrounding them, some of which is reflected on those they allow to approach them, all this

helps to veil them. They remain the nice, the right people, the better sort, the good. Wealth insulates from overt injustice. While the policeman beats up strikers with a rubber truncheon, the factory-owner's son can drink an occasional whisky with a progressive writer. By all the desiderata of private morality, even the most advanced, the rich man could—if only he could—indeed be better than the poor. This possibility, admittedly neglected in reality, plays a part in the ideology of those without it: even the confidence-trickster, who may in any case be preferable to the legitimate corporation bosses, enjoys the fame, after his arrest, of having had such a lovely house, and the highly-paid executive acquires human warmth by serving opulent dinners. The barbaric success-religion of today is consequently not simply contrary to morality: it is the homecoming of the West to the venerable morals of our ancestors. Even the norms which condemn the present world are themselves the fruits of its iniquities. All morality has been modelled on immorality and to this day has reinstated it at every level. The slave morality is indeed bad: it is still the master morality.

⌒～

THE CULTURE INDUSTRY, 1991

Free Time, 1954

The question concerning free time, what people do with it and what opportunities could eventually evolve from it, must not be posed as an abstract generalisation. Incidentally the expression 'free time' or 'spare time' originated only recently—its precursor, the term 'leisure' (*Musse*) denoted the privilege of an unconstrained, comfortable life-style, hence something qualitatively different and far more auspicious—and it indicates a specific difference, that of time which is neither free nor spare, which is occupied by work, and which moreover one could designate as heteronomous. Free time is shackled to its opposite.

Indeed the oppositional relation in which it stands imbues free time with certain essential characteristics. What is more, and far more importantly, free time depends on the totality of social conditions, which continues to hold people under its spell. Neither in their work nor in their consciousness do people dispose of genuine freedom over themselves. Even those conciliatory sociologies which use the term 'role' as a key recognize this fact, in so far as the term itself, borrowed from the domain of the theatre, suggests that the existence foisted upon people by society is identical neither with people as they are in themselves nor with all that they could be. Of course one should not attempt to make a simple distinction between people as they are in themselves and their so-called social roles. These roles affect the innermost articulation of human characteristics, to such an extent that in the age of truly unparalleled social integration, it is hard to ascertain anything in human beings which is not functionally determined. This is an important consideration for the question of free time. It means to say that even where the hold of the spell is relaxed, and people are at least subjectively convinced that they are acting of their own free will, this will itself is shaped by the very same forces which they are seeking to escape in their hours without work. The question which today would really do justice to the phenomenon of free time would be the following: what becomes of free time, where productivity of labour continues to rise, under persisting conditions of unfreedom, that is, under relations of production into which people are born, and which prescribe the rules of human existence today just as they always have done? Free time has already expanded enormously in our day and age. And this expansion should increase still further, due to inventions in the fields of automation and atomic power, which have not yet been anywhere like fully exploited. If one were to try and answer the question without ideological preconceptions, one could not avoid the suspicion that 'free time' is tending toward its own opposite, and is becoming a parody of itself. Thus unfreedom is gradually annexing 'free time', and the majority of unfree people are as unaware of this process as they are of the unfreedom itself.

I should like to elucidate the problem with the help of a trivial experience of my own. Time and time again, when questioned or interviewed, one is asked about one's hobbies. When the illustrated weeklies report on the life of one of those giants of the culture industry, they rarely forego the opportunity to report, with varying degrees of intimacy, on the hobbies of the person in question. I am shocked by the question when I come up against it. I have no hobby. Not that I am the kind of workaholic, who is incapable of doing anything with his time but applying himself industriously to the required task. But, as far as my activities beyond the bounds of my recognised profession are concerned, I take them all, without exception, very seriously. So much so, that I should be horrified by the very idea that they had anything to do with hobbies—preoccupations with which I had become mindlessly infatuated merely in order to kill the time—had I not become hardened by experience to such examples of this now widespread, barbarous mentality. Making music, listening to music, reading with all my attention, these activities are part and parcel of my life; to call them hobbies would make a mockery of them. On the other hand I have been fortunate enough that my job, the production of philosophical and sociological works and university teaching, cannot be defined in terms of that strict opposition to free time, which is demanded by the current razor-sharp division of the two. I am however well aware that in this I enjoy a privilege, with both the element of fortune and of guilt which this involves: I speak as one who has had the rare opportunity to follow the path of his own intentions and to fashion his work accordingly. This is certainly one good reason why there is no hard and fast opposition between my work itself and what I do apart form it. If free time really was to become just that state of affairs in which everyone could enjoy what was once the prerogative of a few—and compared to feudal society bourgeois society has taken some steps in this direction—then I would picture it after my own experience of life outside work, although given different conditions, this model would in its turn necessarily alter.

If we suppose with Marx that in bourgeois society labour power has become a commodity in which labour is consequently reified, then the expression 'hobby' amounts to a paradox: that human condition which sees itself as the opposite of reification, the oasis of unmediated life within a completely mediated total system, has itself been reified just like the rigid distinction between labour and free time. The latter is a continuation of the forms of profit-oriented social life. Just as the term 'show business' is today taken utterly seriously, the irony in the expression 'leisure industry' has now been quite forgotten. It is widely known but no less true therefore that specific leisure activities like tourism and camping revolve around and are organised for the sake of profit. At the same time the difference between work and free time has been branded as a norm in the minds of people, at both the conscious and the unconscious level. Because, in accordance with the predominant work ethic, time free of work should be utilized for the recreation of expended labour power, then work-less time, precisely because it is a mere appendage of work, is severed from the latter with puritanical zeal. And here we come across a behavioural norm of the bourgeois character. On the one hand one should pay attention at work and not be distracted or lark about; wage labour is predicated on this assumption and its laws have been internalized. On the other hand free time must not resemble work in any way whatsoever, in order, presumably, that one can work all the more effectively afterwards. Hence the inanity of many leisure activities. And yet, in secret as it were, the contraband of modes of behaviour proper to the domain of work, which will not let people out of its power, is being smuggled into the realm of free time. In earlier times children were allotted marks for attentiveness in their school reports. This had its corollary in the subjective, perhaps even well-meaning worries of adults that the children should not overstrain themselves in their free time; not read too much and not stay awake too late in the evening. Secretly parents sensed a certain unruliness of mind which was incompatible with the efficient division of human life. Besides, the prevalent ethos is suspicious of anything which is miscellaneous, or heterogeneous, of anything which has not clearly and unambiguously been assigned to its place. The rigorous bifurcation of life enjoins the same reification, which has now almost completely subjugated free time. . . .

Taken in its strict sense, in contradistinction to work, as it at least used to apply in what would today be considered an out-dated ideology, there is something vacuous (Hegel would have said abstract) about the notion of free time. An archetypal instance is the behaviour of those who grill themselves brown in the sun merely for the sake of a sun-tan, although dozing in the blazing sunshine is not at all enjoyable, might very possibly be physically unpleasant, and certainly impoverishes the mind. In the sun-tan, which can be quite fetching, the fetish character of the commodity lays claim to actual people; they themselves become fetishes. The idea that a girl is more erotically attractive because of her brown skin is probably only another rationalization. The sun-tan is an end in itself, of more importance than the boy-friend it was perhaps supposed to entice. If employees return from their holidays without having acquired the mandatory skin tone, they can be quite sure their colleagues will ask them the pointed question, 'Haven't you been on holiday then?' The fetishism which thrives in free time, is subject to further social controls. It is obvious that the cosmetics industry with its overwhelming and ineluctable advertisements, is a contributory factor here, but people's willingness to ignore the obvious is just as great.

The act of dozing in the sun marks the culmination of a crucial element of free time under present conditions—boredom. The miracles which people expect from their holidays or from other special treats in their free time, are subject to endless spiteful ridicule, since even here they never get beyond the threshold of the eversame: distant places are no longer—as they still were for Baudelaire's *ennui*—different places. The victim's ridicule is automatically connected to the very mechanisms which victimize. At an early age Schopenhauer formulated a theory of boredom. True to his metaphysical pessimism he teaches that people either suffer from the unfulfilled desires of their blind will, or become bored as soon as these desires are satisfied. The theory well describes what becomes of people's free time under the sort of conditions of heteronomy, and which in new German tends to be termed *Fremdbestimmtheit* (external determination). In its cynicism Schopenhauer's arrogant remark that mankind is the factory product of nature also captures something of what the totality of the commodity character actually makes man into. Angry cynicism still does more honour to human beings than solemn protestations about man's irreducible essence. However, one should not hypostatize Schopenhauer's doctrine as something of universal validity or even as an insight into the primal character of the human species. Boredom is a function of life which is lived under the compulsion to work, and under the strict division of labour. It need not be so. Whenever behaviour in spare time is truly autonomous, determined by free people for themselves, boredom rarely figures; it need not figure in activities which cater merely for the desire for pleasure, any more than it does in those free time activities which are reasonable and meaningful in themselves. Even fooling about need not be crass, and can be enjoyed as a blessed release from the throes of self-control. If people were able to make their own decisions about themselves and their lives, if they were not caught up in the realm of the eversame, they would not have to be bored. Boredom is the reflection of objective dullness. As such it is in a similar position to political apathy. The most compelling reason for apathy is the by no means unjustified feeling of the masses that political participation within the sphere society grants them, and this holds true for all political systems in the world today, can alter their actual existence only minimally. Failing to discern the relevance of politics to their own interests, they retreat from all political activity. The well-founded or indeed neurotic feeling of powerlessness is intimately bound up with boredom: boredom is objective desperation.

GABRIEL (-HONORÉ) MARCEL

1889–1973

Gabriel-Honoré Marcel was born in Paris on December 7, 1889, the only child of a government official, diplomat, and curator, and a mother who died when he was four, an event which disturbed and inspired him for life. His marriage to Jacqueline Boegner (1919) was a happy one, and they adopted one son (Jean-Marie). Marcel died from a heart attack on October 8, 1973 in his hometown at 83. His father married his sister-in-law following his wife's death, and together with Marcel's maternal grandmother, they raised the boy in a pressure-cooker environment for intellectual achievement which he found increasingly distasteful. He took refuge in travel, and went to Sweden when his father was appointed French ambassador. His lifelong love for travel and exploration of unknown cultures led him to introduce foreign writers into French culture. His father (noted museum and library administrator) was an agnostic Catholic, his stepmother a nonpracticing Jew with strong secular ethics. Later in life he sought clarification of religious sentiments on his own, making up for the speculative dimension that was missing from his boyhood home, all of which eventually leading to his conversion to Catholicism in 1929. His personal odyssey also included musical composition, drama, and philosophy, and his role-models included Bach and Mozart, Pascal and Augustine. His piano improvisations became for him a transcendental act, not only an aesthetic one. Lacking siblings, he wrote plays from childhood concerning imagined companions, and his mature philosophy took a similar line, dealing in real-life crises rather than solving epistemological puzzles, which held no interest for him. His plays are obliquely philosophical in nature, but turn around normal human dilemmas. Marcel lost patience for scholastic thought when he worked for the Red Cross during WWI, attempting to locate missing soldiers, and came face-to-face with the harshest realities of human existence.

His work was most carefully studied in the anglophone sphere during the 50s and 60s, identified then as "theistic existentialism," and perceived to be a complement to Sartre's atheism. Yet Marcel himself repudiated Sartre's position and called himself instead a "neo-Socratic." Before Heidegger's and Jaspers' writings were translated into English, his own version of a phenomenological method and an existentialist ethics were in circulation. One of the excerpts reprinted below comes from perhaps his most famous book, *Man Against Mass Society* (1951), wherein, like Kierkegaard a hundred years before, he wonders whether individual morality is still possible in a society taken over my organs of mass persuasion and institutions of gargantuan size and power.

MAN AGAINST MASS SOCIETY, 1951

The Universal Against the Masses (I)

. . . The universal against the masses: no doubt that should really be the title of this book. But what *is* the universal? What are we to understand by it? Not, of course, it goes without saying, a wretched abstract truth reducible to formulas that could be handed down and learned by rote. The universal is spirit or mind—and spirit or mind is love. On this point, as on so many others, we have to go back to Plato. Not, of course, to the mere letter of a philosophy of which, for that matter, hardly more than the letter, than the outward, unsecret aspect, has come down to us—but to the essential message which that philosophy still has for us to-day. Between love and intelligence, there can be no real divorce. Such a divorce is apparently consummated only when intelligence is degraded or, if I may be allowed the expression, becomes merely cerebral; and, of course, when love reduces itself to mere carnal appetite. But this we must assert, and as forcibly as possible: where love on one side, where intelligence on the other, reach their highest expression, they cannot fail to meet: do not let us speak of their becoming identical, for there can be no mutual identity except between abstractions; intelligence and love are the most concrete things in the world, and at a certain level every great thinker has recognized this or had a presentiment of it.

But in point of fact the masses exist and develop (following laws which are fundamentally purely mechanical) only at a level far below that at which intelligence and love are possible. Why should this be so? Because the masses partake of the human only in a degraded state, they are themselves a degraded state of the human. Do not let us seek to persuade ourselves that an education of the masses is possible: that is a contradic-tion in terms. What is educable is only an individual, or more exactly a person. Everywhere else, there is no scope for anything but a *training.* Let us say rather that what we have to do is to introduce a social and political order which will withdraw the greatest number of beings possible from this mass state of abasement or alienation. One mark of that state is that the masses are of their very essence—I repeat, *of their very essence*—the stuff of which fanaticism is made: propaganda has on them the convulsive effect of an electrical shock. It arouses them not to life, but to that appearance of life which particularly manifests itself in riots and revolutions. Also, of course, it is usual—and I do not know that the essential principle of this necessity has ever been grasped—on such occasions for the very dregs of the population to rise to the surface and take command of events. It is at the lowest level that the crystallization of mass impulses to violence takes place. Yet this is not to say that, if revolutions are bad in themselves, they are without some element of counterbalancing good; they might be compared to certain crises in the development of a living organism, which are pathological in themselves, but which seem to be needed to secure, in a very risky fashion, the future growth of that organism by snatching it from torpor and death.

The Universal Against the Masses (II)

. . . In the world that we know—I make this qualification, for there would be no point in referring to other types of civilization, to which we have not the key—human beings can be linked to each other by a real bond only because, in another dimension, they are linked to something which transcends them and comprehends them in itself. Now, the men who reject have broken with that superior principle, and it is in vain that they attempt to replace it by a fiction wholly lacking in ontological attributes and in any case projected into the future. In spite of all the phrases we make use of in our attempt to confer an appearance of reality on such fictions, all that actually happens is that a reality is displaced and a fiction replaces it.

But what happens at this point is something extremely serious. We know very well that abstractions cannot remain at the stage of mere abstraction. It is just as if they took on concrete life; though an abnormal and unhealthy life, which we could properly compare to that of a cancer-tissue. It is experience alone that can throw light on when, where, and how such life is able to take shape. We should have to look, in the first place, into just how the mass condition is able to come into being, particularly in great urban and industrial agglomerations; and secondly into how these masses—to whom we must refuse all ontological dignity, that is, we must not consider them as having substantial being—can be galvanized and magnetized, invariably, as it would seem, by fanatical groups growing up round a nucleus of dictatorship. I am myself neither a sociologist nor an historian, and so must be broad and sketchy here. However, it would be necessary to transcend such data as history and sociology might provide us with in order to isolate, if not exactly the laws, at least the more or less constant conditions, of a social dynamism which imitates life but reaches its climax only in what we ought rather to call death: that is, in servitude and terror. And no doubt it is from that night of servitude and terror that we ought then to seek once more to rise, like a diver coming up to the surface, if we wished to rediscover the human in its dignity and plenitude. . . .

As soon as I start thinking—and by thinking I mean reflecting, here—I am forced not only to take notice of the extreme danger in which the world today stands but also to become aware of the responsibilities which fall upon myself in such a situation. This should be strongly emphasized: for the very act of thinking, as the whole history of philosophy shows us, brings with it a temptation, that of detachment, that of *self-insulation*. But this temptation only persists where reflection has not yet deployed itself in every possible dimension. I discover that it is a temptation, and by the same act I surmount it, as soon as I have understood that what I call the self is not a source but an obstacle; it is not from the self, it is *never* from the self that the light pours forth, even though, through an illusion which is hard to dissipate, it is of the very nature of our ego to take itself as a projector when it is only a screen. The ego is essentially pretentious, it is its nature to be a pretender in every sense of the word.

But when we have recognized this fundamental responsibility, what sort of effort should we make to face it? In other words, what is the first ethical commandment to which I ought, as a philosopher, to conform? Without any possible doubt it is that I ought not to sin against the light. But what exact meaning are we to give to this term 'light'? I do not say to this metaphor of light; for in fact we are not in possession of any word in relation to which the term can be judged metaphorical. The expression at the beginning of the Gospel according to St John, 'That was the true Light, which lighteth every man that cometh into the world', defines in the most rigorous fashion and in terms of unsurpassable adequacy what is in fact the most universal characteristic of human existence; one can see that clearly if one adds by way of corollary that man is not man except in so far as that light lights him. And if nevertheless, yielding to an almost uncontrollable inner necessity, we do after all attempt to elucidate the meaning of the word 'light', we shall have to say that it denotes what we can only define as the identity at their upper limit of Love and Truth: we should have to add that a truth which lies below that limit is a pseudo-truth- and conversely that a love, without truth is in some respects a mere delirium.

We must now ask ourselves what are the still singular and in many ways mysterious conditions under which we can have access to this light? Leaving on one side Revelation properly so called, which has always remained in relation to any thoughts put forward in this work at, as it were, the horizon, I would say that we all have to radiate this light for the benefit of each other, while remembering that our role consists above all and perhaps exclusively in not presenting any obstacle to its passage *through us*. This, in spite of all appearances to the contrary, is an active role: it is an active role just because the self is a pretender, and a pretender whose duty it is to transcend or to destroy its own false claims. This can only be achieved through freedom and in a sense this is freedom. . . .

It is our duty not only to make the imprescriptible rights of the universal currently recognized, but also to plot out with the greatest care the terrain on which these rights can be effectively defended. In my introduction to this book, I said that the word 'universal' seems fated to give rise to misunderstandings of the very sort most likely to darken and confuse its real meaning. We are almost irresistibly inclined to understand 'the universal' as that which presents a maximum of generality. But that is an interpretation against which one cannot too strongly react. The best course here is for the mind to seek its support among the highest expressions of human genius—I mean among those works of art which have a character of supreme greatness. Being a musician myself, for instance, I am thinking of the last works of Beethoven. How can anybody fail to see that any sort of notion of generality is quite inapplicable here? On the contrary, if a sonata like Opus 111 or a quartet like Opus 127 introduces us to what is most intimate and I would even say most sacred in our human condition, at the level where that condition transcends itself in a significance which is at once self-evident and beyond any possible formulation, at the same time it addresses itself only to a very restricted number of people, without for that reason at all losing its universal value. We must understand that universality has its place in the dimension of depth and not that of breadth. Shall we say that the universal is accessible only to the individual? There again is a notion about which we must be terribly cautious. We have to reject the atomic just as much as the collective conception of society. Both, as Gustave Thibon has so pregnantly remarked, are complementary aspects of the same process of decomposition—I would say of local mortification.

There can be no authentic depth except where there can be real communion; but there will never be any real communion between individuals centred on themselves, and in consequence morbidly hardened, nor in the heart of the mass, within the mass-state. The very notion of inter-subjectivity on which all my own most recent work has been based presupposes a reciprocal openness between individuals without which no kind of spirituality is conceivable.

THE EXISTENTIAL BACKGROUND OF HUMAN DIGNITY, 1963

Mortality, Hope, and Freedom

. . . There is a temptation which seems for many men of our time to be almost irresistible to argue from the fact of man's mortality that he is negligible as an individual, and to transfer to the collective and to society that regard of which he has been judged positively unworthy. But to reason in this way is to follow a road which leads to tyranny and to servitude. Now the paradox which we considered briefly in the preceding chapter is that we can, on the contrary, find in man's finitude itself the principle of his essential dignity. How is this possible? We have to take as a point of departure the fact that man is the only being known to us who knows himself to be mortal. Moreover, in the perspective we have adopted this fact reveals that man transcends the society to which a certain type of "reason" pretends to sacrifice him: for this very society, if it has a destiny, is not conscious of it, is incapable of having a conception of it, and *a fortiori* of mastering it. In the final reckoning, then, the priority rests with the individual.

In any case, we must not fail to note that the fact of this knowledge, of one's own mortality involves the same indeterminateness with regard to value that I drew attention to earlier: from this ambiguous situation we can emerge only on condition that we pass beyond the limits of the ego. In the text of *Les Cœurs avides* which I have cited, Arnaud was meditating not on his own mortality, but on that of his father. And this meditation was suffused with a compassion which was also a form of piety. It is precisely the nature of this piety which is to be accounted for, without, however, assuming that it can be reduced to something simpler and "self-evident" in the Cartesian sense.

I believe that our first obligation is resolutely to avoid the reductionist interpretation which would see in this piety a weakened and faded survival of superstitious fears. Of course, such attempts at derivation will always be possible, but

From *The Existential Background of Human Dignity,* by Gabriel Marcel, p. 136-138, 141-142, 146-147. Cambridge, Mass.: Harvard University Press. Copyright ©1963 by the President and Fellows of Harvard College. Reprinted by permission of the publisher.

they would all be open to the central objection that almost inevitably applies to any claim that "such and such is *nothing* but this or that" in other words, to the denial of the distinctive quality of a given experience in the name of genetic considerations. The truth would seem to be rather that piety toward the dead, or toward those whose death we anticipate, fulfills a demand for compensation, which pertains perhaps to a secret modality of justice. Everything happens as if the pious man—and I take this adjective in the most nonconfessional sense—felt called upon to oppose to this process of deterioration, operating on the level of corruptible flesh, an inverse movement directed upward, or one might say towards exaltation, had that word not lost its noble and etymological connotation. But here we must probe still deeper. What takes place—and that usually beyond the reach of explicit formulation—is the confidence that in death one's being will raise itself to an integrity which life lived would perhaps not have allowed it, because of life's perpetually dispersed, tortured, and torn character. The famous line of Mallarmé, "Tel qu'en lui-même enfin l'éternité le change,"[1] happily renders this accession to eternity.

It is true that what is sometimes disclosed at the end of a life is its fundamental nullity, its inanity, or, what is even worse than nothingness, a perverted will embodied in a chain of actions, a will to destroy everything of man's which makes for communication and peace. But it seems to me that it would always be difficult to hold to such a judgment; inevitably, something comes to attenuate its force and to refocus it into a question. For this same being who seemed to have willed evil was either deprived of love, in which case it is as if at the close of his existence he himself became accuser, or else he was loved, and this love to which he could not respond cannot help but take on the character of an intercession. But it is true that this word "intercession" can have meaning only if it is unspoken, and if the intersubjective consciousness refuses to admit or, *a fortiori*, to proclaim the finality of death. . . .

Generally speaking, philosophers, up to the present time, have paid almost no attention to certain structural characteristics of the human being which allow for the insertion of freedom into the fabric of our existence. Once more, unless one is the champion of a scientific materialism which seems to be plainly dated, I do not see how it can be seriously maintained that survival after death is purely and simply unthinkable. A margin of incertitude remains, and it is open to reflection as an aspect of the mystery involved in our destiny. And surely it would be equally wrong to regard this margin as fixed and constant, and therefore independent of the ways in which we tend to orient our existence in this world. It is plain that the more each one of us takes himself for a center, considering others only in relation to himself, the more the idea of the beyond will be emptied of all meaning, for this world beyond will then appear as a senseless prolongation. That is its character in a perspective like Sartre's where "the other" is thought of primarily as a threat to my integrity, or, in other words, my self-sufficiency. On the contrary, the more the other, or others, will have become an integral part of my experience, the more I will be led to recognize their irreducible value as well as the difficulty *for us* of achieving a lasting harmony here below; and the more necessary it will be to conceive a mode of existence which is different from the one we have known, and which will lead us toward the real and *pleromatic* unity where we will be all in all.

I am by no means underestimating the force of the objection which is unfailingly provoked by such an assertion. It will be ascribed to the kind of wishful thinking which rigorous reflection is obliged to reject.

But it is at this juncture that the reflections on hope which I was led to develop in the midst of the second World War become relevant. I took as my point of departure the idea that desire and hope must be carefully distinguished, and that Spinoza in particular erred in identifying them. I had already observed in *Positions et approches concrétes* that the opposition is not, as Spinoza said, between fear and hope, but rather between fear and desire, and I added that the negative correlative of hope is to adopt the perspective of the worst, as the defeatist does, for example. But ten years after this book was written I tried in a more searching way to cast light on some of the fundamental characteristics of hope, basing my reflection on the situation which was ours as French-men, namely, defeat and oppression by the enemy, or, more plainly still, the situation of prisoners awaiting liberation. What was revealed to me then, in a *syneidesis* like those to which I referred earlier, is that hope is always tied to an experience of captivity: "But I appear to myself as captive if I am conscious not only of being thrown into a situation, but engaged by it—under external constraint—in a mode of existence which carries with it restrictions of all kinds on my own action . . . Such a situation makes it impossible for me to rise to an experienced plenitude either of feeling or of thought." But what I realize correlatively is that the subject of "I hope" is not reducible to the ego which is the subject of desire, or, in other words, that the subject of "I hope" excludes all claims. Such claims are in a certain way present in optimism, as found in someone who, confronted with a tragic situation, declares in the name of a wisdom to which he apparently lays claim, "I tell you that things will work out"—while his defeatist interlocutor will say with the same assurance, "Well, I say that nothing will work out and the worst will happen." It is as if hope were situated in another dimension of which it could be said that it is that of humility and patience, a patience which is perhaps a profound and secret characteristic of life. . . .

In this perspective, freedom would be confused with the suggestibility of the dilettante who is in a certain way curious about everything, but without ever being ready to give himself, to devote himself, to anything. There is, to my mind, no more absurd caricature of what a free man is and must be.

To begin with, we must take note of the significant fact that not one of us can really say, "I am free." There is no meaning in the statement that man is free, and there is of course still less in claiming, with Rousseau, that he is *born* free; there is no more fatal error than that which consists in regarding freedom as an attribute. I am tempted to say that it is exactly the opposite. It is far more appropriate to say that every one of us has to make himself into a free man; that within the bounds of the possible he has to take advantage of the structural conditions of which I have spoken, which make freedom possible. In other words, freedom is a conquest—always partial, always precarious, always challenged. And we should remind ourselves again that it is in the midst of a situation of captivity that freedom can be born, at first in the shape of the aspiration to be free. But the word "aspiration" is misleading; it can correspond to a simple "I should like" which is separated by an abyss from "I want" (*je veux*). And in fact we have seen that hope is itself irreducible to aspiration, since it implies a patience, a vigilance, and a firmness of purpose which are incompatible with a simple "I should like."

To say that the freest man is the one who has the most hope is perhaps above all to indicate that he is the man who has been able to give his existence the richest significance, or stake the most on it. But this is enough to exclude absolutely the pure dilettante, that is, the one who, living only for himself, seeks solely to collect such experiences as will awaken in him, each time with different shades and nuances, a feeling of exaltation which fulfills him for that moment. But from such a flame, can anything remain in the end but ashes?

In the line of thought that I have tried to formulate in the course of this book, it is evident that the stakes I have alluded to here can only be conceived of on the level of intersubjectivity, or, if you wish, fraternity, and perhaps everything that has been said up to now will be clarified if we now postulate that the freest man is also the most fraternal.

Note

1. "As eternity at last gives him back to himself." (Tr.)

C. WRIGHT MILLS

1916–1962

Son of an insurance agent, Charles Wright Mills was the second child and only son, born in Waco, Texas on August 28, 1916, was married three times, and died at 45 on March 20, 1962 in Nyack, New York, having suffered a series of heart attacks in the preceding years. He married Dorothy Helen James in 1937 (divorced 1940), remarried her in 1941, divorced again in 1947 (one child, Kathryn Mills); married Ruth Harper, a statistician, in 1947 (Pamela Mills), divorced her in 1959; and finally married Yaroslava Surmach (Nick Mills). Mills grew up in Sherman, Fort Worth, and Dallas, Texas, graduated from Dallas Technical High School in 1934, and studied philosophy, economics, and sociology at the University of Texas at Austin, receiving both a B.A. and M.A. (philosophy) in 1939. His earliest intellectual enthusiasms were for American pragmatists, institutional economists, Weber, Marx, and Veblen. He further developed these interests at the University of Wisconsin, Madison, where he made particularly fruitful use of the knowledge and linguistic facility possessed by the emigré scholar, Hans Gerth. Their difficult relationship as student-teacher, then co-translators and co-authors, has given rise to much speculation and at least one scholarly monograph. They published *From Max Weber* (1946), the most important anthology of his work ever released, and still selling strong, and they also wrote *Character and Social Structure* (1950), for many readers the most creative and suggestive study in social-psychology ever written on the macro-level. Mills' dissertation, "A Sociological Account of Pragmatism," was finished in 1942, and from 1941 through 1945, he taught at the University of Maryland, at the same time writing for left-liberal magazines like *The New Republic, The New Leader,* and *Politics.* He moved to New York in 1945 and began teaching at Columbia, but was never allowed to teach graduate students, nor was promoted to full professor until 1956. From 1954 through 1956 he lectured at the William Alanson White Institute for Psychiatry. His final heart attack came as he was preparing for a televised debate regarding his Marxist writings about Cuba.

Mills' books have become legendary in sociology and political science. With *The New Men of Power* (1948), *White Collar* (1951), *The Power Elite* (1956), and particularly *The Sociological Imagination* (1959), Mills gave the sedate, scientist sociology of the 50s a great shock to the system, and his striking prose style (more like Mencken than Durkheim) have kept the books in print and in demand for a half-century. His phrase-making was memorable and important (e.g., "cheerful robots" and "abstracted empiricism"), and his spirited attacks on authority and privilege earned him virtual canonization among the Left, especially after his untimely death and his ringing political commentaries of the early 60s. He was "an American original," and for a time the best known American sociologist in the world.

WHITE COLLAR, 1951

The Rhetoric of Competition

As an economic fact, the old independent entrepreneur lives on a small island in a big new world; yet, as an ideological figment and a political force he has persisted as if he inhabited an entire continent. He has become the man through whom the ideology of utopian capitalism is still attractively presented to many of our contemporaries. Over the last hundred years, the United States has been transformed from a nation of small capitalists into a nation of hired employees; but the ideology suitable for the nation of capitalists persists, as if that small-propertied world were still a going concern. It has become the grab-bag of defenders and apologists, and so little is it challenged that in the minds of many it seems the very latest model of reality.

Nostalgia for the rural world of the small entrepreneur now so effectively hides the mechanics of industry that the farmer, the custodian of national life, is able to pursue his cash interests to the point of defying the head of the government in time of war. And while the small urban entrepreneur, as an examplar of the competitive way, suffers exhaustion, the officials of American opinion find more and more reason to proclaim his virtues. 'We realize . . . ' Senator James Murray has said, 'that small business constitutes the very essence of free enterprise and that its preservation is fundamental to the American idea.' The logic of the small entrepreneurs is not the logic of our time; yet if the old middle classes have been transformed into often scared and always baffled defenders, they have not died easily; they persist energetically, even if their energies sometimes seem to be those of cornered men.

Not the urgencies of democracy's problems, but the peculiar structure of American political representation; not the efficiency of small-scale enterprise, but the usefulness of its image to the political interests of larger business; not the swift rise

of the huge city, but the myopia induced by small-town life of fifty years ago—these have kept alive the senator's fetish of the American entrepreneur.

1. The Competitive Way of Life.   Official proclamations of the competitive ways of small entrepreneurs now labor under an enormous burden of fact which demonstrates in detail the accuracy of Thorstein Veblen's analysis. Competition, he held, is by no means dead, but it is chiefly 'competition between the business concerns that control production, on the one side, and the consuming public on the other side; the chief expedients in this businesslike competition being salesmanship and sabotage.' Competition has been curtailed by larger corporations; it has also been sabotaged by groups of smaller entrepreneurs acting collectively. Both groups have made clear the locus of the big competition and have revealed the mask-like character of liberalism's rhetoric of small business and family farm.

The character and ideology of the small entrepreneurs and the facts of the market are selling the idea of competition short. These liberal heroes, the small businessmen and the farmers, do not want to develop their characters by free and open competition; they do not believe in competition, and they have been doing their best to get away from it.

When small businessmen are asked whether they think free competition is, by and large, a good thing, they answer, with authority and vehemence, 'Yes, of course—what do you mean?' If they are then asked, 'Here in this, your town?' still they say, 'Yes,' but now they hesitate a little. Finally: 'How about here in this town in furniture?'—or groceries, whatever the man's line is. Their answers are of two sorts: 'Yes, if it's fair competition,' Which turns out to mean: 'if it doesn't make me compete.' Their second answer adds up to the same competition with the public; 'Well, you see, in certain lines, it's no good if there are too many businesses. You ought to keep the other fellow's business in mind.' The small businessman, as well as the farmer, wants to become big, not directly by eating up others like himself in competition, but by the indirect ways and means practiced by his own particular heroes—those already big. In the dream life of the small entrepreneur, the sure fix is replacing the open market.

But if small men wish to close their ranks, why do they continue to talk, in abstract contexts, especially political ones, about free competition? The answer is that the political function of free competition is what really matters now, to small entrepreneurs, but especially to big-business spokesmen. This ideology performs a crucial role in the competition between business on the one hand and the electorate, labor in particular, on the other. It is a means of justifying the social and economic position of business in the community at large. For, if there is free competition and a constant coming and going of enterprises, the one who remains established is 'the better man' and 'deserves to be where he is.' But if instead of such competition, there is a rigid line between successful entrepreneurs and the employee community, the man on top may be 'coasting on what his father did,' and not really be worthy of his hard-won position. Nobody talks more of free enterprise and competition and of the best man winning than the man who inherited his father's store or farm. Thus the principle of the self-made man, and the justification of his superior position by the competitive fire through which he has come, require and in turn support the ideology of free competition. In the abstract political ranges, everyone can believe in competition; in the concrete economic case, few small entrepreneurs can afford to do so.

Work

. . . The gospel of work has been central to the historic tradition of America, to its image of itself, and to the images the rest of the world has of America. The crisis and decline of that gospel are of wide and deep meaning. On every hand, we hear, in the words of Wade Shortleff for example, that 'the aggressiveness and enthusiasm which marked other generations is withering, and in its stead we find the philosophy that attaining and holding a job is not a challenge but a necessary evil. When work becomes just work, activity undertaken only for reason of subsistence, the spirit which fired our nation to its present greatness has died to a spark. An ominous apathy cloaks the smoldering discontent and restlessness of the management men of tomorrow.'

To understand the significance of this gospel and its decline, we must understand the very spirit of twentieth-century America. That the historical work ethic of the old middle-class entrepreneurs has not deeply gripped the people of the new society is of the most crucial psychological implications of the structural decline of the old middle classes. The new middle class, despite the old middle-class origin of many of its members, has never been deeply involved in the older work ethic, and on this point has been from the beginning non-bourgeois in mentality.

At the same time, the second historically important model of meaningful work and gratification—craftsmanship—has never belonged to the new middle classes, either by tradition or by the nature of their work. Nevertheless, the model of craftsmanship lies, however vaguely, back of most serious studies of worker dissatisfaction today, of most positive statements of worker gratification, from Ruskin and Tolstoy to Bergson and Sorel. Therefore, it is worth considering in some detail, in order that we may then gauge in just what respects its realization is impossible for the modern white-collar worker.

2. The Ideal of Craftsmanship. Craftsmanship as a fully idealized model of work gratification involves six major features: There is no ulterior motive in work other than the product being made and the processes of its creation. The details of daily work are meaningful because they are not detached in the worker's mind from the product of the work. The worker is free to control his own working action. The craftsman is thus able to learn from his work; and to use and develop his capacities and skills in its prosecution. There is no split of work and play, or work and culture. The craftsman's livelihood determines and infuses his entire mode of living.

I. The hope in good work, William Morris remarked, is hope of product and hope of pleasure in the work itself; the supreme concern, the whole attention, is with the quality of the product and the skill of its making. There is an inner relation between the craftsman and the thing he makes, from the image he first forms of it through its completion, which goes beyond the mere legal relations of property and makes the craftsman's will-to-work spontaneous and even exuberant.

Other motives and results—money or reputation or salvation—are subordinate. It is not essential to the practice of the craft ethic that one necessarily improves one's status either in the religious community or in the community in general. Work gratification is such that a man may live in a kind of quiet passion 'for his work alone.'

II. In most statements of craftsmanship, there is a confusion between its technical and aesthetic conditions and the legal (property) organization of the worker and the product. What is actually necessary for work-as-craftsmanship, however, is that the tie between the product and the producer be psychologically possible; if the producer does not legally own the product he must own it psychologically in the sense that he knows what goes into it by way of skill, sweat, and material and that his own skill and sweat are visible to him. Of course, if legal conditions are such that the tie between the work and the worker's material advantage is transparent, this is a further gratification, but it is subordinate to that workmanship which would continue of its own will even if not paid for.

The craftsman has an image of the completed product, and even though he does not make it all, he sees the place of his part in the whole, and thus understands the meaning of his exertion in terms of that whole. The satisfaction he has in the result infuses the means of achieving it, and in this way his work is not only meaningful to him but also partakes of the consummatory satisfaction he has in the product. If work, in some of its phases, has the taint of travail and vexation and mechanical drudgery, still the craftsman is carried over these junctures by keen anticipation. He may even gain positive satisfaction from encountering a resistance and conquering it, feeling his work, and will as powerfully victorious over the recalcitrance of materials and the malice of things. Indeed, without this resistance he would gain less satisfaction in being finally victorious over that which at first obstinately resists his will.

George Mead has stated this kind of aesthetic experience as involving the power 'to catch the enjoyment that belongs to the consummation, the outcome, of an undertaking and to give to the implements, the objects that are instrumental in the undertaking, and to the acts that compose it something of the joy and satisfaction that suffuse its successful accomplishment.'

III. The workman is free to begin his work according to his own plan and, during the activity by which it is shaped, he is free to modify its form and the manner of its creation. In both these senses, Henri De Man observed, 'plan and performance are one,' and the craftsman is master of the activity and of himself in the process. This continual joining of plan and activity brings even more firmly together the consummation of work and its instrumental activities, infusing the latter with the joy of the former. It also means that his sphere of independent action is large and rational to him. He is responsible for its outcome and free to assume that responsibility. His problems and difficulties must be solved by him, in terms of the shape he wants the final outcome to assume.

IV. The craftsman's work is thus a means of developing his skill, as well as a means of developing himself as a man. It is not that self-development is an ulterior goal, but that such development is the cumulative result obtained by devotion to and practice of his skills. As he gives it the quality of his own mind and skill, he is also further developing his own nature; in this simple sense, he lives in and through his work, which confesses and reveals him to the world.

V. In the craftsman pattern there is no split of work and play, of work and culture. If play is supposed to be an activity, exercised for its own sake, having no aim other than gratifying the actor, then work is supposed to be an activity performed to create economic value or for some other ulterior result. Play is something you do to be happily occupied, but if work occupies you happily, it is also play, although it is also serious, just as play is to the child. 'Really free work, the work of a composer, for example,' Marx once wrote of Fourier's notions of work and play, 'is damned serious work, intense strain.' The simple self-expression of play and the creation of ulterior value of work are combined in work-as-craftsmanship. The craftsman or artist expresses himself at the same time and in the same act as he creates value. His work is a poem in action. He is at work and at play in the same act.

'Work' and 'culture' are not, as Gentile has held, separate spheres, the first dealing with means, the second with ends in themselves; as Tilgher, Sorel, and others have indicated, either work or culture may be an end in itself, a means, or may contain segments of both ends and means. In the craft model of activity, 'consumption' and 'production' are blended in the same act; active craftsmanship, which is both play and work, is the medium of culture; and for the craftsman there is no split between the worlds of culture and work.

VI. The craftsman's work is the mainspring of the only life he knows; he does not flee from work into a separate sphere of leisure; he brings to his nonworking hours the values and qualities developed and employed in his working time. His idle conversation is shop talk; his friends follow the same lines of work as he, and share a kinship of feeling and thought. The leisure William Morris called for was 'leisure to think about our work, that faithful daily companion . . . '

In order to give his work the freshness of creativity, the craftsman must at times open himself up to those influences that only affect us when our attentions are relaxed. Thus for the craftsman, apart from mere animal zest, leisure may occur in such intermittent periods as are necessary for individuality in his work. As he brings to his leisure the capacity and problems of his work, so he brings back into work those sensitivities he would not gain in periods of high, sustained tension necessary for solid work.

'The world of art,' wrote Paul Bourget, speaking of America, 'requires less self-consciousness—an impulse of life which forgets itself, the alternation of dreamy idleness with fervid execution.' The same point is made by Henry James, in his essay on Balzac, who remarks that we have practically lost the faculty of attention, meaning . . . 'that unstrenuous, brooding sort of attention required to produce or appreciate works of art.' Even rest, which is not so directly connected with work itself as a condition of creativity, is animal rest, made secure and freed from anxiety by virtue of work done—in Tilgher's words, 'a sense of peace and calm which flows from all well-regulated, disciplined work done with a quiet and contented mind.'

In constructing this model of craftsmanship, we do not mean to imply that there ever was a community in which work carried all these meanings. Whether the medieval artisan approximated the model as closely as some writers seem to assume, we do not know; but we entertain serious doubts that this is so; we lack enough psychological knowledge of medieval populations properly to judge. At any rate, for our purposes it is enough to know that at different times and in different occupations, the work men do has carried one or more features of craftsmanship.

With such a model in mind, a glance at the occupational world of the modern worker is enough to make clear that practically none of these aspects are now relevant to modern work experience. The model of craftsmanship has become an anachronism. We use the model as an explicit ideal in terms of which we can summarize the working conditions and the personal meaning work has in modern work-worlds, and especially to white-collar people.

ROLAND BARTHES

1915–1980

Roland Gerard Barthes was born on November 12, 1915 in Cherbourg, France, the son of a naval officer who was killed in WWI within a year of his birth, and to a mother who raised him and his illegitimate half-brother (born 1927) in genteel poverty, clinging desperately to their status among the petit bourgeois even after being rejected by his mother's family. Barthes was killed by a microbus while crossing a Paris street on March 25, 1980 at the age of 64. At 19 he became tubercular and until he was 31 he was never far from various sanitoria, which meant that during the most important stage of young adult development, he was isolated by disease. Yet like many talented writers before him, he turned this disaster to his advantage by developing an astonishing ability to analyze phenomena of cultural and personal life which escaped the notice of his healthier peers. Due to the declassé condition of his nuclear family, he was particularly alert to the social construction of class differences, and the elaborate machinations by means of which people locate themselves within social structure. He took two degrees at the University of Paris (1939, 1943) and taught briefly in the city, but could not sustain the work due to ill health. He left Paris at 32 to become a librarian and teacher at the French Institute in Bucharest, Romania, but was removed along with his compatriots due to political changes in 1949. From there he went to Alexandria, Egypt in 1950 to teach French at the University, served also as a cultural attaché, and returned to Paris in 1952 to begin his astonishing climb through the academic ranks. An inheritance from his grandmother in 1956 eased his financial strain somewhat, and gave him more time to produce the books for which he became globally famous during the 60s and 70s. He spent 1960 through 1976 as the research director of the École Pratique des Hautes Études, and then reached the pinnacle of French academic status with a chair (in semiology) in the Collége de France to which he was elected in 1976.

Barthes' work was embraced by literary critics, media scholars, social theorists, philosophers, and many other analysts of contemporary social life because he was among the first (along with Marshall McLuhan in Toronto) to take seriously the most "frivolous" aspects of mass culture, and to write about them with penetrating, semiological analysis. Barthes began doing this by means of newspaper columns in which during the 50s he rendered soap commercials, movies, athletic events, movie actors, political scandals, unsolved murders, and other staples of mass circulation magazines and newspapers as subjects worthy of scrutiny. To do this he created a set of rules for semiology, and although it varied significantly from those of Lévi-Strauss, Lacan, Jakobson, Chomsky, and other structuralists, his efforts to see the "reality" beneath the surface of everyday life fit the pattern closely enough that Barthes was unwillingly inducted into this burgeoning academic specialty within the French academy, one which spilled far beyond national borders and became over the succeeding twenty years an international phenomenon. For social theorists, his work on modern myths and political rhetoric infused new life into fields of study that had grown stale after the 30s.

MYTHOLOGIES, 1957

Myth Today

What is a myth, today? I shall give at the outset a first, very simple answer, which is perfectly consistent with etymology: *myth is a type of speech.*[1]

Myth Is a Type of Speech

Of course, it is not *any* type: language needs special conditions in order to become myth: we shall see them in a minute. But what must be firmly established at the start is that myth is a system of communication, that it is a message. This allows one to perceive that myth cannot possibly be an object, a concept, or an idea; it is a mode of signification a form. Later, we shall have to assign to this form historical limits, conditions of use, and reintroduce society into it: we must nevertheless first describe it as a form.

It can be seen that to purport to discriminate among mythical objects according to their substance would be entirely illusory: since myth is a type of speech, everything can be a myth provided it is conveyed by a discourse. Myth is not defined by the object of its message, but by the way in which it utters this message: there are formal limits to myth, there are no 'substantial' ones. Everything, then, can be a myth? Yes, I believe this, for the universe is infinitely fertile in suggestions. Every object in the world can pass from a closed, silent existence to an oral state, open to appropriation by society, for there is no law, whether natural or not, which forbids talking about things. A tree is a tree. Yes, of course. But a tree as expressed by Minou Drouet is no longer quite a tree, it is a tree which is decorated, adapted to a certain type of consumption, laden with literary self-indulgence, revolt, images, in short with a type of social *usage* which is added to pure matter. . . .

Semiology, once its limits are settled, is not a metaphysical trap: it is a science among others, necessary but not sufficient. The important thing is to see that the unity of an explanation cannot be based on the amputation of one or other of its approaches, but, as Engels said, on the dialectical co-ordination of the particular sciences it makes use of. This is the case with mythology: it is a part both of semiology inasmuch as it is a formal science, and of ideology inasmuch as it is an historical science: it studies ideas-in-form.

Let me therefore restate that any semiology postulates a relation between two terms, a signifier and a signified. This relation concerns objects which belong to different categories, and this is why it is not one of equality but one of equivalence. We must here be on our guard for despite common parlance which simply says that the signifier *expresses* the signified, we are dealing, in any semiological system, not with two, but with three different terms. For what we grasp is not at all one term after the other, but the correlation which unites them: there are, therefore, the signifier, the signified and the sign, which is the associative total of the first two terms. Take a bunch of roses: I use it to *signify* my passion. Do we have here, then, only a signifier and a signified, the roses and my passion? Not even that: to put it accurately, there are here only 'passionified' roses. But on the plane of analysis, we do have three terms; for these roses weighted with passion perfectly and correctly allow themselves to be decomposed into roses and passion: the former and the latter existed before uniting and forming this third object, which is the sign. It is as true to say that on the plane of experience I cannot dissociate the roses from the message they carry, as to say that on the plane of analysis I cannot confuse the roses as signifier and the roses as sign: the signifier is empty, the sign is full, it is a meaning. Or take a black pebble: I can make it signify in several ways, it is a mere signifier; but if I weigh it with a definite signified (a death sentence, for instance, in an anonymous vote), it will become a sign. Naturally, there are between the signifier, the signified and the sign, functional implications (such as that of the part to the whole) which are so close that to analyse them may seem futile; but we shall see in a moment that this distinction has a capital importance for the study of myth as semiological schema. . . .

Naturally, everything is not expressed at the same time: some objects become the prey of mythical speech for a while, then they disappear, others take their place and attain the status of myth. Are there objects which are *inevitably* a source of suggestiveness, as Baudelaire suggested about Woman? Certainly not: one can conceive of very ancient myths, but there are no eternal ones; for it is human history which converts reality into speech, and it alone rules the life and the death of mythical language. Ancient or not, mythology can only have an historical foundation; for myth is a type of speech chosen by history: it cannot possibly evolve from the 'nature' of things.

Speech of this kind is a message. It is therefore by no means confined to oral speech. It can consist of modes of writing or of representations; not only written discourse, but also photography, cinema, reporting, sport, shows, publicity, all these can serve as a support to mythical speech. Myth can be defined neither by its object nor by its material, for any material an arbitrarily be endowed with meaning: the arrow which is brought in order to signify a challenge is also a kind of speech. True, as far as perception is concerned, writing and pictures, for instance, do not call upon the same type of consciousness; and even with pictures, one can use many kinds of reading: a diagram lends itself to signification more than a drawing, a copy more than an original, and a caricature more than a portrait. But this is the point: we are no longer dealing here with a theoretical mode of representation: we are dealing with *this* particular image, which is given for *this* particular signification. Mythical speech is made of a material which has *already* been worked on so as to make it suitable for communication: it is because all the materials of myth (whether pictorial or written) presuppose a signifying consciousness, that one can reason about them while discounting their substance. This substance is not unimportant: pictures, to be sure, are more imperative than writing, they impose meaning at one stroke, without analysing or diluting it. But this is no longer a constitutive difference. Pictures become a kind of writing as soon as they are meaningful: like writing, they call for a *lexis*.

We shall therefore take *language, discourse, speech,* etc., to mean any significant unit or synthesis, whether verbal or visual: a photograph will be a kind of speech for us in the same way as a newspaper article; even objects will become speech, if they mean something. This generic way of conceiving language is in fact justified by the very history of writing: long before the invention of our alphabet, objects like the Inca *quipu,* or drawings, as in pictographs, have been accepted as speech. This does not mean that one must treat mythical speech like language; myth in fact belongs to the province of a general science, coextensive with linguistics; which is *semiology.*

Myth As a Semiological System

For mythology, since it is the study of a type of speech, is but one fragment of this vast science of signs which Saussure postulated some forty years ago under the name of *semiology.* Semiology has not yet come into being. But since Saussure himself, and sometimes independently of him, a whole section of contemporary research has constantly been referred to the problem of meaning: psychoanalysis, structuralism, eidetic psychology, some new types of literary criticism of which Bachelard has given the first examples, are no longer concerned with facts except inasmuch as they are endowed with significance. Now to postulate a signification is to have recourse to semiology. I do not mean that semiology could account for all these aspects of research equally well: they have different contents. But they have a common status: they are all sciences dealing with values. They are not content with meeting the facts: they define and explore them as tokens for something else.

Semiology is a science of forms, since it studies significations apart from their content. . . .

In myth, we find again the tri-dimensional pattern which I have just described: the signifier, the signified, and the sign. But myth is a peculiar system, in that it is constructed from a semiological chain which existed before it: it *is a second-order semiological system.* That which is a sign (namely the associative total of a concept and an image) in the first system, becomes a mere signifier in the second. We must here recall that the materials of mythical speech (the language itself, photography, painting, posters, rituals, objects, etc.), however different at the start, are reduced to a pure signifying function as soon as they are caught by myth.

Myth sees in them only the same raw material; their unity is that they all come down to the status of a mere language. Whether it deals with alphabetical or pictorial writing, myth wants to see in them only a sum of signs, a global sign, the final term of a first semiological chain. And it is precisely this final term which will become the first term of the greater system which it builds and of which it is only a part. Everything happens as if myth shifted the formal system of the first significations sideways. As this lateral shift is essential for the analysis of myth, I shall represent it in the following way, it being understood, of course, that the spatialization of the pattern is here only a metaphor:

It can be seen that in myth there are two semiological systems, one of which is staggered in relation to the other: a linguistic system, the language (or the modes of representation which are assimilated to it), which I shall call the *language-object*, because it is the language which myth gets hold of in order to build its own system; and myth itself, which I shall all *metalanguage*, because it is a second language, *in which* one speaks about the first. When he reflects on a metalanguage, the semiologist no longer needs to ask himself questions about the composition of the language-object, he no longer has to take into account the details of the linguistic schema; he will only need to know its total term, or global sign, and only inasmuch as this term lends itself to myth. This is why the semiologist is entitled to treat in the same way writing and pictures: what he retains from them is the fact that they are both *signs*, that they both reach the threshold of myth endowed with the same signifying function, that they constitute, one just as much as the other, a language-object.

Note

1. Innumerable other meanings of the word 'myth' can be cited against this. But I have tried to define things, not words.

⌐◞

WRITING DEGREE ZERO, 1953

Political Modes of Writing

All modes of writing have in common the fact of being "closed" and thus different from spoken language. Writing is in no way an instrument for communication, it is not an open route through which there passes only the intention to speak. A whole disorder flows through speech and gives it this self-devouring momentum which keeps it in a perpetually suspended state. Conversely, writing is a hardened language which is self-contained and is in no way meant to deliver to its own duration a mobile series of approximations. It is on the contrary meant to impose, thanks to the shadow cast by its system of signs, the image of a speech which had a structure even before it came into existence. What makes writing the opposite of speech is that the former always *appears* symbolical, introverted, ostensibly turned toward an occult side of language, whereas the second is nothing but a flow of empty signs, the movement of which alone is significant. The whole of speech is epitomized in this expendability of words, in this froth ceaselessly swept onward, and speech is found only where language self-evidently functions like a devouring process which swallows only the moving crest of the words. Writing, on the contrary, is always rooted in something beyond language, it develops like a seed, not like a line, it manifests an essence and holds the threat of a secret, it is an anti-communication, it is intimidating. All writing will therefore contain the ambiguity of an object which is both language and coercion: there exists fundamentally in writing a "circumstance" foreign to language, there is, as it were, the weight of a gaze conveying an intention which is no longer linguistic. This gaze may well express a passion of language, as in literary modes of writing; it may also express the threat of retribution, as in political ones: writing is then meant to unite at a single stroke the reality of the acts and the ideality of the ends. This is why power, or

Extract from *Writing Degree Zero*, by Roland Barthes, published by Jonathan Cape. Used by permission of the Random House Group Limited, UK.

the shadow cast by power, always ends in creating an axiological writing, in which the distance which usually separates fact from value disappears within the very space of the word, which is given at once as description and as judgment. The word becomes an alibi, that is, an elsewhere and a justification. This, which is true of the literary modes of writing, in which the unity of the signs is ceaselessly fascinated by zones of infra- or ultra-language, is even truer of the political ones, in which the alibi stemming from language is at the same time intimidation and glorification: for it is power or conflict which produces the purest types of writing.

We shall see later that classical writing was a ceremonial which manifested the implantation of the writer into a particular political society, and that to speak like Vaugelas meant in the first place to be connected with the exercise of power. The Revolution did not modify the norms of this writing, since its force of thinkers remained, all things considered, the same, having merely passed from intellectual to political power; but the exceptional conditions of the struggle nevertheless brought about, within the great Form of classicism, a revolutionary mode of writing proper, defined not by its structure (which was more conventional than ever) but by its closed character and by its counterpart, since the use of language was then linked, as never before in history, to the Blood which had been shed. The Revolutionaries had no reason to wish to alter classical writing; they were in no way aware of questioning the nature of man, still less his language, and an "instrument" they had inherited from Voltaire, Rousseau, or Vauvenargues could not appear to them as compromised. It was the singularity of the historical circumstances which produced the identity of the revolutionary mode of writing. Baudelaire spoke somewhere of the "grandiloquent truth of gestures on life's great occasions." The Revolution was in the highest degree one of those great occasions when truth, through the bloodshed that it costs, becomes so weighty that its expression demands the very forms of theatrical amplification. Revolutionary writing was the one and only grand gesture commensurate with the daily presence of the guillotine. What today appears turgid was then no more than life-size. This writing, which bears all the signs of inflation, was an exact writing: never was

language more incredible, yet never was it less spurious. This grandiloquence was not only form modeled on drama; it was also the awareness of it. Without this extravagant pose, typical of all the great revolutionaries, which enabled Guadet, the Girondin, when arrested at Saint-Emilion, to declare without looking ridiculous, since he was about to die: "Yes, I am Guadet. Executioner, do your duty. Go take my head to the tyrants of my country. It has always turned them pale; once severed, it will turn them paler still," the Revolution could not have been this mythical event which made History fruitful, along with all future ideas on revolution. Revolutionary writing was so to speak the entelechy of the revolutionary legend: it struck fear into men's hearts and imposed upon them a citizen's sacrament of Bloodshed.

Marxist writing is of a different order. Here the closed character of the form does not derive from rhetorical amplification or from grandiloquence in delivery, but from a lexicon as specialized and as functional as a technical vocabulary; even metaphors are here severely codified. French revolutionary writing always proclaimed a right founded on bloodshed or moral justification, whereas from the very start Marxist writing is presented as the language of knowledge. Here, writing is univocal, because it is meant to maintain the cohesion of a Nature; it is the lexical identity of this writing which allows it to impose a stability in its explanations and a permanence in its method; it is only in the light of its whole linguistic system that Marxism is perceived in all its political implications. Marxist writing is as much given to understatement as revolutionary writing is to grandiloquence, since each word is no longer anything but a narrow reference to the set of principles which tacitly underlie it. For instance, the word "imply," frequently encountered in Marxist writing, does not there have its neutral dictionary meaning; it always refers to a precise historical process, and is like an algebraical sign representing a whole bracketed set of previous postulates.

Being linked to action, Marxist writing has rapidly become, in fact, a language expressing value judgments. This character, already visible in Marx, whose writing however remains in general explanatory, has come to pervade writing completely in the era of triumphant Stalinism. Certain outwardly similar notions, for which a neutral vocabulary would not seek a dual designation, are evaluatively parted from each other, so that each element gravitates toward a different noun: for instance, "cosmopolitanism" is the negative of "internationalism" (already in Marx). In the Stalinist world, in which *definition,* that is to say, the separation between Good and Evil, becomes the sole content of all language, there are no more words without values attached to them, so that finally the function of writing is to cut out one stage of a process: there is no more lapse of time between naming and judging, and the closed character of language is perfected, since in the last analysis it is a value which is given as explanation of another value. For instance, it may be alleged that such and such a criminal has engaged in activities harmful to the interests of the state; which boils down to saying that a criminal is someone who commits a crime. We see that this is in fact a tautology, a device constantly used in Stalinist writing. For the latter no longer aims at founding a Marxist version of the facts, or a revolutionary rationale of actions, but at presenting reality in a prejudged form, thus imposing a reading which involves immediate condemnation: the objective content of the word "deviationist" puts it into a penological category. If two deviationists band together, they become "fractionists," which does not involve an objectively different crime but an increase in the sentence imposed. One can enumerate a properly Marxist writing (that of Marx and Lenin) and a writing of triumphant Stalinism; there certainly is as well a Trotskyist writing and a

tactical writing, for instance that of the French Communist Party with its substitution of "people," then of "plain folk," for "working class," and the willful ambiguity of terms like "democracy," "freedom," "peace," etc.

There is no doubt at all that each regime has its own writing, no history of which has yet been written. Since writing is the spectacular commitment of language, it contains at one and the same time, thanks to a valuable ambiguity, the reality and the appearance of power, what it is, and what it would like to be thought to be: a history of political modes of writing would therefore be the best of social phenomenologies. For instance, the French Restoration evolved a class writing by means of which repression was immediately given as a condemnation spontaneously arising from classical "Nature": workers claiming rights were always "troublemakers," strike-breakers were "good workmen," and the subservience of judges became, in this language, the "paternal vigilance of magistrates" (it is thanks to a similar procedure that Gaullism today calls Communists "separatists"). We see that here the function of writing is to maintain a clear conscience and that its mission is fraudulently to identify the original fact with its remotest subsequent transformation by bolstering up the justification of actions with the additional guarantee of its own reality. This fact about writing is, by the way, typical of all authoritarian regimes; it is what might be called police-state writing: we know, for example, that the content of the word "Order" always indicates repression.

ROBERT REDFIELD

1897–1958

Son of an attorney, Robert Redfield was born on December 4, 1897 in Chicago, married Margaret Park in 1920, with whom he had two sons and two daughters, and died at the age of 60 from lymphatic leukemia in his hometown on October 16, 1958. After working as a volunteer ambulance driver during WWI, he attended the University of Chicago, taking a B.A. (1920), L.L.D. (1921), and Ph.D. (1928) at this revered institution, soon to become the leading university between either coast. After early work in a Chicago law firm (1921) and a vacation trip to Mexico in 1923 which inspired him to study anthropology, he taught sociology at the University of Colorado in 1925, and then returned to his alma mater as assistant professor of anthropology in 1928. He reached full professor and university dean of social sciences in 1934, then chair of the anthropology department in 1948. He became the Robert Maynard Hutchins Distinguished Service Professor, perhaps the most prestigious chair at Chicago at the time, in 1953. Meanwhile, he held visiting positions at universities in Peking, Frankfurt, and at Cornell, and also worked for UNESCO and the American Council on Race Relations, as director, from 1948. During WWII he advised the War Relocation Authority.

Redfield's dissertation was called *A Plan for a Study of Tepoztlan, Morelos,* and the book he made from it, *Tepoztlan, A Mexican Village* (1930) became a standard part of the American anthropological canon for decades. His work was widely praised for its artistry and narrative power, even though some critics disliked the fact that he offered no standard methodological procedures for those who wished to imitate him. He was opposed to the unreflective quantitativist tendency in the social sciences, and his early death led some observers to note that a vital champion of ethnographic research had been lost. His social anthropology skirted the more archaeological or linguistic approach being practiced by Franz Boas and his students at Columbia. Redfield was keen to understand the ultimate effects of modernization or urbanization upon folk cultures, which makes sense given his Chicago background and his affection for village life in Mexico and Guatemala. He used "ideal-types" of Weber's kind in disentangling these transformations of everyday life. Redfield did not mind mixing cool anthropological analysis with impassioned rhetoric about what he called *The Primitive World and Its Transformations* (1953). For this he paid a professional price among those who wanted to link anthropology more firmly with the natural sciences and their opponents, who viewed the field as necessarily bearing moral implications, both for the student of different cultures and for the people they studied.

THE PRIMITIVE WORLD AND ITS TRANSFORMATIONS, 1953

Primitive World View

. . . So may we not say that in the primary world view the quality of the attitude toward the Not-Man is one of mutuality? The obligation felt is to do what falls to one in maintaining a whole of which man is part.

The third assertion as to the primary world view here to be made brings us back to a conception introduced in the first chapter, the moral order. In the primary world view Man and Not-Man are bound together in one moral order. The universe is morally significant. It cares. What man sees out there, that which is not himself and yet in which he somehow participates, is a great drama of conduct. Whether it be the spirit-inhabited water hole and the still more important powerful sexuality of his own being, as in the case of the Arapesh, or the rain-gods and maize plants of the Zuni, or the divine authorities of the Mesopotamian invisible state, these entities and dispositions are part of a man—including moral system. The universe is spun of duty and ethical judgment. Even where the Not-Man acts not as man should act, where the supernaturals are unjust or indecent, the conduct of these gods is thought about according to the morality that prevails on earth. The universe is not an indifferent system. It is system of moral consequence.

So we find that everywhere in the uncivilized societies—and may therefore attribute the characteristic to the pre-civilized societies also—when man acts practically toward nature, his actions are limited by moral considerations. The attitude of primitive man is mixed, uncertain, to our viewpoint, accustomed as we are to separate purely physical nature toward which we act as expedience suggests. Primitive man is, as I have said, at once in nature and yet acting on it, getting his living, taking from it food and shelter. But as that nature is part of the same moral system in which

man and the affairs between men also find themselves, man's actions with regard to nature are limited by notions of inherent, not expediential, rightness. Even the practical, little-animistic Eskimo obey many exacting food taboos. Such taboos, religious restrictions on practical activity, rituals of propitiation or personal adjustments to field or forest, abound in ethnological literature. "All economic activities, such as hunting, gathering fuel, cultivating the land, storing food, assume a relatedness to the encompassing universe." And the relatedness is moral or religious.

The difference between the world view of primitive peoples, in which the universe is seen as morally significant, and that of civilized Western peoples, in which that significance is doubted or is not conceived at all, is well brought out in some investigations that have been made as to the concept of immanent justice in the cases of American Indian children on the one hand and Swiss children on the other. "Immanent justice" is that retribution for my faults which I believe will fall upon me out of the universe, apart from the policeman or a parental spanking. If I do what I know I should not do, will I, crossing the brook, perhaps slip and fall into the water? If I believe this will happen, I live in no indifferent universe; the Not-Man cares about moral career. . . .

If we compare the primary world view that has been sketched in these pages with that which comes to prevail in modern times, especially in the West, where science has been so influential, we may recognize one of the great transformations of the human mind. It is that transformation by which the primitive world view has been overturned. The three characteristics of that view which have been stressed in these pages have weakened or disappeared. Man comes out from the unity of the universe within which he is orientated now as something separate from nature and comes to confront nature as something with physical qualities only, upon which he may work his will. As this happens, the universe loses its moral character and becomes to him indifferent, a system uncaring of man. The existence today of ethical systems and of religions only qualifies this statement; ethics and religion struggle in one way or another to take account of a physical universe indifferent to man.

Changing Ethical Judgment

If we follow Kroeber, we shall not hesitate to accept the words of Furnas that I have already quoted: "The two sets of cultures (precivilized and civilized) are unmistakably on different levels." The insistence of many anthropologists that all cultures are equivalent allows some qualification. Kroeber, in spite of the refusal of anthropologists to say anything that might sound as if primitive people were earlier than or figuratively ancestral to civilized men, does not hesitate to call the pre-civilized societies "infantile" and the civilized societies "more adult." The standards as to the good have changed with history. The moral canon tends to mature. The change is far from steady, and the future course of the ethical judgment is not, it seems to me, assured to us. But in this sense—that on the whole the human race has come to develop a more decent and humane measure of goodness—there has been a transformation of ethical judgment which makes us look at noncivilized peoples, not as equals, but as people on a different level of human experience.

I find it impossible to regret that the human race has tended to grow up. As in the maturing of the individual, there are losses and gains. There are, especially, new responsibilities. The responsibility to look at the cultures of other peoples in the light of civilized ethical judgment is one of these. I think we do in fact appraise the conduct of primitive people by standards different from those by which we judge civilized people and yet also—and this is harder to say convincingly—according to the historic trend which has tended to make the totality of human conduct more decent and more humane. We do not expect the preliterate person to cultivate and protect individual freedom of thought as we expect civilized people to do. We do not blame the Veddah for failing to have a subtle graphic art. We understand how it is that the Siri-ono husband leaves his wife to die alone in the jungle, and we do not condemn him as we condemn the suburban husband who leaves his wife to die in a snowdrift. We do not expect a people to have a moral norm that their material conditions of life make impossible. On the other hand, when a people surmount the difficulties of their material conditions of life to reach a moral norm which puts

them, by so much, on the road which civilization has taken, we value highly what they do. I praise the Yagua for respecting privacy under conditions of living that make privacy difficult to respect.

We judge the conduct of primitive peoples—as of other people—by their success in acting in accordance with the ideals they have chosen. When my Yucatecan Maya friends caught a wild animal, doused it in gasolene, and set fire to it, I condemned the act strongly, partly for the reason that they have set up ideals of kindliness and compassion to animals too. They have plainly gone wrong. There is an aspect of their act which is more to be condemned than the torture of prisoners by the Huron. At least I can see that torture, which I also condemn, bears some relation, among the Huron, to ideals of fortitude and courage.

For we also judge the conduct of a primitive people by the degree to which the ideals they have chosen conform to the conceptions that have developed in history as to what human beings ought to be. These conceptions, as I have tried to suggest in this essay, are in part local, in part more or less universal. I cannot prove to you that man should act more decently and more humanely. I follow Kroeber in saying that on the whole he has come to. When, now, he does not, it is a worse mistake than when he did not in pre-civilized times. We have come to know better, however "better" is to be justified philosophically. I say only that these changing conceptions are drawn from or confirmed by history. Thus I can see some good in Huron customs while I abominate the torture.

❧

PEASANT SOCIETY AND CULTURE, 1956

The Peasant View of the Good Life

There is such a thing as ethnic temperament. The group-personality of the Chinese is something to investigate and describe, and the results will not correspond with the results of investigations of the group-personality of south Italians. The Maya Indians, peasantry remade, have a group-personality which in important degree must have come about before ever they began to come into relationship with the Spanish-American gentry of the present-day towns. Yet in their case the group-personality that had been developing before the Conquest was already congenial, one may perhaps think, to the conditions of peasant life and, indeed, had partly been developed in the course of their relationships to their own priestly elites. The Comanche if moved to Yucatan would have had to change very much more to become peasantry. So it may turn out that the general circumstances of peasant life do not set aside other influences on character but yet do dispose a people toward the more restrained and sober valuation of sex and violence which I first tried to describe.

Possible explanations of peasant values appear to be numerous and complicated. Even in this brief discussion as to what peasants think of sexual prowess or manly aggressiveness, and as to whether the tone of their lives is sober or passionate, one sees that several explanations might be seriously considered. It may be that the characteristics of peasant life do on the whole dispose people to a sober temper unfavorable to individual exploit in any field of action. It may also be that even within such generally conforming circumstances old-established characteristics of the modal personality may be more congenial to such a result in one place than in others. And it may also be that in some parts of the world the peasantry have been strongly influenced by the gentry and elite with whom their lives are completed and entertain views of what is good, desirable, and ideal that they have taken over from examples provided by the gentry. Is it not the gentry of Spain, for instance, that exhibited most markedly that value called *hombría* which involves a certain approval of male sexual exploit and a touchy pride and use of violence in defense of honor? And yet do not the peasantry also show it? Certainly the rural townspeople of Andalusia show it. Do (or did) the peasants, or the gentry in Italy show the satisfactions in sexual exploit and in manly violence which Professor Tentori calls to our attention? The extent to which a gentry ideal has

influenced a peasantry probably differs from one part of the world to another: I imagine the influence to be been stronger in Spain than in Poland or Russia. . . .

It becomes then, impossible justly to explain the ideals of peasantry without considering the kind and duration of the relationships those peasants have had with their gentry. I think that it is in the relations between the peasant and his gentry or townsman that we shall find much of what makes a peasant different from a primitive person. There is very much in peasant life which is also in primitive, tribal life. Peasant activity too is so organized as to provide for what the people there accept as a good life. A structure of meanings gives the pleasure that comes from a life well lived with little. Satisfactions come from the exercise of unquestioned virtues and the enjoyment of one's own skills and the fruits of one's own labor. What Sturt says about the good life of the English peasantry he knew could be said as well of many an African or American Indian primitive: "By their own skill and knowledge they formed the main part of . . . their own neighborhood. And in doing so they won at least the rougher consolations which that mode of life had to offer. Their local knowledge was intensely interesting to them; they took pride in their skill and hardihood; they felt that they belonged to a set of people not inferior to others . . . ; and all the customs which their situation required them to follow contained their belief in the ancestral notions of good and evil. . . .

And yet the peasant is differently situated from the primitive because peasants know of and are dependent upon more civilized people. There is another dimension of life, outside the village, in that powerful manor or that alarming town. The peasant has given his hostage to the fortunes of a society and mode of life that is both like his and yet alien to it. He keeps the integrity of his traditions by making compromises: by selling his grain in the town, paying his taxes, respecting the priest or the political leader, acknowledging that there are things out there that are perhaps better than his own village. He is not self-sufficient in his moral or intellectual life. Out there, he knows, are people who will baptize my child; people who will, in their courts of law, get me my rights or deprive me of them.

HERBERT MARCUSE

1898–1979

Eldest of three children born to an affluent family (his father, Carl, a textile and real estate dealer, and his mother, Gertrud Kreslawsky, the daughter of a factory owner), Herbert Marcuse was born on July 19, 1898 in Berlin. To compensate for his father's incomplete education, Marcuse was sent to an excellent private school, the Mommsen Gymnasium, in preparation for the university education that would open the doors of elite society to him. His family's Judaism was muted, and Marcuse's first love became German secular culture and the humanities, a pattern familiar to so many assimilated Jews of the era. This idyll was shattered when Marcuse was drafted into the army in 1916, and although prevented from combat by poor eyes, he witnessed the politicization of Berlin via food and draft riots, strikes, and unrest that were new to him. While taking courses at the University, he joined the Social Democratic Party in 1917, then the Sparticist splinter group, finally the Independent SPD before wearying of politics and retiring, for life, to his study. At Humboldt University in Berlin he met Georg Lukács and Walter Benjamin, then left for Freiburg where he completed his doctorate and, meeting Max Horkheimer, the pair attended Husserl's lectures. Husserl and others were impressed when Marcuse defended his dissertation on the German artist-novel in 1922. Returning to Berlin, he worked in the book trade until 1929 with financial help from his father. Marcuse published a uniquely complete Schiller bibliography in 1925, but stunned by Heidegger's *Being and Time* (1927), he returned to Freiburg to study with the author and with Husserl. He married the mathematician Sophie Wertheim in 1924 and had one son with her (Peter, 1935) before her untimely death in 1951. He then married Inge Neumann, the widow of his Frankfurt School colleague, Friedrich Neumann (author of *Behemoth*), in 1954. Following her death in 1974, he married his former student and research assistant Erica Sherover in 1976. Marcuse worked for the O.S.S. (later C.I.A.) during WWII, having fled Germany due to his religion, continued working for the State Department as an expert on the U.S.S.R. (see his *Soviet Marxism*), and finally was given a faculty job at Brandeis University in 1954 at 56 years of age. From there he went to UC/San Diego, retiring in 1976 after a riotous career which involved death threats from the right wing and official chastisement from Governor Ronald Reagan, who regarded him as evil and traitorous. He succumbed to a stroke while visiting Habermas in Starnberg, Germany on July 29, 1979, soon after his 81st birthday.

Marcuse was during the late 60s and early 70s the most famous social philosopher on earth among the disenchanted. Blending ideas of Schiller, Hegel, Freud, Weber, Marx, and Heidegger, his *Eros and Civilization* (1955) and *One-Dimensional Man* (1964) became unofficial bibles for the New Left, anti-war, feminist, and Black Power movements during that time. Even if most of the young people who bought these books could not understand them completely, they got the central argument easily enough: there is a perpetual struggle between the individual's desires and needs, physical and emotional, and the grinding regimentation and bureaucratization that were smothering the human spirit (Freud's notion from *Civilization and Its Discontents*), and that due to mass media manipulation (Adorno and Benjamin) and other Kafkaesque forms of mind control, the very possibility to experience revolutionary "negativity" had been abrogated. "Surplus repression," "repressive desublimation," and "artificial negativity" had brought critical responses to industrialized culture almost to a standstill. In *Negations* (1965; tr. 1968) Marcuse wrote about "Aggressiveness in Advanced Industrial Society," highlighting what had by then become his standard criticisms of the more affluent nations. He believed that the global process of industrialization and the commodification of human relations that necessarily goes along with it provoked "the dehumanization of the process of production and consumption," as well as insufferable "conditions of crowding, noise, and overtness characteristic of mass society." He also noted that "the most conspicuous social mobilization of aggressiveness is the militarization of the affluent society," an observation that seems to grow more germane with each passing season of war. For Marcuse the most promising revolutionaries at the time were college students, women, and blacks, since the working class had been either bought off or culturally sedated. Though showing its age these 45 years later, Marcuse's general line of thought remains vital and his works continue to be read, especially with global economic and cultural crises returning with a vengeance after a blissful period of international growth—now known as "the bubble."

EROS AND CIVILIZATION, 1955

The Transformation of Sexuality into Eros

The vision of a non-repressive culture, which we have lifted from a marginal trend in mythology and philosophy, aims at a new relation between instincts and reason. The civilized morality is reversed by harmonizing instinctual freedom and order: liberated from the tyranny of repressive reason, the instincts tend toward free and lasting existential relations—they generate a new reality principle. In Schiller's idea of an "aesthetic state," the vision of a non-repressive culture is concretized at the level of mature civilization. At this

level, the organization of the instincts becomes a social problem (in Schiller's terminology, *political*), as it does in Freud's pyschology. The processes that create the ego and superego also shape and perpetuate specific societal institutions and relations. Such psychoanalytical concepts as sublimation, identification, and introjection have not only a psychical but also a social content: they terminate in a system of institutions, laws, agencies, things, and customs that confront the individual as objective entities. Within this antagonistic system, the mental conflict between ego and superego, between ego and id, is at one and the same, time a conflict between the individual and his society. The latter embodies the rationality of the whole, and the individual's struggle against the repressive forces is a struggle against objective reason. Therefore, the emergence of a non-repressive reality principle involving instinctual liberation would *regress* behind the attained level of civilized rationality. This regression would be psychical as well as social: it would reactivate early stages of the libido which were surpassed in the development of the reality ego, and it would dissolve the institutions of society in which the reality ego exists. In terms of these institutions, instinctual liberation is relapse into barbarism. . . .

The notion of a non-repressive instinctual order must first be tested on the most "disorderly" of all instincts—namely, sexuality. Non-repressive order is possible only if the sex instincts can, by virtue of their own dynamic and under changed existential and societal conditions, generate lasting erotic relations among mature individuals. We have to ask whether the sex instincts, after the elimination of all surplus-repression, can develop a "libidinal rationality" which is not only compatible with but even promotes progress toward higher forms of civilized freedom.

ONE-DIMENSIONAL MAN, 1964

The Paralysis of Criticism: Society Without Opposition

Does not the threat of an atomic catastrophe which could wipe out the human race also serve to protect the very forces which perpetuate this danger? The efforts to prevent such a catastrophe overshadow the search for its potential causes in contemporary industrial society. These causes remain unidentified, unexposed, unattacked by the public because they recede before the all too obvious threat from without to the West from the East, to the East from the West. Equally obvious is the need for being prepared, for living on the brink, for facing the challenge. We submit to the peaceful production of the means of destruction, to the perfection of waste, to being educated for a defense which deforms the defenders and that which they defend.

If we attempt to relate the causes of the danger to the way in which society is organized and organizes its members, we are immediately con-fronted with the fact that advanced industrial society becomes richer, bigger, and better as it perpetuates the danger. The defense structure makes life easier for a greater number of people and extends man's mastery of nature. Under these circumstances, our mass media have little difficulty in selling particular interests as those of all sensible men. The political needs of society become individual needs and aspirations, their satisfaction promotes business and the commonweal, and the whole appears to be the very embodiment of Reason.

And yet this society is irrational as a whole. Its productivity is destructive of the free development of human needs and faculties, its peace maintained by the constant threat of war, its growth dependent on the repression of the threat of real possibilities for pacifying the struggle for existence individual, national, and international. This repression, so different from that which characterized the preceding, less developed stages of our society, operates today not from a position of natural and technical immaturity but rather from a position of strength. The capabilities (intellectual and material) of contemporary society are immeasurably greater than ever before—which means that the scope of society's domination over the individual is immeasurably greater than ever before. Our society distinguishes itself by conquering the centrifugal social forces with Technology rather than Terror, on the dual basis of an overwhelming efficiency and an increasing standard of living.

To investigate the roots of these developments and examine their historical alternatives is part of the aim of a critical theory of contemporary society, a theory which analyzes society in the light of its used and unused or abused capabilities for improving the human condition. But what are the standards for such a critique? . . .

The attempt to answer these questions demands a series of initial abstractions. In order to identify and define the possibilities of an optimal development, the critical theory must abstract from the actual organization and utilization of society's resources, and from the results of this organization and utilization. Such abstraction which refuses to accept the given universe of facts as the final context of validation, such "transcending" analysis of the facts in the light of their arrested and denied possibilities, pertains to the very structure of social theory. It is opposed to all metaphysics by virtue of the rigorously historical character of the transcendence.[1] The "possibilities" must be within the reach of the respective society; they must be definable goals of practice. By the same token, the abstraction from the established institutions must be expressive of an actual tendency—that is, their transformation must be the real need of the underlying population. Social theory is concerned with the historical alternatives which haunt the established society as subversive tendencies and forces. The values attached to the alternatives do become facts when they are translated into reality by historical practice. The theoretical concepts terminate with social change. . . .

An overriding interest in the preservation and improvement of the institutional status quo unites the former antagonists in the most advanced areas of contemporary society. And to the degree to which technical progress assures the growth and cohesion of communist society, the very idea of qualitative change recedes before the realistic notions of a non-explosive evolution. In the absence of demonstrable agents and agencies of social change, the critique is thus thrown back to a high level of abstraction. There is no ground on which theory and practice, thought and action meet.

Even the most empirical analysis of historical alternatives appears to be unrealistic speculation, and commitment to them a matter of personal (or group) preference.

And yet: does this absence refute the theory? In the face of apparently contradictory facts, the critical analysis continues to insist that the need for qualitative change is as pressing as ever before. Needed by whom? The answer continues to be the same: by the society as a whole, for every one of its members. The union of growing productivity and growing destruction; the brinkmanship of annihilation; the surrender of thought, hope, and fear to the decisions of the powers that be; the preservation of misery in the face of unprecedented wealth constitute the most impartial indictment—even if they are not the *raison d' être* of this society but only its by-product: its rationality, which propels efficiency and growth, is itself irrational.

Note

1. The terms "transcend" and "transcendence" are used throughout in the empirical, critical sense: they designate tendencies in theory and practice which, is a given society, "overshoot" the established universe and action toward its historical alternatives (real possibilities).

JACQUES (MARIE EMILE) LACAN

1901–1981

Jacques Marie Emile Lacan was born in Paris on April 13, 1901, son of a businessman, married Marie-Louise Blondin on January 29, 1934, and with her had two daughters and a son. He then married Sylvia Makles on July 17, 1953 (one daughter), and died of cancer at the age of 80 in his hometown on September 9, 1981. After attending Stanislaus School, he received his M.D. in 1932 from the Paris Medical School in psychiatry, with a thesis called "Paranoiac Psychosis and Its Relations to the Personality." He was in private psychoanalytic practice from 1932 until his death, co-founded the French Psychoanalytic Society (1953–63), founded the Freudian School of Paris (1964–80), and taught at the École Normale Superieure from 1963 until 1981, often drawing huge crowds. He also held an important editorial post in the Editions du Seuil, a publishing house, from 1963 until 1981.

At the age when most people retire, he published *Ecrits* (1966) and was suddenly a French celebrity of the special intellectual sort that was then unique to that country. He combined structuralism from linguistics with more traditional Freudianism, mixed in some practical changes in therapy—most notably the idea of a very short session, sometimes only five minutes rather than the conventional 50 minutes—and because of his heterodox approach to psychoanalysis, he was spurned by the standard professional organizations of practitioners, and therefore set up his own. When he was young he associated with surrealists, especially André Breton, because the unconscious played an essential role in this sect's aesthetic theory and practice, and this formed their common ground. Lacan therefore wrote about schizophrenic writing with unusual insight. In 1938 Lacan delivered what became one of his fundamental documents, "The Mirror State as Formative of the Function of the I," in which he proposed that at about six months of age, the infant notices its own image for the first time, and from this shock begins to comprehend its separateness from its mother. Lacan offered lectures in these matters beginning in 1951 at St. Anne's Hospital, and began going through each of Freud's major texts in hermeneutic fashion, but grafted onto standard interpretations the new ideas of Levi-Strauss and Saussure from the structuralist camp. Because of these influences Lacan delivered in 1953 "Function and Field of Speech and Language," where he argued that the unconscious can be interpreted as a set of signs, and that repression should be understood as a violent break in sense between the signifier and signified. Put another way, the child's libidinous drives are sidetracked when the language of expression in the unconscious divides sets of words used to understand and express these desires from the signified items that were originally attached to them. Psychoanalysis restores the "original" sign by bringing signifier and signified back into contagion with one another. These sorts of notions, entirely foreign to orthodox Freudianism, antagonized Anna Freud and others, so they withheld certification from Lacan's French Psychoanalytic Institute, formed in 1953, which Lacan in turn left himself in 1964. The associated scandal made Lacan increasingly famous, and his lectures drew large crowds despite the fact that his writing is often inscrutable, apparently by design. In the end, he was deposed by his own disciples when he refused to retire at 78, even at the time when becoming a "Lacanian analyst" was a sure road to upward mobility among French therapists.

THE LANGUAGE OF THE SELF, 1956

The Empty Word and the Full Word

Donne en ma bouche parole vraie et estable et fay de moy langue caulte.   —(*L'Internele Consolacion*, XLVe Chapitre: qu'on ne doit pas chascun croire et du legier trebuchement de paroles.)

Cause toujours.   —(Motto of "causalist" thought.)

Whether it sees itself as an instrument of healing, of formation, or of exploration in depth, psychoanalysis has only a single intermediary: the patient's Word. That this is self-evident is no excuse for our neglecting it. And every Word calls for a reply.

I shall show that there is no Word without a reply, even if it meets no more than silence, provided that it has an auditor: this is the heart of its function in psychoanalysis.

But if the psychoanalyst is not aware that this is the way it is with the function of the Word, he will only experience its appeal all the more strongly, and if the first thing to make itself heard is the void, it is within himself that he will experience it, and it is beyond the Word that he will seek a reality to fill this void.

From *The Language of the Self: The Function of Language in Psychoanalysis*, by Jacques Lacan, Anthony Wilden, Trans. Published by Johns Hopkins University Press. Copyright © 1981. Used by permission of Johns Hopkins University Press.

Thus it is that he will come to analyze the subject's behavior in order to find in it what the subject is not saying. Yet in order to obtain an avowal of what he finds, he must nevertheless talk about it. Then he finds his tongue again, but his Word is now rendered suspect by having replied only to the failure of his silence, in the face of the echo perceived of his own nothingness.

But what in fact was this appeal from the subject beyond the void of his speech? It was an appeal to Truth in its ultimate nature, through which other appeals resulting from humbler needs will find faltering expression. But first and foremost it was the appeal of the void, in the ambiguous *béance* of an attempted seduction of the other by the means on which the subject has come compliantly to rely and to which he is going to commit the monumental construct of his narcissism.

"That's it all right, introspection!" exclaims the *prud'homme* who knows its dangers only too well. He is certainly not the last, he avows, to have tasted its charms, if he has exhausted its profit. Too bad that he hasn't more time to waste. For you would hear some fine profundities from him were he to arrive on your couch.

It is strange that an analyst, for whom this sort of person is one of the first encounters in his experience, should still take introspection into account in psychoanalysis. For from the moment that the wager is taken up, all those fine things that were thought to be in reserve slip away. If he does engage in it, they will appear of little account, but others present themselves sufficiently unexpected by our friend to seem ridiculous to him and to stun him into silence. The common lot.[b]

Then it is that he grasps the difference between the mirage of the monologue whose accommodating fancies used to sustain his animated outpourings, and the forced labor of this discourse without escape, on which the psychologist (not without humor) and the therapist (not without cunning) have bestowed the name of "free association."

For free association really is a labor, and so much of a travail that some have gone so far as to say that it requires an apprenticeship, even to the point of seeing in the apprenticeship its true formative value. But if viewed in this way, what does it form but a skilled craftsman?

Well, then, what of this labor? Let us consider its conditions and its fruit, in the hope of throwing more light on its aim and profit.

The aptness of the German word *durcharbeiten*—equivalent to the English "working through"—has been recognized in passing. It has confounded French translators, in spite of what the immortal words of a master of French style offered them by way of an exercise in exhausting every last drop of sense: "Cent fois sur le métier, remettez . . . "—but how does the work [*l'ouvrage*] make any progress here?

The theory reminds us of the triad: frustration, aggressivity, regression. This is an explanation so apparently comprehensible that we may well be spared the necessity of comprehending it. Intuition is prompt, but we should be all the more suspicious of the self-evident that has become an *idée reçue*. If analysis should come round to exposing its weakness, it will be advisable not to rest content with recourse to affectivity—that taboo-word of the dialectical incapacity which, with the verb *to intellectualize* (whose accepted pejorative connotation makes a merit of this incapacity), will go down in the history of the language as the stigmata of our obtuseness regarding the subject[c]

Shall we enquire instead into the source of the subject's frustration? Does it come from the silence of the analyst? A reply to the subject's empty Word, even—or especially—an approving one, often shows by its effects that it is much more frustrating than silence. Is it not rather a matter of a frustration inherent in the very discourse of the subject? Does the subject not become engaged in an ever-growing dispossession of that being of his, concerning which—by dint of sincere portraits which leave its idea no less incoherent, of rectifications which do not succeed in freeing its essence, of stays and defenses which do not prevent his statue from tottering, of narcissistic embraces which become like a puff of air in animating it—he ends up by recognizing that this being has never been anything more than his construct in the Imaginary and that this construct disappoints all his certitudes? For in this labor which he undertakes to reconstruct this construct *for another,* he finds again the fundamental alienation which made him construct it *like another one,* and which has always destined it to be stripped from him *by another.*[d]

This ego, whose strength our theorists now define by its capacity to bear frustration, is frustration in its essence.[e] Not frustration of a desire of the subject, but frustration by an object in which his desire is alienated and which the more it is elaborated, the more profound the alienation from its *jouissance* becomes for the subject. Frustration at a second remove, therefore, and such that even if the subject were to reintroduce its form into his discourse to the point of reconstituting the preparatory image through which the subject makes himself an object by striking a pose before the mirror, he could not possibly be satisfied with it, since even if he achieved his most perfect likeness in that image, it would still be the *jouirsance* of the other that he would cause to be recognized in it. This is the reason why there is no reply which is adequate to this discourse, for the subject will consider as a takedown every Word participating in his mistake.

The aggressivity which the subject will experience at this point has nothing to do with the animal aggressivity of frustrated desire. Such a reference, which most people are content with, actually masks another one which is less agreeable for each and for all of us: the aggressivity of the slave whose response to the frustration of his labor is a desire for death.

It is therefore readily conceivable how this aggressivity may respond to any intervention which, by denouncing the Imaginary intentions of the discourse, dismantles the object constructed by the subject to satisfy them. This is in effect what is called the analysis of resistances, whose perilous side appears immediately. It is already pointed to by the existence of that artless simpleton who has never seen revealed anything except the aggressive signification of his subjects' phantasies.[f]

This is the same man who, not hesitating to plead for a "causalist" analysis which would aim to transform the subject in his present by learned explanations of his past, betrays well enough by his very intonation the anxiety from which he wishes to save himself—the anxiety of having to think that his patient's liberty may be dependent upon that of his own intervention. Whether or not the expedient into which he plunges may possibly be beneficial at some moment or another to the subject, this has no more importance than a stimulating pleasantry and will not detain me any longer.

Rather let us focus on this *hic et nunc* to which some analysts feel we should confine the tactics of analysis. It may indeed be useful, provided that the Imaginary intention that the analyst uncovers in it is not detached by him from the symbolic relation in which it is expressed. Nothing must be read into it concerning the *moi* of the subject which cannot not be reassumed by the subject in the form of the "je," that is, in the first person!

"I have been this only in order to become what I can be": if this were not the permanent fulcrum of the subject's assumption of his own mirages, where could one pick out progress here?

Hence the analyst cannot without peril track the subject down into the intimacy of his gestures, nor into that of his static state, except by reintegrating them as silent notes into his narcissistic discourse—and this has been noted very sensitively, even by young practitioners.

The danger involved here is not that of the subject's negative reaction, but much rather that of his capture in an objectification—no less Imaginary than before—of his static state or of his "statue," in a renewed status of his alienation.

Quite the contrary, the art of the analyst must be to suspend the subject's certitudes until their last mirages have been consumed. And it is in the discourse that, like verse, their resolution must be scanned.

Notes

b. Paragraph rewritten in 1966. [Minor changes were also made in the preceding paragraph.]

c. Previously I had written: "in psychological matters. . . ." (1966).

d. Paragraph rewritten in 1966.

e. This is the crux of a deviation as much practical as theoretical. For to identify the ego with the curbing of the subject is to confuse Imaginary isolation with the mastery of the instincts. This lays one open to errors of judgment in the conduct of the treatment: such as trying to reinforce the ego in many neuroses caused by its overforceful structure—and that is a dead end. Hasn't my friend Michael Balint written that a reinforcement of the ego should be beneficial to the subject suffering from *ejaculatio praecox* because it would permit him to prolong the suspension of his desire? But this can surely not be supposed, if it is precisely to the fact that his desire is made dependent upon the Imaginary function of the ego that the subject owes the short-circuiting of the act—which psychoanalytical clinical experience shows dearly to be intimately linked to narcissistic identification with the partner.

f. This is the same work which I crowned at the end of my Introduction. [Added 1966:] It is clear in what follows that aggressivity is only a lateral effect of analytic frustration, even if this effect can be reinforced by a certain type of intervention; as such, this effect is not the reason for the couple frustration-regression.

HANNAH ARENDT

1906–1975

Daughter of an assimilated Jewish engineer who died of syphilitic insanity when she was 7, Hannah Arendt was born on October 14, 1906 in Hannover, Germany (East Prussia), and grew up in Königsberg (Kant's town). She married Gunther Stern in 1928, divorced him in order to marry the communist, gentile art critic, Heinrich Blücher in 1940, and died on December 4, 1975 in New York City from a heart attack at the age of 66. She told an interviewer in 1964 that the word "Jew" never came up within her family circle when she was young, and that her Jewish identity only became important after she left Germany. Alone with her mother until she was 13, they fled Königsberg before the advancing Russian Army, shortly thereafter acquiring two stepsisters and a new stepfather. Her mother fostered a political awareness in Arendt and encouraged her leftwing activities and her refusal to adopt ready-made identities. Graduating from high school at 18, she attended universities at Marburg, Freiburg, and Heidelberg. After breaking away from Martin Heidegger (35 when she was 18) at Freiburg, with whom she was then and remained for years in love, she brilliantly took her doctorate in philosophy at Heidelberg when only 22 by writing *Love and Saint Augustine* under Karl Jaspers, her lifelong counselor and friend. She moved from Germany to Paris in 1933 because of the Nazis, where she helped find homes in Palestine for orphaned children from Europe, then to New York City in 1941 where she continued working for Jewish aid societies. She also served as editor at Schocken Books, a publisher specializing in Jewish culture, during the late 40s, taught at Princeton as a visiting professor, then at the University of Chicago on the Social Thought faculty from 1963–67, and finally at the New School until her death.

Although already well known in the academy for the monumental *The Origins of Totalitarianism* (1951), Arendt became a household name among the literate masses by writing articles in *The New Yorker* covering Eichmann's trial in Israel (1963), during which she famously coined the troubling term "the banality of evil." This was mistakenly taken to be an excuse for the Holocaust, and she came under vicious attack for an alleged, but altogether false, anti-Semitism. Her attempts to answer this criticism did little good in her lifetime. Sadly, this was not her most important work, yet overshadowed the much more powerful *The Human Condition* (1958), which has become a staple in the modern political philosophy literature virtually since it was published. She also wrote essays on notable intellectuals in *Men in Dark Times* (1968), she introduced English readers to Walter Benjamin by sponsoring his *Illuminations* (1968), and her commentary in *On Revolution* (1963) was highly regarded and debated during the rapid social changes occurring in the 60s. By the time of her death, she had become an iconic figure among younger intellectuals, a status only amplified when her biography began to be explored and her longterm love affair with

Heidegger became widely known. He remarked that she inspired his *Being and Time* (1927) and she could not have written *The Human Condition* without his guidance and pedagogy. She never understood his Nazi sympathies in the 30s, yet tried to make amends with him nevertheless, despite the contrary counsel of Karl Jaspers and her other mentors and friends. Arendt was a uniquely important woman theorist in the field of political theory wholly dominated by men at the time she was working within it, and her influence seems to grow rather than diminish with time.

THE HUMAN CONDITION, 1958

The Social and the Private

What we called earlier the rise of the social coincided historically with the transformation of the private care for private property into a public concern. Society, when it first entered the public realm, assumed the disguise of an organization of property-owners who, instead of claiming access to the public realm because of their wealth, demanded protection from it for the accumulation of more wealth. In the words of Bodin, government belonged to kings and property to subjects, so that it was the duty of the kings to rule in the interest of their subjects' property. "The commonwealth," as has recently been pointed out, "largely existed for the common *wealth.*"

When this common wealth, the result of activities formerly banished to the privacy of the households, was permitted to take over the public realm, private possessions—which are essentially much less permanent and much more vulnerable to the mortality of their owners than the common world, which always grows out of the past and is intended to last for future generations—began to undermine the durability of the world. It is true that wealth can be accumulated to a point where no individual life-span can use it up, so that the family rather than the individual becomes its owner. Yet wealth remains something to be used

and consumed no matter how many individual life-spans it may sustain. Only when wealth became capital, whose chief function was to generate more capital, did private property equal or come close to the permanence inherent in the commonly shared world. However, this permanence is of a different nature; it is the permanence of a process rather than the permanence of a stable structure. Without the process of accumulation, wealth would at once fall back into the opposite process of disintegration through use and consumption.

Common wealth, therefore, can never became common in the sense we speak of a common world; it remained, or rather was intended to remain, strictly private. Only the government, appointed to shield the private owners from each other in the competitive struggle for more wealth, was common. The obvious contradiction in this modern concept of government, where the only thing people have in common is their private interests, need no longer bother us as it still bothered Marx, since we know that the contradiction between private and public, typical of the initial stages of the modern age, has been a temporary phenomenon which introduced the utter extinction of the very difference between the private and public realms, the submersion of both in the sphere of the social. By the same token, we are in a far better position to realize the consequences for human existence when both the public and private spheres of life are gone, the public because it has become a function of the private and the private because it has become the only common concern left.

Seen from this viewpoint, the modern discovery of intimacy seems a flight from the whole outer world into the inner subjectivity of the individual, which formerly had been sheltered and protected by the private realm. The dissolution of this realm into the social may most conveniently be watched in the progressing transformation of immobile into mobile property until eventually the distinction between property and wealth, between the *fungibiles* and the *consumptibiles* of Roman law, loses all significance because every tangible, "fungible" thing has become an object of "consumption"; it lost its private use value which was determined by its location and acquired an exclusively social value determined through its ever-changing exchangeability whose fluctuation could itself be fixed only temporarily by relating it to the common denominator of money. Closely connected with this social evaporation of the tangible was the most revolutionary modern contribution to the concept of property, according to which property was not a fixed and firmly located part of the world acquired by its owner in one way or another but, on the contrary, had its source in man himself, in his possession of a body and his indisputable ownership of the strength of this body, which Marx called "labor-power."

Thus modern property lost its worldly character and was located in the person himself, that is, in what an individual could lose only along with his life. Historically, Locke's assumption that the labor of one's body is the origin of property is more than doubtful; but in view of the fact that we already live under conditions where our only reliable property is our skill and our labor power, it is more than likely that it will become true. For wealth, after it became a public concern, has grown to such proportions that it is almost unmanageable by private ownership. It is as though the public realm had taken its revenge against those who tried to use it for their private interests. The greatest threat here, however, is not the abolition of private ownership of wealth but the abolition of private property in the sense of a tangible, worldly place of one's own.

In order to understand the danger to human existence from the elimination of the private realm, for which the intimate is not a very reliable substitute, it may be best to consider those non-privative traits of privacy which are older than, and independent of, the discovery of intimacy. The difference between what we have in common and what we own privately is first that our private possessions, which we use and consume daily, are much more urgently needed than any part of the common world; without property, as Locke pointed out, "the common is of no use." The same necessity that, from the standpoint of the public realm, shows only its negative aspect as a deprivation of freedom possesses a driving force whose urgency is unmatched by the so-called higher desires and aspirations of man; not only will it always be the first among man's needs and worries, it will also prevent the apathy and disappearance of initiative which so obviously threatens all overly wealthy communities. Necessity and life are so intimately related and connected that life itself is threatened where necessity is altogether eliminated. For the elimination of necessity, far from resulting automatically in the establishment of freedom, only blurs the distinguishing line between freedom and necessity. (Modern discussions of freedom, where freedom is never understood as an objective state of human existence but either presents an unsolvable problem of subjectivity, of an entirely undetermined or determined will, or develops out of necessity, all point to the fact that the objective, tangible difference between being free and being forced by necessity is no longer perceived.)

The second outstanding non-privative characteristic of privacy is that the four walls of one's private property offer the only reliable hiding place from the common public world, not only from everything that goes on in it but also from its very publicity, from being seen and being heard. A life spent entirely in public, in the presence of others, becomes, as we would say, shallow. While it retains its visibility, it loses the quality of rising into sight from some darker ground which must remain hidden if it is not to lose its depth in a very real, non-subjective sense. The only efficient way to guarantee the darkness of what needs to be hidden against the light of publicity is private property, a privately owned place to hide in.

While it is only natural that the non-privative traits of privacy should appear most clearly when men are threatened with deprivation of it, the practical treatment of private property by premodern political bodies indicates clearly that men have always been conscious of their existence and importance. This, however, did not make them protect the activities in the private realm directly, but rather the boundaries separating the privately owned from other parts of the world, most of all from the common world itself. The distinguishing mark of modern political and economic theory, on the other hand, in so far as it regards private property as a crucial issue, has been its stress upon the private activities of property-owners and their need of government protection for the sake of accumulation of wealth at the expense of the tangible property itself. What is important to the public realm, however, is not the more or less enterprising spirit of private businessmen but the fences around the houses and gardens of citizens. The invasion of privacy by society, the "socialization of man" (Marx), is most efficiently carried through by means of expropriation, but this is not the only way. Here, as in other respects, the revolutionary measures of socialism or communism can very well be replaced by a slower and no less certain "withering away" of the private realm in general and of private property in particular.

The distinction between the private and public realms, seen from the viewpoint of privacy rather than of the body politic, equals the distinction between things that should be shown and things that should be hidden. Only the modern age, in its rebellion against society, has discovered how rich and manifold the realm of the hidden can be under the conditions of intimacy; but it is striking that from the beginning of history to our own time it has always been the bodily part of human existence that needed to be hidden in privacy, all things connected with the necessity of the life process itself, which prior to the modern age comprehended all activities serving the subsistence of the individual and the survival of the species. Hidden away were the laborers who "with their bodies minister to the [bodily] needs of life," and the women who with their bodies guarantee the physical survival of the species. Women and slaves belonged to the same category and were hidden away not only because they were somebody else's property but because their life was "laborious," devoted to bodily functions. In the beginning of the modern age, when "free"

labor had lost its hiding place in the privacy of the household, the laborers were hidden away and segregated from the community like criminals behind high walls and under constant supervision. The fact that the modern age emancipated the working classes and the women at nearly the same historical moment must certainly be counted among the characteristics of an age which no longer believes that bodily functions and material concerns should be hidden. It is all the more symptomatic of the nature of these phenomena that the few remnants of strict privacy even in our own civilization relate to "necessities" in the original sense of being necessitated by having a body.

Reification

Fabrication, the work of *homo faber,* consists in reification. Solidity, inherent in all, even the most fragile, things, comes from the material worked upon, but this material itself is not simply given and there, like the fruits of field and trees which we may gather or leave alone without changing the household of nature. Material is already a product of human hands which have removed it from its natural location, either killing a life process, as in the case of the tree which must be destroyed in order to provide wood, or interrupting one of nature's slower processes, as in the case of iron, stone, or marble torn out of the womb of the earth. This element of violation and violence is present in all fabrication, and *homo faber,* the creator of the human artifice, has always been a destroyer of nature. The *animal laborans,* which with its body and the help of tame animals nourishes life, may be the lord and master of all living creatures, but he still remains the servant of nature and the earth; only *homo faber* conducts himself as lord and master of the whole earth. Since his productivity was seen in the image of a Creator-God, so that where God creates *ex nihilo,* man creates out of given substance, human productivity was by definition bound to result in a Promethean revolt because it could erect a man-made world only after destroying part of God-created nature.

The experience of this violence is the most elemental experience of human strength and, therefore, the very opposite of the painful, exhausting effort experienced in sheer labor. It can provide self-assurance and satisfaction, and can even become a source of self-confidence throughout life, all of which are quite different from the bliss which can attend a life spent in labor and toil or from the fleeting, though intense pleasure of laboring itself which comes about if the effort is coordinated and rhythmically ordered, and which essentially is the same as the pleasure felt in other rhythmic body movements. Most descriptions of the "joys of labor," in so far as they are not late reflections of the biblical contented bliss of life and death and do not simply mistake the pride in having done a job with the "joy" of accomplishing it, are related to the elation felt by the violent exertion of a strength with which man measures himself against the overwhelming forces of the elements and which through the cunning invention of tools he knows how to multiply far beyond its natural measure. Solidity is not the result of pleasure or exhaustion in earning one's bread "in the sweat of his brow," but of this strength, and it is not simply borrowed or plucked as a free gift from nature's own eternal presence, although it would be impossible without the material torn out of nature; it is already a product of man's hands.

The actual work of fabrication is performed under the guidance of a model in accordance with which the object is constructed. This model can be an image beheld by the eye of the mind or a blueprint in which the image has already found a tentative materialization through work. In either case, what guides the work of fabrication is outside the fabricator and precedes the actual work process in much the same way as the urgencies of the life process within the laborer precede the actual labor process. (This description is in flagrant contradiction to the findings of modern psychology, which tell us almost unanimously that the images of the mind are as safely located in our heads as the pangs of hunger are located in our stomachs. This subjectivization of modern science, which is only a reflection of an even more radical subjectivization of the modern world, has its justification in this case in the fact that, indeed, most work in the modern world is performed in the mode of labor, so that the worker, even if he wanted to, could not "labor for his work rather than for himself," and frequently is instrumental in the production of objects of whose ultimate shape he has not the slightest notion. These circumstances, though of great historical importance, are irrelevant in a description of the fundamental articulations of the *vita activa*.) What claims our attention is the veritable gulf that separates all bodily sensations, pleasure or pain, desires and satisfactions—which are so "private" that they cannot even be adequately voiced, much less represented in the outside world, and therefore are altogether incapable of being reified—from mental images which lend themselves so easily and naturally to reification that we neither conceive of making a bed without first having some image, some "idea" of a bed before our inner eye, nor can imagine a bed without having recourse to some visual experience of a real thing.

It is of great importance to the role fabrication came to play within the hierarchy of the *vita activa* that the image or model whose shape guides the fabrication process not only precedes it, but does not disappear with the finished product, which it survives intact, present, as it were, to lend itself to an infinite continuation of fabrication. This potential multiplication, inherent in work, is different in principle from the repetition which is the mark of labor. This repetition is urged upon and remains subject to the biological cycle; the needs and wants of the human body come and go, and though they reappear again and again at regular intervals, they never remain for any length of time. Multiplication, in distinction from mere repetition, multiplies something that already possesses a relatively stable, relatively permanent existence in the world. This quality of permanence in the model or image, of being there before fabrication starts and remaining after it has come to an end, surviving all the possible use objects it continues to help into existence, had a powerful influence on Plato's doctrine of eternal ideas. In so far as his teaching was inspired by the word *idea* or *eidos* ("shape" or "form"), which he used for the first time in a philosophical context, it rested on experiences in *poiēsis* or fabrication, and although Plato used his theory to express quite different and perhaps much more "philosophical" experiences, he never failed to draw his examples from the field of making when he wanted to demonstrate the plausibility of what he was saying. The one eternal idea presiding over a multitude of perishable things derives its plausibility in Plato's teachings from the permanence and oneness of the model according to which many and perishable objects can be made.

The process of making is itself entirely determined by the categories of means and end. The fabricated thing is an end product in the twofold sense that the production process comes to an end in it ("the process disappears in the product," as Marx said) and that it is only a means to produce this end. Labor, to be sure, also produces for the end of consumption, but since this end, the thing to be consumed, lacks the worldly permanence of a piece of work, the end of the process is not determined by the end product but rather by the exhaustion of labor power, while the products themselves, on the other hand, immediately become means again, means of subsistence and reproduction of labor power. In the process of making, on the contrary, the end is beyond doubt: it has come when an entirely new thing with enough durability to remain in the world as an independent entity has been added to the human artifice. As far as the thing, the end product of fabrication, is concerned, the process need not be repeated. The impulse toward repetition comes from the craftsman's need to earn his means of subsistence, in which case his working coincides with his laboring; or it comes from a demand for mul-

tiplication in the marker, in which case the craftsman who wishes to meet this demand has added, as Plato would have said, the art of earning money to his craft. The point here is that in either case the process is repeated for reasons outside itself and is unlike the compulsory repetition inherent in laboring, where one must eat in order to labor and must labor in order to eat.

To have a definite beginning and a definite, predictable end is the mark of fabrication, which through this characteristic alone distinguishes itself from all other human activities. Labor, caught in the cyclical movement of the body's life process, has neither a beginning nor an end. Action, though it may have a definite beginning, never, as we shall see, has a predictable end. This great reliability of work is reflected in that the fabrication process, unlike action, is not irreversible: every thing produced by human hands can be destroyed by them, and no use object is so urgently needed in the life process that its maker cannot survive and afford its destruction. *Homo faber* is indeed a lord and master, not only because he is the master or has set himself up as the master of all nature but because he is master of himself and his doings. This is true neither of the *animal laborans*, which is subject to the necessity of its own life, nor of the man of action, who remains in dependence upon his fellow men. Alone with his image of the future product, *home faber* is free to produce, and again facing alone the work of his hands, he is free to destroy.

ROGER CAILLOIS

1913–1978

Roger Caillois (pronounced "Kai-*wah*") was born on March 3, 1913 in Reims, France, married Yvette Billod in 1940 (one daughter), then Alena Vichrova in 1957, dying at the age of 65 in Paris on December 21, 1978. He is an interesting, perhaps unique, combination of a literary critic, anthropologist of play, sociologist, editor, and, above all, surrealist. Caillois joined a surrealist group in Paris (1932–34), received a diploma from the College de France in 1936 and the aggregation (teaching certificate) from the École Normale Superieur in 1937. Like so many intellectuals of his era who were waiting in the queue for a professorship, he taught in a secondary school (lycée), in Beauvais as a young man. He was also a founding member of the so-called *College de Sociologie* in 1938, a collection of gifted intellectuals with broad interests and a remarkably unorthodox sense of cultural humor. Moving to Buenos Aires, Argentina in 1941, there he founded the French Institute, also edited *Lettres francaises,* then moved to London following the war where he became editor of another important literary journal. Between 1948 and 1973 he worked his way up to a top administrative position within the Department of Cultural Activities of UNESCO in Paris. Meanwhile, he also founded and edited *Diogenes* (1953–78), an important international journal for philosophy and the humanities. He gave guest lectures at many universities in the U.S. and Latin America.

Caillois is important to the anglophone world of social thought because of two of his thirty books: *Man and the Sacred* (1939; tr. 1959) and *Man, Play, and Games* (1958; tr. 1961). However, he also wrote untranslated works of note, including a sociology of the novel (1942), studies in contemporary sociology (1943), and an "aesthetic vocabulary" (1946). The principal insight which guided his social theory, as expressed in his *L'Ecriture des pierres* (1970), is that minerals (specifically inscape stones), when cut and polished, reveal patterns that speak to the order and disorder of the human world, despite having no material connection with it. Put another way, the inorganic can illuminate the organic when properly perceived, an idea he took from Baudelaire's theory of correspondence. One critic regarded Caillois as an expert on "the fantastic" in whatever form it took. More sociologically compelling, however, is his book on play. Only Johan Huizinga in *Homo Ludens: A Study of the Play Element in Culture* (1938) can be mentioned as a social analyst who recently developed Friedrich Schiller's idea (1798) that only during play are people truly free and "most human." Caillois expanded on this notion, as revealed in the excerpt reprinted below, where he shows that play and freedom are linked, and that realizing one's true self can only occur in an unfettered state.

MAN, PLAY, AND GAMES, 1961

The Definition of Play, 1958

In effect, play is essentially a separate occupation, carefully isolated from the rest of life, and generally is engaged in with precise limits of time and place. There is place for play: as needs dictate, the space for hopscotch, the board for checkers or chess, the stadium, the racetrack, the list, the ring, the stage, the arena, etc. Nothing that takes place outside this ideal frontier is relevant. To leave the enclosure by mistake, accident, or necessity, to send the ball out of bounds, may disqualify or entail a penalty.

The game must be taken back within the agreed boundaries. The same is true for time: the game starts and ends at a given signal. Its duration is often fixed in advance. It is improper to abandon or interrupt the game without a major reason (in children's games, crying "I give up," for example). If there is occasion to do so, the game is prolonged, by agreement between the contestants or by decision of an umpire. In every case, the game's domain is therefore a restricted, closed, protected universe: a pure space.

The confused and intricate laws of ordinary life are replaced, in this fixed space and for this given time, by precise, arbitrary, unexceptionable rules that must be accepted as such and that govern the correct playing of the game. If the cheat violates the rules, he at least pretends to respect them. He does not discuss them: he takes advantage of the other players' loyalty to the rules. From this point of view, one must agree with the writers who have stressed the fact that the cheat's dishonesty does not destroy the game. The game is ruined by the nihilist who denounces the rules as absurd and conventional, who refuses to play because the game is meaningless. His arguments are irrefutable. The game has no other but an intrinsic meaning. That is why its rules are imperative and absolute, beyond discussion. There is no reason for their being as they are, rather than otherwise. Whoever does not accept them as such must deem them manifest folly.

One plays only if and when one wishes to. In this sense, play is free activity. It is also uncertain activity. Doubt must remain until the end, and hinges upon the denouement. In a card game, when the outcome is no longer in doubt, play stops and the players lay down their hands. In a lottery or in roulette, money is placed on a number which may or may not win. In a sports contest, the powers of the contestants must be equated, so that each may have a chance until the end. Every game of skill, by definition, involves the risk for the player of missing his stroke, and the threat of defeat, without which the game would no longer be pleasing. In fact, the game is no longer pleasing to one who, because he is too well trained or skillful, wins effortlessly and infallibly.

An outcome known in advance, with no possibility of error or surprise, clearly leading to an inescapable result, is incompatible with the nature of play. Constant and unpredictable definitions of the situation are necessary, such as are produced by each attack or counterattack in fencing or football, in each return of the tennis ball, or in chess, each time one of the players moves a piece. The game consists of the need to find or continue at once a response *which is free within the limits set by the rules*. This latitude of the player, this margin accorded to his action is essential to the game and partly explains the pleasure which it excites. It is equally accountable for the remarkable and meaningful uses of the term "play," such as are reflected in such expressions as the *playing* of a performer or the *play* of a gear, to designate in the one case the personal style of an interpreter, in the other the range of movement of the parts of a machine.

Many games do not imply rules. No fixed or rigid rules exist for playing with dolls, for playing soldier, cops and robbers, horses, locomotives, and airplanes—games, in general, which presuppose free improvisation, and the chief attraction of which lies in the pleasure of playing a role, of acting *as if* one were someone or something else, a machine for example. Despite the assertion's paradoxical character, I will state that in this instance the fiction, the sentiment of *as if* replaces and performs the same function as do rules. Rules themselves create fictions. The one who plays chess, prisoner's base, polo, or baccara, by the very fact

From *Man, Play and Games*, by Roger Caillois, Meyer Barash, Trans. Published by the University of Illinois Press. Copyright © 2001. English translation copyright © 1961 by The Free Press, an imprint of Simon & Schuster.

of complying with their respective rules, is separated from real life where there is no activity that literally corresponds to any of these games. That is why chess, prisoner's base, polo, and baccara are played *for real. As if* is not necessary. On the contrary, each time that play consists in imitating life, the player on the one hand lacks knowledge of how to invent and follow rules that do not exist in reality, and on the other hand the game is accompanied by the knowledge that the required behavior is pretense, or simple mimicry. This awareness of the basic unreality of the assumed behavior is separate from real life and from the arbitrary legislation that defines other games. The equivalence is so precise that the one who breaks up a game, the one who denounces the absurdity of the rules, now becomes the one who breaks the spell, who brutally refuses to acquiesce in the proposed illusion, who reminds the boy that he is not really a detective, pirate, horse, or submarine, or reminds the little girl that she is not rocking a real baby or serving a real meal to real ladies on her miniature dishes.

Thus games are not ruled and make-believe. Rather, they are ruled *or* make-believe. It is to the point that if a game with rules seems in certain circumstances like a serious activity and is beyond one unfamiliar with the rules, i.e. if it seems to him like real life, this game can at once provide the framework for a diverting make-believe for the confused and curious layman. One easily can conceive of children, in order to irritate adults, blindly manipulating real or imaginary pieces on an imaginary chessboard, and by pleasant example, playing at "playing chess."

This discussion, intended to define the nature and the largest common denominator of all games, has at the same time the advantage of placing their diversity in relief and enlarging very meaningfully the universe ordinarily explored when games are studied. In particular, these remarks tend to add two new domains to this universe: that of wagers and games of chance, and that of mimicry and interpretation. Yet there remain a number of games and entertainments that still have imperfectly defined characteristics—for example, kite-flying and top-spinning, puzzles such as crossword puzzles, the game of patience, horsemanship, seesaws, and certain carnival attractions. It will be necessary to return to this problem. But for the present, the preceding analysis permits play to be defined as an activity which is essentially:

1. *Free:* in which playing is not obligatory; if it were, it would at once lose its attractive and joyous quality as diversion;
2. *Separate:* circumscribed within limits of space and time, defined and fixed in advance;
3. *Uncertain:* the course of which cannot be determined, nor the result attained beforehand, and some latitude for innovations being left to the player's initiative;
4. *Unproductive:* creating neither goods, nor wealth, nor new elements of any kind; and, except for the exchange of property among the players, ending in a situation identical to that prevailing at the beginning of the game;
5. *Governed by rules:* under conventions that suspend ordinary laws, and for the moment establish new legislation, which alone counts;
6. *Make-believe:* accompanied by a special awareness of a second reality or of a free unreality, as against real life.

These diverse qualities are purely formal. They do not prejudge the content of games. Also, the fact that the two last qualities—rules and make-believe—may be related, shows that the intimate nature of the facts that they seek to define implies, perhaps require, that the latter in their turn be subdivided. This would attempt to take account not of the qualities that are opposed to reality, but of those that are clustered in groups of games with unique, irreducible characteristics.

HAROLD GARFINKEL

1917–

Son of a small furniture store owner who hoped he would take over the business, Harold Garfinkel was born in Newark, New Jersey on October 29, 1917, and grew up there in a large Jewish community. His father and a non-Jewish in-law, thought to be worldly, advised Garfinkel to take on some indispensable profession which, during the Depression, was not easy to identify. Even formerly affluent professionals were reduced to menial work. So Garfinkel, in an effort to prepare himself properly before taking over the furniture business, began studying accounting and business at the unaccredited University of Newark. Luckily for him and the other students in 1935, many courses were offered by brilliant students and junior faculty from Columbia University, including Paul Lazarsfeld and Philip Selznick, so the quality of instruction was high. Fortuitously, the academics with whom Garfinkel studied or who were fellow-students at this time continued to help him throughout his career. Very oddly enough, it was from taking these mundane courses that Garfinkel would eventually invent a new form of theorizing, much of it based on what he called "accounts," but of behavior rather than of financial transactions. Although other theorists, notably Kenneth Burke and C. Wright Mills, used the term "accounts" similarly, it was not from them but from his Newark courses that Garfinkel took the imagery, which springs from double-entry bookkeeping and cost accounting. As in keeping ledgers for business, people similarly, so Garfinkel thought, post their credits and losses in social terms by noting and remembering their interactions with meaningful others, even if less precisely than would be the case when toting up dollars and cents. It was from this set of metaphors that he also took the term "indicators," a term of analysis that has spread throughout a number of literatures in social science.

After college, Garfinkel went south to help build a dam in Cornelia, Georgia, something quite common during the Depression. From there he visited the sociology department at the University of North Carolina, where its chair, Howard Odum, gave Garfinkel a graduate assistantship on sight. Using a car bought for him by his father—a rare gift in those days—Garfinkel drove around North Carolina's courts, collecting records, and writing his master's thesis (1942) in which he showed that homicide cases were quite differently handled depending on their within-race or across-race composition. From UNC Garfinkel went to Harvard to study with Talcott Parsons, who was beginning to fight a career-long battle against scientistic modeling in sociology, one which Garfinkel was happy to join in his unique fashion. He learned about Florian Znaniecki's *Social Action*, now scarcely known but influential at the time, the most comprehensive analysis of the topic then available. He also learned, while at UNC, about phenomenology, and read Parsons' *Structure of Social Action* (1937) the moment it left the presses. Garfinkel's first publication was a short story called "Color Trouble" (in *Best Short Stories of 1940*), where one can divine the outline of his mature social theory regarding social accounts. During WWII Garfinkel was given the peculiar job of training troops for fighting tanks by using imaginary tanks and grenades on a golf course in Miami. All aspects of the training regimen were done imaginatively, which gave him more grist for his theoretical mill. He finished his doctorate at Harvard in 1952, where he was one of a very distinguished cohort of sociologists and social psychologists. Parsons never acknowledged Garfinkel's work as helpful to his own, which pained the younger man throughout his career, since his intention had been to expand and enrich his teacher's theory. Garfinkel taught at Princeton for two years, Ohio State for another year, then to Wichita, Kansas to help with a jury study with Fred Strodtbeck. It was there, in the summer of 1954, that Garfinkel coined the term "ethnomethodology," a Greek-based word indicating a method for studying ordinary events. He then moved to UCLA, where he has been ever since. His only major work is *Studies in Ethnomethodology* (1967), from which the excerpt below originates, where he discusses the meaning of "rationality" in social action.

STUDIES IN ETHNOMETHODOLOGY, 1967

Rational Behaviors, 1960

"Rationality" has been used to designate many different ways of behaving. A list of such behaviors can be made without necessarily exercising the theorist's choice of treating any one or more as definitive of the term "rationality." Alfred Schutz' classical paper on the problem of rationality[2] inventories these meanings and is therefore our point of departure.

When the various meanings of the term which Schutz inventoried are phrased as descriptions of conduct, the following list of behaviors results. In the remainder of the paper, these behaviors will be referred to as "the rationalities."

(1) *Categorizing and comparing.* It is commonplace for a person to search his experience for a situation with which to compare the one he addresses. Sometimes rationality refers to the *fact*

that he searches the two situations with regard to their comparability, and sometimes to his *concern* for making matters comparable. To say that a person addresses the tasks of comparison is equivalent to saying that he treats a situation or a person or a problem as an instance of a type. Thereby the notion of a "degree of rationality" is encountered for the extensiveness of a person's concern with classification, the frequency of this activity, the success with which he engages in it are frequently the behaviors meant by saying that one person's activities are more rational than another's.

(2) *Tolerable error.* It is possible for a person to "require" varying degrees of "goodness of fit" between an observation and theory in terms of which he names, measures, describes, or otherwise intends the sense of his observation as a datum. He may pay a little or a lot of attention to the degree of fit. On one occasion he will allow a literary allusion to describe what has occurred. On another occasion and for the same occurrences he may search for a mathematical model to order them. It is sometimes said, then, that one person is rational while another is not or is less so, by which is meant that one person pays closer attention than does his neighbor to the degree of fit

Studies in Ethnomethodology, by Harold Garfinkel. Reprinted by permission of Pearson Education, Inc., Upper Saddle River, NJ. Copyright © 1967.

between what he has observed and what he intends as his finding.

(3) *Search for "means."* Rationality is sometimes used to mean that a person reviews rules of procedure which in the past yielded the practical effects now desired. Sometimes it is the fact that a person seeks to transfer rules of practice which had a pay-off in situations of like character; sometimes it is the frequency of this effort; at other times the rational character of his actions refers to the person's ability or inclination to employ in a present situation techniques that worked in other situations.

(4) *Analysis of alternatives and consequences.* Frequently the term rationality is used to call attention to the fact that a person in assessing a situation anticipates the alterations which his actions will produce. Not only the fact *that* he "rehearses in imagination" the various courses of action which will have occurred, but the care, attention, time, and elaborateness of analysis paid to alternative courses of action are frequent references. With respect to the activity of "rehearsing in imagination," the competing lines of actions-that-will-have-been-completed, the clarity, extent of detail, the number of alternatives, the vividness, and the amount of information which fills out each of the schemata of competing lines of action are often the intended features in calling a person's actions "rational."

(5) *Strategy.* Prior to the actual occasion of choice a person may assign to a set of alternative courses of action the conditions under which any one of them is to be followed. Von Neumann and Morgenstern have called the set of such decisions a player's strategy.[3] The set of such decisions can be called the strategy character of the actor's anticipations. A person whose anticipations are handled under the trust that his circumstances tomorrow will be like those he has known in the past is sometimes said to be acting with less rationality than the one who addresses alternatively possible future states of his present situation by the use of a manual of "what-to-do-in-case-of's."

(6) *Concern for timing.* When we say that a person intends through his behaviors to realize a future state of affairs, we frequently mean by such an intention that the person entertains an expectation of the scheduling of events. The concern for timing involves the extent to which he takes a position with regard to the possible ways in which events can temporally occur. A definite and restricted frame of scheduled possibilities is compared with a "lesser rationality" that consists of the person orienting the future fall of events under the aspect of "anything can happen."

(7) *Predictability.* Highly specific expectations of time scheduling can be accompanied by the person's paying concern to the predictable characteristics of a situation. He may seek preliminary information about it in order to establish some empirical constants or he may attempt to make the situation predictable by examining the logical properties of the constructs he uses in "defining" it or by reviewing the rules that govern the use of his constructs. Accordingly, making the situation predictable means taking whatever measures are possible to reduce "surprise." Both the desire for "surprise in small amounts" as well as the use of whatever measures yield it are frequently the behaviors intended by the term rationality in conduct.

(8) *Rules of procedure.* Sometimes rationality refers to rules of procedure and inference in terms of which a person decides the correctness of his judgments, inferences, perceptions, and characterizations. Such rules define the distinct ways in which a thing may be decided to be *known*—distinctions, for example, between fact, supposition, evidence, illustration, and conjecture. For our purposes two important classes of such rules of correct decisions may be distinguished: "Cartesian" rules and "tribal" rules. Cartesian rules propose that a decision is correct because the person followed the rules without respect for persons, i.e., that the decider decided as "any man" would do when all matters of social affiliation were treated as specifically irrelevant. By contrast, "tribal" rules provide that a decision is correct or not according to whether certain interpersonal solidarities are respected as conditions of the decision. The person counts his

decision right or wrong in accordance with whom it is referentially important that he be in agreement.

The term rationality is frequently used to refer to the application of Cartesian rules of decision. Because conventions may impose constraints on such decision-making, the extent to which the constraints are suppressed, controlled, or rendered ineffective or irrelevant is another frequent meaning of rationality.

(9) *Choice.* Sometimes the fact that a person is aware of the actual possibility of exercising a choice and sometimes the fact that he chooses are popular meanings of rationality.

(10) *Grounds of choice.* The grounds upon which a person exercises a choice among alternatives as well as the grounds he uses to legitimize a choice are frequently pointed out as rational features of an action. Several different behavioral meanings of the term "grounds" need to be discriminated.

(a) Rational grounds sometimes refer exclusively to the scientific *corpus*[4] of information as an inventory of propositions which is treated by the person as correct grounds of further inference and action.

(b) Rational grounds sometimes refer to such properties of a person's knowledge as the "fine" or "gross" structure of the characterizations he uses, or whether the "inventory" consists of a set of stories as compared with universal empirical laws, or the extent to which the materials are codified, or whether the *corpus* in use accords with the corpus of scientific propositions.

(c) Insofar as the grounds of choice are the strategies of action, as was noted before in point 5, another sense of rationality is involved.

(d) Grounds of a person's choice may be those which he quite literally *finds* through retrospectively interpreting a present outcome. For example, a person may realize such grounds in the course of historicizing an outcome in the effort to determine what was "really" decided at a prior time. Thus, if a present datum is treated as an-answer-to-some-question, the datum may motivate the question that the person seeks it to be

the answer to. Selecting, arranging, and unifying the historical context of an action after its occurrence so as to present a publicly acceptable or coherent account of it is a familiar meaning of "rationalization."

(11) *Compatibility of ends-means relationships with principles of formal logic.* A person may treat a contemplated course of action as an arrangement of steps in the solution of a problem. He may arrange these steps as a set of "ends-means" relationships but count the problem solved only if these relationships are accomplished without violating the ideal of full compatibility with the principles of formal scientific logic and the rules of scientific procedure.[5] The fact that he may do so, the frequency with which he does so, his persistence in treating problems in this way, or the success that he enjoys in following such procedure are alternative ways of specifying the rationality of his actions.

(12) *Semantic clarity and distinctness.* Reference is often made to a person's attempt to treat the semantic clarity of a construction as a variable with a maximum value which must be approximated as a required step in solving the problem of constructing a credible definition of a situation. A person who witholds credence until the condition of approximate maximum value has been met is frequently said to be more rational than another who will lend credence to a mystery.

A person may assign a high priority to the tasks of clarifying the constructs which make up a definition of a situation and of deciding the compatibility of such constructs with meanings intended in terminologies employed by others. On the other hand, the person may pay such tasks little concern. The former action is sometimes said to be more rational than the latter.

(13) *Clarity and distinctness "for its own sake."* Schutz points out that a concern for clarity and distinctness may be a concern for distinctness that is adequate for the person's purposes. Different possible relationships, ideal or actual, between (a) a concern for clarity and (b) the purposes which the clarity of the construct serves reveal additional behavioral meanings of rationality. Two

variables are involved: (1) the respect required for the tasks of clarification and (2) the value assigned by the person to the accomplishment of a project. One relationship between these variables makes the task of clarification itself the project to be accomplished. This is the meaning of "clarification for its own sake." But the relationship between the two variables may be treated by a person as consisting in some degree of independent variability. Such a relationship would be meant when treating as an ideal, "clarification that is sufficient for present purposes." Rationality frequently means a high degree of dependence of one upon the other. Such a dependence when treated as a rule of investigative or interpretive conduct is sometimes meant in the distinction between "pure" and "applied" research and theory.

(14) *Compatibility of the definition of a situation with scientific knowledge.* A person can allow what he treats as "matters of fact" to be criticized in terms of their compatibility with the body of scientific findings. As a description of a person's actions, the "allowed legitimacy of such criticism" means that in the case of a demonstrated discrepancy that what the person treats as correct grounds of inference and action (a meaning of "fact") will be changed by him to accommodate what is scientifically the case. Frequently, a person's actions are said to be rational to the extent that he accommodates or is prepared to accommodate in this fashion to what is scientifically the case.

Frequently rationality refers to the person's feelings that accompany his conduct, *e.g.* "affective neutrality," "unemotional," "detached," "disinterested," and "impersonal." For the theoretical tasks of this paper, however, the fact that a person may attend his environment with such feelings is uninteresting. It is of interest, however, that a person uses his feelings about his environment to recommend the sensible character of the thing he is talking about or the warrant of a finding. There is nothing that prohibits a scientific investigator from being passionately hopeful that his hypothesis will be confirmed. He is prohibited, however, from using his passionate hope or his detachment of feeling to recommend the sense or warrant of a proposition. A person who treats his feelings about a matter as irrelevant to its sense or warrant is sometimes said to be acting rationally, while a person who recommends sense and warrant by invoking his feelings is said to act with less rationality. This holds, however, only for ideally described scientific activities.

Notes

2. Alfred Schutz, "The Problem of Rationality in the Social World," *Economica,* Vol. 10, May, 1953.

3. John von Neumann and Oskar Morgenstern, *Theory of Games and Economic Behavior* (Princeton, N.J.: Princeton University Press, 1947), p. 79.

4. The concept of the *corpus* of knowledge is taken from Felix Kaufmann, *Methodology of the Social Sciences* (New York: Oxford University Press, 1944), especially pp. 33–88.

5. When treated as a rule for defining descriptive categories of action, this property is known as the rule of the empirical adequacy of means.

RAYMOND ARON

1905–1983

Raymond-Claude-Ferdinand Aron was born on March 14, 1905 in Paris, only child of a Jewish law professor, married Suzanne Gauchon on September 5, 1933, with whom he had one son and one daughter, and died at 78 in his hometown on October 17, 1983. He attended the Lycée Hoch in Versailles and the Lycée Condorcet in Paris, graduating in 1924. Like so many others of his intellectual caste, he attended the École Normale Superieure and there was certified to teach philosophy in lycées in 1928, winning the top spot in his class. He spent 1930 through 1933 in Germany (one year in Cologne and two in Berlin), which proved a pivotal intellectual experience. He taught in Le Havre (1933–34) and between 1934 and 1939 worked as a social researcher and professor in Paris at his alma mater. His doctoral dissertation there, *An Introduction to the Philosophy of History* (1938), was widely read in various languages, and is still considered a fundamental source in the area, in which he put to great use his facility in German and the knowledge he acquired while in Berlin. He taught briefly in Toulouse, served in the French air force for two years, and spent most of WWII as part of de Gaulle's government-in-exile in London, editing their official, *La France Libre*. He returned to Paris after the war and took up various academic posts, while also working as a journalist, developing an audience that spanned both politically alert readers among the laity and intellectuals concerned with history, social theory, and politics. His columns in *Le Figaro* appeared from 1947 through 1977, and became an essential part of the French cultural landscape, also appearing in *Les Temps modernes* and *Express,* in which he published a regular column. From 1955 through 1968 he was professor of sociology at the Sorbonne, where one of his assistants was Pierre Bourdieu. He ascended to the position of Professor of Sociology and Modern Civilization at the Collège de France in 1970.

Aron was uniquely positioned to communicate with German, Anglo-American, and French audiences simultaneously. His *Main Currents in Sociological Thought* (1960; tr. 1965/67) was a bestseller in the U.S. for years, his *Peace and War* (1962) became the standard work, and his many works on global peace and diplomacy always found ready audiences, including his temperate defense of the U.S. due to its imperialistic tendencies during Viet Nam. He was distinctly to the right of Sartre, his rival in the public sphere—his *Opium of the Intellectuals* (1955) was a brilliant attack on Marxist orthodoxy—but by today's standards was solidly liberal in the 19th century sense. He also wrote an admired biography of Clausewitz and many works on political prospects for the world system. He continues to be read and esteemed by moderate and mildly rightist theorists.

THE DAWN OF UNIVERSAL HISTORY, 1961

From the beginning of the nineteenth century, every European generation has believed in the uniqueness of its own period. Does the very persistence of this conviction in itself indicate that it was unfounded? Or was it rather a kind of premonition, the truth of which has been borne out by our own generation, and which must, therefore, have been false in the case of our predecessors? If we hesitate to ascribe error to so many generations, or rather to every generation but our own, can we suggest a third hypothesis, namely, that all of them have been right, not individually, but regarded as a whole, and not always in the ways that they thought?

In other words, it would seem to be a fact, or at least a plausible hypothesis, that the last century has seen a kind of revolution, or more precisely a *mutation,* which began before the nineteenth century, but whose rate of change has accelerated during the past few decades.

From the beginning of the last century onwards, every generation and every thinker has tried to define this historical mutation. Saint-Simon and Auguste Comte wrote of 'the industrial society', Alexis de Tocqueville of democratic society and Karl Marx of capitalist society. If we go back to the great theorists of the first half of the last century—from whom we derive our ideologies, if not our ideas—and compare their diagnoses and their prophecies with what has actually happened between their time and our own, we shall be able to reach a tentative definition of what I have called a historical mutation.

Let us begin with the school of Saint-Simon and Auguste Comte, who are now once again becoming fashionable, for the very comprehensible reason that the building up of large-scale industry on both sides of the iron curtain has at last compelled observers to recognize the existence of a certain type of society, of which the Soviet and Western systems represent two different species or variants. Why not describe this form of society

as industrial, since its characteristic is the development of industry?

This was, indeed, the central hypothesis of Saint-Simon and Auguste Comte. Both watched a new society in process of construction before their eyes, a society to which Europe had given birth, and which they described as industrial. The essential characteristics of this new society were more accurately described by Auguste Comte than by either Saint-Simon or even the Saint-Simonians. And although few today read the works of the founder of positivism, and still fewer devote any serious study to them, it is his definition of industrial society which we shall take as our starting point.

Like Saint-Simon, Comte stresses the contrast between producers—industrialists, farmers and bankers—and the political and military *élites* who, in a society devoted to peaceful activities, represent survivals from a feudal and theological past. Industrial society, as indeed all human society, has henceforth as its first objective the exploitation of natural resources. Wars, conquest and Caesars belong to the past. In the view of the philosophers of history, Napoleon, for all his genius, was guilty of the most serious of all crimes—that of being an anachronism. Roman conquests had a meaning. They were creative, because they prepared the way for a unified world in which the Christian religion was to spread, and because communities dedicated to war would at some point achieve peace through the victory of the strongest. In our time, however, conquest cannot be justified, because it no longer serves any purpose, because the spontaneous resistance and ultimate triumph of the people has revealed the error of Napoleon. When he came to power, the peoples of Europe were grateful for all that the French Revolution had done for them, but he transformed that heritage of sympathy into hatred.

Arguing with a dogmatism that some will feel to be characteristic of sociologists, Auguste Comte deduces the consequences, all the consequences, that follow from this change of objective. Henceforth it is labour, not war, which constitutes the supreme good. It is through men's labour that a society's *cadres* and leaders are formed, that individual prestige is generally recognized and individual status assured. There must, therefore, be freedom of labour. There must be no more rigid classification of families on the basis of class or occupation. Mobility must be the rule from one generation to another. Henceforth individuals are entitled to hope that their place in society will be determined on the basis of merit, without reference to the position of their parents. To Comte, the wage-earning class represented, not a modern form of slavery or serfdom, but the promise of individual liberation and of social mobility. Europe, or, more precisely, the nations of Western Europe—England, France, Italy, Spain and Germany—constitute the vanguard. The European nations were in advance of others in the pursuit of what was henceforth to be the common objective, namely, the exploitation of the resources of this planet, the creation of an industrial society and the unification within one single peaceful community of peoples dispersed throughout five continents. According to the high priest of positivism, Europe's advance did not confer privileges so much as impose obligations, and Auguste Comte warned his contemporaries against succumbing to the temptation of colonial adventures. Again and again he denounced the conquest of Algeria and even expressed the hope that the Arabs would 'pursue the French with vigour', if the French lacked the intelligence or the moral sense to withdraw of their own accord . . .

If we agree with Auguste Comte that men do not make war for its own sake or simply owing to their passion for conquest, then we must regard wars today as irrational, even though they have continued to exist. If the major objective of industrial societies is to achieve well-being through work, as spokesmen of both Soviet and Western society allege today, then the two European wars which have occurred during the course of this century were useless and there ought not to be a third.

Let us now consider another great theorist, who belongs to the generation following that of Auguste Comte. Karl Marx also recognized the existence of a historical mutation and, although he used a different vocabulary and different concepts, he emphasized the same essential fact, namely, that the forces of production had developed more rapidly than in any preceding century and this he saw as the achievement of bourgeois capitalism. Within the space of a few decades, the triumphant bourgeoisie had brought about changes in the

conditions and the methods of collective labour greater than any made by the leaders of feudal or military society during the previous thousand years.

There is agreement between the high priests of socialism and of positivism regarding the fundamental difference between modern and traditional societies. Both men consider that the uniqueness of modern society lies in the pride of place accorded to work, to the application of science to the techniques of production, and in the resultant increase in collective resources. The major difference between their two theories is that Marx attaches fundamental importance to the conflict between employers and employed, whilst Auguste Comte considers this to be a phenomenon of secondary importance, a symptom of social disintegration that will be corrected as organization improves.

Marx tends to explain everything—poverty in the midst of plenty in spite of the increased powers of production, the alienation of the workers, the despotism of the property-owning minority—as being due to the conflict between employers and employed, the class struggle between capitalists and the proletariat. His vision of the future of capitalism is, therefore, apocalyptic. The conflict between capitalists and proletariat will be intensified to the point at which an explosion ultimately occurs. Marx then sketches in outline an idyllic picture of the post-capitalist regime. He nowhere describes it, but he points out, by way of contrast, the benefits that it will confer. The specific characteristics of capitalism, namely, private ownership of the means of production, the capitalist minority's possession of economic power and, through intermediaries, of political power, are responsible for social inequalities, the exploitation of man by man and working-class alienation. It follows that, with the elimination of private property, and with the proletarian revolution, the prehistory of humanity will come to an end and a new era will be opened up, in which social progress will no longer depend on violence and political revolutions.

On the essential point of difference between Karl Marx and Auguste Comte, the former seems to me to have been right in the short term, but wrong in the long term. Conflicts between employers and employed, either within the industry or about the distribution of the national income, have not been decisive and they were, on the whole, more serious during the initial phases of industrialization than they have been in mature industrial societies. The working classes, organized in trade unions and protected by social legislation, often represented in Parliament by powerful Socialist parties, continue to press their claims, but they have been converted to peaceful and legal methods. They do not want a revolution which would establish the dictatorship of the proletariat. They are not really clear as to what a proletarian revolution would be. In their view, as in that of most observers, there is clear proof that private ownership of the means of production, as it exists today in Western society, does not prevent either the development of productive forces or a continued rise in the standard of living of the masses. . . .

Sociological theorists have failed to take into account the partial autonomy of the political order and have argued as if history, by which they meant the succession of wars and empires, victories and defeats, was henceforth ended. But the present century seems to me in 1960 to present two distinct faces. On the one hand it has witnessed an intellectual, technical and economic revolution, which, like some cosmic force, is carrying humanity towards an unknown future; on the other it is in many respects very like its predecessors. It is not the first century to have seen great wars. On the one hand, there is the need for progress; on the other there is *history as usual,*[1] with its drama of empires, armies and heroes.

Note

1. In English in the original.

FRANTZ FANON

1925–1961

Born into the middle class but eventually a hero to the globe's downtrodden, Frantz Omar Fanon was born in Fort-de-France, Martinique, French Antilles on July 20, 1925, married Josie Duble in 1952 (one son, Oliver), and died from leukemia in Bethesda, Maryland on December 6, 1961 at only 36. Through a sound, traditionally French education, he became aware of the role that cultural indoctrination plays in the creation and maintenance of racism and the colonialist mentality, something he began to fight early in his adult life. Convinced that colonial domination and the racism that necessarily accompanied it, in his native country and in north Africa were causing mental illness, he became a psychiatrist, educated in Martinique and France. He learned more about everyday racist practices while serving in the French Army in 1944, working with the Free French military apparatus in North Africa and in Europe, but was never allowed to put his full capabilities to the test due to his race. From 1953 through 1956 he was the head of the psychiatric unit at the Blida-Joinville Hospital in Blida, Algeria, where he had the rare opportunity to treat mental breakdowns in both the oppressed and oppressors because a revolution broke out while he was there. He was removed from this position because he became increasingly involved with the Algerian National Liberation Front. With help from like-minded Frenchmen, he was reassigned to a more sympathetic setting, moving to the Manouba Clinic and Neuropsychiatric Centre de Jour de Tunis in Tunisia (1957–59), a newly created independent state. There he became a writer of underground revolutionary literature, and taught at the University of Tunis in the mid-50s, and participated in the First Congress of Black Writers and Artists in Paris in 1956, as well as at the All African People's Conference in Accra in 1958. He served as ambassador to Ghana in 1961 on behalf of the Algerian Provisional Government, the rebel government. Struck by leukemia in 1960, he went to the U.S.S.R. for treatment, but realized that his chances for survival would be improved in the States, so he went to the National Institute of Health near Washington, D.C. With his last days of life, he finished *The Wretched of the Earth* (1961; tr. 1963), his fourth and by far most important work, and one that has inspired everyone in the developing countries, and their sympathizers abroad, who has sought to sever colonial relationships, economic and psychological, and bring the less developed countries into equality with the richer nations. This work brought together his clinical experiences with the ideas of Nietzsche, Sartre, and Marx, giving him particularly sharp insight into the distorting "white mask" under which black peoples labor to realize their ambitions. And *Black Skin, White Masks* (1952; tr. 1967) argued for African unification under black leadership.

THE WRETCHED OF THE EARTH, 1961

Concerning Violence

National liberation, national renaissance, the restoration of nationhood to the people, commonwealth: whatever may be the headings used or the new formulas introduced, decolonization is always a violent phenomenon. At whatever level we study it—relationships between individuals, new names for sports, clubs, the human admixture at cocktail parties, in the police, on the directing boards of national or private banks—decolonization is quite simply the replacing of a certain "species" of men. Without any period of transition, there is a total, complete, and absolute substitution. It is true that we could equally well stress the rise of a new nation, the setting up of a new state, its diplomatic relations, and its economic and political trends. But we have precisely chosen to speak of that kind of *tabula rasa* which characterizes at the outset all decolonization. Its unusual importance is that it constitutes, from the very first day, the minimum demands of the colonized. To tell the truth, the proof of success lies in a whole social structure being changed from the bottom up. The extraordinary importance of this change is that it is willed, called for, demanded. The need for this change exists in its crude state, impetuous and compelling, in the consciousness and in the lives of the men and women who are colonized. But the possibility of this change is equally experienced in the form of a terrifying future in the consciousness of another "species" of men and women: the colonizers.

Decolonization, which sets out to change the order of the world, is, obviously, a program of complete disorder. But it cannot come as a result of magical practices, nor of a natural shock, nor of a friendly understanding. Decolonization, as we know, is a historical process: that is to say that it cannot be understood, it cannot become intelligible nor clear to itself except in the exact measure that we can discern the movements which give it historical form and content. Decolonization is the meeting of two forces, opposed to each other by their very nature, which in fact owe their originality to that sort of substantification which results from and is nourished by the situation in the colonies. Their first encounter was marked by violence and their existence together—that is to say the exploitation of the native by the settler—was carried on by dint of a great array of bayonets and cannons. The settler and the native are old acquaintances. In fact, the settler is right when he speaks of knowing "them" well. For it is the settler who has brought the native into existence and who perpetuates his existence. The settler owes the fact of his very existence, that is to say, his property, to the colonial system.

Decolonization never takes place unnoticed, for it influences individuals and modifies them fundamentally. It transforms spectators crushed with their inessentiality into privileged actors, with the grandiose glare of history's floodlights upon them. It brings a natural rhythm into existence, introduced by new men, and with it a new language and a new humanity. Decolonization is the veritable creation of new men. But this creation owes nothing of its legitimacy to any supernatural power; the "thing" which has been colonized becomes man during the same process by which it frees itself.

In decolonization, there is therefore the need of a complete calling in question of the colonial situation. If we wish to describe it precisely, we might find it in the well-known words: "The last shall be first and the first last." Decolonization is the putting into practice of this sentence. That is why, if we try to describe it, all decolonization is successful.

The naked truth of decolonization evokes for us the searing bullets and bloodstained knives which emanate from it. For if the last shall be first, this will only come to pass after a murderous and decisive struggle between the two protagonists. That affirmed intention to place the last at the head of things, and to make them climb at a pace (too quickly, some say) the well-known steps which characterize an organized society, can only triumph if we use all means to turn the scale, including, of course, that of violence.

You do not turn any society, however primitive it may be, upside down with such a program if you have not decided from the very beginning, that is to say from the actual formulation of that program, to overcome all the obstacles that you will come across in so doing. The native who decides to put the program into practice, and to become its moving force, is ready for violence at all times. From birth it is clear to him that this narrow world, strewn with prohibitions, can only be called in question by absolute violence.

The colonial world is a world divided into compartments. It is probably unnecessary to recall the existence of native quarters and European quarters, of schools for natives and schools for Europeans; in the same way we need not recall apartheid in South Africa. Yet, if we examine closely this system of compartments, we will at least be able to reveal the lines of force it implies. This approach to the colonial world, its ordering and its geographical layout will allow us to mark out the lines on which a decolonized society will be reorganized.

The colonial world is a world cut in two. The dividing line, the frontiers are shown by barracks and police stations. In the colonies it is the policeman and the soldier who are the official, instituted go-betweens, the spokesmen of the settler and his rule of oppression. In capitalist societies the educational system, whether lay or clerical, the structure of moral reflexes handed down from father to son, the exemplary honesty of workers who are given a medal after fifty years of good and loyal service, and the affection which springs from harmonious relations and good behavior—all these aesthetic expressions of respect for the established order serve to create around the exploited person an atmosphere of submission and of inhibition which lightens the task of policing considerably. In the capitalist countries a multitude of moral teachers, counselors and "bewilderers" separate the exploited from those in power. In the colonial countries, on the contrary, the policeman and the soldier, by their immediate presence and their frequent and direct action maintain contact with the native and advise him by means of rifle butts and napalm not to budge. It is obvious here that the agents of government speak the language of pure force. The intermediary does not lighten the oppression, nor seek to hide the domination; he shows them up and puts them into practice with the clear conscience of an upholder of the peace; yet he is the bringer of violence into the home and into the mind of the native.

The zone where the natives live is not complementary to the zone inhabited by the settlers. The two zones are opposed, but not in the service of a higher unity. Obedient to the rules of pure Aristotelian logic, they both follow the principle of reciprocal exclusivity. No conciliation is possible, for of the two terms, one is superfluous. The settlers' town is a strongly built town, all made of stone and steel. It is a brightly lit town; the streets are covered with asphalt, and the garbage cans swallow all the leavings, unseen, unknown and hardly thought about. The settler's feet are never visible, except perhaps in the sea; but there you're never close enough to see them. His feet are protected by strong shoes although the streets of his town are clean and even, with no holes or stones. The settler's town is a well-fed town, an easygoing town; its belly is always full of good things. The settlers' town is a town of white people, of foreigners.

The town belonging to the colonized people, or at least the native town, the Negro village, the medina, the reservation, is a place of ill fame, peopled by men of evil repute. They are born there, it matters little where or how, they die there, it matters not where, nor how. It is a world without spaciousness; men live there on top of each other, and their huts are built one on top of the other. The native town is a hungry town, starved of bread, of meat, of shoes, of coal, of light. The native town is a crouching village, a town on its knees, a town wallowing in the mire. It is a town of niggers and dirty Arabs. The look that the native turns on the settler's town is a look of lust, a look of envy; it expresses his dreams of possession—all manner of possession: to sit at the settler's table, to sleep in the settler's bed, with his wife if possible. The colonized man is an envious man. And this the settler knows very well; when their glances meet he ascertains bitterly, always on the defensive, "They want to take our place." It is true, for there is no native who does not dream at least once a day of setting himself up in the settler's place.

This world divided into compartments, this world cut in two is inhabited by two different species. The originality of the colonial context is that economic reality, inequality, and the immense difference of ways of life never come to mask the human realities. When you examine at close quarters the colonial context, it is evident that what parcels out the world is to begin with the fact of belonging to or not belonging to a given race, a given species. In the colonies the economic substructure is also a superstructure. The cause is the consequence; you are rich because you are white, you are white because you are rich. This is why Marxist analysis should always be slightly stretched every time we have to do with the colonial problem.

Everything up to and including the very nature of precapitalist society, so well explained by Marx, must here be thought out again. The serf is in essence different from the knight, but a reference to divine right is necessary to legitimize this statutory difference. In the colonies, the foreigner coming from another country imposed his rule by means of guns and machines. In defiance of his successful transplantation, in spite of his appropriation, the settler still remains a foreigner. It is neither the act of owning factories, nor estates, nor a bank balance which distinguishes the governing classes. The governing race is first and foremost those who come from elsewhere, those who are unlike the original inhabitants, "the others."

The violence which has ruled over the ordering of the colonial world, which has ceaselessly drummed the rhythm for the destruction of native social forms and broken up without reserve the systems of reference of the economy, the customs of dress and external life, that same violence will be claimed and taken over by the native at the moment when, deciding to embody history in his own person, he surges into the forbidden quarters. To wreck the colonial world is henceforward a mental picture of action which is very clear, very easy to understand and which may be assumed by each one of the individuals which constitute the colonized people. To break up the colonial world does not mean that after the frontiers have been abolished lines of communication will be set up between the two zones. The destruction of the colonial world is no more and no less that the abolition of one zone, its burial in the depths of the earth or its expulsion from the country.

JÜRGEN HABERMAS

1929–

The second of three children, Jürgen Habermas was born in Düsseldorf, Germany on June 18, 1929, his father a business and chamber of commerce leader with doctorate, and his mother the daughter of a brewer. In 1955 he married a teacher, Ute Wesselhöft, and with her had three children, Tilmann (psychologist), Rebecca (historian), and Judith. He grew up in Gummersbach, graduating from its *gymnasium* in 1949. He pursued philosophy, history, psychology, and economics at the universities of Göttingen, Zürich, and Bonn (1950–54). Habermas received the doctorate in philosophy at Bonn in 1954 with a dissertation entitled "The Absolute in History" concerning Friedrich Schelling (1775–1854). He worked as a journalist for the next two years, learning to write very rapidly, a habit he has put to extraordinary use as an academic author. Habermas became Theodor Adorno's assistant in Frankfurt from 1956 through 1959, then wrote an habilitation in 1961 under Wolfgang Abendroth called "Structural Change of the Public Sphere" (since neither Adorno nor Max Horkheimer would agree to sponsor the work). This work, especially after being translated into English in 1984, has proved to be quite influential across social science disciplines, and also gave a particular direction to Habermas's writing for the rest of his career, focusing on the need for openness in public communication. He taught at Heidelberg until 1964, then moved to Frankfurt until 1971 when he resigned because of differences with the ebullient student protest movement. From there he went to the Max Planck Institute in Starnberg, Bavaria until 1982, whereupon he returned to Frankfurt.

Habermas has become a virtual writing machine over the last 30 years, turning out something like a book per annum, some of them very large and complex in nature. Partly this reflects standard European publishing practice, in which favored professors are seldom pared down or edited, but simply publish whatever they write (unlike the U.S. system of manuscript critiques by peers and editors), but it also is a function of Habermas's astoundingly fertile imagination in bringing together disparate streams of thought. While he is not a true expert on Freud, Dilthey, Durkheim, Weber, Hegel, Marx, Mead, or Parsons, he has written at some length about all of them (and scores of other theorists), always with an eye toward furthering his own agenda, which itself is fairly simple. Having matured during the Third Reich, too young to fight but too old to ignore the Nazi regime, he has become literally obsessed with the most propitious grounds whereby rational discourse can occur and despotic thought-control can be avoided. In his masterpiece, *The Theory of Communicative Action* (1977; tr. 1984/85), Habermas goes to extreme lengths in debating previous thinkers in order to show that rationality is a public achievement, and that any future society worthy of serious consideration must be built on open channels of noncoercive communication. His other important works include *Knowledge and Human Interests*

(1968; tr.1971), in many critics' opinion his best book; *Legitimation Crisis* (1973; tr. 1975), with which he reintroduced a term borrowed from Weber and gave it new life; *The Philosophical Discourse of Modernity* (1987), and *Between Facts and Norms* (1996). Habermas's scholarly writing—as opposed to his interviews and journalism—is famously turgid and convoluted, which often obscures the basic simplicity of his views. He is by all reckoning the leading social theorist of the day, and even though in his mid-70s, continues writing at a furious pace.

"THE PUBLIC SPHERE," 1962/73

Concept

By "public sphere" we mean first of all a domain of our social life in which such a thing as public opinion can be formed. Access to the public sphere is open in principle to all citizens. A portion of the public sphere is constituted in every conversation in which private persons come together to form a public. They are then acting neither as business or professional people conducting their private affairs, nor as legal consociates subject to the legal regulations of a state bureaucracy and obligated to obedience. Citizens act as a public when they deal with matters of general interest without being subject to coercion; thus with the guarantee that they may assemble and unite freely, and express and publicize their opinions freely. When the public is large, this kind of communication requires certain means of dissemination and influence; today, newspapers and periodicals, radio and television are the media of the public sphere. We speak of a political public sphere (as distinguished from a literary one, for instance) when the public discussions concern objects connected with the practice of the state. The coercive power of the state is the counterpart, as it were, of the political public sphere, but it is not a part of it. State power is, to be sure, considered "public" power, but it owes the attribute of publicness to its task of caring for the public, that is, providing for the common good of all legal consociates. Only when the exercise of public authority has actually been subordinated to the requirement of democratic publicness does the political public sphere acquire an institutionalized influence on the government, by way of the legislative body. The term "public opinion" refers to the functions of criticism and control of organized state authority that the public exercises informally, as well as formally during periodic elections. Regulations concerning the publicness (or publicity [*Publizität*] in its original meaning) of state-related activities, as, for instance, the public accessibility required of legal proceedings, are also connected with this function of public opinion. To the public sphere as a sphere mediating between state and society, a sphere in which the public as the vehicle of public opinion is formed, there corresponds the principle of publicness—the publicness that once had to win out against the secret politics of monarchs and that since then has permitted democratic control of state activity.

It is no accident that these concepts of the public sphere and public opinion were not formed until the eighteenth century. They derive their specific meaning from a concrete historical situation. It was then that one learned to distinguish between opinion and public opinion, or *opinion publique*. Whereas mere opinions (things taken for granted as part of a culture, normative convictions, collective prejudices and judgments) seem to persist unchanged in their quasi-natural structure as a kind of sediment of history, public opinion, in terms of its very idea, can be formed only if a public that engages in rational discussion exists. Public discussions that are institutionally protected and that take, with critical intent, the exercise of political authority as their theme have not existed since time immemorial—they developed only in a specific phase of bourgeois society, and only by virtue of a specific constellation of interests could they be incorporated into the order of the bourgeois constitutional state.

History

It is not possible to demonstrate the existence of a public sphere in its own right, separate from the private sphere, in the European society of the High Middle Ages. At the same time, however, it is not a coincidence that the attributes of authority at that time were called "public." For a public representation of authority existed at that time. At all levels of the pyramid established by feudal law, the status of the feudal lord is neutral with respect to the categories "public" and "private"; but the person possessing that status represents it publicly; he displays himself, represents himself as the embodiment of a "higher" power, in whatever degree. This concept of representation has survived into recent constitutional history. Even today the power of political authority on its highest level, however much it has become detached from its former basis, requires representation through the head of state. But such elements derive from a prebourgeois social structure. Representation in the sense of the bourgeois public sphere, as in "representing" the nation or specific clients, has nothing to do with *representative publicness,* which inheres in the concrete existence of a lord. As long as the prince and the estates of his realm "are" the land, rather than merely "representing" it, they are capable of this kind of representation; they represent their authority "before" the people rather than for the people.

The feudal powers (the church, the prince, and the nobility) to which this representative publicness adheres disintegrated in the course of a long process of polarization; by the end of the eighteenth century they had decomposed into private elements on the one side and public on the other. The position of the church changed in connection with the Reformation: the tie to divine authority that the church represented, that is, religion, became a private matter. Historically, what is called the freedom of religion safe-guarded the first domain of private autonomy; the church itself continued its existence as one corporate body under public law among others. The corresponding polarization of princely power acquired visible form in the separation of the public budget from the private household property of the feudal lord. In the bureaucracy and the military (and in part also in the administration of justice), institutions of public power became autonomous vis-a-vis the privatized sphere of the princely court. In terms of the estates, finally, elements from the ruling groups developed into organs of public power, into parliament (and in part also into judicial organs); elements from the occupational status groups, insofar as they had become established in urban corporations and in certain differentiations within the estates of the land, developed into the sphere of bourgeois society, which would confront the state as a genuine domain of private autonomy.

Representative publicness gave way to the new sphere of "public power" that came into being with the national and territorial states. Ongoing state activity (permanent administration, a standing army) had its counterpart in the permanence of relationships that had developed in the meantime with the stock market and the press, through traffic in goods and news. Public power became consolidated as something tangible confronting those who were subject to it and who at first found themselves only negatively defined by it. These are the "private persons" who are excluded from public power because they hold no office. "Public" no longer refers to the representative court of a person vested with authority; instead, it now refers to the competence-regulated activity of an apparatus furnished with a monopoly on the legitimate use of force. As those to whom this public power is addressed, private persons subsumed under the state form the public.

As a private domain, society, which has come to confront the state, as it were, is on the one hand clearly differentiated from public power; on the other hand, society becomes a matter of public interest insofar as with the rise of a market economy the reproduction of life extends beyond the confines of private domestic power. The *bourgeois public sphere* can be understood as the sphere of private persons assembled to form a public. They soon began to make use of the public sphere of informational newspapers, which was officially regulated, against the public power itself, using those papers, along with the morally and critically oriented weeklies, to engage in debate about the general rules governing relations in their own essentially privatized but publicly relevant sphere of commodity exchange and labor.

The Liberal Model of the Public Sphere

The medium in which this debate takes place—public discussion—is unique and without historical prototype. Previously the estates had negotiated contracts with their princes in which claims to power were defined on case-by-case basis. As we know, this development followed a different course in England, where princely power was relativized through parliament, than on the Continent, where the estates were mediatized by the monarch. The "third estate" then broke with this mode of equalizing power, for it could no longer establish itself as a ruling estate. Given a commercial economy, a division of authority accomplished through differentiation of the rights of those possessing feudal authority (liberties belonging to the estates) was no longer possible—the power under private law of disposition of capitalist property is nonpolitical. The bourgeois are private persons; as such, they do not "rule." Thus their claims to power in opposition to public power are directed not against a concentration of authority that should be "divided" but rather against the principle of established authority. The principle of control, namely publicness, that the bourgeois public opposes to the principle of established authority aims at a transformation of authority as such, not merely the exchange of one basis of legitimation for another.

In the first modern constitutions the sections listing basic rights provide an image of the liberal model of the public sphere: they guarantee society as a sphere of private autonomy; opposite it stands a public power limited to a few functions; between the two spheres, as it were, stands the domain of private persons who have come together to form a public and who, as citizens of the state, mediate the state with the needs of bourgeois so-

ciety, in order, as the idea goes, to thus convert political authority to "rational" authority in the medium of this public sphere. Under the presuppositions of a society based on the free exchange of commodities, it seemed that the general interest, which served as the criterion by which this kind of rationality was to be evaluated, would be assured if the dealings of private persons in the marketplace were emancipated from social forces and their dealings in the public sphere were emancipated from political coercion.

The political daily press came to have an important role during this same period. In the second half of the eighteenth century, serious competition to the older form of news writing as the compiling of items of information arose in the form of literary journalism. Karl Bücher describes the main outlines of this development: "From mere institutions for the publication of news, newspapers became the vehicles and guides of public opinion as well, weapons of party politics. The consequence of this for the internal organization of the newspaper enterprise was the insertion of a new function between the gathering of news and its publication: the editorial function. For the newspaper publisher, however, the significance of this development was that from a seller of new information he became a dealer in public opinion." Publishers provided the commercial basis for the newspaper without, however, commercializing it as such. The press remained an institution of the public itself, operating to provide and intensify public discussion, no longer a mere organ for the conveyance of information, but not yet a medium of consumer culture.

This type of press can be observed especially in revolutionary periods, when papers associated with the tiniest political coalitions and groups spring up, as in Paris in 1789. In the Paris of 1848 every halfway prominent politician still formed his own club, and every other one founded his own *journal:* over 450 clubs and more than 200 papers came into being there between February and May alone. Until the permanent legalization of a public sphere that functioned politically, the appearance of a political newspaper was equivalent to engagement in the struggle for a zone of freedom for public opinion, for publicness as a principle. Not until the establishment of the bourgeois constitutional state was a press engaged in the public use of reason relieved of the pressure of ideological viewpoints. Since then it has been able to abandon its polemical stance and take advantage of the earning potential of commercial activity. The ground was cleared for this development from a press of viewpoints to a commercial press at about the same time in England, France, and the United States, during the 1830s. In the course of this transformation from the journalism of writers who were private persons to the consumer services of the mass media, the sphere of publicness was changed by an influx of private interests that achieved privileged representation within it.

The Public Sphere in Mass Welfare-State Democracies

The liberal model of the public sphere remains instructive in regard to the normative claim embodied in institutionalized requirements of publicness; but it is not applicable to actual relationships within a mass democracy that is industrially advanced and constituted as a social-welfare state. In part, the liberal model had always contained ideological aspects; in part, the social presuppositions to which those aspects were linked have undergone fundamental changes. Even the forms in which the public sphere was manifested, forms which made its idea seem to a certain extent obvious, began to change with the Chartist movement in England and the February Revolution in France. With the spread of the press and propaganda, the public expanded beyond the confines of the bourgeoisie. Along with its social exclusivity the public lost the cohesion given it by institutions of convivial social intercourse and by a relatively high standard of education. Accordingly, conflicts which in the past were pushed off into the private sphere now enter the public sphere. Group needs, which cannot expect satisfaction from a self-regulating market, tend toward state regulation. The public sphere, which must now mediate these demands, becomes a field for competition among interests in the cruder form of forcible confrontation. Laws that have obviously originated under the "pressure of the streets" can scarcely continue to be understood in terms of a consensus achieved by private persons in public discussion; they correspond, in more or less undisguised form, to compromises between conflicting private interests. Today it is social organizations that act in relation to the state in the political public sphere, whether through the mediation of political parties or directly, in interplay with public administration. With the interlocking of the public and private domains, not only do political agencies take over certain functions in the sphere of commodity exchange and social labor; societal powers also take over political functions. This leads to a kind of "refeudalization" of the public sphere. Large-scale organizations strive for political compromises with the state and with one another, behind closed doors if possible; but at the same time they have to secure at least plebiscitarian approval from the mass of the population through the deployment of a staged form of publicity.

The political public sphere in the welfare state is characterized by a singular weakening of its critical functions. Whereas at one time publicness was intended to subject persons or things to the public use of reason and to make political decisions susceptible to revision before the tribunal of public opinion, today it has often enough already been enlisted in the aid of the secret policies of interest groups; in the form of "publicity" it now acquires public prestige for persons or things and renders them capable of acclamation in a climate of nonpublic opinion. The term "public relations" itself indicates how a public sphere that formerly emerged from the structure of society must now be produced circumstantially on a case-by-case basis. The central relationship of the public, political parties, and parliament is also affected by this change in function.

This existing trend toward the weakening of the public sphere, as a principle, is opposed, however, by a welfare-state transformation of the functioning of basic rights: the requirement of publicness is extended by state organs to all organizations acting in relation to the state. To the extent to which this becomes a reality, a no longer intact public of private persons acting as individuals would be replaced by a public of organized private persons. Under current circumstances, only the latter could participate effectively in a process of public communication using the channels of intra-party and intra-organizational public spheres, on the basis of a publicness enforced for the dealings of organizations with the state. It is in this process of public communication that the formation of political compromises would have to achieve legitimation. The idea of the public sphere itself, which signified a rationalization of authority in the medium of public discussions among private persons, and which has been preserved in mass welfare-state democracy, threatens to disintegrate with the structural transformation of the public sphere. Today it could be realized only on a different basis, as a rationalization of the exercise of social and political power under the mutual control of rival organizations committed to publicness in their internal structure as well as in their dealings with the state and with one another.

~~~

THEORY AND PRACTICE, 1971

Dogmatism, Reason, and Decision

In the major tradition of philosophy, the relation of theory and praxis always referred to the good and the righteous—as well as the "true"—and to the life, both private and collective, of individuals as well as of citizens. In the eighteenth century this dimension of a theoretically guided praxis of life was extended by the philosophy of history. Since then, theory, directed toward praxis and at the same time dependent on it, no longer embraces the natural, authentic, or essential actions and institutions of a human race constant in its essential nature; instead, theory now deals with the objective, overall complex of development of a human species which produces itself, which is as yet only destined to attain its essence: humanity. What has remained is theory's claim of providing orientation in right action, but the realization of the good, happy, and rational life has been stretched out along the vertical axis of world-history; praxis has been extended to cover stages of emancipation. For this rational praxis is now interpreted as liberation from an externally imposed compulsion, just as the theory which is guided by

this interest of liberation is interpreted as enlightenment. The cognitive interest of this enlightenment theory is declaredly critical; it presupposes a specific experience, which is set down in Hegel's *Phenomenology of Mind,* just as it is in Freud's psychoanalysis—the experience of an emancipation by means of critical insight into relationships of power, the objectivity of which has as its source solely that the relationships have not been seen through. Critical reason gains power analytically over dogmatic inhibition.

Reason takes up a partisan position in the controversy between critique and dogmatism, and with each new stage of emancipation it wins a further victory. In this kind of practical reason, insight and the explicit interest in liberation by means of reflection converge. The higher level of reflection coincides with a step forward in the progress toward the autonomy of the individual, with the elimination of suffering and the furthering of concrete happiness. Reason involved in the argument against dogmatism has definitely taken up this interest as its own—it does not define the moment of decision as external to its sphere. Rather, the decisions of the subjects are measured rationally against that one objective decision, which is required by the interest of reason itself. Reason has not as yet renounced the will to the rational.

Now this constellation of dogmatism, reason, and decision has changed profoundly since the eighteenth century, and exactly to the degree to which the positive sciences have become productive forces in social development. For as our civilization has become increasingly scientific, the dimension within which theory was once directed toward praxis has become correspondingly constructed. The laws of self-reproduction demand of an industrially advanced society that it look after its survival on the escalating scale of a continually expanded technical control over nature and a continually refined administration of human beings and their relations to each other by means of social organization. In this system, science, technology, industry, and administration interlock in a circular process. In this process the relationship of theory to praxis can now only assert itself as the purposive-rational application of techniques assured by empirical science. The social potential of science is reduced to the powers of technical control—its potential for enlightenment is no longer considered. The empirical, analytical sciences pro-

From *Theory and Practice,* by Jürgen Habermas. English translation copyright © 1973 by Beacon Press. Reprinted by permission of Beacon Press, Boston.

duce technical recommendations, but they furnish no answer to practical questions. The claim by which theory was once related to praxis has become dubious. Emancipation by means of enlightenment is replaced by instruction in control over objective or objectified processes. Socially effective theory is no longer directed toward the consciousness of human beings who live together and discuss matters with each other, but to the behavior of human beings who manipulate. As a productive force of industrial development, it changes the basis of human life, but it no longer reaches out critically, beyond this basis to raise life itself, for the sake of life, to another level.

But, of course, the real difficulty in the relation of theory to praxis does not arise from this new function of science as a technological force, but rather from the fact that we are no longer able to distinguish between practical and technical power. Yet even a civilization that has been rendered scientific is not granted dispensation from practical questions; therefore a peculiar danger arises when the process of scientification transgresses the limit of technical questions, without, however, departing from the level of reflection of a rationality confined to the technological horizon. For then no attempt at all is made to attain a rational consensus on the part of citizens concerning the practical control of their destiny. Its place is taken by the attempt to attain technical control over history by perfecting the administration of society, an attempt that is just as impractical as it is unhistorical. When theory was still related to praxis in a genuine sense, it conceived of society as a system of action by human beings, who communicate through speech and thus must realize social intercourse within the context of conscious communication. Through this communication they must form themselves into a collective subject of the whole, that is capable of action—otherwise, the fortunes of a society ever more rigidly rationalized in its particular parts must slip away as a whole from that rational cultivation, which they require all the more urgently. On the other hand, a theory which confuses control with action is no longer capable of such a perspective. It understands society as a nexus of behavioral modes, for which rationality is mediated solely by the understanding of sociotechnical controls, but not by a coherent total consciousness—not by precisely that interested reason which can only attain practical power through the minds of politically enlightened citizens.

In industrially advanced society, research, technology, production, and administration have coalesced into a system which cannot be surveyed as a whole, but in which they are functionally interdependent. This has literally become the basis of our life: we are related to it in a peculiar manner, at the same time intimate and yet estranged. On the one hand, we are bound externally to this basis by a network of organizations and a chain of consumer goods; on the other hand, this basis is shut off from our knowledge, and even more from our reflection. The paradox of this state of affairs will, of course, only be recognized by a theory oriented toward praxis, even though this paradox is so evident: the more the growth and change of society are determined by the most extreme rationality of processes of research, subject to a division of labor, the less rooted is this civilization, now rendered scientific, in the knowledge and conscience of its citizens. In this discrepancy, scientifically guided techniques and those of decision theory—and ultimately even cybernetically controlled techniques—encounter a limitation which they cannot overcome; this can only be altered by a change in the state of consciousness itself, by the practical effect of a theory which does not improve the manipulation of things and of reifications, but which instead advances the interest of reason in human adulthood, in the autonomy of action and in the liberation from dogmatism. This it achieves by means of the penetrating ideas of a persistent critique.

⁓

THE PHILOSOPHICAL DISCOURSE OF MODERNITY, 1987

Modernity's Consciousness of Time and Its Need for Self-Reassurance

In his famous introduction to the collection of his studies on the sociology of religion, Max Weber takes up the "problem of universal history" to which his scholarly life was dedicated, namely, the question why, outside Europe, "the scientific, the artistic, the political, or the economic development . . . did not enter upon that path of rationalization which is peculiar to the Occident?" For Weber, the intrinsic (that is, not merely contingent) relationship between modernity and what he called "Occidental rationalism" was still self-evident. He described as "rational" the process of disenchantment which led in Europe to a disintegration of religious world views that issued in a secular culture. With the modern empirical sciences, autonomous arts, and theories of morality and law grounded on principles, cultural spheres of value took shape which made possible learning processes in accord with the respective inner logics of theoretical, aesthetic, and moral-practical problems.

What Weber depicted was not only the secularization of Western *culture,* but also and especially the development of modern *societies* from the viewpoint of rationalization. The new structures of society were marked by the differentiation of the two functionally intermeshing systems that had taken shape around the organizational cores of the capitalist enterprise and the bureaucratic state apparatus. Weber understood this process as the institutionalization of purposive-rational economic and administrative action. To the degree that everyday life was affected by this cultural and societal rationalization, traditional forms of life—which in the early modern period were differentiated primarily according to one's trade—were dissolved. The modernization of the lifeworld is not determined only by structures of purposively rationality. Emile Durkheim and George Herbert Mead saw rationalized lifeworlds as characterized by the reflective treatment of traditions that have lost their quasinatural status; by the universalization of norms of action and the generalization of values, which set communicative action free from narrowly restricted contexts and enlarge the field of options; and finally, by patterns of socialization that are oriented to the formation of abstract ego-identities and force the individuation of the growing child. This is, in broad strokes, how the classical social theorists drew the picture of modernity.

Today Max Weber's theme appears in another light; this is as much the result of the labors of those who invoke him as of the work of his critics. "Modernization" was introduced as a technical term only in the 1950s. It is the mark of a theoretical approach that takes up Weber's problem but elaborates it with the tools of social-scientific functionalism. The concept of modernization refers to a bundle of processes that are cumulative and mutually reinforcing: to the formation of capital and the mobilization of resources; to the development of the forces of production and the increase in the productivity of labor: to the establishment of centralized political power and the formation of national identities; to the proliferation of rights of political participation, of urban forms of life, and of formal schooling; to the secularization of values and norms; and so on. The theory of modernization performs two abstractions on Weber's concept of "modernity." It dissociates "modernity" from its modern European origins and stylizes it into a spatio-temporally neutral model for processes of social development in general. Furthermore, it breaks the internal connections between modernity and the historical context of Western rationalism, so that processes of modernization can no longer be conceived of as rationalization, as the historical objectification of rational structures. James Coleman sees in this the advantage that a concept of modernization generalized in terms of a theory of evolution is no longer burdened with the idea of a completion of modernity, that is to say, of a goal state after which "postmodern" developments would have to set in.

Indeed it is precisely modernization research that has contributed to the currency of the expression "postmodern" even among social scientists. For in view of an evolutionarily autonomous, self-promoting modernization, social-scientific observers can all the more easily take leave of the conceptual horizon of Western rationalism in which modernity arose. But as soon as the internal links between the concept of modernity and the self-understanding of modernity gained within the horizon of Western reason have been dissolved, we can relativize the, as it were, automatically continuing processes of modernization from the distantiated standpoint of a postmodern observer. Arnold Gehlen brought this down to the formula: The premises of the Enlightenment are dead; only their consequences continue on. From this perspective, a self-sufficiently advancing modernization of society has separated itself from the impulses of a cultural modernity that has seemingly become obsolete in the meantime; it only carries out the functional laws of economy and state, technology and science, which are supposed to have amalgamated into a system that cannot be influenced. The relentless acceleration of social processes appears as the reverse side of a culture that is exhausted and has passed into a crystalline state. Gehlen calls modern culture "crystallized" because "the possibilities implanted in it have all been developed in their basic elements. Even the counterpossibilities and antitheses have been uncovered and assimilated, so that henceforth changes in the premises have become increasingly unlikely. . . . If you have this impression, you will perceive crystalization . . . even in a realm as astonishingly dynamic and full of variety as that of modern painting." Because "the history of ideas has concluded," Gehlen can observe with a sigh of relief that "we have arrived at *posthistoire*." With Gottfried Benn he imparts the advice: "Count up your supplies." This *neoconservative* leave-taking from modernity is directed, then, not to the unchecked dynamism of societal modernization but to the husk of a cultural self-understanding of modernity that appear to have been overtaken.

In a completely different political form, namely an anarchist one, the idea of postmodernity appears among theoreticians who do not see that any uncoupling of modernity and rationality has set in. They, too, advertise the end of the Enlightenment; they, too, move beyond the horizon of the tradition of reason in which European modernity once understood itself; and they plant their feet in *posthistoire*. But unlike the neoconservative, the anarchist farewell to modernity is meant for society and culture in the same degree. As that continent of basic concepts bearing We-

ber's Occidental rationalism sinks down, reason makes known its true identity—it becomes unmasked as the subordinating and at the same time itself subjugated subjectivity, as the will to instrumental mastery. The subversive force of this critique, which pulls away the veil of reason from before the sheer will to power, is at the same time supposed to shake the iron cage in which the spirit of modernity has been objectified in societal form. From this point of view, the modernization of society cannot survive the end of the cultural modernity from which it arose. It cannot hold its own against the "primordial" anarchism under whose sign postmodernity marches.

However distinct these two readings of the theory of post-modernity are, both reject the basic conceptual horizon within which the self-understanding of European modernity has been formed. Both theories of postmodernity pretend to have gone beyond this horizon, to have left it behind as the horizon of a past epoch. Hegel was the first philosopher to develop a clear concept of modernity. We have to go back to him if we want to understand the internal relationship between modernity and rationality, which, until Max Weber, remained self-evident and which today is being called into question. We have to get clear on the Hegelian concept of modernity to be able to judge whether the claim of those who base their analyses on other premises is legitimate. At any rate, we cannot dismiss a priori the suspicion that postmodern thought merely claims a transcendent status, while it remains in fact dependent on presuppositions of the modern self-understanding that were brought to light by Hegel. We cannot exclude from the outset the possibility that neoconservatism and aesthetically inspired anarchism, in the name of a farewell to modernity, are merely trying to revolt against it once again. It could be that they are merely cloaking their complicity with the venerable tradition of counter-Enlightenment in the garb of post-Enlightenment.

MARY DOUGLAS

1921–

Mary Tews Douglas was born in 1921 in San Remo, Italy, married James A. T. Douglas, and with him had two sons and one daughter. Despite her Anglo-Saxon name, she is identified as an Italian national. She took her three degrees from Oxford in anthropology. Douglas worked as a British civil servant from 1943 through 1946, then did ethnographic fieldwork in the Congo (1949–50), returning to Oxford as a lecturer in anthropology in 1951, finally moving to the University of London where she rose in the ranks to full professor of social anthropology (1951–77). Since 1977 she has worked for the Russell Sage Foundation in New York City, directing its culture program.

Douglas has written a number of books, including *Peoples of the Lake Nyasa Region* (1950), *The Lele of the Kasai* (1963), *Natural Symbols* (1970), and *How Institutions Think* (1986). She is best known to social theorists, however, for her more speculative essays contained in two books, *Purity and Danger: An Analysis of Concepts of Pollution and Taboo* (1966; rev. 1969) and *Risk and Blame: Essays in Cultural Theory* (1992). Douglas returned to the Bible, specifically Leviticus, chapter 11 and Deuteronomy, chapter 14, as a beginning point for the analysis of taboos used in premodern societies. She argues that one of the essential requisites for the persistence of such societies is their ability to separate and distinguish their members from those who belong to competing groups. They do this by means of rituals and taboos concerning defilement and pollution, particularly relating to special eating ceremonies, food and drink that must be avoided or embraced, totemic badges of various kinds which tribal members must wear in order to illustrate their affiliation, and so on. The point for such people is to show their compatriots and their enemies that they belong to a particular tribe or culture, and that their boundedness is the most significant feature of their lives. Max Weber well illustrates her point when he wrote about the extreme lengths to which Indian Brahmins would go in order to preserve themselves from defilement by lower caste cooks, so that a food preparer not only had to be of the correct caste to make food for a Brahmin, but if a lower caste person touched the food in any way, it became instantly inedible and literally repulsive. Douglas herself gives examples from Mosaic law that illustrate the "logic" of restrictive norms regarding meat eating, such that because the early Jews were pastoralists, they could eat cud-chewing meat, but not pigs or camels because they do not meet this requirement. Avoiding "uncleanness," however defined, becomes a major preoccupation within all societies, as other scholars have demonstrated in putting to analytic use Douglas's ideas.

PURITY AND DANGER: AN ANALYSIS OF THE CONCEPTS OF POLLUTION AND TABOO, 1966

Introduction

The nineteenth century saw in primitive religions two peculiarities which separated them as a block from the great religions of the world. One was that they were inspired by fear, the other that they were inextricably confused with defilement and hygiene. Almost any missionary's or traveller's account of a primitive religion talks about the fear, terror or dread in which its adherents live. The source is traced to beliefs in horrible disasters which overtake those who inadvertently cross some forbidden line or develop some impure condition. And as fear inhibits reason it can be held accountable for other peculiarities in primitive thought, notably the idea of defilement. As Ricoeur sums it up:

> Defilement itself is scarcely a representation, and what representation there is is immersed in a specific sort of fear that blocks reflection. With defilement we enter into the reign of Terror.
>
> (*Symbolism of Evil*, p. 25)

But anthropologists who have ventured further into these primitive cultures find little trace of fear. Evans-Pritchard's study of witchcraft was made among the people who struck him as the most happy and carefree of the Sudan, the Azande. The feelings of an Azande man, on finding that he has been bewitched, are not terror, but hearty indignation as one of us might feel on finding himself the victim of embezzlement.

The Nuer, a deeply religious people, as the same authority points out, regard their God as a familiar friend. Audrey Richards, witnessing the girls' initiation rites of the Bemba, noted the casual, relaxed attitude of the performers. And so the tale goes on. The anthropologist sets out expecting to see rituals performed with reverence, to say the least. He finds himself in the role of the agnostic sightseer in St. Peter's, shocked at the disre-

From *Purity and Danger: An Analysis of the Concepts of Pollution and Taboo*, by Mary Douglas. Used by permission of Routledge, an imprint of Taylor & Francis, Ltd., UK.

spectful clatter of the adults and the children playing Roman shovehalfpenny on the floor stones. So primitive religious fear, together with the idea that it blocks the functioning of the mind, seems to be a false trail for understanding these religions.

Hygiene, by contrast, turns out to be an excellent route, so long as we can follow it with some self-knowledge. As we know it, dirt is essentially disorder. There is no such thing as absolute dirt: it exists in the eye of the beholder. If we shun dirt, it is not because of craven fear, still less dread of holy terror. Nor do our ideas about disease account for the range of our behaviour in cleaning or avoiding dirt. Dirt offends against order. Eliminating it is not a negative movement, but a positive effort to organise the environment.

I am personally rather tolerant of disorder. But I always remember how unrelaxed I felt in a particular bathroom which was kept spotlessly clean in so far as the removal of grime and grease was concerned. It had been installed in an old house in a space created by the simple expedient of setting a door at each end of a corridor between two staircases. The decor remained unchanged: the engraved portrait of Vinogradoff, the books, the gardening tools, the row of gumboots. It all made good sense as the scene of a back corridor, but as a bathroom—the impression destroyed repose. I, who rarely feel the need to impose an idea of external reality, at least began to understand the activities of more sensitive friends. In chasing dirt, in papering, decorating, tidying we are not governed by anxiety to escape disease, but are positively reordering our environment, making it conform to an idea. There is nothing fearful or unreasoning in our dirt-avoidance: it is a creative movement, an attempt to relate form to function, to make unity of experience. If this is so with our separating, tidying and purifying, we should interpret primitive purification and prophylaxis in the same light.

In this book I have tried to show that rituals of purity and impurity create unity in experience. So far from being aberrations from the central project of religion, they are positive contributions to atonement. By their means, symbolic patterns are worked out and publicly displayed. Within these patterns disparate elements are related and disparate experience is given meaning.

Pollution ideas work in the life of society at two levels, one largely instrumental, one expressive. At the first level, the more obvious one, we find people trying to influence one another's behaviour. Beliefs reinforce social pressures: all the powers of the universe are called in to guarantee an old man's dying wish, a mother's dignity, the rights of the weak and innocent. Political power is usually held precariously and primitive rulers are no exception. So we find their legitimate pretensions backed by beliefs in extraordinary powers emanating from their persons, from the insignia of their office or from words they can utter. Similarly the ideal order of society is guarded by dangers which threaten transgressors. These danger-beliefs are as much threats which one man uses to coerce another as dangers which he himself fears to incur by his own lapses from righteousness. They are a strong language of mutual exhortation. At this level the laws of nature are dragged in to sanction the moral code: this kind of disease is caused by adultery, that by incest; this meteorological disaster is the effect of political disloyalty, that the effect of impiety. The whole universe is harnessed to men's attempts to force one another into good citizenship. Thus we find that certain moral values are upheld and certain social rules defined by beliefs in dangerous contagion, as when the glance or touch of an adulterer is held to bring illness to his neighbours or his children.

It is not difficult to see how pollution beliefs can be used in a dialogue of claims and counter-claims to status. But as we examine pollution beliefs we find that the kind of contacts which are thought dangerous also carry a symbolic load. This is a more interesting level at which pollution ideas relate to social life. I believe that some pollutions are used as analogies: for expressing a general view of the social order. For example; there are beliefs that each sex is a danger to the other through contact with sexual fluids. According to other beliefs only one sex is endangered by contact with the other, usually males from females, but sometimes the reverse. Such patterns of sexual danger can be seen to express symmetry or hierarchy. It is implausible to interpret them as expressing something about the actual relation of the sexes. I suggest that many ideas about sexual dangers are better interpreted as symbols of the relation between parts of society, as mirroring designs of hierarchy or symmetry which apply in the larger social system. What goes for sex pollution also goes for bodily pollution. The two sexes can serve as a model for the collaboration and distinctiveness of social units. So also can the processes of ingestion portray political absorption. Sometimes bodily orifices seem to represent points of entry or exit to social units, or bodily perfection can symbolise an ideal theocracy.

Each primitive culture is a universe to itself. Following Franz Steiner's advice in *Taboo*, I start interpreting rules of uncleanness by placing them in the full context of the range of dangers possible in any given universe. Everything that can happen to a man in the way of disaster should be catalogued according to the active principles involved in the universe of his particular culture. Sometimes words trigger off cataclysms, sometimes acts, sometimes physical conditions. Some dangers are great and others small. We cannot start to compare primitive religions until we know the range of powers and dangers they recognise. Primitive society is an energised structure in the centre of its universe. Powers shoot out from its strong points, powers to prosper and dangerous powers to retaliate against attack. But the society does not exist in a neutral, uncharged vacuum. It is subject to external pressures; that which is not with it, part of it and subject to its laws, is potentially against it. In describing these pressures on boundaries and margins I admit to having made society sound more systematic than it really is. But just such an expressive over-systematising is necessary for interpreting the beliefs in question. For I believe that ideas about separating, purifying, demarcating and punishing transgressions have as their main function to impose system on an inherently untidy experience. It is only by exaggerating the difference between within and without, about and below, male and female, with and against, that a semblance of order is created. In this sense I am not afraid of the charge of having made the social structure seem over-rigid.

But in another sense I do not wish to suggest that the primitive cultures in which these ideas of contagion flourish are rigid, hide-bound and stagnant. No one knows how old are the ideas of purity and impurity in any nonliterate culture: to members they must seem timeless and unchanging. But there is every reason to believe that they are sensitive to change. The same impulse to impose order which brings them into existence can be supposed to be continually modifying or enriching them. This is a very important point. For when I argue that the reaction to dirt is continuous with other reactions to ambiguity or anomaly, I am not reviving the nineteenth century hypothesis of fear in another guise. Ideas about contagion can certainly be traced to reaction to anomaly. But they are more than the disquiet of a laboratory rat who suddenly finds one of his familiar exits from the maze is blocked. And they are more than the discomfiture of the aquarium stickleback with an anomalous member of his species. The initial recognition of anomaly leads to anxiety and from there to suppression or avoidance; so far, so good. But we must look for a more energetic organising principle to do justice to the elaborate cosmologies which pollution symbols reveal.

The native of any culture naturally thinks of himself as receiving passively his ideas of power and danger in the universe, discounting any minor modifications he himself may have contributed. In the same way we think of ourselves as passively receiving our native language and discount our responsibility for shifts it undergoes in our life time. The anthropologist falls into the same trap if he thinks of a culture he is studying as a long established pattern of values. In this sense I emphatically deny that a proliferation of ideas about purity and contagion implies a rigid mental outlook or rigid social institutions. The contrary may be true.

It may seem that in a culture which is richly organised by ideas of contagion and purification the individual is in the grip of iron-hard categories of thought which are heavily safe-guarded by rules of avoidance and by punishments. It may seem impossible for such a person to shake his own thought free of the protected habit-grooves of his culture. How can he turn round upon his own thought-process and contemplate its limitations? And yet if he cannot do this, how can his religion be compared with the great religions of the world?

The more we know about primitive religions the more clearly it appears that in their symbolic structures there is scope for meditation on the great mysteries of religion and philosophy. Reflection on dirt involves reflection on the relation of order to disorder, being to non-being, form to formlessness, life to death. Wherever ideas of dirt are highly structured their analysis discloses a play upon such profound themes. This is why an understanding of rules of purity is a sound entry to comparative religion. The Pauline antithesis of blood and water, nature and grace, freedom and necessity, or the Old Testament idea of Godhead can be illuminated by Polynesian or Central African treatment of closely related themes.

❧

RISK AND BLAME, 1992

Risk and Danger

Risk and Society. . . . The probability theorists who developed risk assessment as a purely neutral, objective tool of analysis, must find that it is much transformed as it moves into national and international politics. Though the public seems to be thinking politically in terms of comparative risks, the number-crunching does not matter; the idea of risk is transcribed simply as unacceptable danger. So 'risk' does not signify an all-round assessment of probable outcomes but becomes a stick for beating authority, often a slogan for mustering xenophobia. The Japanese have had parallel experience of the use of the word 'risk' to express international concern for the whale as an endangered species. Since there is no Japanese word for 'risk', national concern about siting of airports and nuclear installations is presumably expressed directly in terms of the moral and political concerns which 'risk' language obfuscates. The dangers are real enough, and terrifying too. Furthermore, action taken to avoid one, provokes another set of dangers. Choices between dangers are not simple and it would usually be preferable to have the choices directly presented as political questions, instead of sanitized and disguised in probability theory terms.

From *Risk and Blame: Essays in Cultural Theory,* by Mary Douglas. Used by permission of Routledge, an imprint of Taylor & Francis, Ltd., UK.

The political need is to see various uncertainties in the context of a whole system of probabilities. The original technical sense of 'risk' suggests that such a holistic presentation would be possible. 'Risk' is the probability of an event combined with the magnitude of the losses and gains that it will entail. However, our political discourse debases the word. From a complex attempt to reduce uncertainty it has become a decorative flourish on the word 'danger'. Without using the word 'risk' the Japanese can discourse very precisely about formal probability, technical limits of certainty, degrees of safety, and, of course, about the most primitive idea of all, danger. They obviously do not need the word 'risk' in its new political sense. It is doubtful whether Europeans or anyone else need it in that sense. When the public are told there is a 10 per cent probability of something bad happening, or 0.01 per cent probability, the formula is a poor guide to action and still poorer when the probabilities are reduced by several orders of magnitude.

To invoke very low probabilities of a particular dangerous event makes surprisingly little difference to the understanding of a choice. This is not because the public does not understand the sums, but because many other objectives which it cares about have been left out of the risk calculation.

Having done without it so far, it is unlikely that the Japanese should want to develop or adopt this word in its present uses. However, a better, more rounded and balanced conception of risk in political analysis would be useful for us all. I will argue that it is specially difficult for Europeans to make available to political debate a concept of technically sound probabilistic comparisons of good and bad outcomes. The reasons lie in the history of the theory of probability, and in the history of the industrializing process. What has gone wrong is that the public response to risk has been individualized. Public perception of risk is treated as if it were the aggregated response of millions of private individuals. Among other well-known fallacies of aggregated choice, it fails to take account of persons' interaction with one another, their advice to one another, their persuasions and intersubjective mobilizations of belief. As I will try to show below, the analysis that fails to register risk perception as a culturally standardized response misses the central part of its problem. Japan might

be a good base for developing a revolution in the social sciences' use of probability. It might also be able to provoke risk perception theorists into studying risk-taking and risk-aversion in a cultural framework. There would be two far-reaching innovations in social thought that could come out of this conference.

Heroic and Bourgeois Fiction.   To make the context for this, permit a digression on the idea of political and professional purity. I select three works of fiction on the theme of personal involvement in politics. Gustave Flaubert's *The Sentimental Education,* written in 1869, sets a student hero in Paris, at the time of the revolutionary turmoils of 1848. Sartre's *Les Mains Sales,* published in 1948, is a comment on the idealism of young French radical revolutionaries. Yukio Mishima's *Runaway Horses* was written about the same theme of compromise and commitment as the other two novels, but with triple emphasis: the student hero lives in the turmoil of Osaka and Tokyo in the 1930s, while action in the story is deliberately plotted upon an earlier failed uprising of 1873, and the author is situated in the aftermath of the world-wide student revolts of 1968. (I apologize for the fact that as a European my interpretation of Mishima's great book must seem inevitably clumsy and even false to Japanese readers.)

All three writers deal with the theme of revolutionary ardour and political compromise. In Flaubert's story the young hero accommodates only too easily to the tarnished loyalties and venal consciences around him. The treatment is unheroic, no one has pure motives or takes personal risks and the country is eventually plunged into war. In Sartre's story the young hero vows to carry out a political assassination to prove to his fellow conspirators his perfect commitment to their common revolutionary cause. He discovers his friends' duplicity and though at the end of the story he commits the promised assassination, his reasons for doing it have changed so that he cannot regard it as an act of patriotism—but it is unscrupulously used as such by the co-conspirators who betrayed him. The treatment is cynical, but with more contained passion than Flaubert musters. For Sartre, as for Flaubert, the society is not admirable in which commitment is scorned.

Mishima's story, about the extreme of total commitment, reserves biting scorn for compromise and self-serving. The Japanese student, brilliant, articulate, and dedicated, finds himself caught in a web of contradictory obligations. In his mind the problem is very simple: Japan is in deep trouble, the Emperor is badly served, the gods are insulted, the farmers are ruined, unemployment is rife. The solution is equally simple: a loyal band must assassinate the enemies of the nation, and give themselves a glorious death by *seppuku*. Through the story successive betrayals and fallings away do not shake the hero's resolution. Then to his dismay he finds that his father has for years been a secret pensioner of the villain he has

vowed to assassinate. Now he faces the dire conflict of duty, impossible to honour his vow without dishonouring his father, and so defiling himself. His dilemma is resolved when he eventually discovers that, it was his own father who originally betrayed him to the police. Then he goes forth with a clear conscience to murder the man who is the cause of all Japan's pain and of his father's dishonour, thus purifying himself and his father at the same stroke. All three tales, Flaubert's, Sartre's, and Mishima's, are social commentaries which condemn the society for which risks are not worth taking.

SUSANNE LANGER

1895–1985

Daughter of an affluent lawyer/banker and enthusiastic amateur musician, Susanne Katherina Knauth Langer was born on December 20, 1895 in New York City, married the distinguished historian William L. Langer on September 3, 1921 (divorced, 1942), had two sons with him (Leonard, 1922 and Bertrand, 1925), and died at 89 on July 17, 1985 in Old Lyme (or New London), Connecticut. A pharmacist's error which resulted in cocaine poisoning when she was an infant weakened her constitution so that health problems plagued her entire life. Yet due to her father's encouragement, she became a serious musician (piano and cello), and it was because of this intimate knowledge of musical forms, plus immersion in symbolic logic, that her writing in philosophy took a particularly distinct path. It's also said that she was reading Kant's *Critique of Pure Reason* in German at 12. She attended Radcliffe College and took her three degrees there in 1920, 1924, and 1926 (dissertation: "A Logical Analysis of Meaning"), while also doing graduate work at the University of Vienna (1921–22). Her first publication was a children's book, *The Cruise of the Little Dipper* (1923). Langer's career took her from Radcliffe College, where she tutored in philosophy (1927–42), to the University of Delaware (1943), then to Columbia as a lecturer (1945–50), and finally to Connecticut College (1954–61, emeritus research professor until 1985). She visited at NYU, Northwestern, Ohio State, University of Washington, and the University of Michigan, all between 1945 and 1954. Langer was lucky in receiving an unrestricted scholarly grant from 1956 through 1981 from the Kaufmann family (Pittsburgh department store fortune, for whom Frank Lloyd Wright's "Falling Water" was built), which allowed her to concentrate on her masterpiece, *Mind: An Essay on Human Feeling* (3 vols., 1967–1982).

Langer studied with Alfred North Whitehead at Harvard, who thought highly of her, and was inspired by him and the works of Ernst Cassirer to write *Philosophy in a New Key: A Study in the Symbolism of Reason, Rite, and Art* (1942), which became the first best-seller in paperback of any book in philosophy, selling over 570,000 copies, probably because she made the unique argument that art should be accorded epistemological status. She also wrote the first logic textbook that covered symbolic logic (1937), but with a much broader scope than the traditional primer. Langer's largest desire, as she put it was to "try to tie together a number of disciplines into a structure that these disciplines—the arts, biology, neurology, psychology, language, anthropology, and others—won't themselves singly support. I am trying to develop basic concepts which underlie all these sciences or fields of study, and which can rule all such thought" (*New York Times*, 5/26/68).

MIND: AN ESSAY ON HUMAN FEELING, 1967–82

Idols of the Laboratory

The social sciences, originally projected by Auguste Comte in his sanguine vision of a world reformed and rationally guided by science, have finally come into recognized existence in the twentieth century. They have had a different history from the natural sciences which grew up chiefly in the seventeenth and eighteenth centuries under the name of "natural philosophy," and gradually took shape as formal and systematic pursuits. Astronomy, mechanics, optics, electronics, all merging into "physics," and the strange kettles of fish that became chemistry, had a free and unsupervised beginning; and the most productive thinkers of those maverick days ventured on some wild flights of fancy. Not so the founders of the "young sciences" today. They cannot indulge in fantastic, hypotheses about the aims or the origins of society, the presence of sentience or intellect in anything but the investigator himself, the sources of fantasy, the measures of animal and human mentality. They began their work under the tutelage of physics, and—like young ones emulating their elders—they have striven first and hardest for the signs of sophistication; technical language, the laboratory atmosphere, apparatus, graphs, charts and statistical averages.

This ambition has had some unfortunate effects on a discipline for which the procedures of classical physics, for instance, the experimental techniques of Galileo, may not be suitable at all. It has centered attention on the ordering and collating of facts, and drawn it away from their own intriguing character as something distinct from the facts encountered by the physicist, and perhaps differently structured. The main concern of the early physicists was to understand puzzling events; each scientific venture grew from a problem, the solution of which threw unexpected light on other problematical phenomena. It was always in such a light that the concepts of physical science were set up. But the chief preoccupation of

the social scientists has been with the nature of their undertaking, its place in the edifice of human knowledge, and—by no means last, though seldom candidly admitted—their own status as scientists. For decades, therefore, the literature of those new disciplines, especially of psychology, has dealt in large measure with so-called "approaches," not to some baffling and challenging facts, but to all the facts at once, the science itself. Every theoretical thinker in the field set out to define and circumscribe this science and propose a strict proper method for its pursuit, until a rotating program committee seems to have had the lion's share in the whole venture. . . .

To speak of "hominid individuals" instead of "persons" and of "verbal behavior" instead of "speech," of a clinical interview as a "stimulus to verbal behavior," and so on, is to translate ordinary thinking into a jargon for literary presentation. Jargon is language which is more technical than the ideas it serves to express. Genuine scientific language grows up with the increasing abstractness or extraordinary precision of concepts used in a special field of work, and is therefore always just adequate to express those concepts. It is not deliberately fixed (with the exception of Latin nomenclature in taxonomy), but may become completely technical if scientific thought moves very far away from ordinary thought. Jargon, on the other hand, is a special vocabulary for common-sense ideation. It is an Idol of the Laboratory, and its worship is inimical to genuine abstractive thinking. A sociologist or psychologist who will spend his time translating familiar facts into professionally approved language must surely have more academic conscience than curiosity about strange or obscure phenomena. We are often told that such exercises are necessary because the behavioral sciences are young, and must establish their formal rules, vocabularies and procedures. Not long ago chemistry was young, too; its modern history only began with Lavoisier, who died in the Reign of Terror. But did any chemist ever write an article to show how a recipe for fudge could be stated in proper chemical form, i.e., without any household words?

Another source of idolatry is the cultivation of a prescriptive methodology, which lays down in advance the general lines of procedure—and therewith the lines of thought—to be followed. According to its canons all laboratory procedures must be isolated, controllable, repeatable and above all "objective." The first three requirements only restrict experimentation to simple responses, more significant in animal psychology than in human contexts; but the fourth is a demon. The Idol of Objectivity requires its servitors to distort the data of human psychology into an animal image in order to handle them by the methods that fit speechless mentality. It requires the omission of all activities of central origin, which are felt as such, and are normally accessible to research in human psychology through the powerful instrument of language. The result is a laboratory exhibit of "behavior" that is much more artificial than any instrumentally deformed object, because its deformation is not calculated and discounted as the effect of an instrument. Here, indeed, is a critical spot where haste to become scientific destroys the most valuable material for investigation. It completely masks the radical phylogenetic change induced by the language function, which makes one animal species so different from others that most—if not all—of its actions are only partially commensurable with those of even the nearest related creatures, the higher primates. For the revelation of subjectively felt activities through speech is not a simple exhibit from which the observer infers the action of external stimuli on the observed organism; in a protocol statement, the dividing line between the observer and his object is displaced, and part of the observation is delegated to the experimental subject. Language, in such a situation, does not belong entirely to the behavioral exhibit; the act of using it is a part of the psychological material, which may or may not be relevant to the intended observation, and so are the

subjective phenomena to which it refers; but the semantic function of the words is part of the perceptual medium, the instrument of observation. The speaker, who is the experimental subject, automatically participates in the work; both he and the experimenter handle the semantic instrument. If his observation or power to report is inadequate the instrument is crude. Many vitally important data have to be treated as insecure because the experimental conditions did not permit a definitive view. This is as true of protocol statements as it is of one-way screens, tachistoscopes and galvanometers. . . .

The fact that I wish to point out here is that to make a fetish of "objectivity" means to assume, in the first place, that some phenomena are intrinsically objective and others intrinsically subjective so that they can be accepted or rejected accordingly, it is one of the tacit assumptions which have frustrating metaphysical implications, and lead some great biologists and pathologists to accept strange philosophical doctrines as the only possible supports for those assumptions. In the second place it means that problems of the relationships between subjective and objective factors in mental activity are removed from the psychologist's proper sphere of investigation. These relationships, and the terms that develop in conjunction with them—symbols, concepts, fantasy, religion, speculation, selfhood and morality—really present the most exciting and important topics of the science of mind, the researches toward which all animal studies are oriented as indirect or auxiliary moves. To exclude such relationships for the sake of sure and safe laboratory methods is to stifle human psychology in embryo.

WALTER BENJAMIN

1892–1940

The eldest of three children born to rich Jewish parents, Walter Benedix Schönflies Benjamin was born on July 15, 1892 in Berlin, married Dora Kellner in April 17, 1917, and one year later had with her one son, Stefan, was divorced, and died by suicide on September 26, 1940 near Port-Bou, Spain, wrongly believing that his capture by the Gestapo was imminent. Like others who became intellectuals, Benjamin began life as a sickly, thoughtful child who could not manage the demanding discipline of the Kaiser-Friedrich-Schule in Berlin, was withdrawn by his parents, allowed to recuperate, then went to a less rigorous country boarding school in Thuringia. After two years he returned to the militarist prep school and graduated in 1912. He formed a friendship with Gustav Wyneken in 1905–07, who inspired him with ideas regarding the German Youth Movement and its role in the regeneration of German culture. Benjamin attended college at Freiburg (April 1912) and then Berlin (where he heard Georg Simmel lecture) and Munich, during which time he published his first pieces, "The Metaphysics of Youth" (1914) and "The Life of the Students" (1915). Here he began to theorize about the role of language in shaping one's worldview and in power relations in the larger society. About this time Benjamin's best friend, the poet Friedrich Heinle, committed suicide along with his girlfriend to protest the opening of WWI, an event which shook Benjamin badly. In the winter term, 1915, Benjamin moved to the Ludwig Maximilian University in Munich where he made the important acquaintances of the world-class poet Rainer Maria Rilke and Gerhard (Gershom) Scholem, his lifelong friend and leading Jewish scholar.

The creative peculiarity of Benjamin's mind began to unveil itself in November, 1916 in Munich when he wrote "On Language as Such and on the Language of Man," a meditation concerning Judaism, Genesis, Georg Hamann's theories (opposing Kant), and a range of related topics having to do with linguisticality that would typify his work throughout his short life. The "self-reflexive" quality of linguistic usage and experience, and the role that language plays in shaping political reality, became his central preoccupations. Benjamin's doctoral dissertation at Bern, "The Concept of Criticism in German Romanticism" (1920), is now regarded as a living classic among Germanists, wherein he introduced the notion of "immanent critique," borrowed from Friedrich Schlegel. Other works that quickly followed include "Fate and Character" (1921), "Critique of Violence" (1921), and "Theologico-Political Fragment" (1921). Although Benjamin was regarded as brilliant, he was also thought to be too unorthodox for inclusion into the rigid hierarchy of German academic life, so he was never offered an academic appointment. Moreover, his habilitation prepared at the University of Frankfurt (where he met Adorno), *The Origin of German Tragic Drama* (1928, tr. 1977), was rejected because his committee could not understand what he had set out to do regarding German baroque drama—which up to

that point had been thought of as a second-rate art form and hardly worth careful interpretation. In 1926–27 Benjamin moved to Moscow to be with the Latvian actress, Asja
Lacis, with whom he'd fallen desperately in love in Capri in June, 1924. Out of this came
the *Moscow Diary* (1986), a study in frustrated non-communication. Returning to Paris in
1927, Benjamin was in financial straits, experimented with hashish and other drugs (*On
Hashish,* 1972), and wrote reviews and periodical articles for money. In 1928 he published
One-Way Street (tr. 1979) and was working on what would be his posthumous masterpiece, *The Arcades Project* (tr. 1999), in addition to writing books on the plays of Brecht and
the poems of Baudelaire. When he killed himself with a morphine overdose in the Pyrenees just short of freedom from the Gestapo, he was not the world-famous critic that he
became after being embraced by the New Left during the 60s, and sponsored by Hannah
Arendt, Susan Sontag, and other notable intellectuals in the U.S. His "The Work of Art in
the Age of Mechanical Reproduction" (1936, tr. 1968) is now regarded as an indispensable classic.

ILLUMINATIONS, 1968

The Work of Art in the Age
of Mechanical Reproduction

When Marx undertook his critique of the capitalistic mode of production, this mode was in its infancy. Marx directed his efforts in such a way as to
give them prognostic value. He went back to the
basic conditions underlying capitalistic production
and through his presentation showed what could
be expected of capitalism in the future. The result
was that one could expect it not only to exploit
the proletariat with increasing intensity, but ultimately to create conditions which would make it
possible to abolish capitalism itself.

The transformation of the superstructure,
which takes place far more slowly than that of the
substructure, has taken more than half a century
to manifest in all areas of culture the change in

Excerpts from "The Work of Art in the Age of Mechanical Reproduction," in *Illuminations,* by Walter Benjamin. Copyright © 1955 by
Suhrkamp Verlag, Frankfurt a.M. English Translation by Harry Zohn.
Copyright © 1968 and renewed in 1996 by Harcourt, Inc. Reprinted
by permission of Harcourt, Inc.

the conditions of production. Only today can it be
indicated what form this has taken. Certain prognostic requirements should be met by these statements. However, theses about the art of the
proletariat after its assumption of power or about
the art of a classless society would have less bearing on these demands than theses about the developmental tendencies of art under present
conditions of production. Their dialectic is no less
noticeable in the superstructure than in the economy. It would therefore be wrong to underestimate the value of such theses as a weapon. They
brush aside a number of outmoded concepts, such
as creativity and genius, eternal value and mystery—concepts whose uncontrolled (and at present almost uncontrollable) application would
lead to a processing of data in the Fascist sense.
The concepts which are introduced into the theory of art in what follows differ from the more familiar term in that they are completely useless for
the purposes of Fascism. They are, on the other
hand, useful for the formulation of revolutionary
demands in the politics of art.

In principle a work of art has always been reproducible. Man-made artifacts could always be imi-

tated by men. Replicas were made by pupils in practice of their craft; by masters for diffusing their works, and, finally, by third parties in the pursuit of gain. Mechanical reproduction of a work of art, however, represents something new. Historically, it advanced intermittently and in leaps at long intervals, but with accelerated intensity. The Greeks knew only two procedures of technically reproducing works of art: founding and stamping. Bronzes, terra cottas, and coins were the only art works which they could produce in quantity. All others were unique and could not be mechanically reproduced. With the woodcut graphic it became mechanically reproducible for the first time, long before script became reproducible by print. The enormous changes which printing, the mechanical reproduction of writing, has brought about in literature are a familiar story. However, within the phenomenon which we are here examining from the perspective of world history, print is merely a special, though particularly important, case. During the Middle Ages engraving and etching were added to the woodcut; at the beginning of the nineteenth century lithography made its appearance.

With lithography the technique of reproduction reached an essentially new stage. This much more direct process was distinguished by the tracing of the design on a stone rather than its incision on a block of wood or its etching on a copperplate and permitted graphic art for the first time to put its products on the market, not only in large numbers as hitherto, but also in daily changing forms. Lithography enabled graphic art to illustrate everyday life, and it began to keep pace with printing. But only a few decades after its invention, lithography was surpassed by photography. For the first time in the process of pictorial reproduction, photography freed the hand of the most important artistic functions which henceforth devolved only upon the eye looking into a lens. Since the eye perceives more swiftly that the hand can draw, the process of pictorial reproduction was accelerated so enormously that it could keep pace with speech. A film operator shooting a scene in the studio captures the images at the speed of an actor's speech. Just as lithography virtually implied the illustrated newspaper, so did photography foreshadow the sound film. The technical reproduction of sound was tackled at the end of the last century. These convergent endeavors made predictable a situation which Paul Valéry pointed up in this sentence: "Just as water, gas, and electricity are brought into our houses from far off to satisfy our needs in response to a minimal effort, so we shall be supplied with visual or auditory images, which will appear and disappear at a simple movement hand, hardly more than a sign". Around 1900 technical reproduction had reached a standard that not only permitted it to reproduce all transmitted works of art and thus to cause the most profound change in their impact upon the public; it also had captured a place of its own among the artistic processes. For the study of this standard nothing is more revealing than the nature of the repercussions that these two different manifestations—the reproduction of works of art and the art of the film—have had on art in its traditional form.

During long periods of history, the mode of human sense perception changes with humanity's entire mode of existence. The manner in which human sense perception is organized, the medium in which it is accomplished, is determined not only by nature but by historical circumstances as well. The fifth century, with its great shifts of population, saw the birth of the late Roman art industry and the Vienna Genesis, and there developed not only an art different from that of antiquity but also a new kind of perception. The scholars of the Viennese school, Riegl and Wickhoff, who resisted the weight of classical tradition under which these later art forms had been buried, were the first to draw conclusions from them concerning the organization of perception at the time. However far-reaching their insight, these scholars limited themselves to showing the significant, formal hallmark which characterized perception in late Roman times. They did not attempt—and, perhaps, saw no way—to show the social transformations expressed by these changes of perception. The conditions for an analogous insight are more favorable in the present. And if changes in the medium of contemporary perception can be comprehended as decay of the aura, it is possible to show its social causes.

The concept of aura which was proposed above with reference to historical objects may usefully be illustrated with reference to the aura of natural ones. We define the aura of the latter as the unique phenomenon of a distance, however close it may be. If, while resting on a summer afternoon, you follow with your eyes a mountain range on the horizon or a branch which casts its shadow over you, you experience the aura of those mountains, of that branch. This image makes it easy to comprehend the social bases of the contemporary decay of the aura. It rests on two circumstances, both of which are related to the increasing significance of the masses in contemporary life. Namely, the desire of contemporary masses to bring things "closer" spatially and humanly, which is just as ardent as their bent toward overcoming the uniqueness of every reality by accepting its reproduction. Every day the urge grows stronger to get hold of an object at very close range by way of its likeness, its reproduction. Unmistakably reproduction as offered by picture magazines and newsreels differs from the image seen by the unarmed eye. Uniqueness and permanence are as closely linked in the latter as are transitoriness and reproducibility the former. To pry an object from its shell, to destroy its aura, is the mark of a perception whose "sense of the universal equality of things" has increased to such a degree that it extracts it even from a unique object by means of reproduction. Thus is manifested in the field of perception what in the theoretical sphere is noticeable in the increasing importance of statistics. The adjustment of reality to the masses and of the masses to reality is a process of unlimited scope, as much for thinking as for perception.

The uniqueness of a work of art is inseparable from its being imbedded in the fabric of tradition. This tradition itself is thoroughly alive and extremely changeable. An ancient statue of Venus, for example, stood in a different traditional contest with the Greeks, who made it an object of veneration, than with the clerics of the Middle Ages, who viewed it as an ominous idol. Both of them, however, were equally confronted with its uniqueness, that is, its aura. Originally the contextual integration of an in tradition found its expression in the cult. We know that the earliest art works originated in the service of a ritual—first the magical, then the religious kind. It is significant that the existence of the work of art with reference to its aura is never entirely separated from its ritual function. In other words, the unique value of the "authentic" work of art has its basis in ritual, the location of its original use value. This ritualistic basis, however remote, is still recognizable as secularized ritual even in the most profane forms of the cult of beauty. The secular cult of beauty, developed during the Renaissance and prevailing for three centuries, clearly showed that ritualistic basis in its decline and the first deep crisis which befell it. With the advent of the first truly revolutionary means of reproduction, photography, simultaneously with the rise of socialism, art sensed the approaching crisis which has become evident a century later. At the time, in reacted with the doctrine of *l'art pour l'art,* that is, with a theology of art. This gave rise to what might be called a negative theology in the form of the idea of "pure" art, which not only denied any social function of art but also any categorizing by subject matter. (In poetry, Mallarmé was the first to take this position.)

An analysis of art in the age of mechanical reproduction must do justice to these relationships, for they lead us to an all important insight: for the first time in world history, mechanical reproduction emancipaces the work of art from its parasitical dependence on ritual. To an ever greater degree the work of art reproduced becomes the work of art designed for reproducibility. From a photographic negative, for example, one can make any number of prints; to ask for the "authentic" print makes no sense. But the instant the criterion of authenticity ceases to be applicable to artistic production, the total function of art is reversed. Instead of being based on ritual, it begins to be based on another practice—politics.

part VII

POSTMODERNISM, GLOBALIZATION, AND THE NEW CENTURY

Pierre Bourdieu *1930–2002*

Michel Foucault *1926–1984*

Michael Oakeshott *1901–1990*

Jacques Derrida *1930–*

Christopher Lasch *1932–1994*

Anthony Giddens *1938–*

Jean-Francois Lyotard *1924–1998*

Niklas Luhmann *1927–1998*

Luce Irigaray *1930–*

Dorothy E. Smith *1926–*

Jean Baudrillard *1929–*

Lewis Coser *1913–2003*

David Harvey *1935–*

Julia Kristeva *1941–*

Judith Butler *1956–*

Immanuel Wallerstein *1930–*

Ernest Gellner *1925–1995*

John Rawls *1921–2002*

Richard Rorty *1931–*

Charles Taylor *1931–*

Alasdair MacIntyre *1929–*

PIERRE BOURDIEU

1930–2002

Ever alert to and wary of the social consequences of economic origins, Pierre Bourdieu was born on August 1, 1930 in Denguin, France, son of a postman and grandson of peasants in a Pyrenees backwater. He married Marie-Claire Brizard on November 2, 1962, with her had three sons, and died of cancer on January 23, 2002 in Paris, age 71. Through the highly competitive French educational system, by dint of intelligence and work, he raised himself from his origins, beginning by attending the École Normale Superieure, nursery for French intellectuals, taking a degree in philosophy in 1954. He then taught at the Lycée de Moulins, and moved to the Faculté des Lettres in Algiers, Algeria between 1958 and 1960 where he carried out ethnographic research, resulting in his first book (*The Algerians,* 1962) and giving him a practical basis for his later theoretical speculations. It was his keen sense of particularity based on anthropological study that gave Bourdieu's theory its earthbound quality, and which protected him from the hyper-abstractions of the poststructuralists with whom he competed for the attention of the French intellectual public. At the same time, however, because of the rarefied atmosphere typical of Parisian elite culture, he was also capable of writing works which hovered above the everyday while at the same time claiming to illuminate the quotidian. Bourdieu rose from assistant professor of sociology in Algiers to similar rank at Lille, but ascended to the director of studies at the École des Hautes Etudes, culminating from 1981 in his professorship in sociology at the Collége de France, the most coveted such position.

Bourdieu's most theoretically adventurous and interesting work is *Outline of a Theory of Practice* (1972; tr. 1977), which offered his theoretical method for overcoming the vexing dualism of subject-object that had dogged social theory since the 18th century. It is an interesting contrast with similar attempts by Giddens a few years later, as well as Habermas. Another influential work was *Reproduction in Education, Culture, and Society* (1970; tr. 1977; co-authored with Passeron) in which Bourdieu illustrates how social origins mixed with prescribed educational trajectories (at least in France) go a long way toward explaining where and how people end up in their particular niche in the social class system. He developed this in much greater detail in his magnum opus, *Distinction: A Social Critique of Judgment* (1979; tr. 1984), from which all the social sciences took his key term, "cultural capital" and lavished upon it the same kind of attention that Habermas received for "legitimation crisis" and Foucault for "episteme." Later in his professional life Bourdieu wrote books about Heidegger, photography, what he called "Pascalian meditations," French literary life in the mid-19th century, the world system, television, the educational upper classes, and what he called *Homo Academicus* (1984), a witty dissection of how the academic system works in France and elsewhere, to the benefit of some and the detriment of many. His native suspicion of Parisian elite life, his dislike of French imperialist behavior in northern Africa, and his ability to write with the creative ambiguity so central to French intellectualism in the last 50 years or so gave him a paramount position from which to dominate sociology in Paris during the last 20 years of his life.

OULINE OF A THEORY OF PRACTICE, 1972

Structures, Habitus and Practices

The habitus, the durably installed generative principle of regulated improvisations, produces practices which tend to reproduce the regularities immanent in the objective conditions of the production of their generative principle, while adjusting to the demands inscribed as objective potentialities in the situation, as defined by the cognitive and motivating structures making up the habitus. It follows that these practices cannot be directly deduced either from the objective conditions, defined as the instantaneous sum of the stimuli which may appear to have directly triggered them, or from the conditions which produced the durable principle of their production. These practices can be accounted for only by relating the objective *structure* defining the social conditions of the production of the habitus which engendered them to the conditions in which this habitus is operating, that is, to the *conjuncture* which, short of a radical transformation, represents a particular state of this structure. In practice, it is the habitus, history turned into nature, i.e. denied as such, which accomplishes practically the relating of these two systems of relations, in and through the production of practice. The "unconscious" is never anything other than the forgetting of history which history itself produces by incorporating the objective structures it produces in the second natures of habitus: " . . . in each of us, in varying proportions, there is part of yester-day's man; it is yesterday's man who inevitably predominates in us, since the present amounts to little compared with the long past in the course of which we were formed and from which we result. Yet we do not sense this man of the past, because he is inveterate in us; he makes up the unconscious part of ourselves. Consequently we are led to take no account of him, any more than we take account of his legitimate demands. Conversely, we are very much aware of the most recent attainments of civilization, because, being recent, they have not yet had time to settle into our unconscious."

Genesis amnesia is also encouraged (if not entailed) by the objectivist apprehension which, grasping the product of history as an *opus operatum,* a *fait accompli,* can only invoke the mysteries of preestablished harmony or the prodigies of conscious orchestration to account for what, apprehended in pure synchrony, appears as objective meaning, whether it be the internal coherence of works or institutions such as myths, rites, or bodies of law, or the objective coordination which the concordant or conflicting practices of the members of the same group or class at once manifest and presuppose (inasmuch as they imply a community of dispositions).

Each agent, wittingly or unwittingly, willy nilly, is a producer and reproducer of objective meaning. Because his actions and works are the product of a *modus operandi* of which he is not the producer and has no conscious mastery, they contain an "objective intention", as the Scholastics put it, which always outruns his conscious intentions. The schemes of thought and expression he has acquired are the basis for the *intentionless invention* of regulated improvisation. Endlessly overtaken by his own words, with which he maintains a relation of "carry and be carried", as Nicolai

Hartmann put it, the virtuoso finds in the *opus operatum* new triggers and new supports for the modus operandi from which they arise, so that his discourse continuously feeds off itself like a train bringing along its own rails. If witticisms surprise their author no less than their audience, and impress as much by their retrospective necessity as by their novelty, the reason is that the *trouvaille* appears as the simple unearthing, at once accidental and irresistible, of a buried possibility. It is because subjects do not, strictly speaking, know what they are doing that what they do has more meaning than they know. The habitus is the universalizing mediation which causes an individual agent's practices, without either explicit reason or signifying intent, to be none the less "sensible" and "reasonable". That part of practices which remains obscure in the eyes of their own producers is the aspect by which they are objectively adjusted to other practices and to the structures of which the principle of their production is itself the product.

One of the fundamental effects of the orchestration of habitus is the production of a common-sense world endowed with the *objectivity* secured by consensus on the meaning (*sens*) of practices and the world, in other words the harmonization of agents' experiences and the continuous reinforcement that each of them receives from the expression, individual or collective (in festivals, for example), improvised or programmed (commonplaces, sayings), of similar or identical experiences. The homogeneity of habitus is what—within the limits of the group of agents possessing the schemes (of production and interpretation) implied in their production—causes practices and works to be immediately intelligible and foreseeable, and hence taken for granted. This practical comprehension obviates the "intention" and "intentional transfer into the other" dear to the phenomenologists, by dispensing, for the ordinary occasions of life, with close analysis of the nuances of another's practice and tacit or explicit inquiry ("What do you *mean*?") into his intentions. Automatic and impersonal, significant without intending to signify, ordinary practices lend themselves to an understanding no less automatic and impersonal: the picking up of the objective intention they express in no way implies "reactivation" of the "lived" intention of the agent who performs

them. "Communication of consciousnesses" presupposes community of "unconsciouses" (i.e. of linguistic and cultural competences). The deciphering of the objective intention of practices and works has nothing to do with the "reproduction" (*Nachbildung,* as the early Dilthey puts it) of lived experiences and the reconstitution, unnecessary and uncertain, of the personal singularities of an "intention" which is not their true origin.

The objective homogenizing of group or class habitus which results from the homogeneity of the conditions of existence is what enables practices to be objectively harmonized without any intentional calculation or conscious reference to a norm and mutually adjusted *in the absence of any direct interaction* or, *a fortiori,* explicit coordination. "Imagine", Leibniz suggests, "two clocks or watches in perfect agreement as to the time. This may occur in one of three ways. The first consists in mutual influence; the second is to appoint a skillful workman to correct them and synchronize them at all times; the third is to construct these clocks with such art and precision that one can be assured of their subsequent agreement." So long as, retaining only the first or at a pinch the second hypothesis, one ignores the true principle of the conductorless orchestration which gives regularity, unity, and systematicity to the practices of a group or class, and this even in the absence of any spontaneous or externally imposed organization of individual projects, one is condemned to the naive artificialism which recognizes no other principle unifying a group's or class's ordinary or extraordinary action than the conscious coordination of a conspiracy. If the practices of the members of the same group or class are more and better harmonized than the agents know or wish, it is because, as Leibniz puts it, "following only [his] own laws", each "nonetheless agrees with the other". The habitus is precisely this immanent law, *lex insita,* laid down in each agent by his earliest upbringing, which is the precondition not only for the coordination of practices but also for practices of coordination, since the corrections and adjustments the agents themselves consciously carry out presuppose their mastery of a common code and since undertakings of collective mobilization cannot succeed without a minimum of concordance between the habitus of the mobilizing agents (e.g. prophet, party leader, etc.) and the dispositions of those whose aspirations and world-view they express.

So it is because they are the product of dispositions which, being the internalization of the same objective structures, are objectively concerted that the practices of the members of the same group or, in a differentiated society, the same class are endowed with an objective meaning that is at once unitary and systematic, transcending subjective intentions and conscious projects whether individual or collective. To describe the process of objectification and orchestration in the language of *interaction* and mutual adjustment is to forget that the interaction itself owes its form to the objective structures which have produced the dispositions of the interacting agents and which allot them their relative positions in the interaction and elsewhere. Every confrontation between agents in fact brings together, in an *interaction* defined by the *objective structure* of the relation between the groups they belong to (e.g. a boss giving orders to a subordinate, colleagues discussing their pupils, academics taking part in a symposium), systems of dispositions (carried by "natural persons") such as a linguistic competence and a cultural competence and, through these habitus, all the objective structures of which they are the product, structures which are active only when *embodied* in a competence acquired in the course of a particular history (with the different types of bilingualism or pronunciation, for example, stemming from different modes of acquisition).

Thus, when we speak of class habitus, we are insisting, against all forms of the occasionalist illusion which consists in directly relating practices to properties inscribed in the situation, that "interpersonal" relations are never, except in appearance, *individual-to-individual* relationships and that the truth of the interaction is never entirely contained in the interaction. This is what social psychology and interactionism or ethnomethodology forget when, reducing the objective structure of the relationship between the assembled individuals to the conjunctural structure of their interaction in a particular situation and group, they seek to explain everything that occurs in an experimental or observed interaction in terms of the experimentally controlled characteristics of the situation, such as

the relative spatial positions of the participants or the nature of the channels used. In fact it is their present and last positions in the social structure that biological individuals carry with them, at all times and in all places, in the form of dispositions which are so many marks of *social position* and hence of the social distance between objective positions, that is, between social persons conjuncturally brought together (in physical space, which is not the same thing as social space) and correlatively, so many reminders of this distance and of the conduct required in order to "keep one's distance" or to manipulate it strategically, whether symbolically or actually, to reduce it (easier for the dominant than for the dominated), increase it, or simply maintain if (by not "letting oneself go ", not "becoming familiar", in short, "standing on one's dignity", or on the other hand, refusing to "take liberties" and "put oneself forward", in short "knowing one's place" and staying there).

Even those forms of interaction seemingly most amenable to description in terms of "intentional transfer into the Other", such as sympathy, friendship, or love, are dominated (as class homogamy attests), through the harmony of habitus, that is to say, more precisely, the harmony of ethos and tastes—doubtless sensed in the imperceptible cues of body *hexis*—by the objective structure of the relations between social conditions. The illusion of mutual election or predestination arises from ignorance of the social conditions for the harmony of aesthetic tastes or ethical leanings, which is thereby perceived as evidence of the ineffable affinities which spring from it.

In short, the habitus, the product of history, produces individual and collective practices, and hence history, in accordance with the schemes engendered by history. The system of dispositions— a past which survives in the present and tends to perpetuate itself into the future by making itself present in practices structured according to its principles, an internal law relaying the continuous exercise of the law of external necessities (irreducible to immediate conjunctural constraints)— is the principle of the continuity and regularity which objectivism discerns in the social world without being able to give them a rational basis. And it is at the same time the principle of the transformations and regulated revolutions which neither the extrinsic and instantaneous determinisms of a mechanistic sociologism nor the purely internal but equally punctual determination of voluntarist or spontaneist subjectivism are capable of accounting for.

◆

DISTINCTION: A SOCIAL CRITIQUE OF THE JUDGEMENT OF TASTE, 1979

The Taste for Necessity and the Principle of Conformity

The specific effect of the taste for necessity, which never ceases to act, though unseen—because its action combines with that of necessity—is most clearly seen when it is, in a sense, operating out of phase, having survived the disappearance of the conditions which produced it. One sees examples in the behaviour of some small craftsmen or businessmen who, as they themselves say, 'don't know how to spend the money they've earned', or of junior clerical workers, still attached to their peasant or working-class roots, who get as much satisfaction from calculating how much they have 'saved' by doing without a commodity or service (or 'doing it themselves') as they would have got from the thing itself, but who, equally, cannot ever purchase it without a painful sense of wasting money. Having a million does not in itself make one able to live like a millionaire; and parvenus generally take a long time to learn that what they see as culpable prodigality is, in their new condition, expenditure of basic necessity.

It tends to be forgotten that to appreciate the 'true value' of the purely symbolic services which in many areas (hotels, hairdressing etc.) make the essential difference between luxury establishments and ordinary businesses, one has to feel oneself the legitimate recipient of this bureaucratically personalized care and attention and to display vis-à-vis those who are paid to offer it the mixture of distance (including 'generous' gratuities) and free-

dom which the bourgeois have towards their servants. Anyone who doubts that 'knowing how to be served' is one component of the bourgeois art of living, need only think of the workers or small clerks who, entering a smart restaurant for some grand occasion, immediately strike up a conversation with the waiters—who realize at once 'whom they are dealing with'—as if to destroy symbolically the servant-master relationship and the unease it creates for them. The worker who sees a watch on sale for two million (old) francs, or who hears that a surgeon has spent three million francs on his son's engagement party, does not envy the watch or the party but the two million, being unable to conceive of the system of needs in which he would have nothing better to do with two million francs than spend it on a watch. When there are 'so many things that come first', as they say, 'you'd have to be crazy' to think of buying a two-million-franc watch. But no one ever really puts himself 'in the place' of those on the other side of the social world. One man's extravagance is another man's prime necessity and not only because the marginal value of those two million francs varies with the number of millions possessed. Many of the expenditures that are called conspicuous are in no way a squandering and, as well as being obligatory elements in a certain style of life, they are very often—like engagement parties—an excellent investment in social capital. . . .

What statistics records in the form of systems of needs is nothing other than the coherence of the choices of a habitus. And the inability to 'spend more', or differently, that is, to rise to the system of needs implied in a higher level of resources, is the best illustration of the impossibility of reducing (theoretically) the propensity to consume to the capacity to appropriate or of reducing the habitus to the economic conditions prevailing at a given moment (as represented, for example, by a given level of income). If everything encourages a belief in the existence of a direct relationship between income and consumption, this is because taste is almost always the product of economic conditions identical to those in which it functions, so that income tends to be credited with a causal efficacy which it in fact only exerts in association with the habitus it has produced. The specific efficacy of the habitus is clearly seen when the same income is associated with very different patterns of consumption, which can only be un-

From *Distinction: A Social Critique of the Judgement of Taste,* by Pierre Bourdieu, pp. 374–375, 377–381, 488–490. Cambridge, Mass.: Harvard University Press. Copyright © 1984 by the President and Fellows of Harvard College. Reprinted by permission of the publisher.

derstood by assuming that other selection principles have intervened. . . .

The principle of the most important differences in the order of life-style and, even more, of the 'stylization of life' lies in the variations in objective and subjective distance from the world, with its material constraints and temporal urgencies like the aesthetic disposition which is one dimension of it, the distant, detached or casual disposition towards the world or other people, a disposition which can scarcely be called subjective since it is objectively internalized, can only be constituted in conditions of existence that are relatively freed from urgency. The submission to necessity which inclines working-class people to a pragmatic, functionalist 'aesthetic', refusing the gratuity and futility of formal exercises and of every form of art for art's sake, is also the principle of all the choices of daily existence and of an art of living which rejects specifically aesthetic intentions as aberrations.

Thus manual workers say more often than all the other classes that they like interiors that are clean and tidy and easy to maintain, or the value for money' clothes which economic necessity assigns to them in any case. The doubly prudent choice of a garment that is both 'simple' ('versatile', 'all-purpose'), i.e., as little marked and as unrisky as possible ('no-nonsense', 'practical'), and 'good value for money', i.e., cheap and long-lasting, no doubt presents itself as the most reasonable strategy, given, on the one hand, the economic and cultural capital (not to mention time) that can be invested in buying clothes and, on the other hand, the symbolic profits that can be expected from such an investment (at least at work—unlike clerical workers, for example). . . .

Thus, although working-class practices may seem to be deduced directly from their economic conditions, since they ensure a saving of money, time and effort that would in any case be of low profitability, they stem from a choice of the necessary ('That's not for us'), both in the sense of what is technically necessary, 'practical' (or, as others would say, functional), i.e., needed in order to 'get by', to do 'the proper thing and no more', and of what is imposed by an economic and social necessity condemning 'simple', 'modest' people to 'simple', 'modest' tastes. The adjustment to the objective chances which is inscribed in the dispositions constituting the habitus is the source of all the realistic choices which, based on the renunciation of symbolic profits that are in any case inaccessible, reduce practices or objects to their technical function, a 'short back-and-sides' or 'quick trim-up' at the barber's, 'a simple little dress', 'solid' furniture etc. Thus nothing is more alien to working-class women than the typically bourgeois idea of making each object in the home the occasion for an aesthetic choice, of extending the intention of harmony or beauty even into the bathroom or kitchen, places strictly defined by their function, or of involving specifically aesthetic criteria in the choice of a saucepan or cupboard. Festive meals and 'Sunday best' clothes are opposed to everyday meals and clothes by the arbitrariness of a conventional division—doing things properly—just as the rooms socially designated for 'decoration', the sitting room, the dining room or living room, are opposed to everyday places, that is, by an antithesis which is more or less that of the 'decorative' and the 'practical', and they are decorated in accordance with established conventions, with knick-knacks on the mantelpiece, a forest scene over the sideboard, flowers on the table, without any of these obligatory choices implying decisions or a search for effect.

This conventionalism, which is also that of popular photography, concerned to fix conventional poses in the conventional compositions, is the opposite of bourgeois formalism and of all the forms of art for art's sake recommended by manuals of graceful living and women's magazines, the art of entertaining, the art of the table, the art of motherhood. In addition to providing a form of basic security in a world in which there can be hardly any assurance, the choice of 'doing the proper thing' or 'the done thing' (the vendors of domestic goods understand the power of 'It's the done thing' over working-class insecurity) has a natural place in an economy of practices based on the search for the 'practical' and the refusal of 'frills' and 'fancy nonsense'.

Even the choices which, from the standpoint of the dominant norms, appear as the most 'irrational' are grounded in the taste of necessity—plus, of course, the entirely negative effect of the absence of information and specific competence which results from the lack of cultural capital. For example, the taste for the trinkets and knick-knacks which adorn mantelpiece and hallways is inspired by an intention unknown to economists and ordinary aesthetes, that of obtaining maximum 'effect' ('It'll make a terrific effect') at minimum cost, a formula which for bourgeois taste is the very definition of vulgarity (one of the intentions of distinction being to suggest with the fewest 'effects' possible the greatest expenditure of time, money and ingenuity). What is the 'gaudy' and the 'tawdry', if not that which creates a big effect for a small price, the 'follies' that are only permissible so long as you can say to yourself, 'They were almost given away'? Street hawkers and sales-promotion specialists know that they must release the brakes and censorships which forbid 'extravagances' by presenting the forbidden goods as 'bargains'—the unfashionable settee which, if you can forget the colour and just think of the price, is exactly the one you had always wanted 'to go in front of the TV', or the unwearable nylon dress you ended up buying because it was reduced in the sale, though you had 'sworn you would never again wear nylon.'

And if it still needed to be proved that resignation to necessity is the basis of the taste of necessity, one only has to consider the waste of time and energy resulting from the refusal to subject the daily management of domestic life to the constraints of rational calculation and formal life-principles ('a place for everything', 'everything in its time' etc.), which only apparently contradicts the refusal to devote time and care to health ('molly-coddling yourself') or beauty ('getting dolled up'). In fact, in these two features of their life-style, working-class women, doubly dominated, show that they do not set sufficient value on their trouble and their time, the only things they can spend (and give) without counting, to be concerned about sparing and saving them, or, to put it another way, that they do not value themselves sufficiently (and they do indeed have a low value on the labour market, unlike bourgeois women with their skilled labour-power and cultivated bodies) to grant themselves a care and attention which always imply a certain indulgence and to devote to their bodies the incessant care, concern and attention that arc needed to achieve and maintain health, slimness and beauty. . . .

The calls to order ('Who does she think she is?' 'That's not for the likes of us') which reaffirm the principle of conformity—the only explicit norm of popular taste—and aim to encourage the 'reasonable' choices that are in any case imposed by the objective conditions also contain a warning against the ambition to distinguish oneself by identifying with other groups, that is, they are a reminder of the need for class solidarity. The gaps between the cultural practices and preferences of the different classes are to a large extent due to the fact that the chances of finding in one's milieu the 'market' in which cultural experiences and the discourses to which they give rise can receive a value vary in much the same way as the chances of having such experiences, and no doubt play a part in determining these chances. The low interest which working-class people show in the works of legitimate culture to which they could have access—especially through television—is not solely the effect of a lack of competence and familiarity: just as supposedly vulgar subjects, such as television, are banished from bourgeois conversation, so the favourite subjects of bourgeois conversation, exhibitions, theatre, concerts or even cinema, are excluded, de facto and de jure, from working-class conversation, in which they could only express the pretension to distinguish oneself. Perhaps the most ruthless call to order, which in itself no doubt explains the extraordinary *realism* of the working classes, stems from the closure effect of the homogeneity of the directly experienced social world. There is no other possible language, no other life-style, no other form of kinship relation; the universe of possibles is closed. Other people's expectations are so many reinforcements of dispositions imposed by the objective conditions.

The 'Taste of Reflection' and the 'Taste of Sense'

What pure taste refuses is indeed the violence to which the popular spectator consents (one thinks of Adorno's description of popular music and its effects); it demands respect, the distance which allows it to keep its distance. It expects the work of art, a finality with no other end than itself, to treat the spectator in accordance with the Kantian imperative, that is, as an end, not a means. Thus, Kant's principle of pure taste is nothing other than a refusal, a disgust—a disgust for objects which impose enjoyment and a disgust for the crude, vulgar taste which revels in this imposed enjoyment: 'One kind of ugliness alone is incapable of being represented conformably to nature without destroying all aesthetic delight, and consequently artistic beauty, namely, that which excites *disgust*. For, as in this strange sensation, which depends purely on the imagination, the object is represented as insisting, as it were, on our enjoying it, while we still set our face against it, the artificial representation of the object is no longer distinguishable from the nature of the object itself in our sensation, and so it cannot possibly be regarded as beautiful'.

Disgust is the paradoxical experience of enjoyment extorted by violence, an enjoyment which arouses horror. This horror, unknown to those who surrender to sensation, results fundamentally from removal of the distance, in which freedom is asserted, between the representation and the thing represented, in short, from *alienation*, the loss of the subject in the object, immediate submission to the immediate present under the enslaving violence of the 'agreeable'. Thus, in contrast to the inclination, aroused by the 'agreeable', which, unlike beauty, is common to humans and animals, is capable of seducing 'those who are always intent only on enjoyment' and 'immediately satisfies the senses—whereas it is 'mediately displeasing' to reason—'pure taste', the 'taste of reflection' which is opposed to the 'taste of sense as 'charms' are opposed to 'form', must exclude interest and must not 'be in the least prepossessed in favour of the real existence of the object'. . . .

The object which 'insists on being enjoyed', as an image and in reality, in flesh and blood, neutralizes both ethical resistance and aesthetic neutralization; it annihilates the distanciating power of representation, the essentially human power of suspending immediate, animal attachment to the sensible and refusing submission to the pure af-

fect, to simple aisthesis. In the face of this twofold challenge to human freedom and to culture (the anti-nature), disgust is the ambivalent experience of the horrible seduction of the disgusting and of enjoyment, which performs a sort of reduction to animality, corporeality, the belly and sex, that is, to what is common and therefore vulgar, removing any difference between those who resist with all their might and those who wallow in pleasure, who enjoy enjoyment: 'Common human understanding . . . has the doubtful honour of having the name of common sense . . . bestowed upon it; and bestowed, too, in an acceptation of the word *common* (not merely in our language, where it actually has a double meaning, but also in many others) which makes it amount to what is *vulgar* (*das Vulgare*) what is everywhere to be met with— a quality which by no means confers credit or distinction upon its possessor'. Nature understood as sense equalizes, but at the lowest level (an early version of the 'levelling-down' abhorred by the Heideggerians). Aristotle taught that different things differentiate themselves by what makes them similar, i.e., a common character; in Kant's text, disgust discovers with horror the common animality on which and against which moral distinction is constructed: 'We regard as coarse and low the habits of thought of those who have no feeling for beautiful nature . . . and who devote themselves to the mere enjoyments of sense found in eating and drinking'.

Elsewhere Kant quite directly states the social basis of the opposition between the 'taste of reflection' and the 'taste of sense':'In the beginning, the novice must have been guided by instinct alone, that voice of God which is obeyed by all animals. This permitted some things to be used for nourishment, while forbidding others. Here it is not necessary to assume a special instinct which is now lost. It could simply have been the sense of smell, plus its affinity with the organ of taste and the well-known relation of the latter to the organs of digestion; in short an ability, perceivable even now, to sense, prior to the consumption of a certain foodstuff, whether or not it is fit for consumption. It is not even necessary to assume that this sensitivity was keener in the first pair than it is now. For it is a familiar enough fact that men wholly absorbed by their senses have much greater perceptive powers than those who, occupied with thoughts as well as with the senses, are to a degree turned away from the sensuous.' We recognize here the ideological mechanism which works by describing the terms of the opposition one establishes between the social classes as stages in an evolution (here, the progress from nature to culture).

Thus, although it consistently refuses anything resembling an empirical psychological or sociological genesis of taste, each time invoking the magical division between the transcendental and the empirical, the theory of pure taste is grounded in an empirical social relation, as is shown by the opposition it makes between the agreeable (which 'does not cultivate' and is only an enjoyment) and culture, or its allusions to the teaching and educability of taste. The antithesis between culture and bodily pleasure (or nature) is rooted in the opposition between the cultivated bourgeoisie and the people, the imaginary site of uncultivated nature, barbarously wallowing in pure enjoyment: 'Taste that requires an added element of charm and emotion for its delight, not to speak of adopting this as the measure of its approval, has not yet emerged from barbarism'.

MICHEL FOUCAULT

1926–1984

Son of a physician and professor of anatomy, Paul-Michel Foucault was the second of three children, born on October 15, 1926 in Poitiers, France, lived from 1960 with Daniel Defert, and died on June 25, 1984 in Paris from AIDS at 57. He attended the Lycée de Poitiers (1936–40), and graduated from the Jesuit Collège Saint Stanislas (1942–43). He studied philosophy and psychology in Paris at the École Normale Supérieure, graduating with degrees in both (1948 and 1949). He joined the French Communist Party in 1950 but left after several years due to their hostility to homosexuals. Foucault studied for several years under the structuralist Marxist Louis Althusser at the ENS, and took a diploma in psychopathology at the Institute for Psychology in Paris (1952). Between 1955 and 1958 he worked in Uppsala, Sweden, where he taught French language and culture, then spent a year in Warsaw, Poland and another year in Hamburg on similar assignments. His first faculty position was at the University of Clermont-Ferrand (1960–66), and he completed his dissertation, *Madness and Civilization* (1961; tr. 1965) while there. In 1965 he took a research trip to Brazil, then served a two-year stint as professor of philosophy at the University of Tunis, Tunisia. In 1968 he was recalled to Paris to become professor at the University of Paris-VIII, Vincennes. In 1969 he entered the Collège de France, and from 1970 until his death was Professor of the History of Systems of Thought. He traveled to Japan and the U.S. during the early 70s and became particularly fond of gay life in San Francisco.

Foucault was famous before his death, but has become virtually canonized after it, particularly in the anglophone academic world, not only for his theories but because of his tragic death. His works are too difficult to have made much of an impression among ordinary readers, but so much of his attitude has been absorbed by other authors who have connected with the mass media that the adjective "Foucauldian" is now common. Foucault resisted recognizing his homosexuality when young and was therefore disturbed to learn just how cruel conventional culture could be when confronted with an unapologetic gay person, particularly one who wrote brilliantly about the ways that worldviews are shaped by their political and cultural environments. Foucault's central theme (which some critics believe he developed from Nietzsche), especially as expressed in *The Birth of the Clinic* (1963; tr. 1973) and *Discipline and Punish* (1975; tr. 1977), was that beginning in the Enlightenment "man" was defined as heterosexual and reasonable along rigid lines, and that deviations from these behavioral prescriptions were harshly punished. He argued that epistemology (of the self) did not exist until the 18th century and effectively died during the 20th. He also worked at a much more esoteric level (in *The Order of Things* [1966; tr. 1971) and *The Archaeology of Knowledge* [1971; tr. 1972]) using terms and conceptual leaps that often befuddled his readers who had come to know his work through the properly historical monographs. Foucault sought to redefine the human sciences away from what he called homocentrism and logocentrism, resulting in an apotheosis of normality and rationality. He was suspicious of received wisdom in the social sciences and philosophy, particularly the neat subdivisions into which knowledge, so-called, had been packaged. Like his contemporary, Derrida, he spent considerable time tearing at these definitions of reality in order to reorder them. Toward the end of his life he gave many interviews, which have become the most popular of his works because of their relative lucidity (e.g., "My entire philosophical development was determined by my reading of Heidegger"), and he also left incomplete a history of sexuality (three volumes were published, 1976, 1984, 1984). His occasional works have been collected in three volumes, one each on ethics (1997), aesthetics (1998), and power (1999).

DISCIPLINE AND PUNISH: THE BIRTH OF THE PRISON, 1975

Panopticism

The following, according to an order published at the end of the seventeenth century, were the measures to be taken when the plague appeared in a town.

First, a strict spatial partitioning: the closing of the town and its outlying districts, a prohibition to leave the town on pain of death, the killing of all stray animals; the division of the town into distinct quarters, each governed by an intendant. Each street is placed under the authority of a syndic, who keeps it under surveillance; if he leaves the street, he will be condemned to death. On the appointed day, everyone is ordered to stay indoors: it is forbidden to leave on pain of death. The syndic himself comes to lock the door of each house from the outside; he takes the key with him and hands it over to the intendant of the quarter; the intendant keeps it until the end of the quarantine. Each family will have made its own provisions; but, for bread and wine, small wooden canals are set up between the street and the interior of the houses, thus allowing each person to receive his ration

From *Discipline and Punish*, by Michel Foucault, Alan Sheridan, Trans. (New York: Pantheon, Copyright © 1977). Originally published in French as *Surveiller et Punir*. Copyright © 1975 by Editions Gallimard. Reprinted by permission of Georges Borchardt, Inc., for Editions Gallimard.

without communicating with the suppliers and other residents; meat, fish and herbs will be hoisted up into the houses with pulleys and baskets. If it is absolutely necessary to leave the house, it will be done in turn, avoiding any meeting. Only the intendants, syndics and guards will move about the streets and also, between the infected houses, from one corpse to another, the 'crows', who can be left to die: these are 'people of little substance who carry the sick, bury the dead, clean and do many vile and abject offices'. It is a segmented, immobile, frozen space. Each individual is fixed in his place. And, if he moves, he does so at the risk of his life, contagion or punishment.

Inspection functions ceaselessly. The gaze is alert everywhere: 'A considerable body of militia, commanded by good officers and men of substance', guards at the gates, at the town hall and in every quarter to ensure the prompt obedience of the people and the most absolute authority of the magistrates, 'as also to observe all disorder, theft and extortion'. At each of the town gates there will be an observation post; at the end of each street sentinels. Every day, the intendant visits the quarter in his charge, inquires whether the syndics have carried out their tasks, whether the inhabitants have anything to complain of; they 'observe their actions'. Every day, too, the syndic goes into the street for which he is responsible; stops before each house: gets all the inhabitants to appear at the windows (those who live overlooking the courtyard will be allocated a window looking onto the street at which no one but they may show themselves); he calls each of them by name; informs himself as to the state of each and every one of them—'in which respect the inhabitants will be compelled to speak the truth under pain of death'; if someone does not appear at the window, the syndic must ask why: 'In this way he will find out easily enough whether dead or sick are being concealed.' Everyone locked up in his cage, everyone at his window, answering to his name and showing himself when asked—it is the great review of the living and the dead.

This surveillance is based on a system of permanent registration: reports from the syndics to the intendants, from the intendants to the magistrates or mayor. At the beginning of the 'lock up', the role of each of the inhabitants present in the town is laid down, one by one; this document bears 'the name, age, sex of everyone, notwithstanding his condition': a copy is sent to the intendant of the quarter, another to the office of the town hall, another to enable the syndic to make his daily roll call. Everything that may be observed during the course of the visits—deaths, illnesses, complaints, irregularities—is noted down and transmitted to the intendants and magistrates. The magistrates have complete control over medical treatment; they have appointed a physician in charge; no other practitioner may treat, no apothecary prepare medicine, no confessor visit a sick person without having received from him a written note 'to prevent anyone from concealing and dealing with those sick of the contagion, unknown to the magistrates'. The registration of the pathological must be constantly centralized. The relation of each individual to his disease and to his death passes through the representatives of power, the registration they make of it, the decisions they take on it.

Five or six days after the beginning of the quarantine, the process of purifying the houses one by one is begun. All the inhabitants are made to leave; in each room 'the furniture and goods' are raised from the ground or suspended from the air; perfume is poured around the room; after carefully sealing the windows, doors and even the keyholes with wax, the perfume is set alight. Finally, the entire house is closed while the perfume is consumed; those who have carried out the work are searched, as they were on entry, 'in the presence of the residents of the house, to see that they did not have something on their persons as they left that they did not have on entering'. Four hours later, the residents are allowed to reenter their homes.

This enclosed, segmented space, observed at every point, in which the individuals are inserted in a fixed place, in which the slightest movements are supervised, in which all events are recorded, in which an uninterrupted work of writing links the centre and periphery, in which power is exercised without division, according to a continuous hierarchical figure, in which each individual is constantly located, examined and distributed among the living beings, the sick and the dead—all this constitutes a compact model of the disciplinary mechanism. The plague is met by order; its function is to sort out every possible confusion: that of the disease, which is transmitted when bodies are mixed together; that of the evil, which is increased when fear and death overcome prohibitions. It lays down for each individual his place, his body, his disease and his death, his well-being, by means of an omnipresent and omniscient power that subdivides itself in a regular, uninterrupted way even to the ultimate determination of the individual, of what characterizes him, of what belongs to him, of what happens to him. Against the plague, which is a mixture, discipline brings into play its power, which is one of analysis. A whole literary fiction of the festival grew up around the plague: suspended laws, lifted prohibitions, the frenzy of passing time, bodies mingling together without respect, individuals unmasked, abandoning their statutory identity and the figure under which they had been recognized, allowing a quite different truth to appear. But there was also a political dream of the plague, which was exactly its reverse: not the collective festival, but strict divisions; not laws transgressed, but the penetration of regulation into even the smallest details of everyday life through the mediation of the complete hierarchy that assured the capillary functioning of power; not masks that were put on and taken off, but the assignment to each individual of his 'true' name, his 'true' place, his 'true' body, his 'true' disease. The plague as a form, at once real and imaginary, of disorder had as its medical and political correlative discipline. Behind the disciplinary mechanisms can be read the haunting memory of 'contagions', of the plague, of rebellions, crimes, vagabondage, desertions, people who appear and disappear, live and die in disorder.

If it is true that the leper gave rise to rituals of exclusion, which to a certain extent provided the model for and general form of the great Confinement, then the plague gave rise to disciplinary projects. Rather than the massive, binary division between one set of people and another, it called for multiple separations, individualizing distributions, an organization in depth of surveillance and control, an intensification and a ramification of power. The leper was caught up in a practice of rejection, of exile-enclosure; he was left to his doom in a mass among which it was useless to differentiate; those sick of the plague were caught up in a meticulous tactical partitioning in which individual differentiations were the constricting effects of a power that multiplied, articulated and subdivided itself; the great confinement on the one hand; the correct training on the other. The leper and his separation; the plague and its segmentations. The first is marked; the second analysed and distributed. The exile of the leper and the arrest of the plague do not bring with them the same political dream. The first is that of a pure community, the second that of a disciplined society. Two ways of exercising power over men, of controlling their relations, of separating out their dangerous mixtures. The plague-stricken town, traversed throughout with hierarchy, surveillance, observation, writing; the town immobilized by the functioning of an extensive power that bears in a distinct way over all individual bodies—this is the utopia of the perfectly governed city. The plague (envisaged as a possibility at least) is the trial in the course of which one may define ideally the exercise of disciplinary power. In order to make rights and laws function according to pure theory, the jurists place themselves in imagination in the state of nature; in order to see perfect disciplines functioning, rulers dreamt of the state of plague. Underlying disciplinary projects the image of the plague stands for all forms of confusion and disorder; just as the image of the leper, cut off from all human contact, underlies projects of exclusion.

They are different projects, then, but not incompatible ones. We see them coming slowly together, and it is the peculiarity of the nineteenth century that it applied to the space of exclusion of which the leper was the symbolic inhabitant (beggars, vagabonds, madmen and the disorderly formed the real population) the technique of power proper to disciplinary partitioning. Treat 'lepers' as 'plague victims', project the subtle segmentations of discipline onto the confused space of internment, combine it with the methods of analytical distribution proper to power, individualize the excluded, but use procedures of individualization to mark exclusion—this is what was operated regularly by disciplinary power from the beginning of the nineteenth century in the psychiatric asylum, the penitentiary, the reformatory, the approved school and, to some extent, the hospital. Generally speaking, all the authorities exercising individual control function according to a double mode; that of binary division and branding (mad/sane; dangerous/harmless; normal/abnormal); and that of coercive assignment, of differential distribution (who he is; where he must be; how he is to be characterized; how he is to be recognized; how a constant surveillance is to be exercised over him in an individual way, etc.). On the one hand, the lepers are treated as plague victims; the tactics of individualizing disciplines are imposed on the excluded; and, on the other hand, the universality of disciplinary controls makes it possible to brand the 'leper' and to bring into play against him the dualistic mechanisms of exclusion. The constant division between the normal and the abnormal, to which every individual is subjected, brings us back to our own time, by applying the binary branding and exile of the leper to quite different objects; the existence of a whole set of techniques and institutions for measuring, supervising and correcting the abnormal brings into play the disciplinary mechanisms to which the fear of the plague gave rise. All the mechanisms of power which, even today, are disposed around the abnormal individual, to brand him and to alter him, are composed of those two forms from which they distantly derive.

Bentham's *Panopticon* is the architectural figure of this composition. We know the principle on which it was based: at the periphery, an annular building; at the centre, a tower; this tower is pierced with wide windows that open onto the inner side of the ring; the peripheric building is divided into cells, each of which extends the whole width of the building; they have two windows, one on the inside, corresponding to the windows of the tower; the other, on the outside, allows the light to cross the cell from one end to the other. All that is needed, then, is to place a supervisor in a central tower and to shut up in each cell a madman, a patient, a condemned man, a worker or a schoolboy. By the effect of backlighting, one can observe from the tower, standing out precisely against the light, the small captive shadows in the cells of the periphery. They are like so many cages, so many small theatres, in which each actor is alone, perfectly individualized and constantly visible. The panoptic mechanism arranges spatial unities that make it possible to see constantly and to recognize immediately. In short, it reverses the principle of the dungeon; or rather of its three functions—to enclose, to deprive of light and to hide—it preserves only the first and eliminates the other two. Full lighting and the eye of a supervisor capture better than darkness, which ultimately protected. Visibility is a trap.

To begin with, this made it possible—as a negative effect—to avoid those compact swarming, howling masses that were to be found in places of confinement, those painted by Goya or described by Howard. Each individual, in his place, is securely confined to a cell from which he is seen from the front by the supervisor; but the side walls prevent him from coming into contact with his companions. He is seen, but he does not see; he is the object of information, never a subject in communication. The arrangement of his room, opposite the central tower, imposes on him an axial visibility; but the divisions of the ring, those separated cells, imply a lateral invisibility. And this invisibility is a guarantee of order. If the inmates are convicts, there is no danger of a plot, an attempt at collective escape, the planning of new crimes for the future, bad reciprocal influences; if they are patients, there is no danger of contagion; if they are madmen there is no risk of their committing violence upon one another; if they are schoolchildren, there is no copying, no noise, no chatter, no waste of time; if they are workers, there are no disorders, no theft, no coalitions, none of those distractions that slow down the rate of work, make it less perfect or cause accidents. The crowd, a compact mass, a locus of multiple exchanges, individualities merging together, a collective effect, is abolished and replaced by a collection of separated individualities. From the point of view of the guardian, it is replaced by a multiplicity that can be numbered and supervised; from the point of view of the inmates, by a sequestered and observed solitude.

Hence the major effect of the Panopticon: to induce in the inmate a state of conscious and permanent visibility that assures the automatic functioning of power.

❧

POLITICS, PHILOSOPHY, CULTURE, 1977–84

The Minimalist Self

STEPHEN RIGGINS One of the many things that a reader can unexpectedly learn from your work is to appreciate silence. You write about the freedom it makes possible, its multiple causes and meanings. For instance, you say in your last book that there is not one but many silences. Would it be correct to infer that there is a strongly autobiographical element in this?

FOUCAULT I think that any child who has been educated in a Catholic milieu just before or during the Second World War had the experience that there were many different ways of speaking as well as many forms of silence. There were some kinds of silence which implied very sharp hostility and others which meant deep friendship, emotional admiration, even love. I remember very well that when I met the filmmaker Daniel Schmidt who visited me, I don't know for what purpose, we discovered after a few minutes that we really had nothing to say to each other. So we stayed together from about three o'clock in the afternoon to midnight. We drank, we smoked hash, we had dinner. And I don't think we spoke more than twenty minutes during those ten hours. From that moment a rather long friendship started. It was for me the first time that a friendship originated in strictly silent behavior.

From *Politics, Philosophy, Culture: Interviews and Other Writings*, 1977-1984, by Michel Foucault. Reproduced by permission of Routledge, Inc., part of the Taylor & Francis Group.

Maybe another feature of this appreciation of silence is related to the obligation of speaking. I lived as a child in a petit bourgeois, provincial milieu in France and the obligation of speaking, of making conversation with visitors, was for me something both very strange and very boring. I often wondered why people had to speak. Silence may be a much more interesting way of having a relationship with people.

S.R. There is in North-American Indian culture a much greater appreciation of silence than in English-speaking societies and I suppose in French-speaking societies as well.

FOUCAULT Yes, you see, I think silence is one of those things that has unfortunately been dropped from our culture. We don't have a culture of silence; we don't have a culture of suicide either. The Japanese do, I think. Young Romans or young Greeks were taught to keep silent in very different ways according to the people with whom they were interacting. Silence was then a specific form of experiencing a relationship with others. This is something that I believe is really worthwhile cul-

tivating. I'm in favor of developing silence as a cultural ethos. . . .

S.R. What was the origin of your decision to become a philosopher?

FOUCAULT You see, I don't think I ever had the project of becoming a philosopher. I had not known what to do with my life. And I think that is also something rather typical for people of my generation. We did not know when I was ten or eleven years old, whether we would become German or remain French. We did not know whether we would die or not in the bombing and so on. When I was sixteen or seventeen I knew only one thing: school life was an environment protected from exterior menaces, from politics. And I have always been fascinated by living protected in a scholarly environment, in an intellectual milieu. Knowledge is for me that which must function as a protection of individual existence and as a comprehension of the exterior world. I think that's it. Knowledge as a means of surviving by understanding.

MICHAEL OAKESHOTT

1901–1990

Son of a civil servant with Fabian political beliefs, Michael Joseph Oakeshott was born in Chelmsfield, Kent, England on December 11, 1901, married an artist, and died on December 18 (or 13 or 17), 1990 in Acton, Dorset at the age of 89. After attending St. George's School, Harpenden (1912–1920), he took a B.A. (1923) and M.A. (1927) at Cambridge, and served in the Royal Artillery during WWII (1940–45), reaching the rank of captain. Oakeshott taught at Gonville and Caius College, Cambridge from 1924 through 1950, then surprised his ideological friends by joining the liberal political science faculty at the London School of Economics. He also spent time at Oxford, University of London, Manchester, Harvard, and elsewhere. Aside from a book (with the historian G. T. Griffith) on how to pick race horse winners (1936), he wrote a series of dense essays and books that championed a sophisticated form of peculiarly British conservatism, beginning with *Experience and Its Modes* (1933). R. G. Collingwood, among others, gave the book a very strong review, claiming that it was so "profound" that it could not be summarized or criticized, but required careful reading. After his death he began to be referred to as the most important British political theorist since Edmund Burke, even though A. J. Ayer and others dismissed him as derivative.

Like most conservatives, Oakeshott objected to a strong central government taking over an increasing share of civic and administrative duties, believing instead that volunteer associations made up of citizens ought to take the major roles in governing themselves through "civil association." As he aged he objected not only to the abstract, bloodless rule-mongering of large governments, to which he gave the philosophical name "rationalism," but he also surprised some of his readers by suggesting that humanity needed some sort of religious base, and could not rely simply on historical process. Although reading Oakeshott can be trying, his supporters argue that the effort is worthwhile because he is very careful in his composition, and aims more for wisdom than for mere information or cleverness. His magnum opus is *Human Conduct* (1975), but he is equally famous for his work on Hobbes, on liberal learning, the role of rationalism in political life, and other matters concerning individual liberty. And although his topics are among the most thoroughly worked over in the literature of political thought, their simplicity is deceptive, since he tries to find the basis or "modality" of political and social action, by its very nature a perplexing task.

ON HUMAN CONDUCT, 1975

On the Understanding of Human Conduct

A performance is an agent disclosing and enacting himself in responding to his understood situation by choosing what he shall do or say. There is, as we know, more to it than this, but thus far we may assume that to understand a substantive performance is to understand a substantive performer; and this is where I shall begin.

Since he falls within the terms of the identity 'agent', we know the performer to be a reflective consciousness; he is capable of error and misunderstanding because he is compact of understandings. He is what he understands himself to be and the world is what he understands it to be. Consequently, he is not what is called a 'genetic' identity which may be diseased but is incapable of error. The conditions in terms of which a performance may become intelligible are not those investigated in a science of human biology: an inspection of the chromosomes of a performer is categorically irrelevant to the understanding of his actions. Further, an agent is not a 'psychological' identity: he is not to be understood in terms of a science of psychology recognized as an inquiry into processes of feeling and thinking.

An agent, then, is a 'character' composed of substantive beliefs, affections, understandings, wants, etc.; that is, exhibitions of intelligence. And the contention we must consider first is that he and his performances are to be understood by relating them to an ideal character, called 'human nature', recognized as an organization of emotional and intellectual dispositions, propensities, inclinations, aptitudes, traits, tendencies, 'humors', demeanours, proclivities, etc.: the contention that to understand an agent and his action is to theorize them in these terms.

Sustained reflection upon 'human nature' understood in thus manner has generated a vocabulary of ideas in which to describe human conduct

and theorems in terms of which to interpret it. The components of this ideal character have been distinguished with tireless care and their interrelations have been investigated as systematically as may be. Within it, special characters have been discerned, such as 'men', 'women', and 'the young', purporting to be particular organizations of dispositions; and it has been differentiated in terms of ideal characters each representing a single dominant demeanour: the Miser, the 'Stoic', the Magnanimous, the Treacherous, the Secretive, the Ambitious Man. The virtue of this understanding of 'human nature' is to have recognized it, not as a process, but as an organization of dispositional capacities, the outcome of learning and education in which the supposed organic needs, appetites, tensions, etc. of the species are wholly transformed and superseded; that is, to have understood it as a practice to be subscribed to. And on any reading of it, this is one of the great achievements of human self-understanding; we call upon it in all our attempts to interpret actions and utterances.

It is, of course, the case that 'human nature' has, alternatively, been understood as a system or process. Thus, for example, Spinoza writes: 'If a man has begun to hate an object of his love, so that love is altogether destroyed, he will, causes being equal, regard it with more hatred than if he had never loved it, and the degree of his hatred will be proportional to the strength of his former love.' Hume observes: 'Suppose that an object concerning which we are doubtful, produces either desire or aversion; it is evident that according as the mind turns itself to one side or to another, it must feel a momentary impression of joy or sorrow.' Bentham formulated what purported to be 'axioms' of human behaviour expressing functional connections between sentiments. And others have held that performances are intelligible only in terms of a 'science of the tendencies of human actions'. The 'humors', the dispositions, the traits which constitute 'human nature', and even the dominant propensities which distinguish special human 'types', have even been recognized as the 'causes' of actions. The dream of a science of 'human nature', a dynamics of human character, has long beckoned those concerned with the theoretical understanding of agents, their actions, and utterances.

But if we put this arithmetic of behaviour on one side (together with the extensions of it which constitute the so-called science of ethology and the extraordinary excursions it has provoked into a theory of good conduct), the reflections of those concerned, not with suppositious 'causes' of performances but with 'human nature' understood as a practice composed of dispositions subscribed to in acting, may be recognized as belonging to a serious engagement to theorize substantive performances. And the question to be considered is: What is the worth of this ideal character, 'human nature', as an instrument for understanding substantive actions?

Understood in terms of this ideal character, an agent is recognized as himself a 'character' (or, to use an expression of Shaftesbury's, a 'self-system') composed of dispositions more or less exactly distinguished; that is, as a particular version of 'human nature' thus understood. This 'human nature' is a practice, and employed as an instrument of understanding it focuses our attention upon an agent in respect of being a practitioner, that is, in respect of being a subscriber to 'human nature'. He is an identity composed of aptitudes. But, although it may be said that an agent's actions and utterances are necessarily conditional upon his dispositional capacities, understanding him in these terms does not carry us far in the direction of a theoretical understanding of any of his substantive performances. Indeed, if nothing more or other than this is recognized, and even if the dispositional properties which compose the ideal character 'human nature' were much more closely specifiable than they are,[1] an action as a chosen response to an understood contingent situation related to an imagined and wished-for outcome and performed in consideration of understood compunctions has altogether escaped attention.

An agent's dispositional capacities, his skill, and the range and quality of the aptitudes which he brings to self-disclosure in action cannot themselves account for his choice to do *this* rather than *that*; and an utterance cannot be understood when it is considered only in terms of its subscription to the language in which it is spoken. Nor can the recognition of the moral disposition of an agent supply an understanding of what he has said and done. There is no dependent relation between a performance as an agent meaning to achieve an imagined and wished-for satisfaction and even the sentiments in which it is performed, much less the disposition exhibited in the sentiments. It is only the meanness of an action which may become intelligible when an agent is recognized to have a mean disposition; and no action is merely mean. No doubt *la donna è mobile*: but it is not the substantive actions and utterance of a woman, it is only their fickleness which is illumined by this dispositional theorem. What distinguishes *this* action from the million others which may be performed ficklely remains unrecognized. To understand an action or an utterance as an illustration of the interplay of 'love' and 'hate' is hardly to be counted as an understanding of what is said or done. In short, 'human nature', even when it is recognized as an ideal character composed of dispositional capacities, is an inadequate instrument for understanding the substantive performances of agents. . . .

As an apparatus for the theoretical understanding of substantive actions this ideal character is a somewhat ramshackle construction. Appropriately enough, it is less often used as an instrument of understanding than as a handy formula in which to recommend, to excuse, or to denigrate what is said and done. And the scrappy collection of so-called 'variables' with which this formula is commonly set up for use makes the operation look like a parody without an original. But this enterprise may be recognized as a plausible attempt to understand the substantive actions of agents when two conditions are satisfied. First, it must be exclusively concerned with the understanding of *conduct*; that is, it must avoid the absurdity of pretending that these 'social circumstances' must be recognized as *one* of the engagements of reflective consciousness and not as itself 'the determinant of reflective consciousness'. And secondly, it must recognize 'social being' as a practice; that is, as an intelligent engagement concerned with responding to understood situations. Where these two conditions are satisfied this proposal for the theoretical understanding of performances is distinguished from the project of constructing a 'science of society' for this purpose, which it would be otiose to mention here were it not that the two are often confused.

This 'science of society' is the counterpart of the 'science of human nature'. In it a 'society' is understood as a process, or structure, or an ecology; that is, as an unintelligent 'going-on', like a genetic process, a chemical structure, or a mechanical system. The components of this process are not agents performing actions; they are birth-rates, age groups, income brackets, intelligence quotients, life-styles, evolving 'states of societies', environmental pressures, average mental ages, distributions in space and time, numbers of 'graduates', patterns of child-bearing or of expenditure, systems of education, statistics concerning disease, poverty, employment, etc. And the enterprise is to make these identities more intelligible in terms of theorems displaying their functional interdependencies or causal relationships or of their cyclical or secular change. It is not an impossible undertaking. But it has little to do with human conduct and nothing at all to do with the performances of assignable agents.

Note

1. Since 'human nature' here is a practice, its dispositional components are imperfectly specifiable and subscription to them is similarly indeterminate, allowing incalculable (but not necessarily unrecognizable) gradations of conformity and disconformity. In this respect they are to be distinguished from the propensities of the components of a process, which are expressed in the 'laws' (probable or determinate) of their functional relationships. Different pieces of glass may have different degrees of brittleness, but brittleness (unlike kindness or miserliness), when used as an instrument for understanding what is going on, is exactly specifiable as a coefficient of elasticity.

JACQUES DERRIDA

1930–

Son of a Sephardic Jewish couple, Jacques Derrida was born on July 15, 1930 in the suburbs of Algiers, El Biar, Algeria, the middle of three surviving children in the family (two died in infancy). He married Marguerite Aucouturier in June, 1957 (in Boston while studying in the Harvard library), with her had two sons (Pierre and Jean), and has been a dominating force in global intellectual life for 30 years. Though he has dismissed the significance of biography for writers, some of his experiences have clearly filtered into his work. For instance, he early on experienced the underside of French anti-Semitism and colonialist tendencies, when, for example, he was disallowed to hoist the French flag each morning in primary school, despite being the best student in the class, to which this honor usually belonged, simply because he was Jewish. He also tells the story (in *The Post Card,* 1987) from 1942 of being sent home from school in order to meet a Vichy-set quota of Jewish students, in line with Nazi doctrine, of course. This meant he was taught in a special school run for and by Jews, which in fact he quit attending. He wanted to become a professional soccer player, did not finish high school as scheduled, and instead taught himself by reading Nietzsche, Rousseau, Paul Valéry, Camus, Sartre, and others, thereby passing the pre-university exam a year late after being tutored and reading Heidegger and other difficult philosophers. He was then able to exit this distant province by means of the French system of national competitive exams, and broke into Parisian culture, but reluctantly, at first failing to gain entry to the École Normale Superieure. But after a nervous breakdown owing to his miserable living conditions, and more study, he was admitted to the prestigious school on his third try, along with other academic stars of his generation (1952–56), and, like Foucault, he studied under Louis Althusser.

Derrida then received instruction with the great Hegelian Jean Hyppolite in studying Husserl's work, and writing his master's thesis, "The Problem of Genesis in the Philosophy of Husserl" (1954). He heard Foucault's lectures the next year, later became his friend, but continued travails prevented him from passing the *agrégation* that is necessary for university teaching. Again, he bounced back and passed, then wrote a doctoral thesis on Husserl, partly by translating the latter's work on the origins of geometry (1962). His critics point out that it was by carefully studying Husserl that he began to understand the literary dimension to philosophizing, the *aporias* (logical discontinuities), that are always at work "behind the scenes" in such texts. This work was interrupted by compulsory military service during the Algerian war, during which Derrida returned to Algiers and taught French and English to soldiers' children. His anti-colonial sentiments were recharged during this time, and he later wrote about the linguistic forces that shape imperialist domination in *The Right to Philosophy* (1990).

The year 1967 was the *annus mirabilis* for Derrida, for he published three major works, *Of Grammatology* (tr. 1976), *Speech and Phenomena* (tr. 1973), and *Writing and Difference* (tr. 1978). After attending a conference at Johns Hopkins in 1966, and meeting Jacques Lacan and Paul de Man, his term, "deconstruction," began to circulate freely throughout the writings of literary critics, philosophers, and eventually all the human sciences. He became an enormous star in the anglophone sphere, but not so much in France, despite his friendship with Foucault (upon whose work he lectured with the author present) and others. Everyone agrees that Derrida is difficult to read, mostly because he refuses to use language in any straightforward way (Oakeshott is the other extreme, one might argue). What has interested him throughout his 30 books is an examination of how words are used, how they unintentionally obscure precisely what they are trying to illuminate, and how the authors and readers of such terms, in an unreflective state, seem not to notice—until Derrida points it out—what is being said and not said in actual fact. A great deal of his charm turns around almost untranslatable French puns and word-play, sad to say.

WRITING AND DIFFERENCE, 1978

Structure, Sign and Play in the Discourse of the Human Sciences

> We need to interpret interpretations more than to interpret things. (Montaigne)

Perhaps something has occurred in the history of the concept of structure that could be called an "event," if this loaded word did not entail a meaning which it is precisely the function of structural—or structuralist—thought to reduce or to suspect. Let us speak of an "event," nevertheless, and let us use quotation marks to serve as a precaution. What would this event be then? Its exterior form would be that of a *rupture* and a redoubling.

It would be easy enough to show that the concept of structure and even the word "structure" itself are as old as the *episteme*—that is to say, as old as Western science and Western philosophy—and that their roots thrust deep into the soil of ordinary language, into whose deepest recesses the *episteme* plunges in order to gather them up and to make them part of itself in a metaphorical

displacement. Nevertheless, up to the event which I wish to mark out and define, structure—or rather the structurality of structure—although it has always been at work, has always been neutralized or reduced, and this by a process of giving it a center or of referring it to a point of presence, a fixed origin. The function of this center was not only to orient, balance, and organize the structure—one cannot in fact conceive of an unorganized structure—but above all to make sure that the organizing principle of the structure would limit what we might call the *play* of the structure. By orienting and organizing the coherence of the system, the center of a structure permits the play of its elements inside the total form. And even today the notion of a structure lacking any center represents the unthinkable itself.

Nevertheless, the center also closes off the play which it opens up and makes possible. As center, it is the point at which the substitution of contents, elements, or terms is no longer possible. At the center, the permutation or the transformation of elements (which may of course be structures enclosed within a structure) is forbidden. At least this permutation has always remained *interdicted* (and I am using this word deliberately). Thus it has always been thought that the center, which is by definition unique, constituted that very thing within a structure which while governing the structure, escapes structurality. This is why classical thought concerning structure could say that the center is, paradoxically, *within* the structure and *outside it*. The center is at the center of the totality, and yet, since the center does not belong to the totality (is not part of the totality), the totality *has its center elsewhere*. The center is not the center. The concept of centered structure—although it represents coherence itself, the condition of the *episteme* as philosophy or science—is contradictorily coherent. And as always, coherence in contradiction expresses the force of a desire. The concept of centered structure is in fact the concept of a play based on a fundamental ground, a play constituted on the basis of a fundamental immobility and a reassuring certitude, which itself is beyond the reach of play. And on the basis of this certitude anxiety can be mastered, for anxiety is invariably the result of a certain mode of being implicated in the game, of being caught by the game, of being as it were at stake in the game from the outset. And again on the basis of what we call the center (and which, because it can be either inside or outside, can also indifferently be called the origin or end, *arche* or *telos*), repetitions, substitutions, transformations, and permutations are always *taken* from a history of meaning *[sens]*—that is, in a word, a history—whose origin may always be reawakened or whose end may always be anticipated in the form of presence. This is why one perhaps could say that the movement of any archaeology, like that of any eschatology, is an accomplice of this reduction of the structurality of structure, and always attempts to conceive of structure on the basis of a full presence which is beyond play.

If this is so, the entire history of the concept of structure, before the rupture of which we are speaking, must be thought of as a series of substitutions of center for center, as a linked chain of determinations of the center. Successively, and in a regulated fashion, the center receives different forms or names. The history of metaphysics, like the history of the West, is the history of these metaphors and metonymies. Its matrix—if you will pardon me for demonstrating so little and for being so elliptical in order to come more quickly to my principal theme—is the determination of Being as *presence* in all senses of this word. It could be shown that all the names related to fundamentals, to principles, or to the center have always designated an invariable presence—*eidos, arche, te-*

los, energeia, ousia (essence, existence, substance, subject) aletheia, transcendentality, consciousness, God, man, and so forth.

The event I called a rupture, the disruption I alluded to at the beginning of this paper, presumably would have come about when the structurality of structure had to begin to be thought, that is to say, repeated, and this is why I said that this disruption was repetition in every sense of the word. Henceforth, it became necessary to think both the law which somehow governed the desire for a center in the constitution of structure, and the process of signification which orders the displacements and substitutions for this law of central presence—but a central presence which has never been itself, has always already been exiled from itself into its own substitute. The substitute does not substitute itself for anything which has somehow existed before it. Henceforth, it was necessary to begin thinking that there was no center, that the center could not be thought in the form of a present-being, that the center had no natural site, that it was not a fixed locus but a function, a sort of nonlocus in which an infinite number of sign-substitutions came into play. This was the moment when language invaded the universal problematic, the moment when, in the absence of a center or origin, everything became discourse-provided we can agree on this word—that is to say, a system in which the central signified, the original or transcendental signified, is never absolutely present outside a system of differences. The absence of the transcendental signified extends the domain and the play of signification infinitely.

Where and how does this decentering, this thinking the structurality of structure, occur? It would be somewhat naïve to refer to an event, a doctrine, or an author in order to designate this occurrence. It is no doubt part of the totality of an era, our own, but still it has always already begun to proclaim itself and begun to *work*. Nevertheless, if we wished to choose several "names," as indications only, and to recall those authors in whose discourse this occurrence has kept most closely to its most radical formulation, we doubtless would have to cite the Nietzschean critique of metaphysics, the critique of the concepts of Being and truth, for which were substituted the concepts of play, interpretation, and sign (sign without present truth); the Freudian critique of self-presence, that is, the critique of consciousness, of the subject, of self-identity and of self-proximity or self-possession; and, more radically, the Heideggerean destruction of metaphysics, of onto-theology, of the determination of Being as presence. But all these destructive discourses and all their analogues are trapped in a kind of circle. This circle is unique. It describes the form of the relation between the history of metaphysics and the destruction of the history of metaphysics. There is no sense in doing without the concepts of metaphysics in order to shake metaphysics. We have no language—no syntax and no lexicon—which is foreign to this history; we can pronounce not a single destructive proposition which has not already had to slip into the form, the logic, and the implicit postulations of precisely what it seeks to contest. To take one example from many: the metaphysics of presence is shaken with the help of the concept of *sign*. But, as I suggested a moment ago, as soon as one seeks to demonstrate in this way that there is no transcendental or privileged signified and that the domain or play of signification henceforth has no limit, one must reject even the concept and word "sign" itself—which is precisely what cannot be done. For the signification "sign" has always been understood and determined, in its meaning, as sign of, a signifier referring to a signified, a signifier different from its signified. If one erases the radical difference between signifier and signified, it is the word "signifier" itself which must be abandoned as a metaphysical concept. When Lévi-Strauss says in the preface to *The Raw and the Cooked* that he has "sought to transcend the opposition between the sensible and the intelligible by operating from the outset at the level of signs," the necessity, force, and legitimacy of his act cannot make us forget that the concept of the sign cannot in itself surpass this opposition between the sensible and the intelligible. The concept of the sign, in each of its aspects, has been determined by this opposition throughout the totality of its history. It has lived only on this opposition and its system. But we cannot do without the concept of the sign, for we cannot give up this metaphysical complicity without also giving up the critique we are directing against this complicity, or without the risk of erasing difference in the self-identity of a signified reducing its signifier into itself or, amounting to the same thing, simply expelling its signifier outside itself. For there are two het-

erogenous ways of erasing the difference between the signifier and the signified: one, the classic way, consists in reducing or deriving the signifier, that is to say, ultimately in *submitting* the sign to thought; the other, the one we are using here against the first one, consists in putting into question the system in which the preceding reduction functioned: first and foremost, the opposition between the sensible and the intelligible. For the *paradox* is that the metaphysical reduction of the sign needed the opposition it was reducing. The opposition is systematic with the reduction. And what we are saying here about the sign can be extended to all the concepts and all the sentences of metaphysics, in particular to the discourse on "structure. " But there are several ways of being caught in this circle. They are all more or less naïve, more or less empirical, more or less systematic, more or less close to the formulation—that is, to the formalization—of this circle. It is these differences which explain the multiplicity of destructive discourses and the disagreement between those who elaborate them. Nietzsche, Freud, and Heidegger, for example, worked within the inherited concepts of metaphysics. Since these concepts are not elements or atoms, and since they are taken from a syntax and a system, every particular borrowing brings along with it the whole of metaphysics. This is what allows these destroyers to destroy each other reciprocally—for example, Heidegger regarding Nietzsche, with as much lucidity and rigor as bad faith and misconstruction, as the last metaphysician, the last "Platonist." One could do the same for Heidegger himself, for Freud, or for a number of others. And today no exercise is more widespread.

<hr/>

LETTER TO A JAPANESE FRIEND

10 July 1983

Dear Professor Izutsu,

At our last meeting I promised you some schematic and preliminary reflections on the word

From "Letter to a Japanese Friend," by Jacques Derrida, from *Derrida and Difference*, David Wood and Robert Bernasconi, Eds. Published by Northwestern University Press. Copyright © 1988. First published 1985 by Parousia Press. Reprinted by permission.

"deconstruction." What we discussed were prolegomena to a possible translation of this word into Japanese, one which would at least try to avoid, if *possible,* a negative determination of its significations or connotations. The question would be therefore what deconstruction is not, or rather *ought* not to be. I underline these words "possible" and "ought." For if the difficulties of translation can be anticipated (and the question of deconstruction is also through and through the question of translation, and of the language of concepts, of the conceptual corpus of so-called Western metaphysics), one should not begin by naively believing that the word "deconstruction" corresponds in French to some clear and univocal signification. There is already in "my" language a serious *[sombre]* problem of translation between what here or there can be envisaged for the word and the usage itself, the reserves of the word. And it is already clear that even in French, things change from one context to another. More so in the German, English, and especially American contexts, where the same word is already attached to very different connotations, inflections, and emotional or affective values. Their analysis would be interesting and warrants a study of its own.

When I choose this word, or when it imposed itself upon me—I think it was in *Of Grammatology*—I little thought it would be credited with such a central role in the discourse that interested me at the time. Among other things I wished to translate and adapt to my own ends the Heideggerian word *Destruktion* or *Abbau.* Each signified in this context an operation bearing on the structure or traditional architecture of the fundamental concepts of ontology or of Western metaphysics. But in French "destruction" too obviously implied an annihilation or a negative reduction much closer perhaps to Nietzschean "demolition" than to the Heideggerian interpretation or to the type of reading that I proposed. So I ruled that out. I remember having looked to see if the word "deconstruction" (which came to me it seemed quite spontaneously) was good French. I found it in the *Littré:* The grammatical, linguistic, or rhetorical senses [portées] were found bound up with a "mechanical" sense *[portée "machinique"].* This Association appeared very fortunate and fortunately adapted to what I wanted at least to suggest. Per-

haps I could cite some of the entries from the *Littré.* "*Déconstruction:* action of deconstructing. Grammatical term. Disarranging the construction of words in a sentence. 'Of deconstruction, common way of saying Construction,' Lemare, *De la maniére d'apprendre les langues,* chap. 17, in *Cours de langue Latine. Deconstruire.* 1. To disasemble the parts of a whole. To deconstruct a machine to transport it elsewhere. 2. Grammatical term . . . To deconstruct verse, rendering it, by the suppression of meter, similar to prose. Absolutely. In the system of prenotional sentences, one also starts with translation and one of its advantages is never needing to deconstruct,' Lemare ibid., 3. *Se déconstruire* [to deconstruct itself] . . . to lose its construction. 'Modern scholarship has shown us that in a region of the timeless East, a language reaching its own state of perfection is deconstructed [*s'est déconstruite*] and altered from within itself according to the single law of change, natural to the human mind,' Villemain, *Préface du Dictionnaire de l'Académie.*"

Naturally it will be necessary to translate all of this into Japanese but that only postpones the problem. It goes without saying that if all the significations enumerated by the *Littré* interested me because of their affinity with what I "meant" *["voulais-dire"],* they concerned, metaphorically, so to say, only models or regions of meaning and not the totality of what deconstruction aspires to at its most ambitious. This is not limited to a linguistico-grammatical model, nor even a semantic model, let alone a mechanical model. These models themselves ought to be submitted to a deconstructive questioning. It is true then that these "models" have been behind a number of misunderstandings about the concept and word of "deconstruction" because of the temptation to reduce it to these models.

It must also be said that the word was rarely used and was largely unknown in France. It had to be reconstructed in some way, and its use value had been determined by the discourse that was then being attempted around and on the basis of *Of Grammatology.* It is to this use value that I am now going to try to give some precision and not some primitive meaning or etymology sheltered from or outside of any contextual strategy.

A few more words on the subject of "the context." At that time structuralism was dominant.

"Deconstruction" seemed to be going in the same direction since the word signified a certain attention to structures (which themselves were neither simply ideas, nor forms, nor syntheses, nor systems). To deconstruct was also a structuralist gesture or in any case a gesture that assumed a certain need for the structuralist problematic. But it was also an antistructuralist gesture, and its fortune rests in part on this ambiguity. Structures were to be undone, decomposed, desedimented (all types of structures, linguistic, "logocentric," "phonocentric"—structuralism being especially at that time dominated by linguistic models and by a so-called structural linguistics that was also called Saussurian—socio-institutional, political, cultural, and above all and from the start philosophical). This is why, especially in the United States, the motif of deconstruction has been associated with "poststructuralism" (a word unknown in France until its "return" from the United States). But the undoing, decomposing, and desedimenting of structures, in a certain sense more historical than the structuralist movement it called into question, was not a negative operation. Rather than destroying, it was also necessary to understand how an "ensemble" was constituted and to reconstruct it to this end. However, the negative appearance was and remains much more difficult to efface than is suggested by the grammar of the word (de-), even though it can designate a genealogical restoration *[remonter]* rather than a demolition. That is why this word, at least on its own, has never appeared satisfactory to me (but what word is), and must always be girded by an entire discourse. It is difficult to effect it afterward because, in the work of deconstruction, I have had to, as I have to here, multiply the cautionary indicators and put aside all the traditional philosophical concepts, while reaffirming the necessity of returning to them, at least under erasure. Hence, this has been called, precipitously, a type of negative theology (this was neither true nor false but I shall not enter into the debate here).

All the same, and in spite of appearances, deconstruction is neither an *analysis* nor a *critique* and its translation would have to take that into consideration. It is not an analysis in particular because the dismantling of a structure is not a regression toward a *simple element*, toward an *indissoluble origin*. These values, like that of analysis, are themselves philosophemes subject to deconstruction. No more is it a critique, in a general sense or in a Kantian sense. The instance of *krinein* or of *krisis* (decision, choice, judgment, discernment) is itself, as is all the apparatus of transcendental critique, one of the essential "themes" or "objects" of deconstruction.

I would say the same about *method*. Deconstruction is not a method and cannot be transformed into one. Especially if the technical and procedural significations of the words are stressed. It is true that in certain circles (university or cultural, especially in the United States) the technical and methodological "metaphor" that seems necessarily attached to the very word "decontruction" has been able to seduce or lead astray. Hence the debate that has developed in these circles: Can deconstruction become a methodology for reading and for interpretation? Can it thus let itself be reappropriated and domesticated by academic institutions?

It is not enough to say that deconstruction could not be reduced to some methodological instrumentality or to a set of rules and transposable procedures. Nor will it do to claim that each deconstructive "event" remains singular or, in any case, as close as possible to something like an idiom or a signature. It must also be made clear that deconstruction is not even an *act* or an *operation*. Not only because there would be something "patient" or "passive" about it (as Blanchot says, more passive than passivity, than the passivity that is opposed to activity). Not only because it does not return to an individual or collective *subject* who would take the initiative and apply it to an object, a text, a theme, etc. Deconstruction takes place, it is an event that does not await the deliberation, consciousness, or organization of a subject, or even of modernity. *It deconstructs it-self. It can be deconstructed. [Ça se déconstruit.]* The "it" [ça] is not here an impersonal thing that is opposed to some egological subjectivity. *It is in deconstruction* (the *Littré* says, "to deconstruct itself *[se déconstruire]* . . . to lose its construction"). And the "se" of "se déconstruire," which is not the reflexivity of an ego or of a consciousness, bears the whole enigma. I recognize, my dear friend, that in trying to make a word clearer so as to assist its translation, I am only thereby increasing the difficulties: "the impossible task of the translator" (Benjamin). This too is what is meant by "deconstructs."

If deconstruction takes place everywhere it [*ça*] takes place, where there is something (and is not therefore limited to meaning or to the text in the current and bookish sense of the word), we still have to think through what is happening in our world, in modernity, at the time when deconstruction is becoming a motif, with its word, its privileged themes, its mobile strategy, etc. I have no simple and formalizable response to this question. All my essays are attempts to have it out with this formidable question. They are modest symptoms of it, quite as much as tentative interpretations. I would not even dare to say, following a Heideggerian schema, that we are in an "epoch" of being-in-deconstruction, of a being-in-deconstruction that would manifest or dissimulate itself at one and the same time in other "epochs." This thought of "epochs" and especially that of a gathering of the destiny of being and of the unity of its destination or its dispersions (*Schicken, Geschick*) will never be very convincing.

To be very schematic I would say that the difficulty of *defining* and therefore also of *translating* the word "deconstruction" stems from the fact that all the predicates, all the defining concepts, all the lexical significations, and even the syntactic articulations, which seem at one moment to lend themselves to this definition or to that translation, are also deconstructed or deconstructible, directly or otherwise, etc. And that goes for the word, the very unity of the word deconstruction, as for every word. *Of Grammatology* questioned the unity "word" and all the privileges with which it was credited, especially in its *nominal* form. It is therefore only a discourse or rather a writing that can make up for the rapacity of the word to be equal to a "thought." All sentences of the type "deconstruction is X" or "deconstruction is not X" *a priori* miss the point, which is to say that they are at least false. As you know, one of the principal things at stake in what is called in my texts "deconstruction" is precisely the delimiting of ontology and above all of the third person present indicative: S *is* P.

The word "deconstruction," like all other words, acquires its value only from its inscription in a chain of possible substitutions, in what is too blithely called a "context." For me, for what I have tried and still try to write, the word has interest only within a certain context, where it replaces and lets itself be determined by such other words as "ecriture," "trace," "differance," "supplement," "hymen," "pharmakon," "marge," "entame," "parergon," etc. By definition, the list can never be closed, and I have cited only names, which is inadequate and done only for reasons of economy. In fact, I should have cited the sentences and the interlinking of sentences which in their turn determine these names in some of my texts.

What deconstruction is not? everything of course!

What is deconstruction? nothing of course!

I do not think, for all these reasons, that it is a *good word [un bon mot]*. It is certainly not elegant *[beau]*. It has definitely been of service in a highly determined situation. In order to know what has been imposed upon it in a chain of possible substitutions, despite its essential imperfection, this "highly determined situation" will need to be analyzed and deconstructed. This is difficult and I am not going to do it here.

One final word to conclude this letter, which is already too long. I do not believe that translation is a secondary and derived event in relation to an original language or text. And as "deconstruction" is a word, as I have just said, that is essentially replaceable in a chain of substitution, then that can also be done from one language to another. The chance, first of all the chance of (the) "deconstruction," would be that another word (the same word and an other) can be found in Japanese to say the same thing (the same and an other), to speak of deconstruction, and to lead elsewhere to its being written and transcribed, in a word which will also be more beautiful.

When I speak of this writing of the other which will be more beautiful, I clearly understand translation as involving the same risk and chance as the poem. How to translate "poem"? a "poem"? . . .

With my best wishes,
Jacques Derrida

*—Translated by David Wood
and Andrew Benjamin*

"GESCHLECHT: SEXUAL DIFFERENCE, ONTOLOGICAL DIFFERENCE, 1987

Of sex, one can readily remark, yes, Heidegger speaks as little as possible, perhaps he has never spoken of it. Perhaps he has never said anything, by that name or the names under which we recognize it, about the "sexual-relation," "sexual-difference," or indeed about "man-and-woman." That silence, therefore, is easily remarked. Which means that the remark is somewhat facile. A few indications, concluding with "everything happens as if . . . ," and it would be satisfied. The dossier could then be closed, avoiding trouble if not risk: it is as if, in reading Heidegger, there were no sexual difference, and nothing of this aspect in man, which is to say in woman, to interrogate or suspect, nothing worthy of questioning, *fragwürdig*. It is as if, one might continue, sexual difference did not rise to the height of ontological difference: it would be on the whole as negligible, with regard to the question of the sense of being, as any other difference, a determinate distinction or an ontic predicate. Negligible for *thought,* of course, even if it is not at all negligible for science or philosophy. But insofar as it is opened up to the question of being, insofar as it has a relation to being, in that very reference, *Dasein* would not be sexed. Discourse on sexuality would thus be abandoned to the sciences or philosophies of life, to anthropology, sociology, biology, or perhaps even to religion or morality.

Sexual difference, we were saying or we heard ourselves saying, would not rise to the height of ontological difference. It changes nothing, apparently, to know that "rising to heights" should be out of the question, since the thought of difference gets on no such high horse; yet there is silence. One might even find this to be, precisely, haughty, arrogant, or provoking in a century when sexuality, commonplace of all babbling, has

also become the currency of philosophic and scientific "knowledge," the inevitable *Kampfplatz* of ethics and politics. Not a word from Heidegger! One might judge this to be rather "grand style," this scene of stubborn mutism at the very center of the conversation, in the uninterrupted and distracted buzzing of the colloquium. In itself it has a waking and sobering value (but what exactly is everyone talking about around this silence?): Who, indeed, around or even long before him, has not chatted about sexuality as such, as it were, and by that name? All the philosophers in the tradition have done so, from Plato to Nietzsche, who for their part were irrepressible on the subject. Kant, Hegel, Husserl all reserved a place for it; they at least touched on it in their anthropology or in their philosophy of nature, and in fact everywhere.

Is it imprudent to trust Heidegger's manifest silence? Will this apparent fact later be disturbed in its nice philological assurance by some known or unedited passage when, while combing through the whole of Heidegger, some reading machine manages to hunt out the thing and snare it? Still, one must think of programing the machine, one must think, think of it and know how to do it. What will the index be? On which words will it rely? Only on names? And on which syntax, visible or invisible? Briefly, by which signs will you recognize his speaking or remaining silent about what you nonchalantly call sexual difference? What is it you are thinking beneath those words or through them?

What would be, in most cases, the sufficient basis for remarking today such an impressive silence? What measure would seem to suffice to allow that silence to appear as such, marked and marking? Undoubtedly this: Heidegger apparently said nothing about sexuality by name in those places where the best educated and endowed "modernity" would have fully expected it given its panoply of "everything-is-sexual-and-everything-is-political-and-reciprocally" (note in passing that the word "political" is rarely used, perhaps never, in Heidegger, another not quote insignificant matter). Even before the statistics were in, the matter would seem already settled. But there are good grounds to believe that the statistics here would only confirm the verdict: about

From "Geschlecht: Sexual Difference, Ontological Difference," by Jacques Derrida, as seen in *Research in Phenomenology,* Volume 13, John Sallis, Ed. Copyright © 1983. Used by permission of Brill Academic Publishers.

what we glibly call sexuality Heidegger has remained silent. Transitive and significant silence (he has silenced sex) which belongs, as he says about a certain *Schweigen* (*"hier in der transitiven Bedeutung gesagt"*), to the path of a word (parole) he seems to interrupt. But what are the places of this interruption? Where is the silence working on that discourse? And what are the forms and determinable contours of that non-said?

You can bet that there's nothing immobile in these places where the arrows of the aforesaid panoply would pin things down with a name: omission, repression, denial, foreclosure, even the unthought.

But then, if the bet were lost, would not the trace of that silence merit the detour? It is not just anything he silences and the trace does not come from just anywhere. But why the bet? Because before predicting anything whatever about "sexuality," it may be verified, one must invoke chance, the aleatory, destiny.

Let it be, then, a so-called modern reading, an investigation armed with psychoanalysis, an enquiry authorized by all of anthropological culture. What does it seek? Where does it seek? Where may it deem it has the right to expect at least a sign, an allusion, however elliptical, a reference, to sexuality, the sexual relation, sexual difference? To begin with, in *Sein und Zeit*. Was not the existential analytic of *Dasein* near enough to a fundamental anthropology to have given rise to so many misunderstandings or mistakes regarding its supposed *"réalité-humaine"* or human reality as it was translated in France? Yet even in the analyses of being-in-the-world as being-with-others, or of care either in its self or as *Fürsorge*, it would be vain, it seems, to search even for the beginning of a discourse on desire and sexuality. One might conclude from this that sexual difference is not an essential trait, that it does not belong to the existential structure of *Dasein*. Being-there, *being there*, the *there* of being as such, bears no sexual mark. The same then goes for the readings of the sense of being, since, as *Sein und Zeit* clearly states (§ 2), *Dasein* remains in such a reading the exemplary being. Even were it admitted that all reference to sexuality isn't effaced or remains implied, this would only be to the degree that such a reference presupposes quite general structures (*In-der-Welt-sein als Mit- und Selbst-sein, Räumlichkeit, Befindlichkeit Rede, Sprache, Geworfenheit, Sorge, Zeitlichkeit, Sein zum Tode*). Yet sexuality would never be the guiding thread for a privileged access to these structures.

CHRISTOPHER LASCH

1932–1994

Christopher "Kit" Lasch was born in Omaha, Nebraska on June 1, 1932, the son of a journalist father and philosophy professor mother. He matriculated at Harvard in 1950, was John Updike's roommate, and received his B.A. in 1954, following which he took his other two degrees at Columbia in 1955 and 1961, all in history. He taught at Williams College, Columbia, and Roosevelt University while a graduate student and began publishing essays even then. After graduate school Lasch worked at the University of Iowa, then Northwestern, and finally landed at the University of Rochester, where he remained, and where he managed to influence a small but lively group of budding New Left intellectuals, most of them linked to the journal, *Telos*. In some ways very much a cultural product of the American Midwest—combining a populist sympathy for leftwing politics with a deeply conservative view of the family and social values—Lasch became a well-known critic of society that took him far beyond his earliest works. His first books—*The American Liberals and the Russian Revolution* (1962), *The New Radicalism in American, 1889–1963: The Intellectual as a Social Type* (1965), and *The World of Nations* (1973) were all well-received by informed readers, all of which concerned American political history. But with *Haven in a Heartless World: The Family Besieged* (1977) and especially *The Culture of Narcissism* (1979), he broke into a much wider orbit and became a target for those at the forefront of causes which disagreed with his own critique of cultural change in the U.S. He was accused of marketing nostalgia for a past that never existed (in his attack upon the social forces that were disrupting and undermining family structure) and of counter-revolutionary sentiments in his commentary on the deleterious effects that so-called narcissism were having upon the individual-societal dialectic that he thought had gone astray. Neither of these works were based on what social scientists call "systematic research," but both hit a chord with the reading public and gave rise to tremendous debate. He was continuing this line of argument with *The Minimal Self: Psychic Survival in Troubled Times* (1984) and *The True and Only Heaven: Progress and Its Critics* (1991) when he died suddenly and unexpectedly of cancer. His sentiments in the former book can be partly summarized with a passage from "The Fantastic World of Commodities": "The psychological effects of consumerism can be grasped only when consumption is understood as another phase of the industrial work routine." Such a sentiment became increasingly bizarre-sounding to those who sported t-shirts which read "Born to Shop" during the Reagan period of anti-unionization and the speculative bubble that followed it. In seconding Marcuse's dim view of the meaning that consumerist society held for its participants, Lasch was harking back to an American past which put more stock by what one could produce rather than what one could accumulate. As he put it, "The consumer's complete dependence on these intricate, supremely sophisticated life-support systems, and more generally on externally provided goods and services, recreates . . . infantile feelings of helplessness." His posthumous work, *The Revolt of the Elites and the Betrayal of Democracy* (1995), reminded his readers how important his voice had been before it was prematurely silenced. Jean Bethke Elshtain wrote in an obituary article, "One strong characteristic of his work was his incisive clarity and his restless and stubborn insistence that he must call things by their correct names." Though more a cultural critic with large issues than a social scientist with a focused agenda, Lasch served an important function in reminding the American middle class through his many jeremiads that it had lost its way during the 70s and 80s. Had he lived, he would surely have found much grist for his mill in the 90s, leading to the inevitable collapse of the bubble economy.

THE CULTURE OF NARCISSISM, 1978

The Narcissistic Personality of Our Time

. . . Theoretical precision about narcissism is important not only because the idea is so readily susceptible to moralistic inflation but because the practice of equating narcissism with everything selfish and disagreeable mitigates against historical specificity. Men have always been selfish, groups have always been ethnocentric; nothing is gained by giving these qualities a psychiatric label. The emergence of character disorders as the most prominent form of psychiatric pathology, however, together with the change in personality structure this development reflects, derives from quite specific changes in our society and culture— from bureaucracy, the proliferation of images, therapeutic ideologies, the rationalization of the inner life, the cult of consumption, and in the last analysis from changes in family life and from changing patterns of socialization. All this disappears from sight if narcissism becomes simply "the metaphor of the human condition," as in another existential, humanistic interpretation, Shirley Sugerman's *Sin and Madness: Studies in Narcissism.*

The refusal of recent critics of narcissism to discuss the etiology of narcissism or to pay much attention to the growing body of clinical writing on the subject probably represents a deliberate decision, stemming from the fear that emphasis on the clinical aspects of the narcissistic syndrome would detract from the concept's usefulness in social analysis. This decision, however, has proved to be a mistake. In ignoring the psychological dimension, these authors also miss the social. They fail to explore any of the character traits associated with pathological narcissism, which in less extreme form appear in such profusion in the everyday life of our age: dependence on the vicarious warmth provided by others combined with a fear of dependence, a sense of inner emptiness, boundless repressed rage, and unsatisfied oral cravings. Nor do they discuss what might be called the secondary characteristics of narcissism: pseudo self-insight, calculating seductiveness, nervous, self-deprecatory humor. Thus they deprive themselves of any basis on which to make connections between the narcissistic personality type and certain characteristic patterns of contemporary culture, such as the intense fear of old age and death, altered sense of time, fascination with celebrity, fear of competition, decline of the play spirit, deteriorating relations between men and women. For these critics, narcissism remains at its loosest a synonym for selfishness and at its most precise a metaphor, and nothing more, that describes the state of mind in which the world appears as a mirror of the self.

Psychology and Sociology

Psychoanalysis deals with individuals, not with groups. Efforts to generalize clinical findings to collective behavior always encounter the difficulty that groups have a life of their own. The collective mind, if there is such a thing, reflects the needs of the group as a whole, not the psychic needs of the individual, which in fact have to be subordinated to the demands of collective living. Indeed it is precisely the subjection of individuals to the group that psychoanalytic theory, through a study of its psychic repercussions, promises to clarify. By conducting an intensive analysis of individual cases that rests on clinical evidence rather than commonsense impressions, psychoanalysis tells us something about the inner workings of society itself, in the very act of turning its back on society and immersing itself in the individual unconscious.

Every society reproduces its culture—its norms, it underlying assumptions, its modes of organizing experience—in the individual, in the form of personality. As Durkheim said, personality is the individual socialized. The process of socialization, carried out by the family and secondarily by the school and other agencies of character formation, modifies human nature to conform to the prevailing social norms. Each society tries to solve the universal crises of childhood—the trauma of separation from the mother, the fear of abandonment, the pain of competing with others for the mother's love—in its own way, and the manner in which it deals with these psychic events produces a characteristic form of personality, a characteristic form of psychological deformation, by means of which the individual reconciles himself to instinctual deprivation and submits to the requirements of social existence. Freud's insistence on the continuity between psychic health and psychic sickness makes it possible to see neuroses and psychoses as in some sense the characteristic expression of a given culture. "Psychosis," Jules Henry has written, "is the final outcome of all that is wrong with a culture."

Psychoanalysis best clarifies the connection between society and the individual, culture and

personality, precisely when it confines itself to careful examination of individuals. It tells us most about society when it is least determined to do so. Freud's extrapolation of psychoanalytic principles into anthropology, history, and biography can be safely ignored by the student of society, but his clinical investigations constitute a storehouse of indispensable ideas, once it is understood that the unconscious mind represents the modification of nature by culture, the imposition of civilization on instinct.

> Freud should not be reproached [wrote T. W. Adorno] for having neglected the concrete social dimension, but for being all too untroubled by the social origin of . . . the rigidity of the unconscious, which he registers with the undeviating objectivity of the natural scientist. . . . In making the leap from psychological images to historical reality, he forgets what he himself discovered—that all reality undergoes modification upon entering the unconscious—and is thus misled into positing such factual events as the murder of the father by the primal horde.

Those who wish to understand contemporary narcissism as a social and cultural phenomenon must turn first to the growing body of clinical writing on the subject, which makes no claim to social or cultural significance and deliberately repudiates the proposition that "changes in contemporary culture," as Otto Kernberg writes, "have effects on patterns of object relations." In the clinical literature, narcissism serves as more than a metaphoric term for self-absorption. As a psychic formation in which "love rejected turns back to the self as hatred," narcissism has come to be recognized as an important element in the so-called character disorders that have absorbed much of the clinical attention once given to hysteria and obsessional neuroses. A new theory of narcissism has developed, grounded in Freud's well-known essay on the subject (which treats narcissism—libidinal investment of the self—as a necessary precondition of object love) but devoted not to primary narcissism but to secondary or pathological narcissism: the incorporation of grandiose object images as a defense against anxiety and guilt. Both types of narcissism blur the boundaries between the self and the world of objects, but there is an important difference between them. The newborn infant—the primary narcissist—does not yet perceive his mother as having an existence separate from his own, and he therefore mistakes dependence on the mother, who satisfies his needs as soon as they arise, with his own omnipotence. "It takes several weeks of postnatal development . . . before the infant perceives that the source of his need . . . is within and the source of gratification is outside the self."

Secondary narcissism, on the other hand, "attempts to annul the pain of disappointed [object] love" and to nullify the child's rage against those who do not respond immediately to his needs; against those who are now seen to respond to others beside the child and who therefore appear to have abandoned him. Pathological narcissism, "which cannot be considered simply a fixation at the level of normal primitive narcissism," arises only when the ego has developed to the point of distinguishing itself from surrounding objects. If the child for some reason experiences this separation trauma with special intensity, he may attempt to reestablish earlier relationships by creating in his fantasies an omni-potent mother or father who merges with images of his own self. "Through internalization the patient seeks to recreate a wished-for love relationship which may once have existed and simultaneously to annul the anxiety and guilt aroused by aggressive drives directed against the frustrating and disappointing object."

ANTHONY GIDDENS

1938–

Anthony Giddens, son of a clerk for the London subway system, was born in a poorer section of the city on January 18, 1938, married Jane M. Ellwood in 1963 (divorced), remarried and again divorced, and had two daughters by his first wife. By means of governmentally sponsored scholarships, he was able to attend the Mincheden School, Southgate and then the University of Hull, graduating in 1959 with honors, followed by an M.A. in 1961 from the London School of Economics (of which he became Director in 1997). Without a doctorate, he began teaching social theory, at the University of Leicester, England (where he was influenced by his famous senior colleague, Norbert Elias) (1961–70), with visiting jobs at Simon Fraser University, British Columbia (1967–68) and UCLA (1968–69), finally moving to King's College, Cambridge in 1970. He finally received a doctorate in 1976 from Cambridge, 17 years after his undergraduate degree had been awarded. Despite writing a raft of books and articles, he was denied promotion to Professor at Cambridge many times over the next 16 years, perhaps as much because of his class origins as by the perceived quality of his work among the more conservative dons. He also founded Polity Press in 1985 with two colleagues, and henceforth was in the enviable position of having a guaranteed outlet for whatever he wrote, which has served him well, though not always his readers. His prolixity has noticeably grown since Polity Press opened its doors.

As with many theorists, his earlier books will probably be regarded as his best. *Capitalism and Modern Social Theory* (1971), a lucid and intelligent textbook treatment of Marx, Durkheim, and Weber, has become a standard in the literature. His *New Rules of Sociological Method* (1976), playing on Durkheim's book of similar title, introduced hermeneutics into contemporary social theory, even if in a malnourished state that did not advance much beyond earlier statements by Dilthey, Gadamer, and Ricoeur. His two essay books, *Studies in Social and Political Theory* (1977) and *Central Problems in Social Theory* (1979) include some first-rate analyses of competing thinkers, particularly Parsons and functionalism. In the latter book Giddens introduced his "theory of structuration," which is still regarded as his signal contribution to social thought. He explained: "The concept of structuration involves that of the *duality of structure,* which relates to the *fundamentally recursive character of social life, and expresses the mutual dependence of structure and agency.* By the duality of structure I mean that the structural properties of social systems are both the medium and the outcome of the practices that constitute those systems" (emphases in original). With similar sentiments expressed at some length, Giddens was able to give post-Parsonian theory some new words (agency, structuration, recursiveness, duality of structure) that were, in fact, conceptually quite close to Parsons' own vocabulary, but seemed to be an improvement due to injections of German philosophy and French social theory on the contemporary scene. Giddens has always been strongest analyzing the French intellectual tradition, and has translated Durkheim's works.

Beginning with *A Contemporary Critique of Historical Materialism* (1981), he began to run neck and neck with Habermas for the title of Grand Theorist of the era, and probably made his most important statement in *The Constitution of Society: Outline of the Theory of Structuration* (1984). A long meditation on how the subject/object dualism so common within earlier social theory might be overcome through the "double hermeneutic" within a "duality of structure," and other forms of reflexivity, this enlarged statement illustrated that Giddens had found particularly congenial to his way of thinking the ground rules established for interactional studies by ethnomethodologists, some of whom he had come to know at UCLA. In this project he was seconding work already done by Bourdieu and Habermas, adding his own twists from Heidegger and other sources, all concerning the "virtual" presence and absence as the social agent interacted with or "instantiated" social structure through action. Although structuration theory has not had too many followers in sociology proper, it has influenced geographers and certain philosophers.

Beginning in 1990 with *The Consequences of Modernity, Modernity and Self-Identity* (1991), and *The Transformation of Intimacy* (1992), Giddens issued a torrent of books, about one a year, which were written with a popular audience in mind, and reflected his new self-awareness, partly based on having undergone therapeutic sessions of a psychiatric type (so he revealed in an interview). These books were less closely tied to serious scholarly arguments and tried instead to speak to ordinary readers at the level of their own existential dilemmas (e.g. from *The Transformation of Intimacy,* a chapter opening: "Is sexuality, in some sense or another, the key to modern civilisation? Many, mostly from the progressive side of the political spectrum, have answered in the affirmative . . . Sexuality generates pleasure; and pleasure, or at least the promise of it, provides a leverage for marketing goods in a capitalistic society.") Finally, in the late 90s, Giddens became an advisor to the British government and a spokesman for the so-called "Third Way" between rapacious capitalism and sclerotic socialism. He wrote and edited many other books, including a large introductory sociology book which sold better in the UK than in the U.S., where it was regarded as opaque to the undergraduate mind. Giddens has for many years now been the leading English-speaking social theorist of the large bore, and even if his major work is long behind him, his presence as writer and publisher has been salutary in the post-Parsonsian environment which he helped create.

MODERNITY AND SELF-IDENTITY: SELF AND SOCIETY IN THE LATE MODERN AGE, 1991

Ontological Security and Existential Anxiety

To be ontologically secure is to possess, on the level of the unconscious and practical consciousness, 'answers' to fundamental existential questions which all human life in some way addresses. Anxiety in a certain sense comes with human liberty, as Kierkegaard says; freedom is not a given characteristic of the human individual, but derives from the acquisition of an ontological understanding of external reality and personal identity. The autonomy which human beings acquire derives from their capacity to expand the range of mediated experience: to be familiar with properties of objects and events outside immediate settings of sensory involvement. With this in mind, we can reinterpret Kierkegaard's description of anxiety as 'the possibility of freedom'. As a general phenomenon, anxiety derives from the capacity—and, indeed, necessity—for the individual to think ahead, to anticipate future possibilities counterfactually in relation to present action. But in a deeper way, anxiety (or its likelihood) comes from the very 'faith' in the independent existence of persons and objects that ontological security implies.

The prime existential question which the infant 'answers' in the course of early psychological development concerns *existence itself:* the discovery of an ontological framework of 'external reality'. When Kierkegaard analyses anxiety—or elemental dread—as the struggle of being against non-being', he points directly to this issue. To 'be', for the human individual, is to have ontological awareness. This is not the same as awareness of self-identity, however closely the two may be related in the developing experience of the infant. The 'struggle of being against non-being' is the perpetual task of the individual, not just to 'accept' reality, but to create ontological reference points as an integral aspect of 'going on' in the contexts of day-to-day life. Existence is a mode of being-in-the-world in Kierkegaard's sense. In 'doing' everyday life, all human beings "answer" the question of being; they do it by the nature of the activities they carry out. As with other existential questions to be mentioned below, such "answers" are lodged fundamentally on the level of behaviour. . . .

A second type of existential question concerns not so much the nature of being as the relations between the external world and *human life.* Here there is also a fundamental temporal aspect, in the guise of human finitude as compared to temporal infinity or the 'eternal'. All humans live in circumstances of what I have elsewhere called *existential contradiction:* we are of the inanimate world, yet set off against it, as self-conscious beings aware of our finite character. As Heidegger says, *Dasein* is a being who not only lives and dies, but is aware of the horizon of its own mortality. This is the 'existential awareness of non-being' of which Tillich speaks,'the awareness that non-being is part of one's own being'. When seen in a purely biological sense, death is relatively unproblematic—the cessation of the physiological functions of the organism. Kierkegaard points out that, in contrast to biological death, 'subjective death' is an 'absolute

uncertainty'—something of which we can have no intrinsic understanding. The existential problem is how to approach subjective death: 'it is the case that the living individual is absolutely excluded from the possibility of approaching death in any sense whatever, since he cannot experimentally come near enough without comically sacrificing himself upon the altar of his own experiment, and since he cannot experimentally restrain the experiment, he learns nothing from it.'

In psychoanalytic theory, the existential horizon of finitude does not have a prominent place in the origins of anxiety—or, rather, the unconscious cannot conceive of its own death, not for the reason given by Kierkegaard, but because the unconscious has no sense of time. Anxiety about death in Freud's theory comes primarily from fear of the loss of others, and is thus directly connected to the early mastery of absence. The discrepancy between these two interpretations, however, is more apparent than real. For if we cannot understand 'subjective death', then death is no more or less than the transition from being to non-being; and the fear of non-being becomes one of the primal anxieties of the developing infant. Threats to the being of the infant in the first instance are feelings or presentiments of loss—the realisation that the constancy of persons and objects is bound up with the stable relations provided by the caretaking agents. The possible loss of the caretakers provides the initiating frame-work from which fears of death and sickness emerge with regard to the self. It may be true that, on the level of the unconscious, the person cannot conceive of her death. As Freud says, unconsciously all of us think of surviving as spectators at our own deaths. But consciousness of finitude, which human beings develop with increasing cognitive mastery of temporal categories, is associated with anxieties of an utterly fundamental sort. . . .

A third category of existential question concerns the existence of *other persons.* No issue was more thoroughly explored in the early literature of phenomenology, but we have to be careful to avoid the philosophical errors to which that literature fell prey. Husserl drew on Cartesian rationalism in his formulation of interpersonal knowledge. Given this position, although the individual can perceive the body of another person, he or she cannot perceive that individual as subject.'I know my own soul better than my own body', Descartes wrote. But I can only know the body of the other, he continued, since I have no access to that person's consciousness. According to Husserl, we are aware of another person's feelings and experiences only on the basis of empathic inferences from our own. As is well known, the inadequacy of this view proved to be one of the intractable difficulties of his philosophy. A transcendental philosophy of the ego terminates in an irremediable solipsism.

The difficulty is avoided in the position of the later Wittgenstein, as well as in the more sophistical versions of existentialist phenomenology. Self-consciousness has no primacy over the awareness of others, since language—which is intrinsically public—is the means of access to both. Intersubjectivity does not derive from subjectivity, but the other way around. How should we expand on this view in developmental terms, however, given that the early experiences of the child predate the acquisition of language? And in what sense is the existence of others an existential problem, if we break with Husserl's standpoint? The answers follow from the arguments already developed in the preceding pages. Learning the qualities of others is connected in an immediate way with the earliest explorations of the object-world and with the first stirrings of what later become established feelings of self-identity. The individual is not a being who at some sudden point encounters others; 'discovering the other', in an emotional-cognitive way, is of key importance in the initial development of self-awareness as such. The subsequent acquisition of language would not be possible were not those early developmental processes well in train by that time.

The 'problem of the other' is not a question of how the individual makes the shift from the certainty of her or his own inner experiences to the unknowable other person. Rather it concerns the inherent connections which exist between learning the characteristics of other persons and the other major axes of ontological security. Trust in others, in the early life of the infant and, in chronic fashion, in the activities of the adult, is at the origin of the experience of a stable external world and a coherent sense of self-identity. It is 'faith' in the reliability and integrity of others which is at stake here. Trust in others begins in the context of individual confidence—confidence in the caretaking figures. But it both precedes an awareness of those figures as 'persons' and later forms a generalised component of the inter-subjective nature of social life. Trust, interpersonal relations and a conviction of the 'reality' of things go hand in hand in the social settings of adult life. The responses of the other are necessary to the sustaining of an 'observable/accountable' world, and yet there is no point at which they can be absolutely relied upon. Social reproduction unfolds with none of the causal determination characteristic of the physical world, but as an always contingent feature of the knowledgeable use of convention. The social world, moreover, should not be understood as a multiplicity of situations in which 'ego' faces 'alter', but one in which each person is equally implicated in the active process of organising predictable social interaction. The orderliness of day-to-day life is a miraculous occurrence, but it is not one that stems from any sort of outside intervention; it is brought about as a continuous achievement on the part of everyday actors in an entirely routine way. That orderliness is solid and constant; yet the slightest glance of one person towards another, inflexion of the voice, changing facial expression or gestures of the body may threaten it.

A fourth type of existential question concerns precisely: *self-identity.* But what exactly is self-identity? Since the self is a somewhat amorphous phenomenon, self-identity cannot refer merely to its persistence over time in the way philosophers might speak of the 'identity' of objects or things. The 'identity' of the self, in contrast to the self as a generic phenomenon, presumes reflexive awareness. It is what the individual is conscious of in the term 'self-consciousness'. Self-identity, in other words, is not something that is just given, as a result of the continuities of the individual's action-system, but something that has to be routinely created and sustained in the reflexive activities of the individual.

An anchoring discursive feature of self-identity is the linguistic differentiation of 'I/me/you' (or their equivalents). We cannot be satisfied, however, with G. H. Mead's formulation of the I/me couplet in relation to self-identity. In Mead's theory, the 'me' is the identity—a social identity—of which the 'I' becomes conscious in the course of the psychological development of the child. The 'I' is, as it were, the active, primitive will of the individual, which seizes on the 'me' as the reflection of social ties. We can agree with Mead that the infant begins to develop a self in response to the social context of its early experience. But the I/me (and I/me/you) relation is one internal to language, not one connecting the unsocialised part of the individual (the I) to the 'social self'. 'I' is a linguistic shifter, which gets its meaning from the networks of terms whereby a discursive system of subjectivity is acquired. The ability to use 'I', and other associated terms of subjectivity, is a condition for the emergence of self-awareness, but does not as such define it.

Self-identity is not a distinctive trait, or even a collection of traits, possessed by the individual. It is *the self as reflexively understood by the person in terms of her or his biography.* Identity here still presumes continuity across time and space: but self-identity is such continuity as interpreted reflexively by the agent. This includes the cognitive component of personhood. To be a 'person' is not just to be a reflexive actor, but to have a concept of a person (as applied both to the self and others). What a 'person' is understood to be certainly varies across cultures, although there are elements of such a notion that are common to all cultures. The capacity to use 'I' in shifting contexts, characteristic of every known culture, is the most elemental feature of reflexive conceptions of personhood. . . .

A normal sense of self-identity is the obverse of these characteristics. A person with a reasonably stable sense of self-identity has a feeling of biographical continuity which she is able to grasp reflexively and, to a greater or lesser degree, communicate to other people. That person also, through early trust relations, has established a protective cocoon which 'filters out', in the practical conduct of day-to-day life, many of the dangers which in principle threaten the integrity of the self. Finally, the individual is able to accept that integrity as worthwhile. There is sufficient self-regard to sustain a sense of the self as 'alive'— within the scope of reflexive control, rather than having the inert quality of things in the object-world.

The existential question of self-identity is bound up with the fragile nature of the biography which the individual 'supplies' about herself. A person's identity is not to be found in behaviour, nor—important though this is—in the reactions of others, but in the capacity *to keep a particular narrative going.* The individual's biography, if she is to maintain regular interaction with others in the day-to-day world, cannot be wholly fictive. It must continually integrate events which occur in the external world, and sort them into the ongoing 'story' about the self. As Charles Taylor puts it, 'In order to have a sense of who we are, we have to have a notion of how we have become, and of where we are going.' There is surely an unconscious aspect to this chronic 'work', perhaps organised in a basic way through dreams. Dreaming may very well represent an unconscious selection and discarding of memories, which proceeds at the end of every day.

Tribulations of the Self

The self in high modernity is not a minimal self, but the experience of large arenas of security intersects, sometimes in subtle, sometimes in nakedly disturbing, ways with generalised sources of unease. Feelings of restlessness, foreboding and desperation may mingle in individual experience with faith in the reliability of certain forms of social and technical framework. In the light of the analysis developed thus far, let us consider the origins of such sentiments. . . .

*'Living in the World': Dilemmas
of the Self*

In conditions of late modernity, we live 'in the world' in a different sense from previous eras of history. Everyone still continues to live a local life, and the constraints of the body ensure that all individuals, at every moment, are contextually situated in time and space. Yet the transformations of place, and the intrusion of distance into local activities, combined with the centrality of mediated experience, radically change what 'the world' actually is. This is so both on the level of the 'phenomenal world' of the individual and the general universe of social activity within which collective social life is enacted. Although everyone lives a local life, phenomenal worlds for the most part are truly global.

Characterising individuals' phenomenal worlds is difficult, certainly in the abstract. Every person reacts selectively to the diverse sources of direct and mediated experience which compose the *Umwelt*. One thing we can say with some certainty is that in very few instances does the phenomenal world any longer correspond to the habitual settings through which an individual physically moves. Localities are thoroughly penetrated by distanciated influences, whether this be regarded as a cause for concern or simply accepted as a routine part of social life. All individuals actively, although by no means always in a conscious way, selectly incorporate many elements of mediated experience into their day-to-day conduct. This is never a random or a passive process, contrary to what the image of the *collage* effect might suggest. A newspaper, for example, presents a collage of information, as does, on a wider scale, the whole bevy of newspapers which may be on sale in a particular area or country. Yet each reader imposes his own order on this diversity, by selecting which newspaper to read—if any—and by making an active selection of its contents.

In some part the appropriation of mediated information follows pre-established habits and obeys the principle of the avoidance of cognitive dissonance. That is to say, the plethora of available information is reduced via routinised attitudes which exclude, or reinterpret, potentially disturbing knowledge. From a negative point of view, such closure might be regarded as prejudice, the refusal seriously to entertain views and ideas divergent from those an individual already holds; yet, from another angle, avoidance of dissonance forms part of the protective cocoon which helps maintain ontological security. For even the most prejudiced or narrow-minded person, the regularised contact with mediated information inherent in day-to-day life today is a positive appropriation: a mode of interpreting information within the routines of daily life. Obviously there are wide variations in terms of how open a given individual is to new forms of knowledge, and how far that person is able to tolerate certain levels of dissonance. But all phenomenal worlds are active accomplishments, and all follow the same basic psychodynamics, from the most local of ways of life to the most cosmopolitan.

'Living in the world', where the world is that of late modernity, involves various distinctive tensions and difficulties on the level of the self. We can analyse these most easily by understanding them as dilemmas which, on one level or another, have to be resolved in order to preserve a coherent narrative of self-identity.

JEAN-FRANÇOIS LYOTARD

1924–1998

Jean-François Lyotard was born on August 10, 1924 in Versailles, France, married Dolores Dzizeck and with her had one son and two daughters, and died on April 21, 1998 from leukemia at the age of 74 in Paris. He was educated at the Sorbonne in the late 40s and finished his exams in 1958. During his youth he wanted to be a Dominican monk, an artist, an historian, or a writer, but gave up fiction at 15 after finishing an unsuccessful novel. History was ruled out due to what he called a weak memory, and his interests in women made a clerical life impossible as well. He worked these events into an autobiography (*Peregrinations,* 1986) where he argued that one is inclined to imagine that plans can be neatly worked out for future work, but they go awry and "fate" takes over. He worked with artists organizing exhibits and writing illustrated books, and published an early piece in Sartre's journal, *Les Temps modernes* where he declared that his generation, the "new" one of the 1920s, ought to throw aside traditional ways of living and find adventure in life. On his second attempt, he passed the *agrégation* exam to teach in 1950 and was assigned to the Lycée Constantine in Algeria (1950–52), lectured at the Sorbonne and in 1966 went to the University of Paris at Vincennes, with later visiting positions at Wisconsin, Sao Paulo, Montreal, Minnesota, and elsewhere. In 1954 he published a study of the German phenomenological movement inspired by Husserl which went through nine French editions. Also in 1954 he joined with Cornelius Castoriadis in publishing *Socialisme ou Barbarie,* a Marxist journal. Like many leftist intellectuals in France during the 50s, he wrote about the Algerian war in an anti-imperialist mode.

Lyotard felt intellectually constrained by conventional leftwing politics, and began to write about "the libidinal body" as existing outside of political structures. He also found the hamfisted Marxist disregard of aesthetics bothersome, since so much of his youth had been concentrated on various artistic activities and ambitions. Being asked in 1978 to evaluate Quebec's scientific culture, he surprisingly wrote his most famous book, *The Postmodern Condition* (1979; tr. 1984). This is by far his most quoted statement in which, among other things, he defines "the postmodern" as a condition of the 20th century during which the "grand narratives" of the 18th and 19th centuries could no longer be regarded as persuasive or even relevant to contemporary history. Those stories—regarding e.g., race, national identity, societal evolution—meant to liberate their initial auditors from the imaginative limitations of medieval conventions, had become stale, according to Lyotard, and could no longer explain or accommodate newer social formations and their aesthetic sensibilities. In Lyotard's own words: "Postmodern science . . . is theorizing its own evolution as discontinuous, catastrophic, nonrectifiable, and paradoxical. It is changing the meaning of knowledge while expressing how such a change can take place. It is producing not the known, but the unknown." Such sentiments put Lyotard circa 1980 at the forefront of social thought and gave rise to an entire industry of postmodernist studies, many of which he would likely have disavowed had he lived long enough.

THE POSTMODERN CONDITION, 1979

The Nature of the Social Bond: The Postmodern Perspective

. . . For brevity's sake, suffice it to say that functions of regulation, and therefore of reproduction, are being and will be further withdrawn from administrators and entrusted to machines. Increasingly, the central question is becoming who will have access to the information these machines must have in storage to guarantee that the right decisions are made. Access to data is, and will continue to be, the prerogative of experts of all stripes. The ruling class is and will continue to be the class of decision makers. Even now it is no longer composed of the traditional political class, but of a composite layer of corporate leaders, high-level administrators, and the heads of the major professional, labor, political, and religious organizations.

What is new in all of this is that the old poles of attraction represented by nation-states, parties, professions, institutions, and historical traditions are losing their attraction. And it does not look as though they will be replaced, at least not on their former scale. The Trilateral Commission is not a popular pole of attraction. "Identifying" with, the great names, the heroes of contemporary history, is becoming more and more difficult. Dedicating oneself to "catching up with Germany," the life goal the French president (Giscard d'Estaing at the time this book was published in France) seems to be offering his countrymen, is not exactly exciting. But then again, it is not exactly a life goal. It depends on each individual's industriousness. Each individual is referred to himself. And each of us knows that our self does not amount to much.

This breaking up of the grand Narratives leads to what some authors analyze in terms of the dissolution of the social bond and the disintegration of social aggregates into a mass of individual atoms thrown into the absurdity of Brownian motion. Nothing of the kind is happening: this point

From *The Postmodern Condition: A Report on Knowledge*, by Jean-François Lyotard, Geoff Bennington and Brian Massumi, Trans. English translation and Foreword copyright © 1984 by the University of Minnesota. Original French language edition copyright © 1979 by Les Editions di Minuit.

of view, it seems to me, is haunted by the paradisaic representation of a lost "organic" society.

A *self* does not amount to much, but no self is an island; each exists in a fabric of relations that is now more complex and mobile than ever before. Young or old, man or woman, rich or poor, a person is always located at "nodal points" of specific communication circuits, however tiny these may be. Or better: one is always located at a post through which various kinds of messages pass. No one, not even the least privileged among us, is ever entirely powerless over the messages that traverse and position him at the post of sender, addressee, or referent. One's mobility in relation to these language game effects (language games, of course, are what this is all about) is tolerable, at least within certain limits (and the limits are vague); it is even solicited by regulatory mechanisms, and in particular by the self-adjustments the system undertakes in order to improve its performance. It may even be said that the system can and must encourage such movement to the extent that it combats its own entropy; the novelty of an unexpected "move," with its correlative displacement of a partner or group of partners, can supply the system with that increased performativity it forever demands and consumes.

It should now be clear from which perspective I chose language games as my general methodological approach. I am not claiming that the *entirety* of social relations is of this nature—that will remain an open question. But there is no need to resort to some fiction of social origins to establish that language games are the minimum relation required for society to exist: even before he is born, if only by virtue of the name he is given, the human child is already positioned as the referent in the story recounted by those around him, in relation to which he will inevitably chart his course. Or more simply still, the question of the social bond, insofar as it is a question, is itself a language game, the game of inquiry. It immediately positions the person who asks, as well as the addressee and the referent asked about: it is already the social bond.

On the other hand, in a society whose communication component is becoming more prominent day by day, both as a reality and as an issue, it is clear that language assumes a new importance. It would be superficial to reduce its significance to the traditional alternative between manipulatory speech and the unilateral transmission of messages on the one hand, and free expression and dialogue on the other.

A word on this last-point. If the problem is described simply in terms of communication theory, two things are overlooked: first, messages have quite different forms and effects depending on whether they are, for example, denotatives, prescriptives, evaluatives, performatives, etc. It is clear that what is important is not simply the fact that they communicate information. Reducing them to this function is to adopt an outlook which unduly privileges the system's own interests and point of view. A cybernetic machine does indeed run on information, but the goals programmed into it, for example, originate in prescriptive and evaluative statements it has no way to correct in the course of its functioning—for example, maximizing its own performance. How can one guarantee that performance, maximization is the best goal for the social system in every case? In any case the "atoms" forming its matter are competent to handle statements such as these—and this question in particular.

Second, the trivial cybernetic version of information theory misses something of decisive importance, to which I have already called attention: the agonistic aspect of society. The atoms are placed at the crossroads of pragmatic relationships, but they are also displaced by the messages that traverse them, in perpetual motion. Each language partner, when a "move" pertaining to him is made, undergoes a "displacement," an alteration of some kind that not only affects him in his capacity as addressee and referent, but also as sender. These "moves" necessarily provoke "countermoves"—and everyone knows that a countermove that is merely reactional is not a "good" move. Reactional countermoves are no more than programmed effects in the opponent's strategy; they play into his hands and thus have no effect on the balance of power. That is why it is important to increase displacement in the games, and even to disorient it, in such a way as to make an unexpected "move" (a new statement).

What is needed if we are to understand social relations in this manner, on whatever scale we choose, is not only a theory of communication, but a theory of games which accepts agonistics as a founding principle. In this context, it is easy to see that the essential element of newness is not simply "innovation." Support for this approach can be found in the work of a number of contemporary sociologists, in addition to linguists and philosophers of language.

This 'atomization' of the social into flexible networks of language games may seem far removed from the modern reality, which is depicted, on the contrary, as afflicted with bureaucratic paralysis. The objection will be made, at least, that the weight of certain institutions imposes limits on the games, and thus restricts the inventiveness of the players in making their moves. But I think this can be taken into account without causing any particular difficulty.

In the ordinary use of discourse—for example, in a discussion between two friends—the interlocutors use any available ammunition, changing games from one utterance to the next: questions, requests, assertions, and narratives are launched pell-mell into battle. The war is not without rules, but the rules allow and encourage the greatest possible flexibility of utterance.

From this point of view, an institution differs from a conversation in that it always requires supplementary constraints for statements to be declared admissible within its bounds. The constraints function to filter discursive potentials, interrupting possible connections in the communication networks: there are things that should not be said. They also privilege certain classes of statements (sometimes only one) whose predominance characterizes the discourse of the particular institution: there are things that should be said, and there are ways of saying them. Thus: orders in the army, prayer in church, denotation in the schools, narration in families, questions in philosophy, performativity in businesses. Bureaucratization is the outer limit of this tendency.

However, this hypothesis about the institution is still too "unwieldy": its point of departure is an overly "reifying" view of what is institutionalized. We know today that the limits the institution imposes on potential language "moves" are never established once and for all (even if they have been formally defined). Rather, the limits are themselves the stakes and provisional results of language strategies, within the institution and without. Examples: Does the university have a place for language experiments (poetics)? Can you tell stories in a cabinet meeting? Advocate a cause in the barracks? The answers are clear: yes, if the university opens creative workshops; yes, if the cabinet works with prospective scenarios; yes, if the limits of the old institution are displaced. Reciprocally, it can be said that the boundaries only stabilize when they cease to be stakes in the game.

This, I think, is the appropriate approach to contemporary institutions of knowledge.

Delegitimation

In contemporary society and culture—postindustrial society, post-modern culture—the question of the legitimation of knowledge is formulated in different terms. The grand narrative has lost its credibility, regardless of what mode of unification it uses, regardless of whether it is a speculative narrative or a narrative of emancipation.

The decline of narrative can be seen as an effect of the blossoming of techniques and technologies since the Second World War, which has shifted emphasis from the ends of action to its means; it can also be seen as an effect of the redeployment of advanced liberal capitalism after its retreat under the protection of Keynesianism during the period 1930–60, a renewal that has eliminated the communist alternative and valorized the individual enjoyment of goods and services.

Anytime we go searching for causes in this way we are bound to be disappointed. Even if we adopted one or the other of these hypotheses, we would still have to detail the correlation between the tendencies mentioned and the decline of the unifying and legitimating power of the grand narratives of speculation and emancipation.

It is, of course, understandable that both capitalist renewal and prosperity and the disorienting upsurge of technology would have an impact on the status of knowledge. But in order to understand how contemporary science could have been susceptible to those effects long before they took place, we must first locate the seeds of "delegitimation" and nihilism that were inherent in the grand narratives of the nineteenth century.

First of all, the speculative apparatus maintains an ambiguous relation to knowledge. It shows that knowledge is only worthy of that name to the extent that it reduplicates itself ("lifts itself up," *hebt sich auf;* is sublated) by citing its own statements in a second-level discourse (autonomy) that functions to legitimate them. This is as much as to say that, in its immediacy, denotative discourse bearing on a certain referent (a living organism, a chemical property, a physical phenomenon, etc.) does not really know what it thinks it knows. Positive science is not a form of knowledge. And speculation feeds on its suppression. The Hegelian speculative narrative thus harbors a certain skepticism toward positive learning, as Hegel himself admits.

A science that has not legitimated itself is not a true science; if the discourse that was meant to legitimate it seems to belong to a prescientific form of knowledge, like a "vulgar" narrative, it is demoted to the lowest rank, that of an ideology or instrument of power. And this always happens if the rules of the science game that discourse denounces as empirical are applied to science itself.

Take for example the speculative statement: "A scientific statement is knowledge if and only if it can take its place in a universal process of engendering." The question is: Is this statement knowledge as it itself defines it? Only if it can take its place in a universal process of engendering. Which it can. All it has to do is to presuppose that such a process exists (the Life of spirit) and that it is itself an expression of that process. This presupposition, in fact, is indispensable to the speculative language game. Without it, the language of legitimation would not be legitimate; it would accompany science in a nosedive into nonsense, at least if we take idealism's word for it.

But this presupposition can also be understood in a totally different sense, one which takes us in the direction of postmodern culture: we could say, in keeping with the perspective we adopted earlier, that this presupposition defines the set of rules one must accept in order to play the speculative game. Such an appraisal assumes first that we accept that the "positive" sciences represent the general mode of knowledge and second, that we understand this language to imply certain formal and axiomatic presuppositions that it must always make explicit. This is exactly what Nietzsche is doing, though with a different terminology, when he shows that "European nihilism" resulted from the truth requirement of science being turned back against itself.

There thus arises an idea of perspective that is not far removed, at least in this respect, from the idea of language games. What we have here is a process of delegitimation fueled by the demand for legitimation itself. The "crisis" of scientific knowledge, signs of which have been accumulating since the end of the nineteenth century, is not born of a chance proliferation of sciences, itself an effect of progress in technology and the expansion of capitalism. It represents, rather, an internal erosion of the legitimacy principle of knowledge. There is erosion at work inside the speculative game, and by loosening the weave of the encyclopedic net in which each science was to find its place, it eventually sets them free.

The classical dividing lines between the various fields of science are thus called into question—disciplines disappear, overlappings occur at the borders between sciences, and from these new territories are born. The speculative hierarchy of learning gives way to an imminent and, as it were, "flat" network of areas of inquiry, the respective frontiers of which are in constant flux. The old "faculties" splinter into institutes and foundations of all kinds, and the universities lose their function of speculative legitimation. Stripped of the responsibility for research (which was stifled by the speculative narrative), they limit themselves to the transmission of what is judged to be established knowledge, and through didactics they guarantee the replication of teachers rather than the production of researchers. This is the state in which Nietzsche finds and condemns them.

The potential for erosion intrinsic to the other legitimation procedure, the emancipation apparatus flowing from the *Aufklärung*, is no less extensive than the one at work within speculative discourse. But it touches a different aspect. Its distinguishing characteristic is that it grounds the le-

gitimation of science and truth in the autonomy of interlocutors involved in ethical, social, and political praxis. As we have seen, there are immediate problems with this form of legitimation: the difference between a denotative statement with cognitive value and a prescriptive statement with practical value is one of relevance, therefore of competence. There is nothing to prove that if a statement describing a real situation is true, it follows that a prescriptive statement based upon it (the effect of which will necessarily be a modification of that reality) will be just.

❧

ONE OF THE THINGS AT STAKE IN WOMEN'S STRUGGLES

In the Form of Writing, the Question of the Relations Between Men and Women is Itself Caught Up in These Relations

It may be that you are forced to be a man from the moment that you write. Maybe writing is a fact of virility. Even if you write as a woman, 'femininely'. Perhaps what we call feminine writing is only a variation on a genre that is masculine and remains so: the essay. It is said that the femininity of writing depends on content. Writing is feminine, for example, if it operates by *seduction* rather than conviction. But the opposition of these two efficacies is itself probably masculine.

To avoid such alternatives, you claim no assignable difference between feminine and masculine, in writing or elsewhere: but this *neutralization* of the question is also very suspect (as when someone says that he's not political, neither on the right nor the left; everyone knows he is on the right).

It is a philosopher who is speaking here about relations between men and women. He is trying to escape what is masculine in the very posing of such a question. However, his flight and his strate-

From "One of the Things at Stake in Women's Struggles." *SubStance 20*, by Jean-François Lyotard, Deborah J. Clark, Trans. Copyright © 1978. Reprinted by permission of the University of Wisconsin Press.

gies probably remain masculine. He knows that the so-called question of a masculine/feminine opposition, and probably the opposition itself, will only disappear as he *stops philosophizing:* for it exists as opposition only by philosophical (and political) method, that is, by the male way of thinking.

In the midst of these aporias, one is tempted to give his pen over to the antonym of the inquisitive adult male, to *the little girl.* But it is said that, like a savage, she doesn't write. And above all, that like savages, she is herself the creation of her so-called opposite, the sober-minded male, who in reality is also her judge: a creation of the jealousy he feels for something he is forbidden to be.

How Intelligence Supposedly Came to Women

The King of Ou says to general Sun-Tse: you who are such a great strategist and who undertake the military training of anyone, take 180 of my women and try to make soldiers of them. Sun-Tse orders them to form two ranks led by the king's two favourites and he teaches them the code of drumbeats: two beats: right face; three beats: left face; four beats: about-face. They laugh and talk instead of obeying. He goes over the lesson several times: giggles, disorder, even as they assure him that they know the code. Fine, he says, you have mutinied; military law calls for death: so you will die. The king is alerted and he forbids Sun-Tse to harm the women, and especially his favourites. Sun-Tse answers: You have charged me with their training, all the rest is my business. And he severs the heads of the two favoured women with his sabre. As soon as the king's favourites are replaced, the exercise begins again: 'and, as though these women had always been soldiers, they become silent and orderly.'

Thus, one way to separate masculine and feminine. *Primo:* virility claims to establish order and femininity is the compulsion to deride order. There is chattering in the gynaeceum and silence among the troops. Contrary to our story, even though comedy may be a masculine genre, it represents the successful stratagem of weakness; comedy makes men laugh like women; the prisoner Rosine makes a fool of Don Bartholo. This is only a momentary concession: Rosine escapes her tutor only to fall under the law of the real master,

the Count Alma-viva. He who laughs *last,* laughs best: the aimless humour of women will succumb to the learned, socratic, teleological irony of men.

Secundo: the ruse of reason (masculine) differs from the snares of sensitivity (feminine): reason *makes use of* death. Sun-Tse kills a few women who laugh: that is sobriety. Women must know the fear of death and must overcome it if they are to be civilized (that is, if they are to be virilized). If not, they give in and are subjugated (but continue to laugh up their sleeves); or they don't, a few of them are killed: these are the dead soldiers who can become heroes. Slaves are never entirely reliable: truly civilized women are dead women, or men.

Tertio: What is pertinent for distinguishing the sexes is the relation to death: a body that can die, whatever its sexual anatomy, is masculine; a body that does not know that it must disappear is feminine. Men teach women of death, the impossible, the presence of absence. Tragedy is a noble genre because one does not laugh: in fact, it shows that there is nothing to laugh about. No way to play the woman. Sun-Tse defines a rite of passage: the feminine is on the side of the child, youth, and nature; death is the ferryman; he shows the way to language, to order, to the consideration of lack, to meaning, to culture.

Sexual Theory and Practice of Men Includes the Threat of Death: Or, Sexuality Makes no Sense without a Signifier

When Freud asks: What does a woman desire? as a man, he is suggesting that she desires nothing since she is passive. And when he says, libido is masculine—here he agrees with the spectator of pornographic films who answers when asked why women aren't interested in such spectacles: Women? Have you ever seen them take an interest in sex? 'Women have no sex'—by libido, Freud means not an instinctual process but an intelligible one, because it desires (*to say*) something. For Lacan, the signifier inscribing its effects as unconscious statements is the phallus, the a priori condition of all symbolic function when this function works on sexually determined bodies. The body has no sex before being traversed by 'the defiling of signifier', i.e., the threat of castration, or death, a mark of Oedipal law.

Difference is established here, they say: the little boy supposedly overcomes the threat of castration to resolve the Oedipus complex, and becomes virile, while the little girl becomes feminine by entering the Oedipus complex under the law of castration. The first must identify with the phallus in spite of the father, the other must content herself with receiving it. Sun-Tse seems to be in agreement with this thoroughly masculine version: a woman is become a man; let her confront death, or castration, the law of the signifier. Otherwise, she will always lack the sense of lack. She thinks herself eternal for this reason and is deprived of sexuality as well as the activity constituting the body's language.

Plato's Socrates says nothing else when he claims that Love is born not only of ruse, cleverness, and Resource (*Poros*) but also of Lack (*Penia*)—that one does not love what one loves but loves impregnating it and reproducing itself in order to become immortal; thus he subordinates love to the effect of an absent signifier, the Idea, supreme paradigm which carries bodies beyond themselves. And *he will die* to bear witness to this. The great virile association of war and sexuality (an association found also in Chinese erotic treatises, which are concurrently manuals of strategy) proceeds from this distribution of the symbolic function: virility has its *price:* life; the body can speak only if it can die and each time it knows pleasure, the body risks becoming lawless and speechless once again—capable only of living and laughing. That is why love is for man a struggle in which his virility, at is, culture, is at stake.

Men (Western men, in any case) want to conquer, not love. They have nothing but disdain and irony for the sensual, for odours, sensations, secretions, *laissez-faire,* music; they call 'artists' those among them that consent to these things. But women are the artists. Men feel undone when they love. They prefer prostitutes whose impassivity protects them. A woman's pleasure remains an enigma for them because they have not found the technical means to produce it in a predictable and guaranteed fashion. They prefer the clitoris, which they consider a trustworthy and homologable agent working for them in the adversary's camp. Vaginal penetration consists 'then' in the occupation of this camp; it is likewise a *cursus* followed by the conquered until she reaches the ultimate degree of pleasure, which the man claims to extract from her.

But for women, to 'come' or not, in the sense of having or not having the spasm men *anticipate* on the basis of their own orgasm—this is *not a question* when women love. The question does not arise and the answer is indifferent. But it concerns virility to not want to know this; for it implies a body whose pieces do not 'speak' but 'work' without having to produce a meaning they supposedly lack. If pleasure comes easily without love and love without pleasure, then sexual and affective manoeuvres would have nothing to do with producing meaning—theoretical (Beautiful, True) or physical (orgasmic 'satisfaction').

NIKLAS LUHMANN

1927–1998

Niklas Luhmann was born on December 8, 1927 in Lüneburg, Niedersachsen, Germany, married Ursula von Walter in 1960 and with her had one daughter and twin boys, and died of cancer at 71 on November 6, 1998 in Oerlinghausen, Germany. Drafted as a boy into an anti-aircraft unit, he was captured by Americans, beaten up, which surprised him, and imprisoned for a short time before the war ended. Personally experiencing the chaos of postwar Germany and the arbitrariness of brute force, he resolved to study law as a social process in order to comprehend how social order could be reconstructed and maintained. He studied law at the University of Freiburg, graduating in 1949, then, like most Germans with law degrees, took a civil service job, in the culture ministry in Lüneburg. His job was to create a card-file system for all the cases in the Higher Administrative Court concerning compensation for victims of Nazism. Not overburdened with formal work, he read Husserl, British anthropologists, Descartes, German poetry, and other works. He worked on a second, more elaborate card system for the rest of his life, despite holding academic appointments. In 1960–61 he studied with Talcott Parsons at Harvard and tried to improve on his teacher's concept of "function," though was unsuccessful in convincing Parsons to alter his scheme. Eventually he moved from civil service to academic life, finishing his habilitation in 1966 under Helmut Schelsky at Münster with a work entitled "Law and Automation in Public Administration." He was given the Adorno chair at Frankfurt in 1969, then moved to the newly formed University of Bielefeld in 1970, and the next year carried out a debate with Habermas which the latter refused to have translated into English. His wife died in 1977 and he moved to Oerlinghausen (where Max Weber had carried out factory research at a family-owned mill 70 years before).

Luhmann's reputation in Germany is large and secure, whereas his reception in the U.S. has been less warm, mainly due to his ungraceful prose style (in translation), and the fact that much of his work on systems theory seems unhappily to remind older readers of Parsons' work from the 50s. This is particularly the case with *The Differentiation of Sociology* (1982) and also his magnum opus, *Social Systems* (1984; tr. 1995). His later work, however, like *Love as Passion* (1986) and *Risk: A Sociological Theory* (1993) have been more broadly read and discussed, as well as *Political Theory in the Welfare State* (1990), from which the excerpts below originate. When Luhmann was able to unburden himself of the quasi-Parsonsian mantle, and shook the trap of systems theory, his imagination led him into realms of theorizing with a much broader appeal.

POLITICAL THEORY IN THE WELFARE STATE, 1990

The Representation of Society Within Society, 1981

. . . My argument is that the problems of the legitimacy of political power are linked with this impossibility of representation. The capacity to represent the entire system within the system, the whole of society within society, is the source of legitimation. Whoever can represent all of society within society is thereby legitimate. Representation gives him the right. It is his right. If it dissolves, then this means that whoever still wishes to rule legitimately must then invoke values and ultimately produce results. Starting from the premise that a part of the whole can represent the whole within the whole, the right of authority is a natural right. In lieu of a contrary case or alternatives, this is the task of the *maiores partes,* who clearly stay within the law and who, in the event of its infringement, must expect justified resistance.

This world has passed and, with it, its semantics of self-observation and self-description. In place of *civilitas* we have civilization; in place of the good life, the difference between values and circumstances; and in place of the representation of unity, the representation of difference. Authority has been dissolved into nothingness. How can this change be explained sociologically? And to what extent do the changes experienced in the meaning of political semantics help us in this?

I believe that the explanation lies in a modification of the primary principle of societal differentiation: in the re-organization of the social system of stratification into functional differentiation. This transformation gives modern society its character. In the eighteenth century this development was more or less clearly grasped, and this is why the conceptual universe of old Europe lost its plausibility.

The problem that forms our point of reference, the representation of the system within the system, plays a role in both social orders. One can thereby compare the old and the new, the traditional and the modern society on the basis of the question of how they are represented within themselves. And the difference appears, on the semantic as well as on the socio-structural level, to lie in the fact that the basic acceptance of a hierarchy in one instance corresponds to reality, and in the other does not.

From a logical viewpoint, there is a paradox in both cases, a refusal of logical levels or "types" which must be produced if one wants to analyze the self-referential relations involved. However, this is not an objection against the possibility of real systems. These do not collapse because of a logical error. Evolution is not a "logical construction (or deconstruction) of the world." All differentiated systems share the problem that they function as a unity in relation to their surroundings. But at the same time they are differentiated internally into partial systems, none of which as a partial system can represent the unity of the whole system. For, as *everything* within, be it a subsystem, a process or an operative element, is *only a part,* they lack the ability to be what they are. They exist notwithstanding their logical impossibility: as a paradox. But as this is clearly possible, one can only ask in what forms does the system experience the paradox of its existence, how can it be elaborated, and how can it nevertheless reproduce itself.

The classical answer to this question is in the form of hierarchy. Hierarchy was the evolutionary achievement produced to resolve this problem. In fact, it was a discovery of genius. The unity of the system was reintroduced into the system as difference, and in fact as a difference which reconstructs the problem with which we are dealing exactly: as a difference of rank. The unity of the system is the difference of ranks, with a double significance: it gives each part a rank, and so lets the part participate by means of the difference. And it uses the same difference to represent itself in the supreme rank at the top of the system. It is unity as difference, since difference permits the representation of the unity of the system through the *maiores et savior pars.* Hierarchy is the paradox dissolved, paradoxicalness reflected within itself, as it were. And it thereby becomes conjoinable. This is the precise sense in which it was discussed in the old European semantics of participation and representation, service and authority. Whoever uses these words today outside this context must be aware that he or she is taking on the responsibility of giving them a new meaning.

We can now only dream of this fine artistic product of social imagination. Socio-cultural evolution has gone far beyond it. It has replaced the stratification of society as the form of primary system differentiation with re-differentiation in terms of function systems. This destroyed the plausibility of the semantic hierarchy. When we experience stratification, we do so as if it was a contingent, not a necessary structure: as class structures, without legitimating power. No function system, not even the political one, can take the place of hierarchy and its top. We live in a society which cannot represent its unity within itself, because this would contradict the logic of functional differentiation. We live in a society without a top and without a center. The unity of society no longer appears within this society. And so, for us, legitimacy is a question of the popularity of the current government.

However, we shall remain romantics and, what amounts to virtually the same thing, we shall remain critics if we have to be satisfied with this explanation. Even if our society can no longer represent itself as a unity, there still remains the paradoxicalness of each differentiated system. And if this paradox no longer takes the form of hierarchy, it remains for us to ask in what other form it will now appear. The basic problem in fact remains unchanged; every operational act, every structured process, every partial system participates in the society, and is society, but in none of these instances is it possible to discern the existence of the whole society. Even the criticisms of society must be carried out within society. Even the planning of society must be carried out within society. Even the description of society must be carried out within society. And all this occurs as the criticism of a society which criticizes itself, as the planning of a society which plans itself and always reacts to what happens, and as the description of a society which describes itself.

With the benefit of two hundred years' hindsight we can perceive the formation and development of reflection-theories which restrict themselves to particular systems of functions and deal with their specific problems. At the beginning, in the eighteenth century, these theories still appeared almost like theories of society; as though they involved jointly providing the reflection of society. This is the reason why Kant sought the road to moral law and systematic organizations in the theory of cognition and, consequently, in his reflections on the conditions of the possibility of science. And by taking this route he achieved an unparalleled influence on movements seeking profound social reform. The Physiocrats also viewed their economic theories as political theory as well as a theory of law. The concept of society is more or less limited to economic relations, so that reflection on the economy can at the same time serve as a theory of society. Marx was perhaps the last to have followed this approach in grand style. The result of his work, however, was only that the theory of society subsequently appeared in sociology as a desideratum and as a coercive, ideological position. . . .

In any event we must begin from this in order to establish our distance from such an approach a precise manner. But then one very quickly sees that there are many more possibilities than the ones provided here. I want to propose only three possibilities which lie, so to speak, on the threshold, and they are:

(1) a perfecting of theoretically oriented *historical analysis,* with the aim of clarifying the identity and difference of modern society in relation to older social formations;

(2) a precise analysis of the problematic area of *self-referential systems* in connection with an interdisciplinary and persistent discussion;

(3) a clarification of the logic and consequences of the *functional differentiation of* the societal system on the premise that it is possible to obtain from this a better understanding of the positive and negative characteristics of the modern one.

⌐⌐⌐

RISK: A SOCIOLOGICAL THEORY, 1993

The Concept of Risk

Risk is addressed nowadays by a wide variety of special research areas and even by different scientific disciplines. The traditional statistical treatment of risk calculation has been joined by economic research. Instrumental in this development has been the brilliant approach taken by Frank Knight. His original aim was to explain entrepreneurial profit in terms of the function of uncertainty absorption. This was no new idea: Fichte had already introduced it in relation to the ownership of land and class differentiation. In the modern context of economics, however, it has permitted the astute linking up of macro and microeconomic theory. Knight's distinction between risk and uncertainty has, however, meanwhile petrified into a sort of dogma—so that conceptual innovation earns the reproach of not having applied the concept correctly. But other disciplines do not face the problem of explaining company profits, nor are they concerned with the differences and connections between theories of the market and the business enterprise. Why should they then draw the concept from this source?

Statistical theories have been joined by applications in the fields of decision and games theory interested in their own controversies—such as the degree of meaningful subjectivization of expectations and preferences. As a sort of countermove, psychologists and social psychologists have established that in reality people do not calculate in the way they should if they put store by earning the attribution 'rational' from the statistician. They commit 'errors', some would say. Others would claim that they act in a manner adapted to the requirements of everyday life. In any case it is striking that such deviance displays both structure and direction. The gap is growing ever wider and deeper. As in continental drift, the disciplines are moving farther and farther apart. We now know that housewives in the supermarket and street children in Brazil can calculate highly successfully—but not the way they learned to do so, or did not learn to do so, at school. We know that values can be quantified—with the result that what was really meant can no longer be recognized. And not only private persons cannot do so or do not make the effort. In positions where rationality is among the duties attributed to the role, where particular care and responsibility in dealing with risks are expected, even in the management of organization—risks are not calculated quantitatively; or at least not in the way conventional decision theory proposes. But if this is the case, what use are

theories of risk that determine their conceptual approach in terms of quantitative calculation? Is the aim, as in certain moral theories, only to set up an ideal to permit everyone to establish that he cannot live up to it—luckily no more than others can? Handling quantity and its practical relevance are at stake—at any rate for specialized areas of research and the academic disciplines.

Still within these models of quantitative risk calculation, which are generally guided by the subjective expectation of advantage, we now realize that an important correction must be made. We shall refer to it as the *disaster threshold*. One accepts the results of such a calculation, if at all, only when it does not touch the threshold beyond which a (however unlikely) misfortune would be experienced as a disaster. For this reason subsistence farmers are highly averse to risk because they are under the constant threat of hunger, of losing their seed, of being unable to continue productions. Under money economy circumstances we find corresponding results: entrepreneurs facing liquidity problems are less willing to take risks than those who are not plagued by this problem when the risk is of a given magnitude. It will probably be necessary to take into account that the disaster threshold will have to be located at very different positions, depending on whether one is involved in risk as a decision maker or as someone affected by risky decisions. This makes it difficult to hope for consensus on such calculation even when dealing with specific situations.

But that is not all. In the meantime the social sciences have discovered the problem of risk as well; but not so to speak in their own front yard, but because it has not been nurtured and watered with enough care in neighbouring plots. Cultural anthropologists, social anthropologists, and political scientists point out—and rightly—that the evaluation of risk and the willingness to accept risk are not only psychological problems, but above all social problems. In this regard one behaves as the pertinent reference group expects one to, or—either in conformity with or in breach of prevailing opinion—in terms of one's socialization. The background to this position, although initially only postulated as a countertheory, is a better understanding of the extent of the problem, inspired above all by the technological and ecological problems confronting modern society. This brings to the foreground the question of who or what decides whether (and within which material and temporal contexts) a risk is to be taken into account *or not.* The already familiar discussions on risk calculation, risk perception, risk assessment and risk acceptance are now joined by the issue of selecting the risks to be considered or ignored. And once again, discipline-specific research can reveal that this is not a matter of chance but that demonstrable social factors control the selection process.

However, these efforts still presuppose an individualistic point of departure. They modify the results of psychological research. If, for example, such research demonstrates that individuals in everyday contexts typically underestimate risks—perhaps because everything has gone well to date and because one overestimates one's capacity for controlling events and underestimates the extent of loss or damage that can be suffered in situations one has yet to experience—then we can pose the question of how communication that seeks to raise the level of risk awareness must be constituted. There is no doubt that by including social contexts and operations, a necessary complementation of psychological insights is provided as well as a convincing explanation of why individuals react differently in differing social situations. As we learn more and more in this respect, however, we finally reach a point where we have to ask ourselves *whether* attribution to individual decision making (whether rational, intuitive, habitual etc.) can still be regarded as tenable at all. Or whether, leaving this aside, we should not attempt a strictly sociological approach, tackling the phenomenon of risk only in the sense of communication—naturally including communication of decisions made by individuals.

Without taking such a radical stance, sociology has finally also turned its attention to the problem of risk; or it has at least laid claim to the term risk. Following the ebbing of anticapitalist prejudice, it now finds a new opportunity to fill its old role with new content, namely to warn society. At present this function is, however, being performed completely without reflection; and by this we mean that sociology is not reflecting on its own role. For even if the sociologist knows that risks are selected: *why and how does he do this himself?* Sufficient theoretical reflection would have to recognize at least the 'autological' component

that always intervenes when observers observe observers. The social determination of all experience and action recognized by sociology also applies *mutatis mutandis* with regard to the discipline itself. It cannot observe society from without, it operates from within society; and of all observers, *it should be the first to realize the fact.* It may all very well adopt the topics of the moment, may support protest movements, may describe the dangerous nature of modern technology or warn against irreparable environmental damage. But others do the same. What ought to go beyond this is a theory of the selectivity of all societal operations, including the observation of these operations; indeed, even including the structures determining these operations. For sociology, the topic of risk ought thus to be subsumed under a theory of modern society, and should be shaped by the conceptual apparatus thereof. But there is no such theory, and the classical traditions that continue to guide the majority of theoreticians in the field of sociology provide few openings for topics such as ecology, technology, and risk, not to speak of the problems of self-reference.

We cannot at this point discuss the general difficulties of interdisciplinary research. There is cooperation at project level, and there are areas of research that could be referred to as 'transdisciplinary' fields, for example, cybernetics and systems theory. Risk research could represent a further possibility. For the moment, however, the negative consequences of participation by numerous disciplines and special research areas are most apparent. There is no definition of risk that could meet the requirements of science. It appears that each area of research concerned is satisfied with the guidance provided by its own particular theoretical context. We must therefore question whether, in individual research areas, and even more so more in interdisciplinary cooperation, science knows what it is talking about. If only for epistemological reasons we may not assume that such a thing as risk exists, and that it is only a matter of discovering and investigating it. The conceptual approach constitutes what is being dealt with. The outside world itself knows no risks, for it knows neither distinctions, nor expectations, nor evaluations, nor probabilities—*unless self-produced by observer systems in the environment of other systems.*

LUCE IRIGARAY

1930–

Luce Irigaray was born in Belgium in 1930, was once married, and had children. She is one of the most highly credentialed theorists working today, beginning with an M.A. in philosophy and literature from the University of Louvain (1955), then moving to Paris for an M.A. at the University of Paris in psychology (1961), then a diploma in psychopathology from the Institute of Psychology there (1962), followed by a doctorate in philosophy from the University of Paris VIII, and finally another doctorate in psychoanalysis from the École Freudienne (1974). She taught high school in Brussels (1956–59), then became a research assistant at the National Foundation for Scientific Research for Belgium (1962–64), and an instructor at the University of Paris VIII, Vincennes (1970–74), making her way up to director of research at the National Center for Scientific Research in Paris. She taught at Erasmus University, Rotterdam in 1982 and has lectured worldwide.

Irigaray has done original research in the language of mental illness, other linguistically based study, philosophy of language, and a great deal of gender-based study of psychopathology. Even her most ardent supporters agree that she is very difficult to read, especially in English translation, partly because she brings into her work the combined lexicons of psychoanalysis, linguistics, psychology, philosophy, and literature—not in itself a unique combination among the French intellectual elite, but one that can easily enough confuse the novice reader who is foreign to this hothouse intellectual orbit. In 1973 Irigaray published *The Language of Insanity* in which she used her clinical experience to describe the peculiar linguistic creations of schizophrenics, part of a life-long study of psychopathology and language. But she first came to relatively wide attention in Paris when her second doctoral dissertation, *Speculum of the Other Woman* (1974; tr. 1985), was viewed as heretical at the Freudian School to which it had been submitted, and she was asked to leave the orthodox Freudian association, and her planned courses were canceled. In this work she questions both Freud and Lacan, the reigning demigods at the time in Paris, by suggesting that their use of terminology and analytic language was terminally phallocentric, and that women needed a language of their own that would originate in imagery more properly attuned to their own bodies and psyches than to that of men. This has since become a common cry among writers such as Judith Butler, Toril Moi, and others with whom Irigaray is often compared. *An Ethics of Sexual Difference* (1984; tr. 1993) is regarded as the most representative and comprehensible introduction to her thought, and it is from this book that one of the excerpts below comes.

AN ETHICS OF SEXUAL DIFFERENCE, 1984

Sexual Difference

Sexual difference is one of the major philosophical issues, if not the issue, of our age. According to Heidegger, each age has one issue to think through, and one only. Sexual difference is probably the issue in our time which could be our "salvation" if we thought it through.

But, whether I turn to philosophy, to science, or to religion, I find this underlying issue still cries out in vain for our attention. Think of it as an approach that would allow us to check the many forms that destruction takes in our world, to counteract a nihilism that merely affirms the reversal or the repetitive proliferation of status quo values—whether you call them the consumer society, the circularity of discourse, the more or less cancerous diseases of our age, the unreliability of words, the end of philosophy, religious despair or regression to religiosity, scientist or technical imperialism that fails to consider the living subject.

Sexual difference would constitute the horizon of worlds more fecund than any known to date—at least in the West—and without reducing fecundity to the reproduction of bodies and flesh. For loving partners this would be a fecundity of birth and regeneration, but also the production of a new age of thought, art, poetry, and language: the creation of a new *poetics.*

Both in theory and in practice, everything resists the discovery and affirmation of such an advent or event. In theory, philosophy wants to be literature or rhetoric, wishing either to break with ontology or to regress to the ontological. Using the same ground and the same framework as "first philosophy," working toward its disintegration but without proposing any other goals that might assure new foundations and new works.

In politics, some overtures have been made to the world of women. But these overtures remain partial and local: some concessions have been made by those in power, but no new values have been established. Rarely have these measures

been thought through and affirmed by women themselves, who consequently remain at the level of critical demands. Has a worldwide erosion of the gains won in women's struggles occurred because of the failure to lay foundations different from those on which the world of men is constructed? Psychoanalytic theory and therapy, the scenes of sexuality as such, are a long way from having effected their revolution. And with a few exceptions, sexual practice today is often divided between two parallel worlds: the world of men and the world of women. A nontraditional, fecund encounter between the sexes barely exists. It does not voice its demands publicly, except through certain kinds of silence and polemics.

A revolution in thought and ethics is needed if the work of sexual difference is to take place. We need to reinterpret everything concerning the relations between the subject and discourse, the subject and the world, the subject and the cosmic, the microcosmic and the macrocosmic. Everything, beginning with the way in which the subject has always been written in the masculine form, as *man,* even when it claimed to be universal or neutral. Despite the fact that *man*—at least in French—rather than being neutral, is sexed.

Man has been the subject of discourse, whether in theory, morality, or politics. And the gender of God, the guardian of every subject and every discourse, is always *masculine and paternal,* in the West. To women are left the so-called minor arts: cooking, knitting, embroidery, and sewing; and, in exceptional cases, poetry, painting, and music. Whatever their importance, these arts do not currently make the rules, at least not overtly.

Of course, we are witnessing a certain reversal of values: manual labor and art are being revalued. But the relation of these arts to sexual difference is never really thought through and properly apportioned. At best, it is related to the class struggle.

In order to make it possible to think through, and live, this difference, we must reconsider the whole problematic of *space* and *time.*

In the beginning there was space and the creation of space, as is said in all theogonies. The gods, God, first create *space.* And time is there, more or less in the service of space. On the first day, the first days, the gods, God, make a world by separating the elements. This world is then peopled, and a rhythm is established among its inhabitants. God would be time itself, lavishing or exteriorizing itself in its action in space, in places.

Philosophy then confirms the genealogy of the task of the gods or God. Time becomes the *interiority* of the subject itself, and space, its exteriority (this problematic is developed by Kant in the *Critique of Pure Reason*). The subject, the master of time, becomes the axis of the world's ordering, with its something beyond the moment and eternity: God. He effects the passage between time and space.

Which would be inverted in sexual difference? Where the feminine is experienced as space, but often with connotations of the abyss and night (God being space and light?), while the masculine is experienced as time.

The transition to a new age requires a change in our perception and conception of *space-time*, the *inhabiting of places,* and of *containers,* or *envelopes of identity.* It assumes and entails an evolution or a transformation of forms, of the relations of *matter* and *form* and of the interval *between:* the trilogy of the constitution of place. Each age inscribes a limit to this trinitary configuration: *matter, form, interval,* or *power [puissance], act, intermediary-interval.*

Desire occupies or designates the place of the *interval.* Giving it a permanent definition would amount to suppressing it as desire. Desire demands a sense of attraction: a change in the interval, the displacement of the subject or of the object in their relations of nearness or distance.

The transition to a new age comes at the same time as a change in the economy of desire. A new age signifies a different relation between:

man and god(s),

man and man,

man and world,

man and woman.

Our age, which is often thought to be one in which the problematic of desire has been brought forward, frequently theorizes this desire on the basis of observations of a moment of tension, or a moment in history, whereas desire ought to be thought of as a changing dynamic whose outlines

can be described in the past, sometimes in the present, but never definitively predicted. Our age will have failed to realize the full dynamic reserve signified by desire if it is referred back to the economy of the *interval,* if it is situated in the attractions, tensions, and actions occurring between *form* and *matter,* but also in the *remainder* that subsists after each creation or work, *between* what has already been identified and what has still to be identified, and so on.

In order to imagine such an economy of desire, one must reinterpret what Freud implies by sublimation and observe that he does not speak of the *sublimation* of genitality (except in reproduction? But, if this were a successful form of sublimation, Freud would not be so pessimistic about parental child-rearing practices) or of the sublimation of the *partial drives in relation to the feminine* but rather of their repression (little girls speak earlier and more skillfully than little boys; they have a better relationship to the social; and so on—qualities or aptitudes that disappear without leaving any creative achievements that capitalize on their energy, except for the task of becoming a woman: an object of attraction?)[1]

In this possible nonsublimation of herself, and by herself, woman always tends *toward* without any return to herself as the place where something positive can be elaborated. In terms of contemporary physics, it could be said that she remains on the side of the electron, with all that this implies for her, for man, for their encounter. If there is no double desire, the positive and negative poles divide themselves between the two sexes instead of establishing a chiasmus or a double loop in which each can go toward the other and come back to itself.

If these positive and negative poles are not found in both, the same one always attracts, while the other remains in motion but lacks a "proper" place. What is missing is the double pole of attraction and support, which excludes disintegration or rejection, attraction and decomposition, but which instead ensures the separation that articulates every encounter and makes possible speech, promises, alliances.

In order to distance oneself, must one be able to take? To speak? Which in a certain way comes to the same thing. Perhaps in order to take, one needs a fixed container or place? A soul? Or a spirit? Mourning nothing is the most difficult. Mourning the self in the other is almost impossible. I search for myself, as if I had been assimilated into maleness. I ought to reconstitute myself on the basis of a disassimilation. . . .[2] Rise again from the traces of a culture, of works already produced by the other. Searching through what is in them—for what is not there. What allowed them to be, for what is not there. Their conditions of possibility, for what is not there.

Woman ought to be able to find herself, among other things, through the images of herself already deposited in history and the conditions of production of the work of man, and not on the basis of his work, his genealogy. . . .

A sexual or carnal ethics would require that both angel and body be found together. This is a world that must be constructed or reconstructed. A genesis of love between the sexes has yet to come about in all dimensions, from the smallest to the greatest, from the most intimate to the most political. A world that must be created or re-created so that man and woman may once again or at last live together, meet, and sometimes inhabit the same place.

The link uniting or reuniting masculine and feminine must be horizontal and vertical, terrestrial and heavenly. As Heidegger, among others, has written, it must forge an alliance between the divine and the mortal, such that the sexual encounter would be a festive celebration and not a disguised or polemical form of the master-slave relationship. Nor a meeting in the shadow or orbit of a Father-God who alone lays down the law, who is the immutable spokesman of a single sex.

Of course, the most extreme progression and regression goes under the name of God. I can only strive toward the absolute or regress to infinity under the guarantee of God's existence. This is what tradition has taught us, and its imperatives have not yet been overcome, since their destruction brings about terrible abandonments and pathological states, unless one has exceptional love partners. And even then. . . . Unhappiness is

sometimes all the more inescapable when it lacks the horizon of the divine, of the gods, of an opening onto a beyond, but also a *limit* that the other may or may not penetrate.

How can we mark this limit of a place, of place in general, if not through sexual difference? But, in order for an ethics of sexual difference to come into being, we must constitute a possible for each sex, body, and flesh to inhabit. Which presupposes a memory of the past, a hope for the future, memory bridging the present and disconcerting the mirror symmetry that annihilates the difference of identity.

To do this requires time, both space and time. Perhaps we are passing through an era when *time must redeploy space?* A new morning of and for the world? A remaking of immanence and transcendence, notably through this *threshold* which has never been examined as such: the female sex. The threshold that gives access to the *mucous.* Beyond classical oppositions of love and hate, liquid and ice—a threshold that is always *half-open.* The threshold of the *lips,* which are strangers to dichotomy and oppositions. Gathered one against the other but without any possible suture, at least of a real kind. They do not absorb the world into or through themselves, provided they are not misused and reduced to a means of consumption or consummation. They offer a shape of welcome but do not assimilate, reduce, or swallow up: A sort of doorway to voluptuousness? They are not useful, except as that which designates a *place,* the very place of uselessness, at least as it is habitually understood. Strictly speaking, they serve neither conception nor *jouissance.* Is this the mystery of feminine identity? Of its self-contemplation, of this very strange word of silence? Both the threshold and reception of exchange, the sealed-up secret of wisdom, belief, and faith in all truths?

Note

1. Cf. Luce Irigaray, *Speculum, de l'autre femme* (Paris: Minuit, 1984). pp. 9–162, trans. Gillian C. Gill, under the title *Speculum of the Other Woman* (Ithaca: Cornell University Press, 1985), pp. 11–129.

THINKING THE DIFFERENCE: FOR A PEACEFUL REVOLUTION, 1990

Equal or Different?

What woman has not read *The Second Sex?* What woman has not been invigorated by it? Become a feminist, perhaps, through reading it? Simone de Beauvoir was in fact one of the first women in our century to remind us of the scale of the exploitation of women and to encourage every woman who was lucky enough to discover her book to feel less isolated and more resolved not to surrender or to be taken in.

So what was Simone de Beauvoir doing? She was telling her life story, and at the same time supporting it with scientific data. She never stopped telling her story, bravely, in all its stages. In so doing she helped many women—and men?—to be sexually freer, notably by offering them a socio-cultural model, acceptable for its time, for living as a woman, living as a teacher, living as a writer, living as a couple. I think that she also helped them to situate themselves more objectively in the different moments of a life.

Simone de Beauvoir did more than that. Her relish for social justice led her to support certain feminists in their actions, on their journey, helping them to emerge socially by signing their petitions, going along with their actions, encouraging the existence of a column in *Les Temps modernes,* prefacing their books, taking part in their television programmes, being their friend . . .

The Era of Psychoanalysis.   Whilst I was one of the readers of *The Second Sex,* I was never close to Simone de Beauvoir. Why not? A question of different generations? Not only that: she did mix with young women. That was not, or not simply, the issue. There are major differences between our positions, and I hoped that they might be

overcome at the level of friendship and mutual help. Concretely, they were not. When I sent her *Speculum,* as though I were sending it to an elder sister, Simone de Beauvoir never replied. I admit that that made me quite sad. I had hoped for an attentive and understanding reader, a sister, who would help me with the academic and institutional difficulties that I was to encounter because of that book. Alas, my hopes came to nothing! The only gesture Simone de Beauvoir made was to ask me for some information about *Le Langage des Déments* (Mouton, 1973) when she was writing on old age. Not a word passed between us about women's liberation.

What are we to make, once again, of this continued distance between two women who could, even should, have worked together? Aside from the fact that I encountered certain difficulties with academic institutions that certain American women, say, encountered, and which she may not have experienced in the same terms, which she did not understand, there are reasons that explain her reserve. Simone de Beauvoir and Jean-Paul Sartre always resisted psychoanalysis. I have trained as an analyst and that is important (even despite existing theories and practices) for thinking a sexual identity. I also belong to a philosophical tradition in which psychoanalysis takes its place as a stage in understanding the self-realization of consciousness, especially in its sexuate determinations.

These two formations mean that my thinking about women's liberation has a dimension other than the search for equality between the sexes. That does not stop me joining and promoting public demonstrations to obtain this or that right for women: the right to contraception, to abortion, to legal support in cases of public or private violence, the right to freedom of expression, etc.

If, however, these struggles are to be waged other than by simply putting forward demands, if they are to result in the inscription of equal (but necessarily different) sexual rights before the law, women—and couples, come to that—must be allowed access to an other identity. Women can only take up these rights if they can find some value in being women, and not simply mothers. That means rethinking, transforming centuries of socio-cultural values.

Women: Equal or Different. Demanding equality, as women, seems to me to be an erroneous expression of a real issue. Demanding to be equal presupposes a term comparison. Equal to what? What do women want to be equal to? Men? A wage? A public position? Equal to what? Why not to themselves?

Even a vaguely rigorous analysis of claims to equality shows that they are justified at the level of a superficial critique of culture, and utopian as a means to women's liberation. The exploitation of women is based upon sexual difference, and can only be resolved through sexual difference. Certain tendencies of the day, certain contemporary feminists, are noisily demanding the neutralization of sex [*sexe*]. That neutralization, if it were possible, would correspond to the end of the human race. The human race is divided into *two genres* which ensure its production and reproduction. Trying to suppress sexual difference is to invite a genocide more radical than any destruction that has ever existed in History. What is important, on the other hand, is defining the values of belonging to a sex-specific *genre*. What is indispensable is elaborating a culture of the sexual which does not yet exist, whilst respecting both genres. Because of the historical time gaps between the gynocratic, matriarchal, patriarchal and phallocratic eras, we are in a sexual position which is bound up with generation and not with *genre* as sex. This means that, within the family, women must be mothers and men must be fathers, but that we have no positive and ethical values that allow two sexes of the same generation to form a creative, and not simply procreative, human couple. One of the major obstacles to the creation and recognition of such values is the more or less covert hold patriarchal and phallocratic roles have had on the whole of our civilization for centuries. It is social justice, pure and simple, to balance out the power of one sex over the other by giving, or restoring, cultural values to female sexuality. What is at stake is clearer today than it was when *The Second Sex* was written.

Unless it goes through this stage, feminism may work towards the destruction of women, and, more generally, of all values. Egalitarianism, in fact, sometimes expends a lot of energy on rejecting certain positive values and chasing after nothing. Hence the periodic crises, discouragement and regressions in women's liberation movements, and their fleeting inscription in History.

Equality between men and women cannot be achieved unless we *think of genre as sexuate* [*sexué*] and write the rights and duties of each sex, insofar as they are *different,* into social rights and duties.

Peoples constantly split into secondary but murderous rivalries without realizing that their primary and irreducible division is one between two genres. From that point of view, we are still living in the childhood of culture. It is urgent for women's struggles, for small, popular groups of women, to realize the importance of issues that are specific to them. These are bound up with respect for life and culture, with the constant passage of the natural into the cultural, of the spiritual into the natural. Their responsibility and their opportunity correspond to a stage in the evolution of the world, and not to some more or less lucid and negative competition within a world undergoing a mutation, in which life is in danger for a variety of reasons.

Making friendly gestures towards Simone de Beauvoir means pursuing the theoretical and practical work of social justice she carried on in her own way, not blocking the horizon of liberation she opened up for many women, and men. . . . Her vision of that horizon was certainly in part inspired by her long, and often solitary, walks in the *garrigue,* in the wilds. Her enjoyment and her accounts of her walks seem to me to be one of her messages that we must not forget.

DOROTHY E. SMITH

1926–

Dorothy E. Smith, born in 1926 (and about whom biographical information is scarce in the public sphere), has become during the last 15 years or so, from her lifelong academic position in Canada, one of the most often cited feminist sociological theorists. She has long worked in the Department of Sociology and Equity Studies in Education at the University of Toronto. Her first theoretically important work appeared in 1987 when she was 61, *The Everyday World as Problematic: A Feminist Sociology,* and, interestingly enough, bears more theoretical kinship with the Frankfurt School critique of modern life than with the more usual feminist sources of ideas. The difficulty that some readers have had with this book stems as much from this theoretical inspiration (recalling the thorny prose of Adorno and Horkheimer) as from the complexity of her ideas themselves. Her later works include *The Conceptual Practices of Power: A Feminist Sociology of Knowledge* (1990) and *Text, Facts and Femininity: Exploring the Relations of Ruling* (1990). Her latest work, *Writing the Social: Theory and Investigations* (1999), illustrates a slight shift into textual analysis rather than examination of social life more directly.

Smith is commonly grouped with several other feminists (Sandra Harding, Nancy Hartsock, sometimes Patricia Hill Collins) as what have come to be called "standpoint theorists." The argument they put forth, from different perspectives to be sure, is that traditional epistemological arguments, going back at least to Descartes, imply a sovereign "ego" that somehow exists above the fray of social power relations and the claims of social class and gender distinctions. They point out that this is an illusion, that one person's "common sense" or normal way of perceiving the world—say, that of a privileged white academic philosopher—is very likely at odds with the viewpoint of that great majority of humans who do not partake of that particular worldview or experience the world through that existential lens. This argument, of course, has infuriated traditional epistemologists, and has even come under attack by some women social theorists, too (e.g., Susan Hekman), yet it has certainly changed the nature of argument about what is "true" and what is not in discussions of the social sphere. Smith wrote that she is concerned with "practices of thinking and writing . . . that convert what people experience directly in their everyday/everynight world into forms of knowledge in which people as subjects disappear and in which their perspectives on their own experiences are transposed and subdued by the magisterial forms of objectifying discourse" (*Conceptual Practices,* p. 4). The selections below give evidence of Smith's insistence that women's perceptions are different from men's.

THE EVERYDAY WORLD
AS PROBLEMATIC, 1987

The critique of established sociological frameworks from the perspective of women's location leaves us with the problem of the structure of the sociological relation as it was described above. It does not, as such, serve to design for us a method of proceeding that offers an alternative to the concepts, relevances, and methods of a discourse that, in its very use, organizes and shapes our work into its own forms and intentions regardless of what we mean to do. We must see this problem, I believe, in how our work returns to, is aimed at, and is repossessed by knowers who are participants in the discourse or in other domains of the ruling apparatus, rather than knowers who are members of the society anywhere in it. Suppose then we began to devise a sociological enterprise not directed primarily toward the discourse and its knower, but capable of providing a sociology for women. We might attempt to develop for women analyses, descriptions, and understandings of their situation, of their everyday world, and of its determinations in the larger socio-economic organization to which it is articulated. Then indeed we would be thinking about how to do a sociology relocating the sociological subject. Such a sociological enterprise presents an alternative conception of a science to that which depends upon a knower theoretically located in an Archimedian, that is, a purely formal space. It is a sociology whose knowers are members of the society and have positions in it outside that abstracted ruling apparatus—as an understanding of the bifurcating consciousness shows us everyone does—and who know the society from within their experience of it as an everyday world. Their experience locates for us the beginning of an inquiry. This is to constitute the everyday world as problematic, where the everyday world is taken to be various and differentiated matrices of experience—the place from within which the consciousness of the knower begins, the location of her null point.

Such a sociology would aim to make available to anyone a knowledge of the social organization and a determination of his or her directly experienced, everyday world. Its analyses would become part of our ordinary interpretations of experience and hence part of experience, just as our experience of the sun's sinking below the horizon has been transformed by our knowledge that the world turns and that our location in the world turns away from the sun—even though from where we are it seems to sink. The sociological knower, then, is not the sociologist as such. The work of the sociologist is to develop a sociology capable of explicating for members of the society the social organization of their experienced world, including in that experience the ways in which it passes beyond what is immediately and directly known, including also, therefore, the structure of a bifurcated consciousness.

Rather than explaining behavior, we begin from where people are in the world, explaining the social relations of the society of which we are part, explaining an organization that is not fully present in any one individual's everyday experience. Since the procedures, methods, and aims of present sociology give primacy to the concepts, relevances, and topics of the discourse, we cannot begin from within that frame. This would be to sustain the hegemony of the discourse over the actualities of the everyday experience of the world. It is precisely that relation that constitutes the break or fault disclosed by the women's movement.

An alternative is to turn this method on its head and to make the everyday world the locus of a sociological problematic. The everyday world is that world we experience directly. It is the world in which we are located physically and socially. Our experience arises in it as conditions, occasions, objects, possibilities, relevances, presences, and so on, organized in and by the practices and methods through which we supply and discover organization. It is necessarily local—because that is how we must be—and necessarily historical. Locating the sociological problematic in the everyday world does not mean confining the inquiry to the everyday world. Indeed, as we shall see, it is essential that the everyday world be seen as organized by social relations not observable within it. Thus, an inquiry confining itself to the everyday world of direct experience is not adequate to explicate its social organization.

One way in which the sociological discourse, has maintained its hegemony over experience has been by insisting that we must begin with a conceptual apparatus or a theory drawn from the discipline, if only because to embark on inquiry without such a conceptual framework exposes us to the wild incoherence of "history" or of the actualities of people's worlds. I am not suggesting, of course, that sociology can be done without knowing how to do it and that we can approach our work with a naive consciousness. Indeed, I believe sociology to be rather more difficult than it has been made to seem. But the implication that the actualities of the everyday world are unformed and unorganized and that the sociologist cannot enter them without a conceptual framework to select, assemble, and order them is one that we can now understand in this special relation of a sociology constituted as part of a ruling apparatus vis-a-vis which the local and particular, the actualities of the world that is lived, are necessarily untamed, disordered, and incoherent. But we can begin from a different assumption when as premises we begin with the activities of actual individuals whose activity produces the social relations that they live. Social phenomena are products of action and interpretation by actual women and men. Rational order itself, order itself, as ethnomethodologists have pointed out, is an accomplishment of members of society. The order, coherence, rationality, and sense of social situations and relations are an active work done prior to the presence and observational work of the sociologist. Further, her work itself is inseparable from such a social relation and in its preliminary phases must be constrained by the enterprise of explicating an organization of relations that is there prior to her inquiry and is to be discovered in its course. . . .

The everyday world is not fully understandable within in its own scope. It is organized by social relations not fully apparent in it nor contained in it. This is the social organization of the sociological problematic in the actual work and practices of real individuals. Earlier forms of society do not have this double character. In simpler social forms, the character and organization of the everyday world are fully visible. The ethnographic techniques of the anthropologist have depended upon this visibility. . . .

The way in which events occur, their odd property or senselessness if our knowledge of them is confined to the everyday world, is not so very extraordinary. It is not out of this world. On the contrary, such events are part of a continual process transforming the environment of our lives, transforming our lives; notice next time, in this context, that hole in the ground so soon to become a high-rise apartment, a gymnasium. Events occurring in this way are happening around us all the time. If we care to, we take them for granted. They are normal features of our world. If we cease to take them for granted, if we strip away everything that we imagine we know of how they come about (and ordinarily that is very little), if we examine them as they happen within the everyday world, they become fundamentally mysterious. If we allow them to stand there as Vonnegut does, they do not make sense within the domain of the everyday world. This is what I mean by a problematic implicit in the social organization of the everyday world.

❧

WRITING THE SOCIAL: CRITIQUE, THEORY, AND INVESTIGATIONS, 1999

The Ruling Relations

A Sociology from Women's Standpoint. The sociology for women I propose begins in the actualities of women's lived experience. Its aim is to discover the social as it comes into view from an experiencing of life that is not already defined within the ruling relations. It does not speak only of women. Rather, it seeks a sociology, a method of inquiry, that extends and expands what we can discover from the local settings of our everyday/everynight living.

The standpoint of women establishes a place to open inquiry that begins with a consciousness

---

located in a particular local site. Hence it problematizes the move into transcendence, the ego that slots into subject positions defined and determined discursively, bureaucratically, administratively, managerially, etc. The theories, concepts, and methods of the discourses in which we participate as intellectuals constitute the objectified standpoints through which we are related to the world as if we stood outside it. The experience of those whose particularizing work in relation to children, spouse, and household forms their consciousness is obliterated. I used to find, using standard sociological approaches, that we'd begin with the honest intention of doing research that was oriented towards people's interests and from their viewpoint, but that in doing the work inexorably, it seemed, our good and competent knowledge of how to do valid research led us into producing accounts which objectified them from a standpoint in the ruling relations. To reconstruct sociology as inquiry into the social from a standpoint in people's everyday experience means reconstructing its methods of thinking.

A sociology from women's standpoint in the local actualities of our everyday lives must be put together quite differently from the traditional objectifying sociologies. Committed to exploring the society from within people's experience of it, rather than objectifying them or explaining their behaviour, it would investigate how that society organizes and shapes the everyday world of experience. Its project is to explicate the actual social relations in which people's lives are embedded and to make these visible to them/ourselves.

This means a sociology beginning in a world of activity, the doings of actual people, and finding the social as the object of sociology's inquiry into how their activities are concerted and coordinated. It explores the social from within the same everyday/everynight world as we experience in its living. The subject/knower of inquiry is not a transcendent subject but situated in the actualities of her own living, in relations with others as they are. Whatever exists socially is produced/accomplished by people 'at work,' that is, active, thinking, intending, feeling, in the actual local settings of their living and in relationships that are fundamentally among particular others—even though the categories of ruling produce particular others as expressions of its order.

Thus the knowing subject of this sociology is located in a lived world in which both theory and practice go on, in which theory is itself a practice, in time, and in which the divide between the two can itself be brought under examination. The entry into text-mediated discourse and the relations of text mediated discourse are themselves actual as activities and the ordering of activities. They happen—always in the time they occurred in and during the time they perdured. Concepts, beliefs, ideas, knowledge, and so on (what Marxists know as consciousness) are included in this ontology of the social (see chapter 1) as practices that are integral to the connecting and coordinating of people's activities.

Thus, discourse, and the ruling relations in general, are, ontologically, fields of socially organized activity. People enter and participate in them, reading/watching/operating/writing/drawing texts; they are at work, and their work is regulated textually; whatever form of agency is accessible to them is accessible textually as courses of action in a text-mediated mode. Society is emphatically, from this viewpoint, *not* an ensemble of meaning. The social *happens;* included in the happening/activities are concepts, ideologies, theories, ideas, and so forth. Their deceitful stasis is an effect of how the printed text enables us to return to them again, find them again, as if nothing had changed. But each such iteration is the actual local practice of a particular individual, reading just where she is, for just the what-comes-next that her reading initiates.

In projecting inquiry into social relations coordinating multiple local sites of activity, the investigation of the text-mediation of social relations is foundational. The reason is this: the standpoint of women locates us in bodily sites, local, actual, particular; it problematizes, therefore, the coordination of people's activities as social relations organized outside local historical settings, connecting people in modes that do not depend on particularized relationships between people. The ruling relations are of this kind, coordinating the activities of people in the local sites of their bodily being into relations operating independently of person, place, and time. In putting in question the making of the extra-local and extra-personal ruling relations, women's standpoint does not proclaim them invalid, but rather recognizes the extra-locality of relations as itself a social organization of actual people's practices. In these relations, the particularity of individuals, their actual situation and site of work, the ephemerality of the lived moment, and so on, disappear; their disappearance is itself an accomplishment of what particular people do, in their actual situations and sites of work, as they live, are active, and experience the evanescence of lived time.

From this standpoint, the ruling relations themselves, including the social organization of knowledge, are problematized for investigation. They too exist in the ongoing concerting of actual people's activities in the particular local sites of our bodily being. How can consciousness operate as if it had no body and were not located in a particular local site, in place and time? What are the specific forms of social relations that provide for the subject's modes of being and action in and through texts? How is it that language and discourse appear as if they were autonomous systems, forgetting the irremediably local historicity of speakers, readers, and writers? How can we take up post-structuralism's discovery of how discourse speaks through us and beyond our intended meaning, while at the same time avoiding its solipsistic confinement to discourse? . . .

Returning to Gender and Women's Standpoint. In delineating the ruling relations, I have focused on the texts as integral to an ontology of capital in contemporary society. Traditional social science ontologies, conforming to disciplinary divisions, write a sharp separation between the social and economic. The version of the social that I have put forward above follows Rubin (1973) in breaking with this practice. The ruling relations as a text-mediated organization of relations extend into the economic sphere and can be investigated as accomplished by and organizing the activities of actual people. It is important, however, to keep in mind that the ruling relations are a more general dimension of the organization of society, extending into its systems of discourse, science, mass media, large-scale organization of all kinds, professional organization, and so on.

The historical trajectory of the ruling relations, from their fragmentary beginnings in the seventeenth and eighteenth centuries to their increasing comprehensiveness and complexity in our own time, has been profoundly gendered. In the middle classes, in particular, gender relations were radically reorganized. The dual consciousness that I experienced, one located in the objectified ruling relations and the other in the particularizing work of childcare and home, is located in this trajectory. The experiencing of these two kinds of consciousness cuts across historical time. Experience is always now and hence embedded in an historical trajectory, coming into being dialogically in the discourse of its time. Historically the division between these two worlds of work and consciousness has been gender-organized. The emerging capitalism of seventeenth-century Europe reorganized women's and men's relation to the economy; indeed, it brought into being the economy as a discrete and specialized system of relations mediated by money. Among the middle classes, the domestic setting became sharply differentiated from the relations of capital and of the public sphere (Davidoff and Hall 1987, Habermas 1989), so that forms of consciousness became differentiated by gender. While women remained at work in the particularities of domesticity, men, particularly of the middle classes, were active in businesses that connected them to the impersonal, extra-local dynamic of the market, and in the clubs and coffee-houses of Europe and the saloons and places of public assembly in North America (Ryan 1993), and, as readers, in the journals, newspapers and books that constituted the discourse of the public sphere. 'The new world of political economy necessitated a new sphere of domestic economy' (Davidoff and Hall 1987: 74).

This, of course, was only a beginning. The gender divide that emerged among the middle classes widened and deepened as the powers, technologies, and scope of the extra-local organization of the relations of the economy, the state, and public discourse increased, while the domestic sphere became increasingly ancillary. This is the historical trajectory of which my experience of these two consciousnesses was a moment.

These foundations to the ruling relations, grounded in capitalist social relations, created a radical division between the spheres of action and of consciousness of men and women. The peculiar out-of-body modes of consciousness of the nascent ruling relations required a specialization of subject and agency. The formation of the middle-class male subject in education and ideology aimed at creating that extraordinary form of modern consciousness that is capable of agency in modes that displace or subdue a local bodily existence. Rousseau's *Emile* designs an educational regime aimed at creating the autonomous male subject of civil society. His complement is a woman equally highly trained, but not for autonomy. It's her role to sop up the bodily needs that are residual to the masculine project; she is never to appear for herself or as herself in the zone of civil society that is his preserve.

During the nineteenth century, in particular, the barriers excluding women from participating as subjects and agents in civil society were policed by parents, educators, and the spokesmen of the public sphere. Middle-class women might be actively deprived of education, particularly of education that would give them the skills needed to participate in the discourse of reason—opportunities to learn philosophy, mathematics, and science. Books were taken away; women who read were told they would go mad if they didn't desist; women of knowledge were ridiculed publicly. Later in the century, as education for women became institutionalized, it was as a gender-differentiating system. In Germany, for example, the rise of an administrative class of civil servants was complemented by an educational system for women emphasizing preparation for the domestic sphere in which the rearing of men was central (Kittler 1990). As universal public educational systems were established in the late nineteenth century in both Europe and North America, they were also created as gender-differentiating systems, developing for the sons of the middle class the moral and intellectual capacities they would need in order to act as agents in the field I'm calling the ruling relations, and among women the skills and ideologies of subordination, passivity, and modes of agency restricted to family, home, and neighbourhood.

The women's movement of the late 1960s and early 1970s was a radical break with this formation of the social consciousness. It created, at least momentarily, a breach between the objectified text-based modes of consciousness of the ruling relations, and what had been formed and institutionalized for middle-class women as their place. Here, then, was a contradictory site of consciousness for women, bridging the intellectual functions of the ruling relations and the local particularizations of women's domestic sphere— woman as mother, as housewife, as neighbour, as sexual partner or object, at work, at play, in sex. It may be indeed that the increasing scope of the ruling relations progressively supersedes differentiations of persons on the basis of bodily being that locates them in particular local sites and in particularized relations, and that the women's movement in North America and Europe seized upon the possibilities, ironies, and frustrations emerging in this situation to seek a remaking of the relations of public discourse. Certainly the standpoint of women systematizes an historical bridging across the historical gap. This sociology traverses it from this, women's side, beginning in the local particularities of people's lives. It seeks to redesign knowledge of the social, recognizing that it is in and of the same world as the one we live in.

JEAN BAUDRILLARD

1929–

Jean Baudrillard, son of a civil servant, was born in Reims in the northeastern part of France, on July 20, 1929. Only fragmentary knowledge exists about his life, by his own design, and with so many websites and conferences being held regarding his work during the last decade, he seems to take particular pleasure in remaining entirely elusive about the basic facts of his existence. In many interviews and a set of published diary entries (called *Cool Memories,* vols. 1–3), he notes that his family was still close to bucolic sentiments even after moving to the city, that despite early academic brilliance, he "ran away" after several months of preparation for admission to the École Normale Supérieure, yet somehow became qualified to teach languages and worked at provincial lycées for ten years, and finally, at an age and by a route quite different from those of his esteemed peers, he was introduced to sociology in the early 60s through the intervention of Roland Barthes and Henri Lefebvre, under whom he wrote his dissertation in 1966. Thus, in October, 1966, he began teaching sociology at Nanterre and remained for 20 years, after which he retired and gave himself exclusively to writing and photography. There are veiled references to a marriage that went bad and gave Baudrillard a new view of life, but no specifics.

Baudrillard's ideas and writing are so heavily embroiled in irony and skepticism of received wisdom, particularly about consumer society and the conventional leftwing critiques of same, that he often plunges from the theoretically comprehensible into a self-mocking posture that verges on the duplicitous. Crowds of 1200 listeners wearing Baudrillard baseball caps have attended his talks, as much one would imagine for the anticipated theatrics as for the opportunity to gain clarity of ideas pertaining to modern life. Interviewers have plodded to his fifth-floor walk-up in Paris to find a short, tough-looking man who lives in a brightly lit, relatively empty apartment in which there was until 1981 no television and still no computer. This writer, who is more closely identified with avant-garde interpretations of what he calls "hyperreality" and the postmodern than any other on the current scene, writes his books with a pen on paper, then transfers them to a typewriter. In short, Baudrillard is a contrary phenomenon himself prior to and after any consideration of his ideas, which, considering the nature of his theorizing, does not prove to be too surprising.

Baudrillard's question for some years (after he went through an early period of criticizing Marx's production-based theory as no longer useful) has been rather simple: how does one separate the "real" from the "surreal" or the "hyperreal"? He believes that "simulacra" now populate our collective imaginations, and that any call for "reality" misses the point of postmodern life, especially as infected and affected by orgiastic consumerism. A question that readers of Baudrillard might ask is to what extent his later works will appear as evanescent in 20 years as the global financial bubble that sent all the richest nations into paroxysms of spending and acquisition for the last half decade of the 20th century, only to see this come to a crashing halt in the first three months of 2000. Baudrillard's theorizing may appear to be an excrescence of the imagination that matches that hysterical economic period to a tee.

<hr>

"CONSUMER SOCIETY," 1970

Today, we are everywhere surrounded by the remarkable conspicuousness of consumption and affluence, established by the multiplication of objects, services, and material goods. This now constitutes a fundamental mutation in the ecology of the human species. Strictly speaking, men of wealth are no longer surrounded by other human beings, as they have been in the past, but by *objects*. Their daily exchange is no longer with their fellows, but rather, statistically as a function of some ascending curve, with the acquisition and manipulation of goods and messages: from the rather complex domestic organization with its dozens of technical slaves to the "urban estate" with all the material machinery of communication and professional activity, and the permanent festive celebration of objects in advertising with the hundreds of daily mass media messages; from the proliferation of somewhat obsessional objects to the symbolic psychodrama which fuels the nocturnal objects that come to haunt us even in our dreams. The concepts of "environment" and "ambiance" have undoubtedly become fashionable only since we have come to live in less proximity to other human beings, in their presence and discourse, and more under the silent gaze of deceptive and obedient objects which continuously repeat the same discourse, that of our stupefied (*medusée*) power, of our potential affluence and of our absence from one another.

As the wolf-child becomes wolf by living among them, so are we becoming functional. We are living the period of the objects: that is, we live by their rhythm, according to their incessant cycles. Today, it is we who are observing their birth, fulfillment, and death; whereas in all previous civilizations, it was the object, instrument, and perennial monument that survived the generations of men.

While objects are neither flora nor fauna, they give the impression of being a proliferating vegetation; a jungle where the new savage of modern times has trouble finding the reflexes of civilization. These fauna and flora, which people have produced, have come to encircle and invest them, like a bad science fiction novel. We must quickly describe them as we see and experience them, while not forgetting, even in periods of scarcity or profusion, that they are in actuality the *products of human activity,* and are controlled, not by natural ecological laws, but by the law of exchange value.

> The busiest streets of London are crowded with shops whose show cases display all the riches of the world: Indian shawls, American revolvers, Chinese porcelain, Parisian corsets, furs from Russia and spices from the tropics; but all of these worldly things bear odious white paper labels with Arabic numerals and then laconic symbols £SD. This is how commodities are presented in circulation.

Profusion and Displays

Accumulation, or *profusion*, is evidently the most striking descriptive feature. Large department stores, with their luxuriant abundance of canned goods, foods, and clothing, are like the primary landscape and the geometrical locus of affluence.

Streets with overcrowded and glittering store windows (lighting being the least rare commodity, without which merchandise would merely be what it is), the displays of delicacies, and all the scenes of alimentary and vestimentary festivity, stimulate a magical salivation. Accumulation is more than the sum of its products: the conspicuousness of surplus, the final and magical negation of scarcity, and the maternal and luxurious presumptions of the land of milk and honey. Our markets, our shopping avenues and malls mimic a new-found nature of prodigious fecundity. Those are our Valleys of Canaan where flows, instead of milk and honey, streams of neon on ketchup and plastic—but no matter! There exists an anxious anticipation, not that there may not be enough, but that there is too much, and too much for everyone: by purchasing a portion one in effect appropriates a whole crumbling pyramid of oysters, meats, pears or canned asparagus. One purchases the part for the whole. And this repetitive and metonymic discourse of the consumable, and of commodities is represented, through collective metaphor and as a product of its own surplus, in the image of the *gift,* and of the inexhaustible and spectacular prodigality of the *feast.*

In addition to the stack, which is the most rudimentary yet effective form of accumulation, objects are organized in *displays,* or in *collections.* Almost every clothing store or appliance store presents a gamut of differentiated objects, which call upon, respond to, and refute each other. The display window of the antique store is the aristocratic, luxurious version of this model. The display no longer exhibits an overabundance of wealth but a *range* of select and complementary objects which are offered for the choosing. But this arrangement also invokes a psychological chain reaction in the consumer who peruses it, inventories it, and grasps it as a total category. Few objects today are offered *alone,* without a context of objects to speak for them. And the relation of the consumer to the object has consequently changed: the object is no longer referred to in relation to a specific utility, but as a collection of objects in their total meaning. Washing machine, refrigerator, dishwasher, have different meanings when grouped together than each one has alone, as a piece of equipment (*ustensile*). The display window, the advertisement, the

manufacturer, and the *brand name* here play an essential role in imposing a coherent and collective vision, like an almost inseparable totality. Like a chain that connects not ordinary objects but *signifieds,* each object can signify the other in a more complex super-object, and lead the consumer to a series of more complex choices. We can observe that objects are never offered for consumption in an absolute disarray. In certain cases they can *mimic* disorder to better seduce, but they are always arranged to trace out directive paths. The arrangement directs the purchasing impulse towards *networks* of objects in order to seduce it and elicit, in accordance with its own logic, a maximal investment, reaching the limits of economic potential. Clothing, appliances, and toiletries thus constitute object *paths,* which establish inertial constraints on the consumer who will proceed *logically* from one object to the next. The consumer will be caught up in a *calculus* of objects, which is quite different from the frenzy of purchasing and possession which arises from the simple profusion of commodities.

✎

"SIMULACRA AND SIMULATIONS," 1981

> The simulacrum is never that which conceals the
> truth—it is the truth which conceals that there is
> none. The simulacrum is true.   —Ecclesiastes

If we were able to take as the finest allegory of simulation the Borges tale where the cartographers of the Empire draw up a map so detailed that it ends up exactly covering the territory (but where, with the decline of the Empire this map becomes frayed and finally ruined, a few shreds still discernible in the deserts—the metaphysical beauty of this ruined abstraction, bearing witness to an imperial pride and rotting like a carcass, returning to the substance of the soil, rather as an aging double ends up being confused with the real

From "Simulacra and Simulations," as seen on pp. 1–13, 23–26 of *Simulations,* by Jean R. Baudrillard, Paul Foss, Paul Patton, and Philip Beitchman, Trans. Sylvere Lotringer Beitchman, Ed. Published by Semiotext(e), New York. Copyright © 1983. Used by permission of Semiotext(e).

thing), this fable would then have come full circle for us, and now has nothing but the discrete charm of second-order simulacra.

Abstraction today is no longer that of the map, the double, the mirror or the concept. Simulation is no longer that of a territory, a referential being or a substance. It is the generation by models of a real without origin or reality: a hyperreal. The territory no longer precedes the map, nor survives it. Henceforth, it is the map that precedes the territory—*precession of simulacra*—it is the map that engenders the territory and if we were to revive the fable today, it would be the territory whose shreds are slowly rotting across the map. It is the real, and not the map, whose vestiges subsist here and there, in the deserts which are no longer those of the Empire, but our own. *The desert of the real itself.*

In fact, even inverted, the fable is useless. Perhaps only the allegory of the Empire remains. For it is with the same imperialism that present-day simulators try to make the real, all the real, coincide with their simulation models. But it is no longer a question of either maps or territory. Something has disappeared: the sovereign difference between them that was the abstraction's charm. For it is the difference which forms the poetry of the map and the charm of the territory, the magic of the concept and the charm of the real. This representational imaginary, which both culminates in and is engulfed by the cartographer's mad project of an ideal coextensivity between the map and the territory, disappears with simulation, whose operation is nuclear and genetic, and no longer specular and discursive. With it goes all of metaphysics. No more mirror of being and appearances, of the real and its concept; no more imaginary coextensivity: rather, genetic miniaturization is the dimension of simulation. The real is produced from miniaturized units, from matrices, memory banks and command models—and with these it can be reproduced an indefinite number of times. It no longer has to be rational, since it is no longer measured against some ideal or negative instance. It is nothing more than operational. In fact, since it is no longer enveloped by an imaginary, it is no longer real at all. It is a hyperreal: the product of an irradiating synthesis of combinatory models in a hyperspace without atmosphere.

In this passage to a space whose curvature is no longer that of the real, nor of truth, the age of simulation thus begins with a liquidation of all referentials—worse: by their artificial resurrection in systems of signs, which are a more ductile material than meaning, in that they lend themselves to all systems of equivalence, all binary oppositions and all combinatory algebra. It is no longer a question of imitation, nor of reduplication, nor even of parody. It is rather a question of substituting signs of the real for the real itself; that is, an operation to deter every real process by its operational double, a metastable, programmatic, perfect descriptive machine which provides all the signs of the real and short-circuits all its vicissitudes. Never again will the real have to be produced: this is the vital function of the model in a system of death, or rather of anticipated resurrection which no longer leaves any chance even in the event of death. A hyperreal henceforth sheltered from the imaginary, and from any distinction between the real and the imaginary, leaving room only for the orbital recurrence of models and the simulated generation of difference.

The Divine Irreference of Images

To dissimulate is to feign not to have what one has. To simulate is to feign to have what one hasn't. One implies a presence, the other an absence. But the matter is more complicated, since to simulate is not simply to feign: "Someone who feigns an illness can simply go to bed and pretend he is ill. Someone who simulates an illness produces in himself some of the symptoms" (Littre). Thus, feigning or dissimulating leaves the reality principle intact: the difference is always clear, it is only masked; whereas simulation threatens the difference between "true" and "false", between "real" and "imaginary". Since the simulator produces "true" symptoms, is he or she ill or not? The simulator cannot be treated objectively either as ill, or as not ill. Psychology and medicine stop at this point, before a thereafter undiscoverable truth of the illness. For if any symptom can be "produced," and can no longer be accepted as a fact of nature, then every illness may be considered as simulatable and simulated, and medicine loses its meaning since it only knows how to treat "true" illnesses by their objective causes. Psychosomatics evolves in a dubious way on the edge of the illness principle. As for psychoanalysis, it transfers the symptom from the organic to the unconscious order: once again, the latter is held to be real, more real than the former; but why should simulation stop at the portals of the unconscious? Why couldn't the "work" of the unconscious be "produced" in the same way as any other symptom in classical medicine? Dreams already are.

The alienist, of course, claims that "for each form of the mental alienation there is a particular order in the succession of symptoms, of which the simulator is unaware and in the absence of which the alienist is unlikely to be deceived." This (which dates from 1865) in order to save at all cost the truth principle, and to escape the specter raised by simulation: namely that truth, reference and objective causes have ceased to exist. What can medicine do with something which floats on either side of illness, on either side of health, or with the reduplication of illness in a discourse that is no longer true or false? What can psychoanalysis do with the reduplication of the discourse of the unconscious in a discourse of simulation that can never be unmasked, since it isn't false either?

What can the army do with simulators? Traditionally, following a direct principle of identification, it unmasks and punishes them. Today, it can reform an excellent simulator as though he were equivalent to a "real" homosexual, heartcase or lunatic. Even military psychology retreats from the Cartesian clarities and hesitates to draw the distinction between true and false, between the "produced" symptom and the authentic symptom. "If he acts crazy so well, then he must be mad." Nor is it mistaken: in the sense that all lunatics are simulators, and this lack of distinction is the worst form of subversion. Against it, classical reason armed itself with all its categories. But it is this today which again outflanks them, submerging the truth principle.

Outside of medicine and the army, favored terrains of simulation, the affair goes back to religion and the simulacrum of divinity: "I forbade any simulacrum in the temples because the divinity that breathes life into nature cannot be represented." Indeed it can. But what becomes of the divinity when it reveals itself in icons, when it is multiplied in simulacra? Does it remain the supreme authority, simply incarnated in images as a visible theology? Or is it volatilized into simulacra which alone deploy their pomp and power of fascination—the visible machinery of icons being substituted for the pure and intelligible Idea of God? This is precisely what was feared by the Iconoclasts, whose millennial quarrel is still with us today. Their rage to destroy images rose precisely because they sensed this omnipotence of simulacra, this facility they have of erasing God from the consciousnesses of people, and the overwhelming, destructive truth which they suggest: that ultimately there has never been any God; that only simulacra exist; indeed that God himself has only ever been his own simulacrum. Had they been able to believe that images only occulted or masked the Platonic idea of God, there would have been no reason to destroy them. One can live with the idea of a distorted truth. But their metaphysical despair came from the idea that the images concealed nothing at all, and that in fact they were not images, such as the original model would have made them, but actually perfect simulacra forever radiant with their own fascination. But this death of the divine referential has to be exorcised at all cost.

It can be seen that the iconoclasts, who are often accused of despising and denying images, were in fact the ones who accorded them their actual worth, unlike the iconolaters, who saw in them only reflections and were content to venerate God at one remove. But the converse can also be said, namely that the iconolaters possessed the most modern and adventurous minds, since, underneath the idea of the apparition of God in the mirror of images, they already enacted his death and his disappearance in the epiphany of his representations (which they perhaps knew no longer represented anything, and that they were purely a game, but that this was precisely the greatest game—knowing also that it is dangerous to unmask images, since they dissimulate the fact that there is nothing behind them).

This was the approach of the Jesuits, who based their politics on the virtual disappearance of God and on the worldly and spectacular manipulation of consciences—the evanescence of God in the epiphany of power—the end of transcendence, which no longer serves as alibi for a strategy completely free of influences and signs.

Behind the baroque of images hides the grey eminence of politics.

Thus perhaps at stake has always been the murderous capacity of images: murderers of the real; murderers of their own model as the Byzantine icons could murder the divine identity. To this murderous capacity is opposed the dialectical capacity of representations as a visible and intelligible mediation of the real. All of Western faith and good faith was engaged in this wager on representation: that a sign could refer to the depth of meaning, that a sign could *exchange* for meaning and that something could guarantee this exchange—God, of course. But what if God himself can be simulated, that is to say, reduced to the signs which attest his existence? Then the whole system becomes weightless; it is no longer anything but a gigantic simulacrum: not unreal, but a simulacrum, never again exchanging for what is real, but exchanging in itself, in an uninterrupted circuit without reference or circumference.

So it is with simulation, insofar as it is opposed to representation. Representation starts from the principle that the sign and the real are equivalent (even if this equivalence is Utopian, it is a fundamental axiom). Conversely, simulation starts from the Utopia of this principle of equivalence, *from the radical negation of the sign as value,* from the sign as reversion and death sentence of every reference. Whereas representation tries to absorb simulation by interpreting it as false representation, simulation envelops the whole edifice of representation as itself a simulacrum.

These would be the successive phases of the image:

1. It is the reflection of a basic reality.
2. It masks and perverts a basic reality.
3. It masks the absence of a basic reality.
4. It bears no relation to any reality whatever: it is its own pure simulacrum.

In the first case, the image is a *good* appearance: the representation is of the order of sacrament. In the second, it is an *evil* appearance: of the order of malefice. In the third, it *plays at being* an appearance: it is of the order of sorcery. In the fourth, it is no longer in the order of appearance at all, but of simulation.

The transition from signs which dissimulate something to signs which dissimulate that there is nothing, marks the decisive turning point. The first implies a theology of truth and secrecy (to which the notion of ideology still belongs). The second inaugurates an age of simulacra and simulation, in which there is no longer any God to recognize his own, nor any last judgement to separate truth from false, the real from its artificial resurrection, since everything is already dead and risen in advance.

When the real is no longer what it used to be, nostalgia assumes its full meaning. There is a proliferation of myths of origin and signs of reality; of second-hand truth, objectivity and authenticity. There is an escalation of the true, of the lived experience; a resurrection of the figurative where the object and substance have disappeared. And there is a panic-stricken production of the real and the referential, above and parallel to the panic of material production. This is how simulation appears in the phase that concerns us: a strategy of the real, neo-real and hyperreal, whose universal double is a strategy of deterrence.

Hyperreal and Imaginary

Disneyland is a perfect model of all the entangled orders of simulation. To begin with it is a play of illusions and phantasms: pirates, the frontier, future world, etc. This imaginary world is supposed to be what makes the operation successful. But, what draws the crowds is undoubtedly much more the social microcosm, the miniaturized and *religious* revelling in real America, in its delights and drawbacks. You park outside, queue up inside, and are totally abandoned at the exit. In this imaginary world the only phantasmagoria is in the inherent warmth and affection of the crowd, and in that sufficiently excessive number of gadgets used there to specifically maintain the multitudinous affect. The contrast with the absolute solitude of the parking lot—a veritable concentration camp—is total. Or rather: inside, a whole range of gadgets magnetize the crowd into direct flows; outside, solitude is directed onto a single gadget: the automobile. By an extraordinary coincidence (one that undoubtedly belongs to the peculiar enchantment of this universe), this deep-frozen infantile world happens to have been conceived and realized by a man who is himself now cryogenized; Walt Disney, who awaits his resurrection at minus 180 degrees centigrade.

The objective profile of the United States, then, may be traced throughout Disneyland, even down to the morphology of individuals and the crowd. All its values are exalted here, in miniature and comic-strip form. Embalmed and pacified. Whence the possibility of an ideological analysis of Disneyland (L. Marin does it well in *Utopies, jeux d'espaces*): digest of the American way of life, panegyric to American values, idealized transposition of a contradictory reality. To be sure. But this conceals something else, and that "ideological" blanket exactly serves to cover over a *third-order simulation:* Disneyland is there to conceal the fact that it is the "real" country, all of "real" America, which *is* Disneyland (just as prisons are there to conceal the fact that it is the social in its entirety, in its banal omnipresence, which is carceral). Disneyland is presented as imaginary in order to make us believe that the rest is real, when in fact all of Los Angeles and the America surrounding it are no longer real, but of the order of the hyperreal and of simulation. It is no longer a question of a false representation of reality (ideology), but of concealing the fact that the real is no longer real, and thus of saving the reality principle.

The Disneyland imaginary is neither true nor false: it is a deterrence machine set up in order to rejuvenate in reverse the fiction of the real. Whence the debility, the infantile degeneration of this imaginary. It is meant to be an infantile world, in order to make us believe that the adults are elsewhere, in the "real" world, and to conceal the fact that real childishness is everywhere, particularly among those adults who go there to act the child in order to foster illusions of their real childishness.

Moreover, Disneyland is not the only one. Enchanted Village, Magic Mountain, Marine World: Los Angeles is encircled by these "imaginary stations" which feed reality, reality-energy, to a town whose mystery is precisely that it is nothing more than a network of endless, unreal circulation: a town of fabulous proportions, but without space or dimensions. As much as electrical and nuclear power stations, as much as film studios, this town, which is nothing more than an immense script and a perpetual motion picture, needs this old imaginary made up of childhood signals and faked phantasms for its sympathetic nervous system.

LEWIS COSER

1913–2003

Lewis A. Coser (Ludwig Cohen), son of a Prussian banker and broker, was born in Berlin on November 27, 1913, married the sociologist Rose Laub on August 12, 1942, and had one son and one daughter with her during a long and professionally productive marriage. He died in Cambridge, Massachusetts at 89 on July 8, 2003. During his youth, the unathletic, unPrussian-style Coser found a world within his father's large but unused private library where he read the great 19th century classics from several countries. At 19 he left home for Paris in order to set his own course, freed of parental dictates. There he became fluent in French, and shortly thereafter spent six months in England toward the same end, rounding out his youthful explorations with a trip to Italy, while also teaching himself Spanish in order to read about its Civil War in the 30s. Coser was always active on the left politically. His autodidacticism was so successful that he was able to bypass undergraduate school almost entirely and went directly to work on his dissertation at the Sorbonne. He attended the Sorbonne from 1934 through 1938, deciding to write about how Victorian novels from England, France, and Germany revealed the sociological workings of their respective societies. From this interest his major professor explained that the most suitable field for such scholarship was sociology, not comparative literature proper. Throughout this period Coser worked as a journalist writing for leftist periodicals, was briefly imprisoned in 1939 in Paris along with 40,000 other undesirables, who were interned in a sports stadium, and like so many intellectuals of his period, found security in the U.S. He was lucky in his new friendships, e.g., being tutored by Dwight Macdonald, with whom he would later work for decades on the important journal, *Dissent.*

Working under Robert Merton at Columbia University, he wrote a stunning dissertation (1954) in which he showed that conflict under certain conditions could serve positive functions in promoting societal solidarity. He taught at Chicago (sharing digs with C. Wright Mills), Brandeis, and SUNY/Stony Brook. He also wrote a history of the American communist party with the literary critic Irving Howe (1957), translated works by Max Scheler and Georg Simmel, published a unique sociology textbook composed of excerpts from great literature (1963), wrote a profound study in the sociology of literature (*Men of Ideas,* 1965), and also produced one of the finest histories of sociological theory of the last generation, *Masters of Sociological Thought* (1972). The excerpt printed below embodies many of Coser's favorite themes: the role of literature and history in the production of civility or brutality, the difficulty of theorizing subtleties across cultures and time, and the need to read much more widely than is usually the case among social scientists.

A HANDFUL OF THISTLES: COLLECTED PAPERS IN MORAL CONVICTION, 1988

The Notion of Civility in Contemporary Society

Ever since the Enlightenment, most intellectuals on the liberal and radical end of the ideological spectrum have tended to stand for a morality and politics of authenticity, sincerity, and naturalness; while their conservative opponents defended the need for decorum, civility, and restraints. These differences were, of course, largely rooted in differing basic conceptions about the nature of the human animal. Traditionally, the conservatives had a pessimistic view of human nature and hence believed that it had to be curbed; they pitted their views against the progressive belief in the basic goodness of humankind that emerged in the eighteenth century. When Rousseau proclaimed in *Émile:* "Coming from the hands of the author of all things, everything is good; in the hands of man, everything degenerates," Bonald, the great critic of Enlightenment thought, answered: "We are bad by nature, good through society. The savage is not a man, he is not even a childish man, he is only a degenerate man."

The main thinkers of the Enlightenment argued, though in a more or less modulated manner, for a liberation of the person from the prison of convention and traditional restraint that had heretofore prevented the blossoming of human potentialities. They stood for a politics and morality of authenticity, of disclosure and nakedness; while their conservative opponents, convinced of the essential sinfulness and nastiness of human beings, argued for the need of decorum and demeanor, the politics of an enclosure of the self behind public masks that would hide the ugly propensities of the unrestrained animal.

The politics of authenticity and of disclosure has for a long time been a weapon of the underdogs in the assault against the pomp and circumstance of the high and mighty. It goes back at least to those messianic medieval sectarians who advocated literal nakedness to recapture Adamite in-

nocence in opposition to the elaborate clothing of the upper classes. Rousseau followed this tradition when in the *Confessions* he attempted to disclose his whole private self, both the reputable and the disreputable parts, to the gaze of the public. He thereby attempted self-consciously to lay the foundations for a truly radical assault against traditional culture and its pieties and conventions. This is why he could argue in the *First Discourse* that "the good man is an athlete who loves to wrestle stark naked; he despises those vile ornaments which cramp the use of his power."

Rousseau was soon answered by the great spokesman for conservative thought, Edmund Burke, who lamented that, in the age of the French Revolution,

> all the decent drapery of life is to be rudely torn off. The superadded ideas, furnished from the wardrobe of moral imagination which [are] necessary to cover the defects of our naked, shivering nature, and to raise it to dignity in our own estimation, are to be exploded as a ridiculous, absurd and antiquated fashion

Burke was rebutted in his turn by Thomas Paine, who wrote in *Common Sense* that "government, like dress, is the badge of lost innocence."

A modern scholar; Stephen Greenblatt, discussing the first images of America among Europeans, argues that the Indians horrified a ruling class "obsessed with the symbolism of dress," their nakedness being perceived as a token of cultural void. Yet that very nakedness was seen by the Rousseauists and the Romantics as a sign of uncorrupted innocence.

Almost invariably, those who stood for nakedness, disclosure, authenticity, belonged to the left wing of the political spectrum; while the defenders of the taming of the natural individual and the need for civilized masking of natural propensities through the powers of convention tended to advocate a conservative tradition. I wish, however, to argue in what follows that civility is too important a notion to be left to the conservatives.

I should like, for a start, to follow the lead of Norbert Elias, one of the most significant sociological thinkers of our day, who is by no means a conservative. Elias shows in his seminal *The Civilizing Process* that, at least in post-classical Europe, whatever progress may be dimly perceived in human culture was achieved by the development of civility, that is, by an effort to tame, restrain, and restrict "natural" propensities.

Elias's book attempts to depict the gradual domestication of human affect and emotion from the Middle Ages to the present. He documents the ways in which the modern individual is a result of gradual efforts at bridling the "natural person." His purpose is to show how the physical makeup of modern men and women differs in significant ways from that of their ancestors. Medieval people, Elias argues, were faced with relatively few barriers to the acting out of affect, be it in the area of aggression or sex, be it at the table or in the bedroom. The advancement of civilization, so Elias argues, involves a progressively stricter control of impulse and emotion, the development of habits of restraint, first imposed by superiors on inferiors and later becoming automatic self-restraints which operate no matter whether the person can be observed by others or not. The growth of civilization—and here Elias follows closely in the footsteps of Freud—involves the gradual intensification of constraints over the centuries.

Ideas similar to these can be found in the work of other writers. What makes for the distinctiveness of Elias's book is his leap of the sociological imagination when searching for evidence. He turned to the various etiquette and manner books that have been steadily written and widely read since the days of Erasmus. Systematically comparing their changing content over time, Elias takes them as guides to the changing life styles and sense of proprieties on the passing historical scene.

Take table manners: already medieval writers tell their readers in quest of refinement of manners that one should not gnaw a bone and then throw it back into the common dish, or that diners should not wipe their noses on their hands or spit into the plate. By the sixteenth century, the time of Erasmus, standards became gradually more demanding, and people more self-conscious. Eating habits became ever more refined. People began to use forks instead of hunting with pieces of bread for chunks of meat in the common pot. They were taught that they should use their knives unobtrusively so as not to threaten their neighbors at table. They learned a whole complicated set of restraints and gradually acquired the

various instruments for "civil" eating that made these restraints possible.

Conduct while eating is, of course, only one of the ways in which people gradually learned to repress "natural" drives and propensities. Elias painstakingly documents how a variety of bodily functions were gradually curbed. To him, all these changes are not just curios; they indicate basic shifts in human relationships and fundamental changes in the way human beings use their body in relation to that of others. Bodily functions were increasingly seen as shameful and not to be displayed in public. An invisible wall gradually grew between one human body and another. The public sphere became distinguished from the private. People now began to mold themselves and others more self-consciously and deliberately than was the wont and use of the Middle Ages. To use Elias's telling phrase, "the embarrassment threshold is raised." Much of what we now consider "second nature" was the result of a century-long process of gradual self-domestication.

In the world of modernity, Elias argues, people have learned reserve in social intercourse and have become attuned to the invisible barriers of polite self-control. The civilizing process with its attendant restrictions softens intercourse between people and leads to forms of reserve and areas of privacy that protect the inner personality from invasion by outsiders. A whole new apparatus of self-controls has gradually replaced the prohibitions and sanctions by outsiders. As a result, the pressures to restrain impulses, and the sociogenetic shame surrounding them, has created a new type of personality: a modern psyche. Repression of spontaneous behavior; the inhibition of aggressive impulses, the distancing of people from their bodily functions—all these involved a taming of "human nature." Elias tends to agree with the great moral critic, Oscar Wilde, who wrote: "The first duty of life is to be as artificial as possible."

I showed earlier that in the past the emphasis on restraint, civility, and demeanor was found most frequently in the conservative camp, but stated that it would be quite foolish to leave the field to the conservatives. It is readily apparent in Burke, in Bonald or in Maistre, that their defense of the politics and morality of restraint was rooted in their prepotent desire to maintain and shore up a society in which hierarchy was to be enshrined forever and in which deference to those in power was to be assured.

Upper-class restraints served to mark the distance between that class and those deemed inferior. The upper classes cultivated refinement in manners, and this refinement served to symbolize their superior status in contrast to the lower classes. We, they seemed to say, eat with knife and fork; these peasants know no better than to eat with their hands. The value of upper-class civility was enhanced by reference to the lack thereof among the inferior breeds. The restrained behavior of the upper classes depended on the lack of restraint of inferiors like a figure depends on its ground. Being based on the notion of contrast, upper-class civility reinforced hierarchical superiority. In addition, of course, cruder sorts of restraints were also imposed on the lower classes so as to make sure that they would keep their place and that the high and mighty could be securely ensconced in the seats of power: What these conservative writers wished to insure above all was that people be kept in their appointed place and that the order of rank and precedent not be disturbed. By reiterating, over and over again, that the human animal was fundamentally vicious, they meant to argue that the common herd needed to be securely policed so that it did not pose a threat to the status quo and the prevalent mode of domination.

It is the recognition of these uses of the rhetoric of restraint and civility that led the bulk of the Enlightenment writers to espouse the cause of nakedness, "naturalness" and exposure. What Hans Speier has written in regard to the concept of honor applies more generally: "From the fact that honor is derived from a concept of excellence, it is inevitable that the process of honoring creates hierarchical distinctions." Manners, civility, demeanor, and the like, whatever they may have meant besides, denoted above all the idea that the order of ranks they symbolize and shore up should be maintained forever. Hence, the *philosophes* and their allies were naturally drawn to see them as 'artificial' contrivances that had to be destroyed by "natural" men intent on reversing the old order of rank and precedent.

Yet, what some of the Enlightenment writers less extreme than Rousseau also saw, and what

should be much more apparent to us today, is that the notion of civility, if it is severed from its connection with the notion of hierarchy, is important for those who plead the cause of individualism and who wish to enhance maximum autonomy of the human being. To put it in a nutshell: autonomous individuals can thrive, and they can only thrive, if and when each human being is accorded by all the others the deference and solicitude which in previous ages was reserved only for the high and mighty.

The intent of conservatives is to restrict and restrain the life spaces of those accorded inferior ranks. Liberals and radicals, on the contrary, wish to widen everyone's life space. This aim, however, can never be achieved by a removal of all "artificial" barriers to the intercourse of human beings. It must be safeguarded by all sorts of contrivances that insure that the life space of one person not be unduly invaded by another. Restraints against the invasion of privacy, against uncivil intrusion of others, are functionally necessary if the values of individuality and autonomy are to be enhanced. Such restraints do not suppress individuality; they make it possible—by providing an inviolable private space that allows of no trespass. Just as a conscientious gardener protects tender sprouts by a variety of "artificial" contrivances so as to allow them to develop unharmed by predators or unfavorable natural conditions, so a society intent upon fostering the autonomous growth of all its members must be concerned with the protective devices that go by the name of civility.

What is more, the politics of "naturalness" and nakedness tend to foster a kind of egalitarian uniformity. As Georg Simmel once put it:

> Concrete man is reduced to general man: he is the essence of each individual person, just as the universal laws of matter in general are embodied in any fragment of matter [. . .] All that is needed to make appear what is common to all men, or man's essence, or man as such, is to free the individual from all historical influences and distortions which hide his deepest nature.

Against this kind of levelling view, as Georg Simmel has also shown, a later conception, partly developed under the influence of romanticism, stressed a different notion of individualism by putting its emphasis not on what all individuals have in common, but on what distinguishes particular individuals from one another. The notion of individualism now came to be associated with the differentiation, rather than the uniformities, among individuals. Or as Oscar Wilde once put it, "there is no one type for man. There are as many perfections as there are imperfect men."

If one holds this view, as I do, then it becomes apparent that not the policies of nakedness, but the utmost diversity in clothing is likely to foster individuality. Not the politics of the least common denominator, human nature as such, but the possibility to develop a life style most fully in accord with one's own autonomous and differentiated life plans will be on top of the agenda when one comes to reflect on what a good society might be

like. Yet, and this, to my mind, sharply distinguishes such a position from current conceits about "doing one's own thing" or "letting it all hang out," such a life style becomes possible only when restraints are so effective that each person suffers a minimum of intrusion from all others.

This might also be conceded by many representatives of the "return to nature" philosophies of the sixties. What they do not see, however, is that the intrusions I have in mind are not only those by puritanical moral entrepreneurs, by the agents of what is called public order or by moralizing busybodies, but also intrusions by those who confuse authenticity with the lack of restraint and lack of civility.

DAVID HARVEY

1935–

David Harvey, a geographer by education and social theorist by inclination, was educated at Cambridge University, receiving his doctorate there in 1962. He began teaching as Lecturer in Geography at the University of Bristol in 1961, and in 1969 moved to Johns Hopkins, where he became full professor in 1973. Between 1987 and 1993 Harvey held the Halford Mackinder chair in geography at Oxford, then returned to Hopkins. He has lectured widely on the topics of postmodernism, political economy, cultural geography, the environment, social justice, and the geographies of difference. His principal audience beyond his own discipline is owed to two main books, *The Limits to Capital* (1985) and *The Condition of Post Modernity* (1993). The latter has had particularly wide influence because, unlike so much of the French literature which putatively deals with the same ideas, Harvey's argument is clear, anchored in historical example, and does not require the adoption of an entirely new vocabulary to understand.

Harvey believes that contemporary social actors experience space and time entirely differently than their forbears due to what he calls "space-time compression." He divides Western history into four epochs: 1500–1840, during which the best average speed of travel was by horse at about 10 mph; 1850–1930, when steam locomotives could deliver 65 mph and ships 36 mph; 1950s, when propeller driven airplanes could hit 400 mph; and the 1960s when jets could achieve 700 mph for standard travel, and much higher for warplanes and experimental craft. He regards this as the most important change in recent history, from what he calls Fordism to flexible accumulation, that is, from modernity to postmodernity. This is a far cry from the sort of hyper-philosophical ruminations that usually accompany discussions of "PoMo" phenomena, which may account for Harvey's popularity among those who want to use the term "postmodern" but would rather not engage in gratuitous abstraction. In the excerpts reprinted below, Harvey considers what new form capital might take in the postmodern environment, and also reflects on Benjamin's idea from the 30s regarding the effect that space/time compression might have on the reproduction of images. Harvey is able to link some of his ideas about new forms of capital accumulation with Baudrillard's notion that simulacra have replaced "real things" in the classical capitalist model of exchange. He says that "the simulacra can in turn become the reality" because most of the human interactions that go into the production of a commodity are obscured, become invisible, as they make their way through the globalized markets. Disruption rather than coherence, far-flung origins rather than provincial attachments, distinguish today's postmodern environment from its origins.

THE CONDITION OF POSTMODERNITY: AN ENQUIRY INTO THE ORIGINS OF CULTURAL CHANGE, 1989

The Transformative and Speculative Logic of Capital

Capital is a process and not a thing. It is a process of reproduction of social life through commodity production, in which all of us in the advanced capitalist world are heavily implicated. Its internalized rules of operation are such as to ensure that it is a dynamic and revolutionary mode of social organization, restlessly and ceaselessly transforming the society within which it is embedded. The process masks and fetishizes, achieves growth through creative destruction, creates new wants and needs, exploits the capacity for human labour and desire, transforms spaces, and speeds up the pace of life. It produces problems of overaccumulation for which there are but a limited number of possible solutions.

Through these mechanisms capitalism creates its own distinctive historical geography. Its developmental trajectory is not in any ordinary sense predictable, precisely because it has always been based on speculation—on new products, new technologies, new spaces and locations, new labour processes (family labour, factory systems, quality circles, worker participation), and the like. There are many ways to make a profit. *Post hoc* rationalizations of speculative activity depend on a positive answer to the question: 'Was it profitable?' Different entrepreneurs, whole spaces of the world economy, generate different solutions to that question, and new answers overtake the old as one speculative wave engulfs another.

There are laws of process at work under capitalism capable of generating a seemingly infinite range of outcomes out of the slightest variation in initial conditions or of human activity and imagination. In the same way that the laws of fluid dynamics are invariant in every river in the world, so the laws of capital circulation are consistent from one supermarket to another, from one labour market to another, from one commodity production system to another, from one country to another and from one household to another. Yet New York and London are as different from each other as the Hudson is from the Thames.

Cultural life is often held to be outside rather than within the embrace of this capitalist logic. People, it is said, make their own story in these realms in very specific and quite unpredictable ways, depending upon their values and aspirations, their traditions and norms. Economic determination is irrelevant, even in the famous last instance. I hold this argument to be erroneous in two senses. First, I see no difference in principle between the vast range of speculative and equally unpredictable activities undertaken by entrepreneurs (new products, new marketing stratagems, new technologies, new locations, etc.) and the equally speculative development of cultural, political, legal, and ideological values and institutions under capitalism. Secondly, while it is indeed possible that speculative development in these latter domains would not be reinforced or discarded according to the *post hoc* rationalizations of profit-making, profitability (in either the narrow or the broader sense of generating and acquiring new wealth) has long been implicated in these activities, and with the passing of time the strength of this connection has increased rather than diminished. Precisely because capitalism is expansionary and imperialistic, cultural life in more and more areas gets brought within the grasp of the cash nexus and the logic of capital circulation. To be sure, this has sparked reactions varying from anger and resistance to compliance and appreciation (and there is nothing predictable about that either). But the widening and deepening of capitalist social relations with time is, surely, one of the most singular and undisputable facts of recent historical geography.

The oppositional relations . . . are always subject to the restless transformative activity of capital accumulation and speculative change. Exact configurations cannot be predicted in advance, even though the law-like behaviour of the transformative force can. Put more concretely, the degree of Fordism and modernism, or of flexibility and postmodernism, is bound to vary from time to time and from place to place, depending on which configuration is profitable and which is not. Behind all the ferment of modernity and postmodernity, we can discern some simple generative principles that shape an immense diversity of outcomes. Yet the latter strikingly fail (as in the case of the serially produced downtown renewals) to create unpredictable novelty, even though the seemingly infinite capacity to engender products feeds all the illusions of freedom and of open paths for personal fulfillment. Wherever capitalism goes, its illusory apparatus, its fetishisms, and its system of mirrors come not far behind.

It is here that we can invoke, once more, Bourdieu's thesis that we each of us possess powers of regulated improvisation, shaped by experience, which allow us 'an endless capacity to engender products—thoughts, perceptions, expressions, actions—whose limits are set by the historically situated conditions' of their production; the 'conditioned and conditional freedom' this secures 'is as remote from the creation of unpredictable novelty as it is from simple mechanical reproduction of the initial conditionings.' It is, Bourdieu suggests, through mechanisms of this sort that every established order tends to produce 'the naturalization of its own arbitrariness expressed in the 'sense of limits' and the 'sense of reality' which in turn form the basis for an 'ineradicable adherence to the established order'. The reproduction of the social and symbolic order through the exploration of difference and 'otherness' is all too evident in the climate of postmodernism.

So where, then, can real change come from? To begin with, the contradictory experiences acquired under capitalism render the novelty a little less thoroughly predictable than was the case in Bourdieu's encounter with the Kabyles. Mechanical reproduction of value systems, beliefs, cultural preferences, and the like is impossible, not in spite of but precisely because of the speculative grounding of capitalism's inner logic. The exploration of contradictions always lies at the heart of original thought. But it is also evident that the expression of such contradictions in the form of objective and materialized crises plays a key role in breaking the powerful link 'between the subjective structures and the objective structures' and thereby lay the groundwork for a critique that 'brings the undiscussed into discussion and the unformulated into formulation'. While crises in the experience of

space and time, in the financial system, or in the economy at large, may form a necessary condition for cultural and political changes, the sufficient conditions lie more deeply embedded in the internalized dialectics of thought and knowledge production. For it is ever the case that, as Marx has it, 'we erect our structure in imagination before we erect it in reality'.

The Work of Art In an Age of Electronic Reproduction and Image Banks

'In principle a work of art has always been reproducible,' wrote Walter Benjamin, but mechanical reproduction 'represents something new.' It made concrete the poet Paul Valéry's prediction:'Just as water, gas, and electricity are brought into our houses from far off to satisfy our needs in response to minimal effort, so we shall be supplied with visual or auditory images, which will appear and disappear at a simple movement of the hand.' The consequences that Benjamin foresaw have been emphasized many times over by the advances in electronic reproduction and the capacity to store images, torn out of their actual contexts in space and time, for instantaneous use and retrieval on a mass basis.

The increased role of the masses in cultural life has had both positive and negative consequences. Benjamin feared their desire to bring things closer spatially and humanly, because it inevitably led to transitoriness and reproducibility as hallmarks of a cultural production system that had hitherto explored uniqueness and permanence. The ease with which fascism could make use of that was a signal warning that the democratization of working-class culture was not necessarily an unmitigated blessing.

What is really at stake here, however, is an analysis of cultural production and the formation of aesthetic judgements through an organized system of production and consumption mediated by sophisticated divisions of labour, promotional exercises, and marketing arrangements. And these days the whole system is dominated by the circulation of capital (more often than not of a multinational sort).

As a production, marketing, and consumption system, it exhibits many peculiarities in the form its labour process takes, and in the manner of linkage between production and consumption. The one thing that cannot be said of it is that the circulation of capital is absent, and that the practitioners and agents at work within it are unaware of the laws and rules of capital accumulation. And it is certainly not democratically controlled and organized, even though consumers are highly dispersed and have more than a little say in what is produced and what aesthetic values shall be conveyed.

This is not the place to launch into any extensive discussion of the various modes of organization of this sector of economic activity, or of the ways in which aesthetic and cultural trends get woven into the fabric of daily life. Such topics have been thoroughly investigated by others (Raymond Williams providing a host of thoughtful insights). But two important issues do stand out as directly relevant to understanding the condition of postmodernity as a whole.

First, the class relations prevailing within this system of production and consumption are of a peculiar sort. What stands out here is sheer money power as a means of domination rather than direct control over the means of production and wage labour in the classic sense. One side-effect has been to rekindle a lot of theoretical interest in the nature of money (as opposed to class) power and the asymmetries that can arise therefrom (cf. Simmel's extraordinary treatise on *The Philosophy of Money*). Media stars, for example, can be highly paid yet grossly exploited by their agents, the record companies, the media tycoons, and the like. Such a system of asymmetrical money relations relates to the need to mobilize cultural creativity and aesthetic ingenuity, not only in the production of a cultural artefact but also in its promotion, packaging, and transformation into some kind of successful spectacle. But asymmetrical money power does not necessarily promote class consciousness. It is conducive to demands for individual liberty and entrepreneurial freedom. The conditions prevailing within what Daniel Bell calls 'the cultural mass' of producers and consumers of cultural artefacts shape attitudes different from those that arise out of conditions of wage labour. This cultural mass adds yet another layer to that amorphous formation known as 'the middle class.'

The political identity of such a social stratum has always been notoriously shaky, varying from the white-collar workers who formed the backbone of German Nazism (see Speier, 1986) to those who played such an important role in reshaping the cultural and political life of late nineteenth-century Paris. While it is dangerous to advance any general rules in this regard, such strata tend to lack 'the reassuring support of a moral tradition that they could call their own' (Speier). They either become 'value parasites'—drawing their consciousness from association with one or other of the dominant classes in society—or cultivate all manner of fictitious marks of their own identity. It is in these strata that the quest for symbolic capital is most marked, and for them that movements of fashion, localism, nationalism, language, and even religion and myth can be of the greatest significance. What I am proposing here is to look carefully at the kind of circularity within the cultural mass which brings together producers held in thrall by pure money power on the one hand, and on the other hand relatively affluent consumers, themselves part of the cultural mass, who look for a certain kind of cultural output as a clear mark of their own social identity. . . .

Second, the development of cultural production and marketing on a global scale has itself been a primary agent in time-space compression in part because it projected a *musée imaginaire*, a jazz club, or a concert hall into everyone's living room, but also for a set of other reasons that Benjamin considered:

> Our taverns and our metropolitan streets, our offices and furnished rooms, our railroad stations and our factories appeared to have us locked up hopelessly. Then came the film and burst this prison-world asunder by the dynamite of a tenth of a second, so that now, in the midst of its far-flung ruins and debris, we calmly and adventurously go travelling. With the close-up space expands, with slow motion, movement is extended. . . . Evidently a different nature opens

itself to the camera than opens to the naked eye—if only because an unconsciously penetrated space is substituted for a space consciously explored. (Benjamin, 1969, 236)

Responses to Time–Space Compression

There have been various responses to the travails of time–space compression. The first line of defence is to withdraw into a kind of shell-shocked, blasé, or exhausted silence and to bow down before the overwhelming sense of how vast, intractable, and outside any individual or even collective control everything is. Excessive information, it transpires, is one of the best inducements to forgetting. The qualities of postmodern fiction—'the flattest possible characters in the flattest possible landscape rendered in the flattest possible diction'—are suggestive of exactly that reaction. The personal world that Wenders depicts in *Paris, Texas* does likewise. *Wings of Desire,* though more optimistic, still replies in the affirmative to the other question which Newman poses: 'Have the velocities of recent change been so great that we do not know how to trace their lines of force, that no sensibility, least of all narrative, has been able to articulate them?'

This aspect of postmodernism has been reinforced by the activities of the deconstructionists. In their suspicion of any narrative that aspires to coherence, and in their rush to deconstruct anything that even looks like meta-theory, they challenged all basic propositions. To the degree that all the narrative accounts on offer contained hidden presuppositions and simplifications, they deserved critical scrutiny, if only to emerge the stronger for it. But in challenging all consensual standards of truth and justice, of ethics, and meaning, and in pursuing the dissolution of all narratives and meta-theories into a diffuse universe of language games, deconstructionism ended up, in spite of the best intentions of its more radical practitioners, by reducing knowledge and meaning to a rubble of signifiers. It thereby

produced a condition of nihilism that prepared the ground for the re-emergence of a charismatic politics and even more simplistic propositions than those which were deconstructed.

The second reaction amounts to a freewheeling denial of the complexity of the world, and a penchant for the representation of it in terms of highly simplified rhetorical propositions. Slogans abound, from left to right of the political spectrum, and depthless images are deployed to capture complex meanings. Travel, even imaginary and vicarious, is supposed to broaden the mind, but it just as frequently ends up confirming prejudices.

The third response has been to find an intermediate niche for political and intellectual life which spurns grand narrative but which does cultivate the possibility of limited action. This is the progressive angle to postmodernism which emphasizes community and locality, place and regional resistances, social movements, respect for otherness, and the like. It is an attempt to carve out at least one knowable world from the infinity of possible worlds which are daily shown to us on the television screen. At its best it produces trenchant images of possible other worlds, and even begins to shape the actual world. But it is hard to stop the slide into parochialism, myopia, and self-referentiality in the face of the universalizing force of capital circulation. At worst, it brings us back to narrow and sectarian politics in which respect for others gets mutilated in the fires of competition between the fragments. And, it should not be forgotten, this was the path that allowed Heidegger to reach his accommodation with Nazism, and which continues to inform the rhetoric of fascism (witness the rhetoric of a contemporary fascist leader like Le Pen).

The fourth response has been to try and ride the tiger of time—space compression through construction of a language and an imagery that can mirror and hopefully command it. I place the frenetic writings of Baudrillard and Virilio in this category, since they seem hell-bent on fusing with time-space compression and replicating it in their own flamboyant rhetoric. We have seen this kind of response before, most specifically in Nietzsche's extraordinary evocations in *The Will to Power*. Compared to that, however, it seems as if Baudrillard reduces Nietzsche's tragic sense to farce (but then postmodernism always has trouble in taking itself seriously). Jameson, for all his brilliance, likewise loses his hold on both the reality he is seeking to represent and on the language that might properly be deployed to represent it in his more protean writings.

Indeed, the hyper-rhetoric of this wing of the postmodern reaction can dissolve into the most alarming irresponsibility. In reading Jameson's account of schizophrenia, for example, it is hard not to impute euphoric qualities to the hallucinogenic rush of intoxicating experience behind the surface appearance of anxiety and neurosis. But as Taylor (1987, 67) points out, Jameson's selective quotations from the autobiography of a schizophrenic girl eliminate the terror that attaches to her unreality states, making it all seem like a well-controlled LSD trip rather than a succession of states of guilt, lethargy, and helplessness coupled with anguished and sometimes tempestuous dislocation. Deleuze and Guattari, applauded by Foucault, likewise recommend that we accommodate to the fact that 'everywhere capitalism sets in motion schizo-flows that animate "our" arts and "our" sciences, just as they congeal into the production of "our own" sick, the schizophrenics.' Revolutionaries, they advise, 'should carry out their undertakings along the lines of the schizo process,' because the schizophrenic 'has become caught up in a flux of desire that threatens the social order.' If this is indeed the case, then I am left contemplating the following account from the Associated Press, 27 December 1987, as a possible epitaph on 'our' civilization:

> Mr Dobben had been diagnosed as a schizophrenic. . . . On Thanksgiving Day, the police say, Mr Dobben took his two sons, Bartley Joel, 2 years old, and Peter David, 15 months old, to the Cannon–Muskegon Corporation foundry where he worked and put them inside a giant ladle used to carry molten metal. He then heated it to 1,300 degrees while his wife, un-knowing, waited outside in the car. Now Bartley James Dobben, 26, sits under suicide surveillance.

In case this be thought a too extreme vision, I quote also Kenny Scharf (an East Village 'Day-Glo' painter) whose sequence of paintings of Estelle escaping time–space compression with a one-way ticket to outer space has her, in the final picture, 'just kind of having fun by herself, floating and watching the world blow up' (Taylor, 1987, 123). And if that is judged too imaginary, then I quote Alan Sugar, Chairman of the Amstrad Corporation: 'If there was a market in mass-produced portable nuclear weapons then we'd market them too.'

JULIA KRISTEVA

1941–

Julia Kristeva (Julia Joyaux) was born in Silven, (Soviet) Bulgaria to middle-class parents on June 24, 1941, married Phillippe Sollers, editor of *Tel Quel* and avant-garde novelist, and had a son with him before they divorced. She attended French-language schools in Bulgaria, took a degree in linguistics from the Literary Institute at the University of Sofia in 1963 and began her career as a journalist. Soviet oppression heightened soon thereafter, so she emigrated to Paris by means of a scholarship, for study at l'Ecole practique des Hautes-Etudes and the University of Paris VII, from which she took a doctorate in linguistics in 1973. She worked as Levi-Strauss's research assistant (1967–73) and studied with Lucien Goldman (Marxist literary critic), Tzvetan Todorov (literary and cultural theorist), and Roland Barthes, who became her sponsor in the 60s hothouse of Parisian intellectual life. She published two books and became a professor of linguistics at her doctoral alma mater immediately upon graduating from it. Kristeva also became a psychoanalyst in 1978 in Paris owing to attending the famous lectures of Jacques Lacan. She was also visiting professor at Columbia University and Toronto. Her global following is substantial due to links that have been forged between her psycholinguistics and feminism, even though the latter group has become chary of her more recent work.

Like nearly all humanist intellectuals of the 60s in Paris, she begins with Saussure's basic proposition about language, abetted by Lacan and a rereading of Freud. In short, the elements of semiotics (the sign, made up of signifier and signified) versus symbols are different orders of experience, and that language, both conscious and unconscious, partakes of both sides of the aisle, the former aiming always toward some form of rational expression while the latter develops according to nonlogical procedures that are more difficult to disentangle. Her interest is in "the poetic," lying at the intersection of the two linguistic zones, and serving as a "threat" to normal discourse in that it draws on irrational sources that resist regimentation. Though beginning on the Left following the events of May, '68, she shifted from Marxist to Freudian analysis, and in the recent past has begun studying the phenomenon of female depression in works like *Black Sun: Depression and Melancholia* (1987; tr. 1989). She has also criticized Lacan, arguing for the centrality of mother-centered language acquisition in the young child, a destabilizing force in "paternally" arranged linguistic conformity. Her most important books in the realm of social theory include *Desire in Language: A Semiotic Approach to Literature and Art* (1969; tr. 1980) and *Strangers to Ourselves* (1988; tr. 1991) about xenophobia, in addition to two compendia, *A Kristeva Reader* (1986) and *The Portable Kristeva* (1997).

"STRANGERS TO OURSELVES," 1989

Toccata and Fugue for the Foreigner

Foreigner: a choked up rage deep down in my throat, a black angel clouding transparency, opaque, unfathomable spur. The image of hatred and of the other, a foreigner is neither the romantic victim of our clannish indolence nor the intruder responsible for all the ills of the polls. Neither the apocalypse on the move nor the instant adversary to be eliminated for the sake of appeasing the group. Strangely, the foreigner lives within us: he is the hidden face of our identity, the space that wrecks our abode, the time in which understanding and affinity founder. By recognizing him within ourselves, we are spared detesting him in himself. A symptom that precisely turns "we" into a problem, perhaps makes it impossible, the foreigner comes in when the consciousness of my difference arises, and he disappears when we all acknowledge ourselves as foreigners, unamenable to bonds and communities.

Can the "foreigner," who was the "enemy" in primitive societies, disappear from modern societies? Let us recall a few moments in Western history when foreigners were conceived, welcomed, or rejected, but when the possibility of a society without foreigners could also have been imagined on the horizon of a religion or an ethics. As a still and perhaps ever utopic matter, the question is again before us today as we confront an economic and political integration on the scale of the planet: shall we be, intimately and subjectively, able to live with the others, to live *as others*, without ostracism but also without leveling? The modification in the status of foreigners that is imperative today leads one to reflect on our ability to accept new modalities of otherness. No "Nationality Code" would be practicable without having that question slowly mature within each of us and for each of us.

While in the most savage human groups the foreigner was an enemy to be destroyed, he has become, within the scope of religious and ethical constructs, a different human being who, provided he espouses them, may be assimilated into the fraternities of the "wise," the "just," or the "native." In Stoicism, Judaism, Christianity, and even in the humanism of the Enlightenment, the patterns of such acceptance varied, but in spite of its limitations and shortcomings, it remained a genuine rampart against xenophobia. The violence of the problem set by the foreigner today is probably due to the crises undergone by religious and ethical constructs. This is especially so as the absorption of otherness proposed by our societies turns out to be unacceptable by the contemporary individual, jealous of his difference—one that is not only national and ethical but essentially subjective, insurmountable. Stemming from the bourgeois revolution, nationalism has become a symptom—romantic at first, then totalitarian—of the nineteenth and twentieth centuries. Now, while it does go against universalist tendencies (be they religious or rationalist) and tends to isolate or even hunt down the foreigner, nationalism nevertheless ends up, on the other hand, with the particularistic, demanding individualism of contemporary man. But it is perhaps on the basis of that contemporary individualism's subversion, beginning with the moment when the citizen-individual ceases to consider himself as unitary and glorious but discovers his incoherences and abysses, in short his "strangenesses"—that the question arises again: no longer that of welcoming the foreigner within a system that obliterates him but of promoting the togetherness of those foreigners that we all recognize ourselves to be.

Let us not seek to solidify, to turn the otherness of the foreigner into a thing. Let us merely touch it, brush by it, without giving it a permanent structure. Simply sketching out its perpetual motion through some of its variegated aspects spread out before our eyes today, through some of its former, changing representations scattered throughout history. Let us also lighten that otherness by constantly coming back to it—but more and more swiftly. Let us escape its hatred, its burden, fleeing them not through leveling and forgetting, but through the *harmonious* repetition of the differences it implies and spreads. *Toccatas and Fugues:* Bach's compositions evoke to my ears the meaning of an acknowledged and harrowing otherness that I should like to be contemporary, *because* it has been brought up, relieved, disseminated, inscribed in an original play being developed, without goal, without boundary, without end. An otherness barely touched upon and that already moves away.

Scorched Happiness

Are there any happy foreigners?

The foreigner's face burns with happiness.

At first, one is struck by his peculiarity—those eyes, those lips, those cheekbones, that skin unlike others, all that distinguishes him and reminds one, that there is *someone* there. The difference in that face reveals in paroxystic fashion what any face should reveal to a careful glance: the nonexistence of banality in human beings. Nevertheless, it is precisely the commonplace that constitutes a commonality for our daily habits. But this grasping the foreigner's features, one that captivates us, beckons and rejects at the same time. "I am at least as remarkable, and therefore I love him," the observer thinks; "now I prefer my own peculiarity, and therefore I kill him," he might conclude. From heart pangs to first jabs, the foreigner's face forces us to display the secret manner in which we face the world, stare into all our faces, even in the most familial, the most tightly knit communities.

Furthermore, the face that is so *other* bears the mark of a crossed threshold that irremediably imprints itself as peacefulness or anxiety. Whether perturbed or joyful, the foreigner's appearance signals that he is "in addition." The presence of such a border, internal to all that is displayed, awakens our most archaic senses through a burning sensation. Vivid concern or delight, set there in these other features, without forgetfulness, without ostentation, like a standing invitation to some inaccessible, irritating journey, whose code the foreigner does not have but whose mute, physical, visible memory he keeps. This does not mean the foreigner necessarily appears absent, absentminded, or distraught. But the insistent presence of a lining—good or evil, pleasing or death-bearing—disrupts the never regular image of his face and imprints upon it the ambiguous mark of a scar—his very own well-being.

For, curiously, beyond unease, such a doubling imposes upon the other, the observer, the feeling that there is a special, somewhat insolent happiness in the foreigner. Happiness seems to prevail, *in spite of everything*, because something has definitely been exceeded: it is the happiness of tearing away, of racing, the space of a promised infinite. Such happiness is, however, constrained, apprehensively discreet, in spite of its piercing intrusion, since the foreigner keeps feeling threatened by his former territory, caught up in the memory of a happiness or a disaster—both always excessive.

Can one be a foreigner and happy? The foreigner calls forth a new idea of happiness. Between the fugue and the origin: a fragile limit, a temporary homeostasis. Posited, present, sometimes certain, that happiness knows nevertheless that it is passing by, like fire that shines only because it consumes. The strange happiness of the foreigner consists in maintaining that fleeing eternity or that perpetual transience.

Suffering, Ebullience, and Mask

The difficulties the foreigner will necessarily encounter—one mouth too many, incomprehensible speech, inappropriate behavior—wound him severely, but by flashes. They make him turn gray, imperceptibly, he becomes smooth and hard as a pebble, always ready to resume his infinite journey, farther, elsewhere. The (professional, intellectual, affective) aim that some set for themselves in such an unrestrained fugue is already a betrayal of strangeness, for as he chooses a program he allows himself a respite or a residence. On the contrary, according to the utmost logic of exile, all aims should waste away and self-destruct in the wanderer's insane stride toward an elsewhere that is always pushed back, unfulfilled, out of reach. The pleasure of suffering is a necessary lot in such a demented whirl, and amateur *proxeni* know it unconsciously as they choose foreign partners on whom to inflict the torture of their own contempt, their condescension, or, more deceitfully, their heavy-handed charity.

The foreigner is hypersensitive beneath his armor as activist or tireless "immigrant worker." He bleeds body and soul, humiliated in a position where, even with the better couples, he or she assumes the part of a domestic, of the one who is a bother when he or she becomes ill, who embodies the enemy, the traitor, the victim. Masochistic pleasure accounts for his or her submissiveness only in part. The latter, in fact, strengthens the foreigner's mask—a second, impassive personality, an anesthetized skin he wraps himself in, providing a hiding place where he enjoys scorning his tyrant's hysterical weaknesses. Is this the dialectic of master and slave?

The animosity, or at least the annoyance aroused by the foreigner ("What are you doing here, Mac, this is not where you belong!"), hardly surprises him. He readily bears a kind of admiration for those who have welcomed him, for he rates them more often than not above himself, be it financially, politically, or socially. At the same time he is quite ready to consider them somewhat narrow-minded, blind. For his scornful hosts lack the *perspective* he himself has in order to see himself and to see them. The foreigner feels strengthened by the distance that detaches him from the others as it does from himself and gives him the lofty sense not so much of holding the truth but of making it and himself relative while others fall victim to the ruts of monovalency. For they are perhaps owners of things, but the foreigner tends to think he is the only one to have a biography, that is, a life made up of ordeals—neither catastrophes nor adventures (although these might equally happen), but simply a life in which acts constitute events because they imply choice, surprises, breaks, adaptations, or cunning, but neither routine nor rest. In the eyes of the foreigner those who are not foreign have no life at all: barely do they exist, haughty or mediocre, but out of the running and thus almost already cadaverized.

Aloofness

Indifference is the foreigner's shield. Insensitive, aloof, he seems, deep down, beyond the reach of attacks and rejections that he nevertheless experiences with the vulnerability of a medusa. This is because his being kept apart corresponds to his remaining aloof, as he pulls back into the painless core of what is called a soul the humbleness that,

when all is said and done, amounts to plain brutality. There, soured of mawkishness, but of sensitivity as well, he takes pride in holding a truth that is perhaps simply a certainty—the ability to reveal the crudest aspects of human relationships when seduction fades out and proprieties give way before the results of confrontations: a clash of bodies and tempers. For the foreigner, from the height of an autonomy that he is the only one to have chosen when the others prudently remain "between themselves," paradoxically confronts everyone with an asymbolia that rejects civility and returns to a violence laid bare. The brutes' encounter.

Not belonging to any place, any time, any love. A lost origin, the impossibility to take root, a rummaging memory, the present in abeyance. The space of the foreigner is a moving train, a plane in flight, the very transition that precludes stopping. As to landmarks, there are none. His time? The time of a resurrection that remembers death and what happened before, but misses the glory of being beyond: merely the feeling of a reprieve, of having gotten away.

A Melancholia

Hard-hearted indifference is perhaps no more than the respectable aspect of nostalgia. We all know the foreigner who survives with a tearful face turned toward the lost homeland. Melancholy lover of a vanished space, he cannot, in fact, get over his having abandoned a period of time. The lost paradise is a mirage of the past that he will never be able to recover. He knows it with a distressed knowledge that turns his rage involving others (for there is always an other, miserable cause of my exile) against himself: "How could I have abandoned them? I have abandoned myself." And even he who, seemingly, flees the slimy poison of depression, does not hold back, as he lies in bed, during those glaucus moments between waking and sleeping. For in the intervening period of nostalgia, saturated with fragrances and sounds to which he no longer belongs and which, because of that, wound him less than those of the here and now, the foreigner is a dreamer making love with absence, one exquisitely depressed. Happy?

Ironists and Believers

Yet, he is never simply torn between here and elsewhere, now and before. Those who believe they are crucified in such a fashion forget that nothing ties them there anymore, and, so far, nothing binds them here. Always elsewhere, the foreigner belongs nowhere. But let there be no mistake about it: there are, in the way one lives this attachment to a lost space, two kinds of foreigners, and this separates uprooted people of all countries, occupations, social standing, sexes . . . into two irreconcilable categories. On the one hand, there are those who waste away in an agonizing struggle between what no longer is and what will never be—the followers of neutrality, the advocates of emptiness; they are not necessarily defeatists, they often become the best of ironists. On the other hand, there are those who transcend: living neither before nor now but beyond, they are bent with a passion that, although tenacious, will remain forever unsatisfied. It is a passion for another land, always a promised one, that of an occupation, a love, a child, a glory. They are believers, and they sometimes ripen into skeptics. . . .

Slaves and Master

Dialectics of master and slave? The amount of strength changes the very balance of power. The weight of foreigners is measured not only in terms of greater numbers (from that standpoint did not slaves always constitute an overwhelming majority?) but is also determined by the consciousness of being somewhat foreign as well. On the one hand, because everyone is, in a world that is more open than ever, liable to become a foreigner for a while as tourist or employee of a multinational concern. On the other hand, because the once solid barrier between "master" and "slave" has today been abolished, if not in people's unconscious at least in our ideologies and aspirations. Every native feels himself to be more or less a "foreigner" in his "own and proper" place, and that metaphorical value of the word "foreigner" first leads the citizen to a feeling of discomfort as to his sexual, national, political, professional identity. Next it impels him to identify—sporadically, to be sure, but nonetheless intensely—with the other. Within this motion guilt obviously has its part but it also fades away to the advantage of a kind of underhanded glory of being a little like those other "gooks" (*métèques*), concerning which we now know that, disadvantaged as they may be, they are running before the wind. A wind that jostles and ruffles but bears us toward our own unknown and who knows what future. There is thus set up between the new "masters" and the new "slaves" a secret collusion, which does not necessarily entail practical consequences in politics or the courts (even if they, too, feel its effects progressively, slowly) but, especially with the native, arouses a feeling of suspicion: Am I really at home? Am I myself? Are *they* not masters of the "future"?

Such a habit for suspicion prompts some to reflect, rarely causes humbleness, and even more rarely generosity. But it also provokes regressive and protectionist rage in others: must we not stick together, remain among ourselves, expel the intruder, or at least, keep him in "his" place? The "master" then changes into a slave hounding his conqueror. For the foreigner perceived as an invader reveals a buried passion within those who are entrenched: the passion to kill the *other*, who had first been feared or despised, then promoted from the ranks of dregs to the status of powerful persecutor against whom a "we" solidifies in order to take revenge.

JUDITH BUTLER

1956–

Judith P. Butler was born in Cleveland, Ohio on February 24, 1956, is the partner of Wendy Brown, and they have adopted a son, Daniel Butler-Brown. She attended Yale for all three degrees (B.A., 1978, M. Phil., Ph.D. in philosophy, 1984, where she worked under the phenomenologist, Maurice Natanson). She then taught at Wesleyan University (1983–86), George Washington University (1986–89), Johns Hopkins (1989–93), and finally landed at Berkeley as the Elliot Professor of Rhetoric and Comparative Literature since 1993. Aside from the usual professional associations, she is also active in the International Gay and Lesbian Human Rights Commission, and her name appears frequently in the popular press, either as author or as iconic figure.

Butler's dissertation was converted into a book, *Subjects of Desire: Hegelian Reflections in 20th Century France* in 1987, in which she interrogated some of Hegel's texts and those of Hyppolite, Kojève, Sartre, Lacan, and others that bore on "the ontology of desire." In surprisingly clear prose, when compared with her later work, she analyzed "desire" not exclusively as a philosophical concept, but more in keeping with post-Freudian views of the centrality of sexual passion in human life. The book sold modestly as one would expect from a serious academic monograph, and gave no hint that its author would soon hit the academic jackpot by producing precisely the right book at the right time, *Gender Trouble: Feminism and the Subversion of Identity* (1990). This slim analysis of gender relations was swept up in the euphoric creation of "queer theory," sometimes identified as the first textbook for that area of teaching, and became thereby extremely well known to college students and their teachers across the country. Butler's line of argument has become so well known, either through her own words or by sympathizers, that it no longer bears the shock value it did a dozen years ago. Accepting Simone de Beauvoir's notion in *The Second Sex* (1950) that gender differences are socially created and not a biological necessity, Butler moved into the zone of linguistic usage and theoretical play. She claims that "there is no gender identity behind the expressions of gender . . . identity is performatively constituted by the very 'expressions' that are said to be its results," a sentiment that reads, dialectically speaking, very much like her original mentor, Hegel. By commenting on Lacan, Freud, Foucault, Kristeva, Monique Wittig, and others, she was able to bring novices into the middle of the queer theory debate efficiently. Her ultimate goal was and is to destabilize gender identities, making room for those people who choose to be more or less male, more or less female, as they wish.

GENDER TROUBLE, 1990

Theorizing the Binary, the Unitary, and Beyond

Beauvoir and Irigaray clearly differ over the fundamental structures by which gender asymmetry is reproduced; Beauvoir turns to the failed reciprocity of an asymmetrical dialectic, while Irigaray suggests that the dialectic itself is the monologic elaboration of a masculinist signifying economy. Although Irigaray clearly broadens the scope of feminist critique by exposing the epistemological, ontological, and logical structures of a masculinist signifying economy, the power of her analysis is undercut precisely by its globalizing reach. Is it possible to identify a monolithic as well as a monologic masculinist economy that traverses the array of cultural and historical contexts in which sexual difference takes place? Is the failure to acknowledge the specific cultural operations of gender oppression itself a kind of epistemological imperialism, one which is not ameliorated by the simple elaboration of cultural differences as "examples" of the selfsame phallogocentrism? The effort to *include* "Other" cultures as variegated amplifications of a global phallogocentrism constitutes an appropriative act that risks a repetition of the self-aggrandizing gesture of phallogocentrism, colonizing under the sign of the same those differences that might otherwise call that totalizing concept into question.

Feminist critique ought to explore the totalizing claims of a masculinist signifying economy, but also remain self-critical with respect to the totalizing gestures of feminism. The effort to identify the enemy as singular in form is a reverse-discourse that uncritically mimics the strategy of the oppressor instead of offering a different set of terms. That the tactic can operate in feminist and antifeminist contexts alike suggests that the colonizing gesture is not primarily or irreducibly masculinist. It can operate to effect other relations of racial, class, and heterosexist subordination, to name but a few. And clearly, listing the varieties of oppression, as I began to do, assumes their dis-

crete, sequential coexistence along a horizontal axis that does not describe their convergences within the social field. A vertical model is similarly insufficient; oppressions cannot be summarily ranked, causally related, distributed among planes of "originality" and "derivativeness." Indeed, the field of power structured in part by the imperializing gesture of dialectical appropriation exceeds and encompasses the axis of sexual difference, offering a mapping of intersecting differentials which cannot be summarily hierarchized either within the terms of phallogocentrism or any other candidate for the position of "primary condition of oppression." Rather than an exclusive tactic of masculinist signifying economies, dialectical appropriation and suppression of the Other is one tactic among many, deployed centrally but not exclusively in the service of expanding and rationalizing the masculinist domain.

The contemporary feminist debates over essentialism raise the question of the universality of female identity and masculinist oppression in other ways. Universalistic claims are based on a common or shared epistemological standpoint, understood as the articulated consciousness or shared structures of oppression or in the ostensibly transcultural structures of femininity, maternity, sexuality, and/or *écriture féminine*. The opening discussion in this chapter argued that this globalizing gesture has spawned a number of criticisms from women who claim that the category of "women" is normative and exclusionary and is invoked with the unmarked dimensions of class and racial privilege intact. In other words, the insistence upon the coherence and unity of the category of women has effectively refused the multiplicity of cultural, social, and political intersections in which the concrete array of "women" are constructed.

Some efforts have been made to formulate coalitional politics which do not assume in advance what the content of "women" will be. They propose instead a set of dialogic encounters by which variously positioned women articulate separate identities within the framework of an emergent coalition. Clearly, the value of coalitional politics is not to be underestimated, but the very form of coalition, of an emerging and unpredictable assemblage of positions, cannot be figured in advance. Despite the clearly democratizing impulse that motivates coalition building, the coalitional theorist can inadvertently reinsert herself as sovereign of the process by trying to assert an ideal form for coalitional structures *in advance,* one that will effectively guarantee unity as the outcome. Related efforts to determine what is and is not the true shape of a dialogue, what constitutes a subject-position, and, most importantly, when "unity" has been reached, can impede the self-shaping and self-limiting dynamics of coalition.

The insistence in advance on coalitional "unity" as a goal assumes that solidarity, whatever its price, is a prerequisite for political action. But what sort of politics demands that kind of advance purchase on unity? Perhaps a coalition needs to acknowledge its contradictions and take action with those contradictions intact. Perhaps also part of what dialogic understanding entails is the acceptance of divergence, breakage, splinter, and fragmentation as part of the often tortuous process of democratization. The very notion of "dialogue" is culturally specific and historically bound, and while one speaker may feel secure that a conversation is happening, another may be sure it is not. The power relations that condition and limit dialogic possibilities need first to be interrogated. Otherwise, the model of dialogue risks relapsing into a liberal model that assumes that speaking agents occupy equal positions of power and speak with the same presuppositions about what constitutes "agreement" and "unity" and, indeed, that those are the goals to be sought. It would be wrong to assume in advance that there is a category of "women" that simply needs to be filled in with various components of race, class, age, ethnicity, and sexuality in order to become complete. The assumption of its essential incompleteness permits that category to serve as a permanently available site of contested meanings. The definitional incompleteness of the category might then serve as a normative ideal relieved of coercive force.

Is "unity" necessary for effective political action? Is the premature insistence on the goal of unity precisely the cause of an ever more bitter fragmentation among the ranks? Certain forms of acknowledged fragmentation might facilitate coalitional action precisely because the "unity" of the category of women is neither presupposed nor desired. Does "unity" set up an exclusionary norm of solidarity at the level of identity that rules out the possibility of a set of actions which disrupt the very borders of identity concepts, or which seek to accomplish precisely that disruption as an explicit political aim? Without the presupposition or goal of "unity," which is, in either case, always instituted at a conceptual level, provisional unities might emerge in the context of concrete actions that have purposes other than the articulation of identity. Without the compulsory expectation that feminist actions must be instituted from some stable, unified, and agreed upon identity, those actions might well get a quicker start and seem more congenial to a number of "women" for whom the meaning of the category is permanently moot.

This antifoundationalist approach to coalitional politics assumes neither that "identity" is a premise nor that the shape or meaning of a coalitional assemblage can be known prior to its achievement. Because the articulation of an identity within available cultural terms instates a definition that forecloses in advance the emergence of new identity concepts in and through politically engaged actions, the foundationalist tactic cannot take the transformation or expansion of existing identity concepts as a normative goal. Moreover, when agreed-upon identities or agreed-upon dialogic structures, through which already established identities are communicated, no longer constitute the theme or subject of politics, then identities can come into being and dissolve depending on the concrete practices that constitute them. Certain political practices institute identities on a contingent basis in order to accomplish whatever aims are in view. Coalitional politics requires neither an expanded category of "women" nor an internally multiplicitous self that offers its complexity at once.

Gender is a complexity whose totality is permanently deferred, never fully what it is at any given juncture in time. An open coalition, then, will affirm identities that are alternately instituted and relinquished according to the purposes at hand; it will be an open assemblage that permits of multiple convergences and divergences without obedience to a normative telos of definitional closure.

⌒

EXCITABLE SPEECH: A POLITICS OF THE PERFORMATIVE, 1997

On Linguistic Vulnerability

When we claim to have been injured by language, what kind of claim do we make? We ascribe an agency to language, a power to injure, and position ourselves as the objects of its injurious trajectory. We claim that language acts, and acts against us, and the claim we make is a further instance of language, one which seeks to arrest the force of the prior instance. Thus, we exercise the force of language even as we seek to counter its force, caught up in a bind that no act of censorship can undo.

Could language injure us if we were not, in some sense, linguistic beings, beings who require language in order to be? Is our vulnerability to language a consequence of our being constituted within its terms? If we are formed in language, then that formative power precedes and conditions any decision we might make about it, insulting us from the start, as it were, by its prior power.

The insult, however, assumes its specific proportion in time. To be called a name is one of the first forms of linguistic injury that one learns. But not all name-calling is injurious. Being called a name is also one of the conditions by which a subject is constituted in language; indeed, it is one of the examples Althusser supplies for an understanding of "interpellation." Does the power of language to injure follow from its interpellative power? And how, if at all, does linguistic agency emerge from this scene of enabling vulnerability?

The problem of injurious speech raises the question of which words wound, which representations offend, suggesting that we focus on those parts of language that are uttered, utterable, and explicit. And yet, linguistic injury appears to be the effect not only of the words by which one is addressed but the mode of address itself, a mode— a disposition or conventional bearing—that interpellates and constitutes a subject.

From *Excitable Speech: A Politics of Performativity,* by Judith Butler. Reproduced by permission of Routledge, Inc., part of The Taylor & Francis Group

One is not simply fixed by the name that one is called. In being called an injurious name, one is derogated and demeaned. But the name holds out another possibility as well: by being called a name, one is also, paradoxically, given a certain possibility for social existence, initiated into a temporal life of language that exceeds the prior purposes that animate that call. Thus the injurious address may appear to fix or paralyze the one it hails, but it may also produce an unexpected and enabling response. If to be addressed is to be interpellated, then the offensive call runs the risk of inaugurating a subject in speech who comes to use language to counter the offensive call. When the address is injurious, it works its force upon the one it injures. What is this force, and how might we come to understand its faultlines?

J. L. Austin proposed that to know what makes the force of an utterance effective, what establishes its performative character, one must first locate the utterance within a "total speech situation." There is, however, no easy way to decide on how best to delimit that totality. An examination of Austin's own view furnishes at least one reason for such difficulty. Austin distinguishes "illocutionary" from "perlocutionary" speech acts: the former are speech acts that, in saying do what they say, and do it in the moment of that saying; the latter are speech acts that produce certain effects as their consequence; by saying something, a certain effect follows. The illocutionary speech act is itself the deed that it effects; the perlocutionary merely leads to certain effects that are not the same as the speech act itself.

Any delimitation of the total speech act in such illocutionary cases would doubtless include an understanding of how certain conventions are invoked at the moment of utterance, whether the person who invokes them is authorized, whether the circumstances of the invocation are right. But how does one go about delimiting the kind of "convention" that illocutionary utterances presume? Such utterances do what they say on the occasion of the saying; they are not only conventional, but in Austin's words, "ritual or ceremonial." As utterances, they work to the extent that they are given in the form of a ritual, that is, repeated in time, and, hence, maintain a sphere of operation that is not restricted to the moment of the utterance itself. The illocutionary speech act performs its deed *at the moment* of the utterance, and yet to the extent that the moment is ritualized, it is never merely a single moment. The "moment" in ritual is a condensed historicity: it exceeds itself in past and future directions, an effect of prior and future invocations that constitute and escape the instance of utterance.

Austin's claim, then, that to know the force of the illocution is only possible once the "total situation" of the speech act can be identified is beset by a constitutive difficulty. If the temporality of linguistic convention, considered as ritual, exceeds the instance of its utterance, and that excess is not fully capturable or identifiable (the past and future of the utterance cannot be narrated with any certainty), then it seems that part of what constitutes the "total speech situation" is a failure to achieve a totalized form in any of its given instances.

In this sense, it is not enough to find the appropriate context for the speech act in question, in order to know how best to judge its effects. The speech situation is thus not a simple sort of context, one that might be defined easily by spatial and temporal boundaries. To be injured by speech is to suffer a loss of context, that is, not to know where you are. Indeed, it may be that what is *unanticipated* about the injurious speech act is what constitutes its injury, the sense of putting its addressee out of control. The capacity to circumscribe the situation of the speech act is jeopardized at the moment of injurious address. To be addressed injuriously is not only to be open to an unknown future, but not to know the time and place of injury, and to suffer the disorientation of one's situation as the effect of such speech. Exposed at the moment of such a shattering is precisely the volatility of one's "place" within the community of speakers; one can be "put in one's place" by such speech, but such a place may be no place.

IMMANUEL WALLERSTEIN

1930–

Immanuel Wallerstein was born on September 28, 1930 in New York City, married Beatrice Friedman on May 25, 1964, and with her had one daughter. He took all three degrees at Columbia University (1951, 1954, 1959), and also studied at Oxford in 1955–56. He served in the U.S. Army between 1951 and 1953, and has also held leadership positions in a number of professional associations for social scientists, including President of the International Sociological Association (1994–98). Wallerstein began his career at his alma mater, rising from instructor to associate professor of sociology between 1958 and 1971, at which point he taught at McGill University in Montreal for 5 years. In 1976 he was made director of the Fernand Braudel Center for the Study of Economies, Historical Systems, and Civilizations at the State University of New York at Binghamton, a position he held until recently when he moved to Yale, even while taking visiting appointments elsewhere.

The world of anglophone scholarship was stunned in 1972 when the great French historian of the Annales School, Fernand Braudel, published his two-volume masterpiece, *The Mediterranean.* To that point the Annales School had been best represented by Lucien Febvre and Marc Bloch, whose *Feudal Society* (1940/61) had set a new standard for sociologically informed historiography, as it remains to this day. Bloch was murdered by the Gestapo near the end of WWII, and his successors were prolific but not as gifted as he, until Braudel's work burst upon the scene during the 70s and 80s. His three-volume work, *Civilization and Capitalism* (1981) inspired many historically-minded sociologists to pursue this new avenue of research.

The connection with Braudel and Wallerstein is an intimate one. Wallerstein was offered the unique opportunity in recent U.S. academic history to head a new program using a new paradigm, with the publishing support of a new journal (*Review*) at a time when risks were being taken institutionally and intellectually, largely owing to the tumult of the 60s. When the Braudel Center opened at Binghamton in 1976, it was amidst great publicity, and Braudel's visit at the inaugural ceremonies was covered in major news magazines. Wallerstein, who to that point had been an Africa specialist, suddenly rose to the challenge of bringing to life an American version of Braudelian history, and published his major work, *The Modern World-System* (3 vols., 1974, 1980, 1989). The first volume was received with tremendous attention from the international scholarly press, and "world-system analysis" became for a time the latest methodological innovation to grace the human sciences. Wallerstein surrounded himself with an extraordinary group of foreign-born experts in the socio-economy of the global system, and a steady stream of books, conferences, and journal articles issued from Binghamton, as new graduate students were trained for the first time in this mode of research. Wallerstein's other important works include *The Capitalist World-Economy* (1979), *Unthinking Social Science* (1991), and a number of volumes co-authored with Samir Amin, Giovanni Arrighi, and André Gunder Frank. Heavily leftist in orientation and qualitative/historical by inclination, the Binghamton program ran in vigorous opposition to the mainstream world of U.S. sociology. Whether the Braudel Center and its program shall outlast its founder remains to be seen, but the amount and breadth of work that the Center sponsored during its first 20 years of existence, and the refreshing attention it drew to global dynamics rather than the traditional parochialism of research aimed only at the U.S. went a long way toward invigorating sociology and its sister disciplines, especially history and political-economy.

UNTHINKING SOCIAL SCIENCE: THE LIMITS OF NINETEENTH-CENTURY PARADIGMS, 1991

World-Systems Analysis: The Second Phase

World-systems analysis has existed under that name, more or less, for about 15 years. Some of its arguments, of course, have longer histories, even very long histories. Yet, as a perspective, it emerged only in the 1970s. It presented itself as a critique of existing dominant views in the various social sciences, and primarily of developmentalism and modernization theory which seemed to dominate social science worldwide during the 1960s.

The worldwide revolution of 1968 did not spare the world of social science, and world-systems analysis shared in, was part of, a wider reaction to the ideologized positivism and false apoliticism that had been the counterpart within world social science of the US hegemonic world view. Although world-systems analysis was only one variant of this critique, it stood out in retrospect by the fact that it broke more deeply with nineteenth-century social science than did other critiques, albeit probably not deeply enough.

It is hard to know how to assess "what we have learned." What I shall do is spell out what I think are the major premises or arguments that I

believe have been reasonably explicated. I choose carefully the verb "explicated." It does not mean these premises or arguments have been widely adopted or that they have not been contested, in detail at least, even among those who think they share in the world-systems perspective. What it means is that there has been enough elaboration of the arguments such that they are familiar beyond the bounds of the initiates (and thus, for example, they might appear in textbooks as reflecting a "viewpoint"), and such that these premises and arguments might be seen as part of the defining characteristics of a world-systems perspective.

I see three such defining characteristics. The first and most obvious is that the appropriate "unit of analysis" for the study of social or societal behavior is a "world-system." No doubt this assertion has led to enormous discussion around the so-called macro-micro problem, which in this case translates into how much of local and/or national behavior is explained/determined by structural evolution at the level of the world-system. I believe this is a totally false problem, but I shall not argue that here. I merely point out that, formally, the macro-micro issue is no different if one decides that the boundaries of a "society" are those of a "world-system" or that these boundaries correlate more or less with those of "nation-states." There still can be said to be the macro-micro issue. The real novelty, therefore, is that the world-systems perspective denies that the "nation-state" represents in any sense a relatively autonomous "society" that "develops" over time.

The second defining characteristic has been that of the *longue durée*. This of course put us in the *Annales* tradition, as well as in that of the burgeoning field of "historical sociology." But I believe the world-systems perspective was more specific than either, and spelled out some elements that are blurry in the other two traditions. Long duration is the temporal correlate of the spatial quality of "world-system." It reflects the insistence that "world-systems" are "historical systems," that is, that they have beginnings, lives, and ends. This stance makes clear that structures are not "immobile." It insists, in addition, that there are "transitions" from one historical system to its successor or successors. It is this pair, the space of a "world" and the time of a "long duration," that combine to form any particular historical world-system.

The third element of world-systems analysis has been a certain view of one particular world-system, the one in which we live, the capitalist world-economy. Let me list the various elements that have been explicated. Some of these were borrowed, directly or in modified form, from other earlier perspectives. Some others were relatively new. But it has been the combination of these arguments that has come to be associated with world-systems analysis. I merely list now the characteristics presumed to be the description of a capitalist world-economy:

1. the ceaseless accumulation of capital as its driving force;
2. an axial division of labor in which there is a core-periphery tension, such that there is some form of unequal exchange (not necessarily as defined originally by Arghiri Emmanuel) that is spatial;
3. the structural existence of a semiperipheral zone;
4. the large and continuing role of non-wage labor alongside of wage labor;
5. the correspondence of the boundaries of the capitalist world-economy to that of an interstate system comprised of sovereign states;
6. the location of the origins of this capitalist world-economy earlier than in the nineteenth century, probably in the sixteenth century;
7. the view that this capitalist world-economy began in one part of the globe (largely Europe) and later expanded to the entire globe via a process of successive "incorporations;"

8. the existence in this world-system of hegemonic states, each of whose periods of full or uncontested hegemony has, however, been relatively brief;
9. the non-primordial character of states, ethnic groups, and households, all of which are constantly created and re-created;
10. the fundamental importance of racism and sexism as organizing principles of the system;
11. the emergence of antisystemic movements that simultaneously undermine and reinforce the system;
12. a pattern of both cyclical rhythms and secular trends that incarnates the inherent contradictions of the system and which accounts for the systemic crisis in which we are presently living.

To be sure, this list is merely a set of premises and arguments that have been articulated, and that have become relatively familiar to many. It is not a list of truths, much less a list of creeds to which we all pay allegiance. No doubt much empirical work needs to be done on each of these items, and there may be in the future much theoretical reformulation of them. But, as a relatively coherent and articulated view of historical capitalism, they exist.

~

THE END OF THE WORLD AS WE KNOW IT: SOCIAL SCIENCE FOR THE TWENTY–FIRST CENTURY, 1999

Ecology and Capitalist Costs of Production: No Exit

Today, virtually everyone agrees that there has been a serious degradation of the natural environment in which we live, by comparison with thirty years ago, a fortiori by comparison with one hundred years ago, not to speak of five hundred years ago. And this is the case despite the fact that there have been continuous significant technological inventions and an expansion of scientific knowledge that one, might have expected would have led to the opposite consequence. As a result, today, unlike thirty or one hundred or five hundred years ago, ecology has become a serious political issue in many parts of the world. There are even reasonably significant political movements organized centrally around the theme of defending the environment against further degradation and reversing the situation to the extent possible.

Of course, the appreciation of the degree of seriousness of the contemporary problem ranges from those who consider doomsday as imminent to those who consider that the problem is one well within the possibility of an early technical solution. I believe the majority of persons hold a position somewhere in-between. I am in no position to argue the issue from a scientific viewpoint. I will take this in-between appreciation as plausible and will engage in an analysis of the relevance of this issue to the political economy of the world-system.

The entire process of the universe is of course one of unceasing change, so the mere fact that things are not what they were previously is so banal that it merits no notice whatsoever. Furthermore, within this constant turbulence, there are patterns of structural renewal we call life. Living, or organic, phenomena have a beginning and an end to their individual existence, but in the process procreate, so that the species tends to continue. But this cyclical renewal is never perfect, and the overall ecology is therefore never static. In addition, all living phenomena ingest in some way products external to them, including most of the time other living phenomena, and predator/prey ratios are never perfect, so that the biological milieu is constantly evolving.

Furthermore, poisons are natural phenomena as well and were playing a role in the ecological balance sheets long before human beings got into the picture. To be sure, today we know so much more chemistry and biology than our ancestors did that we are perhaps more conscious of the toxins in our environment, although perhaps not, since we are also learning these days how sophisticated the preliterate peoples were about toxins and antitoxins. We learn all these things in our primary and secondary school education and from the simple observation of everyday living. Yet often we tend to neglect these obvious constraints when we discuss the politics of ecological issues.

The only reason it is worth discussing these issues at all is if we believe that something special or additional has been happening in recent years, a level of increased danger, and if at the same time we believe that it is possible to do something about this increased danger. The case that is generally made by the green and other ecology movements precisely comprises both these arguments: increased level of danger (for example, holes in the ozone layer, or greenhouse effects, or atomic meltdowns); and potential solutions.

As I said, I am willing to start on the assumption that there is a reasonable case for increased danger, one that requires some urgent reaction. However, in order to be intelligent about how to react to danger, we need to ask two questions: For whom does the danger exist? And what explains the increased danger? The "danger for whom" question has in turn two components: whom, among human beings; and whom, among living beings. The first question raises the comparison of North-South attitudes on ecological questions; the second is the issue of deep ecology. Both in fact involve issues about the nature of capitalist civilization and the functioning of the capitalist world-economy, which means that before we can address the issue of "for whom," we had better analyze the source of the increased danger.

The story begins with two elementary features of historical capitalism. One is well known: capitalism is a system that has an imperative need to expand—expand in terms of total production, expand geographically—in order to sustain its prime objective, the endless accumulation of capital. The second feature is less often discussed. An essential element in the accumulation of capital is for capitalists, especially large capitalists, not to pay their bills. This is what I call the "dirty secret" of capitalism. . . .

From the point of view of capitalists, as we know, the point of increasing production is to make profits. In a distinction that does not seem to me in the least outmoded, it involves production for exchange and not production for use. Profits on a single operation are the margin between the sales price and the total cost of production, that is, the cost of everything it takes to bring that product to the point of sale. Of course, the actual profits on the totality of a capitalist's operations are calculated by multiplying this margin by the amount of total sales. That is to say, the "market" constrains the sales price, in that, at a certain point, the price becomes so high that the total sales profits is less than if the sales price were lower.

But what constrains total costs? The price of labor plays a very large role in this, and this of course includes the price of the labor that went into all of the inputs. The market price of labor is not merely, however, the result of the relationship of supply and demand of labor but also of the bargaining power of labor. This is a complicated subject, with many factors entering into the strength of this bargaining power: What can be said is that, over the history of the capitalist world-economy, this bargaining power has been increasing as a secular trend, whatever the ups and downs of its cyclical rhythms. Today, this strength is at the verge of a singular ratchet upward as we move into the twenty-first century because of the deruralization of the world.

Deruralization is crucial to the price of labor. Reserve armies of labor are of different kinds in terms of their bargaining power. The weakest group has always been those persons resident in rural areas who come to urban areas for the first time to engage in wage employment. Generally speaking, for such persons the urban wage, even if extremely low by world, or even local, standards, represents an economic advantage over remaining in the rural area. It probably takes twenty to thirty years before such persons shift their economic frame of reference and become fully aware of their potential power in the urban workplace, such that they begin to engage in syndical action of some kind to seek higher wages. Persons long resident in urban areas, even if they are unemployed in the formal economy and living in terrible slum conditions, generally demand higher wage levels before accepting wage employment. This is because they have learned how to obtain from alternative sources in the urban center a minimum level of income higher than that which is being offered to newly arrived rural migrants.

Thus, even though there is still an enormous army of reserve labor throughout the world-system, the fact that the system is being rapidly deru-

ralization means that the average price of labor worldwide is going up steadily. This means in turn that the average rate of profits must necessarily go down over time. This squeeze on the profits ratio makes all the more important the reduction of costs other than labor costs. But, of course, all inputs into production are suffering the same problem of rising labor costs. While technical innovations may continue to reduce the costs of some inputs, and governments may continue to institute and defend monopolistic positions of enterprises permitting higher sales prices, it is nonetheless absolutely crucial for capitalists to continue to have some important part of their costs paid by someone else. . . .

The environmental dilemmas we face today are directly the result of the fact that we live in a capitalist world-economy. While all prior historical systems transformed the ecology, and some prior historical systems even destroyed the possibility of maintaining a viable balance in given areas that would have assured the survival of the locally existing historical system, only historical capitalism, by the fact that it has been the first such system to englobe the earth and by the fact that it has expanded production (and population) at a previously unimaginable rate, has threatened the possibility of a viable future existence for mankind. It has done this essentially because capitalists in this system succeeded in rendering ineffective the ability of all other forces to impose constraints on their activity in the name of values other than that of the endless accumulation of capital. It is precisely Prometheus unbound that has been the problem. . . .

I draw from this analysis several conclusions. The first is that reformist legislation has built-in limits. If the measure of success is the degree to which such legislation is likely to diminish considerably the rate of global environmental degradation in say the next ten to twenty years, I would predict that this type of legislation will have very little success. This is because the political opposition can be expected to be ferocious, given the impact of such legislation on capital accumulation. It doesn't follow, however, that it is therefore pointless to pursue such efforts. Quite the contrary, probably. Political pressure in favor of such legislation can add to the dilemmas of the capitalist system. It can crystallize the real political issues that are at stake, provided, however, that these issues are posed correctly.

The entrepreneurs have argued essentially that the issue is one of jobs versus romanticism, or humans versus nature. To a large degree, many of those concerned with ecological issues have fallen into the trap by responding in two different ways, both of which are, in my view, incorrect. The first is to argue that "a stitch in time saves nine." That is to say, some persons have suggested that, within the framework of the present system, it is formally rational for governments to expend x-amounts now in order not to spend greater amounts later. This is a line of argument that does make sense within the framework of a given system. But I have just argued that, from the point of view of capitalist strata, such "stitches in time," if they are sufficient to stem the damage, are not at all rational, in that they threaten in a fundamental way the possibility of continuing capital accumulation.

There is a second, quite different, argument that is made, one that I find equally politically impractical. It is the argument on the virtues of nature and the evils of science. This translates in practice into the defense of some obscure fauna of whom most people have never heard, and about which most people are indifferent, and thereby puts the onus of job destruction on flaky middle-class urban intellectuals. The issue becomes entirely displaced from the underlying ones, which are, and must remain, two. The first is that capitalists are not paying their bills. And the second is that the endless accumulation of capital is a substantively irrational objective, and that there does exist a basic alternative, which is to weigh various benefits (including those of production) against each other in terms of collective substantive rationality.

There has been an unfortunate tendency to make science the enemy and technology the enemy, whereas it is in fact capitalism that is the generic root of the problem. To be sure, capitalism has utilized the splendors of unending technological advance as one of its justifications. And it has endorsed a version of science—Newtonian, determinist science—as a cultural shroud, which permitted the political argument that humans could indeed "conquer" nature, should indeed do so, and that thereupon all negative effects of economic expansion would eventually be countered by inevitable scientific progress.

We know today that this vision of science and this version of science are of limited universal applicability. This version of science is today under fundamental challenge from within the community of natural scientists themselves, from the now very large groups who pursue what they call "complexity studies." The sciences of complexity are very different from Newtonian science in various important ways: the rejection of the intrinsic possibility of predictability; the normality of systems moving far from equilibrium, with their inevitable bifurcations; the centrality of the arrow of time. . . .

The concept of substantive rationality presumes that in all social decisions there are conflicts between different values as well as between different groups, often speaking in the name of opposing values. It presumes that there is never any system that can realize fully all these sets of values simultaneously, even if we were to feel that each set of values is meritorious. To be substantively rational is to make choices that will provide an optimal mix. But what does optimal mean? In part, we could define it by using the old slogan of Jeremy Bentham, the greatest good for the greatest number. The problem is that this slogan, while it puts us on the right track (the outcome), has many loose strings. . . .

No exit? No exit within the framework of the existing historical system? But we are in the process of exit from this system. The real question before us is where we shall be going as a result. It is here and now that we must raise the banner of substantive rationality, around which we must rally. We need to be aware that once we accept the importance of going down the road of substantive rationality, this is a long and arduous road. It involves not only a new social system, but new structures of knowledge, in which philosophy and sciences will no longer be divorced, and we shall return to the singular epistemology within which knowledge was pursued everywhere prior to the creation of the capitalist world-economy. If we start down this road, in terms of both the social system in which we live and the structures of knowledge we use to interpret it, we need to be very aware that we are at a beginning, and not at all at an end. Beginnings are uncertain and adventurous and difficult, but they offer promise, which is the most we can ever expect.

ERNEST GELLNER

1925–1995

Ernest André Gellner was born on December 9, 1925 in Paris, son of a manager, married Susan Ryan on September 24, 1954, with whom he had two sons and two daughters, and died of a heart attack on November 5, 1995 in Prague, Czechoslovakia at nearly 70 years of age. He was educated at Balliol College, Oxford (M.A., 1947) and at the University of London (Ph.D., 1961) in social anthropology. He served in the Czechoslovak Armored Brigade from 1944–45 during WWII. His first academic position was a the University of Edinburgh, Scotland (1947–49), then to the University of London, and the London School of Economics and Political Science, where he was lecturer from 1949 until 1962, then professor until 1984. Thereafter he became the William Wyse Professor of Social Anthropology at Cambridge until his retirement in 1993. From Cambridge he moved to Prague to direct the Center for the Study of Nationalism at Central European University.

A reviewer of Gellner's *Cause and Meaning in the Social Sciences* (1973), writing in the *Times Literary Supplement,* exclaimed: "Gellner's considerable virtues are evident here. His essays are written with clarity, verve, elegance, wit, and an irony and paradox that can budge the reader into deep and rewarding reflection." It is an unfortunate truth associated with the social sciences, particularly in the U.S., that the more "verve, elegance, wit, and irony" that a writer displays in his scholarship, the less likely he or she will be taken seriously by those colleagues upon whose taste and judgment one's reputation inevitably rides. Gellner used his native Central European Jewish drollery to great advantage, whether he was writing about the central High Atlas mountains of Morocco (in *Saints of the Atlas,* 1969) or about today's peculiarly self-deluded notions of what constitutes rational action (*Reason and Culture: The Historic Role of Rationality and Rationalism,* 1992). His first book, *Words and Things: A Critical Account of Linguistic Philosophy and a Study of Ideology,* introduced by Bertrand Russell (1959), was widely discussed, in the same way that Peter Winch's *The Idea of a Social Science and Its Relation to Philosophy* (1958) was closely read, each because they considered the role that Wittgensteinian language analysis should play in the social sciences, particularly anthropology and sociology. Some of his essays have become famous in themselves—"Positivism Against Hegelianism" in *Relativism and the Social Sciences* (1985) is one—but what most readers have expected from Gellner is a refusal to be awed by verbiage or unclear thinking masquerading as profundity. He was for discriminating readers their favorite prose stylist among anthropologists of a deeply philosophical character.

REASON AND CULTURE: THE HISTORIC ROLE OF RATIONALITY AND RATIONALISM, 1992

Rationality as a Way of Life

Reason is not merely the name of a supposed path to the discovery of truth or the legitimation of principles. It is also a life-style. The two aspects are intimately connected. The thinkers who theorized about the nature of this alleged inner cognitive and moral guide, the repository of our identity, were also, in effect, knowingly or otherwise, codifying the rules of comportment of a newly emerging civilization, one based on symmetry, order, equal treatment of claims and of evidence. They were helping to bring about such a civilization. Rationality became a powerful philosophical ideal in a world which was also becoming rationalized by other agencies. The universal validity which philosophers credited to their discoveries was perhaps illusory. Instead, they were perhaps drawing up the Charter, or formulating the Constitutional base, of one social order among others. But it was a very special one. The unique civilization whose foundations they were laying down was in some way or other more rational than all the others. In what way? What exactly is rationalism as a life-style?

A rational person is methodical and precise. He is tidy and orderly, above all in thought. He does not raise his voice, his tone is steady and equal; that goes for his feelings as well as his voice. He separates all separable issues, and deals with them one at a time. By so doing, he avoids muddling up issues and conflating distinct criteria. He treats like cases alike, subjecting them to impartial and stable criteria, and an absence of caprice and arbitrariness pervades his thought and conduct. He methodically augments his capital, cognitive as well as financial. He ploughs back his profits rather than turning them into pleasure, power, or status. His life is a progression of achievement, rather than the static occupancy, enjoyment, and fulfillment of an ascribed status.

The obverse of his avoidance of the arbitrary is the possession of good reasons for what he does and thinks. The requirement of good reasons reinforces orderliness of conduct: if a reason is cogent, it must also apply in all like cases. The insistence on reasons is antithetical both to the acceptance of authority and of arbitrary, ecstatic revelation. Authority unjustified by reason is tyranny, and when supported by reason, it is in a way redundant. Reason alone should suffice. The man of reason ideally needs no additional incentives when the reasons are good. When good reasons are lacking, he does not allow mere rhetoric or ritual theatre to cow him. He is both restrained and self-governing. He is loth to join a multitude in committing folly.

The requirement of rational justification is extended to all life. The reasons themselves must be systematized. The separation of issues leads to the simplification of the criteria of success in any single activity. That in turn, in conjunction with the desacralization of procedures and methods, leads to a habitual, precise, and painstaking assessment of cost-effectiveness, and so to instrumental efficiency. Innovation when beneficial is adopted without undue inhibition. No sacred boundary demarcation of activities hampers its implementation. All of this supports and dovetails with an orderly division of labour, and makes possible a rational accountancy of success and failure. The free, untrammelled choice of means is encouraged both by the clear specification of aims and by the levelling out of the world: all things are equally sacred or equally profane, and so there are no sacred prescriptions or proscriptions to inhibit the choice of methods. They become subject to considerations of efficiency.

Dealings between men are similarly rational, guided by the free choice of clear ends by both partners, and by the coolly assessed advantages inherent in any bargain between them. Contractual relations replace those based on status. Society as a totality comes to be seen in the same light. Its organization is not *given*, but determined by rational contract. It is but the summation of free and rational contracts, entered upon by free and rational individuals.

In recent centuries, such styles of conduct have become more common and pervasive, and eventually dominant. They have come to be prominent in production, in cognition, in politics, in private life, and in culture. Their impact in these various spheres has not been identical:

rationality is not applicable in the same way to all problems and activities. Philosophers have explored the principles and merits of rationality. Sociologists, impressed or appalled by the creeping and pervasive advances of rationality, and by its conquest of social life, have tried to understand the underlying social mechanics of this process. It is important to bring the ideas of the philosophers and the sociologists on this topic together. They constitute two aspects of what is but a single story.

The sociologist who, more than any other, is linked to the attempt to map and comprehend this creeping and pervasive rationality, is Max Weber. We have already sketched out his approach earlier, in the imaginary dialogue between Descartes and modern sociology: Durkheim on his own was incapable of answering Descartes's rebuttals, but was enabled to do so thanks to Weber's assistance. Weber fully perceived the uniqueness and distinctiveness of a rationality-pervaded civilization, and the manner in which it constituted a break with the principles normally governing agrarian societies. He saw its emergence as a mystery which required explanation. Unlike the providentialist Hegelo-Marxists, who saw the emergence of our particular world, with all its qualities, as the manifest destiny of all mankind, as an inherent continuation and culmination of a long and universal development, bound to arise sooner or later whatever happened, Weber saw it as the contingent, fortuitous event in the life of a particular religious tradition, which was its necessary (though not sufficient) condition. Durkheim saw communalistic ritual as the progenitor of the pan-human rationality of conceptual thought; Weber saw puritanical monotheistic nomocratic religion as the progenitor of orderly, symmetrical rationality, which alone makes a modern economy and science possible.

As with so many other thinkers, Weber's importance lies at least as much in the problem he highlighted, as in the solution he has proposed for it. The debate concerning the merit of Weber's partially religious account of the initially gradual, but eventually dramatic, spread of rationality has long been vigorous. It is unlikely to be settled soon. It may not be settled ever.

Recapitulation

The human species has, by some evolutionary mechanism not yet properly understood, developed an astonishing volatility of response. This absence of genetic pre-programming has engendered the need to be constrained socially and conceptually, as a compensation of our volatility: if reaction-systems were really accumulated at random by individual association, and by reaction to idiosyncratic experience, as empiricism had taught, neither a semantic nor a social order would be possible. Meanings and reactions would be too chaotic and unpredictable. No such polymorphous, unstable species could possibly have survived. Providentially, the capacity to respond to social-semantic restraints on conduct has emerged at the same time as the behavioural plasticity. Had it not, we should not be here.

This was part of Durkheim's insight. Socially imposed, internalized compulsion was essential, if we were to be capable of thought, communication, cohesion, and cooperation. Rationality, in the first, Durkheimian or generic sense, can be equated with the submission to socially shared, communally distinctive, and compulsively internalized concepts. In the beginning there was the prohibition. Language is an astonishingly rich system of socially instilled markers, capable of helping to keep members of a community within their cultural bounds or at least indicating what the bounds are; but the built-in genuine principles of language are such that countless languages and cultures are possible. This in turn makes possible cultural diversity, and hence a rate of change far more rapid than genetic transformation on its own could ever be.

The socially instilled concepts generally serve multiple purposes and, like the men who carry them, fail to observe any very orderly and developed division of labour. They are so to speak polyfunctional. They are only rational in the Durkheimian sense: they are socially instilled, and make both cohesion and comprehension possible, by endowing members of a semantic community with the *same* compulsions. They impose both logical and moral order on men.

But they are irrational in the narrower or Weberian sense of rationality: they are not methodical, and they do not serve single, insulated and clearly articulated ends, which alone can permit an accurate assessment of instrumental efficiency. They are not all subject to the same laws; they often serve multiple ends, are subject to plural constraints, and so cannot serve any one of them with ruthless single-mindedness and calculable effect. Though sensitivity to extraneous natural fact is often present, it is almost always but one element amongst many; it is not tidily insulated, nor dominant. In other words, language is not primarily referential, and those parts of it which are referential are not exclusively so. There is no single idiom, no single conceptual currency, which would enable the entire wealth of assertion to be cross-connected and systematized and expanded.

As long as the conceptual life of mankind had this so to speak Durkheimian form, there could be no question of limitless and effective exploration of nature. Similarly, there could be no question of that sustained innovation in productive techniques, in the combination of elements of production, which leads to sustained economic growth. Needless to say, there could also be no question of the combination of these two forms of expansion of human life, and the emergence of a society based on growth and progress. On the contrary, the intellectual life of human societies was an integral part of a tendency to self-perpetuation. In general, it underwrote the stagnation-sustaining domination of agrarian humanity by an alliance of specialists in coercion and in ritual.

The transition from the first, generic rationality of Durkheim, to the more specific rationality which obsessed Weber, is perhaps the biggest single event in human history. We do not really know how it came about, and perhaps we never shall. We do, however, possess, in the work of Max Weber, one fascinating and suggestive hypothesis. Even if in the end it proves false, it has the inestimable merit of highlighting the problem forcefully. The answer, whether or not correct, endows the question with a sharp outline. It helps us understand the distinctiveness of our situation.

The world so engendered contained both rational production and cognition. The rules of both were in due course codified. Two Scotsmen, Hume and Smith, put it all down, one of them taking on cognition, and the other, production. Their views on coercion converged, and they were indeed friends.

In this way the notion of a single, systematic, orderly method of the attainment of truth, incarnate in all and privileged in none, was rounded off, and accorded the name of Reason. It was of course in conflict with the residual element of the privileged-sacred view of things, perpetuated by the very theology which had also brought about the new vision in the first place. This conflict, more than any other, made familiar the notion of Reason. The notion of the exclusive, jealous and orderly deity, which had helped engender rational unificatory thought, itself in the end also sinned against it. The privileged claim that the deity existed, not to mention various more specific and sometimes weird affirmations which remained attached to it, could in the end no longer satisfy the criteria of reason. Reason destroyed its own progenitor. Parricide can now be added to the list of its crimes. It is parricidal as well as impotent and suicidal.

Modern irrationalists are much addicted to the *tu quoque* argument: Reason cannot justify her own procedures without circularity: so are we not all equal, all equally guilty of the sin of circularity and prejudgement? But the rationalist may rightly object to being placed at the same level as the believers. He may well say to them, as the Catholic Church used to say to the Protestants in pre-ecumenical days—you are many, we are one. The carte blanche provided by generic irrationalism validates *all* faiths, the path prescribed by Reason is unique. The *tu quoque* argument justifies all faiths equally, and not any single one of them. It blesses all of them alike, including all possible and-as yet unborn beliefs. In as far as it is an argument at all, it leads, not to genuine conviction, but to an unbridled doctrinal permissiveness.

The *tu quoque* argument brings us to the next stage in the story of Reason. After parricide comes impotence. Descartes and the early rationalists had hoped to deliver their new tool, Reason, as a product Guaranteed by the Makers, not for a year, but for all eternity. The Warranty was to be valid forever. Descartes had indeed been impelled to his efforts to guarantee this tool precisely because other producers of truths were supplying such unutterably shabby goods, accompanied by notoriously boastful, vainglorious, menacingly vindictive, and blatantly mendacious and untrustworthy warranties. Ancient sages sought watertight lifestyles, safe from disappointment. Descartes was also determined to market only goods of the highest quality, accompanied by a totally honest and trustworthy guarantee, though, unlike the sages of old, he sought a foolproof method of inquiry rather than a foolproof life-style. Spinoza adapted his new ideas to the old quest for a self-guaranteeing life-style.

First came the discovery that Reason could not really provide any such warranty. The Impotence of Reason is itself an independent truth of reason. Hume showed that the clear and distinct data did not permit a cogent inference to the kind of world we in fact inhabit and manipulate. A system of inquiry which is effective in the exploration of nature, by breaking up questions and the atomization of evidence and the pursuit of order, cannot, from within its own resources, or without contravening its own principles, establish that such an inquiry *must* be successful. And after impotence came suicide. Reason engenders a unitary, naturalistic world, within which there is no real place for Reason.

Modern irrationalism is by now very seldom the expression of a genuine devotion to extra-rational, extra-natural Authority. That particular debate, between protagonists of Authority and partisans of Free Thought, though not wholly dead, is largely antiquated. In as far as it continues at all, it is muted, and much overlaid by other considerations. The important enemies of reason no longer loudly claim to have access to a source of revelation outside the world. They claim that, *within* the natural world, as laid bare by reason, there are authorities more legitimate than reason, so that reason should not, or cannot, be heeded. Cognition, valuation, social organization, are and ought really to be slaves of intra-mundane forces, whom reason serves not merely as slave, but also as façade or camouflage. Freud's charge of the

practice of sustained disinformation was added to Hume's attribution of inherent slavery. The new attack on reason commends not transcendent, but only this-worldly rival authorities. Tradition, earth, blood, the Dialectic, are the new rivals: they speak from within the world, and not outside it. . . .

After the language of cultural transcendence, there came the Providentialism of Hegel and his progeny, including Marx, and many others. That was simply a fantasy. World history is not a story designed for our benefit, edification, and fulfilment; nor is the world which has emerged with rationality a necessary culmination, or the best of all possible worlds. It has some great merits, and some major defects, and we need to explore both. It only emerged by chance, and there is a heavy price to be paid for the material and social perks it unquestionably offers. The siege mentality introduced by Max Weber—it all emerged by a precarious accident, and the cost is great—is incomparably superior to the complacency of the Hegelo-Marxist tradition. We need to understand both our precariousness and our options, and their price. We can do without the illusion that we are the legitimate heirs, the final end, culmination and purpose of global development, and that it had been designed specifically to produce us. This form of philosophic megalomania we can leave to the Hegelians and their intellectual offspring.

In a stable traditional world, men had identities, linked to their social roles, and confirmed by their overall vision of nature and society. Instability and rapid change both in knowledge and in society has deprived such self-images of their erstwhile feel of reliability. Identities are perhaps more ironic and conditional than once they were, or at any rate, when confident, unjustifiably so. But the very style of knowing which has effected this erosion of confidence is also the basis of a new and different kind of identity. We could in the end seek our identity in Reason, and find it in a style of thought which gives us what genuine knowledge of the world we have, and which enjoins us to treat each other equitably—notwithstanding the lady's mundane roots, precarious base, unequal performance, failure to legitimate herself, and her marked parricidal and suicidal tendencies.

JOHN RAWLS

1921–2002

John Bordley Rawls, son of an attorney, was born on February 21, 1921 in Baltimore, Maryland and died of a heart attack on November 24, 2002 in Lexington, Massachusetts at 81. He married Margaret Warfield Fox on June 28, 1949 and had with her two sons and two daughters, including the sociologist Anne Warfield Rawls. Between 1943 and 1946 he served with the 32nd Infantry Division in the Pacific. Rawls attended Princeton and received his B.A. (1943) and doctorate there (1950), also studying at Cornell from 1947 to 1948 on a fellowship. He was president in 1974 of the American Philosophical Association, Eastern Division, and taught at Princeton (1950–52), Cornell (1953–59), MIT (1960–62), and Harvard (from 1963), becoming James B. Conant University Professor in 1979.

Rawls, often referred to as the most important Anglo-American political philosopher of the 20th century, had an unusual career in that his first and surely most important book appeared when he was 50 in 1971, *A Theory of Justice* (revised in 1999). Since then he has written several additional studies and sets of essays which defend or elaborate the ideas of that book, *Political Liberalism* (1993) and *Justice as Fairness* (2001) being the most important. Scholars within the realm of political theory and ethics have hailed Rawls' work almost without exception, even when they disagreed with his principles. The "high moral seriousness" often mentioned when discussing his work since 1971 seems to reveal much about the widespread admiration for Rawls. In a time when governments in the West have been reducing individual liberties, Rawls took the Quixotic position that the goodness of a society must be measured precisely by how much individual freedom is permitted to its members. But he grafted onto this venerable idea a new one concerning the maldistribution of wealth and privilege in advanced societies, by arguing that a "just society" could only be so named if it protected the least wealthy, the weakest of its members, with the same zeal usually given to the richest and most powerful. As one critic wrote, "a condition of almost childlike innocence about the ways of the world" saturates all of Rawls' ethical writings, which makes taking him seriously extremely difficult for sociologists and political scientists, whose view of the world is much more tied to the "is" than the "ought" of social life.

Rawls' main ideas may have originated in Kant (on whom he lectured regularly at Harvard), who famously predicted that democratic societies would not wage war against each other because they would first resort to a "sphere of public reason" (Rawls' term) before taking up arms. It was therefore in the interest of all nations to encourage and sponsor the development of democratic processes in despotic countries, for only then could discussion supersede armed conflict. Though laudable—as is all of Rawls' writing along these lines—there is a major gap between Rawls' ideas for achieving a "just society" and the actual mechanisms of power as they have been operating at least since Machiavelli. He calls for a "realistic utopia," yet the emphasis falls more on the latter than the former word, for the basis of his most desirable society is that the very rich be willing to give up enough of their wealth so that the very poorest's rights could be protected. One thinks here of many Biblical injunctions for decent behavior that have gone unheeded for 2000 years. Nevertheless, Rawls served a wonderful purpose of holding up for inspection a "city on the hill" that might inspire future generations to reduce (unjust) inequalities and individual constraints on lawful behavior. In the same way that modern readers continue to ponder the normative political suggestions of Jefferson or Mill or Rousseau, even while accepting their utopian dimension, so, too, will they continue to read Rawls.

POLITICAL LIBERALISM, 1993

The Content of Public Reason

1. I now turn to the content of public reason, having considered its nature and sketched how the apparent paradox of honoring its limits may be dissolved. This content is formulated by what I have called a "political conception of justice," which I assume is broadly liberal in character. By this I mean three things: first, it specifies certain basic rights, liberties, and opportunities (of the kind familiar from constitutional democratic regimes); second, it assigns a special priority to these rights, liberties, and opportunities, especially with respect to claims of the general good and of perfectionist values; and third, it affirms measures assuring all citizens adequate all-purpose means to make effective use of their basic liberties and opportunities. The two principles stated in 1:1.1–2 fall under this general description. But each of these elements can be seen in different ways, so there are many liberalisms.

In saying a conception of justice is political I also mean three things (I:2): that it is framed to apply solely to the basic structure of society, its main political, social, and economic institutions as a unified scheme of social cooperation; that it is presented independently of any wider comprehensive religious or philosophical doctrine; and that it is elaborated in terms of fundamental polit-

ical ideas viewed as implicit in the public political culture of a democratic society.

2. Now it is essential that a liberal political conception include, besides its principles of justice, guidelines of inquiry that specify ways of reasoning and criteria for the kinds of information relevant for political questions. Without such guidelines substantive principles cannot be applied and this leaves the political conception incomplete and fragmentary. That conception has, then, two parts:

a. first, substantive principles of justice for the basic structure; and
b. second, guidelines of inquiry: principles of reasoning and rules of evidence in the light of which citizens are to decide whether substantive principles properly apply and to identify laws and policies that best satisfy them.

Hence liberal political values are likewise of two kinds:

a. The first kind—the values of political justice—fall under the principles of justice for the basic structure: the values of equal political and civil liberty; equality of opportunity; the values of social equality and economic reciprocity; and let us add also values of the common good as well as the various necessary conditions for all these values.
b. The second kind of political values—the values of public reason—fall under the guidelines for public inquiry, which make that inquiry free and public. Also included here are such political virtues as reasonableness

and a readiness to honor the (moral) duty of civility, which as virtues of citizens help to make possible reasoned public discussion of political questions.

3. As we have said, on matters of constitutional essentials and basic justice, the basic structure and its public policies are to be justifiable to all citizens, as the principle of political legitimacy requires. We add to this that in making these justifications we are to appeal only to presently accepted general beliefs and forms of reasoning found in common sense, and the methods and conclusions of science when these are not controversial. The liberal principle of legitimacy makes this the most appropriate, if not the only, way to specify the guidelines of public inquiry. What other guidelines and criteria have we for this case?

This means that in discussing constitutional essentials and matters of basic justice we are not to appeal to comprehensive religious and philosophical doctrines—to what we as individuals or members of associations see as the whole truth—nor to elaborate economic theories of general equilibrium, say, if these are in dispute. As far as possible, the knowledge and ways of reasoning that ground our affirming the principles of justice and their application to constitutional essentials and basic justice are to rest on the plain truths now widely accepted, or available, to citizens generally. Otherwise, the political conception would not provide a public basis of justification.

As we consider later in §5, we want the substantive content and the guidelines of inquiry of a political conception, when taken together, to be complete. This means that the values specified by that conception can be suitably balanced or combined, or otherwise united, as the case may be, so that those values alone give a reasonable public answer to all, or to nearly all, questions involving the constitutional essentials and basic questions of justice. For an account of public reason we must have a reasonable answer, or think we can in due course find one, to all, or nearly all, those cases. I shall say a political conception is complete if it meets this condition.

4. In justice as fairness, and I think in many other liberal views, the guidelines of inquiry of public reason, as well as its principle of legitimacy, have

the same basis as the substantive principles of justice. This means in justice as fairness that the parties in the original position, in adopting principles of justice for the basic structure, must also adopt guidelines and criteria of public reason for applying those norms. The argument for those guidelines, and for the principle of legitimacy, is much the same as, and as strong as, the argument for the principles of justice themselves. In securing the interests of the persons they represent, the parties insist that the application of substantive principles be guided by judgment and inference, reasons and evidence that the persons they represent can reasonably be expected to endorse. Should the parties fail to insist on this, they would not act responsibly as trustees. Thus we have the principle of legitimacy.

In justice as fairness, then, the guidelines of public reason and the principles of justice have essentially the same grounds. They are companion parts of one agreement. There is no reason why any citizen, or association of citizens, should have the right to use state power to decide constitutional essentials as that person's, or that association's, comprehensive doctrine directs. When equally represented, no citizen could grant to another person or association that political authority. Any such authority is, therefore, without grounds in public reason, and reasonable comprehensive doctrines recognize this.

5. Keep in mind that political liberalism is a kind of view. It has many forms, depending on the substantive principles used and how the guidelines of inquiry are set out. These forms have in common substantive principles of justice that are liberal and an idea of public reason. Content and idea may vary within these limits.

Accepting the idea of public reason and its principle of legitimacy emphatically does not mean, then, accepting a particular liberal conception of justice down to the last details of the principles defining its content. We may differ about these principles and still agree in accepting a conception's more general features. We agree that citizens share in political power as free and equal, and that as reasonable and rational they have a duty of civility to appeal to public reason, yet we differ as to which principles are the most reasonable basis of public justification. The view I have called "justice as fairness" is but one example of a liberal political conception; its specific content is not definitive of such a view.

The point of the ideal of public reason is that citizens are to conduct their fundamental discussions within the framework of what each regards as a political conception of justice based on values that the others can reasonably be expected to endorse and each is, in good faith, prepared to defend that conception so understood. This means that each of us must have, and be ready to explain, a criterion of what principles and guidelines we think other citizens (who are also free and equal) may reasonably be expected to endorse along with us. We must have some test we are ready to state as to when this condition is met. I have elsewhere suggested as a criterion the values expressed by the principles and guidelines that would be agreed to in the original position. Many will prefer another criterion.

Of course, we may find that actually others fail to endorse the principles and guidelines our criterion selects. That is to be expected. The idea is that we must have such a criterion and this alone already imposes very considerable discipline on public discussion. Not any value is reasonably said to meet this test, or to be a political value; and not any balance of political values is reasonable. It is inevitable and often desirable that citizens have different views as to the most appropriate political conception; for the public political culture is bound to contain different fundamental ideas that can be developed in different ways. An orderly contest between them over time is a reliable way to find which one, if any, is most reasonable.

❧

THE LAW OF PEOPLES, 1999

Public Reason and the Law of Peoples

Law of Peoples not Ethnocentric

In developing the Law of Peoples I said that liberal societies ask how they are to conduct themselves

From *The Law of Peoples*, by John Rawls, pp. 121-126. Cambridge, Mass.: Harvard University Press. Copyright © 1999, by the President and Fellows of Harvard College. Reprinted by permission of the publisher.

toward other societies from the point of view of their *own* political conceptions. We must always start from where we now are, assuming that we have taken all reasonable precautions to review the grounds of our political conception and to guard against bias and error. To the objection that to proceed thus is ethnocentric or merely western, the reply is: no, nor necessarily. Whether it is so turns on the *content* of the Law of Peoples that liberal societies embrace. The objectivity of that law surely depends not on its time, place, or culture of origin, but on whether it satisfies the criterion of reciprocity and belongs to the public reason of the Society of liberal and decent Peoples.

Looking at the Law of Peoples, we see that it does satisfy the criterion of reciprocity. It asks of other societies only what they can reasonably grant without submitting to a position of inferiority or domination. Here it is crucial that the Law of Peoples does not require decent societies to abandon or modify their religious institutions and adopt liberal ones. We have supposed that decent societies would affirm the same Law of Peoples that would hold among just liberal societies. This enabled that law to be universal in its reach. It is so because it asks of other societies only what they can reasonably endorse once they are prepared to stand in a relation of fair equality with all other societies. They cannot argue that being in a relation of equality with other peoples is a western idea! In what other relation can a people and its regime reasonably expect to stand?

Toleration of Decent Peoples

As we have seen, not all peoples can reasonably be required to be liberal. This follows, in fact, from the principle of toleration of a liberal Law of Peoples and its idea of public reason as worked out from a family of liberal conceptions. What conception of toleration of other societies does the Law of Peoples express? And how is it connected with political liberalism? If it should be asked whether liberal societies are, morally speaking, better than decent hierarchical and other decent societies, and therefore whether the world would be a better place if all societies were required to be liberal, those holding a liberal view might think that the answer would be yes. But this answer overlooks the great importance of maintaining mutual respect between peoples and of each people maintaining its self-respect, not lapsing into contempt for the other, on one side, and bitterness and resentment, on the other. These relations are not a matter of the internal (liberal or decent) basic structure of each people viewed separately. Rather, they concern relations of *mutual respect* among peoples, and so constitute an essential pan of the basic structure and political climate of the Society of Peoples. For these reasons the Law of Peoples recognizes decent peoples as members of that larger society. With confidence in the ideals of constitutional liberal democratic thought, it respects decent peoples by allowing them to find their own way to honor those ideals.

Comprehensive doctrines play only a restricted role in liberal democratic politics. Questions of constitutional essentials and matters of basic justice are to be settled by a public political conception of justice and its public reason, though all citizens will also look to their comprehensive doctrines. Given the pluralism of liberal democratic societies—a pluralism which is best seen as the outcome of the exercise of human reason under free institutions—affirming such a political conception as a basis of public justification, along with the basic political institutions that realize it, is the most reasonable and deepest basis of social unity available to us.

The Law of Peoples, as I have sketched it, simply extends these same ideas to the political Society of well-ordered Peoples. For that law, which settles fundamental political questions as they arise for the Society of Peoples, must also be based on a public political conception of justice. I have outlined the content of such a political conception and tried to explain how it could be endorsed by well-ordered societies, both liberal and decent. Except as a basis of a *modus vivendi*, expansionist societies of whatever kind could not endorse it. In their case, no peaceful solution exists except domination by one side or the peace of exhaustion.

Some may find this fact hard to accept. That is because it is often thought that the task of philosophy is to uncover a form of argument that will always prove convincing against all other arguments. There is, however, no such argument. Peoples may often have final ends that require them to oppose one another without compromise. And if these ends are regarded as fundamental enough, and if one or more societies should refuse to accept the idea of the politically reasonable and the family of ideas that go with it, an impasse may arise between them, and war comes, as it did between North and South in the American Civil War. Political liberalism begins with terms of the politically reasonable and builds up its case from there. One does not find peace by declaring war irrational or wasteful, though indeed it may be so, but by preparing the way for peoples to develop a basic structure that supports a reasonably just or decent regime and makes possible a reasonable Law of Peoples.

Reconciliation to Our Social World

Society of Peoples Is Possible

In § 1.1 I said that political philosophy is realistically utopian when it extends what are ordinarily thought of as the limits of practical political possibility. Our hope for the future rests on the belief that the possibilities of our social world allow a reasonably just constitutional democratic society living as a member of a reasonably just Society of Peoples. An essential step to being reconciled to our social world is to see that such a Society of Peoples is indeed possible.

Recall four basic facts to which I have often referred. These facts can be confirmed by reflecting on history and political experience. They were not discovered by social theory; nor should they be in dispute, as they are virtually truisms.

(a) The Fact of Reasonable Pluralism: A basic feature of liberal democracy is the fact of reasonable pluralism—the fact that a plurality of conflicting reasonable comprehensive doctrines, both religious and nonreligious (or secular), is the normal result of the culture of its free institutions. Different and irreconcilable comprehensive doctrines will be united in supporting the idea of equal liberty for all doctrines and the idea of the separation of church and state. Even if each might prefer that the others not exist, the plurality of sects is the greatest assurance each has of its own equal liberty.

(b) The Fact of Democratic Unity in Diversity: This is the fact that in a constitutional democratic society, political and social unity does not require that its citizens be unified by one comprehensive doctrine, religious or nonreligious. Until the end of the seventeenth century, or later, that was not a common view. Religious division was seen as a disaster for a civil polity. It took the experience of actual history to show this view to be false. While it is necessary that there be a public basis of understanding, this is provided in a liberal democratic society by the reasonableness and rationality of its political and social institutions, the merits of which can be debated in terms of public reason.

(c) The Fact of Public Reason: This is the fact that citizens in a pluralist liberal democratic society realize that they cannot reach agreement, or even approach mutual understanding, on the basis of their irreconcilable comprehensive doctrines. Thus, when citizens are discussing fundamental political questions, they appeal not to those doctrines, but to a reasonable family of political conceptions of right and justice, and so to the idea of the politically reasonable addressed to citizens as citizens. This does not mean that doctrines of faith or nonreligious (secular) doctrines cannot be introduced into political discussion, but rather that citizens introducing them should also provide sufficient grounds in public reason for the political policies that religious or nonreligious doctrines support.

(d) The Fact of Liberal Democratic Peace: This is the fact discussed in §5 that, ideally, well-ordered constitutional democratic societies do not go to war against one another, and they engage in war only in self-defense, or in an alliance defending other liberal or decent peoples. This is principle (5) of the Law of Peoples.

These four facts provide an explanation of why a reasonably just Society of Peoples is possible. I believe that in a society of liberal and decent peoples the Law of Peoples would be honored, if not all the time, then most of the time, so that it would be recognized as governing the relations among them. To show this, one proceeds through the eight principles that would be agreed to and notes that none of them is likely to be violated. Liberal democratic and decent peoples are likely to follow the Law of Peoples among themselves, since that law suits their fundamental interests, and each wishes to honor its agreements with the others and to be known as trustworthy. The principles most likely to be violated are the norms for the just conduct of war against aggressive outlaw states, and the duty of assistance owed to burdened societies. This is because the reasons supporting these principles call for great foresight and often have powerful passions working against them. But it is the duty of the statesman to convince the public of the enormous importance of these principles.

To see this, recall the discussion of the role of the statesman in the conduct of war against an enemy state, and the emotions and hatreds the statesman must be prepared to resist. Similarly with the duty of assistance: there may be many aspects of the culture and people of a foreign society living under unfavorable conditions that interfere with the natural sympathy of other societies, or that lead them to underestimate, or fail to recognize, the great extent to which human rights are being violated in the foreign society. A sense of social distance and anxiety about the unknown make these feelings stronger. A statesman may find it difficult to convince public opinion in his or her own people of the enormous importance to them of enabling other societies to establish at least decent political and social institutions.

RICHARD RORTY

1931–

Richard McKay Rorty, son of two writers, was born in New York City on October 4, 1931, married Amelie Oksenberg (a philosophy professor) on June 15, 1954 (divorced, September, 1972), married Mary Rosalind Varney (professor) on November 4, 1972, and had with his first wife a son, and with his second a son and daughter. Unlike more reserved philosophers, Rorty has described his youth in vivid detail in a noted piece called "Trotsky and the Wild Orchids" (in Mark Edmundson's *Wild Orchids and Trotsky,* 1993). There he explains that his parents, both Deweyan leftists of the New York type, held in high regard books like Leon Trotsky's *History of the Russian Revolution* (which he was unable to finish reading) and *The Case of Leon Trotsky.* At 15 he escaped regular beatings by his peers by being sent to the famous "lab school" at the University of Chicago, nursery of future academics. As expected, he continued as an undergraduate at the University of Chicago, which, Rorty reports, had about it an Aristotelian mystical air engendered by Richard McKeon and Mortimer Adler, where Dewey—his parents' hero—was regarded as irresponsibly unprincipled. Rorty seemed to go through regular bouts of worry that some "absolute" or "foundation" ought to be "out there" to anchor his existential drift, whether it be T. S. Eliot's high Anglican religiosity, Tibetan Buddhism, true-believing Marxism, or Platonism. But after many years of fruitless searching (and a doctorate from Yale in philosophy, 1956, plus Army duty in 1957–58), Rorty gave up the noble quest and wrote a very influential book about his tribulations.

He explains the genesis of *Philosophy and the Mirror of Nature* (1979), his first and most important book, by invoking Dewey, Derrida, Foucault, Wittgenstein, Heidegger, Ian Hacking, and Alasdair MacIntyre: "I thought I could fit all these into a quasi-Heideggerian story about the tensions within Platonism." As he himself notes, most philosophers did not like the book because it seemed to cut out from beneath them any claims they could make for apodictic truths, yet a wider academic public found it useful and it became one of the most often quoted philosophy texts during the last part of the 20th century. Rorty caused a furor, too, among the Left, because of his apostasy and because his arguments, viewed in a certain way, seemed to cohere too comfortably with the smugness of privilege now associated with Ronald Reagan's presidency. The piece reprinted below is a fantasy in which Rorty uses the same conceit put to such good use by Edward Bellamy in *Looking Backward, 2000–1887* (1887) or Samuel Butler in *Erewhon* (1872), and shows why Rorty has become one of our leading highbrow social critics, combining savvy reportage of contemporary political and social trends with deeply questioning philosophical commentary.

PHILOSOPHY AND SOCIAL HOPE, 1999

Looking Backwards from the Year 2096, 1996

Our long, hesitant, painful recovery, over the last five decades, from the breakdown of democratic institutions during the Dark Years (2014–2044) has changed our political vocabulary, as well as our sense of the relation between the moral order and the economic order. Just as twentieth-century Americans had trouble imagining how their pre-Civil War ancestors could have stomached slavery, so we at the end of the twenty-first century have trouble imagining how our great-grandparents could have legally permitted a CEO to get 20 times more than her lowest paid employees. We cannot understand how Americans a hundred years ago could have tolerated the horrific contrast between a childhood spent in the suburbs and one spent in the ghettos. Such inequalities seem to us evident moral abominations, but the vast majority of our ancestors took them to be regrettable necessities.

As long as their political discourse was dominated by the notion of 'rights'—whether 'individual' or 'civil'—it was hard for Americans to think of the results of unequal distribution of wealth and income as immoral. Such rights talk, common among late-twentieth-century liberals, gave conservative opponents of redistributionist policies a tremendous advantage: 'the right to a job' (or 'to a decent wage') had none of the resonance of 'the right to sit in the front of the bus' or 'the right to vote' or even 'the right to equal pay for equal work'. Rights in the liberal tradition were, after all, powers and privileges to be wrested from the state, not from the economy.

Of course socialists had, since the mid-nineteenth century, urged that the economy and the state be merged to guarantee economic rights. But it had become clear by the middle of the twentieth century that such merging was disastrous. The history of the pre-1989 'socialist' countries—bloody dictatorships that paid only lip service to the fraternity for which the socialist revolutionaries had

yearned—made it plausible for conservatives to argue that extending the notion of rights to the economic order would be a step down the road to serfdom. By the end of the twentieth century, even left-leaning American intellectuals agreed that 'socialism,' no wave of the future, now looks (at best) like a temporary historical stage through which various nations passed before reaching the great transition to capitalist democracy'.[1]

The realization by those on the left that a viable economy requires free markets did not stop them from insisting that capitalism would be compatible with American ideas of human brotherhood only if the state were able to redistribute wealth. Yet this view was still being criticized as 'un-American' and 'socialist' at the beginning of the present century, even as, under the pressures of a globalized world economy, the gap between most Americans' incomes and those of the lucky one-third at the top widened. Looking back, we think how easy it would have been for our great-grandfathers to have forestalled the social collapse that resulted from these economic pressures. They could have insisted that all classes had to confront the new global economy together. In the name of our common citizenship, they could have asked everybody, not just the bottom two-thirds, to tighten their belts and make do with less. They might have brought the country together by bringing back its old pride in fraternal ideals.

But as it happened, decades of despair and horror were required to impress Americans with lessons that now seem blindingly obvious.

The apparent incompatibility of capitalism and democracy is, of course, an old theme in American political and intellectual life. It began to be sounded more than two centuries ago. Historians divide our history into the 100 years before the coming of industrial capitalism and the more than 200 years since. During the first period, the open frontier made it possible for Americans to live in ways that became impossible for their descendants. If you were white in nineteenth-century America, you always had a second chance: something was always opening up out West.

So the first fault line in American politics was not between the rich and the poor. Instead, it was between those who saw chattel slavery as incompatible with American fraternity and those who did not. (Abolitionist posters showed a kneeling slave asking, 'Am I not a man, and a brother?') But only 40 years after the Civil War, reformers were already saying that the problem of chattel slavery had been replaced by that of wage slavery.

The urgency of that problem dominates Herbert Croly's progressivist manifesto of 1909, 'The Promise of American Life'. Croly argued that the Constitution, and a tradition of tolerant individualism, had kept America hopeful and filled with what he called 'genuine good-fellowship' during its first 100 years. But beginning with the first wave of industrialization in the 1870s and 1880s, things began to change. Wage slavery—a life of misery and toil, without a sense of participation in the national life, and without any trace of the frontiersman's proud independence—became the fate of more and more Americans. Alexis de Tocquevillle had rejoiced that an opulent merchant and his shoemaker, when they met on the streets of Philadelphia in 1840, would exchange political opinions. 'These two citizens,' he wrote, 'are concerned with affairs of state, and they do not part without shakings hands.' Croly feared that this kind of unforced fraternity was becoming impossible.

From Croly to John Kenneth Galbraith and Arthur Schlesinger in the 1960s, reformers urged that we needed some form of redistribution to bring back Tocquevillian comity. They battled with conservatives who claimed that redistributive measures would kill economic prosperity. The reformers insisted that what Theodore Roosevelt had called 'the money power' and Dwight Eisenhower 'the military–industrial complex' was the true enemy of American ideals. The conservatives rejoined that the only enemy of democracy was the state and that the economy must be shielded from do-gooders.

This debate simmered through the first two decades following the Second World War. During that relatively halcyon period, most Americans could get fairly secure, fairly well-paying jobs and could count on their children having a better life than theirs. White America seemed to be making slow but steady progress towards a classless society. Only the growth of the increasingly miserable black underclass reminded white Americans that the promise of American life was still far from being fulfilled.

The sense that this promise was still alive was made possibile, in part, by what the first edition of this 'Companion' called the 'rights revolution'. Most of the moral progress that took place in the second half of the twentieth century was brought about by the Supreme Court's invocation of constitutional rights, in such decisions as *Brown* v. *Board of Education* (1954) and *Romer* v. *Evans* (1996), the first Supreme Court decision favourable to homosexuals. But this progress was confined almost entirely to improvements in the situation of groups identified by race, ethnicity or sexuality. The situation of women and of homosexuals changed radically in this period. Indeed, it is now clear that those changes, which spread from America around the world, were the most lasting and significant moral achievements of the twentieth century.

But though such groups could use the rhetoric of rights to good effect, the trade unions, the unemployed and those employed at the ludicrously low minimum wage ($174 an hour, in 2095 dollars, compared with the present minimum of $400) could not. Perhaps no difference between present-day American political discourse and that of 100 years ago is greater than our assumption that the first duty of the state is to prevent gross economic and social inequality, as opposed to our ancestors' assumption that the government's only *moral* duty was to ensure 'equal protection of the laws'—laws that, in their majestic impartiality, allowed the rich and the poor to receive the same hospital bills.

The Supreme Court, invoking this idea of equal protection, began the great moral revival we know at the Civil Rights Movement. The *Brown* decision initiated both an explosion of violence and an upsurge of fraternal feeling. Some white Americans burned crosses and black churches. Many more had their eyes opened to the humiliations being inflicted on their fellow citizens: if they did not join civil rights marches, they at least felt relieved of guilt when the Court threw out miscegenation laws and when Congress began to protect black voting rights. For a decade or so there was an uplifting sense of moral improvement. For the first time, white and black

Americans started to think of each other as fellow citizens.

By the beginning of the 1980s, however, this sense of fraternity was only a faint memory. A burst of selfishness had produced tax revolts in the 1970s, stopping in its tracks the fairly steady progress toward a fully fledged welfare state that had been under way since the New Deal. The focus of racial hate was transferred from the rural South to the big cities, where a criminal culture of unemployed (and, in the second generation, virtually unemployable) black youths grew up—a culture of near constant violence, made possible by the then-famous American 'right to bear arms'. All the old racial prejudices were revived by white suburbanites' claims that their tax money was being used to coddle criminals. Politicians gained votes by promising to spend what little money could be squeezed from their constituents on prisons rather than on day care.

Tensions between the comfortable middle-class suburbs and the rest of the country grew steadily in the closing decades of the twentieth century, as the gap between the educated and well paid and the uneducated and ill paid steadily widened. Class division came into existence between those who made 'professional' salaries and those whose hourly wage kept sinking towards the minimum. But the politicians pretended to be unaware of this steady breakdown of fraternity.

Our nation's leaders, in the last decade of the old century and the first of the new, seemed never to have thought that it might be dangerous to make automatic weapons freely and cheaply available to desperate men and women—people without hope—living next to the centres of transportation and communication. Those weapons burst into the streets in 2014, in the revolution that, leaving the cities in ruins and dislocating American economic life, plunged the country into the Second Great Depression.

The insurgency in the ghettos, coming at a time when all but the wealthiest Americans felt desperately insecure, led to the collapse of trust in government. The collapse of the economy produced a war of all against all, as gasoline and food became harder and harder to buy, and as even the suburbanites began to brandish guns at their neighbours. As the generals never stopped saying

throughout the Dark Years, only the military saved the country from utter chaos.

Here, in the late twenty-first century, as talk of fraternity and unselfishness has replaced talk of rights, American political discourse has come to be dominated by quotations from Scripture and literature, rather than from political theorists or social scientists. Fraternity, like friendship, was not a concept that either philosophers or lawyers knew how to handle. They could formulate principles of justice, equality and liberty, and invoke these principles when weighing hard moral or legal issues. But how to formulate a 'principle of fraternity'? Fraternity is an inclination of the heart, one that produces a sense of shame at having much when others have little. It is not the sort of thing that anybody can have a theory about or that people can be argued into having.

Perhaps the most vivid description of the American concept of fraternity is found in a passage from John Steinbeck's 1939 novel *The Grapes of Wrath*. Steinbeck describes a desperately impoverished family, dispossessed tenant farmers from Oklahoma, camped out at the edge of Highway 66, sharing their food with an even more desperate migrant family. Steinbeck writes: "'I have a little food" plus "I have none." If from this problem the sum is "We have a little food," the movement has direction.' As long as people in trouble can sacrifice to help people who are in still worse trouble, Steinbeck insisted, there is fraternity, and therefore social hope.

The movement Steinbeck had in mind was the revolutionary socialism that he, like many other leftists of the 1930s, thought would be required to bring the First Great Depression to an end. 'The quality of owning,' he wrote, 'freezes you forever into the "I," and cuts you off forever from the "we."' Late twentieth-century liberals no longer believed in getting rid of private ownership, but they agreed that the promise of American life could be redeemed only as long as Americans were willing to sacrifice for the sake of fellow Americans—only as long as they could see the government not as stealing their tax money but as needing it to prevent unnecessary suffering.

The Democratic Vistas Party, the coalition of trade unions and churches that toppled the military dictatorship in 2044, has retained control of

Congress by successfully convincing the voters that its opponents constitute 'the parties of self-ishness'. The traditional use of 'brother' and 'sister' in union locals and religious congregations is the principal reason why 'fraternity' (or, among purists, 'siblinghood') is now the name of our most cherished ideal.

In the first two centuries of American history Jefferson's use of rights had set the tone for political discourse, but now political argument is not about who has the right to what but about what can best prevent the re-emergence of hereditary castes—either racial or economic. The old union slogan 'An injury to one is an injury to all' is now the catch phrase of American politics. 'Solidarity is Forever' and 'This Land is Your Land' are sung at least as often as 'The Star-Spangled Banner'.

Until the last 50 years, moral instruction in America had inculcated personal responsibility, and most sermons had focused on individual salvation. Today morality is thought of neither as a matter of applying the moral law nor as the acquisition of virtues but as fellow feeling, the ability to sympathize with the plight of others.

In the churches, the 'social gospel' theology of the early twentieth century has been rediscovered. Walter Rauschenbusch's 'Prayer against the servants of Mammon' ('Behold the servants of Mammon, who defy thee and drain their fellow men for gain . . . who have made us ashamed of our dear country by their defilements and have turned our holy freedom into a hollow name . . .') is familiar to most church-goers. In the schools, students learn about our country's history from social novels describing our past failures to hang together when we needed to, the novels of Steinbeck, Upton Sinclair, Theodore Dreiser, Richard Wright and, of course, Russell Banks's samizdat novel, *Tramping the Vineyards* (2021).

Historians unite in calling the twentieth the 'American' century. Certainly it was in the twentieth century that the United States was richest, most powerful, most influential and most self-confident. Our ancestors 100 years ago still thought of the country as destined to police, inform and inspire the world. Compared with the Americans of 100 years ago, we are citizens of an isolationist, unambitious, middle-grade nation.

Our products are only now becoming competitive again in international markets, and Democratic Vistas politicians continue to urge that our consistently low productivity is a small price to pay for union control of the workplace and worker ownership of the majority of firms. We continue to lag behind the European Community, which was able to withstand the pressures of a globalized labour market by having a fully fledged welfare state already in place, and which (except for Austria and Great Britain) was able to resist the temptation to impoverish the most vulnerable in order to keep its suburbanites affluent. Spared the equivalent of our own Dark Years, Europe, still, despite all that China can do, holds the position we lost in 2014: it still dominates both the world's economy and its culture.

For two centuries Americans believed that they were as far ahead of Europe, in both virtue and promise, as Europe was ahead of the rest of the world. But American exceptionalism did not survive the Dark Years: we no longer think of ourselves as singled out by divine favour. We are now, once again, a constitutional democracy, but we have proved as vulnerable as Germany, Russia and India to dictatorial takeovers. We have a sense of fragility, of susceptibility to the vicissitudes of time and chance, which Walt Whitman and John Dewey may never have known.

Perhaps no American writer will ever again begin a book, as Croly did, by saying, 'The faith of Americans in their own country is religious, if not in its intensity, at any rate in its almost absolute and universal authority.' But our chastened mood, our lately learned humility, may have made us better able to realize that everything depends on keeping our fragile sense of American fraternity intact.

Notes

1. From the article 'Socialism', by the labour historian Sean Wilentz, in the first edition of *A Companion to American Thought*, Richard Fox and James Kloppenberg, eds. (London and New York: Blackwell, 1995).

CHARLES TAYLOR

1931–

Charles Taylor was born in Montreal, Quebec on November 5, 1931, the son of an industrialist father and a fashion designer mother. He married Alba Romer, an artist, on April 2, 1956 and with her produced five daughters. Taylor attended McGill University (B.A., 1952) and then Oxford (B.A., 1955, M.A., 1960, D. Phil. in philosophy, 1961). He has taught at McGill since 1961, was at the University of Montreal from 1962–71, became Chichele Professor of Social and Political Theory, Oxford, from 1976, and also served as the Vice-president of the New Democrat Party of Canada from 1965 through 1973. His professorship at McGill is in philosophy and political science, an unusual and fruitful combination of intellectual allegiances.

Taylor has written a number of works that are of particular value to social and political theorists, beginning with *The Explanation of Behavior* in 1964, where he concentrated on the reductionistic limitations of behavioral psychology. He claims instead to be creating a "philosophical anthropology" that is unafraid of staking out terrain which in some quarters is considered antique. For some years his essay, "Interpretation and the Sciences of Man" (1971) was his hallmark statement about the make-up of human societies and how they should be understood. His *Hegel* (1975) has become a standard introduction to the philosopher due to its vigorous clarity, and is particularly good on contextualizing Hegel's thinking. His *Social Theory as Practice* (1983) and *Human Agency and Language* (1985; collected essays) added to his reputation as a philosopher who could address important issues in the social sciences, made even more explicit in his *Philosophy and the Human Sciences* (1985; collected papers). His major work, though, is surely *Sources of the Self: The Making of the Modern Identity* (1989), a large and ambitious study that has become part of the canon of indispensable works on the subject for sociologists, philosophers, psychologists, historians, and others involved in the endless discussions currently being held regarding "identity." Its sane mixture of historically anchored connections with the philosophical past, together with insightful comments pertaining to current questions is what sets the book apart from many screeds in this harried zone of inquiry. Taylor has not been afraid to criticize many writers on the contemporary scene who seem to celebrate normlessness and nihilism, for he favors a more robust and ethically anchored portrait of humankind, one based on an understanding of human interaction as a hermeneutic performance. Though "agency" has become a bad word for many postmodernists, Taylor still believes it is essential to a proper understanding of what constitutes responsible action. He added to the utility of this book with a smaller addendum, *Multiculturalism and "The Politics of Recognition": An Essay* (1992), all of which have made Taylor one of the most useful philosophers writing today regarding social issues. The excerpt reprinted below, from *A Catholic Modernity?*

Charles Taylor's Marianist Award Lecture (1999), illustrates his willingness to speak convincingly about ancient concerns that turn on questions of absolute values and transcendental reality, while at the same time being intimately aware of today's political and cultural struggles that impinge on the Church's ability to cope. For example, "a powerful constitutive strand of modern Western spirituality is involved in an affirmation of life. It is perhaps evident in the contemporary concern to preserve life, to bring prosperity, and to reduce suffering worldwide, which is, I believe without precedent in history."

MARIANIST AWARD LECTURE, 1999

A Catholic Modernity?

. . . The first danger that threatens an exclusive humanism, which wipes out the transcendent beyond life, is that it provokes as reaction an imminent negation of life. Let me try to explain this a little better.

I have been speaking of the transcendent as being "beyond life." In doing this, I am trying to get at something that is essential not only in Christianity but also in a number of other faiths—for instance, in Buddhism. A fundamental idea enters these faiths in very different forms, an idea one might try to grasp in the claim that life isn't the whole story.

One way to take this expression is that it means something like: life goes on after death, there is a continuation, our lives don't totally end in our deaths. I don't mean to deny what is affirmed on this reading, but I want to take the expression here in a somewhat different (though undoubtedly related) sense.

What I mean is something more like: the point of things isn't exhausted by life, the fullness of life, even the goodness of life. This is not meant to be just a repudiation of egoism, the idea that the fullness of my life (and perhaps those of people I love) should be my only concern. Let us

agree with John Stuart Mill that a full life must involve striving for the benefit of humankind. Then acknowledging the transcendent means seeing a point beyond that.

One form of this is the insight that we can find in suffering and death—not merely negation, the undoing of fullness and life, but also a place to affirm something that matters beyond life, on which life itself originally draws. The last clause seems to bring us back into the focus on life. It may be readily understandable, even within the purview of an exclusive humanism, how one could accept suffering and death in order to give life to others. On a certain view, that, too, has been part of the fullness of life. Acknowledging the transcendent involves something more. What matters beyond life doesn't matter just because it sustains life; otherwise, it wouldn't be "beyond life" in the meaning of the act. (For Christians, God wills human flourishing, but "thy will be done" doesn't reduce to "let human beings flourish.")

This is the way of putting it that goes most against the grain of contemporary Western civilization. There are other ways of framing it. One that goes back to the very beginning of Christianity is a redefinition of the term *life* to incorporate what I'm calling "beyond life": for instance, the New Testament evocations of "eternal life" and John 10:10, "abundant life."

Or we could put it a third way: acknowledging the transcendent means being called to a change of identity. Buddhism gives us an obvious reason to talk this way. The change here is quite radical, from self to "no self" (*anatta*). But Christian faith can be seen in the same terms: as calling for a radical decentering of the self, in relation with God. ("Thy will be done.") In the language of Abbe Henri Bremond in his magnificent study of French seventeenth-century spiritualities, we can speak of "theocentrism." This way of putting it brings out a similar point to my first way, in that most conceptions of a flourishing life assume a stable identity, the self for whom flourishing can be defined.

So acknowledging the transcendent means aiming beyond life or opening yourself to a change in identity. But if you do this, where do you stand in regard to human flourishing? There is much division, confusion, and uncertainty about this. Historic religions have, in fact, combined concern for flourishing and transcendence in their normal practice. It has even been the rule that the supreme achievements of those who went beyond life have served to nourish the fullness of life of those who remain on this side of the barrier. Thus, prayers at the tombs of martyrs brought long life, health, and a whole host of good things for the Christian faithful; something of the same is true for the tombs of certain saints in Muslim lands, and in Theravada Buddhism, for example, the dedication of monks is turned, through blessings, amulets, and the like, to all the ordinary purposes of flourishing among the laity.

Over against this, there have recurrently been reformers in all religions who have considered this symbiotic, complementary relation between renunciation and flourishing to be a travesty. They insist on returning religion to its purity, and posit the goals of renunciation on their own as goals for everyone, disintricated from the pursuit of flourishing. Some are even moved to denigrate the latter pursuit altogether, to declare it unimportant or an obstacle to sanctity.

But this extreme stance runs athwart a very central thrust in some religions. Christianity and Buddhism will be my examples here. Renouncing—aiming beyond life—not only takes you away but also brings you back to flourishing. In Christian terms, if renunciation decenters you in relation with God, God's will is that humans flourish, and so you are taken back to an affirmation of this flourishing, which is biblically called agape. In Buddhist terms, Enlightenment doesn't just turn you from the world; it also opens the floodgates of *metta* (loving kindness) and *karuna* (com-

passion). There is the Theravada concept of the Paccekabuddha, concerned only for his own salvation, but he is ranked below the highest Buddha, who acts for the liberation of all beings.

Thus, outside the stance that accepts the complementary symbiosis of renunciation and flourishing, and beyond the stance of purity, there is a third, which I could call the stance of agape/*karuna*.

Enough has been said to bring out the conflict between modern culture and the transcendent. In fact, a powerful constitutive strand of modern Western spirituality is involved in an affirmation of life. It is perhaps evident in the contemporary concern to preserve life, to bring prosperity, and to reduce suffering worldwide, which is, I believe, without precedent in history.

This arises historically out of what I have called elsewhere "the affirmation of ordinary life." What I was trying to gesture at with this term is the cultural revolution of the early modern period, which dethroned the supposedly higher activities of contemplation and the citizen life and put the center of gravity of goodness in ordinary living, production, and the family. It belongs to this spiritual outlook that our first concern ought to be to increase life, relieve suffering, and foster prosperity. Concern above all for the "good life" smacked of pride, of self-absorption. Beyond that, it was inherently inegalitarian because the alleged "higher" activities could be carried out only by an elite minority, whereas rightly leading one's ordinary life was open to everyone. This is a moral temper to which it seems obvious that our major concern must be our dealings with others, injustice, and benevolence and that these dealings must be on a level of equality.

This affirmation, which constitutes a major component of our modern ethical outlook, was originally inspired by a mode of Christian piety. It exalted practical agape and was polemically directed against the pride, elitism, and, one might say, self-absorption of those who believed in "higher" activities or spiritualities.

Consider the Reformers' attack on the supposedly higher vocations of the monastic life. These vocations were meant to mark out elite paths of superior dedication but were, in fact, deviations into pride and self-delusion. The really holy life for the Christian was within ordinary life itself, living in work and household in a Christian and worshipful manner.

There was an earthly—one might say earthy—critique of the allegedly higher here, which was then transposed and used as a secular critique of Christianity and, indeed, religion in general. Something of the same rhetorical stance adopted by Reformers against monks and nuns is taken up by secularists and unbelievers against Christian faith itself. This allegedly scorns the real, sensual, earthly human good for some purely imaginary higher end, the pursuit of which can lead only to the frustration of the real, earthly good and to suffering, mortification, repression, and so on. The motivations of those who espouse this higher path are thus, indeed, suspect. Pride, elitism, and the desire to dominate play a part in this story, too, along with fear and timidity (also present in the earlier Reformers' story, but less prominent).

In this critique, of course, religion is identified with the second, purist stance or else with a combination of this and the first "symbiotic" (usually labeled superstitious) stance. The third, the stance of agape/*karuna,* becomes invisible. That is because a transformed variant of it has, in fact, been assumed by the secularist critic.

Now one mustn't exaggerate. This outlook on religion is far from universal in our society. One might think that this is particularly true in the United States, with the high rates here of religious belief and practice. Yet, I want to claim that this whole way of understanding things has penetrated far more deeply and widely than simply card-carrying, village atheist–style secularists, that it also shapes the outlook of many people who see themselves as believers.

What do I mean by "this way of understanding"? Well, it is a climate of thought, a horizon of assumptions, more than a doctrine. That means that there will be some distortion in my attempt to lay it out in a set of propositions. But I'm going to do that anyway because there is no other way of characterizing it that I know.

Spelled out in propositions, it would read something like this: (1) that for us life, flourishing, and driving back the frontiers of death and suffering are of supreme value; (2) that this wasn't always so; it wasn't so for our ancestors, or for people in other earlier civilizations; (3) that one of the things that stopped it from being so in the past was precisely a sense, inculcated by religion, that there were higher goals; and (4) that we have arrived at (1) by a critique and overcoming of (this kind of) religion.

We live in something analogous to a post-revolutionary climate. Revolutions generate the sense that they have won a great victory and identify the adversary in the previous regime. A post-revolutionary climate is extremely sensitive to anything that smacks of the *ancien régime* and sees backsliding even in relatively innocent concessions to generalized human preferences. Thus, Puritans saw the return of popery in any rituals, and Bolsheviks compulsively addressed people as Comrade, proscribing the ordinary appellation "Mister" and "Miss. "

I would argue that a milder but very pervasive version of this kind of climate is widespread in our culture. To speak of aiming beyond life is to appear to undermine the supreme concern with life of our humanitarian, "civilized" world. It is to try to reverse the revolution and bring back the bad old order of priorities, in which life and happiness could be sacrificed on the altars of renunciation. Hence, even believers are often induced to redefine their faith in such a way as not to challenge the primacy of life.

My claim is that this climate, often unaccompanied by any formulated awareness of the underlying reasons, pervades our culture. It emerges, for instance, in the widespread inability to give any human meaning to suffering and death, other than as dangers and enemies to be avoided or combated. This inability is not just the failing of certain individuals; it is entrenched in many of our institutions and practices—for instance, the practice of medicine, which has great trouble understanding its own limits or conceiving of some natural term to human life.

What gets lost, as always, in this post-revolutionary climate is the crucial nuance. Challenging the primacy can mean two things. It can mean trying to displace the saving of life and the avoidance of suffering from their rank as central concerns of policy, or it can mean making the claim, or at least opening the way for the insight, that more than life matters. These two are evidently not the same. It is not even true, as people might plausibly believe, that they are causally linked in the sense that making the second challenge "softens us up" and makes the first challenge easier. Indeed, I want to claim (and did in the concluding chapter of *Sources*) that the reverse is the case: that clinging to the primacy of life in the second (let's call this the "metaphysical") sense is making it harder for us to affirm it wholeheartedly in the first (or practical) sense.

But I don't want to pursue this claim right now. I return to it later. The thesis I'm presenting here is that it is by virtue of its post-revolutionary climate that Western modernity is very inhospitable to the transcendent. This, of course, runs contrary to the mainline Enlightenment story, according to which religion has become less credible, thanks to the advance of science. There is, of course, something in this, but it isn't, in my view, the main story. More, to the extent that it is true—that is, that people interpret science and religion as being at loggerheads—it is often because of an already felt incompatibility at the moral level. It is this deeper level that I have been trying to explore here.

In other words, to oversimplify again, in Western modernity the obstacles to belief are primarily moral and spiritual, rather than epistemic. I am talking about the driving force here, rather than what is said in arguments in justification of unbelief. . . .

The tragic irony is that the higher the sense of potential, the more grievously do real people fall short and the more severe the turnaround that is inspired by the disappointment. A lofty humanism posits high standards of self-worth and a magnificent goal to strive toward. It inspires enterprises of great moment. But by this very token it encourages force, despotism, tutelage, ultimately contempt, and a certain ruthlessness in shaping refractory human material—oddly enough, the same horrors that Enlightenment critique picked up in societies and institutions dominated by religion, and for the same causes.

The difference of belief here is not crucial. Wherever action for high ideals is not tempered, controlled, and ultimately engulfed in an unconditional love of the beneficiaries, this ugly dialectic risks repetition. And, of course, just holding the appropriate religious beliefs is no guarantee that this will be so.

A third pattern of motivation, which we have seen repeatedly, this time occurs in the register of justice rather than benevolence. We have seen it with Jacobins and Bolsheviks and today with the politically correct left and the so-called Christian right. We fight against injustices that cry out to heaven for vengeance. We are moved by a flaming indignation against these: racism, oppression, sexism, or leftist attacks on the family or Christian faith. This indignation comes to be fueled by hatred for those who support and connive with these injustices, which, in turn, is fed by our sense of superiority that we are not like these instruments and accomplices of evil. Soon, we are blinded to the havoc we wreak around us. Our picture of the world has safely located all evil outside us. The very energy and hatred with which we combat evil prove its exteriority to us. We must never relent but, on the contrary, double our energy, vie with each other in indignation and denunciation.

Another tragic irony rests here. The stronger the sense of (often correctly identified) injustice, the more powerfully this pattern can become entrenched. We become centers of hatred, generators of new modes of injustice on a greater scale, but we started with the most exquisite sense of wrong, the greatest passion for justice and equality and peace.

A Buddhist friend of mine from Thailand briefly visited the German Greens. He confessed to utter bewilderment. He thought he understood the goals of the party: peace between human beings and a stance of respect and friendship by humans toward nature. What astonished him was all the anger, the tone of denunciation and hatred toward the established parties. These people didn't seem to see that the first step toward their goal would have to involve stilling the anger and aggression in themselves. He couldn't understand what they were up to.

The blindness is typical of modern exclusive secular humanism. This modern humanism prides itself on having released energy for philanthropy and reform; by getting rid of "original sin," of a lowly and demeaning picture of human nature, it encourages us to reach high. Of course, there is some truth in this, but it is also terribly partial and terribly naive because it has never faced the questions I have been raising here: what can power this great effort at philanthropic reform? This humanism leaves us with our own high sense of self-worth to keep as from backsliding, a high notion of human worth to inspire us forward, and a flaming indignation against wrong and oppression to energize us. It cannot appreciate how problematic all of these are, how easily they can slide into something trivial, ugly, or downright dangerous and destructive.

ALASDAIR MACINTYRE

1929–

The son of two physicians, Alasdair Chalmers MacIntyre was born on January 12, 1929 in Glasgow, Scotland, married Ann Peri in 1953 (divorced, 1963), then Susan Margery Willans in 1963 (divorced 1977), and Lynn Sumida Joy in 1977, having two daughters with his first wife, and a son and daughter with his second. He graduated from Queen Mary College, London in 1949, then took a masters in 1951 at Victoria University of Manchester (England), and another masters degree at Oxford in 1961. He has taught at many universities, including Victoria University as lecturer in the philosophy of religion (1951–55), University of Leeds, England (1957–61), Oxford University as research fellow (1961–62), Princeton University as fellow of Council of the Humanities (1962–63), University of Essex, England as professor of sociology (1966–70), Brandeis University as professor of the history of ideas (1970–72), Boston University as University Professor of Philosophy and Political Science (1972–80) and, dean of liberal arts (1972–73), Wellesley College as Luce Professor (1980–82), and finally Vanderbilt University as Jones Professor of Philosophy, since 1982.

As evidenced by his departmental appointments, MacIntyre has moved from the philosophy of religion to sociology to history of ideas to political science, and finally back to philosophy, making him surely one of the most diversely affiliated academics on the current intellectual scene. Given his broad interests, though, and his longstanding concern for issues that touch on ethics, religion, philosophy proper, and social theory, this is hardly surprising. MacIntyre first came to wide attention with a book that is virtually worthless regarding its topic, *Herbert Marcuse* (1970), about a famous and then most celebrated former member of MacIntyre's new academic home in the legendary History of Ideas Program at Brandeis during the 60s. It is a truly distorting book if one wishes to know about Marcuse's ideas, but an interesting one in considering MacIntyre's subsequent development as a moral philosopher, for his visceral revulsion at Marcuse's philosophy is really an attack against secularized relativism and what he perceives to be a total breakdown in the ability to discern good from bad behavior. His *Against the Self-Images of the Age* (1971) was also widely reviewed and discussed at the time, because of the author's stubborn refusal to bow to what were then the principal shibboleths of left-liberal thinking, of what had become the reigning orthodoxy on many campuses. But it was with a trilogy of later books that MacIntyre truly came into his own, *After Virtue: A Study in Moral Theory* (1981), *Whose Justice? Which Rationality?* (1988) and *Three Rival Versions of Moral Enquiry: Encyclopaedia, Genealogy, and Tradition,* the Gifford Lectures (1990), which established him as a leading analyst of modern ethical thinking and a reviver of what is now called "virtue theory." Building on ancient natural law traditions, MacIntyre claims that the chaotic condition of moral and ethical thinking can only be remedied if certain favored behaviors are connected with good character, and thus virtue. It is a distinctly Catholic, almost neo-Thomist form of thinking, which in some ways connects MacIntyre with Charles Taylor's ideas. It's also fairly obvious that comparing MacIntyre's ideas with those of John Rawls or Habermas along these lines becomes an almost necessary act in self-clarification for modern ethicists and social theorists.

"RIVAL CONCEPTIONS OF THE COMMON GOOD," 1997

The notion of the common good has been used in so many different ways and for so many different purposes that some preliminary considerations are in order. First, we may justifiably speak of a common good in characterizing the ends of a variety of very different types of human association. The members of a family, the members of a fishing crew and the members of an investment club, the students, teachers and administrators of a school and the scientists at work in a laboratory all share aims in such a way that a common good can be identified as the end of their shared activities. Secondly, among these there are cases in which the common good of an association is no more than the summing of the goods pursued by individuals as members of that association, just because the association itself is no more than an instrument employed by those individuals to achieve their individual ends. So it is, for example, with an investment club, by means of which individuals are able to avail themselves of investment opportunities requiring capital sums larger than any one of them possesses. Participation in and support for such associations is therefore rational only so long as and insofar as it provides a more efficient method of achieving their individual ends than would alternative types of activity open to them.

There are also however kinds of association such that the good of the association cannot be

constructed out of what were the goods of its individual members, antecedently to and independently of their membership in it. In these cases the good of the whole cannot be arrived at by summing the goods of the parts. Such are those goods not only achieved by means of cooperative activity and shared understanding of their significance, but in key part constituted by cooperative activity and shared understanding of their significance, goods such as the excellence in cooperative activity achieved by fishing crews and by string quartets, by farming households and by teams of research scientists. Excellence in activity is of course often a means to goods other than and beyond that excellence, goods of types as various as the production of food and the making of reputations. But it is central to our understanding of a wide range of practices that excellence in the relevant kinds of activity is recognized as among the goods internal to those practices.

The achievement of excellence in activity characteristically requires the acquisition of skills, but without virtues skills lack the direction that their exercise requires, if excellence is to be achieved. So it is characteristic of such practices that engaging in them provides a practical education into the virtues. And for individuals who are so educated or are in the course of being so educated two questions arise inescapably, questions that may never be explicitly formulated, but which nonetheless receive answers in the way in which individuals live out their lives. For each individual the question arises: what place should the goods of each of the practices in which I am engaged have in my life? The goods of our productive activities in the workplace, the goods of ongoing family life, the goods of musical or athletic or scientific activity, what place should each have in my life, if my life as a whole is to be excellent? Yet any individual who attempts to answer this question pertinaciously must soon discover that it is not a question that she or he can ask and answer by her or himself and for her or himself, apart from those others together with whom she or he is engaged in the activities of practices. So the questions have to be posed: what place should the goods of each of the practices in which *we* are engaged have in *our* common life? What is the best way of life for our community?

These questions can only be answered by elaborating a conception of the common good of a kind of community in which each individual's achievement of her or his own good is inseparable both from achieving the shared goods of practices and from contributing to the common good of the community as a whole. According to this conception of the common good the identification of my good, of how it is best for me to direct my life, is inseparable from the identification of the common good of the community, of how it is best for that community to direct its life. Such a form of community is by its nature political, that is to say, it is constituted by a type of practice through which other types of practice are ordered, so that individuals may direct themselves towards what is best for them and for the community.

It is important to observe that, although this type of political society—let us recognize that in it which is Aristotelian by calling it a *polis*—does indeed require a high degree of shared culture by those who participate in it, it is not itself constituted by that shared culture and is very different from those political societies whose essential bonds are the bonds of a shared cultural tradition. A *polis* is at least as different from the political society of a *Volk* as either is from that of a liberal democracy. A *polis* is indeed impossible, unless its citizens share at least one language—they may well share more than one—and unless they also share modes of deliberation, format and informal, and a large degree of common understanding of practices and institutions. And such a common understanding is generally derived from some particular inherited cultural tradition. But these requirements have to serve the ends of a society in which individuals are always able to put in question through communal deliberation what has hitherto by custom and tradition

been taken for granted both about their own good and the good of the community. A *polis* is always, potentially or actually, a society of rational inquiry, of self-scrutiny. The bonds of a *Volk* by contrast are prerational and nonrational. The philosophers of the *Volk* are Herder and Heidegger, not Aristotle.

Enough has now been said for it to be possible to sketch the part that different conceptions of the common good play in different types of political justification. Political justifications are those arguments advanced to show why we, as members of some particular political society, should or should not accept as having legitimate authority over us the commands uttered by someone claiming executive authority over or in that society or the laws uttered by someone or some body claiming legislative authority over or in that society. Consider now the part played by different conceptions of the common good in different types of political justification.

There is, for example, the claim that political authority is justified insofar as it provides a secure social order within which individuals may pursue their own particular ends, whatever they are. Individuals need to cooperate, both in order to pursue their own particular ends effectively and in order to sustain the security of the social order. But all such cooperation is a means to their individual ends. The conception of the common good invoked in this type of justification of political authority is such that the common good is arrived at by summing individual goods. It is a conception at once individualist and minimalist. And justifications which employ it have this important political characteristic: that to the extent that they are believed in a political society, that political society is endangered by them, and this for two reasons.

First, if this is the justification for the acceptance of political authority, then rational individuals will attempt to share fully in the benefits provided by political authority, while making as small a contribution as possible to its costs. It will be rational to be a 'free rider', so long as one can avoid whatever penalties are imposed by political authority for free riding. Secondly, it will correspondingly be contrary to rationality, thus understood, to accept an undue share of the costs of sustaining political authority. But no political authority can be sustained over any extended period of time, unless some of those subject to it are prepared to pay an undue share of those costs and this in the most striking way, since the sustaining of political authority requires that some of those subject to it should be prepared, if necessary, to die for the sake of the security of the political and social order: soldiers, police officers, firefighters.

It follows that no political society can have a reasonable expectation of surviving, let alone flourishing, unless a significant proportion of its members are unconvinced that the only justification for accepting and upholding political society and political authority is individualist and minimalist. Only if they believe that there is some other and stronger type of connection between their own ends and purposes and the flourishing of their political society do they have good reason to be willing, if necessary, to die for the sake of that flourishing. And indeed, only if they believe that there is just such another and stronger type of connection, do they have sufficient reason to resist the temptation to act as 'free riders' on occasions in which they could do so without penalty.

An individualist and minimalist conception of the common good is then too weak to provide adequate justification for the kind of allegiance that a political society must have from its members, if it is to flourish. And any political society whose members hold themselves and one another to account in respect of the rational justification of their actions, including their collective political decision-making, will have to be one in which rational argument can sustain the claim that their practices and institutions exhibit a connection between the goods of individuals and the common good sufficient to afford a justification for their political allegiance. But we must not picture this connection between individual goods and the common good as something that might exist apart from and independently of the rational activity of the members of that society in enquiring and arguing about the nature of their goods. For it is a connection constituted by practically rational activity. Practical rationality is a property of individuals-in-their-social-relationships rather than of individuals-as-such. To be practically rational I must learn what my good is in different types of situation and I can only achieve that through interaction with others in which I learn from those others and they from me. Our primary shared and common good is found in that activity of communal learning through which we together become able to order goods, both in our individual lives and in the political society. Such practical learning is a kind of learning that takes place in and through activity, and in and through reflection upon that activity, in the course of both communal and individual deliberation.

When I speak of practical learning and practical enquiry, I refer to that type of learning and enquiry that takes place in the course of asking and answering practical deliberative questions about some subject matter, whenever there is a serious attempt to answer those questions as adequately as possible and to diagnose and to remedy whatever has been defective in one's past answers. Practical learning and enquiry are therefore features of various kinds of activity. It is found among farmers and fishing crews, in the work of households and in the practice of crafts. What is learned does not have to be formulated explicitly in words, although it may be so formulated. But it cannot take place without some significant transformation of activity. And where deliberation is integral to some type of activity, as it is to any politics of the common good, practical enquiry will be embodied in that type of reflective deliberation to which rational participants in such a politics are committed. Indeed politics will be that practical activity which affords the best opportunity for the exercise of our rational powers, an opportunity afforded only by political societies to whose decision-making widely shared rational deliberation is central, societies which extend practical rationality from the farm and the fishing fleet, the household and the craft workplace, to its political assemblies. It follows that no *Volk* can be such a society. It also follows that, if the political characteristics of advanced Western modernity are as I suggested earlier, and if, as I am now suggesting, claims to political allegiance can be justified only where there is the common good of communal political learning, then modern states cannot advance any justifiable claim to the allegiance of their members, and this because they are the political expression of societies of deformed and fragmented practical rationality, in which politics, far from being an area of activity in and through which other activities are rationally ordered, is itself one more compartmentalized sphere from which there has been excluded the possibility of asking those questions that most need to be asked.

NAME INDEX

Abélard & Héloise, 455
Abendroth, Wolfgang, 621
Achilles, 19, 24, 53
Addams, Jane, 3, 7, 464
Adler, Alfred, 547
Adler, Mortimer, 751
Adorno, Theodor, 542, 564–569, 592, 621, 639, 651, 700
Aeschylus, 475
Aesop, 159, 174
Agamemnon, 24
Agassiz, Louis, 284
Agrippa, Henricus Cornelius, 2
Allport, Gordon, 295
Althusser, Louis, 3–5, 399, 558, 653, 663, 732
Altieri, Charles, 6
Amin, Samir, 735
Antonines, 204
Aquinas, Thomas, 2, 353
Arendt, Hannah, 1, 2, 599–604, 640
Aristotle, 2, 159, 209, 212, 544, 565, 651, 764
Arkoun, Mohammed, 3
Arnold, Matthew, 1, 237–242
Aron, Raymond, 518, 613–616
Aronson, Moses, 544
Arrighi, Giovanni, 735
Astell, Mary, 10, 14–17
Athenians, 31
Atticus, 62
Augustine, Saint, 2, 570
Augustus, Emperor, 30, 476
Austen, Jane, 322
Austin, John L., 85, 732, 733
Avenarius, Richard, 517
Averrös, 2
Avicenna, 2
Ayer, A.J., 659

Babeuf, Gracchus, 300
Bach, Johann Sebastian, 570, 725
Bachelard, Gaston, 583
Bacon, Francis 136, 336, 205
Bakunin, Mikhail, 3
Balzac, Honoré, 580
Banneker, Benjamin, 326
Barnett, H.G., 559
Barthes, Roland, 399, 477, 558, 581–586, 706, 724
Bataille, Georges, 477–482
Baudelaire, Charles-Pierre, 568, 583, 585, 605, 640
Baudrillard, Jean, 706–712, 718, 722, 723
Beatrice & Dante, 456
Beaumont, Gustave de, 169
Beauvoir, Simone de, 3, 698, 699, 729, 730
Beck, Ulrich, 3
Beethoven, Ludwig von, 110, 573

Bell, Daniel, 3, 721
Bellamy, Edward, 751
Benedict, Ruth, 3
Benjamin, Walter, 1, 5, 394, 542, 564, 565, 591, 592, 599, 639–642, 669, 718, 720, 721
Benn, Gottfried, 629
Bentham, Jeremy, 85–87, 159, 656, 660, 739
Berg, Alban, 564
Bergson, Henri, 3, 578
Berkeley, George, 79
Berlin, Isaiah, 1
Bishop Burnet, 14
Bismarck, Otto von, 214, 301
Blackstone, William, 85
Blake, William, 95
Blanc, Louis, 300
Blanchot, Maurice, 668
Bloch, Ernst, 4
Bloch, Marc, 734
Bloom, Allan, 5
Bloom, Harold, 3, 5
Blumer, Herbert, 464
Bly, Robert, 3
Boas, Franz, 587
Bodin, Jean, 2, 600
Bonald, Louis de, 3, 714, 715
Borges, Jorges Luis, 708
Boswell, James, 70
Bourdieu, Pierre, 613, 644–652, 677, 720
Bourget, Paul, 580
Boyle, Robert, 10
Brahms, Johannes, 460
Braille, Louis, 33
Braudel, Fernand, 734
Brecht, Bertold, 640
Bremond, Henri, Abbe, 758
Breton, André, 595
Breuer, Josef, 384
Brody, Fawn, 4
Brown, Norman O., 143
Bruno, Giordano, 359
Bryson, Bethany, 6
Buber, Martin, 276, 448–453
Bukharin, Nikolai, 342, 343
Bunyan, John, 463
Burckhardt, Jacob, 3, 543
Burke, Edmund, 90–94, 131, 549, 659, 714, 715
Burke, Kenneth, 608
Butler, Judith, 694, 729–733
Butler, Samuel, 550, 751

Caesar, 30, 60, 74
Caillois, Roger, 605–607
Caligula, 204
Calin, William, 7

Calvin, John, 2, 511
Calvino, Italo, 6
Camic, Charles, 6
Camus, Albert, 663
Caracalla, 204
Carlyle, Thomas, 135, 139–142, 527
Casement, William, 6
Cassirer, Ernst, 523–529, 636
Castells, Manuel, 2, 3
Castoriadis, Cornelius, 682
Catharine the Great, 33, 85
Cato, 60, 62
Ceneaus, 24
Chamberlain, Houston Stewart, 223
Charlemagne, 26
Charles II, 10
Chateaubriand, François René de, 438
Chicago, University of, 5
Chomsky, Noam, 558, 681
Christ, Jesus, 34
Christine de Pisan, 2
Christy, Henry, 258
Cicero, 2, 22, 35
Clausewitz, Karl von, 613
Cleopatra, 117
Cohen, Hermann, 523
Coleman, James, 628
Coleridge, Samuel Taylor, 159
Collingwood, R.G., 659
Collins, Patricia Hill, 700
Columbia University, 5
Comte, Auguste, 135, 152–158, 218, 276, 295,
    357, 361, 371, 452, 453, 524, 525, 614, 615, 637
Condillac, Etienne de, 66–69
Condorcet, Marquis de, 106–109, 152
Confucius, 2
Cook, Albert S., 6
Cooley, Charles Horton, 319–324, 384, 423, 464, 469
Coolidge, Grace, 418
Cooper, A. J., 7
Cornelius, Hans, 542, 564
Cornell University, 5
Coser, Lewis, 428, 713–717
Coulanges, Fustel de, 250–252, 361
Cournot, Augustin, 287
Craig, John, 54
Croly, Herbert, 753, 755
Cuffe, Paul, 326

d'Alembert, Jean, 3, 33, 106, 135
d'Aragona, Tullia, 2
d'Estaing, Giscard, 683
Dante, 2, 21, 529
Dante & Beatrice, 456
Darwin, Charles, 212, 253–257, 258, 420, 525

DaVinci, Leonardo, 233, 385, 538
DeBeauvoir, Simone, 518, 534
Deena, Seodial F. H., 7
Delbanco, Andrew, 6
Deleuze, Gilles, 723
DeMaistre, Joseph, 131–134, 152, 358, 715
DeMan, Henri, 579
DeMan, Paul, 664
Democritus, 184
Demosthenes, 24, 35, 159, 334
Denby, David, 5
Derrida, Jacques, 477, 654, 663–671, 751
Descartes, René, 10, 18, 79, 141, 530, 534, 689, 700,
    742, 743, 744
Dewey, John, 319, 423–427, 454, 464, 517, 526, 751,
    755
Diderot, Denis, 33–38, 66, 90, 106, 530
Dilthey, Wilhelm, 79, 272–275, 319, 621, 646, 676
Disraeli, Benjamin, 457
Domitian, 204
Douglas, Mary, 630–635
Douglass, Frederick, 179–183
Dreiser, Theodore, 755
Dreyfus, Alfred, 306
Dryas, 24
DuBois, W.E.B., 325–329
Duclos, M., 35
Durkheim, Emile, 90, 281, 290–294, 306, 315, 347,
    361, 428, 442, 493, 500, 504, 522, 554, 576, 621,
    628, 674, 676, 677, 742, 743
Dylan, Bob, 5

Eadie, Jo, 7
Eichmann, Adolph, 599
Einstein, Albert, 253, 361
Eisenhower, Dwight, 753
Elias, Norbert, 433, 492–499, 508, 676, 714, 715
Eliot, T.S., 371, 751
Ellis, John, 5
Elshtain, Jean Bethke, 673
Emmanuel, Arghiri, 736
Engels, Friedrich, iv, 135, 184, 185, 262–264, 521, 582
Epictetus, 2
Epicurus, 2, 184
Erasmus, Desiderius, 2, 492, 715
Erikson, Erik, 3
Ernst, Max, 477
Evans-Pritchard, E. E., 306, 631
Exadius, 24

Fabrice, 535
Fanon, Frantz, 617–620
Febvre, Lucien, 734
Feigl, Herbert, 547
Ferguson, Adam, 50–53, 70

Ferrazzi, Cecelia, 2
Ferry, Anne, 6
Feuerbach, Ludwig, 243, 398
Fichte, Johann, 127–130, 201, 355, 692
Firth, Raymond, 559
Flaubert, Gustave, 361, 518, 634
Fleiss, William, 384
Fonte, Moderata, 2
Ford, Laura, 6
Foucault, Michel, 399, 477, 558, 644, 653–658, 663, 664, 723, 729, 751
Fourier, F.M.C. 143–150, 164, 580
Fox, Evelyn, 506
Franco, Veronica, 2
Frank, André Gunter, 735
Franklin, Benjamin, 100, 240
Frazer, James George, 371–373, 442
Frederick the Great, 23, 177, 351, 355
Frederick II, 177
Frege, Gottlob, 399
Freud, Anna, 384, 596
Freud, Sigmund, 143, 315, 319, 371, 384–388, 403, 421, 443, 444, 492, 493, 497, 504, 506, 507, 508, 510, 518, 547, 562, 591, 592, 621, 626, 637, 666, 674, 678, 694, 696, 715, 724, 729, 744
Fromm, Erich, 508–513, 542
Furnas, Clifford Cook, 589

Gadamer, Hans-Georg, 399, 676
Galbraith, John Kenneth, 753
Galileo Galilei, 359, 637
Galton, Francis, 461
Gandhi, Mohandas, 412–416
Garfinkel, Harold, 608–612
Gates, Henry Louis, 7
Gehlen, Arnold, 628, 629
Gellner, Ernest, 740–744
Genghis-Khan(s), 25
Gentile, Giovanni, 580
George III, 241
Gerth, Hans, 576
Gibbon, Edward, 45, 50, 110
Giddens, Anthony, 3, 492, 644, 676–681
Giddings, Franklin, 319
Gide, André, 537
Gillen, F.J., 528
Gilman, Charlotte Perkins, 7, 303–305
Giraudoux, Jean, 538
Gissing, George, 3
Gladstone, William, 241
Gobineau, J.A. Comte de, 223–227, 527
Godwin, William, 95
Godwin, Mary W., 95
Goethe, Wolfgang, 79, 103, 110 139, 201, 206, 270, 331, 346, 352, 365, 384, 474, 490, 525

Goffman, Irving, 3
Goldman, Lucien, 724
Goldoni, Carlo, 322
Gorak, Jan, 6
Gouldner, Alvin, 500
Goya, Francisco, 657
Graff, Gerald, 7
Gramsci, Antonio, 4, 5, 394–398
Greenberg, Clement, 1
Greenblatt, Stephen, 714
Griffith, G.T., 659
Grimm, Brothers, 79
Grote, George, 85
Grotius, 2
Guattari, Félix, 723
Guillory, John, 6

Habermas, Jürgen, 469, 564, 591, 621–629, 644, 677, 689, 763
Hacking, Ian, 751
Hadrian, 204
Hafiz, 270
Halbwachs, Maurice, 428–432
Hall, G. Stanley, 423
Hallberg, Robert von, 6
Hamann, Georg, 639
Hamlet, Prince of Denmark, 462
Hammurabi, 2, 328
Haraclides, 20
Harding, Sandra, 700
Hartmann, Nicolai, 646
Hartsock, Nancy, 700
Harvey, David, 718–723
Hegel, Georg Wilhelm Friedrich, 5, 59, 79, 110–114, 187, 189, 194, 201, 243, 244, 398, 436, 452, 490, 530, 534, 547, 565, 568, 591, 621, 626, 629, 670, 685, 729, 744, 756
Heidegger, Martin, 2, 518, 537, 570, 591, 599, 600, 644, 654, 663, 666, 670, 671, 677, 678, 695, 697, 751, 764
Heine, Heinrich, 351, 361, 384
Heinle, Friedrich, 639
Heisenberg, Werner, 272
Hekman, Susan, 700
Héloise & Abélard, 455
Hemings, Sally, 4
Henku, 2
Henry, Jules, 674
Heraclitus, 474
Hercules, 20
Herder, Johann Gottfried von, 79–84, 764
Herodotus, 83
Herzen, Alexander, 234–246
Herzl, Theodor, 448
Hirsch, E. D., 5

Hitler, Adolf, 223, 547, 548
Hobbes, Thomas, 2, 27, 43, 276, 501, 502, 659
Hölderlin, Friedrich, 110
Homans, George, 514
Homer, 21, 53, 83, 166, 544, 565
Hoover, Herbert, 417
Horace, 21
Horkheimer, Max, 542–546, 564, 565, 591, 621, 700
Horney, Karen, 5, 508
Howard, 657
Howe, Irving, 713
Huizinga, Johann, 605
Humboldt, Alexander von, 79
Hume, David, 45–50, 70–74, 152, 549, 660, 743, 744
Husserl, Edmund, 389, 469, 518, 534, 537, 591, 663, 670, 678, 679, 682, 689
Hyppolite, Jean, 518, 663, 729

Ibn Khaldun, 2
Irigaray, Luce, 694–699, 730
Isocrates, 159

Jakobson, Roman, 558, 581
James, Alice, 284
James, Henry, Jr., 284, 580
James, Henry, Sr., 284
James, William, 284–289, 320, 321, 384, 403, 423, 464, 493, 517, 526
Jameson, Fredric, 723
Jaspers, Karl, 469, 508, 570, 599, 600
Jaurés, Jean, 290
Jay, Gregory, 6
Jefferson, Thomas, 4, 75–78, 173, 184, 326, 746, 755
John of Salisbury, 2
Johnson, Samuel, 70
Jones, Ernest, 445
Joyce, James, 18
Jung, Carl, 371
Justinian, Emperor, 248

Kansas City Star, 5
Kant, Immanuel, v, 59–65, 70, 79, 90, 103, 110, 127, 152, 201, 204, 294, 346, 353, 355, 389, 423, 435, 505, 523, 542, 549, 636, 639, 651, 670, 691, 696, 745
Kaplan, Carey, 6
Keller, Albert, 336
Kerensky, Aleksandr, 514
Kernan, Alvin, 5
Kernberg, Otto, 674
Keynes, John Maynard, 1, 115, 123
Kierkegaard, Soren, 194–197, 450, 570, 677, 678
King Frederick, 141
Kipling, Rudyard, 431
Knight, Frank, 692

Kojève, Alexander, 729
Koran, 2
Kracauer, Siegfried, 564
Kristeva, Julia, 724–728, 729
Kroeber, Alfred, 418, 589
Kuhn, Thomas, 485

Lacan, Jacques, 558, 581, 595–598, 664, 687, 694, 724, 729
Lambropoulos, Vassilis, 6
Langer, Susanne, 523, 636–638
Lao Tzu, 2
Laplace, Pierre, 164
Lasalle, Ferdinand, 300
Lasch, Christopher, 672–675
Lauter, Paul, 6
Lavoisier, Antoine Laurent, 637
Lazarsfeld, Paul, 486, 608
LeBon, Gustav, 295–298, 470, 473
Lefebvre, Henri, 4, 530–533, 706
Leibniz, Gottfried Wilhelm, 18, 212, 420, 361, 454, 523, 646
Lengermann, Patricia, 7
Lenin, Vladimir, 340–345, 586
Le Pen, Jean-Marie, 722
LePlay, P.G.F., 228–231
Lessing, Gotthold Ephraim, 90
Lévi-Strauss, Claude, 306, 399, 518, 558–563, 581, 595, 666, 724
Lévy-Bruhl, Henri, 361
Lévy-Bruhl, Lucien, 306, 361–364
Lidz, Victor, 506
Lincoln, Abraham, 419
Livy, 22
Locke, John, 1, 2, 10–13, 14, 18, 70, 550, 601
Long, Huey, 545
Louis XIV, 25
Louis XVI, 100, 106
Louis-Napoléon, 169
Löwenthal, Leo, 542
Lucian, 159
Lucretia, 60
Lucretius, 2
Luhmann, Niklas, 689–693
Lukács, Georg, 4, 5, 365–370, 433, 530, 591
Luther, Martin, 2, 270, 382, 383, 403, 511
Lyotard, Jean-Francois, 682–688

Macdonald, Dwight, 713
Mach, Ernst, 517
Machiavelli, Nicolo, 2, 18, 299, 301
MacIntyre, Alastair, 751, 762–765
MacIver, Robert, 451
Madame DeStael, 123, 135

Madison, James, 173, 174
Maeterlinck, Count Maurice, 366
Maine, Henry Sumner, 247–249, 276
Malinowski, Bronislaw, 371, 442–447
Mallarmé, Stéphane, 642
Malraux, André, 477
Malthus, T. R., 115–118
Mann, Thomas, 365, 564
Mannheim, Karl, 433–441, 492
Marcel, Gabriel-Honoré, 570–575
Marcus Aurelius, 2
Marcuse, Herbert, 1, 3, 5, 103, 143, 542, 564, 591–594, 672
Maria Theresa, 177
Marshall, Alfred, 500
Marsilius of Padua, 2
Martineau, Harriet, 7, 152, 218–222, 305
Marx, Karl, iv, 1–3, 18, 45, 111, 123, 143, 184–193, 258, 262, 276, 300, 367, 368, 369, 434, 452, 457, 490, 493, 508, 510, 513, 542, 547, 567, 576, 580, 586, 591, 600, 602, 604, 614, 615, 620, 621, 640, 676, 691, 706, 744
Mauriac, Francois, 538
Mauss, Marcel, 291, 306–310, 361, 428, 559
Mazzini, Giuseppe 358
McCarthy, Eugene, 509
McKeon, Richard, 751
McLuhan, Marshall, 581
Mead, George Herbert, 284, 319, 346, 384, 399, 423, 465–468, 493, 579, 628, 679, 680
Medicis, 25
Mencius, 2
Mencken, H.L., 576
Merleau-Ponty, Maurice, 79, 518, 534–539
Merton, Robert King, 295, 485–491, 514, 713
Michelangelo, 141, 385
Michelet, Jules, 18
Michels, Roberto, 299, 357, 374–377
Mill, Harriet Taylor, 85, 198–200
Mill, John Stuart, 85, 139, 152, 159–163, 198, 272, 454, 549, 746, 757
Millais, John, 232
Millar, John, 54
Mills, C. Wright, 500, 576–580, 608, 713
Milton, John, 529
Miro, Joan, 477
Mishima, Yukio, 634
Moi, Toril, 694
Monroe, James, 100
Montaigne, Michel Eyquem de, 2
Montesquieu, Baron de la Bréde et de, 27–32, 152
Moore, George Edward, 461
More, Thomas, 2
Morgan, Lewis, 3

Morris, William, 579, 580
Morris, G. S., 423
Mosca, Gaetano, 5, 299–302, 357
Moses, 83
Mozart, Wolfgang Amadeus, 139, 141, 570
Mussolini, Benito, 295, 315, 374

Napoleon Bonaparte, 119, 297, 359, 520, 614
Napoleon III, 135, 228
Natanson, Maurice, 729
Nero, 204
Nerva, 204
Nestor, 24
Neumann, Friedrich, 591
Newton, Isaac, 23, 70, 79, 139, 141, 143, 420, 550, 739
Nicholas I, 243
Nicolas of Pusa, 2
Niebrugge-Brantley, J., 7
Nietzsche, Friedrich, 5, 201, 223, 266–271, 276, 346, 352, 448, 451, 474, 530, 542, 653, 663, 666, 670, 686, 723
Nizan, Paul, 530

Oakeshott, Michael, 659–662, 664
Odum, Howard, 608
Ogburn, William Fielding, 417–422
Orpheus, 83
Otto, Rudolf, 403–405
Owen, Robert, 198

Paine, Thomas, 90, 95, 100–102, 714
Pareto, Vilfredo, 1, 315–318, 357, 374, 403, 500
Park, Robert, 464
Parsons, Elsie Clews, 281
Parsons, Talcott, 3, 4, 7, 492, 500–507, 608, 609, 621, 676, 689
Pascal, Blaise, 2, 294, 389, 570
Passeron, Jean-Claude, 644
Pasteur, Louis, 409
Paul, Jean, 205
Pearson, K., 517
Péguy, Charles, 535
Peirce, Charles S., 284, 423
Pericles, 334
Perkin, J. Russell, 7
Petzold, 517
Phillips, Wendell, 179
Piaget, Jean, 319
Picasso, Pablo, 477
Pico della Mirandola, 2
Pitt, William, 458
Plato, 2, 5, 18, 59, 146, 159, 201, 238, 301, 317, 334, 353, 435, 451, 452, 524, 547, 571, 603, 604, 670, 688

Pliny, 83
Plutarch, 25, 29, 73
Poincaré, Raymond, 488
Poincaré, Jules-Henri, 517
Politzer, Georges, 530
Pollock, Friedrich, 542
Polybius, 2
Polyphemus, 24
Pompey, 124
Popper, Karl, 547–552
Princess of Orange, 10
Prometheus, 738
Proudhon, Pierre Joseph, 186, 243, 244, 245, 300, 561
Proust, Marcel, 537
Publilius Philo, 22

Queen Anne, 14
Queen Christina, 141
Quetelet, Adolphe., 164–168

Rabelais, Francois, 530
Radcliffe-Brown, Alfred Reginald, 306
Raphael, 139, 141, 233
Rauschenbusch, Walter, 755
Rawls, John, 745–750, 763
Reagan, Ronald, 5, 591, 672, 751
Redfield, Robert, 587–590
Remarque, Erich, 3
Rembrandt, 346
Renan, Ernest, 357, 358, 359
Renouvier, Charles, 284
Reynand, Jean, 228
Reynolds, Joshua, 322
Ricardo, David, 159, 218
Richards, Audrey, 63l
Richelieu, Cardinal de, 25
Rickert, Heinrich, 469, 508
Ricoeur, Paul, 631, 676
Riegl, Alois 641
Rilke, Rainer Maria, 639
Rivers, W. H. R., 563
Rivet, Paul, 306
Robespierre, 100, 106
Robinson, Lillian, 6
Roheim, Geza, 371
Rolland, Romain, 395
Romains, Jules, 519
Romulus, 21
Roosevelt, Theodore, 753
Rorty, Richard, 751–755
Rose, Ellen C., 6
Rousseau, Jean-Jacques, 1, 5, 33, 39–44, 66, 70, 79, 115, 355, 361, 544, 574, 585, 663, 705, 746
Royce, Josiah, 423

Ruskin, John, 1, 232–236, 237, 412, 578
Russell, Bertrand, 423, 451, 454–459, 460, 518, 550

Sachs, Hans, 508
Saint Augustine, 35
Saint Hilary, 35
Saint Paul, 11, 35
Saint-Simon, Henri C.de, 135–138, 152, 243, 302, 452, 614
Sappho, 334
Sargent, John Singer, 322
Sarton, George, 485
Sartre, Jean-Paul, 3, 518–522, 534, 558, 570, 574, 613, 634, 663, 682, 698, 729
Saussure, Ferdinand de, 399–402, 583, 595, 724
Scharf, Kenny, 723
Scheler, Max, 389–393, 713
Schelling, Friedrich, 3, 110, 243, 621
Schelsky, Helmut, 689
Schiller, Friedrich von, 103–105, 276, 351, 448, 591, 592, 605
Schlegel, Friedrich von, 119, 123, 639
Schlegel Brothers, 79
Schleiermacher, Friedrich, 119–122, 201, 403
Schlesinger, Arthur, 753
Scholem, Gershom, 639
Schopenhauer, Arthur, 201–211, 270, 271, 346, 542, 568, 569
Schumann, Robert, 266
Schurman, Anna Maria von, 2
Schutz, Alfred, 609, 611
Schweitzer, Albert, 518
Seidman, Steven, 7
Sekles, Bernard, 564
Selznick, Philip, 608
Seneca, 146, 361
Shaftesbury, First Earl of, 10, 33, 661
Shakespeare, William, 334, 475, 523
Shaw, Bernard, 340
Shelley, Mary W. 95
Shelley, Percy Bysshe, 457
Shils, Edward, 433
Simmel, Georg, 1, 272, 276, 315, 346–356, 365, 464, 493, 523, 639, 713, 716, 721
Sinaiko, Herman, 6
Sinclair, Upton, 755
Sismondi, J.C.L.S. de, 115, 123–126
Small, Albion, 346
Smith, Adam, 1, 45–49, 50, 54, 59, 70, 79, 123, 159, 218, 425, 489, 743
Smith, Dorothy E., 700–705
Smith, Robertson, 307
Socrates, 44, 197, 357, 366, 451, 524
Solon, 35, 351

Solzhenitsyn, Alexandre, 365
Sombart, Werner, 500
Somerville, Mary, 305
Sontag, Susan, 640
Sorel, Georges, 357–360, 578, 580
Sorokin, Pitirim, 5, 406, 485, 500, 514–517
Soros, George, 547
Spanos, William, 7
Spartacus, 124
Spartans, 31
Speier, Hans, 716, 721
Spencer, Herbert, 212–217, 276, 297, 336, 393, 431, 528
Spengler, Oswald, 5, 474–476, 528, 529
Spinoza, Benedict de, 2, 18, 212, 276, 574, 774, 660, 744
Stalin, Joseph, 340, 342, 423
Stanford University, 5
Stein, Lorenz von, 381, 382, 452
Steinbeck, John, 754
Steiner, Franz, 632
Stendhal, 432
Steuermann, Eduard, 564
Stolypin, P.A., 301
Strabo, 83
Strauss, Leo, 5
Strodtbeck, Fred, 609
Stumpf, Carl 392
Sturt, Charles, 590
Sugar, Alan, 723
Sugerman, Shirley, 673
Sullivan, Harry Stack, 508
Sumner, Charles, 241
Sumner, William Graham, 336–339
Sun-Tse, 687, 688
Swift, Jonathan, 3, 240
Sydenham, Thomas, 10

Tacitus, 18, 29, 35
Taine, Hippolyte, 525
Tamerlane(s), 25
Tarabotti, Arcangela, 2
Tarde, Gabriel, 281–283, 452
Taylor, Harriet, 159
Taylor, Charles, 680, 723, 756–761, 763
Temple of Delphi, 40
Tentori, 590
Terence, 2, 7, 174
Thackeray, William, 232
Thibon, Gustave, 573
Thomas, W.I., 336, 406–410, 464
Thoreau, Henry David, 544
Thurman, Howard, 415
Tiberius, 203

Tilgher, Adriano, 580
Tillich, Paul, 564, 678
Titian, 233
Titus, 204
Tocqueville, Alexis de, 169–178, 223, 321, 322, 614, 753
Todorov, Tzvetan, 724
Tolstoy, Leo, v, 544, 578
Tönnies, Ferdinand, 276–280, 346
Toynbee, Arnold, 553–557
Troeltsch, Ernst, 380, 403
Trotsky, Leon, 340–345, 365, 423, 751
Tse-tung, Mao, 506
Turgot, Anne Robert Jacques, 106, 152
Turner, Victor 560
Turner, J.M.W., 232
Tylor, Edward Burnett, 258–261, 371

Ulysses, 21, 544
Ungar, Frederick, 103
Updike, John, 672

Valéry, Paul, 537, 641, 663, 720
Vauvenargues, Luc de Clapiers, marquis de, 585
Veblen, Thorstein, 311–314, 406, 409, 576, 577
Velasquez, 233
Vico, Giambattista, 18–22, 489, 523
Virgil, 166
Virilio, Paul, 722
Volland, Sophie, 33
Voltaire, 23–26, 45, 106, 141, 549, 585
Vonnegut, Kurt, 702

Wagner, Richard, 270
Wallace, Alfred Russell, 3, 254, 420
Wallerstein, Immanuel, 734–739
Washington, George, 100
Watson, John B., 409
Weber, Alfred, 433, 492, 508
Weber, Marianne, 7
Weber, Max, 5, 164, 267, 272, 276, 315, 330–335, 346, 347, 365, 374, 380, 403, 434, 437, 469, 474, 489, 490, 493, 495, 500, 508, 511, 553, 566, 576, 587, 591, 621, 622, 627, 628, 629, 630, 676, 689, 742, 743, 744
Weil, Simone, 518
Wenders, Wim, 722
Westermarck, Edward Alexander, 443
Wheatley, Phillis, 326
Whitehead, Alfred North, 2, 454, 636
Whitman, Walt, 755
Wickhoff, Franz, 641
Wieland, Christoph, 201
Wilde, Oscar, 715, 717

William the Conquerer, 317
Williams, Raymond, 721
Windelband, Wilhelm, 272
Wirth, Louis, 433
Wittgenstein, Ludwig, 460–463, 679, 751
Wittig, Monique, 729
Wollstonecraft, Mary, 95–99, 220
Wordsworth, William, 95
Wright, Richard, 755

Wundt, Wilhelm, 490
Wythe, George, 75

Xenophon, 159, 238

Yerkes, Robert M. 526

Znaniecki, Florian, 3, 406, 608

SUBJECT INDEX

abnegation, 307
abolitionism, 179, 183, 753
aboriginal cultures, 260
aboriginal people, 75, 442, 543
abortion, 506
absolute interpretation, 435
absolute justice, 302
absolute negativity, 114
absolute spirit, 244
absolute values, 461–62
absolutism, 34, 285
abstraction, 196–97
academic privileges, 567
accounts, 608
achievement, status, 741
acquired characteristics, 419
action, 273
Adamite innocence, 714
adaptation, 348
adaptive culture, 421
adolescent boys, 13
adult education, 276
adumbrations, cultural, 258
advertising, 471, 512–13
aesthetic culture, 365–67
aesthetic life, 194
aesthetic state, 592
aesthetic vocabulary, 605
aesthetics, 232, 721
aesthetics, social, 649
affect, 147
African civilization, 327–28
African slave trade, 36
agape, 758
Age of Machinery, 140–41
agency, 660–62, 676, 705, 756
aggregates, 215, 451
aggression, 80, 508, 592
agrarian labor, 57
aisthesis, 651
alcohol and crime, 167
aleatory impulse, 671
aleatory interest, 338–39
Algiers, 644
alienated labor, 57
alienation, 190–92, 269, 366, 369, 472, 508, 512,
      531–32, 597, 615, 651, 707
alimony, 16
All-oneness, 332
aloofness, 727
altruism, 301, 349, 353–54, 514, 526
ambition, 96, 300
American Communist Party, 713
American Indians, 76–78
American Revolution, 100

anarchism, 532
anarchy, 153–54, 174,, 239
anatta, 757
ancien régime, 759
ancient historiography, 250
ancients vs. moderns, 24–25
anger, 409
animal ecology, 482–83
animal rights, 2
animality, 484
animism, 258
Annales school, 734
anomalies, social, 633
anomie, 290
anti-intellectualism, 259
anti-Semitism, 457, 485, 518, 520, 599
antinomy, 294
ants, 283
anxiety, 291–92, 322, 677
apartheid, 619
aporias, 663, 687
apperception, 206
Arabian sciences, 136
argument, grounds of, 163
aristocracy, 133, 172, 229, 317
arrogance, 268
art education, 233
art, 329, 332
art, authenticity of, 642
art, dialectic of, 532
art, great, 274
art, sociology of, 641
articulated masses, 470–71
artisanal labor, 478–79
arts, development of, 67–68
asceticism, 270–71, 294, 330–34, 412, 432, 486, 566,
      759
atheism, 33, 454, 538
Athenian democracy, 452
Athens, 238
aura, decay of, 642
authenticity, 714
authoritarian personality, 508
authoritarianism, 549, 564
authority, origins of, 21–22
autology, 693
automaton, 509
average man, 165
axiology, 585

banality of evil, 599
barbarism, 259
barter, 368
béance, 596
becoming, 397

Beethoven, late works of, 573
being, for humans, 536
Being and Time, 591, 600
being-in-the-world, 671
beliefs, double character of, 430
ben, 528
beneficence, 48–49
Biblical interpretations, 11
bibliomania, 235
bifurcated consciousness, 701
binary division, 656
biological determinism, 419
blasé attitude, 722
blasphemy, 34
body maintenance, 650
body *hexis*, 647
body-soul, 293
body-subject, 534
bohemians, 408
Bolshevism, 341–42
Bonapartism, 480
bookkeeping, 608
books, future of, 6
boredom, 209, 210, 281, 291, 512
boredom, theory of, 568–69
bourgeois culture, 344
bourgeois mind, 197
bourgeois world, 545
bourgeoisie, 341, 478–79
bourgeoisie, decadent, 531
brain research, 384
brand name, 708
Brazilian Indians, 558
breast feeding, 443–44
British educational system, 237
brothels, 245
brotherliness, 333
brutality, 392
Buddhism, 555
bull fighting, 477
bureaucracy, 188–89
bureaucratization, 214, 376, 544, 684

cabalistic spirit, 147
calling, 331
cannibalism, 38, 289
cannibals, 225
canon change, 1–7
canon wars, 5–7
capital, circulation of, 720–23
capital, logic of, 719–20
capital-accumulation, 736
capitalism, 330–31, 531, 615, 718
capitalism, utopian, 577
capitalist process, 719

capitalist structure, 479
captivity, 575
careerism, 189
caretakers, infant, 678–79
Cartesian rules, 610–11
cash nexus, 719
caste rules, 630
castes, 175
Castrator sect, 333
casuistic scale, 286
categorical imperative, 386, 431
Catholicism, 358, 396, 757–58
causality, 283, 362, 436
celibacy, 245–46, 455
centered structure, 665
central presence, 665
ceremonial consumption, 314
certitude, 359
chance, 197, 205, 502
character, 35, 52, 98, 156, 202–05, 208, 238, 240, 298, 409, 458, 510–11, 660–61
character, types of, 20
charisma, 330
chastity, 270
cheerful robots, 576
chemistry, 10
chiasmus, 696
Chicago School of Sociology, 406, 464
child "abuse," 498
child labor, 221, 323
childhood, history of, 496–98
Chinese agriculture, 521–22
Chlyst, 333
choice, 519
Christian sadism, 181
Christian socialism, 135
Christianity, 136, 229
church and state, 216
church vs. sect, 380
circulation, velocity of, 317
circulation of elites, 316, 377
circulus vitiosus, 513
circumcision, 37–38, 510
citizenship, 22, 101, 622, 632
civil association, 659
civil law, 275
civil rights, 20
civility, 16
civility, duty of, 747
civility, origins of, 714
civilization, growth of, 715
civilization, indicators of, 259
civilizations, 227
civilizing process, 492–499
Civilizing Process, 714–15

class conflict, 615
class-consciousness, 323, 721
class habitus, 647
class morality, 263–64
class rankings, 313
class struggle, 343, 452
classical music, 564
cleverness and wickedness, 550
climate, 35, 72, 73, 76, 80, 82
climate and behavior, 29
climate and crime, 167
climate and culture, 24, 25, 31
clothing vs. nakedness, 714
coalition, political, 731
cocaine, 384
coextensivity, 709
coffee trade, 125
cognitive dissonance, 681
coherence, 665
cold rationality, 335
collective autobiography, 18
collective behavior, 456–57
collective consciousness, 307
collective memory, 428–30
collective mind, 297
collective property, 301
collective unconsciousness, 554
Collège de Sociologie, 477
colonial economics, 125
colonialism, 617
colonization, 216
colonizers, 618–19
comedy, origin of, 20
commodification, 189–91, 365
commodities, 67
commodity fetishism, 368–69, 568
commodity relations, 369
common good, 763–65
common sense, 700
communication, 122, 423–24
communicative action, 628
communicative rationality, 547–48, 621
communism, 262, 300, 485, 594
communist party, 365
Communist Party, French, 530
community, 306, 424
community vs. collectivity, 449–50
comparative analysis, 50
comparative anthropology, 371–73
comparative civilizations, 225–26
comparative history, 160
comparative law, 247, 249
comparative mythology, 249
comparative sociology, 228
comparative study, 27

compassion, 43–44, 46–47, 51–52
competition, 347–48, 577
competition, economic, 190
compulsive consumption, 512
compulsive eating, 412
Comtean sociology, 524–25
concepts, 293
concepts, religious, 404
concrete reasoning, 364
confinement, 656
conflict, human, 556
conformity, 196, 230, 650
Congolese slaves, 37
conjuncture, structural, 645
conscience, 387–88
conscientious objection, 459
consciousness, 292–93, 384
consciousness, origins of, 187, 562
consciousness and society, 185–86
conscription, 239
consecration, 307
conservative thought, 434, 437–38
conservatives vs. liberals, 714
conspicuous consumption, 69, 312–14, 648
constitutions, 187
consumer culture, 545
consumerism, 147, 511–12, 593, 672–73
consumerism, logic of, 708
consumerism, manic, 707–08
consumers, 432
consumption, 331, 580
consumption, useless, 482
contagion, 371, 633
contemplation, 370
contingency, 536–38
convention, 679
conventionalism, 649
core-periphery relations, 736
cosmetics industry, 568
cosmopolitanism, 586
counter-finality, 522
counter-revolution, 131
courtiers, 24, 312
courtly behavior, 492, 494–95
craftsmanship, ideal of, 578–80
craftwork, 604
creativity, 367
credit buying, 512
criminality, causes of, 165–66
criminology, 164
critical theory, 593–94
critique, political, 626
critique of everyday life, 532–33
Critique of Judgement, 542
cross-cultural analysis, 247

crowd psychology, 196
crowds, 296–97
crowds, types of, 296
cruelty, 392
cryogenics, 712
crystalline state, 629
cultivated minds, 24
cultural anthropology, 258
cultural capital, 649
cultural contradictions, 516, 720
cultural criticism, 237
cultural degeneration, 145
cultural subconscious, 371
cultural traits, 418
culture, defined, 238, 366, 394–98
culture, evolution of, 259–60
culture industry, 565
cultured timorousness, 195
custom, 102, 131, 279–80, 337–38
cybernetics, 693
cycles of history, 553

Dasein, 670, 678
de-forestation, 521–22
de-humanization, 516
death, 503–04
death, awareness of, 678
death, denial of, 503
death, human, 536, 687
death, meaning of, 505
death, resistance to, 759
decentering, 757
deception, 274
decision theory, 692
decisionism, 71
Decline of the West, 474–76, 528–29
declining profit rate, 738
decolonization, 618–19
deconstruction, 664, 722
deconstruction, definition of, 667–68
deep ecology, 737
defilement, 630
definition of the situation, 611–12
dehumanization, 125
delegitimation, 685–86
delusional contentment, 543
delusory thinking, 92
democracy, 53, 90, 94, 133, 321, 324, 334, 366, 375–76
democracy, defects of, 172
democratization, 731
democratization of culture, 141, 161
demography, 27, 115
demonic power, 386
density of relationship, 348
deruralization, 738

desacralization, 741
desedimenting structures, 668
desire, 696, 729
Despositum, 383
despotism, 28
destructive forces, 593
determinism, 419
developing countries, 3
deviance, 103, 387
deviationism, 586
devolution, 458
dialectical historical change, 153
dialectics, 111–12, 397–98
dialogue, 448
dictatorship of proletariat, 340–41
Die Christliche Welt, 403
diety, omniscient, 286
différence, 7, 669
differential equations, 315
differentiation, 350, 691
diffusion, 282, 417
dikshita, 307
dilettantism, 575
diminution of life, 197
Ding an sich, 505
dirt, definition of, 631, 633
dirty secret of capitalism, 737
disaster threshold, 692
disciplining, social, 654–55
discontent, 207
discourse, 703
discovery, 83
discursive reasoning, 363
disenchantment, 628
disgust, 651
Disneyland as simulation, 711
disorder, cultural meaning of, 631
disorder/order, 655–56
displacement, linguistic, 684
displays, retail, 708
dispositions, system of, 647
Dissent, 713
dissimulation, 709
distracted minds, 322
diversity, 458
divination, 21
divinity, simulacrum of, 710
division of labor, 54, 56–58, 67–68, 236, 291–92
divorce, Roman, 251–52
Doctor Faustus, 564
domestic gods, 251
domestic violence, 222
double-consciousness, 325–27
double hermeneutic, 677
double-meanings, 111–12, 188, 191

double personality, 289
dowaries, 15
dreams, 362–63
Dreyfussards, 306
drosophila, 419
dualism, 293–94, 353, 537
dualism, cultural, 517
duality of structure, 676
durcharbeiten, 597
duty, 156, 204, 408, 431, 476

East vs. West, 249–50
ecological catastrophe, 736–39
ecology, 80
econometrics, 315
economic determinism, 263, 421
economic forces, 480–81
economism, 510–11
education, 106, 156
education, nationalized, 216–17
education, theory of, 12–13
education and ethics, 12–13
educational rights, 95, 97
effective demand, 115
egalitarianism, 699
egocentrism, 366
egoism, 207, 352–53, 526, 543, 757
egoism, male, 378
elites, 299
elites/non-elites, 316–18
emancipation of slaves, 76, 125
embarrassment threshold, 715
Emile, 714
emotional infection, 393
emotionlessness, 509
emotions, expression of, 256–57
empathy, 46–47, 273, 287, 391, 467, 679
empiricism, 23, 136
ends-means, 611
energy, uses of, 481
English education, 24
Enlightenment, 523, 626
Enlightenment ideals, 23
Enlightenment thought, 154
ennui, 321, 568
entrepreneurs, 577
envy, 203, 471
Epicureanism, 555
episteme, 664
epochs, 129–30
equal rights, 199–200, 412
equality, 20, 25–26, 29, 56, 92, 95, 106, 109, 170–71, 241, 266, 326, 356, 397, 471, 748
equality, gender, 162
equality, types of, 41

equality vs. difference, 699
equitable wealth, 432
erasure, 668
Erewhon, 550
eroticism, 333–34, 472
eschatology, 555
essentialism, 730
estranged labor, 189–90
estrangement, 191–93
eternal life, 757
eternal return, 5
ethics, 285–86, 352, 388, 390, 459, 461–62
ethics, evolution of, 588–89
ethnicity, 589–90
ethnocentrism, 72, 589
ethnography, 587
ethnology, 361
ethnomethodology, 608–12, 647, 702
ethography, 702
ethos, 390
etiquette, 55
etiquette and social class, 716
eudaemonism, 353
eunuchs, 28
everyday world, 700–02
excellence, achievement of, 763
exchange-value, 368
exercise, 240
existentialism, 194
existentialist ethics, 570
exogamy, 443–45
exorcism, 358
expertise, 366
expiration, 307–08
exploitation of labor, 221, 323
expression, 273

factionalism, 350
factory labor, 57
fads, 470
falsifiability, 547
families, types of 230–31
family sociology, 228
famine, Irish, 221
fanaticism, 34
Fascism, 276, 315, 478–80, 547–48, 640, 720, 722
Fascism vs. Marxism, 394
fashion, 279
fashions, 347
fate, 60
Faustian culture, 474–476
Faustian universality, 331
feeling, types of, 390
feeling-in-common, 392
felicific calculus, 85–86

fellow-feeling, 46–47
fellow-feeling, types, 391–92
female depression, 724
feminine character, 304
feminine cunning, 99
feminine traits, 418
feminine writing, 686
feminism, 220, 701, 724
fertility, 116
festivals, 484
festivity, vestimentary, 708
fetishization, 365, 719–20
feudal powers, 623
feudalism, 154, 177–78, 230, 334, 494–95
figurational sociology, 492
finitude, 678
flattery, 91, 268
flexible accumulation, 718
folkways, 277, 336–38
Fordism, 394, 718–19
foreigners, 725
foreignness, 725–27
Foucauldian analysis, 653
four basic instincts, 336
"four wishes," 406–08
Frankfurt School, 492, 508, 542, 700
fraternalism, 752–54
fraud, 501
free association, 596
free love, 150
free riders, 764–65
free time, 566–67
free time vs. work time, 568
free will, 164
freedom, 31, 61, 92, 101, 105, 128, 148, 239, 323,
    326, 354–56, 510, 518–19, 574–75, 601, 677,
    741
freedom vs. dependence, 528
French elite culture, 644–45
French Resistance, 518
French Revolution, 91–92, 585–86
Freudian theory of incest, 443
Freudianism, 406, 694
friendship, 206, 268, 278
From Max Weber, 576
Fronde, 351
frontier mentality, 544
frustration, 597
functional differentiation, 691
functional psychology, 423
functionalism, 213, 526, 567, 689

game theory, 692
gaming, 607

Gaullism, 586
gaze, the, 584, 654
Gefühl, 79, 119
Geisteswissenschaften, 272
Gemeinschaft, types of, 277–78
Gemeinschaft/Gesellschaft, 277–79
gender identity, 729, 731
gender relations, 704
gender roles, 163, 418
general will, 39
general strike, 358, 360
generalized exchange, 560
genius, 202, 209, 419, 640
gentry/peasant relations, 590
geological change, 82–83
German baroque drama, 640
German capitalists, 479
German romanticism, 110
Germanic tribes, 304
Gestapo, 428, 448
gestures, 274, 465–67
gift-exchange, 559
gloating, 320–21
gluts, economic, 123
goblinism, 338
God, defined, 404
God, human interaction with, 555–56
God, rational attributes of, 404
God, simulation of, 711
God and time, 696
Golden Rule, 44, 414
good, defined, 285
good and evil, 263, 358
good reasons, 741
goodness, 300
goods, value of, 763
Gothic art, 344
government, 235–36
government functions, 91
governments, origins of, 19–20
governments and freedom, 155
grace, 383
grammar, origin of, 42
grand narratives, 682–85, 722
grand theory, 500
great man theory, 417, 419–20
great men, 282
greed, 15–16, 515
grief, 47
group antagonisms, 515
group-personality, 590
groups, 35
groups, evolution of, 254
guilt, 387

habit, 209, 210, 337–38, 488
habit of inattention, 321
habitus, 645–47
habitus, coherence of, 648
Hamlet, 523
happiness, 15, 52–53, 62, 123, 219, 291–92, 432
happiness, collective, 133
Harvard sociology, 485
hashish, 640
Hasidism, 448
hearth gods, 252
hedonism, 66, 147
hegemonic discourse, 701
hegemony, 394, 736
Heidegger's lacunae, 670
heirarchy, 690–91
heiroglyphics, 20
Heisenberg's principle, 272
herd mentality, 456–57
hermeneutics, 10–11, 595, 676, 756
hero-worship, 420
heroism, 19–20, 543
heterogeneity, social 478–80
historical consciousness, 535
historical materialism, 185–86
historical mutation, 614–15
historical psychology, 493–94, 524
historical relativism, 495
historical sociology, 492
historicism, 380
historiography, philosophical, 553
history, 26
history, understanding of, 430–31
history, uses of, 134
Hobbesian problem, 501
hobbies, 567
Holocaust, 469
hombria, 590
homo aurignacius, 556
homo consumens, 511–12
homo duplex, 293
homo economicus, 489
homo faber, 602–604
Homo Ludens, 605
homogamy, class, 647
homogeniety, social, 478–79
homogenization of class, 646
homosexuality, 653
honor, 289
honorifics, 313
hope, 575
house morality, 278
human/animal interaction, 483
human breeding, 55

Human Condition, 600
human cruelty, 128
human nature, 40, 104, 128, 215, 229, 300, 397, 524, 537, 554, 660–61, 714
human nature, origins of, 19
human right, 101
humanism, 537
humankind, definition of, 395–96
humiliation, 207
humor, 204
humor, male vs. female, 687
humors, 15
Hungarian drama, 365
hyper-rhetoric, 723
hypergamy, 560–61
hyperreality, 706, 709
hysteria, 384

"I", development of, 320–21
I/Thou, 274, 354, 448–49
"I" vs. "me," 465, 467–68
iconoclasm, 710
idealism, 283, 398
idealism vs. realism, 536
ideals, 288
idealtype, 164
ideational culture, 515
identity, 543, 696, 756
identity politics, 721
ideologies, 398, 434–37, 511, 551
Idol of Objectivity, 638
idolatry, 332
Idols of the Laboratory, 637–38
ignorance, 487–88
illocution, 732–33
illusion, 208–09, 607
image, evolution of, 711
images, danger of, 711
images, reproduction of, 720–21
imagination, 155, 249
imbecility, 92
imitation, 281–83
immanence, 536
immanent critique, 639
immanent interpretation, 435
immanent justice, 588
immigrant workers, 726
immigrants, 409
immigrants, Roman, 248
immiseration of workers, 190
immortality, 118
imperialism, 288
impulse, 353
impulsiveness, 488

Incan *quipu,* 583
incest, 64, 443–44
incest, prohibitions of, 561
Indian land, sale of, 78
Indians, American, 226
indicators, 608
individual morality, 570
individual vs. group, 348–51
individual vs. society, 352–53
individualism, 306, 381, 545, 717
individuality, 350, 544
individuality and social forces, 352
industrialization, 135, 139, 147, 290, 614–15
inequality, 40–41, 241, 359
infant sexuality, 497
infanticide, 496
infantilism, 589
inherited characteristics, 419–20
innovation, 229–31, 281, 420
instinct, human, 525–26
instinct, renunciation of, 388
instincts, 51, 337–38
institutions, intellectual, 141
instrumentalism, 423
intellect, types of, 205
intellectual elite, 157
intellectual culture, 390
intellectualism, 335
intelligence, 224–25
intelligentsia, 398
intentionality, 646
inter-societal conflict, 260
interaction, 267, 273–75
interdependence, 425
interest groups, 172
interiority, 522
interpellation, 732
interpretation, 274, 510
interpretation of action, 660
Interpretation of Dreams, 421
interpretation, types of, 434–47
intersubjectivity, 575, 679
interwar crises, 527
intimacy, 601–02
intolerance, 34–35
intrinsic/extrinsic interpretation, 436
introspection, 526, 596
invention, 84, 282
invisible hand, 45, 488
iron, 328
iron cage, 332, 629
Iron Curtain, 551
iron law of oligarchy, 374–77
irony, 533, 728
irrational, 435

irrationalism, 79, 743–44
irrationality, 288, 331–34, 338, 370, 487, 489, 508, 513, 523, 543, 545, 549, 565–66, 593–94, 615, 649, 724, 743
irrationality and religion, 403–05
Islam and women, 97
Italian capitalists, 479
Italian law, 299
Italian Renaissance, 354

Janus-faced culture, 516
Japanese culture, 634–35
jargon, 637
jealousy, 244, 287
jesuitical behavior, 188–89
Jewish identity, 599
Jews, 73
journalism, 197
joys of labor, 603
judgements, types of, 390
jurisprudence, origins of, 21
Jus Gentium, 249
justice, 71, 48–49, 51, 245, 510, 760
justice, theory of, 747–49
justice vs. charity, 431
justifications, political, 764

Kantian morality, 469
Kantianism, 119
Karman, 309
karuna, 758
kingship, 30, 92
kinship, 278
"Know Thyself," 524
knowing subject, 700, 702
knowledge, social bases of, 439–40
Krishna, 414
Kultur, 493
Kwakiutl, 559–60

Lab School, 423
labor, commodification of, 191
labor, exploitation of, 189
labor, free vs. slave, 124
labor power, 738
labor vs. leisure, 124
laissez-faire doctrine, 216–17
language, 450, 595
language, definition of, 400–01
language, injurious, 732
language, origin of, 20, 41–42, 254
language, uses of, 424
language and ethics, 463
language games, 683
language-object, 584

language use, 399
languages and education, 12
late capitalism, 530
law, 104
law, origin of, 19–22
law of error, 164
law of mental unity, 296
law of nature, 90
Law of Peoples, 748–49
Law of Twelve Tables, 22
laws, 349
laws, origins of, 131
laws of equity, 248–49
Laws of Manu, 252
laws of nature, 207–08
laziness, 329
Le Figaro, 613
leadership, 92, 375–76, 476
legitimacy, political, 747
legitimation, 690–91
leisure, 566
leisure class, 312–13
lepers, 656
Les Temps modernes, 518, 534, 682, 698
letter writers, 268
levelling, 197
lex insita, 646
liberal arts, 57
liberalism, 545
liberty, 30, 91–92, 96, 133
libidinal body, 682
libidinal rationality, 593
libido, 593, 687
life, primacy of, 759–60
life as consumer, 314
life-styles, 649
linguistic philosophy, 740
linguisticality, 639
literacy, 366, 369
lithography, 641
logocentrism, 654
London Vegetarian Society, 412
loneliness, 376
longue durée, 736
looking glass self, 319
Los Angeles, simulated, 712
loss, Freud on, 506–07
love, 15, 52, 97, 148, 150, 155, 278, 347, 353–54, 389, 660
love, loss of, 387
love, technicisation of, 472
love and intelligence, 571
love and politics, 413
love and truth, 572
lowest common denominator, 351

luck, 338
lunatics, 457
lust, 30
luxuries, 68–69
luxury, 50, 53, 55, 64, 124

machinery, idolatry of, 239
magic, 306, 308–09, 339, 371
magic, techniques of, 309
make-believe, 607
maladjustment, 408
male-female differences, 81–82
manhood, 326
manifest/latent content, 421
market economy, 577–78
marriage, 14–17, 81, 209, 244–45, 333
marriage, ancient, 251–52
marriage, avoidance of, 219
marriage, collapse of, 472
martyrdom, 34, 359
Marxian utopianism, 530
Marxism, 397–98
Marxism, demise of, 4–5
Marxism, origin of, 184
Marxist aesthetics, 682
Marxist humanism, 533
Marxist writing, 585
masochism, 286, 727
mass behavior, 349–52
mass communication, 321–22
mass culture, 194, 295, 571
mass movements, 357
mass tastes, 471
masses, 375–76, 470–73, 476
master and slave, 111–14, 727
master and slave relation, 697
materialism, 186, 398, 516–17, 537
mathematical logic, 454
maturation, 13
May 1968, events of, 530
meaning, 287, 465–67, 522, 583
meaning, theory of, 521
meanings, genesis of, 435
means/ends, 413
mechanical determinism, 417
mechanistic society, 139
mechanization, 475
mechanization of life, 103
mediation, 113
mediation, existential, 681
medical rites, 309
medicine, nationalized, 217
medieval love, 456
medievalism, remnants of, 176–77
meditation, 107

Mediterranean, The, 734
melancholia, 392, 727
melancholy, 209
memory, reconstruction of, 429
Mensheviks, 514
menstruation, 386
mental illness, 303
messages, types of, 684
messianism, 342
metalanguage, 584
metaphor, 665, 673
metropolis, 279
micro-macro problem, 735
Middle Ages, 455
Middle Ages, government of, 187
middle class, 239
military discipline, 103
military-industrial complex, 753
military psychology, 710
mind, development of, 156
mind, evolution of, 254
mind, nature of, 83–84
mind/body dualism, 534
Mind, 636
miners, 29
minimalism, ethical, 765
minimum wage, 753
miraculous, 405
miscegenation, 4
miscegenation laws, 753
mob behavior, 295
mobs, 351
modal personality, 590
modern European history, 549–50
modern philosophy, origins of, 10
modernism, 538
modernity, 329, 538, 602, 759
modernity, Western, 765
modernization, 587
modernization theory, 628, 735
modesty, 418
Mona Lisa, 538
monarchy, 28, 101, 106, 133, 153–54, 376, 479–80
monasticism, 331, 455, 758
money, 25, 478–79
money power, 721
monogamy, 64
monopolies, 125–26, 495
monopoly, 189–90
monovalency, 727
moods, 366–67
moral culture, 390
moral evolution, 104, 108
moral laws, 156, 157

moral norms, 222, 632
moral suasion, 157, 407
moral theory, 427
moral codes, types of, 263
morality, 51–52, 61, 117, 146, 263–64, 426–27, 565
morals, science of, 390
mores, 336–38, 391
mores, interactional, 684
mortality, 573
motives, hidden, 297
Mrs. Malaprop, 456
multiplicity of worldviews, 441
musée imaginaire, 721
music, 332
music, sociology of, 330
music and philosophy, 636
musical change, 547
mutual attraction, 696
mutual respect, 749
mysticism, 332, 404, 459
mystification, 369
myth, political, 357–58
myth analysis, 558, 582–83

Nachbildung, 646
narcissism, 507, 596–97, 672–74
narrative, self, 680–81
nation of shopkeepers, 237
nation-state, 101, 104, 495
nation-states, 735
national character, 31, 35, 72–74, 295, 299, 322
national identities, 428
nationalism, 299, 725
natural disasters, 128
natural law, 98, 125, 146, 248
natural rights, 43, 91–92
natural selection, 254–55
nature, 105
Naturwissenschaften, 272
Nazi regime, 621
Nazis, 469
Nazism, 547–48
needs, 509
negation, 112–13
Negative Dialectics, 565
negativity, 591
Negro, slaves, 36–38
Negroes, American, 415–16
Negroes, education of, 326–27
neighborhood, 278
neo-Kantianism, 284, 523
neurasthenia, 323
neuroses, 322
new American type, 322

New Left, 591
Newdigate Prize, 237
newspapers, political, 624
nexum, 248
nihilism, 606, 686, 695, 722, 756
Nobel Prize, 485–86
noble savage, 39
nodal points, societal, 683
nominalism/realism, 283
nonrationality, 405, 472, 764
nonreciprocity, 562
nonviolence, 413–416
normal/abnormal, 656
normative order, 502
norms, 51–52, 203, 442
nostalgia, 279, 577, 711
novelty, 470
numinous, 403

obedience, 131
objectification, 63, 598
objective meaning, 645
objective mental structure, 438
objective mind, 274–75
objective structures, 647
objective values, 353
objectivity, fetish of, 638
objects, humans and, 707
obligation, 286
obligatory leisure, 312
occasionalist illusion, 647
Occidental rationalism, 628
Oedipal complex, 687–88
official violence, 495
one-dimensionality, 366
ontogenesis, 562
Open Society, 547
oppression, 327
optimism, 207, 550
order/disorder, 372
ordinary life, 758
ordo amoris, 389
organic analogy, 215–16
organic attitude, 153, 155
organic intellectual, 394
organic relations, 396
orgiastic consumerism, 706
orgiasticism, 333, 477
orthodoxy, 405
orthography, 402
Osiris, 485
Other, The, 620, 647, 725
otherness, 111, 720, 725–26, 728, 730
ousia, 665

overstimulation, 291
overaccumulation, 719

pain, 53
pain and pleasure, 86–87
panopticism, 654–56
Panopticon, 656
Papal infalibility, 131
paradox, 268
paralysis, 323
parent-child relation, 496–98
parental love, 498
Paris, 27
parish schools, 58
parole, 399–400
part/whole, 293
parvenu, 317
passion, 220, 244, 246, 305, 729
passion-free, 416
passion vs. reason, 40
passions, 12, 34, 47, 96, 146–48
passions, three types of, 147
passive resistance, 412
passivity, 512
patience, 416
patriarchal authority, 252
pauperism, 230
peasant naturalism, 333
peasantry, 340
peasantry, French, 178
pedagogy, 66
pedagogy, theory of, 423
pedantry, 395
peer groups, 456–57
perception, 534
perfectability, 107, 109, 116, 169–70, 213, 355
performatives, 732
perlocution, 732–33
permanent rendition, 340–43
Pernia, 688
person, definition of, 503
personality, 104–05, 209, 352, 382, 420, 468, 674
personality death, 504
personalizing protest, 220
perspectival knowledge, 535
persuasion, 547–48
pessimism, 550
phallocentrism, 684–95
phallogocentrism, 730–31
phallus as signifier, 687
phantom objectivity, 368
pharmakon, 669
phenomenology, 389, 469, 536, 608, 678
phenomenology, German, 682

Phenomenology of Mind, 626
philistinism, 237
philology, 266
philosophical anthropology, 525–27, 756
philosophy and history, 359
phylogenesis, 562
physiognomy of genius, 202–03
pictorial reproduction, 641
pictures, 583
piety, 120–21, 573–74, 758
pity, 44, 46–47, 203, 555
plague rules, 654
planned economy, 214
play, 103, 579, 605–07
play, textual, 664
pleasure, 292
pleasure/pain, 337
pleromatic unity, 574
pluralism, 749–50
plutocracy, 93, 515–16
poetics, 724
poetics of the body, 695
poetry, origins of, 19, 21
poisoning, 37
police-state writing, 586
polis, 451–52, 544, 764
political assassination, 634–35
political classes, 299
political correctness, 6
political language, 585
political revolutions, 101
political theory, 10
political utopia, 138
politicians, qualities of, 300–01
Politics (Aristotle), 544
pollution, 233
poor breeding, 13, 15
poor law, 216
popular culture, 398
positivism, 136, 155, 393, 398, 614–15, 735
positivist reconstruction, 158
possessions, 52, 565
possibility, human, 531–32
post structuralism, 644
post-colonialism, 7
posthistoire, 629
postmodernism, 347, 719–23
postmodernity, 628
postmodernity, definition of, 682
potlatch, 312, 559
poverty, 25, 236, 551
power, 64, 501
power, defined, 451
power, theory of, 454
practical rationality, 765

pragmatism, 389, 423, 464, 576
praxis, 521–22, 538
pre-rationality, 389
precociousness, 159
preconsciousness, 535
predatory employments, 313
prediction, 108, 610
prejudice, 43, 174–76
presence, 665–666
pressure groups, 515
priesthood, secular, 157
priests, 73
primary group, 319
primates, 255
primitive culture, 554
primitive humans, 55
primitive thought, 338, 361–64
primitive worldview, 588–89
principles of expressiveness, 256
prison reform, 173
prisons, 712
privacy, 423, 589
private consciousness, 532
private law, 252
private property, 189–90, 245, 263, 300, 600–01
private/public distinction, 425
private vs. public, 600–02
private vs. public education, 12
probability theory, 106, 633
production, 480–81
production vs. consumption, 432
professions and crime, 167
profit, 719
profit, maximizing, 531
progress, 82, 155, 158, 249
progress, theories of, 259
progress, uneven, 531
progress in history, 556
proletarian culture, 343–44
proletarian morality, 157, 263
proletarian revolution, 616
proletariat, 138, 340, 478–79
Promethean revolt, 602–03
Prometheus unbound, 738
propaganda, 571
prose style, 740
prostitution, 688
Protestant ethic, 320, 511
Protestant Ethic, 489
Protestantism, social meaning of, 382
protocol statement, 638
Providentialism, 743–44
proxeni, 726
Prussian government, 403
pseudo-freedom, 513

psychiatry and racism, 617
psychoanalysis, 444–45, 563, 595–98, 674, 695, 698, 709–10
psychoanalytic Marxism, 509
psychodynamics, 681
psychogenesis, 494–95
psycholinguistics, 724
psychologism, 510, 524–25
psychologist's fallacy, 526
psychology, invention of, 284
psychopathology and language, 694
psychosomatic illness, 504
public intellectuals, 423
public opinion, 470, 622
public/private morality, 459
public reason, 746–50
public relations, 625
public sphere, 140–41, 197, 349, 622–26
public taste, 233
publicness, 623–24
pure art, 642
puritanism, 742
purity/impurity, 631–32
purposive action, 486–87

quantitative methods, 165
quantitativism, 515, 587
queer theory, 7, 729

race relations, 339
racial theory, 223–27
racism, 106, 175, 180–83, 325–29, 415–16, 617
racism/sexism, 736
ranks, social, 690
rational action, 85, 692, 740, 763
rational calculation, 650–51
rational control, 407
rational inquiry, 764
rational order, 702
rationalism, 659
rationalism and action, 741
rationalistic psychology, 354
rationality, 238, 289, 487, 489, 502, 543–44, 609–10, 621–624, 629
rationality and religion, 119
rationality as style, 741
rationality of emotion, 119
rationalization, 145, 333, 370, 405, 473, 497, 611, 627–28
reading, 235
reading, art of, 416
reading, theory of, 11
real, evaporation of, 709
realist science, 187
reality principle, 709, 712

reason, 96–97, 106, 128, 230, 238, 246, 626
reason, belief in, 547–48
reason, codification of, 743
reason, newly defined, 545
reason and action, 12, 19
reason and emotion, 155–56
reason and freedom, 130
reason and unreason, 201
reason as life-style, 741
reason as masculine, 687
reason vs. custom, 133
reason vs. passion, 15, 16, 82, 162, 208, 501
reason vs. sentiment, 70
reason's limits, 44
reasonableness, 549
reciprocal interaction, 112
reciprocity, 559–60, 560, 573
reciprocity, criterion of, 748
recognition, desire for, 409
recursiveness, 676
refeudalization, 625
reflection vs. action, 195
Reformation, 358
regimentation, 449
reification, 63, 365, 367–70, 520–22, 567–68, 602–04, 627
relative values, 461–62
relativism, 285, 510
religion, 15, 19, 92, 546
religion, critique of 532
religion and emotion, 121
religion and intellectuals, 359
religion and marriage, 251
religion and politics, 416
religion and racism, 179–80
religion and society, 121–22
religion vs. art, 332
religion vs. science, 372–73
religiosity, 120–21, 284
religious experience, 403
religious illusion, 384
religious intolerance, 34
religious toleration, 145
renunciation, 331
repetition, 283, 603
representation, political, 690–91
repression, 147
repressive desublimation, 592
reputation and marriage, 16
res publica, 426
resentment, 48
reserve army of labor, 738
resignation, 206
responsibility, 361, 519
revolution, 459

Revolution of 1830, 169
Revolution of 1848, 169
revolutions, 90
rhetoric, 96–97, 585–86, 722
rich citizens, 157–58
rich class, 323
righteous indignation, 760–61
risk, 630, 633–34, 691–93
risk assessment, 693
risk calculations, 634
rites, 308–09, 372
ritual, 642
ritualism, 742
Robinsonades, 435, 531
role-playing, 210
role-theory, 567
Roman economy, 124
Roman law, 21, 27, 247–48
Roman state, 248
romantic love, 455–56
Romanticism, 79, 299, 716
rule by the best, 300
rule-following, 606
rulership, 301
ruling class, 452
ruling class culture, 343
Runaway Horses, 634
rupture, conceptual, 664
Russian Revolution, 340

sacred harlotry, 333
sacred/profane, 307
sacrifice, 307–08
sacrifice, functions of, 307–08
sacrifice of being, 449
sadism, 538
sadism and slavery, 182
salon culture, 334
salvation, religious, 555–56
sanctions, 86
savage life, 260
scarcity, 521
scarcity, negation of, 708
schizo-flows, 723
schizophrenia, 723
scholastic curriculum, 10
scholastic process, 487
science, early forms, 154
science, origins of, 108
science and social control, 627
science vs. religion, 120
scientific argument, 359
scientific elite, 295
scientism, 587, 637
second nature, 369

Second Sex, 697
secondary sex characteristics, 304
secondary narcissism, 675
secrecy, 188, 269, 309
secular disturbances, 165
secular humanism, 760
secular relativism, 762
secularization, 489
segregation, racial, 619
self, 467–68
self, development of, 320–21
self, theory of, 680
self and egoism, 572
self-awareness, 679
self-confidence, 301
self-consciousness, 111–13
self-denial, 206
self-identity, 679–80
self-insulation, 572
self-interest, 204, 205, 210
self-knowledge, 207–08
self-limitations, 210
self-made man, 578
self-perfection, 352
self-presentation, 80
self-preservation, 305
self-purification, 413, 416
self-reflexivity, 639
self-slavery, 28–29
self-worth, 208
selfishness, 156
semantics, political, 690–91
semiology, 401, 595, 581–82, 724
semiperipheral zone, 736
Senegalese slaves, 37
sensate culture, 515
sensitivity as feminine, 687
sensuality, 270
sentiment, 71–72
Sentimental Education, 634
separation of powers, 27
seppaku, 635
seraglios, 28, 30
sex roles, 55, 98, 305, 377–78, 695–97
sexual deviance, 455
sexual differences, 695–97
sexual pollution, 632
sexual slavery, 149–150
sexuality, 62–63, 333–34
sexuality, feminine, 304
sexuality, male vs. female, 688
shadows, 362
shame, 494–97
sign, semiological, 666
signifier/signified, 582, 595, 666

signs, 401, 537, 582
silence, 269, 657
similarity, 350
simulacra, 718, 706, 710
simulacra, precession of, 709
simulation, 710
sin, consciousness of 463
sin, feeling of, 563
sixth sense, 62
Sixties, the, 717
skepticism, 299
slave aggression, 597
slave character, 38
slave labor, 56
slave morality, 566
slave narratives, 179
slavery, 25, 28–29, 76, 106, 174–75, 179–83, 326, 348
slavery, abolition of, 551
slavery and sex, 30
slavery, Northern vs. Southern, 176
slavery, Roman, 124
sloganeering, 722
sloth, 16, 25, 29, 32
small business, 577
social act, 465–67
social action, 487
Social Action, 608
social anthropology, 442
social bond, 683
social capital, 648-
social change, 101, 153, 160–61, 230
social change, theory of, 417, 419
social character, 511
social class distinctions, 716
social classes, 241, 316
social classes, French, 581
social control, 19, 51, 230, 241, 654–55, 715, 742
Social Democrats, 381
social disorganization, 153
social engineering, 407
social equilibrium, 317
social evolution, 67–68, 82, 106, 261, 290, 407
social facts, 522
social harmony, 147
social hierarchy, 632
social mechanics, 164–65
social mobility, 327, 441, 615
social order, 502, 689
social organization, 137–38
social physics, 164, 295, 525
social position, 647
social practices, 521, 645–46, 661–62
social psychology, origin of, 319
social stratification, 54, 55
social systems, 155

social thought, defined, 1ff
social types, 660
social vs. physical sciences, 146, 159
social vs. political life, 451
socialism, 198, 213–15, 276, 283, 323, 360, 395, 452, 615, 752–54
sociality, 80
socialization, 503
societal development, 259
societal disintegration, 515–16
societal malaise, 93
society, dynamics of, 453
society, science of, 137
Society of Peoples, 747–50
socio-economic change, 140
sociogenesis, 494–95
sociology, 50, 452, 691
sociology, animal, 283
sociology, formal, 346
sociology, origin of, 152
sociology as science, 282
sociology of knowledge, 291, 439–40
sociology of religion, 380
sociology of science, 485
sociology of women, 702
sociotechnical control, 627
soldiers, 73
solidarity, 395, 431
solipsism, 679, 704
sophistry, 358
soul, 258, 504
sound and language, 402
sovereignty, 101
space/time, 695–97
space-time compression, 718, 721
Spanish Civil War, 713
speaking-circuit, 400
specialization, 370, 526
species-being, 80–81, 192–93
speculative bubble, 672
speculative narrative, 686
sphere of "between," 450
spiritualism, 476
spirituality, 240
St.Louis Exposition, 276
stages of civilization, 107–08, 143–44
standpoint epistemology, 700
state of nature, 42–43, 67
state, 280
state vs. society, 381
state, theory of, 524
statistical inference, 164
statistics conference, 164
stem family, 230–31
Stoicism, 555

strategy, 610
stratification, 312
stream of consciousness, 320
strenuous mood, 286
stress, 322
structural transformation, 399
structural linguistics, 399, 558
structural-functionalism, 500
structuralism, 399, 581, 667–68
structuralist Marxism, 653
structuration, 676
structure, definition of, 664
Structure of Social Action, 608
style of thought, 439–40
subjectively intended meaning, 434–37
subjectivity, 105, 601
subjectivization, 603
sublation, 685–86
sublimation, 385, 563, 696
subordination, 113
subordination of women, 705
substantive rationality, 739
substructure/superstructure, 3, 620, 640
subversion, 479
suffering, 53
suicidal prophecies, 489, 491
suicide, 269, 290, 323, 486, 504, 519
suicide and ethics, 60–62
suntans as fetish, 568
super-ego, 387–88
superego, 495
superficiality, 322
surplus-repression, 592–93
surrealism, 477, 605, 595
sweetness and light, 238
symbolic logic, 636
symbolization, 465
sympathetic introspection, 319
sympathy, 70, 46–47, 155, 203–04, 255, 269, 285, 326,
    389, 414
synchronic/diachronic, 399
syncretism, 515
syndicalism, 358
syneidesis, 575
syphilis, 477
systemic crises, global, 736

taboo, 385–86, 630
talented tenth, 325–27
talking cure, 384
taste, social origin of, 652
tautologies, 586
tax collecting, 100
technical intellectuality, 475
technocracy, 544

Telos, 665
temperament, 207
temperocentrism, 321
termites, 282
text-mediation, 703
textile mills, 262
textuality and social life, 703
theistic existentialism, 570
theocracy, 19, 229
Theories of Society (Parsons et al.), 4
theory vs. practice, 156
theory/praxis, 626–27
thought, evolution of, 372–73
time, 129
time-space relation, 370
tolerance, 287, 549, 748–49
total man, 533
total speech situation, 732
totalitarianism, 545
totality of relations, 397
Totem and Taboo, 562–63
totemism, 528
trace, 669
trade, 279
tradition, 131, 230–31, 429–30, 437–38
tragedy, sense of, 509
tragic hero, 543
trans-substantiation, 522
transcendent meaning, 758
transdisciplinarity, 693
troubadors, 494–95
trust, 268, 679
truth, 552
truth warranty, 744
tu quoque argument, 743
tyranny, 30–31
tyranny of organization, 214
tyranny of the majority, 169–72, 174

ultima ratio, 528
ultimate values, 489
Umwelt, 681
un-meaning, 438
unanticipated consequences, 486–91
unconscious, 440, 645
unconscious mind, 674
unconsciousness, 297–98
understanding, 35, 273–75
unemployment, 551
unequal exchange, 736
unfreedom, 367, 450, 567
uniformity, 280, 291
uniforms, 313
unionization, 319, 323–24
unions, 214

universal history, 614
universal subject, 524
universal time, 129–30
universality, 572–73
unstable family, 230
use-value, 368, 566
utilitarianism, 85–86, 501–03
utility, 71, 86
utopia, 146, 300, 397
utopian thinking, 289

value complexes, 390
value parasites, 721
vanity, 32, 52–53, 96, 268, 359, 409, 557
variable force, 133
vengeance, 49
Verstehen, 272, 319
vicarious leisure, 314
vicarious consumption, 312–13
vice, 16–17
village life, 328–29
violence, 413, 520–21, 547–48, 618–20
violence, political, 357–60
violence/eroticism, 477
virility, 688
virilization, 687
virtue, 12–13, 16–17, 43, 98, 117, 209, 260
virtue, Roman, 359
virtue theory, 762
vita activa, 603
viziers, 28
vocation, 285
vocation, humanity's, 129
volatility, human, 742
Volk, 764–65
vulgar Marxism, 368
vulgarity, 242, 532
vulgarity, aesthetic, 650–51

wage rates, 234
wage slavery, 753
war, 25, 26, 77, 83, 128–129, 216, 288–89, 426, 519, 551, 615
war, functions of, 445–47
waste, capitalist, 482
Waterloo, 535
weakness, 98
wealth, 64–65, 331
wealth, pursuit of, 332
weapons of mass destruction, 547–48

Weber Circle, 365
weeping, 256–57
Weltanschauung, 279, 433
Western philosophy, origins of, 5
Western history, epochs, 718
Western metaphysics, 667
Why Women Are So, 418
wickedness, 204
will, 201, 207, 210
will, freedom of, 203
will to power, 409
Will to Power, 723
Wissenssoziologie, 433
women, 218–22
women, as political category, 730
women, condition of, 148–50
women, subject of, 162
women, virtues of, 81–82
women and civilization, 148–49
women and marriage, 15–17
women and money, 303
women and Roman law, 252–53
women and sympathy, 156–57
women intellectuals, 377–78
women writers, 2–3
women's education, 14
women's labor, 221–22
women's liberation, 149, 157, 377–78, 602, 699
women's perceptions, 700, 702
women's roles, 55
women's rights, 95, 97–99, 148–49, 221–22
women's standpoint, 704
women's suffrage, 198–99
work, degeneration of, 580
work, gospel of, 578
work and being, 526
working class, 238–39
working class consciousness, 323
working-class culture, 720
world market, 342
world socialist revolution, 342
world-plan, 129
world-system theory, 734–36
World-wide web, 6
worldviews, forming of, 162
writing vs. speech, 584
writing, origins of, 108

Zionism, 448